LINGUISTIC GENOCIDE IN EDUCATION— OR WORLDWIDE DIVERSITY AND HUMAN RIGHTS?

LINGUISTIC GENOCIDE IN EDUCATION— OR WORLDWIDE DIVERSITY AND HUMAN RIGHTS?

Tove Skutnabb-Kangas

2000

LAWRENCE ERLBAUM ASSOCIATES, PUBLISHERS
Mahwah, New Jersey   London

Lawrence Erlbaum Associates, Inc., Publishers
10 Industrial Avenue
Mahwah, NJ 07430

Cover design by Kathryn Houghtaling Lacey

Library of Congress Cataloging-in-Publication Data

Skutnabb-Kangas, Tove.
Linguistic genocide in education or worldwide diversity
    and human rights? / Tove Skutnabb-Kangas.
        p. cm.
    Includes bibliographical references and index.
ISBN 0-8058-3467-2 (cloth : alk. paper) —
    ISBN 0-8058-3468-0 (pbk : alk. paper)
1. Language and education. 2. Language and culture. 3. Language
    policy. 4. Multiculturism. 5. Human rights. I. Title.
P40.8.S58   2000
306.44—dc21
                                99-34376
                                CIP

Books published by Lawrence Erlbaum Associates are printed
on acid-free paper, and their bindings are chosen for strength
and durability.

Printed in the United States of America
10 9 8 7 6 5 4 3

Contents

Preface

OUTLINE OF THE BOOK

What is this book about? Here is a short description.

Languages are today being killed and linguistic diversity is disappearing at a much faster pace than ever before in human history, and relatively much faster than biodiversity. The book starts with a short exposé of the present 'health' situation of the world's languages and the prospects for them during the next few generations. The conclusion is that the future looks grim—if things continue, we may kill over 90 percent of the world's oral languages in the next 100 years.

It is claimed that linguistic and cultural diversity are as necessary for the existence of our planet as biodiversity. They are correlated: where one type is high, the other one is too. There seems to be mounting evidence that the relationship between linguistic and cultural diversity on the one hand and biodiversity on the other hand is not only correlational but might be causal. Theories of human-environment coevolution have been proposed, including the assumption that cultural diversity might enhance biodiversity or vice versa. Therefore it is argued that the preservation of the world's linguistic diversity must be an essential goal in any bioculturally oriented diversity conservation[1] programme.

Indigenous peoples and minorities are the main bearers of linguistic and cultural diversity in the world—over 80% of the world's languages exist in one country only, and the median language has no more than 5,000 speakers. Some of the direct main agents of linguistic (and cultural) genocide today are parts of what we call the **consciousness industry**: **formal educational systems** and the **mass media** (including television, 'cultural nerve gas' as Michael Krauss, 1992: 6, has called it). The book shows that the education of most minorities and indigenous peoples in the world is organised in ways which both counteract sound scientific principles and lead to the disappearance of linguistic and cultural diversity.

Schools are every day committing linguistic genocide. They do it according to the United Nations definition of this phenomenon, in the final draft of what in 1948 became the UN Convention on the Prevention and Punishment of the Crime of Genocide. They also do it by forcibly moving children from one group (indigenous or minority) to another group (the dominant group) through linguistic and cultural forced assimilation in schools. Theories in several fields for understanding how and why this is happening are developed and discussed in some detail, including clarification of concepts like mother tongue, ethnicity, integration. Practices (including educational models) leading to linguistic genocide are described and analysed, with numerous examples from all over the world.

This inevitably includes a consideration of power relations. The book shows how the formal educational systems participate in maintaining and reproducing unequal power relations, here especially between linguistic minorities and others, but also more generally, and how the ways of doing this have changed and are constantly changing, and how control and domination are resisted and alternatives are constantly created and negotiated, managed and controlled, and recreated. The deficiency-based models that are used in most minority education invalidate the linguistic and cultural capital of minority children and their parents and communities. They make the resources of dominated groups seem handicaps or deficiencies, instead of valued and validated non-material resources, or they render them invisible and therefore not possible to convert into material resources and positions of structural power. This happens just as much in global international relations

---

[1]Here is the first transdisciplinary challenge. For biologists, 'conservation' is a positive word: that is what you do to prevent nature from deteriorating; you try to grant it better conditions. For sociolinguists and researchers on culture, 'conserving' a language or culture is preventing it from developing, from dynamic 'natural' change. How do we develop transdisciplinary concepts, combining insights from our disciplines?

and the McDonaldization of the world as it happens in English as a Second Language (ESL) classrooms.

Through glorification, the non-material resources of the dominant groups, including the dominant languages and cultures, and maybe specifically English, are presented as better adapted to meet the needs of 'modern', technologically developed, democratic post-industrial information-driven societies—and this is what a substantial part of ESL ideology is about. English and other dominant languages tend to be projected as the languages of modernity, science and technology, success, national 'unity', democracy, and other such positive features.

The non-material resources of the dominated groups, for instance minorities and indigenous peoples, including their languages and cultures, are stigmatised as being traditional, backward, narrow, and inferior; they are marginalised, deprived of resources for their development and use. In this way they are made invisible, or socially constructed as handicaps rather than resources.

The relationship between the dominant and the dominated, the A-team and the B-team, is rationalised so that what the dominant group and its representatives do is always presented as beneficial for the dominated. This can then serve to legitimate and reproduce the unequal access to power and resources and present those with more access as 'helping' those with less.

Processes of globalisation, the increasing insecurity and the growing gaps between haves on the one hand and have-nots and never-to-haves on the other (a 20%–80% world) are analysed in order to understand some of the macro-level factors in power relationships and contemporary changes. The 'free market' ideology, more a political dogma than an economic system, erodes democracy by shifting power from states and democratically elected bodies to transnational corporations and banks, while 'demanding' homogenisation and killing diversity. Globalisation is a killing agent.

When the present situation in the educational system and some reasons for it have been assessed, alternatives will be looked into. One necessary tool in the remedies could be linguistic human rights (LHRs). It is claimed (following Katarina Tomaševski) that the duty of human rights is to overrule the law of supply and demand and to remove price tags from people and from basic necessities for their survival and for a dignified life, including education, and that linguistic human rights are central to this. Human rights should act as a corrective to the 'free market'. But they are powerless unless two unlikely changes happen. Firstly, major redistribution of the world's material resources and structural power is a prerequisite for **implementation** of human rights. Secondly, for this redistribution to happen, civil society needs to take back the control of economy which has been given away to the transnational corporations and the financial giants in the globalisation process.

Linguistic human rights are a necessary (but not sufficient) prerequisite for the maintenance of linguistic diversity. Violations of linguistic human rights, especially in education, lead to a reduction of linguistic and cultural diversity on our planet. The human rights system is analysed so as to see which linguistic human rights in education are protected today, regionally in Europe, and globally. After a critical look at the formulations in most of the central instruments, the assessment is that language in education systematically gets a poorer treatment than other basic human characteristics. Very few international or regional human rights instruments grant binding educational linguistic human rights, despite pious phrases. The present binding linguistic human rights in education clauses are completely insufficient for protecting and maintaining linguistic diversity on our globe, even if there are a few recent positive developments.

The language (and cultural) rights of linguistic majorities are not being met either: formal education does not make the bulk of dominant-group children high-level multilinguals, or truly multicultural, or even appreciative of linguistic and cultural diversity. Education systems reflect monolingual reductionism or monolingual stupidity/naivety where monolingualism (possibly with some foreign language learning) is seen as normal, inevitable, desirable, and sufficient.

Finally, some very recent more positive human rights instruments are presented. Alternative educational models are described which lead to high levels of bilingualism or multilingualism for both minorities and majorities and which respect linguistic human rights.

The structure of this book is as follows. After an introduction describing some of the philosophical and methodological underpinnings and problems in the book, Part I sets the scene. Chapter 1 describes the present situation of the world's languages, problematising their fate and our lack of knowledge about them. Chapter 2 outlines parallels and links between linguistic and cultural diversity and biodiversity and the threats that all three types of diversity face. Chapter 3 defines and analyses a number of central concepts, such as mother tongue(s), culture, ethnicity, assimilation and integration, right to naming one's linguistic and ethnic identities, and the role of language for control and domination and for resistance and self-determination. Chapter 4 asks what the benefits and drawbacks of linguistic diversity are and analyses the ideology of monolingual reductionism.

Part II sets out to investigate linguistic genocide at a more societal level, analysing state policies and globalisation. Chapter 5 looks at language policies of states, more generally and specifically in education, and describes how linguistic genocide in education happens in practice. It also compares two views on how languages disappear—do they die or are they killed? Chapter 6 discusses power and control, and changes in forms of control in the present phase of globalisation, with special attention to the role of language in domination and control. It outlines how 'free markets' respond to the world's problems and to change.

Part III is about the struggle against linguistic genocide and for linguistic human rights in education. Chapter 7 discusses an alternative response to the problems outlined, namely what human rights have to offer. It scrutinizes human rights instruments to see whether we have sufficient linguistic human right, especially in education, to prevent linguistic genocide and to maintain linguistic diversity. The answer is a negative one—the human rights system is at present completely insufficient. Chapter 8 looks at educational models, asking how formal education should be organised in order to lead to high levels of multilingualism and to respect linguistic human rights. The concluding chapter 9 claims that present indigenous and minority education continues to 'forcibly transfer children of the group to another group', something that qualifies as genocide under the UN Genocide Convention. Several prerequisites for the macro-level political changes which are needed to prevent this are outlined, and it is claimed that they are necessary for the planet to have a future.

The losers, if the changes outlined do not happen, are not only the 80 percent of the world's population, who at present consume only 20 percent of the resources. The losers are humanity and the planet. Quoting Edward Goldsmith, I want to remind you that 'environment' means biological, linguistic, and cultural environment. In his words (1996: 91): 'there is no evidence that trade or economic development are of any great value to humanity ... The environment, on the other hand, is our greatest wealth, and to kill it, as the TNCs [transnational companies] are methodically doing, is an act of unparalleled criminality.' The only hope today seems to be that the TNC leaders might realise that it is not in the interest of their grandchildren either because 'there can be no trade and no economic development on a dead planet'.

HOW TO USE THE BOOK—SOME ADVICE TO THE READER

I have tried to make reading and referencing easier by using several kinds of Boxes for Addresses, Definitions, Reader Tasks, and exemplification of various kinds (Inserts and Info Boxes). The Boxes are numbered consecutively within each chapter and listed separately. A short description follows:

- ■ **Definition Boxes** give short or long definitions of central concepts. Some have been defined in lengthy mini-entries, especially in chapter 3, partly to give some of the basic tools for working with the main issues in this book, partly for conceptual clarity, and because language both signals and helps to construct social reality. Some of the definitions are more 'technical' in the sense that the (precise meaning of the) concepts may not be known outside a narrow professional circle. This is true for some legal definitions, e.g., 'indigenous peoples' and 'minorities', bilingual education models, like 'submersion' or 'immersion', or concepts in Deaf education, like 'oralism'. Some are used in everyday language: All of us 'know' what they mean—but we need more precise definitions here, and it does not help the reader if I simply refer to other sources which they may not have available. 'Mother tongue', 'bilingual', 'integration' and 'assimilation', and even 'sign language' belong to this group. Some can be defined in several different ways, and I want to clarify what I mean. The choice of definition enables or limits possible interpretations.

■ **Address Boxes** support the reader by giving snailmail, email, and Web-page addresses and sometimes phone and fax numbers for getting more up-to-date information about various topics. All of them are accurate when the book goes to print, but changes happen constantly. I also apologise to those who have no access to electronic communications.

■ **Reader Task Boxes** try to engage the readers to reflect on their own experience, to get more information, to think together about complex questions with no definite answers, to apply what they have learned or experienced or thought. Sometimes possible answers are suggested in the text.

■ **Info Boxes** contain more quantitative data or 'hard' data—figures, 'facts', law texts, etc.

■ **Inserts** have more qualitative or 'soft' data, often individual experience and exemplification. A few disclaimers might also be needed. The cases and examples in the Inserts do not 'add up' to a representative description of current approaches or of general trends in public education policies. They are used selectively to illustrate various types of policy' as Rainer Bauböck (1998: 1–2) formulates **his** disclaimer in an article with a similar approach. Often the dividing line between 'hard' and 'soft' is blurred. The status of both types of data as scientific evidence can be equally valid. The Inserts are part of my (and sometimes Robert's) 'butterfly collection', as Peter Mühlhäusler calls quotes he has collected over a long time.

There is only a short list of contents at the beginning of the book. Each chapter starts with a detailed list of contents, including a list of all the Boxes, Inserts, Tables, and Figures.

I have borrowed freely from many of my earlier books and articles where appropriate and acknowledge here collectively my debt to 'my' (and other) publishers.

All translations from Danish, Finnish, German, Norwegian, Sámi, or Swedish from sources which are in the bibliography in languages other than English are mine unless indicated otherwise. My native-speaker husband, Robert, has spent years of his life trying to make my language more like his English, but without much success (not for citation...).

WHO MIGHT WANT TO READ THE BOOK

Who might benefit from this book? The prerequisites have more to do with interest and engagement (but some tertiary education might help with the more formal parts). The audience that I have had in mind includes:

■ Students at all levels, from undergraduate through doctoral level, in applied linguistics, sociolinguistics, ESL/EFL, bilingual and multi- and intercultural education, critical pedagogy, ethnolinguistics, any language departments, human rights, ethnography, social psychology, all over the world; likewise, their teachers

■ Preschool and school teachers and teacher trainees, especially in bilingual education and minority education

■ Teacher educators and in-service trainers

■ Educational administrators, policy planners and implementers and other staff in minority and bilingual education

■ Nurses, midwives and doctors specialized in minority or intercultural affairs

■ Parents of minority children

■ Minority 'leaders', and minority/indigenous lobbyists and activists

■ Politicians

This has been a difficult but necessary book to write. So much (unnecessary) pain and sorrow is included in the experience of many of the people and groups I describe. And still, too much has been excluded: for every story, every quote, every argument, there are tens more; for every reference, I have had to leave out tens and even hundreds of others. But there has been a lot of joy and encouragement too—people are marvels of energy, insight, action, love. Much *is* happening.

I sincerely hope that you, dear reader, will enjoy the book: become angry, desperate, frustrated, as well as reflective, optimistic, and eager to join me and others in demanding, suggesting, creating, and implementing change. Even if/when you do not agree with me, I hope the book will change the way you see at least a few things.

ACKNOWLEDGMENTS

Since this book is a kind of destillation of a lifetime of experience, I should thank thousands of people but can name only a few here. My collective thanks go to all the thousands of parents and teachers, children and youngsters, who have taught me. My first real university teacher, Einar Haugen, with whom I had the privilege of working closely in 1967–1968 and to some extent ever after, taught me, in addition to the importance of an ecological macro-perspective on multilingualism and fascination with language diversity, that it is a duty of older scholars to trust, encourage, and support younger ones, try to see the potential in them, even when they may be absolutely ignorant even about the basics, like I was. I still blush when I think of my bottomless lack of knowledge, awareness, and wisdom when I came to Einar with my newly acquired MA and having collected the materials for my first PhD about bilingualism and school achievement—not even knowing what a phoneme was …

I have been incredibly lucky, having met hundreds of people who have patiently and lovingly taught me, and who continue to do so. One difference as compared to 1967 is that I at least now know how little I know and understand.

Most areas and issues discussed in the book I would know nothing about without good friends. Many friends have enlightened me about Kurdish, Roma, indigenous issues, about Sign Languages, Esperanto, about human rights, economics, literature. About the necessity and joy of combining scholarship, action, life, having colleagues who are dear friends. Some have persisted in forcing me to find counterarguments, most have in addition been thinking and acting together with me, in many cases for decades. I could write several pages about each person, specifying what I would like to thank them for—but you know yourselves. I will here just mention **some** of the names and say a big collective THANK YOU, with hugs, to Alma Flor Ada, Robert Adam, Hugh Africa, Marjut Aikio, Pekka Aikio, Antti and Matti Aikio, Samuli Aikio, Ulla Aikio-Puoskari, Neville Alexander, Rob Amery, Ulrich Ammon, Ole-Stig Andersen, Annamalai, Hugo Baetens Beardsmore, Martin Baik, Asta Balto, Marie Battiste, Jennifer Bayer, Richard and Nena Benton, Dina Berenstein, Asger Bergman, Brian Bernal, Ismail Besikci, Anne Marie Beukes, Constance Beutel, Grete Bille, Detlev Blanke, Colin Bourke, Gulda Bozarslan and family, Mehmet Emin Bozarslan and family, Jan Branson and Don Miller, Birgit Brock-Utne, Sertaç Bucak, Ranko Bugarski, Pirkko Carpenter, Stacy Churchill, Michael Clyne, David Corson, Florian Coulmas, Jim Crawford, Jim Cummins, Probal Dasgupta, Bessie Dendrinos, Zubeida Desai, Rosario

Diaz-Greenberg, Teun van Dijk, David Dolson, Ina Druviete, Hans Dua, John
Edwards, Asbjørn Eide, Hans Erasmus, Mahmut Erdem, Philomena Essed,
Mark Fettes, Joshua Fishman and Gella Schweid Fishman, Ofelia García,
Harald Gaski, Ailo Gaup, Maret Gavppi and Johan Mattis Mikkelsen Gavppi,
Mikkel Gaup and family, John Gibbons and Pauline Gibbons, Francisco
Gomes de Matos, Hartmut, Marilena and Thomas Patrick Haberland and
Margaret Malone, Rainer Enrique Hamel, Cees Hamelink, Nils Erik
Hansegård, David Harmon, Betty Harnum, Amir Hassanpour, Elina Helander,
Eduardo Hernández-Chávez, Kathleen Heugh, Ejnar Hjorth, Veikko
Holmberg, Nancy Hornberger, Christian Horst, Leena Huss, Mustafa Hussain
and Ida Høgsbro, Kenneth Hyltenstam, Edel Haetta Eriksen, Odd Mathis
Haetta, Solveig Haetta, Cristina Igoa, Magdalena Jaakkola, Björn Jernudd,
Markku Jokinen, Deirdre Jordan, Braj and Yamuna Kachru, Tero Kangas,
Timoti Kāretu, Liisa Kauppinen, Jan-Henry Keskitalo, Lachman
Khubchandani, Sevki Kizilocak, Georgy Krushlov, Natalie Kuhlman, Normand
Labrie, Jarmo Lainio, Istvan Lanstyák, Aleksei Leontiev, Pirkko
Leporanta-Morley, C. Eric Lincoln, Anna-Riitta Lindgren, Lilja Liukka, Jo Lo
Bianco, Ravna Magga Lukkari, Luisa Maffi, Ole-Henrik Magga, Kahombo
Mateene, Xola Mati, Jacques Maurais, Antje-Katrin Menk, Ulrike Menk,
Melanie Mikes, Don Miller, Ajit Mohanty, Shahrzad Mojab, Rosa Molinas, Matti
Morottaja, Chris and Mike Mullard, Ingegerd Municio, Peter Mühlhäusler,
Albina Necak-Lük, Ngũgĩ wa Thiong'o, M. A. Numminen, Masaki Oda, Agnethe
Olesen, Lucy Other Medicine, Uldis Ozolins, John Packer, Anne Pakir, Kirsti
Paltto, Christina Bratt Paulston, Debi and Shulakhyana Pattanayak, Anne
Pauwels, Alastair Pennycook, Markku Peura, Theo du Plessis, Peter
Plüddemann, Lada Radoměřská, Birgitte Rahbek, Britt Rajala, Ljubica Rajic,
Mart Rannut, Poul-Erik Rasmussen and Birte Hald, Naz Rassool, Timothy
Reagan, Tom Ricento, Francisca Sanchez and Nicholas Handy Sanchez, Marét
Sara, Svenka Savic, David Shea, Rosa Shim, Naomi Silverman, Sarah Slabbert,
Jurek Smolicz, Laila Somby Sandvik, S. N. and Meena (Kamal) Sridhar, Max
van der Stoel, Vigdis Stordahl, Wilfried Stölting-Richter, Merrill Swain, Andrea
Szalai, György Szépe, Sandor Szilagyi, Shelley Taylor, Patrick Thornberry,
Makhan Tickoo, Jim Tollefson, Katarina Tomaševski, Jennifer Toms,
Humphrey Tonkin, Pertti Toukomaa, Georgios and Sigrid Tsiakalos, Yukio
Tsuda, Joseph Turi, Nils-Aslak Valkeapää, Fernand de Varennes, Taina Varpa,
Kerttu Vuolab, Miranda Vuolasranta, Erling Wande, Joan Wink, Dawn Wink
Moran, Birger Winsa, Ruth Wodak, Sakej Youngblood Henderson, Rosalma
Zubizarreta, Tuula Åkerlund, Jan-Ola Östman, Liv Østmo.
    Naomi Silverman has been a wonderful, supportive editor to work with.
Kathleen Heugh, Timothy Reagan, and Terrence Wiley, gave much more of
their time and care than one can ask. Hartmut Haberland came out to help me
install a new computer when the old one broke down three weeks before the
manuscript was due. Our dear neighbours, Arly and Lene Christiansen,

always there to solve problems, practical and mental, trying to gently remind us to be human and take care of other parts of ourselves too and not just the heads, Arly with loads of grains to chickens, game to be enjoyed (or fox to be skinned and cured, shot next to our chickenhouse—my first task when the manuscript leaves tomorrow is to wash off the alum and salt); Per and Trille Hagemann, with parties and dinners and a tractor-load of new raspberries to be planted out immediately, to prevent me from ruining my computer arm. Thanks for care and tolerance! Grandnephew Sami, allowing me to see the long-term development of the fantastic awareness of a participant in one of Finland's first immersion programmes. Grandchildren, Anna (also in an immersion programme) and Silas, for moments of laughter and relaxation. Jane, my wise and supportive mother-in-law. Thomas and Caspar, both practicing bilingualism in the family. Sister Bjarma, for many years of unfailing support, brother Erik for many years of constructive questioning. Ilka and Kea, my most honest critics and greatest joy and pride. And Robert who shares all my enthusiasms and worries and work and joys of nature and care for our planet, Robert … without whom I would not live or love or write or think or continue the struggle.

Introduction

ASKING WHY-QUESTIONS

Having already described some of the content in the Preface, I want to give you, the reader, another type of declaration of content. It has to do with the scientific paradigm which is the basis for questions asked in this book, including the role of the author.

Despite dedicated work for decades by committed teachers and school authorities and despite massive research efforts, too many indigenous and minority children still 'fail' in the formal educational systems, all over the world. The same is true with many of those children of ordinary, 'non-elite' parents in Africa and Asia who actually attend school—many still don't. Too many children are pushed out early, many are still overrepresented in classes for children with 'special difficulties', and the school achievement of many is at a group level below that of dominant-group children, or elite children as a group. Later on, they do not get higher education to the same extent as dominant-group children. They are often overrepresented in unemployment and youth criminality statistics and other statistics showing results of an unequal society. One of the common denominators for these children is that their own languages are not used as the main languages of teaching and learning in school.

This is the **general** picture, even if there **are** both individuals and groups who are an exception and **are** managing well, sometimes even better than majority children. Mostly, though, they do so **despite** the way their formal education is organised, not **because of** it.

There is a grave mismatch between what the official education goals and the claims of intention for minority education by authorities are and what is in fact happening.

Many teachers who teach indigenous or ethnic minority children, including ESL teachers, show a lot of compassion. In addition, in their teaching many draw on scientific descriptions of second language learning, group dynamics, child psychology, intercultural and anti-racist inclusive pedagogy, and other tools that their training gives them. Nice people are working with good intentions—and still the results are often a disaster. **Why?**

I share with many researchers worldwide the belief that the education of indigenous peoples and minorities in most countries is organised in ways which counteract sound scientific evidence from education and several other disciplines. In many cases we **know** in general terms how education could be organised better. We can show that it works, and often it is not even more costly in the short-term and certainly not in the medium or long-term perspective. But it is not done. **Why?**

Many of the teachers are just like Dom Helder Camara, the former Archbishop in Brazil, giving food to the poor. This is the famous quote: 'When I give food to the poor, they call me a saint. When I ask **why** they have no food they call me a communist.' As soon as you start asking uncomfortable why-questions, warning labels and many other exclusionary strategies to silence you are taken into use. But unless all of us start asking why-questions, the situation is not going to improve. Here are some more of the why-questions that have provoked me into writing this book.

Many linguists and educationists are working hard, with devotion, to make people literate. The United Nations and UNESCO, the Organisation of African Unity, and many other organisations publish scores of resolutions and declarations about their commitment to literacy and Education for All. Still, the world's literacy rates are either not improving or are improving at a much much slower rate than any of the firm and realistic plans have suggested. Even if the percentages of the world's population who cannot read and write are slowly going down, the absolute numbers of 'illiterates' are certainly not; rather the opposite. **Why?** I claim that the wrong choice of medium of education is the main **pegagogical** reason for 'illiteracy' in the world. Still, the right medium is not chosen. And most 'development aid' supports the wrong languages. **Why?**

Many linguists are busy describing the languages of the world. Again, UNESCO, the UN, the European Union, and other organisations publish resolutions celebrating diversity, telling us how important and necessary linguistic, cultural, and biological diversity are, and promising to support all these forms of diversity. Still, biological species are dying and being killed off at an alarming rate while the physical environment, including access to any food, not to speak of healthy food, deteriorates to the extent that children and also adults in many parts of the world are being multihandicapped—with the agents fully conscious of what they are doing when poisoning the world. Languages and, with them, cultures, are dying today at a faster pace than ever before in human history, and prognoses say that 90% of today's oral languages may no longer be around in one hundred years' time. **Why?**

I suggest that starting to ask basic 'why-questions' is at this point of time more necessary than still more sophisticated 'what' or 'how' descriptions of the state of the world.

But when I and others ask **why** indigenous and minority children are not doing as well as they should in school, or when we ask **why** people learn English and other dominant languages **at the cost** of their own languages (many of which then disappear), instead of learning them **in addition** to their own languages (which would lead to high levels of multilingualism and maintenance of diversity), and when we ask what these issues have to do with power relations and widening gaps between haves and have-nots (or never-to-haves, as seems more likely), we are not only being called communists, as was Dom Helder. This labelling has other consequences too.

In trying to silence us, the power elites (also, regrettably, including many academic colleagues), whose ideologies and actions I and others are criticizing, also try to **depoliticize** the issues we are raising. They not only claim that we who ask why-questions are political. They also claim that they themselves are neutral and objective and disinterested. That means that the terms of the discussion are narrowed down—only some questions are allowed as legitimate.

Paul Laverty, from Glasgow, wrote in a letter to the editor (**Guardian Weekly** September 14, 1997, p. 2), referring to Dom Helder Camara, the following:

Both Mother Teresa and Princess Diana did indeed have much in common. That dangerous word 'why' was never on their lips. Perhaps this explains in part their iconic stature. Both are sweet, sincere, but most of all, safe, and in the long run utterly irrelevant to the 35,000 innocents who die every day because we live in a world which violently rejects any notion of sharing wealth in a more equitable manner. I don't doubt that the world needs compassion. But it needs justice more than charity, and perhaps for every embrace it needs the question 'why'.

REPOLITICIZING THE LANGUAGE OF SCHOOLING

In several ways, *not* asking why-questions is part of ESL tradition. Most ESL traditions have done and are still very strongly doing what Freire and others have criticized: attempting to **depoliticize the language of schooling** (Giroux 1985, xiv). This is a dangerous narrowing of the field, staying within technical micro-level questions of the best methodologies and materials, in the best positivist tradition. One part of it is excluding the broader power issues from discussions about the 'language of schooling' in terms of the medium of teaching and learning[1] in formal education. This depoliticization is easy to see in the use of the instrumental allegedly market-driven legitimation of the importance of English that is often used. ESL and EFL are too often discussed as completely free-floating half-humanitarian, technologically perfectable professions, separated or separable from not only other language-related issues but also from economic and political concerns. This is, of course, nonsense. English language teaching is a multibillion business. When Britain no longer rules the waves, the English language does—it is in economic terms 'more precious than North Sea oil'. And English is not getting bigger only because 'it happened to be in the right place at the right time' as David Crystal would have it in his analysis (1997: 8). We have to ask **why** English is getting bigger **at the cost** of other languages, rather than **in addition to** them (as Robert Phillipson, 1992, and others are doing). There are too many debates about methodological microproblems while the house is on fire.

There is also an almost complete refusal to see ESL as just **one** part of a necessary wholistic language learning goal, namely bilingualism or multilingualism, where obviously **both** parts should be discussed and planned **together**. There is a practical **exclusion of mother tongue** or primary language-related concerns in almost all evaluations of allegedly bilingual education programmes in 'core English countries' (countries where native speakers of English are a majority). In most evaluations of minority education results in English and maths dominate and results in the mother tongues of minorities are footnoted, if they exist at all. Concentrating on one of the languages is obviously legitimate, but only if it happens with the understanding that the other languages in the students' repertoire are equally important and the development of **all** of them have to be taken properly into consideration for sound pedagogical methods to be found.

---

[1]Many South African researchers have started using the concept 'the language of teaching and learning' instead of 'the medium of instruction', to emphasize the active, mutual nature of education. I fully agree with the ideology behind the change. As Kwesi Kwaa Prah formulates it (1995b: 13), 'Knowledge cannot be effectively handed down, it must be achieved. It is more taken than given.'

Not doing this also protects two anomalies: that teachers monolingual in the target language, or with no knowledge in their students' mother tongues, can continue to be seen as competent teachers of ESL or EFL; and that many of the great experts on how to make whole populations, e.g. in China or Eastern and Central Europe English-competent, i.e. minimally high-level bilinguals, usually come from countries which are well known for *not* having succeeded in this or not even having tried, such as Britain and the United States. None of this makes pedagogical sense (see chap. 8).

In fact, one of Freire's general claims could be a fairly precise analysis of today's ESL. He says, 'domination is ... expressed by the way in which power, technology, and ideology come together to produce forms of knowledge, social relations, and other concrete cultural forms that function to actively silence people.' (Giroux 1985: xix).

Among the people being actively silenced are the ones who want to broaden the terms of discussion and repoliticize the questions about the language of learning. In addition to parents and teachers, these also include intellectuals. In a hegemonically controlled world they seem to be an important group to silence.

ACKNOWLEDGING FEELINGS, VALUE JUDGEMENTS, AND THE NEED FOR ACTION AS LEGITIMATE PARTS OF RESEARCH

We need a more comprehensive understanding of the role of researchers and other intellectuals in order to locate the discussion (and this book) in an increasingly unequal and unjust world.[2] My type of why-questions are part of specific research paradigms but not of others. They are not part of a positivistic tradition.

If positivism is a 'discourse in which value judgements are eschewed, and in which theoretical propositions are regarded as empirically verifiable or falsifiable' (Bocock 1986: 55), it follows that no **'rational** judgements can be made between political and moral systems according to any consistent version of positivism, because no meaning can be given to the judgements. Moral and political judgements may be seen by positivists as reports upon **a speaker's feelings** about an action' (ibid., 61; emphases added). And a researcher's feelings and moral and political value judgements have nothing to do with research, according to positivism. Bocock quotes (ibid., 61) the

---

[2]This includes distribution of books. Starting with basics, the material: more than 70% of the world's paper is used by the 20% of people living in North America, Western Europe, and Japan. Global per capita use of paper is around 46 kilograms a year; the USA average is 320 kilograms, Japan's 232, Germany's 200. In Brazil it is 31, in China 24, and in India 3 kilograms (Abramovitz 1998: 24). What does this book weigh?

formulation of basic positivistic assumptions in Wittgenstein's **Tractatus Logico-Philosophicus** (1922):

> 6.41 The sense of the world must lie outside the world. In the world everything is as it is and happens as it does. In it there is no value—and if there were, it would be of no value ...[3]

> 6.42 ... there can be no ethical propositions ...

> 6.421 It is clear that ethics cannot be expressed. Ethics is transcendental.

Positivistically oriented researchers on the topics of this book, even when sympathetic towards minorities, would then ask 'what' and 'how' questions to describe how 'everything in the world **is**' (for instance, describe threatened languages, or state that minority students are not doing as well as a group as dominant language-speaking students), but would ask few if any why-questions in their research (and often 'wrong' why-questions at that). They would then present the results for the reader (or politician) to judge, without (thinking that they have) moral or political value judgements about how things **should** (or should not) **be**.

Some of them might also go as far as describing (or, more probably, testing) the feelings that the minorities themselves, whom they study, have about their own situation, but would not (think that they) have any feelings of their own involved. Those positivists would then be like Gramsci's (1971: 418) 'abstract pedants', "studying" popular feelings; he does not feel with them ... ', instead of being real organic intellectuals:

> The popular element 'feels' but does not always know or understand; the intellectual element 'knows' but does not always understand and in particular does not always feel. The two extremes are therefore pedantry and philistinism on the one hand and blind passion and sectarianism on the other. Not that the pedant cannot be impassioned; far from it. Impassioned pedantry is every bit as ridiculous and dangerous as as the wildest sectarianism and demagogy. The intellectual's error consists in believing that one can know without understanding and even more without feeling and being impassioned (not only for knowledge in itself but also for the object of knowledge): in other words that the intellectual can be an intellectual (and not a pure pedant) if distinct and separate from the people-nation, that is, without feeling the elementary passions of the people, understanding them and therefore explaining and

---

[3]An example from the Swedish researcher Ekstrand, with whom I had many battles decades ago. In the 1970s Ekstrand questioned everything Pertti Toukomaa and I wrote about immigrant minority education, claiming that we did not have test results measuring how 'everything is in the world' (even if we had many). In a discussion he claimed that everything in the world could be measured. I questioned this. He asked me to give an example of something that could *not* be measured. I suggested love, or the feeling of powerlessness a minority child felt in a classroom where she did not understand the language. After a while, Ekstrand gracefully admitted that there **might** be a **few** things we could not **yet** measure. But then they were, according to him, outside what a researcher could legitimately be interested in ...

justifying them in the particular historical situation and connecting them dia-
lectically to the laws of history and to a superior conception of the world, scientifically and coherently elaborated, i.e. knowledge. One cannot make
politics-history without this passion, without this sentimental connection between intellectuals and people-nation. In the absence of such a nexus the relations between intellectuals and the people-nation are, or are reduced to,
relationships of a purely bureaucratic and formal order; the intellectuals become a caste, or a priesthood (so called organic centralism) ....

But adding 'feeling' and 'understanding' (or 'interpreting') to 'knowing' is
still not enough for the research paradigm that this book represents. Often
'action' and 'change' need to be added (and Gramsci wanted to do this too).
Many researchers may be guilty of what both old and new philosophies, east
and west, the **Bhagavadgītā** and Marx, criticize. In Marx' terms, in his famous
comment on the **Theses on Feuerbach** (1845) (eleventh Thesis): 'The
philosophers have only interpreted the world in different ways; the point is to
change it.' Or, in Radhakrishnan's (1977: 96) interpretation of and comment
on classical Indian philosophy in the **Bhagavadgītā**: 'our world is not a spec-
tacle to contemplate; it is a field of battle'. In the endangered languages field,
it is not enough to preserve the languages for the future by recording them,
the 'archivist' approach (see Insert 4.7)—the position 'of the scholarly student
of folklore who is permanently afraid that modernity is going to destroy the
object of his study', as Gramsci puts it (1971: 419). In the field of education, it
is not enough to discuss methods of dominant (or even dominated) language
learning, or existing language rights. More is needed.

This means that every researcher has to clarify for herself the relationship of
intellectual knowledge to morality, duties, and struggle, and to come to terms
with what for Wittgenstein is transcendental. And to transcend contemplation
and enter the battlefield we need more than intellectual knowledge and
academic analysis. In the **Bhagavadgītā** (see especially X.10 and X.11), devotion and love are necessary for the destruction of ignorance and to gain
intellectual knowledge. This intellectual knowledge in turn is rendered
luminous by intuitive knowledge, which then leads to understanding and
wisdom. Radhakrishnan tells us to focus **all** our energies, intellectual,
emotional and volitional (1977, 254). He sees the fusion of knowledge, love,
and power in a supreme unification as a prerequisite for unity and universality
of spirit (ibid., 254–255). Many researchers still believe that only the head has
a place in research.

Or, we can use the ideas of the Finnish neurophysiologist, Matti Bergström
(1986: 4, 6, 8, quoted in Skutnabb-Kangas & Cummins 1988: 392). He claims
that in the information society we think that knowledge is all that is needed to
manage, or, more precisely, if you have enough of the combination of
knowledge and energy, meaning 'technology, you will manage everywhere in
the world'. The third resource is neglected, namely the 'system which

chooses, samples, evaluates. It is this apparatus which reflects, which sees the larger contexts, and gives us the opportunity to compare'. Our prospects are in his view bleak if educational philosophy does not change:

> In the schools which usually are thought of as knowledge centred, the students are being stuffed with information constantly. There is no time for evaluation. We neglect the development of the very capacity which criticizes, evaluates, turns things upside down. The result is that we are perhaps creating whole generations who have knowledge and energy but who lack the capacity to know how to use the knowledge and what to do with the energy. And so we educate whole generations to become **value invalids**.[4] Science has tidied away the concept of values. Research is now geared towards knowing, towards getting knowledge. Research is not supposed to contain value judgements, they say, and this is where the danger lies ... If we choose value invalids to have power ... which I fear we have, then we are threatened by a general catastrophe.

To me the heart, the stomach and the spirit have to accompany researchers—and there is no doubt in my mind as to which one should lead this integrated whole.

Kwesi Kwaa Prah (1995b: 50) notes that most African languages make a distinction between knowledge and wisdom (in Venda, 'Ndivho' and 'Vhuthali', respectively, in Tswana 'Tsebo' or 'Kitso' and 'Botlhale', in Xhosa 'Lwazi' and 'Ubulumko', etc.) 'Knowledge is based on learning, information, data, facts, and news, while wisdom derives from prudence, judgement, sense and shrewdness. Knowledge is understood to have a specific focus, and solves definite problems, whilst wisdom or sagacity provides discretion and prudence, encompassing the general approach to life.'

Peter Mühlhäusler has a similar message and has specified it for people working in the languages field. He has given it some of the sceptical-sounding secular packaging that may be necessary in order not to embarrass segmented rationalistic Western researchers too much:

> Linguists hide behind the shield of scholarly objectivity whilst the linguistic diversity that has been in existence for tens of thousands of years is being eroded at an alarming rate... So long as we cannot be certain that the progress we are experiencing is progress in the right direction, to discard diversity for seemingly progressive uniformity seems a very dangerous gamble... In the case of much of linguistics, the range of questions that have been addressed have been unduly narrow, ethnocentric and insensitive to the plight of the languages and their speakers. Moral questions and questions of the consequences of linguistic activity have been notoriously avoided in the mistaken belief that it is possible to engage in an ideologically free linguistics... What is needed now is a new reformed linguistics that addresses some of the fundamental issues of the place of language in human life, of the uses of intellectual and linguistic diversity and of the responsibility linguistics has in helping to maintain and rescue a very fragile linguistic ecology. These issues have barely

---

[4] 'Ethically challenged' they might be called in the newspeak of some North Americans.

begun to be addressed... One hopes that they will move towards the centre of the discipline before it is too late .... (Mühlhäusler 1996: 337–338).

We have to take the big step needed to move issues about linguistic human rights (which is what my book to a large extent is about) towards the centre of not only the discipline of linguistics but also education, law, and several others, before it is too late. With love, devotion, intuition, understanding, and wisdom. This includes, even with the risk of academic (and economic) marginalisation, asking some of the uncomfortable why-questions, shouting them out in fact, and demanding answers. After all, an intellectual in Edward Said's (1994: 17) sense is

> neither a pacifier nor a consensus-builder, but someone whose whole being is staked on a critical sense, a sense of being unwilling to accept easy formulas, or ready-made clichés, or the smooth, ever-so-accomodating confirmations of what the powerful or conventional have to say, and what they do. Not just passively unwilling, but actively willing to say so in public.

For Said, 'there is no question in my mind that the intellectual belongs on the same side with the weak and unrepresented.' These are for him 'human beings considered to have subaltern status, minorities, small peoples and states, inferior cultures and races' (ibid.). Said's 'modern intellectual's role' is truly 'that of disputing the prevailing norms' (1994: 27).

I fully agree with Said. But it is also equally much a duty of intellectuals to start to formulate some tentative **answers** to questions where we know enough, in addition to criticizing. To the extent that we think we can offer something else instead, we have to risk suggesting answers. They obviously have to be tentative, though, because answers which take the form of 'truth claims', 'all too often have the effect of closing down conversations, of asserting arrival at a final account', as Sandra Harding puts it (1998: x). With changing political, economic, and other circumstances, answers may also change (as I have shown in my 1984a book in relation to minority education too: When the German 'guest worker' policy changes to an 'immigrant minority' policy, education also has to organised differently).

Suggesting answers belongs in Paulo Freire's tradition to the 'language of possibility'. Henri Giroux sees Paulo Freire's 'discourse [as] stand[ing] between two radical traditions', **the language of critique**, drawing on the new sociology of education, and **the language of possibility**, drawing on the tradition of liberation theology (Giroux 1985: xiv). I have tried in my own work and in this book to combine the two, critique and possibility. The critique part is a necessary prerequisite for planning the strategies for hope and alternatives and a large part of the book is involved in that critique. When I assess my early work in the light of Freire's legacy, most of it falls within the **language of critique** part of Freire's discourse. I have for three decades been criticizing the assimilation-oriented majority-language dominated L2-medium education that most countries in the world still use in minority education (see, e.g., Skutnabb-Kangas 1972a, b, c, d, 1975, Skutnabb-Kangas & Toukomaa 1976, Toukomaa & Skutnabb-Kangas 1977, Skutnabb-Kangas 1981, 1984a, 1990a). This critique continues in this book, as it is still needed. But I have also wanted to move to some concrete aspects of the **language of possibility** and obstacles to their implementation. I see some of the work on linguistic human rights in education as representing what Freire would call strategies for hope and alternatives. It is important to remember, though, that these alternatives do exist already. The book draws on many concrete examples of them—they are not in the future only, they *are* here.

In the book I will, then, try to place minority and dominated-group education in a wider social and political framework. I will show that the education which many minorities receive serves to maintain an unequal division of power and resources in the world. I will also discuss how this happens, and show how various types of inequality and various -isms (classism, racism, sexism, imperialism) coarticulate, and how they in part make use of similar strategies. My starting point is the experience of those who have been at the receiving end of this power misuse. But I also try to move between epistemological understandings, as the next section describes.

STANDPOINT THEORIES

From many quarters researchers have noted shifts in research focus and attention during recent years, 'from centres to margins, from the homogenous to the heterogenous, from the national to the transnational: borders are no longer the end point but the starting point', as Patrick Stevenson (1998: 102) puts it in his review of the quadrilingual book about language policy in border regions, edited by Roland Marti (1996). In standpoint theories the subordinated borderline positions are turned into resources. When research starts off from the experience and lives of 'people who have been disadvantaged by the dominant conceptual framework' (Harding 1998: 90) (disadvantaged because they have been excluded by these frameworks), the Other starts not only speaking back[5] (criticizing normal

---

[5]'Speaking back' thus does **not** mean correcting the obvious mistakes in 'normal science', even if this is also necessary. An example: John Johnson, curator, Santa Barbara Museum of Natural History (California), claims in an interview as a matter of course that the Chumash in California took scalps in inter-tribal wars (Johnson 1987: 202). (He also claims that there 'was no forced labor. It was an exchange, glass beads for labor' (ibid., 203). See Soft Box 3.16 for this). James A. Lewis, historian, himself an 'Indian of Delaware ancestry' (Lewis 1987: 96) comments on Johnson (ibid., 86): 'I cannot believe that he would be so ignorant about California Indians as to have made this observation. California Indians did not take scalps. The taking of scalps originated on the East coast when Governor Kieft of New Amsterdam offered a bounty on Indian heads. He later changed that to ears, but found he was paying double too often, so finally settled on scalps. It was not a native custom, and was never practiced by California Indians. In the East, Indians later adopted this custom.'

science) and not only creating alternative frameworks (which revalidate the resources of the disadvantaged) but creating **constructive** chaos.

Harding discusses two strands in earlier scholarship on 'difference' that both (radical) feminist and postcolonial standpoint theories are bringing together. I would like to label the two perspectives an '**inside-outside**' perspective (Harding's horizontal one), and a '**below-above**' perspective (the vertical one).

On the one hand there is the tradition noting and studying cultural differences **horizontally**. This could be, for instance, looking at female-male differences, or ethnic (minority and/or majority) groups' cultural differences, trying to describe, explain, and understand the ideologies, behaviours, and feelings the way the people themselves see and experience them, in addition to describing them from the outside. But in this tradition there is a risk of tending to

> lose sight of the global political economy and unequal relations it creates between cultures, as well as of pervasive power relations such as gender relations that create similarities and alliances between, on the one hand, those who can exercise economic and political power and, on the other hand, those who are the object of others' power exercises. (ibid., 91)

The other strand looks at vertical, hierarchical differences, focusing on power relations. The risk here is to overemphasize in a binary way discrete categories of 'the powerful' and 'the powerless' and homogenise the differences **within** the categories (ibid., 91).

To start from the standpoint of the marginalised can **combine** the inside-outside and below-above perspectives. This does not mean that the theorising necessarily uses the discourses and conceptualisations which the marginalised themselves use—after all, they are participating in the hegemonising discourses too. Neither does the theorizing necessarily accept their articulation of problems as **by definition** more valid than others—experiences of oppression do not necessarily and certainly not automatically 'generate counterhegemonic analyses' (ibid., 158–159), as Paulo Freire has also often noted. This does **not** mean, however, that the views 'from the margins' should not be made central, as the quote below claims:

> Indian people have survived efforts at cultural genocide time and again. Regrettably, the assault on Indian cultures includes the perpetuation of false images by non-Indian historians. This being the case, there can be no Indian history, until Indians write it …. Deliberate, gross misrepresentations of native cultures cannot be excused. Indians are still working to overcome historical propaganda, and when they do, it will be the Euro-American tradition of history that must be revised, not Indian history. Indian history should be facilitated, not fabricated. (Jackson 1987: 107)

But standpoint theorists criticize the claims of obejctivism which insist that the only alternative to a 'view from nowhere' (a positivistic 'objective' view posing as neutral) is a special interest bias—which leads to value relativism.[6] In contrast, 'standpoint epistemologies propose that institutionalized power imbalances give the act of starting off from marginalized lives a critical edge for formulating new questions that can expand everyone's knowledge about institutionalized power and its effects' (Harding 1998: 159).

Let us exemplify with one of the many possible questions, about the universality of 'progress' which is a central element in 'Western civilisation'. In development theory there has been a 'development' of successive paradigms, from seeing underdeveloped countries as primitive and savage, through evolutionary and modernism theories (where the countries are 'developing') to core-periphery and dependency theories, to world systems theories (Wallerstein, 1990a, b) and beyond (e.g., Appadurai, 1990). Still, in **all** of them there seems to be a strand about the self-evidence of evolution and progress as necessary and positive, 'a tendency when non-Indians write "Indian history" which has long bothered me ... the implicit "up from darkness" strain of thought ... the view of the inevitability of "enlightenment" or "progress" ', as noted by Professor Alfonso Ortiz, himself Pueblo (quoted in Costo 1987: 25). He continues (ibid., 26):

> Historians and anthropologists who write in this vein treat Indian tribal peoples as if they were also grinding, inevitably, inexorably, up the stepladder of progressive enlightenment and toward greater complexity. To insist on perceiving something that is not there is to distort the true experience of these people.
>
> ... perhaps we Indian people who survived with the essences of our cultures intact really want to make contributions first and foremost to the continued survival and perpetuation of these cultures, rather than to something called "civilization", which is, after all, alien to our traditional cultures, and usually antagonistic to them as well.

Another example of combining the 'inside-outside' and 'below-above' perspectives in discussing 'value relativism', and arriving at the necessity of solidarities from not only a political but a theoretical analysis. Shahrzad Mojab (1998) discusses particularistic theories, ranging from cultural relativism and identity politics to postmodernism, in ways which completely agree with the views in this book. Emphasizing the **differences** that divide human beings and cultures, these theories see notions of 'commonality, solidarity and internationalism' as 'inherently oppressive, Eurocentric, and imperialist', because these for particularists 'represent "Grand narratives", "universalism", "totalization", or "essentialism" ' (1998: 19). Mojab shows elegantly, by examining

---

[6]In the end it can lead to the almost hysterically funny—and serious—incident with Alan Sokal writing a nonsense article posing as the latest multidisciplinary genius and getting this fraud article accepted by a serious scientific journal. See the Sokal & Bricmont 1997 book **Impostures intellectuelles**.

particularist theories in relation to gender relations in the Islamic Republic of Iran, how these theories themselves, using simplistic dichotomies, constructing 'Muslim women' and Islamic societies and their practices as homogenous entities, etc., essentialise, by 'overemphasizing the uniqueness and localism of each and every feminist movement, and opening up great divides among women according to their religion, ethncity, race, nationality, culture and geographic location' (ibid.). Likewise, how these theories 'in the guise of respect for other cultures ... also inescapably endorse the suppression of women's demands for freedom and their subordination to the imperatives of religious, ethnic, and national traditions of patriarchy' (ibid., 19–20). According to her, 'politically, these types of particularism imply either passivism or fragmented and localized micro-initiatives' (ibid., 19). All of this could be applied to an analysis of minority education and the struggle for linguistic human rights too.

LINGUISTIC GENOCIDE, LANGUAGE MURDER— A NOTE ON TERMINOLOGY

Finally, a note on terminology may be needed from the start of the book. The concepts we use participate in constructing our world. The metaphors 'linguistic genocide', 'killing languages', and 'language murder' are very strong. Some scholars recommend that we should eschew the 'loaded terms "murder" and "suicide" in instances of language death' (Dorian, 1994: 118, agreeing with John Edwards' suggestion; Dorian finds it a 'wise proposal' because 'neither metaphor is really helpful'). Despite normally fully agreeing with the essence of Nancy Dorian's descriptions, positions, and arguments (see Dorian in the bibliography), here I disagree.

To me 'language death' is equally loaded (in the sense of taking sides) as are the three other metaphors (I will deal extensively with the two paradigms that the 'death' versus 'murder' represent in chap. 4). When languages cease to be spoken (are pushed into not being spoken), there is the separate issue of researchers disagreeing about the relative role played by outside agents and by the group itself. Here my analysis seems to a large extent to agree with Dorian's view (outside agents often play a decisive role) and profoundly disagree with John Edwards' opinions (the group itself has chosen to stop using their own language, on the basis of a cost-benefit analysis—see also the debate in J. Edwards (ed.), 1994.

But in general, there seem to be two main arguments **against** using the metaphors, and they are related: (1) The metaphors are too strong. To use the same terms as about 'real' (i.e., physical) murder/killing/genocide diminishes the strength of ethical condemnation of horrifying atrocities which have happened when people have been/are collectively physically killed/murdered. The terms should be reserved for this serious **bodily** assault. (2) People who might be allies may react negatively towards such emotionally strong terms.

My contention that the terms **should** be used is based on three types of counterargument.

First, we have the question of physical versus psychological, body and identity.

There is an ambivalent attitude towards bodies and bodiness, especially in western secular cultures. On the one hand, bodies are glorified in at least two senses. Bodies have become commodified, objects to care for, keep young, display, use as both individual and collective identity signs, and so on.

Bodies are also treated as *pars pro toto* (part represents the whole) in rationalistic secularised western thought—they are treated as the only 'real' aspect of humans; all else is seen as part of superstition, myth, religion, transcendental, suspect. You **are** your body, in both these senses. Or your body is you.

To me, the body is just one part of a totality, important but at least for humans also the most 'superficial' one. We are much more than our bodies. Therefore, bodily metaphors are not holier than many others.

On the other hand, many of the things happening to this body are avoided, silenced, embarrassing. Normal bodily functions and physiological changes, especially when we become old, are often partial taboos, again, often in western cultures. This includes biological death where many westerners (except for those in close contact with 'the enemy' in armed forces) are alienated from the more physical aspects of it. Death is sanitized, medicalised, made virtually into a metaphor.

This is not only reflected in language but constructed in and through language. People don't die, they 'pass away' or perform some other euphemistic act. In obituaries, and popular speech, the metaphors about people having died abound. When the ecological agriculture control authorities sent me a letter asking me to slaughter my eight chickens immediately (because their beaks were 'trimmed' when I bought them), they wrote that I should 'put them out' ('sætte ud' in Danish), not 'slaughter them'. Like babies, for wolves to kill, in the old days? Or out to grass? Or what?

To me, naming realities is owning them. Metaphors can hide or enlighten or both. Using some rather than others is always a political act. Many of those who do not want to use the metaphors about 'language murder' are happy with 'language death'. But it is a metaphor at the same level—except for being agentless. It makes languages disappearing sound natural, like dying of old age. They seem to me to be more in the businesses of deception or self-deception than any kind of balanced neutrality.

The shock effect inevitable in calling something 'murder' may in some cases frighten off people, yes. Maybe some of them did not want to know, in the first place?

A second, partly related argument has to do with the comparison between physical and psychological death, torture, pain, genocide, which is a central theme in my book. When the final draft of what became the United Nations Genocide Convention (discussed in several chapters) defined linguistic genocide as 'prohibiting the use of the language of the group in daily intercourse or in schools, or the printing and circulation of publications in the language of the group' (see 5.2.3. for details), many people might think of **physical** prohibition only. Likewise, when reading the part of the Convention which in its Article II (e) includes 'forcibly transferring children of the group to another group' as genocide, most people might think of **physical** transfer only, transfer of the children's bodies.

What I claim throughout the book is that genocide happens equally effectively when a child is **psychologically** (and structurally) prohibited from speaking (and wanting to speak) her own language, and is **psychologically** transferred to another group, made to **want** to identify with a dominat group **instead of**, rather than **in addition to** her own. This reading is confirmed by Article II (b) which includes in genocide 'Causing serious bodily **or mental** harm to members of the group' (emphasis added). Therefore, in order to show the seriousness of the psychological prohibition and transfer (which often **result** in the disappearance of a language), words have to be used which clearly show the similarity of a physical and a psychological process, and which show that the processes are not agentless.

A third argument against using 'language murder' is that it makes language a living organism with a life of its own. This can block our understanding of what happens/is done to languages because we may stretch the metaphor too far. Languages, after all, are not independent entities with their own lives, much as some linguists might like this to be the case. They are completely dependent on users. I accept this argument to a large extent. But then it applies to 'language death' as much as to the other three terms.

I will end on a more personal note. As compared to most academics in my own fields worldwide, I have paid a high price for being critical and asking why-questions. But in the civilised West, critical intellectuals like myself, are not thrown into prison or killed, something that happens to system critics in many countries. Instead, attempts are made to ignore or distort our critique and to invisibilise or marginalise us. And it is not economically safe to ask why-questions: if you are critical, immigrant, and female, there are no jobs for you in academia.

It might also be necessary to remind the reader that I of course have nothing against people learning any languages, including English. Learning dominant languages **additively**, including English for everyone, is OK. It is **subtractive** dominant language learning (where for instance English is learned **at the cost** of the mother tongues, not in addition to them) that kills other languages. This is what I hope my book might make people aware of. That is a starting point for action for diversity.

Part I

SETTING THE SCENE

What Is Happening to the Languages of the World

The Okanagan word for "our place on the land" and "our language" is the same. We think of our language as the language of the land. This means that the land has taught us our language.[1] The way we survived is to speak the language that the land offered us as its teachings. To know all the plants, animals, seasons, and geography is to construct language for them.[2]

We also refer to the land and our bodies with the same root syllable. This means that the flesh that is our body is pieces of the land that came to us through the things that this land is. The soil, the water, the air, and all the other life forms contributed parts to be our flesh. We are our land/place. Not to know and to celebrate this is to be without language and without land. It is to be dis-placed . . . I know what it feels like to be an endangered species on my land, to see the land dying with us. It is my body that is being torn, deforested, and poisoned by "development". Every fish, plant, insect, bird, and animal that disappears is part of me dying. I know all their names, and I touch them with my spirit. (Jeannette Armstrong 1996: 465–466, 470)

Some people have described Kaurna language as a dead language. But Kaurna people don't believe this. We believe that our language is a living language and that it has only been sleeping, and that the time to wake it up is now and this is what we're doing. (Cherie Watkins in **Warranna Purruna—Pa:mpi Tunganar—Living Languages** video, DECS, 1997, quoted in Amery 1998: 1)

---

1. WHAT IS HAPPENING TO THE LANGUAGES OF THE WORLD

This chapter shows that languages are today being killed at a much faster pace than ever before in human history, and relatively much faster than biodiversity. As a consequence, linguistic diversity is disappearing. Some of the direct main agents for this linguistic (and cultural) genocide[3] are, as we shall see in later chapters, part of what is called the **consciousness industry**: **formal education** and the **mass media** (including television, the 'cultural nerve gas' as Michael Krauss, 1992: 6, has called it). Behind them there are of course still more macro-level agents, also to be discussed extensively. Even if formal education is the agent I analyse most in this book, schools alone cannot save languages, as sociolinguist Joshua Fishman has repeatedly pointed out (again in 1998: 414–415)—but schools can kill them more or less alone. Of course schools reflect the rest of society.

The following chapters argue that linguistic (and cultural) diversity are as necessary for the existence of our planet as biodiversity, and that they are related. We as humans are just one part of the planet and its diverse inhabitants, as Jeannette Armstrong so beautifully describes above. Languaging the planet, knowing, using, maintaining, developing further, and cherishing all the languages which over millions of years have developed to describe **specific** lands and environments and **specific** peoples and their cultures, necessarily has to be done in **localised** ways, in **addition** to studies about the universal aspects of each language, and global human experience. Language and languages are an essential aspect—maybe the most essential aspect—of being human. The importance of both language and linguistic diversity is growing, as many of the chapters will show. Acknowledging this importance is hopefully soon bound to make people work against those aspects of globalisation which are killing **all** aspects of diversity, including linguistic diversity. Unless governments not only accept but indeed support diversity and localisation, they are heading for trouble very soon, if we are to believe the quote from the Chilean Commission on Indigenous Peoples below.

> In our times, unity is achieved through diversity. Pluricultural, multiethnic, and multilingual societies rise. The states that don't accept this trend are opting for conflict (1993 Annual Report of the Chilean Commission on Indigenous Peoples [CEPI], quoted in Ekern 1998: 4).

1.1. OUR KNOWLEDGE ABOUT 'LANGUAGE' AND LANGUAGES

1.1.1. Problems in Identifying What Is 'a Language'

If we want to preserve and develop further the world's linguistic diversity, we have to know what to preserve. The first questions then are: What are the languages of the world, how many of them are there, and where are they? The short defensive answer is that we do not really know exactly. The number of 'languages' in the world is not known—and cannot actually be known. Why? There are some good reasons and some bad ones.

The most important 'good' reason is that we don't even properly know what 'a language' is. There are continua of communication (see Chambers & Trudgill 1980). There are no unambiguous criteria for what forms of communication should be called 'two different languages' and what are 'varieties of the same language'. These 'varieties' can be geographical varieties, **dialects**, social varieties, **sociolects**, gender-based varieties, **sexolects** or **genderlects**, age-based varieties, situational or stylistic or subcultural varieties, etc. How can we then differentiate between languages on the one hand and varieties of the same language on the other hand. What are the criteria? What are **your** criteria (Reader Task 1.1)?

Reader Task 1.1
Language or dialect?

Do you remember (or can you think of) a situation where you had (or might have) difficulty understanding what somebody said in (what is supposed to be) a 'dialect' or another variant of **your own** language?

Or the opposite: where you understood something of (what is supposed to be) a **different**, 'foreign' language (one that you have never studied)?

If you did not understand (much of) the 'dialect', would you then call it a different language?

Or if you understood some of the 'foreign' language, would you in fact have to call it a dialect of your own language? Or call your language a dialect of this foreign language?

Why? Why not? What criteria do you use when you label something 'a dialect', or something else 'a language'? List them!

1. _____

2. _____

3. _____

(add more lines if you need them)

Do you know of cases where former 'dialects' of the same language have become different 'languages'. This happened recently, for instance, with what from 1919 to the early 1990s used to be called Serbo-Croat[4]—now it is declared in law to be two different languages, Serbian and Croatian. The reinvention of them is a result of politico-linguistic engineering and the decisions to make the differences as large as possible have been quite explicit. Several linguists are now busy making them more dissimilar, to fit the wishes of many politicians in both Serbia[5] and Croatia (see Jakšić 1996, Jakšić (ed.) 1995). Do you know of other cases? Is 'American' a language (see the Noah Webster quote from 1789 in note 8, chapter 6), or a dialect of English? Are British, Australian, Indian, Nigerian, and American Englishes all dialects of one language, English? Or are there several Englishes? What is 'Ebonics'?

There are no **linguistic** criteria for differentiating between a language and a dialect (or vernacular or patois—see 3.4.2.2.2). **Structural similarity or dissimilarity** can only tell apart very dissimilar languages. Thus it is easy to confirm that, for instance, Chinese and English, or Kurdish and Turkish, are clearly different languages because their linguistic structures are so dissimilar (but see Insert 1.1).

INSERT 1.1 Kurdish and Turkish

The existence of major structural differences does not always guarantee the recognition of separate languages. Turkish propaganda has claimed that Kurds are mountain Turks who have lived isolated in the mountains for so long that they have half-forgotten their mother tongue, Turkish, and now speak a variety that differs slightly from ordinary Turkish. This has then been used to legitimate the assimilation of the Kurds and the oppression of the Kurdish language. Erik Allardt, a distinguished sociology professor who wanted to mention the oppressed Kurds sympathetically in his article in **Contact Linguistics. An International Handbook of Contemporary Research** (Goebl et al. (eds), 1996), wrote, by mistake, relying on some propagandist source, that Kurdish is an Altaic language! Allardt is not a linguist. Kurdish is Indo-European, as far from Turkish—which is Altaic—as Finnish or Chinese are from English, something that is indisputably clear to every linguist. So the Turkish government can now claim that this distinguished professor, Allardt, supports them! It was an error which can really harm the Kurds. Neither Allardt nor the handbook editors had noticed it. They freely admit that it was a complete mistake, and promised to have a note correcting it on the publisher's Web-page. Reader, check if they have!

Despite being structurally very close to each other, Swedish, Danish, and Norwegian are called different languages. Serbian and Croatian may be even closer to each other but they are now (again) called two different languages.

Hindi, Urdu, and Punjabi are structurally and lexically very similar, Kannada and Marathi are structurally almost the same but lexically dissimilar. Structural similarity can thus mainly be used to differentiate between two languages in cases which are so clear that no linguists would be needed anyway to solve the problem. In other cases, linguistic criteria are not of much help.

Mutual intelligibility has also been used as a criterion: if you understand a 'language', A, without being taught that 'language', it is a dialect (or another variety) of your own 'language', B. Or your own 'language' B is a dialect of the one you can understand, A. Or what both of you speak (A & B), are dialects of some third entity, C, which is then called 'a language'. If you don't understand A, it is a different language (but see Insert 1.2).

But the criterion of mutual intelligibility is also far from unambiguous (see Skutnabb-Kangas 1984 for details). Let us say that speaker A under-

> **INSERT 1.2** 'Lappish' and Finnish
>
> Mutual non-intelligibility can also be completely disregarded for political reasons. An early school geography textbook from Sweden (**Geografie för ungdom**, by Daniel Djurberg (1781: 189)) claims: 'In Sweden two main languages are spoken, Swedish and Finnish. Lappish is a dialect of the latter' (my translation). All Sámi ('Lappish') languages are completely non-intelligible for ordinary (i.e., non-linguist) Finns, and Finnish and the Sámi languages have always been considered by linguists as completely separate languages even if both are Finno-Ugric. In my personal view, the difference is, for instance, much greater in terms of mutual intelligibility than that between the two Indo-European Germanic languages, English and Norwegian.

stands B, and speaker B understands C, who in her turn understands D. On the other hand, speaker A does not understand C, and speaker B does not understand D. Where is the boundary then between language and dialect. Or if A understands B but B does not understand A (**non-reciprocal intelligibility**), are A and B dialects of the same language for speaker A who understands both, but two different languages for speaker B who does not understand both?

How well do the speakers need to understand each other? Is '**semi-communication**' enough (Haugen 1966: 102) or must the understanding be '**complete**' (and is it ever complete even between speakers of the same language)?

If we think of the situation where languages are oral (spoken) languages and have not been reduced to writing, people in neighbouring villages often understand each other, either well, or at least to some extent, despite the differences, but they may not understand people from villages much further away. These in turn understand their close neighbours, etc. There is an example in Insert 1.3 which we will also use later.

This means that we have a continuum of 'dialects' where those people whose villages are physically close to each other have learned to understand each other. Usually it has been physical barriers which have created the large differences: mountains, deserts, even oceans—whereas smaller waters have not functioned as barriers for communication; quite the opposite. People learned how to cross lakes and seas before they used horses, donkeys or camels to cover long distances, and they even crossed oceans much before they learned how to fly over mountains. We could call what people in village 25 or village 30 (in Insert 1.3) spoke, 'a dialect' **or** 'a language', and both would be 'correct'. In the early days, just like now, people noticed some differences and variation and some similarities between how they themselves spoke and how others spoke. But they did not necessarily use a specific

---

INSERT 1.3 Dialect/language villages

Let us take an example and start with a village we call **25**, our basic village. The people in 25 understand people from 24 and 23 and from 26 and 27 really well. They understand 22 and even 21 people, and 28 and 29 people fairly well but have to concentrate harder. They understand quite a lot of what 20 and 30 people say but certainly not all, and they have quite a lot of difficulty in understanding 19 and 31. They only understand a bit of what 18 and 32 say, but 17 and 33, and, especially, 16 and 34 are almost impossible. They can only grasp some words of 15 and 35 people's speech.

If we instead start with village 30, we can add and deduct in the same way. These people understand quite a lot of what 25 and 35 people say but certainly not all, and they have quite a lot of difficulty in understanding 24 and 36 and can only grasp some words of what people from 20 and 40 say.

```
10                        20
    12    17                  22        29            31
 11    16                  21        28          30    32
    13    18                  23    27                33
       15                       24  26                          35
    14        19                   25                         34
```

'language' **name**, for instance Spanish or Swedish, or a specific 'dialect' name, for what they themselves or others spoke.

When asked what they call themselves, many people who have not been influenced by outside linguists or ethnographers often use a word that would translate as 'people' or 'humans', e.g. 'Inuit', or Khoe ('khoe-i', person, Louw 1977: 86, quoted in Traill 1995: 4). When asked for a name for what they speak, many reply with a word that would translate as 'language' or 'tongue'. People often do not have a **specific** name for who they are or what they speak but use a generic name. Alternatively, their name for themselves or their language may come from another neighbouring 'dialect' or 'language', because these others have had a need to refer to the neighbours before these needed to do it themselves, and then the people have accepted the neighbours' name for them as their own name (see Insert 1.4).

But even people who move from their original habitat or are in contact with others may give as their mother tongue a name which does not correspond to a name of a specific language in the categorisations of linguists (see Insert 1.5 for examples).

INSERT 1.4   Name 'Kaurna' comes from neighbouring people

Rob Amery explains that the name 'Kaurna' for one of Australia's Aboriginal peoples 'most likely . . . comes from the Ramindjeri or Ngarrindjeri word **kornar** "men; people"' and continues: 'Perhaps a more suitable name for the Kaurna might be **Meyunna** . . . **Meyu** "man; person" is distinguished from corresponding terms in neighbouring languages Nukunu **miṟu**; Ngayawang **meru** (**mera** "men"); Ngarrindjeri **korni**; and Narungga **nipu**. **Meyunna** then would define the Kaurna-speaking region.' (Amery 1998: 4). The Kaurna word **meyunna** means 'people'.

INSERT 1.5   Census returns for 'mother tongue', India

In India, census returns for 'mother tongue' may give the name of a language or regional or social variety of a language. But people did also give as the name for their mother tongue in the 1961 census the name of a writing system, a cast, a religious sect, a place, a profession, a people—or, to use literal translations of some of the most interesting diaspora 'mother tongues': 'My mother tongue is "I-come-from-another-village"' or 'My mother tongue is "I-am-not-a-speaker-of-the-language-which-they-speak-in-the-place-where-I-currently-live"' (the examples are from discussions with Debi Prasanna Pattanayak and Lachman Khubchandani—thanks!).

In the 1961 census, the last one where the mother tongue question was asked—later censuses have classified mother tongues under major language heads or grouped them together—the return gave 388 labels for scheduled languages (see Info Box 5.7), 304 for tribal languages, 336 for non-scheduled and non-tribal languages, 521 for unclassified languages, and 103 for foreign mother tongues, altogether 1,652 'languages' (Pattanayak 1981a: 42). These were then classified into 193 'languages'. The 1951 census listed a total of 845 mother tongues. Grierson, in the earliest attempt to codify linguistic diversity in India, listed 179 languages and 544 dialects in his **Linguistic Survey in India**, carried out between 1886 and 1927 (Sridhar 1996: 328). Chaturvedi & Singh (1981: 49–61) list 367 mother tongues with numbers of speakers.

As Pattanayak puts it: 'Places are not geographical concepts; they exist in people's consciousness. So does the concept of "mother tongue". It is not a language in the general sense of the word, neither is it a dialect. It is an identity signifier waiting to be explained' (1992).

Should the speakers who test the criteria be **monolingual**? It is, for instance, easy for me, knowing other Indo-European languages like Danish, English,

German, Latin, Norwegian, and Swedish, to understand some Dutch, without having ever been taught Dutch. Would Dutch then be a separate language for a monolingual Swedish-speaker who does not understand Dutch, but a dialect of Swedish, or German, or English, for me?

Is **oral** understanding enough, or should we rather use understanding of **writing** as a criterion? Or the opposite: is understanding writing enough, or should one also understand the oral mode? A Finn who has studied Swedish at school, understands some written Danish, but does not understand spoken Danish at all. Is oral Danish then a separate language from Swedish, while written Danish is a dialect of Swedish? And what about the Deaf?

Should the criterion be used only with language **spoken by a native speaker, with normal speed**, or can a **second language speaker** who speaks slowly also be used? When several Namibian SWAPO-teachers were asked after a 2-week workshop in Zambia, conducted in English, whose English was easy and whose difficult to understand, I came out as the easiest one of all to understand, whereas some native speakers of English were almost incomprehensible to them (and English is my fifth language in terms of order of learning). Several factors contribute to this. Among them are (1) speed of delivery (SLUs—second language users—may speak more slowly, carefully, or distinctly); (2) level of formality and repertoire in general, as compared to the learners' competence (SLUs may choose to speak more informally or simply, or may not have access to all those formal registers which NSs (native speakers) have (e.g., 'donorspeak' in the SWAPO case); (3) degree of metalinguistic awareness (SLUs may be more aware, at a general level, than NSs, especially monolingual NSs, of what may make a foreign language difficult to understand (even when the specifics depend on the source and target languages involved). SLUs have themselves learned other languages and also the language in question (here English) as a foreign language and may know more about what is difficult in that language); (4) listeners' own group membership/prejudices/ideologies (which may or may not match those of the speaker).

Age, amount of formal schooling, amount of exposure to the language or to other languages in general, learning styles, courage, motivation, fatigue, etc., obviously also affect intelligibility, in many situations much more than the 'same language/different languages' question.

Mutual intelligibility as a criterion thus discriminates well only in situations with structurally unrelated languages, as was the case with the structural linguistic criterion too.

Neither similarity or dissimilarity of structure, nor mutual inelligibility or lack of it can therefore differentiate between languages. Norwegian and Swedish show close structural similarity and most speakers understand each other and can read each other's languages fairly well (Maurud 1976 reviews the literature and tests the mutual understanding between the three Scandinavian languages). Still they are seen as separate languages. Many variants of Black English, cockney, RP (Received Pronunciation, the way English is pronounced and used by a small elite—3%, some estimates say—in England), Indian, Nigerian, or Appalachian Englishes are all supposed to represent one and the same language, English, even if their native speakers may not always understand each other[6] and there are big systematic structural differences.

The social functions of languages, measured, for instance, by the speakers' own views on what are different languages, are based partly on the two linguistic criteria mentioned above (structural similarity, mutual intelligibility), but mainly on extra-linguistic criteria (for an elaboration see Skutnabb-Kangas 1984: 59–64). In Debi Prasanna Pattanayak's view (1991: 27–28), 'the developed countries treat their respective dominant languages as resources, call them world languages, and use them to further their national interest', while those of the 'Third world elites' who follow the West 'deride the mother tongues' in their own countries 'as dialect, slang, patois, vernacular, and condemn them to marginal use, or completely ignore them' (ibid., 28).

One possible criterion which has been suggested is **standardization**. Only dialects which have been reduced to writing (a prerequisite for standardization) and been standardized are languages, everything else is something else (dialect, vernacular, patois). Peter Trudgill's old definition (1983: 16) reflects this; for him 'languages' were 'independent, standardized varieties . . . with, as it were, a life of their own'. This would drastically reduce the number of 'languages' in the world. Very few indigenous languages and only a handful of sign languages would qualify as languages according to this definition. But it might be understood in a historical context, though, as the following Scandinavian example shows.

It only becomes natural to speak about a language as a specific, discrete unit, distinct from other similar units, when there is a written form of that language, claims Tore Janson, earlier Professor of Latin, now Professor of African Languages, at the University of Gothenburg, Sweden (1997: 125). He describes the development of languages **in Europe**, their written forms and the names for them, as follows (1997: 119–136; the example with the villages continuing from Insert 1.3 is my application). The written forms which were developed for the languages we know today were all based on the model from Latin. This displaced and replaced other ways of writing (for instance the Runic script in Scandinavia). In most cases, a written form came first and a name for the language only afterwards. One or some of the dialects were chosen as the basis for the written form, and the choice was obviously made by those or to benefit those who 'needed' the written form in the first place: the elites, the state builders, the church representatives. Writing was needed for lists, contracts, laws, bureaucracy.

These choices were also decisive for inclusion and exclusion: the acts of rulers—each trying to rule over as large areas as possible—decided where the borders in the dialect continua between what was called one language and what another language would be placed. We could imagine that our villages in Insert 1.3 were in what is now Denmark, Sweden, and Norway. We could designate **village 23** as comprising **Västgötaland**, a county in today's Sweden, the area ruled some 750 years ago by the Older Västgöta Law (*Äldre Västgötalagen*). This law was written in the 1220s and was the first book, written in the Latin alphabet, in what later became Sweden. Västgötaland was by that time ruled by the king of **Svealand**, another county in what is now Sweden (our basic **village 25**). In the Västgöta Law, only the people from Svealand were called **Swedes**. The old Västgöta law was written in the dialect of village 23, Västgötaland. Similar laws for other areas (present-day counties) of Sweden were written later, also in their respective dialects (24, 26). In addition to giving the name to the **people**, the Swedes, our village 25, Svealand, also gave the name to the later **state** of Sweden, and the **language** Swedish. This happened in the first law for the whole country which was passed in 1347. It starts as follows: 'Eet kunungx rike, sum hætir **suærike**, hauer i sik siu biskops døme ok nio laghmanz døme meth landamærum thera' (A kingdom which is called **Sweden** ['Sverige' in modern Swedish], contains seven bishoprics/sees and nine legal districts with their land areas; my translation). The state (*rike*, *Reich*) is the basic ingredient, and it is ruled by the king, who has formed a union with the church and the governors. The state is peopled by 'alz **suirikis** almogha' (all people of the **Swedish state**). The law was written in what the law explicitly calls 'suensko' (Swedish; '*svenska*' in modern Swedish). From 'Sweden' and the 'Swedes' (and also, by analogy, the **Swedish language**) having been only something to designate people from village 25 (and their speech, the dialect of the **Svea**), when the borders were enlarged, Sweden, Swedishness and the Swedish 'language' became what people in all the villages 20–29 had in common. This is how Tore Janson judges it (1997: 128; my translation):

> Swedish is thus here finally established as a separate, independent language which has a privileged status, ordained in law, in the independent state of Sweden. The state shall have a common king, it shall have a common law, and it shall have a common language. The Swedish language gets both a name and an official function in the first common Swedish law. In this case it is unusually clear that the creation of the language is connected with the creation of a political entity, the new Swedish state.

In fact, village 29 which we here designate 'Skåne', the southern part of today's Sweden, alternated between Sweden and Denmark for a long time, and in many respects what is now called the 'Skåne dialect' of Swedish is, according to linguists, much closer to 'Danish' than 'Swedish' (e.g., Bannert 1994, Gårding & Bannert 1979). There is an independence movement in Skåne where some people want to claim Skåne as an independent state.

Today, the more or less arbitrary borders within our dialect continuum above designate what is spoken by people in villages 10–19 as 'Norwegian', what is spoken in 20–29 as 'Swedish', and what is spoken in 30–35 as 'Danish'. Out of a dialect continuum, three 'separate' 'languages', three discrete units, have thus emerged.

In fact the **main criterion** for whether something is a dialect of another language or a separate language (and what is being standardized, what not) is the relative **political power of the speakers of that language/dialect**. The decisions about what *are* 'languages' and what are not are thus political decisions. Political definitions of a language would be:

A language is a dialect (or a vernacular or a patois, see 3.4.2.2.2)

with an army (and a navy)

or

A language is a dialect with state borders

or

A language is a dialect promoted by elites.

The main "good" reason for our ignorance about what a language is and how many languages there are is thus that the difference between a language and dialects/sociolects, and the cut-off points between various languages (if they exist at all) are political and arbitrary.

There might be discrete points between structurally completely unrelated language families, but within each language family, even if they are large (like the Indo-European language family) non-linguistic decisions determine where on the continuum to cut off. 'Our definition of "language" is still based on geopolitical, ethnic or cultural rather than linguistic criteria' says Martin Durrell (1990: 921, quoted in Harmon 1995a: 3), one of many similar formulations. Chambers & Trudgill illustrate this in their 1980 book **Dialectology**, through European dialect continua, showing five of them on a map (p. 7): **Scandinavian** (comprising dialects of Norwegian, Swedish, and Danish), **West Germanic** ('all dialects of what are normally referred to as German, Dutch and Flemish' ibid., 6, and using the example that varieties spoken in Vienna and Ostend—the most western point—are not mutually intelligible, but they are linked by a chain of mutual intelligibility), **North Slavic** (Russian, Ukrainian, Polish, Czech, and Slovak), **South Slavic** (Slovene, Serbo-Croat, Macedonian, and Bulgarian), and **West Romance** (varieties of French, Italian,

Catalan, Spanish, and Portuguese). They also include social dialect continua in their discussion.

Peter Mühlhäusler, Professor of Linguistics in Adelaide, Australia, claims that the existence of separate languages may be a Western myth and substantiates this with examples from the Pacific. The Indian linguist Lachman Khubchandani has for years been saying much the same (see his work in the bibliography). Mühlhäusler (1996: 101) claims that the belief 'that successful communication depends on having a shared grammatical and lexical code is a Western assumption, not a fact.'

This means that, contrary to Peter Trudgill's old definition of languages as necessarily standardized varieties, forcing people to accept shared grammatical rules or excluding certain words or certain ways of pronunciation, or any other ways of standardizing language in general, does not necessarily make oral (spoken) communication more successful—on the contrary, it can harm it. This may of course be different in the case of some written communication. One example is Chinese. There are many Chinese languages ('dialects') where the speakers at least initially understand little of each other's speech, but since they all write the 'same' Chinese, they can communicate in writing and, if they stay in contact, eventually also orally.

Now if Khubchandani and Mühlhäusler are right in their claims about the doubtful existence of one of the very objects we are discussing in this book, namely 'a language', and having said that we don't know what a language is, why do I continue this study at all?

These claims do *not* mean that we should stop speaking about separate languages. The importance of the claims above is that we need to be careful every time people talk about separate languages. We need to ask who has the (political) power to claim that this is a language or that is a dialect. Naming the world is an act of power—an act of and for God(dess) (see section 4.1.1, Who invented language?). The issue of the power involved in naming will be discussed in more detail in many parts of this book.

But even when we might decide for practical purposes what a language is, there are still other gaps in our knowledge, and these reflect the 'bad' reasons.

1.1.2. Our Knowledge About Languages Is Shaky

Ordinary people who are not linguists (see Insert 1.6), including politicians (see Insert 1.7), often have no idea whatsoever of the number of languages in the world.

The Keating quote (Insert 1.7) shows how naive the layperson's image of the number of languages in the world is. Ordinary people, including students,

---

INSERT 1.6   Number of languages in the world is 300,
number of states is 2,000 (a classroom scene, USA)

I asked an American teacher and his senior high school students who work extremely actively with multilingualism, multiculturalism, and language and cultural rights, how many **languages** they thought there were in the world. The teacher's guess was 300, the students' initial guesses varied between 200 and 500. I gave them the 'correct' figure. Then I asked how many **states** they thought there were. After their underestimation of the number of languages, they obviously wanted to be on the safe side. The teacher's first guess was 2,000. This might be seen as a sign of Americocentricity of the US education and mass media: the rest of the world is pretty invisible (see also Chomsky 1987, 1989, Pilger 1998) but, mainly, that language is such a self-evident part of our everyday lives that many of us have no need to find out more about it.

INSERT 1.7   Paul Keating: Australians understand all languages

The former Australian Prime Minister, Paul Keating, stated in his Opening Address to the 1995 Global Cultural Diversity Conference (26–28 April 1995, Celebration of the 50th Anniversary of the United Nations) in Sydney, referring to Australia, that '. . . more than 220 nationalities are represented in our population.' (p. 2). 'We have learned that being among the very few countries whose people understand all but a few of the world's languages and cultures is a very considerable competitive advantage' (p. 11).

Comment: If Keating thinks that nationality is the same as citizenship, then indeed there are no more than a couple of hundred nationalities in Australia (i.e., there may be citizens of most states in the world). But how he from this concludes that these people 'understand all but a few of the world's languages and cultures' is a mystery—it seems that he thinks that there are no more than 200-odd languages and cultures in the world. See Ozolins 1993 for an overview of Australian language policy; see also Lo Bianco 1987.

---

also often know very little about where different languages are spoken or how they are related to each other. The relative visibility and perceived value of various languages have less to do with the languages themselves and their speakers, and more with the ideological and political/economic relationships between the speakers of the respective languages and the states where they live. But test yourself! The questions in Reader Tasks 1.2 to 1.6 come from a study originally conducted by Tom Bloor in Britain (1986). Mark Sebba (1994) replicated parts of Bloor's study at Lancaster University, UK, where first-year students of Linguistics completed the questionnaire at their first

---

Reader Task 1.2
Names of languages?

Indicate which of the following are the names of languages and which are not by ticking the appropriate box.

	Yes	No
Soviet		
Israeli		
Rumanian		
Serbo Croat		
African		
Indian		
Czech		
Chilean		
Hindi		
Korean		

Reader Task 1.3
Most likely to hear the language in country x?

For each language, tick the one country in the right-hand column where you would be *most* likely to hear the language.

Spanish	A. Brazil ☐ B. Argentina ☐ C. Portugal ☐ D. Malta ☐
French	A. Trinidad ☐ B. Algeria ☐ C. Sicily ☐ D. Peru ☐
Urdu	A. Turkey ☐ B. Namibia ☐ C. Pakistan ☐ D. Burma ☐

(Continued)

Reader Task 1.3
(Continued)

Afrikaans	A. North Africa B. South Africa C. East Africa D. West Africa	☐ ☐ ☐ ☐
German	A. Austria B. Belgium C. Netherlands D. Hungary	☐ ☐ ☐ ☐
Gujerati	A. Turkey B. Ghana C. Libya D. India	☐ ☐ ☐ ☐

Reader Task 1.4
Where are Arabic and Chinese widely spoken?

Tick the Yes or No box

Arabic is widely spoken in	Yes	No	*Chinese* (of some type) is widely spoken in	Yes	No
Libya			Hong Kong		
Tanzania			Fiji		
Tunisia			Japan		
Egypt			Taiwan		
Sudan			Bangladesh		
Kenya			Malaysia		
Namibia			Singapore		
Malaysia			Sri Lanka		
			Burma		
			Yemen		

Reader Task 1.5
Widely spoken or official languages?

Name *two* languages which are widely spoken or have official status in the following places.

Cyprus	1. _____	2. _____
Belgium	1. _____	2. _____
Spain	1. _____	2. _____
Canada	1. _____	2. _____
Switzerland	1. _____	2. _____

Reader Task 1.6
Official status for English? other languages?
largest number of speakers?

A. Name *two* languages *apart from English* which have official status somewhere in the **British Isles** (Ireland, Scotland, Wales, England, and off-shore islands).

1. _____   2. _____

B. Name *four* countries outside Europe where English is used for official purposes

1. _____   2. _____
3. _____   4. _____

C. Which language has the largest number of speakers who learn it from their parents as their first language?

_____

---

lecture in the first week of term. I replicated the study with 37 second-year general humanities students at Roskilde University, Denmark, in January 1994, and with 6 professional trainers of teacher trainers in California, USA, in February 1994. Some of their replies have been extracted.

Now you can compare your answers with the correct ones in Info Boxes 1.1–1.5 below. Probably you did not get everything right? You are in good company. You can also compare with how some other people have replied.

❖ Info Box 1.1 ❖

Are These Names of Languages? (See Task Box 1.2)

Name	Correct answer	Got it right (R) %		Got it wrong (W) %			Did not know (?)	
		RUC	CA	Lan	RUC	CA	RUC	CA
Soviet	no	92	67	—	5	—	3	33
Israel	no	56	67	49	39	33	5	—
Rumanian	yes	82	83	—	13	—	5	17
Serbocroat	yes	74	17	51	23	67	3	17
African	no	72	67	25	28	17	—	17
Indian	no	67	67	54	33	17	5	17
Czech	yes	64	67	43	28	17	8	17
Chilean	no	54	50	35	36	17	10	33
Hindi	yes	74	100	—	15	—	10	—
Korean	yes	68	100	22	26	—	8	—

Lan = Lancaster University; RUC = Roskilde University Centre; CA = California trainers of teacher trainers group. The percentages for 'right', 'wrong', and 'don't know' are given from my own studies, Roskilde and California. For Lancaster I only have the percentages of 'wrong' answers.

❖ Info Box 1.2 ❖

Most Likely to Hear the Language in Country X?
(See Task Box 1.3)

				RUC	?	CA	?
Spanish	A.	Brazil	☐	26	10	17	—
	B.	*Argentina*	☐	49		83	
	C.	Portugal	☐	3		0	
	D.	Malta	☐	15		0	
French	A.	Trinidad	☐	10	10	*	—
	B.	*Algeria*	☐	74		100	
	C.	Sicily	☐	3		0	
	D.	Peru	☐	0		0	
Urdu	A.	Turkey	☐	21	15	0	—
	B.	Namibia	☐	3		17	
	C.	*Pakistan*	☐	56		83	
	D.	Burma	☐	5		0	
Afrikaans	A.	North Africa	☐	5	13	0	—
	B.	*South Africa*	☐	69		100	
	C.	East Africa	☐	8		0	
	D.	West Africa	☐	5		**	

(Continued)

				RUC	?	CA	?
German	A.	*Austria*	☐	83	3	67	—
	B.	Belgium	☐	8		17	
	C.	Netherlands	☐	3		0	
	D.	Hungary	☐	3		17	
Gujerati	A.	Turkey	☐	0	44	0	17
	B.	Ghana	☐	28		17	
	C.	Libya	☐	4		0	
	D.	*India*	☐	21		67	

RUC = Roskilde; CA = California; ? = don't know; *1 person gave both A and B; **1 person gave both B and D. The correct alternative is italized. The percentages for correct answers for each language and the percentage of "don't know" (?) are given from my own studies, Roskilde and California. A couple of results from Lancaster are in the text below the table.

After a discussion with my contact person in California, two more languages (Farsi and Mien) were added for the California testees, because the community had many refugees from **Iran** and **Laos**, respectively. The alternatives given were, for **Farsi**, Saudi Arabia, Estonia, Egypt and Iran, and for **Mien**, Vietnam, Laos, Mozambique and Morocco. All of them got Farsi right and all but one got Mien right (the remaining one suggested Vietnam).

Here the adult professional trainers in California did considerably better than the European students for all other countries except Austria, with German. How would you explain and/or interpret this?

32% of the Lancaster students thought Spanish was most widely spoken in Brazil and 13% in Malta. 18% voted in favour of Trinidad for French. 16% thought Namibia and 16% Burma was a home for Urdu. 33% placed Gujerati in Ghana.

❖ **I n f o   B o x   1 . 3** ❖

Where Are Arabic and Chinese Widely Spoken?
(See Task Box 1.4)

For *Arabic*, Yes and No are as follows: **Yes** for Libya, Tunisia, Egypt, and Sudan; **No** for Tanzania, Kenya, Namibia, and Malaysia.

The answers of the **ROSKILDE** students were as follows (C=correct; W=wrong; ?=don't know):

Yes-countries: Libya C82%, W10%, ? 8%; Tunisia C74%, W18%, ? 8%; Egypt C93%, W 0%, ? 8%; Sudan C64%, W18%, ? 18%.

No-countries: Tanzania C72%, W 0%, ? 28%; Kenya C69%, W3%, ? 28%; Namibia C64%, W3%, ? 33%; Malaysia C62%, W8%, ? 31%.

The answers of the **CALIFORNIA** trainers of teacher trainers were as follows:

Yes-countries: Libya C67%, W 0%, ? 33%; Tunisia C33%, W33%, ? 33%; Egypt C83%, W 0%, ? 17%; Sudan C50%, W17%, ? 33%.

(Continued)

No-countries: Tanzania C67%, W 0%, ? 33%; Kenya C83%, W 0%, ? 17%; Namibia C67%, W 0%, ? 33%; Malaysia C50%, W17%, ? 33%.

28% of the **LANCASTER** students thought incorrectly that Arabic was **not** spoken in Tunisia and 16% **not** in Egypt whereas 27% of them thought that it **was** spoken in Namibia.

For *Chinese*, Yes and No are as follows: **Yes** for Hong Kong, Taiwan, Malaysia, Singapore; **No** for Fiji, Japan, Bangladesh, Sri Lanka, Burma and Yemen.

ROSKILDE students replied as follows:

Yes-countries: Hong Kong C95%, W5%, ? 0%; Taiwan C74%, W14%, ? 12%; Malaysia C39%, W39%, ? 23%; Singapore C82%, W8%, ? 10%.

No-countries: Fiji C56%, W23%, ? 21%; Japan C69%, W5%, ? 26%; Bangladesh C62%, W13%, ? 26%; Sri Lanka C59%, W13%, ? 28%; Burma C49%, W26%, ? 26%; Yemen C62%, W8%, ? 31%.

CALIFORNIA teacher trainers replied as follows:

Yes-countries: Hong Kong C83%, W 0%, ? 17%; Taiwan C100%, W 0%, ? 0%; Malaysia C50%, W17%, ? 33%; Singapore C67%, W 0%, ? 33%.

No-countries: Fiji C50%, W17%, ? 33%; Japan C50%, W17%, ? 33%; Bangladesh C67%, W 0%, ? 33%; Sri Lanka C67%, W 0%, ? 33%; Burma C67%, W 0%, ? 33%; Yemen C67%, W 0%, ? 33%.

40% of the Lancaster students thought incorrectly that Chinese was **not** spoken in Malaysia whereas 38% of them thought that it **was** spoken in Fiji.

❖ I n f o B o x 1 . 4 ❖

Languages Widely Spoken or With Official Status
(See Task Box 1.5)

Cyprus: Greek, Turkish, English.
Belgium: French, Flemish/Dutch, German.
Spain: Castilian, Catalan, Basque.
Canada: English, French; in Northwest Territories also Cree, Chipewyan, Dogrib, Gwich'in, Slavey (including North and South Slavey), and Inuktitut (including Inuvialuktun and Inuinnaqtun) (Harnum 1993: 1; see also Northwest Territories Education, Culture and Employment 1994).
Switzerland: French, German, Italian, Romanch.

Most of the European students knew these whereas the Californians had problems with all but **Canada**. 50% of them did not know any of the languages of **Cyprus**; 33% suggested English for **Belgium** and one of them suggested German in addition (correct, of course, but this person did not know any of the big Belgian languages); one knew no other languages except Spanish for **Spain** while another one had French as the other language for Spain; English was suggested by two and 'Swiss' by one for **Switzerland**.

❖ **I n f o   B o x   1 . 5** ❖

Languages Apart From English Which Have Official Status in British Isles
(See Task Box 1.6, A)

Irish, Welsh (not Scottish Gaelic).
Countries outside Europe where English is used for official purposes (Task Box 1.6, B). Table 5.2 lists 75 countries of which only 5 are in Europe. The European students had no difficulty and neither did most of the Californians, but there was one suggestion of Japan, and one person could not mention any other countries (from a list of 70) except South Africa.
The language with largest number of first language speakers (Task Box 1.6, C) is Chinese. 58% of the **Lancaster** students listed Chinese; English got 30%, Spanish 9%, French 1%, and Japanese 1%. 79% of the Danish students in **Roskilde** listed Chinese; Spanish got 13% and 8% did not know. 50% of the **California** trainers of teacher trainers listed Chinese and 50% Spanish. It is interesting that none of the Danes *or* Americans listed English while 30% of the British students did.

Now you might think that I am blaming ordinary people for not knowing enough about languages. Not really; some details are specialist knowledge. But I am worried about **the results** of this ignorance, and also want to analyse causes for it. Tom Bloor (1986: 13–14, quoted in Sebba 1994: 1), who developed the original test, was also worried about the results:

> It is not in itself particularly disturbing that three-quarters of an elite group of language students cannot name a Bantu language or that nearly as many do not know that Turkish is spoken in Turkey, but these isolated facts are symptomatic of an ignorance that is disturbing . . . It is a reflection of the general neglect of language issues, and to some extent of current affairs and social matters, in British education . . . From a very limited vocational point of view, these concerns are peripheral, except to students of language and linguistics, but the centrality of language in human life suggests that it is foolish to ignore them.

As we have seen, it is not only the British educational system that leaves students with patchy knowledge about languages. But the uneven knowledge is also typical of reference works for popular use, as Mark Sebba has shown in an analysis in 'publicly available non-specialist sources of information about language such as atlases and almanacs' (1994: 2). Of the 10 representative reference works he studied,[7] only the **The New State of the World Atlas** by M. Kidron and R. Segal (both versions that he used, 1987 and 1991) were more or less accurate. Sebba also says that the incorrect information in itself is not so troubling: it is, after all, difficult even for a linguist to obtain up-to-date and satisfying information about the linguistic situation in most parts of the world. What *is* troubling is the manifest failure of most of the reference works cited to take language sufficiently seriously . . .

Since most people use language habitually, they take it for granted (just like the air they breathe). For many people language may not seem terribly interesting, as compared to many other issues. Despite 'knowing' that we live in an information society (but see Pilger 1998: 3), and that language plays a major role in mediating information, the role of language in maintaining and reproducing (unequal) power relations and in colonising people's consciousness may not even occur to people.

Also, many people seem to think that they know a lot about language, or at least what is important to know. Many have common sense opinions about aspects of it (for instance about language learning, or bilingual education) which are completely wrong.

This lack of knowledge might also be partially responsible for the fact that few people are interested, or react, when hundreds or even thousands of languages are ceasing to be spoken (= being pushed into not being spoken), partly because these people did not even know that these languages existed in the first place. Or that they were languages. I have often heard people talking about 'all those dialects of the different tribes in Africa' (see chapter 3 about 'us' having languages and nations while 'they' have dialects and tribes).

Still, this knowledge **should** of course be available. As Info Box 1.6 shows, a lot **has** been written.

There have during the last couple of decades been many attempts to catalogue the world's languages for specific areas (e.g., Crozier & Blench 1992 for Nigeria, Wurm et al. 1996 for the Pacific), but we still have basically very little of reliable total data. In terms of basic descriptive facts, it would be not only useful but a minimum requirement for proper work on the maintenance of linguistic diversity to have data for **all** the languages in the world (not only those listed in the **Ethnologue**—Address Box 1.4). We would minimally need:

- Descriptions of the languages and their speakers, and the eco-socio-political situation of them.
- Text samples like the ones in Katzner (see Info Box 1.6), or, rather, sound samples for oral languages, sign samples for sign languages (sign languages are ignored in all the books in Info Box 1.6), and also text samples for those languages which have been reduced to writing.

In addition, it would be interesting to have:

- Citations about the languages, like the ones collected by Joshua Fishman in his 1996 book **In Praise of the Beloved Language. A Comparative**

View of Positive Ethnolinguistic Consciousness which were seen as '"characteristic statements" . . . that "sing the praises of" the language' (ibid., 7–8; Fishman has 141 citations from 76 languages, ibid., 300).

- Stories from all of them telling about the origins of languages, as in the 6 volumes (1957–1963) by Arno Borst, **Der Turmbau von Babel. Geschichte der Meinungen über Ursprung und Vielfalt der Sprachen und Völker** (The building of the tower of Babel. A history of views on the origins and diversity of languages and peoples).

For **concerted action** (i.e., not only description and not only ad hoc action, emergency rescue missions), much more is needed, including finance for implementation. These issues will be discussed later.

It shows something about the low status of knowledge about languages that this kind of proper minimal taxa do not exist. A very small but still impressive start has been made with the LINCOM's (Address Box 1.1) language documentation programme **Languages of the World** which has four series: **Materials** (descriptive grammars); **Dictionaries**; **Text Collections** (texts

---

❖ Info Box 1.6 ❖

*Literature Describing and Classifying
the World's Languages*

See Merritt Ruhlen's **A Guide to the World's Languages** 1991 (where volume 1 is called **Classification**) and C. F. and F. M. Voegelin's **Classification and index of the world's languages** 1977. See also Campbell 1995 (revised edition 1998) **Compendium of the world's languages**; Comrie (ed.) 1987 **The world's major languages**; Comrie, Matthews & Polinsky (eds) 1996 **The Atlas of Languages**; Lyovin 1997 **An Introduction to the Languages of the World**; Meillet & Cohen 1952 **Les langues du monde**; Moseley & Ashley (eds) 1991 **Atlas of the world's languages**; Sebeok (ed.) 1963–1976 **Current trends in linguistics**, Vols. 1–14. See also the volumes utilized in tables below, in chapter 1. See also the journal **Languages of the World** (Address Box 1.1).

Kenneth Katzner's 1975 book **The languages of the world** (3rd edition 1994) also has short texts in the individual languages it describes, 40 from Europe, 33 from the Soviet Union, 9 from the Middle East (Kurdish included but, as is often the case, with a gross underestimation of numbers of speakers), 45 from Asia, 7 from Oceania, 26 from 'the Western hemisphere', here meaning indigenous languages of the Americas, 34 from Africa, and 'an artificial language, Esperanto'[8]), totalling 195 languages. Max Hans-Jürgen Mattusch' recent book (1999), **Vielsprachigkeit: Fluch oder Segen für die Menschheit? Zu Fragen einer europäischen und globalen Fremdsprachenpolitik** describes multilingualism and languages from a similar perspective as this book.

```
* * * * * * * * * * * * * * * * * * * * * * * * * * * * * * * * * * * * * * * *
*                                                                            *
*              Address Box 1.1   The journal Languages of the World          *
*                                                                            *
*   email address <lincom.europe@t-online.de>.                               *
*   A useful online address to publications and projects about languages is  *
*   <http://home.t-online.de/home/lincom.europa>.                            *
*                                                                            *
* * * * * * * * * * * * * * * * * * * * * * * * * * * * * * * * * * * * * * * *
```

with full linguistic analysis); and **Text Library** (collections of texts, in original and translation, mostly to English, from riddles and folktales to political, religious, and everyday texts).

Impressive as this little list may seem, most of the languages of the world have still not been even described. LINCOM's ambitious language documentation programme **Languages of the World**, for instance, proudly announces in their online catalogue that they now have grammars of more than 150 languages. If we count the sign languages too and say that there are, maybe, some 6,500 oral and equally many sign languages, making 13,000 in all, that would be grammars of 1.15 percent of the world's languages . . .

To me this lack of absolutely basic knowledge about languages, even about their basic numbers, shows something about the value judgements behind decisions about the worth of various knowledges and research disciplines—and here we have the main "bad" reason behind the lack of knowledge about our object of study. What kind of knowledge is considered important enough to attract a lot of funding?

Many natural scientists can count in fractions of their basic units, in nanounits (nanoseconds, nanomillimeters, etc.), and use this detailed knowledge for sending space ships to Mars, or splitting sheep or soya bean genes for commercial purposes, or for patenting life, or bioprospecting. But in the case of linguists counting people who speak or use different languages, people who are depositories of the world's most precious resources, our linguistic and cultural capital, **any** basic counts can be questioned, as the rest of the chapter shows. In Denmark, a bacon-exporting country, there are at any one time exact figures for how many pigs of different kinds, ages, and weight classes there are, but no idea of how many or which languages people speak as their mother tongues or what linguistic competencies people living in Denmark have. For pigs, or atoms, we have reasonably reliable figures and descriptions in terms of the basic units; for speakers of the world's languages even our millions can be questioned as the tables in this chapter show. For human capital, the basic human linguistic and cultural diversity unit is an individual, and we should at least know how many individuals there are with the precious resource, the capacity to speak natively Avar or Berber or Cree or Dargin or English or Friulian or Guarani or Hausa or Inuktitut or Jaisalmeri or Kalmyk

UNESCO World Languages Report

The **World languages report** is a UNESCO project whose aim is to describe the linguistic diversity of the world, study the evolution and current state of the languages, and explain the problems which affect them in the different regions of the world. The aim of this action is to draw attention to the need for a proper management of the world's linguistic heritage. The project was approved at the UNESCO General Conference (29th meeting) of 1997, and is financed by the Basque Country. The **World languages report** will be based on two sources of information: a specially-designed survey and a specialised bibliography. The survey will be sent out to experts, research institutes and organisations which can provide information on the situation of languages. The computer processing of the data will make it possible to update the information and produce future periodocal reports on the situation of the world languages. The report will also offer a series of recommendations for the safeguarding and promotion of the linguistic heritage of mankind [sic!]. The **World languages report** will be published in the year 2001. (from the Introduction sheet to the report, 1998)

Address Box 1.2   UNESCO World languages report

UNESCO ETXEA, Alameda de urquijo, 60 ppal.dcha, E-48011 Bilbao, Basque Country (Spain); phone 34-944-276432; fax 34-944-272548; email <unescopv@eurosur.org>; Web-site <http://www.unescoeh.org>.

International Clearing House for Endangered Languages

Works with UNESCO on the Red Books on Endangered Languages (see Address Box 2.2). Functions as a data bank of materials on endangered languages. Publishes a newsletter. See Address Box 1.3.

```
* * * * * * * * * * * * * * * * * * * * * * * * * * * * * * * * * * * * * * * * * * *
*                                                                                   *
*              Address Box 1.3   International Clearing House                        *
*                           for Endangered Languages                                *
*                                                                                   *
*    Department of Asian and Pacific Linguistics, Institute of Cross-Cultural       *
*    Studies, Faculty of Letters, University of Tokyo, Hongo 7-3-1, Bunkyo-ku,      *
*    Tokyo 113, Japan; phone: 81-3-3812 2111 ext. 3797; fax 81-3-5800 3740;         *
*    contact: Prof. Tasaku Tsunoda, Director, email: <tsunoda@tooyoo.l.             *
*    u-tokyo.ac.jp>; Dr. Kazuto Matsumura, Associate Director, email:               *
*    <kmatsum@tooyoo.l.u-tokyo.ac.jp>; Web-site: <http://www.tooyoo.l.              *
*    u-tokyo.ac.jp>; email: <staff@tooyoo.l.u-tokyo.ac.jp>.                         *
*                                                                                   *
* * * * * * * * * * * * * * * * * * * * * * * * * * * * * * * * * * * * * * * * * * *
```

or Luo or Mazhua or Njerep or Ojibway or Portuguese or Quiché or Roraima or Sorani or Tuscarora or Uzbek or Vot or Waghdi or Yeni or Zaza (just to pick a sample of languages in alphabetical order). But we do not know this.

There is some hope of our knowledge increasing, though, with two ambitious UNESCO projects, especially the **World languages report project** which has recently started and expects to publish its report in the year 2001. It 'seeks to provide a complete documented register of all the languages that exist throughout the world. To this end, world-wide research will collect all the data possible on different languages so as to establish a database on the world's linguistic heritage.' (from the Document sheet, describing the project, 1998—see Info Box 1.7 and Address Box 1.2).

The other UNESCO-supported project is **International Clearing House for Endangered Languages**, in Tokyo (Info Box 1.8; Address Box 1.3).

But if the projects are based on existing haphazard knowledge (as they are), it means trying to fit together many detailed but incomplete maps, where hundreds of different ways of drawing the maps have been used, and where only parts of the world are covered. (Terralingua—see Info Box 2.4—has recently started a project trying to improve this mapping). Also, the knowledge flowing in to the UNESCO projects depends to a large extent on both the good will and time of researchers replying to time-consuming questionnaires (with no remuneration for this work) and on the quality of their existing primary, secondary or tertiary knowledge, rather than systematic collection of new primary knowledge.

Many of the questions about languages and linguistic and cultural diversity are not only fascinating but vital for the future of the planet. They influence our (and our children's and grandchildren's) everyday lives in very important ways as we will see.

Ignorance about language(s) is not the main reason for the killing of languages, though—power relations, including structural forces, are. Formal education is, together with mass media, a main killer of languages.

DEFINITION BOX 1.1 Linguicism (Skutnabb-Kangas)

Ideologies, structures, and practices which are used to legitimate, effectuate, regulate, and reproduce an unequal division of power and resources (both material and immaterial) between groups which are defined on the basis of language (see also Definition Box 5.4 with a wider definition).

Formal education and the ideologies about languages which guide it reflect both institutional/structural and also often individual **linguicism** (hierarchisation based on language, akin to biologically argued racism and sexism—see Definition Box 1.1). And linguicism is **not an information question**: once we know more, we act accordingly and the world is saved.

Still, information hopefully at least does not do any harm. After you have read this book, dear reader, you at least cannot claim: 'I did not know'.

With these first warning words, we turn to some of the basic figures about linguistic diversity and its disappearance, the killing of languages.

1.2. THE WORLD'S LANGUAGES: NUMBER OF LANGUAGES AND NUMBER OF SPEAKERS

1.2.1. Number of Languages

1.2.1.1. *Reliability of Statistics*

After the caveats about uncertainties in our definitions and knowledge, we go on to claim that there probably are something between 6,500 and 10,000 **spoken (oral)** languages[9] in the world, and a number of **sign languages** which can be equally large. Below we look at the figures (and the lack of reliable figures) more carefully.

There are many oral languages which are spoken by millions of people. But most languages in the world are in fact spoken by fairly few people. The **median** number of speakers for oral languages is probably some 5–6,000 people (Krauss 1992: 7). And most languages in the world are *not* used for reading and writing on a daily basis. Many different statistics on the number of languages in the history of humankind have been presented (Info Box 1.9).

Statistics change all the time. 'In 1929 the French Academy announced that the number of languages in the world was exactly 2,796', Gunnemark (1991: 102) reports.[10] The principles behind each set of statistics can be discussed and questioned on many counts, as many researchers—for instance Michael Clyne and John de Vries, see bibliography—have repeatedly shown when working with census statistics (see also Gunnemark 1991 and Putseys 1993 for various criticisms; see also Info Box 1.10).

> ### ❖ Info Box 1.9 ❖
>
> #### Differences in Estimates on Numbers of Languages in Prehistoric Times
>
> Here is one example of the variation in statistical estimates. Michael Krauss estimates that the number of (oral) languages in prehistoric times was probably around 10–15,000 whereas Mark Pagel's estimate (quoted in Ostler 1995: 6) is 31,000–600,000, with a middle estimate of 140,000. See section 4.1.3 for a discussion.

> ### ❖ Info Box 1.10 ❖
>
> #### Examples of Difficulty in Getting Reliable Census Figures
>
> An example of the difficulties, given by Valentin Vydrine who did fieldwork in Mali in 1997 among Kagoro-speakers: 'So, in the population census which took place exactly during my stay in the Sebekoro village, Kagoro was not present in the list of Malian languages, and all those who said that their language is Kagoro were listed as Bamana (Bambara)' (1998: 5). Francis Ekka, then Acting Director of the Central Institue of Indian Languages, himself from an indigenous ('tribal' in Indian terminology) people, reported (1995) that he had 'a list of 149 endangered languages whose speakers number below 10,000 and these are not listed in the Census', and discussed their problems in his paper.
>
> One might, somewhat eurocentricly, expect that administratively well-organised countries like Canada, with a manifest interest in languages, would be in an excellent position census-wise. Not so. There is serious criticism, with many examples, of the statistics on native languages in, for instance, Cook 1998 and Drapeau 1998 and in many of Michael Krauss' detailed publications (see also references in them and in Mark Fettes' publications).

I will in the following mainly use the **Ethnologue** (see Address Box 1.4) estimate of some 6,700 oral languages, especially where I have done specific counting myself rather than using other authors' data. Where nothing else is said, it is always the latest online version as per July 1998, i.e. an updated version of the 13th edition of the **Ethnologue**.

Many other sources have also been used (for instance, Krauss 1992, Gunnemark 1991, Crystal 1987, 1995, 1997a, b, McArthur 1998, and others, including figures from international organisations).[11] All of them are not compatible. This means that there may be differences and inconsistencies in the figures in the different tables, and some of these will be shown. Erik Gunnemark's 1991 book **Countries, Peoples and their Languages. The Geolinguistic Handbook** strikes me as a very impressive source but his careful, conservative

```
* * * * * * * * * * * * * * * * * * * * * * * * * * * * * * * * * * * * * * * * * * * * *
*                                                                                       *
*                    Address Box 1.4    The Ethnologue                                  *
*                                                                                       *
*    The so far most comprehensive total (and online searchable) listings of the        *
*    world's (mostly oral) languages are in the 13th edition of Ethnologue, edited      *
*    by Barbara F. Grimes (1996) of the Summer Institute of Linguistics; the            *
*    latest estimates (as of July 1998) can be found in the updated 13th edition        *
*    on the Web: <http://www.sil.org/ethnologue/>; emails <www@sil.org> and             *
*    <editor.ethnologue@sil.org>. The Ethnologue 'is a catalogue of more than           *
*    6,700 languages spoken in 228 countries. The Ethnologue Name Index lists           *
*    over 39,000 language names, dialect names, and alternate names. The                 *
*    Ethnologue Language Family Index organizes languages according to                   *
*    language families.' (from their Web presentation).                                  *
*                                                                                       *
* * * * * * * * * * * * * * * * * * * * * * * * * * * * * * * * * * * * * * * * * * * * *
```

estimates are to be seen as minimum figures, as he himself also acknowledges.[12] **Ethnologue** also assesses the reliability of some of their own information about languages. For threatened languages, the online versions of UNESCO's Red Books on Endangered Languages (parallelling to some extent the Red Lists of threatened animals, plants, etc.—see Address Boxes 2.1 and 2.2), are an invaluable source. Many of the sources are critical and self-critical, and some use various categorisations of the reliability of their own information.

There is no way (even for researchers who *are* specialised in the field—and I am not) to check the accuracy of all the different figures—reliable and comparable census figures do not exist. Both researchers and international organisations (e.g., UNESCO and others who issue statistical yearbooks) publish data about the numbers. The detailed knowledge of linguists should obviously be combined both with overviews from international organisations which can oblige governments of mosts countries in the world to give them the available data, and, of course, with the only 'concrete' source of information, the speakers themselves. Regrettably, though, much of the data has not been gathered in comparable ways. Some of the problems are that the criteria for inclusion, exclusion, definitions, and categorisations differ. Some countries use endo-definitions about mother tongues while others use exo-definitions (see Definition Box 1.2).

1.2.1.2. *Where Are the Languages?*

Of the **Ethnologue** estimate of over 6,700 mostly oral languages:

- ■ **Europe** has only 3% (225 languages). Of these, 94 are 'endangered', i.e., on the Red Book on Endangered Languages (online version, downloaded 10 August 1998; this version is also used in references below).

DEFINITION BOX 1.2 Endo-definitions and exo-definitions (autonyms and heteronyms)

Endo-definition—one's own definition of oneself or of one's own group and language, its name, place, and status.
Exo-definition—a definition of oneself or one's own group and language, its name, place, and status, by outsiders.

UNESCOs **World Language Report** survey (1998)—see Info Box 1.7— uses for endo- and exo-definitions of names of languages (glottonyms[13]), the terms 'autonym' ('name given to the language by native speakers') and 'heteronym' ('name given by the non-native community to the language').

Some official definitions of indigenous peoples combine a criterion by origin with both internal and external identification: an Aboriginal person is someone of Aboriginal descent, who identifies as an Aborigine (endo-definition) and who is accepted by others in the Aboriginal community as an Aborigine (exo-definition at an individual level but endo-definition at a group level). The tendency is, though, towards an endo-definition only for indigenous peoples but not for minorities. See also the legal definitions in chapter 7.

- **Europe and the Middle East together** have only 4% of the world's oral languages (275 according to Krauss 1992: 5).
- All the **Americas** (North, South, and Central) together have around 1,000 of the world's oral languages, 15%. Krauss (1992: 5) reports 900, while Gunnemark (1991: 102) reports the following: US and Canada have at least 200 Indian and Eskimo languages, Latin America at least 700 Indian languages; the total may be up to 1,000–1,100.

  The rest, 81% of the world's oral languages, are in Africa, Asia, and the Pacific.
- **Africa** has

  —over 1,400, according to Gunnemark (at least 1,200, perhaps 1,500 or even more, 1991: 102)

  —close to 1,500, according to Ruhlen (1991: 76)

  —1,900, according to Krauss (1992: 5)

  —2,011, 30% of the world's languages, according to the **Ethnologue**

  Of these, 171 are on the Red Book on Endangered Languages online version.
- Asia has

  —excluding ex-USSR, about 1,600, Gunnemark 1991: 102

—2,165, 32% of the world's languages, according to **Ethnologue**
- **The Pacific** has
    —about 1,200, Gunnemark, ibid.
    —1,302 or 19%, **Ethnologue**
- **Asia and the Pacific together** have
    —3,000 according to Krauss 1992: 5
    —3,467 in the **Ethnologue**)
Of these, on the Red Book on Endangered Languages online version, 14 are extinct or possibly extinct, and 45 are in other endangered categories in Northeast Asia, while 79 are on the Asia-Pacific list.

The distribution for sign languages might follow similar lines—the facts are simply not known (see Definition Box 4.1 and references in it).

1.2.1.3. Megadiversity Countries

There are, according to Krauss (1992: 6), nine countries in the world with more than 200 languages each (Gunnemark's 1991 figure is 6). According to Krauss (1992: 6) they account for more than half the world's languages (Krauss' total is 3,490—see Table 1.1. Krauss uses the 1988 **Ethnologue** figure of 6,000 languages even if he has had some late 1990 updates). The 9 are the two megadiversity countries, Papua New Guinea and Indonesia (850 and 670 respectively, according to Krauss' 1992 figures) and seven others.

Another 13 countries have more than 100 languages each; they are presented in roughly descending order in Table 1.1.

TABLE 1.1
The countries with most languages in the world

Over 500 Languages		Over 200 Languages		Over 100 Languages
1. Papua New Guinea	850	1. Nigeria	410	1. Philippines
2. Indonesia	670	2. India	380	2. Russia
		3. Cameroon	270	3. USA
Total	**1,520**	4. Australia	250	4. Malaysia
		5. Mexico	240	5. China
		6. Zaire	210	6. Sudan
		7. Brazil	210	7. Tanzania
				8. Ethiopia
		Total	**1,970**	9. Chad
		TOTAL for 9	**3,490**	10. Vanuatu
				11. Central African Republic
				12. Myanmar (Burma)
				13. Nepal

Based on figures given in Krauss 1992: 6.

These top 22 countries, just over 10 percent of the world's countries, probably account for some 75 percent (over 5,000) of the world's oral languages.

Table 1.2 also presents some of the differences between different authors; Krauss has been used as the first source for **ranking** the countries. The list contains those 22 countries which according to Krauss have more than 100 languages. Krauss, Gunnemark, and Robinson (1993) present the total number of languages whereas David Harmon's figures (1995a: 14) consist of **endemic** languages only (see Definition Box 1.3). In the **Ethnologue** column I have used the figures for 'living' languages; **Ethnologue** also gives the figures for 'extinct' languages.

The relatively small differences between Harmon's figures and those of the others show that countries high on endemic diversity are also high on general linguistic diversity, i.e. the conditions which have promoted the evolvement of unique languages seem to be the same which promote general linguistic diversity. These conditions will be mentioned below in section 2.4. According to IWGIA (International Working Group on Indigenous Affairs), there are at present perhaps 5,000 linguistic groups that may qualify as indigenous or tribal peoples in the world (see Definition Boxes 7.1 and 7.2 for definitions on Indigenous), and the total number of individuals may approach 300 million (IWGIA 1996). Even when the state borders have often been drawn so that some groups may exist in several countries (e.g., in Latin America), most indigenous peoples are probably endemic.

Here we can also show results of using Robinson's (1993) diversity evaluation (see the discussion in section 2.2). Table 1.3 lists the 10 most linguistically diverse countries, based on not the number of languages in the country but on the **percentage of the population speaking the largest language**.

A comparison with the earlier tables based on defining **diversity in terms of the number of languages in each country** shows that only three of the countries on Robinson's list would qualify as top diversity countries: Papua New Guinea, Cameroon, and Zaire. Even when we take the 22 most diverse countries in terms of number of languages (those with over 100 languages each), only Vanuatu would be added to the three. Six countries from Robinson's list would still be outside. Thus the two ways of evaluating linguistic diversity

---

DEFINITION BOX 1.3   Endemic species & languages

'**Endemic species** are those found in restricted locales and nowhere else' (WRI 1988: 95, quoted in Harmon 1995a: 6).
'**Endemic languages** are those restricted to a single country' (Harmon 1995a: 6—for problems with this definition see Harmon 1995b).

TABLE 1.2
Variations in estimates of number of languages in the most diverse countries

Country	Krauss		Gunnemark		Harmon		Robinson	Ethnologue	
Papua New Guinea	1	850	1	a. 750	1	847	867	1	817
Indonesia	2	670	4	o. 300	2	655	701	2	772
Nigeria	3	410	2	a. 400	3	376	427	3	470
India	4	380	3	a. 350	4	309	405	4	407
Cameroon	5	270	5	o. 200	7	201	275[§]	6	279
Australia	6	250	9	a. 150	5	261		7	234
Mexico	7	240	—	**	6	230		5	289
Zaire	8	210	6	a. 200	9	158	219	8	221
Brazil	9	210	7	o. 150	8	195		10	195
Philippines	10	*	11	o. 100	10	153	168	12	168
USSR	11	*	14	o. 100	20	71[#]		20	104[#]
USA	12	*	8	o. 150	11	143		11	176
Malaysia	13	*	10	a. 120	15	92	141	13	137
China	14	*	—	**	17	77		9	205
Sudan	15	*	12	o. 100	14	97		14	132
Tanzania	16	*	13	o. 100	13	101	131	15	131
Ethiopia	17	*	—	**	16	90	112	21	82
Chad	18	*	—	**	19	74	126	16	127
Vanuatu***	19	*	15	o. 100	12	105	111	19	109
Centr. Afr. Republ.	20	*	—	**	—	##		22	68
Myanmar (Burma)	21	*	16	a. 100	—	##		18	110
Nepal	22	*	—	**	22	68		17	124

Harmon: endemic languages only; the others: all languages

a. = about; o. = over; *numbers not mentioned; **not on Gunnemark's list of 16 countries with over 100 languages; ***earlier New Hebrides; #Russia, not USSR; ##not on Harmon's list of the top 25 most diverse countries; §266 on Robinson's detailed Appendix 3 in the same article; both figures are said to be based on the **Ethnologue** 1992. Sources: Krauss 1992 (Krauss' figures are also repeated in Graddol 1996: 197); Gunnemark 1991; Robinson 1993; Harmon 1995a, **Ethnologue** (I have counted some of the figures on the basis of more detailed ones, specifically those for Indonesia, Malaysia and Russia). In addition to these, Harmon's list of 25 countries (1995a: 14) contains the following (the ranking number precedes the country name): 18. Peru (75), 21. Solomon Islands (69), 23. Colombia (55), 24. Côte d'Ivoire (51) and 25. Canada (47).

TABLE 1.3
The 10 most linguistically diverse countries, according to Robinson 1993

Country	Country pop. (millions)	No. of living lgs.	LLG	No. in LLG	LLG as % of pop.	Official lgs.
1. Papua New Guinea	3.6	867	Enga	164,750	5	English Tok Pisin Hiri Motu
2. Vanuatu	0.143	111	Hano	7,000	5	Bislama English French
3. Solomon Islands	0.3	66	Kwara'ae	21,000	7	English
4. Côte D'Ivoire	12.07	75	Baoule	1,620,100	13	French
5. Gabon	1.069	40	Fang	169,650	16	French
6. Uganda	17.593	43	Ganda	2,900,000	16	English
7. Cameroon	11.9	275	Beti	2,000,000	17	French English
8. Kenya	25.393	58	Gikuyu	4,356,000	17	Kiswahili English
9. Namibia	1.372	21	Ndonga	240,000	17	English
10. Zaire	35.33	219	Ciluba	6,300,000	18	Ciluba Kikongo Kiswahili Lingala French

lgs. = languages, LLG = largest language group
(adapted from Robinson 1993: 55; based on figures in **Ethnologue**, 12th edition; my abbreviations)

really do give very different results. It is also significant that the largest language in the country is an offical language in only one of the ten countries (Ciluba in Zaire) on Robinson's list (but see the discussion in Info Box 2.2).

1.2.2. Number of Speakers of Each Language

From the number of languages in various countries we move to the number of speakers of each language, having already taken this into account in our second measure of linguistic diversity above. Even here the figures can be discussed from several angles, starting from the question of what a language is (see, e.g., Mühlhäusler 1996) and how it can be defined. Is it advisable to bunch together all the Chinese languages, including Mandarin and Cantonese? Treating Hindi/Urdu as one complex, based on linguistic structure (as has been done by some authors), could be used politically to legitimate war.

Likewise, the notion of a 'speaker' (or 'native speaker' or 'mother tongue speaker' or 'first language speaker'—the concept 'mother tongue' is clarified further in chapter 3) of a language is a really murky one, as many authors have noted (e.g., articles in Coulmas (ed.) 1981, Amery 1998, Rampton 1990, Phillipson 1992b, Davies 1991). The numbers are extremely unsure anyway, as mentioned earlier.

The **top 11 oral languages** in the world, in terms of number of mother tongue speakers, are Chinese (Mandarin Chinese accounts for 16% of the world's speakers), English (8%), Spanish (5%), Arabic (all varieties, 4%), Hindi, Portuguese, Bengali and Russian (all 3%), Japanese, French, and German, all around 2% . All have more than or very close to 100 million speakers. But even if they represent only 0.10–0.15% of the world's oral languages, they take half the pie: they account for some 51% of the speakers, i.e. the world's oral[14] population. The figures come from David Harmon's (1995a) figure with the share of the linguistic pie that the big ones take (except I have added German). But even here we already have uncertainty about the numbers of speakers, as will be shown below in the tables.

The first column in Table 1.4 is based on Graddol (1997, Table 1, p. 8), with figures created by his engco model.[15] The rank ordering is here according to the engco model numbers. The **Ethnologue** (second column) figure for the number of Chinese speakers has, for instance, gone up from 1,123 million in the June 1996 13th edition to 1,223 million in the June 1998 revised 13th edition. The third column is based on Gunnemark (1991: 167) and the fourth on Crystal (the first figure on his 1987: 287 and the second on his 1997b, the second edition of **The Cambridge Encyclopedia of Language**; I have extracted the list from his Appendix with almost 1,000 languages with more than 100,000 speakers, pp. 443–451).

As we can see, the authors agree on which languages are the top 10, even if the ranking differs somewhat. Crystal's first figures are obviously some 5 years older than Gunnemark's and 10 years older than **Ethnologue**'s and Graddol's. But this does not explain why the number of native English speakers would in fact have **decreased** in 10 years from Crystal's 350 to **Ethnologue**'s 322 million. It is also interesting that the two British evaluators have the highest figures for English. Since **some** of Crystal's second figures are directly from the **Ethnologue** (Hindi, Spanish), it is also interesting that there are fairly big differences between his and the **Ethnologue** in some of the others (English, Chinese,[16] German, Arabic) where the three others agree much more.

There is much more disagreement about the following dozen languages (Table 1.5). According to Graddol (1997:8), the next three languages—he does not give more—are French (engco 70), Italian (57) and Malay (47). Gunnemark (1991: 167) gives all home languages with at least 35 million speakers. I have again extracted the figures in Crystal's column from his second edition of **The Cambridge Encyclopedia of Language** (1997b: 443–451).

TABLE 1.4
**The top 10 oral languages in terms of number of first language speakers,
all more than 100 million speakers, in millions**

Name of language	L1-speakers, engco, Graddol	First language speakers, Ethnologue	Home language speakers, Gunnemark	Mother tongue speakers, Crystal, 1987; 1997b
Chinese	1. 1,113	1. 1,223	1. o. 1,100	1. 1,100 1. 1,002
English	2. 372	2. 322	2. o. 300	2. 350 2. 400
Hindi/Urdu*	3. 316	6. 182	4. o. 250	4. 200 4. 182
Spanish	4. 304	3. 266	3. o. 300	3. 250 3. 266
Arabic	5. 201	4. 202	5. 200	5. 150 5. 180
Portuguese	6. 165	7. 170	7. o. 160	8. 135 8. 154
Russian	7. 155	7. 170	8. 160	7. 150 7. 155
Bengali	8. 125	5. 189	6. 185	6. 150 6. 162
Japanese	9. 123	9. 125	9. n. 125	9. 120 9. 126
German	10. 102	10. 98	10. n. 100	10. 100 10. 123
Total	2,996	2,947	o. 2,630	2,705 2,750

o. = over; n. = nearly; *Graddol puts Hindi and Urdu together, the other three have only Hindi here.

Except for Urdu, Crystal's estimated numbers of second language speakers (in parentheses) seem to correspond better to Gunnemark's home language speakers than the figures Crystal himself gives for mother tongue speakers. Crystal's figures are in general somewhat lower than Gunnemark's, except for the glaring exception of French (where Gunnemark's figure is close to that of other researchers whereas Crystal's is way above them). The comparison also shows that many of the difficulties in the estimates may have to do with the definitions of the scope of the languages (e.g., for Panjabi, Bhojpuri, and even Gujarati).

If we use Gunnemark's estimates and allow for some growth since his 1991 book, we see that all other languages in the world except around 30 have fewer than 35 million native speakers.

TABLE 1.5
The languages with between 35 and 100 million first language speakers, in millions

Name of language	Gunnemark	Crystal	Ethnologue
Panjabi*	11. o. 90	12. 78	20. 56
Javanese	12. o. 80	13. 75	11. o. 75
Korean	13. n. 70	14. 60	12. 75
French	14. 65	11. 109	13. 72
Tamil	14. 65	17. 50	17. 63
Telugu	14. 65	16. 54	15. o. 66
Vietnamese	17. o. 60	15. 55	14. 67
Marathi	18. 60	17. 50	16. n. 65
Italian	19. n. 60	23. 40 (65)	24. 40
Turkish	20. o. 50	17. 50	18. 59
Persian	21. n. 50	26. 20 (55)	26. n. 35
Urdu	22. o. 45	21. 41 (85)	19. n. 57
Thai	23. 45	25. 25 (50)	25. 35
Ukrainian	24. n. 45	20. 45	23. 41
Polish	25. n. 40	23. 40	21. 44
Bhojpuri	26. o. 35	21. 41	25. 25
Gujarati	27. o. 35	27. 33	21. 44
Total	920	866	919

o. = over; n. = nearly

For Crystal, his estimated numbers of **second** language speakers have been given in parentheses for some languages.

*Both Punjabi and Panjabi are used, also by speakers of the language themselves.

According to Tore Janson (1997: 198), there are around 60 languages with **more than 10 million speakers**, together accounting for far over 4 billion people. In addition to the top 10 plus the 27 between 35 and 100 million above, that would mean an additional list of 23 languages. Using Gunnemark's figures from his list of languages with at least 1 million home speakers (1991: 169–171), Asher's list of the languages of the world (mainly based on the **Ethnologue**, 12th edition; extracted by me from Asher (ed.) 1994: 5189–5240), and Crystal's 1997b list of languages with at least 100,000 speakers as a first language (extracted from pages 443–451), we get the following list of 36 languages (with between 10 and 35 million speakers according to Gunnemark) (Table 1.6). I have also counted the ranking for each.

When thinking of possible African **lingua francas**, it is interesting that the figures in Table 1.6 vary so much, especially for Fulfulde, the language which is spoken both as mother tongue and as a 'community language' (see Defi-

TABLE 1.6
Languages with beween 10 and 35 million home speakers, numbers and ranks

Name	Number of home speakers, Gunnemark		Number of speakers, Asher		Number of first language speakers, Crystal	
Akan	36	10	35	6	35	5.7
Amharic	15	18	15	15	19	14
Assamese	27	o. 12	28	10	9	20
Azerbaijani	19	16	33	6.8	18	14.1
Berber*	30	11	26	11	33	*7.5
Burmese	1	o. 30	7	22	8	22
Cebuano	19	16	22	12	22	12
Czech	35	10	22	12	26	11.7
Dutch	12	20	9	20–21	9	20
Ful/Fulfulde	9	22**	19	13	36	1.8
Greek	31	n. 11	22	12	27	11.5
Hausa	5	30	7	22	4	25 (40)
Hungarian	25	n. 14	18	14.5	17	14.4
Igbo/Ibo	23	15	17	14.7	22	12
Indonesian	1	o. 30	1	o. 35	1	35 (125)
Kannada	1	o. 30	4	27	22	7
Kurdish	33	o. 10	35	6	34	6
Magahi	28	12	28	10	31	10
Malay	32	10.5	12	17.5	12	19 (130)
Malayalam	1	o. 30	2	34	3	26
Marwari/Mewari/ Rajasthani	33	o. 10	33	6.8	21	13.8
Nepali/Gurkhali/ Pahari	24	14	14	16	14	16
Oriya	6	n. 30	3	30	6	23.2
Oromo	17	o. 17	30	8	29	10.6
Pashto	10	o. 20	30	8	16	15.9
Quechua/Quichua	29	o. 11	32	7.9	32	8.4
Rumanian	7	25	6	25	7	23
Rwanda-Rundi	12	20	21 (Rundi 4, 6; Rwanda 8)	12.6	28 (Rundi 5; Rwanda 6, 2)	11.2

(Continued)

TABLE 1.6
(Continued)

Name	Number of home speakers, Gunnemark		Number of speakers, Asher		Number of first language speakers, Crystal	
Serbo-Croatian	16	n. 18	10	20	12	19
Sindhi	22	o. 15	13	17	19	14
Sinhalese	26	13	19	13	25	11.8
Sundanese	7	25	4	27	4	25
Tagalog	17	o. 17	27	10.5	30	10.5 (40)
Uzbek	14	n. 19	15	15	14	16
Yoruba	10	o. 20	10	20	9	20
Zhuang	21	15.5	22	12	22	12

o. = over; n. = nearly.

Based on Gunnemark 1991: 169–171, Asher (ed.) 1994: 5189–5240, and Crystal 1997b: 443–451; the rank numbers added. Gunnemark does not have Maithili where Crystal's figure is 23.8 million.

*Crystal does not have an entry for Berber (which is the outsiders' name of a subgroup of languages from the Hamito-Semitic or Afro-Asiatic family, comprising of Shluh, Tamazight, Riffian, Kabyle, Shawia, Tuareg (Tamashek)—Katzner 1975: 7) but has instead several Berber languages: Kabyle 2.5 million, Tamajeq/Tamashek 900,000, Tamazight 3 million, Tarifit 1 million (see the special number on Berber of the **International Journal of the Sociology of Language**, nr 123, 1997—see also 7.8.2). **The language is called Fulfulde by many of the native speakers. In English it has often been called Fulani, in French Peul. Other names are Fula, Fulbe, and Pular/Pulaar. It is not listed under any of the other names in Crystal's list. Gunnemark (1991: 118) gives the following list for Fulfulde: Nigeria 12 million, Guinea 3, Senegal over 2, Mali over 1, Niger 1, Cameroon 800,000, Burkina Faso over 700,000, Benin 200,000, Mauritania 200,000, Guinea-Bissau nearly 200,000, Gambia over 100,000. Unesco Regional Office for Education in Africa (1985: 32) lists 14 countries where it is spoken (Sierra Leone, Ghana, and Togo in addition to Gunnemark's list; in these countries it is spoken as a family not community language; see Definition Box 1.4). A 'community language' could be spoken by native speakers or second language speakers.

nition Box 1.4) in more countries (to be exact, in 14 countries) than any other African language, according to UNESCO's Regional Office for Education in Africa (1985) (Kiswahili comes second, spoken in 10 countries—in 7 as a community language—and Mandinka third, with 8 countries—in 6 of these as a community language) (see Info Box 1.11).

Gunnemark's list is of course again based on figures that are almost a decade old, but so are many of the entries in the others,[18] and all of them use partially the same common sources, mainly the **Ethnologue**. We get an indication of some relative sizes of some groups, but there are some significant and disturbing differences between the three lists in Table 1.6. These reflect both our ignorance of basic issues in the field of the languages of the world but also of course the complexity of the task, including definitions of 'language' and 'speakers' as discussed earlier. But also agreement between

DEFINITION BOX 1.4 Community language

Community language—'the dominant and general means of communication in a district or province or similar larger area . . . which serve the purposes of general communication over fairly wide areas within countries, are what are referred to as the **community languages** in Africa. The term community language was adopted at the subregional seminar on National languages and Teacher training in Africa, Dar es Salaam, 1979 . . . That seminar gave a five tier categorisation of African languages in relation to development as follows:

- mother tongue languages
- community languages
- national language or languages (i.e. decreed as such)
- languages of African intercommunication
- international languages (i.e. English, or French, etc).' (Unesco Regional Office for Education in Africa 1985: 10)

❖ **I n f o B o x 1 . 1 1** ❖

'Community Languages' in Africa

UNESCO's Regional Office for Education in Africa (1985: 12) identified 159 'community languages' in the 45 sub-Saharan African states (excluding South Africa), estimating the number to no more than 200. Of these, some 23 languages are used as community languages in more than one state, Fulfulde, Kiswahili, and Mandinka/Malinke as the top scorers. If we include in the list of languages spoken in more than one country also family use, we still get the same 23 languages, but more countries. The following list is compiled from the UNESCO publication above, pages 27–48; the number of countries where the language is spoken is indicated after the name of the language: Creole[17] 5, Crioulo 4, Dyula 2, Ewe 3, Fang 4, Fulfulde 14, Hausa 7, Kanuri 4, Kikongo 3, Kiswahili 10, Kpelle 2, Kreol 2, Lingala 2, Lozi 2, Luo 2, Mandinka 8, Setswana 2 (if South Africa had been counted, the figure for Setswana would be 3), Shona 2, Songhay 4, Soninke 3, Tamashek 2, Wolof 3, Yoruba 3. The largest of these in terms of numbers of speakers are Hausa, Creole, Kiswahili, Yoruba, Fulfulde, Lingala, Kikongo, and Shona, all between 7 and 35 million speakers (ibid).

the three lists may be deceptive: at least the figures for Kurdish are to my best knowledge inaccurate in all three. The numbers are much higher in accounts from reliable inside and outside researchers, specialised in Kurdish.[19]

A very small group of the world's languages, numbering **less than 300** (Harmon 1995b; between 200 and 250, Krauss 1992; more than 200, Gunnemark 1991), are spoken by communities of **1 million speakers and above** (see Info Box 1.12 where I have listed and also counted them). A Reader Task (1.7) relates to the Info Box.

❖ I n f o   B o x   1 . 1 2 ❖

Languages With Over 1 Million Home Speakers—Total 208 Languages

Achinese, Afrikaans, Akan, Albanian, Amharic, Arabic, Armenian, Assamese, Aymara, Azerbaijani, Bai, Balinese, Baluchi, Bambara, Bashkir, Batak, Bemba, Bengali, Berber, Bete, Beti, Bhili, Bhojpuri, Bikol, Buginese, Bulgarian, Burmese, Buyi, Byelorussian, Catalan, Cebuano, Chinese, Chokwe, Chuvash, Congo, Czech, Danish, Dinka, Dong, Dutch, Edo-Bini, Efil-Ibibio, English, Estonian, Ewe, Finnish, Fon, French, Ful, Galician, Ganda, Garhwali, Georgian, German, Gisu, Gondi, Greek, Guaraní, Gujarati, Gurma, Hadiyya, Haitian, Hani, Hausa, Haya, Hebrew, Hehe, Hiligaynon, Hindi, Ho, Hungarian, Igbo, Ijo, Iloko, Indonesian, Italian, Japanese, Javanese, Kamba, Kannada, Kanuri, Karen, Kashmiri, Kazakh, Khmer, Kirghiz, Kisii, Konkani, Korean, Kumauni, Kurdish, Kurukh, Kuyu, Lao, Latvian, Li, Lingala, Lithuanian, Low German, Luba, Luhya, Luo, Macassar, Macedonian, Madurese, Magahi, Maguindanao, Maithili, Makonde, Makua, Malagasy, Malay, Malayalam, Malinke, Manipuri, Marathi, Marwari, Mbundu, Mende, Miao, Minangkabau, Mongolian, Mongo-Nkundu, Mordva, More, Mundari, Nahuatl, Nandi, Nandi-Kipsigis, Ndebele, Nepali, Nkore-Kiga, Norwegian, Nuer, Nupe, Nyamwezi, Nyanja, Occitan, Oriya, Oromo, Pampangan, Pangasinan, Panjabi, Pashto, Pedi, Persian, Polish, Portuguese, Quechua, Romani, Romanian, Ronga-Tsonga, Russian, Rwanda-Rundi, Santali, Sasak, Senufo, Serbo-Croatian, Serer, Shan, Shona, Sindhi, Sinhalese, Slovak, Slovenian, Somali, Songe, Songhai, Sotho, Spanish, Sundanese, Swahili, Swazi, Swedish, Tagalog, Tajiki, Tamil, Tatar, Teke, Telugu, Temne, Teso-Turkana, Thai, Tibetan, Tigrinya, Tiv, Tonga, Tswana, Tulu, Turkish, Turkmen, Ukrainian, Umbundu, Urdu, Uygur, Uzbek, Vietnamese, Waray, Welamo, Wolof, Xhosa, Yao (Man), Yao (Chiyao), Yi, Yoruba, Zande, Zhuang, Zulu (source: Gunnemark 1991: 169–171).

In Table 1.7, I give one possible overview of the sizes of (oral) languages. As we can see, there are many gaps in reliable knowledge (mine or in general).

Several of the sources mentioned above have been used and combined for Table 1.7. According to the more detailed lists used here, there should be somewhat over 700 languages with over 100,000 speakers (those in cate-

Reader Task 1.7
Place languages geographically—Eurocentrism?

How many of the languages in Info Box 1.12 can you place geographically? Find one of the larger reference works mentioned above and find out how many speakers each language has. Check whether your knowledge is Eurocentric: find languages from Europe which you can place geographically; then find the languages from other parts of the world which are similar in size (number of speakers) and check whether you can place all of them.

TABLE 1.7
Overview of oral language sizes and numbers

Category	Nr of speakers of each language	Nr of languages	Total Nr of speakers in each group	% of world's languages	% of world's speakers
A. Really Very Big: the top 10	over 100 million	10	between 2,700 and 3,000m	0.10 to 0.15%	ca. 49%
B. Big (see Table 1.5)	between 35 and 100m	ca. 30	920 mill.	under 0.5%	
C. Middle-sized (see Table 1.6, Info Box 1.12)	between 1 and 35m	ca. 170	over 1,174 mill.**	ca. 2.5%	
A + B + C together		*210 to 300**	*over 5 billion*	*under 3%*	*close to 95%*
D. Smallish	between ½ and 1 million	ca. 50		,	
E. Small	between 100,000 and ½ million	ca. 250; *total A–E 708*		*total D+E+F ca. 40%*	
F. Very small	between 10,000 and 100,000				
G. Really small	between 1,000 and 10,000			under 25%	
H. Minimal-sized	fewer than 1,000	*total F–H ca. 6,000*		ca. 28%; *total D–H 95%*	

'world's languages' refers to oral languages only; *a count based on Gunnemark's figures gives 208; several other estimates are between 200 and 300; **is an absolute minimum figure.

gories A to E). Crystal 1997b lists 'nearly 1,000 living languages' for this group.

The top languages in terms of number of speakers are the **really very big killer languages**.[20] **Today**[21] English is the foremost among them. These are the languages whose (native) speakers have arrogated to themselves and to their languages more structural power and (material) resources than their numbers would justify, at the cost of speakers of other languages, and that is partially why their numbers are growing.

The **big** and **middle-sized languages** have between 1 and 50 million speakers (ca. 30 between 35–100 million, probably around or over 40 between 10–35 million, the rest between 1–10 million). Demographically the **less than 300 languages** (the Really Very Big plus the Big and Middle-sized languages) accounted in the early 1990s for a total of over 5 billion speakers,[22] or close to **95% of the world's population**.

But these 95% of the world's **population** speak considerably under 5% of the world's **languages**.[23]

This means that **more than 95% of the world's languages have fewer than 1 million speakers each**. Most of the figures about them are very unsure, and estimates differ.[24] Probably around **40% of the world's languages are spoken by between 1 million and 10,000 speakers each** (the **smallish**, **small**, and **very small** languages).

Somewhat **over half of the world's (oral) languages** (51% or 52% are the figures most often used) and most of the sign languages are spoken by communities of **fewer than 10,000 speakers**. These languages are the **really small** and **minimal-sized** languages.

And half of these, in turn, meaning around **a quarter of the world's languages**, are spoken by communities of **1,000 speakers or fewer** (e.g., Harmon 1995b; LaPolla's online Handout on Endangered Languages 8 April 1998— see Address Box 2.3—says 28%). These **really small and minimal-sized languages** are the most vulnerable oral languages of the world. All sign languages are threatened, except maybe around 200, one per country.[25]

LaPolla notes that around 10% of the world's languages are spoken by fewer than 100 speakers each, counted on the basis of Grimes 1992.

1.3. THE STATE OF THE LANGUAGES: THE 'MORIBUND', THE 'ENDANGERED', AND THE 'SAFE'

Linguists agree that many languages face extinction, at least as far as speaking them is concerned (but see Amery's discussion of this, and on the concepts used in general, 1998: 25–30; see also the quote from Cherie Watkins about the Kaurna language sleeping, at the beginning of this chapter).

Michael Krauss (University of Alaska) is one of the linguists who has worked hard to make the world aware of the threat to languages (e.g., Krauss 1992). Krauss estimates (1992, 1995) the number of oral languages that are assured of still being around in 2100 to only around 600, less than 10 percent of the present oral languages. Again, this count does not consider sign languages. According to this prognosis, then, not only are most of the languages with fewer than 10,000 speakers, over half of today's languages, going to disappear, but also most of the ones which have between 10,000 and 1 million speakers. All this just in the next hundred years. Many linguists agree with him. Even the absolutely lowest estimates are that around half of today's oral languages are likely to disappear in the next hundred years.[26]

Krauss (1992: 5–7) divides the (oral) languages into three groups, the **moribund**, the **endangered**, and the **safe** languages, on the basis of three criteria: **intergenerational transfer from parents to children, numbers**, and **official status**. The basic criterion is whether or not children are learning the language (see Definition Box 1.5).

DEFINITION BOX 1.5   Moribund, endangered & safe languages

moribund—languages which are no longer being learned by children
endangered—languages "which, though now still being learned by
    children, will—if the present conditions continue—cease to be learned
    by children during the coming century" (Krauss 1992: 6)
safe—languages which are neither moribund nor endangered (Krauss
    1992: 5–7)

See also Definition Box 2.4 on UNESCO Red Book definitions.

The **'moribund'** languages, which are **no longer being learned by children**, comprise between 20 and 50 percent of the world's oral languages. They are 'beyond endangerment, they are living dead and will disappear in the next century' (Krauss 1995). But see Insert 1.8 on the concept of 'moribund'.

Several minorities, and researchers[27] object to the term 'moribund'/'dying' about languages. It makes it seem somehow natural and inevitable that languages should disappear (in the same way as 'language death', see section 5.4). Besides, as minority representatives say, the psychological effect of having to hear that one speaks a 'moribund' language may block action and make people feel hopeless—you cannot fight against fate (see also the discussion in section 4.1.3, and, again, the initial quote from Cherie Watkins about the Kaurna language sleeping).

INSERT 1.8 Moribund slaves and languages

Latin 'mors', gen. 'mortis' means death; 'morior', to die; 'moribundus', about
to die. The slaves in the amphitheatre, going to fight the lions or other animals,
greeting the emperor as the people who were to die, with 'Ave Caesar, morituri
te salutant', were as little giving up their lives 'voluntarily' as speakers of
endangered languages are 'voluntarily' giving up their languages. They were
'helped' on their way. Just as speakers of the 'moribund' languages, the slaves
had no objective choice. Some of those slaves who had been prepared for the
fight with the lions for a long time had probably 'accepted' the inevitable and
were even in some curious way proud of it. Just as the talk about 'our boys',
'duty to the fatherland', and so on, later and today may make some young
and older men (and even some women) 'voluntarily' and 'proudly' go and
slaughter fellow humans, and themselves be slaughtered in modern war
'theatres'.

Today's minority parents, killing off their languages by not speaking them
to their children, are also sometimes accepting what is presented to them as
'the inevitable' (= a (false!) choice between language and identity, or jobs)
and depriving their children of their linguistic heritage, 'for their own good',
proud over the children's competence in a dominant language. But most of
them would, given a choice, rather tame the lion (= learn the dominant
language) **and** live (= maintain the mother tongue(s)), given the choice (see
Vuolab, in press, for a beautiful description of this).

Krauss sees the **number of speakers** as the second of the three important
criteria for safeness. Only languages with over 1 million speakers are considered to be 'safe' ('have a good future') by Krauss. Michael Foster (1982,
as reported by Mark Fettes <mfettes@magi.com> in a posting on the email
list 'Endangered Languages', 4 March 1996) calls languages with fewer than
5,000 speakers 'clearly threatened'.

There is a grey area between 'clearly threatened' (under 5,000 speakers)
and 'safe' (over 1 million speakers). When Krauss arrives at his figure of
90% of the world's oral languages disappearing before 2100, he starts with
seeing languages with more than 1 million speakers as 'safe' (200–250 languages). Then he first goes down to half a million (which raises the numbers
with some 50 languages) and then all the way down to 100,000. This gives
around 600 'safe' languages (see Table 1.8). On the other hand, Krauss
mentions Breton, with over a million speakers in living memory, and very
few now, and Navajo, with well over 100,000 speakers a generation ago but
with a very unsure future (1992: 7).

Trond Trosterud of the Barents Secretariat (<http://www2.isl.uit.no/trond/
index.html>—a goldmine for information on endangered languages) likewise
considers that not even languages with millions of speakers are necessarily
safe. Nancy Hornberger (1998: 445), discussing the factors contributing to

the fact that declarations of policies protecting indigenous languages are not enough, mentions 'a growing threat to even such a large indigenous language as Quechua, with its estimated 10 million or more speakers'. Trosterud, like many others, warn that the degree of threat cannot be directly predicted from numbers (see also Bereznak & Campbell 1996). Table 1.8 summarizes some of the definitions and estimates.

In addition to using numbers and whether or not the languages are being learned by children for his prediction, Krauss uses **official state support** as his third criterion (1992: 7). In chapter 5 we look at state support, discussing the legal status of languages as official or not. Later (in chapter 7), legal support through human rights instruments for languages in education will be examined. In chapter 2, Definition Box 2.4, we have the more detailed UNESCO Red Book categories which also use all three criteria even if the first two (children, numbers) are the most important ones.

But knowing that we lack adequate figures even for the numbers of the largest languages, it comes as no surprise that 'we currently lack an accurate assessment of the situation [of endangered languages] in most areas of the world' (Grenoble & Whaley 1996: 210[28]). This lack of reliable information, a dominant theme at the conference Grenoble and Whaley were reporting from in their paper (ibid.), also makes it more difficult to design the community-specific, case-to-case maintenance (or revitalisation or reclamation) programmes which Grenoble and Whaley think are needed (ibid., 211–217). In a perceptive article with many examples, Nancy Hornberger (1998) formulates

TABLE 1.8
Threatened and safe languages, definitions, and estimates

SAFE	■ Not even lgs with millions of speakers; degree of threat cannot be directly predicted from numbers (Trond Trosterud; Nancy Hornberger, etc.)	?
	■ a. lgs with over 1 million speakers (Michael Krauss)	200–250
	■ b. lgs with over 500.000 speakers (Krauss)	250–300
	■ c. lgs with over 100.000 speakers (Krauss)	■ ca. 600 'safe' lgs around 2,100
Threatened	■ 'clearly threatened': lgs with fewer than 5,000 speakers (Michael Foster)	
Endangered	■ lgs 'which, though now still being learned by children, will—if the present conditions continue—cease to be learned by children during the coming century' (Krauss)	
Moribund	■ 'beyond endangerment', 'living dead': not learned by children (Krauss)	20–50% (1,200–3,000) of the 6,000 lgs (Krauss

'two principles that support . . . multilingual ideologies and policies.' Her **second** principle (with regard to educational policy and practice for immigrant (and other) language minority learners) also emphasizes the differences: 'the specific characteristics of the optimal contexts for their learning can be defined only in each specific circumstance or case' (1998: 449). Her **first** principle, though, emphasizes some commonalities. She sees bilingual learning as consisting of several continua (oral-to-literate, monolingual-to-bilingual, productive to receptive skills, micro-to-macro contexts, etc.), and claims that 'the more the contexts of their learning allow bilingual/biliterate learners to draw on all points of the continua of biliteracy, the greater are the chances for their full biliterate development' (ibid., 447; see also Auerbach 1995).

I fully agree with these writers and the principles they espouse. For the purposes of this book the principles can be condensed to one. The necessary context-sensitivity in supporting endangered languages means not only **avoiding the typical either-or stances**: support either L1 or L2, you cannot have both; or, if you concentrate on the macro-level, it means insensitivity to or omission of micro-level factors; or, if you are interested in the medium of education, it means that you ignore content or pedagogy—all these will be exemplified later. It means **moving along continua**, and often **embracing goals along the whole continuum**.

We finish with some concrete examples of languages pushed into disuse.

1.4. EXAMPLES OF LANGUAGES PUSHED INTO DISUSE

There are amazing similarities in what is happening all over the world—many of the basic reasons which the following chapters will elaborate are the same. The final section gives a flavour of the threat, the despair, the sadness, the injustice. Likewise, the struggles, the positive action, people's resilience, courage, energy. Hope?

❖ **I n f o   B o x   1 . 1 3** ❖

None of California's Roughly 50 Native Languages Widely Learned by Children

California has about 50 of the United States' 2-250 indigenous languages and none of them is being learned widely by children. 20 of the languages have already died this century, Leanne Hinton said (as reported in **The Philadelphia Inquirer** 19.2.1995, p. A15), with the last speaker of Northern Pomo (a woman in her eighties) dying a month before the conference reported. In her 1994 book **Flutes of Fire** Hinton states, talking about 'great despair', that in California

---

(Continued)

'nearly 100% of the Native languages . . . are no longer learned by children' (1994: 221) and continues:

> There are those who speak their language of heritage but have no one left to talk to. There are those whose ancestral language has not been spoken by anyone at all for a generation or more. Many people feel the loss of language as a loss of personal history, a loss of identity. There is a sense of loneliness, of yearning for lost meaning, lost values. (ibid.)

Costo and Costo (1987) describe the role of missionaries in California and show how the same ideologies are still alive (see Jackson 1987 and interviews with Johnson, Engstrand, Hornbeck, Mathes, Neuerburg, and Nunis, all in Costo & Costo (eds) 1987).

But there is action too: people 'are forming tribal language committees, school and after-school programs, evening language classes; they are audio-taping and videotaping elders,[29] and researching tapes and field notes from university archives. Along with these linguistic activities, there is also a resurgence of cultural and ceremonial activities' (ibid., 221–222). 'Some people are trying to develop writing systems from scratch; some have more than one writing system in competition,[30] and have to suffer factional struggles over which one should prevail. Some are trying to research and develop oral language techniques, and get away from a dependence on writing. Some people are emphasizing the task of teaching adults the language . . . And some are working with languages long dead, just trying to gather materials and learn what they can' (ibid., 223–224—see also Amery 1998). Hinton also describes interesting Master (sic!)–Apprentice programmes where a younger non-speaker or 'semi-speaker' is paired with a competent older speaker, for up to 20 hours per week, for at least half a year, preferably longer, to learn more of the language and culture.

In Canada, 'the percentage of the population that speaks neither of the two official languages of English and French is rising steadily as immigrants bring their own languages with them, Statistics Canada says. But among aboriginal people, the situation is reversed. Native languages are falling rapidly to the onslaught of English. Of Canada's 53 native languages, 43 were classified as on the 'verge of extinction' in a 1990 report of the House of Commons standing committee on aboriginal affairs. An additional seven were listed as threatened.

(Continued)

Only three—Cree, Ojibway and Inuktitut—are considered to have an excellent chance of survival, said the committee's report, entitled **You Took My Talk: Aboriginal Literacy and Empowerment** (Platiel 1996). According to Mark Fettes (1996), though, the 1988 report took the figures, 'without attribution, from a 1982 paper by Michael Foster, and [they] are simply based on estimated numbers of speakers (any language with fewer than 5,000 speakers is rated as threatened, without any consideration of retention rates or the cultural vitality of the communities involved).' All this was reported by Mark Fettes <mfettes@magi.com> in a posting on the email list 'Endangered Languages', 4 March 1996—see Fettes in the bibliography and his Web-page for more information: <http://infoweb.magi.com/~mfettes/>; see Foster 1982a, b, for the originals. Eung-Do Cook's and Lynn Drapeau's 1998 articles give short overviews of the history and current status of Canada's native languages, and Betty Harnum, who recently completed a 4-year term as the first Languages Commissioner for the Northwest Territories, sums up her experience in Harnum 1998. See also Lipka et al. 1998 for a fascinating account of Yup'ik Eskimo teachers' struggle to reclaim the school.

In Cameroon, the situation is similar (Info Box 1.15).

❖ **I n f o   B o x   1 . 1 5** ❖

Cameroon—Travel 50 Kilometers, Almost a Dozen Languages

Bruce Connell (email address: <connellb@vax.ox.ac.uk>) is a linguist, primarily interested in phonetics/phonology and historical/comparative linguistics, and focuses on African languages. Most of his research has been on the languages of the Cross River/Nigeria-Cameroon borderland region. He gave the following report on the email list on Endangered Languages, on disappearing languages in Cameroon.

I spent last dry season in the Adamawa/Mambila region, ranging from Bankim to Banyo (Adamawa Province)—and mostly from Nyamboya to Banyo—with a brief excursion into adjacent North West Province. In this small area I came across several languages that are now moribund; there are others which may not have more than two or three generations of active life left. I list them here and describe briefly their present state of health.

1. Yeni—once spoken not far north of Mayo Darle village in the area now called Nyalang; apparently all that remains now is a song, sung to me by speakers of another language, Sundani (Kwanja).

(Continued)

2. Kila—a language formerly spoken by blacksmiths, now remembered only by a few old people at Hore Toram Torbi, though it may be the same as the language called Kila (or Somyewe) spoken (or remembered?) nearby in Nigeria. (Kila is the Fulfulde word for blacksmith).

3. Bung—there are apparently only three people left who remember this language, though no one uses it any longer for communicative purposes. It may have been another form of Kwanja.

4. Njanga—also a part of the Kwanja cluster, spoken in the village of Mbonjanga; only two people use it on a more or less daily basis, though other old people know or remember the language.[31]

5. Luo—to the best of my knowledge, there is one speaker left, living in a quartier of Atta.

6. Njerep—there are about 5 speakers left of this language, living in a quartier of the village of Somie. No one uses it any longer for communicative purposes.

7. Twendi—there are about 35 people who still use Twendi, living primarily in the villages of Sanga and Chamba, on the Nyamboya–Somie road, though there are also some individuals living in other villages in the region. It is still spoken on a daily basis by some, though the children are not learning it.

It appears that Twendi, Njerep and Luo, and probably Yeni were all fairly closely related.

8. Vute—the Banyo variety of Vute has about 300 speakers (though in total Vute has perhaps 30,000); this dialect is still used daily, though it seems heavily adulterated by Fulfulde.

9. Wawa—there are three or four dialects of Wawa, with a total of about 3,000 speakers. It is used in the home and is being transmitted to the young, and so is comparatively healthy. However, Fulfulde, the regional lingua franca, is encroaching.

In addition to these there are a number of Mambila dialects which are in better shape, though as yet I have been unable to assess yet whether the smaller ones (i.e., those spoken only in one or two villages, such as Kumchum) are giving way to the larger ones, as is the case with Kwanja. Most people in the region know some Fulfulde and many, especially the young, some French, though neither of these are threatening the local languages as Fulfulde is slightly further north in the Wawa/Vute area.

All of this in a very small region—Nyamboya to Banyo is perhaps 50 km—but even so, I cannot yet be certain there are not others yet to be found. It is also not impossible that there are still speakers of Yeni, or others of Luo, who I didn't manage to find.

In Central Nigeria, the neighbouring country, the conditions are also similar (see Info Box 1.16). Sylvester Omodiaogbe (1992: 21) quotes: 'As one musician singing about the need for a lingua franca has rightly put it, "every kilometre is another language"'. My comment is, though: lingua franca, yes, but additively, not subtractively!

❖ **I n f o   B o x   1 . 1 6** ❖

*Central Nigeria—95 of 100 Languages With Under
200 Speakers 'Completely Undescribed'*

a) there are approximately 250 distinct languages spoken in the Middle Belt

b) of these, at least 100 have under 200 speakers

c) 95 of these remain completely undescribed

d) there is no government policy towards these languages at all

e) the fate of these languages depends largely on the future political history of Nigeria (Blench 1996)

Blench's own prognosis is that 'a number of small communities with only a small number of speakers are likely to disappear soon. Descriptive studies on these languages are unlikely to be conducted before they disappear. Urban populations are likely to form consolidated blocks and large masses of population will speak either English or the urban lingua franca' (Blench 1996)

The disappearance of languages has been extremely fast in areas of European colonisation, as the Californian example showed. Australia probably has the world record, as Info Box 1.17 also shows.

❖ **I n f o   B o x   1 . 1 7** ❖

Aboriginal Peoples in Australia

In 1788 Aboriginal peoples constituted more or less 100% of Australia's population. The pre-colonial population may have been up to one and a half million. In 1861 they were about 13% of the population (Smolicz 1989: 1). When the 'white' colonisers came, they hunted down and killed Aboriginal peoples like animals. These were by some researchers considered to be the missing link between apes and human beings (Jordan 1984, Fesl 1993). The first 'white' formal education was provided by missionaries (see Amery 1998, Fesl 1993)—of course children had had informal education for millennia. Many

---

(Continued)

❖ **I n f o   B o x   1 . 1 7** ❖

(Continued)

children were taken away from their parents to be educated on mission stations. Both then and later, many lost contact with their parents completely, and needed to (try to) find them again as grown-ups (see Coral Edwards and Peter Read's (eds) beautiful, sad 1992 book **The Lost Children.** **Thirteen Australians taken from their Aboriginal families tell of the struggle to find their natural parents**—see also Insert 5.26 for a similar Danish book by Tine Bryld). Many also lost their languages. Even in situations where the missionaries reduced their languages to writing and translated the Bible into (what they believed were) their languages (i.e., often simplified, distorted, constructed versions—see Mühlhäusler 1996, Amery 1998, Bailey 1995a, b, Traill 1995, Fesl 1993), the Aboriginal culture was condemned and the missionaries tried to eradicate it as barbaric and pagan. On the reserves (to which many people, even part-Aborigines, were forcibly removed from towns in the 1930s), the level of education considered appropriate for Aborigines was up to fourth grade of primary school, often taught by untrained people (Fesl 1993). In the towns, Aboriginal children were not free to enter ordinary state schools in New South Wales until 1949 (Jordan 1983: 21). In 1986 the 227,645 Aborigines formed 1.44% of the population (Suter & Stearman 1988: 4). Of the original 200–250 languages with some 600 dialects (or at least 500 languages—see Suter & Stearman 1988: 4), at least 50 languages are now extinct while another 100 or so face imminent death. In the mid-1980s, only 50 languages had more than 100 speakers, 28 of them more than 250 speakers (Lo Bianco 1987: 34), and only 9 of them had more than one thousand speakers (Smolicz 1989: 1). According to the estimates on the basis of the 1976 census, there were only 27,572 people above the age of 5 in Australia who regularly used one of the Aboriginal languages (Clyne 1982, table 5, p. 12). No Aboriginal languages are official (or national) languages in Australia. For later figures, see the **Ethnologue** (Address Box 1.4).

The Sámi are the only indigenous people in the European Union. Revitalisation efforts are similar to those in California, Aotearoa, and Hawai'i.

❖ **I n f o   B o x   1 . 1 8** ❖

Skolt and Ánar Sámi in (the Finnish Part of) Sápmi

Sápmi (the Sámi Country) is divided between Finland, Norway, Russia (the Kola Peninsula), and Sweden. The numbers are estimated to be between 65,000–120,000. There are at least nine Sámi languages, North Sámi being the

(Continued)

absolutely largest (see Korhonen 1998). Skolt Sámi, a nation of some 500 people, now mostly living in the Sevettijärvi and Nellim villages in northern Finland, were moved there when their original lands were lost to Soviet Union in the Second "World" War. Traditionally many of them were multilingual; they used to know Skolt Sámi, western Sámi languages (including North Sámi), Finnish, Norwegian, and Russian—there was a lot of international trade in their areas (**Oktavuohta** 1997: 11).

In the late 1980s there was no teaching of Skolt in schools. Earlier the only teacher who knew Skolt, Satu Mosnikoff (a Finn, married to a Skolt) used to teach early literacy in Skolt. In comparisons (still unpublished as far as I know) where she tested children taught by her and Skolt children taught in Finnish (by a Finnish teacher, for instance in those years when she was on maternity leave), the children taught in Skolt had better test results in the Finnish language than those taught completely in Finnish. She used her own orthography. When this competed with the orthography devised by one of the Skolts, she stopped using hers, and teaching. As a partial result of this, there were no children learning Skolt as their first language, or learning it in school.

In the late 1980s the Skolts heard about the New Zealand Kohanga Reo language nests,[32] and an experiment started in 1993. Lack of finance stopped it temporarily but it started again in 1997, with European Union money. Skolt is now also been taught as a subject in schools, and there is some teaching through the medium of Skolt in Sevettijärvi.

Ánar Sámi is a people of similar size, around 500, and in 1995, 324 claimed to have learned Sámi as their first language. Of them around 10 are of school age, and none under school age. The youngest mother tongue speaker is in 1999 14 years old. A language nest programme started in 1997; the language was taught as a subject in 1996–1997 in six primary schools to a total of 29 students, and to 4 students in upper-secondary school. Lack of materials is a problem. Also the other problems are the ones typical for small language groups: 'there are few knowledgable, active people. The same person is forced to be politician, teacher, journalist, cultural worker, lawyer, artist, linguist, child minder, youth worker . . .', Matti Morottaja writes (1997: 11). He is actually describing himself, and his children are the youngest mother tongue speakers. But the *Anarášskielá servi* (Association for the Ánar language) has around 150 members, that is, a third of the population, so there is hope. Even if the next but last speaker of one of the small Russian Sámi languages died—was shot—in January 1999 (Máret Sara, personal communication). See also **Oktavuohta** 1997, **Sámegiella—skuvlagiella 1998**, Aikio-Puoskari 1998, 1999; Seurujärvi-Kari et al. (1995). Huss 1996 compares Fishman's revitalisation stages with the situation of Lule Sámi on the Norwegian side of Sápmi where there is a language nest in Tysfjord (where both of us have visited); Huss (1999) gives thorough descriptions of the educational situation of all the northern minorities. For more general works about the Sámi and their languages,

(Continued)

❖ **I n f o   B o x   1 . 1 8** ❖

(Continued)

see e.g., Haetta 1996, Lehtola 1997, Ruong 1975, NOU 1980:59, NOU 1985:14, NOU 1987:34; likewise, all references to all Aikio's, Gaski, and Hoëm in the bibliography. Gustavsen 1980, Gustavsen & Sandvik (eds) 1981, and Beach 1995 are examples of criticism of official policy. See also the Web-site of Trond Trosterud of the Barents Secretariat (<http://www2.isl.uit.no/trond/index.html>). The general Swedish Libris data base <http://www.libris.kb.se> has a fair collection of literature on the Sámi in Indo-European languages, even some in Sámi.

A few more descriptions follow in Inserts 1.9 and 1.10.

But it is not only indigenous languages which are being pushed to disuse. And often the speakers themselves who have taken over the negative attitudes of the dominant group are instrumental in pushing their languages in this

---

INSERT 1.9   Last speaker of Tuscarora dies

Helen Salter, 93, lay dying in a Toronto hospital in December, and her passing was to mean more than a family's grief over the loss of a loved one.

When her spirit finally left her body, a language also took a small step closer to death.

Mrs. Salter was believed to be the last person in Canada to speak Tuscarora fluently, those familiar with the language say.

One of the languages of the Six Nations of the Iroquois Confederacy, Tuscarora is one of 2,000 to 3,000 languages around that world that are moving—seemingly inexorably—toward extinction.

In a world fretting about overpopulation, paradoxically up to half of all spoken languages are in danger of disappearing forever.

Source: Platiel, Rudy, in **The Globe and Mail** March 1, 1996, quoted in a posting on the email list Endangered Languages, 4 March 1996, from Mark Fettes (mfettes@magi.com), on 'Tuscarora on the wane'.

INSERT 1.10   I will not for the world give up (Meänkieli, Sweden)

I . . . speak **meänkieli**[33] with my parents, siblings and other people from my village who were born before 1961, the year when the language border was moved from the school gate and ate itself into the home environment of my

---

(Continued)

INSERT 1.10 *(Continued)*

family. In 1971 I was on my way to a conference for young people with the motto 'Unity in diversity'. In the bus I hoped to be able to speak **meänkieli**, protected by the motto of our joint destination. Regrettably, that was not what happened. "Now stop with your **äppuli-suomi**", the person next to me, a fellow Finnish-speaker, said. But . . . I decided that I WILL NOT FOR THE WORLD GIVE UP. How could I otherwise continue in believing in unity in diversity, or, as a feminist recently wrote in the subtitle of her book, 'Diversity in unity', with diversity first. And ÄPPULI became the secret mascot for my soul and kept the courage up. But I had to 'travel' far to find a travel companion who succeeded in giving me the final courage, all the way to East Africa. At a conference (for African authors, writing in English), at Makerere University in Uganda in 1962, somebody called Obi Wali said that every language, regardless of how small it is, deserved its own literature—there were no "maybe" or "if". Equally sure is the Kenyan author Ngũgĩ wa Thiong'o, and I have now finally got the time to write a doctoral thesis about him. AND HE HAS A LOT TO GIVE US. (Inga-Britt Isaksson Faris on an email list for **meänkieli** (<met-vi@egroups.com> 7 January 1999)

---

direction—while others resist. The experiences are similar worldwide—and can be shared (Insert 1.10).

It is indicative that Inga-Britt Isaksson Faris (Insert 1.10) wrote the first part of her contribution to the list in **meänkieli** but then switched over to Swedish, the language she has had her formal education in. Her comment, written in **meänkieli**, was: 'Sorry, there may be many linguistic errors but I cannot resist writing at least a bit in **meänkieli** . . . It is horrible that one is not able to write securely in one's own language, but one can also say that getting out each letter from the ears, linguistic roots, and memory, to one's fingers—for a letter to all of you met-vi-emailers—feels good.' And then, starting in Swedish: 'Now I won't tire you anymore, you who have had the stamina to follow my alphabetisation efforts so far. Now I will write in Swedish, the language I have been technically schooled in.' See also Isaksson Faris, forthcoming.

Most languages in the world are spoken/signed in one country only: just over 83% of all the world's oral languages are endemic to the country, according to David Harmon's (1995a: 6) analysis of the **Ethnologue**'s 12th edition (5,635 out of 6,760). If they also have few speakers, as we have seen they have, what can be provisionally concluded is that the future for linguistic diversity is not bright, also because it is unlikely that many new languages will be born. Latin, for instance, took some 2,000 years to evolve into a dozen or so European languages, Krauss observed (1992).

Next we will have a look at some other parts of the wider ecology within which languages exist and thrive or not. The first aspect of the ecosocial world has to do with biological diversity, and the similarity of threat towards both types of diversity.

NOTES

1. The relationship between language and land is seen as sacred. Most non-indigenous people need a lot of guidance to even start understanding the primacy of land in it. One example from Australia. None of the Aboriginal people participating in the reclaiming of the Awabakal language were descendants of the Awabakal (the last speakers died before 1900) but came from other areas and peoples. Still, they speak about 'our language' and 'our identity' in connection with Awabakal. In Rob Amery's words (1998: 94), 'the revival of Awabakal seems to be based primarily on the association of the language with the land, the language of the place in which a group of Aboriginal people of diverse origins now live'.

2. See also 4.1.1. and 4.1.2. on the origins of language according to the Bible and the Qur'an.

3. When I use this strong term and make this very serious accusation, I am deeply aware of the risk of turning off some people who object to the term—see also Introduction. This problem has been discussed by many others too (Nicholas Ostler 1995: 6 reports about a discussion on tactics, 'Is it effective in the long run to up the ante, and use shock and scandal to make a point?'). I think it is necessary here, though. Those readers who object are invited to start with the United Nations definition of linguistic genocide (Section 5.2.3) and the short history of (lack of) linguistic human rights in the West in section 7.3.

4. Both Serbian and Croatian existed as separate 'languages' prior to 1919 when the Kingdom of 'Jugoslavia' ('the southern Slavs', i.e., Slovenes, Croats, and Serbs) was created. Now the languages are being 'reinvented' as it were.

5. In the Introduction to their edited book **Language Planning in Yugoslavia**, written in July 1991, Ranko Bugarski and Celia Hawkesworth say that 'it is far from clear whether and how long the country can survive as a single state' and express their worry that the 'rising nationalism in all parts of Yugoslavia bodes ill for minorities everywhere, and there are already signs of its adverse effects on the exercise of language rights' (1992: 9). Their Postscript, December 1991 (ibid., 9), reads: 'As this volume goes to press, we wish to dedicate it to the memory of Yugoslavia as described in these pages.' As we know, those trying to defend minority rights in ex-Yugoslavia (like Ranko Bugarski and many other friends), are paying for their ethical stance.

6. 'An additional example of the extreme variation found in English is that in the television show (and videotape) **The Story of English** captions are provided (and needed, for most viewers!) for Scots English' (Timothy Reagan, personal communication, December 1998).

7. These were (Sebba 1994: 12) the following: (1) **Collins New International Atlas** (1982). Collins; (2) Kidron, M. & Segal, R. (1987) **The New State of the World Atlas**. Pan Books; (3) Kidron, M. & Segal, R. (1991) **The New State of the World Atlas**, 4th edition. Simon and Schuster; (4) **Kingfisher Countries of the World: an A–Z Reference Atlas** (1993). London: Kingfisher Books; (5) Middleton, N. (1988) **Atlas of World Issues**. Oxford University Press; (6) **New Concise Atlas of the World**. London: Longman; (7) **Peters Atlas of the World** (1989). London: Longman; (8) **Philip's Geographical Digest 1992–93** (1993). Oxford/London: Heinemann/Philip Atlases; (9) **Third World Guide 89/90**. Montevideo: Instituto del Tercer Mundo; (10) **Whitaker's Almanac** (1993).

8. See section 4.5 on Esperanto; also on terminology about planned languages.

9. David Dalby, director of the Observatoire Linguistique, based at Hebron in Dyfed, and his team are reported in **Guardian Weekly** July 27 1997, p. 1, to have completed 'the first comprehensive classification of world languages and dialects', having 'identified more than 10,000 living languages, some 50% more than previous estimates. The first copy of its 1,600-page global register was to be presented to Unesco this week as a gift to celebrate Britain's decision to rejoin . . . Unesco', the report says. 'The register will form the basis of a computerised map of the world's linguistic communities which Unesco plans to complete by 2001' (ibid.). See Info Box 1.7.

10. In his **A dictionary of language planning terms** Cluver (1993: 17) observes, referring to Eastman, de Vries, and Downes, that it 'is estimated that there are more than 2,976 language in the world', meaning probably that the French Academy's estimate has travelled and a couple of figures have changed places. Cluver's dictionary is in other respects one of the most impressive ones, with thorough definitions, categorisations, good referencing, etc.

11. The interested reader might want to consult other sources too, e.g., Voegelin & Voegelin 1977 **Classification and Index of the World's Languages**; Grimes, Barbara F. (ed.) 1984 **Index to the Tenth Edition of Ethnologue: Languages of the World**; Ruhlen, Merritt 1991 **A Guide to the World's Languages**; see also Info Box 1.6 and Address Box 2.2.

12. It does not make it less reliable that Gunnemark himself translates from 45 languages. Polyglots like Gunnemark and Stephen Wurm are a real asset to geolinguistics (see also Wurm, Mühlhäusler & Tryon 1996).

13. Glottonym comes from the Greek glōssa, glōttis = tongue, language. I use the Latin-based "linguonym" (lingua, tongue, language).

14. From now on I will drop 'oral': when I say 'languages' or 'population', I mean 'oral languages' and 'oral population'—I hope I have made the point about invisibilising sign languages.

15. 'engco' stands for The English Company—see Graddol 1997: 64 and the Internet site <http://www.english.co.uk>.

16. I have counted Crystal's 1997 figure from the Chinese languages he himself refers to: 'Chinese see Gan, Hakka, Mandarin Chinese, Minbei, Minnan, Wu, Xiang, Yue)' (1997b: 444).

17. **Creole**, **Crioulo** and **Kreol** are all **creoles**, meaning languages which were first used as pidgins, means of communication between speakers who had no common language, using whatever means from several languages, and then developing to fully-fledged creole languages when they became first languages of children (see Mühlhäusler 1996 for interesting discussions about pidgins and creoles from a language ecological point of view). The English-oriented **Creole** is known as Aku in the Gambia, Fernandino in Equatorial Guinea, Krio in Sierra Leone, and Pidgin in Cameroon and Nigeria (where it is a lingua franca, not a family language). The Portuguese-oriented **Crioulo**, known (1) in Equatorial Guinea as Annobonés, (2) in Sao Tome/Principe as Saotomense or Principense, (3) in Cape Verde as Capverdien, and (4) in Guinea-Bissau as Guineense, is the only African language in 2 and 3, and has been recognized as a national language in 3 and 4. The French-oriented **Kreol** is known as Mauricien in Mauritius, and as Seychellois in the Seychelles where it is also recognized as the national language (Unesco Regional Centre for Education in Africa 1985: 27, 28, 38).

18. I have not wanted to start updating the figures because there are no accurate figures for many of the entries and changing only some would make the figures less comparable. Who has figures for Rwanda-Rundi after the massacres? Should Serbian and Croatian be listed separately? How do you get census figures for the Kurds when Turkey (where more than half of the Kurds live) still denies their existence as a minority (or even their existence—saying 'the Kurdish people' led as late as in 1998 to one year of imprisonment; see the example of Birdal, Info Box 5.13) and the use of the Kurdish language is still forbidden for all official and many private purposes? (see Inserts 1.1, 4.20, 5.4, 5.9 and 6.6 and Info Box 5.13 for examples). In the latest 1999 update of the **Ethnologue**, Spanish has more speakers than English globally.

19. We (Hassanpour et al., 1996: 368) summarize the estimates as follows: 'The Kurdish population has been estimated at between 25 and 40 million [. . .] Iran (8 million), Iraq (5 million), Syria (1½ million) and Turkey (18–20 million); there are ½ million Kurds in ex-Soviet Union and nearly a million in diaspora, mostly settled in Western Europe. These last estimates come from the 65-member Kurdish Parliament in Exile [. . .] Many researchers estimate that there are 12–18 million in Turkey and between 25 and 30 million altogether.' Leclerc's data (1986: 55, 138) rank Kurdish as the 40th globally in terms of number of speakers. Med-TV, the mainly Kurdish language satellite TV station, broadcasting 18 hours a day, in 5 languages, estimate that they have a 'growing audience - anything up to 30 million people across three continents' (in Europe, Middle East and North Africa; Tabak 1998: 1) (see Address Box 7.2 for Med-TV). The **Ethnologue** figures for Kurdi, Kurmanji, Luri and Zaza for all countries come up to around 20 million but several of the figures are a decade old. See van Bruinessen 1978 for perceptive discussions. See also, e.g., Kirisci & Winrow 1997, McDowall 1996, 1997, Olson (ed.) 1996, Olson 1998, Vali 1996, Wahlbeck 1999.

20. The term 'killer language' (attributed to Anne Pakir, Singapore, about English) is widely used even if it might feel offensive to some. The British linguist, David Graddol (Open University), has 'English as a killer language' as a subtitle in a part of his 1996 article.

21. It might be statistically possible that Spanish has killed off as many as or more languages than English, especially in the period after Columbus but before Europeans colonised Australia, after which English certainly took over as the main killer language. But Spanish is also continuing in what significantly is called Latin America.

22. **Unesco Statistical Yearbook 1997** gives the figure 5,687,174 for the total world population. Most of the sources referred to here for languages have used an earlier figure of 5.3 billion.

23. Not even this do we know—nor are the future trends clear. The world population is expected to be over 6 billion in 1999 and 9.4 billion around 2050, with nearly 60% of the projected growth expected to occur in Asia. On the other hand, Nigeria alone is expected to have 339 million people, more than the entire continent of Africa had 35 years ago. In 1997, only 16 countries had zero population growth (Belarus, Belgium, Czech Republic, France, Germany, Greece, Hungary, Italy, Japan, Netherlands, Poland, Rumania, Russia, Spain, Ukraine, United Kingdom) (all figures from Brown & Mitchell 1997: 174). But there are no prognoses of what this might mean for the world's languages—only some for the big ones (e.g., Graddol 1997).

24. Most of these figures are from Krauss 1992 and Harmon 1995. Harmon's figures are based on the **Ethnologue**, 12th edition.

25. The difference in the threat between spoken and sign languages is that sign language speakers cannot shift to an oral language, say, English. The likely scenario might be that each country will have only one sign language, in addition to signers learning to read and write each country's one dominant oral language and, for some, one or more "international" languages. For oral languages, the nightmare scenario could in the long run involve a strictly diglossic situation, where only some of the top 10 languages would be used in formal domains and all the other languages would be reduced to informal communication, with successively reduced repertoires.

26. The discussion started on a large scale as late as in the early 1990s—a debate in the journal **Language** 68, 1992 (see Hale, Krauss, and Lagefoged, all 1992) played an important role. Since then, many symposia, conferences and publications have debated the issues. Bobaljik et al. (1996) bibliography is a very useful source for literature.

27. For instance linguist Frances Karttunen, at a lecture in Helsinki, Finland, October 1997.

28. See also Hale 1992, Krauss 1996, Wurm 1991 and all references to Maffi in the bibliography; see Ladefoged 1992 for views which take up criticism.

29. The same things are happening in the Roma community in Finland—young and middle-aged Roma organise workshops where they collect the elders, their own parents and grandparents,

and audio- and videotape them—even when the youngsters in many cases do not understand the language which they have just started (re)learning. Miranda Vuolasranta and Tuula Åkerlund have been especially vital for this work, and for Roma education in general.

30. The Nordic Sámi Council accepted a common orthography for North Sámi, the largest Sámi language, in 1979—earlier it had had 13 different orthographies. An orthography for Ánar Sámi (some 500 people) was accepted in October 1996 (**Oktavuohta** 1997: 13). Skolt Sámi almost died because of the struggle about competing orthographies—see Info Box 1.18).

31. This language—Njanga or Njanja—is spoken, however, by thriving communities in Malawi and Mozambique—Kathleen Heugh, personal communication, January 1999.

32. See Info Box 8.1 for these. I had an evening talking with Skolt parents about them.

33. 'Meänkieli' (= our language) is the (Finnish) language spoken in the part of Tornedalen which remained 'Swedish' when what is now Finland became a Grand Duchy under Russia in 1809. It is a variant easily understandable for Finnish-speakers from Finland. Some 'meänkieli'-speakers want it to be accepted as a separate language, not variant. 'Meänkieli' is represented at the European Bureau for Lesser Used languages, EBLUL (see Address Box 2.3). It has many Swedish loanwords, including 'äppuli' (Swedish: äpple/äppel). 'äppuli-suomi'—'apple Finnish' is a derogatory term. See, e.g., Winsa 1997, 1999, forthcoming, Wande 1984, 1988, 1996, Wande & Winsa 1995, for references.

Chapter 2

Connections Between Biodiversity and Linguistic and Cultural Diversity

Each Contraction Party shall, as far as possible and as appropriate . . . [s]ubject to its national legislation, respect, preserve and maintain knowledge, innovations and practices of indigenous and local communities embodying traditional lifestyles relevant for the conservation and sustainable use of biological diversity and promote their wider application with the approval and involvement of the holders of such knowledge, innovations and practices and encourage the equitable sharing of the benefits arising from the utilization of such knowledge, innovations and practices (Art. 8(j), Convention on Biological Diversity).

. . . [T]he dreadful finality of language death—the complete loss of a human idiom from planetary consciousness—will send a shiver of almost personal shame down the spine of any language-sensitive person . . . Which is why protecting endangered languages ought to be a natural "good cause" for language folk. (Nicholas Ostler in **Language International** 9:1, 1997: 5).

Our knowledge is our soul, it is the wisdom that our ancestors gave us. Knowledge about the plants, the animals, the stars, the rivers. It is the collected wisdom of the universe. (said by an indigenous Siriono at a meeting in Santa Cruz, Bolivia, organised by CIDOB, an indigenous lowland organisation, to discuss intellectual property rights; quoted in Oellerrich 1998: 9)

In most of the world, conserving threatened species is as much a cultural as a biological endeavor. (Tuxill & Bright 1998: 56).

While Weinstein, an eminent political scientist looking at the American structure asks "how much diversity can this structure tolerate?", a person in a Third World country must ask "how much uniformity can that structure tolerate?" . . . The Western view is linear and binary, whereas the Eastern is cyclical and spiral. However, the westernized eastern elites, who are in charge of planning, follow essentially the Western world view. (Pattanayak 1991: 31, 19)

Political scientists in the developing Third World, tutored in the theory and methodology of the social science of the West, also join the chorus and repeat ad nauseam that plurality is a threat to the stability of the fragile State. They forget that in these countries freedom is more fragile than the State . . . It is inconceivable that there was a single language for all human beings at any time since human societies were formed. Multiplicity and diversity are the characteristics of nature. (Pattanayak 1981b: 3, vii)

WORDS
Each worldly thing sounds differently,
all objects have their names.
So these too have their designations:
sun, tundra, hut site,
mother, father, river,
earth and village.
From deep down in the age-old earth
clear waters appeared
a spring opened
and joined word to word.
It's like an old man
who's seen his share of life
remembering his youth . . .
A silky flame now eats the firewood
and sorrow fills your heart.
You take a stick
and poke the glowing embers.
Up to the point of hurting memories
you call old words to cross your mind:
Sun, Tundra, Water,
Mother, Father, Earth.
(Oktyabrina Voronova[1] 1996: 103, translated by Pekka Sammallahti)

2. CONNECTIONS BETWEEN BIODIVERSITY AND LINGUISTIC AND CULTURAL DIVERSITY

2.1. OUR THREEFOLD LIVING ENVIRONMENT— BIOLOGICAL, LINGUISTIC, AND CULTURAL— IS THREATENED BY GLOBALISATION

Our thinking about the environment that all things living share can be seen as involving, apart from the **spiritual** environment, at least our **biological** environment, our **linguistic** environment, and our **cultural** environment. The contemporary diversity in all three areas is very seriously threatened.

The threefold environment is of course not a new realisation. For me as a Finn, it is interesting to see that the connection between the three—and power and spirituality—is equally strong in the Finnish national epic **Kalevala** as it is in the worldviews of most indigenous peoples (exemplified in Insert 2.1 by an Algonquian story).

INSERT 2.1 Algonquian and Finnish stories

Jaan Kaplinski (1998: 21), an Estonian poet, renders a North American indigenous, **Algonquian** story[2]: The old man Ugluchopt (or Uglochot) is (just like Vipunen in **Kalevala**) as old as the world, and lives up in the far north. In the indigenous story seven young men travel for nine weeks, walking and paddling, to see him and to get charms. He lies on his side in his wigwam for hundreds of years at a time, until somebody turns him around. When the young men do this, after having lit a fire for him, they notice that he has grown roots. Ugluchopt thanks them for the care and gives them the charms.

In **Kalevala**, the **Finnish** national epic, knowledge and power are also in words. One of the main 'heroes' in **Kalevala**, the old shaman, Väinämöinen, wants to build a new boat without touching it and needs the words to do it. He travels to Antero Vipunen, an ancient shaman who has all the charms (**Kalevala** 1964, Poem 17), 'a mythical giant long since dead but still immensely learned in magic spells' (Magoun 1963: 406). He finds Vipunen lying on the ground, just as Ugluchopt in the Algonquian story:

Vipunen rich in songs,
an old man of great resources,
he is lying stretched out with his lays,
sprawled out with his charms.
An aspen was growing on his shoulders,
a birch rising from his brows,
an alder on the tip of his jaw,
a willow on the end of his beard,
on his forehead a fir, the haunt of squirrels,
a tall evergreen on his teeth.[3]

After a dramatic struggle between the two shamans, Väinämöinen gets many important charms[4] from Vipunen.

The differences between the two stories (the ancient shaman growing trees on top of him, as in **Kalevala**, rather than roots below him, as in the Algonqian story, and the Finnish hero Väinämöinen using force to get the powerful words while the young Algonqian men are using care) are not important for our concerns here. The **relationship between knowledge, nature, language, and**

power is. Knowledge is nurtured by and nurtures nature; it is embodied in charms, expressed in words, in language; language is power. Our world is connected. In post-post-modernity, the great stories are sought out again and are alive.

In human rights instruments the connection between language and culture is also often made, albeit more in ceremonial than substantive ways, and more often in preambles than in binding texts. Boutros Boutros-Ghali, former Secretary General of the United Nations, said in 1995 at one of the celebrations of 50 years of the UN, in an address called 'Unity and Diversity: The Contemporary Challenge': 'The right to live one's culture is among the most basic rights of life' (1995: 3). He continued: 'This, then, is the fundamental approach to culture as found in basic documents of the United Nations: every person has a fundamental right to his or her culture.'

In the Opening Address to the conference, the then Prime Minister of Australia, Paul Keating, **had** included language: 'multiculturalism . . . a policy for managing the consequences of that diversity in the interests of all. This means a policy which guarantees rights and imposes responsibilities. The rights include those of cultural identity—the right to express and share individual cultural heritage, **including language** and religion.' (1995: 9–10, emphasis added).

One of the interesting issues was that Boutros-Ghali also seemed to want to include language, to the extent that he in fact in his **oral** delivery modified important human rights instruments to include language, which is in fact not included in the original documents that he referred to. In the **written** version of his paper, language was, correctly, **not** included. This is what Boutros-Ghali wrote:

> Article 22 of the Universal Declaration of Human Rights states that everyone is entitled to realization of the cultural rights indispensable for dignity and the free development of personality. Thus, the Charter and the Universal Declaration establish **culture** as a fundamental human right. (ibid., 4)

But this is what he **said**[5] in Sydney: '. . . establish **culture and language** as fundamental human rights' (emphases added). Numerous international and regional human rights instruments make it a right **and a duty** for both the peoples concerned and the states to preserve and develop the various cultures (see Info Box 2.1).

There are equally compelling documents about nature, and the worth of biological diversity (see one of the initial quotes at the beginning of this chapter). But it is only very recently that the three are being brought together by international organisations (see section 2.5). One of the claims in this book is that they need to be seen together, mutually influencing each other, if we want lasting solutions. Biological, linguistic, and cultural diversity share the fact that all are, in partially parallel ways, very much threatened by

---

❖ **I n f o   B o x   2 . 1** ❖

Right and Duty to Develop Cultures (UNESCO)

A typical example of formulations on the value of cultural diversity is Article 1 of the UNESCO 'Declaration of the Principles of International Cultural Co-operation', proclaimed at UNESCO's 14th session, 4 November 1966:

1. Each culture has a dignity and value which must be respected and preserved.
2. Every people has the right and the duty to develop its culture.
3. In their rich variety and diversity, and in the reciprocal influences they exert on one another, all cultures form part of the common heritage belonging to all mankind [sic[6]].

---

globalisation in general and by market forces, economic, political, and socio-cultural, in particular. Globalisation and what is called the 'free' market will be discussed in chapter 6, but a couple of remarks about the linguistic market are in place already here.

Access to the linguistic market is as little 'free' as access to the 'free' economic market. Competence in dominant languages can be turned into linguistic capital which secures the 'profit of distinction' to the national and world elites (as Pattanayak 1991 also said, see section 1.1.1). One prerequisite for this process to happen is, according to Pierre Bourdieu (1992: 56) 'the unification of the [linguistic] market'. This means the creation of large areas, spaces (physical and non-material—see section 6.3.1.2; see also Ngũgĩ 1998 on spaces) where a dominant language can be or has to be used. One aspect of this process of unification and homogenisation was discussed in chapter 1 when describing how some 'dialects' became 'languages'. Bourdieu makes the significant sociological connections between economic and political power and the symbolic power of competing forms of language, and of knowledges.

Another precondition for competence in dominant languages to become linguistic capital for linguistic markets is 'the unequal distribution of the chances of access to the means of production of the legitimate competence, and to the legitimate places of expression' (ibid.). The required competence in dominant languages is largely produced in institutions of formal learning, schools. Various sectors of society have differential access to school achievement—schools are still largely middle-class schools, both linguistically and in terms of the types of knowledge, attitudes, and behaviour that they require and teach (see Willis 1977 and references to Bernstein in the bibliography). Even in Social Democrat Sweden, after almost a century of the welfare state and 'the People's Home' (*folkhemmet*) ideology, only 13 percent of children from working class homes continue to college-level education, as compared to around 50 percent of children from middle-class homes. The mother tongue and the variant of it spoken by learners, as compared to the language and variant of instruction[7] in school, is one of the important sorting mechanisms, to ease or complicate or even prevent this access. That is why the educational system is so important for the production of inequality, including access to prerequisites for being able to compete on linguistic markets; this in turn leads to linguistic and other inequality. And it is this inequality which decisively influences which languages and cultures can be maintained, at the same time as the inequality also reproduces the ecosocial and political world in which people negotiate about access to markets (both material and symbolic) in general.

There are other parallels between threats to all three kinds of diversity too, to be discussed later. But first we have to note one difference. We can compare knowledge people have about the loss of languages to their knowledge of some aspects of loss of biodiversity. Many people know about the threat to biodiversity (Task Box 2.1).

Reader Task 2.1
How many organisations do you know for the maintenance of biodiversity? What about linguistic diversity?

Can you mention at least one international and some national organisations working to maintain (some aspects of) biological diversity, and at least one big international conference concerned with biodiversity? Can you mention several? Then think of corresponding organisations and meetings to maintain linguistic diversity. How many do you know of?

Most readers could probably mention at least one organisation and/or conference about biodiversity, and many are worried about its disappearance. But many might have trouble in identifying organisations working to maintain linguistic diversity. Still, languages are today being killed at a much faster pace than ever before in human history and linguistic and cultural diversity are disappearing relatively much much faster than biological diversity, as we will see.

In making comparisons between the disappearance of diversities—and there are parallels—we start with some definitions and go then on to a few figures about the decline of biodiversity.

2.2. LANGUAGE AND SPECIES—DEFINING LINGUISTIC AND BIOLOGICAL DIVERSITY

First we give general definitions of biological and linguistic diversity (see Definition Box 2.1).

DEFINITION BOX 2.1 Biological & linguistic diversity

'**Biological diversity** (or "biodiversity" for short) is the range of variation exhibited by life forms. The term is "commonly used to describe the number, variety and variability of living organisms" and is essentially a synonym for "life on Earth"' (WCMC 1992: xiii).
'**Linguistic diversity** is the range of variation exhibited by human languages' (Harmon 1995a: 9).

One big question is how these rather vague definitions can be operationalised. Often we tend to think that the natural sciences are supposed to be more exact than the social sciences or the humanities. But comparison shows that the problems of defining the objects of study have not been solved in the study of biological diversity either. There are close parallels between the linguistic discussions about language versus dialect (and other varieties) and the biological discussions about species versus variety (see the discussion in Harmon 1995a). 'Species' is no easier to separate from other varieties than 'language'. Still, just as the number of separate languages is used to measure linguistic diversity, the number of separate species is used as one of the measures when measuring biodiversity, as David Harmon shows. The levels in Harmon's analysis below (1995a: 9) also show parallels with the measurement of linguistic diversity. There are

> three fundamental, hierarchically related levels of biological organization at which biodiversity is measured: the **genetic, species**, and **ecosystemic** levels. From an evolutionary perspective, the **genetic** level is probably the most important because evolutionary change ultimately is reflected in gene frequencies . . . From a conservation management standpoint, the **ecosystem** level is arguably the most important because it also includes abiotic (non-living) components of natural communities and thus is the most holistic measurement. In practice, however, biodiversity is usually measured on the **species** level. Moreover, discussion of global biodiversity is typically presented in terms of global numbers of species . . . with the result that the term "biodiversity" has become equated with "species richness." This is a rather loose usage, since the sheer number of species extant is only an approximation of the range of taxonomic variation among them, though it is a good proxy measure nonetheless. (emphases added)

Harmon claims (1995a: 9) that linguistic diversity can be measured on three corresponding levels too: the **structural level**, the **language level**, and the **genetic or lineage level**. The first refers to how large the variation of **structural differences** between languages is and the third to the number of distinct lineages (or **language families**). There are thousands of books and articles describing and classifying languages at both these levels (see Info Box 1.6. for some examples of them).

The middle, 'language', level has to do with 'the range of variation between individual languages across lineages, but the sheer number of distinct languages is a good approximation of linguistic diversity' (ibid.).

The **number of languages (or species)** can, then, be used as **a proxy for linguistic (or biological) diversity**. This is so even despite several unresolved concerns:

- we are still groping for a proper 'hard' definition of both 'language' and 'species';
- 'no single measure of anything so complicated as linguistic or biological diversity is diagnostic' (Harmon 1995a: 10).
- 'languages are not the same as living organisms, though there are parallels' (Amery 1998: 27). We need to be very careful not to overextend the analogy. The difference between 'a language' and 'a biological species' is major because of (a certain amount of) volition or lack of it: 'humans can choose which language or languages to use, whereas volition does not play a role in determining which species an organism belongs to . . . [L]anguages change by cultural selection; species by natural selection' (Harmon 1995a: 2).

A primary difference (not mentioned by Harmon) is the **additive** aspect of languages but not species. You can at the same time be a native speaker of two or even more languages, whereas you cannot be both a cat and a dog. And animals raised with a mother from another species (e.g., in zoos) would still recognize other individuals from their own species and also be able to communicate with them. By comparison, a Basque baby raised by Chinese foster parents would become linguistically completely Chinese and would not be able to communicate with other Basque. The propensity for humans to learn a language, **any** language, is innate, but **which** specific language(s) a child will learn is in no way biologically determined, and the learning can be either additive or subtractive (see Definition Box 2.2—see also further discussion in section 4.1.3).

We can draw a parallel from language to species, even if biologists do not use these concepts. In my view, even if there is no parallel to subtractive and additive language learning in other biological species, biological species can, however, **spread** subtractively or additively, with the introduction of non-native species. Subtractive spreading, ecological imperialism (Crosby 1994; see also Shipek 1987), is one of the reasons for reduced biological diversity. Well-known cases are foxes, rabbits, and goats in Australia, destroying the habitat or other conditions of life for other species, and many

DEFINITION BOX 2.2 Subtractive and additive language learning and language spread; diglossia

Subtractive spread of languages—incoming language first *displaces*, then *replaces* original languages, domain by domain. Often a result of linguistic imperialism (see Phillipson 1992a).

Subtractive language learning—a new (dominant/majority) language is learned **at the cost** of the mother tongue which is displaced, with a diglossic situation as a consequence, and is sometimes replaced. The person's total linguistic repertoire does not show (much) growth as a result of the learning. The concept originally comes from Wallace Lambert (1975).

Additive spread of languages—incoming language is initially used for new functions ('*neoplacement*', Phillipson & Skutnabb-Kangas 1986b) but does not replace original languages which continue to be used and developed, even if some diglossia may occur. Later, terms in the original language may develop for the neoplaced concepts.

Additive language learning—a new language is learned **in addition** to the mother tongue which continues to be used and developed. The person's total linguistic repertoire is extended.

Diglossia—functional differentiation between languages, e.g., using one language or variant (High, Low) at home and in the neighbourhood, and another one for more formal, official purposes, e.g., school and work. The original concept was used about varieties, not different languages, by Charles Ferguson (1959).

plants ("weeds") which have taken over from indigenous plants (see Crosby 1994 and, for instance, articles in Costo & Costo). Subtractive spread has been and is both intentional and 'accidental' (many insects and bacteria spread, for instance, today with exports and tourism). Crosby's (1994) excellent book **Ecological imperialism. The biological expansion of Europe, 900–1900**, gives numerous examples. The introduction of non-native species, which according to the IUCN is a growing threat in all ecosystems (threatening entire ecosystems), often leads to "hybridization, competition for resources, predation, disease, parasites, and the alteration of ecological relationships between species" (from Introduction to the 1996 IUCN Red List of Threatened Animals, downloaded 1 September 1998 from the IUCN Website; see Address Box 2.1).

Additive spread is also possible, and we have at least 2,000 years of **documented** experience of the spread of both plants and animals where at least the intention was additive, but where we often do not know yet how much subtraction has been involved anyway.

An additional serious methodological concern, already mentioned earlier, needs to be discussed. In an article analysing countries with no definite linguistic majorities (in the sense of **one** large group, for instance over 50% of the population), Clinton Robinson (1993: 54) suggests, that

> a ranking of degree of linguistic diversity should not be based on the absolute number of languages in a country, but rather on the percentage of the population speaking any single language. Thus the country where the largest language group represents the smallest proportion of the population would be deemed as the most linguistically diverse, since all the other language groups would represent yet smaller percentages.

It seems to me that both ways of assessing linguistic diversity, absolute number of languages and the percentage of the population speaking the largest language, are useful measures for certain purposes. We clearly have to differentiate between countries with a definite linguistic majority and one or many minorities, and countries consisting of 'minorities' only, without a 'majority'. The first type is prevalent in Europe and neo-Europes, whereas the second type is more common in the rest of the world, even if there are many exceptions (see Info Box 2.2).

Many formulations of minority protection and language rights in international law are based on the 'majority-cum-minorities' model, as is a lot of theorising in scientific disciplines which work with multilingual situations, including, regrettably, much of this book. Robinson's plea for considering alternatives is therefore very much needed. However, there should in most cases not be any conflict between considering both ways of classification, depending on the purpose one has with the diversity assessment. When we in chapter 1 compared the ranking of the 10 most diverse countries in the world with both methods (Tables 1.1 and 1.3), we could see that the results showed major differences. As is often the case, I see a both-and approach as more fruitful than an either-or approach.

2.3. COMPARING THE THREAT TOWARDS BIODIVERSITY AND LINGUISTIC DIVERSITY

2.3.1. Decline of Biodiversity

2.3.1.1. *Numbers and Extinction Rates*

After having defined biological and linguistic diversity, we can start looking in more detail at what is happening to them. The total number of species on earth is not known, and estimates vary much more than for languages, from 5 million to 30 million or even many more. There are some 1.7 million documented species, and these 'represent a relatively small proportion of all

---

❖ I n f o   B o x   2 . 2 ❖

Countries Where No Linguistic
Group Exceeds 50% of the Population

Counting from Robinson's lists in his Appendix 1 (1993: 63–65), we get altogether 44 countries where 'no single language group exceeds 50% of the population' (ibid., 63). Of these, 25 are in Africa, 9 in Asia, 4 in the Caribbean and Latin America, and 6 in the Pacific—but none in Europe, North America, Australia, or New Zealand. Only in 10, less than a quarter, is the largest language one of the official languages: Chad (Arabic), Guinea (Fuuta Jalon), Mali (Bambara), Nigeria (Yoruba), Zaire (Ciluba), India (Hindi), Malaysia (Malay), Philippines (Tagalog), Thailand (Thai), and New Caledonia (French).

The changes in South Africa have after Robinson's 1993 list brought in one more country where the largest language, though not exceeding 50% of the population, is an official language. Of South Africa's population 22.2% have a Nguni language, Zulu, the largest language, as their home language. Nguni languages[8] are so closely related that 'most people will agree that they are all able to communicate with other Nguni speakers' (Kathleen Heugh, January 1999, personal communication). Particularly speakers of Swati and Ndebele feel 'very comfortable with Zulu—occasionally historical political competition with Xhosa speakers complicates perceptions' (ibid.). Counting all the Nguni speakers together gives some 45% of the population who 'are able to communicate in Zulu with native-like or near-native-like ease' (ibid.). See also Alexander 1989, 1992, for suggestions flowing from this fact and Bailey 1995a and b for overviews.

---

species believed to exist on this planet' (Baillie 1998: 13). This is one of several reasons why **extinction rates** are also difficult to determine. Extinction is, it seems, a natural process for biological species, and it is estimated that 95% of all species that ever existed on our planet are now extinct. But on the other hand, the time span has been some 3.5 **billion** years, and during that time there has been a general trend of **increasing species richness** (Baillie 1998: 12).

The average life-span of a species has been estimated to be 5–10 million years. If one uses a fairly low estimate of the number of species, 5–10 million, the background extinction rate should be about one species per year. Even the numbers of **documented** extinctions over the last 400 years (611 species) exceed the background estimates (ibid.), but they represent a minute proportion of what biologists believe are the real extinction rates. Less than 10% of the 1.7 million documented species have been evaluated for extinction; the 1.7 million are a small proportion of existing species, and for most of the evaluated 10%, the figures are relatively recent, i.e., tens of thousands of species may have become extinct during those 400 years without any documentation. The documentation is very heavily biased towards vertebrates (**vertebrates**: mammals, birds, reptiles, amphibians, fishes), and terrestrial vertebrates at that (of the documented 611 species above, 86 are mammals and 104 birds, ibid., 13). But at least 95% of all the known animal species are invertebrates, and many invertebrates are not yet known. Today,

> [c]onservative estimates put the [extinction] rate at more than 5,000 species each year. This is about ten thousand times as fast as prehuman extinction rates. Less conservative estimates put the rate at 150,000 species per year. (Goodland 1996: 214)

If we take the most conservative (**'most optimistic'**) estimate of extinction (5,000/year) and the 'most optimistic' (least conservative) estimate about numbers (30 million), we get an extinction rate of 0.017% per year. With reverse estimates, the **'most pessimistic'** (least conservative) estimate for extinction (150,000/year) and the 'most pessimistic' (most conservative) estimate for the number of species (5 million), the yearly extinction rate would be 3%. As we can see, the difference is huge, mainly because the highest extinction rate estimate is 300 times the lower one. On the other hand, those researchers who use higher extinction rate estimates usually also seem to use higher estimates of numbers of species. For instance, an extinction rate of 150,000/year, with the numbers set at 30 million, would give a yearly extinction percentage of 0.5%. It seems that figures used by many researchers lie somewhere between 0.2% ('pessimistic realistic') and 0.02 ('optimistic realistic'). In Table 2.1, I summarize the variation in estimates.

TABLE 2.1
Extinction rates for biological species, alternative estimates

Number of species		Extinction rate per year		
pess. *PN*	*opt.* *ON*	*pess.* *PE*	*opt.* *OE*	*% extinction rate, various alternatives*
5 million	30 million	150,000	5,000	ON + OE (30m + 5,000) 0.017%
				PN + PE (5m + 150,000) 3.0%
				ON + PE (30m + 150,000) 0.5%
				PN + OE (5m + 5,000) 0.1%
				'pess. realistic' 0.2%
				'opt. realistic' 0.02%

PN/ON = 'Pessimistic'/'Optimistic' estimates of Numbers of species;
PE/OE = 'Pessimistic'/'Optimistic' estimates of Extinction rates.

2.3.1.2. *Threatened Animals*

From extinction rates we move to threat of extinction. The degree of threat of extinction is assessed by international organisations and published in various kinds of Red Lists or Red Books which list species under various categories of threat. The categories used in Red Data Books and Red Lists have recently (1994) been changed, after having been in place, with some modifications, for almost 30 years (see IUCN Red List 1998). Earlier, for instance, **'endangered'** species were defined as 'species that are in imminent danger of extinction' and **'threatened'** as 'species that in the foreseeable future will be in imminent danger of extinction' (Krauss 1992: 7). These were categories which were general enough to be used for languages too, as we see from Krauss' definitions (ibid., and Definition Box 1.4).

The earlier lists included the **Endangered, Vulnerable**, and **Rare** categories, and also **Insufficiently Known** and **Indeterminate** were used. The present categorisation operates with 8 classes: **Extinct** (EX), **Extinct in the Wild** (EW), **Critically Endangered** (CR), **Endangered** (EN), **Vulnerable** (VU), **Lower Risk** (LR), **Data Deficient** (DD), and **Not Evaluated** (NE). Parts of the new definitions are included in Definition Box 2.3. (Compare these later with the categories used at present in the UNESCO Red Books on Endangered Languages, Definition Box 2.4). But see first Task Box 2.2!

Reader Task 2.2
Possible definitions of threats to languages

Before comparing the species/taxa definitions in Definition Box 2.3 to those used about languages in UNESCO Red Books (Definition Box 2.4), the reader is invited to think of and write down possible corresponding definitions about threat and endangerment to languages! Consider what role existence or lack of written or recorded materials might play, and whether there are parallels to existing in 'the wild'?[9] Could reclaiming/recreating a language from written materials be compared to possible recreation of biological species from DNA strings in the future? What might reasonable 'criteria (A to E)' be for assessing languages? Rob Amery has insightful, reflective discussions on the issues of reclaiming languages in his PhD thesis (1998).

In 1990, of the 4,400 **mammal** species, 326 or 7.4% were on either the 'endangered' or the 'threatened' lists. The corresponding figures for **birds** were 231 or 2.7% of 8,600. Krauss reported (1992: 7) that Alaskan biologists claimed underlisting, and estimated the percentages to 10% and 5%, respectively.

The 1996 edition of the **IUCN Red List** (the most comprehensive list of globally threatened animal species ever compiled) includes altogether 5,205

DEFINITION BOX 2.3 New IUCN Red List category definitions on endangered species; U.S. Endangered Species Act definitions

IUCN RED LIST: 'A taxon is . . .'
Extinct (EX): 'when there is no reasonable doubt that the last individual has died'.
Extinct in the Wild (EW): '. . . when it is known only to survive in cultivation, in captivity or as a naturalised population (or populations) well outside the past range. . .'.
Critically Endangered (CR): '. . . when it is facing an extremely high risk of extinction in the wild in the immediate future, as defined by any of the criteria (A to E)'.
Endangered (EN): '. . . when it is not Critically Endangered but is facing a very high risk of extinction in the wild in the immediate future, as defined by any of the criteria (A to E)'.
Vulnerable (VU): '. . . when it is not Critically Endangered or Endangered but is facing a high risk of extinction in the wild in the medium-term future, as defined by any of the criteria (A to E)'.
Lower Risk (LR): '. . . when it has been evaluated, does not satisfy the criteria for any of the categories Critically Endangered, Endangered or Vulnerable'. There are three subcategories: Conservation Dependent (cd), Near Threatened (nt), and Least Concern (lc).
Data Deficient (DD): '. . . when there is inadequate information to make a direct, or indirect, assessment of its risk of extinction based on its distribution and/or population status . . .'
Not Evaluated (NE): '. . .when it has not yet been assessed against the criteria.'

U.S. ENDANGERED SPECIES ACT:
Endangered: plants and animals 'in danger of extinction through all or a significant portion of their range';
Threatened: species may become endangered 'if conditions surrounding the species begin to or continue to deteriorate.' (Source: IUCN Red List 1998, see Address Box 2.1; go to the source to see the criteria A to E).

species threatened with extinction. All known species of both mammals and birds were evaluated whereas the assessments even for other vertebrates are still insufficient. In 1994 there were 2,114 vertebrates in the Endangered, Vulnerable, or Rare categories which loosely correspond to the present threatened categories (CR, EN, and VU above); in 1996 there were 3,314 threatened **vertebrates**. 20% of the evaluated **reptiles** (reptiles are, for instance, crocodiles, tortoises, snakes), 25% of the **amphibians** (for instance, frogs and salamanders) and 34% of the evaluated **fishes** are listed as threatened. Of the few **invertebrates** assessed, more than 500 insects, 400 inland crustaceans (e.g., crayfish) and 900 molluscs (e.g., snails) were classified as threatened.

The latest figures, downloaded 1 September 1998 from the IUCN Red List Web-site (Address Box 2.1), tell us the following:

Birds: 168 (2%) Critically Endangered (CR), 235 (2%) Endangered (EN), 704 (7%) Vulnerable (VU); in total, 11% threatened and an additional 9% near-threatened.

Mammals: 169 (4%) CR, 315 (7%) EN and 612 (14%) VU, in total, 25% threatened and an additional close to 16% near-threatened.

Thus a total of 20% of known birds and close to 41% of mammals are in a risk zone if we also take the Lower Risk categories into account; an alarming increase (see also Tuxill & Bright 1998 in the **State of the World 1998** from the Worldwatch Institute for a general discussion of the significance of the figures).

The countries with the largest numbers of threatened animal species are, in descending order, Indonesia, China, and India. The same countries also have the largest numbers of threatened mammals, followed by Brazil, Mexico, Australia, Papua New Guinea, Philippines, Madagascar, and Peru. For birds, the list is Indonesia, Brazil, China, Philippines, India, Colombia, Peru, Ecuador, the United States, and Vietnam. Of the 20 countries with most threatened mammals, 35% are in Asia, 30% in Africa (with Madagascar only among the top 10—and 73% of its mammals are endemic), and 15% in South America. The corresponding figures for birds are 50% in Asia, 25% in South America and 15% in Oceania—but no African countries (all figures are from Jonathan Baillie's analysis of the 1996 **IUCN Red List of Threatened Animals**).

The majority of the animal species qualify as threatened as a result of human-induced threats. These include, according to IUCN (1996), 'exploitation as a result of harvesting for reasons of commercial value, human subsistence and sport [and because of] pollution and climate change.'

2.3.1.3. Threatened Plants

The **1997 IUCN Red List of Threatened Plants**, compiled by the World Conservation Monitoring Centre in Cambridge, UK (Walter & Gillett, eds), is the first comprehensive international study of the world's threatened plants. It draws on data from more than 200 countries and it took a team of botanists more than 15 years to compile, from some 2,000 data sources. Still, as for animals too, scientific data is seriously lacking from parts of Asia, South America, and Africa, i.e., those parts of the world which are rich in biodiversity.

The Red List estimates that out of the global known total of some 270,000 plants more than 34,000 must be put on the **Red List** of plants facing extinction (Address Box 2.1).

```
* * * * * * * * * * * * * * * * * * * * * * * * * * * * * * * * * * * * * * * * *
*                                                                               *
*                  Address Box 2.1   The Red Lists for animals and plants       *
*                                                                               *
*     The Web-sites for the Red Lists of Threatened Plants and Threatened       *
*     Animals are <http://www.rbge.org.uk/data/wcmc/plants.by.taxon.html> or    *
*     <http://www.wcmc.org.uk/species/plants/plant_redlist.html>; and <http://www. *
*     wcmc.org.uk/species/animals/>.                                            *
*     The lists are monitored by World Conservation Monitoring Centre, 219      *
*     Huntingdon Road, Cambridge CB3 0DL, UK; phone 44-1223-277 314; fax        *
*     44-1223-277 136; email <info@wcmc.org.uk>; more general Web-site          *
*     <http://www.wcmc.org.uk/species/data/index.html>                          *
*                                                                               *
* * * * * * * * * * * * * * * * * * * * * * * * * * * * * * * * * * * * * * * * *
```

A further 6,522 plants are likely to join them in the near future, and many others 'are declining rapidly round the world', the authors say, adding: 'This is a very conservative figure. As information increases the situation will be shown to be worse. We are on the brink of a serious wave of extinction. The situation will deteriorate unless vastly increased action is taken now' (as reported in **The Guardian** April 9 1998: 3).

The highest **absolute numbers** of plants known to be facing extinction are in the USA (4,669; 24% of the known 19,473 plants), Australia (2,245), South Africa (2,215), Turkey (1,876) and Mexico (1,593). Table 2.2 shows some of the countries where the relative percentage of plants threatened is high, and a couple from the other end, with low relative numbers.

Just as for animals, some regions have been more thoroughly assessed than others—for instance the United States, Australia, and South Africa have been subject to detailed reviews for both plants and animals, and may therefore also have proportionally more species listed as threatened than countries in less well studied regions, according to Baillie's estimate (1998: 2). Still, various regions in the world show huge differences in terms of absolute numbers reflecting diversity. We can compare the number of native plants **in the whole of Britain**, a total of **1,623**, with the estimated number of plants in just **one acre** of warm temperate forest: at least **2,000** different plant species (Info Box 2.3).

Of course losing plants also means losing other species which are dependent on the plants: ants, worms, butterflies, birds, mammals. For both animals and plants, habitat reduction or loss, fragmentation and degradation (for instance through pollution), introduction of foreign, non-native species, and overexploitation, leading to serious decline, often threaten entire ecological

TABLE 2.2
World's native plant species facing extinction

| Country | Total number of species | Under threat of extinction | |
		%	number*
1. St. Helena	165	41.2	68
2. Mauritius	750	39.2	294
3. Seychelles	250	31.2	78
4. USA	19,473	24.0	4,669
5. Jamaica	3,308	22.5	744
6. Turkey	8,650	21.7	1,876
7. French Polynesia	959	19.5	187
8. Spain	5,050	19.5	985
9. Pitcairn	76	18.4	14
10. Reunion	546	18.1	99
11. Australia	15,638	14.4	2,245
12. New Caledonia	3,322	14.4	478
13. Sri Lanka	3,314	13.7	454
14. Cuba	6,522	13.6	887
15. Japan	5,565	12.7	707
16. Greece	4,992	11.4	569
17. South Africa	23,420	9.5	2,215
UK	1,623	1.1	18
Ireland	950	0.1	1

Source: The 1997 **Threatened Plants Report**, as reported in **The Guardian** April 9 1998: 3.
*I have counted the numbers from the list of the percentages.

Info Box 2.3

Life in 1 Acre of Warm Temperate Forest—
More Plants Than in the Whole Of Britain

One estimate (reported in Sale 1996: 478) of the biological life of just **one acre** in a warm temperate forest: 50,000 vertebrates, 662,000 ants, 372,000 spiders, 90,000 earthworms, 45,000 termites, 19,000 snails, 89 million mites, 28 million collembola, and some 5,000 pounds of plant life divided into at least 2,000 species.

systems. Tropical forest loss, which reached record levels in 1997, following fires in Indonesia and Brazil, is believed to be destroying up to 27,000 species of plants and animals a year, many of which have not even been named, says a spokesperson for the Worldwide Fund for Nature (as reported in **The Guardian**, April 9 1998: 3). All this 'clearly highlights the importance of maintaining intact ecological systems for the preservation of biodiversity', Baillie concludes (1998: 10).

2.3.2. Endangered and Threatened—Comparison Between Biological Species and Languages

Serious as the decline and loss of biodiversity is, still, as compared to the threat to languages (90% 'moribund', endangered, or threatened), the threat to biodiversity is 'relatively mild', according to Krauss (1992: 7).

In addition to the discussions on threatened languages in chapter 1, we can now compare the threat to biodiversity with data compiled in a somewhat similar way, namely **UNESCO's Red Books on Endangered Languages**. The Red Book for Europe, with its Index, as well as the Databank for Endangered Finno-Ugric Languages have been compiled by Tapani Salminen and the North-East Asia Red Book by Juha Janhunen and Tapani Salminen, whereas the Asia and the Pacific book is by Stephen Wurm and Shigeru Tsuchida, and the book on Africa by Bernd Heine and Matthias Brenzinger. A Russian book (see Kolga et al. 1993; Humphreys & Mits (eds) 1993) and a Uralic (Finno-Ugric) book (Vaba & Viikberg 1997) have been compiled in Estonia (see Address Box 2.2 for the online versions).

```
* * * * * * * * * * * * * * * * * * * * * * * * * * * * * * * * * * * * * * * * * *
*                                                                               *
*                   Address Box 2.2   UNESCO Red Books                         *
*                         on Endangered Languages                               *
*                                                                               *
*    Europe: <http://www.helsinki.fi/~tasalmin/europe_index.html>              *
*    Northeast Asia: <http://www.helsinki.fi/~tasalmin/nasia_index.html>       *
*    Asia and the Pacific: <http://www.tooyoo.l.u-tokyo.ac.jp/redbook/         *
*    asiapacific/asia-index.html>                                               *
*    Africa: <http://www.tooyoo.l.u-tokyo.ac.jp/redbook/africa-index.html>     *
*    Databanks for Endangered Finno-Ugric Languages: <http://www.helsinki.     *
*    fi/~tasalmin/deful.html>                                                   *
*    http://www.suri.ee>                                                        *
*    Russia: <http://www.eki.ee/books/redbook/>                                *
*                                                                               *
* * * * * * * * * * * * * * * * * * * * * * * * * * * * * * * * * * * * * * * * * *
```

Of course a comparison is problematic because the knowledge in all areas is patchy and the definitions used vary to some extent (see Definition Box 2.4).

DEFINITION BOX 2.4 UNESCO Red Books category definitions of endangered languages

(i) **extinct languages** other than the ancient ones;
(ii) **possibly extinct languages** without reliable information of remaining
speakers;
(iii) **nearly extinct languages** with maximally tens of speakers, all elderly;
(iv) **seriously endangered languages** with a more substantial number of
speakers but practically without children among them;
(v) **endangered languages** with some children speakers at least in part of
their range but decreasingly so;
(vi) **potentially endangered languages** with a large number of children
speakers but without an official or prestigious status;
(vii) **not endangered languages** with safe transmission of language to new
generations.

These categories were developed on the basis of Juha Janhunen's earlier categories (i) extinct; (ii) moribund or extinct; (iii) moribund; (iv) endangered or moribund; (v) endangered; (potentially endangered); and (vii)
not endangered. The information is taken from Janhunen & Salminen's
Northeast Asia Red Book (see Address Box 2.2). See also categories in
Hallamaa 1998.

I have made a very simple comparison. For biodiversity, with a very
elementary calculation **for the year 2100**, estimating the rate of extinction
with today's situation as the starting point, we get the following results:
according to the 'pessimistic realistic' estimate above (Table 2.1), **20%** of all
today's biological animal species would be extinct in 100 years' time, while
according to the 'optimistic realistic' estimate the figure would be **2%**. The
corresponding figure for plants would be **under 13%** according to the 'optimistic' figures from the 1997 **Threatened Plants Report** (34,000 out of
270,000), or **15%** if we add the 6,522 likely ones to the 34,000 (see above),
and still somewhat higher if we account for today's lack of knowledge from
some of the most diverse areas.

In contrast, 'in the last 5 hundred years about half the known languages
of the world have disappeared', according to Hans-Jürgen Sasse (1992: 7—
compare this with the **documented** extinction of 611 species over the last 400
years mentioned above), and **90% of today's languages might be extinct or
'on the death row' in 100 years' time**, according to Krauss, and **over half** even
according to the most optimistic estimates (see also articles in Grenoble &
Whaley (eds) 1998).

This shows that there is a very large difference: the threat to languages
is far more serious. Linguistic diversity is today disappearing relatively much
much faster than biological diversity, in the sense that the percentage of

languages that will probably perish/be killed in the next century is much larger than the percentage of all biological species that will be killed during the same period.

It is interesting, then, that loss of biodiversity has had massive attention all over the world—many people are worried about it. But few people talk of loss of linguistic diversity. There are literally thousands of international and national NGOs and other popular organisations in some way fighting decline and loss of biodiversity but extremely few fighting decline and loss of linguistic diversity. Address Boxes 2.3 to 2.5 list some of them—a few have been listed in earlier Address Boxes.

So far, we have discussed linguistic diversity and biodiversity separately, even if some comparisons of definitions and relative numbers have been made. Next we will investigate the relationship between these different types of diversity.

2.4. THE CORRELATION BETWEEN BIODIVERSITY AND LINGUISTIC AND CULTURAL DIVERSITY

Linguistic and cultural diversity on the one hand and biodiversity on the other hand are correlated: where one type is high, the other is too, and vice versa.

Mark Pagel points out that in North America 'languages, like all biological species, get thicker on the ground as you approach the equator' (as reported by Nicholas Ostler in **Iatiku: Newsletter of the Foundation for Endangered Languages** 1, 1995: 6). This seems to be true on the other side of one of the oceans too: there are fewer native languages in the whole of Europe (even when Russia is included) than in just one African country, Nigeria, which is much closer to the equator (see Tables 1.1, 2.3). The most linguistically diverse areas in the world (Indonesia and Papua New Guinea, Tables 1.1, 2.3) are both tropical.

Reporting on the conference 'Endangered Languages, Endangered Knowledge, Endangered Environments' at the University of California, Berkeley (October 1996), Luisa Maffi, President of Terralingua (see Info Box 2.4; Address Box 2.4), also says that there are 'remarkable overlaps between global mappings of the world's areas of biological megadiversity and areas of high linguistic diversity', and likewise a 'correlation between low-diversity cultural systems and low biodiversity'[10] (Maffi 1996).

Conservationist David Harmon (Secretary/Treasurer of Terralingua) has studied the question of the correlation in relation to several species. In Table 2.3 (p. 89) he compares **endemism** (see Definition Box 1.2) in language and in higher vertebrates (mammals, birds, reptiles, and amphibians), taking the top 25 countries for both. Harmon derived the figures for endemic languages

**Address Box 2.3   Organisations working
with endangered languages**

Some of the organisations working either to describe and catalogue threatened or endangered languages or to support their maintenance and development, or both, are listed below.

■ **Anthropologists' Fund for urgent anthropological research**
   P.O. Box A, Phillips, ME 04966, USA; contact: George N. Appel
■ **Fellowships in Urgent Anthropology**
   Royal Anthropological Institute (RAI) and Goldsmith College,
   University of London, New Cross, London SE14 6NW;
   phone: 44-171-919 7800; fax: 44-171-919 7813.
   —Sponsors research on 'currently threatened indigenous peoples,
      cultures, and languages'. Offers fellowships through RAI.
■ **Arbeitsgruppe bedrohte Sprachen** (Work Group on Endangered Languages)
   Institut für Sprachwissenschaft, Universität Köln,
   D-50923 Köln, Germany;
   phone: 49-221-470 2323; contact: Hans-Jürgen Sasse:
   <hj.sasse@uni-koeln.de>; <agbs@uni-koeln.de>
   —A permanent committee of the German Linguistic Society. Goals: to
      draw attention to endangered languages and their maintenance and
      documentation; to promote linguistic fieldwork in academic
      curricula; and to seek sources of funding in support of endangered
      language research.
■ **The Endangered Languages Fund**
   Dept. of Linguistics, Yale University, New Haven, CT 06520, USA;
   contact: Doug Whalen: <whalen@lenny.haskins.yale.edu>;
   <elf@haskins.yale.edu>;
   Web-site: <http://sapir.ling.yale.edu/~elf/index.html>
   —Dedicated to the scientific study of endangered languages, support of
      native communities' language maintenance initiatives, and
      dissemination of research and applied work results. Offers grants
      for both kinds of activities.
■ **Foundation for Endangered Languages**
   172 Bailbrook Lane, Bath BA1 7AA, UK;
   phone: 44-1225-85 2865; fax: 44-1225-85 9258;
   <http://www.Bris.ac.u./Depts/Philosophy/CTLL/FEL/>;
   contact: Nicholas Ostler: <nostler@chibcha.demon.co.uk>
   —Aims to spread information about language endangerment and to
      increase scholarly knowledge about the smaller languages of the
      world. Publishes a newsletter, organizes workshops, and offers
      funds for language documentation.

(Continued)

```
* * * * * * * * * * * * * * * * * * * * * * * * * * * * * * * * * * * * * * * * * * *
*                                                                                   *
*                    Address Box 2.3   (Continued)                                  *
*                                                                                   *
*   ■ Linguistic Society of America, Committee on Endangered Languages              *
*     and their Preservation (CELP), Survey of the world's endangered               *
*     languages                                                                     *
*     1325 18th St. N.W., Suite 211, Washington, D.C. 20036-6501, USA;              *
*     <lsa@lsadc.org>; phone: 1-202-835 1714; fax: 1-202-835 1717; contact:         *
*     Scott Delancey, CELP; <delancey@darkwing.uoregon.edu>;                        *
*     Akira Yamamoto: <akira@kuhub.cc.ukans.edu>                                    *
*     —Calls attention to issues about and fosters field research on the world's    *
*        endangered languages. Conducts a survey of their status and of             *
*        existing scholarly resources on them.                                      *
*   ■ Permanent International Committee of Linguists                                 *
*     Instituut voor Nederlandse Lexicologie, University of Leiden,                 *
*     P.O. Box 9515, 2300 RA Leiden, The Netherlands;                               *
*     phone: 31-71-514 1648; fax: 31-71-527 2115/522 7737;                          *
*     contact: P. J. G. Van Sterkenburg: <sterkenburg@rulxho.leidenuniv.nl>         *
*     —Works with UNESCO on the Red Books on Endangered Languages.                  *
*   ■ UNESCO International Council for Philosophy and Humanistic Studies             *
*     (CIPSH)                                                                        *
*     Contact: Stephen A. Wurm; Australian National University,                     *
*     Dept. of Linguistics, Canberra, ACT 0200, Australia;                          *
*     phone: 61-6-249 2369; fax: 61-6-257 1893                                      *
*     Grants for the Study of Endangered Languages; Contact: M. Maurice             *
*     Aymard, Secretary General, UNESCO, CIPSH, 1, Rue Miollis,                     *
*     75732 Paris, France; fax: 33-1-4065 9480; <cipsh@unesco.org>                  *
*     —Publishes the Red Books on Endangered Languages. Offers grants for           *
*        endangered language research.                                              *
*   ■ World Federation of the Deaf                                                  *
*     13D, Chemin du Levant, 01210 Ferney-Voltaire, France;                         *
*     fax: 33-450-40 01 07; contact: Liisa Kauppinen                                *
*     —Resource development and advocacy for the world's sign languages.            *
*        Publishes a Newsletter (WFD News. Magazine of the World Federa-            *
*        tion of the Deaf) and other materials (see also Address Box 4.1).          *
*   ■ EBLUL, the European Bureau for Lesser Used Languages should also              *
*     be mentioned even if it does not work only with endangered languages.         *
*     Head Office: 10, Sráid Haiste Íocht, IRL-Baile Átha Cliath 2, Ireland;        *
*     phone 353-1-661 2205; fax 353-1-676 6840; email <eblul@indigo.ie>;            *
*     Information Centre: Sint-Jooststraat 49/Rue St. Josse 49, B-1210              *
*     Brussel/Bruxelles, Belgium/Belgique, phone 32-2-218 2590; fax 32-2-218        *
*     1974; email <pub00341@innet.be>. Web-site: <http://www.eblul.org/>            *
*                                                                                   *
* * * * * * * * * * * * * * * * * * * * * * * * * * * * * * * * * * * * * * * * * * *
```

(Continued)

```
* * * * * * * * * * * * * * * * * * * * * * * * * * * * * * * * * * * * * * * * * * *
*                                                                                   *
*                    Address Box 2.3   (Continued)                                  *
*                                                                                   *
*   ■ UNESCO World languages report and International Clearing House for             *
*     Endangered Languages, see Address Boxes 1.2 and 1.3. More addresses,          *
*     including many of the electronic mailing lists discussing endangered          *
*     languages, are given on the Web-sites of these organisations.                 *
*   ■ Terralingua's Web-site (Address Box 2.4) carries a fairly extensive list.     *
*   ■ Randy J. LaPolla's Handout on Endangered Languages                            *
*     <http://ctspc05.cphk.hk/lapolla/el.html> also has a good list.                *
*                                                                                   *
* * * * * * * * * * * * * * * * * * * * * * * * * * * * * * * * * * * * * * * * * * *
```

```
* * * * * * * * * * * * * * * * * * * * * * * * * * * * * * * * * * * * * * * * * * *
*                                                                                   *
*                    Address Box 2.4   Terralingua                                  *
*                                                                                   *
*   Terralingua is a nonprofit international organisation devoted to preserving      *
*   the world's linguistic diversity and to investigating links between biological  *
*   and cultural diversity; Web-site: <http://cougar.ucdavis.edu/nas/terralin/home. *
*   html>. E-mails: Luisa Maffi, President: <maffi@nwu.edu>; David Harmon,           *
*   Secretary & Treasurer: <gws@mail.portup.com>; Tove Skutnabb-Kangas,             *
*   Vice-President: <tovesk@babel.ruc.dk>. See also Info Box 2.4 for Terralin-       *
*   gua's Statement of purpose.                                                     *
*                                                                                   *
* * * * * * * * * * * * * * * * * * * * * * * * * * * * * * * * * * * * * * * * * * *
```

```
* * * * * * * * * * * * * * * * * * * * * * * * * * * * * * * * * * * * * * * * * * *
*                                                                                   *
*                 Address Box 2.5   Electronic Resources on Languages               *
*                            and Language Endangerment                              *
*   ■ Endangered-Languages-List                                                     *
*       List address: endangered-languages-l@carmen.murdoch.edu.au;                 *
*       contact: Mari Rhydwen; email: <white.cloud@bigpond.com>                     *
*       —Discussion of language endangerment, linguistic diversity, and            *
*           indigenous and minority languages.                                      *
*   ■ GeoNative (electronic database of native place names)                         *
*       Web-site: <http://www.geocities.com/Athens/9479>; contact: Luistxo          *
*       Fernandez, Web-site owner, email: <txoko@redestb.es>                        *
*       —Dedicated to 'putting minority languages on the map'; gathers and         *
*           displays native place names in the world's smaller languages.           *
*   ■ Language Documentation Urgency List (LDUL)                                    *
*       List address: <ldul@cis.uni-muenchen.de>; contact: Dietmar Zaefferer,       *
*       Institut für Deutsche Philologie, Universität München, Schellingstrasse 3,  *
*       D-80799 München, Germany; phone: 49-89-2180 2060/2180 3819;                 *
*       fax: 49-89-2180 3871; email: <ue303bh@sunmail.lrz-muenchen.de>              *
*       —Automatic mailbox and database. Provides information on endanger-         *
*           ment status of and need for documentation on the world's languages.     *
*                                                                                   *
* * * * * * * * * * * * * * * * * * * * * * * * * * * * * * * * * * * * * * * * * * *
```

(Continued)

■ **List of Language Lists**
<http://condor.stcloud.msus.edu:20020/docs/lnglstcurrent.txt>; contact:
Bernard Comrie, List co-owner; email: <comrie@bcf.usc.edu>;
Department of Linguistics, GFS-301, University of Southern California,
Los Angeles, CA 90089-1693, USA; phone: 1-213-740 2986;
fax: 1-213-740 9306; contact: Michael Everson, List co-owner,
email: <everson@indigo.ie>
—Inventory of electronic bulletin boards devoted to the study of
    individual languages and groups of languages.
■ **The Ethnologue**—see Address Box 1.4.

Info Box 2.4

Terralingua—Partnerships for Linguistic and Biological Diversity; Statement of Purpose

Terralingua: Partnerships for Linguistic and Biological Diversity

Statement of Purpose

A. Terralingua recognizes:

1. That the diversity of languages and their variant forms is a vital part of the world's cultural diversity;

2. That cultural diversity and biological diversity are not only related, but often inseparable; and

3. That, like biological species, many languages and their variant forms around the world are now faced with an extinction crisis whose magnitude may well prove very large.

B. Terralingua declares:

4. That every language, along with its variant forms, is inherently valuable and therefore worthy of being preserved and perpetuated, regardless of its political, demographic, or linguistic status;

5. That deciding which language to use, and for what purposes, is a basic human right inhering to members of the community of speakers now using the language or whose ancestors traditionally used it; and

6. That such usage decisions should be freely made in an atmosphere of tolerance and reciprocal respect for cultural distinctiveness—a condition that is a prerequisite for increased mutual understanding among the world's peoples and a recognition of our common humanity.

(Continued)

❖ **I n f o   B o x   2 . 4** ❖

(Continued)

C. Therefore, Terralingua sets forth the following goals:

7. To help preserve and perpetuate the world's linguistic diversity in all its variant forms (languages, dialects, pidgins, creoles, sign languages, languages used in rituals, etc.) through research, programs of public education, advocacy, and community support.

8. To learn about languages and the knowledge they embody from the communities of speakers themselves, to encourage partnerships between community-based language/cultural groups and scientific/professional organizations who are interested in preserving cultural and biological diversity, and to support the right of communities of speakers to language self-determination.

9. To illuminate the connections between cultural and biological diversity by establishing working relationships with scientific/professional organizations and individuals who are interested in preserving cultural diversity (such as linguists, educators, anthropologists, ethnologists, cultural workers, native advocates, cultural geographers, sociologists, and so on) and those who are interested in preserving biological diversity (such as biologists, botanists, ecologists, zoologists, physical geographers, ethnobiologists, ethnoecologists, conservationists, environmental advocates, natural resource managers, and so on), thus promoting the joint preservation and perpetuation of cultural and biological diversity.

10. To work with all appropriate entities in both the public and private sectors, and at all levels from the local to the international, to accomplish the foregoing.

---

from the **Ethnologue** 1992 and for species from WCMC 1992: 139–141. The countries which are on both lists are here **BOLDED AND CAPITALISED**.

16 of the 25 countries are on both lists, a concurrence of 64%. According to Harmon (1995a: 6) it 'seems highly unlikely that this is mere coincidence.'

The geographical and environmental characteristics which explain the concurrence include according to Harmon the following three: (1) **Extensive countries** which have **highly varied terrain, climate, and ecosystems** (examples: Mexico, USA, Brazil, China); (2) **Island countries** (examples: Papua New Guinea, Philippines, Solomon Islands); and (3) **Tropical countries** (examples: Cameroon, Zaire, Tanzania) (ibid.). Harmon adds urbanisation to factors promoting **low** diversity. Johanna Nichols (1992: 234; quoted in Harmon 1995a: 9–10) identifies essentially the same factors as promoting high genetic diversity among languages: coastline, tropical to subtropical climate, and mountains. Similarly, 'low density is favored by high latitudes, drier and/or more seasonal continental interiors, and also by the presense of large-scale

TABLE 2.3
Endemism in language and higher vertebrates: comparison of the top 25 countries

Endemic languages	Number	Endemic higher vertebrates species	Number
1. PAPUA NEW GUINEA	847	1. AUSTRALIA	1,346
2. INDONESIA	655	2. MEXICO	761
3. Nigeria	376	3. BRAZIL	725
4. INDIA	309	4. INDONESIA	673
5. AUSTRALIA	261	5. Madagascar	537
6. MEXICO	230	6. PHILIPPINES	437
7. CAMEROON	201	7. INDIA	373
8. BRAZIL	185	8. PERU	332
9. ZAIRE	158	9. COLOMBIA	330
10. PHILIPPINES	153	10. Ecuador	294
11. USA	143	11. USA	284
12. Vanuatu	105	12. CHINA	256
13. TANZANIA	101	13. PAPUA NEW GUINEA	203
14. Sudan	97	14. Venezuela	186
15. Malaysia	92	15. Argentina	168
16. ETHIOPIA	90	16. Cuba	152
17. CHINA	77	17. South Africa	146
18. PERU	75	18. ZAIRE	134
19. Chad	74	19. Sri Lanka	126
20. Russia	71	20. New Zealand	120
21. SOLOMON ISLANDS	69	21. TANZANIA	113
22. Nepal	68	22. Japan	112
23. COLOMBIA	55	23. CAMEROON	105
24. Côte d'Ivoire	51	24. SOLOMON ISLANDS	101
25. Canada	47	25. ETHIOPIA	88
		26. Somalia	88

Source: Harmon 1995a, 14. Figures for Ethiopia include Eritrea. Reptiles are not included for USA, China, and Papua New Guinea.

economies and/or societies such as empires, whose languages spread with their political/economic systems' (ibid.). The final factors in Nichols' list, i.e., those cultural, socio-economic, and political factors which, to put it mildly, are not conducive to diversity, are the topic of much of the rest of the book. A useful systematisation will be presented here, though. On the basis of his experience in Africa, especially central Nigeria, Roger Blench (1996) lists a whole lot of societal **factors** which are **responsible for language death**. He also gives counterarguments for some of them, showing the complexity of any theories one might want to develop. Blench also lists **factors responsible for language maintenance** (and counterarguments) (see Info Box 2.5).

I n f o   B o x   2 . 5

Factors Responsible for Language Death
and Language Maintenance (Blench, Central Nigeria)

Roger Blench (1996) lists a number of **factors responsible for language death** (I have organised them to some extent):

'the growth of the nation state'—but 'demographic growth has increased the likelihood of small languages surviving.'

'the promotion of specific languages'—but 'oppression and neglect creates a situation where language maintenance becomes a tool of resistance.'

■ 'assimilation to larger more powerful groups nearby.'

'assimilation to smaller but culturally dominant groups.'

'assimilation to English.'

'demographic crises caused by labour migration/urbanism.'

Blench also lists **factors responsible for language maintenance** (and counter-arguments), as follows:

'absence of adjacent culturally dominant groups.'

'endogamous marriage practices.'

'maintenance of traditional religion/cultural pride.'

'existence of an orthography' (this should be weighed against Peter Mühl-häusler's several counterarguments, my comment).

■ 'government oppression and neglect.'

■ 'remoteness.'

■ 'access to media.'

■ 'demography.'

■ 'unstable political situation with the infrastructure breaking down.'

■ 'Islam.' Blench thinks Islam has 'had an ambivalent impact on language maintenance' and gives examples of conversion lately having shown a strong relationship with adoption of the Hausa language, while it earlier did not, even in situations where the group was small and was fluent in Hausa.

In the final section of this chapter we will look at one of the very important additional connections between the three types of diversity, namely the possible causal connection. In the next chapter we will continue the analysis of why not only language but a diversity of languages is important, and in chapter 4 we will scrutinize some of the arguments for or against diversity more systematically.

2.5. CAUSAL CONNECTIONS BETWEEN BIODIVERSITY AND LINGUISTIC AND CULTURAL DIVERSITY?

The relationship between linguistic and cultural diversity on the one hand and biodiversity on the other hand is, maybe, not only correlational. There seems to be mounting evidence that it might be causal. The strong correlation need not indicate a **direct** causal relationship, in the sense that neither type of diversity can probably be seen **directly** as an **independent** variable in relation to the other. But linguistic and cultural diversity may be decisive **mediating** variables in sustaining biodiversity itself, and vice versa, as long as humans are on the earth. Of course there was no relationship in the prehuman times, but as soon as humans came into existence, they started to influence nature. Today it is safe to say that there is no 'wild' nature left—all landscapes have been and are influenced by human action, even those where untrained observers might not notice it immediately (see Definition Box 2.6; see also Definition Box 5.3 about the concept Terra nullius, uninhabited or empty land). All landscapes are cultural landscapes.

According to Maffi, ethnobiologists, human-ecologists, and others have proposed 'theories of "human-environment coevolution" ', including the assumption that 'cultural diversity might enhance biodiversity or vice versa' (Maffi 1996).

To make the claim more concrete, I will quote at length Nils Jernsletten, Professor of Sámi Language at the University of Tromsø, Norway, and Head of the Sámi Language Council. He gives beautiful concrete examples of how this 'human-environment coevolution' works, and of threats to it. Jernsletten, now in his mid-sixties, 'grew up in a small Sámi village on the banks of the Tana River, where salmon fishing has long been an important source of income' (from Notes on contributors in Gaski (ed.) 1997: 221).

Jernsletten describes traditional professional Sámi terminology on reindeer, salmon and snow. He states that the 'prerequisite for making a living from nature' is for the hunter, fisherman/woman and reindeer herder 'an intimate knowledge of the landscape' (Jernsletten 1997: 90). Even if modern reindeer herding represents 'a relatively new development over the last four hundred years' (ibid., 86), the reindeer herding culture has preserved a tradition of hunter/gatherers' way of using the environment which is thousands of years old, because hunting, fishing, collecting berries, and so forth, have been important secondary modes of production, well suited to the seasonal moving life of a reindeer family.

DEFINITION BOX 2.5 'Traditional knowledge', 'indigenous peoples' knowledge'

'**Traditional knowledge**' or '**indigenous peoples' knowledge**' 'refers to that knowledge which is acquired and preserved through generations in an original or local society. This knowledge consists of experience in working to secure a subsistence from nature' (Jernsletten 1997: 86).[11]

In 'traditional knowledge' (Definition Box 2.5), observations

are tied to being able to understand phenomena and connections in nature, so that people will be able to use nature for sustenance. This knowledge can be said to be usage-oriented. The Sámi language(s) has (have), for example, words for grasses and plants which have been used as foodstuffs, and which have been important in the grazing of livestock, cattle and reindeer. But there are few terms for flowering plants which, though quite visible in the summer land-scape, are nevertheless not useful. Likewise there are few names for small birds, and of these names many are compound words combining a modifier with *cizáš* (small bird, sparrow). At the same time there is a richer vocabulary having to do with sea and waterfowl, which have been useful as food sources (Jerns-letten 1997: 87).

When a reindeer herd is lost, or when animals from different herds are to be separated from each other, one needs to have immensely sophisticated vocabulary in order to describe details about landscape and specific animals[12] for somebody who subsequently needs to identify them without the describer being present. The prerequisite for transmitting this knowledge to others, when planning and solving problems and when discussing hunting, fishing, the movement of the reindeer in the landscape, etc., and for transmitting it to subsequent generations is 'that the language has exact expressions and precise terms for those concepts which are important for exploiting nature's possibilities to support life.' Likewise a 'large vocabulary makes it possible to describe and remember landscapes and places in rivers and lakes when conversing about hunting and fishing' (ibid., 87, 90). There are several ways for this intimate knowledge about the environment to disappear, abruptly or slowly. Often abrupt disappearance is a result of outside forces, sometimes natural (e.g., earthquake), mostly human, whereas slow disappearance is often either natural (e.g., new Ice Age) or something where the group itself changes.

Fairly **abrupt disappearance of knowledge**, sometimes even in a couple of generations or even some decades, often happens in connection with colonisation as many authors have described (see, for instance Amery 1998 and Mühlhäusler 1996 for Australia and the Pacific). This may happen if a group's habitat is destroyed (compare this with the factors responsible for loss of biodiversity in Info Box 2.5) or they are forced to move. Florence Connolly Shipek (1987) describes in her article about the Franciscan missionaries in California the indigenous agriculture and plant husbandry which was destroyed by the Europeans, at the same time as the culture and languages disappeared (see also Insert 3.16). Definition Box 2.6 describes this

---

DEFINITION BOX 2.6 'Wild nature'—indigenous peoples' agriculture

The 'Indian' agriculture in California produced mixed fields with 'a variety of food producing plants, including the grain, annuals, perennials, shrubs and trees' (Shipek 1987: 34) interplanted—'these included yucca, agave, cacti, sedums, sages, sumacs, manzanita, ceanothus, oaks, pines, wild plums and the native palms' (ibid.). 'Planning for drought years, they sowed seeds which lay dormant in the soil for twenty years or more until the right combination of rain, sun and fire caused them to sprout and produce.[13] Thus some food was produced during drought years when normal rainfall patterns failed . . . providing food when the staple grain, acorns, mesquite, and pine nuts failed' (ibid., 34). 'The Spanish, not understanding a different form of agriculture . . . which lacked cleared or plowed fields, saw the Indian carefully managed and interplanted grain fields as **"natural pastures"** and the interplanted slopes as **wild**, that is, it was thought they were produced by nature. They never realized the labor required to maintain them' (ibid., 35; emphases added).

When the Spanish 'cultivated' this 'wild nature', plowing fields, letting their cattle, sheep and horses graze, introducing European crops, etc., the native food supply was drastically reduced in terms of both quantity and quality.

The same type of misrecognition of areas managed by indigenous peoples has been one of the background factors enabling the creation of the concept of 'Terra nullius', nobody's land, uninhabited or empty land (see Definition Box 5.3). Today, there is *no* 'wild nature' anywhere in the world—every bit of our earth, including mountain tops, deserts, and arctic areas have been molded by human influence. Posey (in press b) stresses in general how the extent of indigenous management of nature has often been misunderstood or completely overlooked, because indigenous techniques mimic natural biodiversity and nature's own 'techniques' in a subtle way. This has helped colonisers to legitimate the colonisation of lands which they labelled as 'wilderness', instead of seeing them as 'cultural landscapes'—see Posey & Dutfield, in press, and note 9 in this chapter. See also Maffi (in pressa, b).

intricate Californian knowledge, which the colonisers did not recognise as knowledge—for them indigenous cultivated fields were 'wild nature' (or 'wasteland', 'untamed land', 'savage,' and 'wilderness', and contrasted 'with "the ordered woods and gardens" descriptions of the English landscape'— Fesl 1993: 30–31). With the language and culture also the knowledge base disappears, as for instance Luisa Maffi has shown in relation to knowledge about plant medicine (Maffi, in pressa, based on Maffi 1994).

In **slow disappearance of knowledge** about environment new ways of sub-sistence develop and some of the old ones disappear. If this development is really slow (in human terms), taking millennia (as in Aboriginal Australia until the colonisers arrived) or at least centuries (like moving from hunting wild reindeer—which ended in the Sámi areas during the 1700s—to reindeer herding, with both coexisting for a long time), there is time to adjust, both for people and for nature.

> The close connection between people's activities and skills and the knowledge preserved in the form of terms and words is also evident when linguistic ex-pressions and terminology disappear alongside the disappearance of the activity with which the knowledge is connected. (Jernsletten 1997: 88)

The knowledge from wild reindeer hunting has disappeared even if some of the old words are still known through dictionaries. When Peter Mühlhäusler (end of section 4.3.1.2) says that 'it takes time to get to know a place', he is not talking about years or even decades but centuries (see Diamond's arguments in section 9.3). Traditional knowledge about environment is never instant, McDonaldized knowledge. And 'knowing a place' in this sense is both a prerequisite for proper maintenance of it and for developing ways of talking about it. In its turn, being able to talk about a place, in a language which has developed ways of talking about it, observing it, in a detailed way, is a prerequisite for maintaining it and for transferring the knowledge about the place and its maintenance to further generations. And maintenance, in its turn, is a prerequisite for having a place to talk about in the first place. Both locally and globally.

This is also where education comes in. For youngsters to acquire tradi-tional knowledge, they must 'partake in work together with someone older who possesses the knowledge and experience' (Jernsletten 1997: 89). The teacher/master does not 'give theoretical introductions in advance', but the pupil learns through observing, experiencing, trying out, learning skills, lis-tening, hearing stories, asking questions, connecting the comments to her/his own experience, and 'systematizing this in linguistic expressions, terms, and professional jargon' (ibid., 89). Thus

> the terms one learns are a rich mix of experiences and associations. As one begins to connect words and terms to one's observations and experiences, this

knowledge is verbalized, systematized, committed to memory . . . the terms are appropriated through an intensive and detailed education where the activity and **the learning of terminology through language** are closely connected. (ibid., 88, 89; emphasis added)

When children were together with their parents and others in work situations, taking part from early on in adult tasks, they

received a gradual introduction to professional knowledge together with training in professional skills. With personal experience in the work they could understand and participate in the conversations and stories of knowledgeable adults during free moments, and in this way they could **broaden their terminology and knowledge**. (ibid., 98; emphasis added)

Jernsletten talks about a central concern of reindeer-herding Sámi today:

their children are taken away from work in reindeer-herding when they enter the Norwegian school system and thus are not exposed to an important introduction to the knowledge that is necessary for one who one day will become a reindeer owner or herder himself/herself . . . an important portion of the content of the Sámi traditional knowledge is lost when the type of insight and understanding is taken away which is tied to a physical approach and experience together with **an introduction to and expansion of terminology**. (ibid., 98, 99; emphasis added)

Comparing to modern physical sciences where a good deal of learning takes place 'with demonstrations, exercises, and practice in laboratories and fieldwork out in nature' (ibid., 99), without which learning is 'unimaginable', Jernsletten claims that the

laboratories of the Sámi and other small societies have been the landscape, the sea, rivers and lakes where the youth have practised and learned. Modern educational methods cannot fully replace this older manner of learning. If scholastic instruction is not supplemented with instruction in the environment where the knowledge belongs, that is, in nature itself, important aspects of that knowledge will be lost. In this sense 'Sámi-schools' are Sámi in name only and are European in content. (ibid., 99)

In Jernsletten's view, 'the use of modern media cannot replace learning combined with practice', and it is self-evident that the people 'who have grown up and lived with traditional modes of production and who have learned from their parents in a traditional manner . . . **must transmit their knowledge through their own language**, Sámi' (ibid., 101; emphasis added).

All Jernsletten's experience, shared with not only other indigenous peoples but everybody who traditionally lives in contact with nature, strengthens our understanding of how the causal connections might work. Research into this area is only in its beginning, but it might prove to be research vital for our future. Luisa Maffi starts her Introduction to her new edited book **Language, Knowledge and the Environment: The Interdependence of Biological and Cultural Diversity** with a quote from Diane Ackerman (1997: xviii–xix) which sums up the seriousness with which this new area should be taken:

> We are among the rarest of the rare not because of our numbers, but because of the unlikeliness of our being here at all, the pace of our evolution, our powerful grip on the whole planet, and the precariousness of our future. We are evolutionary whiz kids who are better able to transform the world than to understand it. Other animals cannot evolve fast enough to cope with us. It is possible that we may also become extinct, and if we do, we will not be the only species that sabotaged itself, merely the only one that could have prevented it.

In this perspective, the first conference investigating this specific relationship between humans and their environment, 'Endangered Languages, Endangered Knowledge, Endangered Environments' (see Maffi, in press) stressed 'the need to address the foreseeable consequences of massive disruption of such long-standing interactions' (Maffi 1996) (i.e., the human-environment coevolution). The processes of language loss also 'affect the maintenance of traditional environmental knowledge—from loss of biosystematic lexicon to loss of traditional stories' (ibid.).

The United Nations Environmental Program (UNEP), one of the organisations behind the 1992 Rio Biodiversity conference, produced a massive book (Heywood (ed.) 1995) on **Global Biodiversity Assessment** that summarizes current knowledge about biodiversity. Now UNEP also acknowledges the connection between biological resources and human resources. It has recently produced a companion volume to the biodiversity book, on **Cultural and Spiritual Values of Biodiversity** (Posey (ed.), in press). The chapter on Linguistic Diversity in it (Maffi, Skutnabb-Kangas & Andrianarivo, in press) argues that 'the preservation of the world's linguistic diversity must be incorporated as an essential goal in any bioculturally-oriented diversity conservation program' (from Executive Summary).

To me it seems important that serious consideration to a study of the possible **causal** relationships will not be curtailed by accusations of essentialism, romanticism, fundamentalism, neo-Darwinism, or any of the other -isms which might prevent serious and solid scholars from entering the field. The issues are too important to be waved away by thoughtless labelling before they have been thoroughly studied. And the interest, and action, have to grow faster than the threats to the planet.

Schooling, in addition to migration, was explored as one of the important causal factors in language loss at the Berkeley conference. Deirdre Jordan (1988: 190) who has compared the impact of formal education on identity among the Australian Aboriginal peoples, the Sámi and Inuits in Greenland and Canada, claims that

. . . history shows that it was not only forces springing from economic bases, and the exploitation of material resources, which, breaking the nexus of indigenous people with their land, acted to destroy their culture and substitute for a positive identity the negative traits with which indigenous people have come to be stereotyped. One of the crucial forces which has acted to destroy the identity and the culture of indigenous people has been that of schooling.

Most indigenous peoples have experienced this.[14] 'Maori people are acutely aware of the devastating role that schooling has played in the demise of their language' (Smith 1993: 218, quoted in Amery 1998: 81). Thus the Berkeley conference recognised what Jernsletten, Jordan, and Smith, together with many others, have noted.

But as is the case with the destruction of biodiversity, also the destruction of linguistic and cultural diversity is not caused by 'ill will' of the destructors (even if that may also be a component). The economic forces which exploit and destroy nature in creating and unifying a homogenous market place, and bringing profit to those who control this market (see Mander 1996a, b), also try to create, at both local and global levels, homogenous linguistic markets, for exchanges (both material and verbal) to flow (as they 'believe'). As Pierre Bourdieu puts it, the groups which possess the dominant linguistic capital (i.e., high formal competence in a/the dominant language),

> are able to impose it as the only legitimate one in the formal markets (the fashionable, educational, political and administrative markets) and in most of the linguistic interactions in which they are involved . . . The position which the educational system gives to the different languages (or the different cultural contents) is such an important issue only because this institution has the monopoly in the large-scale production of producers/comsumers [on the linguistic market, TSK], and therefore in the reproduction of the market without which the social value of the linguistic competence, its capacity to function as linguistic capital, would cease to exist (Bourdieu 1992: 56–57).

But before we move to education, there are still other background aspects that need to be discussed. In the next chapter, we move to some of the prerequisites for understanding why language in general and mother tongues in particular are so important for human existence as humans. In later Chapters the more macro-level importance will be discussed.

NOTES

1. Oktyabrina Voronova (1934–1990) was born in a small Ter Sámi speaking settlement in the far eastern part of the Kola Peninsula. The settlement was abandoned in the 1960s, 'because the Russian authorities felt that it offered no possibilities for development' (from Introduction to authors in Gaski (ed.) 1996: 101). She worked as a librarian and 'published three collections of poetry in Russian, always wishing, however, to use her native language

to give expression to her experience of a life close to nature with the reindeer herders on the tundra' (ibid.). The book **Yealla** (Life) in Ter Sámi from which 'Words' comes was published posthumously and is now in the process of being translated to Northern Sámi, the Sámi language with most speakers.

2. He translated the story into Estonian long ago from a 1925 number of **Journal of American Folklore**.

3. The prose translation is by Francis Peabody Magoun, Jr. (1963: 104), and makes me sad. Even if you don't understand Finnish, compare it with the music of the original, also prose (**Kalevala** 1964, 105), with its alliteration and vowel harmony:

> Itse virsikäs Vipunen,
> mies vanha varaväkevä,
> tuo viruvi virsinensä,
> luottehinensa lojuvi;
> haapa kasvoi hartioilla,
> koivu kulmilla yleni,
> leppä leukaluun nenässä,
> pajupehko parran päällä,
> otsalla oravikuusi,
> havuhonka hampahilla.

4. He gets an expulsion charm; charms against uncertain injuries, natural diseases, a disease or misadventure induced by magic or by another person; charms to restrain injuries; for summoning help; for sending someone home; for revenge, exorcism, imprisonment, and conveyance; for magic ski equipment; for getting under way; for intimidation; and a charm for a time of trouble.

5. Several other sociolinguists sitting close to me at the conference noted the inclusion of language; some of us knew that it is not established as a fundamental human right in the instruments mentioned.

6. I am **TIRED** of needing to write 'sic!' every time we women are being excluded and made invisible as human beings. But I'll probably struggle on . . . my frustration is probably as great as that of some readers needing to see 'sic' repeatedly . . .

7. Many educators—see, e.g., Heugh et al. 1995—have started using the expression '(languages of) learning and teaching', rather than 'instruction', claiming, and rightly so, that 'instruction' implies a one-way process, and also that the learning itself (which in the end is an internal process) may involve languages which are not the same as the teaching languages.

8. The Nguni cluster includes, in addition to the two largest languages in South Africa, Zulu and Xhosa, also Swati and Ndebele; the Sotho cluster includes North Sotho, South Sotho, and Tswana. The more distantly related Tsonga and Venda are also 'Bantu' languages—see Info Box 5.8—and belong to the wider Niger-Kordofanian language family (see Mesthrie 1995, Bailey 1995a, b).

9. See section 2.5 and Definition Box 2.6 for 'wild'. All landscapes are 'cultural landscapes' (Posey, in press a, b)—'wild' nature thus does not exist. 'Cultural landscape' is now a new category of World Heritage, recognised under the 1972 UNESCO Convention Concerning the Protection of the World Cultural and Natural Heritage (The World Heritage Convention). It is defined in the 1995 revised Operational Guidelines for implementing the Convention (UNESCO WHC/2 Revised, Item 38) (see Posey & Dutfield, in press, for elaboration, and links with linguistic diversity).

10. For empirical evidence and an excellent discussion of the complexities of assessing these correlations, see Harmon 1995a, b. A book inspired by the Berkeley conference, edited by Maffi, is in press.

11. There is a useful discussion about the biases in Western education vis-à-vis traditional knowledge in general and educational knowledge of non-European cultures in particular

in Reagan 1996. One of the 'broad common themes in the non-Western educational traditions concerned is that the Western tendency to conflate and confuse "formal schooling" with "education" is less common in non-Western societies; there is a continuum. Education has been more community-based and communal, a social responsibility shared by all adult members of the community, and with relatively little focus on identifying (and training) educational specialists' (from my review, in press, of Reagan's book). Regrettably, one can see this conflation even in the writings of some indigenous scholars themselves. E.g., Asta Balto and Jon Todal write in their article on Sámi bilingual education: 'The history of Saami education begins in the 1700's with the Christian missions that sought to convert the Saamis' (1997: 77). Balto who is the former chair of the Sámi Education Council in Norway is normally extremely aware of the need to get rid of assimilationist thought patterns from the older colonial times . . .

12. Harald Gaski has been in many debates about his language, Sámi: 'Hi there, wait a minute! Didn't you tell us that our language is an inferior one? So what do you call a four-year-old male reindeer with a white spot on its leg, and with the antlers pointing forward? In one word, please?' (Gaski 1997: 218)

13. We (Robert Phillipson and I) heard biologists and conservationists give similar descriptions about the Cape fynbos, the specific flora in an area around the Cape in South Africa.

14. See discussions reported in Reyhner 1996 for alternatives.

Mother Tongue(s), Culture, Ethnicity, and Self-Determination

The voice of the land is in our language. (National First Nations Elders/ Language Gathering, Mi'gmaq Nation, Canada)

NOTHING
Nothing stays longer

in our souls
than the language we inherit
It liberates our thoughts
unfolds our mind
and softens our life.
(Paulus Utsi (born 1918), 1996: 111, translated by Roland Thorstensson)

Words are, of course, the most powerful drug used by mankind.
(Rudyard Kipling, 1923)

It is easier to divest a nation of all its guns than it is to rob it of its language.
Machine-guns will fall silent sooner than the loquacious mouths that raise so
very different words up to the sky. (Kosztolányi 1987: 27)

It was not by chance that in Germany, the murderers in power were burning
books (before burning in crematoriums the corpses of millions of victims). It
was not by chance that the Francoists in Spain shot to death Lorca, who was
poetry itself. (Clancier 1996: 28)

This tongue of mine I use to appreciate taste;
how can one taste with someone else's tongue?
(From a Wolof poem by Useyno Gey Cosaan; quoted in Fishman 1997: 292)

What is thy sentence, then, but speechless death,
Which robs my tongue from breathing native breath?
(From William Shakespeare, Richard II 1.3; Mowbray when sentenced to
banishment from his country and language)

Remember what is good:
Your language.
Your tradition.
Your family, All the relations of the World.
We are not by ourselves,
We are in Unison, Watch . . .
(From a poem by Damon Clarke, Hualapai; quoted in Cantoni 1996: 95)

Tzvetan Todorov, a neighbour from Paris, published a now-famous book
entitled "Nous et les autres". But "Nous et nous", who will be writing this
more complicated book?
    The rest—as a classic says—is literature. (Prelipceanu 1996: 45)

---

3. MOTHER TONGUE(S), CULTURE, ETHNICITY,
AND SELF-DETERMINATION

3.1. CONCEPTUALIZING OURSELVES
AND THE WORLD

Language is a tie, and our mother tongues both form and are symbols of
our identity. Language plays a key role in most aspects of human life ev-

erywhere. Language is also a tool, a mediator and an active creative agent, central to our conceptualization and indeed creation of the world, and for interpreting, understanding, and changing it. Language supports us in organizing our world and frees our energy for other tasks. Words for concepts are like pegs on which we hang the meanings that we inherit, learn, work through, accept and reject, and create, and store in the fluid storehouse of our mind. They are the framework that binds together the experienced details into a totality, a meaningful whole. Verbalising helps us remember, reproduce, and reflect on meaning and thus make sense of reality, participate in creating the changing realities and to try out alternatives in our mind before we act in more concrete ways. Through the verbal socialisation process we also learn much of our own culture's ethics. Together with the words for objects and phenomena, we learn our culture's connotations, associations, emotions, and value judgments which we can then modify. The definition and construction of our ecosocial world, including our individual and group identities, status, and world view, are all reflected in, reflect on, and are partially created and realized through language.

The particular social and ecological circumstances in which different human groups develop over time—the specific relationships each group establishes among its members and with other people around them, as well as with the (material and spiritual) place in which they live—lead to different and historically changing ways of defining, understanding, interpreting, and creating the world via language. The diversity of languages (and cultures) around the world has arisen through these complex and dynamic processes of understanding, coping, and changing.

Conceptualizing the world in childhood mainly happens through the mother tongue of a child (or mother tongues, if she has more than one). Before continuing to discuss the more general importance of language, we need to probe first into some basic definitions, starting with mother tongue and continuing with cultural competence, integration and assimilation, and ethnicity. In all the definitions we look especially at the role played by language. My contention is that many of the concepts discussed can be more profitably understood if they are conceptually treated as socially constructed mutual **relations** between the definer and the defined, rather than as characteristics of the defined. Then we come back to language, dominance, and control, finally discussing self-determination.

3.2. MOTHER TONGUE(S)

3.2.1. Definitions of Mother Tongue(s)

Defining 'mother tongue(s)' is not only an academic exercise—it is necessary also for practical purposes. It is increasingly unclear to many educators what their pupils' mother tongues are. Proper definitions are also needed for many

TABLE 3.1
Definitions of mother tongue

CRITERION	DEFINITION
1. Origin	the language one learned first (the language one has established the first long-lasting verbal contacts in)
2. Identification a. internal b. external	a. the language one identifies with/as a native speaker of b. the language one is identified with/as a native speaker of, by others
3. Competence	the language one knows best
4. Function	the language one uses most

(Source: Skutnabb-Kangas 1984a: 18)

official purposes (census, right to services which are given on the basis of mother tongue, assessment of linguistic qualifications for education, jobs, etc.). The definition exercise also gives us an opportunity to assess whether minority and majority mother tongues have the same rights or whether dominant mother tongues are granted more institutional support (institutions in the abstract sense of laws and regulations, including human rights, and in the concrete sense of day care centres, schools, universities, work places, media, etc.). And many necessary linguistic human rights are centrally connected to mother tongues.

In the literature there are several different ways of defining mother tongues. I have distinguished between four different criteria for the definitions: origin, identification, competence, and function (Table 3.1) (for details, see Skutnabb-Kangas 1984a, chapters 2–4).

For monolingual people, or people who, in addition to their mother tongue, only have limited proficiency in a foreign language, learned in school, it may be difficult to see the importance and consequences of the various definitions. Try out the definitions in a group where there are at least some who are bilingual or multilingual (Task Box 3.1)!

Reader Task 3.1
What is/are your mother tongue(s)?

Do this task in a group. Each should write down what their mother tongue(s) is/are, according to each criterion in Table 3.1. Share your lists and discuss the criteria. (You might want to look at Insert 3.1 with my list if you are monolingual and are doing this alone). Then read the theses about the definitions, and discuss to what extent you have experience of them and agree or disagree with them. What are the consequences of them for some people or situations that you know?

INSERT 3.1 Tove's mother tongues

My mother tongues by **origin** are **Swedish** and **Finnish**, in that order—both my bilingual parents spoke Swedish to me initially but almost everybody else around us spoke Finnish (which was my mother's mother tongue by identification even if she had used both languages from the beginning and was a native speaker of both, the way I am too). I used both languages natively from the very beginning, and I am told that my first long sentence (telling everybody around me that I was able to stand alone and asking them to look) was in Finnish.

My mother tongues by **internal and external identification** are **Finnish** and **Finland Swedish** (i.e., not the variants of Swedish which are spoken by native speakers in Sweden, but the variant spoken by native speakers of Swedish in Finland). I identify with both, and am recognised as a native speaker by both groups.

My mother tongues by **competence** are also **Finnish and Swedish**, with some functional differentiation—there are areas where my vocabulary is bigger in one or the other language because I have lived that theme more in one, typically so that themes I learned in school and did not use much afterwards are much easier to discuss in my school language, Finnish, whereas some leisure activities were dominated by Swedish—and I know many plants best in Latin. But there are also areas which I have worked with mostly in **English,** in international teams, or reading, writing, and lecturing in English, after moving away from Finland, and where I do not know the vocabulary properly in Finnish or Swedish. These are specialised areas, like human rights conventions. If I ever moved back to Finland (or Sweden), or worked much in these countries, I would obviously learn the vocabularies quickly (and they certainly exist in both these languages). My initial university training was in both Finnish and Swedish (in Finland you can choose the medium).

My mother tongues by **function**, which were Finnish and Swedish during the first close to 40 years of my life, are today **English and Danish**. These are my daily languages: I live in Denmark, with a British husband who only speaks English to me (Danish is used at home only when there are Danes present, or other immigrants who prefer Danish to English and do not understand Swedish), and I read, write, and work mostly in English. Still, my competence in these two 'mother tongues' is never going to be anywhere near a native level, especially in terms of pronunciation or vocabulary—and in my view it does not need to be. It is enough that I can write books (like this) in both languages—or, rather, in all four.

Thus I am a good example of the theses about definitions: I have several mother tongues; they are different, depending on which definition one uses; my mother tongues have changed during my life time, most markedly in terms of function but also competence, while my identification is (and will always be) according to my mother tongues by origin. I do not identify with my 'mother tongues' by function—they are foreign languages which I use and like but no more. I can myself decide this because I am in a strong position to negotiate if it becomes necessary—except in census returns, if the country refuses to accept several mother tongues and forces me to choose just one.

3.2.2. Theses About Mother Tongues

Below I first present four **theses about the definitions**. After a discussion about the last one (I have discussed the first three extensively in Skutnabb-Kangas 1884a), I choose my favourite definition. Then I problematise it, and present some additional theses for consideration.

1. The same person can have different mother tongues, depending on which definition is used.
2. A person's mother tongue can change during her life time, even several times, according to all other definitions listed except the definition by origin.
3. A person can have several mother tongues, especially according to definitions by origin and identification, but also according to the other criteria.
4. The mother tongue definitions can be organized hierarchically according to their degree of linguistic human rights awareness. This degree in a society can be assessed by examining which definition(s) the society uses in its institutions, explicitly and implicitly.

3.2.2.1. *Degree of Human Rights Awareness in Definitions*

Some comments about the last thesis. I see the definition by function as the most primitive one. Use of it for minority children does not consider the fact that most of them are forced to use an L2 (= a second or foreign language) because there are no facilities (day care centres, schools, etc.) which function through the medium of their mother tongue, L1 (= first language). The children and their parents have not themselves been given a chance to choose freely, from among existing alternatives, which language they would like to use in day care and school. This is the definition which is, explicitly or implicitly, used in educational institutions in many European immigration countries. It is, of course, important to differentiate between 'dominant language' at an individual level (X is **my** dominant language) and a societal level (Y is the dominant language in country P). Likewise, dominant may be used to mean dominant in terms of function or even competence for individuals (where minority individuals may have the societally dominant language also as their most used or even best known language)—still it does not mean that the societally dominant language would be their mother tongue. Insert 3.2 gives a recent Danish example of an implicit function definition by a politician, where 'dominance' is equated with 'mother tongue'.

Use of a definition of function or competence in educational institutions when defining a minority child's mother tongue is typical of the early phases

---

INSERT 3.2   Mother tongue defined by function (Denmark)

'It is self-evident that refugees who are only going to be in Denmark during a short period should maintain their mother tongue. But when one is born and has grown up in Denmark and will have one's whole existence here, then **the mother tongue is Danish—full stop.**' (Svend Erik Hermansen, Social Democrat Party, chair for the Board of Education and Culture in Høje Tåstrup. Said to **Berlingske Tidende**, reported in **Information** 11 December 1995, p. 7; emphasis added). In this assimilationist definition the politician is probably thinking of the fact that Danish for somebody living in Denmark today will be the language she hears and uses most. (See also section 3.5.3. for an additional analysis).

---

of the history of minority education and reflects cultural and institutional linguicism (see Definition Boxes 1.1 and 5.4). Linguicism can be **open** (the agent does not try to hide it), **conscious** (the agent is aware of it), **visible** (it is easy for non-agents to detect), and **actively action oriented** (as opposed to 'merely' attitudinal). Or it can be **hidden, unconscious, invisible, and passive** (lack of support rather than active opposition), typical of later phases in the development of minority education. In the example in Insert 3.2 it is open, visible and action oriented (here basis for political decisions) but probably unconscious. Those countries which have developed more sophisticated forms of racism (culturally and linguistically argued forms of racism—ethnicism and linguicism—rather than biologically argued racism), also tend to exhibit more covert forms of linguicism which manage to blame the victim in subtle ways.

With a somewhat higher degree of awareness a definition by competence is often used ('the Turkish children could not even count in their so-called mother tongue' said a well-known linguist, implying that Swedish, in which the children had been taught how to count, was their mother tongue, because they knew it better than the language of their parents). Use of this definition fails to consider that lack of proficiency in the original mother tongue (= mother tongue according to the criterion by origin) is a result of not having been offered the opportunity to use and learn the original mother tongue well enough in those institutional settings where many western children spend most of their day (day care centres, schools, organised after-school activities). Lack of use leads to lack of competence, especially with children. A poor competence in the original mother tongue (which is a result of the neglect of the mother tongue in institutions earlier on, i.e., a result of earlier oppression) is then often used to legitimate additional oppression. The child is labelled as a majority language speaker, or she is denied teaching in the original mother tongue on the grounds that she does not know it well enough or because she knows the majority language better and therefore does not 'need' mother tongue teaching. Many indigenous people (Sámi in the Nordic countries, Aborigines in Australia, etc.) may officially not always be counted as members of the group, if they no longer know the original mother tongue (which they have been prevented from learning), or if their parents or grand-parents did not know it. The dwindling numbers can then be used to legiti-mate lack of services offered in the indigenous language (see e.g., Aikio 1988 for the Sámi) which then leads to still less use and competence. The same numbers game is used to deny services in immigrant minority languages. Often denying language rights to both children and adults (in case of adults, for instance the right to information or voting or using the mother tongue in the work place) is implicitly based on a definition of function or competence.

Often a right to use the mother tongue is made dependent on **lack** of competence in a dominant language: one has to declare that one is **deficient** in one's competence in the dominant language in order to be able to have the right to use the mother tongue, or to have the right to an interpreter, as for instance Ole-Henrik Magga, earlier president of the Sámi Parliament on the Norwegian side of Sápmi (The Sámi Country) has pointed out many times.

This also leads to arguments about **cost**: the minority person who demands services through her mother tongue (e.g., interpretation) is seen as **causing** the cost, even if she only demands what the dominant language speaker takes for granted for herself, i.e. the right to use her own language (Skutnabb-Kangas 1991c). It could of course be seen the other way round: we bilin-guals/multilinguals who know several languages, do not cause the costs; it is the monolinguals who cause them, by being able to function in one language only, and thereby forcing everybody else to use the monolingual's only language (see Insert 3.3). See also Insert 3.4 for another note about costs.

Use of a combination of definitions by origin and identification shows in my view the highest degree of awareness of linguistic human rights: **the mother tongue(s) is/(are) the language(s) one has learned first and identifies with**.

3.2.2.2. *Problems with the Definitions*

But a definition combining origin and internal identification implies that the language(s) identified with is/are the same as the original mother tongue(s), the language(s) learned first. It also presupposes that others accept the in-ternal identification of a person. Therefore there are a number of exceptions to seeing this definition as an optimal one. In order to discuss them I present two additional theses:

5. It is possible to claim a mother tongue by identification, even if one knows very little, or sometimes, next to nothing, of the language, and

---

INSERT 3.3   Who causes the costs, bilinguals or monolinguals?
Laila Somby Sandvik (Norway)

Laila Somby Sandvik (LSS), a Sámi educator, high-level bilingual in Sámi and Norwegian, was at a meeting of her County Health Board in northern Norway where all the other members except a medical doctor (Norwegian non-Sámi speaker) were also Sámi. There had been a lot of talk about the costs 'caused' by the Sámi needing interpretation. Usually the meetings were in Norwegian. LSS announced that she was going to speak Sámi from the following meeting on. The doctor: 'Then you will need an interpreter.' Laila: 'I don't, and none of us Sámi does—we are all bilingual—but **you** may need one.' (told to Tove Skutnabb-Kangas by LSS and retold in TSK 1991c, article called 'Who causes the costs?')

INSERT 3.4   Monolinguals cause the costs—they should pay . . .

Causing costs is, of course, also what monolingual English-speakers do: they force us others to use English partly because they do not know any other languages. In addition, they force **other** people to cover the cost: masses of time and vast sums are spent by us others to learn their language, in our schools, courses, for materials, teacher training, etc., and to translate what we write into 'their' language, whereas few of them learn **our** languages. Monolinguals cause the costs, not multilinguals. It would be fair if, for instance, English-monolingual Americans, Brits, Australians, etc. paid much or most of the cost of school systems, courses, teaching materials, and interpretation and translation costs caused by us others needing to learn English and function in English.

---

even when native speakers do not identify one as a native speaker, or even when there are no native speakers. Mother tongue definitions have to be rethought so as to allow for situations where parents and children may not have the same mother tongue, especially by origin; for situations where the mother tongue by origin may not be learned in infancy and may not be taught by the primary care-takers; for situations where lost languages are being reclaimed as mother tongues by identification; and for fluid multilingual situations where multilingualism is the mother tongue,[1] rather than one or two discrete languages.

6. What is accepted as somebody's mother tongue is crucially dependent on who has the right to define it. Mother tongues are relations to be negotiated, not (only) characteristics that people possess, and relations depend on who has more power.

It seems to me that the criterion of origin has to be left out in several cases. This leaves us with the self-identification criterion only.

Firstly, there is the situation of deaf children. Since most deaf children (90–95%) are born to hearing parents who in most cases are **not** competent signers when the child is born, the child may not learn Sign language in infancy. Sign language (see Definition Box 4.1) may in some views not become the child's mother tongue according to the criterion of origin. But we also have to consider whether the child learns **any other** language, or whether Sign language, even if it comes only later, is the first natural language that the child learns properly (see Definition Box 4.1 for some of the basic concepts in relation to deafness).

A deaf child can have the same mother tongue according to all the criteria only in the **best** case: if a deaf child is born to deaf parents who know a Sign language really well and who use it with the child from the very beginning, feel positive about it, and give a child a strong positive identification with the Sign language and the Deaf community; if the child gets both the day care and a large part of her or his education through the medium of Sign language; and if the Sign language is accepted by the rest of the society. Then the Sign language is the child's mother tongue, according to all the criteria. But worldwide this would be a very unusual case.

In the absolutely **worst** case a deaf person may grow up with no natural language as her mother tongue, and not knowing any language properly, ever. This would be in a society where the Deaf are seen as mentally handicapped (e.g., Argentina; see Massone, Curiel & Veinberg 1993: 23); where the deaf person either does not get any formal education at all or is submerged in an education planned for oral communities and where the deaf person therefore does not have a chance to become proficient in any written language; where the person does not meet any competent signers; and where she does not know that Sign language is a fully developed minority language and the Deaf community a linguistically and culturally competent, self-contained minority community. This is sadly still the case with many deaf people, especially but not exclusively in **underdeveloped countries** (i.e., those countries which we so-called whites have consciously underdeveloped and are continuing to underdevelop—see Rodney 1983; also 1969; see Insert 6.1).

Secondly, we have the case of indigenous and other peoples who have not had an opportunity of learning their parents' or grandparents' or ancestors' mother tongue(s), and in extreme cases, where there are no native speakers (or no competent speakers) left. We can have cases with **individual** reclamation or revival of the language (the person wants to learn, or relearn, or learn more of the language, and/or use it more and there are native speakers to learn from) or **collective** revival or reclamation (see Amery 1998 about the differences, and about a case of reclamation of an indigenous Australian language, Kaurna—see also Inserts 4.4 and 5.25). In these cases, the person/group may identify with a language they do not 'know' or know well (there are several examples in Inserts later).

In both cases we also have to ask ourselves: Can a mother tongue be learned from other people and not from the primary care-takers? It is obvious that the situation of the Deaf community forces us to rethink the definitions. If the primary care-takers are unable to provide the child with a fully fledged language, which all oral parents with oral children in principle can do, then the mother tongue of most deaf children is dependent on external, societal factors in relation to **every** definition of a mother tongue, whereas external factors are completely decisive for the mother tongue of oral parents and children, even indigenous and minority parents and children, only in relation to competence and function, but not origin and identification. This means that deaf minority children need linguistic rights to an even higher extent than oral minority children; also because of their history of oppression is still largely unrecognised (see Reagan 1992: 306).

But we also have the opposite, those probably fairly few cases where self-identification can be mistrusted, cases where people with few or no connections to a language or group claim a certain mother tongue by internal identification, for economic or other purposes, and where this identification is in no way acceptable to the guardians of the language (see the example of large numbers of ethnic Finns claiming Sámi identity, section 3.5.3). It is often a difficult task to judge both the motives and the arguments, and few cases are clearcut. Many may also historically be results of shame and earlier linguistic genocide of the type described below.

The last thesis can be exemplified with situations like the one above, where there is a conflict between internal and external self-identification of a mother tongue (or two). But there are more common situations. If a deaf person says that Sign language is her mother tongue, while some people in the surrounding society say that the deaf person does not have any language, the two definitions collide (see Reagan 1997b for a discussion and examples). Whose definition is valid? People in powerless positions have to negotiate about the validity of their internal identification. Many countries still have laws which invalidate deaf peoples' own definition of their mother tongue. Outsiders (even hearing parents of deaf children) might claim that the child's mother tongue is (or at least should be, or become) the oral language that the parents speak, or a manually coded form of it (see Definition Box 4.1), or, in the worst cases, that the child has no language and thus no mother tongue (see Reagan 1995b). We might say that it is the person herself who in a human rights oriented view has the right to decide about her identity, and others have to accept this. But this is naive in the real world.

Just like 'ethnicity' and statehood are not (only) characteristics that an ethnic group or a state possess, but relations (see section 3.5 below), a mother tongue too is not (only) a characteristic that a person possesses. **A mother**

tongue is also a relation. And relations have to be validated by both parties, i.e. a mother tongue needs external validation. If those whose languages are already somehow accepted as languages do not accept that Sign language is a language (which can fulfill all the same functions as other mother tongues), Sign language is invalidated, delegitimised (see Timothy Reagan's 1997b article 'When Is a Language Not a Language? Challenges to "Linguistic Legitimacy" in Educational Discourse'). An invalidated language cannot be a mother tongue, on a par with other mother tongues, and it does not get the same protection as other mother tongues in international law. A similar invalidation of other minority or dominated mother tongues is also common in several ways, as will be exemplified in many of the chapters.

In societies with institutional and cultural linguicism and discrimination, not all minority children are allowed to identify positively with their original mother tongues and cultures. Many minority children are being forced to feel ashamed of their mother tongues, their parents, their origins, their group, and their culture. Many of them, especially in countries where the racism is more subtle, not so openly expressed, internalize the negative views which the majority society has of the minority groups, their languages and cultures. Many disown their parents and their own group and language. They attempt to shift identity, including linguistic identity, 'voluntarily', and **want** to be German/ Dutch/ Anglo-American/ British/ Swedish/ Turkish etc. instead of, respectively, Turkish/ Moluccan/ Mexican/ Pakistani/ Finnish/ Kurdish etc. Wanting to change identity can also be a result of lack of linguistic and cultural competence in the original mother tongue and its concomitant culture, caused by a neglect of these by the school. I have given many examples of this in my 1984 book **Bilingualism or Not: the education of minorities**.

However it often happens that this attempt at identity shift does not work either. The child's new identity (identification with the/a dominant—majority—group and its language(s)) is not accepted by everybody. This is generally expressed more openly in the years after the minority youngsters reach puberty. It is more common with youngsters who do not look like the stereotype of what a 'real' German, Dutch etc. person 'should' look like (and/or with youngsters whose accent does not sound 'native'). The minority youngster then often hears: 'You are not one of us, you are not a real Swede/ American/ Dutch/ German/ Dane etc., you are a Finnish devil/ a Turkshit/ a damn Paki etc.' The child has then 'voluntarily' disowned her original identity, but the new identity is not accepted by everyone in the dominant group either. There is a conflict between the internal and the external identification (endo- and exo-identification). The youngster is not accepted, at least not unconditionally, by the dominant group, with which she has been forced to identify (but whose language and culture she has not always been given the opportunity to learn 'fully'—see Cummins 1984). At the same time the road back to her own group is often closed too. Not only psychologically (= she does not

want to identify with the 'dirty Turks' or 'aggressive silent Finns'), but often also linguistically and culturally. The child no longer knows (or has never had the chance to learn) the original mother tongue well enough to be able to pass as a native or near-native speaker. Nor does she have all the other components of cultural competence in the original culture (see below).

Inserts in later chapters give examples of all these cases. In many of them the non-identification with the mother tongue(s) (with the help of threats, shame, carrots, etc.—see, e.g., Info Box 3.5) mostly leads to an interruption in transgenerational transmission of the language later on, with the result that subsequent generations do not learn the language or know only a little.

This in fact means that **'children from one group have been forcibly transferred to another group'**—and *this is part of UN's definition of genocide.*

Some of them, or their descendants, might at some later point try to go back to their roots and identify or reidentify with the language if the societal pressure lessens or when it is again not only legitimate but maybe even carries a certain status to represent the indigenous or minority group in question.

Last but not least of the problems with mother tongue definitions is that most Western definitions (see summaries in Skutnabb-Kangas 1984a, chapter 2 and Baetens Beardsmore 1982) start from the assumption that a person definitely **has** a discrete mother tongue, or two (or in unusual cases more), and that the mother tongue is an important and relatively independent element of identification. In countries of popular traditional multilingualism the concept seems to be much more fluid and flexible, and combined in complex and multiple ways with other elements. Multilingualism may be the mother tongue, rather than any discrete language, as Lachman Khubchandani rightly points out in several publications. We might have a somewhat similar problem in discussing 'mother tongue' as in discussing 'language', as Khubchandani and others have also emphasized. Western definitions of mother tongues, including my own, may therefore offer an insufficient basis for discussing mother tongue related rights as I have formulated them. This conceptual problem should also be seriously approached, especially by those researchers who, like myself, have grown up with more than one mother tongue. These questions have, as I have pointed out already earlier, also to do with the relative eurocentricity (and Europe here includes Neo-Europes) of research and scientific concepts. In order for us to start formulating **international** linguistic human rights, the concepts we use also need to be truly international. Therefore, definitions taking into consideration the last two theses (and others) need to be developed.

The relationship between the four criteria used in the definitions, origin, identification, competence, and function, is also reflected in how culture and cultural competence (in a broad sense) can be conceptualised and operationalised. Next we shall therefore discuss cultural competence and cultural diversity.

3.3. CULTURAL DIVERSITY
AND CULTURAL COMPETENCE

In parallel with the definition of linguistic diversity (Definition Box 2.1) we will, in rather general terms, define **cultural diversity** as 'the range of variation exhibited by human cultures.' A working definition of culture in this book covers 'the material and ideological ways in which a group organizes, understands and reproduces its life as a group' (Skutnabb-Kangas & Phillipson 1985: 51; for an elaboration, see Skutnabb-Kangas 1987, chapter 3, which this section also draws on). A good definition of culture is also Eric Smith's (in press) 'culture is socially transmitted information.'

In order to be able to discuss cultural diversity we need to look more closely at the basic ingredients of cultures, here in terms of the components of cultural competence. This is similar to looking at the concepts 'language' and 'species' in discussing linguistic and biological diversity.

3.3.1. Components of Cultural Competence: Cognitive, Affective, Behavioural, and Awareness-Related

I have earlier operationalised cultural competence in terms of four components or constituents (Phillipson & Skutnabb-Kangas 1983: 61–68, Skutnabb-Kangas & Phillipson 1985: 50–52): **cognitive, affective, behavioural, and awareness-related**. These cover **knowledge (including language), feelings, behaviour, and metacultural/metalinguistic awareness**. These components correspond partially to the criteria used for mother tongue definitions, where the cognitive component would correspond to 'competence', the affective to 'identification' and the behavioural to 'function'. The 'origin' criterion possibly does not play an equally important role for culture as for mother tongue, partly because all cultures are probably hybrids to a much higher degree than languages, and all environments multicultural, and changes in cultures happen much faster than changes in languages, at least at a system level. These are claims which, of course, can be disputed—even by myself. The metalinguistic and metacultural awareness would partly correspond to the relation and possible tension between internal and external identification.

'Language' is in the analysis below part of culture. But one could also analyse it the other way round: culture is what we describe **and create** through communication (at least a weak but probably also some stronger forms of the Whorf-Sapir hypothesis would be compatible with this view—and so would, somewhat ironically, some post-modernist views be . . .). Yet another way which has been debated extensively is to see culture as part of superstructure in Marxist terminology and language as at least partially outside both base and superstructure. A fourth way might be to look at both as partial components of and constitutive of each other. A possible combination of the last two ways of seeing the relationship between language and culture might in general correspond best to my present inclinations. But it is possible to emphasize the importance of language also within the framework used in the operationalisations below, by positing language as a cultural core value (see below).

The **cognitive**/intellectual/scholastic/literary component of cultural competence relates to **knowledge** about the relevant culture. I see, following Smolicz (1979²), language as a possible core value in many cultures. Therefore the knowledge component of cultural competence includes knowledge of the language(s) pertaining to that culture. The cognitive component also includes some knowledge about the history and traditions of that culture, knowing how different institutions (both concrete and abstract) function, how people behave and react, what they grow, eat, drink and think, what they wear, read, write, and do or do not do, how they pattern their family and communal life, what the relationship between genders and generations is, how they bring up their children, and so forth.

As will become clear below (section 3.5), most definitions of ethnicity include language as one of those cultural traits which belong to defining characteristics of an ethnic group. This is the case even in the face of those exceptions where some kind of ethnic identity remains even when the capacity to speak the language has been lost, the linguistic heritage 'stolen' (see especially Fishman's 1977 discussion of this). Irish and Yiddish/Hebrew have often been quoted as examples. But 'while it is undoubtedly true that competence in Irish can no longer be considered a necessary condition for Irish ethnic identity, at least in the context of contemporary Irish society competence in **Irish English** might well be. In other words, even where the ethnic language has been killed off (or nearly so, as in the case of Irish), linguistic markers of ethnic identity may still be significant' (Timothy Reagan, December 1998, personal communication). Thus claims that a culture can survive even without language (for instance John Edwards 1977, 1985, Bratt Paulston 1982, 1994) should rather be taken as describing exceptions, and not as covert recommendations to neglect support to minority languages and cultures—these recommendations abound (see Insert 3.5 for some examples from Australia). John Edwards likewise does not want to use taxpayers' money to support minority ethnicity and cultures (Insert 3.6).

The Australian suggestions obviously lead to the loss of minority languages (see Info Boxes 8.2 and 8.3 for some empirical studies). Christina Bratt Paulston is very clear about her recommendations: 'Once it is clear . . . whom the children of migrant workers in Europe will marry, the setting of educational policy will be much facilitated. If they commonly marry nationals of the host culture, there will be **no need of special or different educational policies** for their children. If, however, they marry exclusively within their own ethnic group, **learn the national language poorly** and show **other**

INSERT 3.5 It is not part of the Australian policies to sustain
or preserve different cultures (Zubrzycki, Gobbo)

In the eyes of one of the early architects of Australian multiculturalism,
Emeritus Professor Jerzy **Zubrzycki** (1995—see also 1988), 'the polysyllabic
noun "multiculturalism" has outlived its purpose',

> acknowledg[ing] the validity of ethnic cultures . . . should not imply that
> every culture is equally valued and equally legitimate . . . Maintenance
> of cultural identity is not a policy that should be promoted without regard
> to its ramifications . . . An example of this deviation from the ideal of
> pluralism in a liberal democracy is the scheme of grants to ethnic groups
> which in theory should be justified as a necessary, short term measure
> of positive discrimination . . . So the maintenance of cultural identity is
> not a policy that should be promoted . . . The aim should be to ensure
> that all Australians irrespective of their status should be ensured equality
> of access to the nation's resources. But to extend this principle to the
> equality of outcome . . . would do great harm to the very principle of
> liberal democracy. . . . The tolerance of ethnic diversity is the principal
> means available to us to reach this goal [i.e., the goal of developing
> Australia's potential] . . . The Australian policy of multiculturalism is
> more a policy of toleration than a policy of support.

Another important Australian researcher/politician, James **Gobbo**, has this
to say: 'It is not and never has been part of the policies of multiculturalism
as set out in the National Agenda to provide for special funding to sustain
or preserve different cultures; even less is this true of particular religions.'
(Gobbo 1995: 2).

> There is some force in an argument that without resources and
> programs—and no political push—the multicultural policies and objec-
> tives in the National Agenda will not be achieved. But an aggressive
> campaign to increase intervention or to press for widespread affirmative
> action programs may undermine the progress already made. Such
> programs are in any event contrary to the spirit of the National Agenda.
> (ibid., 6)

trends of strong cultural maintenance (arranged marriages with partners from
the home country, **vacations in the home country**, etc.) then a strong case can
be argued for the case of bilingual education' (Paulston 1994: 31, emphases
added). This is a typical 'either-or' stance: assimilation or segregation are
the alternatives (see also Powers 1995). If I go to Finland on vacations, it
can also be taken as a proof of learning Danish poorly? Our grandson (his
mother is Danish) does not need any teaching of English, one of the father's
two mother tongues—he should become Danish-speaking only?

INSERT 3.6 Abolish **dominant** languages and cultures from schools—they are part of a private ethnicity and programmes for their maintenance are misguided? (John Edwards)

In overtly liberal/intercultural rhetoric the implicit assumptions are often covertly assimilationist vis-a-vis integration/ethnicity. It is overtly acknowledged that a migrant minority group may have something to contribute, but it is the host society which decides what of it is accepted as enriching, and thus allowed to exist as part of the 'mainstream' (often ethnic food, dances, clothes, etc.). The rest, meaning many of the more vital non-material group-reproduction-oriented parts of minority cultures, are seen as belonging to the domain of the private sphere. They are labelled parts of the minorities' 'private ethnicity', and 'public institutions' like schools should not 'promote private ethnicity', because 'matters of ethnicity are best left to those directly concerned', as John Edwards puts it (1984b: 299–300).

However, the same attributes are not seen as part of any private ethnicity when it comes to the majority population. Their 'private ethnicity' is of course being supported by public institutions like schools. Majority language schools for majority children 'naturally' maintain their language. But it should logically also be seen as a private aspect of **their** ethnicity. This lack of consistency is a logical consequence of seeing ethnicity as something that majorities are devoid of. Therefore quotes like the following are seen to pertain only to minorities, not to majorities: 'Educational programmes aimed at sustaining ethnic identity through communicative language maintenance are misguided and may even damage those private aspects of ethnicity (i.e., language) which are essentially out of the reach of external intervention.' (John Edwards 1984a: 14). Logically this view should of course not only lead to banishing minority mother tongues from the curricula (something that many countries are busy doing right now) but also to abolishing the use of Danish in Danish schools, the use of English in British schools, etc. Logically one should, then, abolish majority languages and cultures for majority populations completely from all Western schools, because they are part of a private ethnicity, and programmes for their maintenance are misguided . . .

What these examples show is that minority education often reduces or destroys that part of minorities' cultural competence which has to do with the cognitive component in relation to their own mother tongue. This has consequences for their cultural competence as a whole. Several of the researchers worried about loss of linguistic diversity claim, basing themselves on empirical evidence, that a culture cannot survive even for a couple of generations if the language is lost. This is because what has to be transmitted to subsequent generations cannot be reduced to 'folkloric festivals' or 'romantic musings on the past'—'ethnic identity needs a solid cultural substratum', and 'the elimination of linguistic cores reduces the cultures concerned to ethnic remnants or empty shells that lack creative potential or economic value', as Jurek Smolicz formulates it (1990: 74).

The **affective**/empathetic/identificational component relates to deep (positive) **feelings** about and **attitudes** towards a culture, an understanding of it from the inside, internalizing it, and an identification with it or, rather, parts of it, including acceptance of (most of) its norms and values (or feeling so strongly about them that fighting them, rejecting or abandoning them may require a lot of emotional effort). Aspects like dependence on the group for security, solidarity with the group, low levels of anxiety, feeling at ease, naturalness, when being enveloped by the culture, are parts of this (see Giles, Leets & Coupland 1990, Leets & Giles 1995, for some possible ways of systematizing the factors in more detailed ways). Many of the aspects of interethnic cognitive and discourse style differences (e.g., Gudykunst (ed.) 1986, Gudykunst & Ting-Toomey 1990, Ting-Toomey 1988), more general differences between ethnic groups (e.g., Daun 1984, 1989, Daun & Ehn 1988, Ehn & Arnstberg 1980, Hofstede 1980) and motivation studies also belong here. In negotiations between dominant and dominated groups also aspects like competitive or collaborative conflict styles play important roles (e.g., Ting-Toomey 1988; see Daun et al. 1989, Skutnabb-Kangas 1996a, for an exemplification of the differences between Finland and Sweden).

The third component of cultural competence is a **behavioural** component, the capacity to act in culturally appropriate ways with members of a given cultural group. It may often be possible, at least superficially, to act according to the norms of another culture even without accepting its norms and values, if the benefits from doing so are great enough, and if one has the necessary knowledge. A Scandinavian secular woman may thus cover her head and wear long sleeves when going to a village church in Sicily, or abstain from pork and alcohol in an islamist Arab country, without necessarily accepting that god or allah demands it. Being cognitively competent in a foreign culture may lead to adequate behaviour, even if the affective cultural competence, deep understanding, acceptance, and identification, is lacking, as many of the global nomads show. There may in this case be a fair amount of conscious acting when behaving according to the norms of another culture. This may also be experienced within different subcultures of the same culture, when one, for instance, crosses a class border (or age border), and behaves in a way which is alien to one's own class (or even age) culture. But it seems that a certain amount of acceptance and understanding of the norms of the foreign culture, i.e. a certain degree of affective competence, is often needed, in addition to knowledge, in order to behave naturally in ways that are appropriate to another culture. Gallois et al. (1988), Coupland et al. (1991), Leets & Giles (1995) and others, working with social-psychological aspects of language learning and minorities in accommodation and ethnolinguistic vitality theories (see references to Giles in the bibliography; see also Liebkind et al. 1995 for one of the applications—there are dozens), discuss conditions 'under which speakers may **attune** (e.g., converge) or **contra-attune** (e.g., diverge) discoursally, paralinguistically and non-verbally to . . . features of their addressee . . . For example, in an interethnic conversation one person may **contra-attune** to the other person by not adhering to their partner's cultural rules and not being sensitive to the types of words they use and the topics they discuss' (Leets & Giles 1995: 46).

It is also possible to have the cognitive and behavioural competence but to choose **not** to use the competence and not to behave according to the rules of the other culture. Not behaving according to them might thus be a result of not having the knowledge, not having the behavioural competence, not being able to use the knowledge, or not **wanting** to use the knowledge and/or the behavioural competence. This again might be a matter of affective competence, not identifying with the norms which guide behaviour. It might also be part of a conscious (or, as it might be, less conscious) 'ethnic strategy' or power strategy.

The fourth component of cultural competence is **metacultural and meta-linguistic awareness**, an understanding of the distinctiveness and relativity of one's own (and other) cultures, consciously being able to reflect over one's own and other cultures, at times distancing oneself from them and looking at them as objects. Several sections below discuss this Self-Other relationship. Many analysts see border maintenance mechanisms/strategies as central to cultures, and even the border itself or, rather, the existence of it, as the main defining characteristic of a culture. Metacultural/metalinguistic awareness might be taken as an expression of precisely this. A precondition for being able to develop this awareness is at least some knowledge of other cultures with which to compare, to contrast and create 'one's own' Other as consti-tutive of Self: the existence of Thou, and a dialogue between I and Thee, as a necessary component of I (see section 3.4.2.1 below).

One's own culture becomes clearer and one becomes more aware of it when one changes countries, as Eeva Tikka, Carelian speaker in Finland, notes in her poem (my translation):

She was not different
she only happened to get dumped
in the middle of foreigners.
She imagined how it would be
in one's own country
when light would be speaking her language
about water and trees
and would wipe away the cosmic emptiness
from under the skin.
She would have the language
and life.
Would never need to be
The Other.

Rita Liljeström and others from Sweden wrote in a book (1985) about their visit to China, where they studied Chinese pre-school education, that the Swedish group really went to China in order to learn more about **Swedish** pre-school education. Elizabeth Szász, a British translator, married to a Hungarian author, says after 30 years in Hungary that she had 'never realized how much you can learn about your own language through translation' (1996: 188). 'Monocultural' people by definition have a low degree of metacultural awareness (or at least metacultural consciousness, a more verbalised and possibly more politicized version). It is assumed that somebody who lives (her whole life) in a specific culture is fully competent in it according to the cognitive, affective, and behavioural components (just like monolingual people in principle have full command of their only language), but for the fourth component to develop, more contact with Others is needed. Therefore this component of cultural competence is not at the same level as the other three components. The awareness component also functions so as to give more depth to the other components.

One aspect of this component has been discussed in some of the social-psychological literature on ethnic identification in terms of a difference between **ethnic awareness** and **ethnic consciousness**. The former would mean an awareness of one's descent, without necessarily resulting in any kind of conscious evaluation of it, whereas the latter would imply using one's ethnicity as a dynamic force. 'Ethnicity, as a highly conscious, instrumental, outward oriented ideology, is abundantly in evidence in the Western world', according to Fishman (1977: 35), and 'heightened language consciousness . . . mobilizes and solidifies the ethnicity collectivity' (ibid., 34). Thus it seems probable that a group which meets fierce resistance to using its language as a medium of education might as a result develop an (even higher degree of) ethnic consciousness, especially vis-a-vis language, as a part of their metacultural and metalinguistic awareness. In order to parallel the distinction made above we could of course speak of a metacultural awareness and a metacultural consciousness, but I think that the distinction is still too imprecise to warrant that type of differentiation of concepts. Rather I would like to see the metacultural consciousness as implying a component of awareness of the political dimensions of minority ethnicity. Likewise, metalinguistic consciousness might be seen as an awareness of status (planning) aspects of language planning and language policy, rather than just corpus awareness (awareness of forms of a specific language). At a behavioural level, though, use of conscious 'ethnic strategies' might be a result of ethnicity-related metacultural consciousness. It would be important to work in much more multi- and transdisciplinary ways, though, to understand ethnic strategies—neither sociolinguistic nor social-psychological nor sociological (or political science) theories in themselves are enough. Despite many basic differences of approach in particular scholarly traditions, a coming together would be to the benefit of all.

The concepts presented in this section will be used to specify assimilation and integration, initially discussed in general terms.

3.3.2. Assimilation and Integration

Assimilation and integration have to be discussed at both **collective** and **individual** levels, just as (human) rights and duties in general. At a **collective** level, one of the self-evident human rights of indigenous peoples and minorities (and ethnic groups) is the right to exist and reproduce themselves as separate groups (e.g., Alfredsson 1989, 1990, 1991, Thornberry 1987, 1991, de Varennes 1996a). This presupposes a right **not** to assimilate. On the other hand, all these groups also need the right to integrate into the larger units with whom they coexist if this is what they want. Otherwise the world might disintegrate into ever smaller separate **and segregated** units. It has been intensely debated (especially by lawyers, political scientists, and sociologists) whether integration is not only a right but also a **duty** for, especially, minorities and ethnic groups, but the issue is so far unresolved. There is more agreement, it seems, at an international level, on the principle—not the practice—that indigenous peoples do not have this duty; but they have the right to integrate if they so wish.

A closely related issue is the role of an official or dominant language: **is it a duty of (ethnic) minorities to learn the official language**, or is it only a right? Several recent laws and propositions in many countries are trying to make both assimilation (called integration) and the learning of the dominant language a duty, with enforced assimilationist demands. Often the means (e.g., more dominant language medium education and no mother tongue-related rights) in fact work against the goal. Two recent cases in point are the Californian **Proposition 227**, dismantling bilingual education[3] and the Slovak Language Law.[4] The issue of the collective right to self-determination will be discussed further in chapter 7.

Assimilation and integration have been discussed and defined in numerous ways, at least since the 1930s when serious research on the issues started. They have been seen as concepts placed on one continuum (initial segregation, functional adaptation, acculturation, integration, assimilation), or as opposites, or parts of more complex nested continua and hierarchies. Sometimes 'acculturation' has had the characteristics usually labelled as integration, here illustrated by the hierarchical definitions from the **Encyclopaedia Britannica** in Definition Box 3.1.

My definitions of assimilation and integration here are inspired by Drobizheva and Gouboglo (1986) with some modifications. **Assimilation** is

1. disappearance of distinctive features, i.e. objectively the loss of specific elements of material and non-material culture and subjectively the loss of the feeling of belonging to a particular ethnic group;

DEFINITION BOX 3.1 Acculturation, assimilation, no integration
(**Encyclopaedia Britannica**)

Acculturation is defined in **Encyclopaedia Britannica** (1971 version, p.
83) as

> the processes of change in artifacts, customs and beliefs resulting
> from the contact of peoples of different cultural backgrounds. The
> term is also used to refer to the effects of those processes, as in
> "an acculturated Navaho Indian", meaning a Navaho who has
> adopted Anglo-American behaviour while retaining some tradi-
> tional Navajo ways.

The Britannica article distinguishes two major types of acculturation,
incorporation, where 'people of different cultures maintain an interchange
without the exercise of military or political domination by one group over another', and **directed change** where 'one people establishes dominance over
another through military conquest, political domination or other means of
control'. Within directed change the article further distinguishes between
assimilation, blending (also called fusion, accommodation, or syncretism)
and **reaction against aspects of the culture of a dominant group.**
'**Integration**' is not an entry in the **Britannica** at all . . .

2. simultaneously, adoption of traits belonging to another culture, which
   replace those of the former culture, accompanied by the subjective
   feeling of belonging to the second culture.

Integration is defined as formation of a series of common features in an
ethnically heterogenous group. I have my own shorter complementary definitions in Definition Box 3.2.

DEFINITION BOX 3.2 Short definitions of assimilation and integration

Assimilation is enforced subtractive 'learning' of another (dominant)
culture by a (dominated) group. Assimilation means being transferred
to another group.
Integration is characterized by voluntary mutual additive 'learning' of other
cultures. Integration means a choice of inclusive group membership(s).

If the learning of a dominant language is made an unconditional **duty** for a dominated group, we have to do with assimilation, whereas making this learning a **right** is characteristic of integration policies.

The concepts of integration and assimilation have been defined and discussed from numerous points of view. Only a few will be mentioned here.

Integration has been discussed both as a **process** and as a result of a process, a **product**. When integration is discussed as a process, it has often been seen as an active **individual** ('ethnic') strategy, whereby an individual passes into the dominant society by acquiring the 'instruments' needed, i.e. the cultural competence pertaining to the majority culture. The relative openness of a dominant society can be measured in terms of its propensity to let individuals from another culture 'pass'. If integration is discussed as a **collective group** strategy, the openness of a society can be assessed in terms of to what extent it allows groups to become **structurally incorporated** (be treated as equals, with the same rights and duties, economically, politically, socially, educationally, etc., something that often necessitates affirmative action of some kind), at the same time as they are 'allowed' **not to assimilate**, to maintain their cultural distinctiveness (see Schermerhorn 1970, Skutnabb-Kangas & Toukomaa 1976). Being structurally incorporated and culturally integrated entails at a group level in a pluralist society a position as **national ethnic minorities**.

There are two possible outcomes in an **open** society. If it allows individuals to 'pass', some of these individuals might assimilate. But if it is an open society, it permits at the same time groups (and thus individuals as members of these groups) **not** to assimilate. These two are obviously close to end points on one of the continua involved in the integration-assimilation analysis. This distinction reflects an important observation about the complexity of the processes of assimilation/integration.

The most **closed** societies would thus be those which at the **collective** level **prevent structural incorporation**, at the same time as they exert a strong cultural assimilation pressure. This also includes glorification of the dominant culture and not valuing minority ethnicity or culture. But at the **individual** level a closed society would also prevent both assimilation and integration because it would not allow individuals from minorities to 'pass'. **Segregation and apartheid** are results. These countries thus give conflicting messages: in order to get your share of the goods, services, and power of this society, you have to become like us—but we won't allow you, because you are not one of us.

An important aspect of the assimilation-integration discussion is the relative consensus or lack of it about the future of the minorities. Often there is a total disagreement between the dominant majority and the dominated minorities. Most minorities want structural incorporation and cultural, including linguistic maintenance (which includes a goal of bilingualism and biculturalism), whereas the majority may want to prevent structural incorporation and demands assimilation.

In Skutnabb-Kangas & Toukomaa (1976) we described typical stages in a development towards agreement in relation to the goals for minorities. Often there is first a partial agreement about the cultural goal (i.e., integration, not assimilation) while the dominant group still prevents any achievement of structural incorporation and equality. Often agreeing to some cultural rights for minorities is used to legitimate lack of structural equality. Likewise, structural and cultural goals are often falsely seen as an 'either-or' question—a typical dilemma of liberal pluralism. The question here is not about needing to choose between jobs or identity, political power or your own language, but how to 'reconcile the rightful concerns of cultural diversity and identity with the socially legitimate desires and claims to achieve equality', or 'to recognize the competing pressures of the expressive and instrumental dimensions of ethnicity—the latter being concerned with the more material aspects of living, especially the need for economic, social and political power on the part of ethnic minority group members' (Jayasuriya 1986:8, quoted in Skutnabb-Kangas & Cummins 1988: 393). And an agreement between minorities and dominant groups about **both** is where the dilemma lies.

No elites want to change an unequal system. In many countries, the strategy has been to let a few token minority **individuals** ('assimilados') pass, in order to be able to show them off to the rest of the group which can then be blamed for not doing the same, not acquiring the instruments needed for passing.[5] The 'assimilados' can also be used for purposes of legitimation of measures intended to assimilate the rest of the group—they function as token 'spokespeople' for their own groups while in fact being mouthpieces for the dominant group. At the same time strategies which a whole minority **group** could use in order to change its **collective** status and to integrate are fiercely fought.

The term 'integration' is still often used in many countries when in fact 'assimilation' is what is meant. According to the final report from the Swedish State Committee Against Racism and Xenophobia (SOU 1989: 115), a group is not integrated if it 'maintains its ethnic distinctiveness'—they have to lose it and become Swedish in order to integrate, that is, they have to assimilate: 'There is reason to believe that **some groups** of immigrants will little by little **integrate** into Swedish society. But a probable development is also that **other groups** will **maintain** and specifically emphasize **their ethnic distinctiveness**' (emphases added).

The reasoning of German authorities in relation to Turkish children and parents is, despite Germany officially still having a 'guest worker' policy, very similar. The situation of immigrant and refugee minorities in Germany is fairly representative of many of the Western European countries, especially Britain and France. Therefore I provide a fairly long description of it, adding a few observations from other countries. See Info Box 3.1.[6]

❖ Info Box 3.1 ❖

'Foreigners' in Germany 'Have Not Yet Understood' That They Have to Assimilate

At the end of 1993 there were 6.5 million *Ausländer* ('foreigners'/foreign nationals) in Germany (**Arbeitsplatz Deutschland** 2, 1994: 2). There are over 1.5 million 'foreign' children under the age of 18, over 2.5 million under 25. There are around 160,000 'foreigners'[7] over the age of 60 and in 10 years' time there will be more than half a million elderly 'foreigners' (ibid., 3). Of the 'foreigners' 60% have been in Germany more than 10 years, 40% more than 15 years, 25% more than 20 years. Three-quarters of the 'foreign' children and youngsters were born in Germany. There are around 1.4 million people in Germany with at least two citizenships (ibid., 3–4), i.e., double politonymic (see 3.5.2) identity.

Of the 'foreigners' 80% live with their families in Germany. Marriages between Germans and 'foreigners' have gone up from around 28,000 per year in 1980 to almost 40,000 per year in 1990. Of these 55.4% were between German women and 'foreign' men. Two 'foreigners' divorce much less often than two 'Germans', but the divorce rate is higher among mixed marriages than among 'German' marriages. The number of children is going down, but the birth rate is still higher among 'foreigners' than 'Germans': 1.6 children per family in 'German' families, 1.87 for 'foreigners' in general, 2.2 for Turks (who have the highest fertility).

'Foreign' families live in less attractive housing. They are often discriminated against when trying to find places to rent. Only 20% of the 'foreigners' live alone, as compared to over 33% of 'Germans'. 'German' families have over 34.5 square meters per person, 'foreigners' 21.5.

The usual statistics about the difference between the dominant group and the minorities in relation to type of work (more physical labour and services), working conditions (more dirty, heavy and dangerous work, monotonous movements, less independence, long and inconvenient hours, long transport times, etc.), much higher rates of unemployment, and so on, have not changed much during the last decade as one can ascertain by looking at OECD, ILO, etc. reports on migration.

There are many migrant minority children of obligatory school age in all European countries who are not in schools at all. Some are undocumented (e.g., in Switzerland and France), some are children of refugees who do not get full-time schooling while waiting for decision on asylum (e.g., Denmark), some have 'adjusted education' (a Danish term for children in grades 7–9 who only spend a few days per week in school and the rest working as apprentices—needless to say most of them are migrant minorities); many are pushed out[8] before reaching the end of obligatory schooling.[9]

There were over 800,000 'foreign' children and young people in the German primary *allgemeinbildende* schools at the end of 1993, 11.5% of the school population. Young 'foreigners' between the ages of 14 and 19 make up over 14% of the age group but only 7.6% of the school population. Most of those

(Continued)

❖ I n f o   B o x   3 . 1 ❖

(Continued)

'foreigners' who continue their education go to *Hauptschule* (vocational stream) after the comprehensive school, with a slowly growing tendency to go to *gymnasium* (upper secondary school). But many are pushed out without getting a school leaving certificate of any kind, and few get a vocational training.

Why do young 'foreigners' not get *Berufsausbildung* (vocational training)? We will compare what the German editors of the official state publication **Arbeitsplatz Deutschland** (2: 1994) report about what *Fachleute* (professional people) say, with what they themselves think. *Fachleute* give, according to them, the following reasons (ibid., 12; my translation):

• lack of knowledge of the German language
• gaps in the school education (*Schulbildung*)
• *Anpassungsschwierigkeiten* (adjustment difficulties)
• prejudices of the German employers against foreigners.

Then the editors express what the reasons are according to **their opinion**:

• Many foreign youngsters and many parents have not yet understood that vocational training is very important, in many cases even necessary, in order to find a job.
• Many of them do not know to whom to turn in order to get advice and help.
• Many foreign parents still demand of their children that they earn money as soon as possible and help the family. For them, years used on education are a waste of time (*verlorene Zeit*).
• Many foreign youngsters believe that it is possible to manage well in life even without an education, if one only is clever and has good connections. Therefore they seek a job immediately, with relatives or good acquaintances, where they instead of vocational qualifications can acquire a capacity to achieve.
• According to the views of many foreign parents girls do not need to learn a trade because they will marry and have children even without that. (ibid., 12)

This confirms Stacy Churchill's diagnosis in the early 1980s on the reasons for problems which immigrant minorities face (1986; see also Skutnabb-Kangas 1984a, 1988). Blame is squarely placed by these German editors of the official state publication on the minority youngsters, their parents, their culture. **They** are the ones who 'do not know', 'have not yet understood', who have old-fashioned cultural values which prevent their children from achieving and learning. There is not one reason which would hint at the need for the educational system to change, to 'integrate'—changes are required only of the 'foreigners'.

The Danish Ministry of Interior is equally blunt in their definitions. In a 1990 report suggesting measures for better integration of immigrants, their definition of 'immigrants' includes 'only foreign nationals who do not come from the Nordic countries, the countries of the European Common Market and North America and who do not have political asylum in this country' (Indenrigsministeriet 1990: 15). Why? Because the aforementioned groups 'in general are expected to be able to cope on their own' (ibid.). 'Immigrants' are those who are **not** expected to be able to cope, i.e. they are the ones who are deficient and need help.[10] And their major deficiency (which is repeated several times on most pages of the report) is 'their lack of competence in the Danish language'. Consequently, the main recommendations in the report have to do with coaxing, urging, forcing, and threatening the immigrants into learning Danish (and teaching it to their children before these come to school[11]). Minority organisations' severe criticisms of the report (including statistics recording the wish of immigrants to learn Danish and the long queues for Danish courses) have not seemed to lead to much enlightenment in more recent ministerial and other reports emanating from Danish authorities. The immigrants are still the deficient ones to be blamed, the ones who have to change.

The Swedish, German, and Danish reports all exhibit some other features which are typical of how integration has been understood in many official reports and often also in research:

• Integration is seen as a product, a final result of a process where the goal is known and there is a straight path to it. This also reflects a static view of ethnicity (which is attributed only to minorities). 'Ethnics' are seen as some sort of outsiders who are struggling to 'integrate', to become part of the unmarked majority (and its unmarked ethnicity). They go through several phases in this process (initial segregation, functional adaptation, acculturation) and at the end of the road, once they have reached the goal, they **are** integrated and there is no more fuss, they function nicely.

• Integration is seen as something that only the minority (the 'un-integrated') group/individual has to do. They integrate into something that *is* there, waiting ('Swedish/American/German society'). It is the minority's degree of integration (and their 'wish to integrate') that is assessed ('Aborigines in Australia do not want to integrate'), not the majority society's willingness or unwillingness to 'let them integrate' and the majority's willingness to do **their** part of the integration.

• Integration is seen as a characteristic of the group or individual to be integrated ('minority person x or minority group Y is not integrated—or is well integrated—in the Z mainstream society'; 'x/the Y's has/have not done enough to integrate in Z'). '**Not being integrated**' is seen as a negative cultural *characteristic* **in the minority**, which is partly a result of a conscious choice by the minority group/individual. It is often used to legitimate unequal access to power and resources ('the Turks in Germany do not want to integrate, and therefore they should not have the right to vote in municipal elections either'; 'the Finns in Sweden do not want to integrate, they do not take Swedish citizenship. Therefore they cannot be allowed to vote in state elections either').

When integration is understood as a final result of a one-way process, this also has consequences for how the majority society is treated. When those who come as migrants or who are an indigenous minority are seen as the only ones who have to change and to embrace the goals, ideals, and identity of the new country or the dominant society, in order to fit into a virtually unchanged society, this society can continue to regard itself as the mainstream. And the mainstream is always regarded as integrated into 'its own' society. '**Being in the mainstream**'[12] (which includes 'being integrated') is thus also treated as a characteristic, but a *characteristic* **of the majority**, a characteristic which they somehow possess in a natural way. Even in avowedly immigration countries like Australia, dominant group policy may want 'to develop . . . mechanisms that would bring non-English speaking minority groups into recognised relationship with the "main-stream" Australian group life' as Jerzy Zubrzycki (1988), quoting Jean Martin (1971, 1978) presents this 'emasculated pluralism'. Minority groups have to participate 'in the shared and universalistic structures of the wider society' (Australia, 1975: 48–51, quoted in Zubrzycki 1988: 12).

This static and ethnocentric view where the whole burden of integration is on the incomer or the indigenous peoples alone, and where the dominant group's values are presented as somehow 'shared' and 'universal', rather than particularistic and changing, like all values are, still prevails in many countries. When the majority population is presented in this way as an integrated mainstream, homogenously sharing universal cultural values, this characteristic legitimates its access to most of the power and resources (which are, of course, shared unevenly on a class and gender basis within the majority population—but this is often not mentioned when integration is discussed).

The official views in various countries could be analysed in terms of these simple distinctions. Swedish views might, for instance, be seen in this light as combining an emphasis on individual strategies, and on products, more than collective group strategies and processes.

In most cases **assimilation** is forced assimilation. Minorities are forced through the same means which are normally used for control: sticks (physical violence, force, threats), carrots (bargaining, gratifications) and ideas (persuasion) (see chapter 5). In the earlier phases of minority education, minority children were often forced to leave their own languages and cultures through the use of sticks, physical means: separation from parents and physical punishment for speaking their own language. There are descriptions of this from all over the world (see chapter 5). Now the same result of 'forcibly transferring children from one group to another' (from the UN genocide definition) is often achieved through a combination of carrots and ideas, psychological means: positive reinforcement in relation to the dominant languages, and shame, guilt, and ideas of uselessness and traditionalism, non-modern, in relation to the dominated languages and cultures. In recent years, negative sanctions seem to have been on the increase again in many Western countries, though, in the same way as they are increasingly used to control the domestic poor (see Pilger 1998 for examples).

In the present book integration is **not** seen as a final product, nor as a characteristic in the minority individual/group, nor as something that only the minority has to do. Instead, it is seen as a **process** and a socially constructed **relation** which the minority and the majority have to negotiate reciprocally, and where **both** have to change. The hegemonic view is that 'being ethnic', 'being a minority', 'not being integrated' and 'not being European' are characteristics which 'justify' the fact that individuals/groups which are 'different' in these ways (i.e., labelled as 'deficient') not only do have but **should** have less power and (material) resources than 'non-ethnic, integrated, majority-group ("mainstream") Europeans/Australians/Americans', until they have stopped 'being different', i.e. lost their ethnic traits, become integrated into the 'mainstream' and worthy of admission to the European Club or acceptance as 'real Australians/Americans', etc.

A majority can prevent integration by refusing to change itself, regardless of how ready a minority group is for integration. It is the degree of integration (and wish to integrate) of the whole society that has to be assessed. The results of the process of negotiating integration depend crucially on the power relationships between those who negotiate, the dominant group(s) and the minorities.

Integration of societies, not assimilation of dominated groups, is a prerequisite for cultural (and linguistic) diversity to be maintained.

3.3.3. Combining Cultural Competence and Integration

Now we can combine the earlier analysis of components of cultural competence, with the discussion about integration. An immigrant minority or an indigenous people or an autochthonous minority group would be ready for doing **its** part of the integration process when it has formed **common features with** (parts of) **the majority population**, so that they share some of the cultural competence that the majority have, on the level of the three components of cultural competence, cognitive (including language), affective, and behavioural. In addition they have (retained) **common features with the people representing their original culture** (in their country of origin, in the case of immigrant minorities), so that they share some of the cultural competence that these have, on the level of the three components of cultural competence, cognitive (including language), affective, and behavioural. In addition, integration preparedness also entails a higher degree of metacultural and metalinguistic awareness vis-a-vis both cultures than the metacultural and metalinguistic awareness possessed by representatives of the original source culture and the other ('new') culture. This may in time lead to new features in the ethnic minority's culture, so that it develops specific cultural traits not found in any of the source cultures. And of course all these cultures are in constant change anyway—we are thus not talking about any kind of preservation of traditional cultures in museal cultural reserves, but dynamic processes. Likewise, we are not talking about cultures as reified objects with clearcut boundaries, but living constantly renewed socially transmitted and negotiated information.

Thus I see this integration readiness as a necessary (but not sufficient) prerequisite for forming a national ethnic minority. But since integration includes both the majority population (where there is one) and all the other minority groups (common features in an ethnically **heterogenous** group, i.e. a group comprising all the different ethnoses), we cannot speak of real integration before the **majority** or dominant group has also acquired new features. Here too integration should be discussed both as a collective phenomenon and as an individual phenomenon. My contention, to continue the example above, is that many majority group individuals, for instance in Sweden or Germany, or the United States, are willing and have in fact acquired some of these new features in their cultural competence. As a collectivity, though, majorities in Sweden, Germany, and the USA, have changed little, especially in terms of structural societal features and ideologies, on the basis of for them new cultures coming in or becoming more visible, and there do not seem to be many signs of a willingness to change either—except, maybe, in a still more assimilationist direction. Many recent documents and voting results in all countries testify to this (see, e.g., Huss 1999, Lainio 1997, 1978, Municio 1996, Municio-Larsson, in press, Wingstedt 1998, on Sweden). At the most what one can expect seems to be some kind of 'tolerance' towards Others.

The two broad types of theories predicting this tolerance are **conflict theories** and **contact theories**. According to the more socioeconomically oriented **conflict theories**, attitudes to 'foreigners' reflect the threat they are seen to pose on the labour market, in relation to housing, welfare, etc., i.e. competing about scarce goods and services, and the presumed threat in terms of crime, violence, aids, etc. The prediction would then be that attitudes are more negative in times of high unemployment, economic hardship, etc., and that people with less formal schooling and an insecure economic situation would have more negative attitudes. According to the more social-psychologically oriented **contact theories** more knowledge about and contact with 'foreigners' would be a base for more positive attitudes. In terms of the first type of theories, changes towards positive attitudes require socioeconomic changes in society, towards more welfare and less insecurity for the domestic (as well as 'foreign') population, whereas the second would require information and contact opportunities, a change in the ideological climate.

Most recent studies in Scandinavia and elsewhere show—not surprisingly, again—that both-and is required. Magdalena Jaakkola's recent (in press) comparison of the attitudes of representative samples of Finns towards refugees and immigrants (and, for some questions, the domestic national minorities and the indigenous Sámi) shows that the attitudes were very positive in 1987 when unemployment was low, the economic trends positive, and when there were very few refugees and immigrants in Finland as compared to most Western countries. In 1993 when unemployment was extremely high, around 16 percent (one reason being the complete collapse of Soviet trade), and the number of refugees, asylum seekers, and immigrants was rapidly growing, the attitudes were very negative, but in 1998, with a better economic situation, they were again more positive. On the other hand, the results show, just like in many other countries, that the characteristics connected with a likelihood of positive attitudes in all areas are:

- more (vs. less) formal education;
- being a woman (vs. man);
- more (vs. less or no) contacts with people from other countries and cultures;
- religion being important (vs. less or not important) (ibid.).

High levels of formal education seems to be the most important factor in predicting attitudes. It combines explanations from both theories. Referring to several recent Nordic studies, Jaakkola (ibid.) sums up some of them: those who have had many years or formal education have the opportunity of getting more knowledge about other countries, cultures, and peoples and being exposed to teaching about tolerance and respect for other people, and of developing cognitive models for analysing and resisting xenophobic and stereotyping propaganda, for not generalising and for independent thinking. High levels of formal education often also lead to less objective economic insecurity and less need to compete with refugees and immigrants about goods and services. This may also lead to more secure control of one's life situation so that one is less amenable to feeling psychologically threatened. On the other hand, tendencies towards opportunist behaviour may also get strengthened in conflict situations—people with high formal education know that tolerance is expected and may conform to the expectations and know how to hide negative stereotypes, also in interview situations that the studies are based on. More complex models, combining several theories, are also being developed and applied (see, e.g., Berry's (1998: 85) figure with four components, describing official multiculturalism in Canada—see also Mackey's and McRae's 1998 articles in the same book, explaining the prerequisites for the Canadian policies).

But if the interpretation of some tolerance towards Others but not (yet?) much active, positive willingness to change oneself is correct, it means that the unwillingness of the Swedes, Finns, Norwegians, Germans, North Americans, and others to change would be an effective hindrance in the integration process of ethnic minorities. Indeed it might be a hindrance for the development of national ethnic minorities. It would be an extremely efficient strategy for a country which does not want to have national ethnic minorities: first the majority society prevents, by its own unwillingness to change, the integration which is a prerequisite for the development of national ethnic minorities. Then it says to the minority (as has happened in Sweden, see Widgren 1986a, b): **you** have not had the will to form national minorities; **you** do not fulfill the criteria. The strategy of blaming the victim is a familiar one from minority education (see references to Cummins in the bibliography).

One prerequisite for making majority populations see the need for change would be a higher degree of metacultural awareness. This might help Swedes and Americans to see some of those racist features in their own culture which now may prevent them from seeing other cultures and languages as equal. In several Western countries even the modest acceptance there has been of minorities' right to maintain their mother tongues is rapidly decreasing (Info Box 3.2 gives some examples). Enhanced metalinguistic awareness might help majority populations to see in their cultures the linguicist features responsible for lack of a willingness to grant others linguistic human rights which they see as good and take for granted for themselves. One of the prerequisites for this kind of willingness is an understanding of the role of language(s) for identity.

3.4. LANGUAGE(S) FOR MULTIPLE IDENTITIES

3.4.1. Mother Tongue as Identity

'Making oneself conscious' of one's life-conditions and contradictions and taking action against the oppressive elements of reality ('conscientization' in Paulo Freire's terms, Freire 1972), is a powerful tool for counter-hegemonies and liberation, and language is central for this. Language is not, and cannot, by definition, be a neutral, 'objective', disencumbered tool.[13] It is always interpretative and subjective, regardless of whether those using it know or admit it or not. It is both a tool for domination and a tool for change and self-determination. Language is creating and willing the world.

Some scholars are critical of approaches which give prominence to language in general, and to the mother tongue in particular, for identity and other psycho-social purposes. Their position can be labelled some kind of **instrumentalism**. For them languages are instruments, tools only, and mother tongues are in no way seen as special—any language can fulfil the same

❖ Info Box 3.2 ❖

Minorities' Right to Maintain Their Mother Tongue

Two recent representative empirical studies, Maria Wingstedt's doctoral dissertation from December 1998 (1998; Sweden) and Magdalena Jaakkola's comparative study (in press; Finland) show some of the latest Scandinavian results. Wingstedt's results can be compared to earlier studies in Sweden, mainly by Charles Westin and Anders Lange (Trankell 1974, Westin 1984, 1988, Lange & Westin 1981, 1991, 1993), and Jaakkola's with her own earlier studies (1989a, 1995). Some Danish (Körmendi 1986; Togeby 1997, also summarising earlier studies, including her own) and Norwegian studies (Puntervold Bø 1984, Hernes & Knudsen 1990, 1994) have also used partially the same questions. Only a couple of results from these very rich materials will be mentioned.

How many Nordic citizens require assimilation from 'foreigners'? 'If "foreigners" plan to stay in Sweden/Finland, they should in their own interest try to become as like Swedes/Finns as possible'. Percentages of full or partial agreement in Sweden were in 1969 74%, 1981 59%, 1987 63%, 1993 67%; in Finland 1987 36%, 1993 35%, 1998 37%.

Do Nordic citizens wish to grant 'foreigners' the right to maintain their mother tongues?

'It is good that "foreigners" who come to Sweden/Finland maintain their languages and cultures and teach them to their children'. Percentages of full or partial agreement in Sweden were in 1969 45%, 1981 53%, 1987 57%, 1993 63%; in Finland 1987 88%, 1993 84%, 1998 85%. In Norway there was full or partial agreement in 1988 by 23% and in 1993 by 16% with the statement 'We must increase the economic support to immigrants so that they can maintain their cultures'.

'Society must organise for those immigrants who want it, an opportunity to maintain their languages and cultural traditions' got in Sweden full or partial agreement as follows: 1969 71%, 1981 69%, 1987 60%, 1993 59%. In Finland the question was 'Finland should organise teaching through the medium of the languages of the "foreigners" if they so wish'. Full or partial agreement was in 1987 67%, 1993 60%, 1998 60%. The Finnish question is obviously much more demanding—the Swedish one can be understood as involving only teaching the mother tongue as a subject.

Wingstedt discusses in an insightful way the ambivalence and contradictions in the attitudes of Swedes (see Info Box 8.8 on some other results from her study). While 71.3% agreed totally or hesitantly with the statement 'It is good if immigrants to Sweden keep their mother tongues and teach them to their children', 41.2% also agree with 'From the very first, immigrant children ought to learn that Swedish should be their mother tongue'. While 68.5% of them agreed to 'Immigrant parents should speak Swedish with their children as much as possible' (1998: 275), at the same time 91.1% agreed that 'Being able to speak two languages is better than being able to speak one' (ibid., 269), and 92.1%, 96.7%, and 90% agreed with, respectively, 'Your mother tongue is the most important language for expressing your feelings', 'Knowing your mother

(Continued)

❖ I n f o   B o x   3 . 2 ❖

(Continued)

tongue well is important for self-esteem and a sense of identity' and 'Knowing your mother tongue well is important for developing your thinking and intelligence' (ibid., 265).

According to a large new study (June-August 1997, reported by Neij 1998) a majority of Swedes think that Sweden has accepted too many immigrants, that this has been a burden, that immigrants are the main cause for criminality, and that many foreigners come to Sweden in order to exploit the social benefits. At the same time, 76% disagree with the statement that immigrants would be the main cause for unemployment, and close to 60% would not mind if their son or daughter marries an immigrant. On the other hand, almost 70% think that immigrants who plan to stay should in their own interest become as much like the Swedes as possible, and almost 60% disagree with the statement that society should create possibilities for immigrants to maintain their language and cultural traditions. The Swedish Minister of Integration, Leif Blomberg, condemns the study and claims that he knows of other studies which show that Swedes are **very** tolerant.

---

functions. Language is socially constructed learned (or acquired) behaviour, possible to manipulate situationally, almost like an overcoat you can take on and off at will, whereas **primordialists** would see the mother tongue more like your skin and later languages like the overcoats. When an ethnic group sees their own language as important, instrumentalists often see this as a result of manipulation by an ethnic elite which wants, for their own benefit, to exploit any traits which can be used to mobilize a group.

Instrumentalists often label primordial arguments as emotional, romantic, and traditional, and pre-rational or irrational (whereas they themselves 'have' the opposite characteristics).

Primordialists often see the mother tongue as something more 'ascribed' than 'acquired'; we get it more or less with our mother's milk, we are born into a language, we do not choose it. Many primordialists support the Whorf-Sapir hypothesis, either in its strong form (our language is our fate; it decides our worldview) or, more commonly, in a weak form: our languages influence initially the way we interpret and create the world. Most language and ethnicity researchers have traits from both primordialism and instrumentalism, but most can be placed closer to one or the other grouping.

An attachment to one's language or mother tongue as a central cultural core value seems to me to draw, like ethnicity, on primordial, ascribed sources: you are 'born' into a specific ethnic group and this decides what your mother tongue(s) will initially be. But what happens later to your ethnicity, and your language(s), and how they are shaped and actualised, is influenced by (achieved/acquired) economic/political concerns (Fishman 1989, Smolicz 1979), by your social circumstances and later life. This also influences to what extent you are aware of the importance of your ethnicity and your mother tongue(s) and the connection between them.

This also means that I do not agree with those researchers who see both ethnicity and a mother tongue from an instrumentalist point of view, as something you can choose (to have or not have, use or not use), according to your own whims and wishes. Because of the primordial sources, reaching back into infancy and personal history, neither ethnicity nor mother tongue(s) can be treated as things, commodities, which you can choose at will and chuck out like an old coat if that is what you want. On the other hand, this does *not* mean that they are unchangeable givens or impossible to influence or change, either.

What is important to study, then, is: under which circumstances can their ethnicity and their language(s) become positive forces and strengths, sources of empowerment in people's lives?

It seems to me that some of the criticism of the **uses** that an attachment to the mother tongue may be put to, **is** valid. This is true especially when language is used to mobilize negative nationalistic sentiments, often on the basis of the nation-state-language nexus. But I am afraid that a lot of the criticism simply misses the point, by not understanding or by doubting the authenticity of the experience of people whose languages are in some way threatened. Labelling those feelings negatively as 'emotional', 'manipulated', and then dismissing them, does not seem to me to enhance our understanding of what moves people to action.

The quotation from Florian Coulmas in Insert 3.7 seems to me to combine the legitimate worries (*italicized*) with this lack of understanding (**bolded**). It should be possible to see the importance of languages/mother tongues, at the same time as criticizing some of the negative uses, i.e. again a 'both-and' rather than an 'either-or' stance.

Another negative 'either-or' stance is the one where learning of L1 and L2 is presented as involving two more or less exclusive alternatives. There are many extreme versions of this (like US English-inspired argumentation— see Crawford 1998 and for counterarguments also his 1997) but also more subtle ones where one would still hope that the researchers concerned might, with more knowledge and understanding, develop their views. Leets & Giles (1995: 47), formulate Garrett, Giles & Coupland's (1989) views as: 'Also one can argue that the processes enabling proficiency in one's own minority language, on the one hand, will be precisely those fostering a low motivation for learning a majority L2 on the other hand'. This seems to imply an acceptance of 'either-or', rather than the 'both-and' that I have experienced with the tens of thousands of minority people I have been in contact with.

Many linguists have analysed language, that is, mother tongue, as the essence of being human/humane, and as a basis for security (see the examples

---

INSERT 3.7   Coulmas: 'either-or' rather than 'both-and'

Florian Coulmas concludes in his article 'European integration and the idea
of the national language. Ideological roots and economic consequences' (1991)
that issues which must be addressed include the following:

> . . . the ideological dead weight of the nineteenth century must be *dropped*,
> that is *linguistic nationalism*. . . . It will fall upon educators and the media
> to see to it that the Europeans once again **conceive of language as a tool**
> **rather than a myth**. . . . necessary to *part with the idea of the identity of*
> *language, nation and state* which has served as the ideological basis of
> relating language with political loyalty . . . *language must be recognized*
> *and reckoned with as an important factor of economy* . . . A realistic and
> just language policy for the EC can be devised **only** on the basis of *an*
> *understanding of language which is more economically determined* and
> **ridded of ideological cobwebs**. (Coulmas 1991: 27–28, emphases added)

Harald Haarman (1991), on the other hand, does not believe that
'educators and the media' can do the job. Old traditions live embedded in
new identities for centuries or even millennia, and educating whole people to
overcome their national language identities is a hopeless task (the ex-Soviet
Union is an example).

In the same book, Peter Nelde (1991) pleads for 'reducing emotionality'
around questions of language and identity. Reducing politically motivated
emotionality which legitimates language loss, yes. But ridiculing and dismissing people's legitimate emotional attachment to their languages, no.

---

in Fishman 1997; Ehlich 1994). Some examples of what people say about
the importance of their mother tongues follow in Inserts 3.8–3.12.

But an understanding (or lack of understanding) of the importance of the
mother tongue(s) for identity development is only one part of an understanding of the connectedness. It is clear that those who are unaware of the
importance of their own language for themselves also have difficulty in accepting that it is important for others. We co-create Self and Others, to be
both Same and Different.

3.4.2. Creation of Self and Other

3.4.2.1. *Complementary, Non-Threatening I*
and Thou, We and You

With the conflict and/or contact theories in mind, we will next see how the
creation of Self needs Other, i.e. prerequisites for the contact being cooperative rather than conflictual. The more socio-economic considerations as

INSERT 3.8 Language and identity: Ojibway (Canada);
Palawa Karni (Tasmania)

Two indigenous people's views on their language dying (Canada) and being reintroduced (Australia): 'Our language is dying, that is the first sign of deterioration. Our native style of life has to be based on four elements—heritage, culture, values, language—and if you take one away it begins to break down. Then we have the symptoms of this breakdown, alcoholism and abuse' (Randy Councillor, Ojibway, director of a detoxification centre in Ontario, Canada, himself an earlier 'street-drunk', in Richardson 1993: 25).

In Tasmania, Australia, a Tasmanian Aboriginal language called Palawa Karni, is being (re)introduced, a composite language based on the scant written evidence of the 6 to 14 Tasmanian languages over 200 years ago. This is how Gaye Brown of the Tasmanian Aboriginal Centre (quoted in Amery 1998: 96) sees the benefits: 'The re-introduction of our language is restoring our peoples' confidence and identity, which is helping to reverse the devastating effects of assimilation. One of the most important things has been the increasing use of the word 'Palawa'. Before the revival of our language we adopted the word Koori or Tasmanian Aboriginal and seldom used our own word to identify who we are. The name Palawa is now used statewide with pride and has made our identity even stronger.'

INSERT 3.9 Linguistic competence most important aspect
of general education—Kerstin Ekman, author

'What is important to maintain in general education?'

What I still feel is the absolutely most important is linguistic competence, to know your own language. To be able to express oneself in a nuanced way about oneself and one's intentions. And that requires of course that one has them in the first place. To be able to describe one's reality. Without a new description of reality there will be no change. But also to be able, via criticism, to adopt those of others. That is the basis for democracy. The efficient education/training has made people very complete, finished. One can quickly acquire a linguistic code, but one never discovers one's own identity, and does not get a feeling for where one stands oneself in relation to the system. Because there is no time for deepening. [Ekman, Kerstin (1995) Skovens skygger spejler betonstaten (Shadows in the wood reflect the cement state). Interview med Kerstin Ekman. **Information**, 29–30 april 1995]

INSERT 3.10 A person forced to leave her language
loses the meaning of her life (Transylvania, Rumania)

'A person forced to leave her language loses the meaning of her life. A people
has a genetic soul. It is best transmitted in their own language', says Andres
Sütö, Hungarian author from Transylvania, Romania.

'Language is the pinnacle of the culture of every nation, and if assimilation
annihilates identity, then the people too will be annihilated' (Bari 1996:
67—Károly Bari is a Roma poet, and what he says cannot be taken to defend
the ordinary language-nation-state nexus.

INSERT 3.11 With God you speak your emotional language

When the Swiss missionaries in the foothills of Zoutspansberg used Sesotho,
'a Gwamba woman . . . complained to Eugénie Berthoud: "I do not know
how to pray! If God were able to understand Shigwamba I would try, for I
cannot speak to him in Sesotho". The missionary's wife, who seemed unaware
of the political implications of this statement, merely encouraged the woman
to improve her Sesotho' (Harries 1995: 157; quoting letters by the Berthouds
from 1875, published in Lausanne in 1900, p. 259). Not much has changed:

What does one need Finnish parish life for? There are local parishes
everywhere in Germany which welcome newcomers.

Language is one of the reasons. Language is a means for communication
and self-expression. The word heard, spoken, sung in the mother tongue.
Words are more than just thoughts. Often they contain feelings, hidden fears,
horrors from the past, insecurities. Words mediate hopes, joy, and bring
security. A human being can learn many languages, but s/he has one mother
tongue.

Faith also has a mother tongue. The Finnish parish in Germany speaks
this language. In this language we have the childhood and all our life
experience. In our language we have the roots to the God of the church of
our mother and father, our sisters and brothers.

It is difficult to learn to speak about the deepest issues of the heart in any
other language except the mother tongue. One can learn the Creed, one can
sing the hymns and even say Our Father, and listening to the Word of the
Bible may succeed in the foreign language.

What you cannot learn in a foreign language is praying. In Praying you
return securely to the paths of the childhood home and you trust your whole
life and future to God. The mother tongue is the language which creates the
contact to God. (Leading article in **Rengas** (The Link) 6–7, 1998, 5; my
translation from German). **Rengas** is the monthly journal of the Finnish church
in Germany.

INSERT 3.12 'Like an oyster gasping for air'—
French journalist forced to use English

The following start of an interview, conducted by the Danish journalist Peter Tygesen, with Serge July, the main editor of the French intellectual paper **Liberation**, for its Danish partner paper **Information** (16–17 May 1998, p. 10) describes how many of us feel when forced to use a language not our own:

> The editor sighs and inhales air. For a sentence, maybe—a thought. But it does not want to come out. He gives the upper part of his body a shake, a quick forward movement with his head, as if he wanted to shake it loose, shake it out of himself, get it to place. But it stays in his prominent frame.

> He opens up his palms like an oyster gasping for air.
> 'But', he finally says, 'I would be able to be more wise in French . . .'

> It is no use, and he knows it well, it has been clear since this interview was agreed upon that we would be speaking English, but he **has** to say it. Establish that the following will be expressed primitively, all too inelegantly, it will be all too little nuanced, all too . . . **tame** for this man whose flaming speeches were heard from the arrow head of the avantgarde in May '68, and whose will has kept the newspaper **Liberation** going. This year they are celebrating 25 years together.

---

prerequisites for conflicts to become less conflictual will be discussed in chapter 6. The philosopher Marcelo Dascal, Dean of Humanities at Tel Aviv University, offers ontological (see Definition Box 3.3) arguments about the desirability of more equal negotiations.

In his list of "arguments in favor of language multiplicity" (1996, 25–38), Dascal presents the following claims:

1. The reality of the individual depends upon social relationships.
2. There is no 'I' without 'Thou'.
3. There is no 'We' without 'You'.
4. The construction of alterity is also the construction of self-identity.

Dascal extends the Jewish philosopher Martin Buber's argument about the non-existence of an 'I' without the 'Thou' (Buber 1958). What according to Buber 'constitutes ultimate reality is not the individual subject alone but rather the **Zwischenmenschlich**, the Inter-human, the 'We', the community formed through the set of 'I'–'Thou' dialogues' (Dascal 1996: 31). As Manuel Gutiérrez Estévez (see 3.4.2.1) formulates it, 'Everyone invents himself [sic!] by inventing, for that purpose, the others'. Dascal then goes on to propose

---

DEFINITION BOX 3.3   Ontological, epistemological

Ontology deals with the nature of being.
Epistemology is the theory of knowledge and deals with the grounds and
   method of knowledge, conditions under which we acquire knowledge
   and under which knowledge grows.

---

that 'the 'We' in fact cannot exist without the 'You' (Plural)—the 'Other'
community of dialogue which faces the 'We'. This 'We' is the real, enhanced
'(we)^2' (Dascal 1996: 33; emphasis added; '(we)^2' = 'we' squared).

Also Dascal thus treats both 'I' and 'We' (individual identities and group
identities) as relations not characteristics, in the same way as in this book.
These relations require the presence of **both** pairs: in order for 'I' really to exist,
not only does 'Thou' have to exist (or be created) but 'I' and 'Thou' must
become 'We'. Likewise, for 'We' really to exist, not only does 'You' (plural)
have to exist (or be created), but 'We' and 'You' must become '(We)^2'.

Dascal sees 'Thou' **not** as **threatening** 'I' but, on the contrary, as **complementing** and to some extent constituting it. He also sees 'You', the other
community, as not (necessarily) opposed to 'We' but complementing (and to
some extent constituting) it (ibid., 33). This is of course also how the heterogenous
integrated community discussed in 3.2.2 above should be understood. And

> [j]ust as each community is formed and enriched by the plurality of intra-com-
> munity I-Thou pairs, so too humankind as a whole results from the exponential
> growth of inter-community dialogical pairs, here represented 'algebraically' by
> the operation of raising to the square power. (ibid., 33)

There are two initial lessons for us to learn here. The I-Thou and We-You
dialogues are necessarily conducted via language(s), for a relationship to
become truly inter-human (Zwischenmenschlich), which again emphasizes
the importance of language. Secondly, losing any of the possible 'You's,
groups with different languages and cultures, would then diminish the possibility of this exponential growth, i.e. it is a powerful argument for the
necessity of linguistic and cultural diversity.

But instead of Dascal's **equal** inter-human negotiations, most minority-
majority negotiations and most negotiations about survival of linguistic diversity, for instance in schools, involve unequal power relationships between
the negotiators. Instead of I and Thou, We and You complementing each
other, an opposition and subsequent hierarchisation is often created between
them.

This is how Manuel Gutiérrez Estévez (1993, quoted in and translated by Dascal, 1996: 54) describes his own experience of creating the Other as enemy:

> The Spaniards carried with them—in their heads and in their ears, in their myths, in their rituals and festivals, in their proverbs and novels—images and evaluations of other neighboring peoples, of the mediterranian region. Among them, a special place was reserved for Moors and Jews. They elaborated pejorative ethnic stereotypes about Moors and Jews, that served to express, through various oppositions and contrasts, the more positive features of their then enhanced national consciousness. These two peoples are the 'others' with respect to which the Spaniards felt and made themselves imaginarily 'ones'. This has been done by ignoring the many aesthetic, moral and ideological traits that they came to share—as a result of the living together and confrontation of Christians, Moors and Jews of Spain. . . . when I was six years old, I already knew that Moors and Jews were my enemies'.

Edward Said's pioneering book **Orientalism** (1978; see also 1981) is a brilliant analysis of how Other is created in literature, history, research.

3.4.2.2. *Oppositional, Hierarchical Self and Other*

In most -ismic discourses, for instance in a racist or sexist or linguicist discourse, a negative image of the Other (consisting of both Thou and You) is created. At the same time, the discourses also construct Self (I and We) as a positive counter-image of the Other, as mirroring the opposite of the negative Other (see e.g., Miles 1989). This positive Self is constructed as the self-evident norm, towards which the Other should strive. As long as Other is 'different', Other is seen as **deficient**, as an undeveloped or underdeveloped (or, as in the assimilation discussion above, un-integrated) Self. If Other wants to develop and get more power and material resources, it must annihilate itself, by either disappearing or by acceding to being completely subsumed by Self, becoming like Self, assimilating into Self. This is also reflected in the language used to describe Other and Self. Earlier we discussed assimilation from a more sociological point of view. Here we will see how language participates in legitimating a psychological assimilation (and this will be followed up in section 3.5 on ethnicity by a more social psychological view).

Before discussing linguicist discourse, I will start with a few examples from **sexist and racist discourses** where males and 'whites' are defined as Self, as the developed, positive, neutral norm, while women and 'blacks' etc., are defined as Other, as the undeveloped, negative, deficient deviant from the norm. There is, of course, a lot of literature about both sexist and racist Self-Other creation, but the point in presenting a very short and simplified summary here has to do with the parallels between the creation of Self-Other in the three -isms: there are clear parallels from the others to how a **language** is defined in a linguicist discourse, as opposed to how a dialect, a vernacular or a patois are defined.

3.4.2.2.1. *Woman and Man, 'Black' and 'White'*

We see the creation and hierarchization of Self and Other in sexism, where women were earlier and are still sometimes seen as undeveloped men (e.g., 'penis envy', or using male behaviour as the norm, in psychological tests, in clothing—women in male business suits, etc.). The linguistic concomitant is seen in male forms in language being used as 'gender-neutral' (as in Rights of Man, you guys, mankind) or as the unmarked form (heir/heiress; doctor/ lady doctor). 'Man' and many other male forms are in dictionary definitions (see Definition Box 3.4 where I have chosen one of the less hierarchical dictionaries) seen as both referring to males and also sometimes subsuming females, while the opposite is almost never the case. 'Man' is said to mean sometimes a male, and sometimes both male and female, whereas 'woman' only means female and never both female and male. Definitions of males are mostly presented as neutral and independent, and most of the connotations are positive, whereas the connotations of many words denoting females are negative and/or present females as dependent, as mostly existing only in relation to others, as somebody's daughters, sisters, wives, lovers, mothers. There are dozens of studies of dictionaries from many countries and languages and from various periods, and all of them show the same pattern, often also the new ones. Women are invisible or negative, both quantitatively and qualitatively. For an alternative, and references, see, e.g. Kramarae & Treichler 1992, Mills 1991 and for old and recent theoretical overviews, e.g. Thorne & Henley (eds) 1975, Thorne, Kramarae & Henley (eds) 1983, Cameron 1995, (ed.) 1993, Coates (ed.) 1998 (there would be literally thousands of references). For more fun, see Heinämäki & Skutnabb-Kangas article 'When this very prestigeous researcher met Mrs Average Housewife, or: where have all the women gone . . .' (1979).

Thus is a hierarchy between female and male created and reproduced.

Invisibilization also functions to exclude, even without using 'he' or 'man'. We also discovered (Rekdal & Skutnabb-Kangas 1977), that in the four big dictionaries (3 Swedish, 1 Finnish), we studied, females got less space than males—except in their reproductive function: 'mother' got more space than 'father' (see Info Box 3.3)

You, female reader, can you identify and do you feel included when the film director Milos Forman (quoted in Barnet & Cavanagh 1994: 37) explains why people around the world buy the American Dream in pop culture: 'Every child dreams to be a prince; every adult has a secret closet dream to be Rambo and kill your enemy'. I must admit that I never dreamt about any of those things as a child, in my closet or outside.

DEFINITION BOX 3.4 'Woman' and 'man' from one dictionary

'WOMAN: . . . sb. . . . woman, WIFE . . . now only in vulgar or dial[ectal] use . . . 1. An adult female human being. b. generically without article: The female human being: the female sex . . . c. pl. in pregnant use with ref. to (irregular) intercourse with women . . . e. With allusion to qualities attributed to the female sex, as mutability, proneness to tears, or physical weakness; also to their position of inferiority or subjection . . . Provbs. A woman, ass, and walnut tree, the more you beat, the better be . . . Three Women make a market . . . Don't make such a fuss; you're as bad as a woman . . .

WOMAN . . . v . . . b. To make like a woman in weakness or subservience' (**The Shorter Oxford English Dictionary** 1967: 2443).

'MAN: . . . I.1. A human being . . . 2. In generic sense, without article: The human creature regarded abstractly; hence, the human race or species, mankind . . . 3. In biblical, etc. use, with *inner, inward, outer, outward*: The spiritual and material parts (respectively) of a human person . . . II.1 An adult male person . . . 3. In pregnant sense: An adult male eminently endowed with manly qualities . . . Manliness, courage . . . 3. A person of position, importance or note . . . 5. A husband . . . now only . . . in *man and wife*.' (ibid., 1196)

The hierarchization might also prevent males in particular from accepting and cherishing the 'female' side in males (because it is seen as negative) and from seeing the characteristics which males and females share. Unnecessary either-or polarities are created.

❖ **I n f o   B o x   3 . 3** ❖

Women Get Less Space in Dictionaries Than Men—Except as Mothers
(Sweden, Finland)

Space in column centimeters given to females and males in four big dictionaries—for details, see Rekdal & Skutnabb-Kangas (1977):

woman 55.3 cm; **man** 124.3 cm;
girl 29.6 cm; **boy** 70.5 cm;
sister 20.2 cm; **brother** 45.2 cm;
but **father** 32.8 cm; **mother** 47.1 cm

We see the same happening in racist discourse, where for instance the words chosen to describe people on the basis of their presumed skin colour are more ideological than 'realistic'. I have extremely seldom seen a 'black' person, and my own skin colour is certainly not 'white'. The connotations of and synonyms for black are all negative, whereas most of the connotations of 'white' are positive (Definition Box 3.5).

It is probably unnecessary to add a Task Box asking the reader to choose which characteristics she would rather have. Even when many of the meanings are historically explicable, connotations die hard (see Insert 3.13).

Thus, again, a hierarchy between 'white' and 'black' is created.

If, instead of these ideological terms, more realistic labels were used, the connotations would be very different. We so-called whites have often pink or yellowy or greyish or light brown hues in our faces and bodies. What about 'pig-pink' (provided we talk about 'European' domesticated pink pigs rather than the more naturally dark ones . . .)? That might, especially for Muslims or others for whom pigs are unclean animals, create an image which

---

DEFINITION BOX 3.5 'Black' and 'white' from two dictionaries

BLACK: 'lacking hue and brightness, soiled or stained with dirt, gloomy, pessimistic, dismal, deliberately harmful, inexcusable, boding ill, sullen or hostile, threatening, without any moral quality or goodness, evil, wicked, disgrace, grotesque, morbid, unpleasant, undesirable, substandard, potentially dangerous, illegal or underground, deliberately false or intentionally misleading', all these just picked out from one modern dictionary, **The Random House Dictionary of the English Language**, 1987, pp. 215–216. The **Shorter Oxford English Dictionary** 1967: 184, adds the following to the list: dirty, having dark purposes, malignant, deadly, baneful, disastrous, sinister, foul, iniquitous, atrocious, sad, clouded with anger, boding ill, indicating disgrace, censure, etc..

WHITE: 'of the color of pure snow, decent, honorable, dependable, auspicious or fortunate, morally pure, innocent, without malice, harmless' (**Random House** 1987: 2167). The **Shorter Oxford English Dictionary** 1967: 2420, adds the following: of the colour of snow or milk, of a light or pale colour: applied to things of various indefinite hues approaching white, esp. dull or pale shades of yellow, colourless, uncoloured as glass, fair, morally or spiritually pure or stainless, spotless, free from malignity or evil intent, innocent & harmless, esp. as opp. to something characterized as *black*, propitious, auspicious, happy, highly prized, precious, dear, beloved.

INSERT 3.13   Impact of negative labelling, USA

'I don't think anybody really fully understands how negative the influence of slavery on black people was. Our long struggle for equity and social and cultural esteem has time after time been restrained by the inbuilt racism in American society and in the political system. Just take a look at Webster's dictionary or the bible. Everything black is defined as something negative. The black sheep and the black lie. The other way round for white. Come to Jesus whose blood will wash you as pure as a white stone.' (Lawrence Edward Carter, Morehouse College, Atlanta, professor of philosophy and leader of the international chapel for Martin Luther King, in an interview, 'Slaveriet sætter stadig spor' (Slavery still leaves traces), with Danish journalist Martin Burcharth, **Information**, 27–28 June 1998, p. 10). See also C. Eric Lincoln (1961, 1967)—he was the first Black person to really start teaching me, in 1967, about being Black, offering books, reading lists, discussions—thanks, Eric!).

---

might, in terms of connotations, approach the image we have created for 'black'.[14] Linguistic labels thus participate in creating the images of Self and the Other, positing Self as the positive norm and Other as a negative counterpart, hierarchizing Self and Other, and polarizing the relationship towards either-or.

A similar process can be seen in the definitions of **language, dialect, vernacular**, and **patois**. These definitions participate, through their connotations, in creating the opposition between Self, Us (speakers of a language; therefore worth a nation-state of our own as we shall see) and Other, Them (speakers of a dialect/vernacular/patois; therefore to be subsumed under a nation-state) and in hierarchizing them. We, Self, speak languages, They, Other, speak only dialects, vernaculars or patois. Therefore, We have nations, the Other has tribes. We have the right to self-determination, they, the dialect-speaking tribes, don't.

3.4.2.2.2. *Language or Dialect/Patois/Vernacular?*

As we saw in chapter 1, it is not possible to differentiate between languages on the one hand and dialects/vernaculars/patois on the other hand in this hierarchical way on the basis of linguistic criteria, since the main criterion for whether something is a dialect of another language or a separate language is the relative political power of the speakers of that language/dialect. Therefore, it is important to see how those with more political and/or economic power **create** this hierarchical difference in discourse (see also Kramarae et al. (eds.) 1984, O'Barr 1982, Tollefson 1991, 1993, (ed.) 1995). How is the opposition and the hierarchization of Us (speakers of a language) versus Them (speakers of a dialect/vernacular/patois) created? What are the connotations of 'language' as opposed to those of 'dialect/vernacular/patois'. And does it matter, if something is being called 'dialect' or 'patois' or 'vernacular', instead of being called a 'language'? Let's again look at dictionary definitions from one contemporary dictionary (Definition Box 3.6).

Even if the hierarchisation here is much more subtle, we see the same process as earlier with sexism and racism happening in how a **language** is defined, as opposed to how a **dialect**, a **vernacular**, or a **patois** are defined (and, implicitly, how **minority language speakers**—or speakers of indigenous languages—are labelled, as opposed to **dominant language speakers**.

'Languages' are defined positively or neutrally, as the general, abstract, self-evident, and unmarked norm, whereas dialects, vernaculars, and patois are defined partly negatively, with connotations of some kind of deficiency, commonness, lack of cultivation and civilisation, partly as undeveloped or underdeveloped forms of communication, something to be got rid of, to be subsumed under languages, in the same way as female forms or women are (supposed to be) subsumed under male forms or men.

Just as the underdeveloped Other has tribes, we the developed Self have nations. Other has chiefs, Self has presidents or kings. Other has primitive rituals, Self has civilized ceremonies. Other has medicine men (or sometimes even women), Self has doctors. And so we could go on. Try yourself (Reader Task 3.2).

Reader Task 3.2
Observe how Self and Other are labelled; change labels!

Observe how Self and Other are labelled. Write down all examples you find during a specified time. Compare with others. Analyse the connotations. Find alternatives and discuss those strategies which might make others aware of the power of the images that labels create. Try out alternatives and write down people's reactions. Compare, discuss, revise strategies.

When Others comes to our country, Others' children become, in the USA, NEP- or LEP-children (No English Proficiency or Limited English Proficiency—see Wink 1994 for criticism) or, in Australia, LOTEs (Languages Other Than English) or NESBs (Non-English Speaking Background) or, in Denmark, 'fremmedsprogede børn' (foreign-speaking children; see Inserts 3.14 and 3.15).

DEFINITION BOX 3.6 Language, dialect, vernacular, patois, from one dictionary

'LANGUAGE 1. a body of words and the systems for their use common to a people who are of the same community or nation, the same geographical area or the same cultural tradition . . . 3. the system of linguistic signs or symbols considered in the abstract (as opposed to **speech**). 4. any set or system of such symbols as used in a more or less uniform fashion by a number of people, who are thus enabled to communicate intelligibly with one another. . . . 13. a nation or people considered in terms of their speech . . .

LANGUAGE, DIALECT, JARGON, VERNACULAR refer to patterns of vocabulary, syntax, and usage characteristic of communities of various sizes and types. LANGUAGE is applied to the general pattern of a people or race: **the English language**. DIALECT is applied to certain forms or varieties of a language, often those that provincial communities or special groups retain (or develop) even after a standard has been established (**Scottish dialects**) . . . A VERNACULAR is the authentic natural pattern of speech, now usually on the informal level, used by persons indigenous to a certain community, large or small.' (**Random House** 1987: 1081)

'DIALECT 1. **Ling**[uistically] a variety of a language that is distinguished from other varieties of the same language by features of phonology, grammar, and vocabulary, and by its use by a group of speakers who are set off from others geographically or socially. 2. a provincial, rural, or socially distinct variety of a language that differs from the standard language, esp. when considered as substandard . . . 4. a language considered as one of a group that have a common ancestor: **Persian, Latin, and English are Indo-European dialects** . . . Syn[onyms] 2. idiom, patois.' (Random House 1987: 546–547)

'PATOIS . . . 1. a regional form of a language, esp. of French differing from the standard, literary form of the language. 2. A rural, provincial form of speech . . . F[rench] lit. clumsy speech; akin to OF **patoier** to handle clumsily, deriv. of **pate** paw.' (Random House 1987: 1421).

'VERNACULAR . . . 1. (of language) native or indigenous (opposed to **literary** or **learned**). 2. expressed or written in the native language of a place, as literary works: **a vernacular poem**. 3. using such a language: **a vernacular speaker** . . . 5. using plain, everyday, ordinary language . . . 9. the native speech or language of a place . . . 12. the plain variety of language in everyday use by ordinary people. . . . 15. any medium or mode of expression that reflects popular taste or indigenous styles . . . L[atin] **vernacul(us)** household, domestic, native (appar. adj. use of **vernaculus**, dim[inutive] of **verna** slave born in the master's household . . .'
(**The Random House Dictionary of the English Language**, Second Edition, Unabridged, 1987, New York: Random House, pp. 546–547, 1081, 1421, 2114).

INSERT 3.14 Connotations of NEP and LEP

I asked a large group of teacher trainers in California at a course to write down the first thing they thought of when hearing NEP and LEP. This is the collective list: unable, remedial, single parent, deficient, handicapped, copying, cheating (cooperating!), Gate Program, Gifted & talented, immigrant, illegal, potentially English proficient, non-standard, sub-standard, not standard-English proficient, failed the English test, limited, LEP = leprosy, lesser, minority-speaking, non-English-speaker, non-traditional, non-white, poor, second language, sheltered, short(er) attention span, **THOSE** kids, unschooled, alingual, they have no language, alien, Asia Minor, culturally deprived, educationally disadvantaged, dysfunctional, disabled, at risk, below grade level, Chapter 1, culturally disadvantaged, ESL, illiterate, flatlands, have less, ignorant, ignorance, language minority = minor language.

Mühlhäusler (1996: 345) finds it interesting that LOTA (Languages Other Than Aboriginal) is not used—LOTE signals what is unmarked and thus 'normal'.

INSERT 3.15 'I don't speak "foreign", I speak my own language!'

When my (British) husband's children were small, we received the standard letter, sent to parents of minority students in Denmark, presenting the possibility of a few hours of mother tongue teaching per week (in this case 2 hours of English in another local authority, 2 hours' transport each way). The letter was in English, and very literally translated from Danish. It started: 'Dear Parent. You are the parent of a foreign-speaking child . . .' Caspar, then 12, reacted: 'What do they mean, "foreign-speaking"? I don't speak "foreign", I speak my own language!'. The same letter, sent to many Muslim and other parents also asked the parents to provide the child's Christian name.

Children of Others are defined with Self (= dominant language speakers) as the norm, negatively, in terms of what they are not, do not know or do not represent, often as possessing a deficiency, whereas Self is taken as the self-evident norm. What Others **are**, **know**, and **represent**, is made invisible, negated, or reconstructed as a non-resource, a handicap, stigmatised as of less value. We, Self, speak languages, they, Other, speak only dialects, vernaculars or patois.

Is it, though, necessarily the case that all these labels **are** negative? The question is enormously complex as we can see from the following extract— regardless of whether the original connotation of 'vernacular' to 'slave' holds, the present connotations can be stigmatising. This is how the Indian scholar

Nambi Arooran (Professor and Head of the Department of History, Institute of Correspondence Course, Madurai Kamaraj University) discusses the matter (1980), basing himself on his PhD from the School of Oriental and African Studies, University of London, 1976:

In this context it may be pointed out that since the establishment of the British rule in India, in administration as well as in academic usage the term 'vernacular' was generally assigned to all Indian languages with the exception of Sanskrit which was ranked 'classical'. In all academic discussions and classifications of the Madras University syllabuses Tamil was considered a vernacular and this was resented by Tamil scholars and non-Brahmin politicians. The fact that Tamil was a classical language was not recognized until the middle of the 20th century (p. 108)[15] . . .

In the wake of the renaissance of Tamil it was a member from Tamilnad, S. Satyamurti, who raised the objection to the categorization of Indian languages as 'vernacular' in official terminology. During the debate in the Legislative Assembly, Delhi, in September 1936, Satyamurti said that the noun 'vernacular' meant 'tongue of a slave' and he suggested that he had dictionary authority for this meaning. He pleaded for the dropping of the usage of the term 'vernacular'. (note 37: **Madras Mail**, 29 Sep. 1936). Referring to the views expressed by Satyamurti, the **Madras Mail** in an editorial entitled 'Vernacular' said that in Latin 'verna' meant a slave born in his master's house and that emphasis in philological descent had been laid on the place of birth without paying attention to the question of bond or free. The **Mail** further added that Satyamurti was sentimentally extravagant when he suggested that the word was "flavoured with contempt and should be abandoned in favour of a circumlocution". (note 38: Ibid.).

Discussing the etymology of the word 'vernacular', an article appeared in the **Madras Mail**, in which the author observed that "one of the common outcrops of nascent nationalism is (was) the development of a touchiness towards anything even remotely suggestive of offence to its dignity". (note 39: Ibid., 6 Aug. 1938). The author pointed out that the meaning of 'vernacular' had always been used as a synonym for "one's own", "domestic", "homely", **swadeshi**, etc., and that it came from the Latin word **verna** whose etymology was **verna**—root, **vas**—to dwell: Sanskrit **vastu**—house. Further the author said that the word **verna** was specifically appropriated to mean "a homeborn slave", though the adjective "vernacular" always meant "one's own" and that to extend it to mean "a slave's language" or even to "belonging to a slave" would be gratuitous. However, complying to the request made by Satyamurti to drop the usage of the word 'vernacular', the Government of India decided in February 1939 to drop the term in future official publications and correspondence. (note 40: **Hindu**, 5 Feb. 1939. **Madras Mail**, 5 Feb. 1939)

The resentment expressed over the usage of the term 'vernacular' and its eventual dropping by the Government was an indication of the revival of the native languages of India and of the concern shown for a respectable status for Indian languages in official terminology. Such being the resentment over the supposed contemptuous categorisation of Indian languages with the exception of Sanskrit, the resentment among the proponents of Tamil was understandable in view of its classical nature which was not given due recognition during the period under survey (ibid., 109–110).

There are several ways of using the hierarchies created to legitimate linguistic oppression, and we will mention some. For some varieties which are called vernaculars or patois, a corresponding 'higher' variety is thought to exist, and this high variety is then called The Language. For instance, peasants in Bretagne or Normandie in France have been said to speak a French patois whereas professors in Paris speak the French language.

For some vernaculars there is no 'high' variety. This mostly means that the language has not been reduced to writing (see Mühlhäusler 1990 on some of the negative consequences of doing this) or at least not standardized. Mühlhäusler 1996 gives a number of examples of consequences of both, theorizing literacies in terms of linguistic ecology.

The group with enough political power can tell another group: 'What **we** speak is a language, but what **you** speak is only a dialect of our language. Our language is fully developed, modern, rich, logical. But your dialect is primitive, underdeveloped, traditional, with poor vocabulary, emotional, irrational, not fit for education or administration, literature, thinking, or civilization' (for examples, see Phillipson 1992 and Skutnabb-Kangas & Phillipson 1986b, 1989a). This is what the Turks tell the Kurds: Kurdish is an underdeveloped dialect of Turkish. The Kurds were for a long time called mountain Turks by representatives of the Turkish state, and the language they spoke was labelled a distorted dialect of Turkish which had been developing in isolation in the mountains and therefore had some special features not found in proper uncontaminated Turkish (see e.g., Clason & Baksi 1979). Kurdish of course is completely unrelated to Turkish, just as Polish is to Japanese (see Insert 1.1). Here a We **is** created but then hierarchized: we are the same, but **you are a deficient We** and therefore not fit to determine your fate.

The same story can be told about sign languages, and Harlan Lane has told it about France and the United States. In his view,

> Speakers of dominant languages have two ways of attempting to annihilate a nondominant language: replacing it outright or **dialectizing it**. In the latter case, they lead the users of the nondominant language to believe that theirs is a substandard dialect of the dominant language, a "vernacular" that should not be employed for serious purposes such as education and government (Lane 1980: 119; emphasis added).

Lane further notes that 'it has generally been thought that the nondominant language could be dialectized only if it was related to the dominant language' (ibid.), and quotes Heinz Kloss' example comparing Basque and Catalan, where the Spanish governments' attempts to dialectize them did not meet any success with the Basques, 'for there is no possibility that the Basques will ever lose consciousness of the fact that their language is unrelated to Spanish' (Kloss 1967: 46), whereas some Catalan speakers might have been induced into believing that their mother tongue was 'a patois, with Castilian as its natural standard language' (ibid.), because of the close relationship between Spanish and Catalan. Kloss then goes on to discuss other 'spiritually subjugated' speakers (Low German, Occitan/Provençal, Sardinian, Haitian Creole), but clearly sees this as possible only in the case of related languages. Our Kurdish example above shows that this has not necessarily deterred governments from trying. Harlan Lane says that it at first 'might seem improbable that people whose native language is American Sign Language (ASL) could be induced to consider their mother tongue as a patois with the majority oral language, English, as their natural standard language', and the same holds true for French Sign Languages and French. 'Nevertheless, the oral majority in each nation has, from time to time, waged such a campaign of dialectization, using educational institutions for deaf children as the vehicle for indoctrination' (Lane 1980: 120).

Many of the claims about different Englishes (Nigerian, Indian, Black) belong to the same type. Both the We-ness and especially the hierarchization have only fairly recently started to be questioned (e.g., Kachru 1986— see also other references to Kachru in the bibliography; Rickford & Rickford 1995—see also John Rickford's homepage <http://www.stanford.edu/~rickford/>).

In the examples above, the group in power claims that the 'dialect' is **a dialect, vernacular, or patois of their (i.e., the powerful group's) language**.

The group in power can also tell the subordinated group that its language is **just a dialect, vernacular, or patois where no proper corresponding (high) language has been developed at all** (i.e., it is not claimed to be a dialect of **their**, the dominant group's, language). This second type of claim is still being used in relation to thousands of the world's languages which are small in numbers. Robert Dixon (1993) comments that Aboriginal languages were referred to as 'dialects' by a Prime Minister of Australia as recently as 1972. Professor Doyce B. Nunis Jr. says in an interview, defending the genocidal Franciscan misssions in California, that 'the Indians all spoke different dialects. It was a big problem here in California for the missionary fathers' (Nunis 1987: 219).

The group with enough political power can also tell another group the exact opposite: 'What we speak is just in some ways similar to your language, but it is a language of its own. These are two completely separate languages.' Here the dominated group's mode of communication is NOT subsumed under the powerful group's language and any close relationship between the two is rejected.

Here a possible or earlier We is separated into two or more entities, and the existence of two separate entities (two nations, each with a language of their own) is then often used as a legitimation of secession and, often, hierarchization. This is what has happened with Serbo-Croat in the 1990s, as mentioned earlier.

The labelling can also be done at least partially by outsiders who make no claims about how the variant relates to their own language, but who instead claim a status for it in relation to some other language. The way Karelian has been labelled, sometimes as a language (even with official status in the Soviet autonomous republic of East Karelia in 1937–1939, but written in the Cyrillic rather than Roman alphabet), sometimes a dialect or vernacular (with no status at all in the Karelo-Finnish Soviet Socialist Republic, i.e., a union republic, from 1940), has completely followed political developments, rather than any changes in sociolinguistic attitudes to Karelian (McRae 1997: 123[16]).

Labels used thus reflect the power to define oneself, to use endo-definitions, or lack of power to define oneself, having to accept exo-definitions, somebody else's definitions of oneself. In a situation where speakers of maximally 5 percent (probably *much* less) of the worlds languages live in states where their languages are official languages and where they have the power to define themselves (to use their own endo-definitions of themselves) speakers of the majority of the world's languages have to accept an exo-definition. Demanding the right to define oneself and to have this definition accepted and respected by others is one form of self-determination.

When the American teacher and his senior high school students (see Insert 1.6) thought that there were only 300 languages in the world, one can guess that they did not have enough knowledge to counteract the invisibilization of languages. Languages are obviously made invisible if one calls them dialects (and this was what they also did, talking about 'all those dialects in Africa'). This lack of knowledge also makes it difficult for them to counteract, for instance, U.S. English arguments about multilingualism leading to disintegration and conflict (see 6.2.2 on language and 'ethnic' conflict).

Labels are a matter of negotiation. Dominant groups keep a monopoly of defining Others, and it is their labels we see in dictionaries.[17] The 'neutrality' of dictionaries is simply assumed by most people. The social hierarchization process that led to the creation of dictionaries and that maintains the monopoly is largely unanalysed (but see Graddol, Leith & Swann (eds) 1996: 91–94). As long as this is the case, the decolonisation of the mind, needed for real economic, political, cultural, and linguistic decolonisation, is difficult to achieve. Names used about individuals, groups and countries are deeply symbolic, at several levels. In the next section we will look more closely at the relationship between identity and the right to name oneself.

3.4.3. Identities and the Right to Name Oneself

We have an **individual identity** where we recognize ourselves, despite both physical and psychological changes over time. Our identities, our ties with ourselves and others, can be seen as both horizontal (contemporary) and vertical (chronological). They are **horizontal** with others who share the 'same' characteristics and relations (with the We), for instance speaking the same idiom. Our identities are also **vertical**: with ourselves earlier and in the future and with preceding and following generations and often places. Our identities are never static—they are always **changing**.

Likewise, we have a **group identity, a social identity** with a collectivity (or, rather, many collectivities), which also changes, in terms of both which groups we at any time identify with, and how those groups see themselves during various times. The content of our ethnic group's cultural identity, for instance, may have few traces left of what it was 200—or even 50—years ago; what is there is a continuous construction and reconstruction of the **boundaries** that make us feel different from others (see Barth 1969, Berger & Luckmann 1966). Thus neither identities nor cultures can or should be reified (Latin 'res', genitive 'rei', thing). But despite the constant changes, we recognise our earlier selves through the ties, and we experience 'sameness' at the same time with change. This is as much true at the individual as the social identity levels: just as we 'know' that we are at some level 'the same individual' now as we were 50 years ago, and can recognise ourselves, despite the fact that most of our cells have changed (i.e., the biological 'content' of 'me' is not the same), we also 'know' that our ethnic group is X, despite the fact that the content of Xness may bear little resemblance to what we read about our group historically. These ties, binding us together with our earlier identities, are to a large extent maintained through language: information, negotiation, reconstruction.

Our identities are also **multiple**. We may identify at the same time as, say, woman, socialist, ecological farmer, world citizen, mother, daughter, wife, sister, researcher, Finnish, Scandinavian, witch, theosopher, lover of nature and music, and so on. We are at the same time members of a gender group, a generation, an ethnos, a demos, a professional group, a religious (or secular/secularized) group, a geographical area: local, regional, national, up to global, a political group and so on. We can also be members of **two** or even more of some of them at the same time (e.g., **two** language groups or two ethnoses). Many of these multiple identities coexist harmoniously, without necessarily being in conflict with each other (Éva Molnár (1994) gives beautiful examples in her article titled 'You Are a Slovak!—My Mother Said to Me in Hungarian'). Some of them we are not usually aware of. Some identities are more, or less, salient, focussed, and emphasized than others, at different times, and new identities emerge/are added, and some fade or are rejected. Some become focussed, if we gain benefits or are being discriminated against because of them, and we may then become aware of potential conflicts between some aspects of our multiple identities. As a result, we may try to exaggerate some, or to get rid of some of the identities, for instance by denying them, or through assimilation, or we may try to change the negative value placed on them, by redefining them in a positive way (e.g., 'Black is beautiful') and struggling to get this endo-definition accepted by others.

Still, ethnic identities and, especially, **linguistically anchored ethnic identities**, seem to be remarkably resilient. The historian of Rumanian literature, Calinescu, wrote in 1941 in the final chapter of his **History of Roumanian literature from its origin to its present** that ethnicity is 'a hereditary framework that one can neither obtain, nor discard at will' (quoted in Cristea 1996: 155). Ethnicity is not dead at all, quite the opposite. Many of the characteristic features are there whether the label 'ethnicity' is used or not.

Our name, both the individual one and our group's name, symbolizes our self-recognition and self-identification; it is our verbally manifested endo-definition. We will discuss both below. Change of name also means a partially new identity.

If the change is voluntary, as when somebody wants to create or assume a new identity, this may be liberating. Or it may by many be seen as 'the normal thing to do', for instance in societies where the woman takes the husband's name at marriage. On the other hand, if the change of name is enforced, this symbolizes lack of power for self-definition, an endo-definition: the person has to accept an exo-definition because of lack of power. This is often true in relation to women when they have to accept the father's or the husband's name (see Info Box 3.4). It has been and is still often true in relation to indigenous peoples, who have been forced to have the colonisers' names (Insert 3.16 gives some examples). It can also be a question of non-acceptance by a state of the name which the parents want to give to a child (see Insert 3.17 and Skutnabb-Kangas and Bucak 1994, note 2 and Jernudd 1994).

This lack of power is still also often true in relation to immigrants or people wanting to change their citizenship (an example: when applying for USA citizenship, Professor Alma Flor Ada, San Francisco, experienced a lot of pressure from the interviewer, repeated several times, to change her 'un-American' name; personal communication, February 1993).

It is not only speakers of 'small' minority languages who feel invaded and cannot name themselves, as the extract from a letter from Hugo Baetens Beardsmore shows. What is ironical here too is that since the letter was sent

❖ I n f o   B o x   3 . 4 ❖

Married Woman—From Husband's Material Property
to His Symbolic Property (Finland)

The ownership issue was symbolically reflected in a Finnish law in 1929 abolishing male guardianship but imposing change of name. Finnish women had comparatively early a similar legal status to men (we were, for instance, the first women in Europe and third in the world to get the vote, in 1906). But the price married women had to pay, when they gained independent economic status and were no longer under the guardianship of their husbands, was that they had to take their husband's family name on marriage (Kangas 1997: 28). From being the husband's material property until 1929, they became his symbolic property.

INSERT 3.16   Enforced change of names

Most of my Sámi friends have the **coloniser's** Norwegian, Swedish, or Finnish last or even first names: Harald Gaski, Britt Rajala, Ole-Henrik Magga, Pekka Aikio, Liv Østmo, Steinar Pedersen, etc. Most Roma in Finland have Finnish or Swedish names or a combination: Miranda Vuolasranta, Tuula Åkerlund. Many completely Finnish families still have Swedish or Latin names, given to them when the first male was enrolled in the army of the Swedish colonisers, or when the first male went to school. Having the coloniser's name is a common practice also in Africa, even today (think of names like **Desmond** Tutu, **Nelson** Mandela, **Albert** Luthuli). Or the missionaries' name—there are several Finnish names in Namibia (e.g., 'Toivo ja Toivo' ('toivo' in Finnish means 'hope').

Descendants of slaves all over the Americas still have the names of their former 'masters' (see Joel Spring's beautiful discussion with Ronald Roberts in Spring 1998: 1–5). Indigenous peoples in today's USA and Canada are comparable—many who were forced to live on missions lived in slavelike conditions ('For the slightest things they receive heavy floggins, are shackled, and put in the stocks, and treated with so much cruelty that they are kept whole days without a drink of water'—written by one of the Franciscans themselves, Padre Antonio de la Conception Horra in 1799, according to historian H. H. Bancroft, quoted in Castillo 1987: 69), or were indentured or sold (e.g., some 10,000 in California between 1850 and 1863, Norton 1987). Evidence for 'the forced substitution of foreign Spanish names for the native Indian names . . . is to be found in the mission registers' (Costo & Costo 1987: 132; see also Amago 1987). Many immigrant minority children and adults or even national minority children are told to change their names because dominant group representatives cannot remember or pronounce it. (During all my school years—in Finnish-medium schools—I had to write

(Continued)

157

my—Swedish—name on the blackboard every time we got a new teacher; it was 'impossible' for them to even 'hear' it, let alone spell it themselves). Many Māori or Australian or North American indigenous peoples have the intruders' names. See also Insert 5.31, German teachers never learning to pronounce Turkish names correctly.

'If you want to become an officer, you cannot have the name you have now', an officer said to Inga Hubinette's classmate whose name was Uusitalo (a Finnish name which means 'new farm' or 'new house'). 'His brothers changed their name to Nygård (Swedish for 'new farm/house'), but he did not do so. But became an officer anyway.' (Inga Hubinette, a Finnish-speaker from Tornedalen in Sweden, now a teacher in her sixties, told this to me in a workshop in March 1992).

Diglossic[18] naming is common: one official, one at home (Mikkel in passport may be Miihkal at home). Some indigenous peoples now use a **double name**: Sakej James Youngblood Henderson, Eve Mumewa Fesl (compare her 1988 and 1993 in the bibliography!). Some **change back**, or **start using their own original name**: James Ngugi became Ngũgĩ wa Thiong'o (see bibliography). My book **Bilingualism or not** (1984) has many examples.

Enforced change of names is often analysed by the victims as part of and often the final step in complete degradation, as the two Chumash men, Tony and Pete Savala (1987: 145) tell in their interview 'Mission Slavery', where one first tells about his great-uncle's childhood: 'In the missions, it was forbidden to speak Chumash, so even after the missions, this stayed with the people'. The result:

> There are only 200 of us left now, and there were more than 20,000, according to what they have found out. So that is what the Spaniards did to us. They took our culture away, we lost our culture through the Spaniards; we lost our self-esteem . . . And we were one of the largest tribes in the United States at one time, bigger than all of them at that time. Now we have only a little reservation, where we had thousands of miles before the Spanish came and took away our land, our culture, our language **and even our names**. (emphasis added)

This is how the person now called Eva Hoffman describes the name change. She is 13, her sister is 9, and they have just arrived from Cracow to Canada in 1959:

> All it takes is a brief conference between Mr. Rosenberg and the teacher, a kindly looking woman who tries to give us reassuring glances, but who has seen too many people come and go to get sentimental about a name. Mine—'Ewa'—is easy to change into its near equivalent in English, 'Eva'. My sister's name—'Alina'—poses more of a problem, but after a moment's thought, Mr. Rosenberg and the teacher decide that 'Elaine'

(Continued)

is close enough. My sister and I hang our heads wordlessly under this careless baptism. The teacher then introduces us to the class, mispronouncing our last name—'Wydra'—in a way we've never heard before We make our way to a bench at the back of the room; nothing much has happened, except a small, seismic mental shift. The twist in our names takes them a tiny distance from us—but it's a gap into which the infinite hobgoblin of abstraction enters. **Our Polish names didn't refer to us; they were as surely us as our eyes or hands.** These new appellations, which we ourselves can't yet pronounce, are not us. They are identification tags, disembodied signs pointing to objects that happen to be my sister and myself. We walk to our seats, into a roomful of unknown faces, with **names that make us strangers to ourselves.** (1997: 105; emphases added)

And much later, in adulthood:

The tiny gap that opened when my sister and I were given new names can never be fully closed up; I can't have one name again. My sister has returned to her Polish name—Alina. It takes a while for me to switch back to it; Alina, in English, is a different word than it is in Polish: it has the stamp of the unusual, its syllables don't fall as easily on an English speaker's tongue. In order to transport a single word without distortion, one would have to transport the entire language around it. My sister no longer has one, authentic name, the name that is inseparable from her single essence. (ibid., 272)

Luitxo Fernandez from the Basque Country (Spain) has a large data collection of examples on minority place names at <http://www.geocities.com/Athens/9479/>. Stephan A. Grosse, email <solano@compuserve.com> is doing a study on naming and labels.

INSERT 3.17 Turkish state does not accept Kurdish name

Serhat and Gulda are Kurds from the Turkish part of Kurdistan who live in Denmark. They have just had their first child, Mizgin (which means 'good tidings') and want to visit Turkey to show the grandchild to their parents. They need Mizgin's name to be added to their passports. The Turkish Embassy refuses to record the Kurdish name. Mizgin is over 3 years old before the Embassy agrees to do this, as a result of pressure from the Danish Helsinki Committee—and the grandparents have missed the first three years of the grandson's life, because Kurdish names are not allowed in Turkey. (from Phillipson et al. 1994: 18)

on email, what I saw on my screen for one of the important points was this: 'Belgique/Belgi=EB'. As many of us know, 'mainstream' computers speak English too. You, reader, what does '=EB' stand for?

> I very much share your preoccupations with the invasion of English, which may sound the death-knell of many not so small languages. The French, who are often sneered at for their so called "hysterical" reaction towards English were the first to feel the threat, but if only they could understand that French too is now being regarded as a minority language and that it would be in their interest to bundle their efforts with the so-called lesser used languages it might advance the cause of their own. The problem in Western Europe is the same as in India, i.e., one can't blame the Anglo-Saxons so much as ourselves for allowing the insidious and creeping anglicisation to infiltrate our daily lives. I have irrational (or not so) reactions when I now see that in Belgium itself most people now use the English name "Belgium" rather than Belgique/Belgi=EB in their advertising of their own address, that I can no longer find a post card of Brussels with the name Brussel/Bruxelles on it, but only Brussels, and that the homogenisation of the tourist market is helping to destroy the reason for travelling to different countries, by getting a feel of a different language and culture. When do we send up our own WWF before it's too late. I mainly fight back by irritating personal campaigns, as when people write to me in 'Brussels', to which I reply by using things like "Londen/Londres", as more and more people address me as Beardsmore, and ever fewer abbreviate to Baetens (even my own students, something which never happened a few years ago), and so on and so on. (personal communication, 8 March 1995)

All of this is also true in relation to our status as a member of a group, where the name used by ourselves about our group or our language may differ from how others name us. If others call us Lapps or Eskimo or mountain Turks or tribes or populations, whereas we ourselves call ourselves Sápmi or Inuit or Kurds or nations or peoples, respectively, our identity has to be negotiated with significant or powerful others. Or if the UN calls us a 'population' or 'a group' or if researchers and others call us a 'minority' (neither has the right to self-determination according to international law) whereas we call ourselves 'a people' (with the right to self-determination) this may in the long run be decisive for our existence as a separate entity (see Definition Boxes 7.1 to 7.2 and 7.3 about legal definitions of 'indigenous peoples' and 'minorities', respectively).

Often an individual or a group has been forced, by punitive, remunerative, or ideological means (see Table 4.2), to internalize other more powerful groups' exo-definitions of who this individual or group is, for instance that it is a tribe speaking a dialect, instead of a nation or a people speaking a language.

Or that the individual is not part of her own group. Indigenous individuals in Canada could be declared 'white' in the middle of last century (Info Box 3.5).

<hr>

❖ **I n f o   B o x   3 . 5** ❖

Exo-Definitions Making 'Indians' (Canada) or
Japanese and Chinese (South Africa) 'Honorary Whites', or
Khoe and San 'Coloured' (South Africa)

In 1857 'An Act for the Gradual Civilization of the Indian Tribes of the Canadas' was passed. Its object was to remove all legal distinctions between Indians and other Canadians (Richardson 1993: 61), but it did not do this by giving indigenous peoples the same rights that other Canadians had (which would, of course, have included linguistic and cultural rights). On the contrary, it set out to assimilate the indigenous peoples. The law spelled out in detail how aboriginal people could 'be detached from their community, their nation and their race, and become "honorary whites" ' (ibid., 61).

The criteria a male over 21, willing to be enfranchised, had to fulfill were: 'ability to speak, read and write English or French, good moral character, and freedom from debt' (ibid., 61). If the three-person commission (which included at least one missionary) 'found him so, they could recommend to the Governer that such a person "shall no longer be deemed an Indian" within the meaning of the Act.' (ibid., 61).

In South Africa, during the apartheid regime Chinese and Japanese were likewise accorded 'honorary white' status, while people from India were classified 'Asians', as pointed out to me by Timothy Reagan. The socio-economic/political pressures connected with the classification as 'white', 'coloured', 'Indian' or 'black/African/native' have partially caused the 'rapid linguistic genocide of the Khoe and San' (Kathleen Heugh, January 1999, personal communication). By 1980s the Khoe and San would have needed to classify themselves as 'coloured' 'in order to qualify for certain benefits such as old age pensions or limited claims for land' (ibid.). One way to do this was to identify Afrikaans as their home language—which many of them did. The carrots have now been exchanged to shame. Kathleen Heugh (ibid.): 'An old lady in Douglas, Northern Cape, told me last year that her grandchildren laugh at her or tell her to shut up if she speaks Griekwa, a Khoe language, because "it sounds like stones being thrown on the roof of a car".' (Compare this with the opinions on Khoe in Insert 3.31).

<hr>

Richardson thinks that the Canadian measure, 'declaring a person to be of another race than the one into which he had been born, was probably unique in the history of the world' (1993: 61). Be this as it may—for instance in Britain, children in mixed marriages are 'British' if the father is British, despite the mother's 'race' (Bernal 1991)—this **exo-definition** obviously was a clear instance of the **stigmatisation** of the cultures, languages and values of indigenous peoples and **glorification** of the 'civilized'.[19]

The Canadian law of 1857 also reinforced the stigmatisation by providing carrots for those who enfranchised: up to 50 acres of reserve land, and money (Richardson 1993: 62).

Exo-definitions can, just like other types of discrimination, combine racism with sexism, or with classism, as the examples in Info Box 3.6 show.

❖ **I n f o   B o x   3 . 6** ❖

Exo-Definitions Combining Racism With Sexism and Classism (Canada)

The 1869 Enfranchisement Act in Canada—which was repealed only in 1985, after large-scale protests (see an account of them in Silman 1988: see also Sandra Lovelace v. Canada) 'provided that an Indian woman who married a non-Indian would lose status, band membership and annuities, as would her children' (Richardson 1993: 62). The law led to 'the absurdity of tens of thousands of aboriginal people being defined as non-Indian although they lived as Indians, spoke Indian languages, and held to Indian beliefs and values, while thousands of European women who married Indian men were defined as status Indians' (ibid., 62).

The 1876 Act forcibly assimilated those indigenous people who got some higher education: 'any Indian who qualified as a doctor, lawyer, solicitor, notary, minister or priest, or who attained any university degree, would '**ipso facto**' . . . be deemed to be no longer an Indian' (Richardson 1993: 96). This Act then deprived the indigenous peoples their intelligentsia, by law.

Few indigenous people wanted to change their status, though, and this finally led the Government to pass a law in 1920 according to which indigenous people had no choice in the matter of whether or not they wished to continue to be 'Indians'. With the exception of 1922–1931, the law was in effect until 1951 when the pressure became too high. But voluntary enfranchisement was government policy until 1985 (Richardson 1993: 103–104).

As the examples show, our social identity, just like our mother tongue, is not a **characteristic** that we possess. Our identity is a **relationship** between the negotiating parties, enacted in and symbolized by the results of this negotiation (Skutnabb-Kangas 1991b).

If we use Pierre Bourdieu's (1992) concepts 'habitus', 'linguistic capital' and 'linguistic markets', those lasting, durable dispositions, perceptions, and attitudes which form the habitus and which all the time integrate past experience, could be seen as characteristics, whereas habitus itself necessarily is formed in a relationship between these dispositions and the tasks people encounter in the practice of their daily lives. The utterances people produce are 'the product of the relation between a linguistic habitus and a linguistic market' (Thompson 1992: 17). The capacity of both producing these utterances and of evaluating which utterances to produce when, form the linguistic capital. The linguistic capital that people possess (which is unevenly distributed along similar lines to the distribution of other types of capital) is then an outcome of the negotiations about the value of the specific linguistic dispositions of each person and group on the various linguistic markets, starting with that of the home and neighbourhood in early childhood, continuing through informal and formal education and work and social life.

For most groups seeking political self-determination today, this negotiation situation is not Dascal's equal inter-human negotiation, as we noted earlier: on the contrary, it involves unequal power relationships between the negotiators. One of the symbolic outcomes of the negotiations, the labels, at an individual or group level, whether they will, for instance, be called James Ngugi versus Ngũgĩ wa Thiong'o, or tribes versus nations/peoples (or, indeed, states—a state is also a relation—see Info Box 3.7), encapsulate this relationship.

❖ **I n f o B o x 3 . 7** ❖

A State Is a Relation

A state is not a characteristic of the supposed state. It is not enough for PLO or Somaliland or Estonia, Latvia and Lithuania, to proclaim a state (which is an act of self-categorisation, an endo-definition). The state does not 'exist' before (at least some) other states have accepted its existence, meaning exo-categorisations are needed as a validation, and thus ambo-categorisation becomes necessary. The Turkish Cypriot Republic, recognised only by Turkey, is thus not 'a state', and neither were the Bantustans in South Africa, only recognised by the apartheid regime. This is equally true for minorities, who cannot become officially acknowleged, if the negotiation partner does not accept their self-categorisation. As usual, Kurds in Turkey are a case in point. If Turkey (or Slobodan Milosevic' Serbia) refuses to negotiate with what they call terrorists but where the groups call themselves something else, something that **would** be a legally recognised negotiation partner, there is a problem—see below.

We can also see the close relationship between the right to name oneself and political power, if we compare the changes in and and the sliding scales of what groups seeking self-determination or groups oppressing other groups are called. The labels often depend much more on global political relations and intrigues than characteristics of the groups—another example of western hypocrisy. The United Nations and UNESCO use officially the label 'FYR of Macedonia', FYR standing for 'Former Yugoslav Republic', because Greece, a member state of both UN and UNESCO, does 'not accept the concept (or reality) of a non-Greek Macedonia' as Timothy Reagan puts it (personal communication, December 1998). A few additional examples in Definition Box 3.7. also show clearly that labels are results of negotiations—they do not necessarily describe characteristics in those whom they are supposed to define.

DEFINITION BOX 3.7 Who is a terrorist?

When and why did ANC and SWAPO change from being exo-defined as **'terrorists'**, to being called **'freedom fighters'**, and still later, for SWAPO, **'the only legitimate representative of the Namibian people'**? Why (and by whom) are the people fighting for the freedom of the Kurds or the East Timorese or Albanians in Kosova exo-defined terrorists, and when and why will they become freedom fighters (which is their own endo-definition)?

Why are there no international sanctions against Israel, for **apartheid** against Palestinians—there are many parallels to earlier South Africa? Why are there sanctions against Iraq for possessing mass destruction weapons and outcries for sanctions against India and Pakistan for testing them, but not against France when it possesses and tests them, on other people's land and sea? Why can the USA interfere with democratically elected governments and support repressive governments, participating in massacres of literally millions of people, and have their own people killed through gas or injections, or electrocute them, and still endo-define as 'the land of the free' (see, e.g., writer Harold Pinter's 1997 eloquent, devastating article 'Land of the Free? It Never Happened'), and have this endo-definition accepted by many if not most other governments? Why is the country fighting terrorism with terrorizing and bombing civilians in Afganistan or Sudan not exo-defined as a terrorist country?

Historian Frank Furedi (1994: 116) writes that 'any foreign people you don't like . . . become terrorists'. See also George (ed.) 1991, especially articles by Chomsky and Falk.

Nino Nikolov, a Bulgarian poet raised in Hungary, has one of the answers in his question (1996: 34): 'I lived through 1956 and today I still cannot understand why the great powers helped petroleum-rich Egypt and not democracy-rich Hungary'.

The analysis of one's own condition that precedes change, for instance preceding demands for self-determination, must be based on knowing where one comes from and goes to, i.e. the historical context of one's identity construction. In a situation of enforced change of identity, a (new) language, embodying the group's own endo-definitions of who the group is, must be created or recreated. The **decolonisation of the mind** (see Ngũgĩ 1987a) of the group, seeing and defining the world in the multiple ways that correspond more with the interests of the group, is required. Naming one's world differently is often the first step preceding demands for self-determination.

3.5. ETHNICITY AND LANGUAGE

One possible collective identity is conncected to ethnicity. Ethnicity has been proclaimed dead many times during this century, especially after the second 'World' War. **Survivalists** see ethnicity as one of the bases for categorisation that is historically permanent but still dynamic and changing. Ethnicity is seen as corresponding to deep emotional needs for community which states and other modes of organising cannot fulfill. **Evolutionists**, on the other hand, see ethnicity as an outmoded form of social organisation. **Liberal**[20] researchers claimed (and many continue to claim) that it was a traditional, romantic characteristic which would disappear with modernisation, urbanisation, global mobility. Ethnic identities would be replaced by other loyalties and identities: professional, social, gender, interest-group, state-related, global, and so on. **Marxist** researchers claimed that class-related solidarities, even crossing national borders, would replace ethnicity, seen by some as an undeveloped precursor to what would develop into class consciousness and solidarities: the international proletariat would unite (against world capitalism). **Bourgeous** evolutionists saw ethnicity as a primordial mode of organisation which would give way to more rational forms of organising, e.g. political parties (something one can still hear when western politicians talk about African, Arab, and other societies, clans, etc.). **Post-modern/ist** researchers now pronounce that we have (should have?) no lasting identities, only temporary ones. We choose, among alternatives where ethnicity may be one, the identifications which in our cost-benefit analyses momentarily benefit us most.

But ethnicity has refused to die . . .

First we examine who is ethnic according to various writers. Then we define ethnicity and trace some developments in types of definition. We differentiate ethnicity-based definitions from other ways of labelling groups, and finally we use 'Europe' as an example of the distinctions elaborated. The role of language in ethnicity is commented on continuously. It is important also to remember that most definitions of (ethnic) 'minority' attribute to minorities all the traits attributed to an ethnic group, plus some more.

3.5.1. Are Only Minorities 'Ethnic'?

The first distinction is between those for whom everybody has ethnicity (this agrees with my own view) and those who only see minorities as ethnic. Especially in literature emanating from earlier and present Western empires, the term 'ethnic' is often used to denote (numerically or spatially) relatively small communities only. Majority populations in Western countries do not seem to have ethnicity, according to these writers (see Definition Box 3.8).

DEFINITION BOX 3.8 Only minorities have ethnicity,
A Modern Dictionary of Sociology, New York, 1969

The definition in **A Modern Dictionary of Sociology** describes most of the commonly used criteria for ethnicity (see later), but then says: 'Usually the term is **applied only to minority groups** but if there are a number of culturally distinct groups in a society some writers also refer to the dominant cultural group as an ethnic group' (emphasis added).

Implicitly 'ethnic' seems in this type of description to denote formations which are not (yet?) people or nations, while 'nations' would not have any ethnicity. In some countries, groups which in other countries might be called national minorities are called something else: 'nationalities' (as in ex-Yugoslavia), 'an equal part of the population' (as Swedish-speakers in Finland), 'foreigners' or 'guest workers' (as Turkish citizens in Germany), first- and second- and third-generation 'immigrants' (as Turkish citizens in Denmark), 'culturally diverse groups' (as many in the United States)—or simply 'ethnics' (see Insert 3.18). For our purposes, they are all ethnic minorities, while ethnic majorities are equally much ethnic. Even for an advocate of 'open societies' (as in Richard Pratte's (1979) ideology of cultural diversity) where ethnicity would be irrelevant in public decision-making, Anglo-American norms

---

INSERT 3.18 Who is 'ethnic?'?

The Danish researcher Jørgen Christian Nielsen from the Danish National Institute for Educational Research published in August 1998 a third report in a series on a 3-year study of 'bilingual students' in which the reading skills of Turkish students in L1 and L2 had been studied. He informed the participants at a seminar on 20 August 1998 that one of his conclusions was that the Institute should 'develop ethnic language and reading tests' ('udvikle etniske sprog- og læseprøver'). When questioned about his use of 'ethnic' (he did not include tests for Danish mother tongue children), he could not understand the question, even after several attempts by others to explain that Danes were also 'ethnic'. To him, as to many others, a majority population is not ethnic.

seemed to be seen as non-ethnic (thanks to Timothy Reagan for the reference!). This contrasts with Mary Kalantzis' (1995) way of seeing the state as necessarily non-ethnic (see chapter 9).

Another way of understanding why 'ethnic' is used only about minorities in certain traditions is that 'ethnic' in many contexts has replaced 'race' (in the same way as 'of colo(u)r' has). Many of the negative connotations that the earlier term had are attached to the new term, which explains why the dominant group does not want to be included. Using 'ethnic' (or 'of colo(u)r') the way many people now use them makes 'ethnicity' or 'colour' marked. It becomes a characteristic that only the dominated have, i.e. the dominant are made to seem as if they do *not* have this characteristic, **they** are made invisible. They become the unmarked norm against which the (negative) characteristic of the dominated is singled out and 'ethnics' and 'non-ethnics' are hierarchised. In a popular sense, 'ethnic' becomes synonymous with 'foreign' (which can sometimes also be exotic or exciting) and/or 'different'—but also 'powerless'. When members of 'tribes' move to European countries, they become 'ethnics' (see Insert 3.19).

INSERT 3.19 'Ethnic'/'Ethnicity' used as a marked label, Norway, Finland, Denmark

'Had I been coloured I would have had real problems', said a male lecturer whose parents came from Hungary to Norway in 1956, at a Nordic conference 'The tolerant Nordic countries—wishful thinking or reality?', Helsinki, Finland, 9–10 December 1995. 'We now have so many ethnic restaurants', said another lecturer, Janina Andersson, Green MP). Birgül Engin, who presents herself as a '2nd generation immigrant' from Turkey, wrote in her columns 'Etnicitet' and 'Ægteskabets signalværdi' (Signalling value of marriage in the Danish daily **Information** (11.12.1995, p. 6 and 23.1.1997, p. 8) about 'some of the youngsters with an ethnic background . . .', 'the youngsters with an ethnic background born in Denmark . . .', 'I have myself an ethnic background . . .'.

So, pink is not a colour, 'Finnish' restaurants in Finland are not ethnic, and Danes in Denmark do not have an ethnic background. But if Finns and Danes migrate to the USA or Australia they might become ethnic, especially if they celebrated 'in their ethnic costumes'.

As examples in Insert 3.19 show, also representatives of the dominated groups participate in their own labelling. Even people who themselves have suffered from the system have difficulty in finding terms which would not be discriminating in the sense of continuing the two-tier system. Often this happens with the best of intentions. The term 'of colo(u)r' (e.g., 'women of color', instead of 'black' or 'brown' or similar terms), is prevalent in many texts today (Insert 3.20), especially in the United States.

INSERT 3.20 First person 'of color' to play Othello

Sudipto Chatterjee, 'director, actor, poet, playwright, translator', doing his doctorate on 'Bengali theatre in British Calcutta' (from presentation of contributors to Gainor (ed.) 1995) writes about 'the appearance of a Bengali . . . as Othello in a professional English production of the Shakespearean play . . . [in] Calcutta, in 1848 . . . he was probably the first person of color to play the tragic Moor' (Chatterjee 1995, 20).

Every person in the world has some type skin colour (which is, supposedly, what the terms 'black' and 'white' originally referred to—they are now more political terms)—therefore saying 'of colo(u)r' is meaningless—white and shades of pink are also colours, even if darker hues of course have more pigmentation (melanin) and therefore 'more colour'. Trying to substitute a new positive term, instead of an earlier term with negative (racist or sexist) connotations may help raise cosciousness about the need for substantial societal changes, but without those changes the old negative connotations stick to the new term too quickly, or the new term is appropriated by the dominant groups and turned against the dominated—which is what is about to happen with 'ethnic'. Many people use the new terms without seeing that the system has not changed. Speaking about 'ethnic food' or 'ethnic clothes' does not make sense—**all** food and clothes **are** ethnic and outsiders can see them as ethnically marked, even if the people concerned may not. But exo-defining somebody else as ethnic (you are ethnic, I am not) makes us **different** and is part and parcel of constructing that somebody as Other, different from Self. The difference is often used to legitimate the allocation of less power and fewer material resources to that Other: until you, Other, become like us, Self (e.g., 'a real American'), you have no right to the same share as we. Through this demand of assimilation, a majority society can then blame the victim: if you do not have the same benefits as we, it is your own fault. It is because you cling to your traditional language and culture, you do not *want* to fulfill the demands, you want to remain ethnic. An unequal society is legitimated with the help of labels and definitions which make inequalities seem fair. As a strategy, then, it would probably be wise to insist on using ethnicity as an inclusive term.

My 'pig-pink' tries to turn the tables by, first, using a colour label which is somewhat more realistic than 'white'. Please help me find a better label which does the same job (Task Box 3.3)!

Reader Task 3.3
Find alternatives to pig-pink

First do a test: put a sheet of white paper against the face of any 'white' person and compare the colours. I have never seen a white person in my life.

Secondly, try to think of another qualifier to pink (i.e., not **pig**-pink), one which shows what kind of pink many 'white' people's faces resemble (apologies to those who only know darker pigs) but which at the same time has ambivalent connotations, positive for some, negative for others if used about people, and disgusting and unclean for still others (e.g., many Muslims)—just like the connotations of 'black' are varied but mainly negative.

And, thirdly, find other terms altogether for presumably skin-colour-based ones, and argue both ideologically and pragmatically for your choice.

The **system** of hierarchising is the same, even when the methods vary. There are several possibilities.

Sometimes there are **parallel labels** where the connotations attached to the label for the dominated are mainly negative and the connotations attached to the label for the dominant are mainly positive (e.g., 'white', 'black', Definition Box 3.5).

Sometimes there are parallel labels in the sense that the label for the dominant is the positive norm, and the dominated are defined negatively in relation to that norm, in terms of what they are not, do not have, do not represent (**civilized** vs **un**civilized, **educated** vs **un**educated, **literate** vs **il**literate, etc.).

Sometimes the **dominated** are made (negatively) **visible**, by positing the dominant as the self-evident (positive) norm as in the case above (pink is not a colour), and marking the dominated, often attaching **negative connotations to the marked**. Dominant languages are sometimes treated in the same way by their speakers—they are so self-evident that they are not even seen as languages, as the question and answer example from Peace Corps recruitment material shows (Insert 3.21).

Sometimes the **dominated** are made **invisible**, by likewise positing the dominant as the self-evident (positive) norm but, in contrast to the above, not mentioning the dominated at all, pretending that they do not exist or are somehow subsumed under the dominant. When labels for an ethnic groups appear, at first they seem to be, or are presented as, or made to seem as generic—but they are not. This has been and is a strategy which is especially prevalent in relation to women and often ethnicity and gender coarticulate (Insert 3.22).

See Dale Spender's **Invisible women** (1982) and French 1986, Haraway 1991, Harding 1986, 1998, Hellinger 1989, Kramarae & Treichler 1992,

---

INSERT 3.21   Peace Corps: English is not a language

DO I NEED TO KNOW A LANGUAGE?

No, but some countries require people who have studied one year of college level (or two years high school) French or Spanish within the past ten years. You should, however, be prepared to learn another language in the country where you serve. (from Peace Corps recruitment materials 1998, under 'Commonly asked questions')

INSERT 3.22   No women in Israel? Celts were men?
Only males are working class in France?

Talking about different groupings in Israel, Matthew Engel writes: 'Maybe a sixth of the country count as 'ultras'—the black-hat, black-coat, black-bearded Jews; maybe another sixth are what they call the 'knitted *kipa*' class, who cover their heads and observe *kashruth* and the Sabbath without entirely retreating from the 20th century.' From the description (black-bearded, cover their heads) we can see that these two-sixths of the Israeli population are males. Is there, in Engel's Israel, another, female third of the population whose beliefs correspond to these males? No. Indirectly we get a hint that there may be women too in Israel because 'nearly all will have a family dinner at Passover, just as all Britons will have Christmas Dinner'—all those dinners are probably not cooked by the (bearded) men—but otherwise . . . (from Engel, Matthew (1996). In pursuit of the Promised Land. **Guardian Weekly**, June 2, 1996, 23).

'It is altogether likely that many Celts were held as slaves by the conquerors and that many of the Teutons married Celtic women' (Dorian 1991: 87).

Talking about the French distinction between 'a closed, pinched mouth (*la bouche*) . . . associated with the bourgeois and the feminine (e.g., "tight-lipped")' and 'a large open mouth (*la gueule*) . . . associated with the popular and the masculine (e.g., "big mouth", "loud mouth"), John B. Thompson then goes on to claim that 'from this viewpoint, the adoption of an articulatory style of the upper or middle class may appear to some **individuals** from working-class backgrounds as a negation not only of their social identity, but also of **their sexual identity**' (Thompson 1992: 17–18, emphases added).

Spender 1980, for other examples and analyses of and additional references to invisibilizing in general.

Earlier this inexact use of 'ethnic' was particularly common in parts of the British, American, and Australian linguistic and educational literature—

sociologists tried to be somewhat more rigorous—but today it is, with the ideological implications mentioned, common in other parts of the world too.

Riggs (ed.) 1985 is a global glossary on issues on ethnicity and has more entries about ethnicity, including definitions of ethnic groups, than any other contemporary work (see Riggs 1986). It was created in collaboration with Soviet researchers. A thorough treatise of ethnicity by the Soviet Academician, Yu. V. Bromley (1973, 1981, 1984) claims that the term 'ethnos' in Soviet science 'has always denoted not only "small" peoples, but also multi-million communities: Russians, English, French, etc.' (Bromley 1984: 8).

Even if some are of the opinion that the term should be confined to pre-nation formations, Bromley, like the majority of Soviet scholars, thinks that it should be applied to both tribes, nationalities, and nations (ibid., 8), and that in trying to find a definition for 'ethnos' one should try to describe what these formations have in common (ibid., 9).

The narrower interpretation of ethnicity is an understandable result of the fact that the ethnicity of dominant populations is often 'unmobilized and unthreatened' (Fishman 1977: 49) and more difficult to study, because of its lesser degree of saliency, than the conscious ethnicity that often characterizes groups which have to struggle to maintain their ethnicity, i.e. minority groups. Nevertheless, since the unconscious ethnicity of majority or dominant groups influences the way they treat the ethnicity of other groups (and is thus dangerous to us), it is important to include it in the study of ethnicity, as Bromley and others imply.

But as Allardt's discussion below indicates, all of the members of an ethnic minority group do not need to identify with the group for this group to be an ethnic group. Dominant-group Americans in the USA need not **identify** as ethnics—they still are. All the Finns in Sweden or Spanish-speakers in the United States do thus not need to feel as a part of an ethnic minority, nor do they need to give a self-categorisation which indicates membership in the ethnic group. All of them do not even need to have the cultural and linguistic competence for integration preparedness discussed above (section 3.3.3), for the group to be a national ethnic minority group. It is thus also perfectly possible both to accept the view that self-categorisation is an important defining characteristic of an ethnic group, and at the same time also maintain that this need not be expressed verbally, in the labels (all) the group members use of themselves.

A high degree of metacultural awareness is necessary for recognising the specific cultural traits formed by an immigrant minority ethnic group, the traits which set it apart from both the original culture and the new country's dominant culture. This awareness may take a long time to develop. It is often also reflected as a verbalisation of the distinct new ethnic minority identity, also as it expresses itself in labels for self-categorisation.[21] Thus not using a label in self-categorisation which expresses a **national minority** identity does not necessarily mean that the affective component of a double cultural competence would not be present. Becoming aware of it and expressing it verbally may come much later than the existence of it. In this sense, the 'objective criteria' for the existence of a minority group which the UN Human Rights Committee's reinterpretation of Article 27 in its General Comment (see section 7.8.1) implies, must take into consideration that the criteria may be fulfilled even in situations where self-categorisation by (parts of) the group is lacking. This takes us to more detailed definitions of ethnicity.

3.5.2. Exo- or Endo-Definitions—Is Ethnicity a Characteristic or a Relation?

In the development of definitions of ethnic groups and ethnicity one can discern three stages: use of **exo-definitions only** (identification by others), often still used in relation to minorities; a demand for using **only endo-definitions** (self-identification, self-categorisation), the present trend, first in relation to indigenous peoples in legal texts, then also to some extent in relation to minorities and, in some cases, for indigenous peoples in practice. Finally, the third stage would be use of **ambo-definitions** (identification by both, relational identification), so far mainly used in sociological and political science analyses.

Both exo- and endo-definitions may attribute ethnicity to the ethnic group concerned as a characteristic of the group or person, in the same way as 'integration' can be attributed as a characteristic to a minority individual or a minority group (see section 3.3.2). Many of these definitions of ethnicity list characteristics which a group has to possess in order to qualify as an ethnic group.

Exo-definitions define people as members of an ethnic group on the basis of one or more of the criteria, regardless of whether the people themselves self-categorize as members. For instance, the Turkish Constitution (Article 66, Paragraph 1) states: 'Everyone bound to the Turkish state through the bond of citizenship is a Turk.' This means that Kurds and other minorities are exo-defined by the State as Turks. Minorities which have been created through immigration may also be categorized in ways they do not accept themselves. Habitually calling some youngsters 'second- or third-generation immigrants' makes the few moments when their parents or grandparents crossed a state border the most important characteristic in them whereas they themselves might find other characteristics much more important. Terms like 'first- or second-generation Americans/Danes' still focus on the same moments. In education, submersion models (see later), without any component of mother tongue, are often used in this exo-defined phase, but segregation models (with at least some mother tongue teaching, even mother tongue medium instruction) can also be used. The group itself often has little say. As discussed earlier, having to accept somebody else's exo-definition of who you are signifies unequal power relations.

Forced other-categorizations are seen by many researchers (e.g., Liebkind 1984: 19; see also articles in Liebkind (ed.) 1989) as violations of basic human rights. According to a human rights oriented argumentation, it should be the right of every individual and group to have their own definition of their ethnic group membership accepted and respected by others. Consequently, only endo-definitions (definitions by self, self-identification) would be valid. In the initial phases of 'ethnic revival', a minority itself starts to demand this right to an endo-definition, and often language and culture and everything that defines the borders between the minority and the majority are emphasized. Learning the minority language as a subject in school or after school is often important.

But in the same way as 'a state' (e.g., Palestine) does not become a state just by an endo-definition, by proclaiming itself a state, but needs validation (acceptance of its statehood) by other states (i.e., an exo-definition) in order to exist (see Info Box 3.7), ethnicity needs validation from others and cannot be based on self-identification only. If the Kurds in the Turkish part of Kurdistan say that they belong to the Kurdish ethnos, while the Turkish state says that Kurds do not exist, the Kurds are in several senses made invisible as an ethnos. The right to decide yourself who you are, which should be a human right, works only when the power relationships between the parties who negotiate about a group's or an individual's ethnic identity are at least for some aspects equal, as we have seen earlier. If a minority is, by definition, smaller in numbers than the majority and in a non-dominant position, this is hardly likely.

A minority has few instruments for threatening the majority (using a stick) or granting them benefits (using carrots). The only strategy left is persuasion (using ideas, convincing the majority that the minority's views are correct and fair). Clarifying one's own views and arguments is therefore vital for the minority in a revitalisation situation. This includes a clarification of the power relationships between those who negotiate about whose definition of whom is valid, for instance 'the majority' and 'the minorities'.

This way of looking at ethnicity also makes it easier to see why refusing to accept the ethnic self-identification of a group/an individual and forcing the group/individual to take on another ethnic (and linguistic) identity, is a violation, regardless of whether it is done in brutal ways (as Turkey does, killing, imprisoning, and torturing people, even children, who claim Kurdish identity) or in more sophisticated ways, through making a child 'want' to change language, culture, and ethnic self-identification. Ethnic minority groups and languages can be killed both through brutal physical force and through shame and invisibility, and through making the people believe that assimilation is good for them. 'Helping' them, with compassion, to kill their own languages, for their own good. This is the preferred Western strategy in the education of ethnic minority children. It amounts to linguistic genocide. Ethnicism and linguicism are more sophisticated but as efficient weapons as biologically argued racism in committing ethnocide (ethnic and cultural genocide, the destruction of the ethnic socio-cultural identity of a group) and linguistic genocide. Linguistic and cultural human rights are a prerequisite for preventing ethnic and linguistic genocide.

How is then membership in an ethnic group assessed by researchers? Erik Allardt, in his discussion of ethnicity and ethnic revitalisation, shows that there are no criteria for membership in an ethnic group that would hold for all the members (Allardt, Miemois & Starck 1979: 11–12). People can, according to him, belong to the same ethnic group, on different bases (Allardt & Starck 1981: 42). Different persons themselves emphasize different criteria. The criteria themselves also constantly change with the historical situation, and even for each individual the criteria for insertion in an ethnic group or linguistic minority are situation-bound (Allardt, Miemois & Starck 1979: 12). Allardt suggests that the following criteria be used (Definition Box 3.9):

DEFINITION BOX 3.9   Criteria for an ethnic group, Allardt

1. self-categorization (self-identification);
2. common descent (factual or mythical);
3. specific cultural traits, e.g., the capacity to speak a specific language; and
4. a social organization for interaction both within the group and with people outside the group. (Allardt & Starck 1981: 43)

According to Allardt, there are **no** criteria for inclusion in an ethnic group that **all** the members of the group have to fulfill. But it is necessary that **some** members fulfill **all** the criteria, and **every** member must fulfill **at least one** criterion. Often most members fulfill all the criteria, but there are also some ethnic lukewarms and ethnic self-haters who do not categorise themselves as members despite fulfilling all the other criteria except self-categorization and despite being categorized as members by others. There is 'a firm and stable nucleus whereas the boundaries are fluid and constantly changing' (ibid., 12). Paradoxically then, 'the stable features in an ethnic group are not the boundaries but rather the existence of mechanisms which maintain and regulate them' (ibid., 12). One could add here 'and reproduce them'—that is one of the important reasons why minority education issues are so decisive, and why there is so much resistance to schools which use other mother tongues as media of education. Mother tongue medium education enables the group to continue to exist as a group.

Joshua Fishman's three characteristics of ethnicity are 'an actor's descent-related being, **paternity** [sic] and behaving, **patrimony** . . . [and] the meanings that he [sic] attaches to his descent-related being and behaving, **phenomenology**' (Fishman 1977: 23). These might correspond to Allardt's 'descent', 'cultural traits' and, to some extent, 'self-identification', respectively. The (putative) biological origins-related 'paternity' is a concept which 'the notion of ethnicity requires (as) a central concept or chord around which all others can be clustered' (Fishman 1989: 24). 'Patrimony', the 'behavioral or implementational or enactment system' of ethnicity (1989: 27–28), can also be compared to my behavioural component of cultural competence earlier. Fishman's ethnicity 'is viewed as having both inner and outer characteristics and consequences, causes and effects' (1989: 6). Barth's (1969) way of seeing boundaries between ethnicities as the focal point of ethnicity makes the very existence of the boundaries, not their content, the essence of ethnicity. But in the end, the binary oppositions used to constitute a boundary function as characteristics, even if they are constantly changing, and not static characteristics. See also Anthony Smith's (1983, 1991) very reflective discussions of ethnicity and identities in connection with nation building, nationism, and nationalism, and articles in Hutchinson & Smith (eds) 1994.

The definition in **A Modern Dictionary of Sociology** (1969) mentioned above also uses the first three criteria in Allardt's definition, without mentioning social organisation (Definition Box 3.10):

DEFINITION BOX 3.10 Criteria for an ethnic group,
A Modern Dictionary of Sociology

Ethnic Group: a group with a common cultural tradition and a sense of identity which exists as a subgroup of a large society. The members of an ethnic group differ with regard to certain cultural characteristics from other members of their society. They may have their own language and religion as well as certain distinctive customs. Probably most important is their feeling of identification as a traditionally distinct group.

According to Allardt (1981: 43), sociolinguists like Fishman (1977: 16–26) tend to be content with the first three criteria in Allardt's definition (which are **individual** characteristics), while social anthropologists like Barth (1969: 15–16), tend to emphasize the **social organisation** of the group, Allardt's fourth criterion. Allardt thinks that **both** types of criteria, i.e. both individual and group characteristics, should be combined, and that is what he does in his definition.

It is also important to look at definitions from the point of view of how they handle possible conflicts between endo- and exo-definitions. Since for Barth the content of the boundaries between ethnicities is not important, the conflict in negotiating whose content definitions should be valid, does not become salient for him—both groups define the boundaries for themselves and their conceptions of the boundaries do not necessarily need to coincide. It is not a contest about whose boundaries and world views are valid. In the same way as Barth, Fishman sees boundaries (contrast) and fully articulated opposition across boundaries as something that ethnic identity logically requires, but 'there can be no boundaries unless there is a heartland', i.e. characteristics to relate to.

According to Fishman (1977: 22), 'actors' views of their ethnicity are a part of their ethnicity; certainly they are a part of their ethnic identity'. Fishman is also concerned with the relationship between the actors' views and the observers' views. The observer should not merely 'report the ethnicity views of actors' (ibid., 22)—that would make observers 'descriptivists, reporters, cameras' (ibid., 22). Observation must alternate with interpretation, the actor's view with the interpreter's view. But there is also a risk that the interpreter's view has 'little to do with the actors' perceived reality, and if so, what have we explained?' (ibid., 22). Fishman thus sees self-categorisation as a part of the ethnicity, and other-categorisation as something that should be constantly checked against self-categorisation.

Allardt goes even further when he sees self-categorisation and categorisation by others (endo- and exo-definitions) as having logically different structures. This is so because a categorisation by others 'always implies referral to one or several external criteria, like descent, language proficiency, a wish to speak a specific language, other specific cultural traits, etc.' (Allardt & Starck 1981: 43). This is of course inevitable since the observer cannot directly study the 'phenomenology' of ethnicity, in Fishman's terms, only the observable results of it, i.e. the patrimonial part, the behaviour. 'In contrast, self-categorisation only presupposes an explicit wish to belong to or categorise oneself as a member of a group' (ibid., 43). Therefore, categorisation by others is not included in Allardt's criteria. It need not be, because it would only replicate criteria which are included already (but included in a form where they too are defined by the group itself, not by outsiders). Besides, minorities understandably tend to explicitly reject one-sided definitions of the minorities by the majorities, as for instance Henri Tajfel has shown (e.g., 1978a, b).

In this book, ethnicity, just like mother tongue, assimilation and integration, and identity earlier, is seen as a relation, and not as a characteristic of an ethnic group. And this book obviously acknowledges that relations of this kind are very often conflictual, not harmonious. Since ethnicity is here seen as needing validation through interaction between the parties to be defined, the conditions for this interaction are equally important as objects of study as the actors, in this intercultural conflict view. Fishman also discusses ethnicity in relational terms in most of his articles, and recognises fully the power relations involved. However, this recognition of the complexity of ethnic relations seems to lead to an acceptance of an intellectually laudable but at the same time (politically and otherwise) frustrating stance that it is still too early to produce a comprehensive theory of ethnicity (or integration), or even a definition. This seems to lead to a certain avoidance of fully exploiting power relations as causal factors in empirical analyses. Many of the more productive relation-oriented (rather than characterstics-oriented) conceptualisations of both ethnicity and integration, using ambo-definitions, have, despite different types of rhetoric, implicit assumptions of intercultural conflict, even if the conflict may be abstract (between definitions) or concrete (power conflict between groups). Some stop at description, explanation and understanding, some go further to advocacy.

To me it is clear that if there is unequal access to power and resources in the negotiation process, there is a risk that some features are being forcibly imposed as 'universal' and 'common' to all—and these are invariably features of the powerful groups. This can also be seen in labels, as the next section shows.

3.5.3. Ethnonyms, Toponyms, Politonyms, and Linguonyms/glottonyms

Next we look at concepts about group labels, how ethnic (and several other) identities are expressed verbally. Even if you, dear reader, might first feel irritated by the wealth of Latin-based terms, I hope you find them useful later on—they help us make several necessary distinctions and analyse some confusing debates about minority rights, as I will show in later chapters.

The Soviet ethnographer Bromley (1984) sees the self-identification of the group as the first and most important common characteristic when defining 'ethnos'. This can be operationalized in terms of the name that the group gives itself, the **endo-ethnonym** (or auto-ethnonym) (see Definition Box 3.11 summarizing Bromley's definitions). This is a necessary but insufficient characteristic of 'ethnos'. Bromley also makes a sharp distinction between the stable endo-ethnonym and varying **exo-ethnonyms** (hetero-ethnonyms), names given to ethnoses by others. His example is that 'the endo-ethnonym "Deutsch" is named "nemtsy" in Russian, "allemagne" in French, "German" in English, "tedesco" in Italian, etc.' (ibid., 9). This adds an interesting linguistic aspect to characterisations of ethnoses by others.

When arguing for why the existence of endo-ethnonyms is not sufficient as a criterion for ethnos, Bromley distinguishes several other bases for self-identification for communities which do not necessarily denote ethnoses. He talks about **politonyms**, used when denoting 'all people (citizens) living within the boundaries of one or another social organism . . . or political formation' (1984: 10) (for instance Belgians or the French), and about **toponyms**, 'when the group's self-identification originates from the name of the territory it inhabits' (ibid., 10).

DEFINITION BOX 3.11   Toponym, politonym, ethnonym (Bromley); linguonym

'-nym' = name
toponyms names referring to geographical places;
politonyms names referring to political entities;
ethnonyms names referring to the ethnicities and cultures of the people concerned;
linguonyms names referring to people speaking specified languages.

The difference between ethnonyms on the one hand and politonyms and toponyms on the other hand is for Bromley the stability of the self-identification. 'Tribes, nationalities and nations . . . are known to be stable communities existing under one and the same name of their own for many generations' (ibid., 10). But when a group of people move outside the original settlement, both the politonym and the toponym often are not retained by the second and further generations (while the endo-ethnonym might).

Bromley also discusses the possibility of two or three of these coinciding. He claims that 'when the politonym of a group of settlers is retained for several generations, this means that the given self-identification is also the ethnonym. The coincidence of politonym and ethnonym is especially characteristic of relatively mono-ethnical states: for instance, the words "Frenchman" ("Francais") or "Italian" ("Italiano") are both the politonym and the ethnonym.' (ibid., 10). This can be a result of either politonyms turning into ethnonyms or vice versa, ethnonyms turning into politonyms, which makes it more complicated to distinguish ethnic communities from political (and geographical) ones. Politicians and others can also try to make several -nyms coincide. In Insert 3.2 the Danish politician tries to force a toponymic identity also to become an **exclusive** linguonymic identity: if you live in Denmark, your mother tongue is Danish. Turkey tries to force a politonymic identity (Turkish citizen) to become an exclusive ethnonymic and linguonymic identity (you are an ethnic Turk; your mother tongue is Turkish) as our examples show.[22]

For the topic of this book it is significant that Bromley does **not** discuss **linguonyms** (or glottonyms, the term used in UNESCO's World languages report project—see Info Box 1.7), names denoting people who are (native) speakers of a language. The role of language in ethnicity has been a hotly debated issue (see section 3.4.1). Here we first add some reflections on the more legal issues, with Austrian law as an example.

The Austrian 1976 Ethnic Group Act ('Volksgruppengesetz') grants everybody free choice in deciding whether or not to be classified as belonging to a linguistic minority:

> Ethnic groups as defined by this federal statute are groups of Austrian citizens living permanently in parts of the national territory, but having a non-German native language and their own traditional customs. (Art. 2)
>
> The acknowledgement of adherence to an ethnic group is voluntary. No disadvantage shall accrue to any member of an ethnic group through the exercise of rights to which he [sic] is entitled or through the failure to exercise such rights. No person shall be obliged to furnish proof of his status as a member of an ethnic group (Art. 3). (Source: Lüsebrink (no date), 9–10)

Native language is in this Act regarded as one of the main criteria for the definition of an ethnic group.

Just as with many indigenous peoples and even recent immigrant minority groups everywhere (see Wong Fillmore 1991), there are many people in Austria who on the basis of their **origins** would be members of ethnic minorities but who do not know the minority language. Many Slovenes in Austria 'have no knowledge of the Slovene language because their parents opted to speak German in the home, often in the hope of enhancing their children's success in school' (Lüsebrink, 10). Some of these acculturated/assimilated Slovenes claimed nevertheless Slovene ethnic membership in the official census and claimed that 'the criterion of language was an inadequate measure of ethnic identity' (ibid., 10) (see also the discussion on mother tongue definitions, 3.2.2.2).

On the other hand, 'many parents whose native languages are Slovene or Croatian' (ibid., 10–11) opt for monolingual German instruction for their children, despite speaking the minority language at home. The free choice of ethnic identity and ethnic group membership may thus both increase and decrease official minority group membership, regardless of language competence.

On the other hand, the children of those Slovenes and Croats who opt out school-wise, in the sense of opting voluntarily for majority language medium education, even in situations where mother tongue medium education is available, are not likely to learn the language at a formal level, despite speaking it at home. Very probably most of the children of the assimilated relinguified Slovenes will not learn it either (meaning claiming minority ethnic group membership may be a symbolic gesture of solidarity at an abstract level but may not lead to the actual learning of the minority language). This would mean that both actions, despite being superficially opposites, may in the long term lead to the same result: a diminishing of the ethnic minority group (see also Info Box 8.4 on consequences for linguistic competence and intergenerational transmission of various school choices).

A third possibility does not seem to lead to the learning of the 'minority' language either. In Finland, large numbers of ethnic Finns are claiming Sámi identity, including the right to vote in the election for the Sámi Parliament. This seems to be done, probably at least partially, for economic reasons, from a conviction that being indigenous might directly or indirectly make them entitled to European Union support, especially if reindeer herding at some point becomes an exclusive monopoly of the Sámi (which it is not today in Finland). There has been a long, bitter debate, with many racist claims, including biological claims about more or less 'Sámi-ness'. Of course, the debate also highlights the fact that 'blood' type claims, in addition to being completely unscientific (as are 'race' claims—see note 19) and impossible to prove anyway, can be seriously misused. In Insert 3.23 the lawyer is replying to the metonymic, literal level (blood = 'race') rather than to the group membership question—and both were insulting in the situation.

INSERT 3.23 A blood type called 'Māori blood'? 'Indians,
or persons having one fourth or more Indian blood'
could not be witnesses (California)

I was waiting in a lecture hall in Sydney to talk to a Māori lawyer after his lecture while an American journalist finished her discussion with him. She asked how he could represent the Māori—she could see that his 'blood was not hundred percent Māori'. The lawyer smiled and said softly: 'I thought there were only a few types of blood in the world, with A's and B's. I have never heard of there being a blood type called "Māori blood".'

Section 394 of the Act to Regulate the Proceedings in Civil Cases in the court of Justice of this State (from The California Statute, 1851, Chapter Five, Title II; quoted in Norton 1987: 116) defines the persons who could not be witnesses. This included 'those who were of unsound mind and children who were under ten years of age' (ibid.)—and 'Indians, or persons having one fourth or more Indian blood in an action in which a white person was a party' (ibid.).

People have obviously many other additional types of identity-signifying names for themselves and others. In principle, the same kind of analysis of -nyms could, though, be applied to many of the others. Many young people might, for instance, claim that their identities at certain stages in life are more influenced by their music tastes or life styles or clothing than their ethnicity, and discuss the international recognition of and identification with peers from other countries with the same 'characteristics'. They might also analyse the status of their endo-definition in comparison with the exo-definitions of their group by (many) older people, and the factors influencing this. Likewise, one might also profitably use the concepts of glorification, stigmatisation, and rationalisation (introduced later), in similar ways to how I use them in analysing the statuses of various languages and cultures. The four -nyms chosen here are, though, more central for the theme of the book than other alternatives, as will be demonstrated in the example with Europe, which is where we turn to now. In analysing possible future scenarios for Europe I want to combine several of the earlier discussions and also show that our conceptual framework so far might help in analysing the identities of 'Europe' and 'Europeans'.

If an integrated Europe is to be 'an ethnically heterogenous group' (from my earlier definition of 'integration'), one implication of the definition is that also dominant group ethnicities have to be acknowledged and made visible. All groups living in Europe must become conscious of their ethnicity and its implications (also the fact that most majority ethnicities have elements of dominance). Minorities are mostly aware of their ethnicity, possibly with the exeption of migrants who come from former imperialist countries (in Canada 'the British are not considered immigrants', according to Helen Ralston (1988), and my British husband sometimes causes Danish eyebrows to raise when insisting that he is an immigrant in Denmark). Secondly, all groups have to change, not only old or new minorities, or Eastern Europeans now entering what many Western Europeans have defined as 'Europe', and everybody should have the right to contribute on an equal basis. There cannot be any kind of 'mainstream Europeanness', that we 'in the fringe areas', east or north of the self-nominated Euroclub, are invited to join. So who is the 'European'?

3.5.4. Example Europe: Fortress Europe (Exclusion) or 'Integrated Europe' (Inclusion) for Whom?

We will apply the -nymic concepts to the example of 'Europe' and 'European',[23] by asking questions about the validity of particular definitions of concepts like European or ethnically/linguistically non-European. What is the role of language in creating and maintaining identities which are then juxtaposed to other identities in the process of the unequal allocation of societal power and its legitimation? We also want to explore what role language plays in the capacity of dominant groups to set a hegemonic agenda in identity creation and negotiation. In essence it is again a question of who has the power to define and who is being defined. Who/what is included, who/what is excluded through definitions, and how are the criteria and the borderlines constructed? Do we want 'Fortress Europe' or 'Integrated Europe'?

'Europe' has many definitions. During this century there has been a tendency to narrow down the concept more and more. Different 'clubs' have called themselves 'Europe', left other geographically European countries outside, and included geographically non-Europeans (e.g., USA and Canada as members of the OSCE, see later). Many have tried to monopolise the term for their own club. 'The European Community/Union' does not mean a community of all the countries in Europe, nor does 'Council of Europe' mean all the countries in Europe, despite the fact that both organisations use an inclusive 'Europe' when they are in fact only talking about their own club.

These exclusive clubs have noticed, though, that they need a more solid basis in the scramble for the best markets in the new economic and political world order. Therefore they have recently invited some Others to join them. The queue of peoples who are negotiating terms for inclusion in the European Union, ideologically, politically, economically, culturally, and linguistically, is long. This inclusion involves a major reorganisation and rehierarchisation process whereby power and resources are redistributed, not only between and within different European countries but very importantly, probably mainly, between Europe and the rest of the world. The reorganised Fortress Europe then aims at a greater share in the scramble for the power and the resources of the whole world.

The designations of groups of people or places as 'Europe' and 'Europeans' can be be classified following Bromley's categories. But first we apply Bromley's concepts to individuals. Try yourself (Reader Task 3.4)!

Reader Task 3.4
Your own identity in terms of toponym,
politonym, ethnonym and linguonym?

Try to place yourself in terms of the -nyms. Who/what are you toponymically, politonymically, ethnonymically, and linguonymically? Then compare with Robert and me. Try to place your parents, and grandparents. See if there are changes. Why? Are they voluntary, or enforced? What is 'voluntary'? Are your endonyms accepted by significant others, are they also your exonyms?

I will in the discussion use my husband, Robert Phillipson, and me as examples of how the concepts can be used for individuals and how they can help in sorting out where one 'belongs'.

Ethnonymically Robert is British, his parents are/were Brits and he identifies culturally as originally British (even if many other cultures have been added later, including a 'global' identity). I am Finnish and Finland-Swedish, in relation to both parentage and culture. Hyphenated identities (Greek-Australian, Latvian-American) often signal multiple ethnonymic identity. In many (western) countries multiple ethnonymic identities are seen as negative, in many others, especially in Africa and Asia, they are seen as natural.

Toponymically both of us are Danish because we live permanently in Denmark. Robert started off toponymically as Scottish (spending his first years in Scotland because of the war). It is difficult to tell how long and how permanent one's stay has to be in order to change toponymic identity. Likewise, it might according to some people be impossible to have a multiple toponymic identity ('you cannot live permanently in two places at the same time')—but there are many people who do (for instance immigrant minorities who have a summer house in the old country).

It also depends on to what extent all these identites are seen as subtractive or additive. When you get a new one (for instance, move countries, learn a new culture or language), does it replace the old one or is it added to it? I still feel most 'at home' in terms of the landscape with Finnish woods and lakes, but the Danish spring beech wood, white and yellow with anemone and primula, is also part of me, meaning an additive toponymic affective identity. If, for instance, 3 years of residence, would change the toponymic identity, Robert would also have been toponymically Algerian and Yugoslav because he has lived in those countries.

Politonymically we **could** also be Danish (be part of the Danish political entity) at a state level, but are in fact not. Robert is British and I am Finnish, we have not changed our passports (citizenship) to Danish. One of the drawbacks is that we still, after over 20 years of residence, cannot vote in Danish parliamentary elections. On the other hand, we are allowed to vote in municipal elections, that is, we are politonymically Danish at that sub-state level. When we vote for the European Parliament, on the other hand, we do it as politonymic 'Europeans', i.e. as citizens of a state (UK and Finland, respectively) which is a member of the European Union.

We are ourselves responsible for not being politonymically Danish at the state level—we could have changed our passports long ago. On the other hand, we did not do anything ourselves to change our politonymic identity to 'Danes' at sub-state level (for municipal elections) or to politonymic 'Europeans' at supra-state level (for European Parliament elections). Denmark made us politonymic 'Danes' by allowing certain resident immigrants to vote. Our countries made us politonymic 'Europeans', by joining the Union and by letting citizens not living in the country also vote (which Britain did only recently, Finland at the same time as joining). Robert also has the 'European' dark red cover on his passport, I don't yet.

The tendency in Europe so far has been to discourage or not to allow multiple politonymic identities **at the same level** (for instance, having two passports), only at different levels which can be seen as forming concentric circles (you can be at the same time Welsh, British, European, a citizen of the world). Some other countries (e.g., the USA) accept double passports more easily—if you happen to be born in the country you are included in the group of citizens, on toponymic grounds (**ius soli**—see Definition Box 3.12), regardless of whether your parents' country also grants you citizenship or not. The mono-politonymic countries (e.g., Germany until spring 1999), on the other hand, often grant you citizenship more or less only on eth-nonymic not toponymic grounds (**ius sanguinis**—Definition Box 3.12), often regardless of linguonymic identification (many 'Germans' from the ex-Soviet Union, now German citizens, know no German, just like many ex-Soviet 'Jews' now in Israel are reported (e.g., Bernard Spolsky) as knowing nothing about Judaism, Hebrew or Jiddish). And when double citizenship was suggested in 1998 by the new German government, voting behaviour has already shown that the government may have to pay for it.

DEFINITION BOX 3.12   Ius soli versus Ius sanguinis

Solum, genitive **soli**, in Latin means, among other things, 'ground, earth, soil, foundation'—if you are born on the soil of the country you are a citizen. **Ius**, gen. **iuris**, means 'law, right', so **ius soli** is 'the right/law of the soil'. Citizenship is given to everybody born in the country.
Sanguis, genitive **sanguinis**, Latin, means 'blood'; **ius sanguinis** = the right/law of the blood. Citizenship is given on the basis of parents' citizenship or ethnicity.

Linguonymically English is Robert's mother tongue and Finnish and Swedish are mine. But some Danes think that Robert is a native speaker of Danish (an exo-definition) whereas he would never himself (endo-definition) claim native competence in any other language except his mother tongue, even if he speaks several really well. Likewise, I would never do it, even if there are issues within my profession which are easier for me to discuss in English than in Finnish or Swedish (see Insert 3.1). The relationship between 'mother tongue' and '(native) competence' is thus complex and far from one-to-one correspondence (see section 3.2.1).

Many countries demand at least some linguonymic 'identification' for citizenship, mostly meaning a certain level of competence. In some countries the more conservative, often linguicist forces want this 'identification' to be subtractive—people are asked to denounce their mother tongue or it is exo-denounced for them, at least in official usage, sometimes also privately (see

Insert 3.2 for one example of this). Some linguicist countries claim legally that their official language is everybody's language, or that all the citizens have a certain linguistic (France) or ethnic identity or both (e.g., Turkey) just because of the politonymic identity.

From this individual example of how to apply the -nyms, we move to how 'Europe' and 'Europeans' can be analysed with the help of our conceptual tools. A **toponymic** reading of Europe opens up several possibilities. Some of the ex-Soviet Central Asian republics were bidding for support simultaneously from both 'Eastern European' and 'Asian' development banks (Tomaševski 1993a). Is this symptomatic of fluid toponyms and the definitional problems that diversity and multiple identities may give? Can the countries be at the same time both European and Asian? Are the Banks themselves based on a toponymic or a politonymic reading of the 'European' and 'Asian' in their names?

The toponym Europe is often prefaced by a geographical modifier, for instance 'central' or 'western'. But sometimes 'western' Europe refers to both north and west, and may include the south. Where are the eastern and south-eastern borders of the toponymic 'Europe'? Does eastern Europe stretch to the Ural mountains or not, including which former Soviet republics (see Insert 3.24)?

Tolstoy's reading was based on the common 19th century belief in some kind of superior 'European' culture: ' "How is one to recognize this superior culture? The English, the French, the Germans—which of them is at the highest stage of development? Which is to nationalize the other? We see that the Rhine provinces have turned French—is this a proof of inferiority on the part of the Germans?' he cried. 'There must be some other law at work." "I believe that the advantage is always on the side of true culture,' observed Karenin, raising his eyebrows slightly' (ibid., 411). 'Europe' is here confined to the big three, and there is also the usual classist, linguicist hierarcy: "And, in the usual way with Russians when they do not wish the servants to understand what they are saying, he began speaking in French" '(ibid., 486; Count Vronsky).

In popular speech, people from the topographical fringes of Europe such as the British, Danes, and Finns appear to regard their countries as lying outside Europe ('When Blair made his first trip to Europe as Prime Minister . . .', Pilger 1998: 88), but here there may be a blurring between a toponym and a politonym (see examples from Kiernan later). Some blurring is starting to happen at an intra-state level too, so that toponymic and politonymic 'belonging' is enough in some countries to make one in some way ethnonymically 'legal' too, as the Swedish example shows (Insert 3.25)—but not in others (or not when one asks the minorities), as in the Danish example (Insert 3.26)—even if there is some optimism (Insert 3.27)—which I do not share.

INSERT 3.24 Is Russia European? Tolstoy:
big landowners and intellectuals yes, peasants no

As the following excerpts from *Anna Karenina* show, for Tolstoy Russia was
not toponymically part of Europe (examples 1, 2, 3). Ethnonymically, Russian
peasants were not Europeans whereas the Russian aristocracy was (example
4), and politonymically again Russia was not considered part of Europe
(example 5). The emphases are mine:

1. "Oh, rental value!" Levin exclaimed with horror. "There may be such a
thing **in Europe,** where the land has been improved by the labour put into it;
but in this country the land is deteriorating . . ." (pp. 357–358).

2. "But **Europe** is not satisfied with this system."
"No, and is looking for new methods . . ."
"But if it doesn't do **for us?** If it is stupid?" said Levin.
". . . We've found the secret **Europe** was looking for! . . . are you aware of
all that's been done in Europe on the question of the organization of labour?"
(p. 359; Levin, Sviazhsky).

3. ". . . Schools will not help . . ."
"Yet all over Europe education is now compulsory." (p. 362; Levin,
Sviazhsky).

4. "**We** [the Russian landowners] have pushed on in **our own way—the
European way**—a long time, without stopping to consider the nature of labour.
Let us try seeing labour not as abstract man power, but as **the Russian peasant**
with his instincts, and organize our system of agriculture accordingly." (p.
363; Levin)

5. Koznyshev . . . His book, the fruit of six years' labour—Sketch of a Survey
of the Principles and **Forms of Government in Europe and Russia**—had been
finished . . . (p. 803; Levin's brother).

After this initial application of labels to 'Europe' and 'European', we
proceed to looking at the scenarios for a future 'Project Europe', continuing
the scrutiny of inclusion and exclusion through the -nymic concepts used.

'Nazi imperialism included the grand design of a New Order for Europe,
a unified, hierarchical structure which would make the Aryan continent
strong enough, under German leadership, to master the world', the British
historian Kiernan described the goals in 1980 (reprinted in Kiernan 1995:
153). In Fortress Europe, with Schengen and other agreements designed to
keep immigrants and refugees from non-European and, to a large extent,
eastern European countries out, under the European Monetary Union where
the strong German currency plays the tune, in the European Union with its
Lomé trade agreements to continue the exploitation (**Focus ACP** 1:2, 1997),

---

INSERT 3.25 Swedes need not be flax-blond . . .

Under the subtitle 'There are models with various ways of ethnic belonging', Swedish journalist Karin Larsson (1995) says in her article 'En segregerad värld är inte hip. Reklamens etniska enfald är märklig' (A segregated world is not hip. The ethnic stupidity of advertisements is curious; my emphases): 'Sweden no longer is a people with homogenous looks, a flock of flax-blond people from Svealand ["svear"; see chapter 1 on this concept]. No, it is equally Swedish to have African, Asian, Latin American, southern European, Arabic, Sámi traits, yes, any traits. **We are all equally Swedish, because we live in Sweden and are Swedish citizens.** Modern Sweden is diversity.'

INSERT 3.26 . . . but in Denmark darker citizens are in trouble

'Are you a Danish citizen?'

'Yes, I got citizenship in 1991.'

'But you still think that it has something to do with you being a foreigner, that you could not get through with your wishes?' [getting 'no' to training as a tailor, an occupation that he had had in Iran before he fled].

'Of course I cannot prove it, but I can only refer to the fact that those Danes I can compare myself with got better treatment. It was my clear impression that if I had asked for something at a lower level of qualifications it would have been easier—they obviously thought that my goals were too high . . .

I think it has become much more difficult to be a refugee in Denmark during the last few years. It does not change anything whether you are a citizen or not. If you look like a foreigner you are made suspect, in the unemployment system and on the street. One hardly dares to be active in trade unions or politically. In fact the situation in Denmark is such that one can risk getting involved with the police if one is just in the wrong place at the wrong time. It was exactly what I fled from'. (Mahmoud Ghasemi, 33, Iranian refugee, came to Denmark in 1984, unemployed, in an interview in **Information**, 11 December 1995).

---

it seems that the originally Nazi 'grand design of a New Order for Europe, a unified, hierarchical structure which would make the Aryan continent strong enough, under German leadership, to master the world' is closer to fruition than it ever was under Hitler . . .

But Project Europe would not necessarily have needed to become Fortress Europe. There was—maybe still is?—another possible scenario, which many call 'Integrated Europe'. Project Europe is presumably going to result in some kind of acculturation (see Definition Box 3.1). It is a matter of negotiation, which type of Europe we want: one which is based on exchange without domination, with acceptance of complementarity in Dascal's sense (see 3.4.2.1): 'Integrated Europe'. Or do we want a Europe which is based on domination, control and exclusion: 'Fortress Europe'.

Questions we should ask are, for instance: Which Europes are the grandchildren of migrants going to be integrated into—or will they be forced to assimilate in some and be marginalised in relation to others? Are all toponymic Europeans also allowed to be politonymic Europeans: are those who live in 'Europe', whatever that may be, also allowed (or, in some cases, forced) to belong politonymically, i.e. become citizens? Are all toponymic Europeans allowed to maintain their ethnonymic and linguonymic identities (become national ethnic minorities, learn their own languages and cultures, and use them—also in some official contexts, including schools), *in addition* to taking on (some of) the cultures and languages of the dominant groups in the countries where they live? Or are they instead being forced to assimilate to the new ethnonymic and linguonymic identities *subtractively*, at the cost of their own? Are multiple identities allowed in the beautiful multicultural Europe, celebrating diversity—or is the 'European diversity' just nation-state monolingualism and monoculturalism multiplied (as Monica Heller (1997) puts it in her review of Labrie 1993)? 'Fortress Europe' leads the way in ever harsher exploitation of the rest of the world outside the block of Europe, Europeanised countries and a few others. It does it both with more subtle means and with the help of arms (as we have seen in the Gulf war, in the Balkans and in the plans for a 'European army' that at least the three big European countries seem to agree is necessary). 'Fortress Europe' keeps its borders virtually closed to 'outsiders', with the help of the Schengen agreement and others. Kiernan claims, in analysing pre-Great European Civil War[24] Europe, that some are drawn in and some excluded against their will:

> If Britain was suspected of not wanting to be thought part of Europe, Russia was considered by many liberals as well as socialists not fit to be part of it. European Russia shaded off into Asia, and seemed too much on a level with Asia. (Kiernan 1995: 152)

'Fortress Europe' probably has elements of both ethnonym and politonym, conforming to the classic orientalist (Said 1978) mould of Us versus Them, the Others. 'Fortress Europe', run by a small Euroelite, instrumentally multilingual and multicultural but de-ethnicized, widens the gaps in Europe, and the world. Migrant and refugee minorities are, together with the national criminalised poor (see Insert 6.18), at the bottom of the hierarchy. Between them, the bulk of Europeans, East and West, would feel equally much alienated from the practical multiculturalism of migrant minorities and the rhetorical multiculturalism and European integration talk of the elites.

'Integrated Europe' could possibly harbour some of the globally necessary alternatives. One dream is presented by Roberts and Nelson (Insert 3.27).

But there is also in the minds of the analysts in Insert 3.27 a keen awareness of the shallowness and negative traits in what a 'common' 'European' culture

---

INSERT 3.27 Hope for Europe?

The quest for European unity beyond the nation-state presupposes citizens conscious not only of their multiple roles in contemporary society but equally of their multicultural identities (community, region, nation, language, religion, etc.) in an expanding European community and as inhabitants of an ever more threatened planet. At the heart of this project of a new Europe lies the recognition of diversity and pluralism, the mediation of cultural and political identities and allegiances, the ongoing strengthening of civil society, and the creation of democratically accountable transnational institutions capable of steering an autonomous course between the pressures of international capitalism and national sovereignty. (Roberts & Nelson 1992: 5).

---

is at present (I have emphasized these in **bold** type), at the same time as there is still glorification (*italicized*) of what it should or could be:

. . . only a European common ground can ensure the success of economic and political union. At present, however, this **common ground exists only negatively**—as the **"democratic deficit" of unaccountable transnational bureaucracies and as the "educational deficit" of the national school systems**, which have scarcely tackled the European dimensions of our common future, a future that depends upon a shared awareness of our common past, the European *heritage of the free individual and civil society* and all that it comprises: the ideas of *personality, democracy, tolerance, social justice, and human rights.* The identity of a new Europe can only form around common, democratic European institutions (Roberts & Nelson 1992: 6–7; my emphases).

This 'heritage of the free individual' and 'human rights' of course invisibilizes both past and present atrocities, slaveries, genocides. The Roma (so-called Gypsies) have a largely undocumented history of oppression in Europe (e.g., Grönfors 1995, Ollikainen 1995). Their position as slaves in Rumania is described in Insert 3.28.

Eurocrats have intensified the advertising of 'European integration', but it is important to ask which 'Europe' we are supposed to 'integrate' into and who is deciding? The supra-statal **politonymic** 'European' has many partially conflicting interpretations, for example, with 15, 37, or 55 countries. A re-

---

INSERT 3.28   Slavery in Europe (Roma)

'For more than four hundred years, until 1956, Gypsies were slaves in Wallachia and Moldavia, the feudal principalities that with Transylvania now make up modern Romania. Some Transylvanians also owned Gypsies, but only in these principalities was slavery an institution' (Fonseca 1995: 177).

As early as the late 1300s, the rulers of the principalities made gifts of Gypsy families to monasteries (ibid., 177). According to Fonseca, mentions of the Gypsies in Romanian archives look like references to cattle. The slavery was legitimated by claiming that the Gypsies had already been slaves when they first appeared in Romania, 'they came from a pariah class in India; slavery was in their blood.' (ibid., 177–178). Romanian historians saw slavery as 'an improvement on the Gypsies' previous station . . . because here at least they were usefully integrated into society. A certain Dr. Wickehauser, who visited the principalities in the nineteenth century, corroborated the view of earlier and later Romanian historians: Gypsies "wished to become slaves, because this would raise them, if not to the level of human beings, at least to a par with good, domestic working animals." ' (ibid., 178).

In 1837, an 'eloquent liberal statesman and an ardent and influential abolitionist', Mihail Kogălniceanu, wrote, more than 25 years before emancipation in the principalities: '[Europeans] form philanthropic societies for the abolition of the slavery in America, even while in the bosom of their continent, in Europe, there are 400,000 Gypsies who are slaves . . .' (ibid., 186).

Fonseca bases her accounts on the slavery on Potra, George (1939) **Contribuţiuni la istoricul Ţiganilor din Romania**. Bucharest: Fundatia Regele Carol I, according to her 'the only full-length account on slavery—written in Romanian, untranslated and the sole source of every subsequent account' (Fonseca 1995: 175).

Károly Bari, Roma poet, tells: 'Gypsies who survived the Holocaust have related to me how, when they were put into a barracks with other nationalities, the other inmates maltreated them because of their race' (1996: 66).

---

strictive but common one is to interpret 'Europe' as only the 15 countries of The Club, the **European Union**, and this Club tries to appropriate the label 'Europe' for itself as a matter of course.[25] There are conflicting signals in relation to the extent to which the new members who joined this club in 1995, namely the Austrians, Finns, and Swedes, regarded themselves in some sense as 'European' prior to January 1995 (probably the Austrians and Swedes did more so than the Finns who were more uncertain but are now close to overassimilated). And Norway (where the population voted against joining the EU) may or may not still do so. Do those Swedes who claim they would now vote *no* (consistently a great majority of the Swedish population since 1996, around or over 60 percent, depending on the polls) feel that they are now less 'European' than the Finns (where a majority still wants to be members) even if these Swedes do not want to be part of the Union.

Another **politonymic** 'Europe', that of the **Council of Europe**, is much larger than the EU (37 countries, including Turkey which is toponymically not seen as part of Europe). The **OSCE (Organisation for Security and Co-operation in Europe**[26]) included Canada and the US as founding members in 1975, when 35 states were signatories of the Helsinki accords. In 1998 OSCE had 55 member states.

What does the **ethnonym** 'European' culture refer to? Or the 'European' heritage? European Studies (also at universities outside toponymic Europe)? When schools are supposed to teach about 'European' culture or include a 'European' dimension in the curriculum, or inculcate a 'European' identity into the students, we supposedly have to do with an ethnonymic and some-times linguonymic reading of 'Europe'. But are the cultures of all those ethnic groups who toponymically live in Europe or who politonymically claim a 'European' identity really included? Are the literatures and oratures of all the peoples whose languages are spoken in toponymic Europe (reaching at least to the Ural mountains) included in the 'European' heritage that Euro-pean nationals or migrants from outside the toponymic 'Europe' are sup-posed to learn about? Are their own languages and cultures included? To me, Eino Leino's *Helkavirret* is one of the greatest books of poetry in the world, whereas my husband is ignorant of this part of 'European' heritage because it has not been translated from Finnish into any of the seven 'Euro-pean' languages he knows.

Is the borderline between Europe and the Orient a question of Christianity versus Islam and 'alien' faiths? In that case, is Turkey really more European than the Maghreb? If what distinguishes Turkey and Russia from the Maghreb is that the first two are officially secular, is not Turkey then more European than Ireland or southern Italy? And how could the ungodly Soviet Russia qualify? Or, if historically 'among Spain's enemies at least there was a widespread conviction that the country did not really belong to Europe: it was Moorish, African, heroic but barbarous, like an Othello' (which is what the British historian V. G. Kiernan claims, 1995: 148), and if we consider the 'recurrent paradox that the two great leaders of European expansion, after the Spaniards, were Britain and Russia, both of which were regarded by many other Europeans as not fully or genuinely part of Europe' (ibid., 151), then what is left of Europe? And what about the following quote? 'In 1898 all Europe except Britain sympathized with Spain against America; in 1900 all Europe but not America, sympathized with the Boers against Britain' (ibid., 151–152).

Can this observation be used to construct Britain and Spain as the eth-nonymically excluded underdogs, supporting each other and the toponymi-cally excluded America? Or the rest of Europe (excluding both America and the Brits), by supporting a British 'enemy'? Or does it mean that then, as now, ethnonymically constructed identities have been exploited for power purposes and reconstructed at will? Sandra Harding (1998) criticizes the eurocentric histories of science and technology which present European culture as the direct heir of classical Greek culture (dormant during the Dark Ages in Europe) and which work with notions of a 'European miracle' and the 'European scientific revolution', where the emergence and development of modern science in Europe (and not in other parts of the world) is explained by internal features of European culture and societies. As opposed to this, many accounts, including recent postcolonial ones, maintain that the notion of a 'European miracle', calling on the legacy of the classical Greek culture, ignores significant contributions of flourishing Islamic cultures to Europe's sciences. Aristotle's Greece was a part of the Mediterranean and **included** Northern Africa as well as the Near East, and **excluded** in fact peoples lying to the north of Greece, meaning most of Europe. Still, European cultural identity and origins were placed entirely into ancient Greece.

What then of languages, and 'European' as a **linguonym**? Are 'European languages' those that are 'traditionally used within a given territory',[27] when 'tradition' is an unclear concept in a world of change and when the 'territory' where 'European' languages are spoken does not have firm boundaries or coincide with the toponymic Europe? Are Finnish and Estonian as **non-Indo-European** languages more European or less European than Panjabi or Hindi, which **are** Indo-European languages? Or are Panjabi and Hindi only 'European' when the speakers stay outside Europe, and 'non-European' ('ethnic') when the speakers move to the British school system and want their languages to be studied as 'modern European languages'? Are only Indo-European languages or only the toponymically European ones of the Indo-European family real European languages, as is often implicitly claimed? When the architects and drafters of the Maastricht Treaty referred to 'European languages', which languages were they thinking of, only the official EU languages, or all languages spoken natively in 'Europe', and which Europe? Why are European languages 'modern' in education in some countries, 'living' in others and 'foreign' elsewhere? Why in schools is there the widespread pecking-order of modern/foreign languages, with English with the sharpest beak, French and German slightly less greedy but often going hungry, and most other languages, including immigrant minority languages, starving because they are not seen as 'European'? Does a 'European' language have certain characteristics, or is it rather to be found in the eye of the observer (see the example about Khoekhoe languages below in Insert 3.31)?

One possibly positive outcome of discussions about 'European integration' is a higher degree of metacultural and metalinguistic, maybe also metapolitical awareness. Still, most people in 'Europe' probably feel more strongly about being French or Danish than about being European. Efforts to pro-

mote European integration are implicitly and explicitly attempting to reinforce what is **distinctive** (familiarity with one or more specific ('other') languages and countries in Europe) and what is **shared** ('the common European
heritage'), at the same time as major political, economic and cultural forces
are generating new sub-national, national, and supra-national identities. A
supra-national European **political** identity could easily cohabit with a national cultural **and** political identity, Ole Wæver et al. (1993) claim, i.e. people
could be ethnonymically Danish or Italian and still, at least politonymically,
both Danish or Italian **and** European.

By pointing out the multiple denotative and connotative references of
'Europe' and 'European', and suggesting that one needs to consider whether
a designation is toponymic, politonymic, ethnonymic, or linguonymic, I am
keen to demonstrate that in this way we may be able to render more public
and accountable the covert agendas of 'European' 'integration', and the role
of language generally, and of specific languages, in such policies. Definitions
of 'Europe' are often ethnicist or linguicist or classist or, mostly, all of them,
taking the dominant groups and classes and cultures and languages as the
norm and ignoring the rights of others. Such practices may fall into the
pattern of how hegemonic ideologies are reproduced.

Likewise, references in the dominant discourse to 'minorities', 'ethnic
groups' or 'minority languages' are often exclusionary as we have seen: only
minorities or certain minority groups or languages are seen as ethnic, while
majorities are seen as devoid of ethnicity. 'National' languages tend in Europe
to refer to the languages of the dominant group, and coincide with official
languages, while the opposite may be true in Africa or India (see chapter 5).
'All languages of India are national languages. No language is anti-national',
according to Debi Prasanna Pattanayak, former Director of the Central
Institute of Indian Languages (1988: 379).

The processes through which those wanting to join The Euroclub become
included/integrated into 'Europe' show close affinities to the processes
through which minorities are seen to 'integrate into the mainstream majority
societies', i.e. join The National Club, and processes through which the global
reordering takes place. Languages and ethnicities are involved in important
ways.

Worldwide, the negotiations are about common or disjointed futures. This
should involve a negotiation between equal parties, where the languages,
cultures and ethnicities of all negotiating groups should be acknowleged as
resources. Instead, most languages, cultures and ethnicities of humankind
are made invisible or are redefined so that they seem handicaps to integration
rather than resources. This makes Dascal's 'squared We' impossible.

Focussing on identities has been seen by some researchers as fussing about
less important issues (believing exclusively in contact theories—see section
3.3.3.) and diverting people away from the decisive political and economic

questions (i.e., those based on conflict theories). Quite the opposite. Mary Kalantzis has captured the relationship between economic, political and identity struggles in a integral way:

> The global moment is one in which the Cold War has ended. And with it has the politics of East/West boundary drawing, an argument essentially about economic systems. Into the space have stepped arguments that are still about access to social resources, but arguments that are now expressed through a discourse of culture, identity and nation. (1995: 1)

In this 'discourse of culture, identity and nation', the right or lack of right to define who you are decides your share in the economic and political systems. We can see the development in the construction of the definitions discussed in this chapter from a dialectic point of view. The **thesis** is the phase (which still seems to be the most common one) where the dominant groups define (and name) the linguistic, cultural, and ethnic identities of others: only exo-categorisations are valid (this also corresponds to all the assimilationist phases in studying integration, and in organising minority education). The progressive **anti-thesis** is that all, including dominated and minority groups, themselves have the right to define (and name) themselves, that is, only endo-categorisations are valid. During both the thesis and the anti-thesis phase cognitive dissonance, conflict between endonyms and exonyms is possible and often probable in the real world, but since only either one or the other categorisation is seen as valid, the conflict does not become apparent.

The **synthesis** which I develop here, sees the -nyms, the names by which groups are characterised, as signifiers of the power relation between constituencies and stakeholders in the world. Cognitive consonance can be reached and the endo- and exo-categorisations agree only in a situation of balanced power between the parties. The human right to self-definition, a fine principle which I of course support, makes sense only when the parties are equal. But if minorities are defined on the basis of power, not numbers, as most present definitions in international law do—see chapter 7—minorities (and indigenous peoples) and other dominated groups are by definition not equal parties in the negotiation processes about 'their' ethnicities or 'their' degree of integration or their mother tongues. This inequality has to be made explicit. Research about ethnicity and integration should, in my view, mainly study the structural and ideological conditions for the negotiation, including the power relationships between the actors. By concentrating the study of integration (including education and first and second language learning) on researching the migrants/minorities and 'their' characteristics, the conditions for real integration, most importantly the power of the dominant groups to prevent integration, are neglected. Thus the concept of integration is constructed in a way which permits it to be used in legitimating new forms of racism and exclusion, nationally and globally.

The role of researchers in supporting one or the other party in a conflict of this kind is important. By choosing how to define and study 'integration' or 'ethnicity', or 'mother tongue', by treating them as characteristics or as relations, researchers can present evidence to legitimate or delegitimate the results of the unequal power relations between dominated and dominant groups. Researchers can, knowingly or unintentionally, come to function as parts of the repressive state apparatuses, or repressive global power-holder apparatuses, and can ideologically contribute to the support of exploitative ideologies, structures and practices, when they define concepts discussed here (and others) as characteristics of the dominated, characteristics, the lack of which is then used to deny the group access to certain resources which the dominant elites have as groups.

Or we may be able to participate in delegitimating exploitative ideologies and structures, by supporting dominated groups when they try to create the knowledge and awareness necessary for negotiating from a position of the power which a theoretically sound analysis may give. In a world where control, in addition to brutal physical power, is increasingly constructed and maintained with the help of words, research which focuses on whose meanings prevail and why, is more urgently needed than ever.

3.6. LANGUAGE FOR CONTROL AND DOMINATION, RESISTANCE, AND SELF-DETERMINATION

In a hegemonic discourse, inequality and exclusion are legitimated so that both those who do the excluding and those who are excluded feel that exclusion is based on rational arguments and that the actions benefit those who are excluded. Again, the role of language in both achieving this and resisting it is vital. In the prefinal section of this chapter we will introduce three important processes in those hegemonic discourses which legitimate the reduction of linguistic and cultural diversity. Later chapters will exemplify further how they work especially in intergenerational transmission of languages and in the educational system. The final section summarizes some of the areas where language plays a vital role.

3.6.1. Glorification, Stigmatisation, and Rationalisation

A prerequisite for success in persuading individuals to replace their mother tongue by another language is the invalidation of their own languages and cultures. It is achieved through an ideological discourse which presents dominated/minority languages and cultures as deficiencies or handicaps, or makes them invisible. Glorification of the non-material resources of the dominant groups, stigmatisation of the resources of the dominated, and rationalisation of the relationship between the two, the A team and the B team (see 6.1.1.2), represent means for attempts at colonising the consciousness (Fanon 1952, 1963, 1965) of the dominated. The content of the messages about their non-material resources created for minorities and others from the B team, when they are being controlled through ideas in general, can be analysed in terms of these three processes (Table 3.2; partly based on ideas in Preiswerk (ed.) 1980).

TABLE 3.2
Reproduction of unequal power relations through glorification, stigmatisation, and rationalisation

1. **GLORIFY the majority/dominant group**, its language, culture, norms, traditions, institutions, level of development, observance of human rights, etc.

2. **STIGMATISE and devalue the minorities/subordinated groups**, their languages, cultures, norms, traditions, institutions, level of development, observance of human rights etc., so that they are seen as non-civilised, primitive, non-modern, traditional, backward, not fit for or able to adapt to postmodern technological 'democratic' information societies.

3. **RATIONALIZE their relationship** economically, politically, psychologically, educationally, sociologically, linguistically, etc., so that what the dominant group/s do/es always seems functional, and beneficial to the minorities/subordinated groups (the dominant group is 'helping', 'giving aid', 'civilizing', 'modernizing', 'teaching democracy', 'granting rights', 'preventing conflict', 'protecting world peace', etc.)

Here I give only a few examples of each—more follow later. The **glorification** of dominant majority languages has typically involved projecting them as 'the language of God' (Sanskrit, Arabic in the Islamic world, Dutch in South Africa), 'the language of reason, logic, and human rights' (French both before and more generally after the French Revolution), 'the language of the superior ethno-national group' (German in Nazi ideology), 'the language of progress, modernity, and national unity' (English in much post-colonial discourse) or simply as the language of wider currency in the country concerned (most majority languages for immigrant and refugee minorities), or in the world.

One way of conceptualising glorification of the dominant language or dominant variety is Carol Myers-Scotton's concept 'elite closure'. She describes it as follows:

Elite closure is a type of social mobilization strategy by which those persons in power establish or maintain their powers and privileges via linguistic choices. Put more concretely, elite closure is accomplished when the elite successfully employ official language policies and their own nonformalized language usage patterns to limit access of nonelite groups to political position and socioeconomic advancement (1993: 149).

The elite is set off from others in the following ways:

1. If the elites are fluent in varieties different from those that others know, this fluency is an identifying feature of elites.

2. If elites use, especially in public situations, a variety different from the one that others use, then their use patterns are means of identifying members of the elite. That is, their fluency and their use patterns have clear utilitarian value.

3. If the way elites speak is judged positively and therefore has psychological value, there is an obvious incentive for elites to retain this evaluation for themselves by ensuring that their linguistic abilities and use patterns remain distinctive. (ibid., 151)

Stigmatisation of the dominated groups and their non-material resources, here especially invalidating their languages, has typically involved the pattern of labelling dominated languages as mere 'dialects', 'vernaculars' or 'patois' as described earlier (see Definition Box 3.6). Languages have thus been made invisible *qua* languages. The Sámi example below (Insert 3.29) does it more specifically by not acknowledging that there is a group of related languages rather than one language with several dialects. It involves using different criteria for defining a language when talking about smaller as opposed to larger or more widely known entities. A parallel to the Sámi example might be to say that there is one German language, spoken across Germany, Britain, Sweden, Norway, Denmark, Iceland, the Netherlands, and so on, and it exists as several local dialects (which might be named: German, English, Norwegian, etc.).

INSERT 3.29   Just one Sámi language? Not correct.

Even scholars supporting minority languages can participate in stigmatisation through invisibilization. Kaplan & Baldauf, speaking of the nine Sámi languages, call them dialects: 'Sami (Lappish)—a Uralic language—is an indigenous minority language spoken across Finland (Aikio 1991), Norway, Sweden and Russia. It exists as several (nine or more) local dialects' (1997: 226–227). Kaplan and Baldauf are in good company; also Peter Mühlhäusler and even Marjut Aikio (whose doctoral dissertation was about the death of Sámi and who speaks North Sámi) **sometimes** talk about a Sámi language.

Stigmatisation also labels dominated languages as ugly, not human, confused, not capable of being used for abstract thinking, insignificant, not useful, etc. Inserts 3.30 through 3.34 show a few examples—there are many more in later chapters.

INSERT 3.30   Afrikaans—'confused utterance of half-articulated patois' (South Africa)

The English Cape Town newspaper **The Cape Times** wrote 1906: 'Afrikaans is the confused utterance of half-articulated patois' (quoted in Prah 1995a: 7).

INSERT 3.31   Khoikhoi: 'When they speak they fart with their tongues in their mouths' (Southern Africa)

1. 'They sound like . . . the clucking of hens or the clucking of turkeys.'

2. 'When they speak they fart with their tongues in their mouths.'

3. 'They seem to resound always with the very nature, the poetic character of the lands where they were used. The cadences of the wild, of water and earth, rock and grass, roll onomatopoetically along the tongue. Khoikhoi words . . . crack and softly rustle, and click. The sand and dry heat and empty distance of the semi-arid lands where the Khoikhoi originated are embedded in them. But so is softness, greenness. They run together like the very passage of their olden days.'

The three descriptions above of the Khoekhoe[28] languages of South Africa and Namibia (Khoekhoe are click languages), all by outsiders,[29] reflect a possible change in attitudes, which might, in the best case, have some positive consequences for the maintenance of Khoekhoe languages, already thought to be 'dead' in South Africa. The Khoekhoe have been called 'Hottentots' by outsiders (and the San 'Bushmen'), and 'to this day the Shorter Oxford English Dictionary notes that the word Hottentot is used to describe "a person of inferior intellect and culture"' (Koch & Maslamoney 1997: 28). It is easier to rob the lands and kill the languages of peoples if they are constructed as 'inferior', and this is exactly what happened (and is still happening in the world, only now with more sophisticated methods than centuries ago).

Similar descriptions abound. Australian Aboriginal languages were branded as 'primitive', 'heathen gibberish', and 'rubbish languages' (Fesl 1993: 27), Pacific languages as 'rubbish' 'repositories of wickedness and moral degradation' (Mühlhäusler 1996: 196, 140), 'Satan had a special agency in the formation of the Chinese language' (ibid., 141), 'the hideous snapping, barking dialect that passes for speech . . . scarcely like human speech in sound . . . noises like sneezes, snarls, and the prelimary stages of choking' (Rossel Island, ibid., 130–131). Other types of stigmatisation of a language can also make it less palatable, even to its own speakers (Insert 3.32).

INSERT 3.32   Nagamese = dog Assamese? (India)

Rajesh Sachdeva from North-Eastern Hill University, Shillong, India, compares the elite bilingualism with English as one of the languages and the folk bilingualism, involving Nagamese as one of the languages. He reports that it was called 'Assamese/Nagamese [or dog Assamese as Hutton called it to capture the pidginised nature of the language]' (1998: 8). (Hutton is presumably an English speaker). As Satchdeva shows in his empirical study, the negative evaluation of Nagamese has to a very large extent been taken over by its own speakers. Even if many if not most people in Nagaland know it, they do not claim it as a mother tongue: Nagaland, with English as the official language, has the highest percentage of 'minority language speakers in India, 86.06% in 1981 census (Sridhar 1996: 330). Nor do they want it to be used for official or other high status purposes (Satchdeva 1998).

The glorification and stigmatisation also lead to differential knowledge about the glorified and stigmatised languages, respectively (Insert 3.33).

INSERT 3.33   Linguistics students do not know the number of vowels in their mother tongues (India)

University of Hyderabad is a postgraduate university which gets some of the best students in India. Prof. Panchanan Mohanty asked his course of 8 third term linguistics students, with many different mother tongues, how many vowels there are in their mother tongues. Not one of them could give an answer. In contrast, each of them could immediately tell how many vowels and consonants English has, and even allophones. (Source: discussion with Mohanty in his home, 5 January 1995).

One might, of course, claim that the knowledge of the number of vowels is 'the kind of knowledge one is likely to acquire when learning second/additional languages'—this is Timothy Reagan's point (personal communication, December 1998). He adds that he is 'by no means certain that I know the number of vowels in English (arguably my mother tongue, and certainly my dominant language), but I could certainly answer the question for Russian, Spanish or Afrikaans' (ibid.). It seems to me, though, that the knowledge of what a vowel is should be enough to give the answer for the mother tongue, given a couple of minutes, and this knowledge one presumably has if one knows the number of vowels in some other language.

Rationalization of the relationship between the dominant and the dominated has typically involved presenting the dominant group as 'civilizing' and 'helping' the dominated, giving them 'aid', and 'teaching them democracy and human rights'. This rationalising of the relationship where the actions of the dominant are constructed as unselfish and good for the dominated has a long pedigree. Geoffrey Best writes, in an article about the French Revolution and human rights, how these liberating notions were received in lands that Napoleon conquered (1988: 106–107):

> What the French called liberation and what, indeed, met with welcome from Francophone minorities in most countries, was experienced by their national majorities as oppression and exploitation. Revolutionary rhetoric did not deceive them. Satirical parodies of the standard French liberation proclamations were not far from the truth: e.g., 'We have arrived and you are free. Anyone found on the street after sunset will be shot at sight.' . . . The French . . . had a mission, a calling, the duty as well as the right to give other peoples the benefits of the same experience they had given themselves. Beginning as 'liberation', it was in practice scarcely distinguishable from domination.

The rationalization of the relationship between the languages and their speakers shows the dominant group as a benefactor and the dominated one as the one to gain from language shift. As other (minority, dominated) languages are explicitly or implicitly (presented as) deprived of such positive qualities and functions as are attributed to the dominant languages, it is 'logical' that speakers of stigmatised languages can only benefit from using the 'superior' languages.

Most of the development studies paradigms and evolution and modernisation theories are in fact based on these hegemonic processes. Zygmunt Baumann (1997) speaks about 'chronopolitics': everything that was different from the West was put down chronologically, placed on a scale where it was seen as similar to something that might have existed earlier in the West. In the Nordic countries and Germany it used to be common to hear politicians speak about the distance of 150 years which 'guest workers' or 'immigrants' from Turkey had to cover in a couple of days on the bus and plane from a Turkish village via Istanbul to Copenhagen or Stockholm or Berlin. But it was in their own interest to 'catch up and become modern'.

The same linguicist/ethnicist policies which deprive dominated languages and cultures of recognition (delegitimates and invalidates them, see also 3.2.2.2), also deprive them of resources for building on their potential. This happens in clear ways in the educational system. Glorification, stigmatisation, and rationalisation will be discussed and exemplified further in later chapters. It is, though, important to remember that the counterforces, people seeing through the ideologies in the hegemonic processes, likewise have a long pedigree in relation to both languages and cultures, as the example with the great Indian poet Tagore shows (Insert 3.34).

INSERT 3.34 Countering stigmatisation and glorification: Tagore's family

Tagore was born in 1861 and writes here about the late 1870s:

> Looked at from the outside, our family appears to have accepted many foreign customs, but at its heart flames a national pride that has never flickered. The genuine regard my father had for his country he never forsook through all the vicissitudes of his life, and in his decendants it took shape as a strong patriotic feeling. Such, however, was by no means characteristic of the times of which I am writing. Our educated men were then keeping at arm's length both the language and thought of their native land. My elder brothers had, nevertheless, always cultivated Bengali literature. On one occasion when some new connection by marriage wrote my father a letter in English it was promptly returned to the writer. (Tagore 1992: 104–105, originally published in 1911)

This also happened in schools. Lachman Khubchandani, now in his late sixties, related in a discussion (December 1994, Pune, India) that he as a schoolboy, from the age of 12, wrote in every English textbook in school: 'I dream of the time when English will be kicked out of my country'.

3.6.2. Control and Domination—and Resistance

A short summary of some of the uses of language will finish this chapter. Many of them have already been discussed, others will be highlighted in later chapters. Just a few references will be given here, more will follow.

Language has been an important means of control and domination and its importance is rapidly growing.[30] Language has been seen as an essential, homogenizing element in the nation-building of states since the Age of Enlightenment (e.g., Gellner 1983, Hobsbawm 1991). There is also continuous controversy over the role of the 'standard' language ('proper' language) as opposed to other variants (e.g., the Kingman Report in the UK (1988) and its critics, e.g. Cameron & Bourne 1989, Tollefson 1991, 58–67), or as in the recent Ebonics[31] debates in the USA. The enforcement of standard languages has likewise been a powerful method in controlling ordinary people (e.g., O'Barr 1982) and in homogenisation (e.g., Illich 1981). Language has played an important role in maintaining colonial structures[32] and reproducing neo-colonial structures (e.g., Bamgbose 1991, Ngũgĩ 1986). Education through the medium of majority languages or colonial languages has been the most powerful assimilating force for both indigenous children and immigrant/refugee minority children, thus likewise having a homogenizing function.

But as discussed above, language has also become an important means for counterhegemonies and for seeking self-determination at several levels, psychologically, educationally, politically. Language is central for seeing, interpreting, understanding and changing the world, and indeed in creating it. Language is central to the cultural and ethnic identity of most groups (e.g., Fishman 1989, Skutnabb-Kangas 1987, 1990b, 1991a, Smolicz 1979, 1989). The right to naming one's own world, having the right to define how one sees oneself and the rest of the world, is realized through language. The validity of one's own endo-definition of one's own group and its status (as opposed to having to accept an exo-definition, a definition of one's own group and its status from outsiders) is negotiated through language, even when arms and other material resources and structural power set the framework for these negotiations.

Language is one of several important mobilizing factors in struggles for national recognition, whether for indigenous peoples[33] or for groups re-asserting themselves after the disintegration of communist regimes.[34] Control over the destiny of one's own language and maximizing its official use is also of paramount concern to groups seeking self-determination or more cultural rights, before or, indeed, after decolonisation.[35] Language is also central to the demands of many immigrant groups, regardless of whether these are aspiring to become new national minorities or not.[36]

The fate of languages is thus of the utmost importance. And this importance is growing since the struggle over the power and resources of the world occurs increasingly through ideological means, and ideas are mainly mediated through language. Instead of and in addition to using 'sticks'—physical violence and control over the material resources (land, water, natural resources; bodies as producers of profit) of the B team, the A team use 'carrots'—rewards and benefits, and ideas, mediated through language. The world's B team is increasingly being ruled and controlled hegemonically, with their own (partial) consent.

This also partially explains the spread of numerically large languages (English, Spanish, Russian, Chinese, etc.) at the cost of the smaller ones. The ideas of the power-holders cannot be spread, nationally or internationally, unless those with less power understand the power-holders' language (e.g., 'international English' worldwide, or standard Italian in Italy). Therefore the struggle is about whose language is to prevail. The A team want and need the B team to learn the A team's languages but not vice versa.

The division of the world into the haves, have-nots and never-to-haves is partly formed and reinforced on the basis of languages, as even non-linguists start acknowledging, even when they might disagree about everything else (e.g., Huntington 1996 versus Galtung 1996). In this new discourse of culture, identity, and nation (Kalantzis 1995), negotiations about not only the tolerance of but indeed the preservation, promotion, and development of linguistic and cultural diversity are vital for world peace. Language is a necessary prerequisite and a peaceful weapon in the struggle for a more just world. In the light of the importance of language, it might also be easier to see the enormous relevance about the exciting new hypotheses about the (causal) connections with biodiversity discussed in chapter 2. In the following chapter we will be looking at other arguments for or against maintenance of linguistic diversity.

The non-dominant languages and the cultural interpretations and knowledge of the world they are bearers of are a necessary counterweight to the power-holders' homogenising and homogenised languages and messages. Pirkko Leporanta-Morley captures many of the themes from this chapter in her poem about 'Men in Power' (Insert 3.35).

INSERT 3.35   Poem MEN IN POWER by Pirkko Leporanta-Morley

MEN IN POWER
Pirkko Leporanta-Morley

Who gives you
the right to define
our reality?
You offer us 'help'
binding our hands
interpreting our demands as mere ingratitude.
You give us
'progressive changes'
ignoring our true needs
expecting obedience.

You have misunderstood us.
We want our freedom!
You cannot control us
We have our own languages!

(Pirkko Leporanta, came to Sweden as an immigrant from Finland. 'Progressive changes' refers to Mullard 1988).

NOTES

1. Merrill Swain's doctoral dissertation was called **Bilingualism as the first language**.
2. See also Smolicz 1981, 1984, 1985, 1988, 1989, 1994, Smolicz & Secombe 1986, 1989, Smolicz et al. 1990.

3. The **Californian Proposition 227** was passed on 2 June 1998. It was an Initiative Statute by the multimillionaire Ron K. Unz, a high-technology entrepreneur who does not have children himself and has no expertise in education or languages. Unz ran for governor in the 1994 Republican primary and lost to Pete Wilson, a candidate he called 'too moderate'. Unz' positions on other issues are extreme right wing, from 'eliminating workers compensation to cutting taxes for the wealthy to cracking down on welfare mothers' (**NABE News** 21:4, 11).

The co-signer of the initiative, Gloria Matta Tuchman, is a former director of US English, the leading English Only lobby in the USA. This is the organisation which proclaimed that 'California was being taken over by "fast-breeding" Mexican-Americans ("Perhaps this is the first instance in which those with their pants up are going to get caught by those with their pants down!")' and which questioned the 'educability' of Latino children (ibid.). The Proposition takes California back to the period between 1872 and 1967 when California law required all instruction to be in English and when the Hispanic high school drop-out rate was close to 75%. In 1960 the census found that only 50% of the state's Hispanic 18–24 year olds had even completed the eighth grade, one of the many negative results of this English-only educational policy.

The blanket directive is that 'All children [shall] be placed in English language classrooms'. If children know no English, they are allowed to have 180 days of English teaching (according to Unz 'young children can easily learn a new language in a matter of months . . .', ibid., 6). After those 180 days, schools are forbidden to use the native language of the students to facilitate subject matter teaching, and all teachers can be threatened with lawsuits and personal liability for speaking even a few words of a language other than English in class. No professional standards or special ESL or other training is required by those who teach minority children; this has already led to some universities considering scrapping this kind of teacher training. It is proposed that schools are reorganized on the basis of student English proficiency, across age and grade levels, completely ignoring the academic knowledge of students in other subjects. Parent choice is out. Waivers from the English-only instructional mandate may be obtained by some parents, but the procedures are cumbersome and for children under the age of 10 the circumstances allowing a waiver are very limited.

The whole campaign which led to the passing of Proposition 227 was characterized by outright lies and false threats. These have been carefully documented and analysed by many responsible research and educational organizations, both Californian and countrywide. Even before the initiative, it was only 30% of California's minority students who were not yet fully competent in English who had any type of bilingual education. In the overwhelming majority of cases this was of the early-exit transitional type. Now the restrictions mean that California is blatantly violating children's linguistic human rights, as these are interpreted in the Hague Recommendations on Education Rights of National Minorities from the OSCE High Commissioner on National Minorities (see 7.8.3)—and the USA is a member of the OSCE. These human rights violations were confirmed by an international panel of judges in The Hague in May 1999—see 7.8.2. **NABE News** 21:4, February 1, 1998, is a Special Issue on Unz. For more information on the Unz Initiative, see the following Websites: <http://www.noonunz.org> (Citizens for an Educated America: No on Unz); <http://www.nabe.org> (National Association for Bilingual Education); <http://www.smartnation.org> (Smartnation); <http://www.onenation.org> (Ron Unz's Pro-Initiative Organization). See both Jeff MacSwan's (<http://www.public.asu.edu/~macswan/>) and Jim Crawford's Language Policy Web-pages <http://ourworld.compuserve.com/homepages/ jwcrawford>, for references and latest documentation about consequences of the Proposition; see also the Web-page of the National Clearinghouse for Bilingual Education <http://www. ncbe.gwu.edu>; for alternative action, see also the Web-page of the organisation Rethinking Schools <http://www.rethinkingschools.org/>.

4. See Kontra 1996a, b, 1997, 1998a, Lanstyák, in press, Driessen 1999.
5. A close parallel is the 'tiger' economies in Asia—if they could do it, everybody can, so it is the fault of the underdeveloped countries themselves if they 'choose' not to, so the claim goes. But if these 'overassimilados' start questioning the doctrine, a crash follows, and they have to be rebrought under the control of the Bretton Woods and other instruments, as for instance happened to South Korea in 1997–1998. See Pilger 1998.
6. Info Box 3.1 is a slightly revised version of a section in Skutnabb-Kangas & Phillipson 1996a.
7. 'Foreign' is a relational term, not a characteristic of the person or group (or language) described—it posits Me/Us at the centre and constructs everything else as Others, Foreign. And the less power this Foreign has in relation to Us, the more foreign it is and the more it can be invalidated and illegitimated.
8. 'Push-out' is a more realistic term for the customary 'drop-out', in expressing where the changes have to be sought if the children are to be retained in school.
9. We (Rahbek Pedersen & Skutnabb-Kangas 1983: 206–207) showed for instance for the late 1970s, that of those Turkish nationals between the ages of 12 and 15 who were resident in Denmark according to census statistics, less than a third were to be found in the school statistics. There is no reason to believe that the figures have changed considerably since then even if some improvement has taken place. Skutnabb-Kangas 1984a gives a lot of older figures for Germany and Scandinavia, and the changes to the positive are not desperately large. We also showed that it would be perfectly possible—and not more costly—to organise mainly mother tongue medium education for at least some 80% of the immigrant minorities.
10. Marianne Gronemeyer's article 'Helping' (1992) is a real eye-opener in relation to who is being helped by whom—it also makes is almost impossible to use the concept of 'help' without quotation marks. A similar point is made by Leslie Schwartz (1998).
11. There are several cases where the estimation of the Danish authorities in custody disputes between parents where at least one is an immigrant is based on considerations about the person's and the family's competence in the Danish language, as an indication of their 'willingness to integrate'. Families can, for instance, be seen as 'willing to integrate' if a member has attended a course in the Danish language. A family has been seen as 'unwilling to integrate' if a child who has arrived to Denmark as part of a family reunion, 'still' after 6 months does not speak Danish (information from a colleague, February 1999).
12. Or 'malestream', as a Bengali student at our university called it.
13. As quantum physics tells us, nothing can in fact be a disencumbered tool. The observer effect—see e.g., Pagels 1982, Wolf 1991—means not only that the phenomenon to be observed (e.g., 'the world') changes **because** it is being observed, but also that we **create** it (make it happen or materialise) by observing it—this is one of the senses in which some aspects of post-modernism might make more sense. And speaking about something is observing it, through language.
14. Racism and sexism seem to blend in the changes of images here: earlier black was the **positive** colour of life itself: earth, moist caves where life was born, life-giving blood when caked, etc. White was the **negative** colour of death—dead bones of animals and humans, bleached in the sun, people who were ill. When Goddesses became gods with the overtaking of patriarchy, also the colour symbolism changed (see the fascinating book by the archaeologist Marija Gimbutas 1991).
15. In fact Tamil past linguistic glories of more than 2,000 years were being unearthed and revived by scholars and administrators from the middle of the 19th century, resulting in a Tamil Renaissance towards the end of the 19th century (Arooran 1980: 16, 32).
16. Kenneth McRae himself does not problematise this in the sense that there is no doubt for him that Karelian is 'a language': 'The fate of Karelian is a reminder that . . . a language may also be demoted to dialect status by dictatorial fiat' (ibid., 123, note 13). See also Hyry 1995.

17. Sometimes we may see double exo-definitions, as in the case of the Tsonga language, constructed by missionaries (as many other languages were) in the late nineteen hundreds. First the Swiss missionaries used the joint name Gwamba (see Insert 3.11) for a wide variety of dialects/languages (many as distant from each other as French and English, according to Erskine), then replaced Gwamba with Tonga/Thonga, later Tsonga. Tonga 'simply means something which is not Zulu' (Erskine 1875, quoted in Harries 1995: 161). Most of the Tonga/Thonga genericisms (e.g., Ronga—easteners, Djonga—southeners) 'were merely terms of exclusion applied by people to neighbours from whom they wished to distinguish themselves. They were not categories of linguistic inclusion' (Harries 1995: 161). But these exo-definitions by neighbours were then taken over by the missionaries and used about all of the groups, thus uniting them under 'a false degree of separation and cohesion' (ibid.).

18. See Ferguson 1959 for the concept 'diglossia' and Fishman 1967, 1976, for its development and some applications; see also Ferguson et al. 1977. See Definition Box 2.2.

19. It is also interesting for me as an outsider to see who is explicitly defined as not 'white' and what the information is that the USA census 2000, Questions 5 and 6 (Ethnicity and Race) is interested in. For 5, 'ethnicity' there is a very detailed list with 'Mexican, Mexican Am., Chicano [no females?] Puerto Rican, Cuban, other Spanish, Hispanic, Latino'. The formulation of question 6 is: 'What is this person's race? Mark (X) one or more races to indicate what this person considers himself/herself to be'). 'White' is—of course—on top of the possible 'races'; the others are Black, African Am. or Negro; American Indian or Alaska Native; Asian Indian; Chinese; Filipino; Japanese; Korean; Vietnamese; Other Asian (Print race); Some other race (Print race) [this is where I would belong: 'the human race'— this would be the only scientifically correct category]; Native Hawaiian; Guamanian or Chamorro; Samoan, Other Pacific Islander (Print race). The 'Guamanian or Chamorro' is also interesting when knowing that the Chamorro language was completely banned in schools by the Americans in 1922 and all Chamorro dictionaries were collected and burned (Richard Benton 1981: 122, here quoted from Mühlhäusler 1996: 109).

20. 'Liberal' is used in this book as a historical-philosophical term about supporters of liberalism. I am aware that this does not always tally with some popular North American usages.

21. As in many other situations too, the Deaf community is interesting here. Even if endogamous marriages are extremely common (Reagan mentions estimates between 86% to well over 90% for the USA, 1992: 312), only some 10% of deaf children have deaf parents, and thus the children mostly learn sign language from peers, not primary caretakers. This means that the 'descent' criterion is not fully relevant biologically, but culturally it is. Otherwise the Deaf fulfill all Allardt's criteria (Definition Box 3.9) for an ethnic group:—**important cultural traits**, including both norms for culturally appropriate behaviours and language; sign language is the single 'most effective signal of membership in the deaf community' (Erting 1978: 139, quoted in Reagan 1992: 307); 'membership in the deaf community is contingent upon communication competence in ASL' (American Sign Language) (Reagan 1992: 311), and the sign DEAF can be used in an ASL sentence to mean "my friends", which conveys the cultural meaning of "Deaf" ' (ibid., 312);—social organization for interaction both within the group and with people outside the group; and—self-identification as 'Deaf' (a cultural group) rather than 'deaf' (an audiological definition—see Definition Box 4.1).

    Because of the lack of the full descent criterion, though, the Deaf are probably best called a sociocultural minority group rather than an ethnic group.

22. It seems to me that the discussion about **ethnos or demos** as beneficiaries of self-determination, sometimes becomes confused, because **demos** for some people seems to denote a **toponymic** group (especially after the shift in the 1960s and 1970s from ethnicity or language as a basis for the right to statehood to territory as the main basis), for others a **politonymic** group, which in a way should render a discussion of the right to self-determination of a **demos** meaningless. For still others, they denote both **toponymic** and **politonymic** groups.

The discussion of a definition of 'peoples' could also benefit from keeping these concepts apart. It is often difficult because the same word (e.g., a Turk) can be used to designate all four.

Merging the meanings of all four into one concept and/or word can but need not also signify an extreme nation-state ideology, i.e., everybody is a Turk who lives in the territory called Turkey. This Turk is a Turkish citizen, s/he is (= **must** be) ethnically Turkish, and speaks (= must speak) Turkish only.

Internal self-determination can then concern rights to **linguonymic, ethnonymic**, and even **toponymic** groups/peoples, whereas self-determination to **politonymic** peoples leads to external self-determination.

23. See also the discussions on the meaning of 'Europe' in Wæver et al. 1993, 4, 10, Kiernan 1995: 145–170, Pentikäinen 1995.
24. I have only recently noticed, reading several historians, that calling the war which started in Europe in 1917–18, the first 'World War' is again one of the Eurocentric tricks we all have been subjected to. We Are The World! The terminological problem then becomes what to call the 'Second World War'.
25. In 1994 the exclusive use of politonymic 'European' would have meant that the problems faced by the Finnish labour immigrant minority in Sweden (the largest migrant minority group in Scandinavia) would not have been a 'European' dilemma: Sweden and Finland only joined the Union in 1995. But in 1999 it is an 'internal European' dilemma. Whereas the problems that the Baltic states face with the Russian-speaking labour (im)migrant minorities, or that these face with the Baltic states are not supposed to be a 'European' problem—yet. Still, internal Estonian ethnic relations are influenced much more by Russia, the United States, and western Europe than by the ethnic groups in Estonia themselves—see Rannut 1994, 1999. Estonia will probably join the EU in the next round, together with Hungary, Poland, the Czech Republic, and Slovenia. Neither the Russian Federation nor the Baltic states are members yet. But if Russians or Poles or Albanians try to enter the German or Italian labour market, that is a 'European' dilemma.
26. In several 'European' languages the reading of the name is not 'in' but 'of' Europe, including the language OSCE was dreamed up in by the then Finnish President Kekkonen.
27. This formulation is used in Article 1, Definitions, of the European Charter for Regional or Minority Languages, along with exclusions (dialects and migrant languages) and a definition of 'non-territorial languages' aimed at covering the Roma and Jews. The Charter will be analysed in chapter 7.
28. 'Khoekhoe' is the preferred present spelling used by linguists, on linguistic grounds (see Traill 1995—a useful overview of the Khoesan languages—who also refers to Nienaber's (1990) discussion). 'Khoesan' is also 'linguistically misleading because it does not refer to a single family of languages' (Traill 1995: 15, Note i), but 'three genetically unrelated groups of languages' (ibid.). The Central Khoesan group, Khoe languages (Nama, Cape Khoe, Naro, etc.), are mutually non-intelligible with the two groups of San Languages (Northern and Southern Khoesan groups) which again do not constitute a genetic unity. The Northern San include languages like Zhu and !Xung, the Southern includes !Xam, !Xóõ, etc.
29. The first two descriptions are by some of the first colonisers of the Khoekhoe areas, the third by historian Noel Mostert, all quoted in Koch & Maslamoney 1997: 28.
30. See, for instance, Anderson 1983, Apple 1993, Bourdieu 1997, 1992, 1998, Fairclough 1987, 1989, 1991, 1992 (ed.), 1996, Freire 1985, Foucault 1980, Giroux 1992, Habermas 1971, 1984, 1987, Pennycook 1994, 1998a,b, Phillipson 1992, Tollefson 1991.
31. The Web-pages of Jim Crawford (<http://ourworld.compuserve.com/homepages/jwcrawford/>) and John Rickford (<http://www.stanford.edu/~rickford/>) have a lot of information and references. See Lippi-Green 1997, Perry & Delpit (eds) 1998, Rickford & Rickford 1995; see also Kontra & Baugh 1994 for comparisons.
32. E.g., Calvet 1974, 1987, Phillipson 1992, Mühlhäusler 1990, Heath 1972, Hornberger 1988, 1989, 1995.

33. See e.g., Hamel 1994a,b, 1995 on Latin America; Fesl 1988, 1993, Harris 1990, Harris & Devlin 1997, Amery 1998 on Aboriginal peoples in Australia; Magga 1994, Jernsletten 1993, 1997, Gaski 1996, 1997a,b, in press, Stordahl 1997, Eidheim 1997, Keskitalo 1997, Balto (ed.) 1996, Helander (ed.) 1996 on Sámi in Norway; Kāretu 1994, Benton 1996, Durie 1997, Smith 1993, on the Māori in New Zealand; Crawford 1996, 1998b, McLaughlin 1992, McLaughlin & Tierney 1993, Hinton 1994, Vorih & Rosier 1978 on indigenous peoples in the USA; Ekka 1984, Khubchandani 1991, 1994 and Pattanayak 1991 on 'tribals', i.e., indigenous peoples in India; Stairs 1988, Fettes 1992, 1998, Drapeau 1998, Cook 1998, Harnum 1993, 1998, on First Nations in Canada. These are just samples of both countries and references.

34. See e.g., Rannut 1994, 1999 on Estonia; Druviete 1994, in press a, b, on Latvia; Kontra 1995, 1998a, b, on Hungary; Lanstyák in press, Kontra 1996a, b, 1997, Information Centre of the Hungarian Coalition in Slovakia 1997, on Slovakia, Necak Lük 1996, on Slovenia, and articles in Plichtová (ed.) 1992, Tóth & Földeák (eds.) (1996), Tóth (ed.) (1987), and the journal **Regio. A Review of Minority and Ethnic Studies** published in Budapest, which is a real goldmine (e.g., the 1994 number contains several articles central for the concerns of this book).

35. See, e.g., Afolayan 1978, 1984, Akinnaso 1990, 1994, Alexander 1989, 1992, 1995a, b, Bamgbose 1991, Bokamba 1991, Bokamba & Tlou 1980, Bunyi 1997, de Cluver 1994, 1996, Djité 1993, 1994, Heugh 1995a, b, c, Desai 1994, 1995, 1998, Mateene 1980a, b, 1985a, b, Alamin Mazrui 1996, 1997, Ali Mazrui 1975, 1980, Obondo 1997, Phillipson, Skutnabb-Kangas & Africa 1986, Prah 1995a, b, Rubagumya 1990, Twahirva 1994 on Africa; Hassanpour 1992, in press, Hassanpour, Skutnabb-Kangas & Chyet 1996, Skutnabb-Kangas & Bucak 1994 on Kurds; Tickoo 1994 on Kashmiri.

36. See, e.g., articles in Skutnabb-Kangas & Cummins (eds.) 1988, Peura (ed.) 1983, Peura & Skutnabb-Kangas (eds.) 1994, especially Skutnabb-Kangas & Peura 1994.

Linguistic Diversity—
Curse or Blessing?
To Be Maintained or Not? Why?

We multilinguals may in a hundred years' time display voluntarily English-monolinguals (those who could have learned other languages but chose not to) in pathological museums.

'The real issue, therefore, is not whether, how or under what forces does an individual or a group become bilingual; it is whether and at what cost does one become monolingual.' (Mohanty 1987)

'Those of us who love languages, especially if we have devoted our lives to learning or teaching them, find it hard to put ourselves in the right frame of mind to understand the concept of language diversity as a curse. We see in language a source of novel delights and subtle experience, a blessing.' (Haugen 1987: 1)

4. LINGUISTIC DIVERSITY—CURSE OR BLESSING?
TO BE MAINTAINED OR NOT? WHY?

Having discussed the power in naming, labelling, and defining, we start this chapter by exploring how the origins of naming, language and linguistic diversity have been seen in great myths. Then some parallels between the naturalness of the death of biological organisms and languages are explored. We continue exploring ideologies—and agents—responsible for linguistic genocide. And finally, arguments for and against the maintenance of linguistic diversity are presented.

4.1. LINGUISTIC DIVERSITY IN GREAT MYTHS

4.1.1. Who Invented Language, God or Adam—or Eve?

Until approximately the middle of the seventeenth century, most researchers in the West conducted their languages-related studies with the Bible myths in the background. This included studies trying to understand where linguistic diversity came from. Here is the short story:

- the Word created the World (Genesis 1:3–31);
- Adam used language in the process of the naming of the world (animals, plants, etc.).

It is interesting to see the great difference between the two holy books, the Bible and the Qur'ān, in whom they attribute the 'invention' of human language to. The Bible makes Adam invent language himself, on his own. In the more humble version of the Qur'ān, on the other hand, God taught Adam the names of the animals, plants, etc., and then Adam told the names to the angels, repeating what God had taught him (see Info Box 4.1);

- Eve was the first one who used language for **earthly** social purposes—and, after all, language is a social contract. Eve spoke to another earthly being, the serpent (Genesis 3:3–5). Since Adam only used language with God and angels, maybe Eve was the real creator of earthly language. The transcendental man, the earthly, pragmatic woman?;
- there was only one language at least until the Flood.

After the Flood, we get different readings. Genesis 10 (5, 20, 31) speaks of the division of the lands by Japheth, Ham, and Shem, the sons of Noah, and the grandsons, 'every one after his tongue, after their families, in their nations' (so: nation-state + one language?). Genesis 11, on the other hand, assumes that after the Flood 'the whole earth was of one language, and of one speech' (11:1), until the tower of Babel[1] (see Info Box 4.2).

Who Created Language? The Bible, The Qur'ān

The Bible:

And out of the ground the Lord God formed every beast of the field, and every fowl of the air; and brought them unto Adam to see **what he would call them**: and whatsoever Adam called every living creature, that was the name thereof.

And **Adam gave names** to all cattle, and to the fowl of the air, and to every beast of the field . . . (Genesis 2:19–20).

The Qur'ān:

He taught Adam the names of all things and then set them before the angels, saying: 'Tell Me the names of these, if what you say be true.'

'Glory to You,' they replied, 'we have no knowledge except that which You have given us. You alone are wise and all-knowing.'

Then he said to Adam: 'Tell them their names.' And when Adam had named them, He said: 'Did I not tell you that I know the secrets of heaven and earth, and all that you hide and all that you reveal?' (2:31–33; Dawood's translation; emphases added).

❖ **I n f o   B o x   4 . 2** ❖

Number of Languages Between the Flood and the Tower of Babel

4. And they said, Go to, let us build us a city and a tower, whose top may reach unto heaven; and let us make us a name, lest we be scattered abroad upon the face of the whole earth.

5. And the Lord came down to see the city and the tower, which the children of men builded.

6. And the Lord said, Behold, the people is one, and they have all one language; and now nothing will be restrained from them, which they have imagined to do.

7. Go to, let us go down, and there confound their language, that they may not understand one another's speech.

8. So the Lord scattered them abroad from thence upon the face of all the earth: and they left off to build the city.

9. Therefore is the name of it called Babel; because the Lord did there confound the language of all the earth: and from thence did the Lord scatter them abroad upon the face of all the earth.' (Genesis 11:4–9).

Thus Hebrew, the language of the Old Testament, was seen as the '**pro-tolanguage**', the language that at least Adam and Eve and Noah—if not God—spoke, the original language that all the other languages in the world were derived from or related to (see Eco 1995 for a fascinating account).

At the same time as Western linguists, theologicians, mystics, kabbalists, and so on based their ideas of linguistic diversity on the Bible, different peoples in all parts of the world had their own stories of the origins of linguistic diversity. Arno Borst has collected many of these in the six volumes (1957–1963) of his book **Der Turmbau von Babel. Geschichte der Meinungen über Ursprung und Vielfalt der Sprachen und Völker** (The building of the Tower of Babel. History of views on the origins and diversity of languages and peoples).

4.1.2. Many Languages, Good or Bad? The Bible: A Curse; the Qur'ān: Sign of Allah's Omnipotence; Other Myths: Punishment for or Prevention of Quarrelling

Myths and stories have also interpreted the desirability, or otherwise, of diversity. In Western thinking there seems to be a possibly stronger inheritance of seeing homogeneity as positive and natural than in many other parts of the world. The Bible definitely sees, in the Babel tower story, the diversity of languages as a curse, a **punishment for peoples' pride**. Diversity has also been seen as a result of people quarrelling with each other. It could be a **punishment for quarrelling**, as the Dolgan fairytale indicates (see Insert 4.1).

Diversity could also be in order to **prevent** further **quarrelling**, as Iatiku did (see Insert 4.2).

As opposed to the Bible, the Qur'ān 'has established language variation as one of the great signs of Allah on earth', according to Abdussalam (1998: 59). This seems to be true not only for linguistic but also ethnic/racial diversity (see Info Box 4.3).

Many other myths (maybe especially indigenous creation stories?) seem to consider diversity as positive too. Accepting diversity as more positive than homogeneity may also preclude many either-or stances. Choices of a kind where other alternatives are necessarily excluded may make both-and stances impossible—and bilingualism and multilingualism are both-and because they imply adding other languages to one's repertoire rather than learning others at the cost of the original one(s), in a subtractive way (see Definition Box 2.2). Later in the chapter (section 4.2) other notions from scientific mythology will be discussed, including the myths involved in what I call monolingual reductionism/naivety/stupidity.

> **INSERT 4.1**   Dolgan fairytale—many languages
> punishment for quarrelling
>
> A Dolgan fairytale, called 'How the Peoples of the North Came to Speak
> Different Tongues' (retold in **Northern Lights**, 1980) narrates how a man
> started a journey south during a terrible snowstorm to find a warm and sunny
> land which he finally found. He came back and told his people. They started
> the long journey—while the man himself did not go: he 'made himself a warm
> deerskin coat, put it on and sat there, looking like nothing so much as a
> strange, fuzzy bird' (p. 65).
>
> > Meanwhile the people of his tribe journeyed on. They sought the road
> > to the warm land, and they made their way slowly, holding on to each
> > other. Bows and arrows were their only weapons, and, as they went
> > along, they shot game for food, tying eagle feathers to the arrows in
> > order for them to reach their mark better.
> >
> > One day they killed an eagle and began dividing his feathers among
> > themselves, but they could not agree as to who was to get the smaller
> > and who the bigger share.
> >
> > "You have offended me", one would say to another. "You have given
> > me too few feathers. We cannot speak the same language now, nor shall
> > we ever speak it."
> >
> > And so bitterly did they quarrel that they quite forgot that they were
> > on their way to a southern land. So that is how it came to be that there
> > are so many different peoples in the North, the Dolgans, the Yakuts,
> > the Evenks, the Nentsi and many, many others, and that they all speak
> > different tongues. (1980: 65-66).

> **INSERT 4.2**   Iatiku—many languages prevent quarrelling
>
> **Iatiku**, 'the mother goddess of the Acoma tribe of New Mexico . . . caused
> people to speak different languages so that it would not be so easy for them
> to quarrel.' (Gill & Sullivan 1992).

4.1.3. 'Natural' Extinction Rates for Languages?

From the origins of language and diversity we move to the end of them. As
mentioned in chapter 2, biologists estimate that the average life-span of a
biological species has been 5–10 million years, and that some 95% of all
species that ever existed during the last 3.5 billion years are now extinct, but
that during that time there has been a general trend of increasing species

---

❖ I n f o   B o x   4 . 3 ❖

Qur'ān—Diversity Sign of Allah

'Among his other signs are the creation of heaven and earth and the diversity of your tongues and colours. Surely there are signs in this for all mankind.' (Qur'ān 30: 22).

Comment: This is from N. J. Dawood's translation, revised edition 1959, p. 188. Abdussalam (1998: 57) renders the same as: 'Among his signs is the creation of heaven and earth and the variations in your languages (*alsinatukum*) and colours: verily in that are signs for those who know' and comments that *alsinatukum* is interpreted by Al-Zamakhsharī (1977) 'as variation in languages, dialects and modes of expression among groups and individuals' (ibid., 57). The Finnish translation from Arabic, **Koraani**, by Jussi Aro, Armas Salonen and Knut Tallqvist, also supports 'languages' and renders Dawood's 'colours' as 'appearances' (1957: 310), i.e., 'racial' diversity is also seen as positive.

---

richness (Baillie 1998: 12). Would something similar hold for languages? Do languages have a life-span which can be estimated? How many languages have there been in the world and how many have died? Are there more—or fewer—languages now than at any one earlier historical time?

Whereas the number after the tower of Babel was supposed to be 70 or 72 according to the Bible, Michael Krauss' cautious estimate (1995) is 10,000 to 15,000 in prehistoric times.

Mark Pagel (as reported by Nicholas Ostler, 1995: 6), on the other hand, has estimated

> the upper and lower bounds of the number of languages ever spoken, using current hypotheses of the rate of language change and the age of the language faculty in man [sic[2]]. His middle estimate was 140,000—with a low figure of 31,000 and a maximum of 600,000, which puts into some sort of perspective the 5–8,000 we reckon with now.

Tore Janson (1997: 22–23) estimates that some 12,000 years ago when all people were gatherers and hunters, there might have existed one language per every one or two thousand people. There were then people on all continents, and most of the areas peopled now had inhabitants then too, i.e., there were most probably millions of people already then. If there were just one million people, there might have been at least some 500 languages (1,000,000 divided by 2,000). Ten million people would give five thousand languages, and if there were a hundred million people (which is perfectly possible according to Janson—fewer than in today's Russia), we would have had 50,000 languages. Adelaar (1995) estimates that the original number of languages spoken in South America in the year 1500 must have been several times higher than the present number of approximately 600, and quotes Rodrigues 1993, who calculated the original number of languages for Brazil alone at 17,175. Regardless of whose estimates on the total number of languages we believe, all the languages have obviously not existed at the same time and the figures are based on change. Many languages have become extinct, and new ones have come into existence.

Does this then mean that languages, like biological species, have a lifespan? That it is 'natural' for languages to come and go (natural in the same way as for biological organisms)? If so, does it also follow that, at the present time, trying to maintain languages, trying to prevent what might be seen as a 'natural' development, is 'working against nature' and should not be done?

Or can we argue, as this book does, that trying to maintain languages is something we can and should do? That seeing the diversity of languages and cultures as something inherently valuable is as important and necessary for the future of the planet as maintaining biodiversity?

Can we discuss languages and linguistic diversity (linguodiversity) somehow in the same way or at least parallel to biological diversity? Some doubts were expressed about this already in section 2.2. These are very big questions indeed, and our prerequisites for answering them in a fully informed way are still shaky.

One of the problems with my questions above is that a common sense logic seems to say: you cannot have your cake and eat it. **Either** you believe that biodiversity and linguodiversity are somehow similar or parallel, and then you must accept the other parallel too, namely that languages like biological species 'naturally' have a life-span, including death. **Or**, if you believe that languages do not, at least today, die a 'natural' death—they die because of human intervention, because of murdering agents—then it sounds logically contradictory to use an argument about the necessity of biodiversity to support the claim about the necessity of linguodiversity—it has to be established on independent grounds.

You cannot have it both ways, common sense says.

This book expounds the principle that languages **should** be maintained; linguodiversity is not only valuable but necessary for the future of the planet, as is biodiversity—but at the same time, the relationship between them has to be conceptualised in ways which avoid what has been called biologism, and essentialism, and fundamentalism. If we accept this principle, is there then still a logical contradiction in the eclecticism: We draw (some) arguments from **parallels with nature** (= linguodiversity is in some way parallel to biodiversity), at the same time as we are suggesting procedures which would mean **preventing a 'natural' development** (= preventing languages from becoming extinct)? Everything living in nature has a life-span, everything is born, blossoms, withers away, is replaced by the next candidate—so why not languages? Let a natural order prevail!

I do not see any contradiction. There are some parallels, as discussed in the section on the connections between linguistic and biological diversity. Still, in several ways we cannot treat languages at the same level as we treat biological species.

First there is volition, as mentioned earlier in section 2.2. We cannot treat in the same way an individual organism (for instance a specific bird), seen as a representative of a specific biological species and an individual speaking a certain language (e.g., Khoekhoe), seen as a carrier of a specific language. **A biological organism cannot shift** and become a representative of another species (if you are a bird, you cannot decide to become a horse or butterfly), whereas an individual **can** become a speaker of another language, shifting from Khoekhoe to Afrikaans or Sotho, for instance. Even at the cost of Khoekhoe—which obviously is not what this book advocates—but that is at the heart of the difference, as the second argument shows.

Second, you **cannot be at the same time a horse and a bird** (except in myths), whereas you can at the same time be a speaker (even a native speaker) of Afrikaans and Khoekhoe (see also Insert 4.14), or of all three languages mentioned. This means that the parallels have to be between cultural, learned, characteristics of biological organisms, animals, and humans alike (like reindeer learning to eat different foods in the winter and in the summer; people speaking different languages in different domains), rather than treating languages at the same level as biological species. Individuals can be multilingual in the same way as animals can be multicultural in their **learned** food habits, and can adapt to new circumstances and shift back and forth.

Third, we have the **fate of the following generation**. Even if we have the parallel where the individual organism, the bird, dies (but not necessarily the species) and the individual human being dies (but not necessarily the language), there is nothing volitional or transfer-dependent in the next generation of birds becoming or not becoming birds: they do. By contrast, a child is not born (or, rather, conceived) with a specific language, and the 'unfolding' of a specific language depends on which language(s) the child hears in the environment (whereas a baby bird, despite being dependent on the environment for learning, does not become a horse, even with no exposure to other birds and exposure to horses only). On the other hand, a baby not exposed to the language that was the mother's and father's language earlier (e.g., Khoekhoe) will not know Khoekhoe, i.e., human parents' 'choice' and shift has direct consequences for the child.

Another argument, drawing parallels from the natural sciences, goes as follows: in nature the weak (individuals and species which cannot adapt to changing circumstances) die and the strong (those who can adapt) survive.

Does the parallel, linguistic Darwinism, not mean that the languages and cultures which respond to the demands of modernity, technology, the information society, the market economy, survive and spread, while those who cling to traditions, die? That those languages which are threatened and become extinct, were in some way deficient, as compared to the ousting languages? Or that the speakers' 'ethnolinguistic vitality' (see Giles in the bibliography) was lower, so that it was their own fault (or choice, after a cost-benefit analysis, as John Edwards (e.g., 1985, 1994a, b) claims, and the world is better off without these non-sufficient languages and non-vital speakers? The languages were weak because they were reaching the end of their life-span? We could also specify the question in terms of the discussions about language and dialect, and anticipate the discussion about official languages in the next chapter: is it not the case that all or most of those languages which are developed enough (i.e., which **are** languages and not dialects) already are official languages of states? Are not the others more primitive, less developed? Is it not correct to call them dialects (vernaculars, patois)? Maybe those who are monolingual in the present world need not learn other languages because their mother tongues (English, Chinese, Russian, French, etc) are so much better and more developed than other languages? Maybe 'smaller' languages are small because they in fact are somehow more primitive?

Readers scarcely need reminding that **there are no 'primitive' languages** (see Kuper's 1988 book **The invention of primitive society: Transformations of an illusion** for how we invent the concept in general). From a **linguistic** point of view all languages have equal worth. Linguists certainly agree that every idiom in the world, spoken natively by a group of people, is logical, cognitively complex, systematic, and capable of expressing any thoughts and concepts (provided enough resources are being devoted to elaboration, creation of new lexical items, among other things). This does **not** mean that the 'same' concept has the same connotations (= associations, feelings, value judgements) in different languages. But all connotations can be expressed in any language, even if we may need long explanations in language X to express what in language Y is one word (see the example in note 12, chapter 2)—and vice versa. All languages are capable of functioning as media of education or as official languages, provided enough resources are used to develop the vocabulary in the necessary fields (scientific, administrative, etc.). Even languages which have never been written can be used (and have been successfully used) as media of education. Every one of the world's languages could also be developed for official use, provided enough resources are granted for this work. No languages are inherently deficient; some are more complex phonologically, some morphologically, some syntactically, but all are in principle capable of expressing everything in the world in complex, abstract ways.

In Skutnabb-Kangas & Phillipson (1986a: 380–385) we analysed the arguments used to 'sell' English worldwide in terms of Galtung's three-partite division (see 6.1.2), with the **innate** 'being-power' corresponding to *English-intrinsic* arguments (what English 'is'), **resource** power, 'having-power', to *English-extrinsic* arguments (what English 'has'), and **structural** 'position-power' corresponding to *English-functional* arguments (what English 'does', i.e., gives access to). We gave many examples of each, some older, most of them fairly recent—space prevents me from repeating them (some are found in Phillipson 1992). Just a sample follows (for the references, see our 1986a; Bailey 1992 has many more):

English-intrinsic; what English 'is': noble, rich, pliant, expressive, interesting, well-adapted for development and change, a unique non-national, non-regional, non-ethnic stature, talking-point for everyone, a vehicle for the entire developing human tradition, God-given asset . . . Or French, according to Leopold Senghor in **Esprit**, November 1962 (quoted in Prah 1995a: 34): the 'language of good manners and courtesy . . . order and clarity . . . the language of science and diplomacy'.[3]

English-extrinsic; what English 'has': the position of a lingua franca of science, technology and commerce, possesses a great range of rules for the formation of new words, a universal interest in the English language, trained teachers, teacher trainers, teaching materials, literature, dictionaries, multinational publishers, computer software, experts, British Council, BBC . . .

English-functional; what English 'does'or gives access to: has accomplished a linguistic miracle, access to books, journals, research, trade, shipping, aviation, diplomacy, international organisations, media, entertainment, gateway to better communications, better education, higher standards of living, a dominant position, facilitates the administration of a country, offers a neutral language of communication, helps overcome regional differences, unites a country, ensures that no particular advantage is given to one language group . . .

Of all the arguments which have been used to show that some languages are 'better' than others, because of what they 'are', 'have' or 'can do', only some of the 'have'-arguments ('English' **has** more textbooks, literature, teachers, etc.) and a few of the 'can do'-arguments ('Through English you can get access to more information on science and technology') are true.

But even here there are counterarguments: 'It is mother language which affords room for the creative application of human ingenuity. In all developed societies science and technological development is based on the native language, cultivated as the mother tongue. In Africa, the position is different . . . Since the rural masses do not know European languages, obviously the best way of reaching them educationally for purposes of science and technological development is in their languages . . . If Africa is to develop, we need to begin from where we are. Scientific and technological knowledge must come to the masses in forms and in languages which speak to them, and in which they can exploit their native genius.' (Prah 1995a: 46, 48, 77).

The rest of the arguments are simply false and follow the glorification—stigmatisation—rationalisation pattern described earlier[4] (see Ansre 1979, Phillipson 1992, Skutnabb-Kangas & Phillipson 1986a). And the ones which **are** 'true' are a result of the unequal division of power and resources whereby speakers of some languages have had (grabbed) more resources at their disposal for the development of 'their' languages. On linguistic grounds all languages could have the same rights, the same possibility of being learned fully, developed and used in all situations by their speakers. This also applies to sign languages. Linguistic Darwinism does not have any scientific support. When different languages have different political rights, this has nothing to do with any inherent linguistic characteristics, but power relationships.

In his concluding remarks at the end of the first International Symposium on Endangered Languages organised at the opening of the new UNESCO-supported International Clearing House for Endangered Languages (see Address Box 2.3), Professor Shigeru Tsuchida (1995) reported on the one hand the feeling that 'it may be the linguists' duty to attempt to restore and maintain such languages', on the other hand the hesitation expressed about 'whether we are allowed to interfere with **the natural development** of any language' (emphasis added). It could thus be seen as part of a 'natural' development that languages die.

These are questions which will be discussed in several ways in later chapters. But we can already here state two of the general credos in this book:

1. It seems that our present answers are and have to be based not on a dangerous gamble but on considerations like Peter Mühlhäusler's (1996: 337):

> the linguistic diversity that has been in existence for tens of thousands of years is being eroded at an alarming rate . . . So long as we cannot be certain that the progress we are experiencing is progress in the right direction, to discard diversity for seemingly progressive uniformity seems a very dangerous gamble
> . . .

We have to give diversity the benefit of the doubt, also because eroding it is in most cases irreversible (but see Amery 1998). This must be done even if it were to mean 'working against nature'. After all, we do this in so many ways already. Both genetic manipulation and most hospital treatment are 'against nature'. The criterion must be to what extent it is compatible with ethical norms, including human—and animal—rights.[5]

2. Many languages and cultures have died at least during the recent centuries *not* because this has been a 'natural' development, but because they have been 'helped' on their way. They have not 'died' because of old age or lack af adaptability—they have been murdered. Linguistic and cultural genocide, the **extermination of languages**, analogous concepts to (physical) genocide, is in most cases a more accurate name for what has happened (whereas **language death** and **language attrition** would be analogous concepts to natural death). As will be shown, linguistic and cultural genocide are happening every day, at an accelerating speed, and we shall discuss at great length some of the main stages for this murder, the stages where the consciousness industry has a free hand: day-care centres, schools, mass media.[6]

A last note on discussing languages using metaphors of languages as living mechanisms/organisms with a life of their own, irrespective of speakers, and other questions of agency. Despite the ideological differences between researchers who use terminology with either 'death' or 'killing', both metaphors constitute languages as something that have their own lives, as do metaphors with a language sleeping rather than being dead (Amery 1998). It is, after all, speakers and societal forces influencing the speakers that are decisive. On the other hand, recorded or written materials preserve languages beyond the last speaker, and in that sense languages indeed have a life independent of at least present-day speakers. Speakers both do and do not 'own' a language. On the other hand, metaphors which make language 'death' seem natural also often hide the agency and 'naturalize' the process as necessarily a one-way road—just like 'globalisation'—see chapter 6. I have tried to partly use the terminology people themselves use when reporting on other people's views, partly to avoid unnecessarily gloomy and agentless terminology. Thus I in most cases do not want to use terms like 'extinct' or 'moribund' or 'on death row' or 'no longer spoken', but rather 'languages pushed into (temporary?) disuse' and the like. Labelling is important in raising awareness about the need for action.

4.1.4. Simultaneous Killing and Preserving of Diversity—Double Agents?

Some of the complexities of these questions are illustrated in the very actions and texts of **some** of those who try to save languages. Missionaries (especially Christian ones) have been on the one hand agents of linguistic and cultural genocide and imperialism, and on the other hand active in saving a type of written form, however distorted, of languages whose killing as oral languages they have also partly enabled. Likewise, some of those who today claim that they support linguistic diversity or multilingualism, and also often in some ways act to promote these, are or may at the same time be acting against diversity, verbally or in other ways, often (but probably not always) unintentionally. I want to emphasize that the analysis below concerns just **some** actors, by no means all—and I include myself.

4.1.4.1. *Missionaries*

The missionaries have doubtless generally had (and still have) the best of intentions (see Insert 4.3).

INSERT 4.3 No praying—no antibiotics (SIL)

At a conference in 1995 I talked with a woman from the Summer Institute of Linguistics (SIL, the organisation which is also responsible for the **Ethnologue,** Address Box 1.4) who had worked earlier for several years as a missionary in a very poor Asian country, together with another woman who was a nurse. She told me about a situation where a child was very ill and needed antibiotics which the two women had. They asked the father of the child to pray with them for the health of the child, and then they would give him the medicine. The father refused. The child died. She felt bad about the child dying, but also said very categorically that it was the father's fault.

She was telling me at length about the 'primitive customs and traditions' of the people she was working with. She was 'helping' them, unselfishly, and with every good intention.

On the other hand, she was really trying to understand what I meant when talking about the Summer Institute as an agent of imperialism/capitalism (with examples, for instance, from Latin America), and she asked for literature about the topic.

I am sure many people at the SIL will be horrified to read this story and would distance themselves from the attitudes of the two women described (as, for instance, Clinton Robinson did very strongly when I discussed it with him). Still, this is what **also** happens—religious identity is being forced onto people. As Edward W. Said (1995: 238) has so succintly put it, 'Imperialism is the export of identity'. This is a total process:

> Whilst they tried to preserve the language, the missionaries also contributed in a major way to this cultural genocide . . . they attempted to challenge and break down the Kaurna belief systems and to set the young against their Elders. Both the missionaries and the government were responsible for instituting a dormitory system, cutting children off from their families. (Amery 1998: 160)

On the other hand, many languages today exist only in missionary records. 'More than anywhere else, our knowledge of the native languages in south America has been the product of missionary activity. Many grammars and dictionaries of the American languages of South and middle America date from the colonial period of conversation [sic! conversion?] to Roman catholicism', states Willem F. H. Adelaar in a summary of his paper 'The endangered situation of the native languages in South America' (1995)—and this could be repeated almost all over the world. Many who try to revive languages use these records. Without missionary documentation the reclamation of, for instance, Kaurna, an Australian Aboriginal language, and Esselen, an indigenous Californian language, would have been completely impossible (Insert 4.4).

INSERT 4.4   Reclaiming languages using missionary sources:
Esselen (California), Kaurna (Australia)

The **Esselen** language was last spoken in the 1880s in California, USA, and was probably the first indigenous language in California to become extinct after colonisation. It is now being reclaimed/revived. Most of the very meagre information about the language, including much less than 1,000 words altogether, collected between 1786–1936, comes from missionary sources (see the one page description in Amery 1998, based on information from the linguist David Shaul).

In addition to the fairly few words and phrases remembered by today's Kaurna, the **Kaurna** language (Adelaide, Australia) reclaimers use missionary sources as the main information, mainly letters and reports (including a grammar and dictionary) by one person between 1839–1853, Christian G. Teichelmann, archived in Leipzig, Germany, Cape Town, South Africa, etc.—see Amery 1998. Robert Amery has collected all known sources of Kaurna. The main linguistic catalyst in the reclamation process, he works together with the Kaurna community and has documented the reclamation from the very beginning in a unique action research doctoral dissertation (1998).

Without the work of the missionaries, the reclaiming of these and many other languages would simply not be possible. See Harry Hoijer's (1976) 'History of American Indian Linguistics' which is in fact a survey of missionary linguistic studies. The Summer Institute of Linguistics are continuing this missionary work.

Many missionaries used, at least to start with, people's mother tongues in both church and education. In order for people's souls to be saved, the people needed to understand the gospel. Douglas Baynton describes in his book **Forbidden signs: American culture and the campaign against sign language** (1996) how early North American manualists (see Definition Box 4.1), concerned with bringing the Christian gospel to Deaf people, did what missionaries working with hearing people also did: they saw it necessary to use the language of the people they wanted to convert, that is, sign language(s). But from early on, oralists were strong too (see Rebecca Edwards 1997), and the same controversies about assimilation raged as in relation to hearing indigenous peoples and minorities, and with church representatives on both sides (see Harlan Lane's excellent historical article 'A Chronology of the Oppression of Sign Language in France and the United States', 1980). The parallels between on the one hand supporters of mainly L1-medium education versus submersion education through L2 for hearing children, and on the other hand, manualists advocating the use of the L1 of deaf people (i.e., a sign language) and oralists advocating an L2 (i.e., an oral language), are very strong. One important difference is, though, that most deaf children are physically unable to take full advantage of using L2, even in cases where they might have wanted to do it. Rebecca Edwards (1997: 136, quoted in Senghas 1998: 542) quotes a passage from 1885 where George E. Day describes orally trained deaf Germans as being like 'perplexed strangers in a foreign country'. Even where the emphasis on the mother tongue of the Deaf has disappeared (as with oralists), the 'common "missionary" attitude found among hearing professionals in contact with the Deaf' (Penn & Reagan 1990: 94) has not; the education still follows 'a classic colonial model', 'with great resistance to the hiring of deaf professionals', and 'the control of deaf education, at all levels, is firmly in the hands of hearing individuals' (Reagan 1992: 315), with 'an essentially imperialist approach' (ibid., 316). Harlan Lane, one of pioneers in Deaf education, captures this stigmatising rationalisation (see section 3.6.1) in the telling title of one of his books (1992): **The Mask of Benevolence: Disabling the Deaf Community**.

But both earlier and now again the mother tongues are/were also used in churches. Rob Amery (1998) reports that some hymns, translated to Kaurna by missionaries, were sung by children with enjoyment a century and half ago. And again today in Canada, at 'Sunday morning mass, the sounds of ancient Mikmaq chants and songs now ring out across Eskasoni from the parish church on the hill, sung by a congregation that is usually filled with young people, who a few years ago were in the habit of ignoring church. "You have to realize", said Alex Denny, with a satisfied smile, "that in the early '70s a priest told people who were singing the Mass in Mikmaq, 'I don't want any of that trash in my church' " ' (Richardson 1993: 74–75). Later chapters include more examples of missionary activities in education.

4.1.4.2. *Invisibilisers*

Many of us linguists may, as unintentionally as the earlier missionaries, be 'double agents' today. At the same time as we are busy trying to create conditions for (what we think are) the world's languages to survive, we are, by omission and invisibilisation, actively preventing half the world's languages from having a chance of survival because we do not even acknowledge their existence!

Examples of participating in the extinction of languages are Mark Pagel's (above) 'the 5–8,000 [languages] we reckon with now', or Leets & Giles (1995: 37) 'the more than 3,000 languages in the world', or what **most** linguists and sociolinguists routinely say about the number of languages. I have several times written in a similar vein myself: 'the 4–5,000 (or, later: 'the 6–7,000') languages in the world'.

In fact, there are probably more than 10,000, maybe up to 16,000. Do Pagel and Leets and Giles not know that? Did I not know? Very probably not. Or at least we had, at some level, not thought of the consequences of knowing.

What are those unknown languages that double the world's linguistic resources? You, dear reader, do you know?

Of course: **Sign languages**.

There may be as many Sign languages as oral languages—all fully-fledged languages, logical, systematic, capable of expressing everything in the world, provided enough resources are devoted to their development—just as all oral languages are fully-fledged languages, logical, and so on. But the Sign languages have simply not been counted in the figures of 5,000 to 8,000 languages—or at least very few of them have. The **Ethnologue** lists a few of them though.

How do we know that there are so many Sign languages? In fact we don't; we can only estimate (see Branson & Miller in the bibliography. The **WFD News. Magazine of the World Federation of the Deaf** is a good source of information and includes many useful Web—addresses—see Address Boxes 2.3 and 4.1). So far, we do not know of any communities which do not have deaf people. And Deaf people everywhere have developed Sign languages, just like oral people everywhere have developed oral languages. Since they in most cases have lived dispersed among hearing people who have not had any knowledge of any Sign languages[7] and since many of the Deaf have moved around less, been less in contact with other groups, and had much less (if any) formal education (this would today enable contact between them, also on e-mail) than most comparable hearing people, their speech communities have been much smaller than those of hearing people. That means that there might be even more Sign languages than oral languages. In fact we might suspect that some types of Sign languages (not as fully-fledged as the modern ones, though) might be older than oral languages (see the fascinating new series on the history of one Sign language, Auslan (= Australian Sign Language) and of the Deaf Heritage in Australia, by the two pioneers, Jan Branson and Don Miller; see also Lane 1980 for a discussion). In any case, as both deaf researchers and their hearing colleagues start unfolding the structures and the diversity of Sign languages, a process which has barely started, the number of 'known' languages (i.e., described by prestigious outsiders—of course these languages have always been known to their own users!) is rapidly growing—ironically at the same time as these languages, just like the oral ones, but maybe even more so, are being killed at an accelerating pace. Earlier they were mainly killed by oralism (see Definition Box 4.1). Now when some of the Sign languages slowly start getting some recognition, rights and visibility, others are being replaced (and killed) by these recognised, sometimes standardised Sign languages and—surprise surprise—by subtractive spreading of American Sign Language (or carrots masked as 'aid' being used to spread oralism—see Miklós Kontra's horrifying description of British Council in Deaf education in Hungary, in press b—see also Muzsnái, in press). Just like the dominant dialects became 'languages', and dominant official languages displace and replace other languages nationally, in each country where the Deaf start organising, usually only one Sign language becomes recognised. Hearing people, sometimes Sign language teachers but often teachers with no knowledge of any Sign languages, in most cases dominate these linguicist processes. These teachers are also often the ones who mandate the use of manual sign codes for spoken languages, e.g., signed English or signed Swedish, rather than a natural Sign language (see Definition Box 4.1; see also Reagan 1995b). Section 8.3.2.2 on submersion programmes has additional examples.

Address Box 4.1 contains some useful addresses for getting more information about Deaf resources, taken from Alverson 1997: 22–23.

Some other examples of invisibilizing (and therefore not supporting, or actively suppressing) languages are the following:

- Not calling them languages but dialects, patois or vernaculars or using some similar labels (see Insert 1.2 for a typical example).
- Only mentioning some languages in a country, most often dominant languages in terms of power but not necessarily numbers, while pretending that this covers all the languages of the country. Two influential British applied linguists exemplify this. Randolph Quirk et al. (1972: 3) discussed languages in South Africa in their **A Grammar of Contemporary English** as if there are only two, English and Afrikaans, and Quebec as if indigenous languages and other immigrant languages except the two big ones did not exist: 'In several of these countries, English is not the sole language: the Quebec province of Canada is French-speaking, much of South Africa is Afrikaans-speaking . . .'.[9] Chris Brumfit (1995:20) contributes to language policy in an equally Anglo-centric way—only English seems to contribute to harnessing creativity and talent in a peaceful South Africa.[10] Canada is in many if not most accounts presented as a country with two languages and two founding people (nota bene: not only when discussing **official** languages—and even then it would not be correct).

DEFINITION BOX 4.1 Some basics: Pathological versus sociocultural ideologies of Deafness; 'Deaf' vs. 'deaf'; Sign languages vs. manually coded oral languages (Manual Sign Codes); manualists vs. oralists; Total Communication

The **pathological** view sees deafness as an auditory deficiency, a handicap, a medical problem to be remedied so that the deaf person becomes as much like a hearing person as possible. Means used are teaching speech and lip-reading, hearing aids, cochlear implants, etc. The **sociocultural** view sees the Deaf as a sociocultural minority ('different' but not deficient) which shares characteristics with other minorities and where problems the Deaf face can be seen as human rights problems (see Reagan 1995a, and references to Branson & Miller in the bibliography).

In writing, **'deaf'** commonly 'refers to deafness solely as an audiological condition' whereas **'Deaf'** describes deafness 'as a cultural condition' (Reagan 1995a: 240) and the capitalisation is used just like for other cultural/linguistic groups (Hispanic, Greek-Australian). 'Thus, a person can be "deaf" without being "Deaf" (as in the case of an older person who gradually loses his/her hearing)' (ibid.). Likewise, a deaf child of hearing parents who has no contact with any Deaf community is also 'deaf', not 'Deaf'—a tragic situation. And a person can be 'Deaf' without being 'deaf', as a bilingual bicultural person who grew up bilingually, as hearing, but with signing Deaf parents, and therefore as Sign language as (one of) the mother tongue(s). This is the group that the best interpreters often come from. Audiological deafness 'is actually neither a necessary nor a sufficient condition for cultural deafness', as Timothy Reagan formulates it (1995a: 244).

Sign languages are those natural languages that developed in Deaf communities approximately in the same way as spoken languages developed in hearing communities. Examples are AUSLAN (Australian Sign Language), ASL (American Sign Language), or Swedish Sign Language. Even all these are in a way misnomers—they are the dominant, partially standardised, named Sign languages from the three countries concerned, but there are many other Sign languages in those countries. Sign languages are complex, abstract linguistic systems, with their own grammars. They have 'a small closed set of distinctive features, meaningless in themselves which . . . combine in ways peculiar to [each] language to form morphemes, i.e., signs which denote meaning' (Stokoe 1974: 367). Sign languages combine the morphemes into meaningful 'signs':

In analyzing a sign, the equivalent of the phoneme is the chereme. Cheremic variation in individual signs plays precisely the same role in differentiating one sign from another as does phonological variation in distinguishing words from one another. In natural Sign languages, there are five parameters within which cheremic variations occur: (1) handshape(s); (2) location of sign; (3) palm orientation; (4) movement(s); and (5) nonmanual features (e.g., facial expressions, use of shoulders and

(Continued)

DEFINITION BOX 4.1 *(Continued)*

body, and so on) . . . By changing the chereme in any one of these five areas, the meaning of a sign is altered (Reagan 1995b: 135).

Since the majority of signs, just like words in a spoken language, are fundamentally arbitrary, Sign languages are 'no more mutually intelligible or "universal" than would be comparable spoken languages' (Reagan 1995b: 134). This myth of them being mutually intelligible is partially based on a relatively small number of iconic signs which are comparable to onomatopoetic words in spoken languages (like 'hiss' or 'buzz' in English). Even iconic signs may be culture-specific. Timothy Reagan gives as an example the sign for 'basket' in South African Sign languages: white signers indicate a basket carried by hand, while 'many, especially rural, black signers will indicate a basket being carried on the head' (ibid., 136). There is also a partially planned **lingua franca**, International Sign language, to a large extent based on ASL.

   Manual Sign Codes 'seek to represent the lexical items of an oral/aural language', for instance Swedish or English, 'in a gestural/visual linguistic context' (Reagan 1995b: 140). Thus these 'languages' are *not* Sign languages, but manually coded oral languages. It is thus important to remember the distinction between, e.g., **Swedish Sign Language** (the language of the Swedish Deaf community, i.e., a language which has evolved 'naturally' among the community, just as oral languages have, with its own grammar, vocabulary, etc.), and **signed Swedish**, which uses manual sign codes for a spoken language, i.e., trying to imitate or represent spoken Swedish with manual codes. There is some terminological confusion here, because the expression 'signed **LANGUAGES**' is sometimes also used about Sign languages if one needs to emphasize that they are just as complex as oral languages, i.e., to counteract the myth that they would **not** be full languages.

   Manual sign codes are relatively recent, and have in most cases been used to teach a dominant oral language to deaf children. As tools for this second language teaching, they may be appropriate; likewise, they can be used as a **lingua franca** with deaf people who have **lost** their hearing. The ideology behind them, though, is the pathological one, and it hierarchises languages, with oral languages on top, Sign languages at the bottom, and manual sign codes as the in-between code, trying to bridge what is seen as a gap (see Reagan 1995b for a description of manual codes and the ideologies behind them). Most Deaf communities reject the use of manual sign codes (except, possibly, as tools for L2-learning) and see them as 'awkward efforts to impose the structures of a spoken language on sign' (Reagan 1995a: 243) whereas there are various opinions among deaf people. 'In ASL there is actually a sign used to denigrate [sic[8]] a Deaf person who "thinks like a hearing person", roughly comparable in use to the term "Uncle Tom" among African Americans', Timothy Reagan notes (ibid.: 244).

(Continued)

DEFINITION BOX 4.1 *(Continued)*

'**Manualists**' also has at least two meanings. The Latin 'manus' means 'hand', and in the more general meaning, manualists are the ones who see use of manual signs as normal or preferable—but these manual signs can be either Sign languages or, more often, manual sign codes. In the more restricted positive sense (e.g., Senghas 1998: 542), manualists are 'those who consider Sign languages normal or most appropriate for deaf people'. '**Oralists**' (Latin 'os' (genitive 'oris') means 'mouth') try to teach Deaf people to **speak orally**, in a subtractive way, to the exclusion of using Sign language and often forbidding the use of Sign languages.

Both oralists and manualists teach deaf people to lip-read, and to write, oralists subtractively, manualists mostly additively. '**Total communication**' supporters often try to combine lipreading, speaking and manual sign codes with varying amounts of Sign language use. But Sign language often has the same type of ideological status for them as the mother tongue with supporters of transitional bilingual education, i.e., it is used as a tool to make the transition to the dominant language easier and its full learning and use is not seen as a linguistic human right. In Neisser's (1983: 4, quoted in Reagan 1992: 314) terms total communication meant that 'no change in philosophy took place; to all other methods, techniques, training, and curricula, signs were merely added'.

See Appendices 21 and 22 with Resolutions from the XI World Congress of the World Federation of the Deaf, 1991, detailing what the Deaf themselves want (in Skutnabb-Kangas & Phillipson, eds, 1994, 408–412).

■ Only mentioning minority children's or adults' competence in a dominant language, and not in their mother tongue, as in much of North American research; to the extent that they can be labelled as 'having no language' if they are not yet speakers of English. Or, if they are called bilingual, only taking into account bilingualism in a dominant language and their mother tongue, no other types. An example is Christina Bratt Paulston's account (1994: 12) of 'American Indians', where she claims that the 'Indian population probably has been the slowest to become bilingual', mentioning then, quoting Lieberson et al., that 'as recently as 1900 slightly more than 40 percent of the Indian population could not speak English. Many of those who did speak English also maintained their Indian mother tongue' and, quoting Lieberson et al., 'mother-tongue shift was far slower than for the subordinate immigrant groups'. Many accounts show that bilingualism and multilingualism were common among American and many other indigenous peoples[11]—but, alas, if English was not one of the languages

* *

Address Box 4.1   Deaf Resources

General
Deaf World Web <http://deafworldweb.org/>, a comprehensive resource for Deaf people, with news page, a directory of individuals and Deaf organisations worldwide, an events calendar, an online encyclopedia, discussions fora.
The Deaf Resource Library <http://pantheon.yale.edu/~nakamura/deaf/> Deaf culture in the USA and Japan, many links, a search engine.

Sign Language Resources
Singapore Association of the Deaf <http://www.sad.org.sg/resource.htm# sign>.
Animated ASL Dictionary <http://www.feist.com./~randys>.
Standard ASL dictionary <http://www.hoh.org./~masterstech/ASLDict. spml>.
Yamada Web Guide <http://babel.uoregon.edu/yamada/guides/asl.html>, ASL fonts, links (including and interactive Braille and ASL Guide).
The University of Lyon's Sign Language Web Site <http://bonucci.univ-lyon2.fr/home/lsf-univ-lyonII.html>, can be accessed in English, French or Italian; a multilingual sign database, Cybersign, that displays signs in several different languages for a given word; online dictionary of French Sign language; a feature that translates an input word into 5 languages.
The Gesture Language archive <http://peipa.essex.ac.uk/gesture/lang/>, a collection of links to research on the linguistics and theoretical aspects of Sign language.

International organisations
For UN and other documents on the Deaf, see <http://www.igc.apc.org/ habitat/rights> and <http://www.dpa.org.sg/DPA/ESCAP/logo.htm>.

* *

they knew, then they 'were' not bilingual according to this account. In the same way, many adult immigrant have been called 'illiterate' in Denmark if they have used other writing systems, not the Latin one that Danish happens to use.

■ Treating dominant languages separately while lumping dominated languages together, or mentioning them as some kind of afterthought but without enumerating them. The last often happens in presentations of countries like Canada, India, Australia, Nigeria. One example of the first is a language planning report for Namibia (Chamberlain et al.

❖ **I n f o   B o x   4 . 4** ❖

French More Important for Namibia Than 'Indigenous Languages'—
Exo-Planners Views

English as **the** official language for Namibia became the end result of a language planning report for Namibia (Chamberlain et al. 1981) where various languages were assessed by three 'aid experts' in terms of their potential to become official languages in independent Namibia. Afrikaans, German, French, and English were all laboriously assessed at a time when less than 1 percent of the population had any knowledge of French or English, while the fifth 'language' that was assessed was 'Indigenous languages', at a point when, for instance, Oshiwambo (Oshindonga) was the mother tongue of at least 40 percent of the population and many others knew it. With the help of criteria which had to do mainly with the interests of the elites ('United Nations' counting as much as 'Familiarity', for instance), the conclusion does not come as a surprise: 'the choice of English as the main official language seems to be well supported' (Chamberlain et al. 1981: 40). Even when 'Pan Africanism' and 'Wider Communication' were among the criteria, not one African **lingua franca** was among the languages assessed. We added Kiswahili to the table, and while still using the same biased criteria from the assessors' table, it got more points than German and Afrikaans. For details, see our analysis of the document, Skutnabb-Kangas & Phillipson 1986a (developed further in Phillipson 1992a, Chapter 9), Phillipson et al. 1986.

1981) where various languages were assessed in terms of their potential to become official languages in independent Namibia (Info Box 4.4).

■ Using linguonyms about a country or group of countries which only highlight former colonial languages, i.e., make the fact that people have been colonised by a specific country the most important linguistic characteristic of them, at the same time as the false impression is given that most people know and/or use the old colonial language. Examples are 'Francophone countries' in Africa or 'the English-speaking countries in Africa/Asia'. Pattanayak's assessment in 1970 was that in India 'in spite of the massive effort of the past 200 years a mere 1% of the total population of the country may be said to have acquired facility in manipulating English in some manner and . . . this is not compatible with democracy' (1970: 7). In the mid-1990s he assessed that less than 4 percent of the population has **any** knowledge of English (personal communication). Ngũgĩ's assessment of 'English-speaking' countries in Africa is similar: 90% of Africans speak only African languages (1992: 27). Bernd Heine (1992) has some estimates on use of exo-languages in Africa: for English in Nigeria, up to 20%, French in 'francophone'

Africa: no more than 10%, Portuguese in 'lusophone' Africa, 5 to 10% (thanks to Kathleen Heugh for the reference). Thus we would have **more** legitimation to call South Africa a Zuluphone (or Xhosaphone) country, making all the other languages, including Afrikaans and English, invisible, than calling parts of Africa Anglophone, Francophone or Lusophone. Dear reader, try to find **one** legitimate reason for why 'we' do one but not the other . . .

Cultures, peoples, countries, etc. can also be invisibilized, using partially similar means (see Insert 4.5 for some examples).

■ Finally, we could also mention the depressing lack of knowledge about languages (also discussed in section 1.1.2). One expression is using toponymic labels as linguonyms. In newspapers, TV, official reports, school statistics, etc., it is common in many countries to see 'Pakistani', 'Iranian', even 'African' as **language** names. Today when I am writing this (September 5, 1998) my Danish daily, **Information**, a really high-class newspaper, describes two local authorities in Denmark (Århus and Odense, which have together some 3,000 Iranians) withdrawing a licence from the local Iranian TV stations—these have sent (authentic) torture scenes from today's Iran. They are reported as broadcasting 'in Iranian'. Invisibilisation/censorship of both what happens in Iran, and of the Farsi language. Danish papers have several times carried advertisements where authorities are looking for somebody to teach a language called 'Pakistani'.

INSERT 4.5 Invisibilizing cultures, peoples, countries

Uffe Ellemann-Jensen, the former Danish Foreign Minister is quoted in **Universitetsavisen** (nr 16, 14.10.1993) as saying the following: 'We should not be afraid of telling people from other cultures who wish to live in our country: You can keep your own culture, but **keep it to yourselves**. Our society is built on our values. That you must respect if you want to live here' (emphasis added).

Danish journalist Ole Vigant Ryborg reported in an article 'EU-allierede uden forbehold' (European Union supporters have no doubts) that 'The Nordic EU opponents have much more in common than just **belonging to the same language family**. Their opinions on subjects like the environment, health, consumer protection, and so on, are to a large extent identical' (**Information**, 2.12.1996, 2). My comment: Ryborg makes everybody in the Nordic countries who is not a native speaker of one of the languages from the Nordic language family invisible, including some 94% of the population in Finland, meaning both the Finnish-speakers (the Finnish language is not Nordic or Indo-European, while the country **is** Nordic), and **all** minorities and indigenous peoples in **all** Nordic countries.

4.1.4.3. *Triumphalists*

Some researchers, while writing with regret about all the languages which have died, still claim that this, or some languages first displacing and then replacing others, is a 'natural' process. Many linguists who write about the spread of English, without properly analysing the causes, seem to treat English in the same way as nursery owners, specialised in a specific, big plant, treat other plants.

David Crystal is, for instance, first (1997a: 7) very clear in saying, in abstract, that a language 'becomes an international language for one chief reason: the political power of its people—especially their military power'. But his analysis of the spread of a specific language, English, lets us understand that it has just somehow grown naturally because it 'was in the right place at the right time' (ibid., 8), just like the tall shade plants in the example below.[12] Sale (1996: 479), describing an ecological system, says that in nature, there are

> **producers** of energy (plants), **consumers** (from fungi to carnivores), and **decomposers** (from microorganisms to termites); and there must be some sort of circular balance among all of them for the successful life of the system. When one or another species uses an unusual amount of energy, the change will eventually affect all other species and may in time lead to a new configuration of the community. For example, when tall shade plants begin to dominate a grove, using extra energy from sun and soils, they squeeze out certain other mid-sized species no longer able to get sufficient photosynthetic energy, but at the same time they allow many other shade-tolerant species to take root and thrive beneath them.

If one sees the British Council, or an author of English language teaching or reference materials as representing a nursery, profiting hugely from selling the tall shade plant, its negative impact on the ecology of a diverse system (the world's linguistic ecology[13]) is probably underplayed or not mentioned at all, or naturalised as an example of linguistic Darwinism where the 'voluntary' aspect of accepting this plant subtractively, as a result of a cost-benefit analysis, is emphasized.[14] But one might suspect that there are very few other shade-tolerant species in the linguistic nursery.

When other researchers show that there in fact have been plans, suggestions and money, behind the spread of English, triumphalists often label this as 'conspiracy theories', or as 'propaganda', 'nonsense at best, and, at worst, destructive' (Andrew Conrad (1996: 13, 20), when attacking Robert Phillipson's book **Linguistic imperialism**). One influential plan/suggestion for post 'World' War II reconstruction was, for instance, that 'gentlemen teachers of English' should form 'an army of linguistic missionaries' (Insert 4.6).

INSERT 4.6   An army of linguistic missionaries: gentlemen teachers of English

'The British mission in promoting English is not without similarities to a Herrenfolk ideal, as can be seen in a wartime book on **The diffusion of English culture outside England** (Routh 1941). It is a blueprint for English as a "world-language", wrapped in a learned mantle of humanism and Darwinist cultural evolution.

"England will be the dominating force in international politics, the professed and confessed arbiter of liberty" (ibid., 31), the world's leading nation (ibid., 50). Britain has a new responsibility which means that "we not only have a spiritual heritage of our own—a national soul—but that somehow this possession is incomplete unless shared with other nations" (134). A new career service is needed, for gentlemen teachers of English with equivalent status to "the Civil Service, Army, Bar, or Church" (60), an "army of linguistic missionaries" generated by a "training centre for post-graduate studies and research" (12), and a "central office in London, from which teachers radiate all over the world" (13). The new service must "lay the foundations of a world-language and culture based on our own".'

(quoted from the English original of Phillipson 1997a: 49, published in German).

Contemporary linguists can still recognise this description, especially if they have been 'cured from their missionary zeal'. Tony Fairman writes, under the subtitle 'The problem' (1999: 24):

Since being trained in linguistics in the mid-1960s I've helped spread English among users of many other languages. In 1970 I arrived in Uganda with **the normal assumption in the ELT profession** that I was a linguistic missionary bringing the 'true' language (emphasis added).

Another triumphalist expression is treating dominant languages, for instance English, in distinct ways where they are outside all categorisations used for other languages (see Insert 3.21 for an example). They can be placed in a very visible way above all other languages, or the opposite: they can be treated as the unmarked norm. How would you, dear reader, analyse the following example (Task Box 4.1)?

What McArthur manages to give an impression of (Reader Task 4.1), by his placement of 'other' is that English is *not* a 'settler-cum-immigrant language'. Had he said '. . . English . . . and **other** settler-cum-immigrant . . .' it would be a factual statement—after all, English is as much a settler language

---

Reader Task 4.1
English and other languages—same treatment?

In what way has English been treated differently from other comparable languages in Tom McArthur's text? 'In the US, Standard American English co-exists and mixes with regional dialects, with several English-based creoles (such as Gullah), with creole-linked dialects (such as varieties of African-American English), and with two categories of **other language**: indigenous (Aleut, Hawaiian, Iroquois, Navajo, etc.) **and settler-cum-immigrant** (German, Italian, Spanish, etc.).' (McArthur 1998, 39–40; emphasis added).

---

as German. Somehow Tom McArthur's English must have been there always, or somehow English is in a different category. One of the ironies here is, of course, that a substantial Spanish presence as settler-cum-immigrant language in what is now the USA historically predates a substantial English presence, and German was for a very long time a strong language (see, for example, Hernández-Chávez 1988, 1990, 1994).

In several ways, the triumphalist 'naturalising' of the spread of big languages at the cost of smaller ones (i.e., not additively), is similar to the views on the 'natural' fate of indigenous peoples and other groups deemed inferior. Several of the academics interviewed about indigenous Californians and the Franciscan missions had similar views to the ones quoted here: 'The Indians were doomed as a culture' (Iris Engstrand, Professor of History, 1987: 196) or '. . . one point that they constantly make is that the coming of the Spaniards meant the end of the Indian civilization. This is certainly true, but it was inevitable. . . . Their civilization was doomed in any case' (Norman Neuerburg, Professor of Art History, 1987: 214–215). I have dozens of similar quotes from all over the world, both about peoples and about small languages—their fate is 'inevitable' and 'natural'.

It is perfectly possible to have diverse, even conflicting views of English represented at the same time. One can see the English language as 'a vehicle of an often insensitive triumphalist culture' (Brumfit 1995: 14). But one can also see 'in this war . . . one weapon which our enemies cannot use against us, and that is the English language' (George Orwell 1970: 250, quoted by Brumfit, ibid., 15, about 1942 when 'Britain was at war, but was able to commandeer the English language as part of the war effort' (Brumfit 1995: 14).

We will come back to the issues of the spread of English several times, especially when discussing how the supporters of subtractive English and other dominant languages are not only legitimating but rationalising and naturalising monolingualism and linguistic genocide. Sophisticated triumphalism is often difficult to analyse, especially when it coarticulates with often paternalistic well-wishing for small languages.

4.1.4.4. 'Research for Researchers' Sake'?

In his paper on the objectives of linguistic research on the Ainu,[15] Osami Okuda (1995) criticizes linguistic research on the Ainu so far for

> 1.1 Research only for the sake of research or from researchers' individual interests
>
> 1.2 Ignorance of the interests and wishes of the speakers who taught their language to the researchers [compare this to the Kaurna criticism, reported in Amery 1998]
>
> 1.3 Irresponsible in not aiding Ainu's movements for the revival of their language.

In relation to endangered languages, many of the 'archivists' would show similar traits in other parts of the world. '**Archivists**' here are the groups whose main interest is to describe, catalogue and thus 'preserve' languages which they see as endangered, **to the exclusion of working with analyses of and action for changing the power relations which threaten these languages** (see Insert 4.7 for an Australian example—see also criticism in Mühlhäusler 1996).

Of course it is perfectly possible to do both at the same time, describe and act. Amery says in a note (1998, Note 23, p. 93) that one of the linguists he has mentioned, namely Bob Dixon, 'did attempt to teach Yidiny at Yarrabah for a time and has given assistance since to groups, such as the Ngadjan, who wish to revive their languages.' Deborah Cameron, Elizabeth Frazer, Penelope Harvey, Ben Rampton, and Kay Richardson discuss research ethics in sociolinguistics in the introduction to their 1992 book, and

---

INSERT 4.7 'Archivists' in Australia

This is Rob Amery's (1998: 93) description of work by linguists which I would characterise as 'archivism':

> Such linguistic research was usually referred to as "salvage work" and was carried out with a sense of urgency to preserve the languages, oral histories, Dreamings, songs and place names for future generations. However, the need to obtain data for comparative linguistics and the formulation of linguistic theory was the main driving force behind much of this research. Little thought was given to the possibility of reviving or reintroducing these as spoken languages either then or at a future time.

---

present three types of possible relations with the researched: one can do **research on, for, or with somebody**. The typical archivist approach could be 'research on', sometimes legitimating funds with arguments from 'research for' (i.e., it is useful for the speakers themselves). Even if archivists in most cases are completely dependent on native speakers to get any data, from an ethical point of view what many of them do is not 'research with'. For perceptive discussions on the possible cooperation, see the Sámi researchers Gaski 1986 and A. I. Keskitalo 1986. See also my 1990b.

Section 5.3 on the two paradigms, language death or linguicide, continues the exploration of this topic. Next we are going to turn to more detailed scrutiny of some of the ideologies which lie behind linguistic homogenisation and subtractive spread of languages.

4.2. THE IDEOLOGY OF MONOLINGUAL REDUCTIONISM/STUPIDITY/NAIVETY

There are many areas where diversity is presented as inherently good, even by the liberalist 'free' market system. After all, there need to be many players if the market is to be 'free'; diversity enables choice. If diversity is reduced, this would therefore need to be legitimated and rationalised.

An ideology of monolingual reductionism (or monolingual stupidity or naivety) rationalisizes the reduction of the number of languages (which leads logically to linguistic homogenisation). At an intra-state level, the ideology of monolingual reductionism is connected with and supports the mythical homogenous nation-state (a state with one nation and one language which probably does not exist anywhere in the world). At a global level, it is connected with the purported desirability of an efficient global market place, of a global information society, and of international cooperation and peace. It is clear that the accelerating corporate fusions lead to fewer and fewer banks, insurance companies, transnational corporations, etc. monopolising the 'free' markets (see, e.g., Pilger 1998, articles in Mander & Goldsmith (eds) 1996, and Barnet & Cavanagh 1994 for examples). One interesting aspect would be to study the parallels between the arguments in favour of reducing diversity by getting rid of smaller 'units' in the economic and linguistic fields (small companies, small farms, small languages). On the surface the arguments seem very similar, and in both cases the gap between the rhetoric (diversity) and facts (homogenisation) is massive.

Monolingual reductionism is characterized by several myths which glorify monolingualism, stigmatise multilingualism and/or real linguistic diversity, and rationalise linguistic homogenisation. There is an awareness and even acceptance of the fact that there are risks with reductionism *ad absurdum*: that 'one state—one nation—one language' might also be connected with or lead to 'one religion—one culture—one party—one leader', totalitarianism and fundamentalism. The factual linguistic reductionism, the disappearance of linguistic diversity, can, though, be rationalised by presenting diversity as a nice but romantic and unrealistic dream, fit for prefaces in human rights documents and other places for mantras but not for implementation in real life.

Here four of the myths (there are more) are presented. These claim or imply that monolingualism at both the **individual** level and the **societal** level is **normal, desirable, sufficient and inevitable** (unavoidable). I shall summarize these myths (there are many concrete examples of them in other chapters) and also critique them. There is some emphasis on educational aspects of the myths.

4.2.1. The Four Myths

4.2.1.1. *Myth 1: Monolingualism Is Normal*

The Myth: According to the first myth, the nation-state is an ideal formation, (one of) the most highly developed way(s) of social organisation of peoples' lives. Therefore it is the normal goal that all (ethnic) groups strive towards. Since the nation-state is ethnically homogenous, only has one nation, it is also ideally monolingual—the state-constitutive ethnic nation speaks one language. This means that only one official language is accepted at a **societal** level. The myth also claims that most states and people are monolingual (by invisibilising or denying the existence of other groups).

At an **individual** level it means that a monolingual individual is seen as the norm. This has been especially prevalent in testing. Of course she may learn foreign languages at school or when she visits other countries, but not in the family or the neighbourhood. A multilingual individual is seen as an exception. Even Chomsky's[16] 'ideal speaker' (1965: 2) was monolingual (in addition to being impossible to find in the real world in any case, of course): 'Linguistic theory is concerned primarily with an ideal speaker-listener, in a completely homogenous speech-community, who knows its language perfectly and is unaffected by such grammatically irrelevant conditions as memory limitations, distractions, shifts of attention and interest, and errors (random or characteristic) in applying his [sic] knowledge of the language in actual performance.'

Critique: Monolingualism is 'abnormal': a majority of the world's population (individuals) and its states is multilingual (and certainly multidialectal).

In fact monolingualism is **abnormal**, if we by 'normal' mean the way most countries and people are.[17] As discussed earlier, there may be some 10,000 to 13,000 languages in the world but only around 200 states. There are extremely few countries in the world without national minorities, and every

state in the world has speakers of more than one language, where speakers of all but the dominant language(s) are often multilingual—they **have** to be.

Despite the wealth of languages, more than half of the world's states are **officially monolingual**, as chapter 5 shows. English is (one of) the official language(s) in over 70 of these states (see Table 5.2). The number of languages used as media in primary education is probably much less than 500. Speakers of more than 6,500 spoken languages and all signers (Sign language users) thus have to become minimally bilingual, at least to some degree, in order to have any formal education, to read (anything else than the Bible and maybe a few primary text books), to receive any public services, to participate in the political processes in their country, etc. (see also Rassool 1999, in press).

Some of the remaining official or semi-official languages have many speakers and many of these are virtually monolingual (like Chinese, English, Arabic, Hindi, Spanish, Japanese, Russian (see example in Info Box 4.5) and so on. Still, there are probably more multilingual than monolingual **individuals** in the world.

❖ **I n f o   B o x   4 . 5** ❖

Knowledge of Other Former USSR Languages by Russians, Versus Knowledge of Russian by Non-Russian Mother Tongue Speakers

'According to the official census data of 1989, there are some 120 million Russians in the Russian Federation. Only 726,450 (0.637%) of them know another language of the former USSR. 11,802,537 Russians live in [. . .] Soviet Socialist Republics. Only 84,427 (0.7163%) of them fluently speak the official language of the Republic where they live'. On the other hand, the total number of native speakers of the majority languages of the 'title nations' (the Chuvash in the Chuvashian Republic, the Yakuts in Saha-Yakutia, etc.) in 1989 was 9,708,632. Of these, 7,766,761, i.e., 79.99%, speak Russian fluently (Leontiev 1995: 199).

Thus despite monolingual dominant language speakers, claiming that monolingualism is normal is absurd, both at societal level and at individual level.

4.2.1.2. Myth 2: Monolingualism Is Desirable

The myth: It is believed that monolingualism is efficient and economical and that it is causally connected with and leads to rich and powerful **societies**. Several large-scale studies show that (some) officially or semiofficially monolingual states (e.g., the USA) are richer than countries with a lot of autochthonous linguistic diversity (e.g., India). **Individuals** who are mono-lingual can devote all their energies to *one* language, learn it really thoroughly and thus maybe become somehow cognitively better equipped than multi-linguals for learning other things, thus enhancing school achievement. Nu-merous studies show that monolingual majority group children as a group have done better than bilingual children in school. Besides, it is still also believed (by some proponents of monolingualism) that bi- or multilingualism is harmful to a child: it is a burden to have to learn many languages ('Main-taining two extra languages seems too cumbersome a task', Paulston 1994: 33—'extra' in relation to what?), it confuses, prevents the child from learning any language properly. In early studies, before Peal & Lambert's classic study[18] (1962), 'bilingual' children fairly consistently performed at a lower level than monolinguals on many IQ, language and school achievement meas-ures (see overviews in Cummins 1976, 1979, 1981, 1984, Hakuta 1986, Saville-Troike 1973, Skutnabb-Kangas 1972, 1975, 1981, 1984a, Skutnabb-Kangas & Toukomaa 1976, Toukomaa & Skutnabb-Kangas 1977). Bilinguals have also been suspected of lack of loyalty towards their country of residence (one of the backgrounds for internment of Japanese in the USA during the Second World War), of moral depravation, etc. (see a modern example in Insert 4.8—I give many examples in my 1975 and 1984a books).

INSERT 4.8 Monolingualism is desirable (Japan)

A myth which Japan shares in common with other countries is that multilateral loyalties necessarily entail suspicious patriotism or social or educational deficit: "Monolingualism Rules OK". The somewhat bizarre expression in Japanese *hafu* [meaning 'half'] refers to people of mixed ethnic background, insinuating also that one cannot truly comprise both. The field worker in Okinawa inevitably encounters the notion that one should be either one thing or the other; speak one language or another but not both, and that bilingualism is fundamentally problematic . . . Throughout Japan, as Murphy-Shigematsu notes, mothers of hafu have been stereotyped as prostitutes or bar hostesses. (Maher & Yashiro 1995: 7)

Multilingualism has also been claimed to divide a nation whereas one language is supposed to unite it. This question will de discussed in 6.2.2 under 'ethnic' conflict, but we can already here claim that national unity can only be built on respect for the languages and cultures of all the peoples who make up the nation.

Critique: At a **societal** level, it is inefficient and uneconomic to prevent people from getting their education in a language they know thoroughly, from understanding important messages, from understanding the discourse necessary for democratic governance to take place, and to prevent them from using a language they know well. These violations are an inevitable result if a society functions monolingually in all official spheres, and they obviously lead to inefficiency.

There is no **causal** connection between multilingualism and poverty (even if there in many cases may be a correlational one),[19] or between monolingualism and prosperity. Monolingually oriented nations might rather be richer than those who have considerable linguistic diversity because the former follow cultural patterns, built on competition and glorification of power as the highest value, thus enabling them to exploit, with fewer scruples, other (multilingual) countries and peoples with cultural patterns built on more cooperation and humanistic values (see Galtung 1988 and French 1986 for a development of this—one might have some doubts about this polarisation into 'goodies' and 'baddies' though). Likewise, Vandana Shiva (e.g., in her 1993 book **Monocultures of the Mind**) attacks the Western-imposed capitalist monoculturalism with its dominant knowledge, and calls for insurrection of subjugated knowledges and a plurality of paths to knowing the nature and the universe, in ways which remind of Sandra Harding's (1998) similar plea.

Pool (1969: 151–152) formulated his conclusion of a large study like this: 'a planner who insists on preserving cultural-linguistic pluralism had better be ready to sacrifice economic progress.' Kenneth McRae, who has studied multilingual Belgium, Switzerland, Finland, and Canada in depth, is slightly more optimistic (1983: 15, and see his 3 monographs): '. . . high levels of political and economic development are compatible with the existence of two (or possibly more) significant language communities but probably not with extreme linguistic fragmentation.'

Joshua Fishman, who has pursued the question of the relationship between multilingualism and poverty for decades (e.g., Fishman 1966, 1971 (ed.), 1972 (ed.)), wishes with a fairly recent study (Fishman & Solano 1989) to get more support for his hope that 'it is not impossible to pursue (via modern planning methods) BOTH economic development AND ethnolinguistic heterogeneity together, as joint rather than as mutually exclusive goals' (ibid., 5, here quoted from the 1987 manuscript version).

There are in fact examples of prosperous countries and districts with official and informal **multi**lingualism (not just **bi**lingualism), countries like Belgium, Canada, Finland, or Switzerland or parts of the ex-Soviet Union, or districts like South Kanara in India (where the majority of the people use four to five languages, see Chaudhary 1986). Likewise, neither de facto nor official monolingualism has ensured economic prosperity to all countries and districts (for example Portugal, which is de facto monolingual, or many African and Latin American countries where official monolingualism in a former colonial language (which is virtually nobody's mother tongue) has been forced onto a multilingual population). Besides, 'each language is equally economic for the group speaking it', answers Debi Pattanayak (1988: 381) to the question 'Aren't too many languages economically wasteful?' Some of the more recent economic arguments will be presented in section 4.3.2.1.2. In Australia, at the same time when 'almost 87% of the population over the age of five speaks no other language save English in their homes' (Clyne 1988: 22; see also Clyne 1991), the National Agenda for a Multicultural Australia (1988) concluded that this majority of Australia's population were 'disadvantaged by a general lack of facility in other languages' (quoted in Smolicz 1990: 67).

A monolingual state prevents political participation of many of its citizens and an integration of the society. 'If social integration is taken to be a psychological state characterized by positive self/ingroup identity along with positive other/outgroup identification, then bilingualism, both at the individual and at the social levels, seems to promote social integration', Ajit Mohanty (1994a: 163) summarizes his longitudinal studies of the Konds in India (see also Info Box 4.6 and section 6.2.2 on other aspects of the study). A monolingual state ideology often ruins trust and cooperation between different ethnic groups, it often breeds arrogance, ethnocentrism, racism, ethnicism, and linguicism in the majority group and it may breed bitterness and hatred, because of a sense of injustice, in minority groups. It increases waste of talent, knowledge, and experience, and prevents 'free movement of goods, services, people and capital' (the goals of the European Union/Community).

Every normal **child** can become bilingual or multilingual, it is not a strain on children. It may take a little more effort than becoming monolingual, but since we know that much of children's intellectual capacity is underused anyway, it should be no great burden. If all the children in the world (including present monolinguals) were to be helped to develop high levels of bi- or multilingualism through education (a perfectly feasible goal), the 'intelligence' pool of the world would grow.

A monolingual **individual** experiences many drawbacks, compared to a high level bi- or multilingual (i.e., someone who knows two or more languages well). Contrary to what most of the biased early studies claimed, we now have evidence of advantages for bilinguals (see Mohanty 1994a for an excellent overview; see also Hakuta 1986, Barry McLaughlin 1987, Cummins 1989a, 1996). The fact that many multilinguals have done and still do poorly on tests and in school is a result of neglect of one of the languages, normally their mother tongue, a generally badly planned and/or implemented education, and biased research, *not* their bilingualism (see Skutnabb-Kangas 1984a). They have not had a chance to develop into high level multilinguals. If children are allowed to develop their multilingualism properly throughout the educational process (see articles in Skutnabb-Kangas (ed.) 1995), this enhances several aspects of their intellectual development, over and above what would have been probable for them as monolinguals.[20] **High level** bilinguals or multilinguals who know both their languages well, are as a group statistically more likely than a corresponding monolingual group to show better test results on tests measuring the following:

- some aspects of general intelligence
- cognitive flexibility
- divergent thinking
- some aspects of creativity
- sensitivity to and capacity to interpret feedback cues (separating form and content etc.) (see Cummins 1984, 1988 for an overview).
- sensitivity to and interpretation of non-verbal cues and meanings ('body language')
- metalinguistic (and possibly metacultural) awareness
- efficiency in learning further, additional languages (faster and often better) (e.g., Bild & Swain 1989, Swain et al. 1990).

State monolingualism is, then, not a rational imperative and a sign of a mature state which has made substantial progress towards an inevitable goal, one which is at the same time also desirable. Evidence seems to point in the direction of state monolingualism being an irrational and illegitimate state of affairs—a reflection of linguicism? This question is discussed further in connection with the principles behind Universal Primary Education in section 8.3.4.

At the educational/individual level the conclusion is that high levels of bi- or multilingualism are a necessary educational goal for all linguistic minority children, and a desirable goal for all children.

Thus claiming that monolingualism is desirable is false and short-sighted, both at societal level and at individual level.

4.2.1.3. Myth 3: Monolingualism Is Sufficient

The myth[21]: According to the myth, bilingualism is at an **individual** level unnecessary, because what is being said in other languages, is basically the same as what is being said in one's own language ('or in a stronger form, that it is in fact irrelevant or could *better* be expressed in one's own language' (Fettes 1995, personal communication). Macaulay's famous language policy for India is a good example of this attitude (Insert 4.9).

'The whole post-Enlightenment thrust has been to construct secure linguistic walls around the majority of the population, while assuring them that they are missing out on nothing', Mark Fettes claims (personal communication, 1995). Pity pictures are too expensive for critical books. One of my favourites has a couple sunning themselves on a small island, with their boat

---

INSERT 4.9 Macaulay: value of literature in English

'Whoever knows that language [English, my remark] has ready access to all the vast intellectual wealth which all the wisest nations of the earth have created and hoarded in the course of ninety generations. It may be safely said that the literature now extant in that language is of far greater value than all the literature which three hundred years ago was extant in all the languages of the world together' (Trevelyan 1881: 290–291). See, e.g., Khubchandani 1983, Phillipson 1992, and Said 1978 for analysis.

---

next to them. One says to the other, pointing to a notice: 'No worries. If it can't be said in English, it ain't worth saying at all'. The notice reads: 'Accès interdit. Expérimentations nucléaires'.[22]

At a **societal** level, it is believed that 'if there is anything of any importance being said in other languages, it is being said or translated into the so-called world languages, primarily French and English. This is a kind of monolingual escape clause' (ibid.). If something has not been translated into English, it does not exist: it cannot be good or important since it has not been translated. Roger Bowers, former Assistant Director-General of British Council, in speaking about the competence needed in English by non-native speakers in the future does not seem to think that anything **needs** to be translated from other languages to English (Insert 4.10).

Critique: The discussion about to what extent thoughts are influenced by the language they are expressed in is one of the most persistent and vast discussions in psycholinguistics, and I will not enter it here. But it is at least clear that even if it were **possible** to say in English everything important that has been said in cultures represented by other languages, it **has** not been done and **will** not be done. And the importance of what is said/written in other languages is only one (and often not an important) factor when what should be translated from what language/s into others is decided on. Commercial and other (including political) interests are decisive, and translation is often one way, or strongly biased: from big languages to smaller ones.

The individual tragedies which are experienced in families where parents have different mother tongues and where the children only learn one of them, or none of them, are becoming more and more common. Marriages across linguistic and cultural identities are increasing exponentially today, and the long-term consequences of the large-scale challenges involved are still to be seen. The results depend to a certain extent also on how exclusive or inclusive the attitudes of less mobile members of the communities are, or how common multilingual fluid identities and their changes are. Inserts 4.11 and 4.12 have examples.

INSERT 4.10   No need to translate from other languages
to English, British Council

. . . in the language domain we may find there is a small group of
professionals who need full linguistic competence in the language, a small
group of aficionados who seek cultural awareness as well, and a majority
who require a basic and generally passive competence that can be
supplemented where necessary by technological support. For the specialised groups there will be a premium on cultural awareness, depth of
knowledge, **translation into the mother tongue from English**. For the many,
there may be a need for little more than a rudimentary knowledge of
pronunciation, vocabulary, and syntax—enough to press the right
buttons, scan the right bits of text into the automatic translator, and
have the right level of confidence in the results. (Bowers 1997: 5; emphasis
added)

My comment: translation **from** English, but not **to** English, i.e., everything
that is worth bothering is being said/written **in English**, there is no need to
translate **from** other languages **to** English.

Thus claiming that monolingualism is sufficient is a false, socially constructed myth, both at societal level and at individual level.

4.2.1.4. *Myth 4: Monolingualism Is Inevitable*

The myth: According to the myth, bilingualism is at an **individual** level seen
as a (negative) temporary phase on the way from monolingualism in one
language to monolingualism in another language. According to this view,
the first generation Latvian immigrant in Siberia, Canberra, or Vancouver
knows her mother tongue, and learns a little Russian/English. Her children
know Latvian as children, but the language of the new environment, Rus-
sian/English, becomes their main language as an adult. The third generation
Latvian in Siberia, Canberra, or Vancouver maybe knows some words of
the grandparents' language, but is fairly monolingual for all practical purposes, and in the fourth generation nothing is left of the Latvian language.
This is seen as an inevitable/unavoidable (and positive) development, everything else is romantic dreams.

At a **societal** level, it is believed that modernisation and development (see
articles in Sachs (ed.) 1992 for brilliant criticism of these concepts) necessarily
lead to the disappearance of 'lesser used languages' (see section 6.2.2). Having
several languages is seen as uneconomical, traditional and as preventing
development. Linguistic assimilation of groups is mostly seen as voluntary,
good for the individual and necessary for the group if they want to participate

Doris is Czech-German, with parents from Czechoslovakia. Kamalesh Bengali, born in Bangladesh, Hindu brahmin, studied in the Soviet Union. They met in Sweden, and then spoke English together. Now they live in Germany. They speak mostly German to their two daughters, Shanti, 10, and Anja, 12. Doris has learned some Bengali and Kamalesh has also taught Anja and Shanti some.

His mother had always wanted to visit the old Jagannath temple (from 1198) in Puri, India. The temple is one of the four **dhams** (holiest Hindu pilgrimage places in India). Now she is too old, but she wanted her son's family to go. Jagannath is closed to non-Hindus. When Kamalesh and Doris went, Doris was not allowed in. The next day Kamalesh came with one daughter, Anja, only. He was asked who they were and whether they were Hindus. He said that he was a Hindu brahmin and had his daughter with him. They were refused entrance. He spoke to another guard/priest. He was questioned in detail and then asked if the daughters spoke Bengali. Rapid questions in Bengali followed to the daughter who did not understand everything and could not answer in Bengali in a way which would have satisfied the priest. Kamalesh was taken to the superintendent who behaved in an arrogant manner, asking how the daughters could be Hindus if they did not speak Bengali, and asking how Kamalesh could prove that he was a Hindu brahmin. Kamalesh took out his identity card, saying that his name showed that he came from Bengal and that the family were brahmins. Now the daughter was in tears. The superintendent did not even look at the identity card, and said that he advised Kamalesh against entering the temple, and refused to give any reason.

Had the German school supported the daughters' father tongue, would they have been able to see the temple their grandmother so badly wanted to see? Kamalesh said that the daughters' lack of full knowledge of Bengali was only used as a pretext. Had they known Bengali better, they might have been told that they were too fair (source: discussion with the family the day this had happened, in Puri, December 1994; both checked my rendering of their account).

'They grow up in towns and are exposed to English and Swahili. I even doubt if my children know my mother tongue. In fact I don't even doubt, I'm sure that they **don't** know my mother tongue.' Professor S. A. K. Mlacha, Director, University of Dar Es Salaam, Institute of Kiswahili Research, in a discussion we had about the children of elites, Mysore, India, 12 January 1995.

in the economic and political life of the new environment/country. Maintaining the old language is at the cost of structural incorporation. You must choose.

Critique: In fact many minorities **have** kept or tried to keep their old language while learning the new one. Latvians in Siberia, Canberra, and Vancouver have certainly tried. There is no need for subtractive learning of the new languages, at the cost of the old ones, or for 'either-or' solutions (**either** you 'cling to' your old language, and it means you don't learn the new one, **or** you learn the new and it inevitably means losing the old). 'Both-and-and', meaning additive learning of new languages, is better for the individual and for the society. Both are enriched by bilingualism, intellectually, culturally, economically, politically. It is perfectly possible to become a high level bilingual or multilingual if the educational language policy is geared towards it (see articles in Skutnabb-Kangas (ed.) 1995 on how to do it).

Thus claiming that monolingualism is unavoidable is also a false, socially constructed myth, both at state level and at individual level.

At an **individual** level monolingualism is a result of a wrong educational policy, and of linguicism. The patients, i.e., those individuals who suffer from monolingual stupidity (being monolingual voluntarily, when there is a choice), are in need of care, just like any patients.

At a **societal** level monolingualism is a social construction which is unmodern, underdeveloped and primitive. It might have been seen as a necessary concomitant to the development of the first phases of a traditional Western-type nation-state (and even that is doubtful), but now it is definitely outmoded and dangerous. It prevents political and economic global development, justice, equity, cooperation and democracy

Like cholera or leprosy, monolingualism at both societal/state and individual level is a dangerous illness which should be eradicated as soon as possible. Its promotion is dangerous for peace in the world. The centre of the contaminated area is Europe and the Europeanised countries. This centre does its best to spread the disease to other parts of the world (see Phillipson 1992) and has been particularly successful in contaminating the ex-colonies of European states. It juxtaposes in a false way the factual and legitimate interests of diversity in civil society against the interests of the unity of the state, and the security and continuity demands of ethnically and linguistically defined identities against the security and political integrity demands of the state. **Both** are legitimate, and possible to combine (cf. Waever et al. 1993: 19–47), something that will be discussed further in chapter 6.

The only positive aspect of this illness is, however, as I have kept repeating for decades, that it is curable (see also the 1997 number of the trilingual journal **Sociolinguistica**, with the subtitle 'Einsprachigkeit ist heilbar'/'Monolingualism is curable'/'Le monolinguisme est curable').

4.3. ARGUMENTS FOR AND AGAINST LINGUISTIC DIVERSITY

4.3.1. Arguments for Linguistic Diversity

4.3.1.1. Dascal's 'Arguments in Favor of Language Multiplicity'

'Preservation of the linguistic and cultural heritage of humankind' (one of Unesco's declared goals) has been seen by many politicians and also by many researchers as a nostalgic primordialist dream, creating employment for the world's linguists but not much else. Why should the diversity be preserved, then? What would be arguments for and against?

Many have been presented already. In this section we summarise some of the additional arguments (see also Laponce 1993 and Thieberger 1990 for counterarguments). There are many possible ways of organising them. Philosopher Marcelo Dascal whose ontological argument about the necessity of Thou to I, and You (plural) to We we already discussed in connection with language and identity (2.5.1), gives a list of 'arguments in favor of language multiplicity' (1996: 25–38), and I shall initially follow his list. First I shall give Dascal's arguments with their subarguments (and my numbering and lettering), with some more details from those which are less opaque, and then substantiate some of Dascal's arguments or add others. Dascal divides his arguments into **'practical evidence'** and **ethical, ontological, epistemological and cognitive arguments**.

*A. Practical evidence

- A1. Communication across languages *is* possible.
- A2. Translation, albeit imperfect, *is* possible.
- A3. *No* reason to fear Babelian confusion.

Dascal claims, after providing many examples, ranging from the **mutual** hesitation and observation to ultimate communication that he experienced with several Amazonian peoples, that 'cross-linguistic communication thus enhances **understanding, dialogue, tolerance**, rather than conflict and dispute.' One might also add the practical argument that the world in fact **is** multilingual, and the many languages are a fact of life. This should be a starting point for realistic planning.

Dascal then continues with

*B. An ethical argument

- B1. The condition for cross-linguistic and cross-cultural communication is to be able to value the other, the different.

- B2. Rejection of 'invidious comparison'.
- B3. No language is 'primitive'.
- B4. No human being is 'inferior'.
- B5. No way of life or culture is valueless.
- B6. No human suffering can be indifferent for us.

In relation to B, Dascal posits as a precondition for the cross-linguistic and cross-cultural communication that we

> should suspend—at least temporarily—our tendency to consider ourselves 'superior' to the others, a tendency that yields what I call 'invidious comparison': **We** tend to think that we are the representatives of Reason, of Science, of Progress; whereas **they** are poor 'primitives' or dangerous 'barbarians'. And we do so, as we have seen, partly because we consider their different languages unintelligible, and therefore 'inferior'.
>
> If one adopts such a stance, what value can we find in their culture and language, other than 'museum' value? Only if we reject it can we understand that theirs is a way of life as legitimate as ours, and possibly superior to ours in many respects. But, most important, we must stay away of such tendentious comparison altogether, and understand that there are no such things as 'primitive' languages, 'inferior' human beings, 'valueless' ways of life and unimportant human suffering. (Dascal 1996: 30–31)

The ontological argument, C, has already been discussed in 3.4.2.1.:

*C. An ontological (see Definition Box 3.1) argument
- C1. The reality of the individual depends upon social relationships.
- C2. There is no 'I' without 'Thou'.
- C3. There is no 'We' without 'You'.
- C4. The construction of alterity is also the construction of self-identity.

Closely connected to the ontological come Dascal's epistemological (Definition Box 3.1) arguments:

*D. Epistemological arguments
- D1. For the science of language: To know what *language* is we must have data about as many languages as possible.
- D2. For science in general: The importance of alternative theories for the growth of knowledge. The importance of criticism and controversy for the growth of knowledge.

For Dascal, it is important to know what language is because 'the capacity to learn and use language . . . is one of man's [sic!] most important assets' (ibid., 35). In fact it has been claimed by many researchers that the essence of being human (as opposed to some other animal) is precisely the capacity to self-reflect and to use language (i.e., Dascal's ontological and epistemological arguments). For determining the nature of this asset, then, we have to collect data about as many languages as possible, and it is essential to collect this data 'before more languages die' (ibid., 35). Peter Mühlhäusler (1996) has similar arguments, with many examples, and so has Alwin Fill (1993, 1998a, b).

For science in general, intellectual criticism, confrontation of opposed theories, is 'the engine of intellectual progress' (Dascal 1996: 35). Knowledge advances through controversies, and other languages and cultures can be considered as 'alternative theories' to the established ones. These alternatives have the right to be expressed, for the benefit of the growth of human knowledge, and in the languages in which they have been developed (see Jernsletten in chapter 2) and of which they are inseparable. Therefore, with languages dying, the alternative theories embodied in them also die.

Dascal's last set of arguments are cognitive:

*E. A cognitive argument.
- ■ E1. Innovation and creativity require the ability to shift perspective.
- ■ E2. Bilingualism trains the mind for shifting perspective.
- ■ E3. Viewing things from 'the other's point of view' enriches cognition.

We can add some detail to Dascal's list. Drawing on the psychology of bilingualism studies, as was discussed above (section 4.2.1.2), high-level bilinguals have been shown to do better as a group than corresponding monolinguals on several types of test, including some aspects of intelligence, divergent thinking, cognitive flexibility, some aspects of creativity, sensitivity to feed-back cues, sensitivity to non-verbal meanings, metalinguistic and metacultural awareness, and efficiency in learning further languages. The training that bilinguals get when they change between languages and compare them, the metalinguistic awareness, seems to be a probable causal factor in all the other enhanced capacities too, as Ajit Mohanty (1994a, b) has convincingly shown; see Info Box 4.6; see also Skutnabb-Kangas 1995b—a review of Mohanty 1994a).

Linguist John Steckley who has been studying Huron (one of the North American indigenous languages, now being relaimed by a group of 1,500 Huron in Quebec) for 25 years, also teaches Huron at university level, using it as a 'tool . . . for teaching non-Native students in Toronto about other ways of perceiving the world and expressing that perception' (quote from an email from Steckley to Rob Amery 17 April 1998, in Amery 1998: 89). Amery comments that Steckley's role with Huron bears similarities to his own role with Kaurna, an Australian Aboriginal language being reclaimed— he has also been teaching it to non-Kaurna students. Of course some arguments used might resemble those used to legitimate the teaching of Latin and Greek for metalinguistic reasons, but today's arguments have added both metacultural and epistemological aspects.

Mark Pagel has presented 'some suggestive results with neural nets, arguing (by implicit analogy) that if learning different phonological systems can affect the development of our brains, just think of the variety that different grammar and semantics may make; and what the human race will lose, in terms of knowledge of its potential, if the diversity of languages available is markedly reduced' (reported by Nicholas Ostler in **Iatiku: Newsletter of of the Foundation for Endangered Languages** 1, 1995: 6).

Next we add some specifications to Dascal's arguments which relate more directly to earlier chapters.

4.3.1.2. *Relationship Between Linguistic and Cultural Diversity—Languages as Depositories of Diverse Knowledge for Sustainability*

But do cultures disappear if languages disappear? And can't we maintain our planet even with fewer languages? It is important to make it clear that language and culture are not synonymous, nor do they exhibit a one-to-one relationship. Class, gender, or professional cultures and sociolects could of course be used as examples. Elites may globally share much more culturally with other elites speaking other languages than with ordinary people from the same language groups in their own countries. Shared gendered experience may in many situations be more important than difference of language, as international women's conferences have shown. But 'racial' and class differences can of course be divisive here too, and rightly so—just being a woman does not make 'racial' or class differences disappear, as little as being a man does. But sporting or multinational company men across languages barriers may also feel that they share a culture. Often indigenous peoples recognise cultural affinities despite completely different languages. But on the other hand,

> hearing the same music, playing the same globally distributed games, or watching the same global broadcast do not appear to change people's sense of who they are or where they belong. Serbs and Croats, Sinhalese and Tamils, listen to the same Michael Jackson songs as they take up arms against each other. The exotic imagery of music video offers the illusion of being connected to

cultural currents sweeping across the world, but this has little to do with the consciousness philosophers from Kant to Marshall McLuhan have dreamed of, an identification with the whole human species and the welfare of the planet itself (Barnet & Cavanagh 1994: 138–139).

Kenneth Wee from Singapore, 15 at the time of writing the two poems in Insert 4.17 (p. 258), has analysed the conflicts and the 'disease inside'. More concretely, there are growing numbers of groups who speak the same language but have different cultures, starting from families where the parents originally come from different languages and cultural backgrounds, to whole countries where sizable populations speak the same language or where a foreign official language, initially only spoken by a small elite, is spreading, but remains a non-organic 'Auntie Tongue', as Probal Dasgupta (1993) so aptly calls English in India, but where at least some aspects of the cultures are diverse and possibly diverging further. Many books and journals discuss these questions of polycentric languages, mainly English (see, e.g., the journal **World Englishes** and references to Kachrus and Sridhars in the bibliography) but increasingly also other languages (e.g., Ammon 1989a,b, 1991, 1994, 1995, 1997a, 1998, in press, Clyne 1992 (ed.)).

Likewise, there are groups who have approximately the same culture but who speak different languages, i.e., they may be ethnonymically similar but linguonymically different, at least in terms of competence. Ajit Mohanty (1994a) compares two 'tribal' (indigenous) groups in Orissa, India. Both are Konds, but one group is bilingual, speaking both Kui, the language of the Konds, and Oriya, the official state language of Orissa. The other Kond group is monolingual in Oriya and has thus assimilated linguistically—but not culturally (see Info Box 4.6; see also sections 4.2.1.2 and 6.2.2 on other aspects of the study).

But does this mean, then, that linguistic diversity could go and cultural diversity could still remain? It seems doubtful. We can look at the few instances which are always used as examples: the Irish and the Jews are mentioned most often. That language loss has happened on a large scale (even if the languages themselves are still alive), and people have survived, does not mean that it is something that should be recommended. Many of those people who have themselves experienced this, or the results, and who are brave enough to take the pain, or admit that they should not have acted the way they did, bear witness to possible negative results. Many people are also worried about what happens to their culture if peoples' competence in their mother tongues diminishes. Jurek (Jerzy) Smolicz and Margaret Secombe (see bibliography) have investigated the relationship between linguistic competence and cultural core values for decades. Even if they think that overarching cultural values for a whole country are important, they can be additive. Besides, 'a language should not be taught "naked", stripped of the cultural envelope which is so important in understanding Asian society and

---

❖ I n f o   B o x   4 . 6 ❖

The Konds in Orissa, India

The half a million Konds, 1.94% of the population of Orissa, are an economically and politically disadvantaged group, 'extremely poor . . . mostly working
as farm labourers, with very little or no land holding. They also engage in
seasonal gathering from the surrounding forests'.

The Konds live in the Phulbani district, partly spread out, in close contact
with 'non-tribal' Oriya-speakers. The indigenous language of the Konds is Kui,
a Dravidian language (Oriya, the dominant language of Orissa, is an Indo-Ar-
yan language). In the north-east regions of the Phulbani district 'there has been
a complete shift in Kui language, resulting in Oriya monolingualism among
the Konds' (p. 58), whereas there is a relatively stable form of Kui-Oriya
bilingualism in the south-west part of the district: the Konds use Kui at home
and for intra-group communication, and Oriya for intergroup communication.
Almost all Kond children in the bilingual areas are bilingual to different degrees
by school age, learning Kui at home and Oriya in the neighbourhood through
the Oriya-speaking peers and others.

The literacy rate is 12% (as compared to the all-Indian 52.6% in 1991). The
medium of instruction in schools is Oriya, Kui is not used in education. Only
around 30% of the Kond children are enrolled in schools, and the push-out
rate (see chapter 3, note 8 for this concept) is more than 80% by grade V.

Despite the difference in the patterns of language use, the Konds in the
monolingual and bilingual areas

> constitute a close in-group, sharing a common Kond identity and showing
> little difference in terms of socio-cultural and economic parameters . . .
> They share a common culture in all respects, with the same religious beliefs
> and rituals, marriage and child rearing practices, birth and death rites and
> all other social customs and practices . . . Kui is perceived as the language
> of the Konds by everyone, including the Oriya monolingual Konds. Thus,
> the difference in the pattern of language use among the Konds provides
> a unique setting for methodologically valid studies of the effects of
> bilingualism. Unlike other bilingual and monolingual populations most
> often studied, the Konds belong to the same cultural and socio-economic
> milieu, regardless of the differences in their patterns of language use.
> (Mohanty 1994a: 58–59).

---

economy' (Smolicz 1990: 77)—or, any society and economy. A few examples
are given in Inserts 4.13 through 4.17.

The examples show how people think and feel about the language-culture
relationship when the language is threatened or disappears, and this seems
to support Smolicz' views above about the necessity of language for culture

English-medium education:
'We possess insignificant amounts of the cultural capital of Telugu'

We asked our colleague/friend, Dr. Giridhar Rao (Department of English, University of Hyderabad) to summarise his linguistic upbringing. His father's and mother's mother tongue is Telugu. The mother's English is according to Giri 'disastrous' (even if she teaches it):

> Father, a professor of veterinary physiology, served for over twenty-five years at the Haryana Agricultural University in Hisar, some 1800 kilometres from Vijayawada where he, mother and two of us three children were born. The language spoken at home was English and a haryanavi-coloured Hindi, in that order of preference and proficiency. Medium of instruction at school was English, of course. Of course, since the quality of education at the Hindi-medium schools in Hisar was deemed by them as dismal. The school, fairly predictably for small-town India of the seventies, was called St. Mary's School.
>
> One of the major consequences of an English-medium education in Hisar with no Telugu at home has been an almost complete inability to function in Telugu during our short summer visits to Andhra Pradesh. My youngest brother, born in Hisar, is particularly handicapped in the matter. Significantly, we have named him Leo! As a family, we possess insignificant amounts of the cultural capital of Telugu. It is a loss only I who live in Hyderabad feel. The others have acquired to various degrees what their environments have had to offer.

Many Indian intellectuals who use English brilliantly, are linguistically disconnected from the mass of the people among whom they live. Sometimes it is as if they were in permanent diaspora in their own country.

INSERT 4.14 'I have drunk the milk of a strange woman'
(Khoekhoe, South Africa)

Says Hendrik Stuurman, a Khoekhoe Nama who came back to South Africa in the mid-1990s from Namibia where some of his people had gone after a forced removal from their ancestral lands during apartheid: 'Now we have our land back. We are doing well with houses, schools and clinics. We thought that with our land we would be able to heal the culture that is the soul of our people. But we find instead that our language is dying. At least while we were in exile we were able to read and speak our language (Nama is recognised in Namibia). We now realise that, in the act of regaining our land, we may have destroyed our culture.'

As for Stuurman himself, he already belongs to the generation where the intergenerational transmission was incomplete; his main language is Afrikaans. This is how he feels about it: '. . . a feeling deep inside me that something is wrong . . . that I have drunk the milk of a strange woman, that I grew up alongside another person. I feel like this because I do not speak my mother's language.' (quoted in Koch & Maslamoney 1997: 28)

INSERT 4.15 Telugu-speaking grandmother cannot communicate
with her Hindi- and English-speaking grandchildren

An Indian Telugu mother tongue professor of economics worked with the
UN for 17 years and is now retired. I and my husband had breakfast and
dinner with him and his wife several times in January 1995 in the Guesthouse
of the University of Hyderabad (where we all stayed), and also spent a whole
Saturday day with them, going round a fort in Hyderabad. The wife, also a
native speaker of Telugu, who had been a housewife all her married life, knew
almost no Hindi and very little English. The husband spoke Telugu and
English and interpreted between us.

When he was younger, a Sikh on a train asked him something in Hindi
and he said he did not understand Hindi. The Sikh said he should feel ashamed
of himself. This made him decide that he did not want to learn Hindi, and
he never did.

Their only daughter attended English-medium schools, but knows Telugu
orally (not reading & writing). The two grandchildren (3 and 6 in 1995) who
lived in Delhi, knew Hindi, the father's mother tongue, and were in
English-medium schools. The grandfather can speak to the grandchildren in
English, but the grandmother can hardly communicate with them verbally.
The grandfather says she manages somehow, with body language. Both feel
sad about this.

I asked if they knew that this might be the long-term consequence if they
placed their own child in an English-medium school. He answered by
enumerating the benefits of an English-medium school:

- the discipline was better
- they learned to carry on a conversation in English
- English is needed for any good jobs
- the English-medium schools are better equipped, better quality of teaching
- it is a sacrifice one has to make.

When I insisted on having an answer to my question of whether they were
aware of the long-term consequences of the grandmother not being able to
communicate with the grandchildren, both said no. (He was an avid supporter
of women's rights, and we had long discussions on that). When the wife was not
present, he talked about serious psychological problems that she had because of
identity conflicts, and the sad situation with her only grandchildren.

---

to remain vital. The existence of both linguistic and cultural diversity is also
a necessary prerequisite for sustaining the knowledge basis needed for the
discourse of legitimating the support for **maintaining** biodiversity.

Darrell Posey, Director of the Oxford Centre for Environment, Ethics
and Society, writes about the roughly 250 million indigenous peoples of the
world (in press a—here quoted from the manuscript, 1997: 8; IWGIA's 1996

INSERT 4.16　Singapore Prime Ministers regret choice of English as medium and diminishing competence in Chinese

Singapore has often been hailed as The Success Story of both language shift and economics: with the English language, learned in the English medium schools, came the prosperity which made Singapore to one of the richest and most technologically advanced places in the world—and there was a straightforward causal relationship according to dubious outsider analyses. Paulston, applauding the choice of English (1994: 59), claims that for the 'fact' that 'there is no sign of ethnic strife or educational problems . . . the simple explanation is to be found in Singapore's very strong and expanding economy'. Lee Kuan Yew, the Prime Minister of Singapore for over a quarter of a century, since independence in 1965, '. . . in his last National Day rally speech as Prime Minister' when looking back at his work 'expressed regret at the wholesale shift to English in the schools' (Fraser 1997: 25): 'If I had the opportunity to start all over again in 1965, then the system of education would not be the same. I would have preserved the Chinese primary schools . . . I believe that cultural values are our basic strength. If we lose these, then we will not be able to solve our problems (Lee Kuan Yew, translated from Mandarin, from **Straits Times**, 27 August 1990, quoted in Fraser 1997: 25).

Also the present (1998) Prime Minister, Goh Chok Tong, in his National Day speech on 'maintaining Asian Identity', expressed concern that 'educated Chinese families' may be losing their fluency in Mandarin in favour of English: 'In 20 years' time there will be no new generation of Chinese-educated elite, because all schools now teach in English'. Referring to the growing importance of Chinese when China becomes stronger and more influential, he exhorted Singapore to 'find ways to sustain a high level of proficiency in Chinese' and the elite to use more Mandarin socially. The 'Speak Mandarin Campaign' has been successful in 'getting dialect-speaking Chinese to switch to Mandarin', at the same time as children from ethnically Chinese but English-speaking homes have difficulty 'in coping with the mother tongue [i.e., Chinese] in school' and 'some Ministers and MPs too complain that their sons are having difficulty in coping with Chinese' (quoted in **Global English Newsletter** 2, item 9). The same Newsletter also reports on several Asian countries dropping English courses, further teacher training, student grants and other English language support systems, in Hong Kong, Malaysia, and Korea. Even if this is a reaction to the economic crises, it might work in the same direction as the worries reported above.

---

figure is 'may approach 300 million'). Demographically they make up no more than 4 percent of the world's population, but they have around 19% of the earth's surface under their control or management, and the majority of the world's oral languages, 60 to 80% (between 4,000 and 5,000) are spoken by them. In addition, they are 'active stewards of some of the most

'And we think: "I'm proud to be Chinese,"
In English' (Singapore)

Sonnet for the Poor and the Young by Kenneth Wee

Little child, what sort of future have you? /
  Living in clothes given from foreign lands
Dependent on food from a stranger's hands /
  Will all your life be spent in a food queue?
The languages which you speak and learn /
  Are those of another people's country
You will never know your family /
  Why is your culture like so much wood burned?
The sins of those long dead and gone; /
  Why must you suffer, because of them?
O colonial men who exploited them, /
  You help them as the dead are by Charon.
The rebels say rise up and take back your pride /
  How can you, when the disease is inside?

Festival by Kenneth Wee

We sit in a corner, my friends and I / In a house filled with the roaring
  of the
Docks and harbours of our ancestors, and the / Colours of the sun which
  burned their fields.
The old men talk at the tables, / Remembering old times. We know them
Not, nor the language that they speak, / Yet we are relatives, only two
  generations apart.
We watch the television, glued to its screen, / Not knowing the meaning of
  the lotus seeds
We unseeingly eat / They are just more candy to us.
When the dinner is brought on, / With special foods prepared by the elders,
We grimace at the "tasteless" stuff / And think longingly of cheesy pizzas.
Somewhere down the street / Lion dancers twirl to heart thumping music
In my room we, too, dance / But to the latest rock hits.
On my door hang spring couplets: / Quotations from Shakespeare.
Door gods adorn our entrances /Posters of Schwarzenegger and Stallone.
We watch the organised festivities /
  And are reminded of our culture, our roots
And we think: "I'm proud to be Chinese," /
  In English. (Wee 1994: 3–5; written at the age of 15)

biologically and ecologically rich regions of the world' (ibid., 8). The holistic views of these indigenous peoples link 'environmental sustainability directly with individual health and community well-being'. Likewise, they link the diversity of life that provides the cornerstone for sustainability, with 'the knowledge of that diversity enshrined in the laws, sciences, religions, rituals, and ceremonies of human societies. In other words, there is an inextricable link between environmental and cultural diversity' (ibid.). Echoing Jernsletten, Posey maintains that it is 'language that links cultural knowledge to environmental practice. Without language, indigenous concepts of nature, perceptions of environment, and categories of conservation and management would be lost. Traditional knowledge may indeed linger even after a native language is lost, but the richness and diversity of that knowledge cannot survive even one generation of language loss' (ibid., 8).

It should give food for thought to see that 96% of the world's population not only leaves the **responsibility** for 60–80% of our planet's linguistic and cultural resources to a mere 4%, but the elites of those 96% are busy killing those resources.

Peter Mühlhäusler, Professor of Linguistics at the University of Adelaide, Australia, formulates the links between environment, cultural practices for sustainability of life, and language, as follows (in an interview, called 'Landscape language' with Pamela Lyon, in his university newspaper, in January 1998—see also Mühlhäusler 1994, 1997, in press, and Diamond in 9.3):

> There are palpable consequences of not having a language to appropriately describe a landscape . . . The rapid loss of much of Australia's vegetation and animals following European colonisation was, in important ways, the result of the invaders' lack of linguistic resources for understanding what they encountered.
>
> Encoded in their language the colonisers brought with them ways of seeing the world—a culture—which includes notions of what the world contains (including land, flora and fauna) and how humans interact with these things. The European way of perceiving the Australian landscape radically missed the reality. . . .
>
> The Aboriginal inhabitants had languages extremely well fitted to the Australian landscape, but that wasn't always the case. Australia's original inhabitants were once colonisers too. The introduction of the dingo and fire-based land use techniques profoundly altered the environment—what today would be termed 'disasters'.
>
> Ecological disruption also followed the colonisation of New Zealand by Eastern Polynesians, of South Africa first by the Bantus and then by the Dutch, of Mauritius by the French, and so on. Today, however, Maori language reflects a deep understanding of the land, plants and animals of New Zealand.
>
> Languages over time become fine-tuned to particular environmental conditions . . . It is language that allows people to become efficient users of the environment. But it takes time to get to know a place.

4.3.2. Arguments Against Linguistic Diversity

4.3.2.1. *The Cost and Efficiency Argument*

Many arguments relating to various types of cost and efficiency have already been analysed, especially in the section about the myths. Some additional common arguments, as well as counterarguments will be discussed here. First the argument is presented.

4.3.2.1.1. *The Argument*

The argument: **it costs too much. Even if we had the money, it is not cost-effective, the ROI (return on investment) is too low.**
The first and most important cost argument is harsh cash: we cannot afford to develop, reduce to writing, develop materials in, train teachers, bureaucrats, researchers, and so on for all the languages of the world and use them for offical purposes—it is completely unrealistic. The figure of some 40 percent of the administrative budget of the European Union going just to translation and interpretation, with only 11 languages involved, is often mentioned as an example. Likewise, the simple space problem, having interpreter booths for interpreters between all the official languages, was often mentioned (and physically demonstrated) to us in South Africa (11 official languages). When counting up the logistic cost of interpretation to and from all official languages in the EU, Joshua Fishman (1994a) presented figures which must make everyone agree that we face an impossible challenge. When the EU had 9 offical languages (until 1995), there were 70 possible combinations if one translated from each of the languages to every other language. 15 languages would give 210 directions, and 21 likely member states (now there are 15) would give 420 directions. With ex-Yugoslavia and ex-USSR as members (with just some of their present official languages), would for 25 languages, still a very small number, give 600 directions of interpretation (Fishman 1994a: 51–53). This type of argument obviously makes language rights activists seem like stupid, unrealistic romantics.[23] It is not cost-effective, and, knowing the limitations of interpretation and translation, even at the highest levels (see Piron 1994, 1996; see also Phillipson's review of the former, 1997b), it is not efficient; we don't get out enough of our investment.

4.3.2.1.2. *Critique: Costs and Communications*

Critique: When discussing the costs involved in the maintenance of linguistic diversity, it is important to start with a differentiation of what I shall call 'physical' and 'mental' aspects of costs, at two levels, in relation to **communication(s)** and in relation to **power and control**.

First communication. When people 'communicate' with each other, **concrete objects can be moved**: people can travel themselves, or exchange **commodities**, things ('physical communication'). Alternatively, they can **exchange ideas** ('mental communication'). Table 4.1 tries to capture some of the elements. It is a first draft and the readers are invited to improve it!

TABLE 4.1
Communication (physical or mental) as exchange of commodities or ideas

	Physical communication: exchange of commodities (including physical mobility of people)	**Mental communication**: exchange of ideas
Means for communication to flow	Roads, motorways, railways, airports, bridges, tunnels, lakes, seas, ports, etc.	Spoken and signed languages, visual and aural images, telephone cables, satellites, cables, etc.
Tools (vehicles) needed	**Self-reproducing**: legs; horses, donkeys, camels, etc. **Non-self-reproducing**: bicycles, motorbikes, cars, lorries, trains, aeroplanes, boats, ships, etc.	Physical apparatus for hearing, seeing, speaking, signing, reading; paper & pen, board & chalk, typewriters, TVs, phones, computers, radios, music instruments, clothes, food, movement, jewellery, etc.
Cost for material investment by individual	Relatively small for self-reproducing tools; large for anything above bicycle	Relatively small for most basic tools
Cost for material investment by society	Massive (see Means above), for both building and maintenance	Relatively large initially, less for maintenance (materials for language learning, training of teachers & translators, interpretation equipment, etc.)
Cost for mental investment by individual	Relatively large (time & effort)	Relatively large (time & effort for language learning)
Cost for mental investment by society	Massive (research, planning, production, maintenance)	Relatively large (research, planning, interpretation & translation)
Cost for environment	Massive; to large extent irreversible	Negligible
Return On Investment (ROI)	Negative for the world, including environmental effects	Positive

A general conclusion is that while the costs for physical communications are enormous, the return on investment low and negative (except for TNCs, transnational companies), the rationale for much of the movement of commodities non-existent, except for market capitalism, and the effect for equity and peace negative, the costs for mental communications are relatively much lower, the return on investment much higher (also for some TNCs, like Microsoft!) and with few side-effects and the rationale a positive one for peace and democracy (on this, see, e.g., Sachs (ed.) 1992 and Galtung 1996). Several of these issues will be discussed further in chapter 6 on globalisation.

From a communications cost point of view, then, **languages are our most cost-effective communication tools**. In rational communication, ideas should travel globally, with the help of additive multilingualism and translation and interpretation, while most of the production of commodities should be done locally, for local needs. For this to be effective, in terms of ROI, local and global mental communication and the free exchange of ideas must be optimal. Since people receive, reflect on, exchange and create ideas most optimally in languages they know, local languages and thus linguistic diversity are necessary for cost-effective communication. This might be the only way in which the disastrous economic theories about 'comparative advantage' (everybody should produce what they are good at—see Lehman & Krebs 1996 for a critique) do work—using local languages definitely **is** a comparative advantage. The cost involved in people not understanding the messages (also in education) and not being able to fully utilise their potential and creativity, are enormous. This will be discussed further in later chapters.

Creativity precedes innovation, also in commodity production, and in information societies commodities have become lighter and lighter—the travel of ideas weighs little. Multilingualism enhances creativity, and investment follows creativity. The least linguistically diverse parts of the world, Europe and North America, will be overtaken by others very soon. One prognosis (McRae 1997, reported in **Global English Newsletter** 2, item 5) predicts that the share in the world economy of the Big Five (Brazil, China, India, Indonesia, and Russia), now 21%, will rise to 35% by 2020, when they will exceed Europe and North America's share, now 23%. Of these, only India may contribute to the growth of English. David Graddol's (1997: 29) prognosis is that while the 'Big Three' (Europe, North America and Japan) now command 55% of the world's wealth, while Asia has 21% and the rest of the world 24%, by 2050 the Big Three will have shrunk to 12% while Asia is at 60% and the rest at 28%. The growing appreciation in Asia of the relationship between supporting one's own culture and not accepting at least gross linguistic imperialism, maybe even supporting linguistic diversity, certainly influences the prognoses.

The economist François Grin from the Université de Genève states that high proficiency in English is already something a lot of people have, and even more people will have in the future. It is like computer literacy, something that employers see as self-evident. Even if it still may pay off economically, in a few years' time it will not. Grin argues that those with only good English plus their mother tongue will get fewer chances (and less ROI) than **high level multilinguals.** This is especially true for those whose mother tongue is **not** one of the 'big' other-than-English ones. That means that English-German and E-French bilinguals will manage still for a while when E-Danish or E-Finnish or E-Romansch bilinguals are already out.

But in the next century, high levels of **multi**lingualism will be a prerequisite for many high-level and/or high-salary jobs, and also for many of the interesting jobs (see García 1995, García & Otheguy 1994, Lang 1993), regardless of status and cash. ROI is higher for languages other than English.

In a large-scale study in Switzerland (Grin 1995a,b, 1996—see also other references to Grin for economics of multilingualism), French and German speakers were asked in the interview to self-declare their linguistic competence in all languages they knew, according to a 4-point scale where level 1 was no or almost no competence and level 4 perfect/complete or almost perfect competence. Examples were given of all four levels (level 4 included, for instance, being able to manipulate humour). For four 'key' foreign languages (German, French, Italian, and English) the levels were given in all four dimensions of understanding, speaking, reading, and writing. One item also dealt with understanding and speaking the Swiss-German dialect/language (Schwyzerdütsch). People's income was then compared with their linguistic competence, while schooling, profession, age, mother tongue, and other social variables were held constant in the multivariate analyses.

The results show that the higher the level in a second/third language, the higher the earnings. Especially at higher levels of proficiency, the earnings go up the more one goes up in the four dimensions: you earn more if you also speak a language rather than just understanding, still more if you read, and most if you also write it. At some of the lower levels of proficiency, speaking seems to be important and the salary does not grow proportionally as much if one also knows how to read and write the other language(s), whereas good reading skills are very important at the higher levels. For native French-speakers, adding high-level German pays off more than for native German-speakers to add high-level French, i.e., knowledge of German produces more ROI.

Having 'perfect' English (10–15% of the interviewees, depending on the dimension) gives the highest salary level for both German and French speakers (but it is important to remember that they **also** know either German or French at mother tongue level). But having 'only' good competence (level 2) in English pays off **less** well for both German and French speakers than having good competence in each other's languages, French for German speakers and German for French speakers.

Presenting these results to 'my' Danish students for a discussion about the possible consequences of this knowledge for their studies, I argued that they could be interpreted in two different ways:

1. Since it is only the highest level of English, perfect or near-perfect competence, that seems to pay off, we should forget about all the other languages and concentrate on English.

2. Since one does not know whether it is possible to attain this perfect level, it is a safer bet to try to become 'good' (level 3) in **both** English **and** either German or French, or even both (in addition to their mother tongue, Danish). Because good French or German pays off better than good English, the worst possibility is to end up with 'only' good English but not much competence in other foreign languages. If one ends up with near-perfect English anyway (in addition to good French and/or German), fine.

Info Box 4.7 provides an example of typical language competencies in advertisements where people are looking for jobs.

When we take into account prognoses from several countries of English proficiency, even very high levels, becoming more and more common (e.g., Graddol 1997), it seems that the second interpretation is a much safer one. In fairly few years' time, when Europe (including UK), USA, and Canada are lesser and lesser economic players globally, as seems likely (see above), even native-like English takes people nowhere—there will be too many people who possess that qualification. **High competence in English** will be like literacy skills today and computer skills tomorrow, a self-evident, necessary basic prerequisite, but **not sufficient**. Supply and demand theories predict that when many people possess what earlier might have been a scarce commodity, the price goes down. When a relatively high proportion of a country's or region's or the world's population have 'perfect' English skills, the value of these skills as a financial incentive decreases.

Monolingual English speakers will not only lose out. We multilinguals may in a hundred years' time show voluntarily English-monolinguals (those who could have learned other languages but chose not to) in pathological museums.

One additional complexity needs to be pointed out, though (and see Graddol 1997 for some others). Since additional language learning only gives an economic bonus provided there is a relative scarcity of competence in that language, and the economic incentives for individuals would decrease with higher supply, regulating that competence might become a necessity for elites who have the competence themselves. Literacies have certainly been and are still being used in this way (see Naz Rassool's excellent analysis of this, 1999). This means that, for instance, English could be used to legitimate the unequal access to power and resouces in a multidimensional way: elite rep-

---

❖ **I n f o   B o x   4 . 7** ❖

Jobs—Everybody Knows English—You Need More!

This was an exercise in 1997 with 'my' multilingual first year students in Roskilde, Denmark, looking at job prospects. 25 people, each allowed 60 words, were advertising their skills in a number of the weekly paper **The European**, to find jobs. The only ones who say **nothing about their language skills** are the 2 American English-speaking **mono**linguals. The third monolingual, from Britain, says: 'English language only'. Only these 3, 12% of the people, know 1 language only. 20% know 2 languages, 36% know 3, 20% know 4, 8% know 5, 4% know 6 languages.

Everybody, 100%, knows English (E) (even if one wants to improve hers—but then she does not know French (F) or German (G) either—she has Spanish (Sp) and Catalan).

All the 5 **bilinguals** have two 'big' languages: 3 have the combination E+G and 2 E+F.

68% of the people advertising are **tri**lingual or more. Of the **tri**linguals, all but one have **both English and French**. In addition 3 have Italian (It), 2 Spanish (Sp) and one each has German, Russian, and Rumanian. All of these are 'bigger' languages than Danish even if Rumanian is not (yet?) much in demand internationally. Thus most of the trilinguals have 3 fairly 'big' languages. Even if Danish students were to have E+F or E+G in addition to Danish, they would 'only' have 2 'big' languages.

Of the **quadri**linguals, **100% have E+F+G <u>plus</u> one more language**, the fourth language being It, Sp, Greek (Gr), Dutch or Japanese.

Those with **5** languages have E+F+G+Sp+Gr and E+F+Finnish, Swedish, and Portuguese (Po); the one with **6** languages has 'fluent E+F+Po+Sp and good G and It'.

---

resentatives demanding competence in it at levels or in varieties or of discourses which are always just out of reach of ordinary people, while offering access at lower levels or in varieties/discourses that do not pose threats to elites. This seems to be one of the common scenarios in Africa, for instance, but a similar hierarchisation seems to be at work worldwide.

Killing linguistic diversity is, just as the killing of biodiversity, dangerous reductionism. Monocultures are vulnerable, in agriculture, horticulture, animal husbandry, as we see in increasingly more dramatic ways, with more and more resistant (to antibiotics, to Roundups, etc.) crops, animals, and bacteria starting to spread—and we have just seen the tip of the iceberg. With genetic manipulations the problems are mounting rapidly. Even if it might be to stretch the parallel a bit, in terms of the new ways of coping that we are going to need, the new lateral thinking that might save us from ourselves in time, the potential in every language and culture is needed.

One additional cost-related issue needs to be mentioned: the ethical questions connected to intellectual property rights. Many indigenous peoples have raised the questions about outsiders, from transnational companies, bioprospectors, representatives for ethnomedicine, botanical and zoological gardens, to linguists, making money out of indigenous peoples and minorities. Rob Amery reports (1998: 66) that among many Aboriginal people 'there is also a perception that linguists and anthropologists have made a significant amount of money out of Aboriginal languages, money which is not considered rightfully theirs as the languages do not belong to them'.

4.3.2.1.3. *Critique: Costs, and Power and Control*

The second aspect of cost has to do with to what extent power and control are exerted via physical or mental means. These issues will be discussed further in chapter 6, but some preliminaries will be presented here. Despite the large number of armed conflicts in the world (most of them intra-state), there is an ongoing shift in the means used for exerting power and control, from the use of punitive means (arms, physical violence or threats of both) alone, to more remunerative means, with the help of carrots, benefits, rewards, bargaining, and co-optation, and to ideological means, with the help of ideas, persuasion (making the victims feel guilty if they do not obey, and persuading them to believe that it is in their best interest to do so). Of course, the power holders certainly also uphold and develop further the capacity to be able to **threaten** with physical force at the same time.

When the dominated stay dominated with their own (partial) consent, when the consciousness industry creates consent socially, the messages of the rulers to manufacture and negotiate this consent must be mediated through language. (Of course, visual and auditory non-verbal images are used in addition to the purely verbal ones, but this does not invalidate the argument). Language becomes the (main) means of domination—and counterhegemonies. Therefore it is important for the rulers that the dominated understand the language of the rulers, otherwise the dominated cannot be ruled with their own consent, with the help of the rulers' ideas.

This is also one of the reasons why rulers insist on the importance of dominated groups learning the dominant majority languages: the rulers can to a large extent decide on the official messages because they control the media. Understanding the language of the dominator/coloniser is a prerequisite for this type of attempt at control of the mind. This is a main reason for insisting that immigrant minorities learn majority languages. Minorities are made to shift from their own languages to majority languages and cultures through this colonisation of their minds, by making the resources they have seem invisible or handicaps, by depriving their resources of value on the linguistic and cultural market, through the three processes discussed earlier, glorification, stigmatisation, and rationalisation. This is the light in which the spread of the English language worldwide should be seen. The core English countries are not unselfishly 'helping' periphery English countries to teach English, neither are the motives completely altruistic in the present scramble for Eastern and Central Europe, where the English language is presented as a panacea, on a par with the market economy and democracy. Large scale wars become redundant when everybody understands the English in advertisements glorifying coca cola, mcdonalds, and other types of consumerism at the expense of local products and the environment. Table 4.2 summarizes the means, processes, and sanctions in the various ways of exerting power and control, and the details will be concretised in chapter 6. Here I am only commenting on the cost aspect.

One of the reasons for the development towards more remunerative and, especially, ideological control is the cost. When control is exerted through punitive or threatening measures, through a repressive state apparatus and further developments of this, the controller tries to force the controlled to pay the costs (for the military machinery and the whole techno-military complex, the police, the prisons, the mercenaries). The costs are again enormous and the return on investment questionable for most of the world's population. In addition, the resources are prevented from being used for more positive purposes—all of us can cite figures for how a small percentage of the world's military budget would solve all the world's problems with clean drinking water, shelter, health services, and basic education for all, or how much larger the increase in prison budgets in the USA has been than the increase in education budgets (see Info Box 6.16).

Control through carrots gives the controlled rather more of their share of resources than control through sticks.

Control through ideas, symbolic violence in Bourdieu's terms, colonisation of the consciousness in Fanon's terms (1952, 1963, 1965), hegemonic control in Gramsci's terms (1971), is the most important form of control today. In ideological control the controlled themselves pay for most of the control

TABLE 4.2
Exerting power: means, processes, and sanctions

TYPE	PUNITIVE	REMUNERATIVE	IDEOLOGICAL
MEANS	sticks	carrots	ideas
PROCESS	(physical) force	bargaining	persuasion
SANCTIONS	negative external (punishment) negative internal (shame)	positive external (rewards, benefits, cooptation)	internal (guilt; good or bad conscience)

From Skutnabb-Kangas 1990: 16, mostly based on ideas from Galtung 1980.

'voluntarily', through supporting the consciousness industry: education, mass media, religions.

But control through ideas also means that there is more choice: by whose messages do you want your mind to be colonised (see also Freire 1972, 1985)? Hegemonic control creates, permits, and enables resistance, counterhegemonies. In order to understand and critically reflect on the messages, to deconstruct them, one needs to know the language of those messages well. But still more important, peoples' own languages are needed for building up the knowledge and reflection base needed for counterhegemonies. Alternative ideas and ideologies embodied in a variety of cultures are likewise a necessary counterweight to hegemonic ideologies.

Subtractive language learning ruins this. Additive language learning enables the development of counterhegemonies. Multilingual, multiknowledgable populations are less easy to control by ideological means, and control through other means is much more expensive for the elites. In addition, control through physical (and economic) violence also invites physical retaliation—the elites cannot feel safe, even in their 'gated cities', when those sections of the population who have nothing to lose know who 'the enemy' is.

A partially parallel way of discussing power, control, and costs is to look at the hierarchization of groups and the control of access to structural power and material resources in terms of another change from more physical control to control of the mind. Instead of or in addition to colonizing the land, water, and natural resources of the dominated, as under colonialism, and instead of directly colonizing the bodies[24] of the dominated, as under slavery, the modern version of domination is increasingly colonizing minds (Table 4.3), because this also enables a more covert (re)colonisation of both bodies and lands. More plusses in the Table means stronger emphasis on the specific type of control.

Today your and my slaves are not around the corner—they are the millions of children, women, and men who work under miserable conditions on lands,

TABLE 4.3
What is colonised?

	LAND & WATER & NATURAL RESOURCES	BODY	MIND, CONSCIOUSNESS
COLONIALISM (Africa, etc.)	+++	+	+
SLAVERY	NO, or indirectly	+++	+
MINORITIES (via **consciousness industry**: education, mass media, religion, etc.)	NO or indirectly	+ indirectly	+++

in factories, with contract work in homes, often thousands of miles/kilometers from us. Your and my colonised lands produce food, cut flowers, coffee, raw materials for commodities, for you and me, cash crops instead of food to the local population. The human and environmental costs are **externalized** (not counted in the price we pay), many of the victims are (as 'we' are too) told it is their own fault. And since we in the West don't need to see them directly, we are spared their pain, or it is served us as catharsis-producing infotainment with our TV supper. The elites in the underdeveloped countries at least have to face the realities of their oppression face-to-face, to some extent. But we both get our luxury without paying the cost. Our grandchildren will pay. And our slaves and their children and grandchildren are doing it now, and so is the environment.

Thus it is imperative to think of the different types of exertion of power and control and of the different means (including different languages) used for control, in terms of the cost for world peace, environment, biodiversity, and linguistic and cultural diversity, the future of humankind on earth.

Killing the languages and cultures that could be a counterweight and even offer possible alternative ways of thinking and acting, and support us in stopping the madness, carries with it costs.

4.3.2.2. *The 'Choice' Argument*

The argument: Many researchers, especially different types of 'triumphalists', claim that parents who cease to speak their own language(s) to their children are not interested in or oppose mother tongue medium (MTM) education, or send the children to dominant language medium schools. These are all measures which support subtractive language learning and/or disappearance of linguistic diversity. The argument is that they have voluntarily **chosen** this alternative, after careful cost-benefit analysis. This kind of argumentation also mostly goes together with the either-or argumentation discussed earlier. These groups who do not want or do not use mother tongue medium (MTM) education, undoubtedly exist (see Insert 4.18 for an example).

The fact that these parents exist has been used by politicians, school authorities, and many researchers as a legitimation for not offering or for opposing MTM education or for trying to show that proponents of MTM education seek instrumental benefits for elites or for themselves, or work against the interests of the bulk of the minority group or at least their wishes. I will give examples of the range of 'choice' that parents have, and look at the arguments and counterarguments in more detail.

Critique: There are many flaws in this argumentation, and some of the main ones will be enumerated. Initially it is vital to state that many indigenous and minority parents do want mother tongue medium education. Many also want their children to study the mother tongue as a subject. One problem

> **INSERT 4.18** Croats in Austria in Court to
> get German Medium Education
>
> The 1955 Austrian State Treaty (Staatsvertrag) grants in its Article 7.2 the
> right to elementary mother tongue medium (MTM) instruction to the Slovene
> and Croat minorities in Austria. During the 1960s there were several conflicts
> about minority MTM and bilingual education, where the Croat majority in
> the small Bergenland community of Siegendorf went as far as trying—unsuc-
> cessfully—to obtain an injunction permitting the use of German as the sole
> language of instruction in the schools. The reasons the parents gave had to
> do with finance (bilingual education was a financial burden) and the necessity
> of good competence in German (which they thought would be the result of
> German medium instruction). Some parents also thought that bilingualism
> was a heavy burden on their children. Social Democrat groups tended to
> emphasize the financial argument. Conservative Catholic groups wanted
> MTM education (source: Lüsebrink, no date).

has been that parents are very seldom asked. In a recent Danish longitudinal
study (Nielsen 1998) most of the parents of Turkish children stated that it
was more important for the children to study their mother tongue than to
get still more Danish-as-a-second-language lessons. See also Inserts 4.19 and
4.20.

> **INSERT 4.19** Parents Want Mother Tongue in School (Finns in Sweden)
>
> Anna-Lovisa and Mauno Inkinen did a survey of the wishes for the teaching
> of Finnish in comprehensive school in Sweden before there was any such
> teaching, among 780 parents from 19 Finnish Associations; 97.4% of the
> parents wanted Finnish to be taught in school (source: M. Korhonen 1996).

Likewise, for most national minority parents MTM education is a normal
matter, when the group has enough power to have a system of MTM education. English-speaking parents in South Africa have until now chosen
English medium education for their children.[25] Swedish-speakers in Finland,
French-speakers in Canada, many Welsh-speakers in Wales, and Frisian
speakers in Friesland place their children in MTM schools where this alternative exists, as naturally as linguistic majority parents place **their** children
in schools with their own language.

Presenting Bourdieu's work in an editorial introduction to Bourdieu
(1992), John B.Thompson (1992: 16–17) describes agency in the following
way:

INSERT 4.20   Parents want mother tongue in school
(Kurdish Family, Denmark)

The extracts are from a long interview with a Kurdish family, Mother, Father, and son Mizgin, then 6 years (Skutnabb-Kangas 1993, 190–199, my translation). Mizgin's parents speak Kurdish only to him, tell a lot of stories, etc. They read to him in Kurdish, Turkish, and Danish, and help him with words in the other languages. There are too few Kurdish books in the library so they read the same ones over and over again.

Mizgin: 'I know a boy called Firhat, in my preschool class, and he was always late. He does not understand Danish or Turkish. So I have translated it for him, so now he knows he is not supposed to come late . . . Sometimes there is a Turkish lady there and she talks Turkish to the children, and the Danish children do not understand Turkish. The Turkish children do not yet know Danish.'

Mother: 'The support teacher is Turkish and only speaks Turkish and no Kurdish. It means she only helps the Turkish children. There are also Kurdish children from Konya. If she knew both languages, Kurdish and Turkish, she could also help the Kurdish children. The Turkish and Danish teacher can only help the Danish and Turkish children. Who will then support the Kurdish children? . . . Many families in Denmark try to make their children multilingual. Often it is not easy because there is not enough support for it in Danish society. It is difficult in Denmark even to get enough information about how to do it.' . . .

Father: '. . . Mizgin now knows his own language, Kurdish, and it helps him learn other languages. He knows Kurdish well orally but cannot write it yet so I have to help him. Such an opportunity does not exist in Denmark, to learn how to write Kurdish in school. I have asked the school . . . Mizgin will start school next year. In the preschool they asked me: "Will he have Turkish as a subject in school?" We have said no; he is Kurdish and he must learn the Kurdish language. But the school secretary said: "No. We cannot get a Kurdish teacher". Maybe it will not be a problem for Mizgin. But what about Firhat, he is Kurdish, he only knows Kurdish, he does not understand Turkish or Danish? When Firhat arrives late, the adult cannot ask: "Why are you late?". The teacher knows no Kurdish and Firhat does not know Turkish or Danish. They then come to Mizgin and say: "Can you ask him why he is late?" Mizgin then helps him. So now Mizgin is the interpreter of the preschool.'

A family friend, Yasar, comes in. **Yasar**: 'Many people praise Mizgin for the results. Personally I tell many people how well Mizgin knows all the languages. When I talk with others about the necessity of knowing one's own language, I often use him as an example. Language is a cognitive tool. The better the language, the better thinking capacity and the better you can develop your thought. I have also worked as a support teacher. Many children cannot finish their sentences. Mizgin can finish complex sentences, in both Danish and Kurdish.'

(Continued)

INSERT 4.20   *(Continued)*

Mother: '. . . Parents need to see to it that the children first really learn their own language. I would like to help other parents, plan with them. If somebody tells you: "Speak Danish with your children!", you should not believe them.'

Father: '. . . First and foremost everybody has the right to learn their own language, their mother tongue. That right one gets at the moment one is born. It is a right you are born with, a human right. But in Kurdistan it is forbidden. We are deprived of our right to learn our mother tongue when we are born. And therefore those who do it are not real humans even if they look like human beings. In Denmark it might be doctors, nurses, social workers or others who are in contact with us, doing this. To be different from those others, those who deprive us our human right to the mother tongue, they should not oppose teaching of and through the medium of the mother tongue. And this is valid for all, not just for Kurds. Everybody must be given the chance to learn the mother tongue [in school], so that the mother tongue does not disappear, or so that one does not become assimilated. People need to accept each other, maybe help each other. Accept each other's diversity.'

While agents orient themselves towards specific interests or goals, their action is only rarely the outcome of a conscious deliberation or calculation in which the pros and cons of different strategies are carefully weighed up, their costs and benefits assessed, etc. To view action as the outcome of conscious calculation—a perspective implicit in some forms of . . . rational action theory—is to neglect the fact that, by virtue of the habitus, individuals are **already predisposed** to act in certain ways, pursue certain goals . . . Since individuals are the products of particular histories which endure in the habitus, their actions can never be analysed adequately as the outcome of conscious calculation. Rather, practices should be seen as the product of an encounter between a habitus and a field which are, to varying degrees, 'compatible' or 'congruent' with one another . . .

Enduring in many minority parents' habitus may often be their own school experience, which often introduced shame for the mother tongue, or a determination to ensure that their children need not go through what they did. The assessment of the urgent need of the dominant language on the labour market is also part of it (Karin Knudsen's 1999 study from South Africa gives many examples of this in parents' views). This is often coupled with the wrong either-or message from the school and society at large, the claim that high competence in the dominant language is not compatible with parents speaking the dominated language to the child or the school using it as the main medium of education (see Paulston in section 3.3.1, directly after

Insert 3.6). This 'information' often makes it difficult to choose an alternative leading to high levels of multilingualism even in cases where such an alternative might be available. As we see in the next chapter (e.g., Inserts 5.12, 5.32), using sticks and prohibition for generations may make a population participate in its own oppression, especially when it is presented as beneficial to them, and backed up by research. The history of Irish is typical. In 1851 the Irish-speakers were some 18 percent of the population, 40 years later 17 percent. Another factor in diminishing the population was the 'potato famine'—a period during which Ireland in fact exported food to England, despite hundreds of thousands of its own people dying of hunger . . . This is how O'Donoghue (1994: 491–492) describes the decline of the Irish language:

> Until the late 1870s Irish was excluded from all national schools [in Ireland] both as a school subject and as a teaching medium. This was one factor which hastened the rapid decline of the Irish language. In 1851 the total population of the country was over eight million people of whom 1.5 million were Irish-speakers. Forty years later, in 1891, the total population had been reduced to 3,870,000, but the decrease in the number of Irish-speakers was much more precipitous. By this stage there were only 664,000 Irish-speakers left in the country (Fitzgerald, 1981). To highlight this matter, however, is not to argue that the National Board, in promoting instruction through the medium of English and in excluding Irish from the schools, was acting against the wishes of the general population. Indeed, it is arguable that it represented the overwhelming bulk of Irish opinion in seeing the provision of fluency in English as the essential key to the economic and social advancement of the Irish people. . . . In fact, its policy of all-English instruction for the **Gaeltacht** [the western districts with large groups of Irish-speakers] was consistent with the normal prescription of the 'direct method' by educational language theorists at the time. Furthermore, this 'direct method' was also a major approach adopted as a teaching medium to 'revive' Irish among the English-speaking majority and to strengthen the language in the **Gaeltacht** in independent-Ireland in the 1930s and 1940s.

But very often there has never been a choice. No formal education exists in the parents' mother tongue(s), or it is not available where the parents live. See Inserts 4.21 through 4.24 for examples, but discuss first Reader Task 4.2. Often no alternatives exist (Insert 4.21).

In many if not most cases, if parents are making these 'choices' they do not have enough information about the probable long-term consequences of their choices, neither for themselves and their children (or grandchildren) nor for the fate of the language(s). Inserts 4.15 and 4.17 above gave examples. Insert 4.23 (p. 276) tells about why parents do not get the information needed. In Insert 4.24 (p. 277) the famous Indian writer (Nobel literature prize winner in 1913) Rabindranath Tagore compares those for whom the right choice

Reader Task 4.2
How much *real* choice was there?

When reading the examples, please consider how much **real** choice there is/was. What would the alternatives have been? What would the benefits of, and the costs involved in the alternatives be? Are any of the choices either-or choices? What would the preconditions be for making them both-and? Ask these questions also in relation to the contexts where you work or which you know.

INSERT 4.21 No Malayalam available in Hyderabad

'Linguistic Human Right. I belong to a linguistic minority in Hyderabad. I speak MALAYALAM [the dominant language in the state of Kerala]. Therefore, I wish my son to be taught Malayalam in school, as part of his school curriculum. This is denied to me in this city, even if I am prepared to send him to a school 15 or 20 miles away from where I live. There is simply no school that teaches Malayalam. Signed: P.Madhavan'. (Source: this written comment was given to us during our lecture to professional linguists on linguistic human rights at the University of Hyderabad). It should be added that the population of the city of Hyderabad is almost the same as that of Norway or Denmark or Finland so there would have been other Malayalam-speakers.

has NOT been made to those who, like him, had their education through the medium of their own language, in his case Bengali (while also learning Sanskrit and other Indian languages, and, yes, also English, which he later on also used for some of his creative writing).

The long-term consequences sometimes become clear only when parents and children are separated as adults and would need to communicate with each other in writing. In the examples in Insert 4.25 (p. 277), the Indian parents had a choice whereas the Sámi mother in Scandinavia did not—today she would in the Sámi districts in Norway and Finland (but still not in Sweden), but only if the mother tongue was North Sámi.

Often authorities making the decisions know very little about multilingualism, bilingual education, or long-term consequences, even if few of them might be prepared to admit it or admit that they made a mistake, as the long-time Prime Minister of Singapore did (Insert 4.16 above). In addition, many of those in the Western countries who make the decisions about what educational alternatives to offer are themselves monolingual (as in Australia;

INSERT 4.22 From slavery to multiculturalism—parents not heard (Australia); Why do Huaorani continue to clamor for schools, even while blaming them for the destruction of their culture?

Eve Mumewa Fesl's (1993) account of the 'education' for Aboriginal (Koorie) children in Australia shows that there was no choice. When the free criminal labour force was replaced with Aboriginal people, those (few) who got formal education, after having been abducted from the parents, 'were to be taught English to approximately a grade 3 level', by unqualified teachers, after which the 'girls were sent into domestic service' and boys 'to work as labourers for settlers' (p. 101). There are examples of them working as slaves, without wages, in some areas until 1986 (p. 102), in the same way as many people from underdeveloped countries do today in the West. Later when formal state education started, 'Koorie children were excluded from nearly all state schools established for the benefit of invaders' children. Although some attempts had been made to admit Koorie children, usually animosity and objections from parents of the white children had prevented their acceptance' (p. 125). A government-commissioned report by Watts & Gallacher (1973, quoted in Fesl 1993: 126–127) discussed a model with several stages: early education in L1 (which they called 'vernacular'), then using L1 and L2 concurrently, and finally using L2 only, except for the instruction of L1 as a subject (i.e., an assimilationist transitional model). But after 'pondering on the practicalities of teaching in the vernacular, the report disregarded the chances it had discussed for optimum success (that is, the delivery of education in the vernacular) and settled for another option: "That the language of instruction throughout the entire school programme be in English"' (ibid., 127).

Fesl also discusses later developments, likewise characterised by the fact that neither the people directly concerned (i.e., parents) nor the Aboriginal communities' representatives nor Aboriginal planners and researchers were heard in questions about education. How much 'choice' do parents have under those conditions?

In his book **Savages** (1995) Joe Kane poses the same question in relation to the Huaorani/Auca (who live in Yasuní National Park in Ecuador), basing himself on the dissertation by Laura Rival. The portrait 'Rival draws of the educational system **imposed** on the Huaorani is one of immense destruction, of ethnocide, emotional and physical trauma, deracination. But she poses a riddle, as well: Why do so many Huaorani continue to clamor for schools, even while blaming them for the destruction of their culture?' (ibid., 138). Kane also gives tentative answers—his whole book is about the struggle against the big companies, especially oil companies. And education imposed by missionaries, which made indigenous peoples first aware of and later dependent on money economy and commodities and the need for knowledge in the Spanish language, is closely connected to both the causes for this struggle in the first place and also for access to strategies, however imperfect, to lead the struggle. Kane claims that 'it is no secret that the contracted goal of the Summer Institute of Linguistics was to replace the traditional Huaorani life with a life based on school and church' (ibid., 138), and gives a description of how this was done. Again, how much 'choice' do parents have under those conditions?

INSERT 4.23 'Do the parents really know . . . the damage
done to the children' (Pattanayak, India)

'The Constitution, 7th Amendment Act 1956 in India, introduced Article 350A
which says that "it shall be the endeavour of every State and all other local
authority within the State to provide adequate facilities for instruction in the
mother tongue at primary stage of education to children belonging to linguistic
minorities" . . . Today . . . only 47 languages are used as medium of instruction
in the country . . . The growth of English medium schools has been phenomenal
during the last 30 years. The highly educated alienated minority elite continues
to support English in the name of the minority in the firm belief that English
education is equal to modernisation. However, in reality it helps them keep
the control over administration and mass communication' (Pattanayak 1981:
7–8). 'Whatever may be the difference among the elite on the language issue
they are united in their subservience to English' (ibid., 13).

'It is often said that the parents know what is good for the child. Do the
parents really know . . . of the theories about the acquisition of language by
the child? Do they know how language relates to learning? Even learn-
ing/knowing apart such questions which require a great deal of sophistication,
do they even know what is meant by *good, fair, satisfactory* entries in the
child's marks card with reference to his/her language proficiency? The
individual parents, in their anxiety for their children to participate in the
spoil-sharing arrangements of the elitist education, come in conflict with its
social purpose. They are blinded to the inequality perpetuated by the existing
system and the damage done to the children in this process' (Pattanayak 1991:
60).

'virtually all leading politicians are monolingual', interview with Anthony
Liddicoat, Australian National University, Canberra, editor for the **Australian Review of Applied Linguistics** 1991 number on language policy, January
1996; see also Fesl 1993). Even people who have some (positive) experience
themselves about multilingualism may fail to draw the relevant conclusions
(see Insert 4.26). It has always been a mystery to me (and many of my
non-British, non-American colleagues all over the world) how it is possible
that the greatest experts on how to make people still more multilingual with
the help of education (here = learning English as a second, third, or fourth
language) seem to come from countries which have notoriously failed to
teach their majorities even the first elements of another language, let alone
make them high level multilingual with the help of education. Britain and
the USA have an abysmal record, as opposed to most of the countries where
British and American 'experts' are running around. In addition, a fair number
of these 'experts' have never tried or succeeded to do the trick themselves,

INSERT 4.24   Bengali boy taught in English—like an earthquake
in the mouth—the inside remains starved

We began to learn English after we had made considerable progress in our education through Bengali . . . It was because we were taught in our own language that our minds quickened. Learning should as far as possible follow the process of eating. When the taste begins from the first bite, the stomach is awakened to its function before it is loaded, so that its digestive juices get full play. Nothing like this happens when the Bengali boy is taught in English, however. The first bite bids fair to wrench loose both rows of teeth—like an earthquake in the mouth! And by the time he discovers that the morsel is not of the genus stone, but a digestable bonbon, half his allotted span of life is over. While one is choking and spluttering over the spelling and grammar, the inside remains starved; and when at length the taste comes through, the appetite has vanished. If the whole mind is not functioning from the beginning its full powers remain undeveloped to the end. While all around was heard the cry for English teaching, my third brother was brave enough to keep us to our Bengali course. To him in heaven my reverential thanks. (Tagore 1992: 41, 53–54, written in 1911 when Tagore was 50).

INSERT 4.25   Oral versus written communication:
Kannada—English, Sámi—Norwegian

Grandfather is Professor of Kannada literature. Grown-up daughter had English-medium education. She speaks Kannada well—it was always spoken at the home—but cannot write it. When she writes home to the parents, she has to use English, which the grandmother does not understand. The grandchildren only speak English. Had the grandfather been able to anticipate the situation, he would not have acted as he did—information he volunteered in an interview about language policy in Hampi, India, in October 1994.

A Sámi woman working on an oil tanker writes a letter to her mother in Norwegian—she has never learned how to write in her native language. The mother, who does not know much Norwegian, has to ask a neighbour to translate the letter, and her reply. They can communicate orally in Sámi, but transatlantic phone calls are expensive. In one of the richest countries in the world, with officially a 100 percent literacy rate, neither the mother nor the daughter have learned how to write their own language. (Phillipson et al., 1994: 20)

INSERT 4.26 'the most serious problem for the European Union . . . so many languages' (American Ambassador)

At a lunch at Roskilde University in March 1997, the American Ambassador to Denmark, Mr. Elton, said, talking to 'my' multilingual students from our multilingual humanities basic studies, that 'the most serious problem for the European Union was that it had so many languages'; this 'prevented a real integration and development of the Union'. At the same time, Mr. Elton was immensely proud of his little granddaughter who knew several languages already before starting school—this was very positive for the child's development.

---

even if there are many exceptions too. Likewise, too many of the ESL/EFL teachers have never learned other languages. I am reminded of the story of Dan Quayle who visited Latin America as the US Vice-President and apologized for not knowing Latin—or the American headmaster who said to a minority student that if English was good enough for Jesus it was good enough for him.

My conclusion is that there have to be realistic alternatives, and parents have to have enough reliable information about the long-term consequences of various choices, their benefits and drawbacks, before we can say that there has been any choice. When parents have 'voted with their feet' and rejected MTM education, in my experience it has been in situations with very little real choice. There is more discussion and examples refuting the arguments in chapters 6, 7, and 8.

4.4. THE BALANCE SHEET: EPISTEMOLOGICAL ARGUMENTS FOR LINGUISTIC AND CULTURAL DIVERSITY

Traditional positivistic models of science held as their ideal 'that the representations of nature's order that the sciences produce can be mirror-like reflections of a reality that is already out there and available for the reflecting' (Harding 1998: 2). This mirror-like perfection sees the best scientific methods as contributing nothing culturally distinctive to the representations and wants to weed out all social values and interests from research, according to Harding. There is, 'in the "unity of science" form of this epistemology . . . only one "nature", one truth about it, and one science' (ibid., 3).

Linguistic and cultural diversity would, according to this epistemology, in the end not contribute anything to knowledge. Some of the representatives of very small languages might be able to guide researchers to plants or animals unknown to the researchers a bit earlier than these would otherwise notice them, but everything worthwhile to know about these biological organisms would be in the organisms themselves, to be 'discovered' by scientists.

The post-Kuhnian 'constructionist' approaches, on the other hand, in 'charting how sciences (plural) and their cultures co-evolve', claim according to Harding (ibid., 3) that 'the distinctive ways that cultures gain knowledge contribute to their being the kinds of cultures they are; and the distinctiveness of cultures contributes to the distinctively "local" patterns of their systematic knowledge and systematic ignorance.' This could, of course lead to a cultural relativism which could be used to support linguistic and cultural diversity in a purely quantitative way. Since there is no way to evaluate the worth of the knowledges that various cultures produce (and to a large extent encode in their languages), a safe solution is to maintain and record as many as possible.

Harding claims, though, that recognizing the **social, historical relativism** of knowledge claims does *not* mean that one also has to accept **epistemological, judgmental relativism**. Even if 'different cultures' knowledge systems have different resources and limitations for producing knowledge', it does not follow that 'all proposed standards for knowledge are equally good' (ibid., 19). 'Cultures' distinctive ways of organizing the production of knowledge produce distinctive repositories of knowledge and method' (ibid., 20). At the same time as a specific culture produces a certain type of knowledge, it also produces a distinctive type of (systematic) ignorance.

Harding's own standpoint theory view wants to bring into focus

crucial issues that were either invisible, considered unimportant, or delegitimated [and to] advance the growth of knowledge by making visible aspects of nature, sciences, history, and present-day social relations that are hard or impossible to detect from within the ways of thinking, familiar in the dominant European and North American institutions, their cultures, and practices. (ibid., 18)

The argument for linguistic and cultural diversity would, if we apply Harding, be that the small languages and cultures represent the hitherto invisibilized, ignored, and delegitimated ways of thinking, relating and valuing. They are repositories of both new knowledges and new ignorances.

Therefore they also contribute to and advance what Harding calls 'commitment to stronger standards of objectivity and against epistemological relativism' (ibid., 19), because 'starting thought from marginalized lives . . . provide more rigorous, more competent standards for maximizing objectivity' (ibid., 18).

In this chapter we have claimed that linguistic diversity is not only 'a good thing' but a necessity for the planet (as was claimed in the first chapters).

We have also claimed that maintaining everybody's mother tongue(s), while learning additional languages is not only beneficial for the individual but also a prerequisite for ethnic groups and peoples to maintain themselves as groups, which again is a prerequisite for cultural diversity. We have said that all languages are possible to use for all purposes. Use of a language in formal education (which is a prerequisite for the learning of it at high formal levels) depends on state language policies, and that is where we turn next. But before that we shall make an excursion to one very much neglected possibility, and see what Esperanto might have to offer.

4.5. ESPERANTO?

Many linguists and others seem to dismiss Esperanto as an alternative to today's international communication, without actually knowing (almost) anything about it.[26] Of the world's planned languages (see Definition Box 4.2) Esperanto is today the most known and used.

DEFINITION BOX 4.2   Planned languages (including Esperanto)

Planned languages are 'consciously created languages to serve international communication' (Blanke 1997: 319). Other terms have also been used. (a) To emphasize the **origins** of these means of communication and to separate them from ethnic languages, people often speak of "artificial languages",[27] sometimes "constructed languages" or "synthetic languages". (b) The communicative role of these languages is emphasized through labels like "universal language", "international language", "world language", "auxiliary language"' (Blanke 1997: 319; see also Blanke 1996, 1998).

Detlev Blanke also gives combinations of (a) and (b). The most commonly used term today probably is 'auxiliary world language' ('Welthilfsprache', ibid.). See also Blanke 1987 about the term. Blanke 1985 is a comprehensive 'introduction' (408 pages) into planned languages—see also Janton 1993 and Tonkin & Fettes 1996.

Esperanto takes much less time to learn than any 'natural' languages, because it is regular and logical—there are no exceptions. But still you can say whatever you want in Esperanto, because everybody can easily create new words which are immediately understandable for everybody else once the root is explained—the words are relatively transparent. Try yourself (Task Box 4.3).

There are studies showing that learning Esperanto has propaedeutic value for learning later languages—if you have studied Esperanto first, you learn other languages faster. For example, a combination of 2 years of Esperanto plus 1 year of English may take students to the same level in English as 3 years of English with no Esperanto, if all of the students are monolingual when they start (see also Fantini & Reagan 1992 for a research agenda on Esperanto and education). In order to test this type of conclusion from earlier studies more rigorously, a relatively large project called NEIGHBOUR (New Educational Initiative Guaranteeing Heterogeneity and Bilingualism, Observing Universal Rules) is planned by the European Union Language Problem Working Group (the Secretary is Hans Erasmus, <erasmusz@worldonline.nl> and the project leader is Marc van Oostendorp, <oostendorp@rullet.leidenuniv.nl>, Professor of Interlinguistics and Esperanto at the University of Amsterdam, Netherlands).

Where can you get more information about Esperanto? See Address Box 4.2. There are Esperanto associations in most countries, and the members are usually very helpful and supportive (and pedagogical) if you want to learn Esperanto. There are courses, books on how to teach it to yourself, on-line courses for speakers of several languages.

There are already at least a couple of thousand families where one or both parents speak Esperanto to the children, i.e., the children grow up with Esperanto as (one of) their mother/father tongue(s). There are at least two recent edited books about this experience, both in Esperanto but one, proceedings from an international symposium in Graz, also with a German version (see Tišljar (ed.) 1995 in the bibliography). There are also several articles about bilingualism in the family which includes Esperanto—see, e.g., Corsetti 1996.

Detlev Blanke, Humphrey Tonkin, Mark Fettes, Klaus Schubert, Pierre Janton, Alvino Fantini, and Timothy Reagan are some of those who have

---

Reader Task 4.3
Animal names in Esperanto and other languages

Do you want to play a bit? This little exercise comes from the Danish 'Esperanto-nyt', December 1997: 11 and has been compiled by the editor, Ejnar Hjorth. I have added a couple of things and translated it into English. It is about animal names. If you are not a farmer, maybe you don't know all the names of the family members of the animals?

In Esperanto, the general species name ends in -o, just like all **nouns** do in their basic nominative form. 'Kato' is 'cat'. All *male* animals have the prefix vir- (VIRkato is a male cat), all *female animals* the suffix -ino (katINO is a female cat) and all *animal babies* have the suffix -ido (katIDO is a baby cat). Try it out—and you may see how easy Esperanto is to learn . . . If you don't know any Danish or Finnish, put in other languages you know instead. Have fun!

(Continued)

Reader Task 4.3

(Continued)

LANGUAGE	GENERAL	MALE	FEMALE	BABY
ESPERANTO	KATO	VIRKATO	KATINO	KATIDO
DANISH	kat			
ENGLISH	cat			
FINNISH	kissa			
YOUR LG				
ESPERANTO	BOVO	VIRBOVO	BOVINO	BOVIDO
DANISH	kvæg	tyr	ko	kalv
ENGLISH	cattle	bull	cow	calf
FINNISH	nauta	härkä	lehmä	vasikka
YOUR LG				
ESPERANTO	HUNDO			
DANISH	hund			
ENGLISH	dog			
FINNISH	koira			
YOUR LG				
ESPERANTO	ŜAFO			
DANISH	får			
ENGLISH	sheep			
FINNISH	lammas			
YOUR LG				
ESPERANTO		VIRKOKO		
DANISH		hane		
ENGLISH		cock		
FINNISH		kukko		
YOUR LG				
ESPERANTO			ĈEVALINO	
DANISH			hoppe	
ENGLISH			mare	
FINNISH			tamma	
YOUR LG				
ESPERANTO				KAPRIDO
DANISH				gedekid
ENGLISH				kid
FINNISH				kili
YOUR LG				

(Continued)

Reader Task 4.3

(Continued)

When we start combining root morphemes with each other and with the fairly few suffixes (32), affixes (10) and grammatical endings (17; the numbers are from Hjorth 1998: 11), we can build millions of words. Zamenhof, the creator of Esperanto, had 16 basic rules in the language—compare this with the thousands in all other languages. Hjorth (ibid.) mentions a list of over 2,000 words with just the root morpheme 'skrib' (write). The root morpheme 'san' has to do with health, and 'mal' is 'bad' or 'ill'. Adjectives end in -a (and nouns in -o as you learned above). Translate 'kaprino sana' and 'vircevalo malsana'. A baby could suffer from 'infanmalsano' while I am hopefully not getting 'kormalsano' while writing this book ('kor' is 'heart')—then I would need the help of the Danish 'san sistemo' if my 'san stato' was not good.

* *

Address Box 4.2   Esperanto

Universala Esperanto-Asocio (International Esperanto Association), Nieuwe Binnenweg 176, NL-3015 BJ Rotterdam, The Netherlands, phone 31-10-436 1044, fax 31-10-436 1751.

Mark Fettes has a Web-page called 'Esperanto Studies and Interlinguistics', at <http://infoweb.magi.com/~mfettes/studies.html> which also guides the surfer further to other addresses, including to the Center for Research and Documentation on World Language Problems and its journal **Language Problems and Language Planning**. Martin Weichert's Virtual Esperanto Library at <http://www.esperanto.net/veb/> is a useful guide to thousands of other Esperanto-related sites, including bibliographies, library catalogues, etc. This list comes from Blanke 1996 and has been checked by Mark Fettes in September 1998. Thanks to both!

* *

written systematic introductory articles, books, and overviews about Esperanto, also in languages other than Esperanto. For those who are interested in learning more about Esperanto, the bibliography of this book has a separate section on Esperanto, prepared by Mark Fettes.

I see Esperanto as a possible viable alternative to today's languages for international communication. A Working Group on language options in the European Union (manuscript, 1997) looked at what the options are to solve the language problem in a multinational and multicultural community, using the criteria of (1) **equality**, (2) cultural and linguistic **diversity**, (3) **non-discrimination**, (4) **democracy**, and (5) **efficiency**.

The three theoretical options were: (A) **All official languages** have to be treated the same way; (B) **One common language** which takes over and must fulfill the function of inter-ethnic communication, and (C) **Two foreign languages** obligatory for everybody.

After assessing the advantages and disadvantages of each option carefully, they concluded that within the context of the common institutions of the **Union**, the criteria 5, 4, 1, and 3 have to be the main criteria, in that order, whereas within the **educational system**, 4, 2, 1, and 3 were to be foregrounded.

The options were then analysed as to the internal functioning of the Union's own institutions and organisations (where option B, one common language, was seen as the best), and externally, in the Union's communication with the citizens, where option A, all official languages, is seen as the best option, and lack of efficiency and the high price for this option are seen as the price that has to be paid for democracy.

For the educational system, option C with two obligatory foreign languages at school was deemed the best, with one universal language for inter-ethnic communication and one national one for private purposes, understanding the neighbour, professional ambitions or necessary qualifications.

The big question then is what the common language for institutional use and the first foreign language in school for universal use should be (Task Box 4.4). There is no doubt in my mind that a solution with English does not fulfill any of the criteria. Esperanto does. Esperanto is an additive, not subtractive language. Ignorance and prejudices may prevent useful solutions.

Reader Task 4.4
Which language options fulfill the criteria? Assess Esperanto and English

Using the five criteria above, discuss the three options A, B, and C, for your own context (school, institution, company, country). Assess the present choice of languages, and try out others, including Esperanto and English. When your assessment is finished, look at the counterarguments you presented for your preferred solution. What could be done in practice to overcome some of the challenges? Are you going to try? If you need more arguments, in addition to the Web-sites and literature, look up your local Esperanto Association in the phone book.

NOTES

1. See Eco 1995, 7–10 and 40–43 for accounts for and interpretations of this.

2. Being aware of one of the negative -isms in the world, linguicism, apparently does not automatically result in being aware of the others, here sexism. What is meant is human beings . . .

3. But Senghor **also** argues that 'to be ignorant of one's mother tongue is to be uprooted from one's background' (ibid.). Prah has a brilliant analysis of the ambivalence of the westernised African elite in his 1995a.

4. Of course similar arguments, stigmatising other languages, are equally false, regardless of how pretentiously they are formulated. An example of a Zulu intrinsic argument (by Daniel W. Streeter (1926), in his book **Denatured Africa**, p. 31, quoted in Prah 1995b: 31): 'If Dutch is a jargon, Zulu is a riot between the tonsils, adenoids, palate and larynx. It has three tonal qualities: clicks, clacks and gulps. Some of the noises seemed to be jerked up from the lower oesophagus, others from the pyloric regions of the abdomen. It ought to be given a place among dead languages, and every care should be taken to keep it dead.' Or Crummell 1861, in **English Language in Liberia** (quoted in Prah 1995a: 35): 'African dialects . . . there are . . . definite marks of inferiority connected with them all, which place them at the distance from civilised languages . . . harsh, abrupt, energetic, indistinct in enunciation, meagre in point of words . . . inarticulate nasal and guttural sounds . . . few inflections and grammatical forms . . . lowness of ideas . . . the speech of rude barbarians . . . brutal and vindictive sentiments . . . a predominance of animal propensities . . . they lack . . . ideas of virtue, of moral truth . . . distinctions of right and wrong . . . the absence of clear ideas of Justice, Law, Human Rights and Governmental Order—and so we could go on'.

5. In my view much **responsible** hospital treatment is, whereas much genetic manipulation is not—see, e.g., Illich 1977 for the former and Mander & Goldsmith (eds) 1996 for the latter.

6. Religions are also part of the consciousness industry, but they are maybe no longer implicated in linguistic genocide quite to the same extent as they used to be when proselytizing was more common. See, e.g., Mühlhäusler 1996, 1997. But see also the debates in Terralingua Newsletter, e.g., reports about the Akha.

7. But see the fascinating account (Branson & Miller 1997) of a Bali village where the common language in the village is a sign language, also used by the multilingual hearing people in the village. Likewise, see Nora Ellen Groce's study (1985) **Everyone here spoke sign language: hereditary deafness on Martha's Vineyard**.

8. 'Denigrate' is in itself seen by many (black) people as a stimatising term, one more where 'black' is used with negative connotations . . .

9. In the 1985 version of the same book, there is a change for South Africa: '. . . most South Africans speak Afrikaans or Bantu languages . . .'. None of the 'Bantu languages' are mentioned, even if both Zulu (22.0% of the population) and Xhosa (18.13%) have more speakers than either Afrikaans (14.97%) or English (9.52%—all figures from **South Africa Survey 1996/97**, 1997: 24), i.e., they are still less visible than the two originally European-based ones, and Quebec still has not got any other languages except French and English. The earlier version's examples, supposed to be authentic, also changed to less sexist ones— earlier, while 'he got a chair', i.e., a professorship, 'she got a baby' . . .

10. Students know that other languages contribute to creativity and efficiency in learning. Grade 8 students interviewed by Lindiwe Madonci (1997) in Cape Town: 'I am one of those learners that decided to switch over from Afrikaans to isiXhosa because I found Afrikaans to be very difficult and it is not my language. I felt so discouraged because at times I even got 1% in my Afrikaans work. As a result I hated it and lost hope of ever passing or knowing it ever again. What makes me proud about my language isiXhosa as a subject is that my aggregate mark in tests has improved drastically as compared to when I did not take my language as a subject. I feel relaxed in a Xhosa lesson because it is my language and I do not find any difficulty in expressing myself. It is really boring and frustrating to be compelled to speak or learn a language that is not yours all the time.' 'I was also in a Primary School where isiXhosa was offered as a First Language subject. Therefore, it is

just a continuation to me. But the advantage that I experienced in my previous school is that our teachers could translate whatever that we could not understand in other languages, to our own language which is isiXhosa, when explaining issues that we could not understand. But now we only get that opportunity when we are having an isiXhosa period because it's only our Xhosa teacher that can easily switch over to other languages when explaining issues that we do not understand.' Thanks to Lindiwe Madonci for letting me quote from her work!

11. 'Where marriage rules dictate that a person must marry outside his or her clan, Koorie children grow up speaking two languages—their mother's and their father's. Due to the Koories' own interest in language and their interaction with different linguistic groups, multilingualism is, therefore, quite common. (My circle of friends and relations include Koories who speak Dutch, French, German, Greek, Hungarian, Japanese, and Malay as well as Koorie languages)', Eve Mumewa Fesl observes (1993: 20).

12. For a detailed critique of the way this book represents special pleading for English, see Phillipson 1998b, 1999, in press.

13. Einar Haugen was the first linguist who started seriously discussing language ecology—see his 1972.

14. Roger Bowers, formerly Assistant Director General of British Council, tells about 'one of the findings of the British Council's English 2000 global consultation. Of those . . . offered the proposition that "Exposure to and promotion of English and its cultural assumptions endangers other cultures and values", globally only 28% agreed with the proposition, 49% disagreed, and 11% disagreed strongly. In East Asia and Pacific, 66% disagreed or disagreed strongly. In the Americas, 76% disagreed or disagreed strongly' (Bowers 1997: 5). My comment: We are not informed in the article that the people who were asked were **English teachers** of some kind, often expatriates—how could they agree that their own work was endangering others. But one can get the impression from the presentation that it was people in East Asia, etc. themselves who had been asked.

15. See Dechicchis 1995 on the current state of Ainu; see Kubota 1998, Oda, in press, on the risks posed by English in Japan; see also Wei 1998 on language shift in Singapore for relevant factors; compare this with Shea, in press, on Japan.

16. Chomsky is a curious example of a brilliant thinker and analyst, with a tight wall between his linguistic and political analyses, where it seems almost none of the latter informs the former—(male) segmentation?

17. In non-industrial societies multilingualism is widespread. Urbanisation and telecommunications (especially telephones and radio) also contribute to oral multilingualism.

18. There are even earlier studies than Peal & Lambert 1962 showing positive results—see Malherbe's large study from South African Afrikaans-English bilingualism and bilingual education (1946). Malherbe also quotes Reyburn's positive study of bilingualism in the Cape Province in the 1930s.

19. See, e.g., Fishman 1989 who refutes many of these myths about the causal connection, and Pattanayak (1988, 1990 (ed.), 1991, 1992).

20. If we were to choose our leaders and decision makers in a rational way, we would be wise never to choose monolinguals, if we believe that 'intelligence' is a necessary precondition for 'wisdom' (it is not sufficient, and it all depends on whose definitions are used anyway—see French 1986 and Galtung 1988—but that is another story). A rational choice, maximising chances, would be to choose high-level multilinguals. Naturally multilingualism itself is not enough. Both multilingual dictators and great monolingual authors and scientists have of course existed and still do.

21. This myth has been formulated on the basis of discussions with Mark Fettes, and I use many of his ideas here. Thanks!

22. 'Access forbidden. Nuclear experiments.'

23. See, e.g., Ammon 1994, Coulmas 1991, Domaschnew 1994, Fishman 1994a, b, Haberland 1993, Haberland & Henriksen 1991, Haberland et al. 1991, Haselhuber 1991, Labrie 1995, Labrie & Quell 1997, Schlossmacher 1994, 1996, Phillipson & Skutnabb-Kangas 1994, Volz 1994, on language policy in the European Union.

24. Bodies have also been colonised after death as in the desecration of graves (where many demands are being made now for getting the bones back from museums, etc. for burial) and even selling dead bodies or skins or scalps (see Skotnes (ed.) 1996, with a copy of a list of objects offered for sale, including the skin of a 'Bushman' girl).

25. One might hope that this is changing—English has not been and is not a threatened language in South Africa, and the monolingualism or, in case of English-Afrikaans bilinguals, lack of knowledge of any indigenous African languages, harms both the individual and the country. See Heugh et al. (eds) 1995 for visionary analyses. Peter Plüddemann has sophisticated, perceptive analyses of the arguments for (and against) MTM teaching, both generally (e.g., his parts in Leibowitz & Plüddemann 1998) and, together with other members of PRAESA, specifically in relation to South Africa, based on empirical studies (e.g., Plüddemann in press, Plüddemann et al. 1998; see also Desai 1995, 1998, Maharaj & Sayed 1998).

26. Linguists who have worked with and/or known Esperanto, in addition to those mentioned below, include Paul Ariste, E. A. Bokarev, Björn Collinder, W. E. Collinson, Renato Corsetti, Probal Dasgupta, Aleksandr Dulichenko, Otto Jespersen, Sergei Kuznecov, Andre Martinet, Rene de Saussure, Renzo Titone, Mauro de Tullio, John Wells, and Eugen Wuster. But—where are the women?

27. The German original has two terms: 'künstlichen Sprachen' or 'Kunstsprachen' but both have to be translated as 'artificial languages'.

Part II

LINGUISTIC GENOCIDE, STATE POLICIES, AND GLOBALISATION

State Policies Towards Languages—Linguistic Genocide, Language Death, or Support for Languages?

The punishment of a child for speaking their language is the beginning of the destruction of that language. (Representative from Benin to the World Conference on Linguistic Rights, Barcelona, June 1996)

In January 1998 five Finnish-speaking students in Fjädeling school in Borås, Sweden, went on strike because they were forbidden to use their mother tongue, Finnish, during the breaks. The school authorities claimed that this excluded other students. (Roppola 1998: 11)

One horrible day, 1,600 years ago, the wisdom of many centuries went up in flames. The great library in Alexandria burned down, a catastrophe at the time and a symbol for all ages of the vulnerability of human knowledge . . . Today, with little notice, vast archives of knowledge and expertise are spilling into oblivion, leaving humanity in danger of losing its past and perhaps jeopardizing its future as well . . . [when] a language disappears, traditional knowledge tends to vanish with it. (Linden 1991, quoted in Leets & Giles 1995: 37)

The dominant monolingual orientation is cultivated in the developed world and consequently two languages are considered a nuisance, three languages uneconomic and many languages absurd. In multilingual countries, many languages are facts of life; any restriction in the choice of language is a nuisance; and one language is not only uneconomic, it is absurd. (Debi Prasanna Pattanayak 1984: 82)

'my concern . . . is not the loss of languages *per se*, but the loss of specialized registers in otherwise healthy languages as a clear consequence of the global advance of English. (John M. Swales 1997: 376 in his article 'English as *Tyrannosaurus rex*')

[T]he sickness of languages is greatest in areas where English is the official language. (Mühlhäusler 1996: 273)

Ninety percent of the population in Africa today speak only African languages. (Ngũgĩ wa Thiong'o 1992: 27)

Initially the gun was used as a mechanism of control; this was followed by the supply of food as a controlling mechanism . . . Under the "protection legislation" in force in all mainland states by 1911, Koories were confined to reserves, missions and other institutions . . . accelerated the use of education as a tool for disempowerment. (Eve Mumewa Fesl 1993: 179 about Australia)

Soap and education are not as sudden as a massacre, but they are more deadly in the long run. (Mark Twain, 1867, **Facts Concerning the Recent Resignation**)

Berlin of 1884 [when Africa was divided between the European empires, my remark] was effected through the sword and the bullet. But the night of the sword and the bullet was followed by the morning of the chalk and the blackboard. The physical violence of the battlefield was followed by the psychological violence of the classroom. But where the former was visibly brutal, the latter was visibly gentle . . . The bullet was the means of the physical subjugation. Language was the means of the spiritual subjugation. (Ngũgĩ wa Thiong'o, 1987: 9)

5. STATE POLICIES TOWARDS LANGUAGES— LINGUISTIC GENOCIDE, LANGUAGE DEATH, OR SUPPORT FOR LANGUAGES?

The evaluations and definitions of to what extent languages are threatened or endangered operated with three main factors as described in earlier chapters: numbers, whether or not children learn the languages, and official state policies. I have already discussed numbers, and some aspects which influence minority language speaking parents and children in their 'choice' of which languages to use and not use. In this chapter I will first look at state policies towards languages. State policies, severally and combined in globalisation, are behind 'the punishment of a child for speaking their language' and the 'vast archives of knowledge and expertise . . . spilling into oblivion' in the initial quotes. State policies create the framework within which parents and children can choose. Then I present some of the 'choices' that school language policies have offered to indigenous and minority children and parents. And finally I shall consider two ways of looking at what the negative policies have accomplished: is it a question of language death, or of linguistic genocide?

5.1. POSSIBLE STATE POLICIES TOWARDS LANGUAGES/DIALECTS/'NON-STANDARD' VARIANTS/'NON-NATIVE' VARIANTS

It should be clear by now that educational language rights are not merely vital but the most important linguistic human rights for the maintenance of linguistic and cultural diversity on our planet and the development of languages. If children are not granted the opportunity to learn their parents' idiom[1] fully and properly so that they become (at least) as proficient as the parents, the language is not going to survive.

Normally parents (exception: hearing parents of deaf children) transmit their languages to their children. They do it partly by using the language(s) themselves with the children and partly, and increasingly importantly, by choosing their own language as the medium of education for their children or otherwise ensuring that their children get full competence in their language in school.

When more and more children gain access to formal education, much of the more formal language learning which earlier happened in the community must happen in schools. Partly because that is where many children spend a substantial amount of their most active time when awake. Partly because few parents and smaller communities in our more and more complex, diverse, and bureaucratic societies can alone offer children the variety of linguistic situations, inputs, and registers that societies based on the exchange of symbolic capital require. They need to rely on formal education to take responsibility for part of this.

Where the school does not support the intergenerational transmission of the parents' language to children, it **may** of course sometimes be a result of a conscious, voluntary choice by one or both parents. They **may** be aware of the long-term consequences of this non-transmittance, for the children themselves, for the relationship between parents and children, and sometimes even for the future of the language. But in most cases, as was discussed in chapter 4, there may not have been any conscious choice, based on having had access to alternatives. Then it may be a question of linguistic genocide.

If we want to understand what happens to languages in education, we have to start by looking at the macro-level framework for education, here specifically the decisions about which languages are possible to use in schools and which are not. The language policy of a state is a result of (overt or covert) planning at the three levels of status, corpus, and acquisition planning (see Cooper 1989 for these concepts). Acquisition planning has to do with planning which languages can be learned as mother tongues, second languages, and foreign languages in educational institutions. At a more general language policy level this is decided when states form their policies towards (minority) languages.

5.1.1. Taxonomy of State Policies Towards Languages

Juan Cobarrubias (1983) has elaborated a taxonomy of policies which a state can adopt towards minority languages (see Table 5.1).

As will be shown later, the first three policies seem to lead, with few exceptions, to languages dying/being killed. Especially under conditions when all children participate in formal education, only the last two policies seem to make a language potentially safe, because formal education is one of the main killers of those languages which are not used as main media for that education. Therefore we will first analyse how many languages get this kind of official support. But before embarking on this analysis, it is important to problematise the fifth category. There are cases where 'adoption as an official language' is either not enough or not the best possible strategy to support a language. South Africa today is a good example of a situation where,

TABLE 5.1
Taxonomy of state policies towards minority languages

(1) attempting to kill a language;
(2) letting a language die;
(3) unsupported coexistence;
(4) partial support of specific language functions;
(5) adoption as an official language

(From Cobarrubias 1983: 71)

despite the 11 official languages in the Constitution, implementation does not seem to be forthcoming, as many critical voices in South Africa are increasingly beginning to point out: 'everything possible is being done to avoid bringing this to practical reality'; 'government is avoiding the issue at all cost'; 'even with the new language-in-education policy, nothing, not a thing, has been done re-implementation/trialling implementation since July 1997'; 'The policy/principle is useless without an effective implementation plan, spelt out, monitored and regulated—no soft options here at all'; 'what appears to be happening in South Africa is actually that the rhetorical multilingualism of the Constitution is manifested in practice by the increasing domination of English' (from interviews with colleagues).[2] Mark Fettes (1998) describes in an article about Canada's Aboriginal languages a situation where two territories, the Northwest Territories and the Yukon Territory, adopted different approaches, the former but not the latter declaring the Aboriginal languages official. Fettes seems to think that the Yukon approach has been able to adjust better to local needs, and he argues convincingly for approaches which consider and problematize the complexities of each situation rather than importing ready-made solutions from other contexts. A rights-oriented approach, then, has to be localised—Cobarrubias' categories on a continuum have to be placed together with many other continua. Having expressed some need for caution, we proceed to looking at the status-related aspect of relative officialdom of languages.

How many of the around 6,700 oral languages and the equally many sign languages[3] in the world have some kind of official status? The number of states in the world is somewhere above 170 and below 230, depending on which definition of 'a state' or a similar unit in terms of its right to make policy decisions is being used (Info Box 5.1; Definition Box 5.1). A political science oriented definition of a state focusses on the characteristic of the monopoly of violence, external and internal control, i.e., the army and the police; I have used a relational definition: a state is a unit which is accepted by other states as a state.[4] Even smaller units than states can have the right to educational language policy decisions.

If we were to divide the number of languages with the number of states, using, for example, 210 states and 6,700 oral and 6,700 sign languages, each state would on an average have 32 oral and 32 sign languages as official languages. Of course the languages are unevenly distributed between states as Tables 1.1 through 1.3 show. But the majority of the world's around 200 states are **not** officially multilingual, and there is no state which has 32 oral languages as official languages. Not one of the very few states which give sign languages **any** official recognition in the first place, for instance by mentioning a sign language in the constitution, recognises more than one sign language. In fact all of them talk about 'sign language' as if there was only one (see Branson & Miller 1995a, 1996, 1998b). In addition, there is a

---

❖ I n f o   B o x   5 . 1 ❖

How Many States Are There?

Unesco Statistical Yearbook 1997 has a list of countries (i.e., **not** states) which has 56 for Africa, 37 for North and 14 for South America, 54 for Asia, 49 for Europe and 20 for Oceania. In addition, there is one called 'Former USSR'. This totals 231. The **Yearbook 1998** has 52 for Asia and 45 for Europe, totalling 224. UN's **Human Development Report 1998** gives the Human Development Index for 174 countries.

McArthur (1998: 47–48) lists 232 'territories' (see Definition Box 5.1) in his table of the international distribution of English, French, Spanish, and Portuguese.

Most other accounts are somewhere between these. For instance, the telephone company Interoute Danmark has in its 1998 price list 231 countries.

---

lot of repetition in the lists of official languages: the same language functions as official in several states. Let's start by looking at the repetition.

5.1.2. The Big Languages as Official Languages

'The' or 'an' official language was English in 45 countries in 1992 according to Michael Krauss (1992: 7) and in 'over 70' according to David Crystal (1997a). French is the official language according to Krauss in 30 states, both Spanish and Arabic in 20 and Portuguese in 6. In Table 5.2 I have combined information from several sources and listed the states. I have also added some other 'big' languages which are official in more than one state: German, Chinese, Malay, and Tamil. In section 1.2.2. we mentioned African community languages used in more than one country, but not many of them have official status in more than one or two countries. Again, it is interesting that even this type of basic information is so difficult to obtain and that the accounts vary.

In order to check with some of the most recent sources, I also used McArthur 1998: 49–52. The following countries/territories are completely missing from McArthur: American Samoa, Guam, Northern Marianas and Palau. According to McArthur, English is not an official language but only a lingua franca in some of the countries on the list (Bhutan, Nauru, Nepal) or it is only a *de facto* (but not *de jure*) official language (British Virgin Islands, Montserrat, US Virgin Islands) or it is only recognised for higher education and law (Bangladesh) or it is a compulsory second language in education (Malaysia). In addition, McArthur lists separately Turks and Caicos Islands. Tanzania is also differently placed in the sources. French is official in Sudan according to Kaplan & Baldauf (1997: 337) but according

TABLE 5.2
States where English, French, Spanish, Arabic, Portuguese, German, Malay, Chinese, or Tamil have official status (are 'an' or 'the' official language or 'have otherwise official status')

LANGUAGE	Number of states	Where?
English	45 (Krauss) over 70 (Crystal)	1.American Samoa 2. Antigua and Barbuda 3.Australia 4.Bahamas 5.Bangladesh 6.Barbados 7.Belize 8.Bermuda 9.Bhutan 10.Botswana 11.British Virgin Islands 12.Brunei 13.Cameroon 14.Canada 15.Cayman Islands 16.Cook Islands 17.Dominica 18.Fiji 19.Gambia 20.Ghana 21.Gibraltar 22.Grenada 23.Guam 24.Guyana 25.Hong Kong 26.India 27.Ireland 28.Jamaica 29.Kenya 30.Kiribati 31.Lesotho 32.Liberia 33.Malawi 34.Malaysia 35.Malta 36.Marshall Islands 37.Mauritius 38.Micronesia 39.Montserrat 40.Namibia 41.Nauru 42.Nepal 43.New Zealand 44.Nigeria 45.Northern Marianas 46.Pakistan 47.Palau 48.Papua New Guinea 49.Philippines 50.Puerto Rico 51.Rwanda 52.St Kitts & Nevis 53.St Lucia 54.St Vincent & Grenadines 55.Seychelles 56.Sierra Leone 57.Singapore 58.Solomon Islands[5] 59.South Africa 60.Sri Lanka[6] 61.Suriname 62.Swaziland 63.Tonga 64.Trinidad & Tobago 65.Tuvalu 66.Uganda 67.United Kingdom 68.UK Islands (Channel Islands, Man) 69.United States 70.US Virgin Islands 71.Vanuatu 72.Western Samoa 73.Zambia 74.Zimbabwe
French	30 (Krauss)	1.Belgium 2.Benin 3.Burkina Faso 4.Burundi 5.Cameroon 6.Canada 7.Central African Republic 8.Comores 9.Congo 10.Ivory Coast 11.France 12.French Polynesia 13.Gabon 14.Haiti 15.Lebanon 16.Luxembourg 12.Madagascar 13.Mali 14.Mauritius 15.Monaco 16.Niger 17.Panama 18.Rwanda 19.Senegal 20.Seychelles 21.Switzerland 22.Togo 23.Vanuatu 24.Wallis and Futuna 25.Zaire
Spanish	20 (Krauss)	1.Argentina 2.Bolivia 3.Colombia 4.Costa Rica 5.Cuba 6.Ecuador 7.El Salvador 8.Equatorial Guinea 9.Guatemala 10.Honduras 11.Mexico 12.Nicaragua 13.Paraguay 14.Peru 15.Puerto Rico 16.Spain 17.Uruguay 18.Venezuela
Arabic	20 (Krauss)	1.Algeria 2.Comores 3.Egypt 4.Iraq 5.Israel 6.Jordan 7.Kuwait 8.Lebanon 9.Libya 10.Maldives 11.Mauritania 12.Morocco 13.Qatar 14.Somalia 15.Sudan 16.Syria 17.Tunisia 18.United Arab Emirates 19.Yemen
Portuguese	6 (Krauss)	1.Angola 2.Brazil 3.Guinea-Bissau 4.Mozambique 5.Portugal 6.São Tomé and Príncipe
German	6	1.Austria 2.Belgium 3.Germany 4. Italy 5.Liechtenstein 6.Luxembourg 7.Switzerland
Malay	3	1.Brunei 2.Malaysia 3.Singapore
Chinese (some form)	3	1.China 2.Hong Kong 3.Singapore
Tamil	3	1.India 2.Singapore 3.Sri Lanka

Sources: Number of states: Krauss 1992: 7; lists compiled on the basis of: Crystal 1997a: 57–60, 1997b: 359; Kaplan & Baldauf 1997: 325–340; de Varennes 1996: 380–459; Graddol 1997. The category 'have otherwise official status' includes **de facto** officialdom in some countries which do not have any official language, e.g., the English for the United States.

to de Varennes (1996: 447) only Arabic is an official language in the 1973 Constitution. Again, we have to conclude that it seems to be incredibly difficult to get hundred percent reliable information without using vast amounts of time, even about issues which seem as simple as what the official languages of the states of the world are.

There are 141 states altogether on my list of countries which have **at least one of the big languages as official languages** (and had we added Russian there would have been even more). Of these, the following 16 have **two of the big languages** from our list as official languages (many of them have other additional official languages too): Belgium (German and French), Brunei (Malay and English), Cameroon and Canada (French and English), Comores (Arabic and French), Hong Kong (Chinese and English), India (Tamil and English), Lebanon (Arabic and French), Luxembourg (French and German), Malaysia (Malay and English), Mauritius (French and English), Puerto Rico (Spanish and English), Seychelles (French and English), Sri Lanka (Tamil and English), Switzerland (German and French), and Vanuatu (French and English). Singapore has, as the only one, four of the big languages as official languages: Tamil, Malay, Chinese, and English.

This does not leave much room for other languages.

Several important additions to nuance official support to languages will be made in the next two sections.

5.1.3. Legal Hierarchies of Languages: Official, National, Additional, Link, Part of Culture or National Heritage

There are many other, partially complementary ways in which support to languages can be discussed. Many sources use various ways of gauging the support for and importance of the big languages. In his book **The English Languages** (1998) Tom McArthur relates the roles and status of English to the **de facto** and **de jure** (factual and legal) uses. He operates with eight categories, starting with 'English as a **de facto** official language, the standard variety co-occurring with other varieties and other languages' (ibid., 39; with UK and USA as examples; English is not legally/technically an official language at the level of the whole country in either) and ending with English as an 'official language for international purposes' (ibid., 41) with the UN and the European Union as examples). Except for the first **de facto** category with UK and USA, all his categories save one are in fact about English as in some way official. The only vague category is his number 6, 'Not official or with special legal status, but nonetheless significant', where one of his two examples is: 'In Denmark, Norway, Sweden, and the Netherlands, English is the second language, which everyone learns and many use for personal and professional purposes at home and abroad' (ibid., 41).

If 'everyone learns' is equated with 'everyone who goes to school is taught as a subject' (which is the only reading that makes the statement true for the countries mentioned), then most countries in the world could be placed in this category, i.e., it should not be on the same list as the rest, especially as the list does not form a continuum, from strongest to weakest support or status. This is in fact a mild form of the English language triumphalism discussed in section 4.1.4.3.

Tom McArthur lists 'the international distribution of English, French, Spanish, and Portuguese' in various 'territories' (see Definition Box 5.1 for 'territory' and 'significant'). He lists altogether 232 'territories'.[7] The four languages are 'significant for one or more reasons' in them. 'In some they have official status; in others they do not' (1998: 47–48). In his subtotal he gives a total of 183 territories, discounting overlaps (out of the 232 in the world) where one or more of the four big languages is 'significant'.

DEFINITION BOX 5.1   'territories', 'significant' languages (McArthur)

'I use the word *territories* so as to cover not only nation-states but also remote localities deemed part of those states (such as French Caribbean islands) and colonial and other dependencies (such as Gibraltar and the Channel Islands), because many such places have distinctive patterns of language use. I use '*significant*', rather than, say, 'major', so as not to limit the discussion to such matters as population statistics and polito-economic power.' (McArthur 1996: 9).

English is significant in 114[8] territories, French in 54, Spanish in 27, and Portuguese in 12. It is interesting to look at his list of the 'remaining 52 world territories' where in his view none of the four are significant: Afghanistan, Albania, Armenia, Aruba, Austria, Azerbaijan, Belarus, Bosnia-Herzegovina, Bulgaria, China, Croatia, the Czech Republic, Estonia, Finland, Georgia, Germany, Greece, Greenland, Hungary, Iceland, Indonesia, Iraq, Japan, Kazakhstan, Kirghizia, Korea (North), Korea (South), Latvia, Libya, Liechtenstein, Lithuania, Macedonia, Moldavia, Mongolia, Poland, Romania, Russia, San Marino, Saudi Arabia, Slovakia, Slovenia, Taiwan, Tajikistan, Thailand, Turkey, Turkmenistan, Ukraine, Uzbekistan, the Vatican City, Yemen, Yugoslavia.

Some Japanese colleagues might be very happy to see that English is not 'significant' in their country. Yukio Tsuda, an ardent critic of English language imperialism in Japan (see also Tsuda 1986, 1988, 1994) claims that the Japanese suffer from an Angloholic consciousness of an uncritical and unconditional admiration for English and Western culture, while developing a very negative image of their own language and culture, the position of English as the most dominant international language preventing the linguistic and cultural self-determination of the speakers of other languages. (Tsuda 1992: 32)

There has been major resistance and resentment towards the dominance of English in Japan, for instance on the issue of a language teachers' association functioning in English only (Oda 1994)—or in relation to linguistic discrimination of Japanese students in English-medium universities abroad (see Oda, in press, for an example). Why would resistance be needed if English was not 'significant'? Courses of English in China (see Harrell 1993 on linguistics and hegemony in China) and in countries in the ex-Soviet Union's sphere of influence (almost half of the list) have been mushrooming (with generous 'help' from Britain and the USA) and competence in English already plays an important role domestically for hierarchies and career structures. The 1997–1998 economic crisis may change some of this in Asia, though, as mentioned in chapter 4. Several of the countries on McArthur's list of 52 are in the US and/or UK 'sphere of influence', for example, Saudi Arabia (significantly, included in the Fishman et al. (eds, 1997) book on post-colonial English), Indonesia, South Korea, Iraq, and Libya (at least before Gaddafi and Saddam Hussein) and also others.

McArthur's Panel 2.2, 'The worldwide status and roles of English' (ibid., 49) counts 113 territories (the Netherlands Antilles from the earlier Panel discussed above is missing, for no apparent reason). In these English is official, co-official, **de facto** official, lingua franca, additional language (e.g., Israel), often used in government (e.g., Sri Lanka), 'first' second language (e.g., Denmark, the Netherlands, Norway, Sweden), or third language (the Faroe Islands). The list is thus a not very helpful mixed bag, especially since the designation 'lingua franca', ranging from Switzerland[9] via several African countries to many Asian countries, seemingly has more to do with discourses among parts of the elites rather than ordinary people (who in many cases have little knowledge of English—see Schmied 1991 for English in Africa). Likewise, including 'third language', as for the Faroe Islands, would obviously qualify more than half the list which was designated as the 'remaining territories of the world' above.

The criticism above is not meant to detract from the value of the basic desriptive typological work that many of the researchers whose data I utilize are doing. What all of this shows is:

- that there is an urgent need for more work in order to even start understanding the importance of various factors in supporting or not supporting the world's languages—even here we still do not even have a basic pool of factual information that researchers could agree on, let alone theoretical models; and

- that multilingual multidisciplinary teamwork is needed even for collecting the basic information.

We still need to add one more aspect to the discussion of the variation in official support to languages. How are languages being treated in the constitutions of various countries and in some other equivalent official documents? Most of the examples of constitutions come from the Appendix in human rights lawyer Fernand de Varennes' excellent book **Languages, Minorities and Human Rights** (1996).

Many countries **differentiate between official (or state) and national languages** (Info Box 5.2).

❖ **I n f o   B o x   5 . 2** ❖

Differentiation Between Official (or State)
and National Languages (Switzerland)

1. German, French, Italian, and Romansh are the national languages of Switzerland.

2. German, French, and Italian are declared to be the official languages of the Confederation. (Art. 116 from the Constitution of *Switzerland*, 29 May 1874, amended, quoted in de Varennes 1996: 448)

If a country has both, the official language is often an old colonial language and the national languages are more often domestic (e.g., Malay in Singapore). Often (but not always) **the official language has a higher status than the national language** in administration and other public domains, for example, in the parliament (e.g., English in Kenya). Some countries have still finer hierarchisations (Info Box 5.3).

The status hierarchy can also often be seen in the fact that one of the languages is allocated the final arbiter role in cases where there is a conflict in the translation of important documents, for instance the Constitution itself (Info Box 5.4).

But often there is no difference between whether a language is designated 'official' or 'national', especially in cases where only one or the other is mentioned. **The same language can also be both official and national** (Info Box 5.5).

Many countries have **more than one official language** (often the 'an'— rather than 'the'—official language indicates that there are others too). These can have **equal status** (as Finnish and Swedish in Finland—see Info Box 5.6).

Official Language Has Higher Status Than National Language
(Congo, Vanuatu, Sri Lanka)

'. . . The official language is French. The national vernacular languages are Lingala and Munukutuba.' (from Art. 3 from the Constitution of *Congo*, 15 March 1992, quoted in de Varennes 1996: 397)

'1. The national language of the Republic is Bislama. The official languages are Bislama, English and French. The principal languages of education are English and French.' (Art. 3.1 from the Constitution of *Vanuatu*, 30 July 1980, quoted in de Varennes 1996: 454)

Article 18
'1. The official language of Sri Lanka shall be Sinhala.

2. Tamil shall also be an official language.

3. English shall be the link language.

Article 19
The national languages of Sri Lanka shall be Sinhala and Tamil.' (Art. 18 and 19 from the Constitution of *Sri Lanka*, 31 August 1978, quoted in de Varennes 1996: 445)

Language With Final Arbiter Role (Western Samoa)

'The Samoan and English texts of this Constitution are equally authoritative but, in case of difference, the English text shall prevail' (Art. 112 from the Constitution of *Western Samoa*, 1 January 1962, quoted in de Varennes 1996: 456).

   Despite not being uncommon, this constitutional clause is actually self-contradictory.

Same Language Is Official and National (Burundi)

'The national language is Kirundi. The official languages are Kirundi and other languages determined by law' (Art. 8 from the Constitution of *Burundi*, 13 March 1992, quoted in de Varennes 1996: 392).

❖ **I n f o   B o x   5 . 6** ❖

More Than One Official Language (Finland)

The Finnish Constitution of 1919 declares (in Art. 14, Para. 2) that the right of citizens of *Finland* to use their own mother tongue, Finnish or Swedish, before courts and administrative authorities, and to obtain documents issued to them by these authorities in that language, is guaranteed by law, with the rights of both language groups being protected 'according to identical principles'. The same formulation is found in Art. 14, Para. 3, which states that the 'cultural and economic needs' (changed to 'cultural and social needs' in the 1995 revision of the constitution) of the Finnish-speaking and Swedish-speaking populations shall be provided 'according to identical principles' (for the language situation in Finland, see McRae 1997; see also Kotimaisten kielten tutkimuskeskus 1998 for the Language Policy Programme of Finland—this should be compared to the equivalent in Sweden, see Svenska språknämnden 1998).

Or they can have **unequal status** (as Māori and English in *New Zealand*). The official languages can be old colonial languages (even two of them, as in *Cameroon*, with both English and French—therefore Cameroon figures twice in Table 5.2, under both languages) or domestic languages.[10]

Admittedly many of the 141 countries above have other languages than the big ones as official or co-official or additional languages or as national languages. The world champions are **India**, with its 18 languages (Info Box 5.7) (e.g., Khubchandani 1983: 6; 1997: 124; Pattanayak 1991: 4), and **South Africa**, with its 11 official languages (Info Box 5.8).

Still, probably the number of official languages in the world is no higher than the number of states. Kidron & Segal (1991) claim in the caption above one of their maps that only 86 of the existing languages in the world are official. Even if some additional languages have partial official status, regionally or for specific purposes, for example, education, their numbers are probably maximally some hundreds.

Some languages can also get **support by being specifically mentioned in the Constitution** (Info Box 5.9, p. 308).

Another way of guaranteeing support in the Constitution is a **general formulation** about the right to use the native language or any language, **without specifying the names of the languages**. Often the protection is conditional on citizenship or official recognition as a minority or nationality (Info Box 5.10, p. 309).

Some languages may also get recognition in the Constitution as **part of the national culture or cultural heritage** of the country (Info Box 5.11, p. 309).

❖ **Info Box 5.7** ❖

The 18 + 1 Official or Administrative Languages of India

The original 14 languages in the Eighth Schedule in the *India*n Constitution were **Assamese, Bengali, Gujarati, Hindi, Kannada, Kashmiri, Malayalam, Marathi, Oriya, Punjabi, Tamil, Telugu, Urdu,** and **Sanskrit; Sindhi** was added to the list in 1967, and **Gorkhali/Nepali, Konkani, and Manipuri** were added in 1992. *Hindi*, in the Devanagari script, was given the status of the *national official language* while *English* (which is not part of the 8th Schedule) was made an *associate official language* first for a fixed transition time of 15 years and later indefinitely or until other arrangements are made.[11] English is also a national language because it is the state language in four states (Manipur, Meghalaya, Nagaland, and Tripura), and an official language in eight Union territories (the Andaman and Nicobar Islands, Arunachal Pradesh, Chandigarh, Dadra and Nagar Haveli, Delhi, Lakshwadip, Mizoram and Pondicherry). Other languages recognized by the National Academy of Literature, the Sahitya Akademi (seen by many as a step towards entry in the Eighth Schedule—Khubchandani 1997a: 124) are Dogri, Rajasthani and Maithili. For overviews of the language situation, see Chaturvedi & Singh 1981, Ekka 1995, Kachru 1983, 1990; Khubchandani 1983; 1988, 1997a, b, Pattanayak 1986, 1990 (ed.), 1991; Sridhar 1989, 1996; for the legal situation, see Bhat 1993).

❖ **Info Box 5.8** ❖

The Official Languages of South Africa

'The official languages of the Republic are Sepedi, Sesotho, Setswana, siSwati, Tshivenda, Xitsonga, Afrikaans, English, isiNdebele, isiXhosa and isiZulu' (The Constitution of the Republic of *South Africa*, 1996, Chapter 1, 6(1)). Some readers might be more familiar with the forms of the so called Bantu[12] languages where the initial prefix, marker of singular form (which is obligatory in all nouns in these Niger-Kordofanian languages) has been left out: Pedi, Sotho, Tswana, Swati, Venda, Tsonga, Ndebele, Xhosa, and Zulu.[13] Some might also recognize the form Swazi instead of Swati.[14]

5.1.4. Partial Support of Specific Language Functions

The other positive point in Cobarrubias' taxonomy, apart from full official status, is 'partial support of specific language functions'. Some of the formulations above in various constitutions in fact signal this kind of partial

---

❖ I n f o   B o x   5 . 9 ❖

Support for Named Non-Official Languages in the Constitution
(South Africa, Philippines, Uganda)

The Pan South African Language Board must—
(a) promote and create conditions for the development and use of
  (i) all official languages;
  (ii) the Khoi, Nama and San languages; and
  (iii) sign language.
(b) promote and ensure respect for languages, including German, Greek, Gujarati, Hindi, Portuguese, Tamil, Telugu, Urdu, and others commonly used by communities in South Africa, and Arabic, Hebrew, Sanskrit and others used for religious purposes. (From the Constitution of *South Africa*, 1996, chapter 1, 6(5).

Article 14

6. The national language of the Philippines is Filipino . . .

7. For the purposes of communication and instruction, the official languages of the Philippines are Filipino and, unless otherwise provided by law, English.
  The regional languages are the auxiliary official languages in the regions and shall serve as auxiliary media of instruction therein.
  Spanish and Arabic shall be promoted on a voluntary and optional basis. (From Art. 6 and 7 in the constitution of the *Philippines*, quoted in de Varennes 1996: 433)

The State shall . . .

(b) encourage the development, preservation and enrichment of all Ugandan languages;

(c) promote the development of a sign language for the deaf; and

(d) encourage the development of a national language or languages. (From XXIV. Cultural objectives, Constitution of the Republic of *Uganda*, 1995)

---

support, and most regulations about restricted regional rights for a language fall under this umbrella. Media can use languages which are not official, as for instance the Australian and Swedish and many other media do. This may include both indigenous and immigrant minority languages. The educational sphere is often one where we see this kind of support. It can mean that a language which is not an official or national language can be used as a medium of education in certain (mostly lower) grades in school or taught as a subject (see Info Box 5.12, p. 310).

❖ **I n f o   B o x   5 . 10** ❖

Support for Unnamed Non-Official Languages in the Constitution
(Turkmenistan, Vietnam, China)

The state language of Turkmenistan shall be the Turkmen language.
All citizens of Turkmenistan shall be guaranteed the right to use their native language. (Art. 13 from the Constitution of *Turkmenistan*, 18 May 1992, quoted in de Varennes 1996: 450)

. . . All the nationalities have the right to use their spoken languages and scripts, and to preserve and promote their fine customs, habits, traditions, and cultures. (Art. 5 from the Constitution of *Vietnam*, 18 December 1980, quoted in de Varennes 1996: 455)

All nationalities have the freedom to use and develop their own spoken and written languages and to preserve or reform their own folkways and customs. (From Art. 4 in the Constitution of *China*, 4 December 1982, quoted in de Varennes 1996: 395)

❖ **I n f o   B o x   5 . 11** ❖

Language as Part of the National Culture or Cultural Heritage
(Ecuador, Vanuatu)

. . . The official language is Castilian. Quechua and other indigenous languages are recognized as elements of the national culture. (From Art. 1 in the Constitution of *Ecuador*, 10 August 1979, quoted in de Varennes 1996: 401)

1. The national language of the Republic is Bislama. The official languages are Bislama, English and French. The principal languages of education are English and French.
2. The Republic shall protect the different local languages which are part of the national heritage, and may declare one of them as a national language. (Art. 3 from the Constitution of *Vanuatu*, 30 July 1980, quoted in de Varennes 1996: 454)

Teaching any language as a foreign language in schools also gives the language 'partial support'. Thus we mostly have the paradoxical situation where languages completely 'foreign' to the country (in the sense that there are no or few native speakers) get more official 'support' than many of the country's own indigenous or minority languages. This also means that when

---

❖ I n f o   B o x   5 . 1 2 ❖

Partial Support of Specific Functions (India, Russia)

In *India* in the early 1990s, of the over 400 languages, 34 languages were literary languages, 87 were used for publication, and 71 for transmission (radio or TV); 58 languages were used as media of instruction, according to Debi Prasanna Pattanayk (1991: 38), former Director of the Central Institute of Indian Languages. These are listed in Chaturvedi & Singh 1981: 33–34. 21 of them are used in more than one state (ibid., 35), and some schools have up to 5 languages of instruction (ibid., 36).

In the *Russian Federation*, 66 languages, of the more than 120, were 'used in some capacity in education' in 1991, according to Alexei Leontiev (23 as media, 66 as subjects—see the detailed lists in Leontiev 1995: 208–209; see also Leontiev 1994). In 1934, there were 104 languages used as media of instruction in the *USSR*, in 1988–1989 only 44. In *Russia*, there were 32 in 1927–1928, decreasing to 23 in 1991.

---

the main foreign language(s) in schools change, the languages being displaced are in most of these cases also Big Languages. An increasing trend in Africa today may be that one colonial language is being exchanged for another one, as in *Algeria* (see Insert 5.1).

INSERT 5.1   English replacing other Big Languages
as foreign languages taught in schools

According to David Crystal (1997a: 3–4), English is 'now the language most widely taught as a foreign language—in over 100 countries, such as China, Russia, Germany, Spain, Egypt, and Brazil—and in most of these countries it is emerging as the chief foreign language to be encountered in schools, often displacing another language in the process. In 1996, for example, English replaced French as the chief foreign language in schools in Algeria (a former French colony).'

In former communist countries in Central and Eastern Europe, Russian as the first foreign language in schools is being replaced by other languages, mostly English, but German and French are also strong candidates. In many countries (e.g., in Hungary—see Radnai 1993, 1994, 1995, Radnai & Koster 1995) they are needed in business at least as much as English. This is the case also in the Nordic countries; a diversification of school foreign languages has been discussed and to some extent attempted in all of them. Blondin et al. 1998, Kubanek-German 1998, ed. 1996, Euromosaic 1996, and information in the Mercator and Eurydice data-bases and the Council of Europe's language and education oriented databases give a good start (see Address Box 8.1).

Still, if we disregard the nice phrases about vague support to unnamed languages, we can see that the total number of languages which get official state support by being designated official or state or national languages or by getting 'partial support of specific language functions' (Cobarrubias' point 4 above) is small, maximally a few hundred languages on a worldwide basis. This leaves over 90% of the world's oral languages and more than 99.9% of the sign languages without this kind of official support.

Instead of 'official languages', we would do well to keep in mind Kidron & Segal's definition of their term **Languages of Rule** (see Definition Box 5.2) which they use in their **The State of the World Atlas**.

DEFINITION BOX 5.2 'Languages of Rule' (Kidron & Segal) instead of 'official languages'

'A **language of rule** 'is one which is used by the governing classes, and which helps to secure their dominance' (Kidron & Segal 1981: 33).

Designation as official is a function of power relations, just like designation as a language rather than a dialect. One might suspect that it is not only functionality or principles of economy (it would be impossible or impractical or inefficient or too costly to use all the small languages in official function X—for instance in education) which are at work. Besides, many of the functional and most of the economic arguments used against granting smaller languages some official tasks, for example, in education, have little merit, as was shown in the sections on the monolingualism myths and on cost in chapter 4. Additional arguments will be presented in later chapters.

5.2. LINGUISTIC GENOCIDE

5.2.1. Reducing the Number of Languages Is Reducing Prerequisites for Self-Determination

If a minority group or an indigenous people are allowed to learn and transmit further their own language, they also reproduce themselves as a minority group or an indigenous people. As will become clear in later chapters, one of the reasons for linguistic genocide is that it can reduce the number of (potential) nations, meaning peoples who could demand the right to first internal, then external self-determination. Reducing the number of languages and thus prerequisites for potential nation-states is in fact being attempted in a variety of ways. I will mention three ways of reducing the number of languages as prerequisites for nation-states: **physical genocide, linguistic genocide** and, third, **making languages invisible** by labelling them dialects, vernaculars or patois (as has been discussed earlier). The most dramatic way of reducing the number of peoples (and thus languages) is physical genocide.

The prevention and punishment of **physical genocide** is regulated by a UN Convention.[15] Physical genocide is nevertheless still attempted in relation to too many groups. Physical genocide has by no means been only attempted and committed by a dominant group vis-a-vis dominated groups with a different ethnicity, language, or culture, even if this has historically been the most common situation (see Insert 5.2).

Genocide in Tasmania, Australia, and much of the Americas is well documented, as is the European World War II Holocaust. Even where the genocide was not complete, a decimation of the original population was the result.

But many if not most of the situations presented as massive intra-group (e.g., Cambodia) or intra-statal (in Latin America, e.g., Guatemala, Nicaragua) genocide during the last decades, have in fact been engineered or actively supported (via arms sales, through training, politically, etc.), and/or financed (mostly indirectly) by the large Western powers, most aggressively the USA, Britain, and France (see Pilger 1998, Chomsky 1987, 1994, 1996, and George (ed.) 1991 for overviews of this Western state terrorism). Genocide is of course not exclusively a Western responsibility. Elites in other parts of the world have either cooperated or taken the initiative themselves—and still do.

Another way of reducing the number of possible nations (and thereby nation-states) is to commit **linguistic genocide**. This represents (actively) **killing a language without killing the speakers** (as in physical genocide) or (through passivity) **letting a language die** (see Juan Cobarrubias taxonomy in 5.1.1). Unsupported coexistence mostly also leads to minority languages dying.

A third way of enabling the reduction of the number of possible nation-states, by reducing the number of languages, is, as has been shown earlier in section 3.4.2.2, to hierarchize different groups which might want to form a nation and therefore eventually a nation-state, through **labelling** them so that **only some groups are seen as possessing the necessary prerequisite, a language**, whereas others are labelled as not possessing a language, but only a way of communicating, an idiom, which is **not** a language and is then called something else, a labelling process used as one of the joint strategies in many of the -isms regulating power relationships in the world. In the rest of this section the concept of linguistic genocide will be presented and discussed further.

Physical genocide
(from California to the Phillippines to today)

'. . . after the missions began to develop, deaths generally exceeded births among the missionized Indians' (Rev. Francis F. Guest, Member of the Academy of American Franciscan History, about Spanish Franciscan Missionaries in Upper California, in Costo & Costo (eds.) 1987: 227). The May 23, 1863 issue of the **Humboldt Times** 'editorialized, "the Indian must be exterminated or removed . . . this may not be the most christianlike attitude but it is the most practical" ' (Norton 1987: 123). According to Norton (ibid.), the genocide was in no way accidental: the government of the USA, 'as well as the various state, country and municipal governments, have consciously developed and implemented policies resulting in genocide being consistently practiced against the native people' (ibid., 123). And the same policy continued in other parts of the world with American imperialism—Norton quotes the San Francisco newspaper **Argonaut** which made the goal in genocide clear: 'We do not want the Filipinos. We want the Phillippines. The Islands are enormously rich, but unfortunately they are infested by Filipinos. There are many millions there and it is to be feared their extinction will be slow' (ibid., 122). These attitudes were a logical consequence of the fact that American 'Governers, Senators and military commanders had for decades called for the removal or extermination of people who were considered to be "impediments to progress and civilization" ' (ibid., 122). Local California newspapers were continually urging the public to commit genocide; if any crimes were committed by 'Indians', 'no special pain will be taken to find the individual perpetrators. Any ten will be taken and hung if the guilty are not brought forward', **Humboldt Times** commented (April 9, 1862, quoted in Norton 1987: 123), and another headline (April 11, 1963, quoted in ibid.) told that when one white man was killed, thirty-eight 'Bucks' were killed and 'Forty Squaws and Children Taken'.

Diamond's (1991) quotations from American presidents is horrifying reading: 'The immediate objectives are the total destruction and devastation of their settlements . . . essential to ruin their crops on the ground and prevent their planting more' (George Washington); they 'have . . . justified [their own] extermination' (Thomas Jefferson); the continent is 'nothing but a game preserve for squalid savages' (Theodore Roosevelt), and so on.

Still, the attempts at genocide that the USA has been involved in during the last decades have been perpetrated partly directly, partly by proxy, but the numbers killed are far greater than during last century (see, e.g., Pilger 1998).

5.2.2. Don't Shoot the Messenger!

Initially, we have to tackle an emotional question about this strong term, linguistic genocide. Please start with Task Box 5.1!

Is it the messenger one should feel angry with—or the existence of the phenomenon itself?

If linguistic genocide is a reality, why has it not been discussed? Why has no attention been paid to it? Why are international organisations not screaming? Amnesty International, Save the Children Fund, UNICEF, where are they?

Not only have indigenous and minority **languages** been invisibilised. Linguistic genocide itself has been invisibilised. It is a practice of most states—therefore, if a state accuses another state of it, they have to plead guilty themselves too. In addition to showing how state educational language policies have historically committed linguistic genocide we will in the rest of the chapter (and in later chapters) give examples of how these practices continue today, mostly with the help of more sophisticated means.

Finally, we will also look at one of the many strategies of invisibilising linguistic genocide where it is mainly researchers who are the culprits. When results of linguistic genocide (not only those resulting from education, but in general) start showing and languages 'disappear', this can be made to seem 'natural', or 'voluntary shift', or 'inevitable'—therefore, agentless ('The small dialects must be lost . . . they must give way before the stronger and more developed . . . The language of Ambon is disappearing at an increasing rate . . . It is sensible not to oppose such a gradual, natural process'—'Dutch' 'East India', a high-ranking civil servant, A. A. Fokker in 1891, Malay replacing Ambon, quoted in Mühlhäusler 1996: 178). There is nobody to blame, except the people who left their language. Calling linguistic genocide 'language death' is one way of making the **genocide** invisible. This will be analysed in the final section.

5.2.3. UN Definition of Linguistic Genocide

You may never have heard about **linguistic** genocide. It is in fact not discussed, or directly forbidden using that expression, in any human rights conventions. Linguistic genocide **has** been discussed, though. After the Second 'World' War when the United Nations was created as a successor to the League of Nations, one of the urgent tasks was to start work on human rights covenants which would prevent the cruelties and atrocities which the world had experienced. What happened to Jews and to Roma (and, for instance, to many homosexuals, another minority) in German concentration camps was genocide, and it should never be allowed to happen again, it was said.

Reader Task 5.1
Reflections on 'linguistic genocide'

Before you continue reading, please stop for a few moments and think of three questions below. If you have time, write down your reflections. Here are the three questions:

1. What are your feelings when you hear/see the term 'linguistic genocide'?

2. What does 'linguistic genocide' mean? Can you give synonyms which mean approximately the same? How would you define the term?

3. Do you participate in or have you ever participated in committing linguistic genocide? Do you know anybody who has/does?

Next, read the following description (from Wink 1997: 73–74). Joan Wink has first described her own very positive encounters with me. Then she tells a different story, quoting one of her graduate students, Sharon:

> I have noticed that not everyone reacts to Tove the way I did during my initial encounter with her. In fact, sometimes the power of her ideas gives people a tummy ache. Sharon, a teacher/grad student, shares her story:
> "I first met Tove at a conference in San Francisco. I sat in the front row of the enormous auditorium. I didn't want to miss a word, an inference, a smile.
> Soon, an official of the conference introduced Tove Skutnabb-Kangas, and I immediately noticed her rosy cheeks. Everyone applauded as Tove stepped up to the microphone and began talking loudly about education and language. Where was this soft cuddly bunny rabbit[16] I had heard about? I was so confused. I sat up in my chair so I could try to grasp the words. What? I, as a teacher, was cutting off the native language of my bilingual students? Me, who is so dedicated? My preconceived notions exploded! Well, yes it is true, I only speak English, and I don't know the language of my students.
> I sat up even straighter and thought seriously about leaving the room. How could I get out of here? And, my professor was sitting two seats away. This message was not comfortable for me to hear. I mean, how could I be hurting the children?
> I listened painfully and quickly left the room when Tove finished. I was enraged, hurt, confused, and angry. Later that week in class, we talked about the conference. My professor began talking about how wonderful it was to listen to Tove. All of a sudden she said, "Sharon, tell your colleagues about Tove." I could feel my face turning red, and I had to say, "Well, I really didn't care for her. I thought she was very loud and angry."
> For the next year, I read, reflected, mused, read, reflected, mused before I came to terms with my feelings. Tove was not saying that I was a bad teacher, only the fact that I was not meeting the academic needs of multilingual students in their primary language.

(Continued)

Reader Task 5.1
(Continued)

> Yes, I could teach them in English, I could give them love and build their self-esteem. I could not, however, give them what they really needed to succeed in an English-speaking world: literacy and cognitive development. Even as I worked with the students on their oral English development, they would start to fall behind their classmates cognitively and linguistically."

Finally, compare your own reaction to the term 'linguistic genocide' to Sharon's reaction. Then reflect on the Said quote: 'The intellectual is an individual endowed with a faculty for representing, embodying, articulating a message, a view, an attitude, philosophy or opinion to, as well as for, a public. And this role has an edge to it, and cannot be played without a sense of being someone whose place it is publicly to raise embarrassing questions, to confront orthodoxy and dogma (rather than to produce them), to be someone who cannot be easily co-opted by governments or corporations . . . Least of all should an intellectual be there to make his/her audience feel good: the whole point is to be embarrassing, contrary, even unpleasant' (Edward Said 1994, 9–10).

When the United Nations did preparatory work for what later became the **International Convention for the Prevention and Punishment of the Crime of Genocide** (E 793, 1948), linguistic and cultural genocide were in fact discussed alongside physical genocide. All three were seen as serious crimes against humanity (see Capotorti 1979: 37). The Ad Hoc Committee which prepared the Convention had specified the following acts as examples constituting cultural genocide in Article III:

> Any deliberate act committed with intent to destroy the language, religion or culture of a national, racial or religious group on grounds of national or racial origin or religious belief, such as
>
> **(1) Prohibiting the use of the language of the group in daily intercourse or in schools, or the printing and circulation of publications in the language of the group.**
>
> (2) Destroying or preventing the use of libraries, museums, schools, historical monuments, places of worship or other cultural institutions and objects of the group. (emphasis added)

When the Convention was finally accepted by the General Assembly, Article III, which covered linguistic and cultural genocide, was not adopted (see **Official Records of the General Assembly, Third Session, Part I, Sixth Committee**, 83rd meeting). It is thus *not included* in the final Convention of

1948. What remains, however, is **a definition of linguistic genocide**, which most states then in the UN were prepared to accept.

In connection with the later drafting of the Declaration on the Rights of Indigenous Peoples, many of their representatives have also wanted to include ecocide, whereas 'other opinions have argued that cultural ethnocide and ecocide are crimes against humanity, rather than genocide' (Whitaker 1985: 8). But it has been argued forcefully that 'further consideration should be given to this question, including if there is no consensus, the possibility of formulating an optional protocol' (ibid.).

During the debate of the Genocide Convention in the UN, 'it was maintained that such acts would result in losses to humanity in the form of "cultural contributions" for which it was indebted to the destroyed group' (Capotorti 1979: 37). These 'cultural contributions' obviously also included language, in several ways. Indigenous peoples know this too (see Insert 5.3).

The definition of cultural genocide is in some ways more concrete than the definition of linguistic genocide since it concentrates on cultural 'institutions and objects'. These are important, of course, but there are other aspects of immaterial culture which are equally important, as we shall discuss

---

INSERT 5.3 'If you want to destroy a people, you get their language first'; 'get rid of the language and bring in another language, and that brings in another world view' (Canada)

'Some experts argue that moving to a few common languages improves communication and fosters a better understanding among people in the world.

But Joanne Weinholtz, a teacher at the Tuscarora School near Lewiston, N.Y., said language is more than just communication. "It opens up our understanding of how we think."

If the Tuscarora language disappears, Ms. Weinholtz said, a full insight into Tuscarora culture and thinking will be lost forever.

What will also be gone is the diversity of views about the world and life, said Amos Key, the language director of the Woodlands Cultural Centre at the Six Nations Reserve near Brantford, Ont[ario].

Mr. Key said each language reflects a different cultural "world view," and that is what is being lost—sometimes deliberately eliminated—in the drift toward a few common languages.

"If you want to destroy a people, you get their language first. Then there is no mode to transmit ideas or concepts," he said. "If you want to have another world view, you get rid of the language and bring in another language, and that brings in another world view." ' (Source: Platiel, Rudy, in **The Globe and Mail** March 1, 1996, quoted in a posting on the email list Endangered Languages, 4 March 1996, from Mark Fettes (mfettes@magi.com), on 'Tuscarora on the wane')

later. But cultural genocide and ecocide can also be combined, for financial and political purposes. An example is the Inali Dam (one of 22 across the Tigris and Euphrates rivers, part of the Southeast Anatolia Project, GAP) that Turkey is planning to build near the Kurdish city of Batman—it will result in the destruction of the ancient town of Hasankeyf, one of the world's oldest settlements, full of historical treasures. The completed Atatürk dam alone has already displaced 50,000 people. The Ilisu dam will submerge fifty villages and displace 20,000 people, most of them Kurds. The dams will allow Turkey to control the flow of water to Syria and Iraq.

It is interesting that, for example, Denmark, USA, and UK 'opposed the prohibition of cultural genocide' and UK wanted the Convention to be 'defined in the strict sense to the physical extermination of human groups' (Freedman 1992: 89; for Denmark see McKean 1983: 109; he reports (pp. 105–112) on some of the discussions before Article III was finally rejected).[17] Some of the countries which wanted to keep it in were 'the Soviet bloc countries, plus China, Pakistan, and Venezuela' (McKean 1983: 109, note 37). One of the reasons given was that the definition of cultural genocide was too vague, and it 'would be difficult, for example, to estimate the scope of education policy' (ibid., 109). Indeed . . .

Still, it took the USA until February 19, 1986, to endorse the Convention, and even then the Senate's consent to ratification 'was subject to two reservations and five understandings that significantly weakened the document' (ibid.). The USA had thus not ratified the Genocide Convention during the Vietnam war . . .

So far, we have in this chapter mostly described linguistic genocide at an abstract level. Next I want to look into various ways of 'prohibit[ing] the use of the language of the group' in educational practice. What happens in educational institutions is a concretisation of educational state language policies (the state regulates the general frames also for private schools). Ultimately it is states which are responsible, both through what they **are** doing and also because of what they fail to do.

5.3. LINGUISTIC GENOCIDE IN EDUCATIONAL PRACTICE

5.3.1. A Short Overview of How the Education of Minorities and Indigenous Children Has Been Organised

We shall start looking at the different ways of committing linguistic genocide by first giving a very short general overview[18] of how indigenous and minority education has been organised. Then we continue by presenting examples.

The development of education for many indigenous peoples and for ethnic minorities (hereafter: minority education) has followed a similar course in many countries, both in the West and, to some extent, in other parts of the world. It often started with **indifference**. Minorities were not formally educated or, if they were, no concessions were made in relation to language or culture. Often the next stage was **romantic-racist segregation** (the Noble Savage idea) and **pragmatism** (ad hoc-solutions). Some early missionaries knew (some of) the languages of the minorities. Literacy in the minority mother tongue was sometimes attempted, at least for a short time—the way to the soul was through the mother tongue.

With the spread of the nationalist-romantic nation-state ideology and the growing need for some formal education, a concomitant to early industrialisation, demands for educational and linguistic homogenisation rapidly made the official language the (sole) medium of education in the West (Europe and Neo-Europes, e.g., Australia, Canada, New Zealand, USA), starting from the early 1860s and continuing for more than a century. For instance in Swedish state schools it was officially forbidden to use the minority and indigenous languages, Finnish and Sámi between 1888 and 1957, not only as media of education but also during the breaks. 'Civilization' and sometimes defence arguments provided legitimation for these **assimilation** policies. Some Asian countries had more multilingual education systems, especially before and again after colonisation. In most African and Latin American colonies, the colonial language was used in the education of all those who had access to formal schooling, at least after the initial years of primary school but often from the very beginning, regardless of what the children's mother tongues were and regardless of minority or majority status. Autobiographical fiction from all over the world describes punishments for using the mother tongue, both physical and psychological, and some examples are given below.

In the Western nation-state **ideology** states themselves have assumed ethnonymic and linguonymic identities, in addition to the politonymic (monopoly on violence; thus: a state) and toponymic (monopoly on an area: borders) identities. This (assimilatory) 'integration' and homogenisation has been attempted through social engineering and state-initiated reforms where formal education has always played a decisive part. The nationalistic, racist (and classist and sexist) tendencies in this ideology were directed towards all those who had to be forcefully 'uplifted' from their 'otherness'—linguistic minorities, the working class, women, and so on. For a few national minorities (e.g., Swedish-speakers in Finland, English- and Afrikaans-speakers in South-Africa), their right to exist, to endo-categorize, and to reproduce themselves as minorities and, accordingly, to have mother tongue medium education, has been more or less self-evident.

For most minorities who today have (some of) these rights, achieving them is a result of a long struggle. Most minorities do not have them. Most minorities are still exo-categorized, and the problems they (may) face in the educational system are (mis)diagnosed by representatives of the dominant group(s). Typically the minorities themselves have been and are blamed (the 'blame the victim' approach). 'Reasons' for problems in school have been said to be **L2-related** (they do not know the dominant language, e.g., English, well enough), **social** (they represent the lowest social groups, the children do not get enough school-related support at home) or **cultural** (their culture— family patterns, gender roles, relations between the generations—is different from the dominant group's culture). The minorities themselves, their characteristics (including bilingualism), are seen as The Problem. Measures to cure the problems have typically included more L2-teaching, social support and some forms of multicultural or intercultural education (see Skutnabb-Kangas 1988, 1990a for typologies of minority education phases and explanations for problems). Quick assimilation, linguistically and culturally, and acceptance of the dominant group's linguistic, social, and cultural norms, have been official or inofficial goals.

5.3.2. Preventing the Use of the Language Overtly and Directly, as in the 'Old' Days

Our examples of the practices start with some of the more overtly brutal ways of 'prohibiting the use of the language of the group'. Then we look at more 'modern', sophisticated ways of achieving the same, ways which make it more difficult for the children and even the parents to see that it is still a question of linguistic genocide because the 'enemy' is often invisible, and the direct agent (e.g., the teacher) may be nice and friendly, and all of it is done 'in the best interest of the child'. The examples come from all over the world. The presentation, then, follows the means presented in Table 4.2 in chapter 4, sticks, carrots, and ideas. The children in the examples represent indigenous peoples, national minorities, immigrant minorities, refugees, dominated peoples in underdeveloped countries (for the term 'underdeveloped', see Insert 6.1). Short glimpses are given from various periods during the last century and a half; some are recent, and many of the practices are in use today.

5.3.2.1. . . . *Through Physical Punishment*

5.3.2.1.1. *Example: Turkish Kurdistan*

The use of a minority language can be prohibited **overtly and directly**, through laws, imprisonment, torture, killings, beatings, fines, threats, and intimidation, as in Turkey today vis-a-vis the Kurds. What happens in Kurdistan, especially the Turkish part of Kurdistan, is an example of a combination of physical, linguistic and cultural genocide. Info Box 5.13 describes some of these, first at a general level and at the end at an individual level where Aliser Cengaver[19] describes the combination in his own life.

❖ I n f o B o x 5 . 1 3 ❖

Kurds—Human Rights Violations in Turkey

Between 1990–1995 the following human rights violations took place in Turkey (note that 'ordinary' criminality is not counted in these figures): 3,141 cases where torture was claimed; 528 people were 'missing' after having been arrested; 20,974 were arrested; 218 journalists were arrested; 3,710 were imprisoned; 1,526 civilians were killed and 1,153 wounded in police/military actions; 733 were killed under arrest; 1,218 were killed and 52 wounded by 'unknown people'; 2,827 villages were burned down and/or forcibly evacuated, (and forests burned); 12,715 were killed during attacks; 800,226 people were dismissed from their jobs on political grounds; 294 bombings tooks place; 389 cases of journals, trade unions or associations were shut down; 1,249 cases of books or journals confiscated; 225 police razzias against associations, trade unions and journals; 165 imprisoned MPs, trade unionists, authors, researchers, and journalists; 315 executed.

During this period, state courts gave 1,021 years of imprisonment to different people and fines of 86.7 billion Turkish Lire. In cases still pending an additional 1,911 years of imprisonment were demanded by the state prosecutor, in violation of human rights.

The situation is steadily getting worse, and reporting more difficult, as can be seen from how journalists and writers are being persecuted. The following situation was reported by The Turkish Human Rights Association (IHD) for April 1999 alone: 'a total of 220 years of imprisonment and fines amounting to more than 200,000,000 Turkish lira (TL) were imposed in cases involving freedom of opinion and freedom to organize.' Other statistics for April: 'Murders by unidentified assailants 15; extrajudicial executions, death by torture and in policy custody 24; deaths in clashes with the security forces 86; forced disappearances 1; armed actions against civilians 3 dead, 20 wounded; persons put into police custody 7,078; persons tortured 44; persons arrested 256; persons attacked 84; attacks on political prisoners in the prisons 7 wounded; banned organizations 21; police raids on publishers' offices 37; confiscated and banned publications 19; prison terms and fines imposed 220 years; 503,000,000 TL (Hevi, 22.5.99).' (sources: International Association for Human Rights of the Kurds IMK Weekly Information Service, Number 19, 27 May 1999; International Human Rights Division in Istanbul, as reported in Kurdistan Info 1:14, 8 Dec 1996 (KOMKAR, Denmark); information materials from FEY-KURD (the Union of Kurdish Associations in Denmark) 1 Dec 1996; Kurdistan News; online News in English from Med-TV 3 August 1998; see Address Box 7.2).

During the 1990s, the Turkish government has attempted to persuade world opinion that the oppression of the Kurdish language has ended. Study of the Turkish constitution (1982) tells a different story—and this constitution is still valid. The language of Turkey is still Turkish. 'The state of Turkey is in its state territory and state citizens an indivisible whole. Its language is Turkish.' (Constitution, Art. 3). Other formulations that prohibit the use of languages

(Continued)

other than Turkish, are also still valid: 'No language prohibited by law may be used for disclosure or publication of ideas and opinions. Written or printed materials, records, tapes, videotapes as well as other means of expression that are in violation of this prohibition will be confiscated . . .' (Constitution, Art. 26/3). This is clearly aimed at Kurdish. Even if the law 2932 (stating what 'a language prohibited by law' is) was repealed on 12 April 1991, both the constitution and the anti-terrorist law passed 12 April 1991, still prohibit Kurdish (for details of the laws mentioned, see Hassanpour et al. 1996, Phillipson & Skutnabb-Kangas 1996, Rumpf 1989, Skutnabb-Kangas & Bucak 1994; see also Saado 1989; Kurdish Web-pages (see Address Box 7.2) are recommended for up-to-date changes in the laws).

Necati Bayram, member of the Central Board of the Association for Human Rights in Turkey, said at a hearing organised by the subgroup on Turkey of Amnesty International, Denmark, 16 March 1997, that the human rights situation in Turkey has become worse during the last 5 years. 953 people have been killed under torture, 1,339 people have been killed by 'unknown perpetrators', and 782 people have 'disappeared' after they were arrested by police. During the 3 preceding years, 49,380 people had been arrested on political grounds and of these 5,381 were detained. Of these, 3,758 appealed to the Association for Human Rights in Turkey and said that they had been tortured while under arrest. All these figures include only people who dared to tell about what had happened to them (**Kurdistan Info** 2:27, p. 3, 23 March 1997, published by KOMKAR, Copenhagen).

Both Necati Bayram and other Board members who participated in this and other hearings organised by Amnesty, have been repeatedly harrassed by the Turkish authorities, been threatened, given fines and prison terms for their human rights work. During the first half of 1998, there were 247 documented cases of torture (164 criminal, 83 political prisoners; 67 women, 13 children), according to the Human Rights Association's Torture Monitoring Commission's report. In January 1998 two men seriously wounded the Chair, Akýn Birdal, shooting 7 bullets through him. This caused demonstrations where both Kurds and Turks participated. Three months later, Birdal was sentenced to one year of imprisonment because of a speech he had given at a human rights conference. He was found guilty of 'inciting the people to hostility and enmity regarding class, race, and regional difference'. This was for two words: 'Kurdish people'. He had talked about 'the Kurdish and Turkish people' in his address (online News in English from Med-TV 3 August 1998).

There are also hundreds of examples of harassment, beatings, torture, and court cases where heavy penalties (fines and imprisonment) are demanded for activities which Turkey claims are now allowed, like singing Kurdish songs (examples from 1997: during wedding ceremonies, a student camp, a public concert, inauguration of a cultural centre, all just from one issue of **Kurdistan News**, 41–42, 1998), using the Kurdish colours in public, or in private, as at

(Continued)

weddings, or just using a few words of Kurdish in public. Even when **some** of these activities **are** allowed **some** of the time (personal communication, by researcher Kristiina Koivunen, after a visit in the Turkish part of Kurdistan, 15 February 1999, just when the book goes to print; see also Koivunen, forthcoming), anybody can be punished for them any time.

Freedom of expression, opinion, and organisation and freedom of the press are constantly being violated, publications are being confiscated, sellers and agents of books and newspapers (even children) are being harassed, threatened, beaten up, tortured, fined and imprisoned, offices and printing machines smashed. As of August 1998 1,800 cases have been opened against Turkey in the European Court or Commission of Human Rights.

Turkish authorities try to prevent investigations and research into human rights violations as much as they can. The International Association for Human Rights in Kurdistan has recently (July 1998) published a report on 'disappearances' partly in Istanbul and Ankara, partly in the Kurdish regions, with the records of the Human Rights Association of Diyarbakir as a starting point, interviewing relatives where this was possible without causing them additional harm. In metropolitan western Turkey, more than 90% of those who disappeared were (and are) of Kurdish origin, most of them politically active. Since 27 May 1996, a weekly demonstration of 'Wednesday Mothers' protests against the disappearances, despite threats, beatings, and harrassment by the police. Since 1991, at least 2,000 people have 'disappeared' (been taken away by police or, mostly, military or paramilitary forces, often openly, during daytime) in the Kurdish regions. Most of those who have been found have been killed, often tortured to death.

Behind all these figures there are human fates. One account follows.

THE RELATIONSHIP BETWEEN OPPRESSION & EDUCATION:
THE CASE OF THE KURDISH MINORITY IN TURKEY

An Interview with Aliser Cengaver by Shelley K. Taylor

As argued in Hassanpour, Skutnabb-Kangas and Chyet (1996), language-in-education requirements are violated in Kurdistan. The present interview provides an example of how this process affects Kurds at the level of the individual.

Approximately 18–20 million Kurds live in Turkey. Despite these high population figures, for many years the Turkish government has denied the existence of a Kurdish identity. Kurds have experienced both linguistic and cultural persecution. My own educational experience attests to Turkey's denial of the Kurdish identity and persecution of the Kurds.

In Turkey, children begin elementary school at age 6 or 7, secondary school at age 11 or 12, and high school at age 15. I attended school at all

(Continued)

three levels in Kurdistan—the predominantly Kurdish part of Turkey referred to, officially, as the East. In this area, residential schools are widespread. Kurdish children enrolled in residential schools live there for the entire academic year.

My educational experience. I attended residential schools from the age of 7 to 18. It was a 5 or 6 hour walk from my village to school. I only got to go home for summer vacation. There was a strong assimilation policy in my school, as is commonly the case in residential schools in Kurdistan. That is to say, I had to learn Turkish and take up the Turkish culture. The goal of residential schooling is to make Kurdish children's mother tongue and home culture foreign to them.

Residential schools still exist today. Poor families do not understand the meaning of residential schooling. To them, the schools mean free schooling and they want their children to get an education. I am from a family of 10 children: 8 boys and two girls. Four of my brothers also attended residential school. By the time my younger brothers and sisters were of school age, a school had been built in my village. As a result, they were able to live at home. If a school had been built in my village when I began school, I would not have had to leave home so young.

Linguistic oppression: Submersion. Up until the age of 7, I had never heard Turkish. Then I entered a Turkish-medium school. There was a mix of Turkish and Kurdish teachers in my residential school, but even the Kurdish teachers did not allow me to speak my mother tongue. Kurdish children were required to recite the Turkish national poem in Turkish even before they knew the language.

If the children spoke Kurdish, they were punished. Some were beaten on the hands with rulers; others were forced to stand for hours. Some teachers punished children by burning their hands on the stove used to heat the classroom.

It is very difficult for Kurdish children to learn Turkish since Kurdish is an Indo-European language which has nothing in common with Turkish, an Altaic language. Kurdish children have a high drop-out rate. In part, this is due to the problems Kurdish children have in Turkish-medium classes. There are, however, other reasons why they leave the national education system.

Discrimination in educational settings. I went to high school and secondary school in a Kurdish city even farther away from my home village than my residential school. I was enrolled in a high school that had a teacher training program. (At that time, one could teach elementary school as soon as one graduated from a teaching stream in high school. Now one must first go to University before one can become a teacher). I had high marks in math and was encouraged to study engineering at university.

(Continued)

Discrimination was rampant both at High School and University. I come from Dersim province. Kurds from that part of Kurdistan are Alevis. We are much more secular than Sunni Muslims. The majority of Turks are Sunnis. They do not regard Alevis as real Muslims. For that reason, my fellow Alevi students and myself were humiliated by many Sunni students. The teachers allowed this, and humiliated us in turn. Many of my Alevi peers knew they were not wanted and dropped out of the high school system.

While attending University, I was stabbed by right-wing nationalist Turkish students. Fighting between different groups of students was common back in the early 1980s when I attended University. There was a clear division between left-wing and right-wing University students.

Cultural oppression & awareness. While at University, Kurdish students began to gain awareness of their cultural identity. Speaking Kurdish was officially forbidden, and Kurdish music cassettes were contraband, but we listened to them anyway, putting ourselves at risk. We began looking for our Kurdish roots. We knew nothing of the history of the Kurdish people or of Kurdistan, as there were no books or documentation of any sort, but we knew we were Kurds. We were not only aware of the fact, we were never allowed to forget it. We constantly met discrimination and were treated as inferiors.

State oppression: The military coup of 1980. Students also became aware of leftist ideologies at University and joined the labour movement. I was a student leader at the University and organized students to fight for democratic rights and fundamental freedoms. I was also union leader at my workplace. On September 12th, 1980, there was a military coup, and I was arrested on account of my University and work place activities.

For 45 days, I was held by police in a 'Detention Centre'. During that time, and the two and a half months following, which I spent in prison, I was tortured. I survived, but six of my University friends did not. I was 21 years old.

The aftermath: the legacy of oppression. After being released from prison, I continued my University studies and was granted a degree in Engineering. I worked as an engineer for five years before coming to Canada as a Convention Refugee.

Language loss or maintenance? Even at the time of the military coup, my dominant language—the one I spoke with my friends who were tortured to death—was Turkish. My dominant language now is still Turkish, although I still speak 2 dialects of Kurdish, as well as French and English. I have even learned a little Polish since coming to Canada as a Convention Refugee in 1991.

My mother tongue is not my dominant language. It was not the language I was educated in, the language which was promoted (not forbidden),

(Continued)

or the language which was allowed to develop. There are very restricted fields of usage for Kurdish in Turkey. The use of Kurdish is still very limited in Turkey. It is spoken at home, among friends, and in the community, but it is not the language of schooling, communications or technology.

I was able to maintain my mother tongue (the Zaza dialect), despite my educational experience; namely, Turkish submersion. This I did in the summer when I went home from residential school. My parents would always laugh at me when I first got home because I would forget my mother tongue in-between yearly visits home and would speak a very strange-sounding form of Zaza. It always came back to me after a few days, though. Furthermore, I was lucky in that I attended University in a city where many Kurds from my home village lived. I maintained my mother tongue by speaking to them.

Educational prospects of children in Kurdistan today. Other Kurdish children are not as fortunate as I. Many cannot even get an education due to school close-downs in villages where "emergency rule" is in effect. Since 1987, much of Kurdistan has been under martial law, and schools are often commandeered by soldiers for the duration of military operations in the district. Children in these areas do not have the chance to get an education.

Even before the security measures came into effect it was hard for Kurdish children to get an education. This was partly due to the scarcity of schools. Just as Kurdistan as a region has been underdeveloped economically, so have the Kurdish people been underdeveloped educationally.

Presently, there is a policy of depopulating the border regions of Kurdistan (e.g., borders between Turkish, Iraqi, Iranian and Syrian Kurdistan). Many villages are being razed and the inhabitants forced to relocate. People who fear for their future lack the sense of security required to study. This does not bode well for Kurdish children.

Conclusion. School success is not a given for Kurdish children, even ones who attend school. The linguistic and cultural underpinnings of this phenomenon are linked to broader trends of oppression. My own situation is representative of some of the difficulties which face Kurdish children.

Generally speaking, the educational prospects of Kurdish children are not good. It is hard to separate the general oppression of the Kurdish minority from poor educational prospects; it is hard for Kurdish children to get an education in the wake of language difficulties: no mother-tongue education, discrimination in the educational system, school closings and a general state of psychological trauma: a history of oppression.

Even in prisons Kurdish is not allowed (Insert 5.4).

INSERT 5.4　Only allowed to talk to son in prison in a
language mother does not know (Turkey)

'A Kurdish mother in Diyarbakir visits her son in prison. The guard says that
they have to speak Turkish to each other. The mother does not know any
Turkish.' (Phillipson et al. 1994: 20).

Today Turkey is still the country which tries to 'prohibit the use of a
[specific] language' with the most brutal constitutionally and legislatively
authorised means in the world, while at the same time denying that it is
doing it. Several other countries of course commit physical genocide equally
brutally, but often there is little pretense of this being done in a 'legal' way,
as though the state observes the rule of law. For instance in Myanmar/Burma,
an individual can be sentenced to hard labour for 5 years for 'handing out
leaflets calling for democracy', 7 years for 'singing a song the generals don't
like', 14 years for 'speaking to the BBC', and 15 years for 'sending a report
to the United Nations' (Pilger 1998: 161).

5.3.2.1.2. *Other Examples*

It is clear that punishing children physically for speaking their own language
and/or forbidding the use of the language in schools must be seen as an
instance of linguistic genocide according to the UN 1948 definition. Later
we shall also discuss whether the **intentions** of those who did this forbidding
or punishing were negative—did they really intend to commit linguistic
genocide. The answer in most cases would be NO, but this does not change
the fact that their actions fall within the definition ('one is justified regarding
many of the dramatic consequences of mission language practices as
unintended and uncontrolled' (Mühlhäusler 1996: 139)). In later chapters we
will also see how physical punishment and other means used in committing
linguistic genocide fit into theories about power and control, something that
was already discussed to some extent in chapter 4.

This section presents a collection of examples. I claim no statistical representativity for them—they are part of my 'butterfly collection'[20]—but I
could give you, dear reader, literally thousands more of them if there was
space. What always amazes me is the similarity in how linguistic genocide
is committed, across languages and groups and countries, all over the world.

We start with 'sticks', physical punishment, with both short and some
longer accounts. This is the only one of all the means which has disappeared
as **official** policy in **some** countries, understood as teachers punishing children. It still continues as official policy in other countries, and as unofficial

policy in many. Likewise, physical bullying by other students (see Antti Jalava's account of his school days in Jalava 1988; see also 1980, 1993), often with the knowledge and many a time also acceptance by teachers continues in most countries (see Inserts 5.5 through 5.8).

I have examples of the passing of an object and subsequent punishment from over a dozen countries. In addition to the punishment, it also taught children the value of spying on class-mates. Telling the teacher that somebody had used the mother tongue could lead to various kinds of punishment for the culprit (heavy stones on the shoulders or carried in a rope around the neck or a stiff collar which prevented any head movement, caning, writing

---

INSERT 5.5   Swear in Finnish when chopping wood—
ears boxed (Sweden)

In the child work houses for Finnish autochthonous minority children in Sweden in the early 1950s, one of the jobs of the boys was to chop all the wood (while the girls were responsible for cooking and cleaning, together with the matron). These boarding schools were for the children of the poor in the north, and the children had to pay for their upkeep by working (see Lundemark 1980). Once a ten-year-old drove the axe into his knee, which started bleeding profusely. He swore in Finnish and started crying. Rather than seeing to his knee, all the children were lined up to have their ears boxed because Finnish had been used. (Tage Ranängen, now lecturer at the University of Luleå, Sweden, one of the children, personal communication)

INSERT 5.6   Gikuyu in school—caned (Kenya)

In Kenya, English became much more than a language: it was the language, and all the others had to bow before it in deference. Thus one of the most humiliating experiences was to be caught speaking Gikuyu in the vicinity of the school. The culprit was given corporal punishment—three to five strokes of the cane on bare buttocks—or was made to carry a metal plate around the neck with the inscription: I AM STUPID or I AM A DONKEY. Sometimes the culprits were fined money they could hardly afford. And how did the teachers catch them? A button was initially given to one person who was supposed to hand it over to whoever was caught speaking his mother tongue. Whoever had the button at the end of the day was the culprit. Thus children were turned into witch-hunters and in the process were taught the lucrative value of being a traitor to one's immediate community. The attitude to English was the exact opposite: any achievement in spoken or written English was highly rewarded. (Ngũgĩ 1985: 112)

INSERT 5.7 Hausa—caned in school with American principal (Nigeria)

Lilly Krarup worked as a teacher in Nigeria in 1970–1973 in a secondary school where most of the students spoke Hausa as their native language. When they were caught using Hausa in school, they got a "dismerit". For 3 dismerits, they had to work in the school, instead of attending sports and other activities. At the end of every term the dismerits were counted. If somebody had 9 dismerits, they were taken to the nearby prison to be severely beaten by the prison ward. The minimal punishment was hard caning three times (on bare buttocks, with a wet cloth). All the teachers and students had to be present at the caning. The principal who had installed these rules was American, and after 15 years in the country he knew no Hausa whatsoever. But it was mainly the African teachers who imposed this law. At the neighbouring Teacher Training College Hausa was allowed, even if the language of education was English. Here the Principal was Nigerian. (Lilly Krarup is now a teacher of the Deaf. She told me this at an in-service-training course for teachers of the Deaf, 6 November 1995, in Århus, Denmark).

The experience of many deaf children has been similar. 'It has not been at all unusual for deaf children to be punished (including physically) for signing among themselves, even in residence halls and on playgrounds', Timothy Reagan reports (personal communication, December 1998). Branson & Miller, Lane, and others (see bibliography) note similar incidents.

INSERT 5.8 Pass an object to next pupil—last one punished
(Africa, French colonies)

In French colonies there was a comparable system: 'a small object . . . was passed from pupil to pupil if they accidentally expressed themselves in their mother tongue rather than French. The pupil left with it at the end of the day would be punished' (references quoted in Treffgarne 1986: 163).

INSERT 5.9 Kurdish in school—punishment—
silent games only (Turkish Kurdistan)

I was seven when I started in the first grade in 1962. My sister, who was a year older, started school at the same time. We didn't know a word of Turkish when we started, so one felt totally mute during the first few years. We were not allowed to speak Kurdish during the breaks either but had to play silent games with stones and things like that. The teachers watched us all the time in the playground. Anyone who spoke Kurdish was punished. The teachers hit us on the fingertips or on our heads with a ruler. It hurt terribly. That's why we were always frightened at school and didn't want to go. (Clason & Baksi 1979, quoted in Skutnabb-Kangas 1984a: 310)

INSERT 5.10   Count in Polish—punishment—
mother spoke only Danish afterwards (Denmark)

I asked Erik Swiatek, third generation Polish-Danish man, whether he knew
any Polish. Almost none, he said, and told me about his father's school
experience. Erik's grandparents were farm workers and had come to Denmark
as farm labour, just before the First 'World' War. Erik's father went to school,
in 1922, knowing hardly any Danish. When the teacher asked him to count,
he started in Polish: 'jeden, dwa, trzy . . .'. The teacher hit him and told him
to count properly. He came home crying. Erik's grandmother, a very strong
lady, said: 'No Danish school teacher is ever going to hit my child again for
not knowing Danish. From this day on, we speak only Danish at home.' And
this was what happened.

INSERT 5.11   Spanish in school—punishment—mother spoke
only English afterwards (USA)

When I was a child (5 or 6 years old) I used to be hit on my hand with a
ruler by my teacher whenever I spoke Spanish. I only knew Spanish at the
time. My mother, who is bilingual, started then speaking only English to me.
I lost my native language and a big part of my culture. I am not bilingual
but am working hard on it now. I am now teaching at the same school district
that I was raised in. I hope I am making an important difference in changing
attitudes. I am now 41 years old.

   Please do not mention my name—it might make it difficult for me in my
district. (Written and given to me at a course on Minority Education &
Power, in California, 28 January 1994)

---

100 times 'I am stupid' or 'I am a donkey' or 'I will never speak XX',
standing in the corner for hours, or standing in a dark cupboard, or being
deprived of food or warm clothing, being sent home or being sent outside
in cold weather, fines, and so on—see Skutnabb-Kangas 1984a, chapter 12,
for more examples). It also often led to still more concrete rewards for having
betrayed a classmate than being able to get rid of the object to be passed
on to the next one. The betrayer often received extra food, a bit of chocolate,
and so on. Eve Mumewa Fesl (1993) tells of many similar incidents from
Australia. See also Inserts 5.9 through 5.11.

   Part of the legacy of the French Revolution was a monolingual policy
according to which the State makes civil liberties available to all in one
language, the language of the dominant group. This philosophy was exported
worldwide in the colonial age, and has generally been perpetuated by those

in power in former colonies. Inspired by the French homogenisation tendencies, and continuing a Castilianisation policy initiated by Isabella in 1492 (Illich 1981), Philip V issued already in 1716 a decree which forbade Catalan: 'Books in Catalan must be forbidden, nor must it be spoken or written in schools and instruction in Christian doctrine must be in Castilian (Read 1978: 152; see also Siguan 1993). Different generations have experienced different methods. Even in living memory, groups which have been historically oppressed can have the experience of the Catalans, the Basques, or the Welsh, from harsh bans to softer bans to recommendations, as the Welsh example in Insert 5.12 shows—but the long-term consequences for linguistic competence and identity are equally harsh.

INSERT 5.12   Several generations forbidden to speak Welsh

I am Welsh. Years ago my mother went through the card/placard around the neck situation for speaking Welsh in the playground. This was common practice.

Years later when I attended Sunday School my mother received a letter stating that if I was to get on in school I needed to speak only English in the home. This had been verbally stated whilst I was at Junior School and my mother (whose self-esteem at being Welsh was very low) believed it. She would never speak Welsh at home. I grew up alternating between feeling very bitter at not speaking Welsh and feeling almost ashamed at being Welsh. In fact this has taken many years to right and is still a source of great sadness to me. I cannot now pass on the richness and wonder of my heritage to my children (Welsh classes/schools are also not something that one comes upon in England). I have spent years in England and to everyone must appear a 'Typical English Person'. (The schools also very kindly ironed out our Welsh accent by giving us extra elocution lessons).

I feel lost between two cultures—longing to belong to one and sitting very uneasily in another one and never quite touching down into 'the real world' wherever that may be—because **I am in effect not accepted in either**.' (Example given to me at a conference at Brent, UK, November 10 1993, when I asked people to write about their own experience)

Physical punishment for speaking the mother tongue or following one's own cultural norms was sometimes seen as legitimate because it was bad and sinful to use a pagan language or follow primitive customs. But mostly it seems to have been rationalised by the teachers as being the only way to make the children learn the dominant language, i.e., the children were punished in order to help them ('degrading and painful punishment . . . not considered cruel or unchristian, but rather . . . merciful acts performed for the recipients' "ultimate good" because the Aboriginal people were "the children of the devil lost in the great darkness and steeped in sin" '—Fesl 1993: 91), just as they were in some cultures punished by parents when they broke various rules.

The altruistic motives were often very clearly expressed in the other type of physical prevention of the learning of the culture and language, namely physical separation from the parents and the group. Today, 'forcibly transferring children from one (ethnic) group to another group' is forbidden in the UN Genocide Convention, Art. II(e)—but it still happens.

5.3.2.2. . . . Through Separation: Boarding Schools and Adoption

Physically separating minority children from their parents and placing them in schools or boarding schools by force, often against their will, is a form of physical abuse. Separating minority children from their parents, their group, their culture, has been used in most parts of the world. In contrast to elite boarding schools which educate future leaders for the (old or present-day) empires, where the children's language, culture, and background were and are reinforced and where benefits were to follow, boarding schools for minorities **tried to eradicate their language, culture, and background** and 'educated' them for future subordination to the dominant group. This means, that school forcibly transfers the children from one group to another: **genocide**, according to the UN Convention.

In many cases the long-term consequence is that the language is killed, through a combination of separation and physical punishment, and shame (Insert 5.13).

In the Nordic countries, boarding schools were widely used in the northern areas of Sweden and Norway (and to a lesser extent in Finland) up to the Second World War. The goal was to assimilate the minority children (speakers of Finnish and different Sámi languages) by separating them from their parents and placing them in the environment of the dominant language. The examples and ideology could just as well be from USA, Canada or Australia. In 1938/39 3,000 children, 36% of the primary and lower secondary children in the northernmost county of Norway, Finnmark, where the indigenous Sámi, and the Kven (Finnish-speakers) lived, were in boarding schools (Lind Meløy 1980: 81). It was an officially stated goal of the boarding schools in Norway to Norwegianise minority children. 'The building of the boarding schools and the Norwegianisation of Finnmark are closely bound together. Norwegianisation was the goal, and the building of the boarding schools was the means. Both were part of Norwegian educational policy in Finnmark' (ibid., 14; Lind Meløy was himself earlier the headmaster of one of the boarding schools).

In a debate in the Parliament on 15 March 1901, the Norwegian MP Opdahl said that 'it was only through the primary school that the Norwegian language can be spread' (quoted in Lind Meløy 1980: 27). The work of the

---

INSERT 5.13 Tuscarora forbidden in school—
later hide knowledge of mother tongue (Canada)

Mr. Key, who launched a rescue program for Iroquoian languages 10 years
ago, said there are 127 Cayuga speakers left on the reserve, 80 Mohawk
speakers, 36 Onondaga and one Seneca, as well as 245 Oneida at another
reserve near London, Ontario.

He said he had thought Mrs. Salter's brother, Robert Mount Pleasant,
who died in 1994, was the last Tuscarora speaker in Canada. It wasn't until
two months before her death that he discovered that Mrs. Salter, who was
living in Toronto, was the last one in her family to be fluent in the language.
"Now she's gone."

Mrs. Salter's daughter, Pat Turner, said her mother and her older brothers
and sisters spoke Tuscarora among themselves. But while Mrs. Salter's
younger siblings were able to understand the language, they would always
reply in English.

Mr. Key said the reason it is so difficult to track down the last speakers
is that for years many of the elderly often hid the fact that they spoke one
of the Iroquoian languages.

That is a direct result of a century of deliberate policies by the federal
government, church residential schools and the public-education system to
eradicate aboriginal languages, he said.

"I truly believe my people were persecuted, socially, spiritually and
morale-wise. That's why the languages went underground," he said. "My
parents were punished for speaking their language, and they had horror stories
to tell me about strapping.

Mr. Hill said that as a child he spoke only Tuscarora until he was sent to
school and suddenly found it forbidden. "We would hide in a closet to speak
Tuscarora, because if we got caught, we'd be hit." (Platiel, see reference in
Insert 5.3)

---

boarding schools was praised by the central educational authorities: 'It has
been shown that the boarding schools are excellently suited to the promotion
of Norwegianness, therefore we must try to build as many such schools as
possible in the areas under consideration' (quoted in ibid., 52–53). In the
process of Norwegianisation it was the goal of many school administrators
that the Sámi languages should become extinct (e.g., Bernt Thomassen, Superintendent for schools 1902–1920, ibid., 98–99).[21] The few supporters of
these languages, like Hans Vogt, later Vice-Chancellor of the University of
Oslo, were under no illusions about what the goal of official policy was.
Vogt wrote in 1902 (quoted in Lind Meløy 1980: 106) that 'Norwegianisation
has been victorious, a policy which means purely and simply an **intentional
extinction** of the Sámi and Finnish languages' (emphasis added).

In Sweden, 'in the Finnish-speaking areas the **child workhouses** had a special significance as institutions for Swedification, the absolute best of the kind . . . Primary school teaching in the Finnish-speaking areas had a clear goal: to teach the children the Swedish language, Swedish customs and Swedish culture . . . Through according the Swedish language a monopoly in the school, the Torne valley Finns, a backward and culturally undernourished people, would share the Swedish culture. That the Finnish culture had its own value was not known or recognised' (Lundemark 1980: 114, 100, 125). See Insert 5.14 for an example; see also Insert 5.4.

INSERT 5.14 'Hell's smith'—work houses for Finnish children (Sweden)

One boy from one of the remote villages in the vicinity of Junosuando (Sweden) expressed his opinion of the workhouses like this: 'The workhouse is a hell's smith' (in Finnish, my remark) . . . He was probably thinking of the arduous drudgery, but he got no chance to develop his thought. He was beaten up because of swearing. It didn't help matters that he swore in Finnish (Lundemark 1980: 87–88).

Speaking one's mother tongue would of course have been the easiest way for most of the children in the examples to express themselves. 'It was of course simpler to express joy and rage in Finnish', as Inga Hubinette, a Finnish-speaker from Tornedalen in Sweden, now a teacher, in her early sixties, put it in a workshop in March 1992. For instance, most of the Finnish children in Sweden knew no or little Swedish when they came to school, at least until the 1950s, and Sámi and Kven children in Norway knew no or little Norwegian. Teachers often used the same kind of argument for forcing them to use the language they did not know as in the recent British example in Insert 5.15 where the teacher's concerns were more important than the child's.

INSERT 5.15 Teacher more important than student (UK)

'A colleague who is monolingual would not allow 6 year old non English speaking Pakistani boys to speak Punjabi/Urdu in class.

Stated reason: "I can't understand them so they must speak English."

"If they don't speak English how can I check that they are doing what they are supposed to do?"

When it was pointed out that they couldn't yet speak English, she shrugged her shoulders.' (Example from Brent, UK, see Insert 5.12)

The difference in the Sámi and Kven children, when using their own languages and when being forced to use Norwegian, was described by a

Norwegian observer, Bishop Skaar, in 1888: 'It was awful to see how these lively children had been strangled by unfortunate instruction. Their tongues were so fluent in the informal discussions [in their own languages], but stuttering and hampered in the lessons' (quoted in Lind Meløy 1980: 20).

In the USA 'The Bureau of Indian Affairs operates 77 boarding schools, scattered throughout the nation . . . Some 35,000 children are sent to boarding schools . . . In 1966, more than 16,000 Indian children of school age were not attending any school at all' (Cahn & Hearne 1969: 28). The goals were the same as in Scandinavia (Insert 5.16).

INSERT 5.16 'Acculturate the Navajo' (USA)

For nearly a hundred years the policy of the United States government was to acculturate the Navajo, so that the Navajo could be assimilated into the White society. To effect this assimilation Navajo children were taken from the shelter of the family and sent to boarding school. Almost every child who entered the boarding school spoke only Navajo, and most of the people employed at the boarding schools spoke only English. When a Navajo child spoke the language of his family at school, he was punished. (Platero 1975: 57)

Both in the USA and in Canada it was clear that many of the schools were much further away than they needed to be. The explanation often was that they were mission schools, and 'we were sent to Moose Factory in Ontario because we were Anglicans, and the Anglicans had residences for Indian kids only from Ontario to B.B.' (Buckley Petawabano, a Cree man from Mistissini reserve in northern Quebec, quoted in Richardson 1993: 107). So first indigenous peoples were forced to accept the divisions within Christianity which meant nothing to them, they were made 'Anglicans', and then they were punished for it. Sometimes the children were flown thousands of miles away. Or they used other means of transport, as Hyacinth Colomb, a Cree taxi driver describes about his own journey south to a Catholic boarding school at the age of ten—the journey took about a week and a half: 'They would send six men to take the kids out to school, with eight kids in a canoe. When we left Puk every little kid had his own paddle; we had to work our way' (quoted in Richardson 1993: 221).

Hyacinth Colomb's assessment of the school was that 'it was like ten months in jail. We went in August, and came back in July' (ibid., 212). Since his schooling only lasted 5 years (until 1931) and started late, he did not lose his Cree as did many of those children who were taken earlier—but neither did he learn much English. He ponders about the complexities of it all:

'I learned English mostly after I came out from school. I hardly ever talk English. I talk good Cree—of course, that's my language. It's funny: when I went to school, the government sent us out to learn English. The chiefs wanted us to come back and talk Cree. Now the government wants people to talk Cree again . . . Well—that's something you can't understand. My kids talk Cree, but their kids—Well—what's going to happen to these kids?' he said, gesturing at his grandchildren (who were playing noisily in English). 'If I was to talk to these kids in Cree, they wouldn't know what I am talking about. That's one thing that's bad . . . All the Cree language will be forgotten. More than half of it is forgotten now.' (ibid., 212).

In the Turkish part of Kurdistan:

. . . one of the reasons why they began to build boarding schools in 1964 was that they wanted to prevent the children from having contact with their parents. By isolating them in schools far away from their parents for the greater part of the year the authorities hoped to make the children forget their Kurdish. (Clason & Baksi 1979: 75; for more information see Skutnabb-Kangas 1984a, 310, and McDowall 1989).

The Australian experience is the same:

In the case of Australian Aborigines, residential schools were unashamedly seen as the best means of removing children from the influence of their parents. Many children, taken from their parents, completely lost touch with them and in later years set out on a traumatic search for their families. For many, if not most of these people, schooling away from home is remembered as a searing experience, the designation in conversation most often used being 'cruel'. This is often remembered as physical cruelty; the striking of children as a disciplinary measure is not part of the socialization of indigenous peoples. However, it was the psychological cruelty of removal from family and immersion into an alien way of life which was perceived as equally destructive, so that generations of indigenous people internalized negative attitudes to the "whitening" processes employed in the schools (Jordan 1988: 191).

Mission schools fulfilled the same purpose in many underdeveloped countries, regardless of whether all of them were boarding schools or not:

Exclusively the French language is taught . . . Teaching the native children through the medium of French the moral, religious and vocational subjects that they get in the mission schools has a most favourable influence, because they are by this means brought to take over our customs and habits and to accept our authority. (a French official in Gabon 1864, quoted in Moussirou-Mouyama 1985: 79).

And the universitites which were supposed to train teachers for indigenous African languages followed suit:

French colonial administrations discouraged and neglected the study of African languages . . . Centers for applied linguistics established in the mid-sixties in most of these countries (e.g., Centre de Linguistique Appliquée de Dakar,

Institut de Linguistique Appliquée à Abidjan) have focused their research on the improvement of French teaching materials, rather than on the description of the national languages (Bokamba 1991: 204).

The descriptions of what happened in the mission schools and (other) boarding schools could be from any country—the similarities are striking. Some children were taken away 'only' for term time and were allowed to go home for holidays.[22] Others were taken away completely and placed in orphanages and schools or given away to 'white' 'foster parents'. Up to a third of all Aboriginal children in Australia (some 100,000), the 'stolen generations', were forcibly removed from their families between 1910 and 1970 (see also Insert 5.25) and placed in white missions, institutions, foster homes, 'forced into a form of slavery, often physically and sexually abused and denied protection by the state' (Pilger 1998: 240; see Fesl 1993, Edwards & Read (eds) 1992). See also the Danish example in Insert 5.26. Some examples from boarding schools follow in Inserts 5.17 through 5.19.

The children's **culture** did not play any part in the curriculum. Many of its expressions were forbidden, often not only in schools but generally (Inserts 5.20–5.23).

This is still true, even in day schools (Insert 5.22).

INSERT 5.17 'Trail of Tears'—permission to see parents denied (USA)

'For the children, being sent to boarding schools was "a Trail of Tears", a form of compulsory and permanent expatriation . . . In Alaska . . . Indian children are shipped as far away as Oklahoma, 6,000 miles from their parents . . . Once in a boarding school, the children are effectively cut off from their families . . . Permission to see one's own parent is not a "right". It is often granted as a reward for good behavior—or denied as a form of punishment' (Cahn & Hearne 1969: 32–33).

INSERT 5.18 Not allowed to visit parents, Sámi (Norway)

A young Sámi woman (in her thirties) told me at the end of the 1980s about her boarding school experience. She had spoken Sámi several times during the week outside the classroom. On Friday she was told that as a punishment she was not allowed to go home for the week-end. She started crying. She then called her elder brother, who called the school. He managed, with difficulty, to persuade the head of the school that he could come and fetch his little sister.

INSERT 5.19 Lie to ministry to visit parents, Cree (Canada)

'. . . every Friday evening . . . it was time for us to report whether we spoke our language, Cree, during the week. If we confessed to using our own language, we were denied the visit with our parents and younger brothers and sisters which was the only privilege we had. In other words, we had to lie to the ministry in order to visit with our parents and relatives' (Gilbert Faries, Moose Factory, quoted in Jordan 1988: 191).

INSERT 5.20 Ceremonies and rituals forbidden; fines (Canada)

One of the most important ceremonies of indigenous Canadians on the western coast, 'Potlach' or Feast, was forbidden 1884. The missionaries 'considered the Potlach barbarous and debauched, an obstacle to conversion to Christianity.' The government considered the ceremony 'pernicious' . . . Also banned at the same time were the Sun Dances of the prairie nations, rituals of central importance to both the secular and religious realms (which were inseparable in aboriginal thinking) . . . These prohibitions were extended in 1914 to cover almost any performance that an aboriginal person might like to give or attend . . . forbidding Indians . . . from taking part in 'any Indian dance' . . . or in 'any show, exhibition, performance, stampede or pageant in aboriginal costume' . . . Anyone who induced or employed an Indian to perform such things, could be imprisoned for a month and fined, even if the performance never took place (Richardson 1993: 104–105).

INSERT 5.21 'Indian' dance or craft—no food (USA)

Indians (in the USA) were forced to try to live like 'white men'. Indian dances and Indian hand work was forbidden. A family's ration of food was cut off if anyone in the family was caught singing Indian songs or doing Indian hand craft. Children were physically beaten if they were caught speaking Indian languages (Cahn & Hearne 1969: 18).

Some of the minority's own traditions may also have worked against them in the process of the eradication of their languages and cultures. Respecting your elders, regardless of what they said, may have been one of them, in the example in Insert 5.23 where respect for elders, together with fear and helplessness, prevented protest.

But the children (and parents) had structurally next to no chances of escape. In Canada compulsory attendance of all indigenous children at school was

INSERT 5.22 'Never talk about Gaelic football again!'
(Northern Ireland); 'I dont know how he came under
the title Christian Brother' (Ireland)

Place: Newry High School, Newry, Co.Down, Northern Ireland, a state school, mostly protestant. **Time**: end of September 1992. **Persons**: Seán (Catholic boy), Sports Teacher:

The teacher brought Seán (1st year student) into the private study room (I was there). He gave him a book about soccer and told him to copy (by hand) a few pages. 'And never talk about Gaelic football again!' **Comment**: The boy was punished for having mentioned Gaelic football. (Told by Ulrike Menk, Bremen, Germany, who attended Newry High as a guest student for 6 months, autumn 1992)

On the other hand, majority language representatives do not have a monopoly on physical punishment. For David O'Neill, late immersion was every bit as traumatic as submersion programmes are for minority children.

The year was 1972. I was 11 years old, in 5th class in primary school. The school was the C.B.S. (Christian Brothers School), North Brunswick Street, Dublin. The teacher was Brother Mc Manus. From 9am to 4pm he spoke and taught us in Irish. For me it was a wasted term because I hadn't a clue what was going on. He would pick on myself & some other boys. He would call us idiots and he would make fools of us in front of the rest of the class. This went on every day.

I remember one incident. When we were doing maths, he called me up to the black board to finish an equasion in algebra. I was standing with my back to the class, with the chalk in my hands and with no idea what to do. I felt that if I start crying he will let me go without punishing me. Instead he whacked me on the back of the head which caused the front of my head to hit the black board and that certainly gave me a reason to cry. Then he would call you a baby and some of the other boys would be laughing at you.

When I look back now, it was total humiliation. . . .

Those days, every Christian Brother was equipped with a black leather strap which was about 10ins long 2ins wide & half inch thick. They would whack you with this across the hands front or back and if you weren't paying attention it would be thrown at you.

It got so bad for me that I would miss school some days through fear but I was always caught and you would be punished. One day I went into class late. I was so frightened of what would happen so I told him that I was late because my mother was dying. I feel that was the worst thing that anyone could say but I had no choice . . .

Those are just some of the things that happened to me. It makes my blood boil when I think of him. I dont know how he came under the title Christian Brother.

Last year the Christian Brothers made an apology to their past pupils, in the national newspaper, because there were too many complaints.

(Continued)

INSERT 5.22   *(Continued)*

He was from the north of Ireland. I reckon he just hated anything to do with England. I remember once he brought in a rubber bullet to show us what the British army were using on Irish citizens. Remember we were only 11 year olds . . .

It frightens me to think of what I would say or do to him if I ever come across him. Mind you the way he treated people I wouldn't say he had a happy life (sadists . . .).

I think it was because of this that I lost interest in the Irish language. I hope this might help you in some way to understand. It certainly helps me to get it off my chest.

P.S. My name is David O'Neill'

David told this to me on a long taxi drive to the airport in Dublin in October 1998, and I asked him to write it down. PS. After our long discussion, and writing the letter, David has started relearning Irish. He would like his future children to be bilingual.

INSERT 5.23   Respect for elders prevents protest (Canada)

. . . there was fear, when you're in an environment different from the one you're used to, speaking for myself, 90 percent of the time I would act out of fear.

When the principal made this speech to us, saying, 'We're here to teach you English and anyone caught talking any other language will be punished'. That's a pretty heavy statement, but you can't really protest, because when you're in the bush [here meaning: in the indigenous community] you respect who's looking after you, and you have to respect who's looking after you wherever you are. Otherwise you get thrown out. Your parents are in the bush, so where are you gonna go? Survival is survival. When you're a kid you depend on an older person for your survival, and we'd always been taught to respect the person we survived on, and I guess we took it from there, we respected all older people. (Buckley Petawabano, a Cree man from Mistissini reserve in northern Quebec, quoted in Richardson 1993: 108)

---

secured already in 1894, with the 'added provision for "the arrest and conveyance to school and detention there" of any children who might be prevented from attending by their parents or guardians (who, in such a case, would be liable to imprisonment)' (Richardson 1993: 101). Children could be kept in the schools until they were 18. Richardson heard many people describe how the priests in Mackenzie Valley 'would come downriver by barge, in each village seizing Indian children to take to school, and how parents would send the children to hide in the bush' (ibid., 101–102). A combination of threats and carrots was often used: 'Indian Affairs used to threaten people that if they didn't send their kids to school, they wouldn't get any welfare' (Buckley Petawabano, a Cree man from Mistissini reserve in northern Quebec, quoted in Richardson 1993: 107). There are more examples of this combination under 'carrots', section 5.3.3.4 and in chapter 6. In today's Denmark, threats have been suggested by several MPs and local politicians. Not only have there been suggestions that welfare should not be paid to minority parents if the children arrive late to school after holidays in the parents' country, but also that the school should refuse to receive the child at all that year. These are 'exact parallels to the US experience in a number of states' (Reagan, personal communication, December 1998).

As exemplified above and later, the use of the children's language was in most cases either overtly or covertly forbidden. Language, culture, customs, and traditions are not anything we are born with, they have to be lived and taught to be learned (see Jernsletten's Sámi examples in section 2.5). If children are not surrounded by at least some elders from their own group who (are allowed to) teach them their language, stories, customs, traditions, these will not be learned proficiently. Not allowing children to learn their language, preventing them from using it through separation from grown-up proficient users, means 'prohibiting the use of the language of the group in daily intercourse or in schools'.

And the results: the Royal Commission on the Northern Environment in Canada (1978: 207, quoted in Jordan 1988: 193), heard evidence from one area:

> Within those 25 years (during which formal education had been available) the education system had produced in our area only two university graduates, countless elementary, secondary and post-secondary dropouts, a large absenteeism record and indifference to education as a whole by community members.

During the last decade or two, many representatives of the First Nations in Canada have told horror stories about boarding schools and mission stations, stories of rape, severe beatings, being left without food or adequate warm clothing (I heard from a Spanish-speaking teacher in 1994 that she knew of several children who had frozen to death in her childhood in Arizona when trying to escape from boarding school, and not having adequate clothing), and so on. Similar stories exist in all parts of the Pacific, Australia, New Zealand, among the Sámi in Scandinavia, the Welsh, the Basques, Finns in Sweden, Frisians, many groups in colonised Africa, etc. Europe and Europeanized countries have shown extreme cruelty in this, Asia less so (see Skutnabb-Kangas 1984a for more examples).

Biologically based racism was in many cases the foundation for assimilation in the boarding schools, and it was expressed openly, even if many of the policy-makers do not seem to have been aware of the fact that both their opinions about other languages and cultures and their actions were racist. In a few cases this has been openly admitted, and an apology has been offered, as for example in Canada (Insert 5.24).

INSERT 5.24 Apology offered (Canada)

The Oblate Commission, a Roman Catholic Order that ran many of these schools across Canada, still glorified this education when testifying in front of a parliamentary committee in 1947. But in 1991 they offered an apology:

'We wish to apologize for the existence of the schools themselves, recognizing that the biggest abuse was . . . that the schools themselves happened . . . that the primal bond inherent within families was violated as a matter of policy, that children were usurped from their natural communities, and that, implicitly and explicitly, these schools operated out of the premise that European languages, traditions, and religious practices were superior to native languages, traditions, and religious practices.' (quoted in Richardson 1993: 102)

In other cases, official apologies are still forthcoming, like in Australia, even when private apologies have been offered (Insert 5.25).

INSERT 5.25 Only private but not formal
government apologies (Australia)

A national inquiry by the Human Rights and Equal Opportunity Commission, **Bringing Them Home: National Inquiry into the Separation of Aboriginal and Torres Strait Islander Children from Their Families**) found in 1997 that 'the government policy of forced removal was a gross violation of human rights and technically an act of genocide because it had the intention of destroying Australia's indigenous culture by forced assimilation' (Sitka 1998: 25). The Australian Prime Minister John Howard gave his personal apology but has refused to make a formal government apology. This is in keeping with the rest of his policy: his government has more or less reversed the positive development towards at least some reconciliation which got to a start with the Mabo court case (which rejected the **Terra nullius** principle—see Definition Box 5.3) and gave some hope for believing that there might be a serious will to discuss land rights.

In many other cases, there has been no or little discussion about past wrongs and the level of awareness seems to be low, as in Sweden and Denmark, and to a somewhat lesser extent, Norway and Finland (see Boyd 1985, Municio 1994, 1996, Peura 1983, 1993, Lainio 1997, 1998, in press, Huss

DEFINITION BOX 5.3 'Terra nullius'; the Mabo Case

Terra nullius (empty land)—is based on the myth that lands which were colonised were 'empty', unoccupied, nobody lived there or 'owned' the land. Therefore, it was there for the taking. Of course a prerequisite for the concept to be meaningfull at all is a belief that land **can** be owned by people in the first place, something that may be impossible, even unimaginable, in the world views of many indigenous peoples (see articles in Posey (ed.) (in press). See also Definition Box 2.6 for 'wild' nature.

The **Mabo** case refers to the court case initiated by Koiki (Eddie) Mabo and four Torres Strait Islanders in 1982 to establish their traditional ownership of a piece of land. The case ended in 1992, with a decision of the High Court of Australia. The Court established that Mer people had owned their land (i.e., it was not 'empty') prior to annexation by the government of Queensland (the case is described in **Encyclopaedia of Aboriginal Australia** 1994). Similar court cases (Skattefjällsmålet, Sweden, see Lasko 1992) or groundwork for them (Korpijaakko 1989, Hannikainen 1996, Hyvärinen 1977, Finland) have so far had no success in democratic Scandinavia. They are being pursued in New Zealand, Canada, and the United States, against similar odds—but maybe a bit more hope of success than in the Nordic countries (see also Hannum 1988, 1989, 1990, and articles in Clark & Williamson (eds) 1996)?

'A comparable case is that of South Africa, where generations of school children were taught that white colonists (the Boers) arrived in the interior of the country roughly at the same time as the Bantu people. Thus, it was implied, no one was taking anyone else's land, and Black people had no prior claim to the land. This is, of course, absolutely true as long as one considers tens of thousands of years difference to be "roughly the same time" ' (Reagan, December 1998, personal communication).

1999, Wingstedt 1996, 1998, for Sweden; many of them critical of this), despite literary authors who have written autobiographical accounts (e.g., Kieri 1976, Jalava 1980, 1988, 1993, Marainen 1988, for Sweden). No apologies have been contemplated or offered. I doubt, in fact, whether any European power has officially apologised for slavery or colonisation. In Denmark, there have been two cases in 1998 where an apology for past wrongs has been asked for by the wronged parties or their descendants and this has been officially refused by the Prime Minister (Insert 5.26).

And in both these and other cases, not only do the wrongs continue, but new ones are being planned, like in California, where the Proposition 227, accepted by two-thirds of those who voted, will forbid the use of all other languages except English in classrooms for most purposes after an initial transitional period (see note 3 in chapter 3 for references).

INSERT 5.26   Public refusal by Prime Minister to apologise for slavery
or for removing indigenous children from their parents (Denmark)

In connection with a celebration of the freeing of the slaves in the former
Danish colony, now the Virgin Islands (USA), summer 1998, descendants of
the slaves asked for an official apology for slavery from Denmark, from the
Queen and the Prime Minister. This was publicly ridiculed and belittled by
representatives of the Danish government and the request was dismissed as
unnecessary.

A recent Danish book (Bryld 1998) with interviews, and two TV
programmes, September 13, 1998, describe the fate of 22 Inuit children from
Greenland who were taken to Denmark in 1951, aged between 5 and 8 years,
with the explicit goal of teaching them Danish language and culture—they
were to 'become Danish ambassadors' in Greenland on return. They were
placed in Danish families and forgot most of their mother tongue during the
1½ years. Six were adopted by the Danish families and stayed in Denmark.
Even those who **had** parents were placed in an orphanage on return, and
placed in a Danish medium school with Danish children. The Greenlandic
kitchen and cleaning staff at the orphanage were forbidden to speak their
own language with the children, even teaching a few words. They were to
large extent rejected by both communities. Even if some managed, somehow,
there are many stories in the book about moving back and forth, divorces,
alcoholism, suicides, and suicide attempts, identity and other conflicts,
rootlessness—and a lot of pain. The group (or those who are left) have now
asked for economic compensation for the results of the cruel separation which
has ruined the lives of many of them. The Danish Prime Minister publicly
refused on television (4 September 1998) to apologise, to take any responsibility, or to consider any compensation, again belittling what had happened.
After all, the intention was good, to help them, he said.

The story is largely similar for the hunter families who were at short notice
forcibly removed from Thule in Greenland when the American military base
was built there in the early 1950s—compensation claims are only now starting
to be taken seriously, but the compensation—if it is forthcoming at all—seems
to be ridiculously small.

Present policy thus seems to be equally unaware of the racism underpin-
ning it, as the USA and Swedish examples below (Insert 5.42) and others
show. The purpose of minority education is still assimilation, in the United
States and Sweden as well as in Britain and most other Western countries.

Forbidding the use of a language overtly, without necessarily physically
punishing the culprit who still uses it is also part of direct prohibition. Both
students and minority staff can be victims as several Inserts show. But embarrassment, shame, a feeling of doing something 'wrong', and at least doing
something that is not 'good for one' is inculcated through both overt and,

especially, covert prohibitions. When a ban on speaking one's mother tongue is put as the first commandment, as in the British and Norwegian examples in Inserts 5.28 and 5.27, speaking it is made to seem comparable with either 'other' grave sins (you are a bad person if you do it, and God does not like you) or, in addition, it is turned into something uncivilised, like urinating where you are not supposed to, as in the Norwegian example (Insert 5.27). Even if the children had not been physically punished for speaking their own language (corporal punishment was in fact used in Norway) the message would have got through. More examples are given in Inserts 5.29 and 5.30.

Even when the language may not be overtly forbidden, a prolonged experience like the ones in Insert 5.31 below or in the Welsh, Californian, and Catalan examples, may lead to the same result of children not wanting to use the language.

The long-term consequences of many of the bans can still be seen today even in situations where the ban has been lifted long ago. The consequences are both linguistic and cultural (see Insert 5.32; there have been several examples in earlier Boxes).

There is one case, though, where boarding schools are not only legitimate but often the only approach which leads to bilingualism and a strong positive identity; that of deaf children, especially those with hearing families. 'Residential schooling has (despite its many problems) served an important (perhaps essential) role in the transmission of sign language and deaf culture . . . Certainly, in the Deaf community, residential schooling is generally seen as the preferable approach' (Reagan, personal communication, December 1998). See also Reagan 1992, 1995a, b, Reagan & Penn 1997, Penn & Reagan 1990, Baynton 1996, Branson & Miller 1993, 1995a).

INSERT 5.27   Poster: 'Do not speak Sámi or Finnish in your free time. Do not urinate on the stairs' (Norway)

Many Norwegian boarding schools for indigenous Sámi and Finnish minority children used to have the same set of regulations on the wall, guiding the children about what was forbidden:

a) Do not speak Sámi or Finnish in your free time.

b) Do not go shopping or anywhere else without permission.

c) No boys in the girls' room or girls in the boys' room after 8 o'clock in the evening

d) Do not urinate on the stairs or along the walls of the house (Lind Meløy 1980: 68).

Speaking one's mother tongue was thus constructed as something as sinful, barbaric, uncivilised, and shameful as running around pissing indiscriminately.

INSERT 5.28   Poster forbidding speaking other
languages than English (UK)

'Head of Barnet Language Centre put up a poster in her classroom:

You may not speak Gujerati in this classroom.
You may not speak Greek in this classroom.
You may not speak Urdu in this classroom.
You may not speak Chinese in this classroom.
You may not speak Punjabi in this classroom.
You may only speak English in this classroom.

Head of Language Service made Head of Language Centre take the notice down. This was approximately 1976.' (Example from Brent, UK, see Insert 5.12)

INSERT 5.29   Minority teachers forbidden to use their
own language among themselves (UK)

I am a Bengali speaker. I was talking in the staffroom to a colleague of mine who is also a Bengali speaker. We were in one corner of the staffroom. We were told off by the Head for talking in Bengali in the staffroom. I was offended and asked her whether she would tell me off if I were speaking in French/German? Why would my mother-tongue not get the same status with other European languages? She did not answer and left the room. She also instructed me to speak only **English** in the staffroom. (Example from Brent, UK, see Insert 5.12)

INSERT 5.30   Move furniture to prevent minority
staff from sitting together (Sweden)

I experienced the prohibition myself in a school in Sweden which had Finnish-medium classes (see Skutnabb-Kangas 1987 for the research I did in the school). Many of the Finnish-speaking bilingual staff used to sit in one corner of the staff room during breaks, mostly planning teaching. Several Swedish teachers objected to them speaking in Finnish, even when they did not disturb anybody. One morning the two sofas from the corner had been moved to two different places in the staff room, and one single armchair was in the corner instead. When the Finnish teachers started asking about it, some Swedish teachers said: 'now you cannot speak Finnish anymore.'

INSERT 5.31 'neglect of a child's mother tongue at school
is a form of national discrimination' (Germany)

The neglect of a child's mother tongue at school is a form of national
discrimination. The Turkish child must know German in order to make herself
understood, at least to some extent, at school; but no German need learn any
Turkish. It does not even occur to the teachers that they should learn to
pronounce correctly the names of the Turkish children they teach for years
on end, even while they are scolding them for their inadequate grasp of
German. The Turkish child will, of course, know Turkish (more or less), but
knowing Turkish is 'worth nothing', and the child gets no credit for it, no
acknowledgement. (FIDEF, 1978: 18, about Turkish children in the Federal
Republic of Germany)

INSERT 5.32 Sámi **joik** forbidden for generations—in the 1980's
prohibition upheld by some Sámi parents

The distinctive Sámi singing tradition, **joik**, was also forbidden in Norway as
pagan, just as much of the rest of Sámi culture. In the mid-1980s, when some
schools in Norway still had rules banning **joik**, some majority-group
Norwegian teachers tried to get the rules changed and promote **joik**. But now
it was some Sámi parents who did not want **joik**. The message has been
effectively internalised over centuries by a minority of the parents (Gaski
1986), as several other examples also show.

The official recommendations of the World Federation of the Deaf for
Deaf education are also impossible to implement without boarding schools
(see Definition Box 4.1).

From the use of sticks, physical force, negative external sanctions, we
now move to negative internal sanctions, the use of shame and stigmatisation.
Of course strict divisions are impossible—many processes have been and are
often at work at the same time.

5.3.2.3. ... But Also Through Shame and Stigmatisation of the Uncivilised

Some examples of how a language can be stigmatised were given earlier in
the discussion about language as opposed to dialect, vernacular or patois.
But even if a language **is** called 'language', it is possible to stigmatise it, as
several examples have already shown. A stigmatised language of course can-

not (should not) be used as a medium of education. The pattern of stigmatisation almost always combines the three strategies of **glorification, stigmatisation**, and **rationalisation**, presented in chapter 3, Table 3.2. This was what was done in Australia in the example in Insert 5.33: first construct, erroneously, the dominated language (and culture) as deficient; then use its 'deficiency' as a rationalisation for imposing the glorified dominant language (and culture) at the cost of the dominated ones, for committing linguistic genocide, and, thirdly, do all this 'for their own benefit'. As later examples show, part of the rationalisation is also that if 'they' still do not succeed, after receiving all this 'help', it is their own fault (see also examples of this in chapter 3, e.g., in section 3.3.2). This is, in fact, one of the recipes still in use today, all over the world, as other examples also show.

The comments about primitive languages are still well and alive in relation to sign languages. This is also reflected in the fact that so many articles about sign languages need to start by refuting the claims, in fact establishing the 'languagehood', the legitimacy, of sign languages, 'making the case for sign language as "real" language', as Timothy Reagan puts is (personal communication, December 1998). Reagan's 1997b article 'When Is a Language Not a Language? Challenges to "Linguistic Legitimacy" in Educational Discourse' analyses the issue in an interesting way, drawing parallels between the stigmatisation and thus delegitimation through rationalisation of both sign languages and some oral languages, for instance in today's university entrance requirements in the USA.

But as the Australian example in Insert 5.33 showed, even 'in the old days', more sophisticated means than physical punishment or separation,

---

INSERT 5.33 Killing the Kaurna language 'the best means of promoting their civilisation' (Australia)

Rob Amery (1998) tells the story of the killing of the language of the Kaurna, the Aboriginal Peoples around today's Adelaide. 'The colonial authorities had planned for schools, as an integral part of the reserve system and policy of "protection" ', where government policies were 'clearly directed towards imposing English "civilisation" and obliterating Indigenous cultures as quickly as possible' (ibid., 160).

The German missionaries, learning and describing Kaurna (and providing most of the materials for reclaiming the language today), opposed parts of the means for the 'civilizing mission', namely 'that the best way to educate the natives would be to bring them nearer the larger towns' (ibid., 145). 'If the natives blended with the Europeans, the language of the natives could be lost', one of them, Schürmann, claimed in 1838, in the best Noble Savage tradition.

(Continued)

For a few years the missionaries managed to convince the authorities, and Kaurna was used, not only in schools (from December 1839) but also by the governer. To enhance the 'irregular attendance . . . children were "bribed" to attend the school with the provision of food, and blankets were distributed to adults whose children attended' (p. 153).

But already in 1844, Teichelmann, the other missionary responsible for preserving the Kaurna language, wrote that the governer (Grey), '. . . expressed his favourite idea, to speak to the natives only in English' (ibid., 150). Another missionary (Meyer) 'agreed and said to my [Teichelmann's] no small amazement that the language is so lacking in abstract concepts that it would be more advisable to use the English language, even in religious instruction because one could never express anything in their language', something that Teichelmann did not agree with (he thought (and tried to show to Meyer afterwards) that the language had enough abstract concepts;[23] that religious instruction should be in Kaurna, but all other instruction could be in English; ibid., 150).

A French observer, Piesse, made in 1840 similar comments, which Rob Amery (probably the person with the most extensive knowledge of the language today—my comment, not his) labels as 'fallacious and uninformed': '. . . the verbs are spoken only in the present tense; that almost all nouns are the same in the plural and singular numbers, and that there is no pronoun expressing the third person' (ibid., 213).

These linguicist, fallacious and stigmatising linguistic comments were then used to rationalise the factual linguistic genocide, as the example below shows. Cawthorne, another observer, here echoes Piesse (ibid., 213):

It is doubtful whether the native language could be rendered to a grammatical form, we would recommend that the English Tongue be more extensively taught among the Natives as the best means of promoting their civilisation. Their verbs are spoken in the present tense only and nearly all nouns are the same in singular and plural with no pronoun to express the third person.

In 1845, with the first boarding school, the use of Kaurna in school was finished. The English language was imposed as the only language, not only in schools but also otherwise—the missionaries were also forbidden to preach or teach religion through the medium of Kaurna. This took place 'together with [the government] plans to relocate the Kaurna away from their lands and settle them in a mixed community at Poonindie, with a pervading all-English ethos [which] sealed the fate of Kaurna (ibid., 162).

were of course used. The goal of linguistic and cultural assimilation of the uncivilized was openly declared in boarding schools for minorities, and the legitimation used was the low level of development of the minorities and indigenous peoples themselves, their languages and cultures. First some more older examples, then more modern ones—some of the phraseology has changed but the stigmatisation is still there. (See Inserts 5.34 through 5.38.)

We Finns were geographically squeezed between Sweden and Russia, speakers of a Finno-Ugric language surrounded mainly by Indo-European language neighbours, each in turn colonising us. We were the victims of racist stereotypes in slightly different forms from both in the nineteenth century. The French aristocrat Arthur de Gobineau, one of the important

---

INSERT 5.34 'Degeneration, a low cultural level and weak mental capacities, physical and mental stultification' (Sámi, Norway); 'distinguished from beasts only by possessing the bodily human form'; 'so savage, wild and dirty, disheveled, ugly, small and timid that only because they have the human form is it possible to believe that they belong to mankind' (California)

A parish priest, Tandberg, wrote in 1904 in a letter to the Superintendent for Schools in Norway: 'The reason for the instruction not having much effect is, beside truancy, degeneration, a low cultural level and weak mental capacities, physical and mental stultification' (Lind Meløy 1980: 39–40). Another Superintendent, Christen Andreas Brygfjeld, wrote in 1923 about the Sámi that 'those few individuals who still exist of the original Sámi tribe are now so much degenerated that there is little hope of any change for the better for them. They are hopeless, are probably the most backward and most miserable group in Finnmark, and from them comes the largest contingent from this area to mental hospitals and schools for the mentally retarded . . . The Sámi people have no capacity to rise to a higher cultural level themselves without taking the road through the Norwegian language and Norwegian culture' (ibid., 103–104).

Father Pedro Font wrote in his diary in 1775–76 similar assessments about native Californians: they 'live like beasts without making use of reason or discourse, and being distinguished from beasts only by possessing the bodily human form, but not from their deeds'. They were 'among the most unhappy people in all the world . . . In fine, they are so savage, wild and dirty, disheveled, ugly, small and timid that only because they have the human form is it possible to believe that they belong to mankind' (quoted in J. Lewis 1987: 82, 83). In 1800, rationalisation of the slavery by Franciscans was: 'It is evident that a nation which is barbarous, ferocious and ignorant requires more frequent punishment than a nation which is cultured, educated, and of gentle and moderate customs.' (Quoted in Castillo 1987: 7). Fesl 1993 and Mühlhäusler 1996 have many similar examples.

INSERT 5.35 'The Lapps have neither the
capacity nor the wish' (Sámi, Norway)

The problem is not only that the Sámi and Kven cultures are deficient, but
'The Lapps have had neither the capacity nor the wish to use their language
as a written language.' (Brygfjeld, quoted in Eriksen & Niemi 1981: 258.)
Again, Fesl 1993 and Mühlhäusler 1996 have many similar examples.

INSERT 5.36 Norwegianisation of Sámi and Finns for
their own welfare (Norway)

Superintendent of Schools, Bernt Thomassen, Norway, in a letter to the
Ministry of Education in 1917: 'In Norwegianisation—and its implementation
as speedily as possible—I see not only a national mission, but just as much
a question of the welfare of the majority of the Sámi and Finnish people in
Northern Norway. Via Norwegianisation the road can lead to development
and success for them too' (Lind Meløy 1980: 100).

INSERT 5.37 'a people spiritually and physically undernourished'
(Finns and Sámi, Sweden)

Said about the Finns and the Sámi in Sweden in 1915: 'a people spiritually
and physically undernourished . . . the soul of the people dulled into
sluggishness and inertia' (Lundemark 1980: 114).

formulators of biologically argued racism, divided in his **Essai sur l'inégalité
des races humaines** (1853) humanity into three basic races where the Aryan
race was proclaimed to be the highest form of civilization. His classification
lists 'Altaic, Mongol, Finnish, and Tatar branches' of the 'yellow race'. He
also stated that 'the hierarchy of languages corresponds strictly to the hierarchy of races' (quoted in Centassi & Masson 1995: 289). His ideas were
taken up by both of our neighbours (see Insert 5.39) as Kenneth McRae
reports (1997: 145–148).

'The common feature of these Germanic and Russian stereotypes of the
Finns was the Finns' supposed political passivity, their assumed incapacity
for higher cultural development or—what amounted in a nineteenth-century
context to much the same thing—for political independence' (McRae 1997:
147). Just as slaves or colonised peoples in general, Finns were not seen
developed enough to govern themselves—and maybe as never capable to do

---

INSERT 5.38 Incapable of learning, lazy, work is a foreign concept, lacking in initiative (indigenous peoples, North and South)

The organisation of the schooling often assumed that the indigenous peoples were incapable of learning. They were stereotyped as dependent, lazy, lacking in initiative (Jordan 1986, referring to the Canadian First Nations, the Sámi and Australian Aborigines).

Asked about the reasons for the high death rates of 'Indians' on mission stations in California, Professor David Hornbeck mentioned, in addition to the change from 'a high protein diet that the Indians had to one which was a high carbohydrate diet that the Spanish had' (1987: 198), the 'adjustment from never, ever working, never working at all—work is a foreign concept to you—to being part of a communal society where you have to do some part of the labor to ensure that the institution survives. You're given a job . . . Were they overworked? No. Six hours a day, by our standards it was a life of luxury. The Indians were given ample time off . . . So, you have high death rates. But, did the missionaries cause it? Of course not.' (ibid.). This 'life of luxury' involved in fact conditions of slavery—see Insert 3.16.

---

it.[24] The cruel civil war just after independence (1917–1918) of course just proved this . . . just as it does now in relation to Africans. As soon as the British or the French or the Portuguese left . . .

Now we could say: so what? Most of this is past; and we regret. Mea culpa. Children (and adults) **were** prohibited from using 'the language of the group in daily intercourse or in schools', children **were** 'forcibly transferred from one group to another', 'many children were caused 'serious bodily or mental harm' (genocide according to Art. II(b) in the present Genocide Convention). We acknowledge that is **was** genocide. But surely this does not happen today!

But it does.

5.3.3. Preventing the Use of the Language Covertly and Indirectly, by Today's Means

5.3.3.1. . . . Through Structural Means

The use of a minority language can also be prohibited **covertly, more indirectly**, via structural and ideological means, as in the educational systems of most European and North American countries. There are many modern sophisticated ways of committing linguistic genocide.

My claim is that the use of a minority language is in fact prohibited 'in daily intercourse or in schools' (UN definition) every time there are minority

---

INSERT 5.39   Racist stereotypes: Finns 'without an inner life force' and 'without a culture or a national will'

A Stockholm journalist, August Sohlman (1853: 33; quoted in McRae 1997: 146), inspired by Gobineau's ideas, wrote about the Finns: 'Not one of Europe's great family of nations has played so small a part, or shown so little inclination or capacity to appear independently among the nations, as the Finnish race or in general the entire Tschudic race. Ingrians, Ostiaks, Permiaks, Mordevins, Cheremissians, Voguls, and Lapps are all of them declining peoples, without an inner life force and without a distinctive cultural impulse'.

The Russian 'views of the Finns were equally dismissive, particularly among the Slavophiles and Pan-Slavists . . . The general tendency among Russian intellectuals was to see the Finns as a people without a culture or a national will' (McRae 1997: 146–147).

---

children in day care centres and schools, but no bilingual teachers who are authorized to use the languages of the minority children as the main media of teaching and child care. This means that not offering mother tongue medium maintenance-oriented education to indigenous and minority children when there are enough children to make this possible, can be an instance of linguistic genocide. Not offering mother tongue medium education often (of course not always) leads to either that child herself or the next generation changing linguistic and cultural endo-identification. Thus a person has been 'forcibly transferred from one group to another', often causing 'mental harm' (UN definitions). This can also be an instance of linguistic genocide.

This is the situation still today for most immigrant and refugee minority children in all Western European countries and in the US, Canada, and Australia.[25] Immigrant minority education in these countries is thus guilty of linguistic genocide, as defined by the UN. So is the education that most indigenous first nations have had and that many of them still have. This is true even in countries where some indigenous languages may have a strong position (see Insert 5.40).

Likewise, most national minorities, save a few strong ones, are educated in dominant languages.

Birgit Brock-Utne (1993a: 39; see also her 1993b, 1994, 1995, 1996, 1997, 1998, in press, Brock-Utne & Nagel (eds) 1996, Brock-Utne & Garbo (eds) 1999) observes that 'in many of the African countries the majority language is treated in a way that minority languages are treated in the industrialized world', meaning education in an old colonial language can in many if not most cases be seen as linguistic genocide (see also Prah 1995a, b). But even education through the medium of another African language

---

INSERT 5.40 Only Spanish in school—never learn it perfectly—
stop speaking Aymara (Bolivia)

'Many of my contemporaries have only learned Spanish in school, but they
never learn it perfectly. At the same time they stop speaking their own language
which in my case is Aymara. They end up as people without identity, people
who belong nowhere.' (Vice-president Victor Hugo Cárdenas, Bolivia, in an
interview with Steffen Knudsen, in **Zig Zag—en verden i bevægelse**, 26, 1994:
9)

INSERT 5.41 Learning in another language—raped by
the government (Zimbabwe)

'A Kalanga man said to me in English during my time in Zimbabwe: "Every
day my child goes to school and has to learn in Ndebele [as opposed to the
mother tongue, my remark] I feel raped—raped by others, by government,
raped of my relationship with my child" ' (quoted in Ucko 1983: 28).

---

can function in the same way, even if there are some mitigating factors (see
Insert 5.41).

Even if the goal of assimilation is **expressed** in more sophisticated terms
today, the **goal itself** has not changed much. The structural factors will be
discussed further in the next three chapters.

5.3.3.2. . . . Through Invisibilisation

We have already seen many examples of dominated languages, cultures, and
peoples (and the dominated gender), being made invisible, with several different means. Some more examples are given below. In the United States
and Sweden example (Insert 5.42) labels **hide** the dominated groups, also
implying that this is what they want, at the same time as what they themselves
are and have is rendered stigmatised and/or invisible.

Another way of invisibilisation is to **disperse** minority children—and
thereby also their languages. As a result of dispersal, if there are few children
with the same language, it can be legitimated as too difficult to offer them
their mother tongue even as a subject. Many children have, after dispersal,
nobody else in the same class to speak the language with ('I couldn't speak
to anyone because they didn't know my language. The only one I had to
talk to was the hospital cat. He was my friend. I talked language to him'—

INSERT 5.42 'English-speaking nation' and 'good Swedes'—where did the other languages and identities go? (USA, Sweden)

. . . the basic Federal policy concerns . . . recognize the need to prepare language-minority children to function successfully in **an English-speaking nation.** A programme that produces mediocre English performance while **maintaining the home language** skills will be judged a **worse programme** than one that produces better second language performance while **ignoring home language skills.** The justification for this viewpoint is that in the United States any successful education programme must prepare the students to participate in an English-speaking society. Therefore, **the overriding concern** in evaluating instruction for bilingual students **is how well they learn English.** (Baker & de Kanter 1982: 5, emphases added)

My comment: this 'English-speaking' nation has over 30 million inhabitants with mother tongues other than English. Calling it 'English-speaking' means that all the other mother tongues are being made invisible—it is as if they did not exist.

In Sweden, 'migrant children . . . by being allowed to assimilate and incorporate . . . will with time become good Swedes', Christina Bratt Paulston (1982: 65) claims, in a report to the Swedish National Board of Education, implying that migrant minority children **want** to assimilate, even linguistically. And once they have assimilated and are 'Swedes' (rather than hyphenated, e.g., Sweden-Greeks, showing multiple identities), they are of course invisible, in statistics and minds. One researcher that Bratt Paulston drew support from advocates linguicism in pluralist Sweden: 'for some immigrant children, the optimum (in L1) might well be to keep the level a bit above the risk level for complete decay' (Ekstrand 1978: 11).

---

dormitory experience of Roger Hart, Barrow Point language speaker in Australia, Annette Schmidt's example, quoted in Mühlhäusler 1996: 247). That also invisibilises the language. I have met hundreds of dominant group teachers who have no idea what the mother tongues of their students are. Dispersal is often legitimated by referring to avoidance of 'ghettoes' (but surely ghettoes are something you cannot get out from? rather than something where you **want** to be together), or by constructing some imagined threshold which should not be crossed if one wants the children to 'integrate', or if one does not want dominant group children to 'suffer' and their parents to withdraw the children. Insert 5.43 gives examples.

There are similarities in these dispersal policies to Australian early examples (Deirdre Jordan and Eve Mumewa Fesl have quoted many examples of Aboriginal children being moved from schools on demands from 'white' parents).

INSERT 5.43 'avoid undue concentrations of immigrant children'
(UK, Denmark)

Experience suggests . . . that, apart from unusual difficulties (such as a high proportion of non-English speakers), up to a fifth of immigrant children in any group fit in with reasonable ease, but that, if the proportion goes over about one third either in the school as a whole or in any one class, serious strains arise. It is therefore desirable that the catchment areas of schools should, **wherever possible** be arranged to **avoid undue concentrations** of immigrant children. Where this proves to be impracticable simply because the school serves an area which is occupied largely by immigrants, **every effort should be made to disperse** the immigrant children round a number of schools and to meet such problems of transport as may arise. (Department of Education and Science (DES) 1965: 4–5; emphases added; see also other DES reports in the bibliography for the representativity of these views later)

In Denmark, most cities, especially those with a Social Democrat majority,[26] have followed the British example, not only in schools but also in housing, with rules stating 10% or 20% or 30% thresholds for minority presence in a classroom, or similar thresholds in blocks of flats. The housing regulations have been ruled by courts to be illegal, but they are still being followed in several parts of the country, without any sanctions having followed so far. See also Info Boxes 7.13 and 7.14 for other examples where Denmark may violate human rights conventions.

Privatising minority cultures, while majority cultures are seen as legitimate parts of the educational system (Inserts 5.44 and 5.45), is also part of making them invisible, as we saw in the earlier examples in Inserts 3.6 (John Edwards) and 4.5 (Uffe Ellemann Jensen).

It is interesting that all European and Europeanised national education systems not only perpetuate their own national values, but also insist on 'perpetuating the different values' and 'preserving the different cultures' of

INSERT 5.44 National system not to perpetuate the different
values of immigrant groups (UK)

'A national system of education must aim at producing citizens who can take their place in society properly equipped to exercise rights and perform duties which are the same as other citizens. If their parents were brought up in another culture or tradition, children should be encouraged to respect it, but a national system cannot be expected to perpetuate the different values of immigrant groups' (Commonwealth Immigrants Advisory Council 1964: 2).

INSERT 5.45   National Agenda not to sustain or preserve
different cultures (Australia)

'It is not and never has been part of the policies of multiculturalism as set
out in the National Agenda to provide for special funding to sustain or
preserve different cultures; even less is this true of particular religions.' (Gobbo
1995: 2). In fact, the 'denial of the significance of the cultural envelope in
economic growth' and 'neglect of its multicultural complexity is detrimetal to
the needs of the economy, which also coincides with the legitimate aspirations
of a large proportion of Australians from other ancestries who desire to
maintain their cultural and linguistic heritage', according to Jurek Smolicz
(1990: 75).

---

some 'foreigners', to use the terms from earlier Inserts. The 'classical Greek
heritage' or the 'great European literature' are cherished despite being 'foreign' and 'different'—but the values of today's Greek immigrant in Britain
or Australia have no place in **common** curricula in schools.

5.3.3.3. . . . *Still Through Shame and Stigmatisation,*
and Making a Resource Seem Like a Handicap

It takes courage to tell about shame one has been made to feel because of
who one is. Had Eve Mumewa Fesl (Aboriginal Australian) looked and
spoken like Kathleen Heugh ('white' English-speaking South African), she
might have been spared the shame she tells about in Insert 5.46. But being
'white' and speaking English did not help Kathleen Heugh at all in school
in Britain (Insert 5.46). Both Fesl and Heugh have later analysed their own
experience of shame, and the experience and analysis have contributed towards making both champions of equity and linguistic human rights in their
own countries and beyond (see references in the bibliography). Kathleen
Heugh notes that she comes 'from a long and conservative history in South
Africa and one which is rooted in the double-edged denial of South African
identities by the conquered and colonised consciousness of all the various
communities who comprise the greater South African "nation"—in favour
of a desperate desire to be assimilated into the imagined "English-speaking"
international western world' (personal communication, January 1999). She
also feels that the experience has given her 'an understanding of how conquered consciousness works . . . in terms of that which needs to be challenged,
and also how a minority of language workers/activists/educators are beginning to think' in South Africa (ibid.). For Fesl, one of the factors supporting
the emergence of the consciousness was the arrival of immigrants, proud of

---

INSERT 5.46 English or not English—feel ashamed
(Fesl, Australia; Heugh, South Africa)

Because we were not English, we were made to feel ashamed, of our languages, of our cultures, and we were indoctrinated into feeling ashamed of the colour of our skin. When you, your parents and your grandparents arrived, you dared to speak in public, a language other than English, although you were the recipients of abuse, as we had been for decades. By your example of showing pride in your heritage and ignoring those who said that to be different to Anglo-culture was deficit, you made us reconsider OUR position, and to develop in ourselves a pride in being different. You helped us to relearn not to be ashamed of our cultures, our languages and to be proud of being Black. [Eve Fesl, 'the first Aboriginal woman to hold a PhD from an Australian University', in 1988, 'to an audience consisting principally of non-Aboriginal Australians of non-English speaking background' (quoted in Smolicz 1990: 71; see also references to Fesl in the bibliography)]

As a child, I was brought up to believe that I had to speak 'beautifully' like my mother, who had a Southern British RP accent. To my horror, upon arriving to go to school in Britain for three years, I was told that I had a dreadful American accent (actually it was South African English) and that I should not offer to contribute orally in class unless I could 'speak the Queen's English'. This brought me both to attempt to hide my colonial background as well as an intellectual inferiority complex which haunted me for the next two decades, even though I found myself in the top academic stream in that school. (Kathleen Heugh, personal communication, January 1999)

---

their languages and cultures. See further examples in Inserts 5.47 through 5.49, pp. 359–360.

As we have seen, hiding, dispersing, privatising, stigmatising, and making in other ways the child to feel ashamed are powerful strategies in linguistic and cultural genocide. But carrots and ideas are equally powerful—and more difficult for the children (and adults) to analyse.

5.3.3.4. *Carrots (Combined With Sticks, Threats, or Shame)*

Positive reinforcement (carrots) of the **dominant/majority** language and/or culture and identity have been used at the same time as negative reinforcement (sticks or shame) of the mother tongue.

'The political and economic beneficiaries of the adopted language may even prohibit the native language to acquire some of the modernizing features, like the ban of the colonial British Government on publication of books in Indian languages when the printing technology was introduced in

> **INSERT 5.47** Many African children still 'intellectually unable to cope with a foreign language'
>
> For a British Africanist analysing the spread of education in Africa a crucial issue is the question of 'how the state seeks to manage the transition from an elite secondary system' (where high quality English can be guaranteed) to 'a mass secondary system (where there will necessarily be many children intellectually unable to cope with a foreign language)' (King 1986: 451). My comment: Any children with a 'normal' IQ can cope with foreign languages. According to several studies (reviewed in Genesee 1976) of English-speaking children in French-language immersion programmes in Canada, neither working class children nor children with special language difficulties had any difficulty in coping with the foreign language (in addition to developing their mother tongue, English). In the large secondary pupils' survey in Tanzania in 1970 (reported in Hill 1986) which was a representative sample (20%, randomly selected) of the entire first year secondary population in the country, the average number of languages known by the pupils (self-report) was 5. There was not a single one who claimed to be monolingual, and only 3% claimed knowledge of as little as 2 languages. Thus 97% of the secondary pupils could 'cope' with 3 or more languages. Maybe Tanzanians are more 'intellectually able' than the secondary pupils that King perhaps, in monolingual Britain, takes as the norm . . .

India. Thus the underdevelopment of a language may be a consequence of the political power of a developed language'. This is how Annamalai, a former Director of the Central Institue of Indian Languages describes the combination (1989: 8).

To make carrots more concrete, we again start with historical examples. Carrots were used from early on by missionaries (as with food and blankets in the Kaurna example above, Insert 5.33) and by the state educational systems. I continue with Scandinavian examples (Insert 5.50, p. 361).

Today earmarked funds go to the teaching of the dominat language, whereas funds for minority mother tongue teaching (even as a subject; even when regional or international organisations demand or recommed it—see Tosi 1988; also 1984, 1989) are difficult to get, and experience the first cuts (as in Sweden at the beginning of the 1990s—e.g., Lainio 1998, Huss 1999). Minority children may be praised for their knowledge or good pronunciation of the dominant language, whereas the teacher or other adult says nothing about their pronunciation of or competence in their own language[27] (Insert 5.51, p. 361).

Sticks and shame are also often combined, with lasting results. The ban on speaking Finnish, and the Tornedalen accent when speaking Swedish, are two sides of the same coin for Inga Hubinette, a Finnish-speaker from Torne-

INSERT 5.48   Latin & Greek are English for a British researcher

C. P. Hill reports that pupils in the Secondary Pupils' Survey in Tanzania (Insert 5.47) claim high rates for using English for counting and doing sums. In discussing the influence of mathematics being taught through the medium of English he says: '. . . many of the [mathematical] concepts virtually anglicized even in Swahili -items like "graph", and "axis" and "origin" having no real Swahili equivalents but requiring lengthy circumlocutions, so the English forms are used' (Hill 1986: 255).

My comment: 'English' forms? In my ignorance, I thought they were Latin and Greek. We could with equal justification say, about Britain: '. . . many of the mathematical concepts virtually latinised/greekified even in English—items like "graph", and "axis" and "origin" having no real English equivalents but requiring lengthy circumlocutions, so the Latin or Greek forms are used. And this after English has had centuries to develop its own concepts, it still has not managed but relies on concepts borrowed from Latin and Greek.'

One possibly less linguicist way of saying what Hill says might be: 'Like many other languages, among them English, Swahili has also borrowed some of the labels for its mathematical concepts from Greek and Latin (and Arabic?) and uses "graph", "axis" and "origin" (but without distorting the Greek and Latin pronunciation of these words the way English does)'.

INSERT 5.49   'we are [still] the superior race,
you the beaten and inferior race' (USA)

'On the basis of historical facts, we see ourselves as the members of the victorious **and superior** race and you as members of the beaten **and inferior race**.' This was the explanation given by the director of a large American company, Ronald Vertress, when refusing to employ 'Indians', in 1986 (**Ny Tid** 10.7.1986; emphases added).

dalen in Sweden, now a teacher in her sixties. She said in a workshop in March 1992: 'If we said something in Finnish, even during the break, we were not allowed to borrow books from the school library and we could not see the film. When I spoke Swedish, I did not have the ö-sounds pure [a literal translation; it sounds unusual in Swedish too]. "That we have to repair", the teacher said.'

It is interesting that Inga Hubinette, despite now knowing much more about sociolinguistic variation, still uses the terminology that the teacher must have used, i.e., accepting that the dialectal pronunciation was not 'pure' and needed 'repairing'. Likewise, there is a distancing from the ö-sounds that she produced: she did not 'own' her own pronunciation and say '**my**

INSERT 5.50 Rewards for assimilation combined
with sticks (Norway, Sweden)

From 1851 onwards until the 1920s there were funds in the state budget in Norway specifically earmarked for Norwegianisation. Teachers could get a supplement to their salary from these funds if they could document good results in teaching Norwegian to the Sámi and Kven children. Children received grants if they showed good competence in Norwegian, and poor Kven and Sámi parents could be given money for food and clothes if they showed a 'positive attitude' by sending their children to the Norwegian school (Eriksen & Niemi 1981: 48, 53).

Radio licenses were cheaper in the Finnish- and Sámi-speaking areas than in other parts of Norway (ibid., 245)—a reward for listening to the radio programmes (which naturally were all-Norwegian), that is, a reward for assimilation efforts (assimilation because the mother tongue was prevented from developing at the same time). Books, newspapers, and journals in Norwegian were distributed free of charge, while there were severe restrictions on, for instance, books imported from Finland (and libraries in northern Sweden were forbidden to buy Finnish books). People were suspected of lacking loyalty to Norway if they read such unpatriotic literature (ibid., 239). The same was true on the Swedish side of the border too: books and journals in Swedish were distributed free of charge, while the library of Torneå was overtly forbidden to buy Finnish books until 1957 (ibid., 241). All this positive reinforcement followed after a long period of negative reinforcement, when it was insisted that civil servants should not use Sámi or Finnish, on pain of losing their jobs (ibid., 252–253), when Kven and Sámi were not allowed to buy land, and so on. (ibid, 73–76).

INSERT 5.51 'My dad's boss praised us: "Good. Good. You must all
speak English—like "Wasungus" ' '

My father who was the Chief Auditor in the Civil Service in Kenya once invited his 'boss' at home. He made sure we were all smartly dressed up and showed our etiquette before this gentleman. We came and met him, shook hands, etc, but were rather quiet—being very shy.

Seeing this the man said: 'Oh—don't your children speak English, Mr Y?' My father must have got offended or embarrassed, so he asked me to tell my name in English. I said: 'Hello! My name is Santoshi Y. And I am 6 years old.' Similarly my sisters responded. Hearing this, my dad's boss praised us: 'Good. Good. You must all speak English—like 'Wasungus', meaning the Englishmen. Signed: 'Santoshi' (Example from Brent, UK, see Insert 5.12).

ö-sounds were not pure'. In a later discussion she said that a lot of the shame and embarrassment still hurt. I have met hundreds of indigenous and minority people who have started talking about the pain in connection with their school experience only after an intensive course where these issues have been analysed and discussed, saying that it was the first time they could talk about it. It was too painful and had been too painful, often for decades.

At the TESOL conference, Baltimore (March 1994), a person who had produced an English pronunciation CD-Rom, told me that she had produced this **accent-reparation** material . . . Native dialects were of course treated in a similar way in some countries (for instance in Britain), with elocutionist 'repairing' of 'non-standard', non-prestigious pronunciation. Many voices in the Black English/Ebonics debate have also expressed similar opinions (see also Lippi-Green 1994, 1997). Several court cases have been fought on **accent discrimination** in the USA, referring to the Equal Employment Opportunity Act (Title VII of the Civil Rights Act of 1964, 42 U.S.C. & 2000e-2)—see Miner 1998 for an overview; see also Crandall 1992, Lippi-Green 1994, 1997, Sato 1991. This is also an important issue when hiring teachers (see Info Box 8.8). On the other hand, Norwegian school regulations stated for over a century ago that a teacher was not allowed to eradicate or correct a child's dialectal pronunciation—as long as it was Norwegian.

More examples will be given in later chapters. Before moving to look at alternative ways of understanding what happens in linguistic genocide, we shall raise the question of the relative 'efficiency' of the overt as opposed to more covert linguicide.

5.3.3.5. *Sophisticated Linguicism More Effective?* *Resistance?*

The difference between the way that such countries as Turkey on the one hand and, for instance, Sweden, the US, or Canada, on the other hand, commit linguistic genocide today lies in that it is done more openly and brutally in Turkey (see Skutnabb-Kangas & Bucak 1994) whereas it is more covert, subtle and sophisticated in Sweden, the US, and Canada (Skutnabb-Kangas 1991a; see also Schierup 1992, 1995, and Ålund 1992 for critical accounts of Swedish multicultural policy). **Covert linguicide** (e.g., of the type that most Western states use in their educational systems) appears to be extremely effective, as compared to the overt version (as in Turkey). Within two to four generations, there are fewer speakers of most minority languages in these countries than in more openly linguicidal countries. Kurds still speak Kurdish and resist linguistic (and other) oppression,[28] whereas many former Spanish-speakers in the USA have assimilated, i.e., been transferred to another group. It is often more difficult to struggle against covert violence, against the colonization of the mind, where short-term 'benefits' may obscure longer-term losses.

Having one's language overtly forbidden, even when the punishment for speaking it is psychological not physical, may enhance an awareness of the fact that there should be language rights, even if it may take a long time for the awareness to be verbalised. When we discussed the written examples which people gave to me at a conference at Brent, UK, November 10, 1993 (when I had asked them to write about their own experience), many of the minority staff said it had taken them many years to realise that what had happened was not right, and to start formulating their feelings in terms of what rights they or minority children should have had. Insert 5.52 shows an example, an experience which started a reflective process (1) and what this teacher now sees as some important language rights (2, 3).

Following in Insert 5.53 are excerpts from the experiences of two Kurdish young women.

Even at school level, there is a lot of resistance too (Insert 5.54, p. 365).

Fighting the system can have other results too, as the story in Insert 5.55, p. 366, from 1998 shows. It was sent to me by a friend in Rumania but for safety reasons I will not disclose the identity of my friend.

Later my friend also told about the follow-up. In October 1998 Károly Kerekes, an MP from the Hungarian Democratic Alliance (which is a member of the ruling coalition in Rumania) proposed an amendment to the law on civil marriage to the effect that use of the mother tongue should also be allowed when the marriage vow is endorsed. This proposal was rejected by the Government Committee which approves draft laws for the Parliament. This means that the official position of the Government is that Rumanian alone should be used in such situations.

But as Blench (1996) states for Central Nigeria (Info Box 2.5), 'government oppression and neglect' may also enhance language maintenance. Today it

---

INSERT 5.52 Prohibition may enhance awareness about rights (UK)

1. Being reprimanded at school (by a teacher) for speaking in Punjabi with my friend at a time when I was learning English. I felt more secure in speaking in Punjabi then.

2. Have the right to practise their own language and learning their own language at school etc., lessons in mother tongue. All languages should be valued equally, irrespective of the **number** of people speaking them in a country.

3. Providing people the means and support to become **proficient** in the **main** language too of a society so that they participate **actively** and fully in true mainstream society and challenge existing negative attitudes. This should lead to them gaining more rights. (Example from Brent, UK, see Insert 5.12).

INSERT 5.53 Maybe we Kurds can adapt to foreign cultures because we were foreigners even in our country and we had to study in a foreign language

My school start. In the autumn of 1981 I started school in Iran, in a town called Maku. I went to school without a headscarf and noticed that all other girls had them. The female teacher told us girls always to use headscarf in school, otherwise we would be punished. Then she gave us books and started teaching. I did not understand anything of anything because my teacher was Azerbaijani, spoke Azeri and taught in Azeri. The books were in Farsi and I only spoke Kurdish. We were 40 children, only 4 Kurds, the others were Azeri. This was the last year when boys and girls were in the same class even if we had to sit in separate sections.

The next day the teacher went through our homework. Nobody could answer except for two students who were repeating first grade. We others were hit on our hands and taken to higher grade classrooms where the students were commanded to laugh at us 'stupids'.

How could I have done the homework when I could not even tell the languages apart? (Soghra Hasanzadeh).

In the autumn of 1982 I started in the same school as my sister. We arrived at school before 7 and were organised in rows in the school yard where the head girls and boys checked our clothing and finger nails (these not allowed to be long). School started at 7 and we marched in in rows. During the first school day girls and boys were in the same class, but because of Khomeini's revolution in 1979, the new laws finally came into force on our second school day, and girls and boys could neither be in the same class nor be in school at the same time. Most students in my class were Azeri, a couple were Persian and two were Kurds in addition to me.

I remember my mother walking past the school window. I cried and stood up, saying: 'Mother, please take me home, the teacher hits me'. Mother smiled and left. What else could she have done.

The first day we had to translate from Farsi to an easier form of Farsi. At home I cried with the book in my hand. How could I translate when I did not understand a word of the text.

Maybe we Kurds can adapt to foreign cultures because we were foreigners even in our country and we had to study in a foreign language. (Akram Hasanzadeh)

Both these young Kurdish women came to Finland with their parents as political refugees in 1989 when they were 15 and 14, respectively, and quadrilingual. Both learned Finnish quickly, graduated from upper secondary school and are now studying. Soghra wants to become a medical doctor. She has already written a research report based on interviews, together with another young woman, about the information needs of young immigrants in Finland (Mallon & Hasanzadeh 1998). Both wrote these accounts in errorfree Finnish (after I had spent an evening together with them and their mother after a Kurdish conference in Helsinki, September 1998).

INSERT 5.54 Fighting the system—now multilingual (UK)

I came here in 1965. I was 6 years old. On starting school they forced me to let my parents go (my mother for the first time in my life). I screamed, cried, bit, scratched the teacher so much that they had to let me stay with my elder brother. My parents were told to speak in English to us children. My father admits he was wrong to trust the teachers' idea. They said my English was not good enough to do the O'levels. My father wrote several letters and I was allowed to take O'level English which I passed. I feel bitter that they stopped me going to higher education at that age through normal channels. I started BEd Honours at the age of 26 and passed. I lost my languages and cultural identification. English had become dominant. In 1979 I went to Bangladesh; by extremely good luck I learnt Arabic and Bengali and regained my identity a lot more.

At present my languages are: English—degree; Bengali—O'level (includes Sylheti and other dialects); Italian—CSE; Urdu—spoken/understanding; Gujarati—some understanding; Arabic—reading (Quran; Muslim); Shorthand—2 versions.[29] I hope to develop all languages to higher levels. I feel I can now sort of tune into languages. (Yasmin Khatun, Brent Language Services; example from Brent, UK, see Insert 5.12)

---

is some of those European nations/peoples which have been linguistically and culturally oppressed that are at the forefront in the struggle for language rights. They have managed to maintain and/or revitalise their languages and cultures and gain some rights. Now they are demanding linguistic human rights globally. The Catalans have, together with others, taken the initiative to the Universal Declaration of Linguistic Rights (see section 7.6.2, also for critique). The Basques are paying for the World languages report project (Info Box 1.7), with a strong Catalan participation in the implementation.

To both the Catalans and the Basques it has been clear that their languages were not just 'dying' 30 years ago—they were being murdered. But the existence of agents is not equally clear to all.

5.4. LANGUAGE DEATH AND LINGUISTIC GENOCIDE/LINGUICIDE—TWO PARADIGMS?

When languages disappear, the question is: does this happen as a result of language death or are we talking about language murder? We can now continue the discussion from the Introduction of the concept of **linguicide/ linguistic genocide** or **language murder**, as compared to the more passive **language death** (e.g., Dressler 1988, Brenzinger (ed.) 1992) or even **language suicide** (e.g., Denison 1977). The issue can be seen as a question of two

INSERT 5.55   Fighting the system—cannot get married
(Hungarian in Rumania)

I would like to tell you a story, which could interest you.

It happened in our city, Cluj (in Romanian), Kolozsvar (in Hungarian). There are about 380,000 inhabitants; about 74,000 are Hungarian (including me). Our Mayor, Gheorhge FUNAR is famous for his very nationalistic ideas and practices. His office is following him in this domain.

26 of September, one of my young friends, Jeno MATIS, Member of the Romanian Parliament, wanted to get married. They went to the Office of Registrar of Marriages, together with all the people who are usually present at such events. When asked (in Romanian, of course) whether he was willing to marry the young lady, he answered 'da' ['yes' in Romanian] and 'igen' ['yes' in Hungarian]. The officer got very upset, saying that he needed to consult the Dictionary of the Romanian Language, to see whether such a word as 'da-igen' could be found. After checking, he said that no such word was found in the Dictionary, and therefore he refused to register the marriage. So my friend remained unmarried.

Later the Mayor declared that the decision of the officer was correct. To avoid such events in the future, his office will organise Romanian language courses free of charge for those stupid people who are not able to learn just the simple Romanian word 'da'.

I think this can be one of the funny stories in your collection concerning the Linguistic Human Rights.

theoretical, maybe epistemological, approaches to how to theorize the threats posed in the issue of endangered languages. We are not necessarily talking about two complementary ways of seeing the same phenomenon, just with a different focus (a position I would very much like to be able to take) but are probably dealing with different theoretical (and possibly also political) approaches, in fact almost two different paradigms. I optimistically hope that I am wrong in this assessment though. They may be at least partially exclusive of each other, but need to be understood in the sense that the linguistic genocide paradigm can (and in fact must) include and use all of the empirical knowledge of the language death paradigm, whereas many representatives of the language death paradigm might object to the inclusion of the analyses of the linguistic genocide paradigm. I will present the two paradigms in ways which are somewhat overgeneralising, in order to highlight the differences.

The **language death paradigm** seems to hold, as we have observed earlier, that if everything living in nature has a life-span, everything is born, blossoms, withers away, is replaced by the next candidate—then why not languages? Even if we may not like it, let a natural order prevail. Besides, the weak (individuals and species which cannot adapt to changing circumstances) die and the strong (those who can adapt) survive in nature. The concepts 'language attrition', 'language decay', 'language loss' and 'language death' within this paradigm do not necessarily imply a causal agent, other than the speakers themselves. First decay and attrition and then language death are seen as occurring because of circumstances beyond the control of any (outside) agents, even if some description of changing circumstances is often presented. The 'effects', for instance language death as a result of 'modernization', are often regarded as inevitable concomitants of this social change. Language death is thus seen as comparable to the evolution of natural organisms which develop, bloom and wither away, atrophy, and finally die. 'The term "loss" fails to draw attention to the fact that many of the traditional concepts and their lexical forms were not, in fact, lost but taken away and/or destroyed', Peter Mühlhäusler formulates his criticism, giving concrete examples of this (1996: 301ff).

Therefore attempts to counteract it are often seen as romantic or misplaced, trying to prevent a natural development (see e.g., my analysis of how John Edwards does this, in Skutnabb-Kangas 1991b). The worries expressed by Professor Shigeru Tsuchida, summing up the first conference organised by the International Clearing House for Endangered Languages in Tokyo, Japan, in November 1995 ('whether we are allowed to interfere with the natural development of any language', see section 4.1.3) reflect this approach, albeit in a sophisticated manner.

When some liberal economists (e.g., Friedrich List, 1885: 174ff.) a century ago considered that nations had to be of a 'sufficient size' to be viable, it followed that smaller nationalities **and languages** were doomed to disappear, as collective victims of 'the law of progress'. Their speakers were advised to reconcile themselves to 'the loss of what could not be adapted to the modern age' (quoted in Hobsbawm 1991: 29–39).

Several Western European liberal ideologists and Soviet language planners in the early part of this century held that nations (each with their own language) were but one phase in a development towards a unified world which had a world language, coexisting with national languages which would be 'reduced to the domestic and sentimental role of dialects' (ibid., 38).

This liberal ideology of development is still alive and well. When discussing 'small ethnic groups and languages', we are warned not to 'be idealistic and feel blind pity for everything which **in its natural course** is transformed, becomes outdated or even extinct', (Šatava 1992: 80; my emphasis).

Also linguists who may fully appreciate the importance of languages may think that this 'gigantic task' (of maintaining languages) is impossible. The Indonesian linguist Alisjahbana, having poetically described the richness of each language and concluded 'that every language is the complete expression of the life or, as is very often said, "the soul" of the people' (1984: 47), goes on to claim that 'we cannot escape the fact that many of the smaller linguistic and cultural groups will disappear into the larger linguistic and cultural group of the nation. It is very often even in the interest of these groups that they merge with larger groups, in order to participate in the progress of the whole nation' (ibid., 52). Alisjahbana is prepared to let the government 'promote the culture or in most cases the arts of that group' (ibid.), provided that the group's aim is 'of a purely cultural character' (ibid.)—but **not** if they have 'a political aim . . . of political independence or autonomy' (ibid.).

The evolutionist modernisation agenda is expressed clearly where he talks about 'the true world civilization of our time, based on the tremendous progress of science and technology and resulting in economic welfare in the advanced countries' (ibid, 52–53). Most other countries 'have not yet reached this scientific, technological, and economic progress of Western Europe, North America and Japan' but their endeavour is 'to achieve the same aim' (ibid., 53), namely 'this dominating modern culture with its characteristic scientific, technological and rational economic thought and concepts, [where] universities, banks, and factories are the main centre of activities and achievement' (ibid.). And since the 'advanced modern languages' are 'expressing the same ideas and concepts, which form the core of modern culture or civilization', it 'will be a great advantage' 'when the basic notions and concepts of our progressive culture are as far as possible standardized and expressed in the same words deriving from the same root, that they are recognizable in all modern languages' (ibid.). The other languages are not only lacking scientific vocabulary, materials, etc, but 'also the totality of human thought, ideas, and experiences through the centuries'. Therefore the rhetorical question is posed whether they will still be able to 'catch up' (ibid.), and the advice is given: 'Is it not easier and more efficient for these nations to take the existing modern languages as the languages of their modern culture, which is dominated by the progress of science, technology, and economics?' (ibid., 54).

The concept of language death can be associated with this type of liberal ideology, whether in Eastern Europe, North America (the 'English Only' movement[30]), or in aid policies worldwide, these invariably supporting dominant languages while sometimes deploring the effects on smaller languages (but mostly not even noticing). At the individual level, language death would within this paradigm be seen as a result of voluntary language shift by all younger speakers, while the old ones die (see Gal 1996 for an overview of language shift theories). The speakers of minority languages would simply be seen as viewing bigger languages as more useful and functional, and therefore shifting over, in their own best interest, when wanting to 'modernize'—it is cumbersome and inefficient to have so many languages (see the American Ambassador in Insert 4.26). If we accept this type of anthropomorphizing of languages as organisms and believe (as it seems to me many linguists and politicians implicitly do) in some type of neo-evolutionary modernisation theory where 'knowledge of English is perceived as the precondition of all types of progress' (Mühlhäusler 1996: 84) the parallel seems to mean that those languages and cultures which 'respond to the demands' of modernity, technology, the information society and market economies, survive and spread, while those whose speakers 'cling to traditions', die—even if we may deplore this 'development'.

The **linguistic genocide paradigm** (which I hold to) claims, as argued in 4.2.3, that most languages at least today do not die a 'natural' death. Linguicide thus, by contrast, implies that there are **agents** involved in **causing** the death of languages. In the liberal ideology, described above, only an **active** agent with the conscious **intention** to kill languages (the first point in Cobarrubias' typology (see 5.1.1) would cause linguicide, whereas the next two (2 and 3) would fall within the domain of language death. In my view, the agents for linguicide can be **active** ('attempting to kill a language') or **'passive'** ('letting a language die', or 'unsupported coexistence', also often leading to the death of minority languages). And it is in relation to these two 'passive' policies that state policies, especially in education, are decisive today.

Linguistic genocide is one of the results of linguicism (Skutnabb-Kangas 1988: 13), an analogous concept to racism, sexism, classism, and ageism and coarticulating with these. I define them in similar ways (Definition Box 5.4), and will exemplify their coarticulation in chapter 6.

DEFINITION BOX 5.4   Racism, ethnicism, linguicism, sexism, classism, ageism

Ideologies, structures and practices which are used to legitimate, effectuate, regulate, and reproduce an unequal division of power and resources (both material and immaterial) between groups which are defined on the basis of
'race' (in biologically argued **racism**);
ethnicity and/or culture (in culturally argued racism, **ethnicism** (Mullard 1986, 1988) or culturism);
language (in linguistically argued racism, **linguicism**);
gender (in **sexism**);
class or social group (in **classism**); or
age (in **ageism**).

Since 1986, when I introduced the concept linguicism, it has mainly been studied in connection with the education of immigrant and indigenous linguistic minorities and in relation to the prominence of English as a 'world' language and the role of applied linguists in promoting English. Researchers on all continents have taken up the concept and many have found evidence of linguicism in their contexts. Critics of the concept (Davies 1996,[31] Conrad 1996) have done little to invalidate or refine it, whereas many researchers have started using it as a welcomed analytical tool and the evidence of linguicism worldwide is considerable (see, for instance, ironically, the contributions to Fishman et al. (eds) 1996; see also articles in Phillipson, in press). Some politicians have also started using it.[32]

Seen from the perspective of a conflict paradigm (which the linguistic genocide paradigm obviously is), the **causes** of linguicide and linguicism have to be analyzed from both **structural** and **ideological** angles. This covers both the struggle for and practices involved in the distribution of structural power and material resources, and the ideologies (and strategies) involved in legitimation, effectuation, regulation and reproduction of the unequal division of power and resources between groups based on language. Also the **agents** of linguicide/linguicism can be both **structural** (a state, e.g., Turkey vis-a-vis Kurds or Greece vis-a-vis the Turkish minority; an institution, e.g., schools; laws and regulations, e.g., those covering linguistic rights or the position of different languages on time-tables in schools; budgets, e.g., for teacher training or materials in certain languages) and **ideological** (norms and values ascribed to different languages and their speakers). In this chapter we have looked at state educational policy as the structural framework within which ideological agency was analysed. In chapter 6 we will move to macro-structural agency, and then, in chapter 7, to the legal human rights framework, to come back to education in chapter 8.

To conclude provisionally, I shall, rather than starting to build big new theories, present a very preliminary and modest pragmatic but perhaps provocative list, with many fuzzy edges, of some of the empirical differences between the two approaches I have mentioned, a list which could then lead to a development of a framework for properly theorizing the differences. With lots of simplification, one can force the tendencies into just two, one liberal, one radical (Table 5.3—from Skutnabb-Kangas 1999a). An interesting question for debate seems to me to be to what extent post-modernism, which poses in a new guise as a sophisticated alternative to what it calls either outmoded marxism or a mainstream approach, in fact shares several traits with those old evolutionary liberalist approaches which in development studies build on modernisation theories. Many of the overt arguments used by the researchers and politicians who advocate the benefits of homogenisation, and likewise the much more covert arguments behind the theorizing of both the archivists and, especially the postmodern critics of linguistic human rights, are based on some of the evolutionary premises. This is so even if much of post-modernism overtly distances itself from any further evolution whatsoever—History and the Great Stories and Theories are dead. Therefore it may be difficult to see that many post-modernist arguments,

TABLE 5.3
Linguistic genocide & linguistic imperialism versus language death
& liberalist modernisation paradigms/theories

Linguistic genocide and linguistic imperialism	Language death and liberalist modernisation
1. Analyses power relations between the language communities	1. Does not analyse power relations between the lg communities and objects to others doing so (e.g., Conrad 1996)
2. Sees languages as created by and therefore influencable by people	2. Sees languages as organisms with a natural life-span
3. Discusses presence of, support for, and consequences in relation to *both* languages	3. Discusses *either* the dominant lg (TESOL-tradition) *or* the dominated lgs ('archivist' endangered lgs tradition)
4. Wants to change the unequal relations between languages	4. Wants to document the lgs and make records of them before they die
5. Discusses the relationship between languages, including mutual influence	5. Does not discuss the relationship between the lgs, or does it only in linguistic, descriptive terms
6. Description is theory-driven and not sufficient in itself but basis for analysis	6. Descriptions technical and atheoretical; or theories come only from (socio)linguistics
7. More multidisciplinary; analysis impossible without using at least social and political analysis in addition to (socio)linguistics	7. Less multidisciplinary
8. More primordially oriented vis-a-vis the roles of lgs	8. More instrumentally oriented
9. Sees a qualitative difference between the roles of the MTs and later languages	9. Sees a quantitative difference only between the MT and later languages
10. Emphasizes the difference between additive and subtractive learning of later languages	10. Does not differentiate between additive and subtractive learning
11. Supports additive second and foreign language learning and multilingualism	11. Sees subtractive second and foreign lg learning as instrumentally necessary for modernisation, and as beneficial for the learners
12. Sees in most cases language shift as enforced	12. Sees language shift as voluntary, based on cost-benefit analysis by speaker

despite a celebration of multiple diverse choices and identities, and an interest in seeing how **we** create the world through the word (rather than choice for the majority of the world's population still being largely constrained by structural and ideological framing), are still exponents of the same old liberalist discourse.

In order to start checking some aspects of this interpretation, I have looked at some fairly recent books on 'language death' and 'endangered languages', to see whether titles and indexes signal anything about agency (I have **bolded** words which indicate less and *italicized* words which might indicate more of agency). This is, of course, a **very** crude first indication, but language professionals can (maybe?) be held more accountable than others for the labels they use.

In Robins & Uhlenbeck's edited 1991 volume, **Endangered languages**, the titles of the 10 articles talk about 'Language **Death** and **Disappearance**: *Causes* and circumstances' (Wurm), 'Language **Death** in Africa' (Brenzinger et al.), 'The Endangered Languages **Problem**: South America' (Adelaar), 'Endangered languages' (Cuarón & Lastra), 'The **Condition** of Native American Languages in the United States' (Zepeda & Hill), 'The **Decline** of Native Languages in Canada' (Kinkade), 'An Appraisal of Indian Languages' (Mahapatra), 'Endangered Languages of Mainland Southeast Asia' (Matisoff), 'The Endangered Languages of Australia, Indonesia and Oceania' (Dixon), and 'The **Problem** of Endangered Languages in the USSR' (Kibrik) (all emphases added). There is next to nothing in the titles to indicate that there are any outside agents involved: it is a problem that languages are in a sad condition of decline, they disappear and die.

In Matthias Brenzinger's edited 1992 volume **Language Death. Factual and Theoretical Explorations with Special Reference to East Africa**, we find similar agentless titles, with 'theory' or 'social contexts' or 'survey' of 'language death', languages have a 'fate' or 'decay', and many articles discuss 'language shift'. If we try to find entries in the index which might analyse causes related to power relations, the same picture prevails: the entry 'power' only refers to the following two sentences in the book:

> Which of the two languages influences which is a matter of prestige and power; it is also possible that both languages influence each other. (Sasse 1992: 65)

> We only really know that the Vumba must initially have had considerable prestige, and some kind of social, economic, political, or cultural power (it cannot have been military) over the Digo (and Segeju) in order to persuade them to act on their behalf against the Chifundi. (Nurse & Walsh 1992: 204)

The few references to 'dominance' or 'superiority' and the only one to 'subordinate position' in the index are vague, general statements to do with speakers of various African languages dominating each other. 'Colonialism' does not have an entry in the index. 'Genocide' is indexed twice, once in an article by Sasse (1992: 22), in a quote from a typology, secondly in the first sentence of the book where it is understood as physical genocide only and subsequently dismissed as of little interest to Africa:

> Setting aside the rare case of language extinction through genocide (in Africa only reported within the Khoisan language family so far), all instances of

language death are the result of language shift. Investigating processes leading to language death, therefore, means studying language shift situations. (Brenzinger & Dimmendaal 1992: 3)

Language shift is presented as a voluntary choice by the speech community, 'as a response to the changing conditions in the entire environment' (Brenzinger 1992: 224). These conditions seem to have to do with 'language characteristics and their assessment by the community' but 'also other language external factors' where, for 'the Yakoo community . . . environmental changes seem to have played an important role . . .' (ibid.).

In the language death paradigm, thus, either things just happen to the languages, naturally, because of their inherent characteristics (in the same way as 'globalisation' is presented, without active agents, see chapter 6), or, if there are any agents, these are a vague 'environment', without any kind of intentionality, or the speakers themselves who voluntarily shift.

But there is a parallel between the UN definition's 'transferring children' and 'shifting languages'. The main question then becomes: was/is this 'shift' voluntary—or was it forced? Would those who have shifted, rather had chosen the both-and alternative had it existed? Can a situation where there is no choice be labelled 'voluntary'? Earlier, means for people's livelihood were destroyed physically and intentionally, to force people to the mission stations, where their languages and worldviews were forcibly changed. George Washington: 'The immediate objectives are the total destruction and devastation of their settlements . . . essential to ruin their crops on the ground and prevent their planting more' (Diamond 1991) or 'hunting dogs were shot . . . confiscation of hunting implements' (Fesl 1993: 179). Today, globalisation and TNCs (TransNational Companies) destroy people's livelihood both physically and with 'cultural nerve gas' (Krauss 1992:6), to force people to 'modernise'—and this includes subtractive learning of dominant languages and cultures and worldviews, i.e., a shift.

Is using this 'no-alternatives' policy to be interpreted as 'forcibly transferring'? If it is, might it be the duty of the state to offer alternatives, i.e., enable people to get their basic needs fulfilled, without needing to shift? So that people have a **real** choice; so that they do not need to be in a 'no-alternatives' situation? If the state does not do this, does it have any legitimacy? If the state does not protect people against this forcible transfer, is the state guilty of linguistic genocide?

In chapter 6 on globalisation we also look at what the state does and does not do. In chapter 7 we look at a human rights oriented answer to the dilemma. But first we sum up.

There is in my view nothing 'natural' in language death. Languages cannot be treated in an anthropomorphic way, as organisms with a natural life-span. Some languages may have died (and some of the descriptions in, for instance,

Brenzinger's edited book (1992) on **Language Death** may be placed in this category—but certainly not all). Language death has causes, which can be identified and analysed. A great many of the world's languages have been eliminated in recent centuries as a (direct or indirect) result of European settlement and colonisation. The remaining ones have, through linguicist processes, been **hierarchized** so that speakers of some languages and varieties have more power and material resources than their numbers would justify, simply because of being speakers of those languages and varieties.

The analysis necessarily also involves an ethical dimension. Whether humanity has a moral obligation to prevent linguicide, or whether this would be interference in an inevitable process in which only the fittest survive, has been debated at several levels, some partly inspired by primordial romanticism, some by instrumentalist 'modernism'. An attachment to one's language or mother tongue as a central cultural core value seems, just like ethnicity, to draw on primordial, ascribed sources but to be shaped and actualised by (achieved) economic/political concerns. This also means that language shift **can** be 'voluntary' at an individual level: a result of more benefits accruing to the individual who agrees to shift than to someone who maintains her mother tongue. But in most cases of language shift I suspect that either sticks, punishment, or carrots, economic or other benefits, or ideological persuasion, hegemonic mind-mastering as described in this chapter, have been at work—meaning linguicist agents. Later in the book we will also see that when people are forced to shift their languages in order to gain economic benefits of the kind which in fact are bare necessities for basic survival, this is a violation of their linguistic human rights.

Most states participate in committing linguistic genocide in education. We have already mentioned some of the reasons for this. In the following chapters we will continue to look at additional basic macro-level factors.

NOTES

1. Using the term 'idiom' (rather than 'language') signals that it really means 'what the parents speak (or sign)', regardless of whether this is called a language, a dialect, a sociolect, a vernacular, or whatever—it does *not* need to be the standard or official language of the area/country or what people have replied in census questions about mother tongue, or be written.

2. See also discussions in Granville et al. 1997, Joseph & Ramani 1998, Mathew 1997, Tully 1997, as compared to **South Africa's New Language Policy. The Facts** 1994.

3. For sign languages the answer is: **very** few, in less than 10 countries—see examples below.

4. Of course we have to remember that federal states (like Germany or the USA) are here counted as one state.

5. Should Somalia be here? According to Kaplan & Baldauf 1997, 337, Somalia has 4 official languages: Somali, Arabic, Italian, and English. On the other hand, Crystal (1997) does

not have Somalia, neither does de Varennes (1996: 441) who quotes the Constitution (from 1979), Art. 3.2:

> 2. Somali is the language which all Somalis speak and through which they recognise each other, Arabic is the language which links the Somali people with the Arab nation, of whom they are an intergral part, and the two languages shall constitute the official languages of the Somali Democratic Republic.

6. De Varennes (1996, 445) quotes the Constitution, Art. 18:

> 1. The official language of Sri Lanka shall be Sinhala.
> 2. Tamil shall also be an official languages.
> 3. English shall be the link language.

7. It is interesting to see what are—and what are not—counted as territories: 'Europe's' 17 territories where English is significant (and where 3 are shared with French, 1 with Spanish), include 'the 4 parts of the UK', but many other areas which could just as well be labelled 'territories' (they have a distinct language policy; they have their own parliaments) have been omitted. Catalunya and the Basque country are not seen as territories, neither are Åland Islands, whereas the Faroe Islands are—but then they make the 'English' category larger, because Faroes are, together with Denmark, Sweden, and Norway included in the 17 territories in Europe where English is 'significant', whereas Iceland and Finland, with exactly the same position for English as the other Nordic countries, are not. McArthur 1996: 13 lists 228 territories.

8. McArthur writes 112, but his figures give in fact 114.

9. See Jenny Cheshire (1991) and Urs Dürmüller's (1994) completely contradictory accounts of to what extent English is or is not a lingua franca in Switzerland.

10. It is a matter of value judgement how the difference is defined. As far as I know, the only country which has given a time limit for when a minority becomes national (and their language therefore a national or domestic minority language) is Hungary where the legal limit is 100 years. If the time limit were to be higher than 100 years, for instance 250, English would not be a national/domestic language in many countries (for instance Australia, New Zealand and South Africa would not qualify), and if the limit was, say, 600 years, Britain would be alone with English. A sizable presence of native speakers is also often used as a test—English would then be a national or domestic language in Australia, New Zealand, and South Africa—and, for that matter, in Canada and the United States of America—but not in Kenya or Tanzania. If the origins of the native speakers are also taken into account, the question would be whether those countries where most of the native speakers of English are of non-Anglo origin would count or not. If not, for instance India and Nigeria would not qualify.

11. Many Western sources do not seem to get these right; Graddol (1997: 12) in his list of Scheduled languages leaves out Gorkhali/Nepali, Konkani, and Manipuri which were added in 1992, and also spells Telugu as 'Telegu' (and so does de Varennes 1996: 411). Again, I am sure I have similar mistakes.

12. There is an ongoing debate about the appropriateness of the term 'Bantu' in linguistics.

13. These prefixes are particular to each of the languages. Amongst others, Themba Msimang, former Head of the Department of African Languages at UNISA, South Africa's largest university, has pointed out that they are not transferable across languages. When, for instance, Zulu speakers speak in Zulu about the language Venda, they cannot use the prefix 'Tshi' which Venda speakers themselves use when they speak about Tshivenda in their own language. Just like English speakers do not talk about 'Deutsch' (which is what German speakers say about themselves in German), it is not racist/linguicist to drop the prefixes when discussing the African languages in English—the message from the prefix is expressed in other ways in English. Likewise, when a Xhosa speaker refers to the English language

in Xhosa, she will use the term 'isiNgesi', without causing offence. However, Kathleen Heugh (the source of the information above) points out that because of the legacy of apartheid, some non-linguists have misinterpreted the dropping of the prefixes as racist. No linguists were involved in the negotiations when the terms were included in the Constitution with prefixes. Likewise, because of lack of specific linguistic knowledge, several groups are marginalised in the Constitution. It uses the term 'Khoi' rather than the linguistically correct 'Khoe' (see Info Box 5.9 for the exact wording). It mentions specifically 'Khoi, Nama, and San languages'—singling out Nama which is one of the many Khoe languages (see Traill 1995) and thus 'altering constitutionally, through linguistic ignorance, a very contested area, altering reality, and creating space for much unhappiness amongst tiny, already marginalised communities' (Heugh, January 1999, personal communication). See also articles in Mesthrie (ed.) 1995, especially Bailey a and b, and Mesthrie. It also makes reference to only one of South Africa's sign languages, intelligible mainly to Afrikaans and English signers, and calls it South African Sign Language—see also my earlier discussion about recognition of only one sign language per country as official, in the best case; see also Penn & Reagan 1990. See LANGTAG 1996, Ridge 1996, **South Africa Survey 1996/97** for overviews.

14. Again, there is some confusion in the literature, partly because the final names of the languages, now in the new Constitution quoted here, have not been clarified earlier: the Interim Constitution of 1993 had, for instance, in its Article 3(1) on official languages both 'Sesotho sa Leboa' (also called Pedi or Northern Sotho) **and** 'Sesotho'. But there is also some ignorance about the languages, even among scholars. For instance, Kaplan & Baldauf 1997 get the names right in their table, p. 226, but list both North and South Sotho, **and** Pedi in their Appendix on languages in various countries (p. 337) and leave out Tswana so that the number of official languages remains the correct one, 11. No doubt I make similar mistakes myself.

15. International Convention on the Prevention and Punishment of the Crime of Genocide, 9 December 1948, 78 U.N.T.S. 277, entered into force 12 January 1951. The term 'genocide' was coined as late as 1943, by the Polish jurist Raphael Lemkin (Ignatieff 1998: 123). See Capotorti 1979 for details and context and, e.g., Leo Kuper 1984 for an introduction.

16. To Joan I, with my 'round pink cheek', evoked 'this aura of a cuddly Easter Bunny'. She knew that was not everybody's image, and tells about a male colleague's comment, after a discussion I had with him: 'Easter Bunny, huh? Maybe a pink Malcolm X' (Wink 1997: 72–73).

17. There is a very large legal literature about the Genocide Convention and e.g., Freedman's 1992 book has a useful bibliography.

18. The overview is necessarily simplified and the reader is advised to consult more thorough sources. For Sweden, see, e.g., Lainio 1997, Wingstedt 1998, Wande 1988, 1996; for Norway, Balto & Todal 1997, for the USA, Crawford 1995, 1997, Heath 1981, Hernández-Chávez 1988, 1990, 1994, Kloss 1977, McCarty 1997; for Canada, Cummins & Danesi 1990, Cummins & Swain 1986, Genesee 1987, 1996, Gérin-Lajoie 1997, Heimbecker 1997; in general, Cummins & Corson (eds) 1997 and Baker & Prys Jones (eds) 1998 are useful resource books in English. Also more general overviews about indigenous peoples can be useful, as, for example, the Minority Rights Group's reports (e.g., James Wilson on Canada's (1982) and USA's (1986) 'Indians' and Suter & Stearman's (1988) on Aboriginal peoples in Australia. Literature abounds.

19. A pseudonym, necessary for protection of his family in Kurdistan, just like in Insert 4.20.

20. 'Butterfly collection' is the name Peter Mühlhäusler uses of examples he has kept collecting for most of his life, without rigid systematisation. Qualitative representativity might be an end result. He also gives many examples, similar to mine, of physically punishing children in his 1996 book from the Pacific (New Caledonia, Tahiti, New Zealand, Australia, Korea, and dozens of other places).

21. The scale was different, with only three Sámi languages in Norway. In Papua, New Guinea, the Assistant Administrator Gunther is reported as saying in 1958 (Mühlhäusler 1996: 249): 'Teach them English, English and more English, this is what they want [presumably like Samoan parents who believed that "being educated" is learning to speak English, ibid., 248] . . . Only Christianity can replace the original philosophies, legends, pagan practices and supernatural fears that 510 tongues have engendered. It is only by removal of these 510 tongues and the acceptance of a common language that the end of many unnatural behaviours can be achieved.'

22. In some cases, children spent just the weekdays at the boarding school, because of the long distances and went home for the week-end. This would be the only form that would in my view be to **some** extent acceptable.

23. Teichelmann's analysis in his diary, 18 December 1844, of this intellectual cooption and hegemony was quite astute: 'It saddened me that Br [Brother] Meyer expressed his opinion during this evening when I had no opportunity to counter it in this situation, an opinion however false in itself, agreed to only because it fits into the Governor's plan, is siezed upon by him and used as authoritative but which must strike to the disadvantage of our Mission. Mr Meyer's reasoning goes like this: because I have not the necessary abstract concepts ergo they are not in the language ergo it is better to give up using the language altogether.' (quoted in Amery 1998: 150). In Mühlhäusler's (1996: 141) quote from Newbury 1961, Reverend Davies thinks that the 'Tahitian language, as may justly be expected, is destitute of all such words, common among civilized nations, as relate to the arts and sciences, law proceedings, trade and commerce, and most of those made use of in Technology & Science'. Likewise, the Moravian missionaries who had for long 'examined the world in search of the most degraded people and had discovered them in Victoria' (quoted in Fesl 1993: 90), claimed that 'the Australian dialects' were not worth examining as to religious things 'because they have no religion, no worship of any kind, no prayers . . . and therefore no terms to express anything of the kind' (ibid., 90–91).

24. It should be added that Finland is the 6th of the 174 countries in the UN **Human Development Report 1998** in the Human Development ranking index (our neigbours Sweden and Russia are 10th and 72th).

25. For some additions or alternatives, see, e.g., Banks & Banks 1995, Coelho 1998, Derman-Sparks 1989, García 1994, Gill et al. 1992, Igoa 1994, references to Krashen in the bibliograpy, Martin-Jones & Saxena 1995, Oller & Littlebear 1996, Risager, forthcoming. There are many references to alternatives in chapter 8.

26. As these are generally working class districts, they are dominated by the Social Democrats. In more bourgeois areas treatment would most probably be even harsher.

27. This may also be a factor in the US two-way programmes—see references to Donna Christian and Kathryn Lindholm in the bibliography for presentations and their evaluation; Dolson & Lindholm for an overview, and Skutnabb-Kangas & García 1995, García, in press and Wink & Wink, in press for some questions.

28. See, e.g., Ali Bucak 1989, Besikci 1990, Robins 1996, Wahlbeck 1999, Helsinki Watch 1990, Kirisci & Winrow 1997.

29. It is interesting that somebody should include a writing system (shorthand) when counting languages.

30. A good example of insidious pressure is the current movement in the United States to pass 'English only' legislation at State level (as 17 States have already done) and as an amendment to the Constitution. In the USA more than 30 million speak a language other than English in their homes. 'English only' measures create a climate in which speaking any other language than English is construed as unpatriotic and un-American. As a result of this trend, groups which are already marginalized in American society, Chicanas in particular, are likely to be deprived of education which might meet their cultural and linguistic needs, and of the right to vote in a language that they understand (Guerra 1988). Most of the arguments

used to promote 'English only' (see Crawford 1992a, b for these and their early refutation) are quite false, but it is not easy to repulse a populistic policy which builds on monolingual ignorance and societal anxieties and is marketed with a spurious scientific veneer (in addition to earlier references, see also Marshall 1986 and Padilla et al. (1991), early solid research efforts to scrutinize the arguments; see also Wiley 1998 for a comparison with the early position of other languages, especially German. Several of Heinz Kloss' early works are also illuminating—see bibliography. Adams & Brink (eds) 1990, Dicker 1996, Donahue 1995, Ricento 1996, Smalley 1994, should also be consulted.

31. It might be seen as symptomatic of Alan Davies' 1996 'Review Article: Ironising the Myth of Linguicism' that the originator of the concept linguicism is not even mentioned, neither in the article nor in the bibliography, despite the concept being in the title (or should we just take it as the 'normal' invisibilisation of women? He attributes it to my husband . . .). This is also true of some other critics, e.g., Berns et al. 1998.

32. An example: when Dr. B. S. Ngubane, Minister of Arts, Culture, Science and Technology in South Africa announced the establishment of The **Language Plan Task Group** (LANG-TAG) 12 December 1995, 'to advise the Minister . . . on devising a coherent National Language Plan for South Africa' (LANGTAG 1996: i), one of the four goals for the Plan was that 'The African languages which have been marginalised by the **linguicist** policies of the past should be elaborated and maintained' (ibid., iii; emphasis added).

Globalisation, Power, and Control

When everyone thinks alike, no one thinks at all . . . I consider the diversity of Yugoslav reality to be a fact of nature . . . Maintaining a life in tension between your native culture and foreign ones is doubtlessly exhausting since it forces you to examine the validity of your own assumptions. But that is the only productive way. Whenever we try to eliminate the tension, it comes back with a vengeance . . . The Serbian inability to accept differences reared its Medusa's head in Kosovo, long before the outbreak of war. (Debeljak 1996: 77, 79, 84)

Formal education in Africa and Asia in its present form tends to impede economic growth and promote political instability . . . [it] is an obstacle to development. (Hanf et al. 1975)

India occupies the eighth position in the world in book production, but it houses fifty percent of the world illiterate population. One major reason of this paradox is that people's languages are not used either for literacy or for primary education. Indian languages are developed neither as languages of knowledge nor as language of communication. (**Study of Languages** 1986: 25)

The record of the feminist movement shows that the struggle for liberation is multidimensional, with numerous platforms and strategies. Moreover, this struggle is intertwined with other movements which aim at the democratization of society—movements of the working classes, ethnic groups, race groups, etc. A dialectical perspective sees unity and solidarity in this diversity. (Mojab 1998: 28)

Henry Kissinger: 'I don't see why we need to stand by and watch a country go XX because of the irresponsibility of its own people.' (see Reader Task 6.1)

6. GLOBALISATION, POWER, AND CONTROL

In this chapter I try to place minority education in a wider social and political framework, highlighting some of the more macro-societal ideological, political and economic reasons for linguistic genocide. This shows how the education which many minorities receive serves to maintain an unequal division of power and resources in the world. First I will present one of the many ways of analysing forms of power. I analyse the attempts by the world's A team to maintain and reproduce control, and changes we experience in the forms of power and control. I am of course especially interested in the role that language plays in the reproduction of inequality and in intellectual and emotional colonisation—and decolonisation—of the mind more generally. I will also comment on how various types of inequality and various -isms (classism, racism, sexism, imperialism) work together and coarticulate, and how they work partially through similar strategies. Then a main political reason for linguistic genocide, the problematic relationship between 'nation-states' and ethnic groups and their languages, will be discussed, including myths about the role of language in 'ethnic' conflict. Finally, globalisation in several areas is described cursorily, and it is concluded that a 'free market' response to present global changes is a disaster for linguistic and cultural diversity as well as for the environment. A human rights oriented alternative is then discussed—human rights are supposed to act as correctives to the free market. But start with the Reader Task 6.1!

Reader Task 6.1
Democracy—mutual respect for the will of the people?

Fill in the 'right' XX word in the Kissinger quote above. It was said about Chile before the USA organised the murder of the elected president, Allende. Try out different words! Fascist? Capitalist? Democratic? Christian? Free? Muslim? Equality-oriented? Take your favourite hate and love characteristics. Do you agree with the opinion expressed by Kissinger? Do you agree more, or less, when you change the word? Why?

Kissinger's hate word (the 'correct' one in the quote) was 'communist'. If this was/is a guiding principle in American foreign policy, how would the content of democracy be defined? Is democracy 'Us' forcing 'Them' to do what 'I' want? What is the role of reciprocity? Would Castro's Cuba be democratic in the eyes of a Kissinger if Cubans said and acted out Kissinger's opinion above but changing 'communist' to 'capitalist'? How much is democracy about **forms** of governance and how much about content?

If democracy is about **forms** of governance, are a multiparty system and free elections a guarantee of democracy? 'What we've got now in the United States is one party, two names. We've got Republicans and Republicans Lite', according to Jesse Jackson, the Black leader. 'Britain has become a single-ideology state, with two principal, almost identical factions, so that the result of any election has a minimal effect on the economy and social policy. People have no choice but to vote for political choreographers, not politicians. Gossip about them and their petty intrigues, and an occasional scandal, are regarded as political news'—this is John Pilger's analysis (1998: 98), substantiated by evidence in a 678 page book. Are elections 'free' if apathy ('it does not make the slightest difference') makes people stay at home on election day (American presidents are mostly voted into power by a third of the population or less), or if half the time of those voted in goes to collecting money for the next campaign to stay in power (see Insert 6.6).

If democracy is about **content**, who decides what content is acceptable? Is it increased homogenisation? Or does democracy mean maintenance of diversity (or, rather, a combination: simultaneous homogenisation in some areas and even more diversification in others, some of them counteracting or at least not contributing to democracy—like income distribution, or trademarks for tooth paste)? Is linguistic diversity necessarily part of those aspects which need to be homogenised, in terms of both semantic content (like parties are claimed to be above) and form? What are the roles played by language in homogenisation, and in globalisation in general?

6.1. IDEOLOGICAL REASONS—POWER RELATIONS

6.1.1. Who Has the Power and the Material Resources in the World?

6.1.1.1. *The Growing Gaps*

Regardless of which indicators we use, the gaps in the world between the haves and have-nots have grown, and unless really massive changes happen, those have-nots who are already alive will become never-to-haves. Info Boxes 6.1 through 6.5. present some figures and quotes, but similar figures could fill hundreds of books—and they do. It is not a question of us not knowing, it is a question of lack of action, based on lack of political will. The growing gaps suit the A team.

❖ Info Box 6.1 ❖

70 Countries Have Income Levels Lower Than 25 Years Ago

'Despite overall global economic growth, 89 countries are worse off economically than they were 10 or more years ago; in 70 developing countries today's levels of income are less than in the 60s or in the 70s; in 1975–85 global economy grew 40% but only a minority of countries benefited and, at the same time, the number of poor people worldwide increased by 17%' (**HCHR News** 1:8, November 1996: 2); 1.3 billion people still live for less than 1 dollar a day (**Human Development Report** 1998, from UNDP—United Nations Development Program, see Address Box 6.1)).

❖ Info Box 6.2 ❖

Growing Disparity Between Poor and Rich in the USA, Britain and Australia

In the USA the disparity between the haves and have-nots is widening and 'more marked now than it has been for more than 60 years . . . the richest 1% own more than the bottom 90% of Americans', at the same time as '90% of the budget cuts the last Congress passed were taken from the poor' (Walker 1997: 6). A quarter of the adult British population lives in poverty. 'The gap between well-off and poor in Britain and Australia is the same as in Nigeria, much worse than in Jamaica, Ghana or the Ivory Coast and twice as bad as in Sri Lanka or Ethiopia' (according to United Nations Development Program, quoted in Pilger 1998: 104).

'Up to 2 million British children are suffering ill-health and stunted growth because of malnutrition, according to . . . **The Hunger Within**, a report by the School Milk Campaign [which] blames the Government for cutting free and cheap school meals and milk provision—the only source of nutritious food for many poor children' (reported in **Guardian Weekly** 19 January 1997, p. 8). Remember Margaret Thatcher's nickname when she started this: Thatcher the Milksnatcher. 'Poverty on a scale not seen since the 1930s is blamed for the return of rickets, anaemia and tuberculosis' (ibid.). Anaemia from lack of iron 'affects both mental and physical development', and so does rickets, from lack of vitamin D, all now common in Britain.

❖ Info Box 6.3 ❖

What Do the Richest 20% Earn, Own, Use, Eat?

In 1960, the richest 20% of the world earned 70% of the world's income, 30 times as much as the poorest who got 2.0%. In 1991 the share of the richest was 80% and the poorest got 1.4%, according to **Human Development Report 1996**. Now (**HD Report** 1998) the richest 20% earn 82 times as much as the poorest 20%, consume 86% of the total private consumption in the world, eat 45% of all meat and fish, use 58% of the energy, have 74% of all the telephone lines and 87% of transport vehicles. In East and South Asia, there are 5 cars per 1,000 people, in Sub-Saharan Africa 11, and in the industrialised countries 450 (**Human Development Reports** 1996, 1998).

3 Families Have More Private Property Than 48 Countries Together;
225 Billionaires as Much as Half the World's Population

The poorest 48 countries, so called LDC's (Least Developed Countries), have 0.4% of world trade. Taken together, the private assets of Microsoft director Bill Gates, the Walton family (owners of the supermarket chain Wal-Mart) and the Sultan of Brunei or the investor Warren Buffett (equally rich), are bigger than the Gross National Product of the 48 LDCs. The richest 225 individuals in the world have total assets equalling those of the poorest 2.5 billion people, some 45% of the world's population—only 2 years earlier 358 rich exploiters amounted to this (source: **Human Development Report** 1998 from UNDP—United Nations Development Program).

European & American Pet Food Costs Alone ($112 Billion)
Could Finance Basic Health and Food (85) and Education (39)
for All in Underdeveloped Countries

The cost to finance for everybody in underdeveloped countries (in billions of dollars) would be:

   39 for basic education

   59 for water and basic hygiene

   79 for reproductive health and sexual rights for women, birth control, health clinics, etc.

   85 to ensure basic health and food

What did We use in one year, 1997? All of us (W = World), or 'Europeans' (E), or 'Americans' (i.e., USA, A), or both E + A.

   27 for icecream (E)

   53 for cosmetics (A)

   79 for perfumes (E+A)

   112 for pet food (E+A)

   230 on representation (Japanese business)

   329 for cigarettes (E)

   692 for alcohol (E)

   2,635 on drugs (narcotics) (W)

   5,138 on armaments (W)

(Source: **Human Development Report** 1998 from UNDP—United Nations Development Program)

. . . and thus we could go on, and on, and on. A useful source for information of this kind is the United Nations Development Report Office, Address Box 6.1.

```
* * * * * * * * * * * * * * * * * * * * * * * * * * * * * * * * * * * * * * * *
*                                                                            *
*          Address Box 6.1   United Nations Development Report Office         *
*                                                                            *
*     336 E. 45th Street, Uganda House, New York, N.Y. 10017, USA; phone     *
*     1-212-906 3661; fax 1-212-906 3677; Web-site <http://www/undp.org/     *
*     undp/hdro>. The Web-site has links to a number of useful places for    *
*     information on many of the issues in section 6.3.                      *
*                                                                            *
* * * * * * * * * * * * * * * * * * * * * * * * * * * * * * * * * * * * * * * *
```

6.1.1.2. *The A Team and the B Team*

What is abundantly clear is that not one child or adult would need to suffer from hunger, or lack of basic amenities—all could have their basic needs met tomorrow; we do have the resources. Likewise, it is abundantly clear that those who could make the change do not have the political will to make the changes—quite the opposite. What is equally clear is that both material resources and structural power are unequally distributed between different groups in the world. When we look at the background for the various figures above in detail, it is easy to see that the material resources and the power are distributed in ways where people at the low end and people at the high end **at group level** systematically share other 'characteristics' too, in addition to the uneven access to material resources. We can sum up some of these 'characteristics' by listing some of the main indicators of oppositions/conflicts in the world. These are oppositions in the sense that being close to one end of the continuum on the list of 'characteristics' means a higher probability at a group level of having either more, or less, access to material resources and structural power than the size of the group would make fair in a world where these assets were shared equally. They are conflicts as long as the distribution is hugely unequal—even if the world is *not* a zero-sum game (meaning it is not necessarily the case that me getting more always must mean that you get less).

There is thus an 'A team' which has access to more power and material resources than their numbers would justify, and a 'B team' which has access to less power and fewer resources than their numbers would justify (see Table 6.1). The Table should be read as follows: At a group level, people from 'industrialised countries' have more access to material resources and structural power than people from underdeveloped countries (see Insert 6.1). Likewise, at a group level, people with more formal education have more

TABLE 6.1
Who has the power and the material resources in the world?

MORE—A team	LESS—B team
1a. Developed countries; or 1b. Industrialised countries?	1a. Developing countries; or 1b. Underdeveloped countries
2a. 'Whites'; or 2b. 'Pig-pinks'?	2a. 'Black', 'browns', 'reds', 'yellows', etc.; or ?
3a. Educated, literate; or 3b. (Much) formal education; inorate	3a. Uneducated, little or no education, illiterate; or 3b. (Much) informal education; orate
4. Urban middle or upper class	4. Rural or working class
5. Men	5. Women
6. 'Majorities'/dominant groups or layers of society	6. Minorities (national, immigrant, refugee/dominated groups); Indigenous peoples
7. Dominant language speakers	7. Dominated language speakers

INSERT 6.1 'Uneducated', 'illiterate' and 'developing'—setting the norm

Language plays an important ideological role in the construction of the groups to be glorified (i.e., here the A team) and stigmatised (the B team), and in rationalising the relationship between them so that it seems more fair: based on characteristics in each; positive in the A team and negative in the B team. Especially the terms used in the first three columns are clearly ideological. We have already discussed 'white' versus 'pig-pink'.

The American President Harry S. Truman created the 'developing' countries discursally when he in his inauguration speech on September 20, 1949, hierarchised the world, and set the norm, with the USA on top and the 'underdeveloped areas' placed under 'our' guidance, towards 'our' progress and 'our' democracy:

> We must embark on a bold new program for making the benefits of **our** scientific advances and industrial progress available for the **improvement** and **growth** of underdeveloped areas.
>
> The old imperialism—exploitation for foreign profit—has no place in **our** plans. What **we** envisage is a program of development based on the concepts of democratic fair dealing (Truman 1949, quoted in Esteva 1992: 6; emphases added).

(Continued)

The countries were in need of improvement; growth was the answer; it was to be achieved with **our** plans and science (see Harding below in 6.3.1.1 for how much 'ours' it was), so that we could make the fruits of our industrial progress 'available' to them, at a price (i.e., sell to them), and they were to be molded according to **our** concept of democracy. For critical accounts of the construction of the whole concept of 'development', see Escobar 1995, 1992, Esteva 1992, Sachs 1992a, b, Galtung 1980, 1988; also Galtung 1972; for education, e.g., Reagan 1996).

When terms like 'developing' (which followed when 'underdeveloped' was seen as too stigmatising) and 'developed countries' are used, it is clear already from the words who represents the norm (and is thus to be glorified and emulated) and who is deficient in relation to the norm. But in 'developing', the stigmatised Other are not directly blamed (as they were in the 'old' 'underdeveloped'). Now they are promised carrots: if they do X, Y, and Z, they will become like Us and then they will 'deserve' to have more material resources and structural power. As we know, these promises are almost never fulfilled—if the B team starts to approach the norm, the norm is changed (see Reader Task 6.3 for an example).

I use 'underdeveloped' partly in Walter Rodney's sense (1983) in his book **How Europe underdeveloped Africa**. He describes the conscious underdeveloping by Europeans—which still continues, even when it is masked as 'aid' and 'development cooperation' (see Tomaševski 1993b for a critical human rights account of this 'aid', and Rosas 1995c on the right to development). It is a pity that the English language is so poor that the difference between the two senses of 'underdeveloped' has not been lexicalised—many non-Indo-European languages have separate words, depending on whether the agent is the country itself or outside (and/or intentional) forces (like the Finnish: alikehittynyt vs. alikehitetty). In early development—underdevelopment theories (which Rodney represented) the two were causally connected: 'our' development caused underdevelopment in other areas. More sophisticated, less deterministic theories have been developed since and the literature in the area is enormous (see, e.g., Sachs (ed.) 1992 and Escobar 1995 for a good start). It is still unsatisfactory that there are no adequate terms for the so called 'developed' countries—please try to find one! Some more differentiation of the countries is presented later.

Also terms like 'illiterate' (or *'analfabet'* as in the Scandinavian languages) belong to the same ideologised category, defining one group as the unspoken, positive norm, and defining the other group negatively, in relation to what they do *not* know (and additionally, in an ethnocentric way: no other writing systems except (Roman?) alphabets qualify). Since there are positive aspects in both literate and oral cultures, representatives of both should be defined equally: either both positively, in terms of what they know (i.e., literates and orates) or **both** negatively (illiterates and inorates). Literates often pay a price, lose some of the benefits of fully orate cultures (for instance their superior memory strategies[1]) when they become literate.

INSERT 6.1 *(Continued)*

'Education' is likewise often understood as only formal education, and the well-organised informal education systems (like the one described by Jernsletten in chapter 1) are invisibilised, not seen as education (see also Reagan 1996 and my review of it). Still, they often display many of the characteristics that good experimental formal education tries to imitate: low student-teacher ratio, instant application of knowledge and instant task-related gratification, feelings of relevance for the student and the community, combination of cognitive, affective, and behavioural aspects of learning rather than only the head going to school, etc.

---

access to material resources and structural power than people with little formal education, and so on. In Insert 6.1 we look at the role of language in not only constructing the teams but also in legitimating the unequal access and distribution.

Let us nuance and discuss some aspects of this obviously very crude Table. Firstly, it is important to remember that we are discussing **statistical probabilities, at a group level**. We are also in most cases discussing **continua** rather than binary oppositions (which in any case would be simplistic, not very helpful, and not in line with the epistemological paradigm of this book[2]). There are many exceptions, not only at an individual level but also at a group level, and many groups are difficult to place. Internal gaps within each category are also growing, as some Boxes have shown.

Secondly, we could obviously also add several **more oppositions**—there is, for instance, nothing about religion, or age, not because they are not important, and not even because there are no concepts for describing discrimination because of them (there are—e.g., 'ageism'), but because they are to some extent less central to the other concerns of this book.

Thirdly, our general 'characteristics' are, of course, just as our identities, **multiple** (see the discussion about multiple identities in 3.4.3): we are as individuals at the same time members of a gender group, a generation, an ethnos, a professional group, etc., and can also be members of **two** or even more of some of them at the same time (e.g., **two** language groups). We can belong to one team in the Table (e.g., in terms of class) on the basis of **birth and childhood**, and another team in our **adult** life, i.e., we can change teams in terms of some of the 'characteristics'. We can belong to one team **'objectively'** (in terms of our social placement) and another one because of our **opinions and solidarities**.

When we place ourselves in the Table, many of us may therefore belong to **both** the A team **and** the B team, on the basis of our various placements. Try, using Table 6.1 (Task Box 6.2)!

Reader Task 6.2
Do you belong to both the A team and B the team?

1. My country is _____, therefore I represent the ____ team.

2. My skin colour is _____, hence ____ team.

3. My level of formal education is _____, hence ____ team.

4. My social class is _____ and I live in _____, hence ____ team.

5. My gender is _____, hence ____ team.

6. My group is a _____ group, hence ____ team.

7. My language is a _____ language, hence ____ team.

You probably noticed here too that it is in most cases not simple to place people. In 1, many have one **country** of origin and another of residence. For many economic and other purposes, countries are divided on a much more nuanced scale than the binary one in the first pair here, with 'industrialised' and underdeveloped.[3] In 2, biological **race** (in humans, at least) is not a scientific concept anyway and questions of sociological race are in many cases discriminatory and offending and used for control, in addition to mostly measuring people's prejudices rather than anything else (see the discussion about census quoestions in the USA, note 19 in chapter 3). Where the **formal educational level**, 3, should be placed is context-dependent: 10 years of formal education can be a lot (e.g., parts of Africa) or little (USA, Western Europe), depending on where in the world you are. In some countries almost everybody is 'middle **class**' (Scandinavia). '**Rural**' can mean luxury haciendas (A team) or villas (A) or part-time ecological smallholdings, with (A) or without (B) other income, or no land at all (B), and 'urban' can be rich or poor slums.

As we saw earlier, there are at least 44 countries in the world where there are no **linguistic majorities**: no language group represents 50% of the population. Likewise, in many of the countries where a former colonial language is an (or The) official language, the minority of the population who are native speakers or second or even foreign language speakers of this 'minority' language, usually have much more access to power and resources than those who speak a majority language or other minority languages. And so on. We will come back to the list, especially multiple identities, in discussing co-option (6.1.6).

Despite the crudeness of our measures, the differences are there and capture something basic. They construct a framework which influences our life chances.

6.1.1.3. *The Group With Most Power*

We can specify with the help of the characteristics in Table 6.1 who 'the rulers' are. They are the group which has **most power and material resources in the world**. They are the small elite which represents the A team in all respects: 'white' (see Definition Box 3.5), middle class urban males with a high degree of formal education from majority groups in industrialized countries, speaking majority or dominant languages. Centre-Periphery theories (e.g., Galtung 1980) first divide countries into the rich (the Centre) and the poor (the Periphery), roughly corresponding to the North-South divide, and then divide each country into its own Centre (the elites) and Periphery (the ordinary people, the masses). The A team elite, the rulers, are the Centre in the Centre. They are thus also the group which is primarily responsible for the present state of the world (of course together with the Centres in the Peripheries with whom they cooperate): they could alter the causes of war, famine, environmental pollution, torture, etc., just because they are the ones with most power. As a group they do not wish to (see Pilger 1998 for a devastating description). Says Ngũgĩ wa Thiong'o: 'Within nearly all nations today the centre is located in the dominant social stratum, a male bourgeois minority. But since many of the male bourgeois minorities in the world are still dominated by the West we are talking about the domination of the world, including the West, by a Eurocentric bourgeois male and racial minority (Ngũgĩ, 1993: xvii). Ngũgĩ's brilliant critique of the corruption and co-optation of power elites has forced him into exile from his native Kenya, after a year in prison without charges (see (Ngũgĩ 1982, 1987b, 1998). And Walter Rodney was so dangerous for the rulers of his country that he had to be killed.[4] Rodney wrote (1969: 19): '[The] association of wealth with whites and poverty with blacks is not accidental. It is the nature of the imperialist relationship that enriches the metropolis at the expense of the colony i.e., it makes the whites richer and the blacks poorer.'

Those who are **most deprived of power** are the groups which in **all** respects represent the B team: 'black', 'brown', 'yellow' and 'red' working class or rural women, orate or with no or little formal education, from underdeveloped countries, often from minority groups and speaking minority languages. The Periphery of the Periphery. To quote Margarita Papandreou in her welcome speech to participants at the conference 'Building a Europe without frontiers: the role of women' (1992: 12): 'The poorest of the poor are women. It has been called the "feminisation of poverty". And this is why we need a "feminisation of power" '.

Do we know how many people belong to the A team elites? The majority of the world's population is female, despite victims of infanticide being mostly female. 'Industrialised countries' represent, depending on the definition, 20–25% of the world's countries. Taking just the first two 'characteristics', males from 'industrialised countries' thus represent maximally 9–12% of the world's population. For every additional 'characteristic' ('white', urban, middle- or upper class, with much formal education, majority population, dominant language speaker) the numbers go down. Those who really rule us, the Centre of the Centre, are probably just one percent or two of the world's population. There is nothing new about this, though: the number of colonial civil/military servants was small too.

But if there are so few of them, how can they do it? That is actually what many of the chapters in this book have explored. If we wish for a world in which power and resources are distributed more equally, it is necessary to analyze the strategies which are used by the small elite to exclude others from power. The various forms for exerting power and control discussed so far in relation to minority education are one part of the strategies which the small power elite needs to use in order to stay in power. The power relations are regulated by processes captured in several -isms. And language is today central in and for many of these strategies. Other researchers have started to recognise this too (see Definition Box 6.1).

6.1.1.4. *The -isms: Racism, Ethnicism, Linguicism, Classism, Sexism, Imperialism, Neo-Colonialism, and ?*

Some of the main oppositions/conflicts in the world as regards power and material resources are expressed and reflected in -isms like colonialism, imperialism, racism, sexism, classism, ageism, etc. These -isms regulate the processes involved in the relationship between the A team and the B team. They regulate, legitimate, effectuate, and reproduce the unequal division of structural power and material resources in the world between groups which are defined on the basis of the central factor(s) in each -ism: 'race' in biologically argued **racism**, ethnic groups and their cultures in **ethnicism**, language in **linguicism**, gender in **sexism**, age in **ageism**, social class in **classism**, etc. (see Definition Box 5.4, p. 369).

In the conflict between women and men (conflict 5 in Table 6.1) **sexism** is the most important principle (see Jung 1987, 1994, for fascinating accounts). The conflict between different societal groups, as in conflicts 4 and 6 which

---

DEFINITION BOX 6.1 Cultural violence (Galtung)

Peace researcher Johan Galtung (1996: 31) sees cultural violence as serving 'to legitimize direct and structural violence, motivating actors to commit direct violence or to omit counteracting structural violence'. He divides **direct** violence into verbal and physical, harming the body, the mind or the spirit; **structural** violence into political, repressive, and economic, exploitative, and **cultural** violence by content into religion, law and ideology, language, art, empirical/formal science, cosmology, and by carriers into schools, universities, media.

partially overlap, is mainly a question of **classism** (see Joyce (ed.) 1995), whereas conflict 1 is a question of at least **colonialism, imperialism, and neo-colonialism.**

Racism (see, e.g., Banton 1987, Centre for Contemporary Cultural Studies 1982, Cox 1970, Donald & Rattansi (eds) 1992, Gilroy 1987, Miles 1989, Rex 1986, Rex & Mason 1986, Solomos 1989) is an element in several of the conflicts, most brutally in conflicts 2 and 1, but to a high degree in the conflict between majorities and minorities too, conflict 6. 'Imperialism . . . has been about racial domination as much as about who has economic and political power' (Savory 1995: 244). Here too, over and above brutal **biologically argued racism** (Miles 1989), it is often a question of more sophisticated forms of racism, **culturally/ethnically argued racism, ethnicism** (Mullard 1984, 1985, 1986a, 1988; see also Hutchinson & Smith (eds) 1996) and **linguicism.**

To me it is significant that we do not have a word for the -ism where inequality is based on formal education. Many concepts are the special field of intellectuals—we live off producing concepts and analyses, knowledge. This means that we to some extent get **our** unequal share of power and resources on the basis of this capacity. In Britain and many other countries the type ('public school boy') and level of formal education correlate closely with class, but 'educationism' is more than, and different from classism. We have created concepts for analysing those characteristics on the basis of which **others** get more than their share, but we make invisible the one which we ourselves profit from. Reader, find a name for this -ism! Educationism? Intellectualism?

6.1.1.5. *Coarticulation of the -isms*

When analysing an individual's or a group's position in terms of access to power and resources, we have to look at **all** the characteristics. In general, the more A team characteristics, the higher the probability of (unequal positive) access. But the characteristics are weighed differently in different countries and the combination of characteristics has to be contextualised. A few examples may make the complexity clearer.

Reader Task 6.3
Sexism: same trait—different labels

When women and men have the same trait of character or do the same thing, it is often labelled or interpreted differently. The labels in Table 6.2 come from Märta Tikkanen, a well-known Finland Swedish writer, and were used in Sweden in the women's movement campaigns in the 1960s and 1970s. Are they still valid? Continue the list or write your own! Do the same for racism. Compare with the list of labels for LEP/NEP in Insert 3.14. Is it the same phenomenon?

(Continued)

Reader Task 6.3
(Continued)

TABLE 6.2
Are labels the same for SHE and HE?

TRAIT	*SHE is labelled*	*HE is labelled*
stubborn	nagging	resolute
intelligent	domineering	logical, rational
looks ordinary	ugly	cozy
politically active	hysterical	aware, conscious
active	overactive	energetic
successful	full of intrigues	brilliant and hard-working
soft	feminine	?
bitter	?	?
sexually experienced	?	?

To what extent are characteristics where women are starting to overtake men, to fulfill the norm which earlier gave access to high positions and salaries, starting to be eroded and less valued? This seems to be true for, for instance, formal education (in several countries women now have more of it than men, often up to tertiary level—see gender indexes mentioned in Info Box 6.9, p. 400). Are medical doctors (Eastern Europe) and priests (Scandinavia) going to have less status and pay when the majority are women, as they might soon be? Find other examples!

The coarticulation between the -isms also makes it difficult to assess on the basis of which characteristics people are discriminated against most in various situations. Racism, for instance, coarticulates with other -isms (Miles 1989), and because every immigrant also has allegiance and identity in relation to the other identity groups in Table 6.1, it is often difficult to distinguish between the discrimination that an immigrant meets because she is an immigrant and the discrimination that she meets because she is female, or has little formal education, has a working class job (e.g., in an area with high unemployment in general, also for dominant group people), or comes from an underdeveloped country. The same person or group can also be discriminated against on the basis of one or several of her 'characteristics', or different ones in different situations. Sometimes a 'black' woman may be discriminated against in a situation where a 'white' man would also get the same treatment, if both have little formal education, i.e., it may be a question of classism rather than racism or sexism. The coarticulation of 'race', class and gender is often clear and cumulative—see Info Box 6.6. See also Corson 1992, 1993 for analyses of the coarticulation of gender and education, including the role of language.

❖ I n f o   B o x   6 . 6 ❖

Coarticulation of Gender, 'Race', and Class/Formal Education on the Labour Market (USA)

President Clinton said in a speech to the nation 19 July 1995 that unemployment among African-Americans is twice as high as among whites. The figures for Latin-Americans are higher. Women have started to earn more but they still earn only 72% of what men earn in corresponding jobs. The average earnings for a Latin-American woman with a university degree are still lower than the average earnings of a white male with a high-school diploma. In the largest private companies in the country only 0.6% of the top jobs have gone to African Americans, 0.4% to Latin Americans, 0.3% to Asian Americans; women have 3–5% of these jobs. White men form 43% of the labour force but have 95% of these top jobs (source: Thygesen, Erik (1995). 'Hvorfor er der så mange sorte blæsere?' (Why are there so many black wind players?). Interview with Bernie Richter and the basis of new fundamentalism in the USA, **Information**, 15.8.1995).

The coarticulation of racism and sexism is historically well known, as Insert 6.2 reminds us.

INSERT 6.2   Coarticulations of racism and sexism

From the sixteenth to the eighteenth century, it was common in art to depict both Europe and different European countries as female. But also other countries. In Ipswich on the wall in the Butter Market, built in 1567, 'Europe and Asia are both elaborately costumed, Africa and America nearly naked and savage' (Kiernan 1995: 145). (That was the time when the Chinese civilisation was still admired as something at some level equally 'civilized' as European civilisation.)

Both within and outside Europe, from very early on racist stereotypes were combined with sexist stereotypes ('a variant of the machismo that men everywhere have cultivated, with the aid of swords, beards, and other trappings and struttings, to impress and overawe women', as Kiernan (1995: 147) describes it. The 'effeminate peoples of Asia' (written around 1518) were seemingly easy to conquer for Alexander; Europeans were virile and other peoples effeminate, but there were differences also inside Europe: Kaiser Wilhelm II 'assured an Englishman in 1906 that the French were "a female race and a bundle of nerves, not a male race like the Anglo-Saxons and the Teutons"' (quoted in ibid., 148).

In California, the male/female ratio for indigenous peoples was normal when the Franciscan missions started, approximately 1.1 for all missions, according to Cook's 1976 analysis of the annual report statistics for the missions (quoted in Shipek 1987: 37). By 1834, the close of the mission period,

---

(Continued)

INSERT 6.2　*(Continued)*

it had changed to 1.35, i.e., there were 1.35 males for each female. All unmarried girls and women, and widows, were kept at the missions in special compounds, separated from families and from the men who lived outside the mission walls, and locked in at night to 'protect' them. The conditions, food, health status, etc., were much worse than in the villages, and the women could not 'move inland to the dry sunny valleys' during 'the cold, damp weather' and had a very high rate of respiratory diseases. All this reduced 'the number of women for bearing children in the next generations' (ibid., 38), i.e., was part of delayed genocide.

The practices of rape, sterilisation, forced abortions, etc., often coarticulate with racism today, in most parts of the world, and certainly in the West.

Gender and class can work in the same direction, as in Info Box 6.7, or they can partially cut across, as in Info Box 6.8.

❖ **I n f o　B o x　6 . 7** ❖

Coarticulation of Sexism and Classism Reproduced by 'Aid' (Africa)

'Mechanization of agriculture in Africa has tended to marginalize women. Their role as "custodians of earth" is threatened by male prerogatives in new and more advanced technologies' (Ali Mazrui 1996: 135). 'Aid', including IMF and World Bank loans (in 1994, underdeveloped countries paid back 169 billion dollars on their loans while they received 56.7 billion in 'aid'—source: **World Guide 1997/98**); see also Samoff 1998, Büchert 1996 and Brock-Utne in press for educationally oriented analyses), tend to favour larger agricultural units, reproducing and even further enlarging the economic and status and dominance gaps between genders, as captured by the poem (Mazrui, ibid.):

'When you see a farmer/On bended knee/Tilling land/For the family/
The chances are/It is a *she*.
When you see a tractor/Passing by/And the driver/Waves you "Hi"/
The chances are/It is a *he*!'

❖ **I n f o　B o x　6 . 8** ❖

*Gender and Formal Education Can Both Coarticulate
and Cut Across* (Sweden)

A Swedish study by Jan Einarsson (1978: 73–74) analysed markers of degree of trusting one's own knowledge and experience in similar interview data for

(Continued)

❖ **I n f o   B o x   6 . 8** ❖

(Continued)

female and male academics and industrial workers. He categorised expressions indicating **knowing** (know, am sure of, am informed about, have experienced, have discovered, research shows, etc.); **not knowing** (negation of the verbs above: I don't know, am not sure, don't have any experience, etc.); **believing** (I suppose, I think, I have a feeling that, I suspect, etc.) and **thinking, expressing own opinion** (as I see it, in my view, my opinion, I recommend, I disagree, hold, think, etc.). Table 6.3 shows the relative number of expressions of the various kinds when the length of the interview was held constant.

TABLE 6.3
Knowing, not knowing, believing, thinking—gender and education

	KNOWING	*NOT KNOWING*	*BELIEVING*	*OPINION*
Male academics	11.8	12.1	39.3	16.5
Female academics	9.0	28.6	27.1	13.3
Male ind.workers	7.9	13.7	26.2	22.9
Female ind.workers	5.7	30.5	30.3	18.4

Academics of both genders claim more often that they *know* something, as compared to industrial workers. Academics of both genders are more careful in expressing their **own** opinion. But both female academics and female industrial workers very often say 'I don't know', 'I have no idea', 'I cannot answer this question'. Male academics and female industrial workers share careful formulations about believing or suspecting something, but probably for different reasons. The connotations of, especially, 'believing' (*tro*) and 'thinking (*tycka*) are of course culturally context-dependent, and difficult to translate.

Language plays an important role in the coarticulation, as Insert 6.3 shows. In fact, often the same characteristic can be used for both exclusion and discriminatory inclusion, depending on context, as in the example in Insert 6.4.

INSERT 6.3 Coarticulation—speak English, be pink,
you are 'educated'. Read Zulu (or Xhosa)—you are not 'educated'.
Be dark and poor, speaking English does not help

'Some years ago, with an English speaking friend, I was in Germany (Stuttgart) on a working holiday. In order to obtain a work permit I had to queue at the local police station. We were the only English speaking people in the

---

(Continued)

INSERT 6.3 *(Continued)*

queue, most being Turkish or Greek. The police officer in charge perhaps overheard us speaking English. He left his desk and asked us to come to the top of the queue, saying: "Educated girls should not be standing in the queue with **these people**" ' (Example from Brent, UK, see Insert 5.12).

Black students and teachers in South Africa, according to Sarah Slabbert's study (1994; quoted in Kamwangamalu 1997: 243): 'In my school, if you know English, you are everything.' 'We identify an educated person with English. Once you see a person reading Zulu, you think that person is not educated.' Timothy Reagan's comment (December 1998, personal communication): 'True, **unless** the person is white, and then an entirely different (and far more positive) set of assumptions comes into play'. On the other hand, if you don't know English, no amount of formal education helps—white people think education is not education unless it has taught you English: '. . . people like students who are in schooling in Transkei, when they pass their matric—standard 10—and then come here to find a job, it's like they are lying if they [tell] they've passed standard 10, because they can't speak English. Because everything in the Transkei is being done in Xhosa' (from an interview with a parent in a township in Cape Town, Knudsen 1999: 100).

One of my Indian colleagues, Jennifer Bayer, put the contextualisation of exclusionary strategies like this: 'Earlier the poor in India were excluded because they "did not know any English". Now they are excluded because "they speak bad English" '.

INSERT 6.4 Damned if you are—damned if you aren't: Tribals not aboriginal (India)

Professor G. S. Shurye said in 1950 (to an educational committee, when discussing measures to improve 'tribal' education): 'Tribals are not aboriginal, not even tribals; they do not need preferential treatment.' (Frances Ekka, Central Institute of Indian Languages, himself 'tribal', interview, 29 January 1995).

In theory, it is always important for analytic purposes to try, despite the difficulty, to ascertain what the **main** basis of discrimination is, to distinguish between, for instance, the results of racism or linguicism and the results of classism. For educators, one of the distinctions which seems to be notoriously difficult to make is the coarticulation—or, as it may be, not—of problems in school which **may** be influenced by minority-related issues. There are many examples of cases where a child has been referred to special education or psychological treatment because of being minority (see Cummins' analyses in his 1984), but also of the opposite, where a minority child has not received the support needed, for instance, with reading or other problems, because the problem has been wrongly diagnosed as having to do with the minority status (see Lahdenperä 1997 for interpretations). In practice the issue is further complicated by the fact that the strategies used in the various -isms resemble each other and many of the -isms reinforce each other, in addition to coarticulating.

But we also have examples where B team achievements are invisibilised in the hierarchisations. We hear a lot about issues like women being over-represented among the people who do not read and write, and almost all of the 'illiterates' being in 'developing countries', i.e., coarticulation of sexist and classist/imperialist/racist (see Info Box 6.10) structures (1995 figures: world total of 'illiterate': 885 million; of these 565 female and 320 male (and of them 8 and 5, respectively, in industrialised countries) (UNESCO, **Statistical Issues**, October 1994, STE-16, Table 3). But we see much less seldom the figures which indicate, for instance, that many old industrialised countries have more sexist structures than several other groups of countries in other areas (see Info Box 6.9).

❖ **I n f o   B o x   6 . 9** ❖

Coarticulation of -isms—Women in Universities

Women in physics faculties in universities in selected countries in 1990 (Harding & McGregor 1996: 312) show the following order, starting with Portugal (35%), the highest: Portugal, Philippines, USSR (all over 30%), Thailand, Turkey, Italy, China (all over 20%), Brazil, Poland, Spain, France, Belgium, India (all over 10%), South Africa, German Dem. Republic, Austria, Netherlands, New Zealand, Australia, Chinese Taipei, Mexico, United Kingdom, Norway, Korea, USA, Canada, German Fed. Republic, Switzerland, and, as the lowest, Japan.

Likewise, numbers of female staff at universities as percentage of all teaching staff show that the percentages for countries like Canada, German Federal Republic, Norway, and Japan are considerably lower than those for, e.g., South Africa, Swaziland, Egypt, Saudi Arabia, Brazil, Colombia, Bulgaria, Hungary, Poland, and Albania, just to take a few examples (ibid., 314).

Many publications from international organisations give additional interesting information about results of many of the -isms (see, e.g., the gender indexes from UNDR and from OECD education indicators (from CERI, Centre for Educational Research and Innovation, for instance in **Education at a Glance** reports and **Education policy analysis** reports) but regrettably the coarticulation is not often analysed in them, and usually the figures are not given by language in these publications (except for Belgium where the Flemish and French speakers are often separated).

❖ **I n f o   B o x   6.10** ❖

Coarticulation—Less Money to Educate Minority Students

Expenditure per student in schools in Tanzania in colonial times: a Black pupil cost the colonial government 1.9 pounds, a so-called Asian 4.4 and a so-called European pupil 38.0 (Katende 1976, quoted in Yoloye 1986: 1). According to official South African statistics, education expenditure per pupil in Namibia is 232 rands for Blacks, 300 for so-called coloureds and 1.210 for so-called whites (Ellis 1984: 41). According to FIDEF (1978) the resources given to Turkish children in Germany are much smaller than those for ethnic German children, including salaries for teachers. This is true in all Scandinavian countries too: bilingual teachers are, often regardless of their training and competence, put in a different category from 'native' monolingual teachers (instructors, home-language teachers, class helpers)—and paid less.

As Info Box 6.11 shows, the coarticulation is complex indeed. The SAT, 'the closest thing we have to a national IQ test . . . rates a narrow range of academic-oriented skills' (Hacker 1995: 147), according to some 'reflect how adept people are at taking that kind of test' (ibid., 148–9). It is a multiple choice test of the kind that is notoriously biased in terms of the students' class background.

❖ **I n f o   B o x   6.11** ❖

Coarticulation of -isms—Students in USA Taking SAT

TABLE 6.4
Students in USA taking SAT

STUDENTS TAKING SAT 1993		Black	Hispanic	Asian	White
Average scores (AS)		741	803	950	938
AS of students from	N	36,034	25,180	19,827	60,324
Low-income families	AS	693	734	845	872
Family income (FI) $10–20,000	AS	705	753	860	874
FI $30–40,000		760	825	941	907
FI $50–60,000		798	875	999	942
FI $70,000 and over		871	918	1,082	1,006
Point gain: low to high income		194	215	258	140

(Continued)

❖ I n f o   B o x   6 . 1 1 ❖

(Continued)

STUDENTS TAKING SAT 1993		Black	Hispanic	Asian	White
FI over $40,000		24.8%	28.8%	43.5%	60.3%
FI under $20,000		38.4%	37.4%	27.4%	9.8%
Parents attended college		41.4%	38.0%	62.3%	62.7%
English not first language		8.4%	66.5%	70.4%	5.5%

SAT (Scholastic Aptitude/Assessment Test) scores run from 400 to 1,600. AS = average scores; N = number; FI = family income; based on figures in Hacker 1995: 146, 147, 148.

A follow-up of Yale University graduates showed that there was no significant relationship between the SAT scores and honors at the university or the graduates' standing within their occupations (ibid.).

What is interesting from our point here is the relationship of SAT scores to parents' levels of income and formal education, and to the mother tongue. A Reader Task here could be to discuss these relationships at the various income levels, and relate them to racism, ethnicism and linguicism. It is clear that the Black students suffer most of racism whereas classism and linguicism may explain more of the Hispanic scores even if racism/ethnicism are an important factor here too. As usual, the Asian groups overcome all these hurdles to some extent but very probably again **not** because of what the schools have done but **despite** it. For all three groups, the relationship between the parent's level of formal education and their income is fairly low.

The discussion so far has shown that language is important in creating and legitimating some of the -ismic discourses involved in the unequal divisions of power and resources. On the other hand, linguicism is only one of the several -isms. In the next sections we look at the role of language in power and control from other aspects.

6.1.2. Types of Power: Innate Power, Resource Power, Structural Power

It is necessary to proceed somewhat further with issues of power, in order to see the similarities in the power strategies involved in the different -isms and to be able to identify what types of strategies powerless groups, among them minorities, can use so as to obtain their 'rightful' share of the world's power and resources. Again, this is a central sociological and political science question, and theories abound: what is power, where does it come from, how is it used, is it something that 'is' and that individuals or groups can 'have', or not; is it (only?) created in discourse relations, and so on (for different but possibly complementary views see, e.g., Bourdieu 1977, 1992, see also Bourdieu 1998; Foucault 1980, Feldman 1991). I use theories of power developed by the Norwegian peace researcher, Johan Galtung (especially 1980) and develop them further to understand some of the concerns of this book, partially with the help of Bourdieu's thinking.

Galtung differentiates between three types of power: **innate power, resource power, and structural power.** Even if Galtung's model of power may at first sound as if power was something that *is*, rather than something to be negotiated, he sees power as a relational concept, as do I.

Innate power—being-power, we have inherited from our parents: intelligence, muscles, charisma, and so on. Many of the North American discussions about nature-nurture and about reasons for the position of 'black' people, from Arthur Jensen to the Bell Curve and beyond, see innate power as not only innate (see Insert 6.5) and thus difficult to change through the environment, through nurture, but decisive.

INSERT 6.5   Anglo-Americans have democratic
and responsible bones (Thatcher)

Based on an article in **Newsweek** (October 8, 1990), Maher & Yashiro (1995: 6) report on 'Mrs. Thatcher's view that the Anglo-American peoples possessed democratic qualities and world responsibilities "almost in their bones".'

Resource power is **having-power.** Resources can be **material** (capital, weapons, books, houses, cars) or **non-material** (languages, cultures, traditions, experience, education, knowledge, time).

Structural power one has by virtue of one's **position.**

I shall return to innate power and Galtung later and initially concentrate on the two other types.

6.1.3. How Is Power Maintained? The Relationship Between the Forms of Power

6.1.3.1. *Idealistic-Liberal: Power-Holders Have More Being-Power*

In an **idealistic-liberal** view, **innate power** (intelligence, muscles, charisma) is decisive for a person's fate. If one has 'chosen' one's parents well, one has inherited from them intelligence, a capacity for hard work and other characteristics which lead to the acquisition of knowledge and money. Other people trust a person with innate power and elect her/him to various positions, and thus the person acquires structural power. We thus have the power-holders we have earned: they are simply more intelligent, hard-working, etc., than others. The American Dream represents this idealistic-liberal view: if you are intelligent and work hard (= have a lot of innate power) you can achieve anything: you can become a millionaire (= material resource power) and you can become the President of the United States (= structural power)—it is up to You.

6.1.3.2. Materialistic: Resources and Structural Power Are Mutually Convertible

Johan Galtung's view (1980) is a **materialistic** one. Innate power is a social construction, an illusion. It is not, in fact, innate. Only **structural power and resource power** are 'real'.

I agree. Intelligence is a result of cooperation of nature and nurture, and possible to influence. So is the mental set-up of people. Liverpool's (UK) Department of Public Health's Annual Report 1996 'disclosed that one in three children living in the inner cities was suffering "moderate to severe mental health problems" **as a direct result of poverty**' (quoted in Pilger 1998: 111; emphasis added). A person's height, muscles, etc., are also influenced by the environment, for example, by the food (drink, smoke) consumed by the pregnant and breast-feeding mother and the infant, and the environment of mother, father, and child. At present, we are stunting the physical and mental growth of millions of children through malnutrition and environmental pollution, causing damage that is impossible to repair. My nightmares see a world where 'value invalids' (see Introduction) rule and try to control populations brain-damaged and mentally and emotionally stunted through malnutrition and poverty.

In Galtung's (or Bourdieu's, e.g., 1992) analysis, structural power and resource power are convertible into each other. If one has material resources (e.g., money), one can buy immaterial resources (e.g., knowledge, a 'good education', time), and with a good education one can get money (a high salary), i.e., one can convert one type of resource (money) to another type of resource (knowledge, time). A high structural position makes it possible to accumulate more resources, and resources provide enough knowledge about societal power structures (and money for an election campaign, for instance) for a person to be able to get into positions of structural power (see Insert 6.6).

Pierre Bourdieu's (1992) theories similarly posit various forms of 'capital': economic (material resources in our sense), cultural ('knowledge, skills, other cultural acquisitions, as exemplified by educational or technical qualifications' (Thompson 1992: 14); non-material resources in our sense) and symbolic capital ('accumulated prestige or honour', ibid., 14). Bourdieu talks about 'fields' or 'markets', seen as 'structured space[s] of positions in which the positions and their interrelations are determined by the distribution of different kinds of resources or "capital" ' (ibid., 14). An important property

---

INSERT 6.6 'Standing for power is a millionaire's game' (USA)

'Standing for power is a millionaire's game' has got it right. This article by Martin Kettle in **Guardian Weekly** (May 24, 1998, p. 6) relates the ever increasing costs for election campaigns in the USA where a Republican candidate challenging the Democratic senator seat has fundraised more than $10.2 million and is expecting to spend 'a further $15 million of his own money in the race for the Republican nomination alone.' Another millionaire 'has already spent some $30 million of his own money on the campaign for the nomination, we are told—this time to become the Democrat candidate for California governer. 'American electioneering—especially when you are challenging an uncumbent—is a rich man's sport.'

---

of the fields or markets is 'the way in which they allow one form of capital to be converted into another—in the way, for example, that certain educational qualifications can be cashed in for lucrative jobs' (ibid., 14).

6.1.3.3. *Social Construction of Power:*
A Team Constructs Socially B Team
Non-Material Resources as Invisible
or as Handicaps

In order to analyse the strategies which keep the A team in power, I find it necessary to extend Galtung's position of seeing innate power as a social construction. In keeping with Bourdieu and partly also Foucault, I also see resources, especially non-material resources, as social constructions. The 'worth' a painting is seen to have, or the opinion of how a person has to speak in order to get a high status job have very little to do with 'objective' criteria (see, e.g., Crandall 1992, Lippi-Green 1994, 1997, Miner 1998, Sato 1991 on court cases on language). To call a piece of paper 'money' or 'a check' and to be able to convert it to a house or a car whereas other pieces of paper cannot be so converted is likewise a social construction.

I would like to put it as follows. One of the most important A team strategies, used in all -isms, is to socially construct the A team's own resources, especially their non-material resources, so that only **these** are seen as The Resources, to be learned or acquired also by others. This is done by **glorifying the A team resources**, socially constructing the dominant languages (and their speakers) and cultures as Us, as the self-evident norms, the mainstream, valuable resources. Thus **A team resources are validated as convertible** to positions of structural power.

At the same time, the **B team resources**, especially their non-material resources, the linguistic and cultural capital embodied in the languages and cultures of the dominated, **are invalidated through the stigmatisation process**.

Their resources (and the minorities/dominated groups themselves) are socially constructed as Other, and treated as handicaps, deficiencies, rather than resources, as something to get rid of rather than to cherish. They are **constructed as invisible non-resources** which through this invalidation become **non-convertible** to other resources and to positions of structural power (Fig. 6.1).

In my way of theorizing, Bourdieu's 'symbolic capital' is part of the outcome of the validation process which all non-material resources have to go through. When some of them are validated and legitimated, they acquire symbolic capital. Others are invalidated, delegitimated, invisibilised, or made to seem handicaps, that is, they do not acquire symbolic capital. And it is only the non-material resources with symbolic capital which are convertible on the market where we increasingly trade in symbols.

Since only those non-material resources which are seen as valid and valuable, can be converted, the stigmatisation of minority languages and cultures

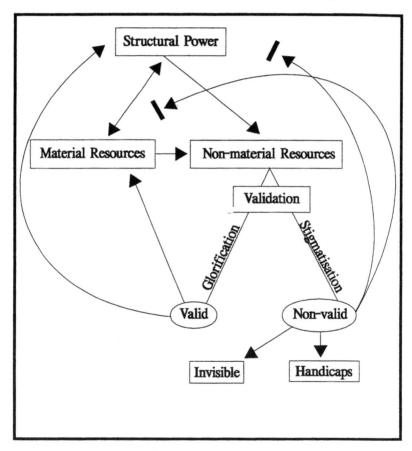

FIG. 6.1. The social construction of non-material B team resources as non-convertible (as handicaps or as invisible).

as non-resources leaves minority children without a starting capital at the outset. In order to start participating in the conversion process, a person needs a 'starting capital' of either valid resources, or structural power, or both. Children acquire their starting capital—or lack of it—from and via their parents, and it reflects the parents' position on the A and/or B teams.

A child with A team parents, with middle class jobs, time to spend with the child, a big house, many books, and so on, already accumulates in childhood many resources: care; enough food; linguistic book-oriented stimuli; formal education; help with home work; knowledge about how sectors of society, important from a power perspective, function; acquaintance with 'important' people; travel, etc. After school, the parents and their friends are, via their connections and knowledge, able to support the youth in finding the first job, which gives a fair salary (material resources) and new knowledge (non-material resources). These resources can later be converted into a better job, with a higher salary and a possibility to acquire more knowledge and connections which can again be converted, etc. etc.

By contrast, a child with working class/dominated group parents inherits the parents' lack of material resources and structural power, and can therefore not convert the non-material resources that the parents and she possess, to other resources or to positions of structural power.

Women's non-material resources are invalidated in both ways: they are either made invisible (e.g., home work is not salaried and is not part of the GNP) or made into handicaps (e.g., PMT, pre-menstrual tension). Barriers to women becoming bomber pilots or top level business leaders are still often legitimated with 'women's characteristics'. Women are still described as more emotional in important decision making situations, or more holistic and empathetic, not 'rational' and cool enough, or 'they don't want responsibility'. On the other hand, the 'female' characteristics are valued and taught (also to men) on high level management courses: empathy, flexibility, 'human qualities', holistic assessments; i.e., it is not the 'characteristics' themselves that matter but the gender of the person who 'has' them, and they are often labelled differently, depending on the owner.

When labour migrants or refugees come to a new country, they have, for obvious reasons, left their material resources behind them, if they ever had any. In most cases, labour migrants had very scarce material resources—the lack of them is usually a major reason for migrating. Some refugees may have had material resources but they may have lost them through their dissenting activities, or used them for the escape. Even when they have managed to convert (some of) them, these resources are not worth as much in the new country. With the money you get when selling a house in Paraguay or Kosova you cannot buy a house in Canada or Australia or Sweden. Usually labour migrants have not had any structural power either in their country of origin. Some refugees have had high positions in the power hierarchy, but in the new country they have little structural power.

What both labour migrants and refugees do have, in contrast, is non-material resources. All of them have their languages, their cultures, their knowledge and skills, in many cases a solid training and sometimes a lot of formal education. These would be a good symbolic starting capital, to start the conversion process into material resources and positions of structural power. But before they can become socially constructed as convertible capital, they have to be validated as such by those who have the monopoly on defining resources in the new country. And this is where the invalidation process starts. The more B team characteristics the migrants and refugees represent, the more their non-material resources, their knowledge and skill, their education and culture and their languages are invalidated.[5]

Since migrant and refugee parents only have these non-material resources, this has serious consequences for their children too: the parents cannot give their children much convertible starting capital in the new country. The only resources that the parents could give them (their languages, cultures, norms, traditions, etc.) are invalidated, and the children are told by the educational system (where their non-material resources are invisible) to get rid of them 'in their own interest', because they prevent the children from acquiring dominant group resources. Under this false belief, many children abandon their languages, cultures, identities etc., as we have seen in earlier chapters. But the educational system, with its submersion programmes for minorities, does not give them full access to dominant group resources either. This prevents minorities from getting access to their fair share of material resources and structural power, at the same time as it prevents them from constructing counterhegemonies, both structurally (through lack of resources) and ideologically (through the colonisation of their minds so that many of them are led to believe that the unequal division of power and resources is due to deficiencies in the dominated group itself, its linguistic and cultural characteristics, norms, traditions, etc.).

The education system invalidates and invisibilises the non-material resources of indigenous peoples in much the same way. Likewise, the non-material resources of the Peripheries in both Centre and Periphery countries are invalidated. The same processes and strategies can be described in the general ideologies in relation to the North-South divide, as well as in the West's attitudes towards the ex-communist countries of Eastern and Central Europe.

6.1.4. Grading of Control: Sticks, Carrots, Shame, and Ideas

Sticks, carrots, shame, and ideas as means of exerting power and control have been mentioned several times, and Table 4.2 presented a summary of the means, processes, and sanctions. Now we come back to them more systematically. First we look at the processes and sanctions involved in using the various means, using several types of concrete illustration to show the similar strategies in the -isms. We also look again at the changes in means used, especially in relation to language in education: starting from the use of punitive **physical** methods of control (physical violence when using the mother tongue) and punitive **psychological** measures (shame). Next we move to **remunerative** means (rewards and benefits in relation to the learning and use of a dominant language) and **ideas** (e.g., guilty conscience) in relation to both L1 and L2, and, especially, the relationship between them. Reasons for the changes are discussed, and the various means are related to the A team strategies. The less you resemble the A team, the more likely it seems to be that the more brutal means are used; the more you resemble the A team and the closer you are to the A team physically and psychologically, the more likely it is that more sophisticated means, including co-option, are used.

6.1.4.1. *Sticks—Physical Force*

The description of the use of sticks, carrots, and ideas below uses concrete, simplified, and generalised examples, without references, to emphasise the fact that these are common processes. The examples could come from anywhere in the world, at many times in history. The reader is invited to use her own examples.

Earlier if the one with less power did not obey the ruler or did not give to the ruler some of the fruits of her labour when the ruler demanded this, the ruler used **physical force** or threatened the use of physical force. A few examples from feudalism, sexism and linguicism.

What happened to a serf who did not want to give the sacks of wheat he produced to the big landowner? A landowner could come with his men and kill or mutilate or beat up the serf, and take all or most of the wheat that the serf had produced. Sometimes it was enough to say: if you don't give them to me, my men will kill you. In the agriculture of many countries similar processes still go on.

What happens to women who do not want to cook and clean and bear children to the husband, wash his clothes, give him sexual services, be nice and kind, i.e., reproduce him biologically and physically and mentally? The husband beats up the wife if she does not obey and 'do her duty', or he threatens to do it. This goes on in all countries. The figures for domestic violence, in all social groups, are growing in many Western countries, and official figures are just the tip of the iceberg.

And finally, what happened earlier to indigenous or minority children who wanted to maintain and develop their languages and cultures in the educational system? There are thousands of examples from all over the world of how minority children have been physically punished for speaking their own languages, even during the breaks, and during the free time in boarding schools, as earlier chapters have shown.

6.1.4.2. *Shame—Psychological Force*

The next phase in the use of power and control is often **shame**. The use of shame presupposes to some extent that at least some norms for proper conduct are shared. These norms can be taught and reinforced either in the extended family or institutionally, through religious teaching and formal education.

If the serf did not give the landowner what he 'owed' to him (the landowner being there instead of God or the King), he was taken to the church and had to sit outside or in the church and repent—and this was often effective.

Women have been and are ruled with the help of shame: when I was young it was scandalous to have a child extra-maritally. Shame was exclusively directed at the woman. For the man it was rather a mixture: stupid not to know how to avoid the consequences, but admiration because of the potency. A girl who became pregnant was often expelled from school whereas the boy father was not. This practice was also suggested by SWAPO (men) in the early 1980s for its first secondary technical school (in Loudima, Congo Brazzaville), until the Womens' Council protested.

To be lesbian was earlier of course even more shameful because the woman then, among other things, declared that she was not dependent on men, i.e., she claimed to be outside their power to control her. And even today, if your curtains are not as white as the neighbours', you are not a proper housewife. Shame on you if your husband looks scruffy or doesn't get proper food, or if your children go to school without having a proper lunch with them or with (unintended) holes in their trousers.

Several countries in the Council of Europe have tried for years to use shame to make Turkey stop at least some of the most brutal human rights violations against the Kurds, to absolutely no avail. Shame is in fact one of the very few means the United Nations can resort to, to enforce compliance. This was true in the first half of the century: 'the only weapons at the disposal of the League [of Nations] were those of moral pressure and wise negotiation' (de Azcárate 1945: 118, quoted in Capotorti 1979: 24). If it had not been so important for the Western powers to show their physical force and try out new weapons, and if they had thought that Iraq was more sensitive to shame, shame could have been used in addition to negotiations, when Iraq occupied Kuwait, and later, instead of the physical means (bombing, later sanctions).[6] The physical means have **not** been used against other countries which have also occupied land or/and developed weapons of destruction (e.g., Indonesia, Israel, or USA, just to take a few examples). Successful use of shame presupposes that the state in question shares the 'international' norms about what a country should not do in order not to lose face in the so-called international community.

By contrast, some other countries are (or are thought to be) more sensitive to being made to feel ashamed in the eyes of the 'international community'. For instance Sweden, which has taken it upon itself to occupy the moral highground in human rights, has several times been made to correct some of the most glaring unjustices (admittedly only small ones), when the wronged party has publicly compared Sweden with countries with a human rights record Swedes feel cannot be compared with theirs (see examples from Sweden and Denmark in Insert 6.7).

INSERT 6.7   Shame sometimes helps (Sweden, Denmark)

The city of Haparanda in Sweden—with 65% Finnish-speakers—mandated an obligatory use of Swedish by the staff in all day care centres in 1991. Complaints to the Ombud of Justice and the Discrimination Ombud did not help. An international letter of protest in which both Turkey and Sweden were simultaneously accused of violating linguistic rights of children caused an immediate withdrawal of the prohibition to speak Finnish.

Likewise in Denmark. In a recent large international comparative study Danish children performed at the same level in reading tests as several underdeveloped countries, for example, Trinidad. The outcry in Denmark expressed shame, not at the performance itself, but the fact that Denmark was in company Danes did not want to be in. Funds which Danish scientific documentation had not been able to release for years were rapidly granted for reading research.

Using one's traditional clothes or speaking one's own language, or even using one's own name has been made to seem shameful for thousands of indigenous and minority children (see Inserts 6.8 and 6.9 for some additional examples). Children have been made to feel ashamed because of their parents, their culture, their language, their accent, their identity. Part of the effectiveness of boarding schools is that even the out-of-school behaviour of the children can be controlled. Johannes Marainen's experience (Insert 8.4) is typical. Antti Jalava has analysed the shame in painful, insightful ways (see references in the bibliography) and so have many minority authors.

INSERT 6.8   'They tell their parents that now they are Turks
and don't want primitive Kurdish parents'

'After a few years the children no longer want to know their parents. The children are forbidden to speak Kurdish at school. They are taught that the Kurds are dirty and primitive. And when they go home to their villages they tell their parents that now they are Turks and don't want primitive Kurdish parents. They want their parents to start speaking Turkish and being civilised' (Clason & Baksi 1979: 75–76, quoted in Skutnabb-Kangas 1984a).

INSERT 6.9   Not understanding 'tables up to 2'—stand the whole day

'In 1952 in India, I was 7 years old and spoke only my mother-tongue (Gujerati). I went to a Convent School at 7 (English medium, i.e., only English). On the first day, I was asked to say my "tables up to 2". I was puzzled and said "table, table", partially understanding. I was made to stand in class the whole day for not understanding English'. Signed 'Asha' (Example from Brent, UK, see Insert 5.12).

Similar incidents happen daily in most western European countries to-day—I could relate hundreds of them.

6.1.4.3. *Remunerative Means: Carrots—Bargaining*

In the **remunerative** phase, the offender is no longer physically **punished for doing** X (or not doing Y) but is **rewarded for not doing** X (or doing Y, respectively). The process here is bargaining: if you do this, I will give you this carrot or you will get that benefit.

The serf was told that he no longer needed to give all his sacks of wheat to the landowner—he could keep a few himself, and his goat was allowed to graze on the landowner's meadow. Other carrots could be added: if he and his wife worked really hard, they would get clean clothes (old, of course) and a Christmas basket from the lady of the manor.

Many Asian, Latin American, and African countries, willing to give some part of their decision-making power over to the Western powers, have been and are 'allowed' to purchase American, British, or French weapons and have Western military expertise to instruct them in the use of them (earlier, the Soviet Union used the same type of carrots). Complying resulted in rewards, arms[7] and training (see, e.g., Pilger 1998). The new carrot for Iraq is 'lifting sanctions', where the conditions for this are close to impossible to fulfill.

If the woman did all the reproductory work for the man, he would 'keep' her, 'give' her children, give her his name, and even give her children a name so that they did not need to be illegitimate. If poor municipalities a century and a half ago promised to use Swedish only as a medium of education, the state took over most of the cost of building the obligatory schools in northern Sweden, with many Finnish and Sámi-speakers. Insert 5.51 has several examples of carrots given for linguistic assimilation in Norway and Sweden: books, radio licenses, food, clothes, additions to teacher salaries, etc. Amery 1998, Fesl 1993, and Costo & Costo 1987, among others, give similar examples of carrots, in combination with sticks, for indigenous peoples. Today Greenland is partially kept under Denmark with financial 'carrots' where the flow may in fact be in the other direction, according to press releases

(**Information** 17 February 1999) about a new report from the London-based Institute for Strategic Studies.

6.1.4.4. *Ideological Means: Ideas—Persuasion*

In a still more sophisticated phase, **persuasion** through ideas is used, meaning this is the attempt at colonisation of the consciousness discussed earlier. Both the reward and the punishment are now internal: a clear conscience if you do what the rulers say; you feel that you are doing the right thing. The reward can also be postponed into the future: you go to heaven not hell, and there you get your just desserts. When the serf has started to believe that the system is fair, he might feel good if he fills the six sacks which go to the landowner a bit higher than his own four sacks—or at least he feels guilty if one of his own sacks has more.

Women and guilt is a sad old story, as fresh today as ever. Everything is my fault. Everything negative that happens with my children, my partner, at my place of work. . . If only I had . . . or If only I had not . . . When women and men do not finish their PhDs in Sweden, men blame everything else, the circumstances, the lousy conditions, the unfair professor, and so on. The women squarely blame themselves: I did not have the guts/the competence/the brains it takes. If you are not the perfect young-looking efficient successful career-woman, the perfect wife and/or companion, the perfect hostess, lover, mom, and so on, you have not tried hard enough.

The school and society is doing *so* much for minority children: ESL classes, extra help, reception classes, bilingual aids, intercultural weeks in school to celebrate their cultures . . . If they still don't make it, it is their own fault.

The whole validation/invalidation of non-material resources is accomplished with the help of ideological persuasion. That is what hegemonic rule is about. Those who have a monopoly of preferred access to official discourses can also make their own ideas into Foucauldian 'regimes of truth' which regulate the kinds of ideas which can be legitimately presented and debated (Bourdieu's 'doxa'). It is also within these broad regimes of truth that the criteria for validation and invalidation of non-material resources are accomplished. What falls outside the discourses permitted by prevalent regimes of truth is not only **labelled** deficient—it simply **is** invisible and invalid. This makes it easier to manufacture the hegemonic consent.

6.1.5. Changes and Reasons for the Changes— Have the Rulers Become Nicer?

To start with, I will sum up three important changes/additions in forms of control. All emphasize the importance of language (Table 6.5).

Firstly, there is a change from colonising the land, water and natural resources, material resources, of the dominated (as in colonialism proper) and from the direct colonisation of the body of the dominated (as in slavery)

TABLE 6.5
From old to new forms of control and oppression

'Old' forms of control	'New' forms of control
biologically argued racism	culturally and linguistically argued racism (ethnicism and linguicism)
overt, conscious, visible, action-oriented; agents individuals or small groups of individuals	covert, unconscious, invisible, passively accepting; ideological and structural agents
physically punitive (sticks, physical violence)	psychologically punitive (shame); remunerative (carrots: benefits, awards); ideological (ideas; conscience, guilt)
colonize land, water & natural resources (colonialism); colonize the body (slavery)	colonize mind, consciousness

towards colonizing the mind, the consciousness, of the dominated (through school, religion, mass media, i.e., the consciousness industry), and thereby **indirectly** also (re)colonizing the body (as labour) and the material resources, also globally (the environment, the air, the water, the planet) (see Table 4.3).

Examples of the new ways of colonising the body have already been mentioned. Hunger affects both physical and mental development, especially of children. We are today consciously producing mental and physical underdevelopment by allowing, encouraging, and directly causing hunger everywhere, with millions of children malnourished, both on a territorial basis, in the Peripheries outside the Centre, and on a class basis within the Centre (see Info Box 6.2). We force the Periphery countries to prefer cash crops, for debt-servicing, instead of food for local consumption; luxury articles for Us instead of food for Them. Cut flowers or fish for mink food, both for Us, instead of nourishment for locals.

Secondly, there is a change (or shift in emphasis, see below) from physically abusive, **punitive means** of control (sticks, physical violence of threat of it) towards psychologically abusive forms of control (shame), **remunerative means**, bargaining (carrots: rewards, benefits, co-option) and **ideological means** of control, negotiation, persuasion through ideas (where individuals who function as agents of oppression can be nice, liberal, well-meaning, even actively opposed to oppression). Ideas are mainly mediated through language. In order to enable the attempts at colonisation of the mind, minorities have to learn the dominant official languages and everybody has to learn (subtractive) English. Wars are a primitive and more expensive means of control, as compared to the consciousness industry.

Thirdly, there is a change from open, conscious, visible, action-oriented, biologically argued racism, with invividuals or small groups of individuals as agents, towards covert, unconscious, invisible, passively accepting, ideological and structural ethnicism and linguicism. Below we will look in more detail at some of these changes, and the reasons for them.

6.1.5.1. The Role of Language: Changes From More Physically Brutal Forms of Control to More Sophisticated and More Psychological Forms of Control

The role of language in exerting power and control worldwide is rapidly growing. Killing a language without killing the people is just one of the changes from more physically brutal forms of control to more sophisticated and more psychological forms of control. Despite the large number of armed conflicts in the world, there is a general ongoing shift, at least a shift of emphasis, in the means used for exerting power and control which many observers have noted. International organisations and multilateral links are, admittedly slowly, and often still together with threat of physical force, entering the scene as important players (compare, e.g., Galtung's early 1972 and 1980 to his 1996 book **Peace by Peaceful Means. Peace and Conflict, Development and Civilization** on this).

For instance Inoguchi, 'in her analysis of the hegemonic stability theory and the recent changes in American-Japanese relations, argues that in the age of a "post-hegemonic system", which she assumes will soon arrive, the relationships among nations will largely be multilateral instead of bilateral. She further claims that the appropriate name for the new age, to replace the term "Pax Americana", should be "Pax Diplomatica", as adjustments by diplomacy rather than rule by power increase in significance in the world of the near future' (quoted in Kishida 1992: 48–49). And diplomacy relies on the use of words.

What Inoguchi optimistically observes is in my view only one part of the manifold changes in global forms of control which are taking place. When powerless groups are being controlled through brutal physical means so that they get less than their fair share of the world's material and non-material resources and structural power, this control happens through a coarticulation of brutal forms of colonialism, imperialism, biologically argued racism and classism (and some forms of sexism). Ten years ago I would have said that all these forms of brutal control are in the process of being **replaced** by more sophisticated, less visible forms of control, which deprive minorities of their fair share of power and resources more indirectly. Now I am not so sure. Looking at the growth in the whole techno-military complex, including the industries of violence, both external and internal, and their increasing integration with other areas (agro-business, biomedicine, computers, research and education, infotainment . . .), I would modify my (optimistic) prediction. Almost half British and US government research funds go to military and arms research. American arms sales increased by 64% during the American troups attacking first Iraq then Somalia at the beginning of the 1990s, and in Britain, by 1994 the 'revitalised arms industry employed one worker in ten and accounted for 20% of the world market' (Pilger 1998: 30). Prisons are the fastest growing business in the USA. In South Africa,

> one of the ANC Government's most impressive achievements has been to restrain black people from protesting against the adaptation of apartheid's social injustices. Since democracy came to South Africa, the amount of public money spent on the police and prisons has risen by as much as a quarter in a country which already had one of the world's biggest internal security systems.[8] Since 1995, deaths in police custody have doubled (Pilger 1998: 604, based on information in the Johannesburg **Mail & Guardian**, May 23, 1997).

This development continues. In an interview December 6, 1998, asked about why he is against death sentence, Nelson Mandela says that there 'is no evidence that death penalty anywhere has brought down the level of crime' (Mandela 1999: 3). Yes! But he then goes on to claim that what brings down this level is 'the knowledge on the part of criminals that if I commit an offence I will end up in jail'; therefore, what is required is 'an efficient police system', and Mandela wants to 'improve the capacity of our police force' and does it with the 'assistance of the FBI and the British foreign service' (ibid.). There is nothing in the interview about improving the living conditions of people so as to prevent crime—the only measures suggested by Mandela have to do with improving the 'capacity of our detectives to detect crime'.

The change might thus rather be that **all** types of control are growing, and all are becoming more sophisticated. It is thus not a question of replacing control by force, but rather the addition of or more emphasis on more consciousness-industry-based control, and more sophistication in all forms of control. Sadly, here: both-and.

Next we move to a discussion of some of the reasons for these changes in emphasis.

6.1.5.2. *Reasons for Changes and Additions*

6.1.5.2.1. *From External Security Threats to Business*

The reasons for changes will be discussed under five headings: from external security threats to business; financial costs; psychological costs; escape possibilities; and the relative visibility/invisibility of the 'enemy'.

Firstly, the phase where the security threat functioned as a motivation or an engine for the development of basic technological and social structures enabling industrialization is over. According to the Swedish peace and conflict researcher Björn Hettne (1990: 38, partly building on Sen 1984), 'military demand for standardized output caused by the constant warfare and mass armies of the seventeeth, eighteenth and early nineteenth centuries hastened factory production'. It was not only a question of producing **arms** for the warfare but also of 'supplying large standing armies with food, equipment, clothing, etc.'. This could not be done without industrialisation, whereas the earlier 'maintenance of decentralized feudal troups' could.

The military impact was not only related to demand factors but also to organizational and technological change. According to Sen, organisational methods advanced at two levels. Partly 'the mass character of military demand stimulated the rationalization of the production process' (1984: 111, quoted in Hettne 1990: 38). On the other hand, 'the army itself provided a model for industrial and social organization' (ibid.).

Since the process of producing more commodities in industrialisation has been replaced in the West by the growth of the tertiary sector and by the advent of what has been called 'the information society' (but see Giddens 1990), the perceived security threats no longer function as engines for the large-scale production of arms in the same way as earlier. Partly, the external security threats of Western countries are more connected to trade shares than to threats to their territories, and here the arms trade is a double-edged weapon. (On the other hand, the large-scale arms trade may be seen as a necessary economic prerequisite to finance the development of the advanced communications technologies which in their turn maintain both Western arms superiority and Western trade shares). Partly, what states perceive as growing **internal** security threats, cannot—so the 'civilised' Western doctrines held **for themselves** at least until Yugoslavia became 'ex-'—be controlled with physical violence as efficiently as with other means. These include information and intelligence technology, repressive laws, both domestic (e.g., the new British, US and Canadian anti-terrorist laws) and multilateral (e.g., the police cooperation within the European Union, see Bunyan (ed.) 1993)—and the remunerative and ideological control discussed above. Thus, control through physical violence has become something that the West has made a big business for themselves, selling arms globally to anybody (see Renner 1998 on examples for 'small' arms), and financing the development of the technology for their own internal control through it. Much internal control has become less visibly physical, partly because prisons are localised and police on the streets are seen by many 'whites' as guaranteeing security, not as a threat, and partly because of the increase in ideological control. In the Periphery physical control is still prevalent.

6.1.5.2.2. Financial Costs

Secondly, to use physical force and to colonise material or physical resources is **financially costly** for the rulers. It requires the maintenance of a private or state machinery of violence (police, paramilitary forces, army, bodyguards, overseers, intelligence, arms industry). When threats of violence are carried out, the rulers often also destroy a part of the basis for their own profit. If the big landowner kills or molests serfs, those serfs will no longer produce profit for the landowner. If the husband beats up the wife so badly that she is out of action, for instance hospitalised for some time, he has to pay somebody else to cook his food and clean the house. Even if some sections of the ruler community in some cases profit from the rebuilding, from a global point of view it is utterly wasteful to ruin and destroy material property and then to have to build it up again, as in wars. The cost of building up again after wars is, though, mainly born by the civilians, not those who caused the cost.

The costs are also the main reason why new weapons are being built which kill the people but don't destroy the material infrastructures, buildings, etc., i.e., the material means of production. It might then become cheaper for the rulers to resort to physical force when other means of control do not seem to work. As long as the industrialised world is dependent on underdeveloped countries for raw materials (or to some extent for depositing their toxic wastes), securing access to those raw materials is important for the rulers in industrialised countries. For this, both physical force and other means (e.g., trade, loans, and 'aid') are used.

But in general using rewards and benefits is cheaper for the ruler than using physical force—the rewards are of course always worth less than what the ruler extracts from the victims. And **the use of ideas is the cheapest alternative**. Even if the cost of gaining and maintaining control over the consciousness industry can be high, the victims are in most cases made to pay these costs themselves, directly, for example, by paying for the school or the television or radio or popular press or music, or indirectly, via taxes.

6.1.5.2.3. *Psychological Costs*

Thirdly, to use physical force and the colonisation of material or physical resources is **psychologically costly** for the relationship between the rulers and the ruled, the more so the closer the relationship is geographically and/or psychologically. The memories of and the bitterness caused by use of physical violence between groups may take decades or even centuries to fade, and they can prevent positive cooperation between the groups involved for a very long time, even if this is not necessarily always the case. This is mainly what the **peace-building** efforts in **An Agenda for Peace** try to address—they are only seen as post(-physical-)conflict measures (e.g., Boutros-Ghali 1992: 11–12).

The historical relationship between Serbs and others in several parts of ex-Yugoslavia has been and will again be coloured by the use of physical force for a long time to come, just as it has been for Hindus and Muslims in India/Pakistan/Bangladesh. Likewise, it will be difficult for Palestinian Intifada-children in refugee camps, in Gaza and the West Bank and elsewhere, to forget. Kurds in Turkey, or Hutu and Tutsi, or people in Burma or Tibet or East Timor or Algeria—regardless of Truth and Reconciliation Commissions, people cannot forget.[9] Insert 6.10 has an example from my own experience in Finland, a classic civil war example.

INSERT 6.10   Class-war 1917–1918 in Finland still remembered

The deep mainly class-based division which was expressed in Finland in the civil war in 1917–1918—a cruel war with torture, hunger, concentration camps—was still very much alive when I was young: children and youngsters knew pretty soon whether a new friend's parents or grandparents had been on the 'red' side or on the 'white' side, and many children were forbidden to play with children who came from the 'wrong' side. Even if somebody in your class tried to hide which side their grandparents had been on, it was revealed at the latest in connection with matriculation: the 'red' students went to the graves of the 'red' fallen in the civil war, and laid their matriculation roses there, and the social pressure to do this was very strong indeed. It is only my children's generation—those born in the 1960s—who in most cases no longer know whether their friends' greatgrandparents were 'red' or 'white', meaning it has taken at least half a century to 'forget' the physical violence. It is only recently that really critical analyses of ideologies leading to the war have started appearing (e.g., Ehrnrooth 1992).

On the other hand, as Robert Phillipson pointed out to me, there are also examples which might lead one to argue the opposite, fairly convincingly in some of the cases, more hesitantly and with other types of explanation (it is happening **despite X, because Y forces are still more powerful**) in others. The French and Germans are no longer shooting each other. American business is taking over Vietnam. Nazis were welcome to the US to build up military capacity. Sarajevo was multi-ethnic, and so on.

Even if battered women often go back to the batterers at least a few times (as centres for battered women in many countries report), relationships which involve use of physical violence are likely to end in separation. Often the physical separation has been preceded by a psychological distancing.

When the world becomes smaller, i.e., communications and trade make countries and groups more interdependent, it will be successively more difficult to ignore the long-term psychological consequences of the use of physical violence, even between groups which are geographically distant. More sophisticated forms of control, carrots and ideas, are therefore needed—even when the 'trade prevents war' slogan is not so much untrue as misleading (see articles in Mander & Goldsmith 1996 for examples).

We could also look at the development of this interdependence in other ways, in terms of the relationship between physical, economic, and psychological barriers to a global market economy which favours the big and homogenising, at the cost of the local and the diversified (see articles in Sachs (ed.) 1992). In this sense, the big bridges and tunnels and megaferries and container ships and jumbojets, all disastrous for the environment, represent the **physical overcoming of barriers**, whereas the toll agreements, disastrous for small-scale local production, are the **economic part**, and the global spread of English (see Kachru 1986, Phillipson 1992), disastrous for the linguistic diversity of the world (when it is subtractive, non-additive), the **mental part** (see also Table 4.1).

6.1.5.2.4. *The Chance to Escape*

The *fourth* reason for the changes is that many individuals/groups can **escape** the type of **control which involves physical violence**. They may be able to leave, run away, hide, fight back, and so on. All these routes were tried in the great Finnish epic **Seitsemän veljestä** (The seven brothers, by Aleksis Kivi) by the grown-up brothers, in order to escape being 'civilised', that is, needing to learn how to read. Often escape may be extremely difficult (e.g., in slavery, in boarding schools). Fortress Europe certainly does its best to avoid receiving those who want to or who have managed to escape.

Also when **shame** is used it is **possible to escape**, if either the victim or the ones to make an individual/a group/a country to feel ashamed, refuse to fulfill 'their' role as either the victim or the punisher. The serf in the stocks outside the church or the minority child put into a corner of the classroom by the teacher for the offence of having said a few words in the mother tongue may refuse to feel ashamed, and instead of shame they may feel defiance. Since control is still external in a culture of shame (it is **not** the **committing** of the offending act itself that is 'bad', but the fact that others **find out** and know about it), the penalty only comes if one's peers agree to participate in the punishment. At least some other serfs filing past the one in the stocks or the minority child's classmates looking at her or him may feel pity and solidarity rather than disgust and a wish to punish, and then punishment by shame also becomes ineffective. This of course presupposes that the rulers and the onlookers, i.e., the ones to do the punishing, by seeing the shame, do not have shared norms about what constitutes an offence. Or at least that the onlookers, even if they agree that not obeying the ruler was shameful, anticipate that they might themselves some day be in the same situation as the one being punished, and do not therefore want to participate in the punishment.

In order to resist, when control is attempted through **rewards and benefits**, the recipients, the victims, have to be materially so **well off** that they do not need the benefits. Or they have to have a **different value system** so that they do not see the rewards as rewards (see Breton 1996 for interesting discussions). Or, alternatively, they have to be so **conscious** of what is happening and so convinced about being right that they can resist co-option. A Sámi friend in his sixties told me what a priest had taught him about '*joik*', the then banned Sámi music, and about swearing, when he was a boy of 12. 'You are **not** allowed to joik or swear. But if you are out in the mountains, completely alone with your God, then you might sometimes do it, and God understands.' A lesson about the difference between shame and guilt, external and internal punishment. In many cases minority parents and children probably have only had different values and also a conviction that they were right, but not always the consciousness needed to see through and analyse the system. Antti Jalava's (1988: 165) analysis of this is acute—this was how he felt in the Swedish medium education where physical punishment and shame had been used to kill his Finnish:

> In the upper grades, one had to apply oneself to one's studies in earnest and compete for the best marks. Others were way ahead of me in knowledge, so I had to study as hard as I possibly could. But it was no use; no matter how hard I tried the meaning of words eluded me; I had to read lines over and over again and still could not understand. My examinations turned out badly; I always got the worst marks. This, again, put me in low spirits, and made me think I was stupid. Paradoxically, however, deep down inside me I had a feeling that I had a head for books. But words mocked me, refused to open up for me; they gave off no odour and seemed to be totally barren; I recognized words but failed to grasp their sense. The depth and diversity of language were lost; this matched the loss of my mother tongue, my Finnish.

Aboriginal peoples in Australia refusing to work for wages probably often had all three: the different values, the conviction, and the consciousness. But often consciousness does not help if the economic means to resist are lacking, and money economy is often forced onto people who used to get what they needed through subsistence economies including bartering, by first making them dependent on petty commodities, given as rewards.

But often the material situation has forced minorities to accept being bought off, as when minority children have been offered food or chocolate or they have escaped punishment when they have agreed to spy on other children and report when these have used the minority language.

'Assimilados' who have been co-opted through majority group rewards, high positions or salaries etc., are often used against minority demands, hailed as representative of minority opinion or as showing that the minority cannot agree among themselves, and therefore the government cannot do anything.

It is only **ideological control** which **can** be **total** and **maximally efficient**. If you have been convinced that the ideas of the ruler are correct, if you have internalised the norms of the ruler, you feel bad when you do not obey, meaning you yourself, not any external ruler, become the punisher. The external physically violent ruler of the earlier phases of control, the enemy, has then moved inside the victim and become part of the victim, so that she no longer knows whose rules and norms she is obeying. The ruler is present every second (without needing to have armies, overseers, etc.); nobody can escape herself, and therefore the control can be both cheap and total.

Of course this does not mean that the 'victims' do not struggle against the rulers' messages—they do, often successfully. Hegemonic control is almost never simplistic or even simple, and never static.

6.1.5.2.5. *The Relative Visibility/Invisibility of the 'Enemy'*

Fifthly, the **relative visibility/invisibility of the 'enemy'** to the victim forms one aspect of the psychological cost of using physical violence. When the rulers use physical violence, the face of the 'enemy' or at least the 'enemy's' agent was clearly visible to the victims. One result of this visibility of the 'enemy' may be that there are more incentives for the victims to try and organise resistance—they know whom to resist. It also means that the rulers may have to live in constant fear of retaliation. Even if the victims are weak, and organised resistance on a larger scale may be impossible or unlikely, the ruler as an individual may be vulnerable. Victims may try to attack, even at the cost of their own lives, and indirect attacks, for example, poisoning etc. are always possible. Large scale more indiscriminate attacks, for example, poisoning a water system or an underground, are also possible as we have seen, even if these weapons have so far not been used much by oppressed groups. Therefore, it is advantageous for the rulers to step back and rule more indirectly. Already in shame culture it is more difficult for the victim to know who the 'enemy' is because the norms may be presented and enacted through an impersonal institution—the church, God, the school, the laws of the country—and because it is one's peers who do the punishing itself. When the landowner's wife offers carrots, the husband grants benefits, the USA offers military advisors, or the teacher rewards the minority child for speaking the majority language (but not the minority language) and tells the parents how hard she is working to teach the child English, the victim feels gratitude rather than fear and hate, because the 'enemy's' face has disappeared. How could somebody who is so nice to me be my enemy?

When the World Bank comes with loans or 'donor' countries with 'aid', the underdeveloped country is supposed to be grateful. It has taken a long time to see that the so called 'development aid' or 'development cooperation', including students from underdeveloped countries who get a grant to study at the university in the 'donor' country, are all part of the scheme whereby underdeveloped countries give huge amounts of developmental aid to the rich industrialised countries, at the same time as the underdeveloped countries' ordinary people pay for having their elites brainwashed (and pay for the higher education costs of the industrialised countries who take over many of the products through brain drain—see Unesco 1971).

When the rulers' norms have been internalised, via the consciousness industry, Self and Other have merged, the face of the 'enemy' has become completely blurred, and the ruler can sleep without nightmares. When the dominated stay dominated with their own (partial) consent, language becomes the (main) means of domination—but also of counterhegemonies. When it is the consciousness industry that socially creates consent, the messages of the rulers to manufacture and negotiate this consent must be mediated through language. (Of course, visual and auditory non-verbal images are used in addition to the purely verbal ones, but this does not invalidate the argument). Therefore it is important for the rulers that the dominated understand the language of the rulers, otherwise the dominated cannot be ruled with their own consent, with the help of the rulers' ideas.

This is also one of the reasons why the rulers insist on the importance of dominated minorities learning the dominant majority languages. This is why ESL programmes get more funding and structural and ideological support and visibility than programmes for the maintenance of minority languages (if they exist at all). This is why the study of the majority language is made obligatory for minority children while the study of their own languages is *not* obligatory, and often not even possible. And this is also the light in which the subtractive spread of the English language worldwide, as an 'international' language, should be seen. External wars might become redundant when everybody understands the English in advertisements glorifying coca cola, mcdonalds, and other types of consumerism at the expense of local products and the environment (even when the power holders may still feel the need to be able to **threaten** with physical force).

In earlier hegemonic control where the legitimation came from a god, the controlled did not necessarily need to understand the overt messages in religions—these were often delivered in a 'sacred' language (Latin, classical Arabic, Sanskrit) not understood (at least fully) by the subjects. In 'cuius regio, eius religio' (the one 'owning' the region also decided about the religion for that region)[10] it was enough to accept the legitimacy of the authority of the power-holder—this was the covert message.

In modern hegemonic control we can modify the thesis to 'cuius lingua, eius cultura'. The one who 'owns' the language can also to some extent determine the content of the hegemonising message. This is of course also part of the rationale for why the messages of McDonaldization (see Definition Box 6.3 (p. 456) for this concept) come in (simplified) English and why everybody worldwide is supposed (and *wants*) to learn English. This enables global hegemonic control and homogenisation.

6.1.6. The Role of Co-Option

When introducing the A team and the B team we also claimed that those who in every respect belong to the A team are numerically a very small minority of the world's population. Because the ones who in every respect belong to the B team are so far almost completely powerless in their role as direct international actors, the A team elite does not need to worry about their resistance having much effect, so far. But the groups which partly belong to the B team, partly to the A team, play an important role in the maintenance of the current distribution of power and resources. The A team elite need in some way to be able to secure their consent, be it voluntary or forced, to remain in power and to continue the exploitation. The more 'characteristics' a group shares with the A team elite, the easier it probably is to manufacture consent, both through the use of ideas and the use of remunerative means. Conversely, the fewer 'characteristics' a group shares with the A team elite, the more likely it is that the more brutal physical means of control will be used to secure their consent, as soon as they are strong enough to be able to offer resistance. Those who belong to both teams seem to experience more attempts at co-opting them the more they resemble the A team elite and partly also the closer they are geographically. The relationship between the genders is a case in point here.

Many of us support the elite in the A team and 'their' ideology, even though we do not ourselves receive as much of the power and resources as those who are all A team. We get enough economic benefits and rewards, and consume much more than the Periphery in the Periphery. A child born in New York, Paris, London, Copenhagen, or Helsinki will in her life-time consume, pollute[11] and waste more than 50 children born in an underdeveloped country (UN **Human Development Report** 1998)—except presumably the children of the elites, the Centre in the Peripheries (see also Info Boxes 6.1 through 6.5). We are also partly pacified to non-caring through ideological persuasion.

But obviously we in the industrialized world would not be able to continue to exploit underdeveloped countries, unless the (mainly male) elites of these countries collaborate with us. When we through 'development aid', for instance offer scholarships to people from Africa, one of the results (and/or causes/motives) is that some Africans will through their education start resembling the power elite of the A team more and more. They will become people of high formal education, urban, middle, or upper class—and in the first place they are often men and from the dominant or majority groups in their own countries (or from the most powerful minority groups in countries which do not have clear-cut majorities). Because of their formal education (and often superior competence in the old colonial language, acquired partially through that education), they will be in powerful positions in their own countries later on. While the scholarship lasts, it will be very difficult for them not to take over (something of) the Western world's view of the superiority of the West and of the causes of underdevelopment. After the acculturation it is easier to get some of them to function as the compradores of the Western A team elite on their return—provided they go back. They are exposed to massive ideological propaganda, while also being rewarded for believing in it. At the same time, elite schools and universities in some of the Periphery countries depend on British and American universities for materials, exams, etc, and prepare their students to function in Centre countries too; there is growing resistance to this also. The same strategies are used vis-à-vis (some) women in industrialised countries, selected immigrants, etc.—co-option is an efficient strategy.

Seen from a researchers' point of view, our own role is also interesting here, as I mentioned in the Introduction. Much more awareness of it is needed.

So far, we have discussed ideological reasons and prerequisites for and the role of language in control leading to linguistic genocide in education. Next we will move to more purely political reasons.

6.2. POLITICAL REASONS—THE 'NATION STATE' 'DEMANDS' ONE LANGUAGE FOR UNITY?

6.2.1. The Mythical Nation State: One State, One Nation, One Language

The traditional stereotypical image of a nation-state saw the nation-state as a product of an evolutionary process starting with small tribal societies and developing via many phases towards higher forms of social organization of people's lives. The nation-states represented the most developed form (the development is described in, e.g., Hobsbawm 1991, A. Smith 1983, 1991). A nation-state comprised one (romantic, Herderian) 'nation', and this imagined community (Anderson 1983) was, especially in the German nationalist tradition, ideally seen as united by one single language. Other nations within this Nation would then either be seen as disruptive, as an anomaly, or, if they are very small in numbers and insignificant in terms of power—as most indigenous nations/peoples have until very recently seen to be—they could (and can still) be seen as colourful, non-threatening remnants from an earlier phase, even positively 'exotic'. But in order not to be seen as disruptive, they have to accept that they 'have no independent future' (Hobsbawm 1991: 35); that they are 'small and backward' (ibid., 34) and 'have everything to gain by merging into greater nations' (ibid., 34), i.e., that they and their languages are 'doomed to disappear' (ibid., 34). This is because of 'the laws of progress' (ibid., 35), because they 'could not be adapted to the modern age' (ibid., 35).

They can also be ignored, or their existence altogether denied.[12] All these are ethnicist and/or linguicist arguments, examples of the glorification, stigmatisation, and rationalisation discussed earlier.

Since the 'natural' development would be for every 'nation' to have its own nation-state with its own language, the existence of **unassimilated** minority groups, having several 'nations' within The Nation, has been feared, because it is seen as leading in a 'natural' way to fragmentation: a complete or partial disintegration of the nation-state, with the formation of several new nation-states or some kind of a federal structure as a result. This results in the demonisation of such countries as India, Belgium, and Canada which have been described as monsters full of ethnic conflict because of support to more than one language (see David Marshall's elegant denunciation, 1986). Since a nation-state is 'indivisible' (e.g., in the Constitution of the Republic of Turkey, 1982, Article 3—or in the French Constitution—see Info Box 7.4), this cannot be allowed.

I will not dwell further on the definitions of states, nations, nation-states or ethnic groups and the relationships between them (see also, e.g., Riggs 1985 but also Gellner 1983, Hannum 1990, Hobsbawm 1991, Hroch 1985, Hutchinson & Smith (eds) 1994, Kallen 1996, A. Smith 1983, 1991 and Tilly (ed.) 1975). But an interesting point about language and self-determination is that all definitions of **state, nation, or nation-state** (or even **state-nation**[13]) which I have checked and which mention anything about communication between the people belonging to the entity in question talk about (a common, unifying, developed, official) **language** for the entity. None of them use 'dialect', 'vernacular' or 'patois' in their definitions, the implication being that people who form a dialect, vernacular or patois (hereafter 'dialect' stands for all three) community do not and/or cannot form a nation or a state or a nation-state (and maybe not even a people?). It is thus possible to hierarchize different groups which might want to form a nation and therefore eventually a nation-state, through **labelling** them so that **only some groups are seen as possessing the necessary prerequisite, a language**.

In order to form a nation or a state you have to have a language. Dialects are not seen as developed enough to fulfill all the linguistic functions of a nation or a state. Having a language (as opposed to a dialect) thus becomes symbolic of a nation and a state (and even a people), in much the same way as a national flag, a national anthem, etc., are or may be symbolic of the state.

When ethnicism and linguicism have socially constructed the languages of powerless groups so that they through being stigmatised are made invisible or are seen as handicaps, this labelling of their languages as 'dialects' (see Haugen 1966, 1991, on definitions), has then been used to exclude powerless peoples' demands for self-determination, by implying or claiming that they do not possess one of the prerequisites for nationhood, a fully developed language. Kurds speak 'mountain Turkish', a 'dialect' (see Insert 1.1).

Thus non-state nations or peoples are **themselves** socially constructed as handicapped, as non-peoples (only a 'group' or only 'a minority' and not 'a people' or even 'a nationality'—see also Thornberry 1987, 1991) and thus made invisible non-actors on the international scene. They are, to use Bromley's terms, restricted to an ethnonymic rather than politonymic existence; they are accepted as some lower-level kind of an **ethnic entity** (= minority) but **not a political entity**. This is the case regardless of whether their inclusion in the larger entity is allowed on the basis of linguistic and cultural assimilation, ethnonymically, as in the German type 'cultural nations' thinking, or on the basis of politonymic assimilation, as in the French type 'political nations of citizens' (i.e., state-nation) thinking. Both demand assimilation in exchange of inclusion and civil and political rights, and in the long run both types of assimilation lead to linguistic and cultural genocide.

At a group level, nations which have their own state obviously have more structural power than non-state nations or peoples. In some states, some idioms may also be invisibilised, even if they are not denied languagehood, by being designated **national** (as opposed to **official**) languages (see examples from constitutions in chapter 5), thus confining them to the type of emotional role envisaged by liberal ideologists in the late 1800s.

Historically it has become a self-fulfilling prophecy—many states have 'tried' to eliminate or their actions have resulted in the elimination of other languages except one. Tore Janson in his discussion about subtractive spread of languages (see Definition Box 2.2) traces the development of the spreading variants in Europe during the middle ages and later (1997: 150): 'To start with, they were just spoken languages, without a name and without any status. Then they became written languages and got their own names, like French, Italian, Swedish, etc. The really successful languages became connected with a state and got the position of national languages'.

Every state thus 'needs' a (highly developed) language which can function as its **official** language (regardless of whether this is formalized in its constitution or not). If it does not have one which is 'developed' enough, it may borrow one from a 'developed' nation-state, often the old colonial power. This is also often done if the state has several candidates, the implication being that a state only must/can have **one** official language to unify it[14] (or two or, at the most, three—see Pattanayak's criticism of this Western idea, 1986; see also Afolayan 1978, 1984, Alexander 1989, 1992, Bamgbose 1991, Bokamba 1991, Bokamba & Tlou 1980, Djité 1993, 1994, Mateene 1980a, b, 1985a, b, Alamin Mazrui 1997, Ali Mazrui 1975, Prah 1995a, b). The other languages, which by implication are not 'developed' enough, may then be designated **national** languages, or they may be designated dialects and not play any official role, or they may be ignored or their existence denied altogether. Cultures and identities are often treated in the same invisibilising reductionist way. Insert 6.11 has an Australian example.

INSERT 6.11 Australia has one language and one fixed identity?

When the Australian Government, on the basis of the 1987 **National Policy on Languages** (Lo Bianco Report), founded the body to supervise the implementation of the policy, it was called The National Languages Institute of Australia. After a Green Paper, issued with the authority of the then Minister for Employment, Education and Training, John Dawkins, called **The Language of Australia**, a heated discussion followed on why the plural in Languages was dropped, and this probably saved the plural in the reorganisation of the Institute. Now (1999) it is called National Languages & Literacy Institute of Australia, but in their publicity (e.g., January 1999) they call themselves 'Language Australia'.

Christine Inglis tells a similar story about identities in an article called 'Multiculturalism and National Identity'. The suggested subject for the symposium from which her article originated was 'Multicultural Australia and national identity'. A book was to be assembled on the topic. The topic first given to her was 'Towards an Australian national identity'. To her this 'suggests that we don't yet have one, that we aspire to one, and (because the article is indefinite) that we have some choice about what it will be. Then the title became just "Australian national identity". Two adjectives and a noun, with no preposition and no article, sounded attractively open. It's since become "The Australian National Identity", having somehow acquired a definite article suggesting solidity: it exists, and there's only one of it.' (Inglis 1991: 13). P.S. The book in which the article finally appeared, is called 'Australian National Identity' . . .

Many of the contemporary national languages in Europe killed off or weakened seriously many of the competitors, such as those in France or Italy, and this led to lower diversity. This was also attempted in relation to Sámi, Finnish, and all other variants of Swedish in Sweden.[15] According to Janson (1997), there were large numbers of languages in Europe 2,000 years ago; most of them are extinct today.

The myth that national unity would demand one language has been criticized or effectively dismantled by many researchers (see, e.g., Alexander 1989 and references above). A few voices will exemplify this.

In an article called 'Monolingual myopia and the petals of the Indian lotus: do many languages divide or unite a nation?', Debi Prasanna Pattanayak (1988: 380) answers a question as to whether a country of many languages is not always threatened by disintegration:

Yes. It is in the same sense that a plural world is always threatened by disintegration. No more, no less. If this leads one to the position that all languages in the world should give way to a single language, all religions should merge into one, all ethnicities should merge and fuse into one, one is arguing in favour of a reductionism which is fraught with serious consequences for the survival of humanity. Ecology shows that a variety of forms is a prerequisite for biological survival. Monocultures are vulnerable and easily destroyed. Plurality in human ecology functions in the same way. One language in one nation does not bring about equity or harmony for members or groups of that nation.

In the Philippines, Enriquez & Protacio-Marcelino (1984: 3) see 'the continued use of English and, with it, an American-oriented curriculum as psychologically and politically inimical to the nationalist and democratic aspirations of the Filipino people . . . it fosters further regionalism and obstructs national unity.'

Also Hans Dua points out that the language policies followed in many underdeveloped countries favour the 'colonial languages of wider communication' and 'ignore the multilingual reality of linguistically heterogenous developing nations by inculcating one-language policy for national unity. The multilingual reality dictates that the developing nations should aim at unity underlying diversity in their educational language planning rather than seek triumph over diversity through uniformizing and stultifying constraints of one-language policy' (Dua 1985: 177).

As analysed earlier (section 2.1), the whole idea of having just one language is to the benefit of those elites who in this way could secure for themselves the 'profit of distinction' for possessing the linguistic capital of proficiency in the one language, and prevent many others from acquiring it altogether, or from acquiring the right variant. The costs in forcing just one language on a multilingual population have also been analysed.

But even if we were to accept that every state 'needs' a language, would the opposite also true? Does every language 'need' its own a state? Does supporting linguistic diversity logically lead to the disintegration of states?

6.2.2. Dismantling the Myth of Nation-States and Ethnic Conflict

We now know that what is needed for minority languages to be maintained over several generations in countries where obligatory education is enforced is overt promotion of these languages ('partial support of specific language functions' or 'adoption as an official language' in Cobarrubias' taxonomy— or often more, see Fettes 1998). The gulf between the good intentions expressed in preambles of international or regional documents and the de facto dearth of linguistic human rights (see chapter 7) can be understood as symptomatic of the tension between on the one hand a wish on the part of states to secure (or give the impression of securing) human rights to minorities, including the right to at least some kind of cultural and linguistic self-determination, and on the other hand states denying linguistic and cultural human rights to minorities, because these rights are decisive for reproducing these minorities as minorities, which is seen as leading to the disintegration of the state.

It is therefore necessary to clarify how (speakers of) threatened languages can be supported without this being perceived as undermining the position of the dominant linguistic group (Grin, 1999) or the integrity of the state. At the same time it is necessary to dismantle the myth of a nation-state as the highest form of social organisation, and indeed renegotiate the concept of a state itself and the need of states.

If we were to believe in the myth of the nation-state as the most developed form of social organisation, and if the principle of self-determination were to be applied fully, so that every language group (every 'nation') were to have their own nation-state, the present states would disintegrate into thousands of states, even if we only count with oral and not sign languages (the Deaf have never, as far as I know, suggested that they want their own state). Since there are speakers of more than one language in every single one of the currently less than 250 states, and since the geographical areas for the maybe 6,800 new nation-states would have to come from the present nation-states, that would mean the disintegration of every state in the present world. As already mentioned, very few nation-states can be expected to voluntarily accept this type of disintegration.

But in fact the conflict between the two principles (self-determination of peoples/minorities/ethnic groups vs. integrity of states) is based on a myth.

There are many different ways of avoiding this presumed disintegration, some negative, some more positive. Many of the negative ones have been discussed earlier, for example, reducing the number of potential nations, including preventing groups from acquiring or maintaining their own languages as one of the central prerequisites needed for nation-building, and the central factor in their reproduction as separate groups—one of the main political reasons for linguistic genocide. Restricting self-determination only to 'old' colonial situations (i.e., claiming that the principle is no longer applicable, all colonies are autonomous or independent), is also a negative one, and was used until recently—but see below.

First a few disclaimers. I do not wish to endorse a crudely primordialist/essentialist view of language. I recognize that the concept 'language' itself is fuzzy, and that linguistic identity interacts and co-articulates with many other factors, particularly those of class and gender. Having said that, I would risk the generalization that **lack** of linguistic rights is one of the causal factors in certain conflicts, and linguistic affiliation is a rightful mobilizing factor in conflicts with multiple causes where power and resources are unevenly distributed along linguistic and ethnic lines. Thus **not** granting linguistic and cultural human rights is today a way of **supporting** what has been called ethnic conflict.

In contemporary processes of integration and disintegration, globalisation and europeanisation, regionalisation and self-determination, the sovereignty of individual states is being re-thought and reorganised, as we also see in the next sections of this chapter. Many states are willing to concede part of their sovereignty, either to supra-statal institutions like the EU (on language policy, see Fishman 1994a, b, Labrie 1993) or internally to autonomous regional authorities (e.g., Catalonia). New states come into existence (e.g., Slovenia, Czechia). A state may wish to concede part of its sovereignty to supra-statal institutions but fiercely oppose internal regional autonomy (e.g., Turkey). Yet other states (e.g., the Baltic states), escaping from one type of overarching structure (the Soviet Union), may wish to join another (the European Union). Thus integration and disintegration, reorganisation, are happening recurrently.

Throughout the cold war and the period of decolonisation there was an uneasy marriage between the principle of the indivisibility of states and the right to self-determination. The relationship is now looser, and the principles should not be irreconcilable, in the view of the ex-Secretary-General of the UN.

> Globalism and nationalism need not be viewed as opposing trends, doomed to spur each other on to extremes of reaction. The healthy globalization of contemporary life requires in the first instance solid identities and fundamental freedoms. The sovereignty, territorial integrity and independence of States within the established international system, and the principle of self-determination for peoples, both of great value and importance, must not be permitted to work against each other in the period ahead. (Boutros-Ghali 1992: 9–10)

A positive strategy to avoid conflictual disintegration which the international community is starting to use at present is to redefine the concept of self-determination (see Hannum 1990, Clark & Williamson (eds) 1996, Eide 1990, 1991, Palley 1984, Rosas 1995a); to see it more as a continumm, ranging from some internal autonomy, all the way to complete external self-determination, i.e., full independence. This opens up possibilities for context-sensitive negotiations about self-determination as a legitimate demand even after the main decolonisation period—even if one can despair at seeing how little is achieved in relation to many of the absolutely legitimate demands—Kurdistan, Kosova, Tibet, East Timor, and so on. See Chapter 7 for further discussion on the right to self-determination.

The nation-state is currently under pressure from globalization, transnational regionalization, and local decentralization (democratic, root-seeking, environment-saving), and may in several of its roles at this point have outlived itself, as will be discussed in later sections. But there can be no doubt that language plays a role in processes of statal, sub-statal and supra-statal formation. This is manifest in the complex mosaic of 'Europe', where identities are currently being refashioned and old certainties challenged. It is equally clear in Africa and Asia, where, for instance 'insurgents in Ethiopia have over the years, placed the use of native languages at the centre of their demands for autonomy and self-determination.' (Prah 1995a: 7). In some cases, the demands are being met:

> A fairly wide agreement today is that ethnicity is a social construct based on a cluster of cultural factors, **language being the most common**, and that its primary function is the assertion of a group's distinct identity . . . Ethiopia . . . a regime that came to power [in 1991] in the aftermath of a long, many-sided, violent conflict, in which ethnicity played a prominent role, is attempting to resolve the dominant problem of modern history of Ethiopia, by confronting the politization of ethnicity in a straightforward manner. The regime maintains it is **the refusal to recognize ethnic claims for political recognition that leads to conflict**. Accordingly, immediately upon taking power in Addis Ababa in 1991, the regime encouraged the formation of ethnic political organizations among Ethiopia's more than 80 ethnic groups . . . Regional and sub-regional units enjoy **complete cultural autonomy**, to the extent of **choosing their own (ethnic) official languages which are also used as the languages of instruction in the local system of education**. All ethnic groups are encouraged to seek political recognition through their own political organization and to claim representation in local government bodies. (Salih 1996: 13; emphases added)

The promotion of just one language, especially an old colonial language, can be seen as an act which **causes** conflict: '. . . I take the defence and promotion of English, or any other language, at the expense of my language, or any other language, as an act of aggression' (Keorapetse Kgositsile, in **The Southern Africa Review of Books**, July/August 1993, quoted in Prah 1995a: 6).

We could also look at the conflict potential in forced assimilation, as opposed to bilingual/bicultural groups. Info Box 4.6 related the example of bilingual Konds and monolingual assimilated Konds in Ajit Mohanty's studies. In 1994 there were serious conflicts with physical violence and killings between Kond 'tribals' and Oriya-speaking 'non-tribals' in the Phulbani district. In a sad and dramatic but convincing way these conflicts validated Mohanty's results. The conflicts occurred **only** in the monolingual areas and did not spread to the bilingual areas despite similar socio-economic and political conditions. When Mohanty asked people why, they explained that people in the bilingual area knew each other better and could talk about things instead of fighting . . . (Mohanty 1994b and personal communication, December 1994). Something for the world leaders to think about?

The Ethiopian solution above, with demands at several interconnected levels, is emphasized by many analysts, regardless of whether they represent political science or peace and conflict research or research into human rights in general, as several quotes will show, starting with Kenneth McRae, the author of probably the most comprehensive analyses ever of the language policies in Switzerland (1983), Belgium (1986) and Finland (1997), all with different models for solving possible and actual conflicts. Thus reducing a conflict where economic and political cleavages coincide with language or ethnicity to 'ethnic conflict' is simplifying the issue:

> One of the most frequently cited propositions of comparative politics is that a conflict based on one type of social cleavage is likely to be reduced or mitigated by the simultaneous presence of another cleavage that crosscuts or intersects the first. The examples most often cited are those involving differences in religion, class, and language (or ethnicity). (McRae 1997: 124)

But when nations, indigenous peoples and minorities try to exercise their right to self-determination, even in a minimalist way, i.e., demanding the right to exist as separate entities, with their own cultures and languages, this is often seen by politicians as **causing** an 'ethnic' conflict. Even some of those researchers whose analyses of ethnic conflict are in other ways subtle may see minorities resisting forced assimilation as the major **cause** for ethnic conflict.

An example is the analysis about conflicts in the ex-Soviet Union by Lars Dencik (1992). He acknowledges the power relationships in ethnic conflicts. He also points out that 'it is decisive to the analysis of a particular conflict who defines it—the actors involved or some external body' (ibid., 143). But then he goes on to define conflict situations completely from external observers' point of view. When the actors see a conflict where an external observer does not, this is according to Dencik because the **actors** are not adequately informed (ibid., 143). Likewise, when the actors perceive the conflict as a zero-sum game whereas the external body describes it as a non-zero-sum conflict, the **actors** may according to Dencik be 'so blinded by their conflict attitudes that they do not perceive the cooperative aspect of the conflict situation' (ibid.). Thus in both cases the external observers' definition of the situation is implicitly taken as the objectively correct one, whereas the actors are seen as inadequately informed or blinded.[16] Dencik also sees it as important to study how the **minority** group changes to 'continuously more instrumental conflict behaviour' (ibid.), whereas the **majority** group's conflict behaviours are not mentioned. Consequently, it is the **minority** group which, according to Dencik, has to change, to become de-ethnicized (i.e., assimilate), in order for the conflict to be solved; it is minority groups 'persisting as distinguished ethnic groups' that becomes The Problem (ibid., 146).

As we see in chapter 7, most Western states have not seriously supported linguistic and cultural diversity and linguistic rights during this century. They have, on the contrary, tried to prevent the acceptance of legally binding international conventions and charters on linguistic rights. But there are very strong reasons why states **should** in fact support linguistic and cultural diversity and linguistic rights, also in the interest of their own elites, i.e., for egoistic reasons, not only for human rights reasons.

'Interethnic cooperation and solidarity' between groups with different languages, 'peaceful coexistence', is 'at least as common and persistent as interethnic conflicts', according to Rodolfo Stavenhagen (1990: 39). But when conflict occurs, language is in many situations one of several factors **separating** the parties. In other conflicts, the parties **share a language** but differ on other counts. Bosnians shared a language with Serbs and Croats, but this did not prevent war. Language is not what separates people in Northern Ireland. Thus there is not even any necessary **correlational** relationship between conflict and differences of language. But when difference of language coincides with conflict, does language play a **causal** role?

In the first place, differences of language can**not** in most contexts be said to 'cause' war or even inter-ethnic conflict. 'If and when ethnic hostility or rivalry occurs, there is generally a specific historical reason for it that relates to **political struggles over resources and power**' is Stavenhagen's assessment (1990: 39; emphasis added).

However, the Swedish peace and conflict researchers Björn Hettne, with extensive experience, especially in Asia, claims (1987: 66–67), that even if

> the economic factor is seldom absent in ethnic conflict, it does **not** usually constitute any kind of triggering factor. Existential problems in a deeper sense are involved. The hatred that an ethnic group can develop against another group probably has less to do with competition per se and more with the risk of having to give up something of oneself, one's identity, in the struggle . . . It is therefore more a question of survival in a cultural rather than a material sense . . . The horror of ethnocide is a more basic impulse than the struggle to reap economic benefits at the expense of another group. . . . To sum up, the problem is not that ethnic groups are different, but rather **the problem arises when they are no longer allowed to be different**, i.e., when they subjectively experience a threat to their own identity, a risk of ethnocide. This is a fundamental cause behind the politicising of ethnic identity.

Linguistic and cultural identity are at the core of the cultures of most ethnic groups (Smolicz 1979). Threats towards these identities can have a very strong potential to mobilize groups as Hettne also notes. Still, in **human rights** contexts, **cultural** concerns, including linguistic concerns, have continued to be neglected, as opposed to economic and social concerns, and, especially, civil and political concerns, Eide claims.

In Asbjørn Eide's analysis, absence of **economic and social rights**, 'the widespread unemployment and poverty' between the two 'World' Wars is seen as having led to 'the political upheavals and the emergence of totalitarian regimes' (Eide 1995a, 29–30). This realization led, according to Eide (who has worked for many years with the UN Human Rights Commission—see bibliography), to a genuine interest in **securing** economic and social rights, not only for their own sake but also for the preservation of individual freedom and democracy. Eide claims that economic and social concerns are 'equally important in the present time, in light of escalating unemployment, increasing poverty and growing disparities in income, not only in the Third World but also in Central and Eastern Europe and in the West' (ibid.). Economic and social concerns have therefore, predictably, received a lot of international attention, for instance at the Copenhagen Social Summit (March 1995), without this leading to any improvement, though. ILO's **World Employment Report 1998** shows that close to one billion people worldwide, i.e., almost a third of the labour pool, are either unemployed (150 million) or underemployed (750 to 900 million) and the figures are still rising (for instance in Asia the number of unemployed increased by 10 million during one year). The figures may underestimate unemployment because of poor statistics, the Director General of ILO, Michel Hansenne, warns (**Information** 27 September 1998).

On the other hand, Eide claims that **cultural rights** have, both in human rights theory and in practice, **lacked** importance and received **little** attention, despite the fact that today 'ethnic conflict' and 'ethnic tension' are seen as the **most important possible reasons for unrest, conflict and violence** in the world.

Just as absence of economic and social rights in the period between the world wars promoted the emergence of totalitarian regimes, absence or denial of linguistic and cultural rights can today be regarded as an effective way of promoting 'ethnic' conflict and violence. This has been acknowledged by many researchers from several fields. For instance Jurek Smolicz (1986b: 96), Australia, formulated it as follows:

> . . . attempts to artificially suppress minority languages through policies of assimilation, devaluation, reduction to a state of illiteracy, expulsion or genocide are not only degrading of human dignity and morally unacceptable, but they are also an invitation to separatism and an incitement to fragmentation into mini-states.

Granting linguistic and cultural human rights is thus a step towards **avoiding** 'ethnic' conflict (Hettne 1987, Stavenhagen 1990), avoiding disintegration of (some) states and avoiding anarchy, where the rights of even the elites will be severely curtailed because of the increasingly civil war-like conditions, especially in inner cities.

I see **lack** of linguistic rights as one of the causal factors in certain conflicts. I also see linguistic affiliation as a rightful mobilizing factor in conflicts with

multiple causes where power and resources are unevenly distributed along
linguistic and ethnic lines.

Summing up, since language is for most ethnic groups one of the most
important cultural core values, a threat to an ethnic group's language is thus
a threat to the cultural and linguistic survival of the group and thus to its
existence as a group, a people. Lack of linguistic rights often prevents a
group from achieving educational, economic and political equality with other
groups. Injustice caused by **failure to respect linguistic human rights** is thus
in several ways one of the important factors which can contribute to inter-
ethnic conflict—and often does.

This means that I see language-related issues as potential causes of conflict
only in situations where groups lack linguistic rights **and/or** political/economic
rights, **and** where the unequal distribution of political and/or economic power
follows linguistic and ethnic lines. Granting linguistic rights to minorities
reduces conflict potential, rather than creating it—we will come back to
this at the end of this chapter and in the next chapter. But conflicts will of
course not disappear just by granting language rights. In the next section
we will address a few issues of economic rights (and wrongs) and globalisation.

6.3. ECONOMIC REASONS—THE GLOBAL 'FREE MARKET'?

6.3.1. Globalisation

Globalisation can be and has been understood in various ways by and even
within various disciplines. Economic globalisation seems to be at the centre
of many of the discussions, but it is imperative to integrate views about and
approaches from all types of globalisation.

George Soros, one of the richest men in the world, made his fortune in
the financial markets. Today, when he says he is going to invest or not invest
in a country, the global stock market reacts within minutes. With his Open
Society Fund, he earlier invested massively to prepare people for the disintegration of communism. Now he thinks that 'the untrammeled intensifica-
tion of laissez-faire capitalism and the spread of market values into all areas
of life is endangering our open and democratic society. The main enemy of
the open society . . . is no longer the communist but the capitalist threat'
(1997: 45). 'Markets reduce everything, including human beings (labor) and
nature (land), to commodities. We can have a market economy but we cannot
have a market society' (1998: 27). I agree with Soros about capitalism and
market values as threats, and the prospect of a 'market society' as horrifying—but I cannot see his logic in not connecting them. Can we in fact have
a market economy? If 'market values' are the ideology of the 'free market',

of 'market economy', they are what leads to a 'market society'. It seems odd to attack the result while approving of the causes.

The evidence showing that we **cannot** have a market economy is compelling. The market economy is, directly or indirectly, responsible for many if not most of the disasters of the planet today. This is not the place to start the systematic accounting that would be needed to analyse the claim. Thousands of books have been written about aspects of globalisation, economic and other (a few references follow). My accounts are necessarily very eclectic and personal, and do not form a general description or coherent narrative or analysis of globalisation. What will be attempted here is only glimpses from some of those aspects which in my view form a necessary minimal background for discussing the main themes of the book. Even this could be done in dozens of different ways, and systematised much more—but then I could use more than a lifetime for it and the book would never be published.

Let me start by concretising globalisation for myself: how does it affect my local life? In Info Box 6.12. I give some facts just from my recent local newspaper reading, in a way which reflects the chaos, angst and worry that

---

❖ I n f o   B o x   6 . 1 2 ❖

(What) Can I Eat and Drink? Can I Protest Legally?
Grandchildren?

What can I eat and drink? At least a half million people in Denmark (out of a population of 5.1 million) suffered from some kind of food poisoning in 1997, most often salmonella (from eggs, chickens, or pork). A routine check of health standards in Copenhagen restaurants showed that 40% were at fault. Of the pigs slaughtered in Danish slaughterhouses—and there are 25 million pigs as opposed to 5 million people in this country—32% show evidence of disease or illness (whereas under 0.5% of those from ecologically run farms do). Of the chickens on chicken farms 10% are unable and another 10% unwilling to walk properly or at all—anatomic misgrowth or constant serious pain in legs as a direct result of being forced to grow too fast. Over 40% of imported turkey is infected with salmonella, mainly from France, Germany, and the Netherlands. The first proven case of someone dying in Denmark from totally antibiotics-resistant bacteria (salmonella DT-104) transferred from eating meat; international biomedical conference is alarmed. A new beef cow breed, the Belgian Blue, is unable to give birth naturally; the calf is too big and a caesarean is needed every time. But the beef tastes good, they say. Over 40% of the Danish ground water which **has** been checked—only a small part has—has unacceptably high levels of various heavy metals and other poisons, including traces of Roundup, a pesticide produced by transnational Monsanto.

(Continued)

A Danish research team has shown that resistance to Roundup **can** spread from gene-manipulated crops to nature, something Monsanto has assured us is impossible. Think of the new generation of strong, resistant weeds we are going to have! How strong will the pesticides be that farmers need to use then? How many are as lucky as Robert and I are, living on an ecological smallholding, producing much of our food, including meat, without pesticides—except we get them through air and rain and groundwater anyway . . .

Legal protest. When I and others try to protest, what happens? Surveillance, registering, end of career. In Denmark, Sweden, Norway, the secret police has, with the acceptance of the (mostly Social Democrat) governments, had tens of thousands of civil spies, 'monitoring' and registering **legal** political activities of 'left-wing' citizens—the scandals are just unfolding while I am writing this. The Danish (Social Democrat) Minister of Justice does not want an open investigation about the illegal registers (whereas the Norwegian and Swedish governments were forced to). Democracy?

Grandchildren? Are Danes going to have any at all? Sperm counts of young men in military recruit health checks show only 20% of the sperm young men had 40 and 50 years ago (while ecological farmers still have almost 'normal' semen). Danish children are much more unhealthy, physically and mentally, than two or three decades ago. Not enough vitamins and minerals—fast food, soft drinks, smoking, alcohol. Every fifth has daily pains (headaches, stomach, back); they are nervous and depressed (14% of the children from highest social groups, more than a third from the lowest ones—but the elite kids drink and smoke more, and bully their peers more). Allergies are growing at an alarming rate, especially in children. Life expectancy figures are going down (Danish women have, with 78 years, the lowest figure in the OECD, men with 72.8 are the 14th of 16 countries). But then Danes eat more than any other people in the world (including for the first time the USA): the mean in 1999 is 3,808 calories per person (Swedes eat 700 and Finns 900 fewer calories). The safety of the Swedish nuclear power station Barsebäck, fully visible from Copenhagen, is extremely questionable according to Swedish experts. What are our grandchildren going to eat? What are their peers in Africa going to eat in 20 years' time, if they have no money to rebuy, each year, the sterile terminator-technology produced seed from Monsanto & Cargill?[17] How many of their peers will be brain-damaged because of undernourishment? Have reduced or no immune defence system, because of gene-manipulated crops? How do we dare to have grandchildren in the first place? Our generation has stolen the world from them.

The world is floods (China, Thailand), hurricanes, fires, CO^2, global warming, air pollution, noise pollution, acid rain, deforestation, deserts growing; all man-made disasters. And if the grandchildren's generation tries to protest, surveillance is easy via computer chips operated into them[18]—they become cyborgs.[19]

some results of globalisation create in the minds of many of us. Everything in the Box has **something** to do with globalisation, directly or indirectly. These are some of my worries—you, reader, write down yours!

I am not trying to **create** The Big Monster—it is here already. The causal connections, direct and indirect, are there, even if they are far from clear. Globalisation is not a brand new monster either—it has just grown exponentially and changed qualitatively. And globalisation is as messy to analyse as the Info Box indicates.

In the following sections I shall be moving back and forth between older and current forms of globalisation to show similarities and differences. Much of it is known to many readers. Still, it is necessary to analyse language and education in this broader context. Globalisation is a causal factor in genocidal and ethnocidal policies—but it may also contain seeds for counterhegemonies and possible strategies for supporting linguistic and cultural diversity, and biodiversity.

6.3.1.1. *Colonialism as an Early Form of Globalisation—A Comparison*

Post-colonial studies have thoroughly analysed the early globalisation implied in colonisation and slavery (even when all forms of slavery did not imply globalisation—now most of them do). Today's globalisation includes neo-neo-colonialism (Galtung 1980) and direct and indirect slavery. Despite decolonisation, the industrial world still has much of the power over what the lands and bodies of Others are used for, and we extract and appropriate both material and non-material resources. We still have the 'desire . . . to achieve ideological as well as military and economic hegemony and conformity, without having to pay the price of permanent conquest' which according to Drake 1991: 34 (quoted in Escobar 1995: 28) characterised US policy during the first third of this century. The Centres (of the Centre and Periphery) have slaves, both in underdeveloped countries (including millions of women and children working in slavery proper or in slave-like conditions) and, increasingly, in the industrialised world (again, women are a majority, working as house-slaves or in sex industry[20]).

Here we shall only comment on two aspects which are central for the concerns of this book, firstly the 'globalisation' of ideas and knowledge, implicated both historically and today in Our appropriation of Their knowledges, often without acknowledgement, and, secondly, the rationalisations involved in the legitimation of the appropriation (which have already been discussed in relation to education).

As noted earlier, in Eurocentric history writing, modern science was (and is) seen as something developed in and by Europe, and 'development' was conceptualised as 'the transfer of European models of industrialization—of European sciences and technologies—to the "underdeveloped" societies in the third World' (Harding 1997: 7[21]). This is of course also exactly what the modernisation paradigm in 'development aid' in the whole Cold War period was about. In fact, 500 years ago Europe lagged in several aspects economically, politically, scientifically and technologically behind other cultural centres,[22] Sandra Harding claims. The beginning of modern science in Europe was a slow gradual process during which European culture was in continual contact and exchange with other cultures around the world, even before but especially after 1492 (i.e., globalisation of knowledge). The Voyages of 'Discovery' and subsequent establishment of colonies contributed greatly to the growth of modern European science. The borrowings from other cultures are claimed by post-colonial science and technology studies to be far more extensive and important for the emergence of the European science (and technologies) than the conventional accounts have indicated.

But the borrowing was not for the benefit of a common One World (see Sachs 1992b). The colonists' science projects were 'first and last, for maintaining Europeans and their colonial enterprises . . . designed especially for increasing the profit Europe could extract from other lands and maintaining the forms of social control necessary to do so' (ibid., 44). This has not changed—see Info Box 6.13.

❖ I n f o   B o x   6 . 1 3 ❖

'Devise a Pattern . . . to Maintain This Position
of Disparity . . . Cease Thinking About Human Rights' (Kennan, USA)

George Kennan, US Cold War planner, wrote in 1948, in the aftermath of the passing of the first parts of United Nations Bill of Rights: 'We have 50 per cent of the world's wealth, but only 6.3 per cent of its population. In this situation, our real job in the coming period is to devise a pattern of relationships which permit us to maintain this position of disparity. To do so, we have to dispense with all sentimentality . . . we should cease thinking about human rights, the raising of living standards, and democratisation' (quoted in Pilger 1998: 59).

According to Harding, the historical accounts reveal an immense unidirectional flow of knowledge **to Europe**, not only **from China, India**, and others in **east Asian and Islamic societies**, but also from cultures of **Africa, pre-Columbian America**, and others. Likewise today, the brain drain from other parts of the world to, especially, Britain and the USA, is unparalleled. In several Western countries, the hospitals would not be able to function without doctors and nurses from other countries, mainly Asia but to an increasing extent today also from Eastern and Central Europe. Recruitment goes on at post-graduate and undergraduate levels. 'For example, in the mid-1990s, fewer than 20% of students from China and Bangladesh enrolled at overseas universities returned home after their studies' (Bennell & Pearce 1998: 26). Interestingly enough, it is not easy to get accurate figures for brain drain (see, e.g., UNESCO 1971)—it is not a category in most of the sources from international organisations I have checked.

The early colonialism in certain parts of the world was made possible by the colonists extracting labour and raw materials and other resources from other parts of the world. Likewise, local scientific and technologial knowledge extracted from one part of the world enabled colonialism in other parts. Indentured labour from country X was used on plantations in country Y for crops transplanted from country Z, all to benefit Europeans. 'Important parts of European organized scientific research were fundamentally in the service of establishing and maintaining colonialism and slavery' (Harding 1997: 45).

There is not much change. Today, too, a large part of not only research but also other budgets and manpower (it is mainly men) goes to military and 'intelligence'[23] purposes, again, especially in the superpower countries and their allies (see Pilger 1998 for some figures). (One of the 'minor' results is that the arms trade, dominated by Western powers, 'and conducted principally with murderous tyrannies, has caused the death of an estimated twenty million people' after the Second World War, an estimate quoted by the Nobel Peace Laureate, José Ramos-Horta, August 14, 1997; Pilger 1998: 7, 611). Technological knowledge is thus used for controlling Them, then as now. The knowledge extracted from Others (and developed further in the industrialised countries, often by the brain drained Others and their offspring) is at **our** disposal whereas the rest of the world often has minimal access, even to knowledge about themselves, as many researchers have shown (see, e.g., Escobar's (1995) discussions on this, and references in Sachs (ed.) 1992, just to name a few).

Colonialism also systematically destroyed competitive local scientific and technological traditions, resources, and knowledge (and educational systems!), both intentionally and unintentionally—just as globalisation does it today (see the examples with the Dumont quote and the Philippines, preceding and after Reader Task 6.2 below). The colonial projects 'permitted Europeans exponentially to increase their ability to organize a disproportionally large share of the world's supply of human and natural "energy" ' for their own benefit' (Harding 1997: 44). And this is still true today.

The earlier colonisation and slavery were legitimated by the 'civilising mission', as shown in the first example in Insert 6.12 and subtly criticized in the second, 6.13, by an indigenous American. Today's slavery is rationalised in similar but more sophisticated ways but it is likewise often presented as beneficial for the victims.

INSERT 6.12 'A race of children . . . the purpose . . . is to bring them forward to the maturity of the adult—if this is possible at all' (Norway)

The Lapps must learn the Norwegian language so that all the goods, spiritual and material, that our country's development has brought our people, can also reach them and in this way they can be raised from the essentially low stage of societal development that they are at . . . The Lapp people are a race of children in more than one sense. As a people, they are at the child's direct, naive, undeveloped stage, and the purpose of Norwegianisation is to bring them forward to the maturity of the adult—if this is possible at all. This is a great and lasting goal to work for. (The rector of Varanger, in a letter to his bishop, 10 December 1886, quoted in Eriksen & Niemi 1981: 57)

Compare this to President Truman's rationalisation of 'development' in Insert 6.1.

INSERT 6.13 'We have a hard trail ahead of us in trying to Americanize you and your white brothers' (USA)

You will forgive me if I tell you that my people were Americans for thousands of years before your people were. The question is not how you can Americanize us but how we can Americanize you. We have been working at that for a long time. Sometimes we are discouraged at the results. But we will keep trying. And the first thing we want to teach you is that, in the American way of life, each man [sic!] has respect for his brother's vision. Because each of us respected his brother's dream, we enjoyed freedom here in America while your people were busy killing and enslaving each other across the water. The relatives you left behind are still trying to kill each other because they have not learned there that freedom is built on my respect for my brother's vision and his respect for mine. We have a hard trail ahead of us in trying to Americanize you and your white brothers. But we are not afraid of hard trails. (Cohen (ed.) 1960: 315–316)

The early 'civilising mission' was, just as the new one, at the same time both cultural and linguistic (see Mühlhäusler 1996), and scientific-technological. According to Frank Furedi, in **The New Ideology of Imperialism** (1994), until the 1930s, 'imperialism and the global expansion of Western powers were represented in unambiguously positive terms as a major contributor to human civilisation' (quoted in Pilger 1998: 38)—just as globalisation is now. Today we want to defend this civilisation in 'splendid isolation'. See Inserts 6.14 and 6.15 for a comparison: the civilising mission has become less openly expressed and more sophisticated in (some) present-day exhortations about cooperation and international understanding, but it can still be seen, as analysed by Treffgarne in Insert 6.15.

INSERT 6.14 NATO defends Western civilisation (Huntington, USA)

According to Professor Samuel Huntington, Director of Harvard's Institute of Strategic Studies (in **The Clash of Civilisations**, 1996), 'we' need to be closed to countries non-Western in their religion and culture, and build trust and co-operation among ourselves. NATO is 'the security organisation of Western civilisation' and its 'primary purpose is to defend and preserve that civilisation'.

INSERT 6.15 'Missions de cooperation' in Francophone Africa
. . . national language education programmes do not
seriously threaten the position of French'

The integrated approach of France's 'mission civilisatrice', in which the political and economic exploitation of its colonies were closely linked to educational policy, was contingent on the exclusive use of French as the embodiment of French civilisation and culture . . . A new emphasis in France's 'missions de cooperation' in Francophone Africa . . . it was widely accepted that the survival of French in Africa was contingent on the evolution of a more complementary relationship with national languages . . . This enlightened policy change seems expedient in circumstances where national language education programmes do not seriously threaten the position of French. (Treffgarne 1986: 144, 155, 156)

Post-Second 'World' War 'development policies' continue these colonial policies—they are 'colonialism by other means' (Harding 1997: 44). As earlier, this is also still applauded for 'civilizational' reasons by some people—see the example in Insert 6.16.

The same 'civilizing mission', discussed earlier, is today also been applied in the 'aid to development' for Central and Eastern Europe. The same model which is causing the growing gaps (see later) is being aggressively exported (despite the fact that western investments have lagged behind Western ideology). The Foreign Ministers of the European Union concluded in September 1998 that the Russian economic crisis is their own fault—never mind the hordes of Western economic advisors whose advice has been followed—and they have to solve their problems without support from the EU. An example of the triumphalism involved is given in Insert 6.17.

INSERT 6.16   Immigrants into Australia still need to be civilized, as do the Kenyans and the migrant to California

A University House Master in Australia told us in October 1994 (when we discussed mother tongue teaching for immigrant minorities) that he was 'convinced that the cultural level of most immigrants is so low that they would be better served learning the high cultures of languages that are closely akin to English, meaning French and German'.

Compare this to the (British) Governor of Kenya who declared in 1955 that 'The task to which we have set our minds is to civilise a great mass of human beings who are in a very primitive moral and social state' (cited in Pilger 1998: 24).

Except civilising 'them' is today too expensive? The California Senator Bill Craven: 'It seems rather strange that we go out of our way to take care of the rights of these individuals who are perhaps on the lower scale of our humanity, for one reason or another' ('Migrants as a burden to local budgets? Hearing gets heated', **The San Diego Union Tribune**, February 6, 1993).

Despite the marginally more careful formulations in Insert 6.17, the resemblance in the Ukrainian example to historical and also many present European attitudes towards Africa and Asia is striking. These people are not developed and civilised, their ways of governance lead to chaos, they need to get advice from western Europeans in order to be able to govern themselves, they know nothing, they have no experts, the experience they have had earlier is not relevant, and their traditional mentality prevents them from modernising, from doing efficient planning, from governing themselves. We must help them, and it is for their own benefit. They will become 'developed' when they act and think like us. It is also instructive to compare this assessment by a Danish 'expert' with what happens in Danish observance of human rights— see the examples in Info Boxes 7.13 and 7.14.

In the next sections we will look further at some of the instruments and ideologies in this new colonialism using the 'development' and 'modernisation' (rather than colonialism) discourse.

6.3.1.2.   *From Pre-Modernity to Modernity With the Help of Bretton Woods: The World Bank, IMF, and Structural Adjustment Programmes*

'Develoment' was supposed to modernise the part of the world which was underdeveloped and pre-modern. Modernity was characterized by **industrialism**'s belief that science (instead of god) could offer solutions to most problems through **rational planning** and action in the transformation of 'na-

---

INSERT 6.17 'Wanted: a "good dictator" '
(a Danish assessment of Ukraine)

Mia Bloch, working for the project **EU-Tacis** (Technical Assistance to the Commonwealth of Independent States), in Ukraine, describes what the project is doing in an article with the title 'Wanted: a "good dictator" '. The project 'tries to make the public administration in Ukraine function better. One of the ways is to train young Ukrainians to work according to western principles. It is no easy task, because the ideology of the earlier empire influences all parts of society, personified in the statue of Lenin rising above the city centre, with his floating coat, while his outreached arm guides the people in the right direction.

Since independence in 1991, Ukraine has passed many laws which live up to European standards. But they are not followed . . . The administration does not see itself as a unified entity, working overall for "the common good". This concept is unknown in Ukrainian society . . . State governance is chaotic . . . Just as the population is completely untrained for voting, the politicians are completely untrained in governing a country with 51 million inhabitants, after having received orders from Moscow for 70 years. It is no longer militant calls for action and slogans that are needed but organisation, planning, budgeting, "realpolitik" and reforms . . . The democracies in western Europe have over a period of centuries built up state governance and the democratic mentality of the people. A woman in her 50s speaks with nostalgia and longing about the Soviet Union, the stable life, payment of salaries on time, and faith in the future. "Is there something that is better now?" I ask. "No. So I naturally voted for the communists." She does not think Ukraine needs western advice, because the country has its own experts. The population of Ukraine has a high educational level, even when compared to western Europe.

But there are no experts within the social sciences, management, economics. In 1991 the economics books were changed, and the first "western" thinking economists have just finished their training.' (Bloch 1998: 8).

---

ture' to 'culture' ('products') and through ordered **division of labour**. It was also characterized by **capitalism**, and by the (further) rise of the **nation-state**, with monopoly of control of the means of violence, including both external wars (the **military**) and internal **surveillance**, which is both overt (the police and secret services) and covert, control of information and 'social supervision' as Giddens calls it (1990: 59). Planning, order, steady progress, and development through rational organisation of society, radiating from industrialised countries to the rest of the world; these were key concepts.

The sociologist Göran Therborn (1995: 4–5) defines the phases in the development from pre-modernity to modernity (and further to post-modernity, see below), on a viewpoint axis where **pre-modernity** is 'looking back, over its shoulder, to the past, to [its] . . . experience and . . . example of wisdom, beauty, glory'. **Modernity** 'looks at the future, hopes for it, plans for it, constructs, builds it.' The changes have been described by many of the sociology classics (Info Box 6.14). For these changes to be implemented

---

❖ **I n f o   B o x   6 . 14** ❖

From Pre-Modernity to Modernity—Sociology Classics

With some classics, the change from pre-modernity to modernity was from military to industrial society (Saint-Simon); from a religious to a 'positive', scientific stage of social evolution (Comte); from Gemeinschaft to Gesellschaft (Tönnies): from mechanical to organic solidarity (Durkheim) and from traditional to rational (Weber).

---

all over the globe, new means were needed. Some of the first economic instruments for today's modern globalisation were put in place at the Bretton Woods hotel in July 1944 when the United Nations Monetary and Financial Conference was held towards the end of the World War II. At this meeting the overt agenda was to create institutions that would secure peace and prosperity globally. One of the not so covert agendas was to make everybody embrace the Unites States' 'elementary economic axiom . . . that prosperity has no fixed limits', as expressed by the president of the conference, the U.S. Secretary of the Treasury, Henry Morgenthau, in his opening speech (quoted in Korten 1996a: 21). The U.S. Council for Foreign Relations, a body with corporate and foreign policy leaders, had already earlier established their vision of this peaceful world, with 'a global economy, dominated by U.S. corporate interests', and with a 'grand area' (minimally 'the Western Hemisphere, the Far East and the British Empire') that the US 'would need to dominate economically and militarily to ensure [raw] materials for its industries' because 'the U.S. national interest required free access to the markets and raw materials' of this area (ibid.)—see again Kennan's formulation of 'our real job' in Info Box 6.13.

By the end of the meeting, the World Bank and the International Monetary Fund (IMF), thereafter called 'the Bretton Woods instruments', had been founded, and the groundwork had also been laid for what later became GATT.

For the pre-modern underdeveloped world the models for modernisation 'naturally' came from Europe and, increasingly, Neo-Europes, especially the USA. In the universalisation of modernity, the old colonial hierarchies were sold under new positive umbrellas, including freedom and democracy, as the Truman quote and some of the earlier civilisation quotes already showed.

The Japanese initial bying of the modernity and democracy discourse is instructive here (see also Spring 1998). Toshiko Kishida (1992) claims that modernisation was often synonymous with 'Westernization' in Japan from the Meiji restoration (1868) until the Second World War: 'The Western world was regarded as manifesting modernity, whereas the non-Western features of Japanese culture and society were seen as being pre-modern and therefore less advanced and less significant' (ibid., 46). After the war, in came 'democratization . . . [which] often paralleled "Americanization", which was again strongly associated with the image of freedom and material wealth' (ibid., 47). The model for 'westernization' was a combination of Europe and America.[24] In Kishida's analysis, it 'represented, in a covert way, Western dominance over the "premodern" Asiatic nations' (ibid., 48).

Economic globalisation still follows principles put in place in Bretton Woods, through economic programmes (Danaher 1994, Dawkins 1994), military threats, and 'development aid' (Hancock 1989). 'Development aid' is still about economic and military control (even if other more humane goals are also part of some of it): it has included 'security aid to military dictatorships facing no external threats', like Nicaragua, El Salvador, Chile, Argentina, Uruguay, and Peru in the 1960s and 1970s (Goldsmith 1996: 258), or later, to other nice 'friends' shunning any kind of democracy (like Saddam Hussein) in Iraq, Uganda, South Africa, Indonesia, and elsewhere. Other UN organisations participate in this, sometimes reluctantly: 'Under American pressure, the World Food Programme handed over $12 millions' worth of food to the Thai Army to pass on to Khmer Rouge.[25] "20,000 to 40,000 Pol Pot guerrillas benefited", according to former Assistant Secretary of State Richard Holbrooke' (quoted in Pilger 1998: 33).

Later, other instruments have been or are being added to the Bretton Woods instruments, both military (NATO, SEATO), and economic (NAFTA, WTO, World Trade Organisation). The latest candidate is MAI—Info Box 6.15.

Homogenisation for rationality and efficiency were among the characteristics which development towards industrialisation and modernity seemed to require in underdeveloped countries. Structural adjustment programmes were and are still one of the expressions for this and they became one of the prices many underdeveloped countries had to pay for getting the 'carrot' of becoming indebted to the World Bank and IMF. Even here one can see that not much has changed; the programmes (see Task Box 6.4) do not seem very different in their function and goals from those expressed a century ago by Dumont, a delegate to the French Association of Industry and Agriculture, in March 1899. The aim of the colonial power, he said, must be 'to discourage in advance any signs of industrial development in our colonies, to oblige our overseas possessions to look exclusively to the mother country for manufactured products and to fulfill, by force if necessary, their natural function,

---

❖ I n f o   B o x   6 . 1 5 ❖

MAI (Multilateral Agreement on Investment)

MAI (Multilateral Agreement on Investment) is an agreement which the 29 states in the OECD have negotiated with each other. What MAI would do in its present form is to protect the foreign investments of companies. The companies could take states to court if regulations in these states were deemed to function in ways which prevent investment and 'free' trade and competition. The types of regulation that companies could question would, for instance, be regulations about the environment, working conditions, or development of the social infrastructure of a country, welfare benefits, etc. But who is it that needs protection? The hundred largest multinational companies in the world control more than half of all foreign investment in the world, which amounts to approximately as much as the total gross national product of Brazil, China and India together (Jespersen 1998: 15; see also Dawkins 1994).

---

that of a market reserved by right to the mother country's industry' (quoted in Goldsmith 1996: 259).

The story (based on some 800 leaked World Bank documents) told by Walden Bello and his colleagues in their book **Development Debacle: the World Bank in the Philippines** (1982), shows how the World Bank, 'in league with the CIA and other U.S. agencies, set out purposefully to destroy the domestic economy of the Philippines so as to create those conditions that best favored TNC interests' (Goldsmith 1996: 260). It is a parallel to what was historically done to the Indian textile industry by the British, and to local products in much of 'French' West Africa. Despite some change in rhetoric over time, **the Bretton Woods institutions by and large continue the projects of colonialism**, only much more efficiently, as massive criticism has shown (e.g., Brock-Utne in press, Danaher (ed.) 1994, Dawkins 1994, George 1992, George & Sabelli 1994, Mander & Goldsmith (eds) 1996, Mulenga 1996, Samoff 1996). Today 'one Filipino child is said to die every hour, in a country where more than half the national budget is given over to paying just the interest on World Bank and IMF loans' (Pilger 1998: 3).

In the planning for future of modernism the small languages and cultures would necessarily have to give way in the name of the efficiency that the structural adjustment programmes purport to represent, as described earlier. **World Bank educational policy, including language policy**, continues to be a disaster (for the areas of this book, see, e.g., Brock-Utne 1993a, in press, Büchert 1996, Alamin Mazrui 1997, Mulenga 1996). Despite some recent rhetoric to the contrary, it does **not support local languages** (Alamin Mazrui 1997), even if a few of the Bank's employees have a goood understanding

---

Reader Task 6.4
Consequences of structural adjustment programmes?

Below are the conditions for getting loans from the World Bank and the IMF that (South) countries typically have to accept, according to Walden Bello (1996: 286), whose recent book, **Dark Victory** (1994) is a critique of structural adjustment programmes. Discuss possible consequences of them (some hints are given) on several countries you know—Russia in the late 1990s might be one good recent example. Which groups of people would lose most? Who might win? Also compare the demands with the century-old goals of colonial powers in the Dumont quote. These are the conditions:

1. Removing restrictions on foreign investments in local industry, banks, and other financial services (restrictions have protected local industries or banks).

2. Reorienting the economy towards exports, e.g., cash-crops (to earn foreign currency required to service the debt); self-sufficiency and diversified local production dimishes.

3. Reducing wages and/or wage increases and radically reducing government spending, also on health, education, and welfare.

4. Cutting tariffs, quotas, and other restrictions to import.

5. Devaluing local currency against hard currencies such as the U.S. dollar.

6. Privatizing state enterprises.

7. Removing government control (that protects labour, the environment, and natural resources) of export-oriented corporations through deregulation, to increase competitiveness.

---

of multilingual education issues (e.g., Dutcher 1982, Dutcher & Tucker 1997). World Bank officials who visited South Africa in 1992 'made it clear that additive bilingualism was not on the World Bank agenda and that funds would not be available to support such programs', Kathleen Heugh observed (1995c: 343). It is perhaps worth noting that these comments by the officials are in direct contradiction to official South Africa government policy which **is** additive bilingualism.

There is mounting evidence for the claim that the economic globalisation instruments for 'development' were and are in most cases, both directly and indirectly, preventing and destroying preconditions for local diversity, in terms of both biodiversity and sustainable development and linguistic and cultural diversity.

What is important to remember here, before we in the next chapter scrutinize some of the United Nations human rights instruments is that the human rights instruments were created to **complement** the Bretton Woods instruments, **not** to counteract them. If the Bretton Woods instruments are 'colonialism by other means', what might the implications be? Dear reader, read once more the quotes about the goals of the Bretton Woods instruments from the beginning of this section, and marvel . . .

Many (not all—see, e.g., Giddens 1990) contemporary analysts claim that we have during the last several decades left modernity behind and moved into the era of post-modernity, and beyond.

6.3.1.3. Shift in Power From 'Nation-States' and Democratically Elected Bodies to the TNCs and Banks

The critique of 'development' as a continuation of colonialism created new labels, to distance itself from the oppressive forms of 'development' and to try to save at least the concept itself, by calling a more radical variant 'another development', 'participatory development', 'socialist development', or the like. Arturo Escobar (1995: 5) criticizes the new labels which, despite being critical, 'were obliged to couch their critique in terms of the need for development', i.e., they did not question the framework within which the discussions were conducted. He accuses the development discourse of having colonised reality itself. Regardless of what additional labels 'development' is tagged with, it has a direction, a goal. Decolonising the development discourse necessitates not only deconstructing the questions about whose development we are talking about (and in whose language(s)), but also who decides what can be legitimately discussed.

Globalisation has in the age of post-modernity replaced the colonialism and imperialisms, universalism and internationalisation, of the ages of pre-modernity and modernity—and the 'development' of modernity. Globalisation needs deconstruction as much as the old forms did. But in addition, as Escobar, Bhabha (1990), Appadurai (1990), Apffel-Marglin 1994, Apffel-Marglin & Marglin (eds) (1990), Brock-Utne (in press), Ngũgĩ (1998) and others argue (with somewhat different meanings, though), both deconstruction and **reconstruction** are needed.

In contrast to pre-modernity's emphasis on the glorious past and modernity's emphasis on the glorious future, post-modernity 'has lost or thrown away any sense of time direction. The past as well as the future and the present have become "virtual realities", or simultaneously combinable elements' (Therborn 1995: 5). Therborn's analysis tallies with that of another early guru/anti-guru of post-modernity, Zygmunt Bauman (see 1973), whose catch phrase 'all that is solid melts in the air' captures (or, ironically, consolidates?) the essence of post-modernity. See Definition Box 6.2 for a difference between post-modernity and post-modernism.

DEFINITION BOX 6.2 Post-modernity versus post-modernism

Even if the two concepts are often used interchangably, '**postmodernity** is more frequently used to refer to phenomena that are taking place in society. The second, **post-modernism**, is more likely to refer to a set of phenomena that characterise social theory . . . and, by implication, policies derived from such theories' (Ó Riagáin 1997: 17). I shall follow this usage, i.e., I am mostly concerned with post-modernity.

Internationalisation, the predecessor of globalisation and one of the desirable contents and goals in modernisation, clearly continued the hierarchisation of the colonial world, even when some countries had started questioning it. To continue the Japanese example, Kishida describes that in Japan since the 1980s, in stepped 'internationalization [which] presupposes an equal status in the global disposition of power, even with the possible implication that Japan has gained a position significant enough to influence the dynamics of world politics' (ibid., 48). Kishida sees Japan as no longer willing to 'enter into a vertical relationship under the hegemony of one nation' and asks whether 'the time has come for Japan to proclaim independence from America, if not entirely, then at least more strongly than in previous decades. This move on the part of Japan will also naturally entail the acknowledgment of various responsibilities expected of an independent nation' (ibid., 48). Kishida's 'internationalization' is thus still not the globalisation of post-modernity, but part of the era of modernity: there is no withering away of the nation-state, as in post-modernity. But at the same time it is 'pre-modern' in its proclamation of Japan being strong and significant enough to influence the world, just as the 'world civilisations' earlier had a firm geographic origin. Instead of being global or international, they were firmly 'rooted in Athens, Rome, Constantinople' (Barnet & Cavanagh 1994: 21) or, later, London, Madrid, Berlin, Washington.[26]

When TNCs and post-modernist nomads today move freely from country to country, without solidarity or ties (or mother tongues or ethnic identities), when the corporate globalisation, with post-modern ideologies, 'celebrates the liberation from passionate attachments to any specific piece of territory' (ibid., 21), and tries to make obsolete the pre-modern states which (like USA or Japan) cling to vertical relations, attached to territories (= their own states), are they then also paving the way for a less hierarchical, more equal world? Is it taking us closer to the universal consciousness that 'poets, philosophers, and prophets have dreamed through the ages' (Barnet & Cavanagh 1994: 21). Quite the opposite. Today's globalisation is creating still more powerful global vertical relations, without even the pretention of democratic control, or 'duties that go with rights' (see the Japanese quote above).

Globalisation means geographical stretching-out (Massey 1993, quoted in Ó Riagáin 1997: 19) of social, economic, environmental, political, and cultural relations—and linguistic relations.

It is not only a fact, as Tony Clarke puts it, that

> 'corporations have achieved effective global governance by virtue of their control of economic processes, of financial markets, of the new global trade bureaucracy, of the media, and, increasingly, of education'. But today 'forty-seven of the top hundred economies in the world are actually transnational corporations [TNCs]; 70 percent of global trade is controlled by just five hundred corporations; and a mere 1 percent of the TNCs on this planet own half the total stock of foreign direct investment' (Clarke 1996: 297, 298)

What has taken place is not only a homogenisation and centralisation of business, but a massive shift in power, 'out of the hands of nation-states and democratic governments and into the hands of TNCs and banks. It is now the TNCs that effectively govern the lives of the vast majority of the people on Earth' (ibid., 298). This is true especially of the largest 500 or so of the 45,000 TNCs. And this is of course what globalisation mainly means. In the new age of transnational economic empires the TNCs have already 'achieved a degree of global integration never achieved by any world empire or nation-state'. This is the assessment of Richard Barnet and John Cavanagh in their book **Global Dreams. Imperial corporations and the new world order** (1994: 15).

But for at least 3.5 to 4 billion people, two thirds of the world's population, the **Global Shopping Mall** and the **Global Financial Network**, two of the four 'intersecting webs of global commercial activity on which the new world economy largely rests' (ibid., 15), might just as well not exist. Two thirds of us are much too poor to participate—we/they are excluded. If they are lucky, some of them might be allowed to sweat for a pittance in the **Global Workplace**, while the **Global Cultural Bazaar**, with TV, radio, films, music, games, toys, t-shirts, reaches them, creating unreachable dreams which always seem to be just around the corner—and pacifies them, or tries, at least, via the 'cultural nerve gas'. 'Panem et circenses', bread and entertainment for the slaves, in Caesar's Rome; cheap beer and football for British workers[27] in Glasgow in 1919 (the closest they ever came to a popular uprising this century); and gene-manipulated soya beans (in the best (!) case) with Murdoch and Time-Warner's Turner (Rupert & Ted) today—and football and the Olympic Games, virtually owned by Coca-Cola, Nike, and other TNCs—all for planned pacification.

But these 'unpeople', as John Pilger (1998) calls them, two-thirds of humanity, are themselves absent in the media world (except as consumers): in

Britain, for instance, 'only 3 per cent of peak-time programmes feature **anything** about the majority of humanity, and almost all of that is confined to the "minority" channels' (Pilger 1998: 2). For some of the facts and discussions about global media as killers of diversity, see, e.g., Herman & McChesney 1997, Raboy & Bruck 1989, Downing 1984, Lewis (ed.) 1996, Tankha (ed.) 1996, Hamelink 1994, 1995, (ed.) 1997, (ed.) 1998.

If the 'unpeople' are absent in the **Global Shopping Mall** (where we as consumers might make decisions?) and the **Global Financial Network** (where the decisions about what might be on the agenda for us as consumers to decide about are made), if they are only consumers without much say in the **Global Cultural Bazaar**, what are the possibilities for them to influence their own lives through negotiations in the **Global Workplace** through trade unions and old-fashioned solidarity? We could characterise one aspect of post-modernity with a few strokes as follows: With Internet, post-modernity and globalisation have left behind not only a fixed 'time' concept, as in Therborn's definitions above, but also the concept of concrete 'places' and 'markets' (see also Giddens 1990). What we have now is 'spaces'. These can be much more decentralised (see van Ermen 1998). Much of the Big Buying and selling happens electronically and often within transnationals,[28] whereas a lot of the small buying happens locally. Many centralised work places may become work spaces too. They can be in homes (with a computer or with actual sub-contracted slavery, children and women sewing footballs, baseballs, shoes, etc.) or in combined local office spaces for many companies.

This development can have aspects of both freedom and isolation. It certainly contributes to hierarchisation. It contributes to both ease in access to knowledge for more people than earlier, and a possibility of contact, organising and counter-hegemonies. At the same time, it contributes to physical isolation, insecurity (Elliott & Atkinson 1998), extreme individualism, and not caring, and also apathy and powerlessness. We will look at a few aspects of conditions for agency, before discussing the role of the 'withering-away' states.

6.3.1.4. *From Active Agents in Universalisation to Agentless Globalisation—It 'Happens' to Us*

In sociologist Zygmunt Bauman's view, in post-modernity globalisation has replaced the **universalism** of the modernisation period (Bauman 1997). **Universalisation** (which of course was also the ideological and cultural legitimation of slavery) was seen by some (idealists?) as positive: 'civilisation' (i.e., Our values) was spread to more and more countries, and differences were going to be levelled out. In fact universalisation also had to do with westernisation and homogenisation, so that is not where the news lies. In Bauman's analysis (1997; see also Bauman 1998a, b), the differerence between the two is that **universalisation** was seen as something with active agents (we **made** it happen) whereas **globalisation** is (constructed as) something that **happens to us**, a 'natural' process that moves by itself. Agentless.[29] Like 'language death'.

In the post-modern era, safety and security of life, connected with controlling it, being agents in it, planning for a future, have disappeared with modernity. Instead, Bauman (1997) claims, we have uncertainty, existential anxiety, Unsicherheit. They are here to stay and we are (or have to be, or become) reconciled to them. The fear is not today a simple fear of natural catastrophes (as much of it might have been in the pre-modern era) but fear of results of human action; it is **manufactured uncertainty** (compare with my fears in Info Box 6.12). Even many of the 'natural' disasters (floods, global warming, etc.) are today often caused or prompted by human action, **inherent** in globalisation.

There is a lack of existential grounding: jobs disappear; traditional skills (or any skills on a long term basis) have no longer a (lasting) market value; human partnerships, including the most intimate ones, are fragile. All is/are on the move. Even if we never leave the place where we were born or where we stay; the ground is moving from under us, despite us. This may be good for some adventurous spirits, but for most of us it means anxiety. All of us have in us both enjoyment of adventure (as the post-modernist ideal has it) but also fear of not being in control. In pre-modernity catastrophes were often 'natural': drought, failed crops, cholera, etc.; and science was supposed to cure them in modernity. Post-modernity represents and has brought back many of the uncertainties of pre-modernity that modernity tried to get rid of; but in a new form.

Rootedness and localisation are one possible answer to the uncertainties, and for most people they are as important as they have ever been—there is no alternative. People's livelihood and well-being are dependent on 'a specific piece of ground and a particular culture and language', Barnet and Cavanagh claim (1994: 21–22). Or languages, in the plural, my comment—some of us have two mother tongues and some territories ('pieces of ground') are multilingual.[30] Even when some countries are vast, and one can experience a lot travelling **within** a country, it is indicative of the lack of some types of globalisation that only 8 percent of the globe's population travelled from their country to another in 1990, and only some 10 percent of the USA's population had a passport (ibid., 29). There are many types of positive localisation, much of it out of necessity, some by choice—this will be discussed further later in the book.

But uncertainty according to Bauman (1997) also creates **fundamentalist, neo-tribal sentiments**: let's **make** the world a bit simpler, more constrained, more secure. This is one of the jobs performed by the consciousness industry, mainly the media, including the pre-censored, pre-digested news (Hamelink

1994, 1995), infotainment. Nationalisms, East and West, North and South, belong to this category—whereas demands for the maintenance of linguistic and cultural diversity do not, when they are expressed in terms of respecting your language and culture too, because one values one's own. Here I will give just one symbolic example, connecting economics and language, of the simplification based on uncertainty (triumphalism often represents this combination). It shows the result of trying to re-create the illusion of pre-modern certainties, in a post-modern world of insecurities, with fundamentalist modernist means.

Dow Templeton Associates, part of one of the powerful transnational complexes, puts their forecast for the next millennium very simply, under the subtitle 'Global village'(**Dow 2000**. Third Quarter, 1997, p. 1): 'Individual value systems, cultures and traditions will be maintained, but English will become the universal language and capitalism will become the dominant social system'. It is interesting that transnational Dow expresses the parallel between a universal/dominant language and a universal/dominant economic system so clearly and simply, not to say simplistically. The development accelerating since the disintegration of the Soviet Union and leading to the triumphalist proclamation of the 'free' market system as The Global System For Ever, has in fact constructed the 'free market' system as a **political** system rather than an economic system only.[31] It is clear that this development is an active agent in killing languages faster than ever, and in that sense there is a causal relationship between the two dominant forces in Dow's proclamation.

There does not seem to be enough reason for this triumphalist prognosis. Dow's image-building claims (in the first part of the quote and elsewhere in their propaganda) draw on individualist post-modern (or at least late modernity-related) ideologies of **mobility, change, and unlimited choice**. But the exact opposite seems to figure prominently in the **lack** of (political and linguistic) choice that it offers: one system, one language. On the other hand, this prognosis, the 'Free Markets For Ever' and 'The Universal Language', symbolizes the early phases of modernity, planning for future with 'rational' means. But according to Therborn and others, that is no longer where we are. The Dow prognosis seems to me to be a perfect little example of a result of the post-modern uncertainty: let's make the world simple, let's have one world language and one world economic system. This is a powerful but at the same time desperate solution: trying to re-create the illusion of pre-modern certainties, with modernist means, in a post-modern world—and ruining the planet as a side-effect. This solution creates certainty for 'Us': We who belong to the neo-tribe of capitalist English-speaking elites will gain and maintain control. We can feel secure because We are able to recognise and feel safe and secure in the McDonaldized World (see Definition Box 6.3 for the concept McDonaldization). Outside, on the streets, We see the same sanitized, safe, predictable, and homogenised and environmentally disastrous

DEFINITION BOX 6.3 McDonaldization (Hamelink, Ritzer)

'Coca-Colaization' (signalling a particular, singular product) seems to be the first name for the phenomenon today discussed under the heading of 'McDonaldization' (taking its name from a more general business franchise). Cees Hamelink, media researcher, and George Ritzer, sociologist, have complementary definitions, and, interestingly enough, none of them figures in the other's bibliography.

For Hamelink, McDonaldization is part of production for global markets where products and information aim at creating the impression of 'global customers that want global services by global suppliers' (1994: 110). McDonaldization involves 'aggressive round-the-clock marketing, the controlled information flows that do not confront people with the long-term effects of an ecologically detrimental lifestyle, the competitive advantage against local cultural providers, the obstruction of local initiative, all converge into a reduction of local cultural space' (ibid., 112).

Ritzer's definition of McDonaldization is: 'the process by which the principles of the fast-food restaurant are coming to dominate more and more sectors of American society as well as the rest of the world' (1996: 1). The 'basic dimensions of McDonaldization' are according to him (ibid., 33) 'efficiency, calculability (or quantification), predictability, increased control through substitution of nonhuman for human technology, and the seemingly inevitable[33] by-product of rational systems [rational in the Weberian sense]—the irrationality of rationality'.

Hamelink is much more critical of the phenomenon and discusses it more from a global and structural point of view, while Ritzer seems to vaccillate between criticism and fascination and individualises McDonaldization in terms of both customers and those who developed the first McDonaldized businesses.

McDonalds[32] and Pizza-Huts everywhere even if We only frequent them in other, unsafe countries, not in our own. Inside, the hotels We stay in in other countries, belong to the same chain, with the same CNN. We don't need to know where in the world we are—the hotel lobbies and rooms and drinks are the same, and we can contact everybody in seconds on our cellocomputer. In our own country, We live in safe, guarded quarters, with smashed glass on the walls of our private ghetto, and a private guard, or in gated cities (Blakely & Snyder 1997), guarded closed villa quarters where our guests have to phone a day in advance to be registered and where our children are driven to school and friends and hobbies because they cannot walk anywhere or play on the streets. And the devil take the rest: Global Apartheid takes care of them. In our own country, We use the localised state for internal control: We put the Others in prisons (see Info Box 6.16), criminalise them as poor

Prisons (USA)

A nation of criminals? The number of people in prison in the United States in 1996 (almost 1¼ million) is four times what it was 20 years earlier, in 1976 (while the costs only doubled between 1976 and 1989, i.e., the conditions in prisons became worse). In relative terms, only Russia and China have more, and in the western world the US is an absolute number one. In 1993, the number of prisoners per 100,000 of population was 89 in Italy, 86 in the United Kingdom, 84 in France, 80 in Germany, 51 in The Netherlands, and 546 in the USA (with Georgia at 730, Texas 700, and New York 519). The costs for prisons are expected to rise so that prison costs alone at the beginning of the next century are close to the US defence budget. Already today the costs for the domestic state machinery for violence (prisons, police) in the US are higher than the defence costs, i.e., attempts to physically control the 'enemy within' cost more than the attempts to control the 'enemy without'.

Within a year, 1 out of 25 grown-up Americans (18 years and over) goes to jail. For men, the figure is 1 of 14, for black men 1 in 4, and for black men between 18 and 34, 1 in 3. For each person in jail in the US, there are two others who are in some way controlled by the criminal law system, e.g., released on parole. More than one man in four has been arrested at least once and is therefore registered in the criminal system. In 1995, 5.4 million Americans were in prison, on parole, or on probation.

At the same time as the costs for prisons doubled between 1976 and 1989, the costs for higher education went down by 6% and the social costs for non-medical purposes went down by 41%. It is more and more difficult and expensive to go to college, and easier and easier (and 'free') to go to prison. If one manages to get to college, it is today, according to Balvig (1996: 8) wiser from the point of view of career and salary prospects to prepare to become a prison guard than a college teacher.[34] The prisons brought down the US unemployment figures by 2 percentage points during the 1990s according to some estimates.

At the same time as almost half the young prisoners in California are 'second generation prisoners' (with a parent who has also been or is in jail), the education for social minorities and ethnic minorities (groups where there is a statistically significant overlap) is disintegrating. In the whole country, Blacks account for 13% of drug users (more or less equivalent to the proportion of Blacks in the population) but a third of those arrested and three-quarters of those imprisoned for drug offences. 'Lock them up' and 'Three strikes and you are out' show that the United States is leading the western world in using brutal physically punitive methods in trying to control people whom the state at the same time itself via its own unemployment, non-housing, non-education, and other policies actively creates as 'enemies'. What the USA has is 'a commercial socio-penal complex designed to monitor and penalise those population groups that refuse to submit[35] to the new economic order, with a gender-based division

(Continued)

```
┌─────────────────────────────────────────────────────────────────┐
│ ┌───────────────────────────────────────────────────────────────┐ │
│ │                     ❖ I n f o   B o x   6 . 16 ❖              │ │
│ │                                                               │ │
│ │                          ( Continued )                        │ │
│ │                                                               │ │
│ │   of labour: the penal element covers males in the main,      │ │
│ │   while the welfare                                           │ │
│ │   component supervises the women and children' (Wacquant      │ │
│ │   1998: 9).                                                    │ │
│ │       It is at the same time perfectly possible to reduce     │ │
│ │   the number of prisoners,                                    │ │
│ │   without increased criminality rates—for instance Finland    │ │
│ │   has reduced the                                             │ │
│ │   numbers by 50% between 1990 and 1996, without any negative  │ │
│ │   consequences                                                │ │
│ │   (sources: Balvig 1996, Wacquant 1998).                      │ │
│ └───────────────────────────────────────────────────────────────┘ │
└─────────────────────────────────────────────────────────────────┘
```

(see below) and keep them otherwise invisible, except when We need to legitimate our control mechanisms, the need for the internal machinery of violence. And in other countries, We use and finance our friends and allies to keep their Others at bay—by their own local states for internal physical violence (with our arms, of course), and by Us, through the dreams that We create via our cultural neo-imperialism.

If ordinary people feel insecure with this direction of 'development', where they may feel that they have not been the agents, where it has 'happened to them' (because surely we did not make it happen?), have we, The People, in some way democratically elected the agents? Are they accountable to us? What is the role of the state that we are citizens in, and loyal to? What is 'our' state doing to protect us, and to protect diversity?

6.3.1.5. *The Role of the Local State in the Globalisation Era—Glocalisation*

Since globalisation is presented as 'natural', states do not need to actively function as its positive agents, according to Bauman (1997, 1998a). The only necessary actions by states are negative: to remove hurdles and obstacles to capitalism from its way: to drop the constraints to the 'free' market (e.g., through WTO), to let capital be flexible, and workers replaceable, movable, and controllable. Bauman uses the claims by Tietmeyer, the German **Bundesbank** director, as an example. According to Tietmeyer the key task for states in the world today is to secure the confidence and trust of investors. The state must remove any obstacles to this confidence. Tietmeyer's claims are accepted at face value; he does not need arguments to support his claims. In his world, the investors are the only volatile element/force.

Behind this lies the collapse of institutions of political control of trade and capital. This control has been handed over from states to transnational capital, including transnational corporations as we saw earlier, and the TNCs often have more representatives than the states where many of the decisions are taken (e.g., about food controls—biotechnology debates are a case in point).

Tietmeyer's investors are in Bauman's view (1997) interested in **weak but sovereign states**.

The tests of the **sovereignty** of a state during modernity had to do with to what extent the state had political control over the economy, the military, and the culture; was self-sufficient and sovereign and could provide for its citizens.

In the globalisation era the post-modern state has no control over the traditional markers of sovereignty; sovereignty has disappeared or is shaky beyond repair. Globalisation has been replaced by **glocalisation**, Bauman and others claim.

There is a **globalisation** of **finance and capital**: they are extraterritorial. In Bauman's view (1997), everybody can buy the same tanks, provided they are 'friends' and 'allies' of the arms producers and can pay, i.e., **military control** has disappeared; UN Security Council is often used as an American rubber stamp. Besides, it is somewhat contradictory that those countries which are supposed to try to secure peace in the world more than any others (i.e., the permanent members of the Security Council) are most dependent on wars continuing—the five members, USA, Britain, France, Russia, and China are 'the world's biggest arms dealers' (Pilger 1998: 123). And American **culture** is everywhere (see, e.g., Herman & McChesney 1997). The legal protection that TNCs have (for instance through GATT, NAFTA, and WTO) over the rights of citizens and states, and the global consumer culture that they create, for instance through advertising, is in Tony Clarkes's words (1996: 300) a 'key element in the new corporate tyranny'. It has been estimated that the sums transnationals spent in advertising already a few years ago were more than half of what the world's states combined spent on education (ibid.). A global monoculture is being created, mainly based on American products and ideologies.

The only area where states are still 'sovereign' in Bauman's (1997) view is the **preservation of local law and order** (see again Info Box 6.16). This represents **localisation**, as opposed to globalisation. States have to be **weak** in order not to be able to prevent the globalisation which transnationals need. But they have to be capable of securing the safety of international businessmen on the streets everywhere, Bauman claims (1997; the information in Info Box 6.16 on prisons and Nelson Mandela's recipe for reducing crime in 6.1.5.1, are indicative of this task) and to control workers, i.e., to have control over the state apparatuses for violence for internal purposes. Most wars today are intra-state wars, not wars between states (and the death toll of war-related causes since 1945 is at least 25 million, of these at least 3.2 million in the first half of the 1990s, Renner 1998: 134).

States use their power to control both the poor who bear the brunt of globalisation, and those who might want to prevent the removal of the obstacles to globalisation. Increasing inequality is one of the necessary and logical consequences of structural changes caused by globalisation (one of the 'stress on people' factors in Figure 9.1). But instead of analysing the structural poverty, resulting from, among other factors, the structural unemployment inherent in the 'free markets', as a result of globalisation, the poor are in the globalisation discourse constructed as being structurally poor and unemployed mostly because of their own inherent characteristics (Insert 6.18), deficiencies within themselves (among these lack of competence in dominant languages). If the **Asian Tigers** could do it, everybody can—if they don't it is their own fault.

INSERT 6.18   Criminalization of poverty

At the same time as poverty is increasing alarmingly (see Info Boxes 6.1 through 6.5), it is denied by Government representatives, regardless of who is in power—most of those on the streets are not poor but criminal, and to be blamed themselves. In Britain, David Maclean, a junior Home Office Tory minister claimed, according to **Guardian Weekly** (19 January 1997, p. 8) that 'most of London's beggars were Scots and were on the streets from choice. There were no "genuine" beggars, he said, because there were plenty of social benefits available.'

Labour has the same policy. Tony Blair, the Labour leader, favours the 'zero tolerance' of crime, obviously counting being poor in the crimes that he wants to get rid of. He wants to 'clear the streets of beggars, vagrants and people sleeping rough' and says that it is 'right to be intolerant of people homeless on the streets', adding that it was 'important to say we don't tolerate the small crimes; that you don't tolerate the graffiti on the wall.' Blair was echoing his shadow home secretary, Jack Straw who promised that Labour would reclaim the streets from 'beggars, winos, addicts and squeegee merchants' (ibid.).

Ironically (?), the Church made a distinction that the political parties did (and do) not make, by not blaming the victims but hinting at social injustice: 'Bishop of Edinburgh gave unprecedented endorsement to the Labour Party when he said it offered "a chance to transform the unjust reality of life in Britain." He accused the Tories of deceitful self-interest and lack of moral vision.' The Head of the Scottish Episcopal Church said in an article in the Church Times that 'the moral vision of socialism has always been higher than that of conservatism, and it was Karl Marx who understood why' (ibid.).

The images of the poor have undergone change over time (see Gronemeyer's excellent analysis of this, 1992). In early Christianity the poor were there to help the rich camels to get through the needle's eye; helping the poor was **beneficial, but for the rich**. There was less stigma attached to being poor, for instance in the Bible: they were poor temporarily, it was not their fault. When, later on, the poor were seen to suffer from temporary illness or unemployment and being just in need of short-term help to become useful and self-sufficient again, some shame was connected with this state, but many poor were helped (and maybe spiritually salvaged) and the rich gained a clear conscience, meaning **both the helper and the helped benefitted**. Industrialisation in the West constructed the poor as poor partly because they did not have the right attitudes or work and food habits or knowledge; in addition to material help, they needed teaching and control. They had to feel shame, be grateful and humble, when the rich were 'unselfishly helping' them (just as they were 'helping' and civilising' in other parts of the world).

Today, because the poor have no spending power, they are bad consumers, and under the 'free' market that is a crime, according to Zygmunt Bauman (1998a, b). The criminalisation of poverty is rapidly spreading from the United States and Blair's Britain to the rest of the Western world. In some other parts of the world the analysis of reasons for poverty is often more astute (see, e.g., Vandana Shiva's or Escobar's analyses, see bibliography[36]).

In some of the most liberal progressive countries—like the Nordic countries—there was a short phase in the 1970s and 1980s when the poor were seen as clients having some basic rights. Today criminalisation, suspicion, and control have taken over again. The criminalisation leads to the poor being 'legitimately' controlled by the state machinery, no longer directly by the rich (in the welfare state by social workers, and increasingly the police). They are no longer 'helped' (see Insert 6.19 for an example of what several Danish analysts have called bonded labour or even slavery for the unemployed and for recipients of social welfare in Denmark).

INSERT 6.19 New Slavery in Denmark?

In the liberal Nordic countries, the latest suggestions from political parties in 1998 on how to get the unemployed and the recipients of social welfare to work in Denmark introduce what some critics have called bonded labour or even slavery. The controlled groups have to accept 'activation' offers, where they are arbitrarily assigned work—not necessarily anything that corresponds to their qualifications. If they refuse, they lose the unemployment benefits or the welfare check. But they are not paid the normal wages for that work—they still only get what the unemployment benefits or the welfare check would be, often much less than minimum wages. No pension rights; no union rights; no rights to complaint. Because of these conditions, the trade union for university graduates in Denmark, Dansk Magisterforening, filed in 1998 a complaint with ILO against the Danish state, for violation of human rights—and lost.

The present labour conditions in many parts of the world, including several European and North American metropoles, represent not ethnic cleansing so much as economic cleansing: townships, bantustans for the poor of the world. There are areas in many of the big cities where 'Third World conditions' prevail in the assessment of several observers (e.g., Barnet & Cavanagh 1994). Thus the local state removes the obstacles for the globalising free market. Signing the half-secretly negotiated MAI (Multilateral Agreement on Investment) will further accelerate this development.

If the glocalisation development continues in the same direction, the state seems to exist rather for control than 'protection' of ordinary citizens.

Several analysts report on contradictory tendencies too—some of these in relation to Asian regrets and worries about identity and the subtractive spread of the English language were reported earlier. Bauman also claims (1997) that if the globalisation of information levels out cultural differences and cultures in general, a policy of fragmentation, implied in localisation, may on the other hand also favour differentiation. You can have whatever cultural values you want but still get Western tanks, computers, etc.; Iraq and Saudi Arabia were earlier good examples. Bauman sees illogicality, a lack of cohesion, in the policy. This seems to me to represent the same illogicality as the one in the initial Soros quote: a post-modern error of treating values, cultural and otherwise, as some kind of free-floating agents where one can pick and choose. This disregards the 'predispositions enduring in the habitus' (Bourdieu) discussed in section 4.3.2.2, and the power of the consciousness industry.

Before looking at other alternatives to this somewhat depressing picture, we will sum up some of the consequences of the issues discussed, for development, education, and linguistic diversity.

6.3.2. Globalisation, Development, Education, and Linguistic Diversity

The development model, with capitalism and English (as in Dow's prognosis above) as both the means and the goals, has been exported worldwide, neo-colonising the 'South' countries. The model is in complete contradiction with the South countries' multilingual realities, and with their own definition of what development is (see Definition Box 6.4), a definition which would also correspond to the human rights and basic needs oriented approach in this book in all other respects except for its advocacy for growth. Development in the sense of this definition is clearly impossible under globalisation, on every account.

The same 'development' model has also operated in a similar fashion domestically in the North's own marginalised, 'underdeveloped' areas. A description of the process in the Arctic areas of the rich Nordic countries

> **DEFINITION BOX 6.4**   Development (South Commission)
>
> A process of self-reliant growth achieved through the participation of the people acting in their own interests as they see them, and under their own control. The primary objective is to satisfy the basic needs of all the people through a democratic structure of government that supports individual freedoms of speech and organization, and respects all human rights (based on the definition provided in **The Challenge to the South**, the Report of the South Commission; Harris 1997: 213).

(Jussila & Segerståhl 1988: 17) could just as well relate to Africa—and, maybe, to central and eastern Europe?

> Economic growth and its implications are present in the modernization process . . . in the marginalised areas. All productive activities have been gradually geared towards markets after the emergence of money economy in these areas. The use of local resources is today a means for acquiring both financial and social prestige, which in turn sets aside ideas of a sustainable use of resources, although the knowledge of sustainability would exist.

What have been the results in Eastern and Central Europe of following Western advise on globalisation and free markets? In a paper called 'The Effects of Globalization on the Economies of the Countries in Eastern Europe', presented at the conference 'Globalisation—on whose terms', the economist Judit Balázs (1999), analyses 'development' in the Visegrad 4 countries (Czech Republic, Hungary, Poland, Slovakia—all but Slovakia to join the European Union in the next round) in terms of several macro-indicators (GDP, capital import, foreign trade balance, wages, etc.). Her general conclusion (see also Balázs 1993) is that there is a growing gap between the dream targets and reality (see Table 6.6).

Ordinary people in these countries are starting to regret, and protest.[37] Just when I am writing this, the news tells about farmers and small-holders protesting in both Namibia and Poland. Subsidised European Union exports destroy the chances of Namibian farmers to export meat to South Africa (where the EU dumps beef that costs South African consumers less than a dollar for 2 kilograms) and the chances of Polish farmers to sell their products in Poland. Tear gas was used in January 1999 by the police against the Polish peasants . . .

The growing gaps, instead of the 'promised land' where benefits are supposed to at least trickle down, are causing increasing disillusionment with the 'development' implied in globalisation, as Balázs shows. The poor and

TABLE 6.6
Growing gaps between dream targets and reality: Visegrad 4 countries

The Target	The Reality
Economic growth	Growing indebtedness
Semantic freedom	Growing demagogy
Restructuring of the economy	Dramatic destruction of the real sphere
Western-style consumption	Shrinking internal market
Democratic social system	Rapid polarisation, impoverishment
Liquidation of the autocracy of the communist elite	Conversion of the former political power into 'money' power
Society based on democratic laws	Organised criminality
Democratic multiparty system	Lack of democratic institutions, emergence of oligarchies in low, middle and upper levels

(Source: Balázs, 1999)

the underdeveloped countries have had the carrot in front of them for a very long time; they have been told that they will start getting their fair share once they 'develop'. The rich North and West countries have always had both the recipes (civilize!, industrialize!, develop!, become like us!) and the means (colonisation, slavery, Bretton Woods, WTO), the paradigms (underdevelopment, modernisation, globalisation), and the cover terms for continued exploitation (including 'structural adjustments', 'comparative advantages', 'free trade', and 'free markets'). This is how Johan Galtung, the Norwegian peace and development researcher, formulated the criticism of not only the modernisation paradigm but also of other economistic development paradigms:

> In development studies . . . development was narrowed down to 'economic growth'; economic growth was then narrowed further down to increase in the gross national product per capita, which is another way of saying that the country should industrialize . . . and do what the western, industrialized, capitalist countries had already done. There were obstacles. Social structures incompatible with this were referred to as 'traditional', any opposing attitude was defined as 'resistance', and sociologists, social anthropologists and psychologists were called in to try to come to grips with such impediments, thus assisting in the study of development economics. (Galtung 1988: 143–144)

Among the 'impediments' or 'handicaps' which many underdeveloped countries 'had', were their 'traditional' cultures and their languages, especially their linguistic diversity, which were seen as preventing both a free flow of information (through education, through mass media) and goods, and the national unity needed to allow for the centralised planning needed for development (without obstinate peasants who clung to the 'economy of affection' as a Swedish development economist (Hyden 1983) has called it.

Two of the basic ideas clearly discernible behind UPE, Universal Primary Education (see 8.3.4) had to do with **nation building** and with **development education** (Takala 1989). UPE was to help in developing an awareness of belonging to one nation, among peoples who had more local or regional loyalties, but who had, mostly because of the European colonizers, come to be lumped together within the same country borders. It was intended also to develop a basic instrument for practising this national unity, namely a common language for people with different mother tongues so that they could communicate with each other.[38] UPE was to include learning (at least one of) the official language(s) of the country.

This means that both basic motivating principles behind **UPE led away from local and regional mother tongues**, because both nation building and development education seemed to 'require' common languages with more currency, even if this was not made explicit in the reports, merely taken for granted. That phenomenon is also understandable, because most of the leaders and planners had, partly through their Western education, been duped into believing in the superiority of the languages of the former colonial powers. As the Ghanaian linguist Ansre puts it (1979: 13), 'linguistic imperialism has a subtle way of warping the minds, attitudes and aspirations of even the most noble in a society and of preventing him [sic] from appreciating and realising the full potentialities of the indigenous languages. Victims of it are often convinced that despite the fact that large numbers of the public may not be able to speak the foreign language it is good for the country . . . '. Debi Pattanayak, then Director of the Central Institute of Indian Languages, wrote: 'Whatever may be the difference among the elite on the language issue they are united in their subservience to English . . . The highly educated alienated minority elite continues to support English in the name of the minority in the firm belief that English education is equal to modernisation. However, in reality it helps them keep the control of administration and mass communication.' (1981b, 13, 8).

Moving then from UPE more specifically to education and language, the modernisation paradigm in development education held that education was one of the main prerequisites for 'modernising' (away from traditional work habits, increasing achievement motivation, long range planning, rational cost-benefit analysis as a basis for action, etc.) and thus for economic growth, which was seen as the panacea for underdeveloped countries. But even after the modernisation paradigm came under increasing attack as an **economic** theory, its arguments were still used (by Unesco, by the World Bank) as a basis for **educational** planning (see, e.g., the World Bank's Education in Sub-Saharan Africa, 1988). Since the idea of 'modernisation' included rapid spread of new technologies and ideas through education and mass media, a common language for this was thought necessary as discussed above.

Now that a common **international** language is claimed to be needed for globalisation for the whole world, it would be instructive to sum up some aspects of earlier **national** experience of 'a common language through education'. Does this 'common, international language' go together with 'Education for All', so that we in the end get 'a common education for all through a common, international language'? where the content of this education is being decided by the A team, for their own benefit? At the Third Oxford Conference on Education and Development, held at New College, Oxford, 21–25 September 1995, the President of the British Association for International and Comparative Education, Sir Christopher Ball, gave an address on 'Towards a global core curriculum' that envisages a globalized education system, complete with 'a global qualifications system and global arrangements for quality assurance in education and training' (quoted from Ball's synopsis). Robert Phillipson analyses it as follows (1998: 103):

> For Ball, an influential British educationalist, the globalization of education must 'focus on seven key domains of learning: (i) learning how to learn, (ii) the world-language, (iii) the mother-tongue (if different from ii), (iv) numeracy, (v) cultural literacy, (vi) social skills, (vii) religion, ethics and values' (ibid.).
>
> His global core curriculum thus involves producing two types of educated people, monolingual English-speakers, and bilinguals who learn English as a second language. In responding to questions after his paper, Ball indicated that he could identify no intellectual or educational arguments for English-speakers to learn any foreign languages. His global core curriculum has little to do with equity, cultural diversity or additive language learning. It is a recipe for global diglossia, an exercise in ante-diluvian myth-making, and ultimately a return to pre-Babel monolingualism ('And the whole earth was of one language, and of one speech', Genesis XI), the difference being that in the new dispensation the whole earth will speak English.

In much of Africa and Asia, the dominant role of English in secondary and higher education, on the route to upward social mobility, remains unchanged, with substantial 'aid' from British and American donors consolidating the position of English. As a result, there is a growing mismatch between actual language use in the society, societal goals, and educational means, with the result that education is largely failing to deliver the goods (Alexander 1995a, 1995b, in press, Brock-Utne 1993a, b, in press, Hartshorne 1995, Heugh 1995a, 1995b, in press, Luckett 1995, Rubagumya 1990). The picture is broadly similar in most former colonies (Haddad et al. 1990). Symptoms of crisis and financial straits make injections of cash from the World Bank more attractive, and the Bank and the IMF seem to have African countries in their pockets.[39]

There are grave grounds for doubting the appropriacy of such development assistance. Why should the western world, in which mass education is fraught with unresolved problems, be able to resolve acute problems elsewhere? (See Kozol 1991 on schools in diverse areas of the USA. In Britain the pattern is equally patchy: 'Half the primary schools and two-fifths of secondary schools are failing to teach children to a satisfactory standard, the Office for Standards in Education said in its annual report on the condition of schooling in England', *Guardian Weekly*, 11 February 1996). Can the new type of colonial decentralised education correspond to local needs where local teachers are made into mediators of Western educational packages (books, videos, radio programmes) and the 'distance educators' who pull the financial and ideological strings (i.e., who are responsible for the materials and equipment used) know neither local cultures nor local languages? These are fundamental ethical questions. Accountability must relate not merely to budgets but to a wide range of cultural and ecological concerns.

It seems to some observers that we today have two almost separate worlds, one for the majority of the world's population, the 'unpeople', another for the rest. The world, created by capitalist interests, is not capitalist for everybody. Paradoxically, what we have, is, in John Pilger's words (1998: 2): 'the "new" system of capitalism for the powerless and socialism for the powerful, under which the former are persecuted and the latter are given billions in public subsidies'. In Pilger's (and many others') view, the rich of the world and the TNCs have probably never pulled as little of their weight as they do now. The richer you are, the less you pay for what you take, and the more public subsidies you get. The poorer you are, the more you have to pay for the pittances you have—there are no fringe benefits or parachutes. The solution to the problems of poverty and the gaps, 'which is the return of vast wealth taken from the poor by the rich' (ibid., 2) is not discussed. We are supposed to live in an information age—but this is a myth: in fact 'we live in a media age, in which the available information is repetitive, "safe" and limited by invisible boundaries', Pilger claims (ibid., 4), quoting Michael Parenti in **Inventing Reality: The Politics of the Mass Media**:

> . . . journalists . . . 'rarely doubt their own objectivity even as they faithfully echo the established political vocabularies and the prevailing politico-economic orthodoxy. Since they do not cross any forbidden lines, they are not reined in. So they are likely to have no awareness they are on an ideological leash'. Thus, the true nature of power is not revealed, its changing contours are seldom explored, its goals and targets seldom identified.

The same analysis, of not even discussing the real problems, the cleavages in society, is shared by Japanese scholars, in general, and in relation to minority communities and their languages:

Public opinion has it that as social classification leads invariably to social discrimination, it should not exist in principle and, therefore, does not in reality. Consideration of social division would lead to its recognition, stabilisation, or imposition, and that is evil from an egalitarian point of view (Honna 1975: 194).

Thus, the post-war efforts to promote social and racial equality have led to a desire to avoid any mention of discrimination and social prejudice. The study of minority languages, such as Korean or Ainu or Okinawan, and the social dynamic which keeps discrimination in place, has been markedly neglected (Maher & Yashiro 1995, 5).

The labels used and the inequalities not discussed are part and parcel of control through ideas, manufacturing consent via linguistic means. However, it is the market forces behind the languages and ideas, behind the relative validation or invalidation of certain ways of seeing, that are important to analyse. What I loosely call 'the "free" market response' inherent in the present phase of globalisation has been centralisation, homogenisation, monocultural 'efficiency'—and the consequences for linguistic diversity have been and are disastrous.

This, then, is the response of market forces to the post-modern problems of their own making. A human rights oriented alternative response to changes during and after modernity could be different. In the final section we will look at what it could consist of, and add a few sociological notes on responses built on respecting diversity, including implementing linguistic human rights.

6.4. 'Free' Markets and Human Rights

If states are weak and have given market forces free range, is there any support to be had from the human rights system? Historically, both **development** and **human rights** are central to UN activities, and figure both separately and together in innumerable declarations, beginning with the Charter of the United Nations. Article 55 commits the members to the promotion of higher standards of living, solutions to international economic, social, health, and related problems and international cultural and educational co-operation, and universal respect for human rights and fundamental freedoms. The same article also outlaws discrimination on the basis of language.

There is though an inherent contradiction between the commitment to 'development' (as promoted by the UN's agencies, and multilateral and bilateral donors) and to human rights, since much of the evidence is that development programmes, for example, the structural adjustment policies of the World Bank and the IMF have 'been found to harm rather than promote human rights' (Tomaševski 1993a: 45). It is an additional paradox that much mainstream 'aid' in the late 1980s was made conditional on human rights observance, particularly political rights, at a time when such 'development aid' was in fact **jeopardizing** human rights. Criticism of the neglect of human rights in 'development aid' has often been expressed by NGOs which, for instance, have documented that the interests of indigenous groups have been sacrificed on the altar of 'economic progress' (ibid., 51; see also Stavenhagen 1990, 1995).

What is then the response of the human rights system to giving market forces free range? Human rights, especially economic and social rights, are, according to human rights lawyer Katarina Tomaševski (1996: 104), to act as **correctives to the free market**.

The first international human rights treaty abolished slavery. Prohibiting slavery implied that **people** were not supposed to be treated as market commodities. ILO (The International Labour Organisation) has added that **labour** should not be treated as a commodity (see below). But price-tags are to be removed from other areas too. Tomaševski claims (ibid., 104) that 'The purpose of international human rights law is . . . to overrule the law of supply and demand and remove price-tags from people and from necessities for their survival.'

These necessities for survival include not only basic food and housing (which would come under economic and social rights), but also basics for the sustenance of a dignified life, including basic civil, political, **and cultural** rights. In Johan Galtung's terms, it is not only material, somatic needs that are necessities for survival, but also non-material, mental needs (see Table 6.7):

TABLE 6.7
Types of basic needs and basic problems

TYPES OF BASIC NEEDS vs Impediments to their satisfaction		
	DIRECT *(intended)*	*STRUCTURAL* *(built-in)*
Material needs *(SOMATIC)*	**SECURITY** vs violence	**WELL-BEING** vs misery
Non-material needs *(MENTAL)*	**FREEDOM** vs repression	**IDENTITY** vs alienation

(Based on Galtung 1988: 147)

Education is part of 'well-being' and 'identity', and a prerequisite for 'security' and 'freedom'. Education, including **basic educational linguistic rights**, is one of the necessities from which price-tags should be removed. A development policy which aims at universal literacy and universal primary education must formulate a policy which puts basic human needs, not economic growth, in focus.[40] This means necessarily a serious reassessment of the educational language policies worldwide which have shown such miserable results.

It seems that both the basic principles behind UPE, those relating to nation building and to development education, have followed economistic, neo-colonial language policies which have in turn **impeded** national unity and development—and literacy. Besides, the principle of UPE itself may not be as soundly conceived in every detail as we would like to believe as will become clear in chapter 8.

The approaches to development which The Human Development Index (HDI), used in the UN **Human Development Reports** and increasingly elsewhere, criticises, are the ones connected to **economic growth** (growth should rather be seen as a means, not an end of development; there is no automatic link between progress in human development and high GNP growth); to **theories of human capital development and human resource development** (because humans are seen as inputs to increasing production, in the way that the slavery treaty and ILO banished long ago—see above); to **the human welfare approach** (because it looks at human beings as beneficiaries rather than participants in the development process), and to **the basic needs approach** (because it focusses on the provision of goods and services that people need— food, shelter, water, health care—rather than the implications that having or not having these goods and services have on human choices).[41] Galtung's 'basic needs' above combine the positive features which the HDI tries to capture— its conceptualisation of 'basic needs' sees the goods and services as only one aspect of human needs, a prerequisite for other equally basic needs.

Accepting Tomaševski's claims above means that it is the duty of each government to create conditions under which people are able to provide the necessities, the basic tools for human development, for themselves. Many people cannot do this, some of the reasons being that the right to work is not a fundamental inalienable individual human right. Neither is the right to fair trade at a collective level. If people cannot provide the necessities themselves, it is the duty of governments, according to human rights principles, to provide the necessities for those unable to do so themselves. If individual governments are unable to do so, it is the duty of the international community, according to Tomaševski (The Hague Recommendations, described in section 7.8.3, also imply that this applies to minority education[42]).

If this really happened, we would not need to worry about the fate of the world's languages. But it does not. Most states are either unwilling or unable to deliver—or both.[43] The unwillingness will be shown below, in scrutinizing the protection of educational language rights in some human rights instruments—which are, after all, signed and ratified by states. The capacity of states to deliver is partially eroded by the restrictions on sovereignty, as discussed above.

According to the analysis above, one of the important tasks for states would be to guarantee the satisfaction of basic human needs for everybody. A human rights oriented answer, different from a market oriented answer, could be accomplished if human rights and economic rights came together, controlled by a democratic political process. Is this likely to happen?

In global **human rights policies** there is a conspicuous silence about economic and social (or welfare) rights, coupled with very vocal anti-welfare policies from many governments. In global and European **economic policies**, human rights are hardly mentioned, except when legitimating economic benefits for the industrialised countries by referring to alleged (and often real) human rights violations in underdeveloped countries. Also, in renegotiating **political, military and economic alliances**, Western countries skilfully play the card of alleged human rights violations.[44]

Tomaševski sums it up (1996: 100): 'the ideology of the free market has exempted economy from public control (sometimes even influence) and thus eliminated the basis for human rights, when these are understood as an exercise of political rights to achieve economic, social and cultural rights'. Globalising access to information has enabled counterhegemonic forces to ensure that there is growing sensitivity to human rights. At the same time there is also a growing inability to secure them by progressive forces in civil society. The gap between rhetoric and implementation is growing, with all the growing inequalities.

The message from both sociologists like Zygmunt Bauman and human rights lawyers like Katarina Tomaševski and many others is that unless there is a redistribution of resources for implementing human rights, nothing is going to happen. It is probably not even of any use to spread knowledge of human rights as a basis for self-directed human development, unless the resources for implementation follow, and that can only happen through a radical redistribution of the world's material resources. Today, knowledge of what human rights **should** and could be sometimes makes one just despair . . .

In the next chapter we look at linguistic human rights, especially in education, as they are, and as they should be. Before we start suggesting present human rights as a possible ally in protecting linguistic and cultural diversity, we need to know in detail what they contain of language rights in education.

NOTES

1. If you carry your whole library in your head, as individuals in orate cultures collectively do, it has to be enormously well organised, for maintenance, easy access, and transmitting it to the next generation, and a lot of mnemonic devices are constructed. If your library is externalised and commodified, as in literate cultures, even many disorganised people with 'bad' memory can get access to knowledge.

2. See, e.g., Henri Giroux's criticism 1992, and Sandra Harding's denunciation of these polarities, and alternatives to them, in her 1986 and 1998.

3. In economic and trade terms, we have, for instance, a division into seven groups of countries: (1) the around 2 dozen rich countries, Australia, Canada, Japan, New Zealand, South Africa, USA, and the western European industrialised countries, (2) the 8 with Argentina, Brazil, India, Mexico, and the 'Asian tigers' Hong Kong, Singapore, South Korea, Taiwan, (3) some 2 dozen 'aspiring', nearly industrial countries (NIC), with China, Indonesia, Malaysia, and Thailand as main examples; (4) ex-Soviet Union and (other) Eastern and Central European countries; (5) the oil-exporting OPEC (Organization of Petroleum Exporting Countries); (6) the around 40 poor countries, some in Asia but the vast majority in Africa and Latin America, mainly exporting raws materials; and (7) the poorest 48 so called Least Developed Countries (LDCs), mostly in Africa (see, e.g., Barnet & Cavanagh 1994: 281–287). It is obvious that the divisions are very crude indeed. In many countries the internal distribution is so uneven that there are groups living in the same country where some (the elites) belong to the 'rich' group 1 whereas the vast majority of the population represent 6 or 7. India and South Africa are typical examples. Core/Centre—Periphery theories discuss this.

4. 'Dr. Walter Rodney was assassinated by agents of the Burnham government of Guyana on June 13th 1980. Dr. Rodney returned home with his wife and three children in 1974 after spending seven years as Professor of African History at the University of Dar es Salaam. Up to the time of his murder he was prevented from taking-up an appointment with the University of Guyana on the intervention of the Burnham Government' (from the back cover of 1983 reprint of Rodney's 1972 book **How Europe underdeveloped Africa**—see also the Publisher's Note, and the Introduction, by Robert Shenton).

5. Interestingly, it seems that the Nordic countries and Europe in general are much worse than Neo-Europes and, for instance, Israel, which at least accept some of the skills that people with high formal education from other countries have.

6. This of course does *not* mean that the Iraqi dictator, Saddam Hussein, is not partially responsible—but most of the ones who suffer from the use of force (the killing of hundreds of thousands of innocent civilians—at least half a million children, according to Pilger 1998: 2), ordinary Iraqi people, are not.

7. On 17 May 1999, the US Congress approved Turkey's purchase of fifty S-70 Black Hawk general-purpose helicopters for a total of $561,000,000 from the US Sikorsky Aircraft Company. The Turkish military forces are planning to buy additional combat helicopters worth $85,000,000,000 from the USA in the coming years and preliminary talks between US firms and representatives of the Turkish government and the Turkish Aviation and Space Industry (TAI) have already taken place. It is not difficult to guess against whom the helicopters are being used. See also The Stockholm International Peace Research Institute, SIPRI; their Yearbooks (published by Oxford University Press) carry a lot of information. See their web-page <http://www.sipri.se>.

8. This is relative, though. In a table with private security and public police in the late 1980s and military armed forces in 1995 from selected countries in the 1998 **State of the World** from the Worldwatch Institute, Israel leads by far, relative to citizenry, having 41 per thousand population of all forces. The United States is second, with 14, then France (12), United Kingdom and Australia, both 11, and then comes South Africa, with 10, as number six (Renner 1998: 135).

9. The intention of the South African Truth and Reconciliation Commission was **not** to make people forget—quite the opposite. 'The point was to make the truth public, and thus allow us to move on in positive and constructive ways rather than continually focusing on past oppression and injustice and being unable to construct a new, better South Africa', Timothy Reagan argues, based on a number of personal discussions with Desmond Tutu (Reagan, December 1998, personal communication).

10. Again one example of how immensely difficult it is to translate into this 'flexible, rich' language, English, even from another very closely related Indo-European language, Latin. 'whose region, his religion'? 'ruler decides religion'? 'owner of the region/place/state decides the religion'? Both German and Danish can do this easily, and so can Finnish: 'jonka valtakunta, sen uskonto'. English flexible?

11. But it is the poor children who are likely to die from the air and water pollution, including the toxic wastes that we dump in their country. Air pollution causes 2.7 million deaths a year, with 80% of the victims in rural poor areas of underdeveloped countries. In Latin America and parts of Asia millions of children risk losing four or more IQ points just because of lead emissions. At the other end, the USA has the least strict sludge control regulations in the industrial world (Gardner 1998), and in California, several parents came late to one of my lectures (in the 1990s) because their children had been exposed to helicopters spraying pesticides over the school yard, near fields.

12. In Japan, 'the Meiji administration's (1871–1912) design for a unified common language was part of the nation's march towards the nation-state. The intensity of the national drive towards cultural and linguistic homogeneity continued up to the end of the war' (Maher & Yoshiro 1995: 3). This 'construction of the ideology of social uniformity (one language, one people) . . . does not merely involve the subjection of peoples and languages but lies in invented tradition of "harmony" ' (ibid., 8). This ' "invented tradition" of social and industrial harmony [was] a pressure-driven political expedience derived from industrial capitalism's need for an ideology of moral order and community which subsequently underpinned the much repeated claim that Japanese "naturally" avoid conflict and possess a culture of harmony' (ibid., 9).

13. In a state-nation the statehood comes first, and the citizens are only later on supposed to start feeling that they form a 'nation'. Many African states, with borders drawn by colonialists disrespecting old ethnic and linguistic borders, are said to be state-nations, but for instance France could also have been characterised as such around the time of the French revolution and after it.

14. '[A] **national language** is a band of **national unity**. Every engine should be employed to make the people of this country **national**; to call their attachments home to their own country; and to inspire them with the pride of national character . . . Let us then seize the present moment, and establish a **national language** as well as a national government' (emphases added), Noah Webster exhorted the American people in 1789, in suggesting a new, 'American' orthography for English.

15. **Gutalagen**, the County Law for the island of Gotland (Sweden: known to many outsider's from Ingmar Bergman's films) was written in the 'dialect' of Gotland in the 13th century. Had Gotland become an independent state (which would have been perfectly possible then, according to Janson (1997: 135), Gutnish ('gutniska' in Swedish) could today be a language. Even the name is a construction by later linguists, i.e., the language did not yet have a name despite being used in writing: the process was 'interrupted' by the creation of the state of Sweden which included Gotland.

16. This also seems to be typical of many press reports about the Kurdish situation and protests at the point when the PKK leader, Abdullah Öcalan, was kidnapped by Turkey—external observer's views prevail.

17. Cargill is the world's largest grain trader, controlling around 60% of the trade. Their income is equivalent to that of the 9 largest sub-Saharan African countries (World Development Movement press release, 2 November 1996), at the same time as 40,000 children under the age of 5 die from malnutrition every day, according to UN's **Human Development Report 1996**.

18. Timothy Reagan (December 1998, personal communication): 'My three cats have all had tiny implants placed under their skin on the back of their necks—and the implants can be scanned by a veterinarian to find out who they are, where they live, and who owns them. For pets, this is a high-tech equivalent of a name tag. When we had this done, I joked

about perhaps doing the same thing with my children; in retrospect, that was not at all funny.' Human cyborgs are already being tested.

19. 'Cyborg' is a blend between a living organism, e.g., a human, and a computer, a CYBernetic ORGanism—see Donna Haraway's book **Simians, Cyborgs, and Women** (1991).

20. There are alarming reports about the growing sex industry where females, including children, in and from Africa, Asia, and, increasingly, Eastern and Central Europe (see Géry 1999), are receiving the Western European malestream under slavelike conditions.

21. The section on the history of globalisation draws on Radoměřská & Skutnabb-Kangas 1998, a book review of Harding 1997.

22. Rolf Jensen, Director for the Danish Centre for Research on Future, referred (Copenhagen, 9 September 1998) at a meeting about theoretical probability figures, accepted by the OECD, to GNPs in Europe and China. These were calculated to be approximately equal in 1500, $525 per capita, i.e., they show in economic terms what Harding notes in terms of knowledge capital. In 1820, Europe was somewhat more prosperous than China (around 620 dollars). Today the GNP per capita in Europe and the USA are around 25,000 to 30,000 while China is around 3,000 and Central Africa around 600 dollars per capita. Source: report in **Information** 10.09.1998, p. 3.

23. I have never understood this specific (mis)use of a concept which, just like many others which I only learned as an adult in or from the USA, obviously strikes me more than those who grew up with them. If 'intelligence' is what CIA and others work with, I am ashamed of being intelligent. If ruining the environment (Sachs 1992c) is called 'developing an area', I do not want to be 'developed'. And so on—see Wink 1994.

24. Joel Spring's (1998) analysis of American attempts to influence Japan, especially the education system, gives a complex picture of Western individualism/egoism as compared to a Confucian authoritarianism/respect for elders, in conflict and also some dialogue (see also Timothy Reagan's 1996 book **Non-Western Educational Traditions: Alternative approaches to educational thought and practice**).

25. The USA was even in other ways supporting Pol Pot.

26. Agnes Heller's point (referred to in Cryle 1993) was that when European colonial powers took their culture worldwide, they were not spreading 'Europeanisation' (let alone universal values) but practices which were specifically British (cricket, horse racing, Kipling) or French (cuisine, linguistic consciousness, Victor Hugo), etc. Peter Cryle (1993) echoes Heller when criticizing the narrowness of what is, falsely, called 'European studies' in Australian education, something that in fact only covers small fragments of the cultures of the French, Germans, and a few others who are 'significant enough to influence', to use Kishida's terms. It is an example of the invisibilisation for Australians of the majority of the cultures in a Europe, limited ethnonymically to just the few, according to our earlier analysis.

27. Britain obviously did not have females, or at least they were not seen as a revolutionary threat . . .

28. Almost half the world's 'free trade' is transactions **within** 189 multinationals. Annual sales of the top 8 companies exceed the Gross Domestic Product of the 50 countries which have over half the world's population (Pilger 1998: 72).

29. The only highlighted agents seem to be the ones who try to prevent positive globalisation—and these vary. The Jews who always had an ambivalent role, have been replaced by successive enemy agents: communism, Saddam Hussein, Islam, terrorists, ecological fundamentalists, etc.

30. This comment refers to the fact that even language rights activists tend to forget this—see the critique of the draft Universal Declaration of Linguistic Rights in section 7.5.3.5.

31. One could almost claim that the 'free market' is no longer an economic system at all anymore, but rather a fundamentalist political-ideological dogma. It has abandoned, 'betrayed' most of its 'father's', Adam Smith's, prerequisites for it to function, as David Korten (1996b) shows in his article 'The Mythic Victory of Market Capitalism'.

32. Meat-eaters may have to rethink when the prices of grain go up because of lack of grains, and this will happen very soon (see **State of the World 1998**; the grain area per person worldwide has already gone down from 0.23 hectares in 1950 to 0.12 in 1997 and is expected to drop to 0.08 hectares in 2030, Brown 1998b: 81; see also Brown 1998a). Sub-Saharan Africa now uses 97% of its grain for food for people, compared with 28% in the United States (Gardner 1998: 98).

33. 'Inevitable', in the same old way: 'Considering colonial systems as inevitable, the Spanish system, for all its faults, was the best available at the time; The most humane, the most progressive in the sense that it was designed to integrate a society . . . The Spanish hoped to make productive subjects out of the Indians, and to teach them how to cope with the outside world' (Mathes 1987: 210 when interviewed about the missions in California).

34. Prisons are 'the fastest-growing business in the United States; more people are now employed in what are known as "prison industries" than in any of the country's top 500 corporations, with the exception of General Motors' (Pilger 1998: 70).

35. Compare this with Oscar Wilde: 'We are told that the poor are grateful for charity. Some of them are, no doubt, but the best among the poor are never grateful. They are ungrateful, disobedient and rebellious. They are quite right to be so. Disobedience, in the eyes of anyone who has read history, is man's [sic!] original virtue' (quoted in Pilger 1998: 99).

36. Vandana Shiva's Web-page is <http://iisd.ca/pcdf//1996/shiva.htm>.

37. In **Information** 8 May 1995, describing the economic situation in Hungary, people are quoted as saying that they now, 'instead of the dictatorship of communism have the dictatorship of the World Bank' and that the living conditions are much worse now (Plöger 1995: 2).

38. Despite this goal, and despite the focus on English-only education, there are for instance in Zambia today fewer people proficient in English than before independence, according to Tripathi (1990). Siatchitema (1992, referred to in Heugh 1995c: 337) and Africa (1980) have similar analyses about Zambia.

39. This was how a South African MP formulated it in an interview 14 November 1997. We (Robert Phillipson & TSK) have heard Hungarian and Baltic colleagues claim the same about their own countries. 'Every year Africa transfers to its creditors—principally northern governments, the World Bank and the IMF—around $10 billion, more than the region spends on health and education combined . . . For every dollar on health, the Ugandan government spends five on debt repayment . . . Zambia is spending 10 times more on repaying the IMF than on primary education.' (Watkins 1996: 14). Watkins also notes that Germany, Japan, Britain, and the US have notoriously rejected proposed plans to alleviate the situation. The partial overlap with a list of countries which have notoriously tried to prevent the acceptance of linguistic human rights is not surprising.

40. This would also tally with the demands Ivan Illich makes in his astute criticism of the concept of 'needs' (1992).

41. The analytical tools which the HDI uses are summarised on the HDR Web-site, <http://www.undp.org/undp/hdro>.

42. Article 4 (1996: 5) states: 'States should approach minority education rights in a proactive manner. Where required, special measures should be adopted by States to actively implement minority language education rights to the maximum of their available resources, individually and through international assistance and cooperation, especially economic and technical.' The Explanatory Note deepens the obligations of both the relevant State and the international community, referring to specific human rights instruments (specifically the OSCE **Copenhagen Document**, Articles 31 and 33, and article 2 of the **International Covenant on Economic, Social and Cultural Rights**).

43. One reason not discussed here is of course that even basic human rights do not apply to all humans, and very clearly not to most of those who are speakers of the most threatened languages.

When the UN Universal Declaration of Human Rights was accepted, UN consisted of only 51 states, as compared to the present number of close to 200 states. But only a minority of the individuals living in those states were deemed "human" in the sense that the Universal Declaration should apply to them—the human beings in colonies and dependent territories were not 'human', according to the vote in UN. In the same sense, migrants are not human today, according to Katarina Tomaševski (1997)—thay have very few human rights and certainly no binding linguistic rights.

44. The concept 'human rights' is often used in international relations arbitrarily and selectively by 'donor' governments so as to attempt to trigger 'democratic' elections or to sanction states that commit gross human rights abuses; in effect it is used as a political tool rather than a rigorous concept rooted in international law (Tomaševski 1997).

Part III

STRUGGLE AGAINST LINGUISTIC GENOCIDE AND FOR LINGUISTIC HUMAN RIGHTS IN EDUCATION

Linguistic Human Rights

Special rights are not privileges but they are granted to make it possible for minorities to preserve their identity, characteristics and traditions. Special rights are just as important in achieving equality of treatment as non-discrimination. Only when minorities are able to use their own languages, benefit from services they have themselves organized, as well as take part in the political and economic life of States can they begin to achieve the status which majorities take for granted. (**Human Rights Fact Sheet 18, Minority Rights**, United Nations, 1998:4)

Depression is widespread in the [Tlingit] communities, long characterized by social dysfunction, substance abuse, domestic and community violence, and suicide. We attribute much of this to unresolved grief (due to **social and legal suppression of ritual** ceremonial grieving through 'potlach') for the death of loved ones, and for the **death of language and culture** (emphases added). (Dauenhauer & Dauenhauer 1995: 109)

In a world where more people are on the move, migrating, than ever before, greater emphasis must be given to the principle of human rights, which could be understood to mean that every person has the right to be born, live, fall sick and die in his or her own language. (Nylund-Oja et al. 1995: 218)

7. LINGUISTIC HUMAN RIGHTS

7.1. INTRODUCING LINGUISTIC HUMAN RIGHTS (LHRs)

In this chapter I make several claims and present evidence for these. I claim that despite fine declarations of the intent to promote diversity, including linguistic diversity, the most important linguistic human rights (LHRs), needed for the maintenance of linguistic diversity, were, until the mid-1990s, absent from binding international human rights instruments, especially in education: mother tongue medium education is not a linguistic human right (LHR). This is not only in conflict with the spirit of the human rights instruments, but is also in contrast to how several other human attributes fare in human rights law. Language gets much poorer treatment in human rights instruments than other important human attributes. This is true especially for LHRs in education. There are also clear signs of Western hypocrisy and double standards in relation to human rights in general and specifically LHRs in education. A few recent trends with positive recommendations might give some hope, though, if one chooses to be optimistic—but mainly still on paper: implementation is still not forthcoming.

7.1.1. Information on Human Rights

The political rights or lack of rights of any language cannot be deduced from linguistic considerations. They are part of the political and societal conditions of the country concerned, including its international situation and relations, and can only be understood in their historical context, studying the forces which have led to the present socio-political division of power and resources in the societies concerned and worldwide.

The notion of rights evolves out of a particular historical socioeconomic and political context (e.g., references to Macías, Van Dyke in the bibliography) and the cultural relativity of the notion has been extensively debated (see articles in An-Na'im & Deng (eds) 1990—see also Shahrzad Mojab's (1998) discussion of cultural relativism in the Introduction).

Throughout history people have struggled for language rights, as the examples below also show. Obtaining substantial support from the human rights system and international law presupposes binding, codified, enforceable linguistic rights which are both individual and collective. In principle, human rights should apply to everyone, without discrimination on grounds of, for example, language. There are as yet no binding international covenants specifically on **linguistic rights**. Most human rights are individual. Most language-related rights are to be found in articles on minority rights, and these have so far also been **individual** (the beneficiaries being 'persons belonging to minorities'). **Collective** minority rights are essential tools through which minorities can get access to those rights which majorities are granted through individual rights.[1]

For minorities and indigenous peoples struggling for language rights today and wanting to find out whether and to what extent they can use the human rights system to argue their case, it is often difficult even to get hold of basic human rights documents, not to mention learning the specific 'human rights language'. For speakers of most languages in the world none of the relevant documents exist in their own languages in the first place—they need to know other, dominant languages really well, even to get started. The area is vast—a recent useful UNESCO overview, the third updated edition (1997) of **Access to Human Rights Documentation. Documentation, Bibliographies and Data Bases on Human Rights** (see Address Box 7.1), informs us that a search on

---

❖ I n f o B o x 7 . 1 ❖

Useful Fact Sheets From the UN Centre for Human Rights

The series of **Fact Sheets** published by the Centre for Human Rights, United Nations Office at Geneva—see Address Box 7.1—give useful overviews of 'basic human rights, what the United Nations is doing to promote and protect them, and the international machinery available to help realize those rights' (from the joint back cover of them). The Fact Sheets (which are revised when changes happen) are free of charge and distributed worldwide. Some of the absolutely central ones for concerns in this book are:

No. 2: **The International Bill of Human Rights**

No. 5: **Programme of Action for the Second Decade to Combat Racism and Racial Discrimination**[2]

No. 9: **The Rights of Indigenous Peoples**

No. 10: **The Rights of the Child**

No. 12: **The Committee on the Elimination of Racial Discrimination**

No. 15: **Civil and Political Rights: The Human Rights Committee**

No. 16: **The Committee on Economic, Social and Cultural Rights**

No. 18: **Minority Rights**

No. 24: **The Rights of Migrant Workers**

'human rights' on the Web came up with over two million references in February 1997, and the list is growing daily.

One way of getting started, once one knows one of the 'big' languages, is to use the UN Centre for Human Rights and UNESCO. Both publish many basic documents pertaining to human rights, with explanations, and sometimes in less technical language. Info Box 7.1 and Address Box 7.1 have some basic references.

```
* * * * * * * * * * * * * * * * * * * * * * * * * * * * * * * * * * * * * * * * *
*                                                                             *
*                Address Box 7.1   Centre for Human Rights,                   *
*                United Nations Offices at Geneva and New York                *
*                                                                             *
*     8–14 avenue de la Paix, 1211 Geneva 10, Switzerland. The Centre publishes *
*     the Human Rights Fact Sheets and has many other tasks related           *
*     to information and education about human rights. The Fact Sheets are also *
*     available from the New York Office: Centre for Human Rights, United      *
*     Nations, New York, N.Y. 10017, USA. The Centre (the UN High             *
*     Commissioner on Human Rights) has a Web-site which is (intended to       *
*     become) the most complete source of information on the Internet on UN   *
*     action for the protection and promotion of human rights: <http://www.   *
*     unhchr.ch>. Many of the UN human rights documents can be downloaded     *
*     from this useful site.                                                  *
*         UNESCO's 1997 overview (see above) can be ordered from Division of  *
*     Human Rights, Democracy and Peace, UNESCO, 7 Place de Fontenoy,         *
*     F-75352 Paris 07 SP, France, phone (33) 01 45 68 38 18, fax (33) 01 45 68 *
*     57 26. UNESCO's Web-page, with many education and human rights          *
*     documents, is <http://www.education.unesco.org/unesco/>.                *
*         Most international human rights organisations, including many non-  *
*     governmental ones (NGOs), have their own home pages on the Web. The     *
*     UN Web Site Locator provides a complete list in alphabetical order by   *
*     agency name, at <http://www.unsystem.org/index8.htm>                    *
*                                                                             *
* * * * * * * * * * * * * * * * * * * * * * * * * * * * * * * * * * * * * * * * *
```

7.1.2. Language Rights + Human Rights = Linguistic Human Rights

Language rights have been discussed and written about for a very long time, but especially since the First 'World' War, after which the Peace Treaties contained some language rights for minorities. Minority rights and language rights figured together fairly prominently during the era of the League of Nations, as we see below. Mostly the experts on language rights were lawyers, writing constitutions and treaties, prompted by politicians and minority movements. The rights were seen as the field of expertise of mainly lawyers, rather than linguists or other language experts.

Human rights are supposed to be rights that every individual has, simply because of being human. In theory they are supposed to be rights which are so fundamental, so inalienable, that no state (or other person) is allowed to violate them. This is of course far from true, even on paper. Not even the right to life is inalienable, as for instance the fact that some states are still 'legally' murdering some of their own people shows.[3] The death penalty is still 'legal', even in some countries which arrogate to themselves the right to criticise other countries for their violations of human rights, for example, the USA. Increasingly, certain collective rights are also being included in the human rights regime.

As compared to language rights, human rights have been studied, discussed, and clarified much more thoroughly. Human rights have been at the centre of a field of both study and politics involving states, international organisations, courts, tribunals, research institutes, monitoring bodies of different kinds, international lawyers, philosophers, and mass movements and NGOs—but, again, so far, very few language experts, except in their roles as ordinary citizens.

This is slowly changing now, though. Language rights and human rights have been brought together as **linguistic human rights** only very recently as we will see from the short historical section below which, regrettably, only covers western countries.

7.1.3. Some Basic Definitions

As some of the examples below will show, further scientific and political work is still greatly needed in this new multidisciplinary field. One sign is that there is confusion and disagreement about many basic concepts and terminology.

A partial reason is that working with linguistic human rights involves cooperation between not only different constituencies but also various experts (including politicians, human rights lawyers, (socio)linguists, writers, philosophers (see Chen 1998) and others, in formulating linguistic human rights. Such cooperation is only just starting—so far this has almost exclusively been an area for lawyers. It is also easy to see from conferences and debates and from some of the latest attempts to formulate rights (e.g., the draft **Universal Declaration of Linguistic Rights** where Catalans, together with the International PEN club, took the initiative) that experts from the various disciplines do not yet talk together well enough (see Kontra et al., 1999, for some critical comments on this) and they do not have enough shared background. And third, there are also several types of ideological conflict about what should go into universal declarations/conventions of linguistic human rights. Various constituencies have different interests, and these have to be fitted together if possible.

Therefore what is needed is (1) concept clarification; (2) providing a shared background through continuous multidisciplinary working teams; and (3) open discussions about ideological conflicts.

One starting point to improve communication is to discuss differences in how several basic concepts are understood, and to negotiate to what extent various experts can put their fingerprint, with their interpretation of the concepts, on the formulation of instruments for linguistic human rights. What may be clear to one group is far from so for another, and vice versa. Often each group also sees concepts in the fields of expertise of other groups as much less problematic than these groups themselves. Some of the uncertainties will be mentioned here and later in the Chapter.

Lawyers may think that concepts like 'language', 'mother tongue', 'learn a language' are relatively simple and unproblematic, whereas sociolinguists claim that they are far from clear (see section 1.1.1., Problems in identifying what is 'a language'). A UNESCO-sponsored workshop on these problems stated in its report (general rapporteur: TSK) that there is a need to clarify concepts central for LHRs, concepts like 'mother tongue', 'first language', 'bilingual', 'official language', 'national language', 'learn a language fully', 'efficient communication', etc. (**Workshop on Human Rights and Languages**, UNESCO, 1992). Most of these concepts can be defined in several different ways, as shown in chapter 3 for 'mother tongue' and chapter 8 for 'bilingual'. It should be stated in LHR instruments which definitions have been used. Also, the background and reasons for why these specific definitions have been chosen rather than others should be included in Explanatory Notes. Some declarations, conventions and charters (for example the **European Charter on Regional or Minority Languages**) start with defining a few of the basic concepts used, whereas others do not define their central concepts.

On the other hand, (socio)linguists may think that clear-cut definitions of 'minority' or 'indigenous' have existed in international law for a long time, whereas lawyers have been debating for decades—and still are— whether it is possible (or even necessary) to define these concepts. For instance, the **Framework Convention for the Protection of National Minorities** does not define the basic concept 'minority'.

Both linguists and lawyers may think that sociologists and others have clarified and operationalised concepts like 'ethnicity' or 'ethnic group' or 'integration' versus 'assimilation', concepts needed if, for instance, the existence of a minority is 'to be established by objective criteria' (see the UN Human Rights Committee's General Comment on Article 27, section 7.8.1). Or that ethnographers have a clear-cut definition of 'culture', or geographers and political scientists of 'territory'.[4] Not so.

Some of these problematic concepts have already been discussed at length earlier in this book. In the next section a few of the additional problematic concepts will be discussed. All could be seen from the point of view of several disciplines. In the earlier sections I analysed definitions of 'ethnic groups' and 'integration/assimilation' from a more sociological point of view. Here I will discuss the concepts 'indigenous peoples' and 'minorities' more from the point of view of international law, hoping that the discussions complement each other. We start with 'indigenous peoples'.

7.1.3.1. *Indigenous Peoples*

The question of defining both 'indigenous peoples' and 'minorities' in a way which can be used in legal documents has not been resolved, despite decades of work. Why is it important?

Only **peoples**, not minorities or populations or (ethnic or other) groups, have the **right to self-determination** in international law. This has led to terminological disputes. The UN Group which worked for over a decade with the **Draft Declaration on the Rights of Indigenous Peoples**, was, for instance, called 'UN Working Group on Indigenous **Populations**', not 'Peoples'). The problem has also led to the formulation of legal exceptions (as in the ILO Convention below which, though using 'peoples', stipulates that the use of the word shall not have any consequences for the rights that lie with 'peoples' elsewhere in international law, i.e. indigenous or tribal **groups** do not have the right to self-determination in the classical sense (= independence).

Gudmundur Alfredsson (1990: 5) sees the criterion of inhabitation of land since 'time immemorial' as the critical factor for defining indigenous peoples. Stener Ekern (1998: 7) asserts that the criterion of descent seems 'to come out as the least significant criterion', especially because of (a) several consecutive colonisations (Africa); (b) many Asian countries in addition claim that all their peoples are indigenous; and (c) many groups (like the Basques, Tuaregs, Kurds) reject the status of 'indigenous'. The decisive factors, according to him, are 'a disadvantageous relation with a national community' and 'readiness to adopt the status of "indigenous" or "tribal" as against the external world. In practice, groups choose to be indigenous if it is politically expedient. If not, it might be better to appear as minorities or colonised nations fighting for self-determination' (ibid.).

Some broad definitions suggest a focus on endo-definitions and on cultural and other differences from the rest of the society, and on the will to transmit them to succeeding generations. These definitions share many characteristics with definitions of minorities. One representative example is the definition below (Definition Box 7.1) by José R. Martinez Cobo, Special Rapporteur appointed by the UN Subcommission on the Prevention of Discrimination and the Protection of Minorities to study the problems of discrimination against indigenous peoples (1987: 4).

DEFINITION BOX 7.1 Indigenous peoples, José R. Martinez Cobo 1987

[I]ndigenous communities, peoples and nations are those which, in having a **historical continuity** with pre-invasion and pre-colonial societies that developed on **their territories, consider themselves distinct** from other sectors of the societies now prevailing in those territories, or parts of them. They form at present **non-dominant** sectors of society and are **determined to preserve, develop and transmit to future generations** their **ancestral territories,** and their **ethnic identity,** as the basis of their continued existence as peoples, in accordance with their own **cultural patterns, social institutions and legal systems** (emphases added; the **focussed** characteristics are in bold).

ILO (International Labour Organisation) **Convention Concerning Indigenous and Tribal Peoples in Independent Countries** (Convention No. 169, 27 June 1989) contains the maybe currently strongest definition of indigenous peoples for legal purposes (Definition Box 7.2).

DEFINITION BOX 7.2 Indigenous peoples, ILO 169, 1989

. . . peoples in independent countries who are regarded as indigenous on account of their descent from the populations which inhabited the country, or a geographical region to which the country belongs, at the time of conquest or colonisation or the establishment of present state boundaries and who, irrespective of their legal status, retain some or all of their own social, economic, cultural and political institutions.

Logically the next Definition Box should contain the definition of indigenous peoples from the UN Draft Declaration on the Rights of Indigenous Peoples—but there is no definition in this document.

Since virtually all indigenous peoples are also at the same time minorities in terms of both numbers and power (less than 50% of the population and non-dominant), they can in principle make use of all the rights that minorities have in international law. But still more important is that most of them have never properly surrendered or abandoned their sovereignty as a people—it has been forcibly taken from them. This is also true in most cases where there have been treaties with the colonisers. Therefore they should be seen as sovereign entities, with the right to negotiate self-determination.

For further references, see Clark & Williamson's edited volume **Self-Determination: International Perspectives** (1996), de Varennes 1996a, b, Hannum 1988, 1989, 1990, Martinez Cobo 1987, Alfredsson 1990, 1991, Thornberry 1987, 1991, 1995, 1997; Patrick Thornberry is also finishing a substantial book on the rights of indigenous peoples in 1999.

7.1.3.2. Minorities

Why is it important whether a group is defined as a minority according to international law or not? In international law, groups accepted as 'minorities' have many more guaranteed rights, also in education, than 'immigrants', 'migrants', 'guest workers' or refugees, who have almost no rights. Therefore many groups strive towards being granted the status of minorities. One of the strategies to force unwilling States to organise minority education better is to make them real duty-holders: to hold them to task under international or regional human rights instruments which they have signed and ratified.

On the other hand, many groups reject labels, not knowing the legal implications. 'Linguistically diverse students' (a recent North American invention) have no rights whatsoever, they are a non-entity in international law, whereas 'minority students' have at least some rights. In much British discourse 'immigrant' is seen as a negative term by many immigrant minorities from former colonies, whereas in Germany being accepted as 'immigrants' (rather than 'foreigners' or 'guest workers') would be positive for Turks. In the USA, on the other hand, 'minority' is seen by many as degrading. From a human rights point of view, especially in relation to legal implications in education, those groups who reject the label (ethnic/linguistic/national) 'minority', are doing themselves a disfavour and, sometimes unknowingly, rejecting rights which they need and want to have.

The definitions of both minority and different types of minorities (indigenous, national, regional, territorial, immigrant, etc.) are notoriously difficult.[5] Most definitions use as defining characteristics a combination of the following:

A. **Numbers;**

B. **Dominance** is used in some but not others ('in an inferior and non-dominant position', Andrýsek 1989: 60; 'in a non-dominant position', Capotorti 1979: 96);

C. **Ethnic or religious or linguistic traits**, features or characteristics, or cultural bonds and ties which are (markedly) different from those of the rest of the population (in most definitions);

D. A will/wish (if only implicit) **to safeguard**, or preserve, or strengthen the **patterns of life** and behaviour, or culture, or traditions, or religion, or language of the group is specifically mentioned in most definitions (e.g., Capotorti 1979: 96). **Language** is included in most but not all definitions (e.g., not in Andrýsek's definition 1989: 60).

E. Citizenship/nationality in the state concerned is required in most definitions in charters and covenants as part of the definition, i.e. minorities are defined so as to give national or regional minorities more rights than to immigrants and refugees (who, by definition, are considered non-national and non-regional). In contrast, academic definitions for research purposes often make no mention of nationality as a criterion (cf. Riggs 1985 (ed.): 155, 102).

Partly the 'minority' concept is also difficult to handle because of the many connotations which place the concept differentially in several hierarchies. Many groups therefore do not wish to be called 'minorities' but prefer other terms. Many indigenous peoples do not see themselves as minorities but as peoples—accepting to be a 'minority' would connote accepting the legitimacy of the jurisdiction of the state which has colonised them, and might prevent certain preferred interpretations of self-determination. Some groups see a hierarchy where nations and nationalities are 'above' minorities—here both nations and nationalities would have a certain right to political self-determination (including having their own state if they so wish) whereas minorities might only have the right to cultural autonomy—this has been the interpretation in several central and eastern European situations under communism. Some groups think that 'minority' necessarily has negative connotations of 'dominated', 'poor', 'less worthy', even 'primitive' or 'backward'—many North American immigrant groups have held this view. On the other hand, other immigrant groups, for example, in northern Europe, have claimed that 'minority' connotes a group which intends to and is allowed to settle permanently and is therefore a preferred label (as compared to 'guest worker' or 'immigrant') for a hyphenated group, e.g. Sweden Finns (Finns in Sweden), Greek-Australians (Australians of Greek origin). Likewise, these groups see that being accepted as a 'national/ethnic' minority confers many more legal rights in international law to a group than the rights which immigrants or refugees have, and therefore becoming a minority has positive connotations.

For purposes of linguistic human rights, I use here a definition of 'minorities' in a general, positive sense. The definition is based on my reformulation of the definition by the Council of Europe Commission for Democracy through Law (91) 7, Article 2.[6] My definition (from Skutnabb-Kangas & Phillipson 1994a: 107, Note 2) is in Definition Box 7.3.

DEFINITION BOX 7.3 Minority (from Skutnabb-Kangas & Phillipson 1994a).

A group which is smaller in number than the rest of the population of a State, whose members have ethnic, religious or linguistic features different from those of the rest of the population, and are guided, if only implicitly, by the will to safeguard their culture, traditions, religion or language.

Any group coming within the terms of this definition shall be treated as an ethnic, religious or linguistic minority.

To belong to a minority shall be a matter of individual choice.

I have in this definition omitted the requirement of citizenship ('who are nationals of that State'), because a forced change of citizenship to my mind cannot be required in order to be able to enjoy basic human rights.[7] As long as many immigration states practise a fairly restrictive policy in granting citizenship (for instance residence requirements which are longer than 3–4 years, and/or linguistic requirements, often based on evaluations by non-language-professionals, or **ius sanguinis**—Definition Box 3.12), it also seems to me that especially children may suffer unduly if they are only granted basic linguistic rights after, in the best case, upwards of 5 years in the new country.

If an individual claims that she belongs to a national minority, and the State claims that there are no national minorities in that State (e.g., Kurds in Turkey, or Finns in Sweden at least until 1998), there is also a conflict, and the State may refuse to grant the minority person or group rights which it has accorded or might accord to national minorities. In most definitions of minority, minority rights thus become conditional on the acceptance by the State of the existence of a minority in the first place, i.e. only exo-definitions of minorities are accepted. According to my definition, minority status does *not* depend on the acceptance of the State, but is either 'objectively' ('coming within the terms of this definition'—but see the discussion about ethnicity as a characteristic or a relation in section 3.5.2) or subjectively verifiable ('a matter of individual choice'). See also Note 4.

Many of the definitions of indigenous peoples also have this combination of 'objective' characteristics and self-identification (e.g., the definitions of Sámi for the purposes of voting rights to the Sámi Parliaments in Finland and in Norway, see Magga 1994). The processes whereby indigenous peoples are (or are not) 'recognised' by the states in which they live still often reflect profoundly paternalistic approaches where exo-definitions only are valid.

The trend, though, seems to be towards self-identification only (endo-definitions), for numerically small groups. Minority definitions can be compared to definitions of ethnic groups—see the discussion in section 3.5.2, and Stavenhagen 1987; Skutnabb-Kangas 1987, 1991a; Riggs 1985 (ed.). One benefit of endo-definitions is that even groups who have lost the mother tongue as a result of (forced) assimilation can still claim minority or indigenous status, because 'language' is not necessarily part of an endo-definition. (We also get the same result if 'mother tongue' is defined on the basis of self-identification, not competence—see the mother tongue definitions in section 3.2.1). Another benefit is that nobody who does not want to belong to a minority is forced to do so. This has been an important consideration in many legal and, especially, political discussions. On the other hand, 'self-identification only' definitions tend to be to some extent paperwork products, describing an ideal situation where power relations are equal or do not influence what happens, i.e. they often work badly in real-life situations where dominant groups can prevent any rights accruing to a self-identifying (minority) group, even very large groups like the Kurds. Likewise, some individuals may in a changing situation endo-define themselves as minority members because of economic benefits only.

We might also mention the relational aspect of definitions from three points of view. The first concerns **the size of the unit of measurement**. If a local or regional unit (or, for instance, a school district) is the unit of measurement, Spanish-speakers in Hayward (Oakland, Calif.) or Russian-speakers in Narva or Sillamäe (Estonia) would be a majority. If the state is the unit of measurement, they are a minority. Native English-speakers are in many urban school districts in the USA a minority; in the whole of the USA they are a majority; on a global scale, again, they are a minority. The second aspect concerns **the dependence on each group on the other**: both 'minority' and 'majority' are concepts that require each other: you can only be a 'minority' if you are compared to another unit which is in some aspect bigger/larger. The third aspect concerns the usual **(power) relation between endo- and exo-definitions**: the power of the respective groups is decisive for who can decide on both the unit of measurement and which comparisons are relevant, and therefore on the validation of the labels.

Finally, we will consider signing and ratifying human rights instruments as a necessary prerequisite for their implementation.

7.1.4. Signing and Ratifying Human Rights Instruments—A Prerequisite for Respect

Many governments applaud of human rights, as long as they can define them in their own way, according to their own cultural norms. Many governments demand that human rights be respected—at least by other countries. One can gauge the seriousness of governments in claiming respect for human rights by checking to what extent they themselves have ratified human rights instruments. Ratification means that the country promises to respect the rights in the documents it has signed (the human rights instruments) and to amend its domestic legislation accordingly.

Of course implementation then needs to follow. There are many examples of countries which have signed and ratified several human rights instruments but which are, nevertheless, violating many basic human rights in their practise. One might also consider the opposite, states implementing human rights but refusing to sign and ratify instruments because they do not accept some aspects of the international system. There is reason to be suspicious of this possibility if one believes in international cooperation and openness.

Even if it is clear that mere ratification is not sufficient, ratification is a starting point for respect. If a state claims that rule of law is important, its own laws should be amended so as to conform to human rights requirements. This is also a precondition for asking other countries to respect human rights. We shall first examine what the ratification situation is worldwide in relation to some of the basic human rights documents.

UNESCO's most recent status report 'concerning the state of ratifications, successions and adhesions to human rights instruments' (1998:3; see UNESCO 1998), published by its Division on Human Rights, Democracy and Peace, lists which countries had by 31 May 1998 ratified the 52 **Universal Human Rights Instruments**. These consist of three groups: 5 **General Instruments**; the 23 **Specific Instruments** (11 concerning prevention of discrimination; 5 on genocide, war crimes, and crimes against humanity; 6 on slavery, traffic in persons, and forced labour and 1 on freedom of information); and the 24 **Instruments Relating to the Protection of Particular Groups** (4 on aliens, refugees, and stateless persons; 8 on workers; 7 on women, children, and family; and 5 on combatants, prisoners, and civilians).

The UNESCO publication gives figures for how many of the 193 countries on the list have ratified each instrument. The **Convention on the Rights of the Child** is a leader, with 191 ratifications, the 2 non-ratifiers being Somalia and the USA. It is closely followed by the 4 main instruments in the Geneva Convention on war, with 188 ratifications.

Interestingly enough, UNESCO does not give the figures for how many instruments each country has ratified—this might be embarrassing for some countries. But this can easily be counted from the information given, and I did this. My list, containing a total of 193 countries, in descending order, is given in Table 7.1—this is the Global Human Rights Olympics . . .

In addition to the **Universal Instruments**, the UNESCO publication also lists ratifications to **Regional Instruments**: 31 from the **Council of Europe**, 3 from the **Organization of African Unity**, and 14 from the **Organization of American States**. These organisations have, respectively, 40, 53, and 35 Member States. The correlation between ratifications of Universal and Regional Instruments seems to be quite high. In Tables 7.2, 7.3, and 7.4 I have counted

TABLE 7.1
**How many of the 52 Universal Human Rights Instruments
had countries ratified by 31 May 1998?**

1. Norway: 46
2. Denmark, Netherlands: 44
4. Finland, Sweden: 43
6. Bosnia and Herzegovina, Croatia: 42
8. Australia: 41
9. Ecuador, Germany, Hungary, Spain: 40
13. Italy, Poland: 39
15. Cyprys, France, Slovenia: 38
18. Argentina, Russian Federation, Yugoslavia, United Kingdom: 37
22. Austria, Bulgaria, Czech Republic, Guinea, Macedonia (The former Yugoslav Republic of), Slovak Republic: 36
28. Algeria, Greece, Phillippines, Romania, Senegal, Tunisia, Ukraine: 35
35. Belarus, Costa Rica, Guatemala, Iceland, Latvia, Luxembourg, Malta, New Zealand: 34
43. Brazil, Cuba, Egypt, Peru, Portugal, Uruguay: 33
49. Mali, Niger, Venezuela, Zambia, Libyan Arab Jamahiriya: 32
54. Azerbaijan, Barbados, Belgium, Bolivia, Canada, Switzerland, Uganda: 31
61. Jordan, Kyrgyztan, Mexico, Yemen, Nicaragua: 30
66. Albania, Cameroon, Chile, Colombia, Israel, Jamaica: 29
72. Mongolia, Panama, Seychelles, Togo: 28
76. Antigua and Barbuda, Armenia, Burkina Faso, Côte d'Ivoire, Ethiopia, Ireland, Lesotho, Morocco: 27
84. Central African Republic, Estonia, Madagascar, Nigeria, Sri Lanka, United Rep. of Tanzania: 26
90. Burundi, Chad, Dominican Republic, Ghana, Paraguay, Sierra Leone, Trinidad and Tobago: 25
97. Benin, Gabon, Guyana, Iraq, Malawi, Rwanda, Suriname: 24
104. Bahamas, Congo, Dominica, El Salvador, Kuwait, Mauritius, Rep. of Korea, Syrian Arab Republic, Turkey: 23
113. Dem. Republic of the Congo, Honduras, India, Liberia, Lithuania, Mauritania, Moldova (Republic of), Turkmenistan, Uzbekistan, Zimbabwe: 22
123. Cape Verde, Fiji, Georgia, Haiti, Mozambique, Nepal, Tajikistan: 21
130. Afganistan, Bangladesh, Iran (Islamic Rep. of), Lebanon, Namibia, Sudan, St. Vincent and the Grenadines: 20
137. Angola, Belize, Botswana, Cambodia, Japan, Pakistan, Saint Lucia, San Marino, Swaziland: 19
146. China, Djibouti, Gambia, Kenya, Solomon Islands, South Africa: 18
152. Lao People's Dem. Rep., Papua New Guinea, Viet Nam: 17
155. Saudi Arabia: 16
156. Comoros, Equatorial Guinea, Guinea-Bissau, Liechtenstein, Somalia, United States of America: 15
162. Bahrain, Grenada, Sao Tome and Principe: 14
165. Malaysia, Monaco, Singapore: United Arab Emirates: 13
169. Indonesia, Myanmar: 12
171. Dem. People's Rep. of Korea, Maldives, Qatar, Samoa, Thailand: 11
176. Holy See 10
177. Brunei Darussalam, Saint Kitts and Nevis: 9
179. Oman, Vanuatu: 8

(Continued)

TABLE 7.1
(Continued)

181. Fed. States of Micronesia, Kazakstan, Kiribati, Palau, Tonga, Tuvalu: 7
187. Andorra, Bhutan: 6
189. Eritrea: 2
190. Cook Islands, Marshall Islands, Nauru, Niue: 1

Counted on the basis of information from UNESCO Division of Human Rights, Democracy and Peace 1998 (Symonides); the numbers of instruments ratified are after the name of the last country in each group.

TABLE 7.2
Number of the 31 Council of Europe Human Rights Instruments ratified by each of the 40 member states

Albania 11, Andorra 7, Austria 19, Belgium 15, Bulgaria 9, Croatia 12, Cyprys 17, Czech Republic 16, Denmark 20, Estonia 15, Finland 22, France 16, Germany 18, Greece 14, Hungary 18, Iceland 15, Ireland 17, Italy 23, Latvia 11, Liechtenstein 15, Lithuania 8, Luxembourg 17, Macedonia (the former Yugoslav Republic of) 13, Malta 15, Moldova (Republic of) 13, Netherlands 24, Norway 24, Poland 16, Portugal 19, Romania 16, Russian Federation 13, San Marino 17, Slovak Republic 16, Slovenia 17, Spain 16, Sweden 24, Switzerland 16, Turkey 13, Ukraine 10, United Kingdom 15

TABLE 7.3
Number of the 3 Organization of African Unity Human Rights Instruments ratified by each of the 53 member states

Algeria 2, Angola 2, Benin 2, Botswana 2, Burkina Faso 3, Burundi 2, Cameroon 2, Cape Verde 3, Central African Republic 2, Chad 2, Comoros 1, Congo 2, Congo (Dem. Republic of the) 2, Côte d'Ivoire 2, Djibouti 1, Egypt 2, Equatorial Guinea 2, Eritrea 0, Ethiopia 1, Gabon 2, Gambia 2, Ghana 2, Guinea 2, Guinea-Bissau 2, Kenya 2, Lesotho 2, Liberia 2, Libyan Arab Jamahiriya 2, Madagascar 1, Malawi 2, Mali 2, Mauritania 2, Mauritius 2, Mozambique 2, Namibia 1, Niger 3, Nigeria 2, Rwanda 2, Sao Tome and Principe 1, Senegal 2, Seychelles 3, Sierra Leone 2, Somalia 1, South Africa 1, Sudan 2, Swaziland 2, Togo 3, Tunisia 2, Uganda 3, United Rep. of Tanzania 2, Zambia 2, Zimbabwe 3

the number of the Regional Instruments ratified by the various Member States, from the UNESCO publication mentioned above. Here I give the countries in alphabetical order, with the number of instruments each member state has ratified.

It may be interesting to note that the USA, posing as The Defender of Human Rights globally, occupies, together with 5 other countries, a shared 156th–161st position of 193, in terms of the number of its own ratifications of Universal Human Rights Instruments—hardly a morally convincing record. Likewise, having only ratified 3 of the 14 American Regional Instruments, it occupies, together with 2 other countries, a shared 22nd–24th place

TABLE 7.4
Number of the 14 Organization of American States Human Rights Instruments
ratified by each of the 35 member states

Antigua and Barbuda 0, Argentina 8, Bahamas 1, Barbados 2, Belize 1, Bolivia 3, Brazil 13, Canada 3, Chile 8, Colombia 10, Costa Rica 11, Cuba 5, Dominica 5, Dominican Republic 8, Ecuador 12, El Salvador 11, Grenada 1, Guatemala 12, Guyana 1, Haiti 8, Honduras 8, Jamaica 1, Mexico 11, Nicaragua 8, Panama 13, Paraguay 10, Peru 11, Saint Kitts and Nevis 1, Saint Lucia 1, St.Vincent and the Grenadines 1, Suriname 5, Trinidad and Tobago 2, United States of America 3, Uruguay 12, Venezuela 9

out of 35. The USA does not recognise the authority of international law over US law, something that can be exemplified by the fact that 'American representatives on the United Nations Security Council vetoed a resolution calling on all governments to observe international law' as Noam Chomsky notes (1991: 16, as quoted in Pilger 1998: 27).

After these examples of some of the problems of definition and prerequisites for implementation we move to further constraints and/or delimitations.

7.2. DELIMITING THE TOPIC–FROM LANGUAGE RIGHTS TO EDUCATIONAL LINGUISTIC HUMAN RIGHTS

In principle, linguistic human rights could have to do with any situation where language is used, and this obviously includes most situations in life. First we have to delimit the situations where the use of language **can** be covered by regulations in general, and then where it **should** be covered, i.e. where there should be language rights and duties. Then we have to limit the topic still further, in order to finally arrive at the main concerns of this book.

7.2.1. What Can and Should be Regulated— Language Rights and Duties

No state is allowed to interfere in what languages people use at home, in their private lives, or in private conversations, even in public places, for instance on the street. Still, even this basic right is violated, for instance by Turkey vis-a-vis Kurds, as several examples in this book show. Both these areas belong to **non-official**, as opposed to **official** language usage (Turi 1994: 112). No language legislation can regulate non-official usage; it is not applicable. Language legislation covering **official usage** can be divided into four categories, according to Turi (ibid.): **official, institutionalizing, standardizing** and **liberal language legislation**, depending on its function. Official legislation makes languages official in the domains of legislation, justice, public administration, and education, and the most common principles used are those of **territoriality** (obligation or right to use specific languages within a territory— e.g., Switzerland) and **personality** (rights inhering in the individual, irrespective of which language she uses, her own language or any language). Various combinations of both principles are also used, e.g., in the Finnish legislation. Institutionalizing legislation covers the unofficial domains of labour, communications, culture, commerce, and business (for further details, see Turi 1994). Vic Webb concretises the distinctions from a more sociolinguistic point of view in reviewing what language rights are needed in South Africa (1996).

Innovative thinking is needed to incorporate necessary rights of speakers of **all** languages into a legal framework, and these need to come from multidisciplinary thinking (see, e.g., Grin 1991b, 1992, 1993, 1994a, 1997; Gromacki 1992). Suggestions like Alexei Leontiev's (1994) on how to combine the rights and obligations of individuals, collectivities, and the state within the educational domain are also needed (e.g., a group has the right to demand mother tongue medium education but at the same time the duty to secure enough students for a class to make it viable, also economically). Few language planning documents written by non-lawyers are exhaustive in a legal sense (but see LANGTAG 1996) but many may discuss areas not considered by lawyers (e.g., Cooper 1989). Again, more multidisciplinary teamwork is needed, also including economists (e.g., Grin 1994b, 1996b, 1999, Grin & Vaillancourt, in press).

7.2.2. Difference Between Language Rights and Linguistic Human Rights

Before continuing the delimitation further, the difference between **language** rights and linguistic **human** rights has to be clarified. The first concept is obviously much broader. There are many language rights which, while important, cannot (and should not) be seen as linguistic **human** rights, i.e. if the scope is extended too much, linguistic **human** rights become meaningless. This has been one of the problems in drafting the present version of the **Universal Declaration of Linguistic Rights**.

There is a significant difference between the need of (speakers of) dominated minority languages for protection in order to ensure their survival and basic justice on the one hand, and, for instance, the urge to promote European unity through foreign language learning or multilingualism for 'international understanding', or the need for everybody to learn English, on the other. It should undoubtedly be a human right to learn one's mother tongue, a right that speakers of the dominant language take for granted for themselves. Is it though, in the contemporary world, a human right to learn several languages in school? A variety of answers is possible to this question, reflecting the complexity of the issues involved.

I have suggested that we differentiate between **necessary** rights and **enrichment-oriented** rights. Necessary rights are rights which, in human rights language, fulfill basic needs and are a prerequisite for living a dignified life (see the discussion about needs in section 6.4 around Table 6.7). The rights in Table 7.5 below are necessary for linguistic, psychological, cultural, social, and economic survival for minorities and for basic democracy and justice—and, of course, for linguistic diversity on earth to be maintained.

In my view the **necessary individual rights** have to do, firstly, with the right to a language-related identity and, secondly, with access to the mother tongue(s). In a civilized state, there should be no need to debate the right to identify with, to maintain, and to fully develop one's mother tongue(s) (the language(s) a person has learned first and/or identifies with). Thirdly, the right of access to an official language should be considered a necessary right. The fourth necessary right has to do with the relationship between the mother tongue(s) and dominant languages (no enforced language shift), and the fifth with language-related access to formal primary education (nobody should be denied access on the basis of language). **Necessary collective rights** have to do with the right for minorities and indigenous peoples to **exist** and to reproduce themselves as distinct groups, with their own languages and cultures. Most linguistic minorities do not have these rights at present.

Individual and collective enrichment-oriented rights have to do with 'extras' for a good life, above basic needs. The right to learn foreign languages in school is oriented towards enriching the linguistic repertoire of both majorities and minorities over and above linguistic necessities.

Only the necessary rights should be seen as linguistic human rights. Enrichment-oriented rights, for instance the right to learn foreign languages, can be seen as **language** rights but I do not see them as inalienable human rights, i.e. they are not linguistic **human** rights.

There are considerable pressures afoot in Europe at present to ensure that all European children learn at least two foreign languages at school. The LINGUA, ERASMUS, SOCRATES, and other programmes (pupil, student, and teacher mobility schemes) are designed to implement such a policy, and disagreement between Britain and its other European partners reflects a major difference in perception of the issues. Britain has refused to agree on a policy of two obligatory foreign languages in schools. The British promote a dominant position for English internationally (see the project English 2000) and seem to assume that if others have two foreign languages, this might be endangered because other strong languages might emerge. Also, Brits are considered to be doing really well if they themselves learn **one** foreign language in the National Curriculum. One way of promoting English is to combine glorification and rationalisation, as in the example in Insert 7.1.

Continental European countries on the other hand wish to ensure that their children learn English **and** (at least) one other foreign language—French/German/Spanish and so on, i.e., the dominant languages of two

---

INSERT 7.1   Deprived if you do not know English?
Enrichment-oriented versus necessary rights

The Burchfield quote below might, for instance, be interpreted so that it should be some kind of language right for any 'literate, educated person' to know English: '. . . Any literate, educated person on the face of the globe is in a very real sense deprived if he [sic] does not know English' (Burchfield 1985: 160–161).

In my interpretation, this could be seen as an enrichment oriented wish, but hardly even a language right, and certainly not a linguistic human right. Hundreds of millions of 'literate, educated' people live happily without knowing English and without knowing that they are 'in a very real sense deprived'—and before they notice, machine translation may have developed so much that many of them might have little need to know English.

---

neighbouring European countries. This also reflects the wish of many Europeans (especially the French) to provide a counterweight to the pervasive influence of English and to bolster the official languages of some other European countries. Still, most 'European' projects support English or one of the official languages. Only the European Bureau for Lesser Used Languages (EBLUL, see Address Box 2.3) works with some of the dominated languages and what can be deemed to be necessary rights for their speakers.

In the rest of the chapter only necessary rights will be considered.

7.2.3. Singling Out Linguistic Human Rights in Education

Linguistic majorities, for instance English-speakers in the United States or Australia, or Swedish-speakers in Sweden, normally take it for granted that their children can be **educated through the medium of their own language.** They also take it for granted that their mother tongue, the majority language, can be **used in all (or most) official situations,** by both children and adults. They see it as self-evident that the school supports the children in **learning the official language** (i.e., their mother tongue) as well as possible. Normally they also take it for granted that they **can identify with their mother tongue and have this identification accepted and respected by everybody, including the school and census authorities.**

Many of the majority members are not aware of the fact that these, for them **self-evident rights are in fact denied to most linguistic minorities in the world,** even when these rights should be seen as fundamental, inalienable linguistic human rights. Neither indigenous peoples nor the Deaf (see Baynton 1996, Branson & Miller 1998a, b, Reagan 1995b) nor other linguistic minorities usually enjoy these rights, with fairly few exceptions worldwide.

Through education we are exposed to both the instruments (= languages) and the ideological messages (= cultural content) which are presently used in attempts to control us. Formal education reinforces the relative importance of different languages and cultures. It does it partly through the way it is organised, where some languages are media of education, some are learned as subjects, and some not at all. It also does it through the ideological content of the instruction: what is said about different languages and cultures, explicitly or implicitly, and which languages and cultures are not mentioned at all. Formal education is decisive for which languages are in fact learned and maintained. Most school systems in the world are both ideologically and organisationally geared towards a norm of monolingualism in dominant majority languages/official languages, possibly with some foreign language learning. On the other hand, non-formal education structures, organised by minorities themselves, have in many places played a large part in the maintenance of minority languages.

Those individuals whose mother tongues do not happen to be official languages in the countries where they live **have** to become bilingual (or multilingual). The majority of multilinguals are in other words *not* multilingual because they thought that multilingualism was so desirable that they consciously wanted to become multilingual. It is rather because all those people whose mother tongues have no official rights in their country have been forced to learn other languages in addition to their own. They have been forced into multilingualism precisely because of their powerless status (which has meant that their demands for official rights for their own languages have not been met, or they have not even been able to make such demands). As a group they thus have less power than those whose native language is an official language. Reagan did not need to know any of the languages spoken in the United States except English, while native Americans and Chicanas **must** learn English in addition to their mother tongues.

If linguistic minority children want to be able to speak to their parents and grandparents, know about their history and culture, and know who they are, they have to know their mother tongue, for **identity** reasons (there are many other reasons too, as we have shown). If they want to get a good formal education (which is usually not available in their own language, at least not to the same extent as in the official language/s) and to participate in the social, economic and political life of their country on an equal basis with speakers of dominant languages, they have to know the official language, for reasons of **equal participation**. (However it is important to note that bilingualism in any two languages is not enough. Minority children need to know at least their mother tongue and its culture, and the dominant language of the wider society and its concomitant culture. Some Aboriginal people in Australia might know their own language and several other Aboriginal languages, but it is not enough: they must know English too).

It should be the **duty of the educational system to enable minority children to become (minimally) bilingual** (in the mother tongue and a dominant language), since bilingualism is a necessity for them, and not necessarily or not usually a matter of personal or free choice. Bilingualism/multilingualism is thus necessary for reasons of **democracy**.

Much of the necessary further development of a mother tongue, especially in the more formal domains, takes place within the school system, as mentioned earlier. Therefore it is vital to see what kind of educational language-related human rights are guaranteed in legal covenants and other declarations of human rights. These rights are of course especially vital for a linguistic minority when the children mostly have to learn their main mother tongue through formal education, as most deaf children do. What kind of reference, if any, is made to language rights in education? Do children, especially minority children, have a right to be educated through the medium of their mother tongues? Do children have a right to become bi- or multilingual?

7.2.4. What Should be Individual LHRs in Education?

In order to prevent linguistic genocide and to counteract linguicism, a **Universal Covenant of Linguistic Human Rights** is needed. Some work has already been done towards one, partly under UNESCO auspices as section 7.6 will show. Here I will ask you, the reader, to reflect on what it should contain and then, as a base line, present some of my own concerns, restricting myself here only to individual **educational** rights.

Even when agreeing that linguistic diversity has to be maintained, and with the restriction to educational rights, there are still many different opinions about which LHRs are so important, so basic and fundamental, that everybody should be granted them unconditionally. You, dear reader, can try it out (Task Box 7.1).

Reader Task 7.1
What should be a child's individual educational LHRs?

If you want to maintain linguistic diversity, what would in your opinion be the basic individual (as opposed to collective) educational LHRs that every child should have? Reflect and write a list. Discuss your list with others, each making their suggestions and justifying them. Also justify what you leave out and why.

In my view, every state should **guarantee** basic linguistic human rights to **all** children in the educational system, in day-care, schools, and institutions of higher education, regardless of whether these children belong to linguistic majorities or minorities and regardless of whether the minority children represent indigenous peoples, traditional national minorities, immigrated minorities, or refugee minorities. Knowing what linguistic human rights are and how to guarantee basic linguistic human rights to everybody should also be an obligatory part of the training of every teacher and of school authorities.

I have formulated one set of proposals for what basic educational LHRs should guarantee at an **individual** level for a child (adults are not included in this proposal). For collective rights, see the discussion below, and also our formulation of them in Phillipson et al. (1994). In my view, universal linguistic human rights should be guaranteed in relation to the **mother tongue**, in relation to an **official language** (and thus in relation to bilingualism), and in relation to **drawing profit from education** as far as the language of education is concerned. I started discussing parts of this proposal in the late 1960s and have summarized the suggestions in Table 7.5. in many publications. This version is from 1997 (published in my 1998a).

TABLE 7.5
What should a universal covenant of LHRs guarantee to individuals?

A UNIVERSAL COVENANT OF LINGUISTIC HUMAN RIGHTS
SHOULD GUARANTEE AT AN **INDIVIDUAL** LEVEL,
IN RELATION TO

THE MOTHER TONGUE(S)

that everybody has the right to
- identify with their mother tongue(s) and have this identification accepted and respected by others;
- learn the mother tongue(s) fully, orally (when physiologically possible) and in writing.[8] This presupposes that minorities are educated mainly through the medium of their mother tongue(s), and within the state-financed educational system;
- use the mother tongue in most official situations (including schools).

OTHER LANGUAGES

- that everybody whose mother tongue is not an official language in the country where s/he is resident, has the right to become bilingual (or trilingual, if s/he has 2 mother tongues) in the mother tongue(s) and (one of) the official language(s) (according to her own choice).

THE RELATIONSHIP BETWEEN LANGUAGES

- that any change of mother tongue is voluntary (includes knowledge of long-term consequences), not imposed.

PROFIT FROM EDUCATION

- that everybody has the right to profit from education, regardless of what her mother tongue is.

Many of my arguments have been given earlier in this book. Here I only add some clarification and reflections on a few details.

In relation to the right to **use the mother tongue in most official situations**, these should minimally include day-care, schools, courts, emergency situations of all kinds, health care, including hospitals, and many governmental and other offices. The educational situations for children and some of the health care situations should involve bilingual staff[9]; in some of the other situations interpretation and translation may be enough and often the only practicable way of granting the rights.

In relation to learning an **official language**, the right to become a high level bilingual presupposes bilingual teachers. In my view, for instance a monolingual English-as-a-second-language teacher in Australia or the United States or Hong Kong is per definition incompetent. An English teacher **must** know both English and the student's mother tongue.

In relation to the **relationship between languages**, it is clear that if parents/guardians, choosing the medium of day-care and education for children, are not offered alternatives or do not know enough about the probable long-term consequences of their choices, the change of mother tongue which mostly is the result of majority-medium education for minorities, cannot be deemed voluntary, meaning it reflects linguistic genocide: the child has been 'forcibly transferred' to the linguistic majority group. The parents **must** know enough about the research results when they make their choices—they must, for instance, know that good MT-medium teaching can also lead to a better proficiency in *both* the dominant language, for instance English, *and* in the mother tongue, than English-medium teaching.

In relation to **drawing profit from education**, 'profit' should be defined in educational terms, not just in terms of having the right to receive marks (as it has been interpreted, for instance in the famous Belgian Linguistic Case, see the report by Sieghart, 1983, especially p. 249).

Examples of issues and formulations in my proposal which have been questioned by some commentators:

■ Why 'through the medium of'?

What is vital for minorities is whether they get the right to education **through the medium of** their own languages, or only **of** their languages. Is their mother tongue a medium, or a subject? We know from many studies that having one's mother tongue as a subject only, in most cases, leads to language shift for minorities (see, e.g., Boyd 1985). It is not even enough to keep the mother tongue at the same level where it was when the child started school, let alone enough to develop it. Teaching a minority mother tongue a few hours a week in a school where a majority language is the medium of education is cosmetic, therapy which can be psychologically beneficial, but which is not enough for language maintenance and development. Having a formulation which only gives a right to the mother tongue as a subject does not help minorities.

■ Why 'according to her own choice'?

One of the examples which has been widely discussed is the situation in Quebec, where the law broadly speaking stated that non-Quebecers had to place their children in French-medium schools and were only allowed to enter them in English-medium schools under specific conditions (for instance if the parents themselves had earlier attended an English-medium school in Quebec). This law was ruled unconstitutional in Canada. In my view, there must be a choice, even when trying to protect minority rights.

   ■ Why 'identify with the mother tongue' and 'have this identification accepted and respected by others'?

As chapter 3 showed, it is necessary to clarify the relationship between internal and external ethnic and linguistic identifications and the verbal expressions for these (endo-ethnonyms and exo-ethnonyms; endo-linguonyms and exo-linguonyms). Treating identification as a relation, as in my formulation above, guarantees that the endo-linguonym and the exo-linguonym can merge. As has been shown, there are many situations where insisting on the validity of one's endo-ethnonym and endo-linguonym (for instance insisting that one identifies as a Kurd and a speaker of the Kurdish language in Turkey) can lead not only to the state insisting on the validity of an exo-ethnonym ('you are a mountain Turk') and an exo-linguonym ('you speak a dialect of Turkish which has developed into an almost non-intelligible dialect because of the isolation in the mountains; a Kurdish language does not exist') but also to imprisonment and torture. **Both** formulations above are needed in order to prevent this type of situation.

On the other hand, alternative formulations need to be discussed. An example of a formulation, suggested in a document discussed at one of the UNESCO-supported conferences working on a draft Declaration, was about having the right to learn the mother tongue 'to a level which enables effective communication'. This can be interpreted in almost any way (as has been the case in Sweden). In countries which do not wish to grant minorities a right to mother tongue medium education, it would most probably be interpreted in a minimalistic way. This type of formulation does not help minorities either. The difficulties involved in the formulations reflect both the need for clarification and varying political opinions mentioned initially in this chapter.

Some people might think that it cannot be a human right to use one's mother tongue in all official situations, for instance. Many people might say that a minority child who has through her education become bilingual in the mother tongue and an official language, can use the official language in official situations, and does not need to have the right to use the mother tongue. This type of argumentation neglects the link between use, competence and identity: if a language cannot be used, it will not be learned, and it is difficult to identify with a language one does not know. Not giving languages any official rights is an indirect way of killing them.

But even if one did not accept that the rights in the suggested covenant are legitimate human rights, there is no way of denying the fact that majority and minority mother tongues do not enjoy the same rights in the educational systems of most countries. Groups defined on the basis of their mother tongues thus get unequal access to educational resources, i.e. these educational systems reflect linguicism.

Before we finally discuss some of the present linguistic human rights, we take a very short look at some aspects of their recent history in the West. A more global coverage would of course be needed but is outside the scope of this book (and my linguistic competence. See e.g. references to Hamel in the bibliography for Latin America).

7.3. A SHORT HISTORY OF LANGUAGE RIGHTS IN THE WEST

One bias in need of correction has to do with the fact that many people from other parts of the world see human rights as a western concept. They **are**, if one thinks of the history and origins of present human rights instruments. There is still vigorous debate on which texts (*nota bene*: of several western ones) were the first public human rights texts: was the first text the English 1689 Bill of Rights, or The North American Bills and Declarations of 1776, or the French Revolution's Declarations of the Rights of Man [sic] and the Citizen, 1789–1795. The American Virginia Bill of Rights of 12 June 1776 offers a typical example of these texts:

> 1. That all men [sic] are by nature created free and independent and have certain inherent rights . . . namely the enjoyment of life, liberty, with the means of acquiring and possessing property, and pursuing and obtaining happiness and safety.

My comment to the 'who was first' debate is that none of these were, of course, if we believe that slaves, people without material property, non-citizens, and even women (or children) are humans. Some or all of them were excluded from these lofty texts and from the practice of enjoying the rights. It is also being debated whether, how and to what extent these Western texts influenced the United Nations Bill of Rights (see, e.g., Best 1988).

Non-western countries played a much smaller role in the development of **The International Bill of Human Rights** than western countries. This is true especially of the first generation of post-1945 instruments, mostly consisting of individual civil and political rights. Many Asian and African countries have contested several aspects of human rights **in their present form**, even if more collective aspects have been added and there has been a more diverse involvement in developing the second (economic, social, and cultural rights) and, especially, the so called third generation (see Rosas 1995b for the concept) of rights, right to peace,[10] development,[11] environmental rights.[12]

But formalised **lack** of language rights is much older than any of the three historical Bills mentioned above. The notion of imposing a single language on all the groups living within the borders of the state was proposed as an instrument of government policy in Spain in the late fifteenth century, the time when the expansive modern European states began to take shape (Illich 1981). The dominant language (often in a standardized form) was seen as a means of securing conformity internally and expansion externally. When Antonio de Nebrija, the author of the first-ever modern grammar of any European language, presented Queen Isabella of Spain with his grammar in 1492, Isabella asked him what it was for. He advised the Queen that Castilian Spanish was 'a tool for conquest abroad and a weapon to suppress untutored speech at home . . . language has always been the consort of empire and forever shall remain its mate' (quoted in Illich 1981: 35). A monolingual doctrine and adherence to the principle of 'one state, one nation, one language' were exported worldwide, and the agenda of control and domination was clear. The Nebrija quote shows an acute awareness of the political implications of linguistic assimilation. The results of this policy can be seen throughout what came to be called the Americas (see Heath 1972 on language policy in Mexico from this period on). In colonial (and neo-colonial) empires, the promotion of the language of the coloniser generally resulted in local languages being deprived of most rights.[13] Linguistic genocide has, for instance in the Americas, resulted in the killing of hundreds of languages.

At the time when Castilian Spanish was being launched on the world scene, English, according to Phillipson 1997a:

> was spoken by approximately the same number of people as currently speak Danish (5 million), and was regarded as unsuitable for scientific writing. Although the French have been relatively more active in claiming superior merits for their language, its 'mission civilisatrice' being inconceivable in any language other than French, English is no exception to the rule of an ideology of linguistic superiority accompanying political power. By the mid-19th century English was being projected as
>
>> a strong, a harmonious, a noble language . . . Before another century has gone by it will, at the present rate of increase, be spoken by hundreds of millions . . . That language is rapidly becoming the great medium of civilization, the language of law and literature to the Hindoo, of commerce to the African, of religion to the scattered islands of the Pacific. (Edwin Guest, 1838, quoted in Crowley 1989: 71–72)

In France less than half the population had French as their mother tongue at the time of the French Revolution (Calvet 1974), but civil liberties were extended to 'all' through the exclusive medium of French, with occasional departure from this principle from Alsace, near Germany (the French language policy has always been unusually colonial—see Calvet 1974, 1987). In Britain, the rights of Welsh-speakers were oppressed for centuries. 'Under **An Act for the English order, habite and Language** [from 1535, Henry VIII, chap. 26], English law sought for many centuries to do away with the Welsh language in Wales', Fernand de Varennes describes it (1996a: 11).

Linguistic expansion of western elites thus went hand in hand with both ideological (e.g., religious) and military, economic, and territorial expansion—and ecological colonialism (see Crosby 1994). It was not only 'cuius regio, eius religio' (owner of the region/place/state decides the religion) but 'cuius regio, eius lingua'—the one who rules over a territory has the right to decide the language. This was why minorities, i.e. those who were not speakers of the ruler's language, needed language rights.

The story of formal treaty-based language rights can be divided into five phases[14] (see Skutnabb-Kangas & Phillipson 1994a that this section partially draws on—it has more details). In all of the phases language rights have been closely connected to or part of minority rights (see, e.g., de Varennes 1996a, chapter 2, Historical Overview of Language and Law, and Vilfan (ed.) 1990 for substantial overviews).

The *first* phase was pre-1815. Language rights were covered in several **bilateral** agreements but not in any international treaties. Here rights concerning minorities were primarily to be found in agreements covering religious minorities (Capotorti 1979), and linguistic minorities did not merit separate mentioning in international treaties. This practice has in fact partially continued, and even in cases where there is a more or less complete equivalence between linguistic and religious minorities, language rights have sometimes been subsumed under or can only be indirectly inferred from religious rights. The Treaty of Lausanne (July 23, 1923, Section III Concerning Protection of Minorities) and the rights granted to religious minorities in Turkey (see specifically Articles 37–39) are a case in point.

The *second* period begins with the Final Act of the Congress of Vienna 1815. It was 'the first important **international** instrument to contain clauses safeguarding national minorities, and not only religious minorities' (Capotorti 1979: 2; emphasis added). Most national minorities are simultaneously linguistic minorities. The Congress concluded the age of Napoleonic expansion and was signed by seven European major powers. Poles in Poznan were granted the right to use Polish for official business, jointly with German. However, most nineteenth century multilateral treaties which involved a large number of European powers accorded no separate rights to linguistic minorities.

During the 19th century several national constitutions and some multilateral instruments safeguarded national linguistic minorities. An early example of the recognition of linguistic rights in a national constitution is the Austrian Constitutional Law of 1867, which contrasts strongly with the monolingualism which other powers were attempting to impose at the same time (see Info Box 7.2).

❖ I n f o   B o x   7 . 2 ❖

Austrian Constitutional Law of 1867, Article 19

All the ethnic minorities of the State shall enjoy the same rights and, in particular, have an absolute right to maintain and develop their nationality and their language. All the languages used in the provinces are recognized by the State as having equal rights with regard to education, administration and public life. In provinces inhabited by several ethnic groups, the public educational institutions shall be organized in such a way as to enable all the ethnic groups to acquire the education they need in their own language, without being obliged to learn another language of the province. (Art. 19, quoted in Capotorti 1979: 3)

During the *third* period, between the two 'World' Wars, the Peace Treaties and **major multilateral and international conventions** worked out under the auspices of the **League of Nations** contained clauses protecting minorities. Many national constitutions also stipulated the rights of linguistic minorities.

The Peace Treaties that concluded the First 'World' War attempted to safeguard the rights of linguistic minorities in Central and Eastern Europe (roughly 20% of the population of the 13 countries affected). A substantial number of international instruments emanated from the Paris treaties (listed in the League of Nations Official Journal, special supplement no. 73 of June 13, 1929), embracing multinational agreements and the national constitutions of many European states (significantly, few Western European states among them). The essential points are summarized as follows (Capotorti 1979: 47):

> As regards the use of the minority language, States which have signed the treaties have undertaken to place no restriction in the way of the free use by any national of the country of any language, in private intercourse, in commerce, in religion, in the Press or in publications of any kind, or at public meetings. Those states have also agreed to grant adequate facilities to enable their nationals whose mother tongue is not the official language to use their own language, either orally or in writing, before the Courts. They have further agreed, in towns and districts where a considerable proportion of nationals of the country whose mother tongue is not the official language of the country are resident, to make provision for adequate facilities for ensuring that, in the primary schools (the Czechoslovak Treaty refers to 'instruction' in general), instruction shall be given to the children of such nationals through the medium

of their own language, it being understood that this provision does not prevent the teaching of the official language being made obligatory in those schools.

Such rights were supposed to prevail in countries like Hungary, Rumania, and Yugoslavia. Similar principles guided the treaties relating to Turkey and the (religious) minorities within its territory. Britain, France and the United States were signatories to the minorities' treaties, but did **not** offer equivalent rights to their own minority group citizens. It is also indicative of the slow progress that **linguistic minorities in most countries in the world still do not have these rights at the turn of the millennium.**

The treaties provided for the right of complaint to the League of Nations (via its Minorities Secretariat), and the International Court of Justice. Initially, it was used extensively (204 complaints were filed in 1930–1931), but since the right of appeal proved to be of limited value, only 4 complaints were filed in 1938–1939 (Boudoin & Masse 1973: 19).

Some countries (Latvia 1922, Lithuania 1925, and Poland 1932, 1933, 1934) proposed universal minority protection within the framework of the League of Nations, but the Supreme Council rejected all the proposals (Andrýsek 1989: 20). A token gesture was made in a League of Nations Assembly recommendation in 1922:

> The Committee expresses the hope that the States which are not bound by any legal obligations to the League with respect to minorities will nevertheless observe in the treatment of their own racial, religious or linguistic minorities at least as high a standard of justice and toleration as is required by any of the Treaties and by the regular action of the Council. (From Protection of Linguistic, Racial or Religious Minorities by the League of Nations, 2nd edition, Document C.8.M.5 I.B.1, Minorities, Geneva, 1931, quoted in Andrýsek 1989: 20)

The *fourth* period, from 1945 to the 1970s, was the period when, within the framework of the **United Nations**, a major effort to legislate internationally for the protection of human rights was undertaken. 'Universal' declarations were elaborated and codified. However, the thrust of promoting **individual** human rights resulted in a **relative neglect of the protection of minorities**, with the exception of broad formulations outlawing discrimination. It was thought that human rights instruments in general provided enough protection for everybody; therefore specific **collective** rights for minorities were unnecessary. Besides, as Eleanor Roosevelt put it, the concept of minority rights was not of universal significance but was a European problem. There was, relatively speaking, a lack of attention to minority rights during this phase. A draft treaty for the protection of minorities submitted by Hungary to the 1946 Peace Conference in London was not accepted. Proposals to include a provision on minorities in the Universal Declaration of Human Rights did not succeed, and the United Nations Charter does not mention minorities at all (**Human Rights Fact Sheet** 18, 1992: 3–4). This is admitted by the UN itself too. The same **Fact Sheet**, on Minorities (No 18, March 1992: 1) states that

> the setting of standards which would create additional rights and make special arrangements for persons belonging to minorities and for the minorities as *groups*—although a stated goal of the United Nations for more than 40 years— has made slow progress.

When civil and political rights were extended in the decolonisation process **from the rights of individuals to the (collective) rights of** oppressed **peoples to self-determination,** the rights of other collectivities also gained new emphasis. The *fifth* period, from the early 1970s onwards, has seen a renewed interest in the rights of minorities, including linguistic rights, and work began on the formulation of several multilateral declarations. This new focus of interest can be seen in the Capotorti report (commissioned by the UN in 1971 and published in 1979), a major survey of juridical and conceptual aspects of the protection of minorities. Information on how minorities are treated *de jure* and *de facto* was solicited for the report from governments worldwide. Capotorti proposed, among other matters, the drafting of a declaration on the rights of members of minority groups and this finally resulted in 1992 in the **UN Declaration on the Rights of Persons Belonging to National or Ethnic, Religious and Linguistic Minorities** which will be analysed below.

The overall pattern in the phases above also reflects the extent to which linguistic human rights are explicitly proclaimed in different instruments— the earlier the stronger. The **strongest** degree of protection, for **some** minorities, is discernible in the types of texts, namely **national constitutions** and relevant legislation, which were the first to guarantee linguistic rights to minorities. There is **less support** in the multilateral but still geographically restricted **regional** human rights instruments (e.g., 'European' or 'African' instruments, mostly covering one continent or parts thereof), and **still less** in **'universal'** ones. And the more general human rights instruments usually mention language only in passing. Language rights are often somewhat more specifically elaborated in instruments which are restricted to certain themes or apply to numerically small groups only, such as instruments relating to education, or genocide, or to minorities, or indigenous peoples. Instruments which specifically concentrate on language have only started to appear in the very late 1980s and early 1990s.

Below I shall look in more depth into a variety of instruments. Here I shall merely reiterate the provisional generalisations from Skutnabb-Kangas & Phillipson 1994a (pp. 78–79 and Notes) about linguistic human rights in the UN framework.

1. It is recognized (for instance in the Capotorti report) that most minorities, not least linguistic ones, are in need of much more substantial protection. Some

of the very recent recognition given to linguistic rights in declarations of intent or other texts with no legal force is laudable (e.g., *UN Human Rights Fact Sheet* 18 (1992: 4) on Minorities:

> Only when minorities are able to use their own languages, run their own schools . . . can they begin to achieve the status which majorities take for granted.

2. The coverage of educational linguistic human rights in existing international instruments reflects the relative neglect of minority rights during the 30-year period after the Second World War.

3. Language has not figured prominently as a concern. It has been thought until very recently that the cultural characteristics of minorities, including language, were adequately covered by general references to 'ethnic, religious and linguistic minorities'.

4. Immigrant minorities were deliberately excluded from consideration in the Capotorti Report, hence from the main thrust of UN efforts to end discrimination against minorities. Migrant workers, refugees, stateless persons and other non-nationals are still 'not true minorities' (UN Human Rights Fact Sheet 18, 1992: 9).

After this short survey, we proceed with contemporary rights, initially their systematization.

7.4. SYSTEMATISING LANGUAGE-RELATED RIGHTS

7.4.1. Combined Efforts at Systematising Needed

This section starts with presenting some of the various ways in which language rights have been systematized, and presents Turkey as an example of overt prohibition of the use of a minority language. Some of the early attempts by sociolinguists include Heinz Kloss (1971), who differentiated between **tolerance-oriented** and **promotion-oriented** rights. David Marshall (1986: 19) similarly discussed the 'right to **freedom from discrimination** on the basis of language' and the '**right to use your language** for the activities of commercial life.' These two represent what lawyers call **negative rights** (non-discrimination; nobody is allowed to do x to/against A on the basis of y1, y2, etc. (y being a certain human characteristic that A 'has') and **positive rights** (A is allowed/has the right to do z; often a dutyholder, e.g., the state, is specified[15] who has to guarantee that A indeed can accomplish z). Juan Cobarrubias' (1983: 71) **taxonomy of official attitudes** toward minority languages was presented in section 5.1.1, see Table 5.1.

It is clear that the systematisations by human rights and constitutional lawyers have been different from the systematisations by sociolinguists and politologists. It seems to be only fairly recently that at least some joint work has started, and more is urgently needed.

7.4.2. Degrees of Promotion-Prohibition and Overtness-Covertness—An Early Attempt to Analyse National and International Instruments

7.4.2.1. *Presentation of the Grid*

In an early attempt to try to capture some of the relevant dimensions of language rights in a range of relevant national constitutions and international covenants (Skutnabb-Kangas & Phillipson 1986b, 1989a, 1994a), my husband, Robert Phillipson, and I developed a grid to gauge to what extent these legal measures provide support for dominated languages and to evaluate educational linguistic human rights. This was also an early attempt to start specifying some aspects of **institutional** (as opposed to individual) linguicism.

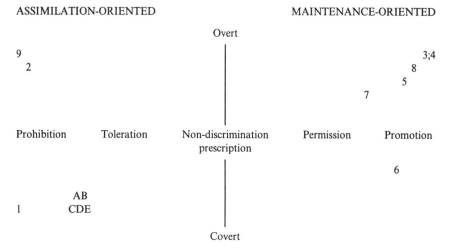

Numbers refer to countries, *letters* to covenants (see text)

1. English Language Amendments to the USA Constitution, senator Huddleston
2. as above, senator Hayakawa
3. ex-Yugoslavia
4. Finland, Swedish-speakers
5. Finland, Sámi
6. India
7. The Freedom Charter of ANC and others, South Africa
8. the Basque Normalization Law
9. Kurds in Turkey

A: The Charter of the United Nations, 1945;
B: The Universal Declaration of Human Rights, 1948;
C: International Covenant on Economic, Social and Cultural Rights, 1966;
D: International Covenant on Civil and Political Rights, 1966;
E: The UN Convention on the Rights of the Child, 1989.

FIG. 7.1 Language rights in selected countries and covenants.

The two dimensions we used were **degree of overtness** and **degree of promotion** (Figure 7.1). On the first dimension, **degree of overtness**, represented in our grid on the vertical axis, one can mark the extent to which laws or covenants are explicit in relation to the rights of minority languages in education (see Info Box 7.3 for an illustration and pp. 523–526 for the numbers and letters in Figure 7.1).

❖ **I n f o B o x 7 . 3** ❖

Examples of Degree of Overtness in Regulations

Laws and decrees can be more or less overt in relation to the rights of minority languages. **Finland**'s regulations (Jansson 1985) about the rights of linguistic minority children from one of the two groups representing official languages (Finnish or Swedish) represents a maximum degree of overtness (the first example), while, for instance, the Council of Europe's **Framework Convention for the Protection of National Minorities** (see analysis below, in section 7.5.3.4) represents a much more covert type of regulation (the second example) and grants hardly any rights. Compare the two:

> According to the law on comprehensive schools, municipalities with both Finnish- and Swedish-speaking students must form a district for [the first 9 years of] comprehensive school education in each language if minimally 13 comprehensive school students[16] have the language of the minority as their mother tongue. This has been interpreted to mean that the municipalities must form either a separate district for education through the medium of the minority language, or a common district with another municipality. (Svenska Finlands Folkting 1991: 17)

If the municipality has a school in the minority language and the number of students falls below 13, the municipality is allowed to discontinue the school only after the number of students had been under 8 during 3 successive years. Even then the municipality has an obligation to pay for the student to have mother tongue medium instruction in another municipality which offers this.

> In areas inhabited by persons belonging to national minorities traditionally or in *substantial* numbers, *if there is sufficient demand*, the parties shall *endeavour* to ensure, *as far as possible* and *within the framework of their education systems*, that persons belonging to those minorities have *adequate* opportunities for being taught in the minority language *or* for receiving instruction in this language (emphases added to the **Framework Convention**).

The **promotion** continuum on the horizontal axis starts with **prohibition** of a language, the goal of which is clearly to force the linguistic minority group to assimilate to the dominant language. It continues via **toleration** of the language, a situation where the language is not forbidden (explicitly or implicitly), to **non-discrimination prescription**, where discrimination of people on the basis of language is forbidden. This can also be done either **overtly** (discrimination is made illegal in a way which is explicit enough not to cause difficulties of legal interpretation and/or where there may be sanctions of some kind) or **covertly** (as part of general legislation on countering discrimination). The next point on the continuum is **permission** to use the minority language. At the other end of the continuum we have **promotion** of the minority language. This is obviously oriented toward maintaining it. Info Box 7.4 shows examples of covert prohibition of rights to minority languages. It is covert because the countries concerned might sign minority protection clauses, but they might still be able to manage to refuse to grant their minorities any protection, because they could/would claim that they have no minorities in the first place. This can, of course, be combined with other regulations which are more overt, as in the case of Turkey.

Before I show how the grid was used to analyse national and international instruments, some aspects of Turkish law and practices are analysed as an example of the most extreme prohibition in the world (see Skutnabb-Kangas & Bucak 1994); Turkey is alone in the top left corner of the grid.

7.4.2.2. An Example of Overt Prohibition of Linguistic Human Rights—Turkey

Many examples of linguistic human rights violations in Turkey have been given already (see Info Box 5.13 with some statistics; there are several Inserts with Kurdish examples from Turkey). Turkish law contained, according to the International Association for Human Rights in Kurdistan, at the beginning of 1996, 156 laws where a total of around 700 Articles prevent freedom of expression. What follows gives first some more examples of commonly occurring violations. This is followed by law extracts, and finally a letter of protest gives some arguments against the violations.

A trial began on 20 November 1997 at the Ankara SSC against nine officials of the teachers' union Egitim Sen charged with 'disseminating separatist propaganda by defending mother-tongue education' in Kurdish in articles in the union's journal. The prosecution demanded prison terms of between one and three years in accordance with Article 8(1) of the LTC [for Article 8(1), see Info Box 7.5]. The defendants stated that education in the mother tongue was guaranteed by international conventions and denied that demanding this right amounted to disseminating separatist propaganda. At the final hearing of the trial on 9 December, the court sentenced the nine defendants to prison terms of one year and four months and fines of 3,000,000 TL, then suspended the sentences.[18] (**Emek**, 21.11.1997; **Gündem**, 10.12.1997)

A trial was launched against Mehmet Sener Sürlü, HADEP Secretary for Aydin province, and Mehmet Nuri Güneş, a member of the party assembly. Sürlü was charged with violating the Law on Political Parties in a speech he had made during the Solidarity Festival held in June by the HADEP chapter for

❖ I n f o   B o x   7 . 4 ❖

Covert Prohibition of LHRs: There Are No Minorities
(Japan, France, Turkey)

If there 'are no minorities' in a country, minorities obviously cannot have any LHRs.

'The now notorious public statement of former conservative Prime Minister Yasuhiro Nakasone in 1986 that "there are no minorities in Japan" became the touchstone for the narrative of official denial and popular *mokusatsu* ("death by silence") regarding minority communities and their languages in the modern era' (Maher & Yashiro 1995: 4).

The 1958 French Constitution does not officially recognise any rights to linguistic minority groups, and the concept of 'minority' does not appear in the relevant French legislation. The legislation only recognises the existence of 'regional languages and cultures' which are seen as part of the national heritage and merit preservation. Four regional languages are specifically mentioned in the law 'relating to the instruction of local languages and dialects', enacted in January 1951, Catalan,[17] Occitan, Basque and Breton, which could be taught on an elective basis and offered to students as subjects, as a choice among several different cultural activities (Claire Lüsebrink; no date).

Article 2 of the French Constitution (stating that the language of the Republic is French) is currently used to oppose any legal improvement in favour of regional or minority languages in France. There have been demonstrations and lobbying for a long time to change the Article and also to make France sign and ratify the European Charter for Regional or Minority Languages, and France did indeed sign 7 May 1999. France first claimed that a ratification would be unconstitutional. The Government commissioned a study into the question of the implications of a possible signature, chaired by Guy Carcasonne. He 'believes that 50 of the 98 points contained within the Charter are compatible with the French Constitution' (reported in the Basque Country's Deputy Ministry for Language Policy's December 1998 number of their Newsletter **Euskararen Berripapera** (Vol. 6, No. 2, p. 2), in an article optimistically titled 'France is to recognise the official nature of Basque in the French Basque Country'.

The Turkish Law No. 2820 on Political Parties, section 81, from 22 April 1983, had the following (close to surrealistic) formulation 'It is forbidden to claim that there exist minorities in Turkey. It is forbidden to protect or develop non-Turkish cultures and languages'. The second part indirectly admits that minorities do in fact exist—no law would be needed to deny protection and development of something that does not exist. The law was repealed on 12 April 1991, the same day as the new Law to Combat Terrorism (No. 3713) came into force. The new law prohibits claims of minority existence equally efficiently but more covertly (see Info Box 7.5).

the Nazilli district in Aydin. In his speech, Sürlü had greeted the audience with the phrase 'Hello, friends!' in Kurdish and made the rest of the speech in Turkish. (**Gündem**, 11.11.1997)

In a press statement Ünsal Öztürk, owner of the Yurt publishing company, and the lawyer Levent Kanat said that the author/sociologist Ismail Besikci has by now spent fifteen years, four months, and 25 days in prison. A total of 105 trials have been launched against Besikci because of his 35 books, as well as his press statements and published articles. He has been sentenced to a total of more than 100 years in prison, and to fines totalling more than 100,000,000,000 TL. (**Radikal**, 13.11.1997)

All three examples are from **Kurdistan News** 43–44, June 1998, pp. 15, 14, and 12; published by International Association for Human Rights in Kurdistan; see Address Box 7.2. Even mentioning the Kurds and advocating peaceful solutions to the problems that Turkish state terrorism causes can lead both Kurds and Turks to imprisonment. In fact, Ismail Besikci (one of the examples above) is himself Turkish, not Kurdish. Despite the brutal physical force used against him for doing what any good and ethically aware sociology professor should be doing, namely analysing the problems in his country and sometimes even suggesting that they might be solved in peaceful ways (which is what Besikci has done), he still believes in the word as a weapon, and in human rights. He wrote to me that the Appendix and articles in our book **Linguistic Human Rights** (Skutnabb-Kangas & Phillipson (eds) 1994a—I sent a set of the proofs to him in prison) were extremely useful for him when he was preparing one of his big defences—he did not have any access to human rights instruments in prison (Besikci, personal communication). Info Box 7.5 presents some aspects of the Law to Combat Terrorism, which several of the examples refer to.

One and 2 years of imprisonment, respectively, was demanded for two Kurds, Yilmaz Camlibel and M. Celal Baykara, who wanted to organise a course in the Kurdish language. A massive international campaign was launched to protest. Info Box 7.6 contains Terralingua's protest letter to the Turkish Prime Minister and Minister of Education. This is one way researchers can try to support speakers of dominated languages. In addition to protesting, the letter also argues why it is not advisable to violate linguistic human rights.

In May 1998, the two were acquitted—but still no Kurdish course can be organised. Kurdish music is supposed to be free, but for instance in 1995 over 70 music cassettes were banned, selectively: they were allowed in Istanbul and Ankara but forbidden in the Kurdish areas. After changes in the law in October 1995, the Court of Appeal converted a 2-year sentence to 1 year, for publishing a book with Kurdish folk songs, i.e. it is still forbidden. The translation of the **Qur'ān** into Kurdish by Mehmet Varle was banned, first with the pretext that it contained several mistakes, then the High Court

The Law to Combat Terrorism (3713), Turkey, Extracts

The Law to Combat Terrorism (3713) has been in force in Turkey since 12 April 1991. I have emphasized some of the formulations which can be used to prosecute a person who claims any linguistic human rights. Most political parties in democratic countries could be considered terrorist organisations according to the Turkish definition. The Law defines in its Article 1 Terrorism and in Article 2 Terrorist Criminals as follows:

1. Terrorism is any kind of action conducted by one or several persons belonging to an organization with the aim of changing the characteristics of the Republic as specified in the Constitution, its political, legal, social, secular and economic system, **damaging the indivisible unity of the State with its territory and nation**, endangering the existence of the Turkish State and Republic, **weakening** or destroying or seizing **the authority of the State**, eliminating fundamental rights and freedoms, or damaging the internal and external security of the State, public order or general health by any one method of pressure, force, violence, terrorization, intimidation, oppression or threat.

An organization as described in this Law is constituted by **two** or more **people gathering under a common aim**.

2. A member of an organization, founded to attain the aims defined in Article 1, who commits a crime in accordance with these aims individually or with others **or a member of such an organization, though not committing** the intended **crime**, is called a terrorist criminal.

Those who are not members of the terrorist organization, but commit a crime in the name of the organization count as terrorist criminals and are punished like members of the organization.

Article 8, Propaganda against the indivisible unity of the State, stipulates, in Article 8(1):

> **Written and oral propaganda and assemblies, meetings and demonstrations aiming at damaging the indivisible unity of the State of the Turkish Republic with its territory and nation** are forbidden, <u>regardless of the method, intention and ideas behind it.</u> Those conducting such an activity are to be punished by a sentence of between 2 and 5 years' imprisonment and a fine of between 50 million and 100 million Turkish lira.

The underlined part, <u>regardless of the method, intention and ideas behind it</u>, was repealed 27 October 1995, after massive international pressure. When Sertaç Bucak (the Chair of the International Association for Human Rights in Kurdistan) and I wrote an article about Turkish violations of the linguistic human rights of the Kurds (Skutnabb-Kangas & Bucak 1994), we used the publishing of that article as an example of how the Law could be (and has been) interpreted in Turkey. We wrote:

> There are two authors, and we have a common aim, to write a scientific article about the linguistic rights of the Kurds. We would be considered

(Continued)

a terrorist organization according to Article 1. Claiming that the Kurds exist and that they should have what is here defined as linguistic human rights is a terrorist crime, as defined in Articles 1, 2 and 8 in Law 3713. If we were Turkish citizens, we could be sentenced under the Anti-Terror law, Article 8, with heavy imprisonment and fines. In addition, both the publisher of this book [Mouton de Gruyter] and the series editor [Joshua Fishman] could be imprisoned and fined severely, and their assets could be confiscated. So could the assets (e.g., buildings) of our places of work (Universities of Bremen and Roskilde) and the publisher's assets. If you, dear reader, wrote a review of this article in a scientific journal and said that you agreed that Kurdish children should have the right to learn Kurdish, or if you joined a local Committee for the Human Rights of the Kurds (as the former Danish Prime Minister Anker Jørgensen who [together with TSK] is on the Board of the Danish Committee), you would likewise be considered a terrorist criminal, and could be imprisoned, according to Article 2, even if you never did anything for the Committee or for the education of Kurdish children.

✤ **I n f o   B o x   7 . 6** ✤

Protest Letter by Terralingua to Turkish Ministers for Violating LHRs

Mr Mesut Yilmaz, Prime Minister of the Republic of Turkey
Basbakanlik, Cankaya, Ankara, Turkey; and
Mr Hikmet Ulugbay, Minister of National Education
Bakanliklar, Ankara, Turkey

We are alarmed at the news that the course in the Kurdish language offered by the Foundation for Kurdish Culture and Research has been banned by Turkish authorities, and proceedings initiated against the Chair and Deputy Chair of the organisation, Yilmaz Camlibel and M. Celal Baykara.

There are at least some 7,000 spoken languages in the world. Kurdish is among the 100 largest languages in the world, even according to minimalist accounts of numbers of Kurdish speakers. 'Globalization carries with it a danger of uniformity [. . .] Peace means diversity [. . .] it means multi-ethnic and multilingual societies', according to UNESCO's **The Human Right to Peace. Declaration by the Director-General**, 1997, p. 9). Denying the existence of several ethnic groups and languages in Turkey is not only counterfactual—these groups DO exist, despite the official denial—but economically disastrous and politically counterproductive, internally and externally. Already now the proportion of the GNP that Turkey uses for the military and the police is among

(Continued)

the largest in the world. Much of the cost goes to fighting the Kurds. Peace and conflict research shows clearly that it is almost impossible for a state to win a war against a people who think that they are being treated unreasonably. Physical force, especially against a group with large numbers, is an expensive undertaking and not cost-effective. Human rights violations in general and especially the lack of linguistic and cultural rights create and feed tension which then becomes 'ethnic' conflict. Granting linguistic and cultural rights to minorities is in no way opposed to protecting national sovereignty and territorial integrity—quite the opposite. We would like to remind you of the premable of the **European Charter for Regional or Minority Languages**, from 22 June 1992. The preamble

- considers 'that the right to use a regional or minority language in private and public life is an inalienable right',
- stresses 'the value of interculturalism and multilingualism' and
- considers 'that the protection and encouragement of regional or minority languages should not be to the detriment of the official languages and the need to learn them' but rather 'an important contribution to the building of a Europe based on principles of democracy and cultural diversity within the framework of national sovereignty and territorial integrity.'

Likewise, the positive impact of linguistic diversity for the economy is getting increasing acknowledgement:

> It is especially important to note that supporting interaction between localities and regions will not only help to build a European identity, but pave the way for a stronger European economy which takes account of cultural and linguistic diversity. An economy, even a strong one, based on these principles will not lead to a greater similarity in European ways of life but will instead reinforce the distinctive traditions and characteristics of Europe's localities and regions (from the Preface, by Pascan Maragall í Mira, to the book **The Diversity Dividend: Language, Culture, and Economy in an integrated Europe**, by Adam Price, Caitríona O. Torna and Allan Wynne Jones, and published by the EBLUL (European Bureau for Lesser Used Languages).

For Turkey, seeking stronger ties with Europe, not only leaving the Kurds alone but in fact encouraging the flourishing of Kurdish language and culture also makes economic sense.

The absence or denial of linguistic and cultural rights are today effective ways of promoting 'ethnic' conflict and violence, of the type which leads to both separatism and the emergence of totalitarian states. This has been acknowledged by many researchers from several fields. Professor Jurek Smolicz from Australia has (in 1986) formulated the argument as follows:

(Continued)

... attempts to artificially suppress minority languages through policies of assimilation, devaluation, reduction to a state of illiteracy, expulsion or genocide are not only degrading of human dignity and morally unacceptable, but they are also an **invitation** to separatism and an **incitement** to fragmentation into mini-states.

It has also been acknowledged by policy makers. Dr. M. Xulu, the South African Deputy Director-General of DACST (Department of Arts, Culture, Science and Technology), said in his opening address on 4 November 1997 at a seminar in Pretoria (where Terralingua's Vice-President was a main speaker) that one of the popular myths that has to be exploded is 'that promoting multilingualism and respecting language rights will lead to language conflict and ethnic conflict'. If South Africans can recognise this as a myth (which they have), Turkey can do so too.

There are strong reasons why states should support rather than try to eliminate linguistic and cultural diversity, not only in the name of human rights, but also in their own political and economic interest. It is in fact the Turkish state itself which 'incites to separatism' and 'incites to racial or ethnic enmity' (Article 312 of your Criminal Code) and transmits separatist propaganda, through violating basic linguistic and cultural human rights. The banning of the Kurdish course and the ensuing proceedings against Mr Yilmaz Camlibel and Mr M. Celal Baykara are examples of these state violations of linguistic human rights where it is these violations themselves which lead to conflict and incite separatism.

Terralingua, Partnerships for Linguistic and Biological Diversity, is a non-profit international organization devoted to preserving the world's linguistic diversity and to investigating links between biological and cultural diversity. Our Board of Directors and Advisory Board consist of some of the most respected researchers in the field worldwide. We work with all other international organisations interested in linguistic, cultural or biological diversity, including UNESCO and UNEP (the UN Environmental Programme).

As an organisation devoted to preserving the world's linguistic diversity, we are of course concerned with the promotion of the teaching and learning of ALL languages in the world, including Kurdish. We urge you to allow the Kurdish language to be freely taught in Turkey, on courses, in schools and universities, to be used as the medium of education in schools and other educational institutions, and to be freely used in media. Likewise, we urge you to drop the allegations against not only Mr Yilmaz Camlibel and Mr M. Celal Baykara but against all those who are imprisoned or face charges for learning and using Kurdish and discussing peaceful solutions to the Kurdish question.

On behalf of Terralingua
Dr. Tove Skutnabb-Kangas
Vice-President

(Continued)

of Religious Affairs (a state institution) just said that it was impossible to publish it in Kurdish. Address Box 7.2 lists some Kurdish electronic resources where the reader can continue.

```
* * * * * * * * * * * * * * * * * * * * * * * * * * * * * * * * * * * * * * *
*                                                                           *
*        Address Box 7.2   Electronic resources on Kurdistan,               *
*              the Kurds, and the Kurdish language                          *
*                                                                           *
*    International Association for Human Rights in Kurdistan, Box 200738,    *
*    D-53137 Bonn, Germany, phone 49-228-362802, fax 49-228-363297; email:  *
*    <IMK-Bonn@t-online.de>.                                                *
*                                                                           *
*    Readers who want more information on human rights in Kurdistan and     *
*    Kurdish questions in general, can get started by consulting the following *
*    Web-sites. Most of the list has been prepared by Siamak Rezaei-Durroei, *
*    Centre for Cognitive Science, Edinburgh, UK <siamakr@cogsci.ed.ac.uk>  *
*    in September 1998 (thanks!).                                           *
*                                                                           *
*    General:                                                               *
*        <http://www.kurdish.com>; Kurdish Worldwide Resources             *
*        <http://www.xs4all.nl/~tank/kurdish/htdocs/>; Kurdish Information  *
*        Network; European site with general data, cultural information, songs *
*        (with audio).                                                     *
*        <http://www.humanrights.de/~kurdweb/>; Kurdistan Web News,        *
*        Information and Documentation Database.                           *
*        <http://www.geocities.com/CapitolHill/9574/armenia.htm>; Yezidi   *
*        Kurds in Armenia.                                                 *
*        <http://members.tripod.com/~zaza_kirmanc/index.html>;            *
*        Zaza/Kirmanc/Dimili Kurds.                                        *
*        <http://home5.swipnet.se/~w-54922/index.htm>; Faili Kurds Homepage. *
*        <http://www.kurdistan.org/>; American Kurdish Information Network  *
*        (AKIN).                                                           *
*        <http://www.clark.net/kurd/>; Washington Kurdish Institute (WKI). *
*                                                                           *
* * * * * * * * * * * * * * * * * * * * * * * * * * * * * * * * * * * * * * *
```

(Continued)

Address Box 7.2 *(Continued)*

News:

■ <http://www.mnsi.net/~mergan95/EnglishN.htm>; The Kurdistan Observer, Daily News in English.

■ <http://home.nordnet.fr/~sdara/>; Kurdistan Tribune, Monthly News and Analysis in English.

■ <http://www.med-tv.be/med/>; Med-TV web-page, News in English from Kurdish Satellite Television (Med-TV); email <med@med-tv.be>.

■ <http://www.ozgurpolitika.org>; Özgur Politika On-Line, Kurdish Daily in Turkish.

■ <http://www.khrp.org/>; Kurdish Human Rights Project, London-based NGO.

Academic and Cultural:

■ <http://www.cogsci.ed.ac.uk/~siamakr/kurd_lal.html>; Kurdish Language and Linguistics (Kurd_lal), Archive and newsletter on Kurdish grammar, linguistics and bibliography.

■ <http://www.deakin.edu.au/~kstudyg/kstudyg.html>; Kurdish Study Group at Deakin University, Australia-based academic site, teaching materials, Newsletter.

■ <http://www.tidalwave.net/~bcks/>; Badlisy Center for Kurdish Studies, US based research organization.

■ <http://www.marebalticum.se/kurd/index.htm>; Kurdish Library and Documentation Center in Stockholm, Sweden (English, Kurmanji, Swedish, Turkish), with links to Kurdish literature, poetry, art, publishers.

■ <http://wwwcip.rus.uni-stuttgart.de/~etk10310/>; Kurdish Poetry Page.

■ <http://home1.swipnet.se/~w-19878/index.html>; ROJBAS, magazine in Kurdish.

■ <http://www.unitype.com/globaloffice.htm> has information on how to use [Microsoft Office—sorry] software to write Kurdish (Soraní, Kurmandjí, Guraní, and Zazakí) as well as Farsi, Arabic and Turkish.

Political parties:

■ <http://www.pkk.org/>; Kurdistan Workers Party (PKK).

■ <http://www.cpiran.org/Ku/index.html>; Komala (Communist Party of Iran).

■ <http://www.puk.org/>; Patriotic Union of Kurdistan.

■ <http://www.kdp.pp.se>; Kurdistan Democratic Party.

■ <http://members.aol.com/kurdis6065/Psk.html>; Socialist Party of Kurdistan.

Newsgroups and Interactive chat:

■ <http://members.xoom.com/pashew/>; Kurdistan, Realtime Interactive Discussion Forum.

Hassanpour (in press) is a perceptive analysis of the Kurdish situation, with some hope. After this example of brutal overt prohibition, we go back to showing how the grid can be used.

7.4.2.3. Using the Grid to Analyse National Constitutions and Some International Instruments

In the original study (1986b) we plotted on to the grid a range of **national constitutions**: **Finland**, for both the **Sámi** (No 5 on the grid) and the **Swedish** (No 4) languages; the then **Yugoslavia** (No 3); **India** (No 6) and **Turkey** vis-a-vis the **Kurds** (No 9) and **proposals for constitutional change**: **English Language Amendments** to the **USA** Constitution (Huddleston No 1, Hayakawa No 2; see Marshall 1986: 36); **The Freedom Charter of the African National Congress (ANC) and others, South Africa** (No 7); the **Basque Normalization Law** (No 8). The examples were elaborated further in Skutnabb-Kangas & Phillipson 1989a. It is interesting to see the changes in a decade, some for the better (Finland, South Africa), some for the worse (Yugoslavia, Turkey, USA), some on paper, some in terms of implementation. India and the Basque Country are the only countries from our original grid which have hardly changed.

Serbia has moved left and down on the grid, scrapping most rights of minorities, including educational language rights, as the example of Kosova so tragically shows. Yugoslavia's earlier Constitution guaranteed to every individual 'the right to instruction in their own language' in the regions they natively inhabit (SFRY Constitution, Article 171, para. 2; see also articles in Bugarski & Hawkesworth (eds) 1992 for details). This was overt maintenance-oriented promotion.

Finland's recent Constitution (1993) has retained the rights of Swedish-speakers and improved the rights of the Sámi (see **Kielilaki** (The Sámi Language Act) 516/91, and **Kieliasetus** (The Language Decree) 1201/91 and 1202/91), and also included the Deaf and other linguistic minorities, albeit in a more covert way.

The new South African Constitution (1996) has, on the basis of the LANGTAG (Language Plan Task Group) report[19] (1996), moved the country on paper to overt promotion for the 11 official languages, rather imprecise but semi-overt permission to use several other languages which are mentioned in the constitution, and at least overt toleration if not covert permission to use any indigenous languages (see the formulations in Info Boxes 5.8 and 5.9). To what extent implementation of the laudable principles will be achieved is still to some extent unsure. Pansalb, Pan South African Language Board, which was given ambitious tasks in the Constitution (1996: 5) (see the list of these in Info Box 5.9), has not yet seemed to be able to have much impact, despite the many excellent people in it.[20]

In Turkey the oppression has in fact become worse,[21] despite a few positive minor changes in laws. There are several other countries which commit all three types of genocide (physical, cultural, linguistic) but without the same detailed constitutional legislative backing that genocide has in Turkey.

For the USA we used the two Amendments to the Constitution which existed at the time (now there are dozens of them). Info Box 7.7 shows how we then classified them.

❖ **I n f o   B o x   7 . 7** ❖

Suggestions for Amendments to the USA Constitution by
Senators Huddleston and Hayakawa

'Section 1. The English language shall be the official language of the United States' (Senator Huddleston's formulation of the English Language Amendment, S.J.R. 167, quoted in Marshall 1986: 36; Example 1 in Figure 7.1), was an example of **covert assimilation-oriented prohibition** of minority languages. It makes no mention of other languages, but implicitly prohibits their use in functions which are carried out in an official language. It forces minority language speakers to use English for all official purposes instead of their own languages.

In Senator Hayakawa's ELA, the same Section 1 (above) is followed by Section 2: 'Neither the United States nor any State shall make or enforce any law which requires the use of any language other than English' (ibid., example 2 in Fig. 7.1). This **overt assimilation-oriented prohibition** could obviously have prevented both voting information and education in Spanish, Chinese, etc. One of my friends who visited a zoo and a botanical garden in one of the around 20 States which have already (1998) passed some form of English Language Amendment reported that the names of the animals and plants can no longer be displayed in Latin . . .

The USA situation has become still worse with the passing of Proposal 227 in California (see note 3 in chapter 3).

I have also placed on the grid some of the results (see Skutnabb-Kangas & Phillipson 1989a: 14–19 for more) of our review of the clauses on educational language rights (i.e., *not* the general clauses) in some international and European conventions and decrees. Some of them will be commented on and evaluated here in relation to the dimensions on the grid, and they and others will be discussed further in later sections of this chapter.

Example A. The Charter of the United Nations (1945) commits its member nations in its **general** articles to promoting

> universal respect for, and observance of, human rights and fundamental freedoms
> for all without distinction as to race, sex, language, or religion. (para. 6.11, 55)

This can be understood as **overt non-discrimination prescription**. But the Charter has no specific article on **education** and thus **nothing on language in education**, implying only **covert toleration**.

The **general** articles in all the following covenants (B–E) can also be characterized as **overt non-discrimination prescription**. For instance, the **Universal Declaration of Human Rights** declares in paragraph 2:

> Everyone is entitled to all the rights and freedoms set forth in this Declaration, without distinction of any kind, such as race, colour, sex, language, religion, political or other opinion, national or social origin, property, birth or other status.

Example B. The **Universal Declaration of Human Rights** (1948), in its paragraph on **education** (26), **does not refer to language**. The main thrust of the paragraph is to ensure free universal education. There are references to the 'full development of the human personality' and the right of parents to 'choose the kind of education that shall be given to their children'. This can be considered **covert toleration**.

Example C. The **International Covenant on Economic, Social and Cultural Rights**, adopted in 1966 and in force since 1976, having mentioned language on a par with race, colour, sex, religion, etc. in its **general** article (2.2) again omits any reference to language in the **educational** article (13). There is an inconsistency here, because the covenant **does** explicitly refer to 'racial, ethnic or religious groups' in the education article, though not 'linguistic' ones (see the formulation in section 7.5.2). This also represents **covert toleration**.

Example D. **International Covenant on Civil and Political Rights** (1966, in force since 1976) does not have any **educational** clauses (i.e., there is **covert toleration**). But Article 27 states:

> In those states in which ethnic, religious or linguistic minorities exist, persons belonging to such minorities shall not be denied the right, in community with other members of their group, to enjoy their own culture, to profess and practice their own religion, or to use their own language.

This represents **overt non-discrimination prescription**, tending towards permission, but does not at least overtly include educational institutions.

This article, which grants the best binding minority language protection so far, has been one of the most important for the protection of linguistic minorities, as both Capotorti (1979, the UN Special Rapporteur on Minorities) and more recent UN reports (Eide 1990, 1991, Palley 1984) confirm. Both the UN Conventions on the Rights of the Child (1959 and 1989), and several Council of Europe and CSCE/OSCE documents have used approximately the same formulation. Still, rights are only granted to individuals, not collectivities. And in the customary interpretation (but see section 7.8.1) 'persons belonging to . . . minorities' only had these rights in states which accept that the minorities exist. See also Capotorti's and de Varennes' (1996a) throrough analyses of Article 27.

Example E. The UN Convention on the Rights of the Child, 1989, stresses the maintenance of identity, including 'nationality' and 'name' (Art. 7 and 8; see also Jernudd 1994, Kontra 1996b, Druviete, 1999). It does not mention language in its general article on **education** (28; i.e., there is **covert toleration**), though it mentions 'development of respect for the child's parents, his or her own cultural identity, language and values' (Art. 29.c), encourages 'the mass media to have particular regard to the linguistic needs of the child who belongs to a minority group or who is indigenous' (Art. 17.d) and decrees that 'due regard shall be paid to the desirability of continuity in a child's upbringing and to the child's ethnic, religious, cultural and linguistic background' (Art. 20.3)—but all these apply only when a child is temporarily or permanently deprived of the family environment. The clause obviously does not refer to daily child care or school. Article 30 is substantially the same as Art. 27 on minorities quoted above in example D ('persons of indigenous origin' have been added, and 'their' has been replaced by 'his or her'). This **overt non-discrimination prescription** implicitly restricts use of the minority language to private minority community use. (This has been extended in the preamble of the **European Charter for Regional or Minority Languages** (see below), which, with reference to Art. 27 (see D above) considers 'that the right to use a regional or minority language in private **and public** life is an inalienable right' (emphasis added).

In sum, many **national constitutions provide more protection** to minority languages in education **than the international covenants** placed on the grid. Conversely, none of the international covenants overtly prohibits the use of minority languages, as some national constitutions do.

On the other hand, our review (1989a) concluded that the five UN conventions (A, B, C, D, and E) have **general** provisions which are apparently an **overt non-discrimination prescription** (A, B, C) or even **overt permission**, mentioning language specifically (D, E), even if no legally binding declarations/covenants were mother tongue maintenance-oriented. But the absence of any overt mention of language under the **education clauses** of those covenants which are binding is in contrast with the **general clauses** on non-discrimination, which relate to the exercise of all human rights. The **education** clauses are no stronger than **covert assimilation-oriented toleration** of minority mother tongues. Minorities are allowed to use their languages in private, but not in schools. The same is also true of other examples from regional covenants.

In the same review (1989a) we also showed that not even overt maintenance-oriented **permission** is enough for minority (or powerless majority) mother tongues to be maintained and developed. What they require is overt maintenance-oriented **promotion**. This necessarily includes the allocation of the economic means for supporting mother tongue medium schools—one of the crucial deficiencies in UNESCO's own Convention against Discrimination in Education. No international covenants guarantee this to any minority groups, or to any individuals (regardless of whether the individuals come from a linguistic minority or majority). What is needed for minority languages to be maintained over several generations in countries where obligatory education is enforced is overt promotion of these languages (minimally 'partial support of specific language functions' or 'adoption as an official language' in Cobarrubias' taxonomy in section 5.1.1—or beyond, as has already been mentioned).

A central conclusion in the review was thus that the existing international or 'universal' declarations and conventions were in no way adequate to provide support for dominated languages. The evidence unmistakably showed that while individuals and groups are supposed to enjoy 'cultural' and 'social' rights, linguistic human rights were neither guaranteed nor protected. This means that despite many many nice phrases about linguistic rights, international covenants analysed which are binding, and where there is a complaint procedure, contain almost no linguistic rights. The policy on educational linguistic human rights seemed to us to be a posture policy, without much content.

In the next section we will first look in more detail at what happens to language rights in education in human rights instruments. Then the most recent instruments, specifically oriented towards language or minority rights, will be analysed further, including the draft **Universal Declaration of Linguistic Rights**, the most comprehensive language rights instrument planned so far. This shows that not nearly enough improvement has taken place. The hypocrisy of Western states in relation to human rights will be discussed, and Denmark will be used as an example of the double standards. Finally, some recent positive developments will be presented.

7.5. WHAT HAPPENS TO LANGUAGE IN EDUCATIONAL INSTRUMENTS?

7.5.1. Language *is* One of the Important Characteristics on the Basis of Which Discrimination is Prohibited . . .

In many international, regional and multilateral post-WW2 human rights instruments language is mentioned in the preambles and in the general clauses as one of the characteristics on the basis of which individuals are not to be discriminated against in their enjoyment of human rights and fundamental freedoms. The other original characteristics are 'race, colour, sex, religion, political or other opinion, national or social origin, property, birth or other status' (from the joint Art. 2, **Universal Declaration of Human Rights**, Art. 2.1, **International Covenant on Civil and Political Rights**, and Art. 2.2, **International Covenant on Economic, Social and Cultural Rights**). Later UN instruments (e.g., The **United Nations Convention on the Rights of the Child**, Art. 2.1) have added 'disability'; the **American Convention on Human Rights**, "Pact of San Jose, Costa Rica" (Art. 1) replaced 'property' with 'economic status' and added 'or any other social condition'. Some later instruments (e.g., the **UN International Convention on the Protection of the Rights of All Migrant Workers and Members of Their Families**, Art. 1) have added 'conviction, nationality, age and marital status', and likewise 'ethnic' was added to 'national or social origin'.

The original and basic four characteristics, in the **Charter of the United Nations**, Art. 13, are "**race, sex, language, or religion**", with signatories committing themselves to promote

> . . . universal respect for, and observance of, human rights and fundamental freedoms for all without distinction as to race, sex, language, or religion.

This suggests that language has been seen as one of the most important characteristics of humans in human rights principles in the key documents that have pioneered the post-1945 UN human rights effort.

7.5.2. . . . But It Disappears . . .

But when we move from the lofty non-duty-inducing phrases in the preambles of the human rights instruments, to the real business, namely the binding clauses, and especially to the educational clauses, something very strange happens. There is a change of position. All or most of the **non-linguistic** human characteristics, and especially the basic ones (race, sex, religion) are still there and get positive rights accorded to them: the clauses or articles about them create obligations and contain demanding formulations, where the states are firm dutyholders and are obliged to ('shall'—see Note 21) act in order to ensure the specified rights (i.e., positive rather than negative rights). Here modifications, opt-out clauses and sliding-scale alternatives are rare.

In binding educational clauses, however, one of two things can often be noted. Firstly, language often disappears completely, as, for instance, in the **Universal Declaration of Human Rights** (1948) where the paragraph on education (26) does not refer to language at all. Similarly, the **International Covenant on Economic, Social and Cultural Rights** (adopted in 1966 and in force since 1976), having mentioned language on a par with race, colour, sex, religion, etc. in its general Article (2.2), does explicitly refer to 'racial,

ethnic or religious groups' in its educational Article (13.1). However, here
it omits reference to language or linguistic groups:

> . . . education shall enable all persons to participate effectively in a free society,
> promote understanding, tolerance and friendship among all nations and all
> **racial, ethnic or religious groups** . . . (emphasis added)

The **European Convention on Human Rights and Fundamental Freedoms** of
1950 is equally silent on not only language rights in education but even more
general minority rights, as Patrick Thornberry (1997: 348–349) notes:

> The Convention does not establish individual minority rights nor collective
> rights of minorities. Case-law has gradually mapped out what the Convention
> demands and permits . . . There is . . . no right to 'linguistic freedom' in the
> Convention. In the *Isop* case, the Commission denied such a right where the
> applicant claimed the right to use the Slovene language before a civil court;
> similar cases have affected, e.g., speakers of Breton, Flemish, and Frisian. On
> access to education in the language of a minority group, case-law indicates
> that the Convention does not guarantee the right to be educated in the language
> of one's parents by public authorities . . . In a number of instances, the Com-
> mission has stated that 'the Convention does not guarantee specific rights to
> minorities' . . . Similarly, there is no right to separate representation of minori-
> ties in legislative bodies . . . nor to self-determination.

Several new Declarations and Conventions to protect minorities and/or
minority languages have been passed in the 1990s. But even in the new
instruments strange things are happening in relation to language and the
Articles about language rights in education; even here language has been
omitted. This is interesting in relation to definitions of racism. It is very clear
that crude biologically argued racism is no longer accepted as official ideology in any state—in its stead have come culturally/ethnically argued racism
(ethnicism) and linguistically argued racism, linguicism. This should of course
also be reflected in recent action-oriented definitions of racism. When the
UN Centre for Human Rights in Geneva wrote a **Model National Legislation
for the Guidance of Governments in the Enactment of Further Legislation
against Racial Discrimination** for the UN Year Against Racism (1996), 'race,
colour, descent, nationality or ethnic origin' were mentioned in the new
definition of racism used, but there was no mention of language (see Info
Box 7.8).

Another example is the 1995 Copenhagen Declaration. Info Box 7.9 presents the Declaration in UN ex-Secretary General Boutros-Ghali's (1995: 8)
words.

In the text itself, recognition and respect is granted to 'cultural, ethnic
and religious diversity' but not 'linguistic diversity'—'linguistic' has been

---

❖ **I n f o   B o x   7 . 8** ❖

Model Law Against Racial Discrimination, UN

1. The purpose of this Act is to prohibit and bring to an end racial discrimination by any person, group of persons, public authorities, public and private national and local institutions and organizations in the civil, political, economic, social and cultural spheres, *inter alia* in employment, education, housing and the provision of goods, facilities and services.

PART I. Definitions

2. In this Act, racial discrimination shall mean any distinction, exclusion, restriction, preference or omission based on **race, colour, descent, nationality or ethnic origin** which has the purpose or effect of nullifying or impairing, directly or indirectly, the recognition, equal enjoyment or exercise of human rights and fundamental freedoms recognized in international law.

3. Racial discrimination shall not include special measures which have the purpose of ensuring adequate advancement of an individual or group of individuals of any particular **race, colour, descent, nationality or ethnic origin**, for the enjoyment or exercise of human rights and fundamental freedoms recognized in international law, provided that such measures do not result in the maintenance of separate rights for different racial groups and that they do not remain in force after the objectives for which they were taken have been achieved (from **Model National Legislation for the Guidance of Governments in the Enactment of Further Legislation against Racial Discrimination**; emphases added).

❖ **I n f o   B o x   7 . 9** ❖

Linguistic Diversity Not Respected by 103 Heads of State?

The recently concluded World Summit for Social Development held in Copenhagen in March 1995 took an important step in this regard. The participating States, including 103 Heads of State and Government, committed themselves to 'Recognize and respect **cultural, ethnic and religious diversity** and promote and protect the rights of persons belonging to **national or ethnic, religious or linguistic** minorities' (emphases added).

---

omitted. I have literally hundreds of examples from various UN, OECD, OSCE, UNESCO, Council of Europe, etc., declarations, resolutions, and various (other) human rights documents where language logically should be there in the list of characteristics—but it is not.

7.5.3. ... Or Is Watered Down by Modifications and Alternatives

If language-related rights **are** included and specified, the Article(s) dealing with these rights, in contrast to the demanding formulations and the few opt-outs and alternatives in the articles dealing with other characteristics, are typically so weak and unsatisfactory that they may be virtually meaningless. All or many of the other human characteristics are still there and get proper treatment and detailed, positive rights. The clauses about them create obligations and contain demanding formulations, where the states are firm dutyholders and 'shall' (i.e., are obliged to[22]) do something positive in order to ensure the rights; there are few modifications, few opt-out clauses and few alternatives on a sliding scale. Many of the other characteristics get their own specific conventions (e.g., conventions to prevent racism or sexism, or to guarantee freedom of religion). But not so for language, especially in education. In the following, most of the recent language-related instruments will be scrutinized.

7.5.3.1. Introduction to Recent Language-Related Instruments

Among the bodies currently codifying language rights for minorities are the Council of Europe, the European Parliament, the OSCE, the UN and UNESCO (Address Box 7.3, p. 536, gives some Web-sites where one can start). In the 12 countries which made up the European Community until 1995, some 50 million of the 320 million **citizens** spoke a language other than the main or official language of the state in which they lived in the mid-1980s (see de Witte 1991 for the rules and Coulmas (ed.) 1991 in general for the policies; see references to Haarmann in the bibliography for some of the historical background). Pressure from these speakers of the 'Lesser Used Languages' led to both the founding of the European Bureau for Lesser Used Languages (EBLUL—see Address Box 2.3) and the passing of several European Parliament resolutions aimed at guaranteeing rights to speakers of dominated autochthonous languages. The most significant was the **Kuijpers Resolution**, adopted on 30 October 1987, which would have represented semi-overt maintenance-oriented support. It 'recommends to Member States that they carry out education measures including: . . . arranging for pre-school to university education and continuing education to be officially conducted in the regional minority languages in the language areas concerned on an equal footing with instruction in the national languages . . .'. It contained similar recommendations on the use of these languages in public and judicial administration and the mass media. European Parliament resolutions like the Kujpers resolutions are not binding on member states; rather their value lies more in creating a climate of awareness of the issues and in the potential they represent for pressurizing national governments. One of the results of this and similar resolutions was that work started to create the **European Charter for Regional or Minority Languages**.

The **European Charter for Regional or Minority Languages** has great symbolic value, but explicitly excludes migrant languages. In addition, the countries signing it can decide which minorities they want to apply it to, that is, even if they accept that a group in their country **is** a minority, they do not necessarily need to extend the rights to this group. The Charter will be analysed more below.

The European Parliament's **Directive on the education of the children of migrant workers** (77/466/EEC of 25.7.77) is fraught with difficulties of interpretation and implementation,[23] as the Parliament's own **Report drawn up on behalf of the Committee of Inquiry into RACISM and XENOPHOBIA** indicates (A3-195/90, PE 141.205/FIN, 111).[24]

The **Council of Europe**'s European Commission for Democracy through Law, drafted a **Proposal for a European Convention for the Protection of Minorities** (CDL 91–7), which could also have applied to those migrants who have changed citizenship (see below), but it included very little on language rights, and was later scrapped altogether. Instead of it the watered-down (see below) **Framework Convention for the Protection of National Minorities** was adopted.

The **Organisation on Security and Cooperation in Europe (OSCE)** states unambiguously in its **Document of the Copenhagen Meeting of the Conference on the Human Dimension of the OSCE** (1990) that national minorities should have the right to maintain their ethnic, cultural, linguistic or religious identity, the right to seek voluntary and public assistance to do so in educational institutions, and should not be subjected to assimilation against their will (OSCE 1990a: 40), but has so far not agreed on any binding conventions. An OSCE High Commissioner on Minorities was appointed in 1992 and is the source of the positive **Hague Recommendations** analysed below.

The UN **Draft Universal Declaration on Indigenous Rights**, 1988 version, would have given indigenous peoples 'the right to all forms of education, including in particular the right of children to have access to education in their own languages, and to establish, structure, conduct and control their own educational systems and institutions.' (Art. 10, E/CN.4/Sub.2/1988/25), if accepted—but see changes below.

It is in striking contrast to the **UN International Convention on the Protection of the Rights of All Migrant Workers and Their Families**, 1990, which accords minimal rights to the mother tongues and is assimilation-oriented (see Hasenau 1990). L2-teaching has a stronger formulation than teaching of the mother tongue ('States . . . *shall pursue* a policy . . . aimed at facilitating the integration of children of migrant workers in the local school system, particularly in respect to teaching them the local language.' (Art. 45.2), as compared to 'States . . . *shall* **endeavour** to facilitate for the children of migrant workers the teaching of their mother tongue and culture . . .' (Art. 45.3) and 'States . . . **may** provide special schemes of education in the mother tongue of children of migrant workers . . .' (Art 45.4; emphases added; *obligating* formulations are italized, **opt-outs** bolded). But even in this minimal form it 'is not yet in force and . . . is unlikely to enter into force for a long time to come.' (Eide 1995a: 35). 'As of 1 January 1994, there were only 3 ratifications, while 20 ratifications are required for the Convention to enter into force.' (ibid., note 45, p. 35). As of August 1997, the Convention had not entered into force (note 25, p. 14, **Minority Rights Fact Sheet** 18 from February 1998). And the latest Unesco 1998 report (Symonides 1998) informs us that there are still only 9 ratifications (Bosnia and Herzegovina, Cape Verde, Colombia, Egypt, Morocco, Philippines, Seychelles, Sri Lanka, and Uganda). It is easy to see that it is necessary for immigrated minorities to become accepted as national ethnic minorities, if they want to use the human rights instruments in order to get educational linguistic rights—these simply do not exist for immigrants. This minority status is something that most states try to prevent at present (for an example—Sweden—see Skutnabb-Kangas 1996a).

7.5.3.2. *The UN Declaration on the Rights of Persons Belonging to National or Ethnic, Religious and Linguistic Minorities*

The **UN Declaration on the Rights of Persons Belonging to National or Ethnic, Religious and Linguistic Minorities** was adopted by the General Assembly in December 1992. The Declaration goes somewhat further in a few overt formulations than the binding Article 27 of the **International Covenant on Civil and Political Rights** (quoted above in section 7.4.2.3, Example D—but see 7.8.1 below). In Article 2 (1), the Declaration replaces 'shall not be denied' from Art. 27 by 'have the right' and adds that these rights apply 'in private and in public, freely and without any form of discrimination'. In Articles 4.1 and, especially, 4.2, there is also an improvement—the Declaration prompts the states to actively promote enjoyment of the rights:

> Persons belonging to national or ethnic, religious and linguistic minorities (hereinafter referred to as persons belonging to minorities) have the right to enjoy their own culture, to profess and practise their own religion, and to use their own language, in private and in public, freely and without interference or any form of discrimination. (Art. 2.1).

> States shall take measures to create favorable conditions to enable persons belonging to minorities to express their characteristics and to develop their culture, language, religion, traditions and customs, except where specific practices are in violation of national and contrary to international standards. (Art. 4.2).

Most of the Articles use the formulation 'shall' (i.e., an obligation) and have few let-out modifications or alternatives—except where linguistic rights in education are concerned. Compare, for example, the unconditional formulation in Article 1 with the education Article 4.3. For clarity, I have added emphases, '*obligating*' formulations in italics, '**opt-outs**' in bold:

> 1.1. States *shall protect* the existence and the national or ethnic, cultural, religious and linguistic identity of minorities within their respective territories, and *shall encourage* conditions for the *promotion* of that identity.
>
> 1.2. States *shall* adopt **appropriate** legislative *and other* measures *to achieve those ends.*
>
> 4.3. States **should** take **appropriate** measures so that, **wherever possible**, persons belonging to minorities have **adequate** opportunities to learn their mother tongue **or** to have instruction in their mother tongue.

Clearly the formulation in Art. 4.3 raises many questions. What constitutes 'appropriate measures', or 'adequate opportunities'? Who is to decide what is 'possible'? Does 'instruction in their mother tongue' mean through the medium of the mother tongue or does it only mean instruction in the mother tongue as a subject?

When we start looking at the history of the UN Declaration, additional interesting details emerge. A (first) draft was submitted by Yugoslavia (UN Doc.E/CN.4/L.1367/Rev.1, 2 March 1978). While 'the principle of equal respect for cultures runs through the whole text' (Thornberry 1997: 344), Article 4.3 'did not figure in the 1990 draft' (ibid.) but was introduced by Austria in December 1991. 'The principal factors weakening the possible wording of the text were those of resources and a concern for State sovereignty' (ibid.). Patrick Thornberry states that the early response of the United Kingdom to the draft Declaration 'was conditioned in part by resource considerations' (ibid., note 120)—the phrases 'have adequate opportunities' and 'have instruction' 'suggest the need for the provision of resources by the State' (ibid.). When the final Draft Declaration (after having been approved by ECOSOC, the UN Economic and Social Council, in Resolution 1992/4) was submitted to the UN General Assembly, the 36 sponsor states of the resolution[25] did **not** include, for instance, France, Turkey, or UK.

Despite the shortcomings,[26] the Declaration represents a step forward in relation to **attitudinal changes**. The 1988 version considered in its Preamble

> that the promotion and protection of the rights of persons belonging to national or ethnic, religious and linguistic minorities contribute to the political and social stability of States in which they live.

This contests the popular but mistaken belief that the existence of minorities is divisive for nation states, as do several of the draft instruments in their preambles. But despite this, the UN Declaration is only **a recommendation**, not a covenant: states do **not** need to comply, not even after the Declaration was reaffirmed by the United Nations World Conference on Human Rights in Vienna, 14 to 25 June 1993, in its Final Document, the Vienna Declaration and Programme of Action (para. 10).

7.5.3.3. *European Charter for Regional or Minority Languages*

We can see a similar pattern of vague formulations, modifications and alternatives in the **European Charter for Regional or Minority Languages** (22 June 1992; see Info Box 7.10 and Address Box 7.3).

❖ **I n f o   B o x   7 . 1 0** ❖

European Charter for Regional or Minority Languages: Signatures and Ratifications

The Charter came into force on 1 March 1998 when seven states had ratified it. These were: Croatia, Finland, Hungary, Liechtenstein, Netherlands, Norway, and Switzerland. In addition to them, the following states have signed it (August 1998; those who have already promised to ratify at the latest within the next couple of years are marked with an asterisk): Austria, Cyprus, Denmark, *Germany, Luxembourg, Malta, Romania, *Slovenia, *Spain, Macedonia, Ukraine. In addition, Italy and Sweden have promised to sign and ratify it. Dear Reader, check the progress on the Web-site given in Address Box 7.3)! For instance, France signed in May 1999.

A state can choose which paragraphs or subparagraphs of the **European Charter** it wishes to apply (a minimum of 35 is required). Again, the formulations in the education Article, 8, include a range of modifications, including 'as far as possible', 'relevant', 'appropriate', 'where necessary', 'pupils who so wish in a number considered sufficient', 'if the number of users of a regional or minority language justifies it', as well as a number of alternatives, as in 'to allow, encourage **or** provide teaching in **or** of the regional or minority language at all the appropriate stages of education' (emphases added).

While the Charter demonstrates the unquestionably real problems of writing binding formulations which are at the same time sensitive to local conditions, just as in the UN Declaration above, its opt-outs and alternatives permit a reluctant state to meet the requirements in a minimalist way, which it can legitimate by claiming that a provision was not 'possible' or 'appropriate', or that numbers were not 'sufficient' or did not 'justify' a provision,

```
* * * * * * * * * * * * * * * * * * * * * * * * * * * * * * * * * * * * * * * * *
*                                                                               *
*       Address Box 7.3   News and/or Details About Some Human Rights           *
*             Instruments (European Charter, Framework Convention,              *
*                         Universal Declaration)                                *
*                                                                               *
*    The European Charter for Regional or Minority Languages <http://www.       *
*    coe.fr./eng/legaltxt/148e.htm>                                             *
*    Framework Convention for the Protection of National Minorities <http://    *
*    www.coe.fr./eng/legaltxt/157e.htm>                                         *
*    Draft Universal Declaration of Linguistic Rights Follow-up Committee,      *
*    c/Canuda, 6, 5è, 08002 Barcelona, Catalunya (Spain); phone 34-93-318 32    *
*    98; fax 34-93-412 06 66; <http://www.linguistic-declaration.org>; email:   *
*    <dud@linguistic-declaration.org>. The Declaration and many other           *
*    materials and documents on language and law can also be downloaded         *
*    from Mercator Linguistic Law and Legislation's Web-page                     *
*    <http://www.troc.es/ ciemen/mercator/index-gb.htm>.                        *
*                                                                               *
* * * * * * * * * * * * * * * * * * * * * * * * * * * * * * * * * * * * * * * * *
```

or that it 'allowed' the minority to organise teaching of their language as a subject, at their own cost.

7.5.3.4. *Framework Convention for the Protection of National Minorities*

A new Council of Europe **Framework Convention for the Protection of National Minorities** was adopted by the Committee of Ministers of the Council of Europe on 10 November 1994 (see Info Box 7.11).

❖ **I n f o B o x 7 . 1 1** ❖

Framework Convention for the Protection of National Minorities: Signatures and Ratifications

The Convention came into force on 1 February 1998. 36 Member States and one non-Member State (Armenia) have signed it. It has been ratified (August 1998) by Austria, Croatia, Cyprus, Czech Republic, Denmark, Estonia, Finland, Germany, Hungary, Italy, Liechtenstein, Macedonia, Malta, Moldova, Romania, San Marino, Slovakia, Slovenia, Spain, Ukraine, and the United Kingdom. Again, check progress on the Web-site!

We again find that the Article covering medium of education is so heavily qualified that the minority is completely at the mercy of the state:

In areas inhabited by persons belonging to national minorities traditionally or in **substantial** numbers, **if there is sufficient demand**, the parties shall **endeavour** to ensure, **as far as possible** and **within the framework of their education systems**, that persons belonging to those minorities have **adequate** opportunities for being taught in the minority language **or** for receiving instruction in this language (emphases added).

The Framework Convention has been criticized by both politicians and even international lawyers who are normally very careful in their comments. A comparison shows that my critique which is more sociologically oriented is shared by human rights lawyers. I will quote at length Patrick Thornberry, Professor of Law at Keele University, UK, a leading expert on minority rights. Firstly, Thornberry thinks that the Framework Convention. '. . . looks rather odd . . .' (Thornberry 1997: 351) and calls it '. . . somewhat belated commitment of the Council of Europe to protection of minorities' (ibid., 351). He quotes the Parliamentary Assembly of Council of Europe:

The Parliamentary Assembly issued strong criticism of the Framework Convention:

The convention is weakly worded. It formulates a number of vaguely defined objectives and principles, the observation of which will be an obligation of the Contracting States but not a right which individuals may invoke. Its implementation machinery is feeble and there is a danger that, in fact, the monitoring procedure will be left entirely to governments (ibid., 352).

In Thornberry's view, 'The preamble wavers in its terminology of purposes and objectives' (ibid., 351). Thornberry also notes that the vagueness is intentional, and that the Explanatory Report on the Convention in fact makes it clear that the provisions are not to be interpreted as real provisions:

The Explanatory Report on the Convention states . . . that 'the purpose of this last recital is to indicate that the provisions of this . . . Convention are not directly applicable . . .'. . . . The effect is to lend a remote, indirect and programmatic element to the Convention, a reading borne out in other areas of the text. The substantive text . . . already gives the States a great measure of discretion on their reading of obligations. (ibid., 352)

This also means that individuals have no right to complain if the provisions are not being met. In Thornberry's words: 'There is no place in such a scheme for a system of applications by individuals' (ibid., 352). One of the problems already mentioned is that states can claim that they have no minorities. The United Nations Human Rights Committee gives new guidelines here in its General Comment on **UN International Covenant on Civil and Political Rights**, Article 27 (see 7.8.1 for the Comment) which states that the existence of a minority does not depend on a decision by the State but requires to be established by objective criteria. The General Comment existed when the Framework Convention was accepted. Still, the Framework Convention does *not* take it into consideration but counteracts it, as is clear from Thornberry's comments: 'There is no explicit reference in the convention to the existence of minorities and thus to the problem of State denial' (ibid., 353). The existence of minorities is closely connected to questions of both collective and individual identity. Forced assimilation into the dominant population is in most cases an important causal factor in linguistic and cultural genocide and in the disappearance of linguistic and cultural diversity as discussed earlier. On the other hand, states which do not want to grant guarantees against this forced assimilation, are often very interested in guaranteeing that nobody is labelled minority 'against their own will'. This is how the Framework Convention formulates the right to identity in Article 5(1):

> The Parties undertake to promote the conditions necessary for persons belonging to national minorities to maintain and develop their culture, and to preserve the essential elements of their identity, namely their religion, language, traditions and cultural heritage.

All traditions are not acceptable though: the Explanatory Report has a disclaimer about them in its paragraph 44: 'The reference to "traditions" is not an endorsement or acceptance of practices which are contrary to national law or international standards.' Thornberry has the following to say about the Framework Convention's identity Article:

> The provision on identity . . . is peculiarly worded . . . the formulation . . . is possibly restrictive compared to other texts . . . Coupled with the weakness of Article 5(1), the level of protection from unwanted assimilationist pressures appears limited (ibid., 353).
>
> The Explanatory Report offers the opinion that 'no collective rights of minorities are envisaged' and that the 'choice of belonging' principle 'does not imply a right for an individual to choose arbitrarily to belong to any national minority'. (ibid., 353)

We might expect to find some more language rights in other Articles—but these are equally vague and weak. Article 9 on freedom of expression is, in Thornberry's view, 'not remarkable . . . The context of access is oddly phrased' (ibid., 355). And when we come to the right to use one's own language in at least some official contexts (Article 10(2)), we find modifications which are as substantial as in the education article:

> In areas inhabited by persons belonging to national minorities traditionally or in substantial numbers, **if those persons so request and the request corresponds to a real need**, the parties shall **endeavour to ensure, as far as possible,** the

conditions which **would make it possible** to use the minority language in relations between those persons and the administrative authorities (emphases added).

Thornberry comments:

> The language is full of qualification, and there is clearly a great deal of hesitancy concerning this particular right (ibid., 355).
>
> The Explanatory Report places a dubious interpretation on some of the phrases in the paragraph, suggesting that the 'existence of "a real need" is to be assessed by the State on the basis of objective criteria', and that 'as far as possible' indicates that various factors, in particular the financial resources of the Party concerned, may be taken into consideration. It is not clear why the text is to be interpreted so that 'need' must be assessed only by the State; the 'resources' question does not imply the legitimacy of a simple refusal of the State to provide. (ibid., 356)

Article 11(3) is, in Thornberry's assessment, 'drafted with the same or worse hesitation as Article 10(2)':

> In areas traditionally inhabited by substantial numbers of persons belonging to a national minority, the Parties shall **endeavour, in the framework of their legal system,** including, **where appropriate,** agreements with other States, and **taking into account their specific conditions,** to display traditional local names, street names and other topographic indications intended for the public **also** in the minority language **when there is sufficient demand for such indications** (emphases added).

The final verdict from Patrick Thornberry about the philosophy behind and the formulation of the Framework Convention, this latest flower on the tree of European Human Rights, is as follows. First two comments on the general philosophy (which is geared towards 'toleration'):

> Minority rights provisions are sometimes characterized as little more than 'tolerance' provisions. Tolerance is an indispensable virtue for living in diversified societies, which is increasingly the case in an age of great human mobility but it is not a virtue which aspires to nobility (ibid., 354).
>
> The Report continues that, in view of various difficulties—financial, technical, etc., the 'provision has been worded very flexibly, leaving the parties a wide measure of discretion'. This is hardly an overstatement. (ibid., 356)

And then the general assessment of the provisions:

> In case any of this [provisions in the Convention] should threaten the delicate sensibilities of States, the Explanatory Report makes it clear that they are under no obligation to conclude 'agreements', and that the paragraph does

not imply any official recognition of the local names. Despite the presumed good intentions, the provision represents a low point in drafting a minority right; there is just enough substance in the formulation to prevent it becoming completely vacuous. (ibid., 356–357)

7.5.3.5. Draft Universal Declaration on Indigenous Rights

Ground-breaking work has been going on on a broad basis within the UN Working Group on the Rights of Indigenous Populations, where language rights have been just one of the many issues. The recent **Draft Universal Declaration on Indigenous Rights** (as contained in documents E/CN.4/Sub.2/ 1988/25 and, in the final form submitted to the UN Commission on Human Rights for its consideration, in Subcommission on Prevention of Discrimination and Protection of Minorities resolution 1994/45, annex), is a pointer in the right direction. As compared to the ILO 1957 and 1989 versions,[27] the draft Declaration formulates language rights in education in more detail— but still not strongly enough. In the 1988 version it established as fundamental educational language rights that all indigenous peoples in the world should have, the following:

9. The right to maintain and use their own languages, including for administrative, judicial and other relevant purposes.

10. The right to all forms of education, including in particular the right of children to have access to education in their own languages, and to establish, structure, conduct and control their own educational systems and institutions.

23. The collective right to autonomy in matters relating to their own internal and local affairs, including education, information, culture, religion, health, housing, social welfare, traditional and other economic activities, land and resources administration and the environment, as well as internal taxation for financing these autonomous functions.

The version which was adopted at the 36th meeting of the Subcommission on Prevention of Discrimination and Protection of Minorities, 26 August 1994, has made substantial changes. The corresponding articles would now be:

14. Indigenous peoples have the right to revitalize, use, develop and transmit to future generations their histories, languages, oral traditions, philosophies, writing systems and literatures, and to designate and retain their own names for communities, places and persons.

States shall take effective measures, whenever any right of indigenous peoples may be threatened, to ensure this right is protected and also to ensure that they can understand and be understood in political, legal and administrative proceedings, where necessary through the provision of interpretation or by other appropriate means.

15. Indigenous children have the right to all levels and forms of education of the State. All indigenous peoples also have this right and the right to establish and control their educational systems and institutions providing education in their own languages, in a manner appropriate to their cultural methods of teaching and learning. .

Indigenous children living outside their communities have the right to be provided access to education in their own culture and language.

States shall take effective measures to provide appropriate resources for these purposes.

31. Indigenous peoples, as a specific form of exercising their right to self-determination, have the right to autonomy or self-government in matters relating to their internal and local affairs, including culture, religion, education, information, media, health, housing, employment, social welfare, economic activities, land and resources management, environment, and entry by non-members, as well as ways and means for financing these autonomous functions.

There are improvements—but not for linguistic human rights in education—these had a somewhat more prominent place in the earlier version. It is interesting that language figures in very few Articles—one can see the same trend in this Declaration as in the others analysed so far. The document can be downloaded from <http://www.unhchr.ch/html/menu4/subres/ 9445.htm>.

The international community seems to appreciate that the rights of indigenous peoples, including their linguistic human rights, should be promoted. But it is highly unlikely that the Declaration would be accepted in the form the Working Group finally accepted it in, according to its chair, Erica Irene Daes (1995). Despite careful negotiations over a decade, several countries, most importantly the United States, are probably going to demand substantial changes which undermine the progress achieved in the Declaration (Morris 1995). If the educational language rights were to be granted in their present form, some 60 to 80 percent or the world's oral languages would have decent legal support. Implementation is, of course, a completely different matter.

7.5.3.6. *General Assessment of Recent Provisions*

Thus the situation has generally not improved despite new instruments in which language rights are mentioned, and in some even treated in great detail.

There is a hierarchy, with different rights, between different groups whose languages are not main official languages in the state where they live (see **Human Rights Fact Sheets** from the UN Centre for Human Rights in Geneva for these). **Traditional/ territorial/ autochthonous/national minorities** have *more language rights* than other groups and most human rights instruments pertain to them. But even their rights in education are in many cases minimal, and they are to a very large extent dependent of the goodwill of the state. **Immigrant/guest worker/refugee minorities** have practically *no language rights* in education in relation to their own language, and only few in relation to learning the official language. The **UN International Convention on the Protection of the Rights of All Migrant Workers and Members of Their Families**, from December 1990 but not yet in force because of a shortage of signatories, in its assimilation-oriented educational language Article (45) accords minimal rights to the mother tongues and is even more vague than the instruments mentioned earlier. **Indigenous peoples** have on paper some rights and more are suggested in the UN **Draft Universal Declaration on Rights of Indigenous Peoples**, but many of them may disappear in the revision process (see 7.5.3.5 above).

7.6. TOWARDS A UNIVERSAL COVENANT ON LINGUISTIC HUMAN RIGHTS?

7.6.1. Paths Leading Towards Recent Draft Instruments

In order to avoid linguistic genocide and to make indigenous peoples and minorities independent of the goodwill of the state in their enjoyment of basic LHRs in education, there is a need for legislation which explicitly promotes minority languages within a maintenance-oriented framework, especially in education but also more generally. Most general human rights declarations tend to be too vague and conceptually confused; both the right of redress and the economic prerequisites for using the rights have been deficient; the duty-holder has been unclear. A specific instrument protecting linguistic human rights, especially in education, has been notably lacking. The recent specialised instruments are not enough, as shown above. There are a few new instruments in the making though. The various paths towards formulation of linguistic human rights instruments have been long and varied. Some will be mentioned.

At an international seminar on Human Rights and Cultural Rights held in October 1987 in Recife, Brazil, organised by AIMAV (the International Association for Cross-cultural Communication; with **Francisco Gomes de Matos** as the main organiser) and UNESCO, a **Declaration of Recife** was adopted. It ended as follows:

> Hence, conscious of the need to provide explicit legal guarantees for linguistic rights to individuals and groups by the appropriate bodies of the member states of the United Nations,
> RECOMMENDS that steps be taken by the United Nations to adopt and implement a UNIVERSAL DECLARATION OF LINGUISTIC RIGHTS

which would require a reformulation of national, regional, and international language policies.

A preliminary Declaration[28] was also adopted by the Seminar (see Info Box 7.12).

❖ **I n f o   B o x   7 . 1 2** ❖

Recife Declaration: Resolution on Linguistic Rights/
Resolucao Sobre Direitos Linguisticos

1. Every social group has the right to positively identify with one or more languages and to have such identification accepted and respected by others.

2. Every child has the right to learn the language(s) of his/her group fully.

3. Every person has the right to use the language(s) of his/her group in any official situation.

4. Every person has the right to learn fully at least one of the official languages in the country where s/he is resident, according to her/his own choice.

There were follow-up gatherings at UNESCO in Paris, France, in April 1989, in Frankfurt, Germany, in October 1989, and in Pécs, Hungary, in August 1991, organized by FIPLV, the Fédération Internationale des Professeurs de Langues Vivantes. The report from Pécs, **Workshop on Human Rights and Languages** (1992) was circulated by UNESCO (see UNESCO 1992). FIPLV followed up with a booklet (Batley et al. 1993).

The presently most promising language-specific draft Declaration is the result of an initiative undertaken by the International Pen Club (Committee for Translation and Linguistic Rights), and CIEMEN (Mercator Programme, Linguistic Rights and Law). The following section will present and analyse this draft **Universal Declaration of Linguistic Rights**.

7.6.2. The Draft Universal Declaration of Linguistic Rights and Its Limitations

7.6.2.1. *General Presentation and Beneficiaries*

The most recent and, despite many shortcomings, so far most promising attempt to promote language rights is the draft **Universal Declaration of Linguistic Rights**, accepted in Barcelona in June 1996 and handed over to UNESCO (see Address Box 7.3). The initiators, the International Pen Club and CIEMEN, have appointed a small Follow-up Committee, 9 people, trying to raise support for the Declaration, and a Follow-up Scientific Council, 29 people, (which TSK is a member of) which is supposed to advise UNESCO on a revision (see Follow-up Committee 1998: 79–80). This section presents and analyses some aspects of the draft Universal Declaration (hereafter UDLR), in particular educational language rights.

The Declaration is the first attempt at formulating a universal document about language rights exclusively. It relates to all the groups mentioned above—although sign language users are not mentioned specifically. It is a vast document which had already gone through 12 drafts before becoming a UNESCO responsibility—and more are needed. Its 52 Articles are wide-ranging and specify many linguistic rights. My analysis uses the version submitted to UNESCO—at the time of writing it is the latest version, and the Scientific Council has not yet been called upon to start the revision work. At present the text is only a draft recommendation that has no immediate prospect of being approved.

The Declaration, UDLR, grants rights to three different entities: **individuals** (which I will call 'everyone' in my comments), **language groups**, and **language communities**. When the beneficiary is 'everyone' unconditionally, the rights are **individual** ('inalienable personal rights', Art. 3.1). When the beneficiary is the language group or community, the rights are **collective**. And when the beneficiary is **a member of** a linguistic group or community, the rights are in most cases individual but conditional. Even in this Declaration, it is clear already in Article 3.1 that educational language rights, in contrast to cultural rights, are not seen as inalienable:

> This Declaration considers the following to be inalienable personal rights which may be exercised in any situation:
>
> - the right to the use of one's language both in private and in public; . . .
> - the right to maintain and develop one's own culture; . . .

These individual rights (including the rest of Art. 3.1) are **the only rights which apply to all without any conditions.**

Collective rights in the Declaration apply to a (historical) language **community** (which includes both traditional national minorities and also all numerically small peoples, such as indigenous peoples, in addition to dominant linguistic majorities). This should be compared to the definitions of indigenous peoples (Definition Boxes 7.1 through 7.2) and minorities (Definition Box 7.3). Some also apply to a language **group**, which is

> any group of persons sharing the same language which is established in the territorial space of another language community but which does not possess historical antecedents equivalent to those of that community. Examples of such groups are immigrants, refugees, deported persons and members of diasporas (Art. 1.5).

7.6.2.2. *Rights of Language Communities and Language Groups*

Communities have more rights in the Declaration than the other two categories. For communities, Article 8.2 states that

> All language communities are entitled to have at their disposal whatever means are necessary to ensure the transmission and continuity of their language.

This could be interpreted to mean that all language communities are entitled to receive from the state the funds needed to organise mother tongue medium education from kindergarten to university. But when we read Article 8.2 alongside the other Articles in the same section, we see that it belongs to the category of pious preamble which everybody can applaud but which carries no legal obligations. No duty-holders are specified for granting the 'means' mentioned in Article 8.2 above or the 'equal rights' or 'necessary steps' mentioned in Articles 10.1 and 10.3 below:

> All language communities have equal rights (Art. 10.1).

> All necessary steps must be taken in order to implement this principle of equality and to render it real and effective (Art. 10.3).

And when we come to the Articles dealing with education, the same piety prevails, while no duty-holder is specified:

> All language communities are entitled to have at their disposal all the human and material resources necessary to ensure that their language is present to the extent they desire at all levels of education within their territory: properly trained teachers, appropriate teaching methods, text books, finance, buildings and equipment, traditional and innovative technology (Art. 25).

> All language communities are entitled to an education which will enable their members to acquire a full command of their own language, including the different abilities relating to all the usual spheres of use, as well as the most extensive possible command of any other language they may wish to know (Art. 26).

> The language and culture of all language communities must be the subject of study and research at university level (Art. 30).

In many ways these 'rights' sound like a dream—and probably that is what they will remain. They are at present completely unrealistic for any except, maybe, a few hundred of the world's language communities, most of them dominant linguistic majorities.

Groups have fewer rights than communities. Article 3.2 spells out collective rights for groups:

> This Declaration considers that the collective rights of language groups **may** include . . . the right for their own language and culture to be taught (emphasis added).

For groups, collective rights to one's own language are thus not seen as inalienable. In addition, Article 3.2 says nothing about where the language should be taught (whether only in private schools, or after school, or in state-financed schools) and for how long. Likewise, it does not specify whether the language is to be taught as a subject or used as a medium—the formulation seems to point to a subject only. Again, no duty-holder is specified.

7.6.2.3. Does 'Everyone' Have Language Rights?

Indirectly the education section forces all others except those defined as members of **language communities** (which roughly correspond to national territorially based minorities) to assimilate. For all others, including 'everyone', only **education in the language of the territory** is a **positive** right, i.e. not education in their own language. There is no mention of bilingual or multilingual territories in the Declaration. Every territory seems to have only one 'language specific to the territory', i.e. territories are seen as monolingual. This means that for those who speak a language other than the language of the territory, education in their own language is not a positive right. 'Territory' is not defined.

In addition, the Declaration grants members of language communities the right to 'the most extensive possible command' of any **foreign** language in the world, whereas the rights granted to 'everyone' include only the (negative—'does **not exclude**') right to 'oral and written knowledge' of one's **own** language. This is clear if one compares the formulations at the end of Article 26 on language communities with Article 29, which spells out the (negative) right of 'everyone':

> All language communities are entitled to an education which will enable their members to acquire a full command of their own language, including the different abilities relating to all the usual spheres of use, as well as **the most extensive possible command of any other language** they may wish to know (Art. 26 on rights of language communities).
>
> 1. Everyone is entitled to receive an education **in the language specific to the territory where s/he resides**.
> 2. This right does not exclude the right to acquire **oral and written knowledge of any language** which may be of use to him/her as an instrument of communication with other **language communities** (Art. 29 on rights of 'everyone', emphases added).

Besides, Art. 29.2 is formulated so as to suggest that 'everyone's' own language can be learned only if it is a useful instrument when communicating with other language communities. This means that it could in principle be excluded if it is not known by any entity defined as a language community, or if it is not used as a **lingua franca** between people where some represent language communities. If it is 'only' known and/or used by language groups or by individuals representing 'everybody', it can be excluded from any provision in Article 26. This is extremely important when considering the fact (chapter 2) that most threatened languages (over 80% of *all* languages) are used in one country only.

It is thus likely that language policies following the principles in the education section, with its lack of rights, will force all those not defined as members of language communities to assimilate. This interpretation of indirect assimilation through education is strengthened when noting the reservations in Articles which otherwise might grant 'everyone' more language rights. According to Art. 23.4, '. . . everyone has the right to learn any language'. 'Any language' **might** also be interpreted as the mother tongue of those who otherwise are not granted positive mother tongue learning rights—except that this right prevails only 'within the context of the foregoing principles' (Art. 23.4) and these support only the languages and self-expression of language communities, i.e. not the languages of 'groups' or 'everyone':

1. Education must help to foster the capacity for linguistic and cultural self-expression **of the language community of the territory where it is provided**.

2. Education must help to maintain and develop **the language spoken by the language community of the territory where it is provided**.

3. Education must always be at the service of linguistic and cultural diversity and of harmonious relations **between different language communities** throughout the world.

4. Within the context of the foregoing principles, everyone has the right to learn any language (Article 23; emphases added).

The Declaration thus clearly gives language communities very extensive rights but leaves 'everyone' with very few rights. This makes the Declaration vulnerable in several respects. As mentioned several times earlier, there are many states which claim that they do not have minority language communities, and which do not want to grant these communities any language rights. Self-determination is not an unconditional right in international law, neither internally (autonomy of some kind), nor externally (secession, independence; see contributions to Clark & Williamson (eds) 1996). This means that a Declaration which grants most of the rights to linguistic **communities**, without specifying firm duty-holders, makes these communities completely dependent on the acceptance of their existence by states, an acceptance that many states are not willing to grant. 'Language groups' are in a still weaker position—these may by many states be seen as individuals only, not representatives of any 'group'. And those individuals who are not members of any language communities of groups, even according to the fairly vague definitions of these entities in the Declaration, are in the weakest position. It is for these reasons that the existence of firm individual rights is enormously important, and would be a logical continuation of the tradition of human rights being individual. But such individual rights are the weakest part of the Declaration.

The UDLR thus does not give any positive **educational** language rights to **all** individuals, regardless of which category the individual belongs to—and this is exactly what individual human rights are supposed to do. If something is to be seen as an individual **human right**, it means, by definition, a right which **every individual** in the world has, simply because that individual is a human being. It means an unconditional, fundamental right that no state is allowed to take away.

The UDLR suggests a monitoring body to be set up by the United Nations, and suggests sanctions against states that interfere with their citizens' rights.

For several beneficiaries (**language communities** and, to some extent, **language groups**) the UDLR represents progress in relation to the other instruments described. But even the educational language rights for language **communities** are formulated in such a way that the whole Declaration runs the risk of being seen as full of pious, unrealistic wishes which cannot be taken seriously. For most African, Asian, and Latin American countries, the rights in the Declaration are at present practically, economically and even politically impossible to realize, as was clearly expressed at the first UNESCO meeting where the Declaration was discussed. It therefore seems extremely unlikely that it will be accepted in its present form.

The draft UDLR, though clearly less than ideal in its present form, represents the first attempt at formulating language rights at a universal level which has reached a stage that permits serious international discussion to start. From the point of view of maintaining the planet's linguistic diversity, the immediate fate of the UN Draft **Universal Declaration on Rights of Indigenous Peoples** is probably more important, though, because it has at least some chance of being accepted, signed, and ratified, even if in a form which reduces the rights granted in the present draft. The **Intersessional Working Group of the Commission on Human Rights for the Drafting of a Declaration on the Rights of Indigenous Peoples** which had the mandate to approve and recommend to the Commission for adoption the draft Declaration, after the text was adopted by the Sub-Commission, had its 2nd session in Geneve 21 October–1 November 1996. The draft Declaration itself had not yet been touched by the States; the debates were still about the procedures. Indigenous peoples were allowed to continue to participate by a special procedure established by the Commission, as they also participated in the Working Group (chaired by Erica-Irene Daes) which worked out the Draft Declaration (source: **UNACT** 11, December 1996, 3).

However, even if indigenous peoples are allowed to attend (normally only NGOs with consultative status with the UN Economic and Social Council are allowed to attend; this was changed by the Commission to allow for indigenous participation), they still cannot participate in the decision making—only States can. Indigenous peoples obviously find this an untenable situation: they are still not allowed to participate in making decisions vital for their lives but have to accept unilateral State decisions. Several resolutions from the Commission on Human Rights have touched upon the issue. The latest (as this book goes to print), the 'unedited text—not official document' 1998/13 (downloaded in March 1999 from <http://www.unhchc.ch/html/menu4/chrres/1998.res/13.htm>), under its point 5, when discussing the Report of the Working Group on Indigenous Populations of the Sub-Commission, '*Invites* the Working Group to continue its consideration of ways in which the expertise of indigenous people can contribute to the work of the Working Group, and encourages initiatives by Governments, organizations of indigenous people and non-governmental organizations to ensure the full participation of indigenous people in the activities related to the tasks of the Working Group'. Yes, and then what . . .

The conclusion is, regrettably, that we have yet to see the right to education through the medium of the mother tongue become a human right. We are still living with basic language wrongs in human rights law, especially in education policy. Denial of linguistic human rights, linguistic and cultural genocide and forced assimilation through education are still characteristic of many states, notably in Europe and Neo-Europes. It is to these countries we turn now, before presenting the few positive recent developments.

7.7. THE HYPOCRISY OF WESTERN STATES

7.7.1. Western States as Guardians of Human Rights?

The Western states have created a myth of themselves as guardians of human rights in the world, including the myth that they respect all human rights themselves. There needs to be more awareness of the fact that human rights violations happen in the West at the same time as we penalize other countries for not living up to their human rights obligations. Therefore our own records need to be scrutinised. The hollowness of the guardianship is clear in the human rights conditionalities in 'development aid', excellently described by human rights lawyer Katarina Tomaševski.[29] Likewise, the double standards can be seen in the demands that the West, for instance via UN, OSCE, Council of Europe and other western-dominated organisations, makes on both African and Asian and Pacific countries and, more recently, on Eastern and Central European countries, in terms of the treatment of minorities and human rights performance in general (for a detailed analysis of this for Estonia, see Rannut 1999).

The West is, directly or indirectly, responsible for most of the linguistic and cultural genocide in the world. Many examples could be used. The recent Proposal 227 by Ron Unz in California which was part of the June 2, 1998, referendum and was passed, also clearly violates human rights as was confirmed by the panel of judges at the international Hearing in The Hague in May 1999—see 7.8.2. It would, among other things, make it possible to fine teachers who speak any other language but English in the classroom, even a few words. For good sources of information around the Proposal see note 3 in chapter 3. Below I give some recent Danish examples. But first some general comments.

There have been numerous suggestions for including in international human rights instruments language-related rights which are **binding**, rather than only recommendations, such as are found in, for instance, OSCE-process documents. Thus far, this has not succeeded. It seems that the same states fairly consistently object to international or regional instruments for protecting minority languages. In addition to the examples we have already seen in earlier sections, I shall mention just a few examples; many more could be enumerated (see de Varennes 1996a).

The victorious states in the First 'World' War, who imposed clauses on language-related minority rights on the losers in the Peace Treaties, did not grant the same rights to minorities in their own countries, and voted down proposed internationally binding rights (Capotorti 1979: 16–26), as mentioned earlier. The same countries participated in voting down Article 3 on linguistic genocide after the Second 'World' War.

When The League of Nations debated the recommendation of its own committee to develop Esperanto as an international language, thirteen states were in favour of such a solution (South Africa, Albania, Belgium, China, Colombia, Finland, India, Iran, Japan, Poland, Rumania, Czechoslovakia, and Venezuela). It was decided **not** to follow the recommendation, and France was the country most vociferously against the proposal, according to Claude Piron (1994).

In the drafting of the Universal Declaration of Human Rights, several proposals were made to include minority rights, even the right to 'establish and maintain, out of an equitable proportion of public funds for the purpose, their schools and cultural institutions' (from the text of the Division of Human Rights, quoted in Thornberry 1987: 6; see also Gromacky 1992, 533ff), and these were likewise voted down, the attacks being led by the

Latin American countries and by the USA, Mrs. Roosevelt denying that the concept of minority rights was of universal significance.

Greece and Turkey, for instance, have not signed the UN **Covenant on Civil and Political Rights** (with Art. 27, still the best legally binding formulation for protecting linguistic rights) which for instance China has promised to sign in 1998. Greece, Turkey, the United Kingdom, and the United States have not ratified its **Optional Protocol** which gives access to complaint procedures. Of the 133 States which **have** ratified ICCPR, the United States, Mozambique, and Haiti are the only ones who have failed to ratify the UN Covenant on Economic, Social and Cultural Rights, which contains some (admittedly not many) linguistic and educational rights.

France, despite claiming to be **the** country of human rights, and despite the very important role of the French representative (René Cassin) in drafting the Universal Declaration of Human Rights (see Best 1988: 113–122), stood out for long 'as the one great power in Europe that would not ratify [the Council of Europe's **Convention on Human Rights and Fundamental Freedoms**] (1950), something that "shocked" Cassin' (ibid., 120).

At the CSCE/OSCE Copenhagen meeting on the Human Dimension (June 1990), Bulgaria, France, Greece, Rumania, and Turkey 'did not agree with some far-reaching formulations for the benefit of minorities' (Suppan & Heubergerová 1992: 68). When the Council of Europe's **European Charter for Regional or Minority Languages** was accepted (June 1992), France, Turkey, and United Kingdom abstained, Greece voted against (**Contact Bulletin** 9:2, 1992: 1).

Thus the United States, Britain, France, Greece, and Turkey have often prevented, or tried to prevent, the granting of linguistic human rights. This has not prevented Britain, France, the United States, and Western countries in general, from portraying themselves as protectors of human rights and minorities, and from criticizing other countries for their treatment of minorities.

I have also chosen to use a few concrete recent Danish examples.

7.7.2. Example Denmark: Violations of Human Rights?

It seems to me to be important that Western violations are documented in more detail; if the West chooses to police other parts of the world, we should be careful to follow the principles we preach to others. Therefore, some recent Danish examples, especially because the Scandinavian countries are by many observers seen as democratic countries which respect human rights. Denmark has incorporated the **European Convention on Human Rights and Fundamental Freedoms** into its domestic law but has not done this with the UN **International Covenant on Civil and Political Rights** even if it contains rights and protections beyond those included in the European Convention. The UN Human Rights

Committee, when examining the Danish report submitted to the Committee, at its session 21 Oct–8 Nov 1996, critisized Denmark for this and 'noted an apparent **eurocentric** approach to human rights' (**HCHR News** 1:8, November 1996: 3). Info Boxes 7.13 and 7.14 have two fairly detailed recent examples of the opposite from Denmark—there are many more, just from 1998 (see Witte 1998). As compared to countries with more blatantly violent physical human rights abuses, they may not be 'spectacular'. What they show, though, is double standards and a worrying open disrespect for international human rights standards and democratic procedures.

To sum up, I present five claims about the conduct of what I loosely call 'Western countries' during this century:

1. Western countries have prevented or tried to prevent the acceptance of legally binding international conventions and charters on linguistic human rights when other countries propose them.

❖ **I n f o   B o x   7 . 1 3** ❖

*Denmark Supports Mother Tongue Medium Teaching
in Bolivia—But Not in Denmark*

The Danish development cooperation agency, Danida, has the following to say about the goal of its support to indigenous peoples' education in Bolivia—and this should be compared to the support—or rather, lack of support, to immigrant and refugee minorities in Denmark:

> The Danish support goes to the central elements in attempts to democratize and to promotion of those specific rights that the Indian peoples emphasize most: the collective ownership to land and **the right to teaching in the mother tongue**. [. . .] In addition, establishment of **ethnic districts is supported**. The goal is to **acknowledge the social structure** which has traditionally been prevalent with the Indian peoples. [. . .] **Teaching through the medium of the mother tongue is supported** through further training of Indian teachers, production of teaching materials and establishing parent councils. A **Danish advisor** will advise the organisations of the Indian peoples and the decentralised departments of the Ministry of Education about the planning of the programme which will also be based on **positive experience** from a corresponding project in Peru, financed by Denmark. (**Danida nyt** 12, 1997: 3; my translation; emphases added)

Compared to what happens 'at home', with **immigrant and refugee minorities in Denmark**, the only shared feature in this amazing piece of laudable news about official Danish policy in **development cooperation** is the presence of the Danish advisor(s). But where the Danish advisor in Bolivia is supposed to acknowledge

---

(Continued)

and support what the people to be supported themselves want, this is the exact opposite to what happens in Denmark.

In Denmark, there is **no** mother tongue **medium** teaching for immigrant or refugee minorities, organised by the Danish state. What is on offer is, in the best case, a few hours a week, out of school hours, of the mother tongue as a **subject**. It has even been suggested on several occasions that the conditional right to have one's mother tongue taught as a subject be scrapped, in conflict with the regulations in the EU Directive of 1977 (see notes 22 and 23 in this chapter), and against the wishes of the parents. Recently, again, the parents' wishes were very clearly confirmed when three large studies, contracted by the Ministry of Education (Nielsen 1998) showed that parents do not want more teaching of Danish at the cost of mother tongue teaching and that they do want mother tongue teaching. Likewise, the study showed very good results from this teaching.

As I write this, the Danish Minister of Education, Margrethe Vestager, is proposing new initiatives to strengthen the teaching of the mother tongue of immigrant minority children, on the basis of the study. Her goal (as reported in the daily paper **Information** 13.8.1998: 4) is to strengthen the children's **Danish**, self-confidence, and identity . . . (see my analysis of the phases in the development of minority education, e.g., 1988: 32–36; Denmark has finally reached the deficit-theory phases where the child is supposed to suffer from an L1-related handicap: 'the child does not know her own language and culture properly, and this leaves her without a firm basis for L2-learning and gives her poor self-confidence'—Skutnabb-Kangas 1988: 32). The Social Democrat Minister of Social Affairs, Karen Jespersen, was perhaps even more frank when she stated on Danish television in March 1998 with the Prime Minister at her side, that the Government is working to abolish mother tongue teaching altogether.

Any 'ethnic districts' in Denmark, however small, are labelled in political discourse as ghettoes, and resented. There are strong attempts to both break up the existing ones and prevent new ones from arising, to the point of breaking both Danish laws about discrimination in housing allocation (as several court cases have shown) and international human rights conventions about free settlement (as the Danish Center for Human Rights has pointed out in its comments (in January 1998) about what then were new draft laws—see Info Box 7.14 below).

Representatives of immigrant minority organisations in Denmark have complained, officially and unofficially, dozens of times, that the system is paternalistic, with Danish politicians, administrators and civil servants having the right to make all the decisions about minorities, without listening to the minorities themselves. Suggestions in the new law on integration ensures Danish majority even in advisory functions and makes the decision-making still more undemocratic.

Denmark Violates the Human Rights of Refugees

Denmark has been to the fore in complaining about human rights violations in other countries, notably China, as long as Danish business interests were not affected. Again, these worries about human rights can be compared to what happens in Denmark. During the summer and autumn of 1997 there was a very lively debate in the Danish media about asylum-seekers, refugees and immigrant minorities, with many openly discriminatory and racist commentaries, especially in a series in the populist right-wing daily **Ekstra Bladet**. As a partial result, the support of one of the two extreme right-wing parties, Dansk Folkeparti (Danish People's Party), with Pia Kjærsgaard as chair, grew rapidly. The chair of the other right-wing party, Kim Behnke (the two split up in 1996) is on record as suggesting on TV that Somali asylum-seekers whose applications for asylum in Denmark had been refused could just be dropped to Somaliland from an airplane, with parachutes. Another representative of the same party applauded but suggested that the cost of the parachutes could be saved. In late autumn polls 1997, Dansk Folkeparti was the third largest political party in Denmark, taking many voters from the Social Democrats.

The response of the Social Democrat Prime Minister, Poul Nyrup Rasmussen, to losing voters was to appoint a new Minister of the Interior, the retired Mayor of Århus, Thorkild Simonsen, who rapidly suggested new strict measures for more strict control of 'foreigners', including two new laws (L154 on changing the law on foreigners, the criminal law and the law on marriage, and L155 on integration of foreigners in Denmark). These laws, which were passed in June 1998, suggest, among many other things, that

- asylum seekers are not allowed to marry while their applications are being processed (something that has in the past taken anything between 6 months up to 3–4 years and even longer);
- refugees have to stay in the municipality to which they have been allocated, during the whole 3-year integration period—if they move, their allowances stop;
- the financial support to refugees should be cut, and be around 2,000 crowns (300 US dollars) lower per month than the minimum social welfare given to Danes;
- measures against 'arranged marriages';

The Danish Centre for Human Rights was extremely critical of the draft laws. In their 'Resume of the Comments on the new draft laws' (14 January 1998), the Centre concluded, in language which can be described as unusually sharp:

- It strikes The Centre as worrying that the Ministry of the Interior only to a limited degree makes use of recommendations, ideas and suggestions from White Papers, committees drafting laws, and research contracted by the state.

❖ **Info Box 7.14** ❖

(Continued)

- The Centre is worried about the fact that the Government seriously violates the principle of predictability in [the interpretation of] the Law on Foreigners, preferencing arbitrary powers for administrative bodies dealing with foreigners;
- The Centre notes a new creation in the law drafting techniques, namely that laws are drafted which are on the verge of violating Denmark's international human rights obligations, and that in explanatory comments a duty is placed on the administrative bodies to ensure that Denmark is not in conflict with human rights conventions. The Parliament divests itself of the responsibility which was clearly emphasized when Denmark incorporated the European Convention on Human Rights [and Fundamental Freedoms] [into national law] (comment 14 January 1998, p. 1).

Twenty-two organisations, among them researchers, sent a complaint to the UN High Commissioner for Refugees (UNHCR) about the laws. The first reply, published 13 August 1998 states clearly that the law on refugees violates human rights. Only one example will be given below. The 1951 UN Convention Relating to the Status of Refugees (adopted on 28 July 1951, General Assembly Resolution 429 (V), entry into force 22 April 1957) states in Article 23 on Public Relief: 'The Contracting States shall accord to refugees lawfully staying in the territory the same treatment with respect to public relief and assistance as is accorded their nationals'. Giving refugees less public relief violates this.

The Minister's reply was that the UNHCR 'had no right to pronounce about the Danish Parliament's decisions'; that 'it was impossible to reject what the Parliament decided, just because of what some people in Stockholm write' (the decision came via the Stockholm office of the UNHCR); that 'we first need to know who it is in UNHCR who has written the legal assessment. It might be somebody recently employed who does not represent the opinion of the Main Office'; and finally the Minister came with a covert threat: 'I shall ask the bosses in Geneva if this is a reasonable way to treat a country which [financially] supports them so much' (reported in **Information**, 14–16 August 1998). As research groups in Denmark (spokesperson Morten Ejrnæs) showed, the Minister subsequently gave false information to the UNHCR about the effect of the laws. The offending laws entered into force at the beginning of 1999.

Denmark has also become a centre for European and international racist and neo-nazi organisations—racist organisations are not forbidden in Danish law, in contrast to, for instance, Germany.

---

2. Western countries exclude linguistically argued racism and/or discrimination on the basis of language from the definition(s) of racism(s) and from many human rights documents, especially the articles on education. Even where some rights are granted, covert biologically and culturally argued

racism can be seen in that several instruments are formulated so as to exclude 'non-Europeans' from the enjoyment of these rights in the West.

3. Western countries create a myth that human rights are respected in the West and that the West therefore has the right to function as some sort of a human rights police force in other parts of the world in the name of democracy.

4. Western countries demand from other countries that they grant minorities rights, especially linguistic human rights, which Western countries do not grant to minorities in their own countries.

5. Western countries use different standards in their own countries and in other countries when defining groups that linguistic rights should be granted to. This is especially clear today in relation to the Baltic countries— the Western countries demand rights for the Russian immigrant minorities that none of them grant to immigrant minorities in their own countries (see Rannut 1999, Ozolins, 1999, Druviete 1994, Marshall 1996, Maurais 1992, Rose & Maley 1994, for exemplification; see also Rupesinghe & Tishkov (eds) 1996). Maurais (ed.) 1998 is a useful recent volume about language policy in the Baltic states, with articles by Marju Toomsalu, Normand Labrie, Leeni Simm, Vello Pettai, Dzintra Hiřsa, Ina Druviete, Aina Blinkena, Albertas Rosinas, Danguolé Mikulèniené, and Jacques Maurais).

I have substantiated my claims with a few examples. Mart Rannut's recent thorough analysis support mine. On the basis of a detailed, multidisciplinary analysis of Estonian language policy 1988–1997, Rannut (1999: 248) concludes about 'the link between international human rights standards and *realpolitik*:

■ **International human rights standards are not applicable by international organisations towards the political power centres**, like Russia, the United States, and China.

■ **Spread of double standards.** This position benefits other politically more powerful European and Europeanized countries, which may ignore the standards or interpret them according to their own convenience without threat of major international condemnation.

■ **The subordination of human rights to reasons of state**, meaning that rights are protected insofar as they are seen as being politically and economically in the national interest.'

In the language rights field all the examples of western hypocrisy work in the same direction: supporting or at least not preventing linguistic and cultural genocide, and preventing the use of the human rights system to support linguistic and cultural diversity, all for reasons which are connected to power relations between and within states, mainly external and internal security. Rannut's term for this is **diplomatic linguicism** (1999: 249).

In the next section we see to what extent any recent developments or new instruments and interpretations promise change. Are there reasons for hope for diversity to have better conditions? There are a few positive developments.

7.8. POSITIVE DEVELOPMENTS

7.8.1. UN Human Rights Committee's General Comment on Article 27

One of the difficulties in earlier provisions has been that states can claim that they have no minorities, and that there thus are no beneficiaries for provisions. This has been, for instance, the stance of France and Turkey, as we have seen. Below we look at the change of interpretation of the **UN International Covenant on Civil and Political Rights**, ICCPR, Article 27, which still grants the best legally binding protection to languages. The Article states:

> In those states in which ethnic, religious or linguistic minorities exist, persons belonging to such minorities shall not be denied the right, in community with other members of their group, to enjoy their own culture, to profess and practise their own religion, or to use their own language.

In the customary reading of Art. 27, rights were only granted to individuals, not collectivities. And 'persons belonging to . . . minorities' only had these rights in states which accepted their existence. This has not helped immigrant minorities because they have not been seen as minorities in the legal sense by the states in which they live. The customary reading of Art. 27 interprets it as:

- excluding groups (even if they are citizens) which are not recognised as minorities by the state;
- excluding (im)migrants (who have not been seen as minorities);
- only conferring some protection from discrimination (= 'negative rights') but not a positive right to maintain or even use one's language.
- not imposing any obligations on states.

On 6 April 1994 the **UN Human Rights Committee** adopted a **General Comment on Article 27**.[30] It reinterprets Article 27 in a substantially broader and more positive way than earlier. The Committee sees the Article as:

- stating that the existence of a minority does not depend on a decision by the State but requires to be established by objective criteria;

- protecting all individuals on the State's territory or under its jurisdiction (i.e., also immigrants and refugees), irrespective of whether they belong to the minorities specified in the Article or not;
- recognizing the existence of a 'right', and
- imposing positive obligations on States.

The importance of the General Comment will become clear when the Sub-Commission on the Prevention of Discrimination and Protection of Minorities (together with the UN General Assembly and the Commission on Human Rights) examine country reports to see to what extent minority rights are respected. These country reports are available from the Document Section of the UN.

7.8.2. Peoples' Communication Charter

The Peoples' Communication Charter (PCC), an NGO-initiative, is also a positive recent development (see Hamelink 1994, 1995)—see Address Box 7.4. It was drafted in 1995 at the initiative of the Third World Network, Malaysia, the Cultural Environment Movement, USA, and the World Association of Community Radio Broadcasters (AMARC). The PCC is the first large-scale international attempt by civil society representatives to start drafting human rights documents outside the international organisations where only states are represented. One of the interesting features is thus also that the Charter attempts to draw signatures from those more directly involved, i.e. not states.

The first international public hearing on the PCC on Languages and Human Rights was held in The Hague 1–3 May 1999. In addition to substantial written documentation submitted in advance, the international Panel of 5 judges heard witnesses and experts on five exemplary cases of threats to linguistic human rights: Creole in St. Lucia, Sign languages, Kurdish, Berber (Tamazigh) and bilingual education in California, especially Proposition 227. The Panel's 'overall impression is that the five test cases are representative of serious, generalized and systematic violations of linguistic rights around the world'. The Panel states that 'while there is substantial variation between the overtly linguicidal policies of countries like Algeria and Turkey, and the covert measures in the USA and Western Europe, the evidence submitted to the panel indicates in all five contexts that there is a serious threat to the cultures and languages of a wide range of peoples'. Summaries of the cases, the criteria used by the Panel, and the full judgement can be downloaded from PCC's Web-page (see Address Box 7.4).

Here only two Articles, central for language rights, will be presented in Info Box 7.15.

```
* * * * * * * * * * * * * * * * * * * * * * * * * * * * * * * * * * * * * * * * * *
*                                                                                 *
*              Address Box 7.4   Peoples' Communication Charter                   *
*                                                                                 *
*   The Charter, including the history of its origins, is available at the Web-site  *
*   <http://www.waag.org/pcc>. It can also be signed there. Discussions, papers,  *
*   etc., in relation to the Charter can be found at <http://commposite.uqam.     *
*   ca/videaz/docs/cehaen.html> and <http://commposite.uqam.ca/                   *
*   videaz/wgl/>. The address to an email discussion list is <pcc-l@dds.nl>; the  *
*   person responsible is Reinde R. Rustema <rrr@dds.nl>.                         *
*                                                                                 *
* * * * * * * * * * * * * * * * * * * * * * * * * * * * * * * * * * * * * * * * * *
```

❖ I n f o   B o x   7 . 1 5 ❖

Peoples' Communication Charter, Language Rights Related Articles

Art. 9. **Diversity of Languages.**
All people have the right to a diversity of languages. This includes the right to express themselves and have access to information in their own language, the right to use their own languages in educational institutions funded by the state, and the right to have adequate provisions created for the use of minority languages where needed.

Art. 11. **Children's Rights.**
Children have the right to mass media products that are designed to meet their needs and interests and foster their healthy physical, mental and emotional development. They should be protected against harmful media products and from commercial and other exploitation at home, in school and at places of play, work, or business. Nations should take steps to produce and distribute widely high cultural and entertainment materials created for children in their own languages.

Since the Charter is not envisaged as being signed by states, states have not been made duty-holders. Rather, those media producers, publishers, educational authorities, etc. who sign, are envisaged as pledging themselves to become duty-holders when signing.

7.8.3. The Hague Recommendations Regarding the Education Rights of National Minorities

The third positive development is the new educational guidelines issued by The Foundation on Inter-Ethnic Relations for the OSCE. In 1992, OSCE (= Organisation for Security and Cooperation in Europe) created the position of a High Commissioner on National Minorities 'as an instrument of conflict prevention in situations of ethnic tension' (Rothenberger 1997: 3)—see Address Box 7.5.

```
* * * * * * * * * * * * * * * * * * * * * * * * * * * * * * * * * * * * * * * * * * *
*                                                                                 *
*          Address Box 7.5   OSCE (= Organisation for Security and                *
*          Cooperation in Europe) High Commissioner on National Minorities        *
*                                                                                 *
*   P.O. Box 20062, 2500 EB, The Hague, The Netherlands, phone: 31-70-312         *
*   5500; fax 31-70-363 5910, email <csehcnm@euronet.nl>; Web-site: <http://      *
*   www.osceprag.cz/>.                                                            *
*                                                                                 *
* * * * * * * * * * * * * * * * * * * * * * * * * * * * * * * * * * * * * * * * * * *
```

In order to prevent ethnic conflict, the High Commissioner, Max van der Stoel, published authoritative guidelines in October 1996 for minority education for the 55 member states (which include Canada and the United States). The High Commissioner, Max van der Stoel (1997: 153) stated when launching **The Hague Recommendations Regarding the Education Rights of National Minorities** (see below) that

> . . . in the course of my work, it had become more and more obvious to me that education is an extremely important element for the preservation and the deepening of the identity of persons belonging to a national minority. It is of course also clear that education in the language of the minority is of vital importance for such a minority.

These guidelines, **The Hague Recommendations**, were worked out by a small group of experts on human rights and education (mainly lawyers and including the author of this book). The guidelines are an interpretation and concretisation of international human rights standards about minority education.[31] Even if the term used is 'national minority', the guidelines also apply to immigrated minorities,[32] and one does *not* need to be a citizen in order to be protected by the guidelines.

In the section 'The spirit of international instruments', bilingualism is seen as a right and responsibility for persons belonging to national minorities (Art. 1), and states are reminded not to interpret their obligations in a restrictive manner (Art. 3). In the section on 'Minority education at primary and secondary levels', mother tongue medium education is recommended at all levels, including bilingual teachers in the dominant language as a second language (Art. 11 through 13). Teacher training is made a duty of the state (Art. 14).

> 11) The first years of education are of pivotal importance in a child's development. Educational research suggests that the medium of teaching at *pre-*

school and *kindergarten* levels should ideally be the child's language. Wherever possible, States should create conditions enabling parents to avail themselves of this option.

12) Research also indicates that in *primary school* the curriculum should ideally be taught in the minority language. The minority language should be taught as a subject on a regular basis. The State language should also be taught as a subject on a regular basis preferably by bilingual teachers who have a good understanding of the children's cultural and linguistic background. Towards the end of this period, a few practical or non-theoretical subjects should be taught through the medium of the State language. Wherever possible, States should create conditions enabling parents to avail themselves of this option.

13) In *secondary school* a substantial part of the curriculum should be taught through the medium of the minority language. The minority language should be taught as a subject on a regular basis. The State language should also be taught as a subject on a regular basis preferably by bilingual teachers who have a good understanding of the children's cultural and linguistic background. Throughout this period, the number of subjects taught in the State language, should gradually be increased. Research findings suggest that the more gradual the increase, the better for the child.

14) The maintenance of the primary and secondary levels of minority education depends a great deal on the availability of teachers trained in all disciplines in the mother tongue. Therefore, ensuing from the obligation to provide adequate opportunities for minority language education, States should provide adequate facilities for the appropriate training of teachers and should facilitate access to such training.

Finally, the Explanatory Note states that

[S]ubmersion-type approaches whereby the curriculum is taught exclusively through the medium of the State language and minority children are entirely integrated into classes with children of the majority are not in line with international standards. (p. 5)

Knowing that **most minority education in the world today is of submersion type** (see chapter 8 for definitions), it is useful to know that **this type of genocidal education is not in line with international human rights standards**. This also means that the children that the Recommendations apply to might be granted some of the central educational linguistic human rights. The questions now are to what extent the 55 OSCE countries will apply the Recommendations and how they will interpret their scope (see the Special Issue volume 4:2, 1996/1997 of **International Journal on Minority and Group Rights** which is about The Hague Recommendations). If we take into account the UN Human Rights Committee's reinterpretation of the scope of Article 27 above, **The Hague Recommendations** could in principle apply to **all** minorities, even the 'everyone' with very few rights in the draft **Universal Dec-**

laration on Linguistic Rights discussed above. Since indigenous peoples are supposed to have at least all the rights that minorities have, they might peruse the Recommendations too while waiting for their own Declaration to be approved. This gives **some** hope. Still, the Recommendations are still recommendations, not binding international law, and no sanctions are envisaged if (when) states violate them—as all states today do.

In conclusion, the concept of rights has often been paired with at least two other concepts, namely **wrongs** on the one hand (as in 'rights and wrongs'), and **duties** on the other hand (as in 'rights and (corresponding) duties'). In the title of an earlier paper ('Human rights and language wrongs', 1998a), I formulated the relationship between rights and wrongs, claiming that what we have now is limited human rights and extensive language wrongs. It also seems that, instead of the customary Western-inspired human rights principle where the citizen has (most of) the rights and the state has (most of) the duties, or the African and Asian-inspired human rights principle where communities, individuals, and the state all have both rights and duties, there has so far been an alternative, negative division of rights and duties in the area of educational linguistic human rights.

A nightmare solution makes the individual and the collectivity the sole firm duty-holders and the state the sole beneficiary. What we seem to have in many of today's international instruments, though, is a typical liberal sophisticatedly assimilationist solution:

- ■ It makes '**humanity**' and the **individual** vague, **conditional beneficiaries** and does not make the learning of L1 a right.
- ■ It makes the **state** a **firm beneficiary** which can demand loyalty, assimilation (termed integration) and L2-learning from minorities.
- ■ Correspondingly, it makes the **state** a vague, **conditional duty-holder**.
- ■ But it makes the **individual** and the **collectivity firm duty-holders** who have to deliver loyalty etc. to the state, as a precondition for being granted the rights which they then do not really have.

The pessimistic (but realistic) assessment by Rodolfo Stavenhagen (1995: 76–77) is:

> Too often, policies of national integration, of national cultural development, actually imply a policy of ethnocide, that is, the wilful destruction of cultural groups . . . The cultural development of peoples, whether minorities or majorities, must be considered within the framework of the right of peoples to self-determination, which by accepted international standards is the fundamental human right, in the absence of which all other human rights cannot really be enjoyed . . . governments fear that if minority peoples hold the right to self-determination in the sense of a right to full political independence, then existing

States might break up ... **State interests thus are still more powerful at the present time than the human rights of peoples** (emphasis added).

Despite the small recent improvements, it seems to be clear that the Western countries have so far not respected what should be basic linguistic human rights, especially in education, and that the world so far does little to prevent linguistic and cultural genocide, with the help of the human rights system or otherwise.

Summing up the last two chapters, then: If human rights, including linguistic human rights, are to be properly implemented so that they can fulfill their function as correctives to the 'free market', removing price tags from people and from necessities for their survival, a radical redistribution of the world's material resources is a necessary prerequisite. For this to happen, civil society needs to take back control of the economy, which has in the 'globalisation' process been 'given' away to transnational companies, the financial giants, the techno-military complex. This does not seem to be happening, quite the opposite.

In the meanwhile, what have schools done and what can they do? Have they become multiparadigmatic, entered the battlefield, taken a moral responsibility? Are schools implementing educational policies which respect linguistic human rights? If not, how could it be done? This is the topic of chapter 8.

NOTES

1. The concepts of individual and collective rights were manipulated in apartheid South Africa in a dangerous way—see e.g., Degenaar 1982, 1987 for analyses. Thanks to Timothy Reagan for the references.
2. The Centre has followed up with other publications for the Third Decade, running from 1993 to 2003, for instance with **Model National Legislation for the Guidance of Governments in the Enactment of further Legislation against Racial Discrimination,** 1996.
3. China is the record holder of 'legal' murder, death sentences executed. The numbers recorded by Amnesty International were for China 4,367 for 1996 and 1,876 for 1997, and for Iran, the second, 143 in 1997. USA has by far the highest figures for Western countries.
4. 'Territory' is, for instance, used in several problematic ways, some disastrous for indigenous peoples, in the draft UDLR. This is extremely worrying from the point of view of indigenous peoples as Luisa Maffi and I have pointed out on behalf of Terralingua.
5. There is, despite many attempts, no legally accepted universal definition; see Andrýsek 1989, Capotorti 1979, Eide 1990, 1991, Palley 1984, Skutnabb-Kangas & Phillipson 1994a, note 2 and references in it, for overviews of the criteria used in different definitions. For definitions and thorough treatises on the legal problems involved, see, e.g., Alfredsson 1990, 1991, Chernichenko 1996, 1997, Deschênes 1985, de Varennes 1996a, Eide 1993, 1996, Gromacki 1992, Packer 1993, Thornberry 1987, 1991, 1995, 1997; see also UN Human Rights Fact Sheet No 18, **Minority Rights,** 1992: 8–10 and the revised version 1998: 13–14.
6. This Draft was never accepted by Council of Europe, and the one that replaced it and became the Framework Convention for the Protection of National Minorities does not define minorities. On criticism of the Framework Convention, see section 7.5.3.4 and Thornberry 1997.

7. This interpretation has since been borne out by the UN Human Rights Commission's General Comment on Article 27—see section 7.8.1.

8. An alternative formulation (instead of referring to sign languages through the 'orally (when physiologically possible)' was suggested by Timothy Reagan (personal communication, December 1998): '. . . learn the mother tongue(s) in natural,, communicative settings, and in writing'. But even this may be misused: some people might claim that a signing community (which might necessitate boarding school education at least for those 90% of deaf children who have hearing parents) is not a 'natural' communicative setting. A task for the reader: find an inclusive formulation which cannot be misused!

9. It is obvious that monolingual teachers are not ideal if the goal is bilingualism or multilingualism. On the other hand, the teacher's competence in the dominated/minority language is in most cases more important than her competence in the dominant language; given that the only choice is between a monolingual Spanish-speaking or monolingual English-speaking teacher for Spanish-speaking students in the USA, provided both are well-trained, the principle of supporting the language which otherwise has less opportunity of developing in formal domains would favour choosing the Spanish-speaker. See chapter 8 on bilingual vs. monolingual teachers.

10. See, e.g., the United Nations publication **The Human Right to Peace. Declaration by the Director General**, 1997.

11. See, e.g., the United Nations publication **The Realization of the Right to Development. Global Consultation on the Right to Development as a Human Right**, 1991; see also Rosas 1995c. **Declaration on the Right to Development**, adopted by the UN General Assembly in 1986 (General Assembly resolution 41/128 of 4 December 1986) was adopted by a vote of 146 to 1 (the United States) and 8 abstentions (Denmark, Finland, Germany, Iceland, Israel, Japan, Sweden, United Kingdom) (Norway abstained in The Third Committee of the General Assembly but changed its voting behaviour in the Plenary)—see Rosas 1995c, 248–249). The Declaration 'provides in its Article 8(1) that States shall undertake, at the national level, all necessary measures for the realization of the right to development and shall ensure, **inter alia**, equality of opportunity for all in their access to basic resources, education . . . employment and the fair distribution of income' (Eide 1995a, 39).

12. See Tomaševski 1995b and Posey (in press a, b) for summaries and references.

13. See Pennycook 1994, 1995, 1998a, b, for perceptive accounts of some aspects of the discourse of English, English language teaching and colonialism; the discoursal construction and deconstruction of oppression—see also references to Tollefson and Phillipson in the bibliography.

14. Issues of linguistic diversity and language policies, including some regulations about them, of course date much further back, to Greece, Rome, China, etc. See e.g., works by Haarmann for references.

15. All enforceable rights must include a duty-holder—they must specify whose duty it is to see to it that the rights are a reality. If a duty-holder is not specified in an international human rights instrument, in most cases statements of rights are empty phrases; likewise, the beneficiary has to be properly specified, including humanity, which as a collective entity is also a legitimate beneficiary—see Skutnabb-Kangas 1998a for exemplification.

16. It should be emphasized that this means 13 students of obligatory school age, between 7 and 15. A school could, for instance, have 2 students aged 7, 3 aged 9, 3 aged 11, 2 aged 13, and 3 aged 14. For Finland Swedish, see also Törnudd 1978, Liebkind & Broo 1985, Liebkind et al. 1995, Sandlund 1976, Finnäs 1982, McRae 1997.

17. For the Catalan and Basque situation in general in Spain, see Siguan 1993, and the interesting new book by Conversi, 1997.

18. In a change to Turkish laws 27 October 1995, a sentence was added to Article 8 in the Law to Combat Terrorism (see Info Box 7.5.) stating that first-time sentences according to this law may be made conditional (suspended). If somebody is sentenced a second time according to the same law, s/he has to serve **both** periods.

19. A summary of the LANGTAG Report is available at <http://www.sacs.org.za/gov/arts&cul/docs/langrep.htm>.

20. For background and assessments of recent South African language policy, see Alexander 1989, 1992, 1995a, b, Cluver 1994, Desai 1995, Heugh 1995a, b, c, Luckett 1995, Webb 1994; also compare with Mansour 1993; see also assessments by some of our colleagues in 5.1.1. See Dalby 1985 for some of the early positive pronouncements on language rights.

21. Just one example of deterioration in the health field as a result of the war against civilians, burning of villages, forcible deportations, etc. According to data from the Malaria Institute of the Ministry of Health, the reported cases of malaria in Turkey rose from 8,680 in 1990 to 82,096 in 1995. At the beginning of 1970s malaria was almost non-existent in Turkey. When the numbers of people with malaria started to increase in the middle of the 1970s, prophylactic measures were taken rapidly.

    In 1978, when 88,000 people had malaria, 8,235,000 received prophylactic treatment. In 1995 only 248,000 people got prophylaxy, despite the number of malaria cases being approximately the same as in 1978, the only difference being that today most of the malaria cases are in the Kurdish provinces in South-East Turkey. Sources used for the statistics are **Statistical Yearbooks of Turkey** 1979: 97; 1991: 142 and 1996: 168. Many other diseases and illnesses which were practically wiped out have increased in an alarming way in the Kurdish provinces. I am greatly indebted to Kristiina Koivunen for letting me have this information from her forthcoming dissertation by email <koivunen@elo.helsinki.fi>. Compare the regional differences with what should be human rights in the area of health, Tomaševski 1995a.

22. Timothy Reagan has pointed out that 'most American readers will completely miss the point [of the 'shall/should' distinction], since in American English the distinction really doesn't exist (the two are generally used as synonyms, with "shall" being a bit more formal and perhaps even pompous). See examples below for the difference between 'shall' and less duty-inducing words.

23. See the description of the origins of the Directive and discussion in Tosi 1984: 14; see also Reid & Reich 1992). It was, according to Tosi, unclear whether the then EEC intended the directive as 'an embryonic "enriching" model for the promotion of EEC languages in the modern languages curricula of member states, or as a compensatory measure for the underprivileged' and its effects will remain unclear until 'governments make a definite pronouncement on their interpretation and define their policies for its implementation' (ibid, 17). The same uncertainty holds for the European Parliament Resolution in question, which does not clarify the Directive. 'According to the report presented on 3 January 1989 on the implementation of this Directive by the Member States ... the results are on the whole quite unsatisfactory' since most countries had not 'made adequate provisions for the teaching of the languages and cultures of origin of the children of migrant workers', and in most 'member States, this Directive was either ignored or given very little attention', according to the European Parliament's own Report mentioned in the text.

24. The Report contains endless accounts of initiatives, plans, suggestions, resolutions etc. on migrant rights with 'no follow-up', 'none of them ever saw the light of day', 'never went beyond issue no 1', 'nothing more was said or done', 'has not been able to go further', 'no further initiatives were taken', 'did not take place' (all these just from a few pages, 104–107). The many instances of non-compliance with the limited language rights of migrants thus seem to place the **implementation** of the Directive close to **covert prohibition**, despite the European Parliament Resolution's points 1 to 4 and 10 above.

25. These were Armenia, Australia, Austria, Belarus, Bulgaria, Canada, Cape Verde, Croatia, Czech and Slovak Federal Republic, Denmark, Estonia, Finland, Greece, Guatemala, Hungary, Italy, Latvia, Liechtenstein, Lithuania, Malawi, Moldova, Morocco, Netherlands, Norway, Poland, Republic of Korea, Rumania, Russian Federation, Rwanda, Samoa, Slovenia, Sri Lanka, Sweden, Tadjikistan, Ukraine, and United States of America.

26. See Thornberry 1993 for an interpretation and critique.
27. Convention No. 107 Concerning the Protection and Integration of Indigenous and Other Tribal and Semi-tribal Populations in Independent Countries, adopted in June 1957 by the International Labor organization (ILO), Article 23:

> 1. Children belonging to the populations concerned shall be taught to read and write in their mother tongue or, where this is not practicable, in the language most commonly used by the group to which they belong.
> 2. Provision will be made for a progressive transition from the mother tongue or the vernacular language to the national language or to one of the official languages of the country.
> 3. Appropriate measures shall, as far as possible, be taken to preserve the mother tongue or the vernacular language.

    The revised version, ILO Convention No. 169, 1989, Article 28 (1): 'Children shall, wherever practicable, be taught to read and write in their own language . . . Measures shall be taken to preserve and promote . . . [these] languages'.
28. The Recife Declaration was based on one version of my provisional declaration (Skutnabb-Kangas 1984a); compare it with the version in Table 7.5. I was in another working group myself in Recife, not the one writing the Declaration.
29. For instance in the books **Development Aid and Human Rights Revisited** (1993b) and **Between sanctions and elections. Aid donors and their human rights performance** (1997; both London: Pinter; see also 1996 and 1997). For the role of education in the World Bank's and IMF's structural adjustment programmes and their catastrophic consequences, see Brock-Utne 1993a, in press, and references given earlier.
30. UN Doc. CCPR/C/21/Rev.1/Add.5.. The text is also contained in Annex 3 in Eide, Krause & Rosas (eds) 1995, and some of the articles in the book comment on details of the reinterpretation and its possible consequences. See also de Varennes 1996a.
31. See Eide, Packer, Packer & Siemienski, Siemienski, Szépe, Stobart, Thornberry & Gibbons, and van der Stoel, all 1997, for background and analyses of the Hague Recommendations.
32. In fact the situation of immigrated minorities was discussed extensively in the drafting group. The term 'national' was added to 'minorities' in the name of the Recommendations only after the drafting group had approved the document.

Linguistic Human Rights in Education?

The national education policy has to be built on a multilingual strategy because

(a) More than one language is necessary for greater mobility and employment opportunity within a State and within the country.

(b) Innovativeness and creative expression of a plural society demands cultivated use of more than one language.

(c) Combating illiteracy, which is one of the major national objectives, cannot be possible without using many languages.

(d) Many languages provide many ways for perceiving the same reality.

(e) Knowledge of more than one language encourages respect for other's point of view and is conducive to national integration.

(f) More than one language provides greater participation of greater number of people in the democratic process.

(g) More than one language is necessary to be recognised for protecting minority languages and cultures. (**Study of Languages. A report**, 1986: 3–4)

8. LINGUISTIC HUMAN RIGHTS IN EDUCATION?

One of the **basic linguistic human rights** of persons belonging to minorities is—or should be—to achieve high levels of bi- or multilingualism through education. Becoming at least bilingual is in most cases necessary for minorities to exercise other fundamental human rights, including the fulfillment of basic needs as presented in Table 6.7. But today the education of both majorities and minorities in most western countries (and also elsewhere) functions in conflict with most scientifically sound principles about how education leading to high levels of multilingualism should be organized. As has been shown, education participates in attempting and committing linguistic genocide in relation to minorities. In relation to linguistic majorities, with the exception of elites, education today in most cases deprives them of the possibility of gaining the benefits associated with really high levels of multilingualism.

Sometimes linguistic human rights in education are, falsely, in my opinion, posited as being in conflict with other human rights.[1] Admittedly situations of great linguistic diversity combined with meager financial resources are complex—but on the other hand there is ample evidence from Africa and Asia and from multilingual immigrant minority education of the fact that unnecessary either-or stances (which the false positioning is often based on) are in the long run both costly and misguided, and tend to perpetuate elite dominance.

If multilingualism is more positive than monolingualism for the patients/victims and for the society as a whole, how can educational language planning help in getting rid of monolingualism? How should education be organised, so as to make **everybody** bilingual or multilingual at a high level? What is important is to develop models which combine the positive aspects of at least three experiences. Firstly, the positive strand in the education of minorities, namely strong forms of 'multilingual' education. Secondly, the positive aspects in the education of both minorities and majorities, involved in anti-racist 'intercultural' education. These two have so far, curiously enough, often had competing goals (see, e.g., Lo Bianco 1994). Thirdly, they should be combined with the positive aspects of elite education. Present monolingually oriented reductionist educational language choices seem rather to combine the negative sides of the first two and none of the positive ones of the last. Today's educational models, with few exceptions, do not support the diversity which is necessary for the planet to have a future.

After defining bilingualism as an educational goal, I first list some of the key fallacies which lead to lack of language rights in contemporary educational language planning for some of the main groups discussed in the book. Then I present educational models which do not lead to high levels of multilingualism (non-forms and weak forms of bilingual education). They will be related to literacy and the lack of Universal Primary Education (UPE), and it is claimed that use of the wrong medium of education (i.e., not using the mother tongue) is the main **pedagogical** reason for lack of success of 'literacy' campaigns in the world (political, economic, and many ideological reasons have been discussed earlier). This is followed by a presentation of strong models of multilingual education. Finally, on the basis of the strong models, I will draw conclusions about prerequisites (also bilingual teachers) and principles which are important to follow if high level multilingualism is the educational goal.

Since hundreds of books and thousands of articles have been written about the subject (I have myself contributed a fair number—see the bibliography for a few of them), I will not give many specific references here and will keep the presentation at a fairly general, programmatic level. There are many specialised bibliographies in the area; several volumes of readers, encyclopedias, Web-sites, etc.—many of these resources are mentioned in the book and the reader is asked to consult them.

8.1. WHAT KIND OF 'BILINGUALISM' IS THE GOAL IN 'BILINGUAL EDUCATION' PROGRAMMES?

We have seen that formal education can play a decisive role in killing minority languages. But is the opposite also true? How important is formal education in maintaining a minority language, in supporting threatened languages, in reversing language shift, or in reclaiming a language? Opinions differ. What we can say, though, is that educational conditions, and changes in the educational system, have often made a community aware of the need for other changes. Some of them the communities may be able to make themselves— for instance, decolonise their own attitudes and reorganise community life so as to use the minority language more among themselves, including in the family—there are many examples of this all over the world. Often most of the changes needed are political and economic, and the minority community cannot effect these on their own. Schools cannot save a language on their own (see Fishman 1989, 1991, 1995, 1996b, 1998) but schools can be an important change agent. When assessing the many factors which influence the successful reproduction of a minority group, one conclusion is that education is often easier to change than many still larger-scale macro-societal and political structures, even when a major struggle is needed for educational change. The medium of education is one, if not the most, decisive factor in the multilingualism and the school achievement of the children of dominated groups—and, again, easier to change than some of the other major factors (the parents' socioeconomic status or their level of formal education, or the child's gender, age, or length of stay in the country in the case of immigrant minority children). One recent example of the influence of education is from Wales. Farrell et al. (1998) analyse census data (1981 and 1991) from anglicised areas of South East Wales and show that 'education has been an effective agency of Welsh language production' (1998: 494). There are 'net gains in the percentages of younger Welsh speakers' (ibid., 489), and it can be shown that these are connected to the presence of Welsh-medium education. Other examples will be provided below.

In the following sections I will classify educational models in general in relation to what is called bilingual education. The classic definition of bilingual education (Andersson & Boyer 1978) requires that the educational system uses two languages as media of instruction, in subjects other than the languages themselves. I will follow Colin Baker's classification into weak and strong forms of bilingual education (e.g., 1993). I have also added a third category, non-forms of bilingual education. Neither weak forms nor non-forms succeed in making children high level bi- or multilingual, whereas strong forms **have** succeeded in this. Since the three categories are based on to what extent the models succeed in enabling children to become **high level bi- or multilinguals**, we have to define this goal first.

When I use the term 'bilingualism', this should generally be understood as 'bi- and multilingualism'. Bilingualism as a goal implies by definition that (at least) two languages are involved. When dominant language representatives use the concept, they seem mostly to confine their interest in bilingualism to one of the languages and one of the groups only: the learning of the majority/dominant language by minority children. The mother tongues of the minority children are in most cases tolerated as parts of the curriculum **only** if the teaching of (or in) them leads to a better proficiency in the majority language—and often they are not tolerated at all (see, e.g., Baker & de Kanter 1982).

As a result of this, it is the minorities themselves who have to put a strong emphasis on the learning of the mother tongue and demand mother tongue learning as a linguistic human right. But minorities do of course want their children to learn the majority languages fully too. We want our children to become bilingual[2] as a minimum, not monolingual or strongly dominant in **either** of the two languages. Insert 8.1. gives an example, at the same time as it also shatters some of the all too frequent myths about immigrant minorities wanting segregation.

In my longitudinal study among Finnish working class parents and their children in Finnish-medium classes in Sweden (1987), I asked both the youngsters and the parents about their wishes and hopes in terms of languages, countries, their future, and identification. I also asked the youngsters what they **thought** the parents wished for them, and the parents what they wished for their children and what they hoped the youngsters wished for themselves. Then I told the parents that the youngsters had in fact already replied, and asked how the parents thought they had replied. I present a summary of parent wishes in terms of the distinctions given in chapter 3.

The parents **wish** that Finnish would be the children's identificational mother tongue in terms of the affective component of cultural competence, but they also wish that the children would have a positive identification with Swedish. They **accept** that Swedish will be the functional first language for the children, the language most used. They **wish** the children to have full cultural competence in Swedish in terms of the knowledge and behavioural components. They would **not** like Finnish to become a second language for the children in terms of the knowledge component—they would like them to have native competence in Finnish too, in addition to Swedish.

On the other hand, they see the relationship between function, competence, and identification: if you do not use a language much (especially in the more formal domains), you do not become fully competent, and low competence may lead to less motivation to use and to affectively identify with the language. The parents thus **accept** and encourage more use of Swedish as long as it does not negatively affect the children's competence in Finnish, and, through that, their affective identification. They **wish** the children to have a positive ethnonymic and linguonymic identification, with both languages. They **hope** that the children have a positive toponymic identification with both countries, a total one with Sweden and at least a localised one with Finland ('holiday country'; the place where the parents came from or where the grandparents live; Finnish nature). They **accept** that the children will have a politonymic identification with Sweden, even if they **hope** that Finland will never be a foreign country for the children.

In fact the youngsters' replies showed a very positive bilingual, bicultural, 'bicountrial' (see Skutnabb-Kangas & Peura (eds) 1994) identity, very much in line with what the parents wished but did not always dare to hope.

I see this very much as a result of the mother tongue medium education that these youngsters had had. The youngsters were **creating many new concepts** (see examples in my 1987) for these positive multiple identities: 'Usually one is of course a bit proud that I know two languages, and that I am from two countries, so to say. Sometimes one ponders of course a bit about which "-countrial" one is. But one must surely be able to be bi-countrial too' (Skutnabb-Kangas 1987: 97).

One of the confusing facts has been that many state educational authorities (representing the majority group) also claim that **they** too want our children to become bilingual. But when this claim is analysed, it often transpires that majorities and minorities use different definitions of bilingualism when they speak of it as the educational goal. That is one of the reasons why it is imperative to define 'bilingual' every time the term is being used. There are literally hundreds of definitions (see, e.g., Baetens Beardsmore 1982, Haugen 1964, 1972, Hoffman 1991, Romaine 1995, Vildomec 1963, Weinreich 1967, for presentations and analyses). I organise them according to the same criteria which I use in the mother tongue definitions, and give a sample in Table 8.1. (See Skutnabb-Kangas 1975, 1984a for references on who has used the various definitions).

When majority group educational authorities talk about bilingualism as a goal for the education of immigrant or indigenous minority children, they often seem to mean either a non-demanding competence definition (for instance 3d or 3e) or the most general function definition (uses two languages). We minorities would prefer to use a combination of 2, 3, and 4, a definition which makes sure that the speaker has the chance to learn and use **both** languages at a very high level and to identify positively with both. The

TABLE 8.1
Definitions of bilingualism

CRITERION	DEFINITION A speaker is bilingual who
1. origin	a. has learned two languages in the family from native speakers from infancy; b. has used two languages in parallel as means of communication from infancy
2. identification - internal - external	a. identifies herself as bilingual/with two languages and/or two cultures (or parts of them); b. is identified by others as bilingual/as a native speaker of two languages
3. competence	a. has complete mastery of two languages; b. has native-like control of two languages; c. has equal mastery of two languages; d. can produce complete meaningful utterances in the other language; e. has at least some knowledge and control of the grammatical structure of the other language; f. has come into contact with another language
4. function	a. uses (or can use) two languages (in most situations) (in accordance with her own wishes and the demands of the community)

(Source: Skutnabb-Kangas 1984a: 91)

definitions used by the majority authorities confirm the picture of linguicism, because there are low expectations and almost no demands made on the minority child's competence in her mother tongue. It is often left to the home to teach it, and it is sometimes declared that 'taxpayers' money' should not go into 'supporting private ethnicity' (e.g., J. Edwards, see earlier), conveniently ignoring the fact that minorities are taxpayers too and that majority children's private ethnicity is supported through all taxpayers' money in schools. Minority taxpayers are required to support majority language and ethnicity in schools, both for majority children, and for their own (minority) children, even when it is subtractive for them.

My own definition (Definition Box 8.1) is specifically designed to describe the needs of indigenous and immigrant and other minority children. The goal of minority education should in my view be to enable the children to become bilingual according to this definition.

DEFINITION BOX 8.1 Definition of bilingualism as an educational goal

A bilingual speaker is one who is able to function in two (or more) languages, either in 'monolingual' or multilingual communities, in accordance with the sociocultural demands made on an individual's communicative and cognitive competence by these communities and by the individual herself, at the same level as native speakers, and who is able to identify positively with both (or all) language groups (and cultures) or parts of them (Skutnabb-Kangas 1984a: 90).

The implications of this definition for the educational system are far-reaching, and should be compared with the implications of less demanding definitions (for more detail see Skutnabb-Kangas 1984a).

'Second language' should also be defined for the purposes of the educational models presented below. Except when clearly indicated, I use 'L2' or second language' to mean the language which is the **second in the order of learning for the student** (as opposed to the first language or a third or fourth language).

For some Deaf students a Sign language might thus be their second language in **this** sense.

One of the other common ways of defining a second language is to define it as a language that the student can hear and use in the immediate environment outside the home, a language which is not the student's mother tongue. In this definition the second language is contrasted with a foreign language, which one does not use daily in the environment.

In this sense a Sign language might never become a mother tongue or even a second language for a Deaf student who has hearing parents and who never lives in a signing community.

After these clarifications we move to educational models. When these are categorised in terms of whether they reach the goal of **high levels of bilingualism** or multilingualism, what is intended is preferably 'bilingualism' according to my own definition above, or at least something very close to it. In addition, at least one, possibly two, or even several other languages can be learned at a high level. I consider it a realistic and feasible goal. It has been shown that in the education of both national minorities and elites, the goal can be reached, without the costs necessarily being higher than those of present educational models which do not reach these goals.

8.2. KEY FALLACIES IN THE EDUCATION OF DOMINATED COMMUNITIES

On the basis of his study of factors influencing English teaching worldwide, especially in colonial and post-colonial education, Robert Phillipson (1992; and an earlier version in Phillipson & Skutnabb-Kangas 1986a) identified what he calls 'the five key tenets of ESL/EFL'. These are

- English is best taught monolingually;
- the ideal teacher of English is a native speaker;
- the earlier English is introduced, the better the results;
- the more English is taught, the better the results;
- if other languages are used much, standards of English will drop.

As we also showed (e.g., Skutnabb-Kangas & Phillipson 1989a), these tenets have in fact guided much of indigenous and immigrant minority education all over the world. All five are scientifically false and can rather be (and have been) labelled as fallacies (for a detailed analysis, see Phillipson 1992, chapter 6). These are then

- the monolingual fallacy;
- the native speaker fallacy;
- the early start fallacy;
- the maximum exposure fallacy;
- the subtractive fallacy.

To these, we could add at least the segregation tenet/fallacy:

- if minorities are taught in their own groups or classes or schools, especially through the medium of their own languages, this prevents integration and leads to/is segregation, ghettoisation.

Many of the myths about monolingualism, discussed in section 4.2 could also be formulated as tenets/fallacies. The 'monolingual' and 'native speaker' fallacies will be commented on below in section 8.6 in the section about bilingual teachers.

The **'early start' fallacy** is obviously closely connected to the 'subtractive' fallacy. Several types of programme have shown that if teaching a foreign language as a subject or teaching through the medium of a foreign language is additive, it **can** start early. Early foreign language teaching in 'mainstream' programmes shows it. On the other hand, a large longitudinal Swedish study (Holmstrand 1980, 1982) showed that the gains of starting a foreign language as a subject early were minimal. The strong models below, **immersion**, and **two-way programmes** (see the definitions below), also show that additive early start with a foreign medium is perfectly possible. We do not yet know enough about the long-term results of **double immersion** (using two foreign languages as partial media of education; see Artigal 1995).

On the other hand, if the learning of another language is **subtractive** (as it is in all the non-forms and weak forms of bilingual education), the earlier it starts the worse.

The **'maximum exposure' tenet** (the label comes from Jim Cummins, see bibliography), is maybe the intuitively most understandable of the tenets: the more the child uses L2, the better she learns it. It has also been shown to be a complete fallacy. If the quality of the instruction in L2 is the same in two models, one with maximum exposure, the other with little exposure to a dominant language, and provided that minority children receive high quality mother tongue medium instruction in the model with little exposure to L2, then there have been two types of result.

Either there is no relationship between time-on-task and results in the dominant language, meaning both groups perform equally well in L2, despite the mother tongue medium group having had much less exposure.

Alternatively, there is a reverse relationship: the **less** time is used on instruction through the medium of the dominant language, the **better** the results, again provided that the time is instead used on both good mother tongue medium teaching and good subject teaching of L2, given by bilingual teachers. For instance the Ramirez study in the USA (see both Ramirez et al. 1991 entries in the bibliography) is fairly clear on this (see also Ramirez 1992, Dolson & Mayer 1992, and Cummins 1992 and references in them for a discussion of the methods and findings). Several of Jim Cummins' recent publications have given overviews of the research findings in relation to maximum exposure—see bibliography.

The **subtractive fallacy** is an old one. We find formulations about the subtractive tenet in many of the regulations which have been discussed in earlier chapters. For instance, the Norwegian School Law of 1880 (which has been called the 'Magna Carta of Norwegianisation'), paragraph 3, says: 'Instruction in the school is in the Norwegian language. The Lappish or Finnish languages are used only as a means of helping to explain what is impossible to understand for the children'. Every paragraph after this contains detailed instructions on how to restrain the use of Sámi and Finnish.

> Even if the majority of the children in a group do not understand Norwegian, the teacher must always keep the above regulations in mind and remember that it is imperative that the Lappish and Finnish languages are not used more than absolutely necessary ... When the teacher converses with the children to make them understand, use of the Lappish or Finnish language must be avoided as much as possible; it should be noted in particular that whole sentences and continuous passages of the Norwegian text must not be translated into Lappish or Finnish unless it is has been shown that this cannot be avoided without harm to comprehension. (quoted in Lind Meløy 1981: 122–123)

It is instructive to compare this with the policy offered to children in Africa and Asia almost 100 years later, in the pedagogical tradition which still dominates English teaching: 'The teaching of vocabulary should be mainly through demonstration in situations. When, however, a very brief explanation in the mother tongue is sufficient to ensure that the meaning is fully and accurately understood, such explanation may be given.' (Makerere Report 1961: 13, a report of the Commonwealth conference on the teaching of English as a second language, probably the most influential document on policy and methods for teaching English in ex-colonial countries). For analysis of the monolingual approach in teaching English as a foreign/second language see Phillipson 1992, chapter 6.

After the passing of the Proposition 227 in California, minority children will be placed in English-medium instruction after the first school year. If teachers give even the little support in the two examples above, this may lead to trouble because teachers may be fined if they use other languages.

Californian school authorities might learn from the mistakes of the Norwegians. It was important for the central and local authorities in Norway to control in a more detailed manner whether the teachers really refrained from the use of Sámi and Finnish. According to Karl Aas, Superintendent for Schools, in a communication to the Department of Education in 1899, there were many people who thought that the time had come to forbid the use of Sámi and Finnish as auxiliary languages and 'in addition to the teachers, competent men like the business people and civil servants have here voiced that opinion'. Ron Unz, the engineer behind Proposition 227 in California, is a business man. . .). In Norway, most of these 'competent men' were ethnic Norwegians. One of the Heads of Department in the Ministry had suggested in 1877 that only 'Norwegian' teachers should be appointed, because 'experience seems to have shown that teachers of pure or mixed Sámi or Finnish ancestry are not capable of advancing the Norwegianisation among their compatriots with the success hoped for' (ibid., 19, 21). The teachers and the staff in the boarding schools were to be 'nationally minded' (Eriksen & Niemi 1981: 257). In 1931 the then Superintendent wrote that it was 'completely unnecessary for teachers in Finnmark to have any education in Sámi or Finnish' (Lind Meløy 1981: 27). This seems to be the Californian present stance too.

To counteract the **segregation fallacy** two distinctions are helpful, those between **physical as opposed to psychological segregation/integration** and between **segregation as a goal or a means**. For many dominated groups at least initial physical segregation from dominant group members seems to be a necessity in order to enable later integration psychologically and competence-wise. If physical segregation ensures that the students have a better chance of acquiring the prerequisites for integrating themselves both psychologically and physically later, then the initial physical segregation is used as a positive means towards a later integrationist goal. Minority students are, of course, psychologically integrated in their own classrooms, with other children with whom they share a mother tongue. Here they have a better chance of being appreciated for who they are and what they know, rather than the system defining them as deficient or below the norm, as is often the case when they are physically 'integrated' in dominant group classes (see the labels about minority students in Insert 3.14). Forced initial physical integration into a dominant language and dominant group classroom may prevent dominated group students from acquiring the competencies they need, in their own language and culture, in the dominant language and culture, and in terms of content matter (I have discussed this in several chapters in my 1984a and, especially, in 1986, a book which has been translated into several languages, English not being among them[3]). Insert 8.3, p. 586, shows a clear example of 'segregation' being beneficial, and several other examples in the book indicate the same.

The beliefs in a monolingual L2-teaching methodology, monolingual teachers, maximum exposure, and the either-or thinking which results in forbidding the minority language or restricting its use, have today developed from the earlier more crude forms to their present more sophisticated forms. These are at least equally effective in committing linguistic genocide as have been shown. It is extremely important to recognise that the ideology is still the same. In addition to what has be described in earlier chapters, I will, when discussing the models below, give a few examples where I directly compare the earlier and contemporary ideologies.

8.3. 'NON-FORMS' AND 'WEAK FORMS' OF BILINGUAL EDUCATION

8.3.1. Listing and Defining the Models

I divide the types of education which have been **labelled** as bilingual education into three different groups: **non-forms, weak forms**, and **strong forms** of bilingual education.[4]

The **non-forms** are so termed because although some of them go under the name of 'bilingual education', these do not properly fall within the terms of the classic definition—they do not use two languages as media of teaching and learning. They are types of education where saying 'bilingual' is sheer rhetoric. Other non-forms represent 'traditional' education on the majority's premisses, despite having many minority or indigenous children in the programmes, and they do not even pretend to be bilingual education programmes.

In western countries, non-forms usually lead to virtual monolingualism in the majority language, regardless of whether these forms are used with minority children or majority children. Unless there, for majorities, is further exposure to minority languages outside school, they do not learn much of them. Unless there, for minorities, are massive extra efforts outside school, non-forms are genocidal, they transfer minority children linguistically to the majority group. Even with a lot of effort in the family and community, many of the minority children in these subtractive non-forms may become virtually monolingual in the majority language—non-school efforts seldom succeed alone in maintaining and developing further a mother tongue, especially if it has low status.

In the rest of the world where grassroots multilingualism is common, schooling has sometimes, especially for the elites, been influential in **eradicating** multilingualism (as some of the Inserts have shown). For most ordinary people, a few years in school have not changed their linguistic repertoire much. In Annamalai's words (1994), 'Language development in India has by and large remained a governmental programme and not people's programme'. What can change quickly, though, is attitudes towards various languages, as Mubanga Kashoki (quoted in UNIN 1981: 41) has noted: 'Africans have been psychologically conditioned to believe that only European languages are structured to aid development'. Likewise Pattanayak (1991: 32): 'Replacing many languages by one will not only make many otherwise literate people illiterate, it will also deprive them of access to their own cultural heritage'.

The **weak** forms of bilingual education have monolingualism, strong dominance in one of the languages, mostly the majority language, or limited bilingualism, as their linguistic aim rather than multilingualism and multiliteracy. Some of them do belong to the category of bilingual education in its classic sense because they use two languages as media of instruction. This is true of all transitional models.

The **strong forms** of bi- and multilingual education have as their linguistic aim to promote (high levels of) multilingualism (or, minimally, bilingualism) and multiliteracy for **all** participants in the programme, regardless of whether these represent linguistic minorities or majorities.

It is only the strong forms of bilingual education that are recommended here, because the scientific evidence shows that they can reach the desired goals. But for comparison it is important to review also non-forms and weak forms to some extent. It is also done because there is a lot of confusion about the various programme types. As an example, even when both the founder of immersion programmes, Wallace Lambert, Merrill Swain, and many others (see, e.g., the excellent series of books by California (State) Department of Education, CDE 1981, CDE 1982, CDE 1986, and here especially CDE 1984) have for decades countless times emphasized that the immersion concept cannot be used for the USA submersion programmes, these are still often called 'immersion' (e.g., 'structured immersion'). Likewise, late-exit transitional programmes are often called maintenance programmes. Or two-way programmes are called 'two-way immersion' or 'dual immersion', even if they only imply immersion for the participating majority group children but not for the minorities. An overview of the programmes is presented in Info Box 8.1.

❖ I n f o   B o x   8 . 1 ❖

*Overview of Non-Forms, Weak Forms
and Strong Forms of Bilingual Education*

A. NON-FORMS which lead to virtual monolingualism: 1. **'Mainstream' monolingual programmes with foreign language teaching**; 2. **Submersion programmes** (sink-or-swim); 3. **Segregation programmes**.

B. WEAK FORMS which lead to very strong dominance in one language: 4. **Transitional early-exit programmes**; 5. **Transitional late-exit programmes**.

C. STRONG FORMS which lead to high levels of bilingualism or multilingualism: 6. **Language (/mother tongue) maintenance** or **language shelter programmes**; 7. **Immersion programmes**; 8. **Two-way bilingual (dual language) programmes**; 9. **Alternate days programmes**; 10. **European Union Schools** (plural multilingual) **model**.

As a short summary, programmes 1–5 do not lead to high levels of bilingualism or educational success at group level; 6–10 often do. Programmes 1–4 violate linguistic human rights of minorities grossly, 5 somewhat less; 6–10 respect linguistic human rights.

8.3.2. 'Non-Forms' of Bilingual Education

The educational starting point in a monolingually oriented western country is usually **monolingual instruction through the majority language to both majorities** (who stay monolingual) **and minorities** (who at a group level do not become high level bilinguals). In section 5.3.1, the development from indifference to romantic-racist to segregational educational 'ideologies and programmes' for indigenous peoples and also minorities was traced.

Later, when large-scale societal changes 'demanding' a more literate and later more highly educated population (i.e., with more **formal** education) occur, **majorities** are still taught **through the medium of their own languages**, with the teaching of foreign languages as subjects. In most cases they stay fairly monolingual, with few exceptions (such as the Nordic countries and the Benelux countries).

8.3.2.1. *'Mainstream' Monolingual Programmes With Foreign Language Teaching*

A 'mainstream' monolingual model with foreign language teaching is the programme most linguistic majority populations have in countries where their mother tongue is the/an official language. The children are taught through the medium of their mother tongue and are taught foreign languages as subjects (by teachers who in most cases are native speakers of the same language as the students, i.e., bilingual). In several countries with numerically small official languages and well-qualified teachers this model may lead to a good level of competence in one or two foreign languages for majority populations (e.g., the **Nordic countries, Netherlands**), in others (e.g., **Britain, France, Germany, Italy, Russia**) the results are less than impressive (and in the USA even worse—see Reagan & Osborn 1998 for some analyses). The goal is (some/good/excellent) competence in foreign languages, not bilingualism according to any of the more demanding definitions. In countries which achieve good results, foreign language teaching is well organised, and young Western Europeans often have additional extensive exposure to the language outside school (media, travel, exchanges, etc.).

In business, politics, and several other areas, many leading figures in Europe have during the last decade voiced their concern that there are not enough people with high levels of competence in all the languages and cultures which would be needed. Market shares are being lost, important political negotiations are made more difficult, and so on.[5] Competence in English alone seriously disables communication. Several possible solutions have been discussed (see Address Box 8.1 for some references and resources). One of them is starting the learning of foreign languages earlier. 'Early foreign language learning', which is being campaigned for energetically in Europe, is a policy initiative that largely derives from a recognition that foreign language learning in the 'mainstream' formal education is insufficiently successful. It is assumed that this is due to the age at which foreign language learning began, rather than, for instance, because teachers were under-qualified, or the teaching aimed at passing written exams rather than communication, or could have been organized differently. The proposed solution, say starting at age 8 rather than 12, is thus based on a partial diagnosis of the problem only, an inadequate understanding of differences, similarities, and interrelationships between L1 and L2 learning and between informal and formal language learning. It embodies an unscientific hope that the education system can deliver the goods without major changes. This also has implications for budgets and training. In Australia, Japanese and Indonesian are among the most popular foreign languages in schools (that is where the markets are) and Chinese is also rapidly gaining ground, but the results have so far being disappointing (see, e.g., references to Lo Bianco and Smolicz in the bibliography). Exposing all children to another language for a few years in school does not seem to make much difference in terms of achieving bilingualism, without extensive teacher training, streaming of groups on the basis of earlier competence and exposure, etc. (see Phillipson & Skutnabb-Kangas 1997).

8.3.2.2. *Submersion Programmes*

Many of the experiences in the Inserts in this book represent **submersion programmes** (Definition Box 8.2).

DEFINITION BOX 8.2 Submersion

A **submersion** or **sink-or-swim** model is a programme where linguistic minority children with a low-status mother tongue are forced to accept instruction through the medium of a foreign majority/official language with high status, in classes where some children are native speakers of the language of instruction, where the teacher does not understand the mother tongue of the minority children, and where the majority language constitutes a threat to the minority children's mother tongue (MT), which runs the risk of being displaced or replaced (MT is not being learned (at a high level); MT is 'forgotten'; MT does not develop because the children are forbidden to use it or are made to feel ashamed of it)—a **subtractive** language learning situation.

Submersion programmes are the most common method in the present world for educating dominated group minority children. They are used for most immigrant and refugee minority children and some indigenous and national minority children[6] in all **Western European countries** and in **Neo-**

Europes. They are likewise used for many Deaf children (instead of Sign language medium education).

In another variant of a submersion programme, powerless majority children (or groups of minority children in a country with no decisive numerical and/or power majorities) are forced to accept instruction through the medium of a foreign (often former colonial) high-status language (because mother tongue medium education does not exist). This often happens in mixed mother tongue classes, mostly without native speakers of the language of instruction. But it also happens in linguistically homogenous classes, sometimes because MT-medium education does not exist and sometimes because the school or the teachers hesitate to implement a MT-medium programme. The teacher may or may not understand the mother tongue of (some of) the children. The foreign language of instruction is not learned to a high level, at the same time as the children's mother tongues are being displaced and not learned either (at all or properly) in formal domains (for instance literacy is not achieved). Often the children are made to feel ashamed of their mother tongues, or at least to believe in the superiority of the language of instruction (see, for instance, Ngũgĩ's writings on this; see also articles in Pütz (ed.) 1995 for attitudes leading to this). Many **African, Latin-American, Asian, and Pacific** countries use such programmes. Two additional contemporary long examples from submersion programmes for groups which have been discussed throughout the book, the Deaf and indigenous Sámi, will be given below.

Some national minorities have their own mother tongue medium schools. The Deaf Communities are also national linguistic minority communities. In some countries, the Deaf also have their own schools, but unlike other national minorities who also have their own schools, the Deaf have in the majority of cases not had much influence on how the education has been organised. Hearing 'experts', teachers, school authorities, social workers, and others have decided—and oralism has in most cases been the result. Most Deaf children who are in schools at all are in regular submersion programmes ('integrated') or are taught through oralist methods (see references to Branson & Miller and Reagan in the bibliography). There are very few schools in the world teaching Deaf children through the medium of Sign languages (see, e.g., Honna & Kato, in press for the difficulties in Japan). Insert 8.2. describes the various sociolinguistic situations of the Deaf, drawing on a classification from Japan. A recent Swedish study (Insert 8.3) shows that submersion for Deaf students seems to produce low self-evaluation and isolation—still there are strong moves in several countries towards an 'inclusive' submersion education.

Two current Sami examples show two different ways of reacting to the assimilation pressure of a submersion programme. Both suffered seriously, both have analysed the causes, and both are fighting the assimilationist system.

The sociolinguistic situations of the Deaf communities and the repertoires among them and in their communication with hearing people show more variation than the corresponding situations and communication among the hearing. The following list of types of situation and repertoires draws on but extends considerably the list describing this diversity in Maher and Yashiro (1995: 8). They use Japanese and JSL (Japanese Sign Language) as examples, but any spoken language can be exchanged for Japanese and any Sign language for JSL to make the list universally valid. Demographically it has to be remembered that some 90–95% of Deaf children are born to hearing parents.

Sociolinguistic situations

1. Usually the most competent signers are **Deaf children of signing Deaf parents. Sign language** is their undisputed **first language** (or mother tongue). They get access to all the benefits of high levels of multilingualism, if they can also have their education through the medium of their Sign language and become additively bilingual or trilingual. This implies learning to read and write another language (e.g., Japanese) or two (e.g., English, Indonesian, Korean, Ainu, etc.). It may possibly also involve learning how to lip read, maybe also speak, to some extent. They can also add other Sign languages (e.g., Auslan, Australian Sign Language, or International Sign) to their repertoire, and for some purposes also Signed Japanese or Signed English. These are varieties which, instead of following the grammar of a Sign language, follow the grammar of a spoken (or written) language but signing them.[7]

2. **Non-deaf children of signing Deaf parents** have also acquired Sign language as their mother tongue but some of them may also have acquired a spoken language very early, either simultaneously (often in families where one parent is Deaf and the other one hearing) or consecutively, and many can thus have two mother tongues. This is the group that the most competent Sign language interpreters often come from.

3. The **Sign language is a second language**. This is true for several groups of signers:

- those who are **postnatally deaf** and acquired oral Japanese as their first language and Sign only afterwards when they became deaf.

- those non-deaf who have learned Sign language later in life out of interest or necessity. A large group is **parents of deaf children** who have learned to sign after the child's deafness was diagnosed. Partners, other family or friends of Deaf people come into this category also. Many teachers and interpreters are also drawn from this group.

(Continued)

• those **deaf people who have not had a chance to learn any Sign language in their early childhood** and/or who have been exposed to orality-oriented approaches where parents, teachers, etc. have tried to teach them to speak and have considered a spoken language as their first language/mother tongue.

It is disputable whether it is possible to call a language somebody's mother tongue that that person cannot have full access to. I have discussed this with many Deaf people who learned to sign only as adults. My own general impression is that most of them feel that their thinking was confused and difficult before they learned to sign; they felt alingual; many express bitterness because they were not given access to Sign language, and many also think that their 'real life' as the individuals they are started with the learning of Sign.

Repertoires:

1. There are varieties of bilingualism, because signers have 'varying degrees of proficiency along the Japanese-JSL interface' (Maher and Yashiro 1995: 8).

2. Pidgins are used for communication between the Deaf and hearing: very few hearing people have learned anything about or of Sign languages, and many Deaf are innovative and flexible in trying to communicate by whatever means they have at their disposal. Pidgins are often the only means of communication between those Deaf children and their hearing parents where the diagnosis of deafness is not (yet) clear or/and where there is no or little contact with Sign languages or the Deaf community, or where the children are exposed to oracy.[8] Pidgin communication is a positive attempt at communicating where no other means are at disposal but it is a crime to force a Deaf child not to have access to a Sign language or otherwise deprive the child of access. Still, this is what is often done (see Muzsnái 1999, for an example from Hungary).

3. There is often a diglossic situation where different languages are used for different purposes. Maher and Yashiro (1995: 8) claim that Japanese is the H (high) language for the bilingual Deaf and JSL is the L (low) language.

All of this shows the low status and lack of linguistic human rights of the Deaf community and Sign languages. The situation of the Deaf is further complicated if a further medium such as signed English or signed Japanese is added—neither of these are 'natural' languages. Likewise, use of 'total communication', e.g., a simultaneous use of oral language and signing, may make communication difficult. The simultaneous use changes the signing so much that it is in fact doubtful whether the signing in 'total communication' can be understood by those Deaf who are not proficient at lip reading or when the spoken language is one which is unsuited for lip reading (as for instance tone languages are).

INSERT 8.3   Continuous 'segregated' education beneficial for Deaf
and hearing-impaired students (Lawenius & Andersson, Sweden)

'Deaf or hearing-impaired youngsters need a stable educational process with
continuity, in order to feel group belonging and social identity.' (Lawenius &
Andersson 1998: 12). A large Swedish empirical study followed 648 secondary
school students in Örebro, 95 deaf and 41 hearing-impaired in what the authors
call 'segregated' schools (i.e., special schools for these groups, schools with
language shelter or language maintenance programmes, see Definition Box
8.5), 24 hearing-impaired in 'integrated' schools (i.e., in submersion programmes, together with hearing students), and 488 hearing students.

The deaf students' self-appreciation in terms of social relations was lower
than that of the other students, and their understanding of written texts was
not as well developed as that of the others. But the 'segregated' (maintenance
programme) students, both Deaf and hearing-impaired, self-evaluated their
knowledge level in relation to school achievement higher than the 'integrated'
students or the hearing students. The 'integrated' students were also more
pessimistic about their own school achievement-related capacities. The
'integrated' (submersion) students were clearly **more socially isolated** than their
hearing peers.

There were many more among the 'segregated' group, especially among
the Deaf students, with a positive identification with the Deaf community,
whereas very few among the 'integrated' group had this identification. Many
of them identified with the hearing, while many at the same time saw their
hearing impairement as a handicap in their communication with the rest of
the world. Those with the most positive self-evaluation often seemed to have
experienced **continuity** in their educational process, whereas the more
ambivalent ones had often had several breaks and changes, with a lack of
correspondence between their own mode of communication and that of the
(educational) environment. All in all, it seems that a continuous 'segregated'
education (i.e., a language shelter programme) was beneficial for Deaf and
hearing-impaired students.

Johan Mathis Mikkelsen Gavppi, son of the last traditional shaman in
the Nordic countries, refused to assimilate, despite extreme pressure. The
only alternative was to play truant from a school which did nothing to teach
him in a meaningful way (he knew no Norwegian when he started and the
teacher knew no Sámi). The long-term result was 'illiteracy' and financial
hardship. He could not be confirmed, or do his military service, because of
not being able to read. He tried as a grown-up to reclaim what the school
had prevented him from learning. He learned how to read and write in
Norwegian, together with his children, from their elementary readers, with
the help of his wife, because he felt ashamed at not being able to help his
children with elementary reading and maths.

He decided that he wanted to read at least one whole book, even if it would be the only book he read during his life-time. His choice fell on the perfect one: **Makt og kunnskap** (Power and knowledge) by Anton Hoëm. This is a doctoral dissertation about the history of Sámi education. It took him about a year to read the book.

He decided to learn how to read and write Sámi too. Learning mother tongue literacy improved his Norwegian considerably, he claims, and also enabled him to study for A-levels where he passed in most subjects required. He was accepted at the University of Alta with a dispensation. His MA thesis was one of the best at the university.[9]

He also wanted the assimilationist society to compensate for his loss. He started the first court case in the world in which a representative of an indigenous minority claimed compensation from the state for his loss of language (and culture). He lost the case in all three Norwegian courts—the case was deemed obsolete. The European Commission on Human Rights refused to hear it on the same grounds (see Skutnabb-Kangas 1989 and Skutnabb-Kangas & Phillipson 1989a, Chapter 11, 'The Gávppi court case', for details of the case). Sámi is a Finno-Ugric language. In contrast to the Germanic epics and sagas (Edda, Niebelungenlied, etc.), in the Finnish national epic **Kalevala** all the mythical fights are fought with words not arms—see also Insert 2.1). To me it is symptomatic that it was the son of a shaman who started this struggle about language in court, with the help of words. The father, Mikkel Gaup, of course supported his son, and both have also been active in making their peers aware of land rights.

Maybe a younger person goes to court with a similar claim, demanding compensation for the loss of their language—dear reader, please support indigenous people in your country who might consider going to court!

Johannes Marainen (Insert 8.4) was forcibly assimilated during his school time, and started only later in life to question the assimilation. He also tried to reclaim his heritage, mainly working on his own on recovering his mother tongue and identity, but without asking the assimilationist society for compensation through courts for his loss.

More examples of submersion education and its results will follow when the change from submersion to mother tongue medium education is discussed. Likewise, the discussion about the constant postponing of reaching UPE (Universal Primary Education) below has examples. But first we define the last non-form, segregation, and the transitional weak forms of bilingual education.

8.3.2.3. *Segregation Programmes*

Under apartheid, **Namibian** and **South African** programmes in the mother tongues of the children were prototypes of segregation. So were the mother tongue medium classes and schools for Turkish children in many German

Johannes Marainen 'grew up in Saarivuoma, one of the Sami villages within Kiruna, in northernmost Sweden. It is no use to look for this village on the maps, it isn't there. Sami villages are of no interest to the Swedes, they exist in reality only for us Sami. Actually they are not villages but large areas within which groups of Sami move with their reindeer' (Marainen 1988: 179). Johannes Marainen now works as a researcher for the Sami Instituhtta (The Nordic Sámi Institute). The following extracts come from a short story called 'Returning to Sami identity' (1988: 179–185).

As a child I had the opportunity to live and grow in an intact Sami environment. All of us in my village depended solely on our herds of reindeer, and our way of living was still fairly uninfluenced by the Swedish society. We had our own language and our own culture and lived our own lives.

When I started school I took my first step away from my Sami environment . . . I went to first grade in a summer- or tent school. The school looked exactly like my own home. It was a tent, made of canvas, stretched over tall slender birch poles with an opening for the smoke in the middle. We sat on boughs around the open fire with a slate or a book on our outstretched legs . . .

Culturally and linguistically the school was a shock to me. "Mother tongue" was the dominating subject during the first school years, but I did not understand until much later that "tongue" means language. The word "mother tongue" did not mean anything to me, I just accepted that it meant Swedish. "Eatnangiella", my mother's language, it definitely was not.

Like all the other beginners I did not understand a single word of the "mother tongue" and it would take many years before I was able to speak it. During school time we were not allowed to use our own language, not even during recess. We were supposed to become "mother tongued" as soon as possible . . .

I soon learned that outside of school it was better for me to demonstrate my Sami roots as little as possible. Despite that, I was called 'Sami devil' every day. I tried to pretend that I did not hear, but each time a thorn stuck into my heart, and eventually I carried inside me a whole forest of thorns. I tried to supress my feelings and wrapped all the thorns into all kinds of excuses, so they wouldn't hurt anymore. The worst of it was that all this Sami hate was concealed, nobody wanted to show their contempt openly. There were lots of Kiruna dwellers, who were unaware that it existed and who would have been hurt if someone had mentioned that there was Sami hate in Kiruna . . .

The "mother tongue" became our language when we were together in town. Our own language was used only in our boarding rooms and in the Lapp Inn, which was the only hotel in those days which accepted Sami, and the Lapp cafe.

(Continued)

Thus I felt like a stranger among the Swedes and, unfortunately, felt a little bit like a stranger with my people who remained in the Sami village . . . I was no longer sharing their lives as active reindeer herders. They, on their side, were ignorant of my experiences in my new school.

We Sami in town learned fast that the best, and certainly the easiest, way to cope was to adapt, and as far as possible become Swedish. Unfortunately this drove many of us to self-denial. Once I saw some Sami youths purposely avoiding their parents in order not to demonstrate their Sami origin. It hurt me unbelievably and filled me with feelings of shame. To be absolutely honest, it could have been me who felt forced to act the same way! It is painful to remember that it was quite often necessary for me to force myself not to deny myself, which to me felt extremely humiliating. I continued my studies and accepted myself as more or less Swedish . . . In time I became teacher of the "mother tongue" in a high school in Gothenburg, and I felt quite content with my life. I had not been discriminated against. I had received the same good education as other Swedes. I had a job which I liked. Did I have anything to complain about?

I soon realized that as a Sami, I was considered an exotic being in Gothenburg. There were requests that I give lectures on Sami. I hesitated long before I dared to stand up and talk, because in reality I knew nothing about Samis, nothing about my people. All I knew about were my own experiences.

At last, I agreed to give a lecture, and in order to remedy my ignorance, I went to a library and borrowed a book about Samis. As I was reading the book I realized for the first time that we Sami indeed had our own history! I had not been allowed to read my history in nomad school. I had learned about King Karl, the young hero, and other brave Swedish kings, who had made the Swedish name fly in honor over the earth. For my history, it might possibly even have been favourable if the tyrant Danish King Christian had kept Sweden.

Well, my father happened to be visiting when I held my first lecture on Sami in Gothenburg. As we were returning home, I asked him what he had thought of my speech. He answered: "Well, I did not understand much of what you said, but they did applaud, so I assume that it was good." The answer did not surprise me, and I decided to translate my speech into Sami language for him. It was then that I got my life's greatest shock! I realized that "mother tongue" had taken over my "eatnangiella". I realized in horror that I COULD NO LONGER IN MY OWN LANGUAGE RELATE THE MOST COMMON AND EVERYDAY MATTERS!

That was the first time since I grew up that I realized the negative sides of my becoming Swedish. I started to comprehend that the Swedish

(Continued)

Educational System had robbed me of something valuable, yes, maybe the most valuable thing I had owned: my language.

I can no longer talk to Father! This fact made me shiver. I became desperate, despondent. And then I became angry.

I had imagined that I still knew the Sami language, but due to the disrupted contact with my Sami environment and culture, my language had not developed in a natural way. I realized that I stood on a level comparable to a 7-year old's linguistic capabilities. I could still talk about certain matters in Sami, but I was not able to keep a conversation or a discussion going.

As I was unable to develop my language in natural daily contact with other Sami, the school should have given me a chance to study my language. But what had it done instead?

It had forced a new "mother tongue" upon me. I had been robbed of my language, my own history and my own culture. The school had substituted something that was now well known to me. What was foreign to me was I, myself. I felt cheated!

I realized that the first thing to do was to study my own language. I asked for leave of absence in order to study Sami, but that was not granted. A "mother tongue" teacher asking for time off in order to study his mother tongue! Unthinkable! So, instead, I studied my language at night as I kept working and teaching . . .

The most difficult part of my journey to my roots remained. I had to find my way to my Sami identity. I felt obliged to go back and analyze my development. I had to understand how the transformation from Sami to Swede had happened. I forced myself to remember all the bitter experiences which had made me choose the easiest road: accepting myself as Swedish and living like other Swedes. I went through all the painful memories as I tried to understand and realize what had happened. I no longer tried to erase, forget, and hide, nor did I pretend not to hear any more.

It was hard enough to accept myself, but it was harder still to explain myself to others. I felt shame and guilt because I had betrayed my people. My people and myself. It hurt to remember and it was painful to tell others. I did it because I felt it was necessary for me, and maybe I could help others who were looking for THEIR identity . . .

I am a Sami among Swedes. I do not feel that I belong with them the way I feel with Sami from Norway or Finland. Our Samiland is divided by national borders, yet *Samieatnam*/Samiland does not know of any borders between all of us Sami in the North. There are no borders on our maps.

(Continued)

INSERT 8.4 *(Continued)*

In my warm, mild mother tongue foreign words intertwine.
Become a memory you trampled earth
where my tent stood and I played.
The sound of the bells hanging around the necks of my Father's reindeer
has remained in the bottom of my soul.
Grown into my retina is our reindeer mark.
Everything I felt is part of my heart.
Remain in my memory; Father's staff,
lasso of sinew, loop in the edge of the sleigh,
the round-up and moving of the deer, the sled with the fare
Down by the river is the half load waiting for the baby.
Still moving up the valley,
remember the slender bow above the neck of the pack reindeer
Hold on to the land you inherited with all your heart!

But the right to the land, you have lost.
[poem by] Paulus Utsi.

---

inner cities, for instance in Bavaria, in 'guest worker' education (see my 1984a for descriptions).[10]

DEFINITION BOX 8.3   Segregation

A **segregation** model is a programme where linguistic minority children with a low-status mother tongue are forced to accept instruction through the medium of their own mother tongue in classes with minority children (with the same mother tongue) only, where the teacher may be monolingual or bilingual but is often poorly trained, where the class/school has poorer facilities and fewer resources than classes/schools for dominant group children (see Info Box 6.10), and where the teaching of the dominant language as a second/foreign language is poor or non-existent.

In several aspects, segregation programmes give the children at least some chance of learning their own language to some extent, i.e., they may be a better alternative than submersion programmes. This means that apartheid South Africa gave Black children **in some respects** a better chance than what Canada or the USA or Denmark or Finland today give to immigrant minority children. In several books and articles (e.g., 1984a, 1986, 1988, 1990a) I have compared the factors influencing the outcomes of various programmes, and segregation certainly has a somewhat better record than submersion.[11] It does not make children high level bilingual, though, and many of the societal consequences are disastrous.

Among the main differences between the two mother tongue medium programmes, segregation and maintenance, are the following (for details, see, e.g., my 1990: 17–21):

- existence of alternative programmes (no for segregation, yes for maintenance);
- well-trained teachers (segregation programmes usually do not have them, maintenance usually do);
- culturally appropriate materials (segregation programmes often do not have these; materials are either racist, as in South Africa, or they are imported from the country of origin and do not describe the children's reality. Maintenance programmes often produce their own materials);
- negative (segregation) or positive (maintenance) learner-related affective factors, in relation to anxiety, motivation, self-confidence, teacher expectations, etc.;
- good subject matter teaching, also in both languages (not usual in segregation, often present in maintenance);
- opportunity to practice L2 in peer group contexts outside school (in segregation usually prevented by racism or lack of L2 peers or not enough knowledge of L2, while this is often specifically organised in the early years in maintenance, often through cooperation agreements etc.).

Often politicians and policy-makers who block or argue against mother tongue medium maintenance programmes, do so under cover of a fear of segregation (the 'segregation fallacy' above). In some cases, the fear may be genuine, and the policy-makers are completely ignorant about the differences between the two programme types. In many if not most cases, the reasons lie elsewhere and 'segregation' is just a convenient pretext.

8.3.3. Weak Models of Bilingual Education— Transitional Early-Exit and Late-Exit Programmes

Next we move to weak models of bilingual education.

A transitional programme is a more sophisticated version of submersion programmes, a more 'humane' way of assimilating. Early-exit programmes are used to some extent in the education of migrant minority children in some of the settings where there is broad opposition against submersion and some political space for trying out alternatives. There are a few programmes in Sweden, the Netherlands, USA, Australia, and so on (see, e.g., Reid & Reich

DEFINITION BOX 8.4   Transitional early-exit and late-exit

A **transitional** programme is a programme where linguistic minority children with a low-status mother tongue are initially instructed through the medium of their mother tongue for a few years and where their mother tongue is taught as though it has no intrinsic value, only an instrumental value. It is used only in order for the children to learn the majority language better, and so as to give them some subject matter (content) knowledge while they are learning the majority language. In **early-exit** programmes, children are transferred to a majority language medium programme as soon as they can function to some extent in the majority language orally, in most cases after 1 or 2, at the most 3, years. In **late-exit** programmes they may continue to have at least some of their education, sometimes up to half of it, in L1 up to the 5th or 6th grade, and sometimes the mother tongue may be taught as a subject even after that.

1992 for Europe). They are also used in parts of India, 'anglophone' Africa, Latin America, etc. Late-exit programmes for immigrant minorities are still very rare but somewhat more common for national minorities and some indigenous peoples—but even for these, submersion is the most common model used.

It may be harsh for some educationists who work in transitional programmes (which they have really fought to get started—see Insert 8.5 for an example) that the programmes are seen as assimilationist.

Still, assimilation and strong dominance in the majority language have in most cases been the goals of school authorities in all transitional programmes.

INSERT 8.5   Means used to get a transitional programme
started in Calistoga, California

In Calistoga, California, a rural community of some 3,500 people, the parents and teachers wanted bilingual education, the School Board and the Superintendent did not. One response was that teachers were formally forbidden to use any Spanish in the classroom. Parents and teachers had to enlist the help of the District Parent Advisory Committee, lawyers from California Rural Legal Assistance, and others, file a complaint with the USA Office for Civil Rights, charging the district with discriminatory practices, try to force the unwilling California State Department of Education to enforce compliance with State law, force the Superintendent of Schools to resign as a face-saving measure, and so on. In the end, the parents and teachers succeeded in implementing transitional bilingual education for the initial years of schooling (see Curtis 1988).

This inevitably happens at the cost of the dominated mother tongues. Sometimes the goal is openly acknowledged by the school authorities, often not. Often false (negative) conclusions have been drawn about what is called 'bilingual education' on the basis of early-exit transitional programmes.

Minorities and indigenous peoples, the dominated groups, have often had as their goal the maintenance of their own languages and good learning of the dominant languages, i.e., high levels of bilingualism or multilingualism. In Australia, for instance, in the mid-1970s

> bilingual programs were introduced into schools throughout the Northern Territory, but language maintenance was not a primary goal of these programs, at least not from the perspective of the NT Education Department. Rather, they were transitional bilingual programs and as such were fundamentally assimilationist, their primary aim being to facilitate the acquisition of English. Later on, however, especially as Aboriginal peoples gained more control over education and schools in their communities, language maintenance did become a main aim (Amery 1998: 93).

At the beginning of 1999, a decision was made to close down the bilingual programmes in NT. A lot of protests have followed, also internationally.

Early-exit transitional programmes show often (but not always) better results than submersion programmes, as, for instance, several Dutch, Swedish and North American evaluations show. But the positive results are often limited to psychological gains: self-confidence, security, better home-school cooperation. Often the programmes are phased out so early that they make virtually no difference for the children's school achievement or linguistic competence (not even in the mother tongue and even less in L2). On the other hand, these are not often measured.

Late-exit progammes show, almost without exception, better results than submersion. But few large-scale evaluations have been made. This is partly because the programmes are still rare. Partly the type of evaluation which lives up to positivistic criteria is not only very costly but also difficult or close to impossible to organise in many if not most countries. In a large American longitudinal study (Ramirez et al. 1991) those Spanish-speaking children who had most Spanish-medium and least English-medium education were the best ones in English language tests. The Ramirez study has been presented and its details and implications discussed extensively in the United States (including whole journal numbers—e.g., a double number, 16:1&2, 1992, of **Bilingual Research Journal**, and symposia devoted to it). Dutcher & Tucker 1997 give a solid overview of some early- and late-exit programmes worldwide, as did Dutcher 1982. Anne-Sophie Oudin (1996) gives a thorough overview of multilingual programmes in European Union countries which includes transitional programmes. Jenniges (ed.) 1997 is a very useful bibliography.

The non-forms and weak forms of 'bilingual education' will in the following section be related to literacy and Universal Primary Education (UPE).

8.3.4. Universal Primary Education (UPE)
and the Non-Forms and Weak Forms

There is massive evidence to support the claim that use of the wrong medium of education (i.e., non-forms or weak forms of bilingual education, rather than mother tongue medium education) is the main **pedagogical** reason for 'illiteracy' in the world.[12] Global figures for 'illiteracy', both absolute and functional,[13] are notoriously both unreliable and extremely difficult to interpret. Definitions of all types of literacy and 'illiteracy' and the uses these are being put to are also becoming much more sophisticated (see, e.g., Street 1994). The general picture is that while the percentages of 'illiterates' are slowly going down in most countries, the absolute numbers are increasing. A large proportion of the world's orates are female, but the gender gap is diminishing somewhat. According to the **UN Human Development Report 1998** (see Address Box 6.1), presenting the 1995 figures, the 64 countries labelled 'high human development' have a mean adult literacy rate of 95.69% (95.23% for women, 96.16% for men). The rate for the 66 'medium human development' countries is 83.25% (W 76.93%, M 89.53%) and that for the 44 'low' countries is 50.85% (W 38.34%, M 62.96%). The world mean for the 174 countries in the Report is 77.58% (W 71.48%, M 83.71%).

Unesco's **Statistical Yearbook 1998** gives another set of figures, the estimated number of adult illiterates distributed by region and gender for 1995 (the latest estimate) as follows: Sub-Saharan Africa 140.5 million (women form 62% of the illiterates, men 38%); the Arab States 65.5m (W 63%, M 37%); Eastern Asia/Oceania 209.9m (W 71%, M 29%); Southern Asia 415.5m (W 62%, M 38%); Latin America/Caribbean 42.9m (W 55%, M 45%); Developed Countries 12.9m (W 62%, M 38%). The earlier Unesco **Yearbook 1997** presented the general information on 'illiteracy' only for 132 out of the 231 countries and territories. The **Yearbook 1998** has altogether 224 countries and territories, and it gives estimates for illiteracy only for 137 countries, i.e., not many more than the 1997 version. The 1995 estimate information is missing for 7 countries in Africa, 12 in North America (including the USA), none in South America, 17 in Asia (including Japan), all 41 in Europe, and 10 in Oceania, totally 87 countries, but there are statistics from the countries themselves, for most of them (the Nordic countries and a few others are totally missing). There is a more detailed Unesco **Compendium of statistics on illiteracy, Edition 1995**.

'Illiteracy' is rapidly increasing in many of the 'developed' countries (like Sweden, UK, USA, France, West Germany), mainly because of the immigrant population. Many adults, especially women, have immigrated as orates and have either not had any literacy classes in the new country or else reading and writing has been attempted in the L2, a situation which has notoriously been a failure. And young immigrants have been and are being miseducated, as this book shows.

There is no direct language-related information on 'illiteracy' in the Unesco Statistical Yearbook. Indirectly, some countries give language-related information, by excluding what they call 'tribal', 'nomadic' or 'Indian' populations. But that is all. We thus lack even basic global statistical information on the mother tongues of the world's 'illiterates'.

There are many analyses of causes of 'illiteracy', of what could be done and what is being done. What is still lacking is reliable information about how large a percentage of the 'illiterates' in the world belong to populations who, if they were to go to schools or courses, would have to accept instruction through the medium of a second or foreign language and how many are absolutely or, especially, functionally 'illiterate' because they have been taught through the medium of a foreign or second language. Still, it is reasonably safe to estimate that the wrong educational language planning policy, which results in education through the medium of a foreign language, has been and is the main **pedagogical** cause for 'illiteracy' in the world (economic, political, and social factors are of course decisive for people to get any formal education in the first place).

This also means that functional 'illiteracy' in particular will not be eradicated unless most of the mother tongues in the world are developed, at least to some extent, as languages for literacy. This is a huge but absolutely necessary task, and the issue is complex. Peter Mühlhäusler, for instance, shows convincingly that reducing what people speak to writing also contributes to reduction of linguistic diversity (1996). Certain varieties are chosen for the standardisation needed for the reduction to writing, and others are thus excluded. I am sure he is right. The question is whether there are alternatives. Could, for instance, some kind of functional differentiation between maintenance of diversity of spoken languages and learning of written school languages work in communities with a strong enough multilingualism and multilingual ethos (see Khubchandani for this concept)? I doubt it—that kind of diglossia is exactly what has killed spoken mother tongues.

The whole concept of 'literacy' is also a murky one, and has undergone several redefinitions, from simple reading and writing, to UPE to functional literacy and now also to basic computer literacy (e.g., Street (ed.) 1993, Rassool 1999). Just like 'development', or 'knowledge of the English language', 'literacy' has been held up in front of people from underdeveloped countries as a panacea: once you reach this, most of your problems will be solved. The point is, of course, that as soon as enough people from the B team reach the goal so that the rewards should start coming, a new goal is presented for them—they suffer from a new deficiency, and once they have overcome that one . . .

When former colonial countries became independent, one of the most important educational goals was the achievement of Universal Primary Education (UPE), including literacy, as soon as possible. Many hoped that the educational damage from the colonial period could be remedied fast. For instance India wrote in the Constitution of 1947 that a general 8-year education for all was the goal by 1960. In the 1960s most regions of the world where UPE did not exist formulated their goals at ministerial meetings, initiated by Unesco. For Asia they were formulated in Karachi 1960, for Africa in Addis Ababa in 1961, for Latin America in Santiago in 1962 and for the Arab world in Tripoli in 1966. UPE should be achieved by 1980, according to most plans, for Latin-America already by 1970. UPE was seen as a human right, which had been formulated already in Article 26 of the UN **Declaration of Human Rights**, which essentially affirms everybody's right to education. This has to be both free and obligatory at the elementary stage. Today, in 1999, UPE has again been postponed, this time until the year 2015 . . .

But the Declaration of Human Rights does not specify in which language(s) this education should be conducted. Neither do many planning reports. We can take Africa as an example. The historical record tell us (see Phillipson 1992 and Cawson 1975 for overviews) that there was a focus on mother tongue literacy earlier. Many reports in the colonial period stressed the mother tongue. Unesco's 1953 report **Vernacular languages in education**, based on an expert meeting in 1952, saw it as axiomatic that the mother tongue was the best medium for education, at least during elementary education (UNESCO 1953: 6). The Unesco experts used linguistic, psychological, pedagogical, and sociological arguments in order to show why the mother tongues were to be used. The critics of the Unesco recommendation, on the other hand, in the lively debate which followed the publication of Unesco's report, accused the recommendation of naivety and used mainly political and economic arguments (see, e.g., Bull 1955). These political and economic arguments can now, with hindsight, be summed up as belonging under the leaky umbrella of nation-building and development education, respectively.

With this focus on literacy through the medium of the mother tongues in mind, it is amazing that there is not one word about language in the main body of the 1961 Addis Ababa report. Countrywise African educational reports 'either ignored the language situation altogether or made a few routine references to improving the teaching of English' (Cawson 1975: 412; this article comes from the most comprehensive survey of aid policy in underdeveloped countries in the language and education field, conducted for the Ford Foundation). The reports for Malawi 1960 (3 pages out of 360 on language), Uganda 1963 (3 of 83), Ghana 1967 (1 of 160), Nigeria 1960 (5 lines of 8,000) (ibid., 412–413) do not mention the 1,200 to 2,000 African mother tongues in their countries at all. The few remarks on mother tongues in the Kenya report 1964–1965 (5 paragraphs out of 531 on language) are 'negative, and a reversal came only in 1976. One explanation (but there are many) of the language policy in the Kenya Report 1964–65 is that the majority of those who submitted views were expatriates in the education system and in policy making positions in 1964/5', writes the Kenyan linguist/educationist Anna Obura (personal communication). Still, it must have been clear to policy planners, that 'a great deal of drop-outs and failure cases in schools in Africa are due to lack of ability to manipulate the language of education adequately' as Gilbert Ansre points out in an article where he shows that the arguments for maintaining European languages as media of education in Africa are false (1979: 13). Kwesi Prah, Neville Alexander, Kathleen Heugh, and many others have also shown this many times, echoing what Debi Prasanna Pattanayak, Annamalai, and others have said for India.

It seems that many literacy experts also have a somewhat shaky knowledge about language matters. One of Unesco's main experts in the 1980s, Professor H. S. Bhola, wrote, for instance, in his book **Campaigning for literacy** (1984), on the only page devoted to language, that 'literacy in a language other than the national language may doom those involved to a limited, parochial and marginal existence' (1984: 191). This could of course be labelled the **parochial fallacy**'. In claiming that 'a single language of literacy has contributed to the success of mass literacy campaigns in Burma, China, Cuba, the United Republic of Tanzania and Somalia, to give only a few examples' (ibid., 191) he has chosen some of the few countries with either few linguistic minorities or else an extremely widely understood lingua franca. He has 'forgotten' that this type of a situation does not apply in the large majority of the world's countries. The single language of literacy succeeds only in countries which have a very large majority speaking that language either as their native tongue, or as a really well known lingua franca, i.e., the success can be attributed to mother tongue literacy rather than single language literacy. A single language of literacy is a disaster in most multilingual contexts, as many quotes from Pattanayak in this book have shown. Bhola also claims (p. 191) that there are in India 'some fourteen languages spoken . . . , each by millions of people', meaning he acknowleges less than 1 percent of the 1652 languages listed by the 1961 census (see Info Boxes 1.5 and 5.7 for some figures on languages in India).

We know that UPE is still very far from being a reality. The net enrollment ratio in elementary education among the 6–11 year olds was 63% for Africa, 66% for Asia, and 81% for Latin America in 1980 (Coombs 1985: 80). In 1980, the gross enrollment ratio for elementary education (which can be 15–20% higher than the net enrollment ratio, because of the discrepancy between the appropriate age for every class level) was under 50% in 15 countries (mostly in Africa) and under 80% in 35 countries (Unesco 1983). In addition to the children who never come to school, reaching the goal of (absolute or functional) literacy is hindered by the large numbers of children who drop out before finishing their primary education. It has been assessed that achieving a lasting minimal level of literacy requires at least 4 years of schooling (Simmons 1980: 44–45). This was, in fact, conventional wisdom already back in the 1950s, when the Nuffield Foundation & Colonial office (1953: 77) concluded their large review of West and East African educational policies and practices by estimating that 'for children who completed less than four years of schooling, no lasting literacy benefits materialised and the experience of school could well be psychologically damaging'. According to Unesco statistics (see UNESCO 1980) the proportion of children who drop out before grade 4 was over 50% in 12 countries and between 25–50% in 32 countries. On the other hand, there are no clear-cut correlations between the rate of drop-outs on the one hand and the gross enrollment ratio or the gross national product on the other (Wastage . . . 1984, World Bank 1980).

The figures become even more disturbing if functional literacy is defined as including 6 years of education (which is the most common current usage, but figures of up to 12 years have been suggested—see also the series of books from the Unesco Institute for Education (Hamburg) on Post-literacy and Continuing Education).

It is claimed here that one of the main reasons for the minimal success of UPE and global literacy has been the linguicist educational policy, where, in the name of the political and economic arguments of 'nation building' and 'modernisation', education has been attempted through the medium of a language foreign to a majority of the pupils, against pedagogical, psychological, linguistic, and sociological arguments. Paradoxically, then, Unesco has been supporting a policy which its own expert groups already in the early 1950s saw as unfit. Yet the political and economic arguments used against mother tongue medium education seem to have been more naive than the 'naive', 'romantic' and 'utopian' linguistic, psychological, pedagogical, and sociological arguments for mother tongue medium education.

Without acknowleging the decisive role of mother tongues, and without a more informed assessment of language questions in general, there is little hope to achieve Universal Primary Education and functional literacy. This having been said, reaching global literacy and UPE is of course a complex goal where the medium of education, despite its vitality, is just one of the causal factors and has to be combined with analyses in many areas. The difficulties involved in doing this can also be seen in most books dealing with literacy—see, for example, Coulmas (ed.) 1984.

Alternative theories, looking at multiliteracies and the uses people make or do not make of them (see Street 1993, 1994, Rassool 1999), have been and are being developed. Some of these question the usefulness of mother tongue literacy or even literacy in general for speakers of numerically small threatened languages, if the speakers want to maintain their languages (see Mühlhäusler 1990, 1996). Others question formal education as a road towards development or the role of literacy in getting access to books and literature. Already a quarter of a century ago, Hanf et al. (1975: 76) claimed that

'optimistic assumptions about the contribution of formal education to the building of modern nations are questionable with regard to the functions of education in political recruitment, socialization and integration', and claim that 'formal education in Africa and Asia in its present form tends to impede economic growth and promote political instability; in short, education in Africa and Asia today is an obstacle to development' (ibid., 68).

Ivan Illich, in his long introductory essay in Debi Pattanayaks book **Multilingualism and Mother-Tongue Education**, discusses the development of silent reading, which in fact is a recent invention. Earlier, books were read aloud, as a natural continuation of oracy, and they often had a large audience:

> In most of the languages of India, the verb that translates into 'reading' has a meaning close to 'sounding'. The same verb makes the book and the vina [kind of violin] sound. To read and to play a musical instrument are perceived as parallel activities. The current, simple-minded, internationally accepted definition of literacy obscures an alternate approach to book, print, and reading. If reading were conceived primarily as a social activity as, for example, competence in playing the guitar, fewer readers could mean a much broader access to books and literature. (Illich 1981: 13)

Other alternative theories want, for instance, to put 'satisfying basic human needs' instead of 'economic growth' as the goal in development policy (as described in 6.4). These may seem to some equally naive and utopian as the UNESCO expert group recommendations about mother tongues as the axiomatically best media of education seemed to some critics. But that is where the hope lies. Utopias may in the long run be our most realistic alternative if we want the planet to survive.

If strong forms of multilingual education were used, literacy rates would climb up in hitherto unprecedented ways. Implementing these forms is not utopian at all as the next section shows.

8.4. STRONG FORMS OF BILINGUAL AND MULTILINGUAL EDUCATION

Many people might agree that indigenous and minority children **in principle** should enjoy the same linguistic and educational human rights which most linguistic majority children enjoy. But when one makes some of these rights **concrete** and suggests that the Hague Recommendations should be implemented (for instance: all Kurdish children in Germany should have their basic education, at least primary and lower secondary education, through the medium of their mother tongue, Kurdish), counterarguments suggest that this is impossible **in practice**. It is therefore important to show that strong forms of multilingual education in fact work in practice—it is not just something that romantic but naive researchers have dreamed up.

8.4.1. Language (Mother Tongue) Maintenance or Language Shelter Programmes

First we define the strong programmes.

DEFINITION BOX 8.5 Language (mother tongue) maintenance or language shelter

A **language maintenance** programme or **language shelter** programme is a programme where linguistic minority children (often with a low-status mother tongue) voluntarily choose (among existing alternatives) to be instructed through the medium of their own mother tongue, in classes with minority children with the same mother tongue only, where the teacher is bilingual (almost always in the case of immigrant and refugee minorities and indigenous peoples; not always (but often) to the same extent in the case of national minorities) and where they get good teaching in the majority language as a second/foreign language, also given by a bilingual teacher.

The purpose of this type of multilingual programme is to ensure that language minority children continue to maintain and develop their mother tongue up to either a native level (national minorities, indigenous peoples) or at least near-native level (immigrant minorities); that they learn the majority language at a native (immigrant minorities; indigenous peoples) or near-native (national minorities) level; become biliterate; and achieve academically. In a European context, they typically also learn additional foreign languages.

For a few national minorities, maintenance programmes are a self-evident, 'normal' way of educating their children, a natural human right—many of them never think of the fact that they are in a maintenance programme. It is revealing that most minorities of this type, for example, the Swedish-speakers in Finland, Afrikaans- and English-speakers in South Africa, or Russian-speakers in Estonia, Latvia, and Lithuania, are either former power minorities and/or are in a transitional phase where they have to accept the fact that they no longer have the power to impose their will on a numerical majority, but where they still have the power to organize their own children's education through the medium of their own language.[14] Several European countries have maintenance programmes for the most established national minorities,[15] and the Nordic countries are building them up for indigenous Sámi. The European Charter for Regional or Minority Languages can provide some support for national minorities, but it is an open question whether all national minorities will be accepted as such. Several countries are contesting the principle for some minorities (e.g., Italy for Sardinians, France (until 1998) and Greece for most, and the Turks deny that they have any minorities, at any rate when this book goes to press).

Those who want to know how mother tongue medium education works for minorities when it is well established, should look into the education of the national minorities. A good example is Finland Swedes, Swedish-speakers in **Finland** (less than 6% of the population). Swedish is their medium of education (see Info Box 7.3 on the number of students needed for this), and they/we learn both languages, but the competence in Finnish, the dominant language, depends to a large extent on the demography of the place where they live, and on peer-group contact with Finnish-speakers outside school. They do as well as Finnish-speakers in their A-level matriculation exam (where both groups, Finnish and Swedish speakers, also have to take an exam in each others' languages), and they do better in English than Finnish-speakers, despite in most cases starting English 2 years later than the Finnish-speakers. As high level bilinguals learn a third language better and faster than corresponding monolinguals or low level bilinguals (e.g., Swain et al. 1990), this is to be expected. Of course it also helps that their mother tongue, Swedish, is related to English: both are Indo-European.

Of course, it should be a fundamental, self-evident linguistic and educational human right for **any** ethnolinguistic minority to use its own language as the main medium for teaching and learning. But in fact most minorities in the world do not have this basic right. For indigenous and immigrant minorities getting access to maintenance programmes has been and is a struggle where few have succeeded so far.[16] A few indigenous peoples (who are mostly numerically a minority in their own countries) have maintenance programmes.[17] Most of them do not (see, e.g., Hamel 1994a, b). Most immigrant and refugee minority children do not have access to maintenance programmes either. A few European countries have maintenance programmes for some immigrated minorities. The programmes are contested in most countries and have to struggle to survive. Australia does not have full maintenance programmes for any minorities or indigenous peoples in the state-financed education system.

Info Boxes 8.2 through 8.6. give examples from one indigenous people (Māori in Aotearoa) and one immigrant minority (Finns in Sweden) moving from submersion to early-exit to late-exit transitional programmes, and finally to maintenance programmes. There are also two examples of protection of educational language rights for indigenous peoples (James Bay Cree and Inuits in Quebec, Canada) and for national minorities (Hungary).

Maintenance models naturally lead to high levels of linguistic competence in the minority language. The results in the dominant language depend on several factors (see the tenets/fallacies in 8.1).

In my longitudinal study (see Insert 8.1; also Insert 5.30) I used CALP-type language tests in both languages. They differentiated extremely well (with a scale from 1–13, the means were around 5,5, with fairly high standard deviations—see Skutnabb-Kangas 1987 for details). After 9 years in a Finnish-medium maintenance programme, the Finnish working class immigrant minority children in **Sweden** showed somewhat better results ($M = 5.68$) on the Swedish language test than Swedish middle class children in parallel

The Māori in Aotearoa/New Zealand

The only indigenous numerical[18] minority group in the world which has succeeded in getting its language accepted as a full official language is Māori in Aotearoa/New Zealand (Sámi has regional official status in Norway and Finland). It received official status in 1987, by the Māori Language Act (1987, No. 176). The situation of the Māori was better than that of the Aboriginal peoples in Australia from the beginning of the colonisation—there were negotiations and treaties. When a 'Westminster-style government was established after 1852 its proceedings were recorded both in Māori and in English' **(Finding of the Waitangi Tribunal . . . 1986: 12).**

Still, the same type of demographic development can be seen initially in both contexts. When Europeans first went ashore in the 18th century in Aotearoa, there were 220,000–250,000 Māori (Macdonald 1985: 4). In 1840, when the Treaty of Waitangi was signed, the Europeans comprised less than 1% of the population. 20 years later, at the time of the Land Wars, the European and Māori populations were more or less equal. By 1896 'the Māori population of New Zealand had declined from well over 100,000 people to 42,100. It seemed that the Māori was dying out' **(Finding of the Waitangi Tribunal . . . 1986: 12).**

The Māori population started to increase rapidly from the beginning of this century, due, among other things, to better health control, and had increased to 385,000 in 1981 (ibid., 13). In the early 1980s, the prediction was that within a generation, the Māori population (then around 10%) might account for over 30% of New Zealand's population (ibid., 21), with the present definition of Māori (a person with Māori ancestry who feels himself/herself to be Māori). This has not happened—in the 1991 census 12.9% of the population identified as Māori (Benton 1996: 64).

The Māori language continued to decline, though, and education played a decisive part in this, including the practice of corporally punishing the children when they spoke Māori, even in the playground (Benton 1979, 1981, **Finding of the Waitangi Tribunal . . . 1986: 13).** In 1913, 90% of Māori school children could speak Māori. In 1953 the figure had dropped to 26%, and in 1975 it was less than 5% (ibid., 15). The survival of Māori depended on the existence of isolated rural communities and traditional villages. According to Dr. Richard Benton's testimony (ibid., 16–17; see also Benton 1986, 1996) it was 'apparent that the expectation that the language would survive because of those villages is not realistic'.

Today there is a strong revitalisation movement for the Māori language and education plays a vital part in it. 1982 was a turning point. The first 50 'Kōhanga Reo' pre-schools, 'language nests', using the Māori language as the medium, and building on Māori culture, started in December 1982, and by

(Continued)

(Continued)

March 1988 they had increased to 521, reaching 15% of Māori children under 5 and aiming to increase this to 75% within the next 10 years (Te Whakamatau ... 1988: 19). Māori elders are also teaching young parents the Māori language and culture in Kōhanga Reo. In 1993 there were 809 of these centres, with 14,514 students (Benton 1996: 79).

At the same time, Māori Language Commission, headed by Professor Timoti Kāretu, 'prepared the whole New Zealand official society to function bilingually' (see the Commission's first full-year report to the Government, Minister of Māori Affairs—Māori Language Commission 1989).

But when the first Kōhanga Reo children started elementary schools, the parents saw the earlier good work being undermined by the English-saturated linguistic and cultural school environment. 'They argue that they have put too much time and energy into their children to risk placing them in compromised options' (ibid., 44). Māori-medium education thus started in elementary schools too. In 1993 there were totally 74 schools (none of these secondary), with 3,176 students, giving the education 100% in Māori, and an additional 64 schools (among them 6 secondary schools) where 81 to 99% was in Māori (Benton 1996: 81).

Today, the Ministry of Education sums up the education offered (1995: 2, quoted in Durie 1997: 18–19):

> Kōhanga Reo are early childhood centres which offer programmes based on the total immersion in Māori language, culture and values of children from birth to school age. Māori language learning in schools is offered at three levels: Taha Māori programmes where students learn Māori songs, greetings and simple words; Māori language (Te Reo Māori) taught as a separate subject; and Māori medium education, where students are taught other curriculum subjects in both Māori and English (bilingual), or in Māori only (immersion) as well as learning Te Reo Māori.

In 1993, only 10.3% of primary Māori students and 20% of non-Māori students did not have any Māori in their education; for secondary school students the corresponding figures were much higher: 50.5% and 88.6%, respectively (Benton 1996: 80). The 'Māori-agenda' **kura kaupapa Māori** schools have rejected the type of 'bilingual education' where Māori and English would have equal position as classroom languages, and they clearly want maintenance programmes (ibid., 79–80). See Benton 1996 and Durie 1997 for up-to-date overviews—see also Linda Smith 1993.

Finns in Sweden

Finns in Sweden are the largest labour migrant group in Scandinavia (see Jaakkola 1983 and my 1996a for a description). Sweden is by many observers thought to have the most liberal immigrant educational policy in the world (see Municio 1983, 1987, for descriptions of the 'home language reform' which played a large role in these images). Still Finns as a group used to show equally poor results in and after schools as those of migrants in other parts of the world. Finnish children often reacted to the submersion with silence (extreme shyness, mutism—Takač 1974) or physical violence or playing truant (Toukomaa 1973), and were highly over-represented in 'special education' (Kuusela 1973). They showed low results in language tests in both languages and in school achievement. There was a pattern of little further education, and of unemployment and suicides. The parents started worrying, and Finnish medium transitional education started on a small scale in 1970 in Gothenburg. The number of Finnish-medium elementary classes grew rapidly, in many cases despite opposition by Swedish politicians and school authorities: there were 88 of them in 1975, 85% of all the 104 mother tongue medium classes in Sweden; 414 in 1980 (76% of the total of 542 classes) and 468 in 1981 (out of 600). In many local authorities there were serious conflicts, with school strikes, organised by parents (see Honkala et al. 1988) and sometimes teachers, to get more mother tongue medium education. Often the continuation of mother tongue medium classes was a result of a struggle every single year, but some local authorities also supported mother tongue medium education and obtained good results (see, e.g., Hagman & Lahdenperä 1988)—but often only after strikes and other protests (see Jaakkola 1989b, Honkala et al. 1988 and my 1988b for a description of the longest one of them in Rinkeby, suburb of Stockholm).

Government-commissioned research was used against the parents at several different levels (just as lack of research results had been used earlier, in the 1920s and 1930s, together with a refusal to grant money for research, despite many well-founded requests and despite research results being claimed as the backbone of Swedish social engineering—see Municio 1996). Lainio 1997, Hyltenstam & Tuomela 1996, Skutnabb-Kangas 1996a, 1997, and my and Pertti Toukomaa's reports for Unesco, among others, present some of the history of this education in English—there are hundreds of accounts in Finnish and Swedish. A few aspects of some studies will be summarised here. What is important to note is the extent to which submersion and transitional programmes might enable minorities to maintain their own language, to become bilingual and to reproduce themselves as minorities.

First I compare a few aspects of two studies of Finnish children, Sally Boyd's (1985) study of Swedish medium **submersion** classes, and Roger Källström & Vuokko Malinen's study (1985; Källström 1988 summarizes it in English) in mainly Finnish medium **transitional** classes. The submersion students used much more Swedish with parents (mother 14%, father 17%), siblings (72%)

(Continued)

and friends (71–84%), than the transitional students (mother 0%, father 7%, siblings 9%; with friends 80% both languages). Submersion students rated their Swedish competence slightly higher and their Finnish competence slightly lower than the transitional students. But while none of the transitional students rated their Swedish as 'poor', 7% of the submersion students did (compare this with my 1987 study below).

Källström concluded with a typical Swedish understatement that 'the comparison does not give us reason to suspect any dramatic differences in language proficiency'. Boyd concludes that Swedish medium instruction with 2 weekly hours of mother tongue subject teaching could not do much to prevent language shift. Källström states that a comparison of their results with Boyd's 'does not contradict the claim that truly bilingual education (e.g., in home language classes) is more effective in supporting active bilingualism than all-Swedish instruction supplemented by a few hours of home language target instruction' (1988: 196).

Hill's ethnographic study (1995) was with 42 17-year olds from several ethnic minority groups in the first grade of upper secondary school ('gymnasie-skolan'), with a dozen mother tongues, chosen amongst 'immigrant children' in Gothenburg born in 1977 who had had 'home language training' in preschool. She divides the youngsters in three groups: those who had had mother tongue teaching throughout their comprehensive school without any break (group A), those who had had at least a few years of it in comprehensive school (group B) and those who stopped it earlier, before grade 3 (group C). (There are some similarities with the tri-partite division in the Ramirez et al. study in the USA, see, e.g., Faltis 1997; likewise, with the continuity or lack of it which was emphasized in the Lawenius & Andersson (1998) Deaf study in Insert 8.3). 81% of all the children came from the lowest social groups. In brief, those who showed the **best results** (school achievement, Swedish language compe-tence, identity, capacity to express abstract concepts, etc.) were the ones with continuous mother tongue teaching from preschool throughout the compre-hensive school, group A. The **lowest scoring group**, with difficulties in Swedish according to both their own and the researcher's evaluation, and with negative scores on all the other measures, were the ones with **most Swedish**, group C.

Several other recent studies can be interpreted in a similar vein, or at least as showing that MTM education or teaching of the MT as a subject has not had any adverse effect on the children's Swedish or educational achievement (e.g., Bergman 1993, Eriksson 1994, Skolverket 1993, Virta 1994; Hyltenstam & Tuomela give a critical overview in their 1996).

A few other researchers (e.g., Linde 1989, Linde & Löfgren 1988, Löfgren 1991, Löfgren & Ouvinen-Birgerstam 1980) have argued that Finnish and other minority students should be in largely Swedish medium classes. However, the data which they base this recommendation on provide little support for it. All

(Continued)

their studies can thus be interpreted differently from what the authors themselves do. Hyltenstam & Tuomela (1996), for example, point out that the very high degree of heterogeneity of the participating students, shown in one of the sub-studies in Löfgren 1991 can have played a role for all the results (not only in this but also in the other sub-studies). They list some of the heterogeneity, where on the one hand some students did not yet know much Swedish whereas others who were monolingual in Swedish were also included, because of the definition of 'immigrant students' used in the project (1996: 82). According to Hyltenstam & Tuomela (ibid., 83) it is 'not impossible that it is conditions of this kind which, when one [= the authors] looks at the group as a whole, are responsible for the result being that mother tongue teaching does not have any impact' (my translation). Furthermore, Linde and Löfgren found that grade 8 Finnish students who had received the bulk of their education through Finnish were performing just as well in Swedish as similar students who had been educated predominantly in Swedish, i.e., maximum exposure was shown to be a fallacy. See also Honkala et al. 1988 and Hagman & Lahdenperä 1988 for the struggle for language rights in education.

Despite all the evidence against submersion, almost 80% of the Finnish children and most other immigrant minority children in Sweden are still today in submersion programmes, with a couple of weekly hours of the mother tongue as a subject, at best. There was a serious backlash in the early 1990s: cutbacks as a result of a weak Swedish economy (was made to) hit minority education to a much larger extent than dominant group education. It killed off large numbers of mother tongue medium classes—the local councils' cutbacks hit them especially hard. The Finnish response was to start founding private schools, something that suddenly became possible, after several decades of struggle, with a change of government. A conservative government allowed what social democrat governments had refused for several decades—it was impossible to have a law which would only have allowed the elite schools that the government was interested in.

There are today 11 Finnish schools in Sweden, all with maintenance programmes. Despite many problems, not least economic ones, the results show, as expected, high levels of multilingualism, together with all the other positive aspects described earlier as goals. Most of the problems that these schools experience are of the same type that any urban schools in western countries experience. Readers who might be interested in sampling what happens, could start with the Web-site of the Finnish school in Upplands Väsby, in metropolitan Stockholm: <http://www.sverigefinskaskolan.se>. (See Table 3, pp. 246–249 in Skutnabb-Kangas & García 1995 where this school, together with La Luz, Dade County, Florida, represents a maintenance model.)

Private but partially state-financed ethnic minority schools of this kind, with the minority language as the main medium of education, are showing excellent results in terms of high levels of multilingualism and multiculturalism

(*Continued*)

❖ **I n f o B o x 8 . 3** ❖

(Continued)

and academic success. The Swedish government suspected that ethnic minority schools could contribute to increased social, cultural, and economic segregation, and asked a Swedish research group to investigate the schools. The official report, published by the National Board of Education in October 1997 (Skolverket 1997) concludes that there is no reason to suspect that the schools lead to segregation. There is criticism in the report of some Muslim schools—most of which do **not** use Arabic as the main medium of education—in terms of the very traditional content of the education and sometimes of low teacher qualifications. But the minority language medium maintenance schools (which the Swedes call 'the linguistically oriented schools' in the report) get high praise for the levels of knowledge and bilingualism attained, the enthusiasm and active engagement of parents, children and teachers, and the social, linguistic, and cultural integration of the students. The Swedish team was looking for problems in these schools, in order to be able to suggest solutions. But they claim, with surprise, that they found no problems—and therefore there is no reason to suggest any solutions. Instead, 'they have to agree with a student we interviewed who claimed that his school gave him as much as any [Swedish-medium] public school could give—plus some more!' (my translation).

TABLE 8.2
Results in dominant language after 9 years of a maintenance programme for an immigrant minority; Competence in Swedish after 9 years in Finnish mother-tongue medium classes; own evaluation and test results (working class Finns, middle class Swedes, 2 Stockholm suburbs; from Skutnabb-Kangas 1987).

	Own evaluation of Swedish competence *(scale 1–5)*		Swedish test results *(scale 1–13)*	
	M	*SD*	*M*	*SD*
Finnish co-researchers	4.50	0.41	5.68	1.86
Swedish controls	4.83	0.26	5.42	2.23

classes in the same schools ($M = 5.42$) (see Table 8.2). It was also interesting that the Swedish youngsters' own evaluation of their Swedish competence was higher ($M = 4.83$) and somewhat more even (standard deviation 0.26) than that of the Finnish youngsters ($M = 4.50$, sd = 0.41). Still, the test results went in the opposite direction, i.e., the Finnish youngsters got better test results in Swedish than the Swedish youngsters. The standard deviation showed that the Finnish children, with 1.86, were somewhat more even than the Swedes ($sd = 2.23$).

In the study above, the Finnish youngsters' Finnish was at almost the same level as that of Finnish control groups in Finland, whereas Finnish children in Swedish-medium education show extremely poor results in Finnish.

It seems clear that if the goal is not only high levels of multilingualism and school achievement, together with a positive development of multiple identity (see my 1991d), but also support for the right of minorities to exist and reproduce themselves as minorities, mother tongue medium education is necessary.

This has been borne out for the Finnish minority in Sweden in a longitudinal study by Pirjo Janulf in her 1998 PhD-thesis (see Info Box 8.4).

❖ **I n f o B o x 8 . 4** ❖

'None of Those Who Had Been in the Swedish Classes Spoke Finnish With Their Children' (Pirjo Janulf)

Janulf's longitudinal study had three bilingual groups and two 'monolingual' control groups in Finland and Sweden, altogether 1,389 students. One of the bilingual groups represented a national minority, with a normal **maintenance** programme: 411 Finland Swedish minority students from Åbo, Finland (Group A; my designation). The two other bilingual groups represented an immigrant minority: there were a total of 560 second generation Sweden Finns from Botkyrka, Sweden [the same local council where one of the two schools in my 1987 study was]. Of them 273 were in Finnish medium classes (FM) in a **transitional** programme (group B); 287 were in Swedish medium classes (SM) in a **submersion** programme (group C). There were also 'monolingual' control groups in both Finland (group D) and Sweden (group E). Questionnaires and tests were used and essays collected in 1980 and 1995. Reading and writing skills in both languages were compared. Table 8.3 (based on information given in Janulf 1998) presents an overview of the groups:

TABLE 8.3
Overview of subjects in Janulf 1998

Group N	Country	Mother tongue	Medium of education
A. $N = 411$	Finland	Swedish	Swedish
B. $N = 273$	Sweden	Finnish	Finnish
C. $N = 287$	Sweden	Finnish	Swedish
D. $N = 133$	Finland	Finnish	Finnish
E. $N = 285$	Sweden	Swedish	Swedish

(Continued)

❖ **I n f o   B o x   8 . 4** ❖

(Continued)

The **most bilingual** group was A (those in a full **maintenance** programme, in an officially bilingual city in Finland where Swedish-speakers are a small minority). They achieved better results on the Swedish tests than any other groups, including the Swedish-speaking Swedish-educated control group E in Sweden. Group A had considerably better results in Finnish tests than group C, even if these are native speakers of Finnish. Compared to group B, group A students read Finnish just as well or better but wrote less well.

Comparison of the results from 1980 and 1995 in terms of the use of both languages at home and in school showed the following changes. Group C used much more Swedish in 1995 than in 1980, while group B to a larger extent used both languages in 1995, as compared to 1980.

In one sub-study, '41 former Sweden Finnish informants with an average age of 27 were revisited. Those who had been in the Swedish medium submersion classes [group C] tended to let Swedish take over at home while those who had been in the transitional Finnish medium classes [group B] used both languages.

Sixteen of the former informants had children of their own. The language chosen when speaking to their children correlated with their own language skills and the language of their partner.' (Janulf, Abstract). **None of those who had been in the Swedish medium submersion classes [C] spoke Finnish with their children**. Among those who were in Finnish classes [B] various combinations of languages were applied: 40% spoke Finnish, 25% spoke both languages and 33% spoke Swedish. Nearly 90% of those who had been in Finnish classes [B] wanted their children to learn Finnish in school (Janulf 1998).

Janulf's conclusions and their implications will be discussed in chapter 9.

The difference between a transitional programme and a maintenance programme is *not* **mainly** in the number of hours through the medium of the MT of the students or whether the transition happens in grade 7 or 9 or later (or not at all—it is not necessary). It is in the *status* of the minority mother tongue and the ideology behind this. Is it seen as a linguistic human right to be educated through the medium of the MT, or is the MT used for instrumental majority-language-learning purposes or as a necessary concession to a minority?

In a seminal article about minority education Richard Ruiz (1984) distinguished between three ways of seeing language: language as a **problem**, language as a **right** and language as a **resource**. Transitional programmes use a defensive argumentation for legitimating the minority language. They are, in terms of Ruiz' divisions, ideologically mostly based on **constantly having to prove that the minority language, used as a medium, is *not* a problem**. On the contrary, those maintenance programmes I know use a combined 'rights and resource' approach. We minorities are not the problem, we and our language are part of the solution. **It is a human right for us to use our own languages as the main media of education, and doing this provides both us and the society as a whole invaluable resources.**

In Sweden, even the shaky legal protection for the few minority-medium schools can be changed from one day to the next, especially as regards the state subsidy. There are so far **no** maintenance programmes in Sweden for national minorities, or for the indigenous Sámi.

As opposed to Sweden, in Canada[19] some indigenous peoples have succeeded in getting legal support for their maintenance programmes. This is a result of a long struggle. Info Box 8.5 gives an example of the positive legal regulations.

❖ **I n f o   B o x   8 . 5** ❖

Legal Provisions for Maintenance Programmes:
James Bay Cree and Inuits in Québec

Two other examples of good practice with legal provisions are from the James Bay Cree and from Inuits in Québec (source: James Bay and Northern Québec Agreement and Complementary Agreements. 1991 Edition. Les Publications du Québec Legal Deposit—3rd Quarter 1991. Bibliothéque nationale du Québec. ISBN 2-551-14501-5[20]). The regulations about Cree and Inuit education are as follows:

The teaching languages shall be Cree and with respect to the other languages in accordance with the present practice (in the Cree Communities) in the Territory. The Cree School Board will pursue as an objective the use of French as a language of instruction so that pupils graduating from its schools will, in the future, be capable of continuing their studies in a French school, college or university elsewhere in Québec, if they so desire.

After consultation with the parents' committee, and having regard to the requirements of subsequent education, the commissioners shall determine the rate of introduction of French and English as teaching languages (para 16.0.10, p. 270 Section 16, Cree Education).

The teaching languages shall be Inuttituut and with respect to the other languages in accordance with the present practice in the territory. The Kativik School Board will pursue as an objective the use of French as a language of instruction so that pupils graduating from its schools will, in the future, be capable of continuing their studies in a French school, college or university elsewhere in Québec, if they so desire.

After consultation with the parents' committee, and having regard to the requirements of subsequent education, the commissioners shall determine the rate of introduction of French and English as teaching languages. (para 17.0.59, p. 285, Section 17, Education (Inuit)

In Canada, the French-speaking national linguistic minority (which in legal terms is a 'founding people' on a par with the English-speaking linguistic majority, i.e., they are, just like Swedish-speakers in Finland, **legally** not a minority), has a very strong legal basis for their own maintenance programmes, especially in Quebec. On the other hand, Canada does **not** have proper maintenance programmes for any immigrant minorities, even if the languages of some of them (e.g., Ukrainian) are used as media of education, but in immersion programmes, where Ukrainian-speakers themselves can participate on a par with monolingual English-speakers.

In Hungary, minority protection also includes education.[21] Info Box 8.6 summarizes some of it.

The Hungarian Act LXXVII of 1993 on the Rights of National and Ethnic Minorities (included in the first **Bulletin (Kisebbségi értesítÖ)** of **The Office for National and Ethnic Minorities** (1993; no date) makes it 'mandatory to organize and maintain a minority class or study group' (section 43 (4) of the Act) if the parents of 8 children so wish. The Act also states, simply, that the additional costs incurred for this 'are to be covered by the state or by the local government' (Section 44). This is to my knowledge the best educational minority protection in the world—no wonder that the Council of Europe Newsletter quoted below does not get it quite right, despite the summarizer being Hungarian . . .

Despite the **legal** protection, there are inevitably problems in both Canada (see Martel, in press) and Hungary.[22] In Hungary, it is mainly two minority groups which suffer from insufficient educational (and other) rights, the Deaf (see Kontra 1998, Muzsnái 1999) and the Roma (see Szalai 1999, Kontra et al. 1999). Still, educational (and other) minority rights in Hungary are among the best in the world.

8.4.2. Immersion Programmes

Maintenance programmes for minorities are a first step, necessary for human rights. But if we are interested in peaceful coexistence and a more just society, we have to how go further and also look at how **majority** children can be helped out of monolingual stupidity and become minimally bilingual (and this also helps us in planning for future programmes where **all** children can become multilingual **together**). The only educational programmes where bilingualism for majorities has been achieved on a really large scale, are the immersion programmes, started by Wallace Lambert in Canada (Definition Box 8.6).

Canada has been the pioneer of immersion programmes (see, e.g., Genesee 1976, 1985, 1987, 1996, Lambert & Tucker 1972, Swain 1997, Swain & Lapkin 1982, 1986). Tens of thousands of pages have been written about immersion and this is not the place to describe the syllabuses or results in detail. Immersion programmes typically involve ethnolinguistic majority chil-

❖ I n f o B o x 8 . 6 ❖

Legal Provisions for Maintenance Programmes:
National Minorities, Hungary

In **Hungary**, the new Law on Public Education, in force since September 1993, has the following to say about the education of minorities, here summarized by Enikö Kulcsár-Szabó, based on document DECS/Rech (94) 59, and prepared for the Council of Europe (source: **Council of Europe Education Newsletter** 3, 1994: 24).

The 13 minorities (Gypsy, German, Croatian, Slovak, Romanian, Bulgarian, Greek, Polish, Armenian, Ruthenian, Serbian, Slovenian, Ukrainian) have the right to education in their mother tongues. The teaching language of language and literature, history, geography and culture must be the mother tongue. At the same time, minority pupils should have the possibility to become acquainted with Hungarian language and culture, while those who do not belong to the given minority should have the possibility to acquaint themselves with the culture of the local minority. [Observe, not language; my remark].

If the language of kindergarten or school education is that of the local minority, or more than half of the pupils study both in the minority language and Hungarian, the director or head teacher must speak the language of the given minority. In the case of more than one applicant having comparable qualifications for such a post, the person belonging to the minority has an advantage.

The Law on Minorities, passed in summer 1993, also states that individuals belonging to minorities have the right to take part in education in their mother tongues, while minority communities have the right to initiate education in the mother tongue or in the mother tongue and partially in Hungarian at all educational levels, as well as to establish a network of institutions of their own. Moreover, the local minority authorities have the right to found and/or support public education institutions.

It is the parents (or legal representatives) who decide if their children should attend a school where the teaching language is the minority language. Provided that the parents (or legal representatives) of **eight children** belonging to the same minority declare their wish, a minority class or group must be started and/or supported [see p. 612—the formulation here is not correct!].

The State should provide the training of teachers able to teach minority languages or in minority languages ... At teacher training institutions (universities and colleges) all minority languages have their departments. Students whose speciality is a minority language can study any of the other subjects in addition. .... Textbooks and teaching materials necessary for minority education must be provided by the State.

There is ... also special section on Gypsy minority (emphasis added).

DEFINITION BOX 8.6 Immersion

An **immersion** programme is a programme where linguistic majority children with a high-status mother tongue voluntarily choose (among existing alternatives) to be instructed through the medium of a foreign (minority) language, in classes with majority children with the same mother tongue only (but see below) where the teacher is bilingual so that the children can at the beginning use their own language, and where their mother tongue is in no danger of not developing or of being replaced by the language of instruction—an *additive* language learning situation.

---

dren, although there are some exceptions.[23] The majority of immersion programmes are still in French, but there are programmes in other languages too, especially in Ukrainian and Spanish but also some in Hebrew, German, Chinese, Arabic, etc. Some trilingual programmes also exist (see Genesee 1986, Taylor 1993, Artigal 1995). And of course trilingual programmes should be the rule in multilingual areas (see Bull 1995)—see also Annamalai 1995 on the Indian three language formula. Close to a million children in Canada have gone through or are in these programmes.

Immersion programmes have spread from Canada to the United States. Most of the US programmes are in Spanish (75 schools in 1994–1995) and French (38 schools), but also in Japanese, German, Hawai'ian, Cantonese, Mandarin, Arabic and Russian.

Increasingly, immersion has also spread to other countries. Catalunya and Finland[24] were the first European countries starting immersion programmes on a large scale and the numbers are growing. Early, late, or partial immersion programmes (which have been studied and reported on) exist, for example, in Australia (e.g., Clyne (ed.) 1986—but see also Clyne et al. 1997, Gibbons 1997, Gibbons et al. 1994), Catalunya (e.g., Arnau 1997 and references to Artigal in the bibliography), Finland (e.g., Helle 1994, Laurén 1991, 1997), Hungary (e.g., Duff, 1991), USA. The Basque country, Holland, Hungary and Germany (see <http://www.goethe.de>) have early immersion, and late immersion exists in a number of additional European countries and elsewhere (e.g., in Brunei, Jones 1997). Oudin 1996 and Jenniges (ed.) 1997 are good starting points, as is the Eurydice (European Education Information Network) Web-site <http://www.eurydice.org>. It is interesting that other Nordic countries have been very slow, and, e.g., the only Danish immersion programme (ages 15–18) was discontinued after 4 years. Some programmes are in minority or neighbouring languages (e.g., many in Catalunya and Finland), many are in 'big' languages. A project on the early learning (from the age of 6 years) of foreign languages was, for instance, started in 1991/92 in primary schools in Zagreb, Rijera, and Split, in Croatia. In the same year, the Ministry of Education decided to open bilingual schools (Croatian-German, Croatian-English, Croatian-French), where 30–50% of subjects are taught in the foreign language (**Council of Europe, Education Newsletter** 3, 1994: 13). Many countries are implementing some type of immersion but without much research follow-up. Others are planning them or are just starting, for example, Estonia (see Ülle Rannut 1992, Rannut & Rannut 1995). The first Estonian immersion preschool (in Estonian, for Russian-speaking children) started in January 1999 (Ülle Rannut, personal communication) and it combines immersion with the teaching of early reading. Still others (e.g., Switzerland) are investigating the possibilities of starting up. Literature about immersion is enormous (see Johnson & Swain 1997, Baker & Prys Jones 1998, and references in them, for international overviews; see Kubanek-German (ed.) 1996 for mainly European immersion projects initiated at the beginning of the 1990s; see also Hermans 1997, Kubanek-German 1998, Trim (ed.) 1992 and Blondin et al. 1998 for more general European overviews on early foreign language teaching). There are international associations for immersion researchers and parents, email lists, international conferences, data bases, summer courses, teacher training, etc. The most up-to-date information about new programmes is on the email lists and Web-pages of immersion researchers and practitioners (see Address Box 8.1 for a few of these resources).

* *

**Address Box 8.1   Resources about early foreign language learning
including immersion and two-way programmes**

The Centre for Information on Language Teaching and Research (CILT) in London, UK, with a wealth of materials and an information service for language professionals: <http:/www.CILT.org.uk/>.

The National Clearinghouse for Bilingual Education in Washington, D.C., USA, has similar resources <http://www.ncbe.gwu.edu>, and so does the Center for Applied Linguistics <http://www.cal.org>.

The European Education Information Network in Brussels, Belgium, has in its Eurydice base <http://www.eurydice.org/> detailed information about the education systems of European countries, including foreign language learning. For German, the Goethe Institute <http://www.goethe.de> is a good source.

Children can find partner schools for Internet and email exchanges at <http://partbase.eupro.se>. Documentation and news about the European

* *

(Continued)

* *

Address Box 8.1 *(Continued)*

Language Portfolio (see Christ 1998a, b) and the Common European framework for language learning, teaching and assessment (see Coste et al. 1998), both to be officially launched in 2001, officially designated as the European Year of Languages, are available on the Council of Europe's Web-site <http://culture.coe.fr/lang>, or at Directorate of Education, Culture and Sport, Modern Languages Section, Council of Europe, F-67075 Strasbourg, France, email <decs.lang@coe.fr>.

Eurobarometer surveys assess the self-evaluated competence of people to speak other languages in addition to their mother tongues. In 1997 71.3% of young people in the European Union were able to speak another language 'well enough to have a conversation in it' (the figures for Sweden and Finland were 97.4% and 96%, respectively). The latest report, **Young Europeans**, can be obtained by clicking on 'opinion survey' at <http://europe. eu.int/en/comm/dg22/youth.youth.html>.

The email list at <lime@garbo.uwasa.fi> is a discussion list on immersion.

More general applied linguistics resources, with a lot of links, are provided at <http//www.ex.ac.uk/~TLearmou/lib/linguistics.html>; specifically for teachers at the Foreign Language teaching Forum <http://www.cortland. edu/www_root/flteach/flteach.html>.

My absolute favourite for links of any kind in applied linguistics which makes a lot of the others unnecessary is from University of Jyväskylä, Finland: <http://www.jyu.fi/tdk/kkkk/yhteinen/linkit/start.htm>. After all, Finns have more computers per person than people in any country (including the USA) . . .

* *

Two languages are used as media of instruction in immersion, initially the students' second language, and the teachers are bilingual, even if they only speak the students' L2 in class. Early, partial and late immersion models aim to make students bilingual (or, in Europe, multilingual) and biliterate so that they can function in (and draw benefit from) plural societies.

Results from early immersion programmes, the most common model, show that the students' **mother tongue competence** is initially not on a par with students with the same L1 in L1-medium programmes, but as soon as instruction in L1 starts (often from third grade), they catch up, and are usually at the latest in grade 5 at the national norm level in their L1—or higher. Their **school achievement** is on a par with non-immersion students, often even somewhat higher. The **competence in their L2** often reaches up to near-native level in listening and reading comprehension. In productive L2 skills, speaking and especially writing, the students usually make more mistakes, are not as fluent as native speakers and generally lag behind. Despite this, their productive L2 is at a much higher level than anything reached by good foreign language teaching. In Canadian studies the students have been especially good in situations where they can themselves choose the topic and the level of formality of the discourse. The **attitudes**, for instance in the early Canadian studies towards French language and culture and towards francophones in Canada have been positive, but maybe not quite as positive as many people might hope or expect.

Some of the weaknesses in immersion programmes have to do with the fact that the students have often had little (informal or formal) contact with other students (or indeed adults) who speak the target language as their native language. The Canadian immersion programmes have mostly been located in English-speaking schools, without any French-speakers. Some of the difficulties in producing fully 'correct' French may also be due to the fact that French has not been taught as a subject, it has 'only' functioned as the medium of education. There are several critical accounts about the weaknesses, and suggestions for how to overcome them (e.g., Cummins 1994a). Experiments and suggestions abound, and the immersion area seems generally to inspire a lot of enthusiasm.

Trying to overcome the weaknesses of immersion programmes mentioned above, together with a belief in the importance of cross-lingual and cross-cultural contacts for attitude formation, have influenced the development of the European Community 'European school' model and partly also the two-way programmes in the United States. Of course the reasons for starting these programmes have been school-external, as for immersion too—this will be discussed below in section 8.5.

8.4.3. Two-Way Bilingual (Dual Language) Programmes

There are over 200 schools with two-way programmes in the USA.

Most of the US two-way programmes are Spanish/English, but there are also programmes with French, Cantonese, Haitian Creole, Japanese, Korean, Navajo, Portuguese, and Russian. Dolson & Lindholm 1995 is an excellent overview of the goals, set-up and preliminary results of these programmes, Lindholm 1997 is a recent overview, Christian 1994, Christian & Mahrer 1992, 1993, and Christian & Montone 1994 give detailed yearly overviews and some comparisons of existing programmes and Christian et al. 1997 also discussions about results. See also references to Lindholm in the bibliography for some of the evaluations. Neither Europe nor Australia has proper two-way programmes (and no variant of the European Schools model exists in

DEFINITION BOX 8.7 Two-way bilingual (dual language) programmes

Two-way bilingual (dual language) (also called 'dual immersion' in the USA—see 8.3.1 for why this is a misnomer) models are models with approximately 50% majority students and 50% minority students (with the same mother tongue) who voluntarily choose to be instructed by a 'completely' bilingual teacher, initially mainly through the medium of a minority language (the 90%–10% model) or through the medium of both languages (the 50%–50% model), with the dominant language taught as a subject (at the beginning separately to both groups: mother tongue English to native English-speakers and English as a second language to minority language speakers in the USA). The percentage of instruction in the dominant language increases in all 90–10% models, in some to 40–50% or even 60% by grade 6, whereas it stays the same in the 50–50% model (something that actually would place them in the transitional models category). Two-way models thus combine in one classroom a maintenance model for minorities (especially in the 90–10% model) and an immersion model for the majority while maximizing peer-group contact in the other language for both groups.

Australia, Canada or the USA). Some South African English-Afrikaans programmes might be characterised as variations of a two-way model, and Malherbe's early evaluation study (1946) shows excellent results in terms of bilingualism. Many Indian programmes are also a variant (see Chaturvedi & Singh 1981, Annamalai 1995) but there are few if any systematic evaluations. Some of the results and problems will be discussed in connection with the comparison of programmes below. Two-way teachers and researchers also have yearly conferences, email lists, etc. Some information is included in Address Box 8.1 above.

8.4.4. Alternate Days Programmes

There are very few alternate days programmes but I have wanted to present them anyway because they illustrate some important principles, discussed in 8.6.

In the alternate days programme in Calistoga, **California** (in English and Spanish), the (bilingual) Spanish mother tongue teacher was responsible for the teaching on Mondays, in Spanish, and the (bilingual) English mother tongue teacher supported especially those children who did not understand all the instruction. On Tuesdays they changed roles, and therefore the main teaching language also changed. Again, Wednesdays were in Spanish, Thursdays in English and Fridays in both languages, mostly Spanish. Jan Curtis,

---

DEFINITION BOX 8.8   Alternate days' programmes

An **alternate days model** could be seen as a sub-category under two-way programmes. There are both majority and minority students in a class with a bilingual teacher (or two bilingual teachers with different mother tongues). Both languages are used as media of instruction with both groups, with a strict separation of the main languages of teaching by weekday.

---

who was instrumental in starting the programme in Calistoga, has written a description of it (1988), from its inception to its preliminary but temporary death—it is now functioning in Calistoga again. Tucker et al. 1970 have an early description of this type of programme in the **Philippines**, with Tagalog and English. There are several less strict variations of separating the languages: by subject, by space (Spanish-medium and English-medium 'work-stations' in the same classroom), morning/afternoon, conscious topic-motivated code-switching (Rodolfo Jacobson's edited book 1998 gives references), etc. There are few evaluations.

8.4.5. European Union Schools
(Plural Multilingual) Model

The **European Union schools** model (Plural multilingual model) schools (10 of them, in 6 countries, with roughly 16,000 pupils and 1,200 teachers in 1998) are controlled by the education authorities of the **member states of the European Union**. The schools have subsections for the 11 different official languages of the 15 member states (few of the schools have all subsections, though[25]) and they lead to the European Baccalaureate. The students differ in nationality and language background—therefore 'plural'. Several languages—all subsection languages—are used as media for instruction, according to a carefully planned progression; teachers and the rest of the staff are bilingual as a minimum; and the goal is that all students become not only bilingual but multilingual—therefore 'multilingual'.

In the European Union Schools an attempt is made to combine good features of maintenance programmes for minorities and immersion programmes for majorities, and to avoid the few weaknesses which these models may have. Summarising the model: The subsections' languages are the main media of education in all cognitively demanding decontextualised subjects (subjects loading heavily on CALP) during the first 7 years, and even in the later grades in several subjects. The teaching of the first foreign language as a subject starts in grade 1 and it becomes the medium in a few cognitively less demanding context-embedded subjects already in grade 3 and increasingly thereafter. Instruction through the medium of the first foreign language in CALP-heavy subjects in the later phases often takes place in mixed groups, but in obligatory subjects **without** native speakers of that language. In contrast, in elective subjects students can be mixed in any combination. At least the first two (often three) languages are both studied as subjects and used as media of instruction.

Since this model seems to fulfill most of the formal criteria for success (see later), is is described below in some detail, mainly based on Baetens Beardsmore 1995 (see also the other references to his work in the bibliography) but also other sources, including my visit to one of the Brussels schools.[26]

The first school was started in Luxembourg in 1953 by the forerunner of the European Union, the European Coal and Steel Union. The second, the first 'European School' as they are called, K–12 (Kindergarten through grade 12, in 1998 with some 3,500 children), was founded in Uccle, a suburb of Brussels in 1958 for children of European Community officials. Everybody who works for the European Union can in principle have their children in these schools: cleaners, ministers, janitors, secretaries, interpreters. If there is room, local children can attend if their parents can afford the fees: one of the schools has many children of former miners, another one has immigrant steel-workers' children. European Community officials' children do not pay fees whereas local children pay a fee which varies between around 900 to 1,400 pounds. 'Outsiders', for example, children whose parents work for member governments or companies, pay a fee five to seven times higher.

The goal is to 'guarantee the development of the child's first language and cultural identity' and to 'promote a European identity through instruction for all pupils in at least 2 languages, compulsory learning of a 3rd as a subject matter, and options regarding a 4th language' (Baetens Beardsmore 1993: 8), to 'eliminate prejudice and nationalistic antagonisms', and 'use multilingualism as a tool for both scholastic achievement and harmonious ethnolinguistic relations' (ibid.)

All or most official languages of the European Union (EU) function as the principal medium of education initially in their own subsections in every school where there are enough children for this. Normally a child attends a subsection for her own mother tongue, that is, Danish, Dutch, English, Finnish, French, German, Greek, Italian, Portuguese, Spanish, or Swedish. There are some children from other language groups, and these attend the subsection the language of which they know best. Most Arabic-speakers are for instance in the French language subsection.

The **medium of education** is initially the child's mother tongue (= the language of the subsection), and **all** cognitively and linguistically demanding decontextualised subjects continue to be taught through the medium of the mother tongue (first language, L1) at least up to grade 8.

All lessons/periods last for 30 minutes in grades 1–2 and 45 minutes from grade 3 upwards. The **mother tongue** is taught as a subject 16 periods per week (hereafter 16p) in the first two grades, 9p in grades 3–5, 5p in grades 6–7 and 4p in grades 8–12. The **second language** (L2) also starts as a subject in grade 1 and has 5p in grades 1–7, 4p in grade 8 and 3p in grades 9–12. The pupils can choose between English, French or German as their L2 (meaning the children in these three subsections only have a choice between two languages whereas all the other children have three choices). All the teachers are native speakers of the languages which they teach, but the absolute majority of teachers are bi- or multilingual—this also applies to the other staff in the schools: the adults must be good models of multilingualism. Every child thus has adults in the school who speak their language.

From grade 3 a couple of **subjects are taught in mixed groups** and they may be taught **through the medium of L2**. The subjects chosen are always cognitively and linguistically less demanding and context-embedded, e.g., 1p physical education, including swimming, and 3p 'European Hours' with excursions, planning of parties, etc. 'European Hours' could, for instance, be taught through French to a group of 5 Italian, 3 Danish, 6 Greek, 7 German and 5 Portuguese children, and through German to 6 English, 5 French, 4 Spanish, 2 Greek, and 3 German children. The medium of education is mostly an L2 for all the children, but there may also be some children present for whom the language is an L1.

From grade 6 the amount taught through L2 increases, so that, e.g., music (2p), arts (2p), physical education (3p) and complementary activities (2p—handicrafts, computers, photography, electronics, typing, painting, etc.) are taught in mixed groups. But **until grade 8 all subjects taught in mixed groups through the medium of L2 are cognitively and linguistically less demanding and context-embedded**.

In grade 8 a **3rd language** (L3) starts as a subject, with 4p. (in grades 9–12 3p), and the pupils can choose between every subsection's language: all are offered. If, for instance, a Greek and a Danish child have become friends, having been taught physical education together through French since grade 3, they can choose to study each other's languages from grade 8.

In **grade 8 L2 becomes the medium of instruction also in** one or two **cognitively demanding decontextualised subjects** (e.g., history, 3p), **often in mixed groups but without mother tongue speakers** of the medium of instruction. The teachers use multilingual dictionaries or word lists and ensure understanding in several ways. The subject matter has often been discussed earlier through the medium of the respective mother tongues of the pupils so the concepts are familiar.

In **grades 9–10**, physical education, history and geography are taught through L2, the other compulsory subjects (there are not many) through L1. Of the elective courses, only Latin and classical Greek are taught through

L1, everything else through L2. The 4th language (L4) starts as an elective subject in grade 9, with 4p (in grades 11–12 3p).

In **grades 11–12**, only L1 and L2 are compulsory while L3 and L4 are optional. Philosophy and mathematics are taught through L1, all other compulsory subjects through L2 (or L3). Of the elective subjects, Latin, classical Greek, physics, chemistry, biology, and advanced courses (including one in L1 as a subject) are taught through L1, everything else through L2 (or L3 or even L4). In grades 9–12, those elective courses which are not prescribed as courses to be taught through the medium of L1, are taught in mixed groups, and the language of instruction can thus be a pupil's L2 or L3 or L4, or, as it may sometimes be, L1.

The **results** seem to show that the children learn at least **two languages at a native level, both receptively and productively, both orally and in writing**. They are supposed to be able to take content matter tests in both L1 and L2 at a native level, and many take some subjects through L2 in the European Baccalaureate. Some even do it in their L3. Many of the children reach high levels in L3, and some even in L4. The results in the final exams are above medium, with, for instance, 95.5% of the 1,002 candidates passing the European Baccalaureate in 1992 (see Baetens Beardsmore 1993, Table 8).

When immersion pupils reach a near-native level in L2-reception, European School pupils seem to reach a native level in L2-reception *and* production, in addition to, for many, high levels in a 3rd and sometimes also a 4th language. Pilot research on attitudes (by Alex Housen) also shows positive results.

8.5. STRONG MODELS AND LANGUAGE POLICY GOALS: EQUALITY, ECONOMICS, AND ENRICHMENT

Having presented the strong models, I assess to what extent they support positive language policy goals. As economic growth in human development should be seen as means to an end (see section 6.4), in education too models or programmes have goals which are more macro-level than high levels of multilingualism and school achievement. There are many possible ways of assessing the broader goals, and I have used several myself. One was broadly differentiating between linguistic and societal goals (e.g., in my 1984a: 127, Table 3, and in another way in 1990a: 18, Table 4). Another was differentiating between the majority's and the minority's views and agreement on the minority's future in relation to structural incorporation and integration/assimilation (e.g., Skutnabb-Kangas & Toukomaa 1976 where the differentiation was partly based on Schermerhorn 1970; see section 3.3.2 above). Structural incorporation was defined in terms of equity in educational outcomes, in housing, on the labour market, for social services and duties and political participation. Yet another assessed the goals for the future of the minority in terms of whether and for how long it was going to exist and continue to speak the minority language (my 1988: 34–35, Table 1.4 and 1990a: 23, Table 5). Education is a means and is supposed to give prerequisites for all these goals, and various models can fulfill the requirements more or less well. One of the difficulties is that the minority's own goals are often different from those of the majority—this is what Pertti Toukomaa and I tried to address when comparing these two in our 1976 report. Another one is that the goals which one can derive from long-lasting practices, where there has been enough background knowledge and evaluation so that changes could have been made but have not been made, do not always tally with the officially expressed goals. Sometimes these function as a smokescreen, in vintage doublespeak.[27] These gaps between the official mantras and reality are of course glaring in many other areas too (see, e.g., Katarina Tomaševski's brilliant critiques in several human rights areas 1993, 1996, 1997a, 1997b), not just linguistic human rights in education.

I shall briefly relate the models to several of these goals. Although the strong forms of multilingual education have different sociolinguistic realities with regard to the linguistic background of the students and the language(s) of the classroom, and different sociopolitical realities with regard to the power relations between the groups attending and the rest of society, they all share an aim of cultural and linguistic pluralism, with the multilingualism and multiliteracy (or minimally bilingualism and biliteracy) of students as an avowed minimum **linguistic** aim. Thus we can concentrate here on their **societal** goals.

The **reasons** for choosing bilingual or multilingual education often vary for diverse groups. Some have recognized multilingual education as a means to make their own children bilingual and thereby improving opportunities for doing business, getting ahead, and maintaining privileges. Immersion programmes, the European Schools and International Schools are examples of this approach.

For other groups, multilingual education represents a means to better understanding of other ethnolinguistic groups with which they are in contact. Immersion programmes and, especially, two-way programmes may have an element of this 'integrative' motivation.

For others, such as threatened ethnolinguistic groups, multilingual education represents a means of linguistic survival. Maintenance/language shelter programmes or revitalization programmes for minorities, for example, the Frisian schools in the Netherlands or the Finnish schools in Sweden or Kōhanga Reo programmes in New Zealand, are of this type.

Yet another use of bilingual education has been the provision of education in the mother tongue to ethnolinguistic groups which had previously been excluded from equal educational opportunity. Again, maintenance and two-way programmes may belong in this category. Mother tongue medium education in some African countries might be considered a type of maintenance programme.[28]

Thus the reasons for using two languages in education vary greatly, as do the goals, among which are ethnolinguistic survival, and an increase of knowledge and potential economic gains, improved educational opportunity, or increased mutual understanding. Many programmes are multipurpose and combine several of the goals.[29]

For comparative reasons, I shall here mainly relate the models to one of the few existing explicit state language policy documents, the Australian **National Policy on Languages** (Lo Bianco 1987) which describes the social goals of Australian language policy. These goals relate to what have been called **'the four E's': equality, economics, enrichment, and external** (Lo Bianco 1990b). **Equality** refers to the correlation between language on the one hand and social and economic equality or lack of it on the other, with language policy needing to correct any systematic injustice. The **economic** goal has to do with multilingualism as a productive asset. The **enrichment** goal uses arguments about the benefits deriving from multilingualism. The **external** goals were about beneficial relations with other countries, in Australia's case mainly the other Asian countries (but on Australia's extreme double-speak in this see Pilger 1992, 1998).

We shall thus briefly consider criteria for multilingual education policy by relating the main four strong forms of educational models (the European Union schools plural multilingual model, the immersion model, the two-way dual language model—with the alternate days' model as a subtype—and the maintenance model) to three of the four E's—the 'external' goals in the Australian localised sense are not relevant here (whereas in a broader sense of 'external' goals they are of course the very topic of this book).

The societal aim of the **plural multilingual** model, with the **European Union schools** as a prototype, and of **immersion** programmes, is clearly one of **enrichment** for the participants themselves. It is more tricky to assess to what extent the enrichment is for the whole society, except in the general sense of societies always benefitting when more individuals become multilingual. As long as the schools cater for a socially selected clientele, they may enrich more the upper strata of society. On the other hand, as Joshua Fishman has pointed out many times, minorities will hardly have education leading to high levels of multilingualism on a large scale before dominant groups (and especially their elites) realise that multilingualism is also positive for their own children. In this sense, the European Schools and immersion education may be doing a great attitudinal job.

But it must be admitted that the societal goals in both these programmes have hitherto related less to **equity** than to middle class populations maintaining advantages and privileges or gaining new ones. This includes **economic** advantages. It is obvious that those who want to be included in the new globalised elites need to be multilingual, as earlier sections have shown. Therefore, the children of the A team and those who aspire to remain or get into the highest 20% in the 20–80 world model see to it that their children participate in education which makes this more likely. For them multilingualism means enhanced symbolic capital and, through a conversion process, economic and political capital. 'International Schools' have a similar goal even if they do not use several languages as media of instruction (see Carder 1995 on International Schools).

In the **two-way dual language** model, with the two-way schools in California and elsewhere in the United States as the prototype, the objective again is **enrichment**, this time for both the majority and the minority group. Some of the programmes, especially the ones with immigrant minority children from lower socioeconomic strata have had **equality** goals at least for the minority population participating. Sometimes this can be the case also for the 'majority' population which in several schools has reflected a wider range of groups than 'WASPs', for example, Black students have participated. Alternate days programmes, a sub-category of two-way programmes, are much more uncommon, and the Calistoga programme has certainly had elements of equality as one of its aims, in addition to enrichment. In relation to the minority populations in two-way programmes, both they themselves and society at large benefit **economically**; the groups themselves because the students get much better education than they would in a submersion programme, which otherwise would be the likely alternative, and society because these students are not being miseducated and their potential can be put to use in society. Dominant group students benefit economically in the same way as in immersion programmes.

Maintenance classes/schools are mostly organized and/or requested by an ethnolinguistic minority community. This type of multilingual programme **enriches** not only the participating individuals but society at large, by ensuring that minorities gain access to the linguistic and educational prerequisites for social, economic and political integration. This is also **economically** beneficial for both them and the rest of society, in the same way as for minorities in two-way programmes. Maintenance programmes work towards **equality**, both for the individuals involved, and for society at large, closing some gaps for indigenous and immigrant minority participants between dominant and dominated groups. For national minority groups they can either do the same (if the groups are not properly structurally incorporated), or they may work for equality only indirectly, by ensuring the observance of linguistic and cultural human rights in society.

In sum, the models can be characterized, admittedly oversimplifying somewhat, as follows:

Immersion programmes may do little to contribute towards the equality goal. They support the enrichment goal and the economic goal for the par-

ticipants in the programmes but less so for the rest of society: to the extent
that their intake is socially biassed, they 'give' to those who already have.

Maintenance programmes support the equality goal and the enrichment
goal for the minorities themselves, and help them economically. Indirectly
majorities benefit because maintenance models aid a better integration of
minorities into the broader society, as Mohanty (1994a) shows.

Two-way programmes and the European Schools plural multilingual models could also function as one positive solution for the educational system,
supporting all four goals, but certain preconditions have to be met first.
These will be outlined below when discussing the general principles, and in
the final section.

8.6. PRINCIPLES FOR EDUCATIONAL MODELS
WHICH RESPECT LINGUISTIC HUMAN RIGHTS

I said in the introduction to this book that it is more important to ask
why-questions than yet more sophisticated what- or how-questions, and most
of this book has emphasized why-questions. In this summary of possible
principles to follow, more narrow how-questions will be dealt with. They
should be seen in the context of what has been said about the broader goals
of various educational models.

In earlier sections the necessity of context-sensitivity and the need for
case-to-case designs were stressed when planning maintenance education for
minorities. Nancy Hornberger claims (1998: 449) that 'there is no one "program"—or even three programs, or ten, or twenty—that will necessarily
provide the best learning context for all biliterate learners'. I agree. Still,
Hornberger asserts (ibid., drawing on her earlier work, e.g., 1991, but see
other references to her work in the bibliography too) that 'there is accumu-
lating consensus, in both research and practice, that enrichment models of
bilingual education . . . offer much potential for both majority and minority
learners' academic success' (1998: 449), and mentions immersion and two-
way programs as examples of such enrichment models, recognising that there
are others too. My contention is that we know enough to start drawing some
broad conclusions about general principles which have to a large extent been
followed in most of those experiments which have reached the best results
(i.e., high levels of bi- or multilingualism, a fair chance of success in school
achievement, and positive intercultural identities and attitudes). I have formulated the principles as 8 recommendations which form one possible base-
line when assessing to what extent educational systems really support multilingualism. I will present them here with very few comments—they form
part of my introduction to the book **Multilingualism for All** (1995) which
compares many different types of successful experiments (i.e., the principles
are based on more types than the ones presented here) and draws conclusions

on the basis of them (see also Skutnabb-Kangas & García 1995 which works them out in much more concrete detail).

Here I assess only the strong models, and do it in a more or less polarized way, giving them pluses or minuses in the tables, in terms of whether they follow the principles below. I have added a 'utopian' model which gets a positive rating on all counts. First the principle is stated, then I comment on to what extent some of the models do or do not follow the 8 principles.

1. **Support (= use as the main medium of education, at least during the first 8 years) the language (of the two that the child is supposed to become bilingual in initially) which is least likely to develop up to a high formal level.**

This language to be supported is for all minority children their own mother tongue. For majority children, it should be a minority language.

The European Schools do not follow this principle completely. In each school, the children in the subsection(s) corresponding to the official language(s) of the country where the school is placed, are majority children. But the schools also teach these majority children initially through the medium of their mother tongues. For instance, Italian-speaking children in the European School **in Italy** are initially taught through the medium of Italian, rather than a minority language.

Alternate days programmes do not support the minority language on those days when they teach in the dominant language.

LANGUAGE SHELTER	IMMERSION	ALTERN. DAYS	EUROP. SCHOOLS	TWO-WAY	UTOPIAN
+	+	+/–	MI+ MA–	+	+

2. In most successful experiments, **the children are initially grouped together with children with the same L1**. Mixed groups are not positive initially, and certainly not in cognitively demanding decontextualised subjects.

Spanish-English two-way (and alternate days) programmes in the USA do not follow this principle: they have mixed in the same class 50% minority, 50% majority children. All are initially taught through the medium of the minority language, later through both.

This may be a relevant factor in accounting for the Spanish-speaking children's **sometimes** relatively less impressive gains in **both** languages, compared to English-speaking children in the same programmes. The mere presence of majority language children in the same classroom may be too overwhelming for minority children, despite the minority language being the medium of education. When there are speakers of a high status language in the class, this may also lead to teachers adjusting the linguistic level in the teaching more to the competence of the dominant group representatives, both when they teach through the medium of Spanish and when they teach in English. This might in some cases mean that the Spanish level is too low (or sometimes too formal, as it may be) for the Spanish speakers, and that English is taught either at too high a level or not contrastively enough for the Spanish speakers. Also some teachers have themselves observed that they tend to take it for granted that the Spanish speakers become bilingual. They may notice more the gains of English speakers (because it is more unusual that English-speakers become bilingual), and also praise **them** more for their bilingualism, for example, 'show them up' to visitors, etc.

All this speaks for the soundness of initial physical separation.

LANGUAGE SHELTER	IMMERSION	ALTERN. DAYS	EUROP. SCHOOLS	TWO-WAY	UTOPIAN
+	+	–	+	–	+

3. **All children are to become high level bilinguals**, not only minority children.

This seems to be especially important in contexts where majority and minority children are mixed. This is one of the positive aspects of both two-way and alternative days programmes, as well as the European Schools model.

LANGUAGE SHELTER	IMMERSION	ALTERN. DAYS	EUROP. SCHOOLS	TWO-WAY	UTOPIAN
+	+	+	+	+	+

4. **All children have to be equalized vis-à-vis the status of their mother tongues and their knowledge of the language of instruction.**

Nice phrases about the worth of everybody's mother tongue, the value of interculturalism, and so on, serve little purpose, unless they are really followed up in how the schools are organised.

There has to be equality in the demands made on the children's and the teachers' competencies in the different languages involved, so that the same demands are made on everybody. Both minority and majority children and teachers must be or become bi- or multilingual.

There has to be equality in the **status and roles** that the languages are accorded on the schedules and in higher education, in testing and evaluation, in marks given for the languages, in the physical environment (signs, forms, letters, the school's languages of administration, the languages of meetings, assemblies, etc.), in the status and salaries of the teachers, in their working conditions, career patterns, etc.—see Skutnabb-Kangas & García 1995 for details; see also García 1992, in press.

It is possible to equalize the children vis-à-vis their **knowledge of the language of instruction** in several different ways:

A. **All children know the language of instruction** (maintenance programmes, European Schools initially);
B. **No children know the language of instruction** or everybody is in the process of learning it (immersion programmes, European Schools in certain subjects in a late phase);
C. **All children alternate between 'knowing' and 'not knowing' the language of instruction** (two-way programmes in a late phase, but not initially; alternate days programmes, European schools).

LANGUAGE SHELTER	IMMERSION	ALTERN. DAYS	EUROP. SCHOOLS	TWO-WAY	UTOPIAN
+ A	+ B	+ C	+ A, C	–	+

5. **Foreign languages should be taught through the medium of the children's mother tongue and/or by teachers who know the children's mother tongue.**

No teaching in foreign languages as subjects should be given through the medium of **other** foreign languages (for instance, Turkish children in Germany should not be taught English through the medium of German, but via Turkish).

LANGUAGE SHELTER	IMMERSION	ALTERN. DAYS	EUROP. SCHOOLS	TWO-WAY	UTOPIAN
varies	+?	?	varies	?	+

6. **All children must study both L1 and L2 as compulsory subjects through grades 1–12.**

Both languages have to be studied in ways which reflect what they are for the children: mother tongues, or second or foreign languages. Many minority children are forced to study a majority language, their L2, as if it was their L1. Often they are also evaluated in it on the same grounds as L1-speakers.

LANGUAGE SHELTER	IMMERSION	ALTERN. DAYS	EUROP. SCHOOLS	TWO-WAY	UTOPIAN
+	–	+?	+	–	+

7. **Both languages have to be used as media of education in some phase of the children's education, but the progression in how and how much each is used seems to vary for minority and majority children.**

For *majority children* the **mother tongue** must function as the medium of education at least in some cognitively demanding, decontextualized subjects, at least in grades 8–12, possibly even earlier.

Majority children can be taught **through the medium of L2** at least in some (or even all or almost all) cognitively **less** demanding context-embedded subjects from the very beginning, and L2 can also be the medium of education, at least partially, in cognitively demanding decontextualized subjects, at least in grades 8–12.

For *minority children* the **mother tongue** must function as the medium of education in all subjects initially. At least some subjects must be taught through L1 all the way, up to grade 12, but the choice of subjects may vary. It seems that the following development functions well pedagogically:

- transfer from the known to the unknown, a general pedagogical principle;
- transfer from teaching in a language (as a subject) to teaching through the medium of that language;
- transfer from teaching through the medium of L2 in cognitively less demanding, context-embedded subjects, to teaching through the medium of L2 in cognitively demanding decontextualized subjects.

LANGUAGE SHELTER	IMMERSION	ALTERN. DAYS	EUROP. SCHOOLS	TWO-WAY	UTOPIAN
+	+	+?	+	+?	+

The progression used for all children in the European Schools seems close to the ideal for minority children. The progression in relation to the **(minority) mother tongue** is as follows:

1. All subjects are taught through the medium of the mother tongue during the first 2 years.
2. All cognitively demanding decontextualized core subjects are taught through the medium of the mother tongue during the first 7 years.
3. There is less teaching through the medium of the mother tongue in grades 8–10, and again more teaching through the medium of the mother tongue in grades 11–12, especially in the most demanding subjects, in order to ensure that the students have understood them thoroughly.
4. The mother tongue is taught as a subject throughout schooling, from 1–12.

The progression in relation to the **second language** is as follows:

1. The second language is taught as a subject throughout schooling, from 1–12.

2. The second language becomes a medium of education already in grade 3, but only in cognitively less demanding context-embedded subjects. The teaching can be given in mixed groups, but ideally together with other children for whom the language is also an L2.

3. Teaching in cognitively demanding decontextualized subjects only starts through the medium of L2 when the children have been taught that language as a subject for 7 years (grades 1–7) and have been taught through the medium of that language in cognitively less demanding context-embedded subjects for 5 years (grades 3–7). Children should not be taught demanding decontextualized subjects through L2 with other children for whom the language of instruction is their L1 before grade 8. In European Schools this is mostly not done even in grades 9–12 in compulsory subjects, only in elective courses.

8. **All teachers have to be bi- or multilingual**. Thus they can be good models for the children, and support them in language learning (through comparing and contrasting and being metalinguistically aware, also vis-à-vis those aspects of the languages which correspond to the common underlying proficiency—see Cummins).

Every child in a school has to be able to talk to an adult with the same native language.

This demand is often experienced as extremely threatening by majority group teachers, many of whom are not bilingual.

Of course all minority group teachers are not high level bilinguals either. But it is often **less** important that the teacher's competence in a dominant majority language is at top level, for instance in relation to pronunciation, because all minority children have ample opportunities to hear and read native models of a dominant majority language outside the school, whereas many of them do *not* have the same opportunities to hear/read native **minority** language models in formal contexts.[30] A high level of competence in a minority language is thus more important for a teacher than a high level of competence in a majority language.

LANGUAGE SHELTER	IMMERSION	ALTERN. DAYS	EUROP. SCHOOLS	TWO-WAY	UTOPIAN
+ (ma ?)	+	+	+	+	+

Since the support that teachers can give (or withhold) for linguistic human rights in education is so vital and the issue of their linguistic competence decisive, I want to look into it in somewhat more detail. There are two important issues involved.

The first, to what extent a monolingual teacher (or a teacher who does not know both languages involved in students' bilingualism) can support a student optimally, has already been discussed extensively in several chapters. I will only repeat here that I think there is enough evidence for the claim that **a monolingual teacher teaching students who are to become bilingual or multilingual is by definition an incompetent teacher for those students**, except as an occasional guest teacher.

Here I want to dwell on the second issue: does a teacher of L2 have to be a native speaker of that language or not? To what extent and for what aspects of teaching, for instance, ESL, might native speaker and standard language speaker/writer English teachers have advantages over second or foreign[31] language speakers or non-standard speakers/writers. There are literally hundreds of possible relevant criteria.

One could start by asking whether there are any arguments for why native speakers/writers (hereafter NS) or standard language speakers/writers, would be 'better', as compared to non-native or 'non-standard' speakers, or speakers with a 'non-native' accent, on a number of accounts. For each, one could review the literature (see Lippi-Green 1997), and come with a claim. I will present **some** of the questions and my tentative claims. Are NS better as models? Easier to understand for learners? Better in understanding learner output? Better in understanding and analysing what learners need to know and better in enabling learners to develop high levels of metalinguistic awareness?

■ Are native speakers of English (NS) better as **models** than second (SLS) or foreign language speakers (FLS)?

Not necessarily. It seems, among other things, to depend on how many (other) NS models and how rich a variation is available to learners, in addition to the teacher. Access to NS models is important in foreign language contexts, but they can be live or taped; in second language contexts NS models are in the environment. The difference between second language vs foreign language contexts is also important vis-à-vis the complexities of the relationship between input and intake. All that is heard/taught, is not learned. What is learned can be for many different purposes and levels. It can also be for reception, or for production. Is input processing meant to result mainly in comprehension, or is it for productive acquisition/intake/integration? To what extent does the learner need to attend to and to process **details** of linguistic form (converting input to intake, creating new mental rules and structures, input becoming part of an acquired linguistic system).

In second language contexts, often a NS teacher has few advantages. In FL contexts there are some, depending on the access to NS models, live, on tape, video, TV etc.

■ Are NSs easier to understand than SLSs or FLSs?

Not necessarily. It depends on the NS's own experience, degree of meta-linguistic awareness and awareness of what is difficult in a language and

---

❖ **I n f o   B o x   8 . 7** ❖

Students Prejudiced Against Understanding Non-Native Teachers—Try to Improve Students' Attitudes (Rubin); *Make Them Aware of the Subordination Model and Standard Language Ideology* (Lippi-Green)

'Vindication may be nigh for foreign teaching assistants whose students whine about the unintelligibility of their instructors' accents' (Wilson 1993: 6). According to a study by Donald Rubin, Professor of Language Education and Speech Communication at the University of Georgia, 'the communication gap may have less to do with fractured vowels than with how their students feel about foreigners' (this and the following quotes are from Wilson 1993: 6–7). Rubin tape-recorded a four-minute lecture given by an Ohio-born 'white' woman, then played the tape back to two separate groups of undergraduates in two different rooms. In each room he projected a slide of a woman he identified as the lecturer; in one room the woman pictured was 'white', in the other she was Chinese. 'To avoid confounding ethnicity with physical attractiveness,' Rubin wrote in his report, 'both models were similarly dressed, were of similar size and hairstyle, and were photographed in the same setting and pose (standing at a lectern in front of a chalkboard).'

The students who thought the lecture was being given by the Chinese woman scored lower on a listening-comprehension test than those who thought the lecture was given by a 'white' woman. The first group scored about the same as a third group that had listened to a lecture actually given by a Chinese teaching assistant with what Rubin calls a **heavy** accent. The students who thought the speaker was foreign also rated her teaching skills lower than those who thought that she was 'American'.[32]

In another experiment, Rubin had two Chinese teaching assistants record short lectures twice, first exaggerating their accents, then downplaying them. He found that undergraduates who listened to the tapes couldn't tell the difference.

'Rubin's findings may affect more than the egos of teaching assistants, since many universities have by now invested significant amounts of time and money in "pronunciation-improvement" programs for their foreign teaching assistants. Pronunciation workshops are often mandatory. A Professor of Speech & Language Pathology at Northeastern University recently developed a talking software program that has foreign teaching assistants sitting at Macintoshes and imitating, over and over, a standard English "model voice." Many states in the US have even passed laws requiring colleges and universities to test the proficiency of all teaching assistants' English, and to arrange remedial education for those who flunk.

(Continued)

❖ I n f o   B o x   8 . 7 ❖

(Continued)

Rubin thinks these efforts may miss their mark. "There's no point in trying to teach the teaching assistants to sound like Tom Brokaw," he says. "It won't happen, and even if it did, their students would still be prejudiced against understanding them." A better solution, he says: "Try to improve students' attitudes about being taught by foreigners. After all, today's teaching assistants are tomorrow's professors." '

In Rosina Lippi-Green's terms, awareness of the standard language ideology might help the students to analyse their own stereotypes about foreign speakers, stereotypes which often cause them to refuse to accept their fair share of the 'communicative burden'. This refusal may often lead to a failure to understand a non-native speaker—of course there are many other reasons too.

Lippi-Green's excellent analyses (cf. especially 1997) clearly show that many minorities in the USA are often believed to have 'foreign' accents when they do not: racism is often externalised through claims of non-comprehension (just as sexism is externalised). Often non-native speakers may accept this exo-definition of their English, thereby submitting to the 'subordination model' which Lippi-Green describes. The same is often true for native speakers who do not conform to the standard so called 'mainstream' pronunciation (terms which themselves, through statistical and ideological normalisation, legitimate (upper) middle class speech).

---

how to simplify or enhance understanding. I give some examples in Info Box 8.7.

The importance of relating accent evaluation and awareness to power relations and symbolic capital cannot be overestimated—just telling people to 'be nice' to each other is hardly a productive strategy, and awareness alone does not necessarily change value judgements . . .

■ Are NSs better in understanding learner output than SLSs or FLSs? Linguistically maybe, culturally maybe not.

■ Are NSs better in understanding and analysing what learners need to know than SLSs or FLSs? Probably the opposite, and especially if they are monolingual.

■ Are NS better in enabling learners to develop high levels of metalinguistic awareness than SLSs or FLSs? Again, probably the opposite, especially if they are monolingual.

In addition to asking whether NSs or standard speakers are better than SLSs/FLSs/NNSs, we could unpick the metaphor 'native speaker' in another way and do what Ben Rampton suggests. When educationalists have communicative aspects of language in mind (language as an instrument of communication, rather than language as a symbol of social identity), accomplished users of a language should be called 'experts' rather than 'native speakers', he suggests (1990: 98–99). Rampton presents the following list of the **advantages of expertise rather than nativeness** for considering language proficiency.

1. Although they often do, experts do not have to feel close to what they know a lot about. Expertise is different from identification.

2. Expertise is learned, not fixed or innate.

3. Expertise is relative. One person's expert is another person's fool.

4. Expertise is partial. People can be expert in several fields, but they are never omniscient.

5. To achieve expertise, one goes through processes of certification, in which one is judged by other people. Their standards of assessment can be reviewed and disputed. There is also a healthy tradition of challenging 'experts'. (Rampton 1990: 99)

The great benefit in unpicking the notion of 'native speaker' is, according to Rampton (1990: 99), that 'the notion of "expert" rather than "native speaker" shifts the emphasis from "who you are" to "what you know", and this has to be a more just basis for the recruitment of teachers'. I agree.

It is important, though, to emphasize that expert knowledge also includes knowledge of sociolinguistic questions of what is necessary for minority languages to be maintained and sociopolitical questions of the consequences of different educational choices—otherwise teachers in, for instance, transitional programmes may do what Ofelia García warns against: '. . . how these Latino teachers think they're contributing to the maintenance of Spanish when, in fact, they're only accelerating the group's shift to English' (1993: 25).

A third practical way of approaching the issue might then be to continue unpicking the **expertise** in terms of the capacities/proficiencies good teachers have, in terms of learner needs, and then compare NSs and SLSs/FLSs with them. Some of the capacities/proficiencies learners need from teachers in relation to our topic could be the following where I paraphrase some of Phillipson's discussion (1992b: 15) and relate it to our concerns:

■ High levels of functional competence in the target language. Both NSs and SLSs/FLSs can have that. It is likely that NSs have a higher competence in idiomatic pronunciation—but in second language situations this is not important. They may also be more competent in semantic fields and in terms of idiomatic expressions, but not necessarily.

■ High levels of analytical competence in the target language. Both NSs and SLSs/FLSs can have that, but it is more likely that a *trained* SLS/FLS teacher has it.

- Insight into the linguistic and cultural background and needs of their learners. It is (much) more likely that SLSs/FLSs have that if they teach students from their own group.
- A detailed awareness of how the mother tongue and the target language differ and what is difficult for learners. It is **much** more likely that SLSs/FLSs have that if they teach students from their own group.
- First-hand experience of having learned and of using a second or foreign language. SLSs/FLs (almost) always have it; NSs can have it but it is more unusual.

Phillipson's own conclusion is:

> It is arguable, as a general principle, that non-native teachers may, in fact, be better qualified than native speakers, if they have gone through the complex process of acquiring English as a second or foreign language, have insight into the linguistic and cultural needs of their learners, a detailed awareness of how mother tongue and target language differ and what is difficult for learners; and first-hand experience of using a second or foreign language. (Phillipson 1992b: 15)

Peter Medgyes' 1994 book **The non-native teacher** is an excellent discussion about the matter.

It seems, though, that resistance towards having non-native speaker teachers may be one of the hardest problems to overcome. I have had the experience in many countries when presenting the eight principles that the principle of bilingual teachers, who know the students' mother tongue (which often in practice means non-native speakers of the dominant language even if this is by no means a necessity) evokes very strong negative feelings among the audience, especially among dominant group teachers. Sometimes all international solidarity and a lot of the normal rational argumentation disappears when it is a question of one's own job, and realising that somebody else might be more qualified. This seems to hold equally strongly in the case of teachers of the Deaf—in most countries most of the teachers are hearing; few teachers of the Deaf are themselves confident and proficient users of a sign language (see, e.g., Reagan & Penn 1997: 6 for South Africa)—see also section 4.1.4.1 on missionary attitudes and hearing control of Deaf education). Info Box 8.8 shows that these feelings are shared by non-teachers too.

Back to principles guiding educational models which succeed in enabling high levels of multilingualism. Alternatives, further developments and discussions about both possible principles and, especially, concrete experience, are vital, and some new trends are emerging, even for seeing the benefits of bilingual teachers.[33]

❖ Info Box 8.8 ❖

Resistance Towards Non-Native Teachers
(Wingstedt, Sweden; Jaakkola, Finland)

Maria Wingstedt asked in her representative study in Sweden: 'Is it acceptable that a person in the following professional categories speaks Swedish with a (foreign) accent? (on the understanding that the speech is **understandable**). Responses: Yes/Maybe/No/Don't know' (1998: 217). The 12 occupations represented variability on three dimensions: **social status** (bus driver versus doctor), **national-symbolic function** (prime minister versus carpenter), and **verbal load** (social welfare officer versus hospital orderly). The responses below (from Wingstedt 1998: 280, Table 8.4 here prepared on the basis of her Table 24) show that the occupation where least people accept 'a foreign accent', i.e., a non-native speaker, is a teacher of Swedish. Your doctor, police officer, other teachers, your TV news reader, and even your prime minister can be non-natives, but NOT your dominant language teacher (see Wingstedt 1998 for details).

TABLE 8.4
Is foreign accent acceptable? Wingstedt

Foreign accent acceptable?	Yes	Maybe	No	Don't know
carpenter	86.1	12.1	1.5	0.3
bus driver	75.2	20.3	4.2	0.3
hospital orderly	73.3	17.0	9.1	0.6
doctor	71.5	16.4	11.5	0..6
social welfare officer	57.0	20.0	20.9	2.1
civil servant	53.6	21.2	23.3	1.8
police officer	53.5	19.1	26.1	1.2
teacher of a subject other than Swedish	50.5	29.2	18.5	1.8
tele-marketing operator	47.9	26.2	24.4	1.5
TV news reader	26.7	18.8	54.1	0.3
prime minister	22.5	18.8	58.7	0.3
teacher of Swedish (in schools)	14.2	17.0	67.6	1.2

Some part of Wingstedt's results can be compared with Jaakkola's (in press) study from Finland about **contact with 'foreigners' in various roles**, i.e., **not** accents (see section 3.3.3 for some of Jaakkola's results; her questions are identical or comparable to her own 1987 and 1993 studies and to Lange & Westin 1991 in Sweden). If one combines Jaakkola's two positive categories for contact with 'foreigners' in various roles ('very or somewhat pleasant/acceptable', as compared to 'not very or not at all pleasant/acceptable)', the percentages for positive categories in Finland were, in descending order: cleaner 85%, friend

(Continued)

❖ **I n f o   B o x   8 . 8** ❖

(Continued)

83%, work mate 83%, neighbour 77%, taxi driver 76%, your children's teacher 74%, doctor 69%, your boss 67%, spouse of your relative 65%, child minder 64%, unemployment officer 59%, police 58%, social welfare officer 57%, spouse 48%. On the other hand, Jaakkola's 'contact' may require much more 'tolerance' than just accepting an accent as in Wingstedt's study.

But what we can already now say is that observing the principles which I have outlined also includes respecting linguistic human rights in education. If all education were to follow principles honouring LHRs, high levels of multilingualism would be likely to follow for both minorities and majorities.

8.7. CONTEXTUALISING IS NECESSARY . . . BUT NOT ENOUGH

Trying to summarise extremely complicated educational matters has necessarily entailed huge overgeneralisations, and the argumentation is to some extent crude. There are no simple solutions. Still a few generalisable trends emerge.

Education (or lack of education) is one of the most decisive factors in determining the life chances and human development of today's children (regardless of which opinion we have about the relative utility or futility of literacy and formal education). Of the factors decisive for educational success, choice of medium of education is one of the most important ones among those which can be changed.

High levels of multilingualism and multiculturalism benefit every child, but for minority children bilingualism is a necessary minimum. It is possible to achieve, if the main principles outlined above are followed.

The language to be supported in everyone's education, the language which otherwise does not get the chance to develop, is for minority children their mother tongue, and for 'simple' majorities (who are majorities in terms of both numbers and power, like English-speakers in Canada) a minority language. These are the 'easy' cases: ethnolinguistic minority children should be educated through the medium of their mother tongues, and majority children should be educated mainly through the medium of a minority language. But what about the others?

If several minorities together form the majority, the choice of medium of education needs to reflect the current power relations between the minority groups and the group whose language they want to learn as their second or foreign language. The weaker the minority groups, the stronger the emphasis on their own language should be. If economic and political relations change, for instance if the minority groups get relatively more power, more emphasis can be put on the learning of the second language without this necessarily harming the development of the minority languages.

Being educated through the medium of one's own language but wanting to become bilingual (i.e., wanting to learn another language too) necessitates either much contact with that second language or good teaching in it, given by bilingual well-trained teachers. In many contexts there may be little (or possibly almost no personal) contact with the second necessary language in the environment, though, and especially with native variants of the language. Even when a language is an official language, if it is an old colonial language with fairly few native[34] speakers in the country (like in much of Africa), learning that language may resemble a foreign language learning situation. Extremely good teaching in that language is then needed if high levels of bilingualism are to be reached—and this is something that most African countries do not have. The situation may be very different if the second language one wants to learn is a dominant regional language which one can hear in the environment. It might also be easier to train competent teachers of African lingua francas.

'Good teaching' also involves critically assessing what variety of an L2 should be the goal and for what purposes it should be taught (see Pakir 1991 and articles in Tickoo (ed.) 1991 for discussions). The stigmatisation of African languages during the colonial period and contemporary neo-colonial economic politics and concomitant ideologies have produced a widespread colonised consciousness. African languages are in a weak position (and need all the support schools can give), even when the former colonial power is no longer physically present with armies. The situation is broadly similar in several other ex-colonial contexts too, and many types of contextualised solution have been proposed.[35] A colonised consciousness can make it necessary to treat a group which could otherwise be seen as a simple majority (and be educated in a foreign language) as a powerless majority (which should be educated through the mother tongue/s). This seems to apply in most sub-Saharan African states where the choice of a foreign medium of education at present reflects linguicism and where change is urgently needed.

But again, situations can change rapidly, as we have seen in many parts of the world recently (e.g., Eastern Europe—see Marshall 1996, Marti (ed.) 1996, Ozolins 1996, Rannut 1999—or Southern Africa—see references to Alexander and Heugh). Learning priorities are sensitive to sociopolitical contexts. Wallace's views on what kind of learning priorities are important in the educational systems in various historical politico-ideological phases are instructive here. According to Wallace (1961; see Table 8.5), groups undergoing **revitalisation** are in a revolutionary phase. In this phase, **moral**

TABLE 8.5
Learning priorities in Revolutionary, Conservative, and Reactionary Societies

REVOLUTIONARY PHASE	CONSERVATIVE PHASE	REACTIONARY PHASE
Morality	Technique	Morality
Intellect	Morality	Technique
Technique	Intellect	Intellect

(Source: from Wallace 1961)

learning will always be stressed. If we apply Wallace to languages, the mother tongue may be seen as an aspect of this moral learning, while language skills in other languages, for instance the dominant majority language for a minority, can in this phase be seen as an aspect of technique: it is necessary for instrumental reasons.

If a revitalisation movement takes place in a **conservative** society, where what Wallace calls 'technique' has the highest learning priority, there is bound to be conflict, because 'in conservative societies schools prepare people not for sacrifice[36] but for jobs' (R. Paulston 1972: 478). Minority groups, both indigenous and immigrant, in a revolutionary phase, where they have started demanding rights, are mobilising and often stress the importance of the mother tongue, as a necessary (often primordial) bond both between the group's members, and between the group and its history and culture. Even if the learning of the dominant language may be important, it is seen as a technical skill where not much of the group's emotional strength is invested. Thus there is often a conflict between the group and the majority society— this could, for instance, explain the bad results in the learning of the Russian language in Eastern and Central Europe.

When the minority group itself is in a conservative phase, the learning of a language may be a matter of mere 'technique' (but important technique, a high learning priority, for instrumental purposes), like Russian in principle could have been for a federal-career-minded Uzbek or Estonian before the new popular movements and (re)-independence. This could also be exploited by the Turkish state to make Kurds learn Turkish—and it has. Learning some other language could in a conservative phase be part of a competence for the 'intellectual' purpose of becoming educated, as the mother tongue, Uzbek or Estonian, could have been for the person above.

This can during a new revolutionary revitalisation phase change so that **both** languages become part of moral learning. Then resisting or unlearning Russian, and learning Uzbek and Estonian could become a high priority because it could be seen as part of 'morality'.

In a reactionary phase, like the Third Reich in Germany, the German language might for fascists again have become a moral high priority, whereas other languages which could have been used for the purpose of getting access to an intellectual analysis of what was happening, could have had a low educational priority. This way of analysing might also be used to explain the difference between an emphasis on the mother tongue in the educational system for reactionary nationalist purposes (reactionary phase), and for liberation and empowerment (revolutionary phase).

It is possible that many African states, on the other hand, may after independence, which required struggle and sacrifice, be closer to a conservative phase, trying to stabilise their development. In this type of society, technical skills like the learning of the official language (where it is not a local language) may for some time have a much higher priority than learning the mother tongue (a fact which makes the operation of linguicism easier).

On the other hand, Africa seems in many senses to have lagged even further behind during the decade since the disintegration of the Soviet Union which redirected some of the development cooperation flows and investments away from Africa. This has been happening during the financial crises in many parts of the world which have reinforced the lack of investment in Africa and caused the still worsening trade conditions. The many internal African wars are part of this. This may again in time lead to a more revolutionary phase, if not for any other reason except the situation is so desperate, and Africa cannot reckon on much outside support

In fact there are signs of a reorientation happening in the language-in-education field. An example is the fairly recent Harare Declaration by an Intergovernmental Conference of Ministers on Language Policies in Africa, Harare 20–21 March 1997), recommending mother tongue medium teaching (reproduced in **New Language Planning Newsletter** 11:4, 1997, 2–4). The Minister of State for Basic Education and National Language of Senegal, Mamadou Ndoye, writes in UNESCO's education journal **Prospects** (1997), in an article called 'Globalization, Endogenous Development and Education in Africa', that 'endogenous development postulates the promotion of cultural identity . . . To that end, it is vital to bring African national languages into education systems' (1997: 83). He then goes on to argue why it is necessary to use the African languages as media of education. Kwesi Prah has argued strongly for the same in several books and articles (e.g., 1995a, b), and many similar voices are being heard more and more strongly.

Attitudes may also lag behind in abrupt large-scale changes. When a former power majority, like Russian speakers in the Baltic countries, suddenly become a minority, it may take a long transition time before they get used to seeing themselves as a minority. The Russian language in the Baltics must, for instance, probably during a fairly long transitional period be treated as a majority language for all educational purposes (including organising immersion programmes for Russian speakers), whereas the Baltic languages, Estonian, Latvian, and Lithuanian, must for educational purposes be treated as minority languages, in need of protection. **Russian** is thus **a majorized**

minority language (a minority language in terms of numbers, but with the power of a majority language), whereas **the Baltic languages** are **minorized majority languages** (majority languages, in need of the protection usually necessary for threatened minority languages—see references to Druviete and Rannut in the bibliography; see also Ozolins 1999, and my 1994b).

I and Robert Phillipson (1989: 465) have also suggested that

> belonging to a dominant group, economically, politically, and linguistically, may be comparable to being in a permanent conservative phase. Some kind of revitalization may be what is needed before dominant linguistic groups become aware of the importance of their mother tongues . . . Many Western linguicists may never have experienced cross-linguistic interactional reciprocity. Not experiencing situations with equal relations between languages, and always being linguistically unthreatened may dull sensitivity to language issues. Being linguistically blinkered may contribute to permanent conservatism. It may prevent one from seeing the relativity of one's own vision, or from knowing that one has a vision in the first place, especially when one profits from linguicism economically and politically. Thus we agree with Khubchandani (1986: 26) when he says that 'identification through a particular language label is very much a matter of social awareness on the part of the individual'.

Still another way of contextualising is to see minorities and majorities as more or less secure in their roles (Moscovici & Paicheler 1978). If a **majority** is **mature and secure**, it does not feel threatened by the existence of minorities and can afford to grant minorities protection. If a **majority** is **insecure**, it tries, mostly by physical or psychologcal force, to get rid of minorities: to make them leave the country (as happened around both World Wars in Europe), to commit genocide, to assimilate or to segregate minorities. This might have applied to Russians during the Soviet era, but it is puzzling if English-speakers in the USA need to feel insecure (or have to be judged as less mature) in this sense—still movements like English Only can easily be analysed from this angle.

If a **minority** is **secure**, its members are proud of their language and culture, at the same time as they want to learn the dominant language and culture, become bilingual and bicultural. A secure minority is loyal towards the state where it lives, in exchange for rights. An **insecure** minority self-segregates or tries to assimilate.

The most positive combination is that of a secure majority and a secure minority. The situation of the Swedish speakers in Finland can today be seen as an example but it has by no means always been problem-free (see McRae 1997). The lethal combination is one where both are insecure. An example would be the Russian speakers in at least Estonia and Latvia, possibly also Lithuania, at the beginning of the 1990s—today the situation is better (see Rannut 1999, Ozolins 1999, Druviete 1999). The insecurity in the whole Central and Eastern European situation is still to some extent worrying, as President Václav Havel analysed it in the same terms as here (1992). Today's South Africa has similar traits if we take all the African nations together as representatives of a majority (and the English and especially Afrikaans-speaking 'white' groups will need a long transition period to become real minorities—there is still a lot of majorisation in their attitudes).

An insecure majority combined with a secure minority also leads to massive problems—Slovakia of the late 1990s is an example (see Lanstyák, in press). There may be fewer problems with a secure majority and insecure minorities but then this would be an unusual case.

Many similar distinctions could be made. This means that every solution has to be constantly contextualized in the historical situation in which it is being proposed, and its efficiency and meaningfulness re-evaluated when the political situation changes. It also means that even when many psychological, linguistic, pedagogical, and sociological factors which guide a child's learning remain the same, their relative importance in relation to political priorities has to be separately assessed in each situation.

What we should demand, however, is that the criteria guiding decisions should be opened up to debate, especially in situations where what is sound and good for children from a psychological, linguistic, pedagogical, or sociological point of view, is rejected for political reasons—as it is in the non-education offered to most minority children in the world today. The political reasons should be made explicit, so that they can be debated and questioned, instead of being hidden behind quasi-arguments of a psychological or linguistic kind, as is mostly the case today.

Very few educational programmes in Europe for migrant minorities try to make the children bilingual, even if many claim that they do. They practise linguicism, as we have shown. But why do they do that? If we as linguists tell them that all languages are of equal worth, and make them aware of the problems, might they not change? If we tell them how minority children should be educated in order for them to reach high levels of bilingualism and to achieve at school, would they not organise education accordingly? Likewise, if we tell the decision-makers in underdeveloped countries what the role of the mother tongues is in achieving literacy and universal primary education and in supporting children's multilingualism through schools, would they not organise the education differently, and choose different 'experts'? Is it not a question of lack of information?

The answer is a simple no.

Western industrial countries will need cheap labour at home in the future too. The shitwork still needs to be done by somebody **in** Western countries.

Underdeveloped countries produce much of the raw materials, food, clothing, and equipment that we use. The exploitation of those countries now just takes different, more invisible forms from earlier types of slavery and colonisation, but it is at least equally severe. We can, in cooperation with the elites in underdeveloped countries, force the bulk of their populations to continue to support and 'help' us.

But we cannot export all of our cleaning, cooking, sweeping, public transport, and washing up, or our sick and old, to be taken care of **in** underdeveloped countries, as easily as we export capital.

Therefore, the industrial world needs to educate the children of the migrants, the greatgreatgrandchildren of the slaves from the colonies, for these jobs (e.g., Castles & Kosack 1973, Castles 1980, Castles et al. 1984).

Therefore minority education and the education of powerless majorities need to be racist and linguicist—and minimal and based on monolingually oriented norms: in order to force the greatgrandchildren of the slaves to continue to do the shitwork for us in living Europe and Neo-Europes. Regardless of whether they do it in their own countries or as labour migrants or refugees in other underdeveloped countries or in overdeveloped countries. In this the education has so far succeeded.

Therefore education also has to prevent (most of) its victims from seeing that they are victims and to make them blame themselves. Therefore it also has to prevent those among the minorities and the powerless majorities who do not believe that failure to be their own fault, from doing anything about it. In these two tasks education has not succeeded quite as well.

And therefore the education of majorities in Europe and Neo-Europes needs to be racist, in order to keep the majorities in the state of monolingual stupidity, unaware of how they through their elites exploit the rest of the world. In this it has almost succeeded too.

Knowing one's mother tongue(s) and achieving high levels of multilingualism does **of course** not in itself change the world's power relations, and that is what is needed (see the Robert Miles quote finishing this book).

But language is necessary for analysing power relations, and action must be based on thorough analysis. This analysis includes an analysis of how issues about language in education dovetail with many other dimensions of social reproduction of a hegemonic order, for example the media, mcdonaldizing life styles, etc. Metalinguistic and metacultural awareness associated with high levels of multilingualism may make the choice between different possible alternatives more informed, both cognitively and affectively. Therefore, they are dangerous for those who at present have more than their fair share of our world's power and resources. Granting everybody linguistic human rights might be a start in trying to acquire instruments for analysis and understanding. And change.

Those minority rights which support the maintenance and reproduction of minorities as minorities are one way of correcting the imbalance of power in minority-majority relations where the future, homogenisation or diversity, is being negotiated. 'Minority rights are part of a democratic system. Through guaranteeing that minorities are treated fairly the majority is protecting itself; it is protecting stability and peace in the the country' (Papandreou 1992: 10).

NOTES

1. For instance Jean D'Souza, herself a native English-speaker, advocates regional language medium or English medium education, rather than mother tongue medium education, for Indian minority language child workers (in press; I am here referring to the pre-final manuscript). She seems to see as the only two possibilities for them **either** no formal education at all, which involves a continuation of their miserable human-rights-violating conditions, **or** at least a few years of formal education, but given either in a regional language or in English. She also seems to take the learning of some surface fluency in the (foreign) medium of teaching as sufficient for school achievement, quoting, without problematising, teacher opinions about children learning a new language in three months. This reasoning leaves out the third possibility, advocated by most Indian scholars who have done extensive research in the area, namely supporting education through the medium of the children's own languages (see references to, e.g., Mohanty, Annamalai, and Pattanayak in the bibliography—see also the conclusions of the **Study of Languages** report 1986 from India, quoted above).

2. The concept 'bilingual' can of course also be misused. In the USA (and Denmark, 'tosproget') it sometimes has the same negative connotations as LEP and NEP (see Insert 3.14)—it is used about minority children in the phase where they are still in the early phases of learning the dominant language. See Eva Hoffman's (1997) simply wonderful book about how she learned the new country—I have never seen any description that comes even close to it in sophistication.

3. See my Web-page for the references: <http://babel.ruc.dk/~tovesk/>.

4. The following two sections build partially on Skutnabb-Kangas & García 1995, developing Baker's distinction between weak and strong models of multilingual education. For these and typologies of bilingual education, see Baker 1993: 153ff, and Skutnabb-Kangas 1984a, chapter 6, which Baker in turn developed.

5. Just one example: Rolf Stomberg, the only German on the Board of BP Oil International, says in **Welt am Sonntag** (19 October 1997, Nr. 42, p. BR 1) in an interview about prerequisites for an international career, titled 'Sprachkenntnisse und Respekt vor der fremden Kultur', that the main issue in a culture is the language. Therefore, BP 'only employs graduates who master minimally three languages', one of them being English. He also emphasizes attitudes of respect towards other cultures, thinking of 'younger colleagues who go, for instance, to Turkey with the image of meeting an "underdeveloped" people. Then I can only say: these people have no idea about history or human beings.'

6. For instance a quarter of the children from the Hungarian minority in Slovakia were in Slovak medium schools in the mid-1990s. In an interesting study comparing a total of 1,604 students ('monolingual Hungarian students in Hungary and bilingual Hungarian students in Slovakia in both Hungarian and Slovak medium schools), István Lanstyák and Gizella Szabómihály (1997; see also their 1996) found that Slovak medium educated students used many more badly stigmatized varieties of Hungarian that both monolingual and bilingual students in Hungarian medium education (see review by Kontra 1998c).

7. There has been and is still a lively debate about the use of Signed oral languages (manual sign codes—see Definition Box 4.1), especially in the education of Deaf children. Many Deaf schools use manual sign codes, not Sign languages. These are by definition not ex-

ploiting the full possibilities of signing. For the Deaf, any Sign language corresponds to full communication while manual sign codes correspond to very partial, 'handicapped' communication. Because written languages are linear (you proceed from one place to the next, in a fixed order, you don't go back, you cannot write (or speak) several things at the same time, etc.), Signed languages also become linear, instead of being able to use all the possibilities that proper Sign Languages have of, for instance, doing several things at the same time, communicating in several modes simultaneously.

8. In classical terms use of pidgin presupposes that each communicator has a fully developed mother tongue (whatever this may mean). Some deaf children without access to signers may not have it.

9. This was an evaluation by some of the staff—I was naturally curious to know since I had been instrumental in securing his dispensation.

10. Submersion can sometimes be combined with segregation, as when immigrant minority children are taught in what otherwise is a segregation programme but where the medium of instruction is the official/national language of their country of origin—e.g., Kurdish children from Turkey taught through the medium of Turkish as opposed to Kurdish in Bavaria, Germany.

11. An interesting detail is that under apartheid, signing was traditionally only allowed in Black schools for the Deaf—see Penn & Reagan 1990.

12. This section draws heavily on Skutnabb-Kangas 1990.

13. What is functional 'illiteracy'? An example. '. . . I thort that I might beabel to improove my spelling and reading. It as bean veary interesting we have hadto torc infrunt of a groop of peapel witch I think is veary inportent.' This is what one of the participants in an Adult Literacy and Basic Education Unit course (for road workers, in paid company time, in the workplace) in Australia wrote after 6 weeks. The article describing the project (Compton 1989) does (maybe typically) not say anything about the mother tongues of the participants, but many of the participants in the picture (p. 9) have dark hair and look as if they could have other mother tongues than English. The extract above shows an acute metalinguistic phonological awareness—still the writer could be considered functionally illiterate according to some criteria. Some 10% of Australian adults 'have significant difficulty with reading, writing and basic mathematics', ranging 'from being unable to read food labels, street names, bus destination boards or stories to their children, to being reasonably literate—able to read with difficulty most items in a newspaper and write simple sentences—but avoiding these activities because of lack of confidence' (Compton 1989: 7). Of the Australian population 3.7% is officially defined as functionally illiterate (Lo Bianco 1987) but we do not know even here what proportion of them have other mother tongues than English.

14. This is recognized, for instance, in Estonian regulations on education where, even in the future, Russian-speakers can have their entire education, including secondary schools, through the medium of Russian if they so wish, and study Estonian as a second language (Rannut & Rannut 1995, Rannut 1999). This is important to note because of the misinformation about the Baltic states that is common in some Russian propaganda.

15. See, e.g., Section 2 in Cummins & Corson's 1997 edited book, where there are articles on bilingual education for the Basque Country (by M. Carmen Garmendia & Imanol Agote), Slovenia (Sonja Novak Lukanovič), Friesland (Durk Gorter), Ireland, Scotland, and Wales (Colin Baker), Ladino in Italy (Paolo E. Balboni) and Sorbian in Germany (Beverley Hall).

16. See, e.g., Skutnabb-Kangas 1987 and articles in Peura & Skutnabb-Kangas (eds) 1994, for examples of Finnish migrant minority children in maintenance programmes in Sweden. See also Eriksson 1994, Janulf 1998. Ethnic mother-tongue schools in the United States can be of this type, but most of them can better be labelled transitional—see Fishman 1980, García 1988, García and Otheguy 1988.

17. See, e.g., Balto (ed.) 1996, Balto & Todal 1997, Black 1990, Durie 1997, Stephen Harris 1990, Harris & Devlin 1997, Kāretu 1994, Khubchandani 1997b, Lotherington 1997, Magga

1994, Daniel McLaughlin 1992, McLaughlin & Tierney (eds) 1993, Stairs 1988, Svonni 1996, Vorih & Rosier 1978 for some examples.

18. Quechua and Aymara are not minority languages numerically but in terms of (lack of) power.

19. For a recent overview on indigenous protection in Canada, see Maurais 1996. See also Burnaby 1996.

20. Thanks to Grand Chief Matthew Coon Come and to the legal advisor of the Cree who had a long breakfast with me in Sydney in April 1995. They also lent me several relevant publications, including the source for the education information.

21. For minority protection in Hungary, see, e.g., Radó 1994, Retí 1995.

22. In the Expert Report which Professor Patrick Thornberry and I wrote for Max van der Stoel, the OSCE High Commissioner on National Minorities, after accompanying him on a mission to Hungary and Slovakia in January 1996, we pointed out several minor gaps in minority education provision in Hungary and massive problems in Slovakia.

23. See, e.g., Taylor 1993, on indigenous Mi'kmaq children in Canadian French immersion. See also Genesee 1976, Swain et al. 1990, Swain & Lapkin 1991. It seems that immersion programmes may produce better results with minority children than submersion, even if the medium of instruction is equally much a foreign language in both submersion and immersion. This can be explained by a number of factors, among them the fact that the medium is an L2 for **all** children in immersion, i.e., also for majority students. The teaching is therefore better adapted to the students' linguistic level in the foreign language. The norm is a student who is learning the language, not one who already knows it, as in typical submersion; the expectations are high but realistic; stress levels can therefore be low. See also articles in Cenoz & Genesee (eds) 1998 on multilingual programmes.

24. Finland could have started 10 years earlier. I suggested immersion programmes in Finland in 1972 (Skutnabb-Kangas 1972e), directly after Wallace Lambert had presented them in Europe for the first time at a small expert meeting at UNESCO, Paris, which I attended. There was interest and the plans had advanced quite far, when the Director of the National Board of Education changed; the new Director was not interested. The first programme in Finland started 10 years later, on the initiative of Christer Laurén.

25. There are, for instance, somewhat over 800 Danish children in the schools. Of these, 450 were in the Uccle school in Brussels and 350 in the school in Luxembourg in 1998, i.e., no other schools had a Danish subsection.

26. I would like to thank Hugo Baetens Beardsmore and Alex Housen for organising the visit, and the teachers in the school, especially Joanna Sancha and Julia Leigh for giving so much of their time to enlighten me and for sharing their delights and concerns.

27. See Skutnabb-Kangas 1988, 1991b, the introduction and final comments by the editors in Skutnabb-Kangas & Cummins (eds) 1988; see also Municio 1983, 1987, 1994, 1996, Hyltenstam & Tuomela 1996, Wingstedt 1996, Mullard 1985, 1986, Sivanandan 1982, Annamalai 1994, 1995, 1998.

28. See, e.g., Obura 1986, Akinnaso 1993. Birgit Brock-Utne's assessment (1993, 39) is that in many African countries the majority language is treated in the way minority languages are treated in the industrialized world. Therefore most African language speakers need much more educational support for their mother tongues, i.e., maintenance programmes.

29. For the varied aims of multilingual education, see, e.g., Baker 1993; Ferguson, Houghton and Wells 1977; Fishman 1976a, b; Hornberger 1991; Lo Bianco 1990a; Mohanty 1994; Skutnabb-Kangas & García 1995.

30. This is one of the main pedagogical differences between majority/minority situations on the one hand, and situations in multilingual countries with no definite majorities on the other hand. It is also one of the main differences between the dominant language being a language spoken by a numerical majority in a country (the situation for most indigenous peoples and all immigrant minorities) and the dominant language being an old colonial language

where there are few native speakers in the students' environment. In the contexts where the dominant language is not spoken by a majority in the children's environment (or the region or country) and where teachers thus are the most important linguistic role models, the teachers' competence in L2 is of course important.

31. In this section I use 'second language' as opposed to 'foreign' about a language which is habitually used by native speakers in minority childrens' environment.

32. Gender differences work in the same way. In a Swedish study by Jan Einarsson and Tor Hultman, students and teachers evaluated a text about the training of mother tongue teachers of Swedish, assessing the argumentation and the author in general. Half of them got it in a version where the person who argues is presented as the departmental director (at the Ministry of Education) Ingvar Lind and mentioned several times as *he*. The other half got the same argumentation, presented by a person with the same title but called Ingvor Lind, *she*. The informants were asked to evaluate the argumentation, and the person on a scale from 1 to 5. The results are given in Table 8.6 both for everybody and in terms of the gender of the evaluator:

TABLE 8.6
Whose argumentation is more competent and trustworthy?

	Total	Total	Female evaluator	Female evaluator	Male evaluator	Male evaluator
	Ingvor	Ingvar	Ingvor	Ingvar	Ingvor	Ingvor
TRUSTWORTHY	3.4	4.7	3.5	4.5	3.4	4.9
NONCHALANT	2.5	2.5	2.3	2.7	2.6	2.4
HUMANE	3.3	2.7	3.8	3.2	2.7	2.9
COMPETENT	3.3	3.9	3.3	3.7	3.0	4.3

How does it influence women, if we know that even if we say/write exactly the same as men do and in the same way (which we don't) we are being evaluated as much less competent and trustworthy, especially by men but also by other women? How does it influence men if they know that they are evaluated by females as a bit less humane, regardless of what they say/write?

Another study by Jan Einarsson: The same dialogue between a female (Margareta) and a male (Jörgen) from a play by Ingmar Bergman was presented to informants. Half of them got the original play, half got the reverse where Margareta says Jörgen's lines and he says her lines. The informants were asked to evaluate them as persons on a number of traits. Regardless of whose lines they say, their own or those of the other, Jörgen, the male, is evaluated as being more successful, dominant, humorous, nonchalant, difficult to understand, and passive than Margareta. Margareta, the female, is being evaluated as more aggressive, serious, emotional, logical, personal, romantic, gossiping, open, and submissive. Which results are in agreement with other research results? Or your own stereotypes? Which are not? Could these be replicated with ethnic group stereotypes?

33. TESOL (Teachers of English to Speakers of Other Languages) now has a Caucus of 'Nonnative English Speakers' (contacts George Braine <georgebraine@cuhk.edu.hk> and Jun Liu <junliu@u.arizona.edu>), and their anthology **Non-Native Educators in English Language Teaching** is in press with Lawrence Erlbaum (Braine 1999: 6). Even Henry Widdowson suggests, here summarised by Kip Cates (1999: 11) 'a reconsideration of translation, relating what the English students learn to the language they know. This also demands that we rethink the status of native and nonnative speaker teachers and the issue of pedagogical

competence. Although native speakers clearly possess communicative competence, they do not know English "as a foreign language" the way nonnative speaker teachers do'.

34. The model in, say, Nigeria, should obviously be good Nigerian speakers of English, not necessarily native speakers (even if there are native Afro-Saxon speakers of, for instance, Nigerian English) and certainly not native British or North American speakers of English.

35. For discussions see, e.g., Afolayan 1978, 1984, Akinnaso 1991, 1993, Angula 1984, Annamalai 1986a, b, c, d, 1993, 1995, 1998, Bailey 1998, Bokamba & Tlou 1980, Brock-Utne in press, Dalby 1985, Kalema 1980, 1985, Mateene 1980a, 1980b, 1985a, 1985b, Alamin Mazrui 1996, Ndoye 1997, Phillipson 1992, Phillipson & Skutnabb-Kangas 1985, 1994c.

36. In reactionary societies (e.g., many societies in or preparing for war, east and west—Israel, Iran, most western countries before and during the 'world' wars, etc.) education may prepare boys to sacrifice their lives.

Chapter **9**

Alternatives to Genocide
and Dystopia

There are three main types of distributional policies: those which envisage distribution from growth, those which plan for distribution with growth, and those which demand redistribution of the existing assets so as to promote economic growth.

Distribution from growth follows the logic of the 'trickle-down' approach—growth first, distribution later. Distribution with growth introduces a balance between promoting growth and addressing its distribution. Redistribution as a precondition for growth aims to ensure equal access to resources, hence challenging the acquired property rights. There are no human rights norms which would require countries to follow a specific distributional policy.[1]

651

Promoting growth, while neglecting distribution, increases inequality. (Tomaševski 1996: 108)

---

9. ALTERNATIVES TO GENOCIDE AND DYSTOPIA

9.1. WEAK FORMS AND NON-FORMS OF 'BILINGUAL' EDUCATION AMOUNT TO GENOCIDE BY 'FORCIBLY TRANSFERRING CHILDREN OF THE GROUP TO ANOTHER GROUP' (FROM THE UN GENOCIDE CONVENTION)

The United Nations Convention on the Prevention and Punishment of the Crime of Genocide does **not** forbid **linguistic** (or cultural) genocide directly since the General Assembly, as we noted in 5.2.3, rejected Article III. But it **does** forbid in its Article II(e) 'forcibly transferring children of the group to another group'. As I said in the Introduction, this transfer can be physical (as in the case of the Australian Stolen Generation which was pronounced as genocide by the court, see Insert 5.25). But as I have shown, the same result can also be accomplished through education.

Pirjo Janulf (see Info Box 8.3), having stated that 'None of those who had been in the Swedish classes spoke Finnish with their children', concludes on the basis of her large-scale partly longitudinal study of Sweden Finnish immigrant minority students (1998):

Judging from the results of the study, attendance in Finnish classes was of great significance for the preservation of Finnish in Sweden because only this program seemed to guarantee many-sided language skills in Finnish. The number of pupils in Finnish classes has decreased sharply since 1980, and nowadays such classes exist only in a few places in Sweden. Swedish school political practices have contributed strongly to the difficulties Finnish is having and will have surviving beyond the coming two or three generations. (ibid.)

There is a lot of similar experience in other countries. You, dear reader, think of your own friends and acquaintances. How many of them had grandparents or parents who spoke other languages which your friend no more knows today? It seems that we have enough evidence, worldwide, to be able to claim that, for minorities and probably also most indigenous peoples, only proper full maintenance programmes lead to high levels of bilingualism at a group level. Submersion and transitional programmes, at least early-exit transition, **lead to language shift**.

This is something that the states organising the education know, and often applaud.

This means that if there are no alternative educational models within a state organised system, no choices (which is the situation for most indigenous and immigrant minorities in the world), education through the medium of a foreign/second, dominant language, amounts to 'forcibly transferring children of the group to another group'. Submersion education is thus included in the 'mental harm' which is defined in Article II (b) as genocide: 'Causing serious bodily **or mental** harm to members of the group' (emphasis added).

I am waiting for the first group to start a court case accusing the state of knowingly committing genocide in education.

9.2. MINORITY LANGUAGE—BOTH RIGHT AND RESOURCE IN STATES WITH CIVIC PLURALISM AND NO ETHNIC STATE IDENTITY

Minority languages in education can be treated as a problem, a right, or a resource, with Richard Ruiz' (1984) alternatives, introduced in chapter 8. In several readings of Ruiz, all three have been seen as **competing** views, rather than the last two being complementary (and Ruiz himself does little to prevent this ambivalent interpretation). One result has been that some of those educationists and sociolinguists who emphasize that (minority) languages should be seen as resources, not as problems or handicaps, have dismissed 'language as a right'-oriented approaches as being in contradiction to seeing languages as resources. This is to the detriment of both those seeking language rights and those who see languages as a resource. It prevents those who are interested in making languages function as parts of positive cultural-linguistic capital from making use of the human rights system in the struggles of linguistic minorities for self-empowerment. It seems that the researchers who take this view do so partially because they lack adequate knowledge about linguistic human rights and cannot see the potential that a human rights oriented approach **may** offer.

The **problem** in connection with languages is **not** the existence of minority languages or a diversity of languages. Rather the problem is that many institutions of state (the educational system, social services, etc.) do not see the existence of linguistic diversity and *all* languages as resources to be cherished, maintained, and developed, or, minimally, as something not to be destroyed. Rather, many of them **construct** linguistic diversity and the presence of many languages and minority language speakers as a problem, both for the speakers themselves (who are constructed as deficient, suffering from lack of knowledge of the dominant language, rather than as owning a positive resource, another language, or multilingual skills) and for the state (which has to cater for them, offer them 'extra' services, 'help' them, etc.).

'Linguistic human rights' can in the framework of 'problem or resource' be understood in two ways which have superficially opposing but in fact complementary goals.

First, people need linguistic human rights in order to **prevent their linguistic repertoire from either becoming a problem or from causing** them problems. This is a defensive use of LHRs.

And second, people need to be able to exercise language rights in order for their linguistic repertoire to be treated as or to **become a positive, empowering resource**. This is a more assertive way of using LHRs.

A combination of these approaches is clearly visible in maintenance programmes but not in transitional programmes, despite some rhetoric in that direction.

After all, a 'minority' person is a normal human being who, from the state's point of view, may just happen to be in the 'wrong' place in the sense that her/his first language (L1) is not the L1 of the majority in the state where s/he lives. And this 'wrong' place can only become 'right' when the ideology of monolingual nation states disappears.

It is only **when the state and educational authorities stop being a problem** that maintenance programmes become a natural human right, and minority languages a resource. What we need is Civic Pluralism. According to the Greek-Australian researcher, Mary Kalantzis (1995: 2) who herself has gone back to relearning her mother tongue, Civic Pluralism

> means that all people have access to political power, economic resources, social services, and, most importantly, cultural symbols regardless of their cultural affiliations and styles. This cultural symbols point is in some important respects the key to the others. **The State can no longer have an 'ethnic' identity** as it did in the era of traditional nationalism. Under Civic Pluralism, the nation's cultural symbols are open and inclusive. One shouldn't any longer have to take on the cultural **and linguistic** demeanour of the so called 'mainstream' in order to enjoy access to political power, economic resources, social services and the symbols of nation.
>
> Far from fostering tribalism or fragmentation, Civic Pluralism is their only antidote. It is a means to create a postnationalist sense of common purpose. (emphases added).

But there are requirements for what a new generation of human rights must fulfill if a new 'social contract', with Civic Pluralism, is to result, one which can be used to support democracy and fight the tyranny of casino economy and mafia capitalism, capitalism-run-wild:

- human rights have to supplement **representative** democracy with mechanisms with further **direct democracy**. Direct democracy cannot function without linguistic human rights and support to linguistic and cultural diversity, neither in general nor in schools (see Apple 1993, Giroux 1992,

Corson (ed.) 1994, Pratte 1977)—local negotiations need to be done in local languages.

- human rights have to acknowledge the rights of future generations. These rights include the right to biodiversity and linguistic and cultural diversity in the future too. It is the only safe alternative.
- human rights have to regulate the relationship between civil society and the business world. We need a 'proper' (i.e., not neo-liberal) stakeholder economy (Wheeler & Sillanpää 1997), combined with economic democracy, in addition to political democracy. Political democracy functions today more and more as an excuse for a new type of feudalism where the transnational corporations have replaced the feudal lords. Business must serve civil society, not vice versa.
- human rights have to be implemented, not stay on paper.

If we want to use the human rights system to prevent genocide and biocide and support linguistic and cultural diversity and biodiversity, several macro-level choices are necessary. I will sketch out some.

9.3. DIVERSITY OR HOMOGENISATION?
LOCALISATION OR GLOBALISATION?

The market economy, and the creation of larger and more centralized economic, administrative, and political units has, despite a rhetoric of democracy and local participation, been the order of the day, in the 'first' and 'third' worlds. It is also emerging in the former 'second' world. The socio-economic, techno-military, and political, structural changes which have been connected with the 'modernisation' and 'globalisation' processes have caused unprecedented stress on both **nature** and on **people**, on our socio-economic conditions of life, and our languages and cultures (Fig. 9.1). These processes have resulted in an accelerated **environmental degradation** (= nature under stress), and **growing gaps** between the haves and the never-to-haves, and in the **linguistic and cultural genocide** we have discussed in this book (= people under stress).

We need as humans to decide whether the choices we make are through markets and monocultural efficiency, or through diversity. An important priority for both politics and research would be to define policies for preservation and development of environmental, linguistic and cultural, economic and political diversity (but see 'Tolerance' below). This would also include studying the role of human rights in the different responses.

This is also the context in which I think we need to see the spread of certain languages at the cost of others. Subtractive language spread does not

Alternative responses to changes

BACKGROUND REASONS

Socio-economic, techno-military and political structural changes

RESULT in

Environmental degradation	Linguistic and cultural genocide	Growing gaps between haves and have-nots

CREATES STRESS UPON

NATURE	PEOPLE	
	Languages and cultures	Socio-economic conditions of life

THESE RESPOND, ALTERNATIVELY,

THROUGH MARKETS & MONOCULTURAL EFFICIENCY: Economic efficiency first priority; larger and more centralized economic and political units; OR	THROUGH DIVERSITY: Sustainability through diversity first priority: flexible, resilient, and democratic economic and political units

WHICH RESULTS, ALTERNATIVELY, in

biodiversity	linguistic and cultural diversity	living conditions	biodiversity	linguistic and cultural diversity	living conditions
disappears	disappears; homogenisation	deteriorate; polarisation	maintenance	maintenance, development	sustainable; democratistion

(This figure is partially inspired by the flow chart in Jussila & Segerståhl 1988: 18.

FIG. 9.1 Alternative responses to socio-economic, techno-military, and political structural changes.

only kill other languages, it is often connected with many of the other factors which are included in the flow chart in Fig. 9.1 but not specified. The Japanese scholar Yukio Tsuda (1994) analyses the spread of English in terms of a 'diffusion of English' paradigm where he sees several other **factors related to this diffusion** (Maher & Yashiro's 1995 description about Japan seems to identify similar concomitants to the spread of English in Japan; so do Masaki Oda's writings; see also Honna 1995).

As an alternative he proposes an 'ecology of languages' paradigm which includes minimally bilingualism but hopefully multilingualism for all. Robert Phillipson and I have worked further on Tsuda's original suggestions (see our discussion in Phillipson & Skutnabb-Kangas 1996b). Table 9.1 presents both

TABLE 9.1
Diffusion of English and ecology of languages paradigms

The diffusion of English paradigm	Ecology of languages paradigm
1. monolingualism and linguistic genocide	1. multilingualism and linguistic diversity
2. promotion of subtractive learning of dominant languages	2. promotion of additive foreign/second language learning
3. linguistic, cultural, and media imperialism	3. equality in communication
4. Americanisation and homogenisation of world culture	4. maintenance and exchange of cultures
5. ideological globalisation and internationalisation	5. ideological localisation and exchange
6. capitalism, hierarchisation	6. economic democratisation
7. rationalisation based on science and technology	7. human rights perspective, holistic integrative values
8. modernisation and economic efficiency; quantitative growth	8. sustainability through promotion of diversity; qualitative growth
9. transnationalisation	9. protection of local production and national sovereignties
10. growing polarisation and gaps between haves and never-to-haves	10. redistribution of the world's material resources

paradigms in my latest version, where I have added several new dimensions to Tsuda (see also his 1998). Obviously the list is very much of a 'goodies' and 'baddies' type. Still, too often there seems to be a correlation between ideologies and practices which follow each approach. Again, it is important to remember that learning of English can be included in **both** paradigms.

We can compare the two end points on the diffusion of English and ecology of languages continuum with how colleagues from other disciplines conceptualise their similar worries even if they may not have linguistic diversity uppermost on their minds. In fact, the killing of diversity is not at all in pact with nature either, as some researchers would like us to believe. Bioregionalists who try to extract basic tenets for a sustainable life, both from nature and from earlier, often more balanced ways of interacting with (the rest of) nature, are sure that, in order to have a chance of saving the planet, we have to 'abandon the notion of controlling and remaking the world in the name of global monoculture' (Sale 1996: 472). Many of them advocate self-reliance at the level of bioregions. Sale (1996: 475) summarizes the basic tenets of the bioregional and industrio-scientific paradigms as follows (Table 9.2):

TABLE 9.2
Basic tenets of the bioregional and industrio-scientific paradigms

	BIOREGIONAL PARADIGM	INDUSTRIO-SCIENTIFIC PARADIGM
Scale	Region Community	State Nation/World
Economy	Conservation Stability Self-Sufficiency Cooperation	Exploitation Change/Progress Global Economy Competition
Polity	Decentralization Complementarity Diversity	Centralization Hierarchy Uniformity
Society	Symbiosis Evolution Division	Polarization Growth/Violence Monoculture

Source: adopted from Sale 1996: 475.

Jared Diamond examines in the chapter 'The Golden Age That Never Was' in his 1992 book the evidence for people and cultures before us having completely ruined the prerequisites for their own life by destroying their habitats or having exterminated large numbers of species. This has happened in many places and it makes the 'supposed past Golden Age of environmentalism look increasingly mythical' (Diamond 1992: 335). If we want to learn from it, and not make it happen on a global basis (this is our obvious risk today), we better heed his advice. Diamond claims (ibid., 335–336) that

> small long-established, egalitarian societies tend to evolve conservationist practices, because they've had plenty of time to get to know their local environment and to perceive their own self-interest. Instead, damage is likely to occur when people suddenly colonize an unfamiliar environment (like the first Maoris and Eastern Islanders); or when people advance along a new frontier (like the first Indians to reach America), so that they can just move beyond the frontier when they've damaged the region behind; or when people acquire a new technology whose destructive power they haven't had time to appreciate (like modern new Guineans, now devastating pigeon populations with shotguns). Damage is also likely in centralized states that concentrate wealth in the hands of rulers who are out of touch with their environment.

As we can see, we have the perfect global prerequisites for ruining our planet beyond repair. Long-established small societies are breaking up, and people encounter new environments, with urbanisation and migration. New technologies are more destructive than ever, and results of biochemical and other experiments are taken into use before we know anything about the long-term effects on nature or people. We have growing gaps and alienated elites. And we do not have the new planets to move to when we have damaged this one . . .

Finally, we could relate the concerns to some parts of Anthony Giddens' comparisons between pre-modern and modern cultures on the one hand and his conceptions of post-modernity and what he calls 'radicalised modernity' on the other hand (Giddens 1990 passim—see Giddens' Tables 1 and 2, and Figures 1–7). Giddens finds questions about whether modern institutions are capitalistic or industrial, reductionist. Instead he works with four 'institutional dimensions' or 'organisational clusters' (ibid., 55) of various systems, expressed differently in various phases and all influencing each other. The four are in *modernity* (1) **surveillance** (control of information and social supervision); (2) **military power** (control of the means of violence in the context of the industrialisation of war); (3) **industrialism** (transformation of nature: development of the 'created environment'); and (4) **capitalism** (capital accumulation in the context of competitive labour and product markets) (ibid., 59). Correspondingly, the dimensions of *globalisation* are (1) **nation-state system**; (2) **world military order**; (3) **international division of labour**; and (4) **world capitalist economy**. Giddens then compares the environments of trust and risk. In 'pre-modern' cultures the sources of trust are in kinship systems, the local community as a place, religious cosmologies, and tradition, whereas the risks come from nature, threat of human violence (marauding armies, local warlords, robbers, etc.), and from falling from religious grace, or of malicious magic. In 'modern' cultures, the sources of trust are personal relationships, abstract systems, future-oriented thought as a mode of connecting past and present. Threats and dangers come from the reflexivity of modernity, threat of human violence from the industrialisation of war, and threat of personal meaninglessness (see Table 1, p. 102 and Giddens' discussion of the concepts). Most of these phenomena have already been discussed in earlier chapters. Giddens then goes on to describe the four dimensions in terms of *'high consequence risks of modernity'* (ibid., 171) which correspond to the stress and disaster poles in our 'response through markets & monocultural efficiency' (Figure 9.1), the 'diffusion of English paradigm' (Table 9.1) and the 'industrio-scientific paradigm' (Table 9.2). Giddens' dimensions here are (1) **growth of totalitarian power**; (2) **nuclear conflict or large-scale war**; (3) **ecological decay or disaster**; and (4) **collapse of economic growth mechanisms**. Next Giddens goes on to compare conceptions of 'post-modernity' and what he calls 'radicalised modernity' (Table 2, p. 150) in a perceptive way which has many similarities to, for instance, Harding's and Escobar's (and Galtung's 1996) analyses.

In counteracting the risks of modernity, Giddens postulates an important role for *social movements* which he relates to the four dimensions: (1) **free speech/democratic movements**; (2) **peace movements**; (3) **ecological movements** (counterculture); and (4) **labour movements** (ibid., 159). These might, in the *contours of a post-modern order*, lead to (1) **multilayered democratic partici-**

pation; (2) **demilitarisation**; (3) **humanisation of technology**; and (4) **a post-scarcity system** (p. 164), and the dimensions of this system could be (1) **coordinated global order**; (2) **transcendence of war**; (3) **system of planetary care**; and (4) **socialised economic organisation** (p. 166). And, finally, Giddens' dimensions of *utopian realism* are (1) **life politics** (politics of self-actualisation[2]); (2) **politicisation of the global**; (3) **emancipatory politics** (politics of inequality[3]); and (4) **politicisation of the local**.[4]

As we can see, there are many similarities in how language and culture-oriented, biologically oriented, and sociologically oriented researchers see some of the main problems in today's world, and also possible alternatives.

Paradoxically, then, linguistic and cultural **homogenising** seem to be at the core of the growing spread of free market nomadism and the ensuing ideological chaos which precludes joint action and legitimates it with the help of sophisticated intellectual games . . .

9.4. 'Promoting Linguistic Tolerance and Development'?

There are additional caveats to be added to optimistic scenarios. There are no longer any 'bad' or 'good' solutions, only relatively better or worse solutions to the world's problems. According to Zygmunt Bauman (1997), both the bipolar possibilities (either **universality**—universal ideas, ideologies, solutions—or **tolerance of diversity and pluralism**) have certain benefits and certain dangers.

Believing in 'universal truths' (like 'communism' or 'capitalism' or 'free market') can in the worst case lead (and has led) to genocides.

On the other hand, Bauman claims, 'tolerance' can also lead to tolerating genocide without doing anything (e.g., Bosnia, Nigeria). 'Tolerance' can also be expressed in demands for autonomy of choice, in an individualistic neo-liberal way, in consumer societies, where any kind of restrictions or limits are seen as negative.

This would be the WTO (World Trade Organisation) and MAI (Multilateral Agreement on Investment) line. This wrongly understood 'freedom of choice' might also include the prevention of any kind of positive intervention to achieve the 'regulated context' which Grin (1999) sees as necessary for harnessing market forces for preservation of at least some linguistic diversity, and which Tomaševski argues is a necessary counterweight for human rights to be implemented.

My critique of 'tolerance' would include still more. I have earlier criticised the 'free market' response to change as disastrous, and the human rights oriented response as completely insufficient. Likewise I have criticised the role of the state in both, for having given away the control to the TNCs and for undermining and misusing human rights.

What about states in cooperation with those NGOs which try to make states their allies? This is where 'toleration' and 'development' really rule.

In October 1993 at the Vienna Summit, the Heads of State and Government of the member states of the Council of Europe reacted to '. . . the increase in acts of violence, notably against migrants and people of immigrant origin . . .' (from the Preamble to Appendix III), by adopting a Declaration and a 'Plan of Action on combating Racism, Xenophobia, anti-Semitism and **Intolerance**' (emphasis added).

The same 'tolerance' also figures in the **World Declaration on Education for All** (to be found on UNESCOs Web-page, Address Box 7.1) from the Jomtien World Conference on Education for All in March 1990. Part 2 of Article 1, after having asked individuals (significantly **not** states) to have 'responsibility to respect and build upon their collective cultural, linguistic and spiritual heritage', asks them 'to be **tolerant** towards social, political and religious systems which differ from their own' (emphasis added; see Joel Spring's (1998: 190–216) and Birgit Brock-Utne's (in press) analyses of this document in relation to human rights and development—their views are similar to mine).

At an international conference, organised by the Canadian Centre for Linguistic Rights, called 'Towards a language agenda: futurist outlook on the United Nations' (see Léger, ed. 1996), the title given to my presentation by the organisers was 'Promotion of linguistic **tolerance** and development' (emphasis added; see my 1996c).

Even if some of the official resolutions and texts mention mutuality and the need for **everybody** to be tolerant, after reading the bulk of them, one is left with a strong impression that those who should **be 'tolerated'** are those who are 'different' in relation to an unspecified mainstream, namely minorities (national, immigrant, and refugee) and indigenous peoples. Those who are asked to **do this tolerating** are the majority populations, the so called 'mainstream'. 'Promotion of tolerance' seems, for instance, in a Council of Europe interpretation, to mean 'counteracting the intolerance of majority populations in Europe and Europeanised countries towards some of their fellow citizens'. In parallel, in 'promoting linguistic tolerance', speakers of dominant languages are then presumably asked to tolerate linguistic diversity, the existence of smaller languages and maybe also the ways the speakers of other languages (and other varieties) use the dominant languages, in ways which do not completely tally with how the speakers of these dominant languages (or rather the formally educated middle class sections) themselves use them. Again, it is the linguistically dominant groups who are asked to tolerate that the dominated languages and groups using them exist, and are different from the dominant ones. Finally, 'development' in 'promoting linguistic development' can be understood in the same sense as in 'the developed countries' and 'the developing countries'. This is the familiar evolutionist paradigm, where it is clear who constitutes the norm, and where it is only some who need to develop (to undergo structural adjustment programmes) because they are still deficient in relation to the norm.

Does 'promoting linguistic development' imply that we also have already developed languages which are the norm for the aspiring developing languages (or developing dialects or vernaculars), in the fashion envisaged by Alisjahbana (in section 5.4)? Are these 'underdeveloped' languages then promised more important roles in education and administration once their 'linguistic development' has been 'promoted' enough?

Do we all have to become monolinguals (with a sprinkling of Japanese or other languages, good for trade, learned in school), in order to become 'linguistically developed'? Do we all have to 'suffer from monolingual stupidity' in order to be considered linguistically developed, instead of being 'blessed with multilingual brains'?[5]

Is 'promotion of linguistic tolerance and development' the best way to support linguistic and cultural diversity and linguistic rights? It depends on how these concepts are defined and whose definitions of them are validated. The way they seem to be interpreted now, 'tolerance' and 'development' do not prevent but may support linguistic and cultural genocide.

In my view it is high time to start a major reversal of the questions and start asking who should tolerate whom, and who or what is developed towards what goals. These are questions I need to ask, in addition to the why-questions which have filled the pages of this book:

For how long are we multilingual and multicultural individuals and groups going to tolerate the monolingual, monocultural reductionism that characterises the ideologies of 'nation states' and homogenising elites? For how long are we going to tolerate that the power-holders have appropriated a monopoly to define the world for us in ways which try to homogenise diversity? How long are we going to tolerate the linguistic and cultural genocide that dominant groups are committing, not only through economic and political structural policies but also, and increasingly, through the consciousness industry? How long are we going to tolerate that our languages are being stigmatised as backward and primitive, tribal and traditional, as vernaculars and patois and dialects (rather than languages), as not adapted to post-modern technological information societies? How long are we going to tolerate that the richness of all our non-material resources, our norms and traditions, family patterns and institutions, our ways of living, our languages and cultures, our cultural capital, are being invalidated by the power-holders; that they are made invisible and stigmatised as handicaps and thus made non-convertible into other resources and into positions of political power? Rather than made visible and celebrated, validated as valuable resources and convertible into other resources and into positions of political power? How long are we going to tolerate the widening gaps between the ever more grim realities, with linguistic and cultural genocide for us and monolingual stupidity for many majorities? How long are we going to tolerate the posture politics, the nice phrases about toleration and celebration of diversity?

For how long are the poor in the world (both in the North and, especially, in the South) going to tolerate the excessive exploitation which is called development, help, and aid? For how long are we ordinary people going to tolerate the grave misuse of power of most political parties in the world? How long are we going to tolerate the accelerating destruction of the planet? And—the most important question—how long can the planet tolerate this 'development'?

I give a couple of examples of the reversal in Inserts 9.1 and 9.2.

INSERT 9.1   Culture of tolerance and silence

A research report, called "Culture of tolerance and silence" (1992) tells about peasant women in Giza, 20 km from Cairo in Egypt. Many of the women have been married off at the age of 9 or 10. They have many miscarriages and bear many children. They are afraid that the husband will take another wife unless they produce enough children. They labour in the fields and the house from early morning til late in the evening, and **they tolerate these conditions in silence.**[6] The report discusses how to support the women in **overcoming** the 'culture of tolerance and silence' which is theirs. Maybe the women rather need to learn how to **stop** being tolerant and silent? Exactly the same conclusion is reached by Anees Jung in her books about women in South Asia (e.g., 1987, 1994).

INSERT 9.2   'Get off my toes, you bloody bastard!'

A Sámi friend, Liv Østmo, once talked about the culture of tolerance. She described the situation of the ignorance, ethnocentrism, and often unintended racism that majority group representatives often display toward the Sámi. She said that she was tired of always having to be the tolerant teacher, patiently trying to develop some awareness in the majority representatives. Tired of always needing to smile and to try and explain to the clumsy intruder, stepping on her toes, that this person really is standing on the toes of the indigenous person, and if the majority representative tried to imagine herself in the same situation, she might understand that it hurts, and might consider moving a bit. Instead of Liv pushing the intruder and screaming: 'get off my toes, you bloody bastard!', as she **sometimes** felt like doing. Liv claimed that she does not have as much tolerance left as she used to—her people have tolerated racism long enough for some to get accustomed to it. She thinks they need to unlearn toleration, and to start treating the majority population as adults who should be responsible for their own learning rather than rely on indigenous peoples and minorities continuing to be their tolerant teachers, patiently waiting for a little development, decade after decade.

What has been promoted especially by some of the powerful Western states so far during this century has been their own linguistic and cultural lack of awareness, their intolerance of linguistic and cultural diversity, and a conscious underdevelopment and killing off of the world's linguistic and cultural resources and diversity. So far, those representing the bulk of this 'underdeveloped' diversity have been much too patient and tolerant of the ignorance, of the attempts at linguistic and cultural genocide and its concomitant economic and political consequences.

Maybe what we rather need is to learn how to **stop** being tolerant and silent? Maybe oppressed groups (including the women in Insert 9.1) rather need a UN Year of Intolerance or Zero Tolerance of the prevailing ideologies of monolingual reductionism.[7]

We also need to develop two kinds of support system. One support system is for these patients who suffer from monolingual reductionism to diversify, to get rid of their illness, dangerous not only for themselves but for world peace.[8] Education can play a major role in the cure. If you, reader, are a teacher, you can start tomorrow! The second support system needed is to protect and support those who are healthy, the multilinguals, so that we are not infected by the illness virus; so that we can stay healthy and can see clearly that **we** are the healthy ones. Legally binding guarantees in international and national laws, protecting basic linguistic human rights, especially in education, are part of this support system.

9.5. DO ARGUMENTS HELP?

Does it help to show, with the help of rational arguments, that the costs are lower if a country, groups of countries (like the EU or the NAFTA or the ACP) or world organisations (like UNESCO) have rational language policies which include multilingualism (and Esperanto as one part of this) and respect linguistic and cultural human rights? Is language policy going to be changed with the help of rational arguments which show that it is better for the future of the whole planet to support linguistic and cultural diversity (in addition to biodiversity) than to enhance homogenisation as one of the results of linguistic and cultural genocide?

I am afraid rational arguments have not counted so far. A summary of experience:

1. If linguistic and cultural diversity and multilingualism were to be promoted as part of a rational language policy, this would mean respecting linguistic human rights, including protecting and promoting minority languages. So far, dominant Western states have tried to prevent the acceptance of international and/or regional human rights instruments on language rights, especially language rights in education.

2. We know approximately how education should be organised to result in high levels of multilingualism for all. So far, education has to a large extent been organised against most scientific evidence. It has involved linguistic genocide for linguistic minorities and monolingual reductionism for linguistic majorities, coupled with inefficient foreign language teaching, and in both cases blaming the victims for the results.

3. 'Illiteracy' could be eradicated within a decade. A wrong educational language policy in underdeveloped countries, in many cases promoted, advocated, and partially financed by the West with its experts, is the most important pedagogical reason for 'illiteracy' in the world, and the most efficient way of preventing the grassroots from organised resistance to continued neocolonial exploitation.

4. Promoting diversity is an accepted principle in declarations. Still, Western language policies have to a large extent been based on **false either-or thinking** (you need to choose **between** languages, you cannot have both this language and that language and maybe others too). It has promoted **subtractive** rather than **additive** language learning and subtractive spread of English and other dominant languages: the learning of a dominant language has been presented as necessarily happening at the cost of a dominated language, instead of in addition to it. Diversity is killed.

If Western states have led and continue to lead the way in irrational language policies which result in linguistic and cultural genocide and in prevention of linguistic human rights, and if the West is trying to spread the ideas in this irrational language policy to other parts of the world (with a fair success), how likely is it that Western and international organisations, dominated by the same states, change their policies because of rational arguments?

Not likely, is my claim. Just like biologically argued racism—or, for that matter, sexism, classism, imperialism, neocolonialism, etc.—are *not* matters of getting the right information, linguicism is not mainly a question of lack of information. It is a question of power relations. In analysing power relations one has to analyse **who benefits**. Purely human rights oriented approaches are naive if they disregard power relations—and many of them do. Some of them are themselves well on their way to rather becoming part of the oppressive system, rather than a solution.

In addition to rational arguments, there has to be a certain element of both carrots and perceived or actual threats, before the power elites start rethinking. We have to present future scenarios with both these elements—and alternatives. Only if we can show to the power elites that not only can **they** themselves benefit from more rational language policies but that their own privileges and present benefits are going to be severely curtailed if they do not adopt a more rational policy can we do something. The costs of the present-day power politics will be high for the elites themselves too in terms of constraints on their own life conditions—after all, they breathe the same air and have to eat the same polluted food as we others, and the 'safe' havens to barricade oneself in are shrinking. Violence breeds violence.

9.6. TO CONCLUDE

Firstly, we have to analyse the role of states and international organisations. Who controls them, and for whose benefit do they work? We cannot rely on the states, controlled by elites, to be nice and rational. Linguistic human rights arguments are true and beautiful, but futile in a negotiation situation of unequal power. Unless power relations are equalised and balanced, power holders (= representatives of monolingual reductionism) can invalidate (= socially construct as non-resources) any minority arguments. The pressure has to come from the grassroots.

Secondly, we have to relativize the question of costs. What are necessary communications? What are necessary costs for necessary communications? Physical communication costs enormous sums, pollutes the planet, transports often unnecessary things, often unnecessarily. We have to make it cheaper to produce food and commodities locally where it is possible and instead use the moneys for improved mental communication. This includes supporting linguistic and cultural diversity and the learning of languages. Physical control is also costly; ideological control is cheaper. Counterhegemonic ideas can also spread from grassroots to other grassroots, without physical revolutions necessarily needing to take place everywhere. Words are weapons. They can be used for control, or for sharing, cooperation.

Thirdly, we who are multilingual must stop being tolerant of the voluntary monolingualism of linguistic majority populations in the big dominant countries. **They** are the ones who cause much of the costs. But we pay, because so far we have agreed to learning **their** languages in order for communication to work, while many of the Brits and North Americans and French and Russians and Chinese have not learned our languages. We need mutuality. We have to start a zero tolerance campaign where we stop tolerating both monolingual reductionism and subtractive diffusion of English.

One way of forcing voluntary monolinguals to see what their monolingualism costs the rest of the world is that we multilinguals for a while give them back their own medicine. First we could have a policy whereby in all official situations nobody is allowed to use their mother tongue. Everybody has to use a second/foreign language.[9] Nothing new in that for us who have always had to use other languages (may I remind you that I am writing this in my fifth language. . .). Might be more difficult for some heads of state or TNCs to formulate diplomatic lies in a foreign language. Then stop learning (or at least using with them) their languages. Learn Esperanto instead or in addition. Maybe they might learn it too, rational and relatively easy as it is. And many of today's monolinguals are not voluntary monolinguals—they might want to escape if they were given a chance. You, reader, if you are an involuntary monolingual, stop tolerating the educational language policies in your country!

Fourthly, we have to show the controlling elites that the world is not a zero-sum game. It is not necessarily so that if we win, they have to lose. Both can win from a rational languages policy which respects linguistic human rights. Or, at least: everybody, including the dominant elites, loses if the irrationality continues. And they may have more to lose.

Finally, it is, of course, typical of academics who write books, to believe, after all, that information at least does not harm, even if inequalities are not a result of lack of information. Linguicism does, mistakenly, 'make sense of the world', just like racism does:

> [R]acism can successfully (although mistakenly) make sense of the world and thereby provide a strategy for political action for sections of different classes. It follows that to the extent that racism is an attempt to understand a specific combination of economic and political relations, and is therefore grounded in those relations, **strategies for eliminating racism should concentrate less on trying exclusively to persuade those who articulate racism that they are 'wrong' and more on changing those particular economic and political relations**. (Miles 1989: 82, emphasis added)

Writing books ('trying to persuade') is useless, unless it is combined with more overt political action (see again the Marx and **Bhagavadgītā** reminders in the Introduction). The question then is whether the action needs to be done by the same people who do the persuading. I believe it is necessary.

NOTES

1. It is noteworthy, however, that the Draft Charter on Human and people's rights in the Arab World demands an equitable distribution as a component of human rights: "The State shall guarantee an equitable distribution of the national income among its citizens" ' (Tomaševski 1996: 108).
2. Giddens relates this to the old distinction between 'freedom from' and 'freedom to', i.e., negative or positive rights in our terms, non-discrimination only or affirmative rights. Life politics necessitates LHRs in the sense they have been discussed in this book.
3. This means liberation from inequality.
4. Giddens talks about diversity in a general way but does not discuss linguistic diversity specifically. I would like to go back to the two paradigms, 'language death' or 'language murder', and relate the two approaches to Giddens.

   'Language murder' type theorising combines some of the sources of localised trust from the 'pre-modern' environment, with transcending the limitations of especially post-modernity (aesthetic-oriented post-modernity in Giddens' terminology), into 'radicalised modernity'.

This radicalised modernity again might offer a source of trust needed in two of Giddens' utopian scenarios, 'Utopian Realism' and even 'Post-scarcity System'. A success for these utopian scenarios presupposes linguistic and cultural diversity.

On the other hand, it seems that 'language death' type theorizing is not a source of **any** trust. In the worst case it can have a twofold negative influence. Under 'modernity', it can contribute to the **threats** in Giddens' 'environment of risk'. In the post-modernist guise, it can at a group level lead to a certain apathy (which is an almost inevitable part of post-modernism). At an individual level it can become part of sceptical hedonism. At both levels, it can lead to fragmented, dissolved, disempowered acceptance of the 'inevitabilities' which characterises Giddens' 'post-modernity' (ibid., Table 2).

5. Both these are modifications of slogans on T-shirts. Some Californian teachers used to give T-shirts to their high-level bilingual students, with 'BLESSED WITH BILINGUAL BRAINS'. I have a T-shirt (given by Portuguese-American friends) with the text 'I DO NOT SUFFER FROM MONOLINGUAL STUPIDITY'.

6. Reported by Inge Schrøder, in **Soldue** 18, March 1995, pp. 10–11, in an article called 'Med Koranen som facitliste' ('The Qur'ān as the facit').

7. Mark Fettes pointed out that the concept of Zero Tolerance is not only a call to minorities/dominated groups to show less tolerance towards overt and covert linguicism (and other types of -isms, racism, sexism, classism etc.). It is also a call for majorities/dominant groups 'to show less tolerance for those among their own group who practise such mistreatment' (from an email letter from Mark Fettes, 10 May 1995). I fully agree.

8. See also articles in Schäffner & Wenden (eds) 1995.

9. This suggestion comes from Theo van Els, vice-chancellor of the University of Nijmegen, the Netherlands. The European Union could reduce the number of working languages (now 11) to the Big Three, on the condition that nobody is allowed to use their first language.

Bibliography

Abdussalam, Ahmad Shehu (1998). Human language rights: an Islamic perspective. In Benson et al. (eds), 55–62.

Abramovitz, Janet N. (1998). Sustaining the World's Forests. In **State of the World 1998**, 21–40.

Adams, K. & Brink, D. (eds) (1990). **Perspectives on Official English: The Campaign for English as the Official Language of the U.S.A.**. Berlin: Mouton de Gruyter.

Adelaar, Willem F. H. (1995). The endangered situation of the native languages in South America. Abstract of the paper presented at the International Symposium on Endangered Languages, November 18–20, 1995, University of Tokyo. [can be downloaded from <http://www.tooyoo.l.u-Tokyo.ac.jp/linguistics/newsletters/newslet1.html>].

Afolayan, A. (1978). Towards an Adequate Theory of Bilingual Education for Africa. In Alatis, James E. (ed.) **International Dimensions of Bilingual Education**. Washington, D.C.: Georgetown University Press.

Afolayan, A. (1984). The English Language in Nigerian Education as an Agent of Proper Multilingual and Multicultural Development. **Journal of Multilingual and Multicultural Development** 5:1, 1–22.

Africa, Hugh (1980). **Language in education in a multilingual state: a case study of the role of English in the education system of Zambia**, Ph.D. dissertation, University of Toronto.

Aikio, Marjut (1988). **Saamelaiset kielenvaihdon kierteessä. Kielisosiologinen tutkimus viiden saamelaiskylän kielenvaihdosta 1910–1980** (The Sami in the screw of language shift. A sociolinguistic study of language shift in five Sami villages 1910–1980). Helsinki: Suomalaisen Kirjallisuuden Seura.

Aikio, Marjut (1991). The Sami language: Pressure of Change and Reification. **Journal of Multilingual and Multicultural Development** 12:1 & 2, 93–103.

Aikio, Pekka, Linkola, Martti, Nuorgam-Poutasuo, Helvi & Saressalo, Lassi (1985). The Sami people in Finland. In Pentikäinen & Anttonen (eds), 45–71.

Aikio-Puoskari, Ulla (1998). Sámi language in Finnish Schools. In Kasten, Erich (ed.). **Bicultural Education in the North. Ways of Preserving and Enhancing Indigenous Peoples' Languages and Traditional Knowledge.** Münster, New York, München/Berlin: Waxmann, 47–57.

Aikio-Puoskari, Ulla (1999). Saamen kielen ja saamenkielinen opetus Suomessa (Teaching of and through the medium of Sámi in Finland). Manuscript (Soaḍegilli/Sodankylä: Sámediggi (Sámi Parliament).

Akinnaso, F. Niyi (1990). The Politics of Language Planning in Education in Nigeria. **Word** 41, 235–253.

Akinnaso, F. Niyi (1991). Toward the development of a multilingual language policy in Nigeria. **Applied Linguistics** 12:1, 29–61.

Akinnaso, F. Niyi (1993). Policy and experiment in mother tongue literacy in Nigeria. **International Review of Education** 39:4, 255–285.

Akinnaso, F. Niyi (1994). Linguistic unification and language rights. **Applied Linguistics** 15:2, 139–168.

Alexander, Neville (1989). **Language Policy and National Unity in South Africa/Azania**. Cape Town: Buchu Books.

Alexander, Neville (1992). South Africa: Harmonising Nguni and Sotho. In Crawhall (ed.).

Alexander, Neville (1995a). Models of multilingual schooling for a democratic South Africa. In Heugh et al. (eds), 79–82.

Alexander, Neville (1995b). Multilingualism for empowerment. In Heugh et al. (eds), 37–41.

Alexander, Neville (in press). Language policy and planning in South Africa: some insights. In Phillipson (ed.).

Alfredsson, Gudmundur (1989). The United Nations and the Rights of Indigenous Peoples. **Current Anthropology** 30:2, 255–259.

Alfredsson, Gudmundur (1990). **Report on Equality and Non-Discrimination: Minority Rights**. Strasbourg: Council of Europe.

Alfredsson, Gudmundur (1991). Minority Rights: Equality and Non-Discrimination. In Krag, Helen & Yukhneva, Natalia (eds). **The Leningrad Minority Rights Conference Papers**. Copenhagen: The Minority Rights Group in Denmark, 19–41.

Alisjahbana, S. Takdir (1984). The problem of minority languages in the overall linguistic problems of our time. In Coulmas (ed.), 47–55.

Allardt, Erik (1996). Dominant autochthonous groups. In Goebl et al. (eds), 342–351.

Allardt, Erik & Starck, Christian (1981). **Språkgränser och samhällsstruktur. Finlandssvenskarna i ett jämförande perspektiv** (Language borders and societal structure. The Finland Swedes in a comparative perspective). Stockholm: Almqvist & Wiksell.

Allardt, Erik, Miemois, Karl Johan & Starck, Christian (1979). Multiple and Varying Criteria for Membership in a Linguistic Minority. The Case of the Swedish Speaking Minority in Metropolitan Helsinki. Research Reports No 21. University of Helsinki: Research Group for Comparative Sociology.

Alverson, Brigid (1997). Deaf Culture on the World Wide Web. **WFD News** 10:1, 22–23.

Amago, Marvin (1987). Families Were Separated. Interview in Costo & Costo (eds), 140.

Amery, Rob (1998). **Warrabarna Kaurna! Reclaiming Aboriginal Languages from Written Historical Sources: Kaurna Case Study**. Unpublished Ph.D. thesis, Linguistics, University of Adelaide. xxv, 489pp., 3 Appendices. [forthcoming in the series Multilingualism and Linguistic Diversity, Lisse: Swets & Zeitlinger].

Ammon, Ulrich (1989a). Schwierigkeiten der deutschen Sprachgemeinschaft aufgrund der Dominanz der englischen Sprache. **Zeitschrift für Sprachwissenschaft** 8:2, 257–272.

Ammon, Ulrich (1989b). Towards a Descriptive Framework for the Status/Function (Social Position) of a Language Within a Country. In Ammon (ed.), 21–106.

Ammon, Ulrich (1991). **Die internationale Stellung der deutschen Sprache**. Berlin: Walter de Gruyter.

Ammon, Ulrich (1994). The Present Dominance of English in Europe. With an Outlook on Possible Solutions to the European Language Problem. **Sociolinguistica** 8, 1994, 1–14.

Ammon, Ulrich (1995). **Die deutsche Sprache in Deutschland, Österreich und der Schweitz. Das Problem der nationalen Varietäten**. Berlin/New York: Walter de Gruyter.

Ammon, Ulrich (1997). National-variety purism in the national centers of the German language. In Pütz (ed.), 161–178.

Ammon, Ulrich (1998). **Ist Deutsch noch internationale Wissenschaftssprache?** Berlin/New York: Walter de Gruyter.

Ammon, Ulrich (ed.) (1989). **Status and Function of Languages and Language Varieties.** Berlin/New York: Walter de Gruyter.

Ammon, Ulrich (in press). Towards more fairness in International English: Linguistic rights of non-native speakers? In Phillipson (ed.).

Ammon, Ulrich, Dittmar, Norbert & Mattheier, Klaus (eds) (1988). **Sociolinguistics: an international handbook of the science of language and society.** Berlin: Walter de Gruyter.

Ammon, Ulrich, Mattheier, Klaus J. & Nelde, Peter (eds) (1994). **Sociolinguistica 8. English only? in Europa/ in Europe/ en Europe.**

Ammon, Ulrich, Mattheier, Klaus J. & Nelde, Peter (eds) (1997). **Sociolinguistica 11. Einsprachigkeit ist heilbar / Monolingualism is curable / Le monolinguisme est curable.**

An-Na'im, Abdullahi Ahmed & Deng, Francis M. (eds) (1990). **Human rights in Africa: Cross-cultural perspectives.** Washington, D.C.: The Brookings Institution.

Anderson, Benedict (1983). **Imagined communities: Reflections on the Origins and Spread of Nationalism.** London: Verso.

Andersson, Theodore & Boyer, Mildred (1978). **Bilingual Schooling in the United States.** 2nd edition. Austin, Tex.: National Educational Laboratory Publishers.

Andrýsek, Oldrich (1989). **Report on the Definition of Minorities.** Amsterdam: Netherlands Institute of Human Rights.

Angula, Nahas (1984). English as a Medium of Communication for Namibia: Trends and Possibilities. In Commonwealth Secretariat & SWAPO (eds). **English language programme for Namibians.** Seminar Report, Lusaka, 19–27 October 1983. London & Lusaka: Commonwealth Secretariat & SWAPO, 9–12.

Annamalai, E. (1986a). A Typology of Language Movements and their Relation to Language Planning. In Annamalai et al. (eds), 6–17.

Annamalai, E. (1986b). Bilingualism through schooling in India. In Abbi, Anvita (ed.) (1986). **Studies in bilingualism.** Delhi: Bahri Publications.

Annamalai, E. (1986c). Comment: legal vs social. **International Journal of the Sociology of Language** 60, 145–151.

Annamalai, E. (1986d). The sociolinguistic scene of India. **Sociolinguistics** XVI:1, 2–8.

Annamalai, E. (1989). Modernization of language: the case of Tamil, Paper presented at the 7th International Conference of Tamil, Mauritius, December 1989, manuscript.

Annamalai, E. (1993). Planning for Language Survival. **New Language Planning Newsletter** 8:1, 1–2.

Annamalai, E. (1994). Multilingual development: Indian experience. Paper at the UNESCO-OAU conference, Addis Abeba, 21–25 November 1994, "The definition of strategies for the promotion of African languages in a multilingual environment", manuscript.

Annamalai, E. (1995). Multilingualism for all—an Indian perspective. In Skutnabb-Kangas (ed.), 215–220.

Annamalai, E. (1998). Language choice in education: conflict resolution in Indian courts. In Benson et al. (eds), 29–43.

Annamalai, E., Jernudd, Björn & Rubin, Joan (eds) (1986). **Language planning, Proceedings of an Institute.** Mysore & Honolulu: Central Institute of Indian Languages & East-West Center.

Ansre, Gilbert (1979). Four rationalisations for maintaining European languages in education in Africa. **African Languages /Langues Africaines** 5:2, 10–17.

Apffel-Marglin, Frédérique (1994). **Decolonizing Knowledge: From Development to Dialogue.** Oxford: Clarendon Press.

Apffel-Marglin, Frédérique & Marglin, Stephen (eds) (1990). **Dominating Knowledge: Development, Culture, and Resistance.** Oxford: Clarendon Press.

Appadurai, Arjuna (1990). Disjuncture and difference in the global cultural economy. In Featherstone (ed.), 295–310.

Apple, Michael W. (1993). **Official knowledge. Democratic education in a conservative age.** New York/London: Routledge.

Armstrong, Jeannette (1996). "Sharing One Skin": Okanagan Community. In Mander & Goldsmith (eds), 460–470.

Arnau, Joaquim (1997). Immersion Education in Catalonia. In Cummins & Corson (eds), 297–303.

Aro, Jussi, Salonen, Armas & Tallqvist, Knut (1957). **Koraani** (The Qur'ān). Translated from Arabic. Helsinki: Werner Söderström.

Arooran, K. Nambi (1980). **Tamil Renaissance and Dravidian Nationalism 1905–1944.** Madurai: Koodal Publishers.

Artigal, Josep Maria (1991a). **The Catalan Immersion Program: an European point of view.** Norwood, N.J.: Ablex.

Artigal, Josep Maria (1991b). The Catalan immersion program: the joint creation of shared indexical territory. **Journal of Multilingual and Multicultural Development.** 12:1 & 2, 21–33.

Artigal, Josep Maria (1992). Some considerations about why a new language is acquired by being used. **International Journal for Applied Linguistics** 2:2, 221–240.

Artigal, Josep Maria (1993). Catalan and Basque Immersion programmes. In Baetens Beardsmore (ed.), 30–53.

Artigal, Josep Maria (1994). The L2 kindergarten teacher as a territory maker. In Alatis, James A. (ed.). **Georgetown University Round Table on Languages and Linguistics.** Washington, D.C.: Georgetown University Press, 452–468.

Artigal, Josep Maria (1995). Multiways towards multilingualism: the Catalan immersion programme experience. In Skutnabb-Kangas (ed.), 169–181.

Asher, R. E. (ed.) (1994). **The Encyclopedia of Language and Linguistcs,** Volume 10. Oxford/New York/Seoul/Tokyo: Pergamon Press.

Auerbach, Elsa Roberts (1995). The politics of ESL classroom: Issues of power in pedagogical choices. In Tollefson (ed.), 9–33.

Baetens Beardsmore, Hugo (1982). **Bilingualism. Basic Principles.** Clevedon, UK: Multilingual Matters.

Baetens Beardsmore, Hugo (1988). Who's Afraid of Bilingualism? In **Euskara Biltzarra/Congreso de la Lengua Vasca,** vol. II, Vitoria-Gasteiz, 75–90.

Baetens Beardsmore, Hugo (1990a). The Multilingual School for Mixed Populations: A Case Study. In Baetens Beardsmore 1990b, 1–51.

Baetens Beardsmore, Hugo (1990b). **Bilingualism in Education: Theory and Practice.** Brussel/Bruxelles: Linguistic Circle of the Vrije Universiteit Brussel and the Université Libre de Bruxelles.

Baetens Beardsmore, Hugo (1993). **The European School Experience in Multilingual Education.** Brussel/Bruxelles: Vrije Universiteit Brussel and Université Libre de Bruxelles.

Baetens Beardsmore, Hugo (1994). Language policy and planning in Western European countries. **Annual Review of Applied Linguistics** 14, 92–110.

Baetens Beardsmore, Hugo (1995). The European School experience in multilingual education. In Skutnabb-Kangas (ed.), 21–68.

Baetens Beardsmore, Hugo (1996). Education plurilingue en Europe. In Goebl et al. (eds), 465–473.

Baetens Beardsmore, Hugo (ed.) (1993). **European Models of Bilingual Education.** Clevedon, UK: Multilingual Matters.

Baetens Beardsmore, Hugo & Anselmi, Gulia (1991). Code-Switching in a Heterogeneous, Unstable, Multilingual Speech Community. In **Papers for the Symposium on Code-Switching in Bilingual Studies; Theory, Significance and Perspectives.** Vol. II. Strasbourg: European Science Foundation, 405–436.

Baetens Beardsmore, Hugo & Kohls, Jürgen (1988). Immediate Pertinence in the Acquisition of Multilingual Proficiency: the European Schools. **The Canadian Modern Language Review** 44:2, 240–260.

Baetens Beardsmore, Hugo & Lebrun, Nathalie (1991). Trilingual Education in the Grand Duchy of Luxembourg. In García (ed.), 107–122.

Baetens Beardsmore, Hugo & Swain, Merrill (1985). Designing Bilingual Education: aspects of Immersion and 'European School' Models. **Journal of Multilingual and Multicultural Development** 6:1, 1–15.

Bailey, Richard (1995a). The Bantu languages of South Africa: towards a sociohistorical perspective. In Mesthrie (ed.), 19–38.

Bailey, Richard (1995b). Sociolinguistic evidence of Nguni, Sotho, Tsonga and Venda origins. In Mesthrie (ed.), 39–50.

Bailey, Richard W. (1992). **Images of English. A cultural history**. Cambridge: Cambridge University Press.

Bailey, Richard W. (1998). Majority Language, Minority Misery: The Case of Sri Lanka. In Kibbee (ed.), 206–224.

Baillie, Jonathan (1998). Analysis. Reprinted from 1996 IUCN Red List of Threatened Animals. [can be downloaded from <http://www.iucn.org/themes/ssc/redlist/analysis.htm>]. [IUCN = International Union for Conservation of Nature and Natural Resources].

Baker, Colin (1993). **Foundations of Bilingual Education and Bilingualism**. Clevedon/Philadelphia, PA: Multilingual Matters.

Baker, Colin & Prys Jones, Sylvia (1998). **Encyclopedia of Bilingualism and Bilingual Education**. Clevedon/Philadelphia: Multilingual Matters.

Baker, Keith A. & de Kanter, Adriana A. (1982). **Federal Policy and the Effectiveness of Bilingual Education**, manuscript. [Published as **Effectiveness of Bilingual Education: A Review of the Literature. Final Draft Report**. Washington, D.C.: Department of Education. Office of Planning, Budget, and Evaluation].

Balázs, Judit (1993). Aftermath of the Gulf War for Europe. In Boulding, Elise (ed.). **Studies in the Interconnectedness of Peace in the Middle East and the World: Perspectives from Europe, Africa and Latin America**. Budapest: Társadalomkutató Intézet.

Balázs, Judit (1999). The effects of globalisation on the economies of the countries in Eastern Europe. In Brock-Utne & Garbo (eds), 40–50.

Baldauf, Richard B. & Luke, Allan (eds) (1990). **Language planning and education in Australasia and the South Pacific**. Clevedon, UK: Multilingual Matters.

Balto, Asta (ed.) (1996). **Kunnskap og kompetanse i Sápmi. 'En samisk skole i emning'. Forhold fra den samiske utdanningssektoren** (Knowledge and competence in the Sámi country. A Sámi school in making. Issues in the Sámi educational sector). Forskningsserie fra SUFUR. Karasjok: Kunnskapsbilder.

Balto, Asta & Todal, Jon (1997). Saami Bilingual Education in Norway. In Cummins & Corson (eds), 77–86.

Balvig, Flemming (1996). Det amerikanske eksperiment. **Information**, 2.12.1996, 8.

Bamgbose, Ayo (1991). **Language and the nation. The language question in Sub-Saharan Africa**. Edinburgh: Edinburgh University Press.

Bancroft, H. H. (1886–1890). **The History of California**. 7 volumes. San Francisco: The History Company.

Banks, James & Banks, Cherry (eds) (1995). **Handbook of research on multicultural education**. New York: Macmillan.

Bannert, Robert (1994). **På väg mot svenskt uttal** (Towards Swedish pronunciation). 2.upplagan. Lund: Studentlitteratur.

Banton, Michael (1987). **Racial Theories**. Cambridge: Cambridge University Press.

Bari, Károly (1996). On being a gypsy and a poet—reflections on tradition, poetry and prejudice. In Tóth & Földeák (eds), 60–70.

Barnet, Richard J. & Cavanagh, John (1994). **Global Dreams. Imperial corporations and the new world order.** New York: Simon & Schuster.

Barth, Fredrik (1969). Introduction. In Barth, Fredrik (ed.). **Ethnic Groups and Boundaries. The Social Organization of Culture Difference.** Oslo: Universitetsforlaget, 9–38.

Batley, Edward, Candelier, Michel, Hermann-Brennecke, Gisela & Szépe, György (1993). **Language policies for the world of the twenty-first century,** Report for UNESCO. World Federation of Modern Language Associations (FIPLV).

Bauböck, Rainer (1998). Cultural minority rights in public education? Religious and language instruction for immigrant communities in Western Europe. Paper prepared for the conference Discourse and Racism, Institute for linguistics, University of Vienna, May 14–16.1998. In press, in Reisigl, Martin & Wodak, Ruth (eds).

Bauman, Zygmunt (1973). **Culture as praxis.** London: Routledge & Kegan Paul.

Bauman, Zygmunt (1997). Universalism and Relativism—Reaching an Impossible Compromise. Keynote lecture presented at the conference Development and Rights, Roskilde University, 8–10 October 1997.

Bauman, Zygmunt (1998a). **Globalization. The Human Consequences.** Cambridge: Polity Press.

Bauman, Zygmunt (1998b). **Work, consumerism and the new poor.** London: Open University Press.

Baynton, Douglas C. (1996). **Forbidden signs: American culture and the campaign against sign language.** Chicago, Ill.: University of Chicago Press.

Beach, Hugh (1995). The new Swedish Sámi policy—a dismal failure: concerning the Swedish government's proposition 1992/93:32, Samerna och samisk kultur m.m. (Bill). In Gayim, Eyassu & Myntti, Kristian (eds). **Indigenous and tribal peoples' rights.** Rovaniemi: Northern Institute for Environmental and Minority Law, University of Lapland, 109–129.

Bello, Walden (1996). Structural Adjustment Programs. "Success" for Whom? In Mander & Goldsmith (eds), 285–293.

Bello, Walden, Kinley, David & Elinson, Elaine (1982). **Development Debacle: the World Bank in the Philippines.** San Francisco. ISBN 0-935028-12-9.

Bello, Walden, with Shae Cunningham and Bill Rau (1994). **Dark Victory: The United States, Structural Adjustment and Global Poverty.** London: Pluto Press.

Bennell, Paul, with Terry Pearce (1998). **The Internationalisation of Higher Education: Exporting Education to Developing and Transitional Economies.** Working Paper 75. Brighton: Institute of Development Studies at the University of Sussex, Brighton.

Benson, Phil, Grundy, Peter & Itakura, Hiroko (eds) (in press). **Access to Language Rights.** Amsterdam/Philadelphia: John Benjamins.

Benson, Phil, Grundy, Peter & Skutnabb-Kangas, Tove (eds) (1998). **Language rights.** Special volume. **Language Sciences** 20:1, 1998.

Benton, Richard A. (1979). **The legal status of the Māori language: current reality and future prospects.** Wellington: Maori Unit, New Zealand Council for Educational Research.

Benton, Richard A. (1981). **The Flight of the Amokura: Oceanic Language and Formal Education in the South Pacific.** Wellington: New Zealand Council for Educational Research.

Benton, Richard A. (1986). Schools as Agents for Language Revival in Ireland and New Zealand. In Spolsky (ed.), 53–76.

Benton, Richard A. (1996). Language policy in New Zealand: Defining the Ineffable. In Herriman & Burnaby (eds), 62–98.

Bereznak, Catherine & Campbell, Lyle (1996). Defense Strategies for Endangered Languages. In Goebl et al. (eds), 659–666.

Berger, Peter L. & Luckmann, Thomas (1966). **The social construction of reality. A treatise in the sociology of knowledge.** Harmondsworth: Penguin.

Bergman, Pirkko (1993). Att undervisa på två språk (To teach through the medium of two languages). In Viberg, Åke, Tuomela, Veli & Bergman, Pirkko (eds). **Tvåspråkighet i skolan**

(Bilingualism at school). BAS-rapport 1. Rapporter om tvåspråkighet 9. Stockholm: Stockholms universitet, Centrum för tvåspråkighetsforskning.

Bergström, Matti (1986). Den glömda resursen (The forgotten resource). **Fredsposten** 6, 4–8.

Bernal, Martin (1991). **Black Athena. The Afroasiatic Roots of Classical Civilization.** London: Vintage.

Berns, Margie et al. (1998). Review Essay. (Re)experiencing hegemony: the linguistic imperialism of Robert Phillipson. **International Journal of Applied Linguistixs** 8:2, 271–282.

Bernstein, Basil B. (1971). **Class, Codes and Control. Volume 1: Theoretical Studies towards a Sociology of Language.** London: Routledge & Kegan Paul.

Bernstein, Basil B. (1975). **Class, Codes and Control. Volume 3. Towards a Theory of Educational Transmissions.** London/Boston: Routledge & Kegan Paul.

Bernstein, Basil B. (1996). **Pedagogy, Symbolic Control and Identity: Theory, Research, Critique (Critical Perspectives on Literacy and Education).** London: Taylor & Francis.

Bernstein, Basil B. (ed.) (1973). **Class, Codes and Control. Volume 2. Applied Studies towards a Sociology of Language.** London/Boston: Routledge & Kegan Paul.

Berry, John (1998). Official multiculturalism. In J. Edwards (ed.), 84–101.

Besikci, Ismail (1990). A Nation Deprived of Identity: The Kurds. Report to Minority Rights Conference. In **Minority Rights, Policies and Practice in South-East Europe.**

Best, Geoffrey (1988). The French Revolution and human rights. In Best, Geoffrey (ed.). **The Permanent Revolution. The French Revolution and its Legacy 1789–1989.** London: Fontana, 101–128.

Bhabha, Homi (1990). The Other Question: Difference, Discrimination, and the Discourse of Colonialism. In Ferguson, Russell et al. (eds). **Out There: Marginalization and Contemporary Cultures.** New York: New Museum of Contemporary Arts & Cambridge, MA: MIT Press, 71–89.

Bhagavadgītā—see Radhakrishnan 1977.

Bhat, P. Ishwara (1993). **A Comparative Study of the Language Provisions in the Constitutions of Canada and India from the Perspectives of Equal Liberty of All.** Mysore: Department of Studies in Law, University of Mysore.

Bhola, H. S. (1984). **Campaigning for literacy. Eight national experiences of the twentieth century, with a memorandum to decision-makers.** Paris: Unesco.

Bible = **The Holy Bible** (1864). London: George E. Eyre and William Spottiswoode.

Bild, Eva-Rebecca & Swain, Merrill (1989). Minority language students in a French immersion programme: their French proficiency. **Journal of Multilingual and Multicultural Development** 10:3, 255–274.

Bilingual Research Journal (1992), 16:1–2.

Black, Paul (1990). Some Competing Goals in Aboriginal Language Planning. In Baldauf & Luke (eds), 80–88.

Blakely, Edward J. & Snyder, Mary Gail (1997). **Fortress America: Gated Communities in the United States.** CA: Brookings Institute.

Blanke, Detlev (1985). **Internationale Plansprachen. Eine Einführung.** Berlin: Akademie Verlag.

Blanke, Detlev (1987). The term 'Planned Language'. **Language Problems & Language Planning** 11:3, 335–349.

Blanke, Detlev (1996). Wege zur interlinguistischen und esperantologischen Fachliteratur. **Language Problems and Language Planning** 20:2, 168–181.

Blanke, Detlev (1997). Zur Plansprache Esperanto und zur Esperantologie im Werk von Eugen Wüster. In Eichner, Heiner, Ernst, Peter & Katsikas, Sergios (hrsgs). **Sprachnormung und Sprachplanung. Festschrift für Otto Back zum 70. Geburtstag.** Wien: Verlag Edition Praesens.

Blanke, Detlev (1998). Plansprachen als Fachsprachen. Article 91. In Hoffmann, Lothar, Kalverkämper, Hartwig & Wiegand, Herbert Ernst (eds). **Fachsprachen. Languages for Special Purposes. Ein internationales Handbuch zur Fachsprachenforschung und Terminolo-**

giewissenschaft. An International Handbook of Special-Language and Terminology Research. Vol. I. Berlin/ New York: Walter de Gruyter, 875–880.

Blench, Roger (1996). Handout for paper Language Death in Central Nigeria, SOAS, December 5, 1996, sent on email December 5, 1996 to Endangered Languages List.

Bloch, Mia (1998). 'God diktator' søges (Wanted: a 'good dictator'). Information 16.6 1998, 8.

Blondin, Christiane, Candelier, Michel, Edelenbos, Peter, Johnstone, Richard, Kubanek-German, Angelika & Taeschner, Traute (1998). Foreign Languages in Primary and Pre-school Education: Contexts and Outcomes. A Review of Recent Research within the European Union. Report for DG22. Brussels: European Commission [also London: CILT; also German and French versions].

Bloor, Tom (1986). University students' knowledge about language: some aspects of language awareness prior to instruction in university courses. British Association for Applied Linguistics, CLIE (Committee for Linguistics in Education, Linguistics Association of Great Britain) Working Papers No. 8.

Bobaljik, Jonathan David, Pensalfini, Rob & Storto, Luciana (1996). A Prelimary Bibliography on Language Endangerment and Preservation. MIT Working Papers in Linguistics, vol. 28. Papers on Language Endangerment and the Maintenance of Linguistic Diversity. Cambridge, MA: MIT. [Available from Terralingua's Web-site <http://cougar.ucdavis.edu/nas/terralin/home.html>].

Bocock, Robert (1986). Hegemony. Series Key ideas, Open University. Chichester, London & New York: Ellis Horwood & Tavistock.

Bokamba, Eyamba G. (1991). French colonial language policies in Africa and their legacies. In Marshall (ed.), 175–213.

Bokamba, Eyamba G. & Tlou, Josiah S. (1980). The Consequences of the Language Policies of African States vis-a-vis Education. In Mateene & Kalema (eds), 45–66.

Borst, Arno (1957–63). Der Turmbau von Babel. Geschichte der Meinungen über Ursprung und Vielfalt der Sprachen und Völker. 6 vols. Stuttgart: Hiersemann. [reprinted in München in 1995; 2,320 pages].

Boudoin, Jean-Claude & Masse, Claude (1973). Étude comparative et évolutive des droits linguistiques en Belgique et en Suisse, Étude E15, la commission d'enquête sur la situation de la langue française et sur les droits linguistiques au Québec. Québec: l'éditeur officiel du Québec.

Bourdieu, Pierre (1977). The Economics of Linguistic Exchange. Social Science Information 16:6, 645–668.

Bourdieu, Pierre (1992). Language & Symbolic Power. Edited and introduced by John B. Thompson. Cambridge: Polity Press.

Bourdieu, Pierre (1998). La domination masculine. Paris: Seuil.

Boutros-Ghali, Boutros (1992). An Agenda for Peace. New York: United Nations.

Boutros-Ghali, Boutros (1995). Unity and Diversity: The Contemporary Challenge. Paper given at Global Cultural Diversity Conference, Strength in Diversity—an Investment in Our Future, Conference to celebrate the 50th Anniversary of the United Nations, organised by the Australian Prime Minister's Office, Sydney, 26–28 April 1995.

Bowers, Roger (1997). New purposes, new paths. TESOL Matters 7:4, August/September 1997, 1, 5, 16.

Boyd, Sally (1985). Language Survival. A study of language contact, language shift and language choice in Sweden. Gothenburg monographs in linguistics, 6, Department of Linguistics. Göteborg: University of Gothenburg.

Braine, George (1999). Nonnative English Speakers in TESOL Caucus Formed. TESOL Matters 9:1, February/March, 6.

Branson, Jan & Miller, Don (1989). Beyond integration policy—the deconstruction of disability. In Barton, L. (ed.). Integration: Myth or reality. Brighton: Falmer Press, 144–167.

Branson, Jan & Miller, Don (1993). Sign Language, the Deaf and the Epistemic Violence of Mainstreaming. Language and Education, 7:1, 21–41.

Branson, Jan & Miller, Don (1995a). Sign Language and the Discursive Construction of Power over the Deaf through Education. In Corson, David (ed.) **Discourse and Power in Educational Settings**. Creskill, N.J.: Hampton Press, 167–189.

Branson, Jan & Miller, Don (1995b). **The Story of Betty Steel. Deaf Convict and Pioneer.** Australia's Deaf Heritage, Vol. 1. Sydney: Deafness Resources Australia.

Branson, Jan & Miller, Don (1996). Writing Deaf subaltern history: is it a myth, is it history, is it genealogy? is it all, or is it none? In Vollhaber, T. & Fischer, R. (eds). **Collage. Works on international Deaf history**. Hamburg: Signum Press, 185–194.

Branson, Jan & Miller, Don (1998a). National Sign Languages and Language Policies. In Wodak & Corson (eds), 89–98.

Branson, Jan & Miller, Don (1998b). Nationalism and the linguistic rights of Deaf communities: Linguistic imperialism and the recognition and development of sign languages. **Journal of Sociolinguistics** 2:1, 1998: 3–34.

Brenzinger, Matthias (1992). Lexical retention in language shift: jaaku/Mukogodo-Maasai and Elmolo/Elmolo-Samburu. In Brenzinger (ed.), 213–254.

Brenzinger, Matthias (ed.) (1992). **Language death: factual and theoretical explorations with special reference to East Africa**. Berlin: Mouton de Gruyter.

Brenzinger, Matthias & Dimmendaal, Gerrit J. (1992). Social contexts of language death. In Brenzinger (ed.), 3–5.

Breton, Roland (1996). The dynamics of ethnolinguistic communities as the central factor in language policy and planning. **International Journal of the Sociology of Language** 118, 163–179.

Brock-Utne, Birgit (1993a). **Education in Africa. Education for self-reliance or recolonization?** Rapport Nr. 3. Oslo: University of Oslo, Institute for Educational Research.

Brock-Utne, Birgit (1993b). Language of instruction in African schools. A socio-cultural perspective. **Nordisk Pedagogik** 13, 225–246.

Brock-Utne, Birgit (1994). Reconstruction of Curricula in Africa—a Feminist Perspective. In Takala (ed.), 243–262.

Brock-Utne, Birgit (1995). **The teaching of Namibian languages in the formal education system**. Study for the Ministry of Basic Education and Culture in Namibia. December 1995. Windhoek, manuscript.

Brock-Utne, Birgit (1996). Internationalisierung des Bildungswesens—eine kritische Perspektive. Paper for the Conference Bildung zwischen Staat und Macht, XV Kongress der deutschen Gesellschaft für Erziehungswissenschaft. Halle an der Saale, März 1996, manuscript.

Brock-Utne, Birgit (1997). The language question in Namibian schools. **International Review of Education** 43:2 & 3, 241–260.

Brock-Utne, Birgit (1998). **Multicultural Education and Development: Similarities with, and Challenges to, Peace Education**. AFB-Texte Nr. 1/98. Bonn: Arbeitsstelle Friedensforschung Bonn/ Information Unit Peace Research.

Brock-Utne, Birgit (in press). **Whose Education for All? Recolonizing the African Mind?** New York: Garland.

Brock-Utne, Birgit & Garbo, Gunnar (eds) (1999). **Globalization on Whose Terms?** Oslo: University of Oslo, Institute for Educational Research.

Brock-Utne, Birgit & Nagel, Tove (eds) (1996). **The Role of Aid in the Development Education for All**. Report No. 8. Oslo: University of Oslo, Institute for Educational Research.

Bromley, Yu.V. (1973). **Ethnos and Ethnography**. Moscow: Nauka Publishers.

Bromley, Yu.V. (1981). **Present-Day Problems of Ethnography**. Moscow: Nauka Publishers.

Bromley, Yu.V. (1984). **Theoretical Ethnography**. Moscow: Nauka Publishers.

Brown, Lester (1998a). The Future of Growth. In **State of the World 1998**, 3–20.

Brown, Lester (1998b). Struggling to Raise Cropland Productivity. In **State of the World 1998**, 79–95.

Brown, Lester & Mitchell, Jennifer (1998). Building a New Economy. In **State of the World 1998**, 168–187.

Brumfit, Christopher (1995). English 2000: the professional issues. In **Best of ELTECS**. Manchester: The British Council, 14–24.

Bryld, Tine (1998). **I den bedste mening** (With the best of intentions). Nuuk: Atuakkiorfik.

Buber, Martin (1958). **I and Thou**. Translated by R. G. Smith. New York: Macmillan.

Bucak, Ali (1989). The Turkish Penal Code and the Kurds. In **Human Rights in Kurdistan**, 122–133.

Bucak, Sertaç (1998)—see Internationaler Verein für Menschenrechte der Kurden.

Büchert, Lene (1996). The concept of Education for All—what has happened after Jomtien? In Brock-Utne & Nagel (eds), 73–98.

Bugarski, Ranko & Hawkesworth, Celia (eds) (1992). **Language Planning in Yugoslavia**. Columbus, Ohio: Slavica Publishers.

Bull, Tove (1995). Language Maintenance and Loss in an Originally Trilingual Area in North Norway. **International Journal of the Sociology of Language** 115, 125–134.

Bull, W. E. (1955). Review of Unesco (1953). **International Journal of American Linguistics** 21, 288–294.

Bunyan, Tony (ed.) (1993). **Statewatching the new Europe. A handbook on the European state**. London: Statewatch.

Bunyi, Grace (1997). Language in Education in Kenyan Schools. In Cummins & Corson (eds), 33–44.

Burchfield, Robert (1985). **The English Language**. Oxford: Oxford University Press.

Burnaby, Barbara (1996). Language Policies in Canada. In Herriman & Burnaby (eds), 159–219.

Cahn, Edgar S. & Hearne, David W. (eds) (1969). **Our Brother's Keeper: The Indian in White America**. New York: New Community Press.

Calvet, Louis-Jean (1974). **Linguistique et colonialisme: petit traité de glottophagie**. Paris: Payot.

Calvet, Louis-Jean (1987). **La guerre des languages et les politiques linguistiques**. Paris: Payot.

Cameron, Deborah (1995). **Verbal Hygiene**. London/New York: Routledge.

Cameron, Deborah (ed.) (1990). **The Feminist Critique of Language**. London/New York: Routledge.

Cameron, Deborah & Bourne, Jill (1989). No common ground: Kingman, grammar and the nation. **Language and Education** 2(3), 147–160.

Cameron, Deborah, Frazer, Elizabeth, Harvey, Penelope, Rampton, M. B. H. & Richardson, Kay (1992). **Researching language. Issues of power and method**. London/New York: Routledge.

Campbell, G. L. (1995). **Compendium of the world's languages**. London: Routledge. [revised version 1998].

Cantoni, Gina (ed.) (1996). **Stabilizing Indigenous Languages**. Flagstaff: Northern Arizona University, Center for Excellence in Education. [can be downloaded from <http://www.ncbe.gwv.edu/miscpubs/stabilize/>].

Capotorti, Francesco (1979). **Study of the Rights of Persons Belonging to Ethnic, Religious and Linguistic Minorities**. New York: United Nations.

Carder, Maurice (1995). Language(s) in international education: a review of language issues in International Schools. In Skutnabb-Kangas (ed.), 113–157.

Castillo, Edward (1987). Cultural Chauvinism Offered to Justify Serra Canonization. In Costo & Costo (eds), 67–80.

Castles, Stephen (1980). The social time-bomb: education of an underclass in West Germany. **Race and Class** XXI:4, 369–387.

Castles, Stephen (with Heather Booth and Tina Wallace) (1984). **Here for good. Western Europe's new ethnic minorities**. London/Sydney: Pluto Press.

Castles, Stephen & Kosack, Godula (1973). **Immigrant Workers and Class Structure in Western Europe**. London: Oxford University Press.

Cates, Kip (1999). New Directions in EFL. **TESOL Matters** 9:1, February/March, 11.

Cawson, Frank (1975). The international activities of the Center for Applied Linguistics. In Fox, Melvyn J. (ed.). **Language and development: a retrospective survey of Ford Foundation language projets, 1952–1974.** (Vol. 1, report; Vol. 2, case studies). Vol. 2. New York: The Ford Foundation, 385–434.

CDE (1981). = California State Department of Education (1981). **Schooling and Language Minority Students: A Theoretical Framework.** Los Angeles: Evaluation, Dissemination and Assessment Center, California State University.

CDE (1982). = California State Department of Education (1982). **Basic principles for the education of language minority students, an overview.** Sacramento: Office of Bilingual Bicultural Education.

CDE (1984). = California Department of Education (1984). **Studies on Immersion Education: A Collection for U.S. Educators.** Sacramento: Bilingual Education Office.

CDE (1986). = California Department of Education (1986). **Beyond Language: Social & Cultural Factors in Schooling Language Minority Students.** Los Angeles: Evaluation, Dissemination and Assessment Center, California State University.

Cenoz, Jasone & Genesee, Fred (eds) (1998). **Beyond Bilingualism: Multilingualism and Multilingual Education.** Clevedon, UK: Multilingual Matters.

Centassi, René & Masson, Henri (1995). **L'homme qui a défié Babel.** Paris: Ramsay.

Centre for Contemporary Cultural Studies (1982). **The Empire Strikes Back. Race and racism in 70s Britain.** London: Hutchinson, in association with the Centre for Contemporary Cultural Studies.

Centre of African Studies (1986). **Language in education in Africa.** Seminar proceedings 26, Proceedings of a seminar at the Centre of African Studies, University of Edinburgh, 29–30 November, 1985. Edinburgh: Centre of African Studies.

Chamberlain, Richard, Diallo, Amenita & John, E. J. (1981). **Toward a Language Policy for Namibia. English as the Official Language: Perspectives and Strategies.** Lusaka: United Nations Institute for Namibia.

Chambers, J. K. & Trudgill, Peter (1980). **Dialectology.** Cambridge: Cambridge University Press.

Chatterjee, Sudipro (1995). Mise-en-(colonial) Scéne: The Theatre of the Bengal Renaissance. In Gainor (ed.), 19–37.

Chaturvedi, M. G. & Singh, Satvir (1981). **Third All-India Educational Survey: Languages and media of instruction in Indian schools.** New Delhi: National Council of Educational Research and Training.

Chaudhary, S. C. (1986). Survey of English: South Kanara District, Hyderabad: Central Institute of English and Foreign Languages.

Chen, Albert H. Y. (1998). The philosophy of language rights. In Benson et al. (eds), 45–54.

Chernichenko, Stanislav (1996) and (1997). Definition of minorities. E/CN.4/Sub.2/AC5/1996/WP.1. and E/CN.4/Sub.2/AC5/1997/WP.1. New York: United Nations.

Cheshire, Jenny (ed.) (1991). **English Around the World: Sociolinguistic Perspectives.** Cambridge: Cambridge University Press.

Chomsky, Noam (1965). **Aspects of the theory of syntax.** Cambridge, Mass.: The M.I.T. Press.

Chomsky, Noam (1987). **On power and ideology: The Managua lectures.** Boston: South End Press.

Chomsky, Noam (1989). **Language and Politics.** Montreal: Black Rose Books.

Chomsky, Noam (1994). **World Orders Old and New.** New York: Columbia University Press.

Chomsky, Noam (1996). **Power and Prospects: Reflections on Human Nature and the Social Order.** Boston: South End Press.

Christ, Ingeborg (1998a). European Language Portfolio. **Language Teaching** 31, 214–217.

Christ, Ingeborg (1998b). Europäisches Portfolio für Sprachen—Eine Initiative des Europarates. In Landesinstitut für Schule und Weiterbildung (ed.). **Wege zur Mehrsprachigkeit—Informationen zu Projekten des sprachlichen und interkulturellen Lernens** 2. Soest, 5–11.

Christian, Donna (1994). Students learning through two languages. Paper presented at 28th Annual TESOL Convention, Baltimore, Md., March 12, 1994.

Christian, Donna & Mahrer, Cindy (1992). **Two-Way Bilingual Programs in the United States, 1991–1992**. Washington, D.C.: National Center for Research on Cultural Diversity and Second Language Learning.

Christian, Donna & Mahrer, Cindy (1993). **Two-Way Bilingual Programs in the United States, 1992–1993 Supplement**. Washington, D.C.: National Center for Research on Cultural Diversity and Second Language Learning.

Christian, Donna & Montone, Chris (1994). **Two-Way Bilingual Programs in the United States, 1993–1994 Supplement**. Washington, D.C.: National Center for Research on Cultural Diversity and Second Language Learning.

Christian, Donna, Montone, Chris, Lindholm, Kathryn & Carranza, I. (1997). **Two-Way Bilingual Education: Students Learning Through Two Languages**. Washington, D.C., & McHenry, Ill.: Center for Applied Linguistics & Delta Systems.

Churchill, Stacy (1986). **The education of linguistic and cultural minorities in the OECD countries**. Clevedon, UK: Multilingual Matters.

Clancier, Georges Emmanuel (1996). In the darkness: poetry as promise and hope. In Tóth (ed.), 27–32.

Clark, Donald & Williamson, Robert (eds) (1996). **Self-Determination: International Perspectives**. London: Macmillan & New York: St. Martin's Press.

Clarke, Tony (1996). Mechanisms of corporate rule. In Mander & Goldsmith (eds), 297–308.

Clason, Elin & Mahmut Baksi (1979). **Kurdistan. Om förtryck och befrielsekamp** (Kurdistan. On oppression and liberation struggle). Stockholm: Arbetarkultur.

Cluver, August D. de V. (1993). **A dictionary of language planning terms**. Pretoria: University of South Africa.

Cluver, August D. de V. (1994). Preconditions for language unification. **South African Journal of Linguistics**, supplement 20, 168–194.

Cluver, August D. de V. (1996). A futurist outlook on the languages of Southern Africa. In Léger (ed.), 173–204.

Clyne, Michael (1982). **Multilingual Australia**. Melbourne: River Seine.

Clyne, Michael (1985). **Australia—Meeting Place of Languages**. Canberra: Pacific Linguistics, Australian National University.

Clyne, Michael (1988). Community Languages in the Home: a First Progress Report. **Vox**, 1, 22–27.

Clyne, Michael (1991). **Community Languages. The Australian experience**. Cambridge/New York/Port Chester/Melbourne/Sydney: Cambridge University Press.

Clyne, Michael (ed.) (1986). **An Early Start. Second Language at Primary School**. Melbourne: River Seine.

Clyne, Michael (ed.) (1992). **Pluricentric Languages. Differing norms in different nations**. Berlin: Mouton de Gruyter.

Clyne, Michael (in press). Promoting multilingualism and linguistic human rights in the era of economic rationalism and globalization. In Phillipson (ed.).

Clyne, Michael, Fernandez, Sue, Chen, Imogen Y. & Summo-O'Connell, Renata (1997). **Background Speakers: Diversity and its Management in LOTE Programs**. Canberra: The National Languages and Literacy Institute of Australia.

Coates, Jennifer (ed.) (1998). **Language and Gender. A reader**. London, UK/Malden, MA: Blackwell.

Cobarrubias, Juan (1983). Ethical issues in status planning. In Cobarrubias, Juan & Fishman, Joshua A. (eds). **Progress in language planning: international perspectives**. Berlin: Mouton, 41–85.

Coelho, Elisabeth (1998). **Teaching and Learning in Multicultural Schools**. Clevedon, UK: Multilingual Matters.

Cohen, Lucy Kramer (ed.) (1960). **The Legal Conscience: Selected Papers of Felix S. Cohen.** New Haven: Yale University Press.

Compton, Elizabeth (1989). Taking Basic Education to Work. **Vox** (The Journal of Australian Advisory Council on Languages and Multicultural Education), 2, 7–9.

Comrie, Bernard (ed.) (1987). **The world's major languages.** London: Routledge.

Comrie, Bernard, Matthews, Stephen & Polinsky, Maria (eds) (1996). **The Atlas of Languages.** New York: Facts on File.

Conrad, Andrew W. (1996). The international role of English: The state of the discussion. In Fishman et al. (eds), 13–36.

Conversi, Daniele (1997). **The Basques, The Catalans and Spain. Alternative Routes to Nationalist Mobilisation.** London: C. Hurst & Co.

Cook, Eung-Do (1998). Aboriginal languages: history. In J. Edwards (ed.), 125–143.

Coombs, P. (1985). **The World Crisis in Education—The View from the Eighties.** New York: Oxford University Press.

Cooper, Robert L. (1989). **Language planning and social change.** Cambridge: Cambridge University Press.

Cooper, Robert L. & Spolsky, Bernard (eds) (1991). **The Influence of Language on Culture and Thought. Essays in honor of Joshua A. Fishman's Sixty-Fifth Birthday.** Berlin/New York: Mouton de Gruyter.

Corsetti, Renato (1996). A Mother Tongue Spoken Mainly by Fathers. **Language Problems & Language Planning** 20:3, 262–273.

Corson, David (1992). Language, Gender and Education: a critical review linking social justice and power. **Gender and Education** 4:3, 229–254.

Corson, David (1993). **Language, Minority Education and Gender. Linking Social Justice and Power.** Clevedon/Philadelphia/Adelaide: Multilingual Matters.

Corson, David (ed.) (1994). **Discourse and Power in Educational Settings.** Cresskill, N.J.: Hampton Press.

Coste, D., North, J., Sheils, J. & Trim, J. L. M. (1998). Language learning, teaching, assessment. A common European Framework of Reference. **Language Teaching** 31, 136–151.

Costo, Rupert (1987). The Indians Before Invasion. In Costo & Costo (eds), 9–28.

Costo, Rupert & Costo, Jeannette Henry (eds) (1987). **The Missions of California: A Legacy of Genocide.** San Francisco: Indian Historian Press.

Coulmas, Florian (1991). European integration and the idea of the national language. Ideological roots and economic consequences. In Coulmas (ed.), 1–43.

Coulmas, Florian (ed.) (1981). **A Festschrift for native speaker.** The Hague: Mouton.

Coulmas, Florian (ed.) (1984). **Linguistic Minorities and Literacy. Language Policy Issues in Developing Countries.** Berlin: Mouton.

Coulmas, Florian (ed.) (1991). **A Language Policy for the European Community. Prospects and Quandaries.** Berlin/New York: Mouton de Gruyter.

Coupland, Nikolas, Coupland, J., Giles, Howard & Wiemann, J. M. (eds). (1991). **The Handbook of Miscommunication and Problematic Talk.** Clevedon, UK: Multilingual Matters.

Cox, Oliver G. (1970). **Caste, Class and Race.** New York: Monthly Review Press.

Crandall, Susan Emlet (1992). Speaking Freely: A Constitutional Right to Language. **The CATESOL Journal** 5:2, 7–18.

Crawford, James (1992a). **Hold your tongue: Bilingualism and the Politics of "English Only".** Reading, Mass.: Addison-Wesley.

Crawford, James (1992b). **Language Loyalties: A source book on the Official English controversy.** Chicago, Ill.: University of Chicago Press.

Crawford, James (1995). **Bilingual Education: History, Politics, Theory and Practice.** Los Angeles: Bilingual Educational Services. [1989. Trenton, N.J.: Crane Publishing Company].

Crawford, James (1996). Seven hypotheses on language loss: causes and cures. In Cantoni (ed.).

Crawford, James (1997). Best Evidence: Research Foundations of the Bilingual Education Act. Washington, D.C.: National Clearinghouse for Bilingual Education. [can be downloaded from <http://www.ncbe.gwu.edu>].

Crawford, James (1998a). Anatomy of the English-Only Movement: Social and Ideological Sources of Language Restrictionism in the United States. In Kibbee (ed.), 96–122.

Crawford, James (1998b). Endangered Native American Languages: What Is to Be Done, and Why? In Ricento & Burnaby (eds), 151–165.

Crawhall, Nick T. (ed.) (1992). **Democratically Speaking: International Perspectives on Language Planning.** Cape Town: National Language Project.

Cristea, Dan (1996). The ethnic group as a measure. In Tóth & Földeák (eds), 153–157.

Crosby, Alfred W. (1994). **Ecological imperialism. The biological expansion of Europe, 900–1900.** Cambridge: Cambridge University Press.

Crowley, Tony (1989). **Standard English and the Politics of Language.** Urbana: University of Illinois Press.

Crozier, David & Blench, Roger M. (1992). **Index of Nigerian Languages.** 2nd edition. Dallas, Tex.: Summer Institute of Linguistics.

Cryle, Peter (1993). The European reference. In Schulz (ed.), 130–135.

Crystal, David (1997a). **English as a global language.** Cambridge: Cambridge University Press.

Crystal, David (1997b). **The Cambridge Encyclopedia of Language.** 2nd edition. Cambridge: Cambridge University Press. [1987; 1995].

Cummins, Jim (1976). The influence of bilingualism on cognitive growth: a synthesis of research findings and explanatory hypotheses. **Working Papers on Bilingualism,** No 9.

Cummins, Jim (1979). Linguistic interdependence and the educational development of children. **Review of Educational Research** 49, 222–251.

Cummins, Jim (1981). The Role of Primary Language Development in Promoting Educational Success for Language Minority Students. In CDE 1981, 3–49.

Cummins, Jim (1984). **Bilingualism and Special Education: Issues in Assessment and Pedagogy.** Clevedon, UK: Multilingual Matters.

Cummins, Jim (1988). From multicultural to anti-racist education. An analysis of programmes and policies in Ontario. In Skutnabb-Kangas & Cummins (eds), 127–157.

Cummins, Jim (1989a). **Empowering Minority Students.** Sacramento: California Association for Bilingual Education.

Cummins, Jim (1989b). Language and literacy acquisition in bilingual contexts. **Journal of Multilingual and Multicultural Development** 10:1, 17–32.

Cummins, Jim (1991). Conversational and academic language proficiency in bilingual contexts. In Hulstijn, Jan H. & Matter, Johan F. (eds) (1991). **Reading in two languages.** AILA Review 8. Amsterdam: Free University Press, 75–89.

Cummins, Jim (1992a). Bilingual Education and English Immersion: The Ramírez Report in Theoretical Perspective. **Bilingual Research Journal** 16:1–2, 91–104.

Cummins, Jim (1992b). Knowledge, Power and Identity in Teaching English as a Second Language. In Genesee (ed.).

Cummins, Jim (1994a). The discourse of disinformation: the debate on bilingual education and language rights in the United States. In Skutnabb-Kangas & Phillipson (eds), 159–177.

Cummins, Jim (1994b). From Coercive to Collaborative Relations of Power in the Teaching of Literacy. In Ferdman, Bernardo, Weber, Rose-Marie & Ramirez, Arnulfo G. (eds). **Literacy Across Languages and Cultures.** Albany: State University of New York Press, 295–331.

Cummins, Jim (1994c). The socioacademic achievement model in the context of coercive and collaborative relations of power. In de Villar, Faltis & Cummins (eds), 363–390.

Cummins, Jim (1995). Reflections on the European Schools Model in relation to French Immersion Programs in Canada. In Skutnabb-Kangas (ed.), 159–168.

Cummins, Jim (1996). **Negotiating Identities: Education for Empowerment in a Diverse Society.** Ontario: California Association for Bilingual Education.

Cummins, Jim & Corson, David (eds) (1997). **Bilingual Education.** Vol. 5. **Encyclopedia of Language and Education.** Dordrecht/Boston/London: Kluwer Academic Publishers.

Cummins, Jim & Danesi, Marcel (1990). **Heritage Languages. The Development and Denial of Canada's Linguistic Resources.** Toronto: Our Schools/Our Selves Education Foundation.

Cummins, Jim & Swain, Merrill (1986). **Bilingualism in Education: Aspects of theory, research and practice.** London/New York: Longman.

Curtis, Jan (1988). Parents, schools and racism: Bilingual education in a Northern California town. In Skutnabb-Kangas & Cummins (eds), 278–298.

D'souza, Jean (in press). Language and education: the rights of the child. In Benson et al. (eds).

Daes, Erica-Irene (1995). Redressing the Balance: The Struggle to be Heard. Paper to the Global Cultural Diversity Conference, Sydney [see Boutros-Ghali].

Dalby, David (1985). The life and vitality of African languages: a charter for the future. In Mateene, Kalema & Chomba (eds), 29–34.

Danaher, Kevin (ed.) (1994). **Fifty Years is Enough: The Case Against the World Bank and the International Monetary Fund.** Boston: South End Press.

Danish Centre for Human Rights (1998). Notat & Resume af Notat vedrørende lovforslag L 154 om ændring af udlændingeloven, straffeloven og ægteskabsloven samt lovforslag L 155 om integration af udlændinge i Danmark (14 januar 1998). København: Det danske center for menneskerettigheder.

Darnell, Frank & Hoëm, Anton (1996). **Taken to extremes: education in the Far North.** Oslo/Stockholm: Scandinavian University Press.

Dascal, Marcelo (1996). **Endangered Languages.** Tel Aviv: Lester & Sally Entin Faculty of Humanities, Tel Aviv University, manuscript.

Dasgupta, Probal (1993). **The Otherness of English: India's Auntie Tongue Syndrome.** Delhi: Sage.

Dauenhauer, Nora & Dauenhauer, Richard (1995). Oral literature embodied and disembodied. In Quasthof, Uta M. (ed.). **Aspects of Oral Communication.** Berlin: Walter de Gruyter.

Daun, Åke (1984). Swedishness as an Obstacle in Cross-Cultural Interaction. **Ethnologia Europea** XIV:2, 95–109.

Daun, Åke (1989). **Svensk mentalitet.** Stockholm: Raben & Sjögren.

Daun, Åke & Ehn, Billy (eds) (1988). **Blandsverige** (Mixed Sweden). Stockholm: Carlssons Bokförlag.

Daun, Åke, Mattlar, Carl-Eric & Alanen, Erkki (1989). **Personality traits characteristic for Finns and Swedes.** Stockholm: Ethnologia Scandinavica.

Davies, Alan (1991). **The Native Speaker in Applied Linguistics.** Edinburgh: Edinburgh University Press.

Davies, Alan (1996). Review Article: Ironising the Myth of Linguicism. **Journal of Multilingual and Multicultural Development** 17:6, 485–496.

Dawkins, Kristin (1994). **NAFTA, GATT and the World Trade Organization: The Emerging New World Order.** Westfield, N.J.: Open Media.

Dawood, N. J. (1959). **The Koran.** London: The Whitefriars Press. [See also **Koraani**].

de Azcárate, P. (1945). **League of Nations and National Minorities: An Experiment.** Washington, D.C.: Carnegie Endowment for International Peace.

de Gobineau, Arthur (1967). **The inequality of human races.** New York: Fertig. [translation of **Essai sur l'inégalité des races humaines**, 1853]

de Varennes, Fernand (1996a). **Language, Minorities and Human Rights.** The Hague/Boston/London: Martinus Nijhoff.

de Varennes, Fernand (1996b). Minority aspirations and the revival of indigenous peoples. **International Review of Education** 42:4, 309–325.

de Villar, Robert A., Faltis, Christian, J. & Cummins, James P. (eds). **Cultural diversity in schools: From rhetoric to practice**. Albany, N.Y.: State University of New York Press.

de Vries, John (1990). On coming to our census: A layman's guide to demolinguistics. In Gorter et al. (eds), 57–76.

de Vries, John (1991). Towards a Sociology of Language Planning. In Marshall (ed.), 37–52.

de Vries, John (1995). Language policy and regional characteristics of minority language communities. In Fase et al. (eds), 135–151.

de Witte, Bruno (1991). The impact of European Community rules on linguistic policies of the Member States. In Coulmas (ed.), 163–177.

Debeljak, Aleš (1996). Odi et amo in the land of Southern Slavs. In Tóth (ed.), 73–88.

Dechicchis, Joseph (1995). The current State of the Ainu Language. In Maher & Yashiro (eds), 103–124.

Degenaar, Johann (1982). **The roots of nationalism**. Pretoria: Academica.

Degenaar, Johann (1987). Nationalism, liberalism and pluralism. In Butler, J., Elpick, R. & Welsh, D. (eds). **Democratic liberalism in South Africa: Its history and prospects**. Cape Town: David Philip, 236–249.

Dencik, Lars (1992). Processes of ethnification and de-ethnification of social conflicts. In Plichtová (ed.), 140–147.

Denison, Norman (1977). Language death or language suicide? **International Journal of the Sociology of Language** 12, 13–22.

Department of Education and Science (DES) and the Welsh Office (1990). **Modern foreign languages for ages 11–16**. The Harris Report. London: HMSO.

Department of Education, Ministry of Human Resource Development, Government (1993). **Education for all: the Indian scene**, A synopsis, Delhi: Government of India.

Derman-Sparks, Louise (1989). **Antibias Curriculum: Tools for Empowering Young Children**. Washington, D.C.: National Association for the Education of Young Children.

DES (1965). = Department of Education and Science (1965). **The education of immigrants** (circular 7/65). London: HMSO.

DES (1971). = Department of Education and Science (1971). **The education of immigrants** (Education survey no. 13). London: HMSO.

DES (1975). = Department of Education and Science (1975). **A language for life** (The Bullock Report). London: HMSO.

DES (1981a). = Department of Education and Science (1981a). **Directive of the Council of the European Community on the education of the children of migrant workers** (circular 5/18). London: DES.

DES (1981b). = Department of Education and Science (1981b). **The school curriculum**, London: HMSO.

DES (1985). = Department of Education and Science (1985). **Education for all**. The Swann Report. London: HMSO.

DES (1988). = Department of Education and Science (1988). **Report of the Committee of Inquiry into the teaching of the English language**. The Kingman Report. London: HMSO.

DES (1989a). = Department of Education and Science (1989). May 19, Circular No. 9/89. **Education Reform Act (1988).: Modern and Foreign Languages in the National Curriculum**. London: HMSO.

DES (1989b). = Department of Education and Science (1989). **English from 5–16**. The Cox Report. London: HMSO.

Desai, Zubeida (1994). Praat or Speak but Don't Thetha: On Language Rights in South Africa. **Language and Education** 8:1–2, 19–29.

Desai, Zubeida (1995). The evolution of a post-apartheid language policy in South Africa: an on-going site of struggle. **European Journal of Intercultural Studies** 5:3, 18–25.

Desai, Zubeida (1998). Enabling policies, disabling practices. Paper presented at the Tenth World Congress of Comparative Education Societies, Cape Town, 16 July 1998, manuscript.

Deschênes, Jules (1985). Proposals concerning a definition of the term minority. E/CN.4/Sub.2/1985/31, 14 May 1985. New York: United Nations.

Diamond, Jared (1991). **The Rise and Fall of the Third Chimpanzee**. London: Vintage.

Dicker, Susan J. (1996). **Languages in America: A pluralist view**. Clevedon/Philadelphia: Multilingual Matters.

Dixon, Robert M. W. (1993). Australian Aboriginal languages. In Schulz (ed.), 71–82.

Djité, Paulin (1993). Language and development in Africa. **International Journal of the Sociology of Language**, 100 & 101, 149–166.

Djité, Paulin (1994). **From language policy to language planning**. Canberra: National Languages and Literacy Institute of Australia.

Djurberg, Daniel (1781). **Geografie för Ungdom**. Stockholm: A. Nordström.

Dolson, David & Lindholm, Kathryn (1995). World class education for children in California: A comparison of the two-way bilingual immersion and European School model. In Skutnabb-Kangas (ed.), 69–102.

Dolson, David P. & Mayer Jan (1992). Longitudinal Study of Three Program Models for Language Minority Students: A Critical Examination of Reported Findings. **Bilingual Research Journal** 16:1 & 2, 105–158.

Domaschnew, Anatoli (1994). Englisch als die einzige Verkehrssprache des zukünftigen Europa? Eine Stellungnahme aus osteuropäischer Sicht. In Ammon et al. (eds), 26–43.

Donahue, Thomas S. (1995). American language policy and compensatory opinion. In Tollefson (ed.), 112–141.

Donald, James & Rattansi, Ali (eds) (1992). **'Race', culture and difference**. London: Sage.

Dorian, Nancy C. (1981). **Language death: The life cycle of a Scottish Gaelic dialect**. Philadelphia: University of Pennsylvania Press.

Dorian, Nancy C. (1993a). Small languages and small language communities. **International Journal of the Sociology of Language** 103, 197–202.

Dorian, Nancy C. (1993b). Discussion note. A response to Ladefoged's other view of endangered languages. **Language** 69:3, 575–579.

Dorian, Nancy C. (1994). Choices and values in language shift and its study. **International Journal of the Sociology of Language** 110, 113–124.

Dorian, Nancy C. (ed.) (1989). **Investigating Obsolescence: Studies in Language Contraction and Death**. New York: Cambridge University Press.

Downing, John (1984). **Radical Media**. Boston: South End Press.

Drake, Paul (1991). From Good Men to Good Neighbours: 1912–1932. In Lowenthal, Abraham F. (ed.). **Exporting Democracy: The United States and Latin America**. Baltimore: John Hopkins University Press, 3–41.

Drapeau, Lynn (1998). Aboriginal languages: current status. In J. Edwards (ed.), 144–159.

Dressler, Wolfgang (1988). Spracherhaltung - Sprachverfall - Sprachtod. In Ammon et al. (eds), 1551–1563.

Driessen, Bart (1999). The Slovak State Language Law as a trade law problem. In Kontra et al. (eds), 147–168.

Drobizheva, L. & Gouboglo, M. (1986). Definitions. Appendix to papers given by the authors at the symposium Multilingualism: Aspects of Interpersonal and Intergroup Communication in Plurilingual Societies, Brussels, 13–15 March 1986.

Druviete, Ina (1994). Language Policy in the Baltic States: a Latvian Case. In **Valodas politika Baltijas Valsīs/Language Policy in the Baltic States**. Rīga: Krājumu sagatavojis, Latvijas Republikas Valsts valodas centrs, 151–160.

Druviete, Ina (1999). Language Policy in a Changing Society: Problematic Issues of Implementation of Universal Linguistic Human Rights Standards. In Kontra et al. (eds), 263–278.

Druviete, Ina (in press). The Latvian language law debate: Some aspects of linguistic human rights in education. In Phillipson (ed.).

Dua, Hans (1985). **Language Planning in India**. New Delhi: Harnam.

Dua, Hans (ed.) (1996). **Language Planning and Political Theory**. **International Journal of the Sociology of Language**, Vol. 118. Special Issue.

Duff, Patricia A. (1991). Innovations in Foreign Language Education: an Evaluation of Three Hungarian-English Dual-Language Schools. **Journal of Multilingual and Multicultura¹ Development** 12:6, 459–476.

Durie, Arohia (1997). Maori-English Bilingual Education in New Zealand. In Cummins & Corson (eds), 15–24.

Dürmüller, Urs (1994). Multilingual Talk or English Only? The Swiss Experience. In Ammon et al. (eds), 44–64.

Durrell, Martin (1990). Language as geography. In Collinge, N. E. (ed.). **An encyclopaedia of linguistics**. London/New York: Routledge, 917–955.

Dutcher, Nadine (1982). **The Use of First and Second Languages in Primary Education: Selected Case Studies**. World Bank Staff Working Paper No. 504, January 1982. Washington, D.C.: The World Bank, Education Department.

Dutcher, Nadine, with the collaboration of G. Richard Tucker (1997) [no date]. **The Use of First and Second Languages in Education: A Review of International Experience**. Pacific Islands Discussion Paper Series 1. East Asia and Pacific Region, Country Department III. Washington, D.C.: The World Bank.

Eco, Umberto (1995). **The search for the Perfect Language**. Oxford, UK/Cambridge, USA: Blackwell.

Edwards, Coral & Read, Peter (eds) (1992). **The Lost Children. Thirteen Australians taken from their Aboriginal families tell of the struggle to find their natural parents**. Sydney/Auckland/New York/Toronto/London: Doubleday.

Edwards, John (1977). Ethnic Identity and Bilingual Education. In Giles (ed.), 253–282.

Edwards, John (1984a). Introduction. In J. Edwards (ed.), 1–16.

Edwards, John (1984b). Language, Diversity and Identity. In J. Edwards (ed.), 77–310.

Edwards, John (1985). **Language, Society and Identity**. Oxford: Blackwell.

Edwards, John (1994a). Ethnolinguistic pluralism and its discontents: a Canadian study, and some general observations. **International Journal of the Sociology of Language** 110, 5–85.

Edwards, John (1994b). Canadian update, and rejoinder to the comments. **International Journal of the Sociology of Language** 110, 203–219.

Edwards, John (ed.) (1984). **Linguistic Minorities. Policies and Pluralism**. London: Academic Press.

Edwards, John (ed.) (1998). **Language in Canada**. Cambridge, UK/New York/Melbourne: Cambridge University Press.

Edwards, Rebecca Anne Rourke (1997). **Words made flesh: Nineteenth-century Deaf education and the growth of Deaf culture**. Dissertation. University of Rochester, N.Y. [quoted in Senghas 1998].

Ehlich, Konrad (1994). Communication disruptions: On benefits and disadvantages of language contact. In Pütz, Martin (ed.). **Language contact and language conflict**. Amsterdam/Philadelphia: John Benjamins, 103–122.

Ehn, Billy & Arnstberg, Karl-Olov (1980). **Det osynliga arvet. Sexton invandrare om sin bakgrund** (The invisible inheritance. Sixteen immigrants about their background). Stockholm: Författarförlaget.

Ehrnrooth, Jari (1992). **Sanan vallassa, vihan voimalla. Sosialistiset vallankumousopit ja niiden vaikutus Suomen työväenliikkeessä 1905–1914** (Ruled by the word, empowered by hate. Socialist revolutionary doctrines and their influence in the Finnish workers' movement 1905–1914). Helsinki: Societas Historica Finlandiae.

Eide, Asbjørn (1990). **Possible ways and means of facilitating the peaceful and constructive solution of problems involving minorities. Progress report submitted to UN Sub-Commission on Prevention of Discrimination and Protection of Minorities at its 42nd session** (E/CN.4/Sub.2/1990/46). New York: United Nations.

Eide, Asbjørn (1991). **Preliminary report submitted to UN Sub-Commission on Prevention of Discrimination and Protection of Minorities at its 43rd session** (E/CN.4/Sub.2/1991/43). New York: United Nations.

Eide, Asbjørn (1993). **Possible ways and means to facilitate the peaceful and constructive solution of problems involving racial minorities.** E/CN.4/Sub.2/1993/34 and Add.1–4. New York: United Nations.

Eide, Asbjørn (1995a). Economic, social and cultural rights as human rights. In Eide et al. (eds), 21–40.

Eide, Asbjørn (1995b). Cultural rights as individual human rights. In Eide et al. (eds), 229–240.

Eide, Asbjørn (1996). **Classification of minorities and differentiation in minority rights.** E/CN.4/Sub.2/AC5/1996/WP.2. New York: United Nations.

Eide, Asbjørn (1997). The Hague Recommendations Regarding the Education Rights of Minorities: Their Objective. **International Journal on Minority and Group Rights**. Special Issue on the Education Rights of National Minorities 4:2, 1996/1997, 163–170.

Eide, Asbjørn, Krause, Catarina & Rosas, Allan (eds) (1995). **Economic, Social and Cultural Rights. A Textbook**. Dordrecht/Boston/London: Martinus Nijhoff.

Eidheim, Harald (1997). Ethno-Political Development among the Sami after World War II: The Invention of Selfhood. In Gaski (ed.), 29–61.

Einarsson, Jan (1978). Språk och kön i skolan, projekt (The project Language and gender in school). Rapporter. 1978–1985. Malmö: Lärarhögskolan i Malmö.

Ekern, Stener (1998). Development Aid to Indigenous Peoples is an Exercise in Crossing Boundaries. In Stokke, Hugo, Suhrke, Astri & Tostensen, Arne (eds). **Human Rights in Developing Countries. Yearbook 1997**. The Hague/London/Boston: Kluwer Law International & Oslo: Nordic Human Rights Publications, 3–34.

Ekka, Francis (1984). Status of Minority Languages in the Schools of India. **International Education Journal** 1:1, 1–19.

Ekka, Francis (1995). Endangered languages in India: Problems and Prospects for Survival. Abstract of the paper presented at the International Symposium on Endangered Languages, November 18–20, 1995, University of Tokyo. [can be downloaded from <http://www.tooyoo.1.u-Tokyo.ac.jp/linguistics/newsletters/newslet1.html>].

Ekstrand, Lars Henric (1978). **Bilingual and Bicultural Adaptation**. Ph.D. dissertation. Stockholm: University of Stockholm.

Elliott, Larry & Atkinson, Dan (1998). **The Age of Insecurity**. London: Verso.

Ellis, Justin (1984). **Education, repression, and liberation**. Namibia, London: Catholic Institute for International Relations and World University Service.

Encyclopaedia of Aboriginal Australia (1994). Edited by the Institute of Aboriginal and Torres Strait Islander Studies. Canberra: Aboriginal Studies Press.

Engstrand, Iris (1987). Interview with Dr. Iris Engstrand. In Costo & Costo (eds), 192–195.

Enriquez, Virgilio G. & Protacio Marcelino, Elisabeth (1984). **Neo-Colonial Policies and the Language Struggle in the Phillippines**. Quezon City: Phillippine Psychology Research and Training House.

Eriksen, Knut Einar & Niemi, Einar (1981). **Den finske fare. Sikkerhetsproblemer og minoritetspolitikk i nord 1860–1940** (The Finnish danger. Security problems and minority policy in the north 1860–1940). Oslo: Universitetsforlaget.

Eriksson, Riitta (1994). **Biculturalism in Upper Secondary Education. The Long Term Effects of Finnish Language Programs on Students' Educational and Occupational Careers—A Swedish Case Study**. Stockholm: Stockholm University, Institute of International Education.

Erting, Carol (1978). Language policy and deaf ethnicity in the United States. **Sign Language Studies** 19, 19–152.

Escobar, Arturo (1992). Planning. In Sachs (ed.), 132–145.

Escobar, Arturo (1995). **Encountering Development. The making and unmaking of the Third World**. Princeton, N.J.: Princeton University Press.

Esteva, Gustavo (1992). Development. In Sachs (ed.), 6–25.

Euromosaic (1996). **The production and reproduction of the minority language groups of the European Union.** Nelde, P. H., Strubell, M. & Williams, C. (eds). Brussel: Research Centre of Multilingualism.

Fairclough, Norman (1987). Register, power and socio-semantic change. In Birch, David & O'Toole, Michael (eds). **Functions of Style.** London/New York: Pinter, 111–125.

Fairclough, Norman (1989). **Language and Power.** Harlow: Longman.

Fairclough, Norman (1991). **Discourse and Social Change.** Cambridge: Polity Press.

Fairclough, Norman (1996). Border Crossings: Discourse and social change in contemporary societies. In Coleman, Hywel & Cameron, Lynne (eds). **Change and Language.** Clevedon, UK: British Association for Applied Linguistics in association with Multilingual Matters, 3–17.

Fairclough, Norman (ed.) (1992). **Critical language awareness.** London: Longman.

Fairman, Tony (1999). Schooled and open Englishes. **English Today** 57, 15:1, 24–30.

Falk, Richard (1991). The Terrorist Foundations of Recent US Policy. In George (ed.).

Faltis, Christian (1997). Bilingual Education in the United States. In Cummins & Corson (eds), 189–198.

Fanon, Frantz (1952). **Peau noire, masques blancs.** Paris: Seuil.

Fanon, Frantz (1963). **The Wretched of the Earth.** New York: Grove Press.

Fanon, Frantz (1965). **A Dying Colonialism.** Harmondsworth: Penguin.

Fantini, Alvino & Reagan, Timothy (1992). **Esperanto and education: Toward a research agenda.** Washington, D.C.: Esperantic Studies Foundation.

Farrell, Shaun, Bellin, Wynford, Higgs, Gary & White, Sean (1998). The Distribution of Younger Welsh Speakers in Anglicised Areas of South East Wales. **Journal of Multilingual and Multicultural Development** 18:6, 489–495.

Fase, Willem, Jaspaert, Koen & Kroon, Sjaak (eds) (1995). **The state of minority languages. International perspectives on survival and decline.** European Studies on Multilingualism, 5. Lisse: Swets & Zeitlinger.

Featherstone, Michael (ed.) (1990). **Global Culture: nationalism, globalization and modernity.** London: Sage.

Feldman, Allen (1991). **Formations of violence. The Narrative of the Body and Political Terror in Northern Ireland.** Chicago/London: The University of Chicago Press.

Ferguson, Charles A. (1959). Diglossia. **Word** 15, 325–340.

Ferguson, Charles A., Houghton, Catherine & Wells, Marie H. (1977). Bilingual Education: An International Perspective. In Spolsky, Bernard & Cooper, Robert (eds). **Frontiers of Bilingual Education.** Rowley, Mass.: Newbury House, 159–174.

Fesl, Eve D. (1988). Language Loss in Australian Languages. Paper presented to the Conference on the Maintenance and Loss of Minority Languages, Institute of Applied Linguistics, University of Nijmegen, The Netherlands.

Fesl, Eve Mumewa D. (1993). **Conned! A Koorie perspective.** St Lucian, Queensland: University of Queensland Press.

Fettes, Mark (1992). **A Guide to Language Strategies for First Nations Communities.** Ottawa: Assembly of First Nations.

Fettes, Mark (1998). Life on the Edge: Canada's Aboriginal Languages Under Official Bilingualism. In Ricento & Burnaby (eds), 117–149.

FIDEF (1978). **Bericht zur Bildungssituation türkischen Kinder in der BRD**, dem Kongress zur Bildungssituation türkischer Kinder in der BRD am 11/12 Februar (1978) in Gelsen-Kirchen vom Bundesvorstand den FIDEF vorgelegt. Frankfurt am Main: FIDEF.

Fill, Alwin (1993). **Ökolinguistik. Eine Einführung.** Tübingen: Gunter Narr Verlag.

Fill, Alwin (1998a). Ecolinguistics—State of the Art 1998. In AAA—Arbeiten aus Anglistik und Amerikanistik, Band 23, Heft 1. Tübingen: Gunter Narr Verlag, 1–16.

Fill, Alwin (1998b). Ecologically Determined Choices and Constraints. In Schulze, Rainer (ed). Making Meaningful Choices in English. On Dimensions, Perspectives, Methodology and Evidence. Tübingen: Gunter Narr Verlag, 61–76.

Finding of the Waitangi Tribunal relating to Te Reo Maori and a claim lodged, by Huirangi Waikerepuru and Nga Kaiwhakapumau I Te Reo Incorporated Society (1986). Wellington: Government Printer.

Finnäs, Fjalar (1982). Språkgruppsidentifikation och kunskaper i finska i Svensk-Finland (Language group identification and knowledge of Finnish in Swedish Finland). MOB No. 11, Ethnicity and Mobility. Åbo: Åbo Akademi.

Fishman, Joshua A. (1966). Some contrasts between linguistically homogenous and linguistically heterogenous polities. **Sociological Inquiry** 6, 146–158 (reprinted in Fishman, Joshua A., Ferguson, Charles A. & Das Gupta, Jyotirindra (eds) (1968). **Language problems of developing nations**, New York: Wiley, 53–68).

Fishman, Joshua A. (1976a). Bilingual education: What and why? In Alatis, J. E. & Twaddell, K. (eds). **English as a second language in bilingual education**. Washington, D.C.: TESOL, 263–272.

Fishman, Joshua A. (1976b). **Bilingual Education: An International Sociological Perspective**. Rowley, Mass.: Newbury House.

Fishman, Joshua A. (1977). Language and Ethnicity. In Giles (ed.), 15–57.

Fishman, Joshua A. (1989). **Language & Ethnicity in Minority Sociolinguistic Perspective**. Clevedon/Philadelphia: Multilingual Matters.

Fishman, Joshua A. (1991). **Reversing Language Shift. Theoretical and Empirical Assistance to Threatened Languages**. Clevedon, UK: Multilingual Matters.

Fishman, Joshua A. (1994a). On the limits of ethnolinguistic democracy. In Skutnabb-Kangas & Phillipson (eds), 49–61.

Fishman, Joshua A. (1994b). "English only" in Europe? Some Suggestions from an American Perspective. In Ammon et al. (eds), 65–72.

Fishman, Joshua A. (1995). Good conferences in a wicked world: on some worrisome problems in the study of language maintenance and language shift. In Fase et al. (eds), 311–317.

Fishman, Joshua A. (1996a). Introduction: Some empirical and theoretical issues. In Fishman et al. (eds), 3–12.

Fishman, Joshua A. (1996b). Maintaining Languages: What Works and What Doesn't? In Cantoni (ed.).

Fishman, Joshua A. (1997). **In Praise of the Beloved Language. A Comparative view of Positive Ethnolinguistic Consciousness**. Berlin/New York: Mouton de Gruyter.

Fishman, Joshua A. (1998). Review of Tove Skutnabb-Kangas (ed.). Multilingualism for All. **Language in Society** 27:3, 413–415.

Fishman, Joshua A. & Fishman Schweid, Gella (in press). Rethinking language defence. In Phillipson (ed.).

Fishman, Joshua A. & Solano, R. (1989). Societal factors predictive of linguistic homogeneity/heterogeneity at the inter-polity level. **Cultural Dynamics** 1, 414–437.

Fishman, Joshua A. (ed.) (1971). **Advances in the Sociology of Language**, Vol. 1. The Hague: Mouton.

Fishman, Joshua A. (ed.) (1972). **Advances in the Sociology of Language**, Vol. 2. The Hague: Mouton.

Fishman, Joshua A., Conrad, Andrew W. & Rubal-Lopez, Alma (eds) (1996). **Post-Imperial English. Status Change in Former British and American Colonies, 1940–1990**. Berlin & New York: Mouton de Gruyter.

Focus ACP. The Magazine for the African, Caribbean and Pacific Group of States 1:2, March 1997. Theme: What future for Lomé?

Follow-up Committee 1998—see **Universal Declaration of Linguistic Rights**.

Fonseca, Isabel (1995). **Bury Me Standing. The Gypsies and Their Journeys**. London: Chatto & Windus.

Foster, Michael (1982a). Canada's indigenous languages: Present and future. **Language and Society/Langue et société** 7 (Winter 1982), 7–16. Ottawa: Commissioner of Official Languages.

Foster, Michael (1982b). Indigenous languages in Canada. A 10-page offprint from **Language and Society/Langue et société** 7 (Winter 1982). Includes a fold-out map and list of 53 Aboriginal languages with speaker estimates. Ottawa: Commissioner of Official Languages.

Foucault, Michel (1980). **Power/Knowledge: Selected Interviews and Other Writings, 1972–1977**, edited by Colin Gordon. New York: Pantheon Books.

Fraser Gupta, Anthea (1997). Moral English. **English today** 49, 13:1, January 1997, 24–27.

Freedman, Warren (1992). **Genocide: A people's will to live**. Buffalo, N.Y.: William S. Hein & Co.

Freire, Paulo (1972). **Pedagogy of the oppressed**. Harmondsworth, Middlesex: Penguin Books.

Freire, Paulo (1985). **The Politics of Education. Culture, Power and Liberation**. Introduction by Henry A. Giroux. Translated by Donaldo Macedo. Houndsmills/London: Macmillan.

French, Marilyn (1986). **Beyond Power: On women, men and morals**. London: Abacus.

Furedi, Frank (1994). **The New Ideology of Imperialism**. London: Pluto Press.

Gainor, J. Ellen (ed.) (1995). **Imperialism and Theatre. Essays on world theatre, drama and performance**. London/New York: Routledge.

Gal, Susan (1996). Language Shift. In Goebl et al. (eds), 586–593.

Gallois, Cynthis, Franklyn-Stokes, A., Giles, Howard & Coupland, Nikolas (1988). Communication accommodation in intercultural encounters. In Kim, Young Yun & Gudykunst, William B. (eds). **Theories in Intercultural Communication**. Newbury Park, CA: Sage.

Galtung, Johan (1972). Notes on the Long Term Development of Peace Research. In Höglund, Bengt & Ulrich, Jörgen Wilian (eds). **Conflict Control and Conflict Resolution**. Interdisciplinary Studies from the Scandinavian Summer University, Vol. 17. Copenhagen: Munksgaard, 202–216.

Galtung, Johan (1980). **The True Worlds. A transnational perspective**. New York: The Free Press.

Galtung, Johan (1988). **Methodology and Development. Essays in Methodology**, Vol. III. Copenhagen: Christian Ejlers.

Galtung, Johan (1996). **Peace by Peaceful Means. Peace and Conflict, Development and Civilization**. Oslo: International Peace Research Institute & London/Thousand Oaks/New Delhi: Sage.

García, Ofelia (1988). The education of biliterate and bicultural children in ethnic schools in the United States. In **Essays by the Spencer Fellows of the National Academy of Education**, Vol. IV, (19–7), 8.

García, Ofelia (1992). Societal multilingualism in a multicultural world in transition. In Byrne, Heidi (ed.). **Languages for a Multicultural World in Transition**. Illinois: National Textbook Company, 1–27.

García, Ofelia (1994). Que todo el pluralismo es sueño, y los sueños, vida son: ethnolinguistic dreams and reality. **International Journal of the Sociology of Language** 110, 87–103.

García, Ofelia (1995). Spanish language loss as a determinant of income among Latinos in the United States: Implications for language policy in schools. In Tollefson (ed.), 142–160.

García, Ofelia (in press). Minority educators' use of minority languages and cultures in the urban classroom. In Phillipson (ed.).

García, Ofelia & Otheguy, Ricardo (1988). The bilingual education of Cuban American children in Dade County's ethnic schools. **Language and Education** 1, 83–95.

García, Ofelia & Otheguy, Ricardo (1994). The value of speaking a LOTE [Language Other Than English] in U.S. Business. **Annals of the American Academy of Political and Social Science** 532 (March), 99–122.

García, Ofelia (ed.) (1991). **Bilingual education: Festschrift in honor of Joshua A. Fishman on the occasion of his 65th birthday.** Amsterdam/Philadelphia: John Benjamins.

Gardner, Gary (1998). Recycling Organic Wastes. In **State of the World 1998**, 96–112.

Garrett, P., Giles, Howard & Coupland, Nikolas (1989). The contexts of language learning: extending the intergroup model of second language acquisition. In Ting-Toomey, Stella & Korzenny, Felipe (eds). **Language, Communication, and Culture.** Newbury Park, CA: Sage.

Gaski, Harald (1986). **Den samiske litteraturens rötter. Om samenes episk poetiske diktning** (The roots of Sámi literature. On Sámi epic poetry). Tromsö: Institutt for sprog og litteratur, Universitetet i Tromsö.

Gaski, Harald (1996). Introduction. In Gaski (ed.), 9–42.

Gaski, Harald (1997a). Voice in the Margin: A Suitable Place for a Minority Literature? In Gaski (ed.), 199–220.

Gaski, Harald (1997b). Introduction: Sami Culture in a New Era. In Gaski (ed.), 9–28.

Gaski, Harald (in press). The reindeer on the mountain, the reindeer in the mind: On Sami yoik lyrics. In Phillipson (ed.).

Gaski, Harald (ed.) (1996). **In the Shadow of the Midnight Sun. Contemporary Sami Prose and Poetry.** Kárášjohka, Norway: Davvi Girji. [ISBN 82-7374-309-8; address: Davvi Girji, P. O. Box 13, N-9730 Kárášjohka, Norway; fax: (+47) 78 46 72 51].

Gaski, Harald (ed.) (1997). **Sami Culture in a New Era. The Norwegian Sami Experience.** Kárášjohka/Karasjok: Davvi Girji.

Gellner, Ernest (1983). **Nations and nationalism.** Oxford, UK/Cambridge, USA: Blackwell.

Genesee, Fred (1976). The Suitability of Immersion Programs for All Children. **Canadian Modern Language Review** 32:5, 494–515.

Genesee, Fred (1985). Second language learning through immersion: A review of U.S. programs. **Review of Educational Research** 55:4, 541–561.

Genesee, Fred (1987). **Learning Through Two Languages: Studies of Immersion and Bilingual Education.** Cambridge, Mass.: Newbury House.

Genesee, Fred (1996). Second Language Immersion Programs. In Goebl et al. (eds), 493–501.

Genesee, Fred (ed.) (1992). **The teaching of ESL.** New York: Newbury House.

George, Alexander (ed.) (1991). **Western State Terrorism.** London: Polity Press.

George, Susan (1992). **The Debt Boomerang. How Third World Debt Harms Us All.** London: Pluto Press.

George, Susan & Sabelli, Fabrizio (1994). **Faith and Credit: The World Bank's Secular Empire.** London: Penguin.

Gérin-Lajoie, Diane (1997). French Language Minority Education in Canada. In Cummins & Corson (eds), 167–176.

Géry, Yves (1999). The dark side of Europe: Women for Sale. **Le Monde Diplomatique** February 1999, 12.

Gibbons, John (1997). Australian Bilingual Education. In Cummins & Corson (ed.), 209–216.

Gibbons, John, White, William & Gibbons, Pauline (1994). Combating educational disadvantage among Lebanese Australian children. In Skutnabb-Kangas & Phillipson (eds), 253–262.

Giddens, Anthony (1990). **The Consequences of Modernity.** Stanford, CA: Stanford University Press.

Giles, Howard, Bourhis, R. Y. and Taylor, D. M. (1977). Towards a Theory of Language in Ethnic Group Relations. In Giles (ed.), 307–348.

Giles, Howard, Coupland, Nikolas, Williams, Angie & Leets, Laura (1991). Integrating theory in the study of minority languages. In Cooper & Spolsky (eds), 113–136.

Giles, Howard, Leets, Laura & Coupland, Nikolas (1990). Minority Language Group Status: A Theoretical Conspexus. In Gorter et al. (eds), 37–56.

Giles, Howard & Smith, P. M. (1979). Accommodation theory: optimal levels of convergence. In Giles & St. Clair (eds), 45–65.

Giles, Howard & Wiemann, J. M. (1987). Language, social comparison and power. In Berger, C. R. & Chaffee, S. H. (eds). **Handbook of Communication Science**. Newbury Park, CA: Sage, 350–384.

Giles, Howard (ed.) (1977). **Language, Ethnicity and Intergroup Relations**. London: Academic Press.

Giles, Howard & St. Clair, Robert (eds) (1979). **Language and Social Psychology**. Oxford: Basil Blackwell.

Gill, Dawn, Mayor, Barbara & Blair, Maud (eds) (1992). **Racism and education: Structures and strategies**. London: Sage.

Gill, Sam D. & Sullivan, Irene F. (1994). **Dictionary of Native American Mythology**. New York: Oxford University Press. [1992].

Gilroy, Paul (1987). **"There Ain't No Black in the Union Jack". The cultural politics of race and nation**. London: Hutchinson.

Gimbutas, Marija (1991). **The language of the Goddess**. San Francisco: Harper Collins.

Giroux, Henry A. (1985). Introduction. In Freire, Paulo. **The Politics of Education. Culture, Power and Liberation**. Houndsmills/London: Macmillan, xi–xxv.

Giroux, Henry (1992). **Border Crossing. Cultural Workers and the Politics of Education**. New York/London: Routledge.

Gobbo, James (1995). Criticisms of multiculturalism. Paper to the Global Cultural Diversity Conference, Sydney [see Boutros-Ghali].

Goebl, Hans, Nelde, Peter Hans, Starý, Zdeněk & Wölck, Wolfgang (eds) (1996). **Kontaktlinguistik. Contact Linguistics. Linguistique de contact. Ein Internationales Handbuch zeitgenössiger Forschung. An International Handbook of Contemporary Research. Manuel international des recherches contemporaines**. Berlin/New York: Walter de Gruyter.

Goldsmith, Edward (1996). Global trade and the environment. In Mander & Goldsmith (eds), 78–91.

Goodland, Robert (1996). Growth has reached its limit. In Mander & Goldsmith (eds), 207–217.

Gorter Durk, Hoekstra, Jarich F., Jansma, Lammert G. & Ytsma, Jehannes (eds) (1990). **Fourth International Conference on Minority Languages**, Vol. 1: General Papers. **Journal of Multilingual and Multicultural Development** 11:1 & 2, Special volume.

Graddol, David (1996). Global English, global culture? In Goodman, Sharon & Graddol, David (eds). **Redesigning English, new texts, new identities**. London/New York: The Open University & Routledge.

Graddol, David (1997). **The Future of English?** A guide to forecasting the popularity of the English language in the 21st century. London: British Council.

Graddol, David, Leith, Dick & Swann, Joan (eds) 1996. **English history, diversity and change**. London & New York: The Open University & Routledge.

Gramsci, Antonio (1971). **Selections from the Prison Notebooks of Antonio Gramsci**, edited and translated by Q. Hoare & G. Nowell Smith. London: Lawrence & Wishart.

Granville, S., Janks, Hilary, Mphahlele, M., Ramani, Esther., Reed, Y. & Watson, P. (1997). English with or without g(u)ilt: a position paper on language-in-education policy for South Africa. Paper presented at the English Teachers' Connect International Conference, University of the Witwatersrand, Johannesburg, South Africa.

Grenoble, Lenore A. & Whaley, Lindsay J. (1996). Endangered Languages: Current Issues and Future Prospects. **International Journal of the Sociology of Language** 118, 209–223.

Grenoble, Lenore A. & Whaley, Lindsay J. (eds) (1998). **Endangered Languages: Current Issues and Future Prospects**. Cambridge: Cambridge University Press.

Grierson, G. A. (1927). **Linguistic Survey of India**. Vol. 1, Part I. Delhi: Motilal Banarasidas.

Grimes, Barbara F. (ed.) (1984). **Index to the Tenth Edition of Ethnologue: Languages of the World**. Dallas, Tex.: SIL (Summer Institute of Linguistics).

Grimes, Barbara F. (ed.) (1992). **Ethnologue: languages of the world**. 12th ed. Dallas, Tex.: SIL (Summer Institute of Linguistics).

Grin, François (1991a). The Estonian Language Law. Presentation with Comments. **Language Problems & Language Planning** 15, 191–201.

Grin, François (1991b). Territorial Multilingualism. **Linguistic Decisions** 15. Washington: Center for the Humanities, University of Washington.

Grin, François (1992). Towards a Threshold Theory of Minority Language Survival. **Kyklos** 45, 69–97.

Grin, François (1993). European Economic Integration and the Fate of Lesser-Used Languages. **Language Problems & Language Planning** 17:2, 101–116.

Grin, François (1994a). Combining immigrant and autochthonous language rights: a territorial approach to multilingualism. In Skutnabb-Kangas & Phillipson (eds), 31–48.

Grin, François (1994b). The economics of language: match or mismatch? **International Political Science Review** 15: 25–42.

Grin, François (1995a). The economics of foreign language competence: a research project of the Swiss National Science Foundation. **Journal of Multilingual and Multicultural Development** 16:3, 227–231.

Grin, François (1995b). La valeur des compétences linguistiques: vers une perspective économique. **Babylonia** 2, 59–65.

Grin, François (1996a). Valeur privée de la pluralité linguistique. Cahier No 96.04, Département d'économie politique. Genève: Université de Genève.

Grin, François (1996b). Economic approaches to language and language planning: an introduction. **International Journal of the Sociology of Language** 121, 1–16.

Grin, François (1997). Amémagement linguistique: du bon usage des concepts d'offre et de demande. In Labrie, Norman (ed.). **Etides récentes en linguistique de contact**. Bonn: Dümmler, 117–134.

Grin, François (1999). Market forces, language spread and linguistic diversity. In Kontra et al. (eds), 169–186.

Grin, François & Vaillancourt, François (in press). On the financing of language policies and distributive justice. In Phillipson (ed.).

Groce, Nora Ellen (1985). **Everyone here spoke sign language: Hereditary deafness on Martha's Vineyard**. Cambridge, Mass.: Harvard University Press.

Gromacki, Joseph P. (1992) The Protection of Language Rights in International Human Rights Law: A Proposed Draft Declaration of Linguistic Rights. **Virginia Journal of International Law** 32:471, 515–579.

Gronemeyer, Marianne (1992). Helping. In Sachs (ed.), 53–69.

Grönfors, Martti (1995). Finnish Rom: a forgotten cultural group. In Pentikäinen & Hiltunen (eds), 147–162.

Gudykunst, William B. & Ting-Toomey, Stella (1990). Ethnic identity, language and communication breakdowns. In Giles, Howard & Robinson, W. Peter (eds). **Handbook of Language and Social Psychology**. Chichester: Wiley.

Gudykunst, William B. (ed.) (1986). **Intergroup Communication**. London: Edward Arnold.

Guerra, Sandra (1988). Voting Rights and the Constitution: The Disenfranchisement of Non-English Speaking Citizens. **Yale Law Journal** 97, 1419–1437.

Guest, Francis F. (1987). Excerpts from A Special Article by Rev. Francis F. Guest, O.F.M. In Costo & Costo (eds), 223–233.

Gunnemark, Erik V. (1991). **Countries, Peoples and their Languages. The Geolinguistic Handbook**. Gothenburg: Geolingua.

Gustavsen, John (1980). **Samer tier ikke lenger: om ytringsforbud i Sameland** (The Sámi are no longer silent: on prohibition of speech in Sápmi). Bodø: Egil Trohaug.

Gustavsen, John & Sandvik, Kjell (eds) (1981). **Vår jord er vårt liv**. En antologi laget i samarbeid mellom Samebevegelsen, Kunstnernes Aksjonskommite og Folkeaksjonen (Our land is our life, an anthology prepared in cooperation with the Sámi Movement, Artists' Action Committee and Peoples' Action). Oslo: Forfatterforlaget.

Gutiérrez Estévez, Manuel (1993). Mayas, espanoles, moros y judios en baile de máscaras. Morfología y retórica de la alteridad. In Gosse, Gary H., Klor de Alva, J. J., Gutiérrez Estévez, M. and León-Portilla, M. (eds) **De Palabra y Obra en el Nuevo Mundo, vol. 3, La Formación del Otro.** Madrid: Siglo XXI de Espana, 323–376.

Gårding, Eva & Bannert, Robert (1979). **Optimering av svenskt uttal** (Optimizing Swedish pronunciation). Projektrapporter. Serie praktisk lingvistik. Lund: Institutionen för lingvistik, Universitetet i Lund.

Haarmann, Harald (1979–1984). **Elemente einer Soziologie der kleinen Sprachen Europas.** Bd. 1, (1983).; Bd. 2, (1979).; Bd. 3, (1984). Hamburg: H. Buske.

Haarmann, Harald (1991a). Language politics and the new European identity. In Coulmas (ed.), 103–119.

Haarmann, Harald (1991b). Monolingualism vs. selective multilingualism: On the future alternatives for Europe as it integrates in the 1990s. **Sociolinguistica** 5, 7–23.

Haarmann, Harald (1992). Measures to increase the importance of Russian within and outside the Soviet Union—a case of covert language spread policy (a historical outline). **International Journal of the Sociology of Language** 95, 109–129.

Haarmann, Harald (1996). Identität. In Goebl et al. (eds), 218–233.

Haberland, Hartmut (1993). Probleme der kleinen Sprachen in der EG: Beispiel Dänisch. **Heteroglossia** 5, 83–131.

Haberland, Hartmut & Henriksen, Carol (1991). Dänisch—eine kleine Sprache in der EG. **Sociolinguistica** 5, 85–98.

Haberland, Hartmut, Henriksen, Carol, Phillipson, Robert & Skutnabb-Kangas, Tove (1991). Tak for mad! Om sprogæderi med dansk som livret (Thanks for the meal! On the gobbling up of languages, with Danish as the favourite dish). In J. N. Jørgensen (ed.). **Det danske sprogs status år 2001—er dansk et truet sprog?** Copenhagen, Danmarks Lærerhøjskole, 111–138).

Habermas, Jürgen (1971). **Knowledge and Human Interests.** Translated by Jeremy J. Shapiro. Boston: Beacon Press. [**Erkenntnis und Interesse**, Frankfurt am Main: Suhrkamp, 1968].

Habermas, Jürgen (1984). **The Critical Theory of Jürgen Habermas.** Edited by Thomas McCarthy. Cambridge: Polity Press, in association with Basil Blackwell.

Habermas, Jürgen (1987). **The philosophical discourse of modernity: twelve lectures.** Cambridge: Polity Press, in association with Basil Blackwell.

Hacker, Andrew (1995). **Two nations. Black and white, separate, hostile, unequal.** New York: Ballantine Books.

Haddad, W. D., Carnoy, M., Rinaldi, R. & Regel, O. (1990). **Education and development: evidence for new priorities.** Discussion paper 95. Washington, D.C.: World Bank.

Haetta, Odd Mathis (1996). **The Sámi, an Indigenous People of the Arctic.** Guovdageaidnu: Davvi Girji.

Hagman, Tom & Lahdenperä, Jouko (1988). 9 years of Finnish medium education in Sweden—what happens afterwards? The education of immigrant and minority children in Botkyrka. In Skutnabb-Kangas & Cummins (eds), 328–335.

Hakuta, Kenji (1986). **Mirror of language: The debate on bilingualism.** New York: Basic Books.

Hale, Ken (1992). On endangered languages and the safeguarding of diversity. **Language** 68:1, 1–3.

Hallamaa, Panu (1998). Scales for evaluating language proficiency and language viability. In Shoji, Hiroshi & Janhunen, Juha (eds). **Northern Minority Languages: Problems of Survival.** Senri Ethnological Studies. Osaka: National Museum of Ethnology.

Hamel, Rainer Enrique (1994a). Indigenous education in Latin America: policies and legal frameworks. In Skutnabb-Kangas & Phillipson (eds) 271–287.

Hamel, Rainer Enrique (1994b). Linguistic rights for Amerindian people in Latin America. In Skutnabb-Kangas & Phillipson (eds), 289–303.

Hamel, Rainer Enrique (1995). Indigenous language loss in Mexico: the process of language displacement in verbal interaction. In Fase et al. (eds), 153–172.

Hamelink, Cees J. (1994). **Trends in world communication: on disempowerment and self-empowerment**. Penang: Southbound & Third World Network.

Hamelink, Cees J. (1995). **The Politics of World Communication. A Human Rights Perspective**. London/Thousand Oaks/New Delhi: Sage.

Hamelink, Cees J. (ed.) (1997). **Ethics and Development. On making moral choices in development co-operation**. Kampen, The Netherlands: Kok.

Hamelink, Cees J. (ed.) (1998). **Gazette. The International Journal for Communication Studies**. Special volume, **Human Rights** 60:1.

Hancock, Graham (1989). **Lords of poverty. The free-wheeling lifestyles, power, prestige and corruption of the multi-billion dollar aid business**. London: Macmillan.

Hanf, T., Amman, K., Dias, P. V., Fremerey, M. & Weiland, H. (1975). Education: an obstacle to development? Some remarks about the political functions of education in Asia and Africa. **Comparative Education Review** 19, 68–87.

Hannikainen, Lauri (1996). Legal status of minorities, indigenous peoples and immigrant and refugee groups in the Nordic countries. In **Minorities and Conflicts**. Report from the Minority Days on the Åland Islands, 18th–23rd October 1995. Meddelanden från Ålands Högskola nr 9. Mariehamn: Ålands Högskola, 57–74.

Hannum, Hurst (1988). New Developments in Indigenous Rights. **Virginia Journal of International Law** 28, 649–678.

Hannum, Hurst (1989). **The Limits of Sovereignty and Majority Rule: Minorities, Indigenous Peoples, and the Right to Autonomy**. Philadelphia, Pa.: University of Pennsylvania Press.

Hannum, Hurst (1990). **Autonomy, Sovereignty and Self-determination: The Accommodation of Conflicting Rights**. Philadelphia: University of Pennsylvania Press.

Haraway, Donna J. (1991). **Simians, Cyborgs, and Women. The reinvention of Nature**. London: Free Association Books.

Harding, Sandra (1986). **The Science Question in Feminism**. Ithaca/London: Cornell University Press.

Harding, Sandra (1998). **Is Science Multicultural? Postcolonialisms, feminisms, and epistemologies**. Bloomington/Indianapolis: Indiana University Press.

Harding, Sandra & McGregor, Elisabeth (1996). Science by whom? In **World Science Report 1996** (ed. Howard Moore). Paris: Unesco, 305–319.

Harmon, David (1995a). Losing Species, Losing Languages: Connections Between Biological and Linguistic Diversity. Paper presented at the Symposium on Language Loss and Public Policy, Albuquerque, N.M., June 30–July 2 1995. In press, in **Southwest Journal of Linguistics** 15.

Harmon, David (1995b). The status of the world's languages as reported in the **Ethnologue**. **Southwest Journal of Linguistics** 14:1 & 2, 1–28.

Harnum, Betty (1993). **Eight Official Languages: Meeting the Challenge. First Annual Report of the Languages Commissioner of the Northwest Territories for the year 1992–1993**. 2nd edition. Yellowknife, NWT [no place mentioned]: Northwest Territories Legislative Assembly.

Harnum, Betty (1998). Language in the Northwest Territories and the Yukon Territory. In J. Edwards (ed.), 470–482.

Harrell, Stevan (1993). Linguistics and hegemony in China. **International Journal of the Sociology of Language** 103, 97–114.

Harries, Patrick (1995). Discovering languages: the historical origins of standard Tsonga in southern Africa. In Mesthrie (ed.), 154–175.

Harris, Phil (1997). Glossary. In Golding, Peter & Harris, Phil (eds). **Beyond Cultural Imperialism. Globalization, communication & the new international order**. London/Thousand Oaks/New Delhi: Sage, 208–256.

Harris, Stephen (1990). **Two-way Aboriginal Schooling. Education and Cultural Survival.** Canberra: Aboriginal Studies Press.

Harris, Stephen & Devlin, Brian (1997). Bilingual Programs Involving Aboriginal Languages in Australia. In Cummins & Corson (eds), 2–14.

Hartshorne, Ken (1995). Language policy in African education: a background to the future. In Mesthrie (ed.), 306–318.

Haselhuber, Jakob (1991). Erste Ergebnisse einer empirischen Untersuchung zur Sprachsituation in der EG-Kommission (Februar 1990). **Sociolinguistica** 5, 37–50.

Hasenau, M. (1990). Setting norms in the United Nations system: the draft Convention on the Protection of the Rights of All Migrant Workers and their Families in relation to ILO in Standards on Migrant Workers. **International Migration** XXVIII:2, 133–157.

Hassanpour, Amir (1992). **Nationalism and Language in Kurdistan (1918–1985)**. New York: The Edwin Mellen Press.

Hassanpour, Amir (1999). Language rights in the emerging world linguistic order: The state, the market and communication technologies. In Kontra et al. (eds), 223–244.

Hassanpour, Amir (in press). Theory and practice in language rights for the Kurds. In Phillipson (ed.).

Hassanpour, Amir, Skutnabb-Kangas, Tove & Chyet, Michael (1996). The non-education of Kurds: A Kurdish perspective. In Labrie & Churchill (eds), 367–379.

Haugen, Einar (1964). **Bilingualism in the Americas: A Bibliography and Research Guide.** 2nd printing. Drawer: University of Alabama Press. [1956].

Haugen, Einar (1966). Dialect, language, nation. **American Anthropologist** 68, 922–935.

Haugen, Einar (1972). **The ecology of language. Essays by Einar Haugen.** Edited by A. S. Dil. Stanford, CA: Stanford University Press.

Haugen, Einar (1987). **Blessings of Babel: Bilingualism and language planning. Problems and Pleasures.** Berlin: Mouton de Gruyter.

Haugen, Einar (1991). The "mother tongue". In Cooper & Spolsky (eds), 75–84.

Havel, Václav (1992). A freedom of a prisoner. In Plichtová (ed.), 14–17.

Heath, Shirley Brice (1972). **Telling Tongues. Language Policy in Mexico. Colony to Nation**. New York/London: Teachers College Press.

Heath, Shirley Brice (1981). English in our language heritage. In Ferguson, Charles & Heath, Shirley Brice (eds). **Language in the USA**. Cambridge: Cambridge University Press, 6–20.

Heimbecker, Connie (1997). Bilingual Education for Indigenous Groups in Canada. In Cummins & Corson (eds), 56–66.

Heinämäki, Orvokki & Skutnabb-Kangas, Tove (1979). When this very prestigeous researcher met Mrs Average Housewife, or: where have all the women gone . . . **Journal of Pragmatics** 3, 507–519.

Heine, Bernd (1992). Language Policies in Africa. In Berbert, R. (ed.). **Language and Society in Africa**. Johannesburg: Witwatersrand University Press.

Helander, Elina (ed.) (1996). **Awakened Voice. The Return of Sami Knowledge.** Guodvageaidnu: Nordic Sami Institute.

Helle, Tuija (1994). Directions in bilingual education: Finnish comprehensive schools in perspective. **International Journal of Applied Linguistics** 4:2, 197–219.

Heller, Monica (1997). Normand Labrie: "La Construction linguistique de la Communauté Européenne". **Multilingua** 16:2 & 3, 270–272.

Hellinger, Marlis (1989). Revising the patriarchal paradigm—language change and feminist language politics. In Wodak, Ruth (ed.). **Language, Power and Ideology**. Amsterdam: John Benjamins, 274–288.

Helsinki Watch (1990). **Destroying ethnic identity. The Kurds of Turkey. An update**, September 1990. New York/Washington, D.C.: Helsinki Watch.

Herman, Edward & McChesney, Robert W. (1997). **The Global Media: The New Missionaries of Corporate Capitalism**. London: Cassell.

Hermans, Stefaan (1997). Promoting foreign language competence in the European Community: The LINGUA programme. **World Englishes** 16:1, 45–55.

Hernández-Chávez, Eduardo (1988). Language policy and language rights in the United States: Issues in bilingualism. In Skutnabb-Kangas & Cummins (eds) 45–56.

Hernández-Chávez, Eduardo (1990). The role of suppressive language policies in language shift and language loss. **Estudios Fronterizos, Revista del Instituto de Investigaciones Sociales**, VII:VIII: 18 & 19, 123–135.

Hernández-Chávez, Eduardo (1994). Language policy in the United States: a history of cultural genocide. In Skutnabb-Kangas & Phillipson (eds), 141–158.

Hernes, Gudmund & Knudsen, Knud (1990). **Svart på hvitt. Norske reaksjoner på flyktninger, asylsøkere og innvandrere** (Black on white. Norwegian reactions on refugees, asylum seekers and immigrants). FAFO-rapport nr. 109. Oslo/Stavanger: Fagbevegelsens senter for forskning, utredning og dokumentasjon.

Hernes, Gudmund & Knudsen, Knud (1994). Klimaskifte? Norske reaksjoner på flyktninger, asylsøkere og innvandrere 1988–1993 (Change of climate? Norwegian reactions on refugees, asylum seekers and immigrants). **Tidskrift for samfunnsforskning** 35:3, 319–342.

Herriman, Michael & Burnaby, Barbara (eds) (1996). **Language policies in English-dominant countries: six case studies**. Clevedon, UK: Multilingual Matters.

Hettne, Björn (1987). **Etniska konflikter och internationella relationer**. Stockholm: DEIFO.

Hettne, Björn (1990). **Development Theory and the Three Worlds**. Harlow: Longman.

Heugh, Kathleen (1995a). From unequal education to the real thing. In Heugh et al. (eds), 42–51.

Heugh, Kathleen (1995b). The multilingual school: modified dual medium. In Heugh et al. (eds), 79–82.

Heugh, Kathleen (1995c). Disabling and Enabling: Implications for language policy trends in South Africa. In Mesthrie (ed.), 329–350.

Heugh, Kathleen (in press). Giving good weight to multilingualism in South Africa. In Phillipson (ed.).

Heugh, Kathleen, Siegrühn, Amanda & Plüddemann, Peter (eds) (1995). **Multilingual Education for South Africa**. Johannesburg: Heinemann.

Heywood, V. H. (ed.) (1995). **Global Biodiversity Assessment**. Cambridge/New York: Cambridge University Press & UNEP (United Nations Environmental Program).

Hill, C. Peter (1986). Patterns of Language Use among Tanzanian Secondary School Pupils 1970: A Benchmark. In Centre of African Studies, 231–276.

Hill, M. (1995). **Invandrarbarns möjligheter. Om kunskapsutveckling och språkutveckling i förskola och skola** (Immigrant children's prospects. On development of knowledge and language in preschool and school). Göteborg: Institutionen för pedagogik, Göteborgs universitet.

Hinton, Leanne (1994). **Flutes of Fire**. Berkeley: Heyday.

Hjorth, Ejnar (1998). Hvor mange ord findes i Esperanto? (How many words are there in Esperanto?). **Esperanto-nyt** 1, 11.

Hobsbawm, E. J. (1991). **Nations and nationalism since 1780. Programme, myth, reality**. Cambridge: Cambridge University Press.

Hoëm, Anton (1976). **Makt og kunnskap** (Power and knowledge). Oslo: Universitetsforlaget. [first published as a dissertation 1971].

Hoëm, Anton & Tjeldvoll Arild (eds) (1980). **Etnopolitik som skolepolitik: samisk fortid, norsk framtid?** Utdrag av kopibøkker etter Finnmarks første skoledirektør, Bernt Thomassen, embetstid 1902–1920 (Ethnic policy as school policy: Sámi past, Norwegian future?). Oslo: Universitetsforlaget.

Hoëm, Anton (1996)—see Darnell.

Hoffman, Charlotte (1991). **An Introduction to Bilingualism**. London: Longman.

Hoffman, Eva (1997). **Lost in Translation. A Life in a New Language**. London: Minerva. [1989].

Hofstede, Gert (1980). **Culture's consequences: International differences in work-related values.** Beverly Hills, CA: Sage.

Hoijer, Harry (1976). History of American Indian Linguistics. In Sebeok, Thomas A. (ed.). **Native Languages of the Americas,** Vol. 1. New York/London: Plenum Press, 3–22.

Holmstrand, Lars (1980). **Effekterna på kunskaper, färdigheter och attityder av tidigt påbörjad undervisning i engelska** (The effects on knowledge, skills and attitudes of early teaching of English). Pedagogisk forskning i Uppsala 18, Uppsala: Pedagogiska institutionen, Uppsala Universitet.

Holmstrand, Lars S. E. (1982). **English in the Elementary School. Theoretical and Empirical Aspects of the Early Teaching of English as a Foreign Language.** Acta Universitatis Upsaliensis, Uppsala Studies in Education 18. Stockholm: Almqvist & Wiksell International.

Honkala, Tuula, Leporanta-Morley, Pirkko, Liukka, Lilja & Rougle, Eija (1988). Finnish children in Sweden strike for better education. In Skutnabb-Kangas & Cummins (eds) 239–250.

Honna, Nobuyuki (1975). Cultural Pluralism in Japan: A sociolinguistic outline. In **Proceedings of the Eighth Annual International Bilingual Bicultural Education Conference.** Tex.: International Clearinghouse for Bilingual Education, 44–55 (quoted in Maher & Yashiro 1995: 5).

Honna, Nobuyuki (1995). English in Japanese Society: Language within Language. In Maher & Yashiro (eds), 45–62.

Honna, Nobuyuki & Kato, Mihoko (in press). Establishing Sign Language in Deaf Education in Japan. In Benson et al. (eds).

Hornbeck, David (1987). Interview with Dr. Hornbeck. In Costo & Costo (eds), 195–201.

Hornberger, Nancy H. (1988). **Bilingual education and language maintenance. A southern Peruvian Quechua case.** Dordrecht: Foris Publication.

Hornberger, Nancy H. (1989). Can Peru's rural schools be agents for Quechua language maintenance? **Journal of Multilingual and Multicultural Development** 10:2, 145–160.

Hornberger, Nancy H. (1991). Extending enrichment bilingual education: Revisiting typologies and redirecting policy. In García (ed.), 215–234.

Hornberger, Nancy H. (1994). Literacy and language planning. **Language and Education** 8, 75–86.

Hornberger, Nancy H. (1995). Five vowels or three? Linguistics and politics in Quechua language planning in Peru. In Tollefson (ed.), 187–205.

Hornberger, Nancy H. (1997). Literacy, language maintenance, and linguistic human rights: Three telling cases. **International Journal of the Sociology of Language** 127, 87–103.

Hornberger, Nancy H. (1998). Language policy, language education, language rights. Indigenous, immigrant, and international perspectives. **Language in Society** 27, 439–458.

Hornberger, Nancy H. (ed.) (1996). **Indigenous literacies in the Americas: Language planning from the bottom up.** Berlin: Mouton de Gruyter.

Hroch, Miroslav (1985). **Social Preconditions of National Revival in Europe.** Cambridge: Cambridge University Press.

Human Rights and Equal Opportunity Commission (1997). **Bringing Them Home: National Inquiry into the Separation of Aboriginal and Torres Strait Islander Children from Their Families.** Sydney.

Human Rights in Kurdistan. Documentation of the international conference on human rights in Kurdistan, 14–16 April 1989. Initiative for Human Rights in Kurdistan. Bremen: Hochschule Bremen.

Humphreys, Andrew & Mits, Krista (eds) (1993). **The Red Book of the Peoples of the Russian Empire.** <http://www.eki.ee.books/redbooks/index1.shtml>.

Huntington, Samuel P. (1996). **The Clash of Civilisations and the Remaking of World Order.** New York: Simon & Schuster.

Huss, Leena (1996). Erste Hilfe für eine bedrohte Sprache: Wiederbelebungsmassnahmen bei den norwegischen Lulesamen. In Larsson, Lars-Gunnar (ed.). **100 Jahre finnisch-ugrischer**

Unterricht an der Universität Uppsala. Vorträge am jubileumssymposium 20.–23. April 1994. Lapponica et Uralica, Acta Uralica Upsaliensia 26. Uppsala: Uppsala universitet, 71–78.

Huss, Leena (1999). **Reversing Language Shift in the Far North. Linguistic Revitalization in Scandinavia and Finland.** Acta Universitatis Upsaliensis. Studia Uralica Upsaliensia 31. Uppsala: Uppsala University.

Hutchinson, John & Smith, Anthony D. (eds) (1994). **Nationalism.** Oxford Readers. Oxford/New York: Oxford University Press.

Hutchinson, John & Smith, Anthony D. (eds) (1996). **Ethnicity.** Oxford Readers. Oxford//New York: Oxford University Press.

Hyden, Göran (1983). **No Shortcuts to Progress. African Development Management in Perspective.** London: Heineman.

Hyltenstam, Kenneth & Tuomela, Veli (1996). Hemspråksundervisningen (Home language teaching). In Hyltenstam (ed.), 9–109.

Hyltenstam, Kenneth (ed.) (1996). **Tvåspråkighet med förhinder? Invandrar- och minoritetsundervisning i Sverige.** (Bilingualism with obstacles? Immigrant and minority education in Sweden). Lund: Studentlitteratur.

Hyry, Katja (1995). The Karelians in Finland. In Pentikäinen & Hiltunen (eds), 84–100.

Hyvärinen, Heikki (1977). **Saamelaisten historialliset oikeudet maahan ja veteen** (Sámi historical rights to land and water). Helsinki: Suomen antropologi 2.

IATIKU: Newsletter of the Foundation for Endangered Languages (ed. Nicholas Ostler) 1, 1995.

Ignatieff, Michael (1998). Your genocide—my self-defence. **Granta** 63: 121–150.

Igoa, Cristina (1994). **The Inner World of the Immigrant Child.** New York: St. Martin's Press.

Illich, Ivan (1977). **Limits to medicine. Medical nemesis: the expropriation of health.** Harmondsworth: Penguin.

Illich, Ivan (1981). Taught Mother Language and Vernacular Tongue. Foreword, in Pattanayak 1981, 1–39.

Illich, Ivan (1992). Needs. In Sachs (ed.), 88–101.

Indenrigsministeriet (1990). **Integration af indvandrere i Danmark. Beskrivelse og forslag til bedre prioritering** (Integration of immigrants in Denmark. Description and suggestion for better priorities). København: Indenrigsministeriet.

Information Centre of the Hungarian Coalition in Slovakia (1997). **The Hungarians in Slovakia.** Bratislava (Pozsony): Information Centre of the Hungarian Coalition in Slovakia.

Inglis, Christine (1991). Multiculturalism and National Identity. In Price, Charles A. (ed.). **Australian National Identity.** Canberra: The Academy of the Social Sciences in Australia, 13–31.

Inoguchi, Kuniko (1987). Pakkusu Americana o koete (Beyond Pax Americana). **Sekai,** March 1987, 152–172. [quoted in Kishida 1992, 48–49].

Internationaler Verein für Menschenrechte der Kurden (1998). **'Verschwindenlassen'. Ein Begriff des Schreckens. Menschenrechtsbericht über das 'Verschwindenlassen' in Kurdistan und der Türkei.** Written by Sertaç Bucak, edited by Leopold Müller. Bonn: Internationaler Verein für Menschenrechte der Kurden.

Isaksson Faris, Inga-Britt (forthcoming). **Gateways to Forsaken Languages. Lexical codeswitching and culture-specific images in Ngūgī wa Thiong'o's fiction.** Ph.D. dissertation. Uppsala: Department of English, Uppsala University. [<ibifaris@hotmail.com>].

IUCN Red List (1998) = IUCN Red List Categories, Prepared by the IUCN Species Survival Commission. As approved by the 40th meeting of the IUCN Council, Gland, Switzerland, 30 November 1994. Introduction. Preamble. Definitions. The Categories. The Criteria for Critically Endangered, Endangered and Vulnerable. 1996 International Union for Conservation of Nature and Natural Resources. [can be downloaded from <http://www.wcmc.org.uk/species/data/index.html>].

IWGIA 1996. **IWGIA Yearbook** (1996). Copenhagen: IWGIA (International Working Group on Indigenous Affairs).

Jaakkola, Magdalena (1983). **Finnish immigrants in Sweden: Networks and life-style**. Research Report No. 30. Helsinki: Research group for comparative sociology, University of Helsinki.

Jaakkola, Magdalena (1989a). **Suomalaisten suhtautuminen ulkomaalaisiin ja ulkomaalaispolitiikkaan** (Finnish attitudes towards foreigners and foreigner policy). Työvoimaministeriö, Suunnitteluosasto, Siirtolaisuustutkimuksia 21. Helsinki: Valtion painatuskeskus.

Jaakkola, Magdalena (1989b). **Den etniska mobiliseringen av sverigefinnarna** (The ethnic mobilisation of Sweden Finns). Stockholm: CEIFO.

Jaakkola, Magdalena (1995). **Suomalaisten kiristyvät ulkomaalaisasenteet** (The deteriorating Finnish attitudes towards foreigners). Työministeriö, Työpoliittinen tutkimus 101. Helsinki: Valtion painatuskeskus.

Jaakkola, Magdalena (in press). **Suomalaisten suhtautuminen maahanmuuttajiin vuosina 1987, 1993 ja 1998**. (Finnish attitudes towards immigrants in 1987, 1993 and 1998). Helsinki: Valtion painatuskeskus.

Jackson, Thomas L. (1987). Father Serra Meets Coyote. In Costo & Costo (eds), 99–110.

Jacobson, Rodolfo (ed.) (1998). **Codeswitching worldwide**. Berlin/New York: Mouton de Gruyter.

Jakšić, Božidar (1996). Conference paper 'Nationalism and language', published in Serbo-Croation in Bosanska vila 7–8, 1998 (Sarajevo), 42–54. Also in **Filozofija i drustvo XI**, 1997 (Beograd), 83–94.

Jakšić, Božidar (ed.) (1995). **Interkulturalnost/Interculturality**. Beograd: Savo Bjelajac.

Jalava, Antti (1980). **Asfaltblomman** (Asphalt flower). Stockholm: Norstedts.

Jalava, Antti (1988). Mother tongue and identity. Nobody could see that I was a Finn. In Skutnabb-Kangas & Cummins (eds), 161–166.

Jalava, Antti (1993). **Sprickan** (The Crack). Stockholm: Norstedt.

Janson, Tore (1997). **Språken och historien** (Languages and history). Falun: Norstedts.

Jansson, Jan-Magnus (1985). Language Legislation. In Uotila, J. (ed.). **The Finnish Legal System**. Helsinki: Finnish Lawyers Publishing Company, 77–89.

Janton, Pierre (1993). **Esperanto. Language, Literature, and Community**. Albany: State University of New York Press.

Janulf, Pirjo (1998). **Kommer finskan i Sverige att fortleva? En studie av språkkunskaper och språkanvändning hos andragenerationens sverigefinnar i Botkyrka och hos finlandssvenskar i Åbo**. (Will Finnish survive in Sweden? A study of language skills and language use among second generation Sweden Finns in Botkyrka, Sweden, and Finland Swedes in Åbo, Finland). Acta Universitatis Stockholmiensis, Studia Fennica Stockholmiensia 7. Stockholm: Almqvist & Wiksell International.

Jayasuriya, D. L. (1986). Ethnic minorities and issues of social justice in contemporary Australian society. Keynote address at Australian Adult Education Conference 'Learning for Social Justice', Australian National University, Canberra, 7–9 December 1986.

Jenniges, Wolfgang (ed.) (1997). **Select bibliography on minority languages in the European Union**. 2nd revised edition. Brussels: European Bureau for Lesser Used Languages.

Jernsletten, Nils (1993). Sami language communities and the conflict between Sami and Norwegian. In Jahr, Ernst Håkon (ed.). **Language Conflict and Language Planning**, Trends in Linguistics, Studies and Monographs 72, Berlin/New York: Mouton de Gruyter, 115–132.

Jernsletten, Nils (1997). Sami Traditional Terminology: Professional Terms Concerning Salmon, Reindeer and Snow. In Gaski (ed.), 86–108.

Jernudd, Björn (1994). Personal names and human rights. In Skutnabb-Kangas & Phillipson (eds), 121–132.

Jespersen, Jørn (1998). Mandatene er miljø og social udvikling. **Information** 29.5.1998, 15.

Johansson, Henning (1993). **På väg mot aktiv tvåspråkighet. Utvärdering av det pedagogiska klimatet i utvecklingsverksamheten för finskspråkiga elever i grundskolan i 18 kommuner** (On the way towards active bilingualism. An evaluation of the pedagogical climate in developing the teaching of Finnish language students in comprehensive schools in 18 local authorities). Luleå: Högskolan i Luleå.

Johnson, John (1987). Interview with John Johnson. In Costo & Costo (eds), 201–206.
Johnson, R. K. & Swain, Merrill (1997). **Immersion education. International perspectives.** Cambridge: Cambridge University Press.
Jones, Gary M. (1997). Immersion Programs in Brunei. In Cummins & Corson (eds), 234–250.
Jordan, Deirdre (1984a). Aborigines and Education. Dept. Education, University of Adelaide, manuscript.
Jordan, Deirdre (1984b). The Social Construction of Identity. The Aboriginal Problem. **The Australian Journal of Education** 28:3.
Jordan, Deirdre (1988). Rights and claims of indigenous people. Education and the reclaiming of identity: the case of the Canadian natives, the Sami and Australian Aborigines. In Skutnabb-Kangas & Cummins (eds), 189–222.
Joseph, Michael & Ramani, Esther (1998). The ELT specialist and linguistic hegemony: a response to Tully and Mathew. **ELT Journal** 52:3, 214–222.
Joyce, Patrick (ed.) (1995). **Class**. Oxford Readers. Oxford/New York: Oxford University Press.
Jung, Anees (1987). **Unveiling India. A Woman's Journey.** New Delhi: Penguin Books.
Jung, Anees (1994). **Seven Sisters. Among the Women of South Asia.** New Delhi: Penguin Books.
Jussila, Heikki & Segerståhl, Boris (1988). **Cultural and societal change in the North—the role of innovation in development**. Working Papers 56, October 1988. Oulu: Research Institute of Northern Finland.
Kachru, Braj B. (1983). **The Indianization of English**. New Delhi: Oxford University Press.
Kachru, Braj B. (1986a). ESP and non-native varieties of English: toward a shift in paradigm. **Studies in the Linguistic Sciences** 16:1, 13–34.
Kachru, Braj B. (1986b). **The alchemy of English: the spread, functions and models of non-native Englishes**. Oxford: Pergamon.
Kachru, Braj B. (1986c). The power and politics of English. **World Englishes** 5:2 & 3, 121–140.
Kachru, Braj B. (1990). **The Alchemy of English**. Urbana, Ill.: University of Illinois Press.
Kachru, Braj B. (1996). The paradigms of marginality. **World Englishes** 15:3, 241–255.
Kachru, Braj B. (1997). World Englishes and English-using communities. **Annual Review of Applied Linguistics** 17, 66–87.
Kachru, Braj B. (1997a). English as an Asian Language. In Bautista, Maria Lourdes S. (ed.). **English is an Asian Language: The Philippine Context**. Manila: Macquerie Library Pty Ltd..
Kachru, Braj B. & Nelson, Cecil L. (1996). World Englishes. In McKay, Sandra Lee & Hornberger, Nancy (eds). **Sociolinguistics and Language Teaching**. Cambridge: Cambridge University Press, 229–241.
Kachru, Yamuna (1996). Culture, variation, and languages of wider communication: the paradigm gap. In Alatis, J. E. et al. (eds). **Linguistics, language acquisition, and language variation: Current trends and future prospects**. Washington, D.C.: Georgetown University Press, 178–195.
Kalantzis, Mary (1995). Coming to Grips with the Implications of Multiculturalism. Paper to the Global Cultural Diversity Conference, Sydney [see Boutros-Ghali].
Kalema, John (1980). Report on Functions and Activities of the OAU Inter-African Bureau of Languages. In Mateene & Kalema (eds), 1–8.
Kalema, John (1985). Introduction. In Mateene, Kalema & Chomba (eds), 1–6.
Kalevala (1964). Uuden Kalevalan kahdeskymmenesneljäs painos (the 24th edition of the New Kalevala). Helsinki: Suomalaisen Kirjallisuuden Seura.
Kallen, Evelyn (1996). Ethnicity and Self-Determination: A Paradigm. In Clark & Williamson (eds), 113–123.
Kalpaka, Annita & Räthzel, Nora (Hrsg.) (1992). **Rassismus und Migration in Europa**. Hamburg: Argument-Verlag.
Kamwangamalu, Nkonko M. (1997). Multilingualism and Education Policy in Post-Apartheid South Africa. **Language Problems & Language Planning** 21:3, 234–253.
Kane, Joe (1995). **Savages**. New York: Alfred A. Knopf.

Kangas, Ilka (1997). Many years of hard work. Women's status and elderly women in Finland. In Kangas, Ilka (ed.). **Sew—Situation of Elderly Women. Four lifestories of grandmothers on the fringes of the European Union.** Helsinki: National Research Centre for Welfare and Health, 21–70.

Kaplan, Robert B. & Baldauf, Richard B. Jr. (1997). **Language Planning: from practice to theory.** Clevedon, UK: Multilingual Matters.

Kaplinski, Jaan (1998). Pohjoisen ukko Ugluchopt ja Vipusessa käynti (The old man Ugluchopt in the North and the visit to Vipunen). **Hiidenkivi** 2: 21.

Kãretu, Timoti (1994). Mãori language rights in New Zealand. In Skutnabb-Kangas & Phillipson (eds), 209–218.

Katzner, Kenneth (1994). **The languages of the world.** 3rd edition. London: Routledge. [1975 New York: Funk & Wagnalls].

Keating, Paul (1995). Opening Address. Paper to the Global Cultural Diversity Conference, Sydney [see Boutros-Ghali].

Keskitalo, Alf Isak (1986). Research as an inter-ethnic relation. In **The First Nations. Indigenous Days /Álgoálbmotbeaivvit /Urbefolkningsdager '84.** Tromsö: Keviselie Productions, 55–82. [ISBN 82-90482-07-8].

Keskitalo, Jan-Henry (1997). Sami Post-Secondary Education—Ideas and Realities. In Gaski (ed.), 155–171.

Khubchandani, Lachman M. (1983). **Plural Languages, Plural Cultures: Communication, Identity and Sociopolitical Change in Contemporary India.** An East-West Center Book. Honolulu: The University of Hawaii Press.

Khubchandani, Lachman M. (1991). **Language, culture and nation-building. Challenges of modernisation.** Shimla/New Delhi: Indian Institute of Advanced Study, in association with Manohar Publications.

Khubchandani, Lachman M. (1994). Demographic Indicators of Language Persistence Among Tribals. **Lokayan Bulletin** 10:5 & 6, 67–78.

Khubchandani, Lachman M. (1997a). **Revisualizing Boundaries. A Plurilingual Ethos.** New Delhi/Thousand Oaks/London: Sage.

Khubchandani, Lachman M. (1997b). Bilingual Education for Indigenous Groups in India. In Cummins & Corson (eds), 67–76.

Khubchandani, Lachman M. (ed.) (1988). **Language in a Plural Society.** Delhi: Motilal Banarasidas.

Kibbee, Douglas A. (ed.) (1998). **Language Legislation and Linguistic Rights.** Amsterdam/Philadelphia: John Benjamins.

Kidron, Michael & Segal, Ronals (1991). **The State of the World Atlas.** London/Sydney: Pan Books. [1981].

Kieri, Gunnar (1976). **Av dig blir det ingenting** (You will become nothing). Lund: Arbetarkultur.

Kiernan, V. G. (1995). **Imperialism and its contradictions.** Edited & introduced by Harvey J. Kaye. New York/London: Routledge.

King, Kenneth (1986). Postscript. In Centre of African Studies, 445–454.

Kipling, Rudyard (1923). Speech, February 14, 1923, reported in **The Times (London) February 16, 1923.** [quoted in Mazrui 1975: 209].

Kirisci, Kemal & Winrow, Gareth M. (1997). **The Kurdish question and Turkey: an example of a trans-state ethnic conflict.** London: Frank Cass.

Kisebbségi értesítÖ. Bulletin of the National and Ethnic Minorities in Hungary 1 [1993; no date]. Budapest: Nemzeti és etnikai kisebbségi hivatal (Office for National and Ethnic Minorities).

Kishida, Toshiko (1992). Europe and Japan: Problems of 'Internationalization'. In Nelson et al. (eds), 44–54.

Kivi, Aleksis (1964). **Seitsemän veljestä** (The seven brothers). Tampere: Suomalaisen kirjallisuuden seura.

Kloss, Heinz (1967). Bilingualism and nationalism. **Journal of Social Issues** 23, 39–47.

Kloss, Heinz (1971). The language rights of immigrant groups. **International Migration Review** 5, 250–268.

Kloss, Heinz (1977). **The American Bilingual Tradition**. Rowley, Mass.: Newbury House.

Kloss, Heinz et al. (1989). **The written languages of the world. Vol. 3: Western Europe**. Québec: Les Presses de l'Université Laval.

Knudsen, Karin J. L. (1999). **On the Other Side of the Railway Line. A study of language and education in South Africa**. Module 3 report, English Studies. Roskilde: University of Roskilde.

Koch, Eddie & Maslamoney, Siven (1997). Words that click and rustle softly like the wild. **Mail & Guardian**, September 12 to 18, 1997, 28–29.

Koivunen, Kristiina (forthcoming). **In the Shadow of Genocide—Turkish Kurdistan**. Licenciate dissertion. Helsinki: Department of Social Policy, University of Helsinki.

Kolga, M. Tõnurist, I., Vaba, L. & Viikberg, J. (1993). Vene impeeriumi rahvaste punane raamat (The Red Book of the Peoples of the Russian Empire). Tallinn.

Kontra, Miklós (1995). Sociopolitical and linguistic aspects of post-communist Hungarian contact linguistics. In Muikku-Werner, P. & Julkunen, K. (toim.). **Kielten väliset kontaktit** (Contacts between languages). AFinLAn julkaisuja no. 53, Jyväskylä: AFinLA, 7–23.

Kontra, Miklós (1996a). English Only's Cousin: Slovak Only. **Acta Linguistica Hungarica** 43:3 & 4, 1995/1996, 345–372.

Kontra, Miklós (1996b). The Wars Over Names in Slovakia. **Language Problems & Language Planning** 20:2, 160–167.

Kontra, Miklós (1997). On the right to use the language of one's choice in Slovakia. **Canadian Centre for Linguistic Rights Bulletin** 4:1, 5–8.

Kontra, Miklós (1998a). Language Rights Arguments in Central Europe and the USA: How Similar Are They? In Kibbee (ed.), 142–178.

Kontra, Miklós (1998b). Final Report to the Research Support Scheme on the Sociolinguistics of Hungarian Outside Hungary, submitted 23 February 1998. Budapest: Linguistics Institute, Hungarian Academy of Sciences. [<email: kontra@nytud.hu>].

Kontra, Miklós (1998c). Review of Lanstyák & Szabómihály 1997. **Journal of Sociolinguistics**, 142–145.

Kontra, Miklós (1999a). 'Don't Speak Hungarian in Public!'. A Documentation and Analysis of Folk Linguistic rights. In Kontra et al. (eds), 81–98.

Kontra, Miklós (in press a). British Aid for Hungarian Deaf Education from a Linguistic Human Rights Point of View. Paper at the Fourth Biennial Conference of the Hungarian Society for the Study of English, Budapest, 28 January 1999. In press, in conference proceedings.

Kontra, Miklós (in press b). Which contacts breed conflicts? In Phillipson (ed.).

Kontra, Miklós & Baugh, John (1994). Should They Give up Their Language and Culture Voluntarily? An Interview. **Regio. A Review of Minority and Ethnic Studies** 1994, 158–174.

Kontra, Miklós, Phillipson, Robert, Skutnabb-Kangas, Tove & Várady, Tibor (eds) (1999). **Language: a right and a resource. Approaching Linguistic Human Rights**. Budapest: Central European University Press.

Kontra, Miklós, Skutnabb-Kangas, Tove, Phillipson, Robert & Várady, Tibor (1999). Introduction. In Kontra et al. (eds), 1–24.

Koraani (1957)—see Aro et al. See also The Qur'ān.

Korhonen, Matti (1996). Esitelmä RSO:n 25–vuotisjuhlassa. **Tiedote** 6, 4–6.

Korhonen, Olavi (1998). Samiskan som språk och traditionskälla (Sámi as a language and a source of tradition). In Korhonen & Winsa, 53–106.

Korhonen, Olavi & Winsa, Birger. **Språkliga och kulturella gränser i Nordskandinavien. Två uppsatser** (Linguistic and cultural borders in Northern Scandinavia. Two essays). Kulturens frontlinjer. Skrifter från forskningsprogrammet Kulturgräns Norr, 7. Umeå: Kulturgräns Norr.

Korpijaakko, Kaisa (1989). **Saamelaisten oikeusasemasta Ruotsi-Suomessa. Oikeushistoriallinen tutkimus Länsi-Pohjan Lapin maankäyttöoloista ja -oikeuksista ennen 1700-luvun puoliväliä** (On the legal status of the Sámi in Sweden-Finland). Rovaniemi: Lapin korkeakoulu.

Korten, David C. (1996a). The failures of Bretton Woods. In Mander & Goldsmith (eds), 20–30.

Korten, David C. (1996b). The Mythic Victory of Market Capitalism. In Mander & Goldsmith (eds), 183–191.

Kosztolányi, Dezsö (1987). The place of the Hungarian language on the earth. Open letter to Monsieur Antoine Meillet, professor of the Collège de France. In Tóth (ed.), 21–37. [1930]

Kotimaisten kielten tutkimuskeskus/Forskningscentralen för de inhemska språken (1998). **Kotimaisten kielten tutkimuskeskuksen kielipoliittinen ohjelma.** (The Language Policy programme of the Research Centre for the Domestic Languages). Helsinki: Kotimaisten kielten tutkimuskeskus. [can be downloaded from <http://www.domlang.fi/>].

Kozol, Jonathan (1991). **Savage inequalities. Children in America's schools.** New York: Harper.

Kramarae, Cheris, Schulz, Muriel & O'Barr, William M. (eds) (1984). **Language and Power.** Beverly Hills, CA: Sage.

Kramarae, Cheris & Treichler, Paula A. (1992). **Amazons, Bluestockings and Crones. A Feminist Dictionary.** London: Pandora Press.

Krashen, Stephen (1981a). **Second Language Acquisition and Second Language Learning.** Oxford: Pergamon.

Krashen, Stephen (1981b). Bilingual education and second language acquisition. In CDE (1981), 51–70.

Krashen, Stephen & Biber, Douglas (1988). **On Course: Bilingual Education's Successes in California.** Sacramento, CA: California Association for Bilingual Education.

Krauss, Michael (1992). The world's languages in crisis. **Language** 68:1, 4–10.

Krauss, Michael (1995). As reported in **The Philadelphia Inquirer** 19.2.1995.

Krauss, Michael (1996). Status of Native American Language Endangerment. In Cantoni (ed.).

Kubanek-German, Angelika (1998). Primary foreign language teaching in Europe—trends and issues. **Language Teaching** 31, 193–205.

Kubanek-German, Angelika (ed.) (1996). **Immersion—Fremdsprachenlernen—Primarbereich.** München: Goethe Institut. [distributor: München: Hueber Verlag].

Kubota, Ruyko (1998). Ideologies of English in Japan. **World Englishes** 17:3, 295–306.

Kuper, Adam (1988). **The invention of primitive society: Transformations of an illusion.** London: Routledge.

Kuper, Leo (1984). **International Action Against Genocide.** London: The Minority Rights Group.

Kurdistan Info 2:27, 23 March 1997. Copenhagen: KOMKAR.

Kuusela, Jorma (1973). **Finnar i Sverige. En studie av assimilation och anpassning** (Finns in Sweden. A study of assimilation and acculturation). No. 4. Stockholm: Sociologiska institutionen vid Stockholms universitet.

Källström, Roger (1988). Bilingual education and bilingualism in the Swedish comprehensive school. In Jørgensen, J. N. et al. (eds). **Bilingualism in Society and School.** Copenhagen Studies in Bilingualism, Vol. 5, Clevedon, UK: Multilingual Matters, 189–199.

Källström, Roger & Malinen, Vuokko (1985). **Det tvåspråkiga högstadiet i Göteborg läsåret 1984–85** (The bilingual lower secondary grades in Gothenburg 1984–85). SPRINS-rapport 30, Göteborg: SPRINS-gruppen, Institutionen för lingvistik.

Körmendi, Eszter (1986). **Os og de andre. Danskernes holdninger til indvandrere og flygtninge** (Us and the others. Danish attitudes towards immigrants and refugees). Publikation 153. Copenhagen: Socialforskningsinstituttet.

Labrie, Normand (1993). **La construction linguistique de la Communauté Européenne.** Paris: Honoré Champion.

Labrie, Normand (1995). Reciprocity agreements as a language planning instrument for the maintenance of minority languages. In Fase et al. (eds), 187–199.

Labrie, Normand & Churchill, Stacy (eds) (1996). **International Review of Education** 42:4. Special issue **The Education of Minorities**. Hamburg: Unesco Institute for Education.

Labrie, Normand & Quell, Carsten (1997). Your language, my language or English? The potential language choice in communication among nationals of the European Union. **World Englishes** 16:1, 3–26.

Ladefoged, Peter (1992). Another view of endangered languages. **Language** 68:4, 809–811.

Lahdenperä, Pirjo (1997). **Invandrarbakgrund eller skolsvårigheter?** (Immigrant background or educational problems?). Stockholm: HLF Förlag.

Lainio, Jarmo (1997). Swedish Minority Language Treatment and Language Policy—Positive Public Rhetoric vs. Grassroots Struggle. In Ammon et al. (eds), 29–42.

Lainio, Jarmo (1998). From guest workers to an ethnolinguistic minority. The case of Sweden Finns and their languages. In Bombi, Raffaella & Graffi, Giorgio (eds). **Ethnos e comunitá linguistics: Un confronto metodologico interdisclipinare / Ethnos and Linguistic Community: An interdisciplinary methodological approach**. Udine: Forum S.r.l., 333–369.

Lainio, Jarmo (in press). From historical shame to present struggle. In Phillipson (ed.).

Lambert, Wallace E. (1975). Culture and language as factors in learning and education. In Wolfgang, Aaron (ed.) (1975). **Education of immigrant students**. Toronto: Ontario Institute for Studies in Education, 55–83.

Lambert, Wallace E. & Tucker, Richard G. (1972). **Bilingual Education of Children. The St. Lambert Experiment**. Rowley, Mass.: Newbury House.

Lane, Harlan (1980). A Chronology of the Oppression of Sign Language in France and the United States. In Lane, Harlan & Grosjean, François (eds). **Recent Perspectives on American Sign Language**. Hillsdale, N.J.: Lawrence Erlbaum Associates, 119–161.

Lane, Harlan (1992). **The Mask of Benevolence: Disabling the Deaf Community**. New York: Alfred Knopf.

Lang, Kevin (1993). Language and economists' theories of discrimination. **International Journal of the Sociology of Language** 103, 165–183.

Lange, Anders & Westin, Charles (1981). **Etnisk diskriminering och social identitet. Forsknings-översikt och teoretisk analys**, Stockholm: Diskrimineringsutredningen.

Lange, Anders & Westin, Charles (1991). **Ungdomen och invandringen** (Youth and immigration). CEIFO Report 29. Stockholm: CEIFO, University of Stockholm.

Lange, Anders & Westin, Charles (1993). **Den mångtydiga toleransen** (The multivalent tolerance). Stockholm: CEIFO, University of Stockholm.

LANGTAG (1996). **Towards a National Language Plan for South Africa**. Summary of the Final Report of the Language Plan Task Group (LANGTAG), Presented to the minister of Arts, Culture, Science and Technology, Dr B. S. Ngubane, 8 August 1996. [can be downloaded from <http://www.sacs.org.za/gov/arts&cul/docs/langrep.htm>].

Lanstyák, István (in press). Bilingual versus bilingual education—the case of Slovakia. In Phillipson (ed.).

Lanstyák, István & Szabómihály, Gizella (1996). Contact varieties of Hungarian in Slovakia: a contribution to their description. **International Journal of the Sociology of Language** 120, 11–130.

Lanstyák, István & Szabómihály, Gizella (1997). **Magyar nyelvhasználat—iskola—kétnyelvüség** (Hungarian language use—schools—bilingualism). Pozsony/Bratislava: Kalligram Könyv-kiadó.

Laponce, J. A. (1993). Do languages behave like animals? **International Journal of the Sociology of Language** 103, 19–30.

Larsson, Karin (1995). En segregerad värld är inte hip. Reklamens etniska enfald är märklig (A segregated world is not hip. The ethnic stupidity of advertisements is curious). **Dagens Nyheter** 24.5.1995.

Lasko, Lars-Nila (1992). **Skattefjällsmålet. Högsta Domstolens dom** (The Skattefjäll case. Judgement by Supreme Court). Guovdageaidnu: Nordiskt Samisk Institut.

Laurén, Christer (1991). A Two-Phase Didactics for School. **Journal of Multilingual and Multicultural Development** 12:1 & 2, 67–72.

Laurén, Christer (1997). Swedish Immersion Programs in Finland. In Cummins & Corson (eds), 291–296.

Lawenius, Maria & Andersson, Egil (1998). Döv eller icke döv? Om socialisationsprocess och social identitet (Deaf or not Deaf? On socialisation processes and social identity). **Social forskning** 1, 12–13.

Leclerc, Jacques (1986). **Langue et Société**. Laval: Media éditeurs.

Leets, Laura & Giles, Howard (1995). Dimensions of minority language survival/non-survival: intergroup cognitions and communication climates. In Fase et al. (eds), 37–73.

Léger, Sylvie (ed.) (1996). **Vers un agenda linguistique: regard futuriste sur les nations unies/ Towards a language agenda: futurist outlook on the United Nations**. Ottawa: Canadian Centre for Linguistic Rights, University of Ottawa.

Lehman, Karen & Krebs, Al (1996). Control of the World's Food Supply. In Mander & Goldsmith (eds), 122–130.

Lehtola, Veli-Pekka (1997). **Saamelaiset. Historia, yhteiskunta, taide** (The Sámi. History, community, art). Jyväskylä: Kustannus-Puntsi.

Leibowitz, Brenda & Plüddemann, Peter (1998). 'Advocacy of the mother tongue as medium of instruction is a red herring'—a debate, manuscript, University of Western Cape & University of Cape Town. [<pp@education.uct.ac.za>].

Leino, Eino (1952). **Helkavirsiä**. Helsinki: Otava. [2nd edition, 11th reprint of the 12th reprint of the 1st edition].

Leontiev, Alexei A. (1994). Linguistic human rights and educational policy in Russia. In Skutnabb-Kangas & Phillipson (eds), 63–70.

Leontiev, Alexei A. (1995). Multilingualism for all—Russians? In Skutnabb-Kangas (ed.), 199–214.

Lewis, James A. (1987). The Natives as Seen by the Missionaries: Preconception and Reality. In Costo & Costo (eds), 81–98.

Lewis, Peter (ed.) (1996). **Alternative Media**. Paris: Unesco.

Liebkind, Karmela (1984). **Minority Identity and Identification Processes: a Social Psychological Study, Maintenance and Reconstruction of Ethnolinguistic Identity in Multiple Group Allegiance**. Commentationes Scientiarum Socialium 22. Helsinki: Societas Scientiarum Fennica.

Liebkind, Karmela (ed.) (1989). **New identities in Europe. Immigrant ancestry and the ethnic identity of youth**. Aldershot: Gower Press.

Liebkind, Karmela & Broo, Roger (1985). The Swedish-speaking minority. In Pentikäinen & Anttonen (eds), 72–113.

Liebkind, Karmela, Broo, Roger & Finnäs, Fjalar (1995). The Swedish-speaking minority in Finland: a case study. In Pentikäinen & Hiltunen (eds), 48–83.

Liljeström, Rita, Noren-Björn, Eva, Schyl-Bjurman, Gertrud, Örn, Birgit, Gustafsson, Lars H. & Löfgren, Orvar (1985). **Young Children in China**. Clevedon, UK: Multilingual Matters. [1982, translation of **Kinas barn och våra**].

Lincoln, C. Eric (1961). **The Black Muslims in America**. Boston: Beacon Press.

Lincoln, C. Eric (1967). **Sounds of the Struggle: Persons and Perspectives in Civil Rights**. New York: William Morrow & Company.

Lind Meløy, L. (1980). **Internatliv i Finnmark. Skolepolitikk 1900–1940** (Boarding school life in Finnmark. School policy 1900–1940). Oslo: Det Norske Samlaget.

Linde, Sylvia G. (1989). **The relationship between medium of instruction and school achievement for Finnish-speaking students in Sweden**. Malmö: Lärarhögskolan i Malmö.

Linde, Sylvia G. & Löfgren, Horst (1988). The relationship between medium of instruction and school achievement for Finnish-speaking students in Sweden. **Language, Culture and Curriculum** 1:2, 131–145.

Linden, E. (1991). Lost Tribes, Lost Knowledge. **Time**, September 23, 46–56.

Lindholm, Kathryn J. (1990). Bilingual immersion education: Educational equity for language-minority students. In Barona, Andres & Garcia, Eugene (eds) (1990). **Children at Risk: Poverty, Minority Status and Other Issues in Educational Equity**. Washington, D.C.: National Association of School Psychologists, 77–89.

Lindholm, Kathryn J. (1991). Theoretical assumptions and empirical evidence for academic achievement in two languages. **Hispanic Journal of Behavioral Sciences** 13, 3–17.

Lindholm, Kathryn J. (1992a). Two-way bilingual/immersion education: theory, conceptual issues, and pedagogical implications. In Padilla, Raymond V. & Benavides, Alfredo H. (eds). **Critical Perspectives on Bilingual Education Research**. Tempe, Ariz.: Bilingual Review Press/Editorial Bilingüe, 195–220.

Lindholm, Kathryn J. (1992b). Relationship Between Language Proficiency, Academic Achievement and Cognition: Outcomes from Bilingual/Immersion Programs. Paper presented at the National Association for Bilingual Education Conference, Albuquerque, N.M., January 1992.

Lindholm, Kathryn J. (1992c). **The River Glen Elementary School Bilingual Immersion Program: Student Progress after Five Years of Implementation**. Evaluation Report 1990–1991. California: River Glen Elementary School.

Lindholm, Kathryn J. (1994). Promoting positive cross-cultural attitudes and perceived competence in culturally and linguistically diverse classrooms. In de Villar et al. (eds), 189–206.

Lindholm, Kathryn J. (1997). Two-Way Bilingual Education Programs in the United States. In Cummins & Corson (eds), 271–280.

Lindholm, Kathryn J. & Aclan, Zierlein (1991). Bilingual proficiency as a bridge to academic achievement: Results from bilingual immersion programs. **Journal of Education** 173, 99–113.

Lindholm, Kathryn J. & Fairchild, Halford H. (1989). **Evaluation of an "exemplary" Bilingual Immersion Program**. Technical Report No 13. Los Angeles, CA: UCLA Center for Language Education and Research.

Lipka, Jerry, with Mohatt, Gerald W. and the Ciulistet Group (1998). **Transforming the Culture of Schools**. **Yup'ik Eskimo Examples**. Mahwah, NJ & London: Lawrence Erlbaum Associates.

Lippi-Green, Rosina (1994). Accent, standard language ideology and discriminatory pretext in the courts. **Language in Society** 18, 213–234.

Lippi-Green, Rosina (1997). **English with an accent: language, ideology, and discrimination in the United States**. London/New York: Routledge.

List, Friedrich (1885). **The National System of Political Economy**. London: Longmans. [reprinted in 1966, New York: Kelley].

Lo Bianco, Joseph (1987). **National Policy on Languages**. Canberra: Australian Government Publishing Service, Commonwealth Department of Education.

Lo Bianco, Joseph (1990a). A Hard-Nosed Multiculturalism: Revitalising Multicultural Education? **Vox** 4, 80–94.

Lo Bianco, Joseph (1990b). Making language policy: Australia's experience. In Baldauf & Luke (eds), 47–79.

Lo Bianco, Joseph (1994). Australian Experiences: Multiculturalism, Language Policy and National Ethos. Manuscript. Canberra: The National Languages and Literacy Institute of Australia.

Lo Bianco, Joseph (1995). Pluralist Nations, Pluralist Language Policies? Paper to the Global Cultural Diversity Conference, Sydney [see Boutros-Ghali].

Lotherington, Heather (1997). Bilingual Education in the South Pacific. In Cummins & Corson (eds), 87–95.

Louw, J. A. (1977). The adaptation of non-click consonants in Xhosa. In Traill, Anthony T. (ed.). **Khoisan Linguistic Studies** 8, 8–21.

Luckett, Kathy (1995). National additive bilingualism: towards a language plan for South African education. In Heugh et al. (eds), 73–78.

Lundemark, Erik (1980). **Arbetsstugorna** (The Workhouses). Luleå: Tornedalica 30.

Lüsebrink, Claire [no date]. **From Assimilation to Apartheid: Paradoxes and Contradictions of the Right to Mother Tongue Education in French, Italian and Austrian Law,** manuscript.

Lyovin, Anatole (1997). **An Introduction to the Languages of the World.** Oxford/New York: Oxford University Press.

Löfgren, Horst (1991). **Elever med annat hemspråk än svenska: en jämförande studie mellan invandrargrupper och en svensk jämförelsegrupp** (Students with a mother tongue other than Swedish: a comparative study on immigrant groups and a Swedish control group). Pedagogisk orientering och debatt Nr 95. Malmö: Lärarhögskolan i Malmö.

Löfgren, Horst & Ouvinen-Birgerstam, Pirjo (1980). **Försök med en tvåspråkig modell för undervisning av invandrarbarn** (An experiment with a bilingual model for teaching immigrant children). Pedagogiska rapporter 22. Lund: Pedagogiska institutionen, Lunds universitet.

Macdonald, Robert (1985). **The Maori of New Zealand.** Report No. 70. London: Minority Rights Group.

Macías, R. F. (1979). Choice of language as a human right. Public policy implications in the United States. In Padilla, Raymond V. (ed.). **Bilingual education and public policy in the United States. Ethnoperspectives in bilingual education research.** Vol. I. Ypsilanti: Eastern Michigan University, 39–75.

Mackey, William F. (1998). The foundations. In J. Edwards (ed.), 13–35.

Madonci, Lindiwe (1997). Action research report conducted for Further Diploma in Education, Multilingual Education, University of Cape Town, PRAESA. Manuscript.

Maffi, Luisa (1994). **A Linguistic Analysis of Tzeltal Maya Ethnosymptomatology.** Ph.D. dissertation, University of California, Berkeley. [UMI order # 9504901].

Maffi, Luisa (1996). Language, Knowledge and the Environment: Threats to the World's Biocultural Diversity. **Terralingua Newsletter** 2 December 1996.

Maffi, Luisa (1996). Position Paper for the Interdisciplinary Working Conference 'Endangered Languages, Endangered Knowledge, Endangered Environments'. Terralingua Discussion Paper 1. [can be downloaded from Terralingua's Web-site <http://cougar.ucdavis.edu/nas/terralin/home.html>].

Maffi, Luisa (in press a). Introduction. In Maffi (ed.).

Maffi, Luisa (in press b). Linguistic and biological diversity: the inextricable link. In Phillipson (ed.).

Maffi, Luisa, Skutnabb-Kangas, Tove & Andrianarivo, Jonah (in press). Linguistic diversity. In Posey (ed.).

Maffi, Luisa (ed.) (in press). **Language, Knowledge and the Environment: The Interdependence of Biological and Cultural Diversity.** Washington, D.C.: Smithsonian Institute Press.

Magga, Ole Henrik (1994). The Sámi Language Act. In Skutnabb-Kangas & Phillipson (eds), 219–233.

Magoun, Francis Peabody, Jr. (1963). **The Kalevala or Poems of the Kaleva District,** compiled by Elias Lönnrot. A Prose Translation. Cambridge, Mass./London, UK: Harvard University Press.

Maharaj, A. & Sayed, Yusuf (1998). Policy contestation and conflict in the democratisation of school governance in South Africa. Working paper, Western Cape College of Education & University of Western Cape [<ysayed@education.uwc.ac.za>; can be downloaded from <http://www.sun.ac.za/edupapers/volume1/Ysuf.html>].

Maher, John C. & Yashiro, Kyoko (1995). Multilingual Japan: An Introduction. In Maher & Yashiro (eds), 1–17.

Maher, John C. & Yashiro, Kyoko (eds) (1995). **Multilingual Japan**. Special Issue, **Journal of Multilingual and Multicultural Development**, 16:1 & 2.

Makerere Report (1961). **Report on the conference on the teaching of English as a second language**. Entebbe: Commonwealth Education Liaison Committee.

Malherbe, E. G. (1946). **The bilingual school: a study of bilingualism in South Africa**. London: Longmans Green.

Mallon, Nina & Hasanzadeh, Soghra (1998). **Maahanmuuttajanuorten tiedon lähteillä** (Sources of information for immigrant youth). Helsinki: Helsingin kaupungin nuorisoasiainkeskus & kulttuuriasiainkeskus.

Mandela, Nelson (1999). Interview by John Carlin. 'President Nelson Mandela on Human Rights and Responsibilities.' **Indaba** (published by the South African Embassy in Denmark) 4:1, 1–.

Mander, Jerry (1996a). Facing the Rising Tide. In Mander & Goldsmith (eds), 3–19.

Mander, Jerry (1996b). The Rules of Corporate Behavior. In Mander & Goldsmith (eds), 309–322.

Mander, Jerry & Goldsmith, Edward (eds) (1996). **The case against the global economy and for a turn toward the local**. San Francisco: Sierra Club.

Mansour, Gerda (1993). **Multilingualism & Nation Building**. Clevedon/Philadelphia/Adelaide: Multilingual Matters.

Māori Language Commission (1989). **Annual Report to the Government (Minister of Maori Affairs)**. Wellington: Māori Language Commission, manuscript.

Maragall í Mira, Pascan (1998). Preface. In Price, Adam, O Torna, Caitríona & Wynne Jones, Allan (1998). **The Diversity Dividend: Language, Culture, and Economy in an Integrated Europe**. Dublin: EBLUL (European Bureau for Lesser Used Languages).

Marainen, Johannes (1988). Returning to Sami identity. In Skutnabb-Kangas & Cummins (eds), 179–185.

Marshall, David F. (1986). The question of an official language: language rights and the English Language Amendment. **International Journal of the Sociology of Language** 60, 7–75.

Marshall, David F. (1996). A politics of language: language as a symbol in the dissolution of the Soviet Union and its aftermath. **International Journal of the Sociology of Language** 118, 7–41.

Marshall, David F. (ed.) (1991). **Language planning. Focusschrift in honor of Joshua A. Fishman on the occasion of his 65th birthday**. Amsterdam/Philadelphia: John Benjamins.

Marta, Claudio (1979a). **A Group of Lovara Gypsies Settle down in Sweden**. IMFO-gruppen, Institute of Education, 1979:2. Stockholm: University of Stockholm.

Marta, Claudio (1979b). **The Acculturation of the Lovara**. IMFO-gruppen, Institute of Education, 1979:3. Stockholm: University of Stockholm.

Martel, Angéline (1999). Heroes, rebels, communities and states: Reflections on language rights activism in Canada and Quebec. In Kontra et al. (eds), 47–80.

Marti, Roland (ed.) (1996). Language Policy in Border Regions/ Polityka jezykowa na pograniczach. Saarbrücken: SDV Saarbrücker Druckerei und Verlag Gmbh.

Martinez Cobo, José R. (1987). **Study of the Problem of Discrimination Against Indigenous Populations**. New York: United Nations.

Martin-Jones, Marilyn & Saxena, Mukul (1995). Supporting or containing bilingualism? Policies, power asymmetries, and pedagogic practices in mainstream primary classrooms. In Tollefson (ed.), 73–90.

Marx, Karl [1845] **Theses on Feuerbach**. From the collection Bottomore, T. & Rubel, M. (1971). **Karl Marx on Sociology and Social Philosophy**. Harmondsworth: Penguin.

Massone, Maria Ignacia, Curiel, Mónica & Veinberg, Silvana C. (1993). Laws do not protect the rights of deaf persons. **WFD News. Magazine of the World Federation of the Deaf** 2 July 1993, 23–24.

Mateene, Kahombo (1980a). Introduction. In Mateene & Kalema (eds), VI–VII.

Mateene, Kahombo (1980b). Failure in the obligatory use of European languages in Africa and the advantages of a policy of linguistic independence. In Mateene & Kalema (eds), 9–41.

Mateene, Kahombo (1985a). Colonial languages as compulsory means of domination, and indigenous languages, as necessary factors of national liberation and development. In Mateene, Kalema & Chomba (eds), 60–69.

Mateene, Kahombo (1985b). Reconsideration of the Official Status of Colonial Languages in Africa. In Mateene, Kalema & Chomba (eds), 18–28.

Mateene, Kahombo & Kalema, John (eds) (1980). **Reconsideration of African linguistic policies.** Publication 3. Kampala: OAU Interafrican Bureau of Languages.

Mateene, Kahombo, Kalema, John & Chomba, Bernard (eds) (1985). **Linguistic liberation and unity of Africa.** Publication 6. Kampala: OAU Interafrican Bureau of Languages.

Mathes, Michael (1987). Interview with Dr. Michael Mathes. In Costo & Costo (eds), 209–212.

Mathew, Rama (1997). English in India: a response to Mark Tully. **ELT Journal** 51:1, 165–168.

Mattusch, Max Hans-Jürgen (1999). Vielsprachigkeit: Fluch oder Segen für die Menschheit? Zu Fragen einer europäischen und globalen Fremdsprachenpolitik. Frankfurt am Main, Berlin, Bern, New York, Paris, Wien: Peter Lang.

Maurais, Jacques (1992). Redédinition du statut des langues en Union Soviétique. **Language Problems and Language Planning** 16:1, 1–20.

Maurais, Jacques (1996). **Quebec's aboriginal languages: history, planning and development.** Clevedon, UK: Multilingual Matters.

Maurais, Jacques (ed.) (1998). **Les politiques linguistiques des pays baltes.** Special issue, **Terminogramme,** July 1998.

Maurud, Øivind (1976). **Nabospråksforståelse i Skandinavia. En undersøkelse om gjensidig forståelse av tale- og skriftspråk i Danmark, Norge og Sverige** (Understanding of neighbouring languages in Scandinavia. A study of mutual intelligibility of spoken and written languages in Denmark, Norway and Sweden). Nordisk Utredningsserie 1976:13. Stockholm: Nordiska rådet.

Mazrui, Alamin M. (1996). Language policy and the foundations of democracy: an African perspective. **International Journal of the Sociology of Language** 118, 107–124.

Mazrui, Alamin M. (1997). The World Bank, the language question and the future of African education. **Race and Class** 38:3, 35–48.

Mazrui, Ali A. (1975). **The Political Sociology of the English Language. An African Perspective.** The Hague: Mouton.

Mazrui, Ali A. (1980). **The African condition: the Reith lectures.** London: Heinemann.

Mazrui, Ali A. (1996). Language planning and gender planning: some African perspectives. **International Journal of the Sociology of Language** 118, 125–138

McArthur, Tom (1996). English in the world and in Europe. In Hartmann, Reinhard (ed.). **The English Language in Europe.** Oxford: Intellect, 3–15.

McArthur, Tom (1998). **The English Languages.** Cambridge: Cambridge University Press.

McCarthy, Teresa L. (1997). American Indian, Alasca Native, and Native Hawaiian Bilingual Education. In Cummins & Corson (eds), 45–56.

McDowall, David (1996). **A modern history of the Kurds.** London: Tauris.

McDowall, David (1997). **The Kurds.** 7th edition. London: The Minority Rights Group.

McKean, Warwick (1983). **Equality and Discrimination under International Law.** Oxford: Oxford University Press.

McLaughlin, Barry (1987). **Theories of second-language acquisition.** London: Arnold.

McLaughlin, Daniel (1992). **When literacy empowers. Navajo language in print.** Albuquerque: University of New Mexico Press.

McLaughlin, Daniel & Tierney, William G. (eds) (1993). **Naming silenced lives: personal narratives and the process of educational change.** New York: Routledge.

McRae, Kenneth D. (1983). **Conflict and compromise in multilingual societies, Switzerland.** Waterloo, Ontario: Wilfrid Laurier University Press.

McRae, Kenneth D. (1986). **Conflict and compromise in multilingual societies, Belgium**. Waterloo, Ontario: Wilfrid Laurier University Press.

McRae, Kenneth D. (1997). **Conflict and Compromise in Multilingual Societies. Finland.** Waterloo, Ontario: Wilfried Laurier University Press.

McRae, Kenneth D. (1998). Official bilingualism: from the 1960s to the 1990s. In J. Edwards (ed.), 61–83.

Medgyes, Peter (1994). **The non-native teacher**. London: Macmillan.

Meillet, Antoine & Cohen, Marcel (1952). **Les langues du monde**. Paris: Champion.

Mesthrie, Rajend (1995). Introduction. In Mesthrie (ed.), xv–xx.

Mesthrie, Rajend (ed.) (1995). **Language and Social History: Studies in South African Sociolinguistics**. Cape Town: David Philip.

Miles, Robert (1989). **Racism**. London: Routledge.

Mills, Jane (1991). **Womanwords. A Vocabulary of Culture and Patriarchal Society**. London: Virago.

Miner, Susan (1998). Legal Implications of the Official English Declaration. In Ricento & Burnaby (eds), 171–184.

Minority Rights, Policies and Practice in South-East Europe. Reports for the Conference at Christiansborg. Copenhagen, March 30th–April 1st (1990). Copenhagen: The Danish Helsinki Committee & The Minority Rights Group.

Mohanty, Ajit K. (1987). Social psychological aspects of assimilation/integration in a language contact situation. Paper presented in the thematic panel on Language and National Integration, XII Indian Social Science Congress, Mysore, India, manuscript.

Mohanty, Ajit K. (1994a). **Bilingualism in a Multilingual Society. Psycho-social and Pedagogical Implications**. Mysore: Central Institute of Indian Languages. [final date of publication: 1995].

Mohanty, Ajit K. (1994b). Bilingualism in a Multilingual Society: implications for cultural integration and education. Keynote address, 23rd International Congress of Applied Psychology, July 17–22 1994, Madrid, Spain, manuscript.

Mojab, Shahrzad (1998). 'Muslim' women and 'Western' feminists: the debate on particulars and universals. **Monthly Review** 50, December 1998, 19–30.

Molnár, Éva (1994). You are a Slovak!—My Mother Said to Me in Hungarian. **Regio. A Review of Minority and Ethnic Studies**, 141–157.

Morottaja, Matti (1997). Inarinsaamelaiset. **Oktavuohta**, 11.

Morris, Glenn T. (1995). 12th Session of UN Working Group on Indigenous Peoples. The Declaration Passes and the US Assumes a New Role. **Fourth World Bulletin. Issues in Indigenous Law and Politics**. University of Colorado at Denver, 4:1 & 2, 1ff.

Moscovici, S. & Paicheler, G. (1978). Social comparison and social recognition: two complementary processes of identification. In Tajfel (ed.).

Moseley, C. & Ashley, R. E. (eds) (1991). **Atlas of the world's languages**. London: Routledge.

Moussirou-Mouyama, Auguste (1985). Die Einführung der französischen Sprache in Gabun: die Philosophie der Glottophagie. In Pleines (ed.), 75–90.

Mühlhäusler, Peter (1990). 'Reducing' Pacific languages to writings. In Joseph, J. E. & Taylor, T. J. (eds). **Ideologies of language**. London: Routledge, 189–205.

Mühlhäusler, Peter (1994). Language teaching = linguistic imperialism? **Australian Review of Applied Linguistics** 17:2, 121–130.

Mühlhäusler, Peter (1996). **Linguistic ecology. Language change and linguistic imperialism in the Pacific region**. London: Routledge.

Mühlhäusler, Peter (1997). Language ecology—contact without conflict. In Pütz (ed.), 3–15.

Mühlhäusler, Peter (in press). Language rights for the language of Norfolk Island. In Phillipson (ed.).

Mulenga, Derek (1996). The 1995 World Bank's priorities and strategies for education: implications for education in sub-Saharan Africa. In Brock-Utne & Nagel (eds), 99–133.

Mullard, Chris (1984). **Anti-Racist Education: The Three O's**. Cardiff: The National Association for Multi-Racial Education.
Mullard, Chris (1985). **Race, Power & Resistance**. London: Routledge & Kegan Paul.
Mullard, Chris (1986). **Pluralism, Ethnicism and Ideology**. CRES Working Paper 2. Amsterdam: CRES (Centre for Race and Ethnic Studies), Universiteit van Amsterdam.
Mullard, Chris (1988). Racism, ethnicism and etharcy or not? The principles of progressive control and transformative change. In Skutnabb-Kangas & Cummins (eds), 359–378.
Municio, Ingegerd (1983). **Hemspråk i förskolan. En undersökning om genomförande** (Home language in preschool. A study on implementation). EIFO-rapport 21. Stockholm: EIFO.
Municio, Ingegerd (1987). **Från lag till bruk—hemspråksreformens genomförande** (From law to use—the implementation of the home language reform). Stockholm Studies in Politics 31. Stockholm: Department of Political Studies, University of Stockholm.
Municio, Ingegerd (1994). Medpart, motpart eller icke-part? Finska föräldrar som brukare i svensk skola. (Cooperators, adversaries, or non-parties? Finnish parents as consumers in the Swedish school). In Peura & Skutnabb-Kangas (eds), 18–72.
Municio, Ingegerd (1996). The return of the repressed 'Other'—linguistic minorities and the Swedish nation-state from the 1840's to the 1990's. To be published in Westin, Charles (ed.). Stockholm: CEIFO, University of Stockholm.
Municio-Larsson, Ingegerd (in press). Science and policy—when does science matter? In Phillipson (ed.).
Muzsnái, István (1999). Recognition of sign language: a threat or a way to solution? In Kontra et al. (eds), 279–296.
Myers-Scotton, Carol (1993). Elite closure as a powerful language strategy: the African case. **International Journal of the Sociology of Language** 103, 149–163.
Ndoye, Mamadou (1997). Globalization, Endogenous Development and Education in Africa. **Prospects. Quarterly Review of Comparative Education** (Unesco) XXVII:1, 79–84.
Necak Lük, Albina (1996). Language as an indicator of interethnic relations. **Razprave in Gradivo—Treatises and Documents** 31. Ljubljana: Institute for Ethnic Studies, 11–24.
Neij, Jeanette (1998). Stor opinion mot invandrare (Large opinion against immigrants). **Svenska Dagbladet**, 21 January 1998, E15.
Neisser, Arden (1983). **The Other Side of Silence: Sign Language and the Deaf Community in America**. New York: Knopf.
Nelde, Peter Hans (1991). Language conflicts in multilingual Europe—prospects for 1993. In Coulmas (ed.), 59–73.
Nelson, Brian, Roberts, David & Veit, Walter (eds) (1992). **The Idea of Europe. Problems of National and Transnational Identity**. New York/Oxford: Berg.
Neuerburg, Norman (1987). Interview with Dr. Norman Neuerburg. In Costo & Costo (eds), 214–217.
Ngugi, James (1994). **Grain of Wheat**. London: Heinemann. [reprinted].
Ngũgĩ, wa Thiong'o (1982). **Devil on the Cross**. London: Heinemann.
Ngũgĩ, wa Thiong'o (1985). The language of African literature. **New Left Review** April–June, 109–127.
Ngũgĩ, wa Thiong'o (1987a). **Decolonising the mind. The politics of language in African literature**. London: James Currey.
Ngũgĩ, wa Thiong'o (1987b). **Detained. A Writer's Prison Diary**. London: Heinemann.
Ngũgĩ, wa Thiong'o (1988). **Petals of Blood**. London: Heinemann.
Ngũgĩ, wa Thiong'o (1998). **Penpoints, gunpoints and dreams: Towards a Critical Theory of the Arts and the State in Africa**. Oxford: Clarendon Press.
Nichols, Johanna (1992). **Linguistic Diversity in Space and Time**. Chicago: University of Chicago Press.
Nielsen, Jørgen Chr. (1998). Presseinformation om Danmarks Pædagogiske Instituts undersøgelser af tosprogede elever i perioden 1995–1998 (Press release on the studies by the Danish

National Institute for Educational Research on bilingual students in 1995–1998). København: Danmarks Pædagogiske Institut.

Nikolov, Nino (1996). Poet between doctrines. In Tóth & Földeák (eds), 33–35.

Northern Lights. Fairy tales of the peoples of the North (1980). Moscow: Progress Publishers.

Northwest Territories Education, Culture and Employment (1994). **People: Our focus for the future. Education, Culture and Employment. A strategy to 2010.** Yellowknife, NWT: Ministry of Education, Culture and Employment. [no place, no publisher].

Norton, Jack (1987). The Path of Genocide: From El Camino Real to the Mines of the North. In Costo & Costo (eds), 111–125.

NOU (1980:59). = **Samisk i grunnskolen** (The Sámi language in comprehensive school). Norges offentlige utredninger 1980:59. Oslo: Universitetsforlaget.

NOU (1985:14). = **Samisk kultur og utdanning** (Sámi culture and education). Norges offentlige utredninger 1985:14. Oslo: Universitetsforlaget.

NOU (1987:34). = **Samisk kultur og utdanning: de enkelte sektorer; administrasjon** (Sámi culture and education: the various sectors; administration). Norges offentlige utredninger 1987:34. Oslo: Universitetsforlaget.

Nuffield Foundation & The Colonial Office (1953). **African education: A study of educational policy and practice in British tropical Africa.** Oxford: Oxford University Press.

Nunis Jr., Doyce B., Interview with Dr. Nunis. In Costo & Costo (eds), 217–222.

Nylund-Oja, Marja, Pentikäinen, Juha, Horn, Frank, Jaakkola, Magdalena & Yli-Vakkuri, Laura (1955). Finnish emigration and immigration. In Pentikäinen & Hiltunen (eds), 173–226.

O'Barr, William M. (1982). **Linguistic evidence: language, power and strategy in the courtroom.** New York: Academic Press.

O'Donoghue, Thomas A. (1994). Bilingual Education at the Beginning of the Twentieth Century: The Bilingual Programme of Instruction in Ireland 1904–1922. **Journal of Multilingual and Multicultural Development** 15:6, 491–505.

Ó Riagáin, Pádraig (1997). Postmodernity and Language Policy: A Need to Refocus? In Ammon et al. (eds), 16–28.

Obondo, Margaret Akinyi (1997). Bilingual Education in Africa: An Overview. In Cummins & Corson (eds), 25–32.

Obura, Anna (1986). Research issues and perspectives in language in education in Africa: an agenda for the next decade. In Centre of African Studies, 413–444.

Oda, Masaki (1994). Against linguicism: a reply to Richard Marshall. **The language teacher** 18:11, 39–40.

Oda, Masaki (in press a). Applied Linguistics in Japan: The Dominance of English in the Discourse Community. In Benson et al. (eds).

Oda, Masaki (in press b). Linguicism in action: language and power in academic institutions. In Phillipson (ed.).

Oellerrich, Annie (1998). De vilde vil vide, hvad de hvide vil (The wild ones want to know what the white ones want). Zigzag 65, November 1998, 9–11.

Oktavuohta/Teemalehti saamelaiskulttuurista (Thematic number about Sámi culture) (1997). Anár/Inari: Sámediggi/Saamelaiskäräjät.

Okuda, Osami (1995). On the Objectives of Linguistic Research on the Ainu. Abstract of the paper presented at the International Symposium on Endangered Languages, November 18–20, 1995, University of Tokyo. [can be downloaded from <http://www.tooyoo.l.u-To-kyo.ac.jp/linguistics/newsletters/newslet1.html>].

Oller, John & Littlebear, Richard (facilitators) (1996). November Roundtable: Education Group Abstract. Education Group Summary. In Cantoni (ed.).

Ollikainen, Marketta (1995). **Vankkurikansan perilliset. Romaanit, Euroopan unohdettu vähemmistö** (Heirs of the caravan people. Romany, Europe's forgotten minority). Ihmisoikeusliitto r.y.:n julkaisuja 3. Helsinki: Helsinki University Press.

Olson, Robert (1998). **The Kurdish question and Turkish-Iranian relations: from World War I to 1998.** Costa Mesa, CA: Mazda Publishers.

Olson, Robert (ed.) (1996). **The Kurdish Nationalist Movement in the 1990s.** Kentucky: The University Press of Kentucky.

Omodiaogbe, Sylvester A. (1992). 150 years on: English in the Nigerian school system—past, present and future. **ELT Journal** 46:1, 19–28.

Orwell, George (1970). **Collected Journalism and Letters.** Vol. 2. Harmondsworth: Penguin.

Ostler, Nicolas (1995). Editor's report. **Iatiku: Newsletter of of the Foundation for Endangered Languages** 1, 6–.

Ostler, Nicolas (1997). Comment. **Language International** 9:1, 5.

Oudin, Anne-Sophie (1996). **Immersion and Multilingual Education in the European Union. Inventory of educational systems in which teaching is provided partly or entirely through the medium of a regional or minority language.** Luxembourg: The European Bureau for Lesser Used Languages. [no date; ISBN 1 87067507X; see also <http://www.eblul.org>].

Oxford = **The Shorter Oxford English Dictionary** (1967). Prepared by Little, William, Fowler, H. W. & Coulson, J. Revised and edited by Onions, C. T. 3rd edition, revised with addenda. Oxford: Oxford University Press (Oxford at the Clarendon Press).

Ozolins, Uldis (1993). **The Politics of Language in Australia.** Cambridge/New York/Melbourne: Cambridge University Press.

Ozolins, Uldis (1996). Language policy and political reality. **International Journal of the Sociology of Language** 118, 181–200.

Ozolins, Uldis (1999). Separating Language from Ethnicity: The paradoxes of strict language policies and increasing social harmony in the Baltic states. In Kontra et al. (eds), 245–262.

Packer, John (1993). On the Definition of Minorities. In Packer & Myntti (eds), 23–65.

Packer, John (1997). The Content and Aim of Minority Education from the Perspective of International Instruments. **International Journal on Minority and Group Rights. Special Issue on the Education Rights of National Minorities** 4:2, 1996/1997, 171–174.

Packer, John & Myntti, Kristian (eds) (1993). **The Protection of Ethnic and Linguistic Minorities in Europe.** Åbo: Institute for Human Rights, Åbo Akademi University.

Packer, John & Siemienski, Guillaume (1997). Integration Through Education: The Origin and Development of The Hague Recommendations. **International Journal on Minority and Group Rights. Special Issue on the Education Rights of National Minorities** 4:2, 1996/1997, 187–198.

Padilla, Amado M., Lindholm, Kathryn J., Chen, Andrew, Durán, Richard, Hakuta, Kenji, Lambert, Wallace & Tucker, G. Richard (1991). The English-Only Movement. Myths, Reality, and Implications for Psychology. **Journal of the American Psychological Association** 46:2, 120–130.

Pagel, Mark (1995). As reported by Nicholas Ostler in **Iatiku: Newsletter of of the Foundation for Endangered Languages** 1, 1995, 6.

Pagels, Heinz R. (1982). **The Cosmic Code. Quantum Physics as the Language of Nature.** Toronto/New York: Bantam Books.

Pakir, Anne (1991). The status of English and the question of 'standard' in Singapore: A Sociolinguistic Perspective. In Tickoo (ed.), 109–130.

Palley, Claire (1984). **Possible ways and means to facilitate the peaceful and constructive resolution of situations involving racial, national, religious and linguistic minorities.** Working paper submitted to UN Sub-Commission on Prevention of Discrimination and Protection of Minorities at its 41st session (E/CN.4/Sub.2/1984/43).

Papandreou, Margarita (1992). The changing role of women within a changing Europe. In European Conference **"Building a Europe without frontiers: the role of women".** 27–30 November (1992). Athens, Greece: European Network for Women's Studies & Ministry of Education and Science, The Netherlands, 9–12.

Pattanayak, D. P. (1970). **Language Policy and Programmes.** Delhi: Ministry of Education and Youth Services, Government of India.

Pattanayak, D. P. (1981a). **Multilingualism and Mother-Tongue Education**. Delhi: Oxford University Press.

Pattanayak, D. P. (1981b). **Language and Social Issues**. Mysore: Central Institute of Indian Languages.

Pattanayak, D. P. (1986). Educational use of the mother tongue. In Spolsky (ed.), 5–15.

Pattanayak, D. P. (1988). Monolingual myopia and the petals of the Indian lotus: do many languages divide or unite a nation? In Skutnabb-Kangas & Cummins (eds), 379–389.

Pattanayak, D. P. (1991). **Language, Education and Culture**. Mysore: Central Institute of Indian Languages.

Pattanayak, D. P. (ed.) (1990). **Multilingualism in India**. Clevedon, UK: Multilingual Matters.

Pattanayak, Debi Prasanna (1992). Mothertongue awareness. Lecture given at Cambridge University, UK, September 1992. Manuscript.

Paulston, Christina Bratt (1975). Ethnic Relations and Bilingual Education: Accounting for Contradictory Data. **Working Papers on Bilingualism** 6, 1–44.

Paulston, Christina Bratt (1982). **Forskning och debatt om tvåspråkighet. En kritisk genomgång av svensk forskning och debatt om tvåspråkighet i invandrarundervisningen i Sverige från ett internationellt perspektiv**. En rapport till Skolöverstyrelsen, Stockholm: Skolöverstyrelsen. [English—not identical—version (1983): **Swedish Research and Debate about Bilingualism**. Stockholm: Swedish National Board of Education].

Paulston, Christina Bratt (1994). **Linguistic Minorities in Multilingual Settings. Implications for language policies**. Amsterdam/Philadelphia: John Benjamins.

Paulston, Rolland (1972). Cultural Revitalization and Educational Change in Cuba. **Comparative Education Review** 16:3.

Peal, Elisabeth & Lambert, Wallace E. (1962). The relation of bilingualism to intelligence. **Psychological Monographs** 76: 27, 1–23.

Penn, Claire & Reagan, Timothy (1990). How do you sign 'apartheid'? The politics of South African Sign Language. **Language Problems & Language Planning** 14:2, 91–103.

Pennycook, Alastair (1994). **The cultural politics of English as an international language**. Harlow: Longman.

Pennycook, Alastair (1995). English in the world/The world in English. In Tollefson (ed.), 34–58.

Pennycook, Alastair (1998a). **English and the discourses of colonialism**. London/New York: Routledge.

Pennycook, Alastair (1998b). The right to language: towards a situated ethics of language possibilities. In Benson et al. (eds), 73–87.

Pentikäinen, Juha (1955). Finland in Europe: a cultural-historical approach. In Pentikäinen & Hiltunen (eds), 227–238.

Pentikäinen, Juha & Anttonen, Veikko (eds) (1985). **Cultural Minorities in Finland. An Overview towards Cultural Policy**. Publication No. 32. Helsinki: Finnish National Commission for Unesco.

Pentikäinen, Juha & Hiltunen, Marja (eds) (1995). **Cultural minorities in Finland. An overview towards cultural policy**. Publication No 66. Helsinki: The Finnish National Commission for Unesco.

Perry, Theresa & Delpit, Lisa (1998). **The real Ebonics debate: Power, language, and the education of African-American children**. Boston: Beacon Press.

Peura, Markku (1983). Invandrar- och minoritetsforskning ur minoritetspolitisk synvinkel (Immigrant and minority research from a minority policy viewpoint). In Peura (ed.), 3–9.

Peura, Markku (1993). Ruotsinsuomalaisen koulutuksen läpimurto (The breakthrough of Sweden-Finnish education). In Vuonokari, Erkki & Pelkonen, Juha (eds). **Luokan kynnyksen yli. Ruotsinsuomalaiset kirjoittavat kouluhistoriaa** (Crossing the class/room threshold. Sweden Finns write educational history). Jyväskylä, Finland & Stockholm, Sweden: Gummerus & Sverigefinländarnas Arkiv, 245–255.

Peura, Markku (ed.) (1983). **Invandrarminoriteter och demokratisk forskning** (Immigrant minorities and democratic research). Stockholm: Riksförbundet Finska Föreningar i Sverige.

Peura, Markku & Skutnabb-Kangas, Tove (eds) (1994). **'Man kan vara tvåländare också'. Den sverigefinska minoritetens väg från tystnad till kamp.** ('You can be bicountrial too'. The road of the Sweden-Finnish minority from silence to struggle). Stockholm: Sverigefinländarnas Arkiv.

Phillipson, Robert (1992a). **Linguistic imperialism.** Oxford: Oxford University Press.

Phillipson, Robert (1992b). ELT—the native speaker's burden? **ELT Journal,** Special IATEFL 25th Anniversary number, 46:1, 12–18.

Phillipson, Robert (1997a). Geschichte der britischen Sprachpolitik. In Sporrer, Susanne & Weber, Mirjam (red.). **Sprachenpolitik in Europa—Sprachenpolitik für Europa.** Materialen zum Internationalen Kulturaustausch. Stuttgart: Institut für Auslandsbeziehungen, 46–52.

Phillipson, Robert (1997b). Review of Claude Piron 'Le défi des langues: du gâchis au bon sens' (The languages challenge: from waste to common sense). **Language in Society,** 26:1, 143–147.

Phillipson, Robert (1998a). Globalizing English: are linguistic human rights an alternative to linguistic imperialism? In Benson et al. (eds), 101–112.

Phillipson, Robert (1998b). Review of 'English as a global language' by David Crystal. **The European English Messenger** (Newsletter of the European Society for the Study of English) VII:1, 53–56.

Phillipson, Robert (1999). Voice in global English: unheard chords in Crystal loud and clear. Review article on 'English as a global language' by David Crystal. **Applied Linguistics** 20:2, 288–299.

Phillipson, Robert (in press). A rejoinder to David Crystal's "On trying to be Crystal-clear: A response to Phillipson". **The European English Messenger.**

Phillipson, Robert, Rannut, Mart & Skutnabb-Kangas, Tove (1994). Introduction. In Skutnabb-Kangas & Phillipson (eds), 1–22.

Phillipson, Robert & Skutnabb-Kangas, Tove (1983). **Cultilingualism—papers in cultural and communicative (in)competence.** ROLIG-papir 2. Roskilde: Roskilde University Centre.

Phillipson, Robert & Skutnabb-Kangas, Tove (1985). Applied linguists as agents of wider colonisation: the gospel of International English. In Pleines (ed.), 159–179.

Phillipson, Robert & Skutnabb-Kangas, Tove (1986a). **Linguicism Rules in Education.** 3 volumes. Roskilde: Roskilde University Centre.

Phillipson, Robert & Skutnabb-Kangas, Tove (1986b). English: the language of wider colonisation. In Phillipson & Skutnabb-Kangas 1986a, 344–377.

Phillipson, Robert & Skutnabb-Kangas, Tove (1994a). English—Panacea or Pandemic? In Ammon et al. (eds), 73–87.

Phillipson, Robert & Skutnabb-Kangas, Tove (1994b). Language rights in postcolonial Africa. In Skutnabb-Kangas & Phillipson (eds), 335–345.

Phillipson, Robert & Skutnabb-Kangas, Tove (1995). Linguistic rights and wrongs. **Applied Linguistics** 16:4, 483–504.

Phillipson, Robert & Skutnabb-Kangas, Tove (1996a). Colonial language legacies: the prospects for Kurdish. In Clark & Williamson (eds), 200–213.

Phillipson, Robert & Skutnabb-Kangas, Tove (1996b). English Only Worldwide, or Language Ecology. **TESOL Quarterly.** Ricento, Thomas & Hornberger, Nancy (eds). **Special-Topic Issue: Language Planning and Policy,** 429–452.

Phillipson, Robert & Skutnabb-Kangas, Tove (1997). Lessons for Europe from language policy in Australia. In Pütz (ed.), 115–159.

Phillipson, Robert & Skutnabb-Kangas, Tove (1999). Englishisation as one dimension of globalization. **AILA Review.** Special number on 'English in a changing world'. Gradddol, David & Meinhoff, Ulrike (eds), 19–36.

Phillipson, Robert, Skutnabb-Kangas, Tove & Africa, Hugh (1985). Namibian educational language planning: English for liberation or neocolonialism? In Mateene et al. (eds), 42–59 [also in Spolsky (ed.), 77–95].

Phillipson, Robert (ed.) (in press). **Rights to language. Equity, power and education**. Mahwah, N.J.: Lawrence Erlbaum Associates.

Phillipson, Robert, Kellerman, Eric, Selinker, Larry, Sharwood Smith, Mike & Swain, Merrill (eds) (1991). **Foreign/second language pedagogy research: a commemorative volume for Claus Faerch**. Clevedon, UK: Multilingual Matters.

Pilger, John (1990). **A Secret Country**. London: Vintage.

Pilger, John (1998). **Hidden Agendas**. London: Vintage.

Pinter, Harold (1997). Land of the Free? It Never Happened. **Z Magazine**, February 1997, 9–10.

Piron, Claude (1994). **Le défi des langues: du gâchis au bon sens**. Paris: L'Harmattan.

Piron, Claude (1996). Une solution á étudier: l'Espéranto. In Léger (ed.), 631–657.

Platero, Dillon (1975). Bilingual Education in the Navajo Nation. In Troike, Rudolph C. & Modiano, Nancy (eds). **Proceedings of the First Inter-American Conference on Bilingual Education**. Arlington, Va.: Center for Applied Linguistics, 54–61.

Pleines, Jochen (ed.) (1985). **Sprachenkonkurrenz und gesellschaftliche Planung: das Erbe des Kolonialismus**. Osnabrücker Beiträge zur Sprachtheorie 31. Osnabrück.

Plichtová, Jana (ed.) (1992). **Minorities in Politics—Cultural and Languages Rights**. The Bratislava Symposium II/1991. Bratislava: Czechoslovak Committee of the European Cultural Foundation.

Plöger, Angela (1995). Den sociale nød vokser i Ungarn (The social misery is growing in Hungary). **Information**, 8.5.1995, 2.

Plüddemann, Peter (in press). Multilingualism and education in South Africa: one year on. **International Journal of Education Research**.

Plüddemann, Peter, Mati, Xola & Mahlalela-Thusi, Babazile (1998). Problems and possibilities in multilingual classrooms in the Western Cape. Final Research Report. September 1998. PRAESA: University of Cape Town, manuscript [<pp@education.uct.ac.za>].

Pool, Jonathan (1969). National Development and Language Diversity. **La Monda Lingvo-Problemo** 1, 140–156.

Pool, Jonathan (1993). Linguistic exploitation. **International Journal of the Sociology of Language**. 103, 31–55.

Posey, Darrell A. (in press a). Introduction: Culture and nature—the inextricable link. In Posey (ed.).

Posey, Darrell A. (in press b). Biological and cultural diversity: The inextricable, linked by language and politics. In Maffi (ed.).

Posey, Darrell A. & Dutfield, Graham (in press). Conservation of Biological and Cultural Diversity: An Inextricable Link. In Posey (ed.).

Posey, Darrell A. (ed.) (in press). **Cultural and Spiritual Values of Biodiversity**. New York: UNEP (United Nations Environmental Programme) & Leiden: Intermediate Technologies, Leiden University.

Powers, Faith (1995). English as official language: An act of unification or segregation? **TESOL Matters** June/July 1995, 1–.

Prah, Kwesi Kwaa (1995a). **Mother Tongue for Scientific and Technological Development in Africa**. Bonn: Zentralstelle für Erziehung, Wissenschaft und Dokumentation (ZED) (German Foundation for International Development, Education, Science and Documentation Centre).

Prah, Kwesi Kwaa (1995b). **African Languages for the Mass Education of Africans**. Bonn: Zentralstelle für Erziehung, Wissenschaft und Dokumentation (ZED) (German Foundation for International Development, Education, Science and Documentation Centre).

Pratte, Richard (1977). **Ideology and education**. New York: David McKay Company.

Preiswerk, Roy (ed.) (1980). **The slant of the pen: racism in children's books**. Geneva: World Council of Churches.

Prelipceanu, Nicolae (1996). We in the mirror. In Tóth (ed.), 27–32.

Puntervold Bø, Bente (1984). **Naboholdninger til innvandrere** (Attitudes of neighbours towards immigrants). Nabolagsundersøkelsen, Delrapport III. Forskningsrapport nr. 13. Oslo: Diakonhjemmets sosiale høgskole.

Putseys, Yvan (1993). The world's languages—how many speakers? **English Today** 36:9,4, October 1993, 4–12.

Pütz, Martin (ed.) (1995). **Discrimination through language in Africa? Perspectives on the Namibian experience.** Berlin/New York: Mouton de Gruyter.

Pütz, Martin (ed.) (1997). **Language choices. Conditions, constraints and consequences.** Amsterdam: John Benjamins.

Quirk, Randolph, Greenbaum, Sidney, Leech, Jeffrey & Svartvik, Jan (1972). **A Grammar of Contemporary English.** London: Longman.

Quirk, Randolph, Greenbaum, Sidney, Leech, Jeffrey & Svartvik, Jan (1985). **A Comprehensive Grammar of the English Language.** London/New York: Longman.

Raboy, Marc & Bruck, Peter (1989). **Communication For and Against Democracy.** Montreal: Black Rose Press.

Radhakrishnan, S. (1977). **The Bhagavadgītā. With the Introductory Essay, Sanskrit Text, English Translation and Notes by S. Radhakrishnan.** Bombay, Calcutta, Madras/New Delhi: Blackie & Son (India) Ltd.

Radnai, Zsófia (1993). The language situation in Hungary 1990–1991. In Ager, Dennis, Muskens, George & Wright, Sue (eds). **Language education for intercultural communication.** Clevedon, UK: Multilingual Matters, 109–113.

Radnai, Zsófia (1994). The educational effects of language policy. **Current Issues in Language & Society** 1:1, 1994 [identical with Wright, Sue (ed.) **Ethnicity in eastern Europe. Questions of Migration, language rights & education.** Clevedon, UK: Multilingual Matters], 65–92.

Radnai, Zsófia (1995). Research in Primary School Language Education: the Situation in Hungary. Written for Edelenbos, P. (ed.). **Research in Primary School Language Teaching.** London: CILT.

Radnai, Zsófia & Koster, C. (1995). The Pécs Language Survey: language use and needs in Pécs and the region. Written for **Proceedings of the Budapest Conference on LSP.** London: CILT.

Radó, Péter (1994). The Public Use of Minority Languages in Hungary. **Regio. A Review of Minority and Ethnic Studies** 1994, 130–140.

Radoměřská, Lada & Skutnabb-Kangas, Tove (1998). Book review of Harding, Sandra (1997). **Is Science Multicultural? Postcolonialisms, feminisms, and epistemologies. Journal of Multilingual and Multicultural Development** 19:3, 244–247.

Rahbek Pedersen, Birgitte & Skutnabb-Kangas, Tove (1983). **God, bedre, dansk? Om indvandrerbørns integration i Danmark** (Good, better, Danish? On the integration of immigrant children in Denmark). Copenhagen: Børn og unge.

Ralston, Helen (1988). The lived experience of South Asian Immigrant Women in Atlantic Canada. In **New Frontiers in Social Research: Conference Session IV, The (Re)presentation of Ethnic Identity.** CRES Publication Series, Occasional Paper No. 11. Amsterdam: CRES (Centre for Race and Ethnic Studies), Universiteit van Amsterdam.

Ramirez, J. David (1992). Executive Summary. **Bilingual Research Journal** 16:1 & 2, 1–62.

Ramirez, J. David, Pasta, David J., Yuen, Sandra D., Billings, David K. & Ramey, Dena R. (1991). **Longitudinal study of structured immersion strategy, early-exit, and late-exit bilingual education programs for language minority children (Vols. 1–2).** San Mateo, CA: Aguirre International.

Ramirez, J. David., Yuen, Sandra D. & Ramey, Dena R. (1991). **Executive Summary: Final report: Longitudinal study of structured English immersion strategy, early-exit and late-exit transitional bilingual education programs for language-minority children, Submitted to the U.S. Department of Education.** San Mateo, CA: Aguirre International.

Rampton, M. B. H. (1990). Displacing the 'native speaker': expertise, affiliation, and inheritance. **ELT Journal** 44:2, 97–101.

Rannut, Mart (1994). Beyond linguistic policy: the Soviet Union versus Estonia. In Skutnabb-Kangas & Phillipson (eds), 179–208.

Rannut, Mart (1999). **Estonian Language Policy 1988–1997**. Ph.D. Thesis, University of Tartu, Estonia. Forthcoming.

Rannut Mart & Rannut, Ülle (1995). Bilingualism—a step towards monolingualism or multilingualism? In Skutnabb-Kangas (ed.), 183–198.

Rannut, Ülle (1992). **Keelekümblus** (Immersion). Keeleameti toimetised nr 3. Tallinn: Keeleamet.

Rassool, Naz (1998). Postmodernity, cultural pluralism and the nation-state: problems of language rights, human rights, identity and power. In Benson et al. (eds), 89–99.

Rassool, Naz (1999). **Literacy for Sustainable Development in the Age of Information**. Clevedon, UK: Multilingual Matters.

Rassool, Naz (in press). Identifying language rights as an arena of cultural and political struggle in a changing world. In Phillipson (ed.).

Read, Jan (1978). **The Catalans**. London: Faber & Faber.

Reagan, Timothy (1992). The Deaf as a Linguistic Minority: Educational Considerations. In Hehir, Thomas & Latus, Thomas (eds). **Special Education at the Century's End: Evolution of Theory and Practice Since 1970**. Cambridge, Mass.: **Harvard Educational Review** 1992, 305–320. [**Harvard Educational Review** 55:3, August 1985].

Reagan, Timothy (1995a). A sociocultural understanding of Deafness: American Sign Language and the culture of Deaf people. **International Journal of Intercultural Relations** 19:2, 239–251.

Reagan, Timothy (1995b). Neither Easy to Understand Nor Pleasing to See: The Development of Manual Sign Codes as Language Planning Activity. **Language Problems & Language Planning** 19:2, 133–150.

Reagan, Timothy (1995c). Language planning and language policy in South Africa: a perspective on the future. In Mesthrie (ed.), 319–328.

Reagan, Timothy (1996). **Non-Western Educational Traditions: Alternative approaches to educational thought and practice**. Mahwah, N.J.: Lawrence Erlbaum Associates.

Reagan, Timothy (1997a). The Case for Applied Linguistics in Teacher Education. **Journal of Teacher Education**, 48:3, 185–196.

Reagan, Timothy (1997b). When Is a Language Not a Language? Challenges to "Linguistic Legitimacy" in Educational Discourse. **Educational Foundations**, Summer 1997, 5–28.

Reagan, Timothy & Osborn, Terry A. (1998). Power, Authority, and Domination in Foreign Language Education: Toward an Analysis of Educational Failure. **Educational Foundations**, Spring 1998, 45–61.

Reagan, Timothy & Penn, Claire (1997). Language Policy, South African Sign language, and the Deaf: Social and Educational Implications. **Southern African Journal of Applied Language Studies** 6:1, 1–13.

Reid, Euan & Reich, Hans (eds) (1992). **Breaking the Boundaries. Migrant Workers' Children in the EC**. Clevedon, UK: Multilingual Matters.

Rekdal, Olaug & Skutnabb-Kangas, Tove (1977). Om androgyn (både-och/varken-eller) lingvistikk. (On androgyn (both-and/neither-nor) linguistics). In Rekdal, Olaug & Skutnabb-Kangas, Tove (eds) (1977). **Vardagsskrift = Arkikirja = Hverdagsskrift til Jan och Jens i anledning det året dom närmade sig 31 og till alle dere andre som tycker om vardagsuppmuntran, utgitt med kram av TSK og OR** (Everyday-schrift to Jan and Jens, on the occasion of the year when they approached 31, and to all you others who like everyday support, edited by TSK and OR, with a hug). Uppsala: Uppsala University, Dept of Nordic Languages, 63–78.

Renner, Michael (1998). Curbing the Proliferation of Small Arms. In **State of the World 1998**, 131–148.

Retí, György (1995). Hungary and the problem of national minorities. **The Hungarian Quarterly** XXXVI:139, 70–77.

Rex, John (1986). **Race and Ethnicity**. Milton Keynes: Open University.

Rex, John & Mason, David (eds) (1986). **Theories of Race and Ethnic Relations**. Cambridge: Cambridge University Press.

Reyhner, Jon (1995). American Indian languages and United States language policy. In Fase et al. (eds), 229–248.

Reyhner, Jon (1996). Language Activists Panel Summary. In Cantoni (ed.).

Ricento, Thomas (1996). Language Policy in the United States. In Herriman & Burnaby (eds), 122–158.

Ricento, Thomas & Burnaby, Barbara (eds) (1998). **Language and Politics in the United States and Canada. Myths and realities**. Mahwah, N.J./London: Lawrence Erlbaum Associates.

Richardson, Boyce (1993). **People of Terra nullius. Betrayal and Rebirth in Aboriginal Canada**. Vancouver/Toronto: Douglas & McIntyre.

Rickford, John R. & Rickford, Angela E. (1995). Dialect Readers Revisited. **Linguistics and Education** 7:2, 107–128.

Ridge, Stanley G. M. (1996). Language Policy in a Democratic South Africa. In Herriman & Burnaby (eds), 15–34.

Riggs, Fred W. (1986). What is ethnic? What is national? Let's turn the tables. **Canadian Review of Studies in Nationalism** XIII:1, 111–123.

Riggs, Fred W. (ed.) (1985). **Ethnicity. Intercocta Glossary. Concepts & Terms Used in Ethnicity Research. International Conceptual Encyclopedia for the Social Sciences**. Vol. 1. Honolulu: Dept of Political Science & International Social Science Council, University of Hawaii.

Risager, Karen (forthcoming). **Language, Culture and Globalization. Towards a Universalist and Critical Language and Culture Pedagogy**. Roskilde. Roskilde University Centre.

Ritzer, George (1996). **The McDonaldization of Society. An Investigation into the Changing Character of Contemporary Social Life**. Revised edition. Thousand Oaks, CA/London/New Delhi: Pine Forge Press.

Roberts, David & Nelson, Brian (1992). Introduction. In Nelson, Brian, Roberts, David & Veit, Walter (eds) 1992. **The Idea of Europe. Problems of National and Transnational Identity**. New York/Oxford: Berg, 1–11.

Robins, Philip (1996). More apparent than real? The impact of the Kurdish issue on Euro-Turkish relations. In Olson, Robert (ed.) **The Kurdish Nationalist Movement in the 1990s**. Kentucky: The University Press of Kentucky, 114–132.

Robins, Robert H. & Uhlenbeck, Eugenius M. (eds) (1991). **Endangered Languages**. Oxford/New York: Berg.

Robinson, Clinton D. W. (1993). Where minorities are in the majority: language dynamics amidst high linguistic diversity. In de Bot, Kees (ed.). **Case Studies in Minority Languages**. AILA Review 10, 52–70.

Rodney, Walter (1969). **The Groundings With My Brothers**. London: Bogle-L'Ouverture Publications.

Rodney, Walter (1983). **How Europe Underdeveloped Africa**. London: Bogle-L'Ouverture. [1972].

Romaine, Suzanne (1995). **Bilingualism**. Oxford: Blackwell.

Roppola, Veikko (1998). Toistuuko Pajalan koululakko? (Will the Pajala school strike be repeated.). **Koulumaailma** 1, February 1998: 11.

Rosas, Allan (1995a). The Right of Self-determination. In Eide et al. (eds), 79–86.

Rosas, Allan (1995b). So-Called Rights of the Third Generation. In Eide et al. (eds), 243–246.

Rosas, Allan (1995c). The Right to Development. In Eide et al. (eds), 247–256.

Rose, Richard & Maley, William (1994). Conflict or Compromise in the Baltic States? **RFE/RL Research Report** 3:28, 15 July, 26–35.

Rothenberger, Alexandra (compiler) (1997). **Bibliography on the OSCE High Commissioner on National Minorities: Documents, Speeches and Related Publications**. The Hague: The Foundation on Inter-Ethnic Relations.

Routh, H. V. (1941). **The diffusion of English culture outside England. A problem of post-war reconstruction.** Cambridge: Cambridge University Press.

Rubagumya, Casmir M. (1990). **Language in education in Africa: A Tanzanian perspective.** Clevedon, UK: Multilingual Matters.

Ruhlen, Merritt (1991). **A Guide to the World's Languages.** Volume 1: Classification. London/Melbourne/Auckland: Edward Arnold.

Ruiz, Richard (1984). Orientations in language planning. **NABE Journal** 8:2, 15–34.

Rumpf, Christian (1989). The Turkish Law Prohibiting Languages Other Than Turkish. In **Human Rights in Kurdistan,** 69–87.

Ruong, Israel (1975). Historisk återblick rörande samerna (A historical retrospective view on the Sámi). In **Samerna i Sverige. Stöd åt språk och kultur. Bilagor.** SOU 1975: 100. Stockholm: Statens offentliga utredningar, 375–433.

Rupesinghe, Kumar & Tishkov, Valery A. (eds) (1996). **Ethnicity and Power in the Contemporary World.** Tokyo/New York/Paris: United Nations University Press.

Saado, Hussain (1989). Document on the United Nations and the Kurdish Question. In **Human Rights in Kurdistan,** 171–179.

Sachdeva, Rajesh (1998). Towards an explicit language policy in education for Nagaland. Manuscript. [address of author: Department of Linguistics, North-Eastern Hill University, Mayurbhanj Campus, Shillong, 793 014, India].

Sachs, Wolfgang (1992a). Introduction. In Sachs (ed.), 1–5.

Sachs, Wolfgang (1992b). One World. In Sachs (ed.), 102–115.

Sachs, Wolfgang (1992c). Environment. In Sachs (ed.), 26–37.

Sachs, Wolfgang (ed.) (1992). **Development Dictionary. A Guide to Knowledge as Power.** London: Zed Books.

Said, W. Edward (1978). **Orientalism.** Harmondsworth: Penguin.

Said, W. Edward (1981). **Covering Islam: How media and the experts determine how we see the rest of the world.** London: Routledge.

Said, W. Edward (1994). **Representations of the intellectual.** London: Vintage.

Said, W. Edward (1995). On Jean Genet's late works. In Gainor (ed.), 230–242.

Sale, Kirkpatrick (1996). Principles of Bioregionalism. In Mander & Goldsmith (eds), 471–484.

Salih, Mohamed (1996). Ethnicity and the State with Special Reference to Ethiopia. **News from Nordiska Afrikainstitutet** 3, October 1996, 13–14.

Sámegiella—skuvlagiella 1998. Dieđihandblađđi sámegielat ja sámegiela oahpahusas (Sámi language—school language. Newsletter about about the Sámi language and Sámi language education). Anár/Inari, Guovdageaidnu/Kautokeino & Johkamohkki/Jokkmokk: Sámediggi, Sámi Oahpahusrađđi & Sámi Skuvlastivra.

Samoff, Joel (1996). Aid and education—transforming the policy making process. In Brock-Utne & Nagel (eds), 10–72.

Sandlund, Tom (1976). **Social classes, ethnic groups and capitalist development—an outline of a theory.** Research Reports No. 24. Åbo: Svenska Litteratursällskapets Nämnd för samhällsforskning.

Sandra Lovelace v. Canada. UN Doc. A/36/40, Fifth Annual report of the Human Rights Committee Covering its Activities at its Eleventh, Twelvth and Thirteenth Sessions. In **Yearbook of the Human Rights Committee 1981–1982,** vol. II, 320–323.

Sasse, Hans-Jürgen (1992). Theory of Language Death. In Brenzinger (ed.), 7–30.

Šatava, Leoš (1992). Problems of national minorities. In Plichtová (ed.), 78–81.

Sato, Charlene (1991). Sociolinguistic variation and language attitudes in Hawai'i. In Cheshire (ed.), 647–663.

Savala, Tony & Savala, Pete (1987). Mission Slavery. Interview in Costo & Costo (eds), 145–146.

Saville-Troike, Muriel (1973). **Bilingual Children: A Resource Document.** Arlington: Center for Applied Linguistics.

Savory, Elaine (1995). Strategies for survival: Anti-Imperialist Theatrical Forms in the Anglophone Caribbean. In Gainor (ed.), 243–256.

Schermerhorn, R. A. (1970). **Comparative ethnic relations. A framework for theory and research.** New York: Random House.

Schierup, Carl-Ulrik (1992). Konstruktion und Krise des schwedischen Multikulturalismus. In Kalpaka & Räthzel (Hrsg.), 163–173.

Schierup, Carl-Ulrik (1995). Multiculturalism, Neo-racism and Vixissitudes of Contemporary Democracy. In Hjarnø, Jan (ed.). **Multiculturalism in the Nordic Societies.** Proceedings of the 9th Nordic Seminar for Researchers on Migration and Ethnic Relations. Final Report. TemaNord 1995:516. Copenhagen: Nordic Council of Ministers, 10–29.

Schlossmacher, Michael (1994). Die Arbeitssprachen in den Organen der Europäischen Gemeinschaft. Methoden und Ergebnisse einer empirischen Untersuchung. In Ammon et al. (eds), 101–122.

Schlossmacher, Michael (1996). **Die Amtssprachen in der Organen der Europäischen Gemeinschaft.** Frankfurt am Main: Lang.

Schmied, Josef (1991). **English in Africa. An introduction.** London/New York: Longman.

Schulz, Gerhard (ed.) (1993). **The languages of Australia.** Canberra: Australian Academy of the Humanities.

Schwartz, Leslie (1998). **Culture and mental health: A southern African view.** Cape Town: Oxford University Press.

Schäffner, Christina & Wenden, Anita L. (eds) (1995). **Language and Peace.** Aldershot: Dartmouth.

Sebba, Mark (1994). **Putting language on the map.** Centre For Language In Social Life Working Paper Series, 55. Lancaster: Department of Linguistics and Modern English Language, Lancaster University.

Sebeok, Thomas A. (ed.) (1963–76). **Current trends in linguistics,** Vols. 1–14. Mouton: The Hague.

Sen, G. (1984). **The military origins of industrialization and international trade.** London: Frances Pinter.

Senghas, Richard J. (1998). Review of Baynton, Douglas C. (1996). **Forbidden signs: American culture and the campaign against sign language.** Chicago, Ill.: University of Chicago Press. **Language in Society** 27:4, 541–544.

Seurujärvi-Kari, Irja, Morottaja, Matti, Saressalo, Lassi, Pentikäinen, Juha, Hirvonen, Vuokko & Aikio-Puoskari, Ulla (1995). The Sami people in Finland. In Pentikäinen & Hiltunen (eds), 101–146.

Shea, David (in press). The Discourse of Homogeneity and the Language Rights of Cultural Minorities in Japan. In Benson et al. (eds).

Shenton, Robert (1983). Introduction. In Rodney 1983, ii–ix.

Shipek Connolly, Florence (1987). The Franciscan Missionaries of California. In Costo & Costo (eds), 29–47.

Shiva, Vandana (1991). **Biodiversity: Social and Ecological Perspectives.** London/New Jersey: Zed Books.

Shiva, Vandana (1993). **Monocultures of the Mind. Perspectives on Biodiversity and Biotechnology.** London/New Jersey: Zed Books.

Shiva, Vandana (1997). **Biopiracy: The Plunder of Nature and Knowledge.** Boston: South End Press.

Shiva, Vandana & Hola-Bar, Radha (1996). Piracy by Patent. The Case of the Neem Tree. In Mander & Goldsmith (eds), 146–159.

Siatchitema, A. K. (1992). When nationalism conflicts with nationalist goals: Zambia. In Crawhall (ed.).

Sidiropoulos et al. (1997)—see **South Africa Survey 1996/97.**

Sieghart, Paul (1983). **The international law of human rights.** Oxford: Oxford University Press.

Siemienski, Guillaume (1997). Report on the Vienna Seminar on Minority Education Issues, 22–23 November 1996. **International Journal on Minority and Group Rights. Special Issue on the Education Rights of National Minorities** 4:2, 1996/1997, 175–185.

Siguan, Miquel (1993). **Multilingual Spain.** Lisse: Swets & Zeitlinger.

Silman, Janet (1988). **Enough is Enough: Aboriginal Women Speak Out.** Toronto: Womens Press.

Simmons, J. (1980). **The Education Dilemma.** New York: Pergamon Press.

Sitka, Chris (1998). A sorry business. **Guardian Weekly** June 7, 1998, 25.

Sivanandan, A. (1982). **A Different Hunger. Writings on Black Resistance.** London: Pluto Press.

Skolverket (1997). **Barn mellan arv och framtid. Konfessionella, etniska och språkligt inriktade skolor i ett segregationsperspektiv** (Children between heritage and future. Confessional, ethnic and linguistically oriented schools in a segregation perspective). Dnr 97:810, 29 September 1997.

Skotnes, Pippa (ed.) (1996). **Miscast. Negotiating the Presence of the Bushmen.** Cape Town: University of Cape Town Press.

Skutnabb-Kangas, Tove (1972a). Om forskningen kring tvåspråkighet och skolframgång (On research about bilingualism and school achievement). **Folkmålsstudier,** Meddelanden från Föreningen för nordisk filologi, XXII, 83–97.

Skutnabb-Kangas, Tove (1972b). Forskning, ideer och debatt om tvåspråkighet och barnens skolspråk (Research, ideas and debate on bilingualism and children's medium of education). In Loman, Bengt (utg.). **Språk och samhälle 1,** Språksociologiska problem. Gleerups: Lund, 135–152.

Skutnabb-Kangas, Tove (1972c). Nuorisoasteen kieltenopiskelun uudistuksesta ja sen edellytyksistä (On language learning reform for secondary schools and its prerequisites). In Aukia, Pekka (toim.). **Nuorisoaste valinkauhassa.** Otava: Helsinki, 111–118.

Skutnabb-Kangas, Tove (1972d). Kommunikationssvårigheter mellan forskare och lärare (Communication difficulties between researchers and teachers). In Lindgren, Birgitta, Loman Bengt & Marell, Anders (red.). **Språkforskning i relation till språkundervisning.** Stockholm: Nordiska Sommaruniversitetet, 250–256.

Skutnabb-Kangas, Tove (1972e). Hur tvåspråkighet tidigt lärs in (How bilingualism is learnt early). **Hufvudstadsbladet** 24.03.1972.

Skutnabb-Kangas, Tove (1975). **Om tvåspråkighet och skolframgång** (On bilingualism and school achievement). Forskningsrapport nr 20. Åbo: Svenska Litteratursällskapet i Finland, Nämnd för samhällsforskning.

Skutnabb-Kangas, Tove (1981). **Tvåspråkighet** (Bilingualism). Lund: Liber Läromedel [revised version in English: TSK 1984a].

Skutnabb-Kangas, Tove (1984a). **Bilingualism or Not—the education of minorities.** Clevedon, UK: Multilingual Matters.

Skutnabb-Kangas, Tove (1984b). Children of Guest Workers and Immigrants: Linguistic and Educational Issues. In J. Edwards (ed.), 17–48.

Skutnabb-Kangas, Tove (1986) (under medverkan av Ilka Kangas och Kea Kangas). **Minoritet, språk och rasism** (Minority, Language and Racism, with assistance from Ilka Kangas and Kea Kangas). Malmö: Liber.

Skutnabb-Kangas, Tove (1987). **Are the Finns in Sweden an Ethnic Minority—Finnish Parents Talk about Finland and Sweden.** Research project The Education of the Finnish Minority. Working Paper Nr 1. Roskilde: Roskilde University Centre.

Skutnabb-Kangas, Tove (1988a). Multilingualism and the Education of Minority Children. In Skutnabb-Kangas & Cummins (eds), 9–44.

Skutnabb-Kangas, Tove (1988b). Resource power and autonomy through discourse in conflict—a Finnish migrant school strike in Sweden. In Zavala, Iris M., Diaz-Diocaretz, Myriam & van Dijk, Teun (eds). **Approaches to discourse, poetics and psychiatry.** Critical theory 4. Amsterdam & Philadelphia: John Benjamins, 25–38. [also in Skutnabb-Kangas & Cummins (eds), 251–277].

Skutnabb-Kangas, Tove (1989). Har ursprungsbefolkningar rätten till språk och kultur? (Do indigenous peoples have the right to language and culture?). **Mennesker og Rettigheter, Nordic Journal on Human Rights** 1, 53–57.

Skutnabb-Kangas, Tove (1990a). **Language, literacy and minorities**. London: Minority Rights Group.

Skutnabb-Kangas, Tove (1990b). Wer entscheidet, ob meine Sprache wichtig für mich ist? Minderheitenforschung zwischen Sozialtechnologie und Selbstbestimmung. In Dittrich, Eckhard J. & Radtke, Frank-Olaf (Hrsg.) **Ethnizität. Wissenschaft und Minderheiten**. Wiesbaden: Westdeutscher Verlag, 329–351.

Skutnabb-Kangas, Tove (1991a). Swedish strategies to prevent integration and national ethnic minorities. In García (ed.), 25–40.

Skutnabb-Kangas, Tove (1991b). Legitimating or delegitimating new forms of racism—the role of researchers. In Gorter et al. (eds), 77–100.

Skutnabb-Kangas, Tove (1991c). Vem kostar? (Who causes the costs?). In Gaup, Johanne (ed.). **Tospråklighet i samiske kommuner i Indre-Finnmark**. Guovdageaidnu: Sámi Instituhtta, 92–100.

Skutnabb-Kangas, Tove (1991d). Bicultural Competence and Strategies for Negotiating Ethnic Identity. In Phillipson et al. (eds), 307–332.

Skutnabb-Kangas, Tove (1993). Identitet og strategier i flersprogede familier. Interviewer (Identity and strategies in multilingual families. Interviews). In Skutnabb-Kangas, Tove, Holmen, Anne & Phillipson, Robert (eds). **Uddannelse af minoriteter** (Education of minorities). Københavnerstudier i tosprogethed 18. København: Center for multikulturelle studier, Danmarks Lærerhøjskole, 190–199.

Skutnabb-Kangas, Tove (1994a). Sverigefinnar förhandlar om etnisk identitet. (The Sweden Finns negotiate about ethnic identity). In Peura & Skutnabb-Kangas (eds), 98–128.

Skutnabb-Kangas, Tove (1994b). Linguistic human rights in education. In **Valodas politika Baltijas Valsīs/Language Policy in the Baltic States**. Rīga: Krājumu sagatavojis, Latvijas Republikas Valsts valodas centrs, 173–191.

Skutnabb-Kangas, Tove (1995a). Introduction. In Skutnabb-Kangas (ed.), 7–20.

Skutnabb-Kangas, Tove (1995b). Book review of Bilingualism in a Multilingual Society: Psycho-social and Pedagogical Implications, Ajit K. Mohanty. **TESOL Quarterly** 29:4, Winter 1995, 775–780.

Skutnabb-Kangas, Tove (1995c). Language, Racism and Linguistic Human Rights. Paper to the Global Cultural Diversity Conference, Sydney [see Boutros-Ghali].

Skutnabb-Kangas, Tove (1996a). The colonial legacy in educational language planning in Scandinavia—from migrant labour to a national ethnic minority? In Dua (ed.), 81–106.

Skutnabb-Kangas, Tove (1996b). Educational language choice—multilingual diversity or monolingual reductionism? In Hellinger, Marlis, & Ammon, Ulrich (eds), **Contrastive sociolinguistics**. Berlin/New York: Mouton de Gruyter, 175–204.

Skutnabb-Kangas, Tove (1996c). Promotion of linguistic tolerance and development. In Léger (ed.), 579–629.

Skutnabb-Kangas, Tove (1997a). Bilingual Education for Finnish Minority Students in Sweden. In Cummins & Corson (eds), 217–227.

Skutnabb-Kangas, Tove (1997b). Language Rights as Conflict Prevention. In Wölck, Wolfgang & de Houwer, Annick (eds). **Recent Studies in Contact Linguistics**. Plurilingua Series XVIII. Bonn: Dümmler, 312–324.

Skutnabb-Kangas, Tove (1998a). Human rights and language wrongs— a future for diversity. In Benson et al. (eds), 5–27.

Skutnabb-Kangas, Tove (1998b). Communication and Power—A Rational Perspective. In Fettes, Mark & Bolduc, Susanne (eds). **Al lingva demokratio/ Towards Linguistic Democracy/ Vers la démocratie linguistique**. Proceedings of the Nitobe Symposium of International Organizations, Prague, 20–23 July 1996. Rotterdam: Universala Esperanto-Asocio, 143–149.

Skutnabb-Kangas, Tove (1998c). Human rights and language policy in education. In Wodak & Corson (eds), 55–65.

Skutnabb-Kangas, Tove (1999a). Language attrition, language death, language murder—different facts or different ideologies? In Christidis, A. F. (ed.). **Proceedings of the Conference: 'Strong' and 'Weak' Languages in the EU: Aspects of Linguistic Hegemonism.** Thessaloniki: Centre for the Greek Language, Aristotle University of Thessaloniki, 59–73.

Skutnabb-Kangas, Tove (1999b). Linguistic diversity, human rights and the 'free' market. In Kontra et al. (eds), 187–222.

Skutnabb-Kangas, Tove (1999c). The Globalisation of Language Rights. In Brock-Utne & Garbo (eds), 168–198.

Skutnabb-Kangas, Tove (in press). Review of Reagan, Timothy (1996). **Non-Western Educational Traditions: Alternative approaches to educational thought and practice.**

Skutnabb-Kangas, Tove & Bucak, Sertaç (1994). Killing a mother tongue—how the Kurds are deprived of linguistic human rights. In Skutnabb-Kangas & Phillipson (eds), 347–370.

Skutnabb-Kangas, Tove & Cummins, Jim (1988). Concluding remarks: Language for empowerment. In Skutnabb-Kangas & Cummins (eds), 390–394.

Skutnabb-Kangas, Tove & García, Ofelia (1995). Multilingualism for All—General Principles? In Skutnabb-Kangas (ed.), 221–256.

Skutnabb-Kangas, Tove & Peura, Markku (1994). Den sverigefinska minoriteten i världen (The Sweden Finnish minority from a global point of view). In Peura & Skutnabb-Kangas (eds), 154–170.

Skutnabb-Kangas, Tove & Phillipson, Robert (1985). **Educational strategies in multilingual contexts.** ROLIG-papir 35. Roskilde: Roskilde University Centre. [also on ERIC microfiche, ED 345 566].

Skutnabb-Kangas, Tove & Phillipson, Robert (1986a). The legitimacy of the arguments for the spread of English. In Phillipson & Skutnabb-Kangas 1986a, 378–415.

Skutnabb-Kangas, Tove & Phillipson, Robert (1986b). Denial of linguistic rights: the new mental slavery. In Phillipson & Skutnabb-Kangas 1986a, 416–465.

Skutnabb-Kangas, Tove & Phillipson, Robert (1987). Cultilinguistic imperialism—what can Scandinavia learn from the Second and Third Worlds. In Wande, Erling, Anward, Jan, Nordberg, Bengt, Steensland, Lars & Thelander, Mats (eds). **Aspects of Multilingualism, Proceedings from the Fourth Nordic Symposium on Bilingualism (1984).** Uppsala: Acta Universitatis Upsaliensis, Studia Multietnica Upsaliensia 2, 167–190.

Skutnabb-Kangas, Tove & Phillipson, Robert (1989a). **Wanted! Linguistic human rights.** ROLIG-papir 44. Roskilde: Roskilde University Centre.

Skutnabb-Kangas, Tove & Phillipson, Robert (1989b). 'Mother tongue': the theoretical and sociopolitical construction of a concept. In Ammon (ed.), 450–477.

Skutnabb-Kangas, Tove & Phillipson, Robert (1994a). Linguistic human rights, past and present. In Skutnabb-Kangas & Phillipson (eds), 71–110.

Skutnabb-Kangas, Tove & Phillipson, Robert (1994b). Linguicide. In **The Encyclopedia of Language and Linguistics.** Pergamon Press & Aberdeen University Press, 2211–2212.

Skutnabb-Kangas, Tove & Phillipson, Robert (1996a). Minority workers or minority human beings? A European dilemma. In Labrie & Churchill (eds), 291–307.

Skutnabb-Kangas, Tove & Phillipson, Robert (1996b). Linguicide and Linguicism. In Goebl et al. (eds), 667–675.

Skutnabb-Kangas, Tove & Phillipson, Robert (1997). Linguistic Human Rights and Development. In Hamelink (ed.), 56–69.

Skutnabb-Kangas, Tove & Phillipson, Robert (1998). Linguistic human rights. In Hamelink (ed.), 27–46.

Skutnabb-Kangas, Tove & Toukomaa, Pertti (1976). **Teaching migrant children's mother tongue and learning the language of the host country in the context of the sociocultural situation of** the migrant family, **Report written for Unesco**. Research Reports 15. Tampere: Dept of Sociology and Social Psychology, University of Tampere.

Skutnabb-Kangas, Tove (ed.) (1995). **Multilingualism for All**. Series European Studies on Multilingualism 4. Lisse: Swets & Zeitlinger.

Skutnabb-Kangas, Tove & Cummins, Jim (eds) (1988). **Minority education. From shame to struggle**. Clevedon, UK: Multilingual Matters.

Skutnabb-Kangas, Tove & Phillipson, Robert (eds, in collaboration with Mart Rannut) (1994). **Linguistic Human Rights. Overcoming Linguistic Discrimination**. Contributions to the Sociology of Language, 67. Berlin/New York: Mouton de Gruyter.

Slabbert, Sarah (1994). A re-evaluation of the sociology of Tsotsitaal. **South African journal of linguistics/Suid Afrikaanse Tydskrif vir taalkunde** 12:1, 31–41.

Smalley, William A. (1994). **Linguistic Diversity and National Unity**. Chicago/London: Chicago University Press.

Smith, Anthony D. (1983). **Theories of Nationalism**. 2nd edition. London: Duckworth.

Smith, Anthony D. (1991). **National identity**. London: Penguin.

Smith, Eric A. (in press). On the coevolution of cultural, linguistic, and biological diversity. In Maffi, Luisa (ed.).

Smith, Linda (1993). From Maori Education—A Reassertion. In Ihimaera, Witi (ed.). **Te Ao Mārama—Regaining Aotearoa: Māori Writers Speak Out**. Vol. 2. **He Whakaatanga o Te Ao—The Reality**. Auckland: Reed Books, 218–222.

Smolicz, J. J. (1979). **Culture and Education in a Plural Society**. Canberra: Curriculum Development Centre.

Smolicz, Jerzy J. (1981). Core Values and Cultural Identity. **Ethnic and Racial Studies** 4:1, 75–90.

Smolicz, Jerzy J. (1984). Multiculturalism and an Over-Arching Framework of Values: Some Educational Responses for Ethnically Plural Societies. **European Journal of Education** 19:2, 22–24. Reprinted in Poole M. E., de Lacey, P. R. & Randhawa, B. S. (eds) (1985). **Australia in Transition: Culture and Life Possiblities**. Sydney/London: Harcourt & Brace Jovanovich, 76–90.

Smolicz, Jerzy J. (1985). Greek Australians: A Question of Survival in Multicultural Australia. **Journal of Multilingual and Multicultural Development** 6:1, 17–29.

Smolicz, Jerzy J. (1986a). National Policy on Languages. **Australian Journal of Education** 30:1, 45–65.

Smolicz, Jerzy J. (1986b). National Language Policy in the Philippines. In Spolsky (ed.), 96–116.

Smolicz, Jerzy J. (1988). **Ethnicity and Multiculturalism in the Australian Catholic Church**. New York: Centre for Migration Studies.

Smolicz, Jerzy J. (1989). **Who is an Australian? Identity, Core Values and Resilience of Culture**. Adelaide: Multicultural Education Coordinating Committee.

Smolicz, Jerzy J. (1990). Language and economy in their Cultural Envelope. **VOX** (The Journal of the Australian Advisory Council on Languages and Multicultural Education) 4, 65–79.

Smolicz, Jerzy J. (1994). Australia's language policies and minority rights: a core value perspective. In Skutnabb-Kangas & Phillipson (eds), 235–252.

Smolicz, Jerzy J. & Secombe, Margaret J. (1986). Italian Language and Culture in Australia. In Bettoni, C. (ed.). **Italians Abroad—Altro-Polo**. Sydney: University of Sydney, 27–60.

Smolicz, Jerzy J. & Secombe, Margaret J. (1989). Types of Language Activation and Evaluation in an Ethnically Plural Society. In Ammon (ed.), 478–514.

Smolicz, Jerzy J., Lee, Lilian, Murugaian, Malathi & Secombe, Margaret J. (1990). Language as a Core Value of Culture among Tertiary Students of Chinese and Indian Origin in Australia. **Journal of Asian Pacific Communication** 1:1, 229–246.

Sokal, Alan & Bricmont, Jean (1997). **Impostures intellectuelles**. Paris: Editions Odile Jacob. [Also in English: Sokal & Bricmont (1997). **Fashionable nonsense: Postmodern intellectuals' abuse of science**. New York: Picador].

Solomos, John (1989). **Race and Racism in Contemporary Britain**. London: Macmillan.

Soros, George (1997). The Capitalist Threat. **The Atlantic Monthly** February 1997, Vol. 279:2, 45–58.

Soros, George (1998). Toward a Global Open Society. **The Atlantic Monthly** January 1998, Vol. 281:1, 20–32.

SOU 1974:69 (1974). **Invandrarutredningen. Invandrarna och minoriteterna** (Immigration report. The immigrants and the minorities). Stockholm: Statens offentliga utredningar.

SOU: 1983:57 (1983). **Olika ursprung—gemenskap i Sverige** (Different origins—togetherness in Sweden). Stockholm: Statens offentliga utredningar.

SOU 1989:13 (1989). **Mångfald mot enfald. Slutrapport från kommissionen mot rasism och främlingsfientlighet.** Del I. (Diversity against homogeneity/stupidity. Final report from the commission against racism and xenophobia. Part I). Stockholm: Statens offentliga utredningar.

South Africa's New Language Policy. The Facts (1994), published by the Department of National Education, Pretoria [ISBN 0-7970-2971-0, no date].

South Africa Survey 1996/97. By Sidiropoulos, Elisabeth, Jeffery, Anthea, Mackay, Shaun, Forgey, Herma, Chipps, Cheryl & Corrigan, Terence (1997). Johannesburg: South African Institute of Race Relations.

South Commission (1990). **The Challenge to the South.** Oxford: Oxford University Press.

Spender, Dale (1980). **Man Made Language.** London: Routledge & Kegan Paul.

Spender, Dale (1982). **Invisible Women. The Schooling Scandal.** London: Writers and Readers Publishing Cooperative Society.

Spolsky, Bernard (ed.) (1986). **Language and education in multilingual settings.** Clevedon, UK: Multilingual Matters.

Spring, Joel (1998). **Education and the rise of the global economy.** Mahwah, N.J.: Lawrence Erlbaum Associates.

Sridhar, Kamal K. (1989). **English in Indian Bilingualism.** Delhi: Manohar.

Sridhar, Kamal K. (1996). Language in Education: Minorities and Multilingualism in India. **International Review of Education** 42:4, 327–347.

Sridhar, Kamal K. & Sridhar, S. N. (1986). Bridging the paradigm gap: second language acquisition theory and indigenized varieties of English. **World Englishes** 5:1, 3–14.

Sridhar, S. N. & Sridhar, Kamal K. (1994). Indigenized Englishes as second languages: toward a functional theory of second language in multilingual contexts. In Agnihotri, R. K. & Khanna, A. L. (eds). **Second Language Acquisition: sociocultural and linguistic aspects of English in India.** London: Sage, 41–63.

Stairs, Arlene (1988). Beyond cultural inclusion: An Inuit example of indigenous educational development. In Skutnabb-Kangas & Cummins (eds), 308–327.

State of the World 1998. A Worldwatch Institute Report on Progress Toward a Sustainable Society (1998). New York/London: W. W. Norton & Company.

Stavenhagen, Rodolfo (1987). Human Rights and Peoples' Rights—The Question of Minorities. **Nordic Journal on Human Rights** 5:3, 16–26.

Stavenhagen, Rodolfo (1990). **The Ethnic Question. Conflicts, Development, and Human Rights.** Tokyo: United Nations University Press.

Stavenhagen, Rodolfo (1995). Cultural rights and universal human rights. In Eide et al. (eds), 63–77.

Stobart, Maitland (1997). The Importance of Minority Education Rights in the New Europe. **International Journal on Minority and Group Rights. Special Issue on the Education Rights of National Minorities** 4:2, 1996/1997, 156–162.

Stokoe, William (1974). Classification and Description of Sign Languages. In Sebeok, Thomas A. (ed.). **Current trends in Linguistics,** Vol. 12. Mouton: The Hague, 345–371.

Stordahl, Vigdis (1997). Sami Generations. In Gaski (ed.), 143–154.

Street, Brian (1994). What is meant by local literacies? **Language and Education** 8:1–2, 9–17.

Street, Brian (ed.) (1993). **Cross-cultural approaches to literacy**. Cambridge: Cambridge University Press.

Study of Languages. A report. (1986). Prepared by Working Group on the Study of Languages. New Delhi: National Council of Educational Research and Training.

Suppan, Arnold & Heubergerová, Valeria (1992). States and Minorities in the Danube Region (1945–1990). In Plichtová (ed.), 61–72.

Suter, Keith D. & Stearman, Kaye (1988). **Aboriginal Australians**. London: The Minority Rights Group.

Svenska Finlands Folkting (1991). **Vad säger lagarna om språkliga rättigheter** (What do the laws say about linguistic rights). Finlandssvensk Rapport nr 16. Helsingfors: Svenska Finlands Folkting.

Svenska språknämnden (1998). **Förslag till handlingsprogram för att främja svenska språket**. (Swedish language board. Proposal for a programme of action for the promotion of the Swedish language). Stockholm: Svenska språknämnden. [can be downloaded from <http://193.14.172.34/ssn/default.html>].

Svonni, Mikael (1996). Skolor och språkundervisning för en inhemsk minoritet—samerna (Schools and language teaching for a domestic minority—the Sámi). In Hyltenstam (ed.), 148–186.

Swain, Merrill (1972). **Bilingualism as a First Language**. Ph.D. Thesis, University of California at Irvine.

Swain, Merrill (1984). A review of immersion education in Canada: Research and evaluation studies. In CDE (1984), 87–112.

Swain, Merrill (1997). French Immersion Programs in Canada. In Cummins & Corson (eds), 261–270.

Swain, Merrill & Lapkin, Sharon (1982). **Evaluating Bilingual Education: a Canadian case study**. Clevedon, UK: Multilingual Matters.

Swain, Merrill & Lapkin, Sharon (1986). Immersion French in secondary schools: "The goods" and "the bads". **Contact** 5:3, 2–9.

Swain, Merrill & Lapkin, Sharon (1991). Heritage language children in an English-French bilingual program. **Canadian Modern Language Review** 47:4, 635–641.

Swain, Merrill, Lapkin, Sharon, Rowen, Norman & Hart, Doug (1990). The Role of Mother Tongue Literacy in Third Language Learning. **VOX** (The Journal of the Australian Advisory Council on Languages and Multicultural Education) 4, 111–121.

Swales, John M. (1997). English as 'Tyrannosaurus rex'. **World Englishes** 16:3, November 1997, 373–382.

Symonides et al. 1998—see UNESCO 1998.

Szalai, Andrea (1999). Linguistic human rights problems of the Romani and Boyash speakers in Hungary. In Kontra et al. (eds), 297–316.

Szász, Elizabeth (1996). British "au pair" in Hungarian culture. In Tóth & Földeák (eds), 187–190.

Szépe, György (1997). Some Remarks on the Education Rights of National Minorities. **International Journal on Minority and Group Rights. Special Issue on the Education Rights of National Minorities** 4:2, 1996/1997, 105–113.

Tabak, Hikmet (1998). Welcome to the first issue. **Med-Tv stêrka med 1**. July 1998, 1.

Tagore, Rabindranath (1992). **My Reminiscences**. New Delhi: Rupa & Co.. [1917].

Tajfel, Henri (1978a). Social categorization, social identity and social comparison. In Tajfel (ed.).

Tajfel, Henri (1978b). **The Social Psychology of Minorities**. Report 38. London: Minority Rights Group.

Tajfel, Henri (ed.) (1978). **Differentiation Between Social Groups: studies in the social psychology of intergroup relations**. London: Academic Press.

Takač, Mirko (1974). **Tvåspråkighet hos invandrarelever. Del 1. Emotionella och sociala effekter. Pedagogiska angreppssätt** (Immigrant students' bilingualism. Part 1. Emotional and social effects. Educational measures). Göteborgs skolförvaltning: Skolpsykologbyrån.

Takala, Tuomas (1989). **Kehitysmaiden koulutusongelmia** (Educational problems in developing countries). Helsinki: Gaudeamus.

Tankha, Brij (ed.) (1996). **Communication and Democracy: Ensuring Plurality.** Montreal: Videazimut.

Taylor, Shelley K. (1993). Trilingualism by design? Contextual factors in the educational experience of Mi'kmaq pupils in French Immersion. Invited Paper presented at **Lancaster University Conference on Bilingual Classroom Discourse, July 1993.** Lancaster: Lancaster University, Centre for Language in Social Life, manuscript.

Te Whakamatau a te Kawana i te Kohanga Reo/ Government review of te Kohanga Reo (1988). Wellington: Government Review Team.

The Hague Recommendations Regarding the Education Rights of National Minorities & Explanatory Note; for the use of the OSCE High Commissioner on National Minorities, Max van der Stoel. October 1996. The Hague: Foundation on Inter-Ethnic Relations.

The Holy Bible—see Bible.

The International Association for Human Rights in Kurdistan—see also Internationaler Verein für Menschenrechte der Kurden, and Bucak, Sertaç.

The Qur'ān—see Dawood. See also Aro et al.

The Random House Dictionary of the English Language (1987). 2nd edition, Unabridged. New York: Random House.

The Shorter Oxford English Dictionary—see Oxford.

Therborn, Göran (1995). **European Modernity and Beyond. The Trajectory of European Societies 1945–2000.** London: Sage.

Thieberger, Nicholas (1990). Language maintenance: why bother? **Multilingua** 9:4, 333–358.

Thompson, John B. (1992). Editor's Introduction. In Bourdieu (1992), 1–34.

Thornberry, Patrick (1987). **Minorities and Human Rights Law.** The Minority Rights Group Report No. 73. London: The Minority Rights Group.

Thornberry, Patrick (1991). **International Law and the Rights of Minorities.** Oxford: Clarendon Press.

Thornberry, Patrick (1995). The UN Declaration on the Rights of Persons Belonging to National or Ethnic, Religious and Linguistic Minorities: Background, Analysis and an Update. In Rosas, Allan & Phillips, Alan (eds). **Universal Minority Rights.** Åbo: Åbo Akademi University Institute & London: The Minority Rights Group, 13–76.

Thornberry, Patrick (1997). Minority Rights. In Academy of European Law (ed.). **Collected Courses of the Academy of European Law.** Vol. VI, Book 2. The Netherlands: Kluwer Law International, 307–390.

Thornberry, Patrick & Gibbons, Dianna (1997). Education and Minority Rights: A Short Survey of International Standards. **International Journal on Minority and Group Rights. Special Issue on the Education Rights of National Minorities** 4:2, 1996/1997, 115–152.

Thorne, Barrie & Henley, Nancy (eds) (1975). **Language and Sex: Difference and Dominance.** Rowley, Mass.: Newbury House.

Thorne, Barrie, Kramarae, Cheris & Henley, Nancy (eds) (1983). **Language, Gender and Society.** Rowley, Mass.: Newbury House.

Tickoo, Makhan L. (1994). Kashmiri, a majority-minority language: an exploratory essay. In Skutnabb-Kangas & Phillipson (eds), 317–333.

Tickoo, Makhan L. (ed.) (1991). **Language and Standards: Issues, attitudes, case studies.** Singapore: SEAMEO Regional Language Centre.

Tilly, C. (ed.) (1975). **The Formation of National States in Western Europe.** Princeton, N.J.: Princeton University Press.

Ting-Toomey, Stella (1988). Intercultural conflict styles: a face-negotiation theory. In Kim, Young Yun & Gudykunst, William B. (eds). **Theories in intercultural communication.** Newbury Park, CA: Sage.

Tišljar, Zlatko (hrsg.) (1995). **Internationale Familie—Utopie oder Realität? Akten des internationalen Symposiums, Graz 1994.** Maribo: Inter-Kulturo. [ISBN 961-9075-08-X].

Togeby, Lise (1997). **Fremmedhed og fremmedhad i Danmark—teorier til forklaring af etnocentrisme** (Alienness and xenophobia in Denmark—theories for explaining ethnocentricity). Copenhagen: Columbus.

Tollefson, James W. (1991). **Planning language, planning inequality.** Harlow: Longman.

Tollefson, James W. (1993). Language policy and power: Yugoslavia, the Philippines, and Southeast Asian refugees in the United States. **International Journal of the Sociology of Language** 103, 73–95.

Tollefson, James W. (ed.) (1995). **Power and Inequality in Language Education.** Cambridge: Cambridge University Press.

Tolstoy, L. N. (1984). **Anna Karenin** (translated and with an introduction by Rosemary Edmonds). Penguin: Harmondsworth, Middlesex.

Tomlinson, John (1991). **Cultural Imperialism.** Baltimore: John Hopkins University Press.

Tomaševski, Katarina (1993a). Aid to Eastern Europe. In Andreassen, Bård-Anders & Swinehart, Theresa (eds). **Human Rights in Developing Countries.** Copenhagen, Lund, Oslo & Åbo/Turku: Nordic Human Rights Publications, 21–50.

Tomaševski, Katarina (1993b). **Development Aid and Human Rights Revisited,** London: Pinter.

Tomaševski, Katarina (1995a). Health Rights. In Eide et al. (eds), 125–142.

Tomaševski, Katarina (1995b). Environmental Rights. In Eide et al. (eds), 257–269.

Tomaševski, Katarina (1996). International prospects for the future of the welfare state. In **Reconceptualizing the welfare state.** Copenhagen: The Danish Centre for Human Rights, 100–117.

Tomaševski, Katarina (1997a). **Between sanctions and elections. Aid donors and their human rights performance.** London: Pinter.

Tomaševski, Katarina (1997b). Development Aid and Human Rights. Keynote lecture presented at the conference 'Development and Rights', Roskilde University, 8–10 October 1997.

Tonkin, Humphrey & Fettes, Mark (1996). **Esperanto Studies: An Overview.** Esperanto Document 43A. Rotterdam: Universala Esperanto-Asocio.

Tosi, Arturo (1984). **Immigration and Bilingual Education.** Oxford: Pergamon Press.

Tosi, Arturo (1988). The jewel in the crown of the modern prince. The new approach to bilingualism in multicultural education in England. In Skutnabb-Kangas & Cummins (eds), 79–103.

Tosi, Arturo (1989). **Feasibility Study No. 1: Bilingualism in the IB.** London: International Baccalaureate and Institute of Education, University of London. Unpublished report.

Tóth, Éva (ed.) (1987). **Today. An Anthology of Contemporary Hungarian Literature.** Budapest: Corvina.

Tóth, Éva & Földeák, Iván (eds) (1996). **Odi et Amo. Writers on the love and hate of foreign nations and cultures.** Budapest: Hungarian P.E.N. Club.

Toukomaa, Pertti (1973). **Korutonta kertomaa. Suomalaisperheet ruotsalaisessa teollisuusyhteiskunnassa** (Straight talk. Finnish families in the Swedish industrial society). Tampere: Tampereen yliopiston sosiologian ja sosiaalipsykologian laitoksen tutkimuksia 1.

Toukomaa, Pertti & Skutnabb-Kangas, Tove (1977). **The intensive teaching of the mother tongue to migrant children of pre-school age, Report written for Unesco.** Research Reports 26. Tampere: Dept of Sociology and Social Psychology, University of Tampere.

Traill, Anthony (1995). The Khoesan languages of South Africa. In Mesthrie (ed.), 1–18.

Trankell, Arne (1974). Svenskars fördomar mot invandrare (Swedish prejudices against immigrants). Invandrarutredningens huvudbetänkande, bilaga 4. In SOU 1974:70, 121–212.

Treffgarne, Carew (1986). Language Policy in Francophone Africa: Scapegoat or Panacea? In Centre of African studies, 141–170.

Trevelyan, George Otto (1881). **The Life and Letters of Lord Macaulay**, by his nephew George Otto Trevelyan, MP. New edition. London: Longmans, Green, and Co.

Trim, John (ed.) (1992). **Language learning and teaching methodology for citizenship in a multicultural Europe**. Strasbourg: Council of Europe.

Tripathi, P. H. (1990). English in Zambia: The nature and prospects of one of Africa's 'new Englishes'. **English Today** 6:3, 34–38.

Trudgill, Peter (1983). **Sociolinguistics: An Introduction to Language and Society**. Harmondsworth: Penguin.

Tsuchida, Shigeru (1995). Concluding remarks at the International Symposium on Endangered Languages, November 18–20, 1995, University of Tokyo. [can be downloaded from <http://www.tooyoo.l.u-Tokyo.ac.jp/linguistics/newsletters/newslet1.html>].

Tsuda, Yukio (1986). **Language, inequality and distortion in intercultural communication. A critical theory approach**. Amsterdam/Philadelphia: John Benjamins.

Tsuda, Yukio (1988). **Language, education and intercultural communication**. Policy Research Project on Internationalization of Japanese Economy. Faculty of Economics, Nagasaki University.

Tsuda, Yukio (1992). The dominance of English and linguistic discrimination. **Media Development** 1, 32–34.

Tsuda, Yukio (1994). The Diffusion of English: Its Impact on Culture and Communication. **Keio Communication Review** 16, 49–61.

Tsuda, Yukio (1998). The Japanese and the English Language. An Interdisciplinary Study of Anglicized (Americanized.) Japan. **Japan Review** 10: 219–236.

Tucker, Richard G., Otanes, Fe T. & Sibanes, B. P. (1970). An Alternate Days Approach to Bilingual Education. In Alatis, James A. (ed.). **Bilingualism and Language Contact: Anthropological, Linguistic, Psychological, and Sociological Aspects**. Report of the Twenty-first Annual Round Table Meeting on Linguistics and Language Studies. Washington, D.C.: Georgetown University Press, 281–300.

Tully, Mark (1997). English: an advantage to India? **ELT Journal** 51:1, 157–164.

Turi, Joseph (1994). Typology of language legislation. In Skutnabb-Kangas & Phillipson (eds), 111–119.

Tuxill, John & Bright, Chris (1998). Losing strands in the web of life. In **State of the World** 1998, 41–58.

Twahirva, André (1994). **Politiques et pratiques linguistiques en Afrique: Rapport d'un travail réalisé pour l'UNESCO**. Paris: UNESCO, Division of Arts and Cultural Life.

Törnudd, Klaus (1978). **Svenska språkets ställning i Finland** (The position of the Swedish language in Finland). Helsingfors: Holger Schildts Förlag.

Ucko, P. J. (1983). The Politics of the Indigenous Minority. **Journal of Biosociological Sciences**. Supplement 8, 25–40.

UNESCO (1953). **The use of the vernacular languages in education**, Monographs on fundamental education VIII. Paris: Unesco.

UNESCO (1971). **Scientists abroad. A study of the international movement of persons in science and technology**. Paris: Unesco.

UNESCO (1980). **Wastage in primary and secondary education: a statistical study of trends and patterns in repetition and drop-out**. Paris: Unesco, Office of Statistics.

UNESCO (1983). **Trends and projections of enrollment by level of education and by age 1960–2000**. Paris: Unesco, Office of Statistics.

UNESCO (1992). **Workshop on Human Rights and Languages**. Pécs (Hungary), 15–16 August 1991, Final Report, July 1992 (Rapporteur: Tove Skutnabb-Kangas). Paris: Unesco.

UNESCO 1998 (1998). **Human Rights. Major International Instruments. Status as at 31 May 1998.** Prepared by Symonides, Janusz & Volodin, Vladimir. Paris: Unesco, Division of Human Rights, Democracy and Peace.

UNESCO Regional Office for Education in Africa (1985). **African community languages and their use in literacy and education. A regional survey.** Dakar.

UNESCO Statistical Yearbook 1997 (1997). Paris: Unesco Publishing & Bernan Press.

UNESCO Statistical Yearbook 1998 (1998). Paris: Unesco Publishing & Bernan Press.

UNIN (United Nations Institute for Namibia) (1981). **Toward a language policy for Namibia. English as the official language: perspectives and strategies.** Lusaka: UNIN.

Universal Declaration of Linguistic Rights (1998). Barcelona: Follow-up Committee for UDLR. [Not for sale. See Address Box 7.3.].

Utsi, Paulus (1996). As long as we have waters. In Gaski (ed.), 109–117.

Vaba, Lembit & Viikberg, Jüri (1997). **The Endangered Uralic Peoples. Short Reference Guide.** Compiled by Vaba, Lembit & Viikberg, Jüri; edited by Anders Heinapuu. [can be downloaded from <http://www.suri.ee>].

Vali, Abbas (1996). **Kurdish nationalism: identity, sovereignty and the dialectics of violence in Kurdistan.** London: Tauris.

van Bruinessen, Martin M. (1978). **Agha, shaikh and state. On the social and political organization of Kurdistan,** Utrecht: University of Utrecht. [also published 1992 by Zed Books, London].

van der Stoel, Max (1997). Introduction to the Seminar. **International Journal on Minority and Group Rights. Special Issue on the Education Rights of National Minorities** 4:2, 1996/1997, 153–155.

van Ermen, Raymond (1998). Tyranni antager mange former (Tyranny takes many forms). **Information** 31.8.1998, 8.

Van Dyke, V. (1974). Human rights and the rights of groups. **American Journal of Political Science** 18, November 1974, 225–241.

Van Dyke, V. (1976). Human rights without distinction to language. **International Studies Quarterly** 20:1, 3–27.

Van Dyke, V. (1977). The individual, the state, and ethnic communities in political theory. **World Politics** 29:3, April 1977, 343–369.

Vildomec, Veroboj (1963). **Multilingualism.** Leyden: A. W. Sythoff.

Vilfan, Sergij (ed.) (1990). **Ethnic Groups and Language Rights. Comparative Studies on Governments and Non-Dominant Ethnic Groups in Europe 1850–1940.** New York: European Science Foundation & New York University Press.

Virta, Erkki (1994). **Tvåspråkighet, tänkande och identitet. Studier av finska barn i Sverige och Finland** (Bilingualism, cognition and identity. Studies on Finnish children in Sweden and Finland). Stockholm: Psykologiska institutionen, Stockholms universitet.

Voegelin, C. F. & Voegelin, F. M. (1977). **Classification and index of the world's languages.** New York: Elsevier.

Volz, Walter (1994). Englisch als einzige Arbeitssprache der Institutionen der Europäischen Gemeinschaft? Vorzüge und Nachteile aus der Sicht eines Insiders. In Ammon et al. (eds), 88–100.

Vorih, Lillian & Rosier, Paul (1978). Rock Point Community School: An Example of a Navajo-English Bilingual Elementary School Program. **TESOL Quarterly** 12:3, 263–269.

Voronova, Oktyabrina (1996). Our Life. In Gaski (ed.), 101–107.

Vuolab, Kerttu (in press). Such a treasure of knowledge for human survival. In Phillipson (ed.).

Vydrine, Valentin (1998). Kagoro: a language transforming into a dialect? **Ogmios.** Newsletter of the Foundation for Endangered Languages 8, Spring/Summer 1998, 3–5.

Wacquant, Loic (1998). From welfare state to prison state. Imprisoning the American poor. **Le Monde Diplomatique,** September 1998, 8–9.

Wahlbeck, Östen (1999). **Kurdish diasporas: a comparative study of Kurdish refugee communities.** New York: St. Martin's Press in association with Centre for Research in Ethnic Relations, University of Warwick, UK.

Walker, Martin (1997). Progressives make their presence felt. **Guardian Weekly,** 19 January 1997, 6.

Wallace, Anthony (1961). Schools in Revolutionary and Conservative Societies. In Gruber, F. C. (ed.). **Anthropology and Education.** Philadelphia: University of Philadelphia Press, 38–39.

Wallerstein, Immanuel (1990a). Culture as the Ideological Battleground of the Modern World System. In Featherstone (ed.), 31–55.

Wallerstein, Immanuel (1990b). Culture is the World-System: A Reply to Boyne. In Featherstone (ed.), 63–66.

Walter, Kerry S. & Gillett, Harriett J. (eds) (1998). **1997 IUCN Red List of Threatened Plants.** Cambridge: World Conservation Monitoring Centre.

Wande, Erling (1984). Two Finnish Minorities in Sweden. **Journal of Multilingual and Multicultural Development** 5, 225–242.

Wande, Erling (1988). Från 1809 till 1988. Svenska Tornedalens språk- och utbildningspolitiska historia. In Svanberg, Ingvar & Tydén, Mattias (red.). **Multiethnic Studies in Uppsala.** Uppsala Multiethnic Papers 13. Uppsala: Centre for Multiethnic Research, Uppsala University, 121–140.

Wande, Erling (1996). Tornedalen. In Horn, Frank (ed.). **Finska språkets ställning i Sverige och svenska språkets ställning i Finland.** Juridica Lapponica 14. Rovaniemi: Rovaniemen Yliopisto.

Wande, Erling & Winsa, Birger (1995). Attitudes and behaviours in the Thorne [sic!] Valley. In Fase et al. (eds), 267–292. [should be 'Torne'].

Wastage in primary education from 1970 to 1980 (1984). **Prospects** XIV:3, 347–367.

Watkins, Kevin (1996). IMF holds a gold key for the Third World. **Guardian Weekly,** June 16, 1996.

WCMC [World Conservation Monitoring Centre] (1992). **Global biodiversity: status of the Earth's living resources.** London: Chapman & Hall.

Webb, Vic (1994). Language policy and planning in South Africa. **Annual Review of Applied Linguistics** 14, 254–273.

Webb, Vic (1996). Language planning and politics in South Africa. **International Journal of the Sociology of Language** 118, 139–162.

Webster, Noah (1789). An essay on the necessity, advantages and practicability of reforming the mode of spelling, and of rendering the ortography of words correspondent to the pronunciation. In **Dissertations on the English language.** Extracts in Graddol et al. (eds) 1996, 91–94.

Wee, Kenneth (1994). **Sonnet for the Poor and the Young** and **Festival.** In Pakir, Anne & Goh, Doreen (eds). **Eye on the World. Making Waves.** Singapore: UniPress, The Centre for the Arts, National University of Singapore, 3–5.

Wei, Li (1998). Language Shift in the Teochew Community in Singapore: A Family Domain Analysis. **Journal of Multilingual and Multicultural Development** 18:5, 364–384.

Weinreich, Uriel (1967). **Languages in contact. Findings and problems.** Fifth printing. The Hague: Mouton & Co. [1953].

Westin, Charles (1984). **Majoritet om minoritet. En studie i etnisk tolerans i 80-talets Sverige** (Majority about minority. A study of ethnic tolerance in the Sweden of the 80s). Stockholm: Liber.

Westin, Charles (1988). **Den toleranta opinionen. Inställningen till invandrare 1987** (The tolerant opinion. The attitude towards immigrants in 1987). DEIFO-rapport 8. Stockholm: DEIFO.

Wheeler, David & Sillanpää, Maria (1997). **The Stakeholder Corporation: a blueprint for maximizing stakeholder value.** London: Pitman.

Whitaker, B. (1985). Prevention and Punishment of the Crime of Genocide. **Studie- en Informatiecentrum Mensenrechten Newsletter** 12, October 1985, 3–33.

Widgren, Jonas (1986a). Interview. 'Widgren ehdottaa itsetutkiskelua: "Vähemmistöasema ei ole ajankohtainen" '. (Widgren suggests self-reflection: "Minority status is not prevalent"). **Ruotsin Suomalainen** 1.1986

Widgren, Jonas (1986b). Interview in Ruotsin Suomalainen 21 August (1986).

Wiley, Terrence G. (1998). The Imposition of World War I Era English-Only Policies and the Fate of German in North America. In Ricento & Burnaby (eds), 211–241.

Willis, Paul (1977). **Learning to Labour.** Westmead: Saxon House.

Wilson, James (1982). **Canada's Indians.** London: The Minority Rights Group.

Wilson, James (1986). **The Original Americans: US Indians.** London: The Minority Rights Group.

Wingstedt, Maria (1996). **Language Ideology and Minority Language Policies: a History of Sweden's Educational Policies towards the Saami, including a Comparison to the Tornedalians.** Rapporter om tvåspråkighet 11. Stockholm: Centrum för tvåspråkighetsforskning, Stockholms universitet.

Wingstedt, Maria (1998). **Language Ideologies and Minority Language Policies in Sweden. Historical and contemporary perspectives.** Dissertations in Bilingualism. Stockholm: Centre for Research on Bilingualism, Stockholm University.

Wink, Joan (1994). I am not a LAP. **TESOL Matters,** February/March.

Wink, Joan (1997). **Critical Pedagogy. Notes from the Real World.** New York: Longman.

Wink, Joan & Wink, Dawn (in press). Rethinking bilingual immersion. In Phillipson (ed.).

Winsa, Birger (1997). Från ett Vi till ett Dem—Torne älv som kulturgräns (From a We to a They—Torne river as a cultural boundary). In Korhonen & Winsa, 5–52.

Winsa, Birger (1999). **Attitudes Form Collective Identity: The effects of linguistic policy and practice in the Swedish Torne Valley.** Canberra: Applied Linguistics Association of Australia.

Winsa, Birger (forthcoming). The socio-economic status of the Tornedalians. In Grin, François & Winsa, Birger (eds). **The Socioeconomics of Bilingualism.**

Witte, Mikael (1998). **Menneskeretskrænkelser i Danmark** (Human rights violations in Denmark). Copenhagen: Husets Forlag.

Wittgenstein, Ludwig [1922] (1960). **Tractatus Logico-Philosophicus.** London: Routledge & Kegan Paul.

Wodak, Ruth & Corson, David (eds) (1998). **Language Policies and Political Issues in Education.** Vol. 1. **Encyclopedia of Language and Education.** Dordrecht/Boston/London: Kluwer Academic Publishers.

Wolf, Fred Alan (1991). **The Eagle's Quest.** New York: Simon & Schuster.

Wong Fillmore, Lily (1991). When Learning a Second Language Means Losing the First. **Early Childhood Research Quarterly** 6, 323–346.

World Bank (1988). **Education in sub-Saharan Africa. Policies for adjustment, revitalisation and expansion.** Washington, D.C.: World Bank (summarized in **Comparative Education Review,** February 1989).

World Bank education sector policy paper (1980). Washington, D.C.: World Bank.

World Guide 1997/1998 (1997). **The World Guide 1997/98: A view from the South.** Oxford: Oxfam Publishers.

WRI [World Resources Institute and International Institute for Environment and Development] (1988). **World resources 1988–89.** New York: Basic Books.

Wurm, Stephen A. (1991). Language Death and Disappearance: Causes and Circumstances. In Robins & Uhlenbeck (eds), 1–18.

Wurm, Stephen A., Mühlhäusler, Peter & Tryon, D. T. (eds) (1996). **Atlas of Languages of Intercultural Communication in the Pacific Hemisphere.** Berlin: de Gruyter.

Wæver, Ole, Buzan, Barry, Kelstrup, Morthen & Lemaitre, Pierre (1993). **Identity, migration and the new security agenda in Europe.** London: Pinter Publishers.

Yoyole, E. A. (1986). **The role of research in curriculum development in anglophone Africa.** Occasional papers 15, Edinburgh: Centre for African Studies, Edinburgh University.

Zubrzycki, Jerzy (1988). Australia as a Multicultural Society. **Siirtolaisuus/Migration** 4, 9–16.
Zubrzycki, Jerzy (1995). The Evolution of the Policy of Multiculturalism in Australia 1968–1995.
Paper to the Global Cultural Diversity Conference, Sydney [see Boutros-Ghali].
Ålund, Aleksandra (1992). Immigrantenkultur als Barriere der Kooperation. In Kalpaka &
Räthzel (Hrsg.), 174–188.

BIBLIOGRAPHY OF ESPERANTO STUDIES AND INTERLINGUISTICS

prepared by Mark Fettes

The following is a selection of materials primarily in English, French, German and Russian.
Researchers should be aware that high quality work exists in various smaller national languages,
and above all in Esperanto. The web site <http://www.esperanto.net/veb/> includes up-to-date
links to on-line catalogues and web pages on interlinguistics.

Periodicals, Series, and Bibliographies

Bibliography of Linguistic Literature (BLL). Frankfurt: Klostermann. (Section: Plansprachen/Artificial languages).
Bibliographie linguistique de l'année . . . et complément des années précédentes. Ed. Comité
International Permanent des Linguistes. Utrecht: Spectrum. (Section: Interlinguistics
[planned languages] - Interlinguistique [langues planifiées]).
Duličenko, Aleksandr (1983). Sovetskaja interlingvistika. Annotirovanaja bibliografija za
1946–1982 gg. Tartu: Tartuskij gosudartstvennyj universitet.
Esperantic Studies. Washington, DC: Esperantic Studies Foundation. ISSN 1084-9831.
Interlinguistics (regular section in **Language Problems & Language Planning**). Amsterdam: John
Benjamins. ISSN 0272-2690.
Interlinguistische Informationen. Berlin: Gesellschaft für Interlinguistik e.V. ISSN 1430-2888.
Informilo por Interlingvistoj. Rotterdam: Centro de Esploro kaj Dokumentado pri la Monda
Lingvo-Problemo. ISSN 1385-2191.
Interlinguistica tartuensis (1982–). Subseries of Acta et commentationes Universitatis Tartuensis
(Tartu, Estonia).
MLA international bibliography of books and articles on the modern languages and literatures,
vol. 3, Linguistics. New York: Modern Languages Association of America. (Section:
Auxiliary languages. International languages).
Stojan, Petr. E. (1973). Bibliografio de Internacia Lingvo. Hildesheim-New York: Olms.
Symoens, Edward F (1989). Dissertations on Esperanto and interlinguistics. Rotterdam:
Universala Esperanto-Asocio. See also the 1993 Supplement.
Tonkin, Humphrey (comp.) (1977). Esperanto and international language problems: a research
bibliography, 4th edn. Washington, DC: Esperantic Studies Foundation.

Monographs on Planned Languages

Blanke, Detlev (1985). **Internationale Plansprachen**. Berlin: Akademie-Verlag. Thorough survey
of attempts to design an international language, with strong emphasis on social aspects.
Couturat, Louis & Leau, Léopold (1979). **Histoire de la langue universelle. Les nouvelles langues
internationales**. Hildesheim-New York: Olms. Classic typological survey from 1902–6.

Duličenko, Aleksandr (1990). **Meždunarodnye vspomogatel'nye jazyki**. Tallinn: Valgus. Ency-
clopedic survey of over 900 projects.
Eco, Umberto (1993). **La ricerca della lingua perfetta**. Roma: Laterza. Includes chapter on
international auxiliary languages.
Haupenthal, Reinhard (Hrsg.) (1976). **Plansprachen. Beiträge zur Interlinguistik**. Darmstadt:
Wiss. Buchgesellschaft. Collection of important articles.
Kuznecov, Sergej Nikolaevič (1987). **Teoretičeskie osnovy interlingvistiki**. Moskva: Universitet
družby narodov. Sociolinguistic foundations.
Large, [J.] Andrew (1985). **The artificial language movement**. Oxford: Blackwell: Popular
exposition covering 17th–20th centuries.
Sakaguchi, Alicja (1998). **Interlinguistik. Gegenstand, Ziele, Aufgaben, Methoden**. Frankfurt/M.
etc.: Peter Lang. Ambitious theoretical work emphasizing semiotic aspects.
Schubert, Klaus (ed.) (1989). **Interlinguistics: aspects of the science of planned languages**. Berlin:
Mouton de Gruyter. Psychological, literary, grammatical, terminological, and engineering
studies.
Serta gratulatoria in honorem Juan Régulo, vol. 2: Esperantismo (1987). La Laguna: Universidad
de la Laguna. Articles in various languages on Esperanto movement, literature, language.
Szerdahelyi, István (ed.) (1980). **Miscellanea interlinguistica**. Budapest: Tankönyvkiadó. Multilingual reader for university courses.
Tonkin, Humphrey (ed.) (1997). **Esperanto, Interlinguistics, and Planned Language**. Lanham
etc.: University Press of America. Articles from Language Problems and Language Planning,
1986–1994.

Interlinguistics and Language Policy

Fettes, Mark (1997). Esperanto and language policy: Exploring the issues: **Language Problems
& Language Planning** 21, 66–77.
Fettes, Mark & Suzanne Bolduc (eds) (1998). **Towards Linguistic Democracy / Vers la démocratie
linguistique / Al lingva demokratio**. Rotterdam: Universal Esperanto Association.
Glossop, Ronald (1988). Language policy and a just world order. **Alternatives**, 13, 395–409.
Humblet, Jean E. (1984). The language problem in international organizations. **International
Social Science Journal**, 36, 143–55.
Mattusch, Max Hans-Jürgen (1999). **Vielsprachigkeit: Fluch oder Segen für die Menschheit? Zur
Fragen einer europäischen und globalen Fremdsprachenpolitik**. Frankfurt am Main: Peter
Lang. Well-argued plea for multilevel language planning framework including planned
languages.
Müller, Kurt E. (ed.) (1992). **Language as Barrier and Bridge**. Lanham: University Press of
America. Papers from the Conferences on Language and Communication, New York.
Müller, Kurt E. (ed.) (1996). **Language Status in the Post-Cold-War Era**. Lanham: University
Press of America. Papers from the Conferences on Language and Communication, New
York.
Pool, Jonathan (1991). The official language problem. **American Political Science Review**, 85
(2). Proves mathematically that a language policy can be both efficient and fair.

Preface to Indexes

Indexes are always ideological, and subjective choices are inevitable in large indexes. A few of the choices I made are mentioned here. In the *Author/Person Index* I have honoured oracy: it includes several 'authors' of oral testimonies. In the *Languages and Peoples Index*, I have to a large extent, followed the labeling and spelling of my sources and apologise in advance to those people whose names and/or languages do not follow their own endodefinitions. Sometimes my own lack of knowledge is the culprit. Needless to say, this is a very imperfect list. It should also be unnecessary to say it but it probably has to be said: just as oral languages, the various sign languages are to be found under their specific names, rather than being lumped together as subheadings under 'Sign Languages'. I have dropped the prefixes usual in many African languages—they are not necessary in English. Thus, Xitsonga is to be found under Tsonga, Sepedi under Pedi, Setswana under Tswana, Kiswahili under Swahili, Oshindonga under Ndonga, etc. Since the English language is referred to on almost every page, I omitted it from the Languages index; specifics are to be found in the *Subject Index*. These 'people' in the *Languages and Peoples Index* are mostly indigenous or minority; that is, I have listed specific peoples and groups at sub-state (and sometimes supra-state) levels. Linguistic majority groups are mostly found in the *Countries/States Index*, especially when their names (ethnonyms, linguonyms) are related to the names of the countries (toponyms). The *Countries/States Index* contains   the 193 UN member states and some additional countries and territories or parts of countries. The names are politonymic or toponymic, not necessarily ethnonymic. There are several grey areas historically and politically and many classification decisions have been pragmatic rather than ideological. Earlier names are sometimes in parenthesis. In the *Subject Index*, I have to a large extent left out references to general information on specific countries or phenomena—there is too much of it. Likewise, many entries contain more specialized information than the title might indicate, especially for entries where most of the book would otherwise need to be listed (like 'linguistic human rights' or 'minority education'). The indexes should be used together with the detailed contents at the beginning of each chapter.

Author/Person Index

Languages and Peoples Index

(languages, dialects, variants, varieties; language families;
speakers, groups, peoples)

Countries/States Index

Subject Index